Five Ballets from Paris and St. Petersburg

Five Ballets from Paris and St. Petersburg

Giselle | Paquita | Le Corsaire |
La Bayadère | Raymonda

DOUG FULLINGTON AND MARIAN SMITH

OXFORD
UNIVERSITY PRESS

OXFORD
UNIVERSITY PRESS

Oxford University Press is a department of the University of Oxford. It furthers
the University's objective of excellence in research, scholarship, and education
by publishing worldwide. Oxford is a registered trade mark of Oxford University
Press in the UK and certain other countries.

Published in the United States of America by Oxford University Press
198 Madison Avenue, New York, NY 10016, United States of America.

© Oxford University Press 2024

Library of Congress Control Number: 2023039579
ISBN 978-0-19-094451-3 (pbk.)
ISBN 978-0-19-094450-6 (hbk.)

DOI: 10.1093/oso/9780190944506.001.0001

Paperback printed by Integrated Books International, United States of America
Hardback printed by Bridgeport National Bindery, Inc., United States of America

for Carl and Rich

Contents

List of Illustrations

1. *Giselle*, Act One, No. 4. Adolphe Adam's autograph score, 1841. Bibliothèque Nationale de France, Département de la Musique, MS-2644, fol. 22r.

2. Carlotta Grisi as Giselle, Act One. Etching published by Hautecoeur-Martinet, Paris, 1841. Bibliothèque Nationale de France, Bibliothèque-Musée de l'Opéra, BMO C-261 (15-1474).

3. Sketch of Giselle's Act Two costume attributed to Paul Lormier, 1841. Bibliothèque Nationale de France, Bibliothèque-Musée de l'Opéra, D216-13 (81).

4–5. Costume drawings by Paul Lormier of Duke Albert, Acts One and Two, 1841. Pencil, pen, watercolor. Bibliothèque Nationale de France, Bibliothèque-Musée de l'Opéra, D216-13 (77–78).

6–9. Drawings from "Grise-Aile" (satirical parody of *Giselle* by Lorentz), *Musée Philipon*, Paris, 1842–1843, pages 68–70. Bibliothèque Nationale de France, Bibliothèque-Musée de l'Opéra, ESTAMPES SCENES Giselle (12).

10. *Giselle*, Act One, No. 2, Titus *répétiteur*, 1841/1842. St. Petersburg State Museum of Theatre and Music, GIK 7114/8a, pages 6–7.

11–12. Costume drawings by Alfred Albert of Bathilde and a page in travesty, 1863. Crayon, watercolor. Bibliothèque Nationale de France, Bibliothèque-Musée de l'Opéra, D216-22 (10 & 4).

13. Page from the Mariinsky Theater manuscript volume of production documents describing the stage setting and properties for *Giselle*, Act One, 1889. St. Petersburg State Museum of Theatre and Music, GIK 16917, page 76.

14. *Giselle*, Act Two, Nikolai Legat partnering Anna Pavlova by the wings. Photograph by Ernst Schneider, Berlin, 1909. St. Petersburg State Museum of Theatre and Music, NVM 1211/25.

15–16. Costume drawings by Henri d'Orschwiller depicting Georges Elie as Inigo and Carlotta Grisi as Paquita, Act One. Pencil, watercolor, 1846. Bibliothèque Nationale de France, Bibliothèque-Musée de l'Opéra, D216-15 (80–91).

17. Caroline Lassia in the *Pas des manteaux* from *Paquita*. Lithograph published by Martinet, Galerie Dramatique, 1846. Bibliothèque Nationale de France, Bibliothèque-Musée de l'Opéra, C-261 (19,267).

18. Costume drawing (unsigned) depicting Hussards (of seven regiments) in *Paquita*, 1846. Pencil, watercolor. Bibliothèque Nationale de France, Bibliothèque-Musée de l'Opéra, D216-15 (80–91).

19. Press illustration by H[enry Augustin] Valentin depicting action from *Paquita*, Act Two, Scene I, 1846. Bibliothèque Nationale de France, Département des Arts du Spectacle, 4-ICO THE-2795.

Archives and Collections

Library of Congress
    Léo Delibes music manuscripts, 1857–1890, ML96.D39
New York Public Library for the Performing Arts, Jerome Robbins Dance Division
    Ballet Foundation Collection of Orchestral Scores and Parts, ca. 1938–1962
    Cia Fornaroli Collection

Introduction

Oral and written tradition

When an orchestra prepares to play a nineteenth-century symphony, its players all learn their parts from written scores—scores that were created as the symphony was conceived. But when a ballet company prepares to perform a nineteenth-century ballet, its dancers nearly always learn their parts from other dancers, in person in the studio (and perhaps on video as well), without referring to original source documents.

Choreographic scores for many nineteenth-century ballets—created relatively soon after the ballets' premieres—*do* exist. The best known of these, of course, are those spirited out of Russia by Nikolai Sergeyev in 1918 and ultimately sold to the Harvard Theatre Collection. Written using Stepanov notation, these documents (now comprising part of what is known as the Sergeyev Collection) preserve step-by-step choreographic instructions for such works as Marius Petipa's *La Bayadère*, *Sleeping Beauty*, and *Raymonda*.

A less-known set of documents was created over the course of several decades by one Henri Justamant, who served as ballet master in Paris, Lyon, and Brussels (among other cities). He made detailed staging manuals for at least 130 ballets, including *Giselle*, *Paquita*, and *Le Corsaire*, and most of them today are to be found in libraries in Paris, Cologne, and New York.

Still less known are rehearsal scores (*répétiteurs*) in which a ballet's mime and action scenes were described with annotations written between or above the staves of music. Though not all *répétiteurs* are thus annotated, a good many are, and they show how the mime scenes were coordinated with the music. When the instructions are followed, the scenes come back to life in unexpected and compelling ways. Such annotated rehearsal scores are now scattered among various libraries and theater collections.

The fact that all of these astonishingly rich and informative documents are tucked away in archives, of course, makes them unlikely to be seen except by those passionate enough to seek them out. Too, many prospective readers do not read Stepanov notation, the Russian or French languages, or music. But the most important reason these documents have dwelt largely in the dark is custom: ballet is handed down in person, from dancer to dancer. This generation-to-generation oral transmission is a time-honored, appropriate, effective, and practical approach. Some might even argue that consulting musty old documents in archives is likely to lead to musty performances and therefore is to be avoided. The living, breathing dancers who serve as culture-bearers, this argument goes, are the better source of information.

Yet, we believe—with due respect to oral tradition—that some latter-day productions have quite lost sight of the strong characterizations, variety, choreographic interest, theatrical effect, and narrative power that made the nineteenth-century ballet classics so successful in the first place. And we count ourselves among those passionate enough to

Five Ballets from Paris and St. Petersburg. Doug Fullington and Marian Smith, Oxford University Press.
© Oxford University Press 2024. DOI: 10.1093/oso/9780190944506.003.0001

have chased down manuscript sources, in our case with the hope of restoring some of those qualities to these old ballets.

Referring back to the written record need not impede creative artistry in the present day, nor preclude the vital in-person coaching—the passing of the torch—that must take place in the studio. But, given the existence of *extensive instructions about how so many of the now-classic story ballets were performed in the nineteenth century*, one must ask: Why ignore them? Why not nurture the art form of ballet with both the living tradition *and* the written record?

We were inspired to write a book by seeing first-hand how effective the lessons of these nineteenth-century ballet manuscripts can be. Over and over, our experience was this: we followed the instructions, even if they at first seemed peculiar or odd, and the effect produced turned out to be excellent. For example, in *Giselle* there is a short scene in Act Two featuring young men in the woods. We did not know what to make of it. It turned out to be a comic respite from the relentless lugubriousness of the Wilis. Audiences responded favorably to the scene, which was not only fun to watch, but made the overall story arc of the second act far more effective.

This book, however, is not meant as a handbook for reconstruction, though of course any reader interested in applying information herein to current-day revivals may find it useful or be inspired to consult the manuscripts themselves. Our goal, rather, is to give the reader a fuller picture of nineteenth-century ballet in Paris and St. Petersburg by exposing to the light of day some of the vital contents of these manuscripts. For we, personally, have found their disclosures revelatory. Taken together, these sources bring into view a ballet culture that is both familiar and strange: one that produced works alive with variety, playfulness, endlessly inventive choreography, and a theatrically savvy coordination of music and movement, one that reflected the racist values of its day in its portrayals of non-white characters and its unapologetically Western colonialist perspective; one that prized female leading characters who were powerful and assertive; one that could still occasionally adhere to the Ancien Régime custom of gendering the sides of the stage; one in which many of the practices we still follow today were becoming established. By learning more about that world and its ballets, we stand to better understand what we have inherited from it, what we have lost, what we have gained, and how its lessons may be applied in the writing of dance history, the staging of the nineteenth-century story ballets, and even in the creation of new ballets.

The Manuscripts

Let us begin with an introduction to the three types of manuscripts that underlie this study.

Annotated *répétiteurs*

Ballets traveled extensively in the nineteenth century and were enthusiastically received in cities far and wide, including (to name a few): Paris, Bordeaux, Nantes, Lyon, Marseille, Berlin, Munich, Vienna, London, Rome, Venice, Naples, Milan, Copenhagen, Stockholm, Warsaw, Brussels, Moscow, St. Petersburg, New York. Dancers, ballet masters, and musical scores were mobile, and many theaters produced ballets for their own

stages and also sent them forth into the world—the Paris Opéra was particularly bounti-
ful in this regard, its busy copy shop systematically reproducing many of its ballet music
scores for other houses and selling them to private individuals, too, including Marie
Taglioni.[1]

One type of musical score, the *répétiteur*, was an arrangement of the orchestra score for
one or two stringed instruments. When annotated with the choreographer's instructions
for mime and stage actions, a *répétiteur* was useful for anyone who wished to transmit a
ballet from one house to another.[2] *Répétiteurs*—sometimes well annotated—were also
employed at rehearsals in the house for which the ballet was created in the first place and
in performances, too, by the violinist-conductor, whose job was made easier by knowing
what to expect on stage.[3] The reader of these annotated *répétiteurs* in the present day, of
course, can learn not only what sorts of actions, silent utterances, and mime was called
for, but can also gain a good deal of information about how the music in ballet scores was
coordinated thereto and thus identify a vocabulary of meanings that ballet composers
and audiences relied on.

Today, the largest known collection of annotated *répétiteurs* is preserved at the
Archives de la Ville de Bruxelles; these scores were sent incrementally by the Paris Opéra
to the Théâtre de la Monnaie in that city. Thanks to the work of David A. Day, this rich
and informative collection has been catalogued, and some of the scores (along with
thousands of other important ballet and opera documents from multiple collections)
have been posted on the website and portal "Opera and Ballet Primary Sources."[4]

---

[1] The Opéra's copy shop, under the supervision of M. LeBorne, made (for instance) a copy of *La Tempête*
"for London," one full score of *La Sylphide* for Moscow, another for Lyon, and another for Taglioni, as well as
parts for the ballet for Brussels; a full score of *La Révolte des femmes* for Taglioni, some sort of *Giselle* score for
Marseille, a *répétiteur* of *Giselle* for Bordeaux, and for Fanny Elssler, *répétiteur* scores and parts of *La Tarentule*
and *Le Diable boiteux*. Bibliothèque-Musée de l'Opéra, RE 235, microfilm SR 97/576.

Not every restaging of the Opéra's ballets, however, employed the original score that had been tailor-made
at the Paris Opéra. On the Italian peninsula, local composers often provided new scores for imported ballets.
As Ornella di Tondo writes, in Italy "exorbitant costs generally made it impossible to acquire a ballet score
from elsewhere, and it was far less expensive to commission a new score from amongst the numerous composers and arrangers of ballet music, or from a local musician already on the payroll of the theater. August
Bournonville for example, for his 1836 Danish version of *La Silfide*, found it less expensive to commission an
entirely new score in Copenhagen. Further, local musicians offered the added benefit of being familiar with
the taste of local theatregoers." Ornella di Tondo, "The Italian *Silfide* and the contentious reception of ultra-
montane ballet," in *La Sylphide: Paris 1832 and Beyond*, ed. Marian Smith (Alton, UK: Dance Books, 2012),
204. And Elise Henry, in a letter to her brother Louis [Luigi], mentioned the high cost of buying a *Giselle*
répétiteur in Paris and proposed that she barter drama lessons given to Coralli's sister for a copy of the *répétiteur*. Bruno Ligore, "Le lettere di Louis Henry e di Élise Henry-Vallier," in *Danza e ballo a Napoli, un dialogo
con l'Europa (1806–1861)*, ed. Paologiovanni Maione and Maria Venuso (Napoli, Turchini Edizioni 2020),
183–185.

[2] An examination of the annotated *répétiteurs* used at the Paris Opéra (and today found in the Bibliothèque-
Musée de l'Opéra, along with the orchestra parts for ballets) shows that they are less densely annotated, in
general, than scores used by ballet masters restaging a ballet in a different house (for example, the *Giselle*
répétiteur taken by Antoine Titus to Russia and the *répétiteurs* sent to Brussels by the Paris Opéra).

[3] David A. Day notes that "the practice of annotating these parts with the choreographers' instructions as an
aid for the ballet orchestra violin-conductor" was followed in the early nineteenth century by Jean Dauberval
and his students at Bordeaux. "As Dauberval's repertory and influence spread to Paris, Brussels, and other
major ballet centers, so did the practice of annotating these *violon répétiteur* parts with instructions for mime,
stage actions, and even occasional dance configurations." David A. Day, *The Annotated* violon répétiteur *and
Early Romantic Ballet at the Theatre Royal de Bruxelles (1815–1830)* (PhD diss., New York University, 2007), 2.

[4] See "Opera and Ballet Primary Sources," https://sites.lib.byu.edu/obps/, which provides links to scans
of libretti, scores, and other documents in several archives, including Music Special Collections in the
Harold B. Lee Library at Brigham Young University and the fonds of the Théâtre de la Monnaie conserved
at the Archives de la Ville de Bruxelles. See also "BYU Brussels Opera and Ballet" at https://archive.org/
details/byubrusselsoperaballet and David A. Day, "Digital Opera and Ballet: A Case Study of International
Collaboration," *Fontes Artis Musicae* 61, no. 2 (April–June 2014): 99–106.

Other such collections of *répétiteurs*, though not as extensive, may be found at the Bibliothèque-Musée de l'Opéra in Paris and the Bibliothèque Municipale de Bordeaux.[5] The St. Petersburg State Museum of Theatre and Music houses at least one such score, that for *Giselle*, used in 1842 by Antoine Titus when he staged the ballet in St. Petersburg, and the Central Music Library of St. Petersburg's Mariinsky Theater surely houses many more. The New York Public Library Music Division has a *répétiteur* of the ballet *La Somnambule*. Others are preserved in private collections.[6]

On the Italian peninsula, as Ornella di Tondo reports, "if ballet music was at all successful, it was printed." Such scores, though rarely reproducing the complete ballet, did often provide interlined descriptions of action.[7] They were published for the use of piano amateurs, usually in two-hand or four-hand arrangements.

Justamant's staging manuals

Though little remembered now, Henri Justamant (1815–1890) was a successful dancer, ballet master, and choreographer. When he was a young man, his career took him to various cities, including London, Berlin, Brussels, Lyon, and Marseilles. After 1866, he produced ballets in no fewer than thirteen houses in Paris, including the Théâtre de la Porte-Saint-Martin, the Théâtre de la Gaîté, the Renaissance, and the Opéra.

Justamant not only created new choreographies and staged the works of others; he also took it upon himself to record an enormous number of ballets in lengthy manuscript staging manuals, including *Le Diable à quatre* and *Le Diable amoureux*, in addition to those mentioned above. He did the same for ballets that had been incorporated into operas, too, including *Guillaume Tell*, *Robert le diable*, and *Les Vêpres siciliennes*. As one observer put it, Justamant came up with

a new method of writing that makes [the ballets] . . . clear to even the most ignorant, and would enable a newcomer to mount [them].[8]

---

[5] See Day, "The annotated *violon répétiteur*," 6. See also Day, "An Inventory of Manuscript Scores at the Royal Opera House, Covent Garden," *Notes, the Quarterly Journal of the Music Library Association* 44, no. 3 (March 1988): 456–462; and Bruno Ligore, "Violin Conductor's Scores and Pantomimic Encoding in the First Half of the Nineteenth Century: Some Methodological Approaches," in *Times of Change: Artistic Perspectives and Cultural Crossings in Nineteenth-Century Dance*, ed. Irene Brandenburg, Francesca Falcone, Claudia Jeschke, and Bruno Ligore (Bologna: Massimiliano Piretti, 2023), 305–330.

[6] For instance, an annotated *violino principale* part for Antonio Pallerini's *Nerone* (1884) is in the collection of Madison U. and Debra H. Sowell; a photocopy of an annotated 1835 violin *répétiteur* for *La Sylphide* once belonging to Victor Bartholomin, of the Théâtre de la Monnaie, was given by Alexander Bennett to Marian Smith (the whereabouts of the original are unknown). See Alexander Bennett, "Regarding the 1835 Brussels Manuscript of *La Sylphide* (the 'Bartholomin score')," in Smith, *La Sylphide*, 334–336. See also Elizabeth Aldrich, Sandra Noll Hammond, and Armand Russell, *The Extraordinary Dance Book T B. 1826: An Anonymous Manuscript in Facsimile* (Stuyvesant, NY: Pendragon Press, 2000). And see Morris S. Levy and John Milton Ward, *Italian Ballet 1637–1977 from the John Milton and Ruth Neils Ward Collection* (Cambridge, MA: Harvard University Press, 2005). Here, one may find scores with interlined instructions. Also, it is known that Jules Perrot brought with him to Russia a violin *répétiteur* of Adam's score for *La Filleule des fées* during the 1849–1850 season; the orchestra parts failed to arrive, as Ivor Guest reports, and the conductor Konstantin Lyadov was commissioned to supply a new orchestration. Ivor Guest, *Fanny Elssler* (Middletown, CT: Wesleyan University Press, 1970), 237–238. This is noteworthy because it shows that sometimes an attempt was made to send orchestra parts and use original orchestration rather than reorchestrating from a *répétiteur*.

[7] di Tondo, "The Italian *Silfide*," 205.

[8] Louis Le Bourg, *Paris-Journal*, 28 June 1882. We thank Helena Kopchick Spencer for bringing this article to our attention.

Justamant's hand was neat, his drawings meticulous and tidy, his words clearly written (though some of his spellings are phonetic). His manuscripts overall are detailed, orderly, and easy to make sense of. He depicted dancers and other characters with simple line drawings, using just a few strokes—females are in red ink, males in black ink—and in those strokes managed to convey hints of human energy, which can make the notations gratifying and even amusing to read. In most cases, Justamant represented both male and female figures with a diamond-shaped upper body and a lower body that looks like a skirt. He showed floor patterns and described choreography in prose, naming particular dance steps in recording each enchaînement (some of the terms he used have fallen from our vocabularies; others are familiar but may not reflect current usage[9]). He also wrote out the text of the mimed conversations in script format and listed details about the music—staves with key and time signatures as well as the number of bars allotted to each passage of dance or action—along the right-hand edge of each page. (In some cases he did not fill in all of the keys and time signatures.) And he provided at the beginning of each manuscript a notation key, dates, names of theaters, casts, lists of dances, and sometimes, elsewhere in the manuscripts, properties lists, lighting instructions, librettos, costume drawings, newspaper clippings—all information that documented a particular production and also could serve as a guide for restaging.

Thus did Justamant create practical records for his own use, and perhaps for other ballet masters (though the intended purpose of the manuals is not clear[10]), and left as his legacy a gold mine for anyone today wishing to learn, in fine detail, about the substance and dramaturgy of ballet as it was found in a variety of genres—comic operas, grand operas, ballet-pantomimes, ballet-féeries, and plays—on a good many important stages in the second half of the nineteenth century in western Europe. Justamant's *oeuvre* of manuals (listed in Appendix B) also presents, needless to say, endless opportunities for restaging.[11]

---

[9] Sandra Noll Hammond, "Dancing *La Sylphide* in 1832: Something Old or Something New?" in Smith, *La Sylphide*, 31–56.

[10] Justamant also seems to have made presentation copies, including one of the "Ballet de *La biche au bois*" (1869) given on 22 May 1870 as "souvenir amical et artistique" to "Monsieur Gabet" (a pencilled-in marking says "Charles, 1821–1903"). It is now in a private collection.

[11] The Justamant manuscripts have attracted little attention in the latter day, and heretofore, no list of his extant manuscripts has been compiled. A few of the manuals, however, have been examined and put to practical use. These include *La Esmeralda*, of which excerpts have been staged by Claudia Jeschke and Robert Atwood—see *Sensuality & Nationalism in Romantic Ballet*, DVD, directed by Claudia Jeschke (Dallas: Dancetime Publications, 2012); *Giselle*, the stagings of which at Pacific Northwest Ballet in 2011 and the Bolshoi Ballet in 2019 were based in part on the Justamant manual, and the mad scene of which was staged by Dawn Urista—see "Giselle's Mad Scene: A Demonstration and Comparison of 21st Century and 19th Century Paris Opéra Stagings" (Master's project, University of Oregon, 2011); and *Paquita*, of which excerpts have been staged by Claudia Jeschke and Francesca Falcone at the Accademia Nazionale di Danza, Rome—see "Henri Justamant's 'Pas des manteaux' (1854): Dealing with a Choreographic Topic of (Trans) National Relevance," in Brandenburg, Jeschke, Falcone, and Ligore, *Times for Change*.

For further published research on Justamant, see Claudia Jeschke and Robert Atwood, "Expanding Horizons: Techniques of Choreo-Graphy in Nineteenth-Century Dance," *Dance Chronicle* 29, no. 2 (2006): 195–214; Claudia Jeschke, Gabi Vettermann, and Nicole Haitzinger, *Les Choses Espagnoles: Research into the Hispanomania of 19th Century Dance* (Munich: epodium, 2009)—see also the longer German edition (same authors), *Interaktion und Rhythmus: zur Modellierung von Fremdheit im Tanztheater des 19. Jahrhunderts* (Munich: epodium, 2010); Linièle Chane-Yue-Chiang, *Pas en variations: Henri Justamant, entrée dans une écriture singulière: Partitions en Cinétographie Laban* ([Paris]: Linièle Chane-Yue-Chiang, 2015); Doug Fullington, "Elementos de danza española en dos producciones de 'Paquita'," in *Marius Petipa: Del Ballet Romántico al Clásico*, ed. Laura Hormigón (Madrid: Asosiación de Directores de Escena de España, 2020), 105–120; and Marian Smith, Sarah Gutsche-Miller, and Helena Kopchick Spencer, "Justamant's *Le Bossu* and Depictions of Indigenous Americans in Nineteenth-Century French Ballet," in *America in the*

Only a little is known of Justamant's life.[12] Born in Bordeaux, he became a dancer as an adolescent, studying with Alexis Blache and Louis Henry.[13] In 1845, at the age of thirty (as he later told his friend Louis Le Bourg), he paused before a mirror in the theater "in the midst of my frolics" and "I found myself very ugly and very ridiculous."[14] He did continue performing for several more years, however, and while still appearing on stage also began his long career as ballet master; he worked in that capacity at several houses.[15]

Justamant could display extreme impatience in rehearsals, as we are told by his frequent collaborator, the musician Albert Vizentini, who also comments on Justamant's notable way of dressing and his excellence as a choreographer:

> [Justamant is] a rager *par excellence* who tears out his hair, loses his temper and removes his clothes little by little as the rehearsal advances. He creates his own clothes or trousers, laces up his shoes, never leaves the house without a golden-knobbed cane, carries quite a large walking stick by night, and is without equal in arranging the most beautiful ballets in the world.[16]

We know, too, that he left his post at the Opéra in 1869 (after just one season as first ballet master) partly out of frustration at its administrators' refusal to allow him to start a dance class there.[17] And we are left, by the journalist Louis Le Bourg, with a charming description of Justamant making his notations:

> Justement [sic] is always composing and setting up, in his lovely retreat in Champigny, *danseuses* in red and blank ink who, on paper, dance the most prettily in the world.

Three years after Justamant's death, his considerable collection of staging manuals was put up for auction,[18] and most of it eventually wound up in four major collections:

French Imaginary, 1789–1914: Music, Revolution and Race, ed. Diana Hallman and César Leal (Woodbridge, UK: Boydell & Brewer, 2022), 49–99.

See also Paul Ludwig's invaluable annotated inventory of Justamant holdings in Wahn and biographical notes in *Henri Justamant (1815–1890), Kommentiertes Bestandsverzeichnis seiner Ballett-Notationen in der Theaterwissenschaftlichen Sammlung Schloß Wahn, Gefördert von der Fritz Thyssen Stiftung, Köln, und der Studienstiftung Niessen* (Köln, 2005).

[12] See Gabi Vettermann, "In Search of Dance Creators' Biographies: The Life and Work of Henri Justamant," in Jeschke et al., *Les choses espagnoles*, 124–136.

[13] *Catalogue de livres anciens et modernes et des manuscrits originaux des ballets et divertissements de M. Henri Justamant* [vente à Paris, Hôtel des commissaires-priseurs, salle 10, 15 mai 1893, Mr Maurice Delestre, commissaire-priseur] (Paris: 1893), 15. Bibliothèque Nationale de France, Département Littérature et art, DELTA-41165, available online at https://gallica.bnf.fr/ark:/12148/bpt6k3211558. This catalog is reproduced in Paul Ludwig's *Henri Justamant, Kommentiertes Bestandsverzeichnis*, 14–20.

[14] Le Bourg wrongly credited Justamant, perhaps tongue in cheek, with having single-handedly accomplished the "near complete suppression of men in the corps de ballet" in 1868 during his tenure as ballet master at the Paris Opéra. When Le Bourg asked Justamant about his "anti-masculine" attitude, Justamant replied by telling him the story about seeing himself in the mirror, and added, "dancing, that is to say grace, should be left to women." Le Bourg, *Paris-Journal*, 28 June 1882.

[15] For instance, he played a leading role in a revival of Milon's *Le Carnaval de Venise* in Lyon in 1850 when he was thirty-five. See http://gallica.bnf.fr/ark:/12148/bt]=[v1b10537843d/f6.image.

[16] Albert Vizentini, *Derrière la toils, flyers, coulisses et comédiens* (Paris: Achille Faure, 1868), 206, qtd. in Vettermann, "In Search of Dance Creators' Biographies," 128. We have modified the translation.

[17] Letter from Henri Justamant to Émile Perrin (November 1869), Paris, Archives nationales, AJ[13] 1004, qtd. in Vettermann, "In Search of Dance Creators' Biographies," 129–131.

[18] *Catalogue de livres anciens et modernes et des manuscrits originaux des ballets et divertissement de M. Henri Justamant.*

The Theater Studies Collection (TWS) of the University of Cologne, at Wahn Castle (Theaterwissenschaftliche Sammlung der Universitat Köln, Schloß Wahn)

The Library-Museum of the Paris Opéra (Bibliothèque-Musée de l'Opéra), Bibliothèque Nationale de France, Paris

The Collection Georges Douay at the Bibliothèque de l'Arsénal (Département des Arts du Spectacle), Bibliothèque Nationale de France, Paris

Jerome Robbins Dance Division, New York Public Library for the Performing Arts

The Deutsches Tanzarchiv in Cologne houses one Justamant manuscript, that for *Giselle*; most fortunately it has been published in facsimile.[19]

Choreographic notations using the Stepanov system

A collection of choreographic notations made according to the Stepanov system is one of the main means by which ballets in the repertory of the St. Petersburg Imperial Theaters were brought West during the first half of the twentieth century. This assemblage, together with musical scores and other performance-related sources, is today housed in the Harvard Theatre Collection at Harvard University's Houghton Library and known informally as the Sergeyev Collection, for it was for more than three decades in the possession of Nikolai Sergeyev. A former *régisseur* of the Imperial Ballet, Sergeyev took a mass of choreographic notations from St. Petersburg when he emigrated West in 1918 and used them to stage productions for dance troupes in France, Latvia, and England.[20] Though a complete biography chronicling the life and work of Sergeyev has yet to be written, Roland John Wiley and, more recently, Sergey Konaev have provided much pertinent information about him as well as the early history of the Stepanov notation system. We will briefly summarize their findings here.

History of the Stepanov notation system: Stepanov, Gorsky, Sergeyev, and the Sergeyev Collection.[21] The genesis of the Stepanov system dates back to 1889, when Vladimir Stepanov, an Imperial Ballet dancer, began studying anatomy and anthropology at the University of St. Petersburg. His interest in the facility of the human body led him to develop a system of movement notation, "an attempt to create a kind of alphabet for choreographers and all others who require to record human movements."[22] In 1891,

[19] Deutsches Tanzarchiv Köln, Item Number 52915, published in facsimile as *Giselle, ou, Les Wilis: Ballet Fantastique en deux actes*, ed. Frank-Manuel Peter (Hildesheim: Georg Olms Verlag, 2008) [hereafter, Justamant, *Giselle*]. Vettermann also refers to holdings in Grenoble and at the British Library; these are not staging manuals. "In Search of Dance Creators' Biographies," 127n8.

[20] Nikolai Sergeev Dance Notations and Music Scores for Ballets, 1888–1944 (MS Thr 245). Harvard Theatre Collection, Houghton Library, Harvard University. The finding aid is available online, along with a number of digitized items, at https://id.lib.harvard.edu/ead/hou01987/catalog.

Notations and other materials relating to the ballet *Swan Lake* are housed as Nikolai Sergeev Choreographic and Music Scores for the Ballet *Swan Lake*, 1905–1924 (MS Thr 186), Houghton Library, Harvard University. The finding aid for the *Swan Lake* materials is available online at https://id.lib.harvard.edu/ead/hou01289/catalog.

Additional examples of Stepanov notation are preserved in the Alexander Gorsky archive (*fond* 1) of the Museum of the State Academic Bolshoi Theater (GABT), Moscow. See Ekaterina Churakova, Elena Frolova, Tatiana Saburova, and Sergey Konaev, *Aleksandr Gorskiy: baletmeyster, khudozhnik, fotograf* [Alexander Gorsky: choreographer, artist, photographer] (Moscow: Kuchkovo Pole, 2018).

[21] A lengthy discussion by Wiley of the history and early use of the Stepanov system, its proponents, and its detractors can be found in his preface to Alexander Gorsky, *Two Essays on Stepanov Dance Notation by Alexander Gorsky*, tr. Roland John Wiley (New York: Congress on Research in Dance, 1978), ix–xviii.

[22] This quotation is from the introduction to Vladimir Stepanov's *Alphabet of Movements of the Human Body*, tr. Raymond Lister (Cambridge, UK: Golden Head Press, 1958), 9. See note 24 in this chapter.

after demonstrating the system to a committee of ranking artists of the Imperial Ballet (including Marius Petipa), Stepanov was awarded a stipend to continue his studies in Paris with the neurologist Jean Martin Charcot.[23] Stepanov published his work in 1892 as *Alphabet des mouvements du corps humain*.[24] He then secured permission from the committee in 1893 to use the system to notate the theater's ballet and opera ballet repertory. That same year, he also began to teach the notation system in the Theater School.[25]

Early projects (now apparently lost) involving Jules Perrot's ballet *Le Rêve du peintre* and (likely) Lev Ivanov's ballet *The Magic Flute* were rendered as part of the notation approval process.[26] Extant notations of Marius Petipa's one-act ballet *The Awakening of Flora* and the divertissement *Le jardin animé* from his staging of *Le Corsaire* (see Chapter 8) appear to be other such early projects, as an examination of the scribal hands and formatting suggests.[27]

After Stepanov's untimely death in 1896, he was succeeded as notation teacher by another Imperial Ballet dancer, Alexander Gorsky.[28] Gorsky refined Stepanov's system and in 1899 published two essays, *Table of Signs for the Notation of Movements of the Human Body According to the System of the Artist of the Imperial St. Petersburg Theaters V.I. Stepanov* and *Choreography: Examples for Reading*.[29] Gorsky was transferred to Moscow in January 1901, where he was first appointed *régisseur* then ballet master. His successor in St. Petersburg was Nikolai Sergeyev, who had been working with him as an assistant since 1897.[30]

Sergeyev had graduated from the Imperial Theater School and joined the Imperial Ballet in 1894; he was named *régisseur* in 1903. He continued to teach notation and also supervised the ambitious project of notating the ballets and opera ballets in the St. Petersburg Imperial Ballet repertory. He was aided during some of those years by two assistants, Alexander Chekrygin (beginning in 1903) and Viktor Rakhmanov (beginning in 1904).[31] (A recent suggestion that Sergeyev had two additional assistants is

---

[23] Roland John Wiley, *The Life and Ballets of Lev Ivanov* (New York: Oxford University Press, 1997), 155, and Gorsky, *Two Essays on Stepanov Dance Notation*, x.

[24] V[ladimir] I[vanovich] Stepanov, *Alphabet des mouvements du corps humain; essai d'enregistrement des mouvements du corps humain au moyen des signes musicaux* (Paris: Impr. M. Zouckermann [Librairie P. Vigot], 1892). A copy is preserved in the Sergeyev Collection, MS Thr 245 (269). The system was published in Russia as *Tablitsa znakov dlya zapisyvaniya dvizhenii chelovecheskogo tela po sisteme Artista Imperatorskikh S.-Peterburgskikh Teatrov, V.I. Stepanova* [Table of Signs for the Notation of the Movements of the Human Body According to the System of the Artist of the Imperial St. Petersburg Theaters, V.I. Stepanov] (St. Petersburg [n.d.]). An English translation by Raymond Lister was published in 1858 as *Alphabet of Movements of the Human Body*. See note 22.

[25] Roland John Wiley, "Dances from Russia: An Introduction to the Sergejev Collection," *Harvard Library Bulletin* 24, no. 1 (Cambridge, MA: Harvard University, 1976), 104, and Gorsky, *Two Essays on Stepanov Dance Notation*, x.

[26] See Wiley, *Lev Ivanov*, 155–157; "Dances from Russia," 104n26; and Gorsky, *Two Essays on Stepanov Dance Notation*, xiii–xiv. *The Magic Flute* was notated again at a later date, very likely in less detail than the original. See MS Thr 245 (58).

[27] MS Thr 245 (45) and (1), respectively.

[28] About Gorsky, see Churakova et al., *Aleksandr Gorskiy*, especially 14–16, and Gorsky, *Two Essays on Stepanov Dance Notation*, x–xi.

[29] *Tablitsa znakov dlia zapisyvaniia dvizhenii chelovecheskago tela po sisteme V.I. Stepanova* and *Khoreografiia, primery dlia chteniia* [Choreography: Examples for Reading] (Imperial St. Petersburg Theater School. Installment I. 1899). A copy is part of the Sergeyev Collection; MS Thr (268). For an English translation, see Gorsky, *Two Essays on Stepanov Dance Notation*. See note 21.

[30] Sergeyev was designated teacher of the "Theory of Notating Dances" on 1 September 1900. See Gorsky, *Two Essays on Stepanov Dance Notation*, xi, note 14. Gorsky was sent to Moscow on 9 September 1900 (ahead of his official transfer) to begin his *régisseur* duties. See Churakova et al., *Aleksandr Gorskiy*, 16.

[31] Wiley, "Dances from Russia," 98 and 106n34.

not supported by documentation.[32]) Promoted to *régisseur general* in 1914, Sergeyev remained in that position until losing his post in the wake of the 1917 revolution.

Leaving Petrograd, Sergeyev took with him a large number of notation scores as well as musical scores and other performance-related documents. These would provide him with his future livelihood in the West. He continued to add materials (mostly musical scores) to this collection during his subsequent European travels. From 1921 until shortly before his death in 1951, he used the documents to stage productions that ultimately became the basis for most Western productions of the classical ballet repertory.[33]

Sergeyev's stagings included, among others, *The Sleeping Princess* (that is, *The Sleeping Beauty*) for Serge Diaghilev's Ballets Russes in London (1921); *Giselle* for the Paris Opéra (1924), the Camargo Society in London (1932), Vic-Wells Ballet (1934), and the Markova-Dolin Ballet (1935); *Coppélia* for the Vic-Wells Ballet (1933) and Ballet Russe de Monte Carlo (1938); and *The Nutcracker* (1934), *Swan Lake* (1934), and *The Sleeping Princess* (1939), all for the Vic-Wells Ballet.[34]

Sergeyev was ballet master for the Latvian National Opera in Riga (1922–1924) and Opera Privé de Paris (1927–1930). In 1934, he founded and directed his own Russian Ballet in England.[35] Following his years with the Vic-Wells Ballet in the 1930s, he was hired by Mona Inglesby, the English ballerina and dance producer, to serve as *régisseur* for her International Ballet from 1941 to 1948. Sergeyev's stagings for the International Ballet included *Coppélia*, *Giselle*, the *Polovtsian Dances* from the opera *Prince Igor*, *The Sleeping Princess*, and *Swan Lake*.[36]

Upon Sergeyev's death in 1951, his collection of notations, musical scores, and other materials passed to an uninterested party, but Inglesby—a firm believer in its historical and practical value—managed to persuade her businessman father to buy it. She then tried, without success, to interest Leningrad's Kirov Ballet and London's Royal Ballet in the collection, and finally sold it to Harvard University in 1969.[37]

[32] In a 2011 essay, Natalia Zozulina posited that Imperial Ballet dancers Nikolai Kremnev and Sergei Ponomarev were additional notation assistants to Sergeyev. See Natalia Zozulina, "Soglyadkoy na istoriyu (N.G. Sergeyev i zapisi russkikh baletov iz garvardskoy kollektsii)" ["With an eye to history (N.G. Sergeyev and recordings of Russian ballets from the Harvard collection)"], *Baletom i operoy* [Ballet and Opera] (online forum), 18 February 2001, http://forum.balletfriends.ru/viewtopic.php?t=3510, note 33. Zozulina cites the inclusion of Kremnev's and Ponomarev's names in the choreographic notation of *The Fairy Doll*, MS Thr 245 (13), as proof of scribal authorship. Upon inspection of the notation, we find nothing resembling a scribe's signature on any of the pages (the notations appear to be in Sergeyev's hand). Ponomarev is listed as the performer of a waltz with Agrippina Vaganova. We have not identified Kremnev's name among the many artists listed as performers in the notation. (Andrew Foster has confirmed that both Kremnev and Ponomarev made debuts in *The Fairy Doll* on 21 February 1907 at the Mariinsky Theater: Kremnev took over the role of the Black Woman, alongside Vasily Stukolkin, and Ponomarev performed the Chinese dance with Vaganova.) To our knowledge, this assertion is not supported by any other documentation. We surmise that confirmation of additional notation assistants was sought in order to account for the various scribal hands found in the notations and to support the false notion that Sergeyev was not one of the notation scribes.

[33] About Sergeyev, see Wiley, "Dances from Russia," 94–103; Jane Pritchard, "Nicholas Sergeyev," *International Dictionary of Ballet*, ed. Martha Bremser, vol. 2, 1275–1277 (Detroit: St. James Press, 1993); and Sergey Konaev, ed., "My vse visim v vozdukhe . . . Pis'ma N.G. Sergeyeva k A.K. Shervashidze (1921–1933)" [We are all hanging in the air . . . Letters from N.G. Sergeev to A.K. Shervashidze (1921–1933)], *Mnemozina* 6 (Moscow: Indrik, 2014), 555–584, available online at http://teatr-lib.ru/Library/Mnemozina/Mnemoz_6/ Mnemoz_6.pdf. See also Beth Genné, "Creating a Canon, Creating the 'Classics' in Twentieth-Century British Ballet," *Dance Research* 18, no. 2 (Winter 2000): 132–162.

[34] For a fuller list of productions, see Pritchard, "Nicholas Sergeyev."

[35] See Jane Pritchard, "Bits of *Bayadère* in Britain," *Dancing Times* 79, no. 948 (September 1989): 1120–1121.

[36] For a description of Sergeyev's work with Inglesby and International Ballet, see Mona Inglesby with Kay Hunter, *Ballet in the Blitz* (Debenham, UK: Groundnut, 2008).

[37] See Ismene Brown, "Keeper of Old Scores," *Daily Telegraph* (3 August 2000), https://ismeneb.com/artic les-indexed/ewExternalFiles/Inglesby%2C%20Keeper%20of%20old%20scores%20Aug00.pdf. See also

The Sergeyev Collection includes choreographic notations of ballets and opera ballets, violin *répétiteurs*, piano reductions, orchestra scores and parts, printed programs, librettos, and miscellany, including photographs and drawings, relating to the repertory of the St. Petersburg Imperial Theaters in the late nineteenth and early twentieth centuries.[38] The collection has been used by scholars and practitioners to research and remount ballets from the St. Petersburg Imperial Ballet repertory.[39] In recent years, an increasing number of digitized documents have been posted on the Harvard Library website.

The Stepanov system and extant examples. Stepanov notation is a precise system that uses Western musical notation as its basis, with noteheads and stems (augmented by a series of additional symbols) written on three different staves to indicate positions of the head, neck, and torso (two-line stave), arms and hands (three-line stave), and legs and feet (four-line stave), and how each moves rhythmically.[40] Taken together, the notated positions describe classical (and character) step vocabulary. Notation manuscripts that document the choreography and action of a ballet include ground plans (showing the position of dancers on stage) that correspond to a series of notated measures (the rhythmic equivalent of musical measures), most containing one *enchaînement*. Mime conversations are written out in prose along with annotations that describe action and other details.

Although most of the extant notations are incomplete and unfinished, the high level of detail found in the earliest surviving examples suggests that a finished, prescriptive document was the original goal of the notation project. These include the aforementioned notations of *The Awakening of Flora* and *Le jardin animé*, as well as the notation of *La Bayadère* (although the latter is made solely in pencil, rather than at least partly in ink, and is primarily a record of the ballet's ensemble dances). Moreover, it seems a musical score was, in the early stages of the project, intended to be part of the notation

---

Inglesby and Hunter, *Ballet in the Blitz*, 74, and Ismene Brown, "Time to Get Authentic," *Dance Now* 16, no. 1 (Spring 2007): 34–39.

[38] For a description of the collection and its genesis, see Wiley, "Dances from Russia." See also the online finding aid for the Sergeyev Collection, http://oasis.lib.harvard.edu/oasis/deliver/~hou01987.

[39] The notations lay essentially undisturbed for more than two decades (save for handling by cataloguers and archivists) until Wiley, then a Harvard doctoral student in musicology, made a study of them for his 1974 dissertation. In 1984 Wiley and the choreographer Peter Wright staged a production of *The Nutcracker* for the Royal Ballet in England that incorporated dances and other elements from the notations. The Royal drew on the collection again for its 1987 production of *Swan Lake*, for which Wiley provided the research.

Sergei Vikharev was a leader in the field of historically informed ballet revivals, assisted by historian Pavel Gershenzon. Beginning with *Sleeping Beauty* in 1999, Vikharev's revivals using the Stepanov notations included *La Bayadère* (2001) and *The Awakening of Flora* (2007) for the Mariinsky Ballet, *Coppélia* (Novosibirsk, 2001; Bolshoi Ballet, 2009), and *Raymonda* (La Scala, 2011). All of these productions included recreation of original (or period) scenic and costume designs, and *La Bayadère* featured the restoration of the musical score by Ludwig Minkus. When it was presented in 1999, Vikharev's *Sleeping Beauty* was the first of its kind—an attempt to present a large-scale, nineteenth-century Russian ballet as it would have been performed at its premiere.

In 2014, Alexei Ratmansky staged a historically informed production of *Paquita* for Bayerisches Staatsballett, assisted by the musicologist Maria Babanina as well as by the authors of this volume. The goal of the collaborators for this production, who drew on a wide variety of source materials, was to adhere as faithfully as possible to the information provided in the Stepanov notation of the ballet. Ratmansky, assisted by his wife Tatiana Ratmansky, has since staged historically informed versions of *Sleeping Beauty* (American Ballet Theatre, 2015), *Swan Lake* (Zurich Ballet, 2015), *Harlequinade* (American Ballet Theatre, 2018), *La Bayadère* (Staatsballett Berlin, 2018), and *Giselle* (Bolshoi Ballet, 2019).

[40] For a discussion of the Stepanov system as it is described in the publications by Stepanov and Gorsky, see Sheila Marion with Karen Eliot, "Recording the Imperial Ballet: Anatomy and Ballet in Stepanov's Notation," in *Dance on Its Own Terms*, ed. Melanie Bales and Karen Eliot (New York: Oxford University Press, 2013), 309–340.

document: both *The Awakening of Flora* and *Le jardin animé* feature a two-violin *répétiteur* copied in ink on the uppermost staves of each notation system.

The majority of the extant notations, however, are descriptive accounts, that is, unpolished eyewitness records of dance and action as rehearsed in the studio or performed on stage—in-house documents that could be used to restage ballets by those already familiar with them.[41] Nevertheless, these documents impart crucial information about the choreography, mime, action, and other details of the ballets recorded. They are notated in pencil, mostly on vertical-format sheets comprising six notation boxes (read from left to right and from top to bottom) consisting of a set of notation staves below an open square used for ground plans and annotations.[42] The level of documented detail found in these notations varies from dance to dance and scene to scene.

Sergeyev's reputation as notator and stager. Nikolai Sergeyev's reputation has been sullied over the years, and shadows of doubt about his abilities persist to this day. Though it is beyond the scope of this book to explore the motives of Sergeyev's detractors (as Roland John Wiley and Tim Scholl have done) or reassess his abilities and aspects of his professional demeanor (as Sergey Konaev and Alexei Ratmansky have begun to do[43]), we would like to say enough about Sergeyev to confirm the merits and significance of the notations that are preserved at Harvard, most of which are in his hand.

In his seminal study of the Sergeyev Collection, written in 1976, Wiley provided essential details of Sergeyev's life and outlined Soviet-era criticisms of Sergeyev that sought to minimize his contributions to the documentation of Imperial-era ballets.[44] Of particular importance to the present volume are assertions that Sergeyev was an incompetent dance notator who was responsible for little or none of the actual notation work undertaken by the Imperial Ballet.[45] Add to this Fedor Lopukhov's and Ninette de Valois's negative assessments of Sergeyev's abilities as a teacher of notation (Lopukhov) and stager of ballets using notation (de Valois), which served to further notions that he was ineffective, at best, or completely inept, at worst.[46]

---

[41] Andrei Galkin has referred to these unpolished notations as "drafts." Andrei Galkin, "Choreographic Notations from 'N.G. Sergeyev's Collection' as a Source of Reconstruction of Ballet Performance," *Marius Petipa on the World Ballet Stage: Materials of the International Conference* (St. Petersburg: St. Peterburg State Museum of Theatre and Music, 2018), 42. Furthermore, Wiley has noted: "With few exceptions the notations show no evidence of being intended as complete records of the ballets involved, but are instead reminders for dancers already familiar with the choreography. Nor, apparently, were the manuscripts meant to be considered finished works of art in themselves. Many erasures and strikeovers show them to be practical documents." Wiley, "Dances from Russia," 107.

[42] Wiley describes three types of paper formatted specially for Stepanov notation. Wiley, "Dances from Russia," 106.

[43] See Konaev, "*My vse visim v vozdukhe . . .*" In an interview with Alastair Macaulay about Ratmansky's 2015 staging of *Sleeping Beauty* for American Ballet Theater using the Stepanov notation of the ballet, Ratmansky describes adjustments made by Sergeyev to the choreographic text of *Sleeping Beauty* when staging it in the West for ensembles smaller than the Imperial Ballet: "[The record of adjustments made] shows him to be a very capable and tactful editor, while the notations of the original text are proof of his complete understanding and command of the material." Alastair Macaulay, "Further Annals of *The Sleeping Beauty*: A Questionnaire," *Ballet Review* 43, no. 4 (Winter 2015–2016): 86. In addition, describing the sources he used to restage Petipa's *Harlequinade* at American Ballet Theater in 2018, Ratmansky has discussed the practical use of extant Stepanov notations for restaging ballets, what the notations reveal about ballet technique and pantomime, and how the notations can be utilized with additional sources to create a fuller picture of how a ballet was presented on stage. See Alexei Ratmansky, "Staging Petipa's *Harlequinade* at ABT," *Ballet Review* 47, nos. 1–2 (Spring–Summer 2019): 45–55.

[44] Wiley, "Dances from Russia," 94–103. See also Gorsky, *Two Essays on Stepanov Dance Notation*, xi–xii and xvi–xvii.

[45] These assertions are cited in Wiley, "Dances from Russia," 97–98.

[46] Fedor Lopukhov, *Khoreograficheskie otkrovennosti* [Candid Remarks About Choreography] (Moscow: Iskusstvo, 1972), 81–82, tr. in Wiley, "Dances from Russia," 98, and Ninette de Valois, *Come Dance with Me: A Memoir, 1898–1956* (London: Hamish Hamilton 1957), 110–112, cited in Wiley, "Dances from

More recently, Tim Scholl has described in greater detail the entrenched and multi-faceted rejection of Sergeyev that developed in Leningrad early in the Soviet period.[47] As did Wiley, Scholl drew from Mikhail Borisoglebsky's 1939 bicentennial study of the St. Petersburg Theater School, which contains a biography of Sergeyev.[48] Noting the "hostility" and "yellow journalism" present in Borisoglebsky's account, Scholl explains how the author attempts to discredit Sergeyev by documenting his "tyranny in the treatment of the company's dancers, his fawning to his superiors, his general stupidity and unsuitability for the position of regisseur of the ballet."[49] These ad hominem attacks against Sergeyev were surely political, for he was a ranking employee of the Imperial regime who left the country with written records of its prized ballet repertory. Borisoglebsky's description of Sergeyev stands in stark contrast to the admiring appraisal written by Vladimir Telyakovsky, director of the Imperial Theaters from 1901 to 1917:

> Nikolai Sergeyev, who replaced [Nikolai] Aïstov as *regisseur* in 1903, proved to be most suitable for this task. He was somewhat rough in his dealings with people, but was certainly a truthful and energetic man. He would argue impartially and equally with both artists and the Director. One had to yield to him quite often, as he always talked sense. He was not liked, but he was respected—more and more with the passing of time.[50]

The notations themselves, as Tim Scholl writes, "whenever discussed in Soviet dance writings, were reviled."[51] Why they were reviled is a complex matter, but one reason, as Scholl argues, is that

> from 1921, when he staged *Sleeping Beauty* in London for Diaghilev, until 1939, when the same ballet was restaged for the Sadler's Wells Ballet [...], Sergeyev staged a number of Russian ballets, from notations, in Europe and England: *Giselle*, *Coppélia*, *Nutcracker*, and *Swan Lake*. In other words, as Soviet productions began to diverge

Russia," 103n23. See also Karen Eliot, "Dancing the Canon in Wartime: Sergeyev, de Valois, and Inglesby and the Classics of British Ballet," in *Dance on Its Own Terms*, ed. Melanie Bales and Karen Eliot (New York: Oxford University Press, 2013), 13–42. Eliot discusses positive and negative assessments by Sergeyev's contemporaries of him and his abilities, but she ultimately uses negative terms to describe him, in language similar to that of de Valois (see note 64 in this chapter), as "a rather sad little man" (p. 27).

In addition to de Valois' recollections, other Western accounts of Sergeyev and his work warrant further examination. For example, Anton Dolin's assertion that Sergeyev, when staging *The Sleeping Princess* for Diaghilev, "took offense and withheld his services before the first performance" in response to "alterations in the traditional choreography" (recounted in Eliot, "Dancing the Canon in Wartime," 19), is proved false by Sergeyev's letters to his colleague Alexander Shervashidze, in which he shared both his satisfaction with the production and that he remained with the Ballets Russes until *The Sleeping Princess* closed early in 1922, after which Sergeyev and his wife, the dancer Evgenia Poplavskaya, went to Riga. See Wiley, "Dances from Russia," 99, citing Anton Dolin, *The Sleeping Ballerina* (London: Frederick Muller, 1966), 24, and Konaev, "My vse visim v vozdukhe...," 563–565. See also Macaulay, "Further Annals of *The Sleeping Beauty*, 86.

[47] Tim Scholl, *Sleeping Beauty: A Legend in Progress* (New Haven and London: Yale University Press, 2004), 49, 59–63.

[48] Scholl summarizes and quotes (in English translation) from Sergeyev's biography in Mikhail Borisoglebsky, *Proshloe baletnogo otdelenija peterburgskogo teatral'nogo uchilishcha, nyne Leningradskogo Gosudarstvennogo Khoregraficheskogo Uchilishcha. Materialy po istorii russkogo baleta* [The Past of the Ballet Division of the Petersburg Theater School, now the Leningrad State Choreographic School. Materials for the History of Russian Ballet], ed. Mikhail Borisoglebsky, 2 vols. (Leningrad, 1938–1939), vol. 2, 76–79.

[49] Scholl, *Sleeping Beauty*, 60.

[50] Vladimir Arkad'evich Telyakovskii, *Vospominaniya* [Memoirs] (Moscow and Leningrad, 1965), 156, tr. in V.A. Telyakovsky, "Memoirs: Part 2," tr. Nina Dimitrievitch, *Dance Research* 9, no. 1 (Spring 1991): 31–33; also qtd. by Wiley (in his own translation) in "Dances from Russia," 95–96.

[51] Scholl, *Sleeping Beauty*, 61.

from their Petipa stagings, and Sergeyev purported to stage these same works authentically in the theaters of the capitalist West, his work represented a very real threat to Soviet claims of the uniqueness and authenticity of their nineteenth-century ballet inheritance.[52]

Let us consider two comments that speak directly to Sergeyev's merit as a notator, both made by Borisoglebsky. First, he claimed that Chekrygin and Rakhmanov, Sergeyev's assistants, did most of the actual notating at the Imperial Ballet (a fabrication repeated as fact in Natalia Roslavleva's 1966 volume and given credence again in a 2013 study).[53] Second, said Borisoglebsky, the reason Sergeyev did so little of the notating himself was that he "understood almost nothing about the notation of dances."[54] The implication here is that, even though the notations were sound—because they were made by the two competent assistants—Sergeyev's understanding of them was dismal. And therefore, by extension, he was incapable of putting the notations to practical use in the West and staging the "true" Mariinsky versions of the ballets.

These two claims are easy to refute. First, simply stated, the large majority of notations held at Harvard are in Sergeyev's hand.[55] Konaev has suggested what seems to be the obvious reason for this: when Sergeyev left Russia, he took the notations he had access to, most of which were his own work.[56] While the Sergeyev Collection includes notations in other hands—mostly individual dances, some of which are filed with Sergeyev's notations of the same ballet; others are filed in "excerpts" folders—the majority of the work done by Sergeyev's assistants is presumed to be lost.[57] Wiley has identified two notation manuscripts in the collection that bear the signatures of Chekrygin and Rakhmanov.[58] Based on the scribal hands of these examples, we are able to identify the handful of notations discussed in this volume that appear not to be in Sergeyev's hand. The rest—aside from a few examples signed by students and others (filed in the "excerpts" folders) for which we have not identified the scribe—appear to be Sergeyev's work.[59] These range from finished copies (the notation of *La Bayadère*, mentioned above) to hasty sketches

---

[52] Ibid., 60–61. The Vic-Wells Ballet was renamed the Sadler's Wells Ballet and then the Royal Ballet.

[53] See Wiley, "Dances from Russia," 98. Roslavleva stated that Sergeyev "was given two assistants, A. Chekrygin and S. [sic] Rakhmanov, who carried out the actual notation of ballets." Natalia Roslavleva, *The Era of Russian Ballet* (London: Victor Gollancz, 1966), 172; see also 173, 197–198. In their recent work, Marion and Eliot have restated the allegations of some of Sergeyev's critics (as quoted by Wiley) as uncontested fact without mentioning Wiley's caveat that assessments of Sergeyev, particularly those made by Soviet writers, were often not impartial. See Marion with Eliot, "Recording the Imperial Ballet," 311–312, 334.

[54] Continues Borisoglebsky, he "merely 'philosophized,' and sprinkled his speech with incomprehensible terminology." And he asserts that Sergeyev had never been truly interested in dance notation in the first place, having taken it up to avoid conscription into the armed services. See Scholl, *Sleeping Beauty*, 60. As Wiley argues, this claim attributes to Sergeyev "a motive with connotations of particular asperity for Soviets when Borisoglebsky's study was published on the eve of World War II." Wiley, "Dances from Russia," 98–99.

[55] This can be verified by comparing the documents in question with notations and other documents made by Sergeyev after he left Russia. For example, his much-reduced version of the Kingdom of the Shades scene from *La Bayadère*, dated 1930 in Paris. See MS Thr 245 (106). This document is discussed in Chapter 9.

[56] Konaev, "My vse visim v vozdukhe…," 555.

[57] Ibid.

[58] Wiley, "Dances from Russia," 107n36. The signature "A. Ch.," likely Alexander Chekrygin, is found in the notation of Petipa's ballet *Halt of the Cavalry*, MS Thr 245 (12), page 45, and the signature "V. Rakhmanov" is found in the notation of dances from Verdi's opera *Aida*, MS Thr 245 (216), page 533.

[59] See Wiley, "Dances from Russia," 107n36. The three files of "Ballet excerpts," which contain notations of variations and excerpts from larger dances, are MS Thr 245 (227–229). The scribal hand for a number of excerpts in these files appears to us to be similar to Chekrygin's hand, but further investigation is required to make a determination. Regarding the examples signed by students, one can imagine that Sergeyev would chose to preserve well-wrought student notations of variations.

of ground plans with minimal annotations. Most of the surviving notations lie midway along this continuum: Sergeyev provided notated movements for legs and feet, plus direction of hips (movements and positions of the upper body are only sometimes documented), supplemented by ground plans and prose annotations.

Second, as for the idea that Sergeyev understood "practically nothing of dance notation": the extant Stepanov notation documents speak for themselves, revealing Sergeyev to have been an accomplished notator who possessed a thorough understanding of the Stepanov system. Eyewitness accounts of ballets that were documented by Sergeyev (such as those by dance writer and critic Akim Volynsky) describe dances that closely resemble those preserved in his notation manuscripts. That Sergeyev was engaged as a stager in the West for a period of nearly thirty years following his emigration also supports his competence as a transmitter of the information contained in the notations, although he was more than once described as lacking in creativity and dynamic personality. Reporting on the 1924 Paris Opéra revival of *Giselle*, André Shaikevich noted,

> Sergueyev, who was otherwise skilled in his work, was incapable of the smallest inspiration to the spirit. He succeeded in mounting the choreography with exactitude, as it was given in his note-books, but he knew no way of transmitting to the dancers even the slightest breath of enthusiasm.[60]

Bronislava Nijinska was also critical of Sergeyev's rehearsal methods during his time as *régisseur* in St. Petersburg, recalling,

> Neither the ballet master, [Nikolai] Legat, nor Sergeyev, demonstrated anything in the dances, nor did they correct the artistic interpretation. They watched only to see that there were no mistakes in the *pas* and that the *pas* came exactly on the musical beat.[61]

George Balanchine may have put it best when he said, "I don't think Sergeyev was incompetent, he was simply uninteresting."[62] Even de Valois, who found Sergeyev insensitive, inconsistent, and unmusical as a stager, and went so far as to say that he "went haywire when he was producing things," did concede that "he'd learned the notations, so he must have had the knowledge."[63] Her faith in Sergeyev's notations, despite her

[60] André Schaikevich, *Olga Spessivtseva, magicienne envoutée* (Librairie Les Lettres: Paris, 1954), [page number not given], tr. in Clement Crisp, "*Giselle* Revived: [D] An Eye-witness Account of the Production," *Dance Research* 13, no. 2 (Winter 1995): 57.

[61] Bronislava Nijinska, *Early Memoirs*, tr. and ed. Irina Nijinska and Jean Rawlinson (New York: Holt, Rinehart and Winston, 1981), 246. See also 311 and Lynn Garafola, *La Nijinska: Choreographer of the Modern* (New York: Oxford University Press, 2022), 2–3 and 83–84.

[62] Solomon Volkov, *Balanchine's Tchaikovsky*, tr. Antonina W. Bouis (New York: Simon and Schuster, 1985), 167.

[63] Genné, "Creating a Canon," 140. Regarding Sergeyev's musicality, Beth Genné summarizes and quotes de Valois's comments: "Often [Constant] Lambert and de Valois would work around the temperamental [Sergeyev], restoring cut passages during his lunch or tea breaks and changing the relationship of the music and choreography if it didn't seem to fit. 'He changed a lot of things, we know (from the notes), and if anything was "madly unmusical" I would discuss it with Constant and we would just change the beats.'" Fixing perceived problems of musicality were not the only changes made behind Sergeyev's back, according to Stanley Hall, a young dancer in the company, who later recalled that as *Sleeping Beauty* was being mounted in 1939, Frederick Ashton removed character steps when Sergeyev was out for lunch. Interview with Marian Smith, April 1994.

apparent reservations about Sergeyev himself (and belittling remarks in her memoir[64]), may explain the fact that she employed him for eight years, from 1931 to 1939, and as mentioned above made his stagings the foundation of the classical repertory of the Vic-Wells company (which later became the Royal Ballet).

Whatever Sergeyev's deficits as a stager, there can be no doubt of the importance of his achievements as a notator, his diligence in continuing the notation project at the Mariinsky that had been begun by Stepanov, and finally his guardianship of so many of the materials that had been created. As Konaev has recently written, Sergeyev "went down in history because under his supervision the ballet repertory of the Mariinsky Theater was recorded in the notation system of V[ladimir] I[vanovich] Stepanov and has been preserved as an archive."[65]

The Stepanov notations were made during the period that spans the end of Marius Petipa's career and the beginning of the transition to a younger generation of dancers and choreographers, many of whom went on to have influential careers in the West—in other words, a crucial time in the history of ballet. Sergeyev played an integral role in documenting and preserving this repertory. His notations provide us with a practical view of the nineteenth-century repertory of the St. Petersburg Imperial Ballet as it stood at the turn of the twentieth century.

Additional sources

Aside from the three types of manuscripts we have described above (*répétiteurs*, Justamant manuals, Stepanov notations), there exist an array of other vital sources that can enrich our knowledge of nineteenth-century ballet. These include musical scores (orchestra scores, short scores, piano reductions, and orchestra parts), production documents (stage plans, lists of props, etc.), drawings, memoirs, reviews, photographs, posters (*affiches*), and programs (leaflets—usually folded in half—listing production credits, casting, and names of dances and performers). Ballet librettos constitute another important source; they offer detailed recountings of the plot (in fifteen to thirty pages), though because they were generally completed before the start of the rehearsal period (during which the story was sometimes altered), they cannot be taken as impeccable guides to what actually transpired on stage.

Most of these valuable documents are held by libraries and museums. Others are in private collections. Some have been published. We will call on a host of these sources as we describe the five ballets we examine in this volume. We do not claim, however, that we have been able to examine every germane source; further pertinent documents certainly exist (though some, including those held by the Central Music Library of the Mariinsky Theater, are currently unavailable to most scholars) and surely more are waiting in archives and attics, yet to be discovered.

We must also admit that our study is focused on music, staging, and choreography; scenery and costumes fall outside the scope of our closest attentions. Further, we limit ourselves mainly (in the core chapters) to ballets produced at the Paris Opéra and the St. Petersburg Imperial Ballet, but without meaning to suggest that ballet everywhere

---

[64] De Valois' description begins with her observation that "Sergueeff was a strange little man." See de Valois, *Come Dance With Me*, 110–112.
[65] Konaev, "My vse visim v vozdukhe . . .," 555.

else—and opera houses across Europe as well as in popular-entertainment theaters—
had ceased to flourish or that the practices we describe in this book were limited strictly
to French and Russian ballets.

Finally, a few words about the term "French ballet," which we use extensively in this
book, usually to refer to the style of ballets created at the Paris Opéra. Such "French" ballets reflect the myriad influences of artists at that house who had learned or practiced
their craft elsewhere. These included the Austrian Fanny Elssler, the Italian Carlotta Grisi,
and the French-born child of Bolognese parents, Jean Coralli, who with his practical
knowledge of the Italian school (gotten in Milan and Vienna) and expertise gained at the
Théâtre de la Porte-Saint-Martin played a vital (and often unheralded) role in the success
of the Opéra's ballets during his tenure there as ballet master (1831–1850) and beyond.[66]

Some practical matters

Dance descriptions

The step vocabulary featured in the ballets under discussion primarily represents the
danse d'école—academic, or classical, dance taught and performed in the nineteenth century. Some of the choreography also features character dance and social dance (some
of it historic, like the gavotte), both of which were important genres within nineteenth-
century ballet.[67]

When providing accounts from Justamant's manuals, we often quote his terms for
ballet steps directly and, with few exceptions, do not attempt to translate those terms
using more modern vocabulary, calling to mind Sandra Noll Hammond's cautionary advice regarding analysis of nineteenth-century ballet choreography and identification of
steps: "Look for similarity of position or movement, not necessarily similarity of nomen-
clature, for ballet terminology can vary at different times and different locations."[68] That
is, rather than attempting to translate Justamant's terms for steps into more modern and
familiar language, we leave them as they are, with the caveat that their meaning may be
hard to know. The Stepanov method, on the other hand, employs a set of symbols to document choreography. Therefore, we use terminology to describe the movements, while
acknowledging that many familiar steps continue to be identified using a variety of terms.
Gail Grant's *Technical Manual and Dictionary of Classical Ballet* has been our main source
for terminology.[69] Sometimes, however, in the case of Stepanov notation, we simply describe the movement or provide the prose terms used in accompanying annotations.

[66] Coralli served as second ballet master from 1 May 1831 to 1837 and first ballet master from 1837 to 1
June 1850. Nicole Wild, *Dictionnaire des Théâtres Parisiens au XIXe Siècle* (Paris: Aux Amateurs de Livres,
1989), 315. His contract of 1837 styled him *maître de ballet en chef* (ballet master in chief). Vannina Olevesi,
"Entre discretion et quête de reconnaissance: Jean Coralli à l'Opéra, une ascension professionnelle au défi
de la standardization du ballet (1830–1854)," in *Giovanni Coralli, l'autore di Giselle*, ed. José Sasportes and
Patrizia Veroli (Canterano: Gioacchino Onorati editore, 2018), 135–136. On Coralli's tenure at the Théâtre de
la Porte-Saint-Martin, see Maria Zhiltsova, "Jean Coralli au Théâtre de la Porte-Saint-Martin (1825–1829)," in
Sasportes and Veroli, *Giovanni Coralli*, 105–122.
[67] See Lisa C. Arkin and Marian Smith, "National Dance in the Romantic Ballet." *Rethinking the Sylph: New
Perspectives on the Romantic Ballet* (Hanover, NH: University Press of New England, 1997): 11–68, 245–252.
[68] Hammond, "Dancing *La Sylphide* in 1832," 36. See also, Sandra Noll Hammond, "Steps Through Time:
Selected Dance Vocabulary of the Eighteenth and Nineteenth Centuries," *Dance Research* 10, no. 2 (1992):
93–108. According to Hammond, ballet masters had vocabularies of their own, and authors of treatises could
use varying terms for the same step.
[69] Gail Grant, *Technical Manual and Dictionary of Classical Ballet*, 3rd ed. (New York: Dover, 1982). We describe position of the arms according to the French school. See Grant, *Technical Manual*, 132.

Several terms require particular definition or explanation:

Arabesque: Most *arabesques* or *demi-arabesques* notated in the Stepanov method feature a raised leg that is bent forty-five degrees at the knee. Rather than identifying this position as *attitude allongée*, we refer to it as *arabesque*.

Bourrée: Although we generally avoid using a step name as a verb, we do employ the term *bourrée* as a verb—a shortened version of Grant's *pas de bourrée suivi* (Justamant refers to this movement as "a continuous *pas de bourrée*").[70]

Demi: We use the prefix *demi-* to refer to half-height of the leg, or forty-five degrees. (Ninety degrees is the maximum extension notated in the Stepanov method.) For example, *demi-emboîté devant* refers to an *emboîté* in which the leg is raised forty-five degrees to the front, whereas *emboîté devant* refers to an *emboîté* in which the leg is raised ninety degrees (or full height) to the front.

Demi-valse: This term refers to a two-part movement that begins with a *tombé* followed by a step on *demi-pointe* with the other foot (usually the back foot in fifth position). *Demi-valse* is usually performed multiple times in succession and employed as a traveling step. We will find that Petipa used *demi-valse* in any number of variants, particularly in dances that combine character and *danse d'école* step vocabulary. We thank Jean-Guillaume Bart for his suggestion of this term. Alexei Ratmansky has also shared with us that what we call *demi-valse* is a characteristic step in Russian dance called *pripadanie* (pl., *pripadaniya*).

Pointe: Justamant uses the phrase "sur l'orteil" to indicate dancing "on the toe," while *pointe* and *demi-pointe* are differentiated by two different notation symbols in the Stepanov method. In our step descriptions we will quote Justamant but use the terms *pointe* and *demi-pointe* when describing dances recorded in Stepanov. In the latter method, *pas de bourrée* is notated on both *demi-pointe* and *pointe*, though we do not always include the distinction in our descriptions.

Our step descriptions are not intended as guides for revival but rather to give the reader an idea of the step vocabulary of the period and the way enchaînements were put together. Some of our descriptions of enchaînements include connecting steps—such as *tombé, coupé, glissade, pas marché*—while others mention only primary steps.

Finally, please note that we have published previously a few of the observations made in this book. These are generally identified in the relevant chapters; see also the bibliography in this volume.

Notes on style

Russian dates before 1918 are given in Old Style, that is, twelve days behind the Western (Gregorian) calendar in the nineteenth century (through 1900) and thirteen days behind the Western calendar from 1901 through 1917. We have in most cases followed the Library of Congress system for transliteration of Cyrillic. Names are generally spelled as they appear in printed programs, although we have made an exception for French

[70] Grant, *Technical Manual*, 78.

names, usually preferring to provide the French spelling rather than the phonetic Russian spelling. We also have usually opted for French or English versions of ballet titles.

We have regularly adopted source abbreviations used by Wiley in his book *Tchaikovsky's Ballets*, including Rep (for *répétiteur*), CN (for choreographic notation), and PR (for piano reduction).

Acknowledgments

It is a pleasure to acknowledge the assistance to this project provided by the Center for Ballet and the Arts, directed by Jennifer Homans, in 2016. During our summer fellowship there, we laid out our plans and drafted the first chapters. We also thank Stephanie Schroedter, who in 2015 had jolted us into action by informing us of the full extent of the Justamant holdings at Wahn Castle.

As the book took shape, Kyle Davis, with skill and enthusiasm, assisted Doug in identifying notated steps in the Stepanov manuscripts and selecting the best terms to describe them. Lisa Arkin puzzled through and danced the Spanish steps as notated by Justamant. And the esteemed dancer and scholar, Sandra Noll Hammond, in the beautiful setting of her home in Dillon Beach, tapped into her vast knowledge of the history of ballet technique, demonstrated many steps for us, and helped put the Justamant notations into historical perspective.

Maria Babanina generously permitted us to use her piano transcriptions of the scores of *Paquita* and *Le Corsaire*. Andrew Foster answered endless questions about ballet personnel and casting in St. Petersburg and elsewhere around the turn of the twentieth century and through the Diaghilev era. Robert Puff expertly set the musical examples. Helena Kopchick Spencer provided information and inspiration of all sorts.

Many others freely provided support and expertise or generously shared copies of source material: Antonia Banducci, Jean-Guillaume Bart, Sergey Belenky, Marvin Carlson, Willa Collins, Germaine Curie, Edmund Fairfax, Olga Fedorchenko, Lynn Garafola, John Gray, Robert Greskovic, Rebecca Harris-Warrick, Laura Hormigón, Sergey Konaev, Peter Koppers, Emily Korzeniewski, Anne-Marie Lebas, Bruno Ligore, Alastair Macaulay, Carol Marsh, Nadine Meisner, Simon Morrison, Lars Payne, Sue Peabody, Jane Pritchard, Alexei Ratmansky, Holly Roberts, Andrea Salvatore, Carol Silverman, Madison and Debra Sowell, Roland John Wiley, and Natalia Zozulina. Thank you, all.

Lisa Arkin, Carol Marsh, Ornella di Tondo, Andrew Foster, Richard Greene, Peter Koppers, and Marina Harss read portions of the manuscript and offered helpful advice. The anonymous readers for OUP offered insightful comments that helped us improve the manuscript greatly. Linda Roppolo created a cover that delighted us. And we could not be more grateful to Norm Hirschy, who provided welcome encouragement from the very beginning.

We are also happy to acknowledge our debt of gratitude to the following archives and their hospitable staffs: the A.A. Bakhrushin State Central Theatre Museum, the Archives Nationales, the Bibliotheque-Musée de l'Opéra (especially Romain Feist), the Harvard Theatre Collection at Houghton Library (especially Irina Klyagin and Dale Stinchcomb), the Library of Congress, the National Library of Russia, the St. Petersburg State Theatre Library, the St. Petersburg State Museum of Theatre and Music (especially Alexandra Shtarkman and Oksana Sklyarova), the Theaterwissenschaftliche Sammlung der

Universität Köln, Schloß Wahn (especially Hedwig Müller and Charlene Fündgens), and the Victoria and Albert Museum (especially Jane Pritchard).

We also offer grateful thanks to those who provided translations and untanglements. Marc Vanscheewijck, with infinite patience and good humor, made sense of near-illegibilities in the Titus manuscript and phonetic spellings by Justamant. Géraldine Poizat-Newcomb translated Justamant's manual for *Le Corsaire* and made astute remarks about the characters therein. Anastasia Shmytova, Stephan Sveshnikov, and Kaleriya Maslyak gave us a much greater understanding of the Russian-language sources we have consulted not only through their translations but by their perceptive comments about the texts. (Transliteration of names and translation of much of the information found on posters and in printed programs in Russian is, for the most part, our own, as are translations from the French and Italian unless otherwise stipulated.) Graciously, Willa Collins provided her translation of the libretto for *Le Corsaire* (Paris, 1856) and Roland John Wiley his translations of the librettos of *Paquita* (St. Petersburg, 1847), *La Bayadère*, and *Raymonda*. These appear in the appendices.

Versions of Chapters 8 through 10 formed part of Doug's recent doctoral dissertation at the University of Washington, Seattle. We acknowledge the support of the University of Washington School of Music and the guidance of JoAnn Taricani, Doug's longtime mentor, and Anne Searcy, who chaired Doug's committee after JoAnn's passing.

Finally, we thank our families, especially Richard Greene and Carl Woideck, who have always supported our love for music and dance.

1

What Made Nineteenth-Century Ballet So Successful?

The five ballets under consideration in this volume—*Giselle*, *Paquita*, *Le Corsaire*, *La Bayadère*, and *Raymonda*—were created in France and Russia in the nineteenth century over the course of about sixty years. They are among the handful of works from that ballet-mad century to have lived on into the modern repertory, survivors from an era in which the *story* ballet reigned supreme and thrived in opera houses across Europe, many of them smaller than the capacious theaters in which ballet is often performed today, giving the audience a close look at the dancing, facial expressions, and interactions between characters.

We chose these five ballets in particular not only because of their ongoing importance in today's repertory but for the richness of the extant archival sources that document them, allowing us to assemble detailed descriptions of productions in Paris and Lyon, circa 1840–1870, and St. Petersburg, from 1842 (the year *Giselle* first came to Russia) through the early years of the twentieth century.

These five works represent the creative output of some of the best-known makers of nineteenth-century ballet—Adolphe Adam, Jules Perrot, Jean Coralli, Marius Petipa, Ludwig Minkus, and Alexander Glazunov—and some currently lesser known: Eduoard Deldevez and Joseph Mazilier, to name only two. In these ballets we find choreography that represents the French school, the Italian school (in St. Petersburg in the final decades of the century), and the combination of mime and dance in the *pas d'action*, which could be both intimate, as used by the Romantic-era choreographers, and grand in scale, as it was later developed by Petipa. And the scores exemplify evolving approaches to composing for ballet, including music that hewed closely to the action, music that set a mood, and music that provided continuity through the use of recurring melodies. Together these five ballets reveal a throughline that connected France and Russia for the whole of the century.

Before proceeding to the particular ballets that are the focus of this volume, let us first consider what in general made these ballets—and others like them—so successful. For story ballets were created in great numbers; they traveled widely; audiences flocked to them. Why?

We identify four reasons: their wide-open accessibility to the audience, their enticing settings in faraway places, the presence of appealing females in their casts (including charismatic star ballerinas), and the great variety of music, movement styles, and scene types that each ballet offered. Let us consider each of these in turn.

Accessibility

Making the story easy to follow. Ballet was not an esoteric art form aimed at the cognoscenti. It was meant to entertain and give pleasure to general audiences. And certainly

Five Ballets from Paris and St. Petersburg. Doug Fullington and Marian Smith, Oxford University Press.
© Oxford University Press 2024. DOI: 10.1093/oso/9780190944506.003.0002

its plots—even far-fetched ones—with their intrigues, strong situations, dilemmas, surprises, and resolutions, were meant to be readily followed.

Much of the comprehensibility of ballets' plots came from the convincing performances by the lead actors, who demonstrated their emotions in their dancing, delivered heartfelt monologues, and "spoke" to one another extensively in mime scenes that revealed their motivations. Too (as we were quite surprised to discover when we read the staging manuals and choreographic notations), characters occasionally addressed the audience directly—sometimes from downstage near the footlights—expressing their feelings, offering explanations, letting the audience in on a joke, commenting on the stage action. For example, Hilarion takes the audience into his confidence early in *Giselle* (Paris, 1841), tells them about his heartache, and points out the dwelling places of his beloved and his rival. In *Paquita* (Paris, 1846), right after the Spanish Governor Don Lopez de Mendoza agrees to give his sister's hand in marriage to Lucien d'Hervilly, he complains in an aside that "this is a political marriage that is involuntary." And in *Raymonda* (St. Petersburg, 1898), the antagonist Abderrakhman twice declares to the audience, "She must be mine," as he schemes to apprehend the French countess. Thus could ballet characters, like those in spoken drama and opera, frankly acknowledge the presence of the spectators and establish a direct connection with them.

Another tool that helped audiences follow the plot was the detailed printed libretto, which explained the action scene by scene and included some of the lines of "spoken" text that were mimed by the actors. These librettos (fifteen to thirty pages long) could be purchased by spectators, who could consult them during the performance. (Eight such librettos are reproduced, in English translation, in the appendices to this volume.)

And let us not forget that ballet composers played a role of great importance in helping the audience follow the action. It is a mistake to suppose that the main purpose of nineteenth-century ballet music was to supply attractive tunes for dancing, for ballet composers were dramatists, just as the choreographers and librettists were, and they deployed many techniques for telling the ballet's story through music. *Parlante* music, for example, provided an abstracted musical version of the human voice, as when the Queen in *Sleeping Beauty* (St. Petersburg, 1890) "speaks" kindly to her husband (in Act One, in a bassoon solo) on behalf of the knitting ladies, persuading him to grant them clemency. Borrowed songs were also used occasionally by ballet composers, because a familiar melody could bring its text or its general mood into the minds of the audience at a relevant moment. Case in point: Adolphe Adam's use (as we shall see) of the tune "Mes rêves de jeune fille" when Giselle unwittingly meets her rival. And recurring melodies signifying particular characters, situations, or ideas were used by ballet composers. They were sometimes developed and transformed to match the changing circumstances in which characters found themselves. One need only watch the *Star Wars* films to know that this technique is still alive and well.

Another possible aid to comprehensibility: In our examination of the Justamant manuals, we discerned (to our surprise) that stage left was associated with power and stage right with relative weakness. This, we are conjecturing, is a continuation of an older approach. In the eighteenth century, as the musicologist Antonia Banducci has shown, the stage could be gendered, with stage left as the more powerful, male side and stage right as the weaker, female side.[1] A rare 1748 prompt book for the opera *Tancrède* (Paris,

---

[1] Antonia Banducci, "Staging a *tragédie en musique*: A 1748 Promptbook of Campra's 'Tancrède,'" *Early Music* 21, no. 2 (May 1993): 180–190. The production in question was staged at a temporary theater at

1702) led her to this conclusion, for the male and female leads made nearly all of their entrances and exits from, respectively, stage left and stage right. (The "male" side was designated as such because the king's box was on that side of the house; the "female" side was on the side of the queen's box.) Tancrède makes all of his entrances and exits from King's side until he is rendered powerless by a magician in Act Four, who calls forth demons to torment him. Thereafter, the devitalized Tancrède exits Queen's side and continues in the final act to occupy the Queen's side, which symbolizes his continued weakness and predicts his ultimate downfall.[2]

Though the pervasiveness of the practice of assigning a higher symbolic weight to the King's side has been little studied, and it remains to be seen how long this practice endured, we shall see there are indications in Justamant's manuals that it was still alive to some degree in the French productions of *Giselle*, *Paquita*, and *Le Corsaire* that he documented.[3] This power-sidedness may be among the many features of ballet that helped make it accessible to audiences of the time (perhaps imparting a sort of order, even subconsciously) though the practice has by now fallen altogether from collective memory.

A mirror of the audience. Ballet characters, whether sultans, peasants, pirates, or bayadères, experienced many of the same emotions that the audience did and thus were easy for the audience to relate to. (The same was true too, of course, for characters in other types of stage drama.) No matter what the setting—from Saragossa to Switzerland, from the Himalayas to Krasnovodsk—ballet characters experienced the recognizable pleasures and challenges of love and family life. Giselle flirts with her boyfriend despite her mother's disapproval. The Silberhaus family celebrates Christmas in their parlor in *The Nutcracker* (St. Petersburg, 1892). Hamsatti becomes distraught when she discovers her fiancé loves another in *La Bayadère* (St. Petersburg, 1877). Raymonda anticipates with pleasure the homecoming party she has planned for her fiancé.

Social dancing. Characters on stage not only bore many of the traits of everyday people and engaged in behavior that audiences could relate to. They also performed *the same popular social dances* that members of the public did (though the theatrical versions were sometimes more elaborate and technically difficult, especially those choreographed for leading dancers). The esteemed social-dance master Henri Cellarius even lamented that social and theatrical dance were often confused for one another.[4]

Versailles. Note that the terms "King's side" and "Queen's side" were replaced after the revolution by (respectively) "Cour" (stage left) and "Jardin" (stage right). These new terms referred to the courtyard near stage left and the gardens near stage right at the Théâtre des Tuileries.

[2] As Banducci puts it, "He learns that he has mortally wounded his beloved Clorinda.... He attempts suicide, his soldiers restrain him, and the opera ends." Banducci, "Staging a *tragédie en musique*," 184.

[3] In Alexander Dean's classic textbook, *Fundamentals of Play Directing* (New York: Farrar & Rinehart, 1941), 132–134, Dean asserts that—contrary to what we are arguing here—stage right (the spectator's left) is stronger than stage left, in part because of our practice of reading from left to right (which he believes compels audiences at curtain-up to look automatically to the left). Marvin Carlson has written in a personal communication (21 March 2021) that "it seems to be a question of far less concern today than it was before the development of modern lighting, when normally the actors would mostly perform in a line across the stage just behind the footlights. The center position was clearly the strongest, but it would make a big difference after that whether the second actor came down right or left." He added, in answer to a query from Marian, that "perhaps the court side had a higher symbolic weight precisely because it was the court side [King's side], but I have no evidence of that." We believe that the evidence brought forth by Banducci, as well as the Justamant manuals we have examined, do provide such evidence. We thank Professor Carlson for his helpful answer to Marian's query.

[4] Henri Cellarius, *La danse des salons*, 2nd ed. (Paris: Chez l'auteur, 1849), 11.

The availability of sheet music to the public, which enabled them to play and dance to melodies they had heard in ballets, made onstage social dance all the more easy to relate to kinetically.[5]

What particular dances were favored? In Paris in the 1840s and beyond, the waltz, polka, mazurka, and galop were typical fare both on stage and in real-life ballrooms, salons, and commercial dance studios. Too, the quadrille stayed in the mix both onstage and off, though as Cellarius averred in 1847, it had taken third place to the new and wildly popular waltz and polka in the real-life ballroom. (He also pointed out disapprovingly that quadrille dancers at parties had abandoned the once-required *entrechats* and *ronds de jambe*, choosing instead to walk their way through the figures, "dancing absolutely as if they were crossing a promenade or a sidewalk."[6])

Similarities between ballroom and theater include these: Props—a handkerchief, a scarf, flowers—could be used in both settings, bringing into social dance, in some instances, a sense of character and drama (as when a cavalier gives a flower to a lady he wants to dance with).[7] Figures used in the ballroom for group dances were used in the theater, too—examples include the *moulinet* and *ronds* (circles) (found both in Antoine Titus's instructions for *Giselle* and Cellarius's discussions of figures recommended for social-dance parties).[8] Also, in St. Petersburg, the polonaise, the stately procession that frequently opened the ball, was sometimes performed in ballets by groups as they came onstage—the children before their mazurka in *Paquita* and the fairy-tale characters as they open the last act of *Sleeping Beauty*, for example. (George Balanchine recalls the polonaise in his *Theme and Variations* and *Diamonds*.) The mazurka, a staple of the Russian ballroom, was also frequently included in Marius Petipa's ballets, in part because he had at his disposal the great Felix Kshesinsky, known as the "King of the Mazurka," whose fiery performances of this dance could bring the house down.[9]

Further, one must note a basic similarity between the sets of music for onstage divertissements and the sets of music for ballroom dances: both consisted of a series of dance pieces of various types, the last often a rousing galop (a lively $\frac{2}{4}$, sometimes with a prominent back-beat).[10] In the ballroom, the crowd frequently danced the galop step to this fast, spirited closing music. But on the stage, even if the galop step was not danced, the galop music, familiar from the ballroom, signaled to the audience that this was the finale. The custom of the closing galop on stage remained in place until the end of the century.[11]

---

[5] See Maribeth Clark, *Understanding French Grand Opera through Dance* (PhD diss., University of Pennsylvania, 1998), 180–226.

[6] Cellarius, *La danse des salons*, 24. See also Chapter 4, note 16.

[7] Ibid., 131 ff.

[8] Titus *répétiteur* for *Giselle*, 62–63 (see Chapter 2, note 79) and Cellarius, *La danse des salons* 128–130, 138–140. Because we do not have Titus's choreographic notebook, we cannot tell how similar the *moulinet* figure on stage was to the one described by Cellarius. Both were likely rotating wheels.

[9] For example: "The benefit artist Mr. Kshesinsky danced with Miss [Vera] Lyadova the mazurka *Souvenir de Varsovie* with such animation that the auditorium, electrified, demanded an encore and showered the dancers with deafening applause." *Savernaya pchela*, 23 April 1860, 362, qtd. in Wiley, *Lev Ivanov*, 27. The Kshesinsky family excelled as mazurka dancers. As Wiley points out, in the Act Two mazurka in *Swan Lake*, "Felix Kshesinsky, 'the king of the mazurka,' appeared as partner to his daughter Julia, and with his son [Iosif] dancing among the additional couples." Wiley, *Lev Ivanov*, 175.

[10] Exceptions include the final waltz in *The Nutcracker* and in the divertissement in *La Bayadère* Act Two, Scene III.

[11] Examples of closing galops may be found in: the codas of the *pas de deux* and final mazurka in *Sleeping Beauty* Act Three, the *Raymonda* finale, the harvest festival in *Giselle*, the coda of what we know as the Black Swan *pas de deux* in *Swan Lake*, the finale of Drigo's *Harlequinade* (St. Petersburg, 1900), the finales of Delibes' *Coppélia* (Paris, 1870) and *Sylvia* (Paris, 1876), the *Pas de Gulnare* in *Le Corsaire* (Paris, 1856), and the finale of Delibes' *Le pas des fleurs* in *Le Corsaire* (Paris, 1867). Many more examples of galop finales may be found in the music of dance divertissements composed for French Grand opera.

Another echo of the real ballroom in staged divertissements was the entertainment intermittently performed by expert dance soloists and ensembles as the merrymakers took a break from their own dancing to watch appreciatively from the sidelines. (The dance selections might consist of character dances, ballet, social dance.) This practice duplicated in broad outline the customs of the ballroom, making for a familiar display that required no leap of imagination to accept. (Today, the danced scene with onlookers may seem like a cliché—and such scenes have been known to bore or evince giggles from the corps members who help comprise the onstage audience—but they are based on a onetime real-life ballroom custom.)

Enticing settings

Nearly all of ballets during the period in question were set in appealing faraway locales (far away from Paris and St. Petersburg, that is). Thus could ballet-goers take an imaginary trip to a foreign land simply by going to the theater, satisfying a seemingly insatiable appetite for foreign culture (no matter how inauthentically presented) that was also catered to by the numerous travelogues and illustrated newspapers that were being published at the time.

Racism. Let us be clear, though, that the ballets under discussion in this volume reflect the values of two powerful nineteenth-century institutions, the Paris Opéra and the Imperial Theaters, and the royal crowns that governed them. Therefore, it is not surprising to find that Others and Elsewhere are seen through the lens of imperialist superiority: faraway and exotic places are viewed with a certain fascination and curiosity, but at the same time, characters who are non-white and non-Christian are subject to suspicion. Specifically, in the ballets we explore, Black people, Jewish men, Muslims, Romani people, and Hindu religious in India are presented as inferior or even evil. (Notably, however, one of the female leads, Medora in *Le Corsaire*, is Jewish, and she is depicted sympathetically.) And the instructions for the seemingly humorous abuse of Isaac Lanquedem in *Le Corsaire* in Justamant's manual surely stand as one of the most detailed extant accounts of how antisemitism was enacted on the nineteenth-century stage.

In the course of our discussions of the five ballets in this book, we take note of pejorative terms used in librettos, production plans, choreographic notations, and staging manuals. In the case of the term "Saracen" (used to refer to a Middle-Eastern Muslim), we restrict our use to quotations from the original sources. In other cases we relegate the offensive terms to footnotes or quote a nineteenth-century offensive term once before reverting to a word that we believe to be more respectful (for instance, "Jew" for the Russian "zhid" and "Roma" for "Gypsy").

Women

It is no secret that many in the audience were drawn to ballet by the presence therein of good-looking female dancers. But what—aside from her looks—made the female dancer appeal to the audience?

The leading ballerina. Let us consider first the leading ballerina, who in all five of the ballets in this study—and most nineteenth-century ballets in general—carried on her shoulders the responsibility for the ballet's overall success. For no matter how capable her leading man and the other players, it was the ballerina who was usually given the most extensive miming and dancing role in the ballet and whose charismatic and forceful character was placed at the center of the action. She therefore drew the lion's share of attention from the spectators, who after all were following the plot of a story. (And because the character was always put in some sort of predicament, she usually garnered their sympathy as well.)

Moreover, the ballet masters who created these works tailored their choreography to the talents and strengths of the lead ballerina, so the role was closely identified with her and her alone. She was expected to appear in every performance of the ballet that was given at that opera house, or nearly so. (Later, with the introduction of multiple casting, this close association faded somewhat.) Understudies were rare: when Carlotta Grisi injured her foot during a performance of *Le Diable à quatre* in February 1846, the ballet was taken out of the repertory for a few weeks until she recovered. And no understudy was assigned to either of the two lead roles in *Le Corsaire*, which had been debuted by Carolina Rosati and Domenico Segarelli, who appeared in all sixty-three of the ballet's performances in its initial run from 1856 to 1858. They were appearing in other ballets at the same time, too—a typical circumstance.[12] Their departure from the Opéra in 1858 ended the run, and the ballet left the repertory for nine years until the young Adèle Grantzow, deemed worthy of the role, was hired to play Medora in 1867.

It is easier to understand the powerful effect of these lead ballerinas when one realizes how high-spirited, how full of life were the characters they played. As the manuscripts make clear, all of the five female leads discussed in the present volume are strong, brave, and resourceful. With the exception of Raymonda, whose personality is less distinctive and whose role was built around the technical (rather than dramatic) prowess of its first interpreter, these lead characters were also feisty, goal-oriented, assertive, and—in the cases of Giselle, Paquita, and Medora—even clever and witty.[13] We found this surprising, because such characteristics (to put it mildly) are not always emphasized in modern-day performance. But the appeal of these admirable and compelling characters, coupled with the fact that they were played by ballerinas with star power, makes all the more understandable their popularity with audiences.

Another ballerina. Often a second and even sometimes a third high-ranking ballerina was included in the cast, ensuring more star power, variety, and interest. She might appear briefly as a soloist in a divertissement, like Nathalie Fitzjames in the Peasant *pas de deux* in *Giselle* or Lubov Radina, who came onstage for a captivating few minutes to perform the Hindu dance in *La Bayadère*. Or she could play a role as an important character: Myrtha in *Giselle*, Gulnare in *Le Corsaire*, Hamsatti in *La Bayadère*, Henriette or Clémence in *Raymonda*.

Women in travesty. Another attraction (for awhile) in French ballet, according to backstage and insider accounts, was the presence of curvy-figured women (with

---

[12] Willa Collins points out that these two were performing not only in *Le Corsaire* in those two years, but that "the Opéra featured Rosati in *Jovita* (1855); Segarelli with Amalia Ferraris in *Les Elfes* (1856); Rosati, Ferraris, and Segarelli in Auber's ballet *Marco Spada* (1857); and in 1858, the Opéra revived *La Somnambule ou L'arrivée d'un nouveau seigneur* (1827), featuring Rosati in the principal role of Thérèse." Willa Collins, *Adolphe Adam's Ballet* Le Corsaire *at the Paris Opéra, 1856–1868: A Source Study* (PhD diss., Cornell University, 2008), 150.

[13] In keeping with the standards of the day, of course, they did all aspire to marry, and some of their resourcefulness was dedicated to the attainment of that aspiration. (Giselle died because of her unrequited love and—like other ballet heroines in ballets outside the scope of this study—willingly relinquished her lover to a woman of his own social class.)

"voluptuous chests and thighs") dressed as male pages.[14] Though we cannot know for sure if all of the women playing pages were voluptuous, a good many travesty pages did appear at the Opéra in the 1830s and 1840s, including four in the first act of *Giselle*.[15] And after the sensational success at the Opéra in 1845 of the visiting children's troupe of Petites Danseuses Viennoises, some of the Opéra's new ballets imitated the Viennoises' practice of dressing half of a female (adult) ensemble as males.[16] For instance, in *Paquita*, twenty women performed in the aforementioned Spanish *Pas des manteaux*, ten of them in male costume "brandishing voluminous red cloaks with which they enveloped themselves and their partners."[17] Six young females in travesty also appeared as cabin boys in *Betty* (Paris, 1846) and six in the Paris production of *Le Corsaire* as "young eunuchs."[18]

By the 1880s female travesty dancers were appearing regularly in the corps de ballet at the Opéra and in a few ballets even played the male lead (in *Coppélia*, 1870; *Gretna-Green*, 1873; and *Les Deux pigeons*, 1886)[19]. In Parisian music-hall ballet (as Sarah Gutsche-Miller has shown), females in travesty were typically featured in the leading

---

[14] Robert Quinault, tr. from the unpublished memoir *La danse en France sous la Troisième République* in Sarah Gutsche-Miller, *Parisian Music-Hall Ballet 1870–1913* (Rochester, NY: University of Rochester Press, 2015), 191.

[15] To be specific: there were four travesty pages in *Le Diable boiteux* (1836), eighteen in *La Chatte métamorphosée en femme* (1837), and seven in *La Jolie fille de Gand* (1842). See Marian Smith, "The Disappearing Danseur," *Cambridge Opera Journal* 19, no. 1 (2007): 52–53. It was Louis Gentil (writing as "une Habilleuse") who pointed out that Duponchel hired "women of a certain air, a certain form who make one cry out, 'Ah! She over there will make a fine page!' Do not believe that the slender, casual form of a young girl would satisfy our requirements. On the contrary, we prefer pronounced forms protruding under the pants of white or sky blue silk that show them to advantage in opposition to all the principles of theatrical illusion. We want to force the spectators to recognize with the first glance and without any help from their opera glasses that the woman is nothing but a woman dressed as a little boy." Tr. in Maribeth Clark, "Bodies at the Opéra: Art and the Hermaphrodite in the Dance Criticism of Théophile Gautier," in *Critics Reading Critics: Opera and Ballet Criticism in France from the Revolution to 1848*, ed. Roger Parker and Mary Ann Smart (New York: Oxford University Press, 2001), 245.

Gentil's substantive and gossipy insider account of life at the Opéra has been published with extensive annotations by Jean-Louis Tamvaco (and an introduction by Ivor Guest) as *Les cancans de l'opéra: Chroniques de L'Académie Royale de Musique et du théâtre, à Paris sous les deux Restaurations: Première édition critique intégrale du manuscrit Les cancans de l'opéra, ou, Le journal d'une habilleuse, de 1836 à 1848*, vol. 2 (Paris: CNRS Editions, 2000). For a review, see Marian Smith, "Backstage at the Paris Opéra in the 1830s," *Dance Chronicle* 27, no. 3 (2004): 427–431.

Note that the custom of having curvy-figured women as pages had not yet taken hold in 1830, when the pages in the ballet *Manon Lescaut* (created that year) were played by males. But Robert Quinault, a *premier danseur* of the Opéra Comique, much later in the century, wrote in an unpublished memoir that the female travesty dancer of his acquaintance was of "uncertain technique, but with voluptuous chests and thighs, and [. . .] immensely pleasing to the *abonnés* of the orchestra stalls. Male dancers became nothing more than mere accessories, supporting here, supporting there, but almost never dancing." See note 14 in this chapter.

[16] On the Danseuses Viennoises, see Ivor Guest, *The Romantic Ballet in Paris*, 2nd ed. (London: Dance Books, 1980), 238–242. Note further that Fanny and Thérèse Elssler often performed *pas de deux* together, with Thérèse (the taller of the two) in travesty. On another sister act, Elena and Elizabetta Menzeli, see Ann Barzel, "Elizabetta Menzeli," *Dance Chronicle* 19, no. 3 (1996): 278.

[17] This description is Guest's in *Romantic Ballet in Paris*, 2nd ed., 253. The dance is titled *Pas des manteaux* in the Justamant staging manual for this ballet. (The term is not used in the Paris libretto of 1846.) The critic for *La France musicale*, 5 April 1846, stated outright that the "gypsy festival" was "inspired by the ensembles danced last year by the Danseuses Viennoises." Tr. in Cyril W. Beaumont, *Complete Book of Ballets* (Garden City, NY: Garden City Publishing, 1941), 188. Note, further, that the eight hussards in the ball scene of the second act of *Paquita* (according to the Paris libretto of 1846) were performed by women.

[18] *Betty* libretto (Paris: Mme Ve Jonas, 1836); *Le Corsaire* libretto, see Appendix E (i).

[19] Gutsche-Miller, *Parisian Music-Hall Ballet*, 191 and 328n49. As she points out, this custom continued past 1900: two early twentieth-century ballets at the Opéra, *Bacchus* (1902) and *La ronde des saisons* (1905), featured a woman in travesty as the male lead. At the same time, these works included roles for many men. See also Sarah Gutsche-Miller, "Liberated Women and Travesty Fetishes: Conflicting Representations of Gender in Parisian Fin-de-Siècle Music-Hall Ballet," *Dance Research* 35, no. 2 (2017): 187–208.

male role, as well as in all-female ensemble dances with half the group in travesty.[20] (This custom stood from the early 1870s until the First World War.)

In St. Petersburg, following what Mazilier had done in Paris, Frédéric (Pierre Frédéric Malavergne) and Petipa, in their version of *Paquita* in 1847, included a *Pas des manteaux* featuring an all-female cast, half in travesty. The *Danse des Corsaires* in *Le Corsaire* was also a travesty-couples dance in St. Petersburg until 1899; the *Panadéros* in Petipa's *Raymonda* was similarly cast.[21] Male-to-female performers also appeared from time to time in St. Petersburg, as (for instance) the mothers in *Giselle* and *La Fille mal gardée* and Mère Gigogne in *The Nutcracker*.[22]

Women of the corps de ballet. The appearance of numerous corps de ballet women, dressed becomingly, posing in groups, and performing prop dances, certainly enhanced the attractions of ballet. We shall mention only one particular such alluring scene type, drawing from an important study by Helena Kopchick Spencer.[23] Here, we are calling it the "females-at-play" scene. Many such displays of femininity took place in a natural setting or a garden. And if the action were set in the Middle East, the corps de ballet women were likely to be odalisques, like the ones in *Le Corsaire*, who are gathered in beguiling groups at curtain-up of Scene III until one of their number says, "Let's dance for pleasure!" whereupon two of them perform solos for their female companions' (and the audience's) delectation.[24]

Female corps de ballet characters in these scenes were frequently associated with water—they might bathe in it, swim in it, live in it, or at least find themselves in close proximity to a lake or pond or a burbling fountain. For instance, in the opening scene of *Sylvia* (Paris, 1876), Diana "seats herself on a bough and swings slightly over the water" as some of her nymphs recline on the greensward and others bathe in the stream, none of them realizing that the shepherd Aminta is watching them.[25] In *The Pharaoh's Daughter* (St. Petersburg, 1862), Aspicia descends peacefully to the bottom of the Nile, where Father Nile places her in the charge of naiads, who later partake with undines in a grand underwater *ballabile*.[26] In *The Little Humpbacked Horse* (St. Petersburg, 1864),

---

[20] Gutsche-Miller, *Parisian Music-Hall Ballet*, 185–186.

[21] *Raymonda* libretto, see Appendix G (i). The choreographic notation of the *Pas des manteaux* in the St. Petersburg *Paquita* calls for "12 women and 12 cavaliers in men's costumes." MS Thr 245 (28). The notation of the *Panadéros* in *Raymonda* also indicates that women performed the male roles in that dance. MS Thr 245 (67).

[22] Enrico Cecchetti performed Mother Simone in *La Fille mal gardée* in 1894 and Berthe in *Giselle*. The original Mère Gigogne in *The Nutcracker* was Nikolai Yakovlev. Diaghilev's *Giselle* of 1910 featured Nicholas Kremnev, husband of Lydia Sokolova, as Berthe.

[23] See Helena Kopchick Spencer, *The jardin des femmes as Scenic Convention in French Opera and Ballet* (PhD diss., University of Oregon, 2014), 348–352 and *passim*. Spencer points out that many female ensemble scenes, taking place in garden settings, are to be found in nineteenth-century French opera and ballet. She notes five types of gardens: private gardens of the queen or other noblewomen, aristocratic pleasure gardens, seraglio gardens, magic/fairy gardens, and demonic/haunted gardens.

[24] This according to Justamant. In the Paris libretto, they emerge from the baths in the gardens of the Pasha's palace to braid their long hair, sport among themselves, adorn themselves with flowers and pearls as they gaze into mirrors, or (dressed in peignoirs) choose from the selection of gowns that are presented to them. See Appendix E (i). But see Chapter 6, note 93, in which we point out that Justamant noted that they did not have either a pool or a fountain. Similarly, in Petipa's *Le Roi Candaule*, before "a bathing pool of pink and white marble, adorned with a fountain and surrounded with flowers," Nisia is attended by female slaves, who dress her hair and remove her jewels. Beaumont, *Complete Book*, 403.

[25] *Sylvia, ou La nymphe de Diane*, libretto summarized in Beaumont, *Complete Book*, 491.

[26] In the ballabile, various rivers—Guadalquivir, Thames, Rhine, Hong Ho (Huang Ho, or Yellow River), Neva, and Tiber—"flow in and perform character dances of the countries through which they run." *The Pharoah's Daughter* libretto, tr. in Wiley, *Century*, 229.

the Tsar-Maiden emerges from the ocean on a dolphin-shaped seashell as a lead-in to the *grand ballabile* with her court of rusalkas.[27] And *Le Roi Candaule* (St. Petersburg, 1868) features a bathing-pool scene, in which Nisia is attended by female slaves who dress her hair and "take up a series of attitudes" to the music of harps.[28]

Another conceit was to feature the female corps (although not necessarily frolicking) in a dream, as in the Kingdom of the Shades scene of *La Bayadère*, in which Solor dreams he is surrounded by the ghosts of maidens who have descended from the Himalayas. Similarly, women and girls appear in Raymonda's dream, surrounding Jean de Brienne and his knights; naiads swirl around Prince Désiré in the vision scene of *Sleeping Beauty*, Act Two.

The music for such scenes was often feminine in instrumentation (matching the gender of the cast and the alluring femininity of the subject matter), featuring flutes, high strings, harps, and, in the case of the Waltz of the Snowflakes in *The Nutcracker*, a chorus of high voices. A telling exception to this rule comes when the Wilis in *Giselle* reveal the cruel side of their personalities after first appearing to be sweet, attractive, and harmless ghosts. Trombones give voice to their loud satanic laughter, replacing the *pianissimo* strings and woodwinds that had begun the scene and quickly dispelling the sweetly gentle mood.

The Wilis were not the only corps de ballet characters to gang up cruelly on a hapless solo man, though surely they were the most murderous; the harem women in *Le Corsaire*, for instance, bully the Eunuch in a comic scene.

Variety: Four movement styles

Surely one of the greatest virtues of nineteenth-century ballet was that it offered the spectator tremendous variety within the two or three hours the ballet took to perform. Let us start with the simple fact that it called for four distinct movement styles—classical (or academic) dance, character dance, social dance, and mime—and used each of them extensively.[29] Of course, these categories could overlap. But whether mixed with another style or executed on its own, each mode of movement carried its own dramatic weight, meaning, and visual appeal. And taken together they gave the audience an enticing variety that was considered a *sine qua non* of ballet—a variety that, when removed, can flatten a nineteenth-century ballet's narrative and visual interest and quickly exhaust its movement and step vocabulary, particularly if the revival in question limits its performers to classical dance alone.

Let us now consider each of these movement styles in turn.

Classical (or academic) dance. In the 1830s and 1840s in Paris, classical dance was characterized by balances, adagios and poses, and buoyant and seemingly effortless jumps and leaps, and made up of a vast step vocabulary that entailed both *terre à terre* (in

---

[27] *The Little Humpbacked Horse* libretto, tr. in Wiley, *Century*, 245–246.

[28] *Le Roi Candaule*, libretto summarized in Beaumont, *Complete Book*, 403.

[29] Sometimes, social dance is included under the umbrella of character dance, as is rustic dance, dances by older characters, novelty dances like the hoop dance in *The Nutcracker* (Dance of the Buffoons, see note 90, later in this chapter), and dances that show a character's occupation (soldiers, sailors, bakers). In this book, however, we use the term "character dance" mostly as a synonym for "national dance."

which the feet scarcely leave the ground) and *petit allegro* (calling for quick footwork and small jumps) enchaînements.[30]

Dancers underwent rigorous training and were increasingly expected, unlike their forebears, to combine virtuosic technique with grace, leaving behind the old system wherein dancers essentially specialized in one or the other.[31] As Sandra Noll Hammond has pointed out, this new blending of great technique and elegance was the goal of a dancer's training not only in Paris, but also in Milan at La Scala, in the classes of Carlo Blasis, and in Naples at the ballet school of the Teatro San Carlo, which was directed by Salvatore Taglioni.[32]

What exactly did the dancers do in class? According to Giovanni Léopold Adice, their regimen was an arduous one. A dancer and then instructor at the Opéra (from the early 1840s until 1867), Adice left a written record—some of it unpublished—that has been carefully examined by Hammond. She reports that barre work alone, according to Adice's recollection, could include

> 128 *grands battements*, 96 *petits battements* (analogous to today's *battements tendus*), 64 slow *battements sur le cou de pied* and 120 rapid ones, as well as some 256 *ronds de jambes* of various kinds and speeds.[33]

Many of these exercises were repeated in the center floor, away from the barre, before the dancers executed

> lengthy series of set combinations designed to develop "aplomb," the ability to sustain movements of balance in a variety of poses. The combinations would progress into turning variations and finally light springs could be added, always keeping the classical ballet forms as established in the slower exercises. Following these were lengthy combinations of many different kinds of *pirouettes*. Finally, the class concluded with the "*tems terre à terre*," quick small steps woven into *enchaînements* (combinations) performed in different directions, and then the "*tems de vigeur*," the jumps which could be embellished with multiple beats, *ronds de jambe*, and turns.[34]

Given this rigorous training, dancers could perform *petit allegro* passages with great velocity in those days—for instance, "pas de bouré dessus-dessous en face, du pied droit en enchainant, pas de bouré dessous et briser croiser en avant, fermer précipiter entrechat quatre, et trois echapés sur les orteils," all rendered by Carlotta de Vecchi within

[30] The information in the following paragraphs is from Hammond, "Dancing *La Sylphide*," as well as Sandra Noll Hammond, "Dances Related to Theatrical Dance Traditions," in Aldrich, Hammond, and Russell, *The Extraordinary Dance Book*, 31–50.

[31] The three categories of noble, demi-character, and comique (and the sometimes-used fourth category, the grotesque) were of particular importance at the Paris Opéra in the eighteenth century. See Hammond, "Dancing *La Sylphide*," 33.

[32] Carlo Blasis (1795–1878), was an Italian dancer, teacher, choreographer, dance theorist, and author of *The Code of Terpsichore*. Salvatore Taglioni, an Italian dancer who studied in France, and the brother of Filippo Taglioni, established a ballet school at the Teatro San Carlo in Naples in 1812.

[33] Hammond, "Dancing *La Sylphide*," 34.

[34] Ibid. See also Sandra Noll Hammond, "Ballet's Technical Heritage: The *Grammaire* of Léopold Adice," *Dance Research* 13 (Summer 1995): 33–58; Léopold Adice, *Théorie de la gymnastique de la danse théâtrale* (Paris: Chais, 1859), 74–75; and Adice, *Histoire et théorie de la danse Théâtrale*, 6-vol. manuscript (unpublished), 1873, Bibliothèque Nationale de France, Bibliothèque-Musée de l'Opéra, RES-1184 (1–6).

about six seconds according to Justamant's staging manual for *Giselle*.[35] (Today, the jumps in such passages are often bigger, the *pliés* between steps deeper, and the sheer number of steps therefore reduced.) Time travelers whisked back to the age of *Giselle*, however, if impressed by the speed of the *petit allegro*, would also surely notice that dancers' leg extensions rarely went higher than hip level, a practice that remained intact throughout the century (and is beautifully depicted in the works of Edgar Degas from the 1870s and 1880s).[36] Indeed, higher extensions in classical dance, though sometimes executed in performance, were frowned upon well into the *twentieth* century; the 1922 guide to the Cecchetti method declared that

> on no account should the foot be raised higher than at right angles to the hip, for then the exercise tends to become an essay in acrobatics, which is opposed to the laws of the dance.[37]

These "laws"—though the book is not specific about what they are—may be best understood as a set of guidelines intended to help dancers express the classic aesthetic on which ballet was based. This makes sense when one recalls that nineteenth-century ballet found particular inspiration in the statues of antiquity that emphasized balance, symmetry, clarity. Therefore, the downstage diagonal trajectory—whether broadly traversing the stage or in a narrower zigzag—is the most frequently used ground plan in the sources we have consulted because it was clearly felt to show the body, executing appropriate poses and movements, to its best three-dimensional advantage.

These same values led choreographers to ensure that most enchaînements are repeated one or more times; this created symmetry and balance, important features of the

---

[35] Original spelling. De Vecchi performed this combination in two measures, repeated it to the other side, and then repeated it again to each side. Justamant staging manual for *Giselle*, Deutsches Tanzarchiv Köln, Item Number 52915, 75, "Variation de Giselle (celle de Mlle Carlotta [de Vecchi])." See Hammond, "Dancing *La Sylphide*," 40–41. Hammond points out that, when restaging a ballet passage with enchaînements calling for more steps than seemingly can be fit into the allotted music, one solution is to reduce the size of the movements. Another is to nearly eliminate or reduce the size of the *plié* customarily done in preparing for, or landing from, small *allegro* steps. This latter strategy might at first seem surprising, but "[t]his did not mean that the legs were stiff or that they were straight all the time. For example, the 'commencement' of a step usually involved some bend of the supporting leg before the weight was taken onto the other leg or onto both legs, either by means of a rise or a spring. If the spring involved higher jumping movement, then the landing would usually require some give or bend of the knees. However, the knees should quickly straighten, the 'few exceptions' being when another spring or jump was to immediately follow. Recalling her training, Marie Taglioni stated that springing must come from the heels, without any movement from the body, and the knees involved very little. Therefore, she said, one did not jump very high in these steps, but such '*élan*' gave her a delightful sense of vibrating in the air just above the ground." Hammond, "Dancing *La Sylphide*," 41. For the passage on Marie Taglioni, Hammond refers to "La leçon de Marie Taglioni," cited in Léandre Vaillat, *La Taglioni ou la vie d'une danseuse* (Paris: Albin Michel, 1942), 76.

In the same vein, Knud Arne Jürgensen, in a comparison of Bournonville's step phrases to those of Hans Beck, executed to the same music, found that "Bournonville had a step for almost every musical beat; Beck had fewer steps spread over many beats." (August Bournonville served both as a dancer and ballet master for the Danish Ballet during the years 1830 to 1877, and he continued to work there off and on even after his retirement. Hans Beck was ballet master of the Danish Ballet from 1894 to 1915.) Hammond, "Dancing *La Sylphide*," 45, referring to Patricia McAndrew, "Bournonville, August," in *International Encyclopedia of Dance*, vol. 1, 512.

[36] Hammond, "Dancing *La Sylphide*," 39. See also "In the Dance Classroom with Edgar Degas: Historical Perspectives on Ballet Technique," in *Imaging Dance: Visual Representations of Dancers and Dancing*, ed. Barbara Sparti, Judy Van Zile, Elsie Ivancich Dunin, Nancy Heller, and Adrienne L. Kaeppler (Hildensheim: Georg Ohms, 2011), 123–146.

[37] Cyril W. Beaumont and Stanislas Idzikowski, *A Manual of the Theory & Practice of Classical Theatrical Dancing (Méthode Cecchetti)*, 2nd ed. (London: C.W. Beaumont, 1932; New York: Dover, 1975), 42, qtd. in Hammond, "Dancing *La Sylphide*," 39.

geometry of any given dance, whether a solo variation or group dance. A soloist may travel down the diagonal from upstage right, then move upstage left to travel down the opposite diagonal, thus creating symmetry and balance in the use of the space. An ensemble may assemble in multiple rows to create a block formation and then reassemble into a circle or into balanced lines at either side of the stage.

Note, further, that the frequent repetition of enchaînements imbues them with a rhetorical significance, emphasizing the particular features of a given step or sequence of steps. It also allows the viewer the opportunity to see a set of movements enough times to let it register in the mind and thus better perceive the balance that is being created over time. These principles of repetition, symmetry, and balance are fundamental to the choreography we will encounter in our study.

Character dance. "Her shoulders spoke; she glided like a swan … and in every way resembled a real Russian maiden."[38] This description by an observer of Fanny Elssler reminds us of the subtlety and perceived authenticity of character dance, as well as its high standing, for it was performed not just by the corps de ballet and the occasional "foreign" entertainers who appeared for a one-off (like the "Arabians" who entertain Clara in the Land of Sweets in *The Nutcracker*), but in many cases by lead characters who were often moved to dance in the style of their own native place or that of an honored guest—for instance, Raymonda dances a *czardas* at her wedding.[39] Other such character dances, or "national" dances include the mazurka, bolero, styrien, cachucha, sicilienne, anglaise, allemande, jig, tarantella, and so on.[40]

Character dance, aside from being pleasurable and intriguing to watch, served other purposes, too. It could help establish the geographic and historical setting of a ballet. It could show the social status or ethnicity of a ballet's characters, from the corps de ballet to the principal dancers. It could "build the dramatic excitement of the ballet" as Mikhail Baryshnikov has pointed out.[41] It could introduce contrast to classical dance not only with its costumes, step vocabulary, and body postures, but at a deeper structural level as well. The bacchanalian Hindu dance in *La Bayadère*, to name one instance, established symmetry as the counterpart to the relative serenity of the Kingdom of the Shades scene, thus expressing the fundamental conflict of the ballet's plot.

How were character dances created for the ballet stage? And to what extent were they truly derived from folk or popular dances observed in nontheatrical settings? Certainly, many professional ballet dancers and ballet masters did make a point of watching, and learning from, specialist dancers from outside the ballet world. Carlo Blasis, in *The Code of Terpsichore*, admonishes dancers to study the "characteristic steps, … attitudes, and movements" of various national dancers and instructs ballet masters to "remark the customs and manners peculiar to different countries, even to their particular features, and whatever other mark of distinction is remarkable between them."[42] These "marks of distinction" were then distilled to a certain repertory of steps, poses, and gestures that were

---

[38] *Moskovskiye vedomosti* (no date given), tr. in Guest, *Fanny Elssler*, 245. The performance was given on 12 January 1851 (Guest gives the New Style date as 24 January 1851).

[39] Raymonda's court seems to be in Provence, but the locale of her wedding is undisclosed—all we know is that it takes place at Jean de Brienne's castle in the Alps. Hungarian dance is performed in honor of King Andrei II.

[40] See Arkin and Smith, "National Dance in the Romantic Ballet."

[41] Alan Jones, "Character Dance Returns with Panache," *New York Times*, 19 June 1983, Section H, 20.

[42] Carlo Blasis, *The Code of Terpsichore* (London: James Bulcock, 1828; New York: Dance Horizons, 1976), 91–92 and 180, qtd. in Arkin and Smith, "National Dance in the Romantic Ballet," 36–37.

deployed when a character dance was created and performed on the ballet stage. But these dances were *theatricalized* versions of folk dance, drawing inspiration from dances in the "field" when possible but not intended as ethnographically exact reproductions of them.

The character dancer and teacher Alexander Shiryaev, along with his colleagues Andrei Lopukhov and Alexander Bocharov, codified character dance as it was performed on the Russian stage at the end of the nineteenth century and into the early twentieth century.[43] Shiryaev describes the process in his memoirs and also editorializes about the merit of Marius Petipa and Lev Ivanov's contributions to character dance.[44]

As for character costume: designers devoted careful effort down to the smallest detail to make them look "authentic." Critics delightedly described character costumes in their reviews; lithographers depicted star dancers wearing them. In some cases, the famous soloists of the period furnished their own, having had them tailor made in the place from which the dances derived.[45]

Further, composers wrote "national" music—meant to sound Spanish, or Indian, or whatever was required—to furnish the all-important sonic complement to the costumes and choreography. They usually achieved this effect by mixing in a few signifying touches, like bolero rhythms for Spanish scenes, oboes for Indian scenes (imitating the sound of the *shehnai*), and so forth.[46] The idea was not to reproduce music faithful to the locale or the nationality of the character being depicted on stage, but, rather, to create a theatrical effect using conventional musical markers that audiences understood.

(A reminder: in this book, we use the term "character dance" as a synonym for "national dance." Note that the latter term was often used in the nineteenth century.)

Social dance. (See discussion earlier in this chapter.)

Mime. Mime and action scenes figured prominently in nineteenth-century ballets. And when one considers that Parisian audiences in the 1820s could enjoy silent, mimed versions of witty and loaded dialogues in Molière's *Monsieur de Pourceaugnac*, one can imagine that they could also be engaged by mime scenes in story ballets at the Opéra in the succeeding years.[47] But because so many mime scenes have been downplayed or eliminated in latter-day revivals, audiences today rarely expect ballet performers (whose primary training is in dance) to excel as mimes, as actors.[48]

Nineteenth-century audiences, though, did expect excellent acting and miming, and we are given a beguiling glimpse into what they saw by eyewitness descriptions. For

---

[43] See A[ndrei] Lopukhov, V[asilievich], A[lexander] V[iktorovich] Shiryaev, and A[lexander] I[lyich] Bocharov, *Osnovy kharakternogo tantsa* [The Fundamentals of Character Dance] (Leningrad: Iskusstvo, 1939), published in English as *Character Dance*, tr. Joan Lawson (London: Dance Books, 1986). Citations will refer to the English translation.

[44] See Birgit Beumers, Victor Bocharov, and David Robinson, *Alexander Shiryaev: Master of Movement* (Pordenone: Le Giornate del Cinema Muto, 2009), 109–110, 121–123.

[45] Marie Taglioni had a mazurka costume made for herself in Krakow. Vaillat, *La Taglioni*, 394–94, 398.

[46] On the portrayal in European performing arts of people and places considered "exotic," see Ralph Locke, *Musical Exoticism: Images and Reflections* (Cambridge: Cambridge University Press, 2009) and *Music and the Exotic from the Renaissance to Mozart* (Cambridge: Cambridge University Press, 2015).

[47] Jean Coralli, as *maître de ballet* at the Théâtre de la Porte-Saint-Martin, was the creator of a ballet version (which apparently succeeded mightily) of Molière's farcical comédie-ballet. Zhiltsova, "Jean Coralli au Théâtre de la Porte-Saint-Martin," 108–110.

[48] Note that French ballet librettos of the nineteenth century customarily list the players as *acteurs*; Russian librettos of the nineteenth century list characters under the heading *dramatis personae* (or "characters").

instance, Carlotta Grisi's performance in the "dramatic and violent scenes" of *La Jolie fille de Gand* (Paris, 1842) is described by Théophile Gautier:

> Her demure shock at the sight of all the orgies and quarrels, her keen sensitivity, her energetic reaction in the duel scene, her horror, depicted with such realism and pathos, at her father's curse, left nothing to be desired.[49]

And here is Virginia Zucchi in her St. Petersburg debut in *An Extraordinary Journey to the Moon*, according to Konstantin Skalkovsky's account in 1885:

> Her entire figure was elegant; her head, with its whimsically tousled hair, vivified by the eyes which took on, when necessary, an astonishing, passionate expression; for all that her mime was not of the eyes alone, but of the entire body.[50]

Other highly regarded mimes include Timofei Stukolkin, St. Petersburg's first Don Quixote and Dr. Coppelius, and the original Drosselmeier,[51] and Pavel Gerdt, *premier danseur* and the original Abderrakhman in *Raymonda*.

Good miming was compelling in itself. But of course the verbal substance of mime scenes was also vital to the telling of a ballet's story. That is why the mime texts were written down, often with scrupulous care, both in staging manuals and, to a lesser extent, choreographic notations. From mime scripts, we can confirm that characters held substantive conversations, engaged in monologues (some of them quite lengthy), uttered asides, and sometimes recollected events or narrated tales that held onstage listeners rapt, as when Berthe in *Giselle* tells the story of the Wilis to the frightened village girls; when Paquita narrates the tale of the Governor's perfidy to a crowd of ball-goers; when in *Le Corsaire* Medora recounts the ordeal of her kidnapping to Conrad, exposing the traitorous Birbanto; when in *Raymonda* the Countess Sybille, Raymonda's aunt, tells her courtiers the history of the White Lady, patroness of the House of Doris; when in *La Bayadère* the jealous Brahmin reports a conversation (on which he had eavesdropped) to the Rajah in a "lively" narrative.[52] Such mimed storytelling scenes, vital to the plot, called for a star turn from the actor, and could be a high point in a ballet.[53]

How exactly particular words and concepts were mimed is hard to discern. In the syntax of the mime texts (as rendered in the choreographic notations and Antoine Titus's

---

[49] *La Presse*, 2 July 1842, tr. in Théophile Gautier, *Gautier on Dance*, ed. and tr. Ivor Guest (London: Dance Books, 1986), 111.

[50] Konstantin Apollonovich Skalkovsky, in *V teatral'nom mire* [In the Theatre World] (St. Petersburg, 1899), tr. in Roland John Wiley, *A Century of Russian Ballet* (New York: Oxford University Press, 1990), 319. Zucchi danced this ballet at the Sans Souci in St. Petersburg in 1885. See also Jennifer Homans, *Apollo's Angels: A History of Ballet* (New York: Random House, 2010), 273.

[51] See Wiley's translations from *Recollections of T. A. Stukolkin, Artist of the Imperial Theatres* (1895) in Wiley, *Century*, 107–134.

[52] *La Bayadère* libretto. See Appendix F (i).

[53] Gautier's description of such a plot-turning mime scene, in *La Tarentule*, is compelling: "All of a sudden Laurette reappears, pale, trembling, scared, and in a state of terrified agitation. Everyone crowds around her, asking the reason for her despair. 'Luigi has just been bitten by a tarantula.' [. . .] At this point the miming of Mlle Elssler attained the very height of sublime tragedy. With terrifying exactitude she conveyed the progress of the bite and the nature of the patient's dance as it grows increasingly convulsive. The most detailed account, loudly declaimed, could not have been clearer than the 'speech' she delivered in gestures." *La Presse*, 1 July 1839, tr. in Gautier, *Gautier on Dance*, 71.

Giselle répétiteur), at least, one can see the order in which the gestures—whatever they were—were meant to be deployed. For example:

> *Giselle*, Titus *répétiteur*:
>
> > *Hilarion to Giselle*: I told you that he's a Prince, a great lord.
> > But he is my fiancé, says Bathilde.
> > *Giselle*: Your fiancé, yours?
> > Yes, mine.[54]

> *Swan Lake*, choreographic notation:
>
> > *Siegfried*: Who are you here?
> > *Odette*: I am here, a swan queen.
> > *Siegfried*: I bow to you, but why are you a swan?
> > *Odette*: Look there. It is a lake. My mother cried and cried.[55]

We lack hard information about particular gestures used, for the tantalizing accounts given by nineteenth-century newspaper writers tended to focus more on the actor's effectiveness rather than particular gestures. Occasional exceptions to this rule, like this derogatory description of Mazilier's portrayal of Stenio in *La Gipsy* (Paris, 1839) do give us specifics:

> You may have noticed the expressions [...] Stenio SAYS, etc. Well, Stenio, instead of SAYING, rotates his two arms like a windmill in a frightening manner, and then he socks the first Bohemian in the eye. Literal translation: "I have strong arms."
> Then he caresses the backs of his legs in a friendly manner, as if he feels an itch; he [...] pinches his waist, he rubs his chin, he lightly curls his forelock [...] Translation: "I am young."
> Then he draws his sword, if he has one, and frightens two or three small children posted near the wings. [...] Translation: "I am courageous."
> Then he strikes a haughty pose in the manner of Caesar [...]. Translation: "Would you like me to join you?"
> The thirty or forty Bohemians first stamp their left feet, holding their right feet in the air, [...] then they stamp the right feet, holding their left feet in the air [...] they roll their eyes in a scary manner—ah, these strapping blades! They gesticulate with an extraordinary vehemence, and they throw their forearms as though they wanted to unhitch the painted canvas that furnishes them a cloudless sky. Translation: "But who are you? Who are you?"[56]

In general, the evidence of the manuscripts and eyewitness accounts—skimpy though it is when it comes to specific gestures—suggests an acting style similar to that of early silent film: a mix of codified gestures with freer, naturalistic movements.[57]

---

[54] Titus *répétiteur* for *Giselle*, 77.

[55] *Swan Lake* choreographic notation, MS Thr 186 (11), 52, Harvard Theatre Collection, Houghton Library, Harvard University.

[56] *La France musicale*, 3 February 1839. See also Marian Smith, *Ballet and Opera in the Age of Giselle* (Princeton, NJ: Princeton University Press, 2000), Ch. 4: "Ballet-Pantomime and Silent Language," 97–123.

[57] As Sarah Gutsche-Miller has pointed out, three types of gestures and movements used in theatrical dance were identified by Berthe Bernay, a choreographer at the Olympia in Paris in the second half of the nineteenth

Codified gestures. Today's vocabulary of codified gestures is an inheritance from the past that has been handed down, generation to generation, for an unspecified period of time. (Does it hearken back to the era of the Ballet Russe de Monte Carlo? of Diaghilev's Ballets Russes? of the Imperial Ballet? of Jules Perrot? of August Bournonville? of *commedia dell'arte* in the eighteenth century or earlier? to Italy? It is hard to trace.[58])

As we seek to understand the world of nineteenth-century ballet, we may well ask if the standardized gestures generally used today are the same as the gestures used then. But answers are not easy to find. In the simple line drawings of Justamant manuals, at least, one may find a few gestures that tend to crop up from ballet to ballet in action scenes—and thus seem to be standardized—including these common-sense gestures: the cupping of the ear while leaning (or stepping) in one direction to indicate "listening," the placement of hands by a man on a woman's waist to indicate serious amorous intentions, and a firm stance with arms crossed in front of the chest, elbows up, to indicate what we might term "fierce defiance." The "fierce defiance" gesture may also be seen in at least one photograph from the late nineteenth century in Russia—Marie Petipa, photographed as Medora in *Le Corsaire*, deploys it—and it apparently could exert an extremely powerful effect on the defiant character's interlocutors. (Of this, more will be said later.)

Freer, naturalistic movements. Of course, ballet acting required much more than a series of standard poses and gestures, and the drawings in the Justamant manuals and the prose descriptions in the Stepanov notations show—not surprisingly—that a good deal of action happened, taking the characters all over the stage. For instance, as Justamant tells us, Hilarion approaches Giselle angrily after watching her flirt with Albert; Hilarion crosses from midstage center to downstage right, saying, "and me, who loves you, you reject me, oh! I will get my vengeance" and raising his arms menacingly. Giselle, afraid, crouches down quickly. Soon thereafter, she rises back up and "with a fierce look" stands

century, and the author of *La danse au théâtre* (Paris: E. Dentu, 1890). Gutsche-Miller writes that Bernay "described three types of pantomime, which she termed 'natural,' 'artificial,' and 'conventional.' According to Bernay, natural pantomime is that which comes naturally to actors from their own feelings; artificial pantomime has specific rules and must be learned; and conventional pantomime consists of natural gestures that have become stock gestures through repetition in the theater." Gutsche-Miller, *Parisian Music-Hall Ballet*, 314n8.

[58] The dance historian and critic Giannandrea Poesio writes that early twentieth-century publications about mime were inspired by Italian dancers like Virginia Zucchi, Pierina Legnani, and Enrico Cecchetti, who had "joined foreign companies and theatres in Europe" at the end of the nineteenth century, popularizing "balletic mime." Giannandrea Poesio, *The Language of Gesture in Italian Dance from Commedia Dell'arte to Blasis* (PhD diss., University of Surrey, 1993), 274.

Such early twentieth-century publications on mime include, according to Poesio, Mark Edward Perugini's series in *The Dancing Times* in 1914 "on the language of gesture as part of the ballet tradition" (Poesio, 274, citation not given), a later book by Perugini's wife, Irene Mawer, *The Art of Mime* (London, Methuen, 1932), and Gertrude Pickersgill, *Practical Miming* (London: Pitman,1936). Later books include Joan Lawson, *Mime, the Theory and Practice of Expressive Gestures* (London: Pitman, 1957; New York: Dance Horizons, 1963); Kathrine Sorley Walker, *Eyes on Mime: Language Without Speech* (New York: John Day, 1969); and Beryl Morina, *Mime in Ballet* (Winchester Hants, UK: Woodstock Winchester Press, 2000). See also the film *Mime Matters*, directed by Ross MacGibbon (London: Landseer Films Production for Royal Academy of Dance, 2002).

Informative nineteenth-century publications about mime include Frances A. Shaw, *The Art of Oratory: System of Delsarte, from the French of M. L'abbé Delomosne* (Albany: Edgar S. Werner, 1882); Henry Davenport Northrop, *Delsarte Manual of Oratory: Containing the Choicest Recitations and Readings [...]* (Cincinnati: W.H. Ferguson, 1895); and Andrea De Jorio, *La Mimica Degli Antichi Investigata Nel Gestire Napoletano* (Napoli: Del Forno, 1832), tr. in Andrea De Jorio and Adam Kendon, *Gesture in Naples and Gesture in Classical Antiquity: A Translation of La Mimica Degli Antichi Investigata Nel Gestire Napoletano, Gestural Expression of the Ancients in the Light of Neapolitan Gesturing* (Bloomington: Indiana University Press, 2000).

See Poesio's discussion of mime treatises and his extensive bibliography thereof (and plates from selected treatises) in Poesio, *Language of Gesture*, 304–312. See also Dene Barnett, *The Art of Gesture: The Practices and Principles of 18th Century Acting* (Heidelberg: C. Winter, 1987).

firmly, looking Hilarion directly in the face. Then, crossing her arms in front of her (in the fierce defiance pose), she walks toward him, forcing him to retreat all the way from the right wing to the left wing, downstage. (Meanwhile, Loys looks on, amused.)[59]

In *La Bayadère*'s final act, the wedding of Solor and Hamsatti, the choreographic notations similarly show that the performers were actively moving about the stage as the drama required, not rooted in place nor restricted to standardized poses. They tell us the shade of the bayadère Nikia "roughly pushes through Hamsatti and Solor," then "runs away behind the curtain." Later, Nikia re-enters and again "roughly pushes apart Solor and Hamsatti." Hamsatti is next described as "running up to Solor" and "embracing Solor," who is "holding the waist of the bayadère [Nikia]." "[L]etting go of the bayadère," Solor is next "embracing Hamsatti." For a third time, Nikia is "roughly pushing apart Solor and Hamsatti" before she exits the stage.[60]

Photographs from the Petersburg *Paquita* also convey a strong sense of movement, even though they are posed still shots. One series of photographs from the second scene of the ballet—in which Paquita foils Inigo's plot to kill Lucien—is notable for the characters' strong and mobile facial expressions (showing worry, bravado, and amorousness as needed), and the off-balance, vigorous positions they are in, demonstrating that they are not at rest, but ready to spring into action (until the end of the scene, when Inigo has fallen asleep untidily in a chair, the victim of a sleeping potion).[61]

More variety

Aside from the four movement types described above, ballets also offered audiences a great variety of scene types, character types, and moods. Indeed, ballet, like opera, was nothing if not a variety show. A single ballet, for instance, could feature intimate conversations between lovers, angry confrontations between foes, large public celebrations, seriousness, comedy (perhaps even some slapstick), violence, prop dances, solos, and all manner of small-ensemble dancing, special stage effects, spectacle, and characters old, young, and in between. Let us consider a few of the various elements the audience was likely to encounter in ballet.

Humor. The subject matter of many ballets was serious. But ballets could be funny, too, sometimes featuring broad physical comedy of the sort that was carried on in American vaudeville, for example, in the early twentieth century and remains alive today in some quarters.

Consider this scene from *Le Diable à quatre* (Paris, 1845), a rollicking body-switching comedy about class difference: Mazourka, a dance-loving Polish peasant who finds herself in the body of a haughty Countess, botches her lesson with an elegant dance-master. Before the lesson even starts, she gives him a hard tap on the shoulder and says, "I'm ready," surprising the onlookers with her informality. Then, after watching with keen interest as he holds his violin and bow and performs an adagio combination (lifting his leg to the right *à*

---

[59] Justamant, *Giselle*, 23–25.

[60] *La Bayadère* choreographic notation, MS Thr 245 (105), 130–134.

[61] This series of photographs, dated circa 1900, features Marie Petipa as Paquita, Sergei Legat as Lucien, and Alexei Bulgakov as Inigo. Copies are preserved at the St. Petersburg State Museum of Theatre and Music and include GIK 3062/854, 3074/118, 3074/637, 3074/638, 3074/639, and 3837/46. These images are also available online at https://goskatalog.ru/.

la seconde, switching to *arabesque allongée*, and then putting his then right foot down *à la quatrième devant*), she loses patience and bursts out into a rustic mazurka instead.[62]

Another such broadly comic scene, this one from *Les Mohicans* (Paris, 1837), is described by Jules Janin thus (note that Georges Élie, who played the role of Jonathas, later played Inigo in *Paquita*):

> In the second Act, Jonathas is going to be eaten by the Mohicans; not only eaten but cooked, cooked and eaten. "The unfortunate Jonathas, trembling in all his limbs, cries, begs . . . shows the savages his arms, meager and thin, his long legs, his skinny body."[63] [. . .] In the end [. . .] the savages understand that Jonathas would be too tough to cook. They will not eat Jonathas, and Jonathas performs a comic dance with an old savage.[64]

Comic parody could play a role in ballet, too, including a send-up of the *Giselle* mad scene in *Les Tribulations d'une ballerine*. Here, a ballerina and her troupe traveling between cities are halted by bandits.[65] The ballerina offers to give a performance instead of money, and the bandits watch attentively as she enacts the mad scene from *Giselle*. Instead of running toward her mother in the scene, though, "Giselle" runs toward one of the bandits, Forza, a tippler with a big red nose. Later, as she de-petals the daisy, the bandits surround her, moved to tears. Forza pulls out his handkerchief but then quickly hides it and wipes his tears away on his coat sleeve instead.

Several light comedic ballets of the Russian school feature fops who attempt to woo the heroine (to the satisfaction of her parents) and keep her from marrying her true love. In *Don Quixote* (Moscow, 1869) the foolish nobleman Gamache attempts to win Kitri's hand, while in *The Magic Flute* (St. Petersburg, 1893) it is the gout-ridden Marquis who declares his love for Lise, and in *Harlequinade* (St. Petersburg, 1900) the rich old man Léandre is Cassandre's choice of groom for his daughter Columbine.

Even ballets that were not full-out comedies from start to finish could feature scenes with humor, ranging from mild to slapstick. Here are a few examples:

> In *Ondine* (London, 1843), Beppo asks his fellow fishermen if they, too, had seen Ondine on the half-shell, floating toward the shore. He re-enacts the scene in which she did so, himself striking the pose she had taken when she made her first appearance. The fishermen smile amongst each other at the sight.[66]
> In *Paquita*, the villain Inigo poisons the wine of Lucien, the hero. Paquita, in a scene around the dinner table with both hero and villain, manages to communicate to Lucien the danger of drinking his wine, distract Inigo by dropping a stack of plates on the floor, switch the men's goblets, and—while performing a table-side Spanish dance with Inigo at his behest—try to convey to the lovesick and oblivious Lucien how many assassins are on their way and the hour of their arrival.[67]

---

[62] See Justamant's staging manual for *Le Diable à quatre*, TWS Inventory Number 70-443.

[63] Here, Janin is quoting from the libretto: Guerra, *Les Mohicans* (Paris: Imprimerie de L.B. Thomassin et Comp., 1837).

[64] *Le Journal des débats*, 10 July 1837, qtd. in John V. Chapman, "Jules Janin: Romantic Critic," in *Rethinking the Sylph: New Perspectives on the Romantic Ballet*, ed. Lynn Garafola (Hanover, NH: University Press of New England, 1997), 227.

[65] See Justamant's staging manual for *Les Tribulations d'une ballérine*, TWS Inventory Number 70-487.

[66] This is summarized from Justamant's staging manual for *Ondine*, TWS Inventory Number 70-471.

[67] Summarized from the Paris 1846 *Paquita* libretto (see Appendix D (i)) and Justamant's staging manual for *Paquita*, TWS Inventory Number 70-479.

In *Giselle*, the gamekeepers, a congenial, rustic group, arrive in the woods at night, a few at a time, to set up camp. They greet each other and drink convivially. Their merry mood (despite Hilarion's repeated warnings) does not fully dissipate until the clock strikes midnight. The rustics fearfully count the strikes on their fingers then move from one side of the stage to the other in a frightened clump as will o' the wisps menace them. Finally, they run away, pell mell.[68]

In *Le Diable amoureux* (Paris, 1840), Urielle performs a tarantella for the Vizir (who is seated on a rug on the floor). She plays the tambourine so close to his face that he reels backward.[69]

In *La Bayadère*, which is not a funny ballet at all, the *Manu* dance is somewhat humorous: two mischievous young girls try to tease a drink of milk from a woman preoccupied with balancing a jug on her head.[70]

In *Raymonda*, which like *La Bayadère* features very little in the way of comedy, after Countess Sybille chides the young courtiers for their idleness and play, they make her dance with them until (in a mildly humorous moment) she falls exhausted in a chair.[71]

Violence (or threat of violence), comic and otherwise. Some comic scenes were (in the manner of *The Three Stooges*) far from gentle. In *Harlequinade*, for example, Pierrette mocks and laughs at Pierrot and finally gives him a smack after he complains that she is giving too much attention to her mistress Columbine and not enough to him.[72] And here are some scenes that entailed the ridiculing of a man by a group of women, who sometimes become physically aggressive:

In *Les Nymphes amazones* (Brussels, 1864), a comic character named Boufonio admires a group of Amazon women. They dance with him, telling him that he can choose one of them. He chooses Zalia and tries to take her by the waist, but she rejects him. Going down the line of women, he is rebuffed by all of them, one by one (in what is perhaps a comic reference to the cruel treatment of Hilarion by the Wilis). The last woman pushes him into the middle of their circle. Laughingly, they alternately expand and tighten the circle around him, pinching and beating him. In response, he crouches and contorts himself. Then, they force him into dancing with them. Suddenly Boufonio is let go, and he runs away in a grotesque fashion, as fast as he can. Now, Francesco (the handsome young male lead) emerges from another hiding place and laughs at the scene that has just transpired.[73]

In *Le Corsaire*, when the Eunuch appears (at the back of the stage) at a gathering of the odalisques, the sight of him makes the women laugh. He comes downstage very slowly and "with an impassive face." Gulnare sneaks behind him and taps on his right shoulder. He turns to his right, and Gulnare turns behind him so that he cannot see her. She then taps him on his left shoulder and slips away as a group of

---

[68] Summarized from Justamant, *Giselle*, 133.

[69] Summarized from Justamant's staging manual for *Le Diable amoureux*, TWS Inventory Number 70-453. This tarantella takes place in Act Three in the bazaar scene.

[70] Summarized from the choreographic notation of *La Bayadère*.

[71] Summarized from the choreographic notation of *Raymonda*, MS Thr 245 (67).

[72] Summarized from the scenario included in the printed piano reduction. Riccardo Drigo, *Les Millions d'Arlequin* (Leipzig: Jul. Heinz. Zimmermann, 1901), 16.

[73] Summarized from Justamant's staging manual for *Les Nymphes amazones*, TWS Inventory Number 70-469.

odalisques comes running up to him. They surround him, entreating, pinching, mocking, and caressing him. He puts up as much of a struggle as he can.[74]
A blindfolded Galifron, Prince Désiré's tutor in *Sleeping Beauty*, encounters churlish female aristocratic coquetry in a game of Blind Man's Buff. (They slap him, hit him with a riding stick, tickle his face with their muffs, and so on.)[75]

In some cases, if the threatened victim is a woman, she shows her mettle and can be violent herself.[76] The Countess in *Le Diable à quatre*, for instance, gives Mazourki a slap; then, after he hits her with a switch, she grabs it and breaks it into pieces.[77] And in *Le Corsaire*, the pirates pull Medora's hair when they are attempting to kidnap her. She ends up stabbing Birbanto, who then drags her by the hand.[78]

Non-comic violence (or threats thereof) could also figure in ballet plots, as in *Giselle*, wherein the title character threatens to kill herself with a sword.[79] Inigo, in the 1881 St. Petersburg version of *Paquita*, is stabbed to death by the assassins he had hired, who mistake him for the intended victim. In *Le Corsaire*, Conrad strikes Lanquedem on the head before stealing away with Medora, and armed pirates attack the guards. In *La Bayadère*, Nikia, wielding a dagger, rushes toward her rival Hamsatti. In *Raymonda's* dream, Abderrakhman threatens her with a dagger and pulls her by her neck. Ultimately, he is slain in a duel with Jean de Brienne. And there is, of course, the gently doleful aftermath of the battle scene in *The Nutcracker* which finds the wounded bandaged and placed on stretchers in the Silberhaus' parlor after mice have devoured the gingerbread soldiers.[80]

The presence of children; large cast size. Children were quite often featured in nineteenth-century ballets, a practice not habitually followed in today's productions of the same ballets, with the notable exception of *The Nutcracker*.[81] (Even *La Sylphide* in its original form in 1832 featured girl sylphides who inhabited the Scottish woods along with their older counterparts.) In France in the 1840s and 1850s, children tended to appear in ensemble scenes along with adults—as villagers, cabin boys, "petits esclaves" (little slaves), and so forth.[82] Many of these children's roles were likely non-dancing

---

[74] Summarized from Justamant's staging manual for *Le Corsaire*, TWS Inventory Number 70-441.

[75] Summarized from the libretto, tr. in Wiley, *Tchaikovsky's Ballets*, 178–179.

[76] The haughty and unsympathetic (and violence-prone) Countess in *Le Diable à quatre* is an exception to the rule: unprovoked, she breaks the violin of a humble musician (who, as it turns out, has magic powers).

[77] Justamant staging manual for *Le Diable à quatre*, TWS Inventory Number 70 443.

[78] Choreographic notation of *Le Corsaire*, MS Thr 245 (1).

[79] See pp. 90 and 102.

[80] Wiley, *Tchaikovsky's Ballets*, 373, and Wiley, *Lev Ivanov*, 244.

[81] One may imagine, further, that onstage appearances made for excellent on-the-job training for these children, just as it did for children in other opera houses in Europe. George Balanchine, among other children at the Imperial Theater School in St. Petersburg, was an heir to this practice, beginning his ballet career as a child performer in operas and ballets on the stage of the Mariinsky Theater. A study dedicated to children's presence on the nineteenth-century ballet stage has yet to be undertaken; suffice it to say for now that audiences were accustomed to seeing them there. See George Balanchine and Francis Mason, *Complete Stories of the Great Ballets*, rev. ed. (Garden City, NY: Doubleday, 1977), 746–748; Alexandra Danilova, *Choura: The Memoirs of Alexandra Danilova* (New York: Knopf, 1986), 13–49; Tamara Karsavina, *Theatre Street: The Reminiscences of Tamara Karsavina*, rev. ed. (London: Dance Books, 1981), 48–135; Mathilde Kschessinska, *Dancing in Petersburg: The Memoirs of Kschessinska*, tr. Arnold Haskell (Garden City, NY: Doubleday, 1961), 22–31; Wiley, *Century*, 108–169; and Wiley, *Lev Ivanov*, 5–20.

French operas in which children appeared, as the Justamant staging manuals attest, include *Faust* (nine female students from the school, Paris Opéra, 1869), *Le Prophète* (Lyon, 1869), and *Les Huguenots* (Paris Opéra production of 1868). We thank Helena Kopchick Spencer for sharing these findings with us. See Helena Kopchick Spencer, "Le divertissement dansé," in *L'Histoire de l'opéra français, vol. 2, Du Consulat aux débuts de la Troisième République*, ed. Hervé Lacombe (Paris: Fayard, 2020), 316–324 and 364–365.

[82] In Justamant's staging manual for *Le Corsaire* (Lyon, 1857), children are listed as playing the roles of little moors, little slaves, and cabin boys. Justamant, *Le Corsaire*.

ones. But students from the Paris Opéra ballet school did perform choreography in a
new *pas des fleurs* in the 1867 Paris Opéra revival of *Le Corsaire*;[83] the next year in St.
Petersburg, girls and boys performed in *Le jardin animé*, a divertissement based on *Le
pas des fleurs* that Petipa added to his revival of *Le Corsaire*.[84] Eleven senior girls, as well
as sixteen young girls and twelve boys, participated in the first production of the celebrated Kingdom of the Shades scene in Petipa's *La Bayadère*, and twenty-six student
girls performed the Lotus dance in the ballet's final act.[85] And for his new production of
Paquita in 1881, Petipa choreographed the much-celebrated children's mazurka, which
is performed by twenty-four student girls and boys in the ball scene of the final act.

Indeed, nineteenth-century Russian ballets virtually always called for children and
senior students, who figured, for instance, in all four acts of *Sleeping Beauty*, in all four
scenes of *Raymonda*, and in *Harlequinade*, in which a large cast of them performed elaborate dances. And in *The Mikado's Daughter* (St. Petersburg, 1897), children performed
in no fewer than eight dances, including a pantomime titled "*Chiu-Shingoura* (Legends
of the fidelity of *ronin*)" after entering in a "brilliant ceremonial procession" during a
grande marche.[86]

Nineteenth-century ballet casts featured not only more children, but more adults as
well. And the better funded the opera house, the bigger the casts. In any case, far more
people appeared in the nineteenth-century productions of ballets than one typically
sees in today's versions of the same ballets. (There were thirty-two vinegatherers in
Giselle, and twenty-four children. According to the cast list in the 1856 Paris libretto, the
opening scene of *Le Corsaire* included nearly 150 characters on stage. And the *Valse villageoise* in *Sleeping Beauty* featured eighty adult and child participants.) One effect of their
presence—aside from providing visual variety in large ensembles, like street festivals,
bazaars in Eastern lands, ballroom scenes, village gatherings, wedding celebrations—
was to make ballet's imaginary world a bit more like the real one in that it was populated
by people of varying ages. For scenes both large and small, choreographers could draw
from stables of performers of various ages and skill levels, including students, specialists
in mime and comedy, former dancers, and extras.

Spectacle; special effects; horses. Scenic and costume designers, machinists, and specialists in lighting and fireworks also contributed to the visual aspect of ballet with
as much lavishness as budgets allowed, and in some cases the budgets were generous
indeed. Wilis in *Giselle* were enabled by see-saws, wires, and traps to float, fly, and
sink into the ground (respectively); a rotating fireplace in *Paquita* allowed the heroine
and her lover to escape the bandits; lightning struck thanks to a *fil de la foudre* and
cables and wires made the ship in *Le Corsaire* roll in the "waves"; descending black
gauze curtains made it disappear into the sea.[87] ("The settings alone have an irresistible attraction," wrote one critic of *Le Corsaire* after its premiere. "[A]ll Paris will go
to see the scene of the ship sinking beneath the waves amid the lightning flashes and
violence of the storm. It is a fantastic sight and the most moving that has yet been seen

---

[83] Collins, "*Le Corsaire*," 319–320n109; see also 285.

[84] According to the notations of the scene made in the 1890s, twelve girls and twelve boys participated in
the scene.

[85] See Appendix F (ii).

[86] See Wiley, *Lev Ivanov*, 272, and for the story of the pantomime, 277–278.

[87] Important machinists include Clément Contant (at the Paris Opéra from 1832 to 1849) and Andrei
Roller (at the Imperial Theaters, St. Petersburg, from 1834 to 1879). See Clément Contant and Joseph de
Filippi, *Parallèle des principaux théâtres modernes de l'Europe et des machines théâtrales français, allemandes et
anglaises* (Paris: A. Levy, 1860).

on the stage."[88]) Horses, too—though only rarely seen on today's ballet stages—were frequently enough employed at the Paris Opéra (in both ballets and operas) to warrant the maintenance of a tack-making shop at that house. (Riders included the Prince and Bathilde in *Giselle* and Lauretta in *La Tarentule*.)

Russian ballet productions were splendid, too, reproducing the effects of French imports (as in, for instance, *Giselle, Paquita, Le Corsaire*) and creating new ones for original works, including the magically appearing castle and the collapsing temple in *La Bayadère*. Visually rich ballets became even richer after the mid 1880s, when the féerie—a genre popular in France and Italy that emphasized extravagant special effects and sudden transformations over plot—arrived in St. Petersburg. Ivan Vsevolozhsky, the ambitious director of the Imperial Theaters from 1881 to 1898, recognized the appeal of the féerie's extraordinary *mise en scène* and sought to bring that element together with the "dance-intensive grand ballet long favoured in Petersburg," as Wiley has put it.[89] The moving panorama in the second act of *Sleeping Beauty* exemplifies this trend well; it proved to be an especially impressive feature of the ballet.

Props; prop dances. Flowers, swords, baskets, books, necklaces, and all manner of objects were held, cherished, hidden, lost, found, brandished, and passed from character to character in nineteenth-century ballets. Some objects had magic power (like Myrtha's rosemary branch); some held crucial information (Paquita's medallion); some embodied a threat (Birbanto's *yatagan*). Some reflected a character's hopes for love (Medora's *selam*, a bouquet of flowers); some simply extended the line or shape of the choreography (the scarves that Nikia, in *La Bayadère*, and Raymonda held, which also added a dreamy quality to their danced solos. (Nikia holds hers during the Shades scene and Raymonda at nighttime just before she falls asleep.)

In *ensemble* prop dances, on the other hand, the objects held by the dancers were generally less powerful, less charged with meaning. They served instead to enhance the visual appeal and choreographic interest of the number and to help set its tone, like the swords and shields of the eponymous warlike women in *Les nymphes amazones*, the coconut shells in the Dance of the Arab Boys in *Raymonda*, the lotus-blossom garlands handled by the girls in the Lotus dance in *La Bayadère*, and the four types of flower props in the *Sleeping Beauty* Act One *Valse villageoise* ("Garland dance"): large, flexible garlands; small, stiff garlands; loose garlands; and flower baskets.[90]

Processions. Though sometimes downplayed or forgotten in today's stagings, processions quite often appeared in nineteenth-century ballets. Some were long; some were short; some were magnificent; some were simple and plain. Each of the five ballets we focus upon in this book featured at least one of them, in keeping with custom.

---

[88] *La France musicale*, date not cited, tr. in Beaumont, *Complete Book*, 215.

[89] Wiley, *Lev Ivanov*, 106. See also Lynn Garafola, "Russian Ballet in the Age of Petipa," in *The Cambridge Companion to Ballet*, ed. Marion Kant (Cambridge: Cambridge University Press, 2007), 156–157. On the *mise en scène* at the Paris Opéra, see, for instance, Karin Pendle and Stephen Wilkins, "Paradise Found: The Salle le Peletier and French Grand Opera," in *Opera in Context: Essays on Historical Staging from the Late Renaissance to the Time of Puccini*, ed. Mark A. Radice (Portland, OR: Amadeus Press, 1998), 171–207; Rebecca Wilberg, *The mise en scène at the Paris Opéra-Salle Peletier (1821–1873) and the staging of the first French Grand Opera: Meyerbeer's* Robert le diable (PhD diss., Brigham Young University, 1990); and Catherine Join-Diéterlé, *Les décors de scène de l'Opéra de Paris à l'époque romantique* (Paris: Picard, 1988).

[90] A celebrated prop dance was the Dance of the Buffoons, first choreographed for (and performed in) *The Nutcracker* by Alexander Shiryaev. Shiryaev and subsequent interpreters (including the eighteen-year-old George Balanchine) received great acclaim for their performance of this dance with a hoop. See Beumers et al., *Alexander Shiryaev*, 102 and 107 (photo); Akim Volynsky, *Ballet's Magic Kingdom*, ed. and tr. Stanley J. Rabinowitz (New Haven and London: Yale University Press, 2008), xxxiii; Wiley, *Tchaikovsky's Ballets*, 216; and Wiley, *Lev Ivanov*, 138.

The great stage popularity of the procession was surely owed in part to its real-life currency, for audiences were accustomed to seeing processions of various kinds both in the city and the village and therefore likely able to appreciate a procession's inherent theatricality and to read its meaning. On the ballet stage, processions—aside from being entertaining to watch—could be used effectively to serve a variety of dramatic functions. These include enhancing local color (like the *marche champêtre* in *Nathalie* and the caravan with young bayadères on camels in *The Pharoah's Daughter*), creating dramatic irony (as when the dejected Benedict in *La jolie fille de Gand* is left behind by Beatrix just as the festive Kermesse procession makes its merry entrance), and displaying contrasts of class (as in the opera *La Juive*).[91] Processions were also useful for introducing magical, mythological, or fantastic characters, as in, respectively, *Sleeping Beauty*, *The Awakening of Flora* (St. Petersburg, 1894) and *Cinderella* (St. Petersburg, 1893). And, of course, spectacular processions were good for flaunting the wealth and power of the presenting theater, as in the case of the massive Japanese procession in *The Mikado's Daughter*, in which large numbers of cast members portrayed Japanese and other Asian people. (Six hundred costumes were created for this ballet.[92])

Though we cannot know much about the manner of the participants in these processions or their facial expressions, one eyewitness to performances at the Paris Opéra in 1837 avers (intriguingly) that ballet masters coached the "processionists" in operas into a sort of precision-style ensemble acting:

> The procession of the opera [Paris Opéra] . . . is a well drilled pantomimic army, schooled to display every shade of wholesale emotion: say to the procession "pray!" and the procession kneels as one man—command it to be gay, and you have the mad populace of the Venetian carnival before you—do you desire to close your eyes and awake amid the pageants of bygone centuries? speak and the procession appears in full panoply, on horseback, and armed in steel—do you seek to be thrilled with a display of storied horrors? the procession stalks before you, arrayed in gloomy habiliments of the auto-da-fé. [. . .] [A]t a certain bar of the music, the procession of the opera smiles, three minutes after, it looks sad; all these symptoms of emotion are regulated by the ballet master—and a well-drilled chorister would be much more likely to sing one, two, three, or a dozen false notes, than would one of the *processionists* of the Grand Opera to smile or sadden out of time.[93]

The staging manuals and choreographic notations also indicate, in a few cases, that the participants did not simply walk, but moved forward with *glissades* and *jetés ordinaires*.[94] Further, we know that at least one—the procession of Badrinata in Act Two,

[91] See Marian Smith, "Processions in French Grand Opera," in *Bild und Bewegung im Musiktheater. Interdisziplinäre Studien im Umfeld der Grand Opéra.* (Image and Movement in Music Theatre. Interdisciplinary Studies around Grand Opéra), ed. Roman Brotbeck, Laura Moeckli, Anette Schaffer, and Stephanie Schroedter (Schliengen: Argus 2018), 43–50. Note, also, that some of the codas of Petipa's divertissements were processions of a sort in which all dancers, having participated in a divertissement, made final stage appearances in quick succession.

[92] See Wiley, *Lev Ivanov*, 194. Wiley asks, "Might [Ivanov's] *The Mikado's Daughter* have represented an emergent *genre nouveau* to the eyes of 1897, compared to the *vieux genre* of Petipa's steadfastly classical dance variations?" He posits that "Ivanov's ballet takes on a new significance in this light, with *Raymonda* to follow two months later, as new style to old, as the still imperfect realization of a balletic spectacle which was to dominate the early twentieth century."

[93] John Walsh, "The Grand Opera of Paris," *American Quarterly Review* XXI (June 1837): 183–184.

[94] This is true for Justamant's staging of the third-act procession in *Les Huguenots* (Paris Opéra, 1868) and the first-act cortège in *Le Dieu et la Bayadère* (Grand Théâtre, Lyon, 1853). See Justamant's staging manual for *Ballets du Dieu et la Bayadère*, TWS Inventory Number 70-458.

Scene III of *La Bayadère*—called for each of six groups to perform its own characteristic steps, including one group traveling backward.[95]

French lineage in Russia and the historiography of Marius Petipa

We would like to close this chapter on what made nineteenth-century ballet successful with a discussion of one of the century's most celebrated choreographers, Marius Petipa, whose place in history, we noticed in the course of our studies, merits some clarification.

His name, of course, is attached to most of the ballets in today's repertory of nineteenth-century "classics." For it was through Petipa's hands (either in revivals or as original works) that these canonic works—*Giselle, Le Corsaire, La Bayadère, Don Quixote, Coppélia, Swan Lake*, and several more—were passed down to us.

Too often, though, Petipa is depicted as a singular genius who not only remade the old-fashioned French ballets, ensuring their palatability, but virtually invented Russian classical ballet on his own, creating new formal structures, devising a new step vocabulary, conceiving lifts that had not existed before his time.

While recognizing Petipa's undeniable virtues as a choreographer (and even his genius), we reject this broad-stroke depiction of his ballets as the products of *sui generis* brilliance. Let us bear in mind that in nineteenth-century Russia (with St. Petersburg as its central hub of creativity), ballet was guided by French (or, in the case of the Taglionis, French-influenced) ballet masters, from Charles Didelot to Jules Perrot, Arthur Saint-Léon, and, finally, Marius Petipa.[96] Petipa's long tenure in Russia overlapped, in the early years, with his immediate predecessors and he drew extensively on the rich inheritance of Perrot, Mazilier, Saint-Léon, and the other older colleagues with whom he worked closely. He performed on stage with them, danced in their ballets, staged their ballets, and—just as they had done—made contributions to the slowly evolving traditions of ballet.

One of the benefits of examining, in the same frame, both Justamant (documenting French ballets that later went to Russia) and Stepanov manuscripts (documenting much of the repertory of the St. Petersburg Imperial Ballet as performed at the turn of the twentieth century) is that it has allowed us to see Petipa's work in a new light. Specifically, it reveals that Petipa and his colleagues (including Lev Ivanov, for example) continued not only to adhere to the principles of dance design of their French predecessors but to use much of the same step vocabulary as well. The notion that Petipa's choreography

---

[95] Choreographic notation of *La Bayadère*. See Chapter 9 and Appendix F (i). We know, further, that in the first act of the opera-ballet *La Muette de Portici* (1828), a group of "huit dames dansant la guarrache" (eight ladies dancing the guarrache) were among the eight groups of characters entering the stage in a procession. (Other groups included Neapolitans, nobles, pages, and piqueurs.) M. Solomé, *Indications Générales et observations pour La Mise en scène de* La Muette de Portici [...] (Paris: Duverger, n.d.), reprinted in H. Robert Cohen, ed., *The Original Staging Manuals for Twelve Parisian Operatic Premières* (Stuyvesant, NY: Pendragon Press, 1991), 13–72.

[96] Wiley provides a succinct history of the era, greatly informed by translations of memoirs, librettos, and reviews, in *A Century of Russian Ballet*. For other English-language accounts, see Natalia Roslevleva's Soviet-era account of Russian ballet history, *Era of the Russian Ballet*, which provides a jumbled and biased history omitting substantive detail about training and choreography; Beumers et al., *Alexander Shiryaev*, 81–128; Wiley, *Lev Ivanov*, 3–72; and Sandra Noll Hammond, "History of Ballet Technique: Ballet in the Late Eighteenth and Early Nineteenth Centuries," and "History of Ballet Technique: Ballet since the Mid-Nineteenth Century," in *International Encyclopedia of Dance*, vol. 1, 344–349.

"represented a break from the vocabulary and syntax of Romantic Ballet" (a recent observation based on criticism of Petipa by one of his ballerinas, Ekaterina Vazem) is not corroborated by the sources.[97] Take, for example, Aurora's entrance in Act One of *Sleeping Beauty*, choreography originally devised in 1890—Petipa was seventy-one years old—for the Italian ballerina Carlotta Brianza and notated around 1903.[98] These steps are similar in style to those recorded by Justamant for other, earlier ballets (for instance, the steps performed by Carlotta de Vecchi in *Giselle*, see above). That is, though they are used by Petipa in a late-nineteenth-century ballet, they can be found with regularity in Justamant's manuals earlier in the century. For easy comparison, we have deciphered Petipa's steps as they are preserved in Stepanov notation and describe them here in prose, using the same format Justamant uses. Aurora enters and performs the following:

> *Pas de chat, pas de bourrée dessous, pas marché de côté sur l'orteil, pas tombé*
> The same *pas* on the other foot
> Two times again the same *pas* on each foot
>
> She goes upstage backward doing 8 times *pas marché en arrière en demi-pointe,*
>   *pas tombé*
>
> *Pas de chat, rond de jambe en l'air* the right leg, *coupé dessus en demi-pointe, pas*
>   *marché de côté* the left foot, *plier à la 4ᵉ, relevé sur l'orteil* the left foot, a turn to
>   the right, the right foot $\frac{3}{4}$ *devant, pas tombé, emboîté derrière*
> The same *pas* 3 times again
>
> *Pas marché en arrière en demi-pointe,* a turn to the right, *coupé dessous, jeté en*
>   *avant, pas de bourrée dessus en tournant*
> The same *pas,* beginning from *jeté en avant,* 3 times again
>
> Finish with *pas marché en tournant* to the right 3 times and end facing the public[99]

Compare this with the step vocabulary in the second half of Giselle's solo (as performed by de Vecchi) from the Act One *pas de deux* for Giselle and Loys as described in Justamant's manual (circa 1858):

---

[97] Nadine Meisner, *Marius Petipa: The Emperor's Ballet Master* (New York: Oxford University Press, 2019), 169. Meisner bases her observation on Vazem's lament that Saint-Léon's "fine, 'beaded' steps" requiring "genuine filigree work" were replaced by Petipa's "coarser" style. This passage from Vazem's 1937 memoirs, during which she unfavorably compares Petipa to Saint-Léon, has also been translated by Wiley: "Although a true adherent of classical ballet, as, of course, were all choreographers of his time, Petipa knew classical dance far more superficially than St-Léon, many *pas* that St-Léon used being completely unknown to him. With the departure of St-Léon [in 1869], those fine 'minute' *pas*, which required genuine filigree work from a dancer, forever vanished from our stage. Variations in a composition by Petipa were monotonous and, I would say, 'cruder' than those of St-Léon." Qtd. in Wiley, *Century*, 281. This passage, in which Vazem's terms "coarser" and "cruder" may have been a reference to Italian step vocabulary employed by Petipa in his choreography from the mid-1880s onward, presumably led Meisner to state that Petipa's enchaînements, which "articulate a spare and linear classicism," were "[u]nique to nineteenth-century Russia." Meisner further separates Petipa from his predecessors by stating that "nobody can ever be sure whether Petipa's early vocabulary was closer to the fleet-footed, filigree dance of the Romantic Ballet, exemplified by Perrot, Saint-Léon, and Bournonville [we note the omission of Mazilier!]" and suggests this was unlikely because "it seems more probable that Petipa found his movement language early on." Meisner, *Marius Petipa*, 169.

[98] See Wiley, *Tchaikovsky's Ballets*, 165.

[99] *Sleeping Beauty* choreographic notation, MS Thr 245 (204).

To go upstage, she does *entrechat quatre*, with the foot that is behind, *petit battement sur le cou-de-pied*, closing behind, and [beginning with] the foot that is in front 4 *petits battements*, closing behind

The same *pas* on the other foot

One time again on each foot

3 times altogether, an *entrechat quatre*, [*relevé*], turn *sur l'orteil* and put the foot down in front

She goes to place herself while doing *glissades naturelles*

Beginning on the left foot, she does *pas de bourrée dessus dessous en tournant*, *assemblé derrière*, two *échappés sur les orteils*, two [*tours*] to the right on the left toe, *jeté dessus*

2 times again the same *pas*

Finish with [multiple] *pas marché en tournant* and end *en position* [in a pose][100]

A close study of the sources (both French and Russian) reveals that, in general, Petipa's work can best be seen as existing on the same continuum as that of his French predecessors, and very much a part of the slow process by which the structures and content of classical dance were altered over time. A comparison of Justamant's staging manuals and the Stepanov notations (both of which represent the work of multiple choreographers) reveals that both sources feature complex enchaînements using a wide step vocabulary, as well as partnering that included overhead lifts. A single enchaînement from the coda of the *Pas de trois des odalisques* in *Le Corsaire* (notated in the early years of the twentieth century) demonstrates that choreographic complexity, delicacy, and *batterie* were alive and well in early twentieth-century St. Petersburg: *sissonne ouverte double rond de jambe* into *ballotté*, *coupé dessous*, *gargouillade* (with a single *rond de jambe* in each leg), and *glissade*, *piqué de côté*, *coupé dessus*, *tombé* twice, all performed three times to alternate sides (the opening *sissonne* becomes a *double demi-gargouillade* for the second and third iterations of the enchaînement).[101] This brilliant enchaînement may have been choreographed by Perrot as early as 1858 or by Petipa at some point in the intervening years before it was notated (see Chapter 7). Whatever the case may be, this combination of steps was still being performed at the end of Petipa's career even though it can be identified as stylistically congruent with choreography from much earlier in the nineteenth century. To suggest that Petipa worked apart from a continuously developing tradition minimizes that which came before Petipa and distances him from the lineage of choreographers from which he descended.

---

[100] Justamant, *Giselle*, 76.

[101] *Le Corsaire* choreographic notation, MS Thr 245 (1). "Demi-gargouillade" is a term coined by Alexei and Tatiana Ratmansky to denote a *pas de chat* with a *rond de jambe en l'air* that is performed only with the leading leg, a step found throughout the Stepanov notations and performed by both women and men. See Macaulay, "Further Annals of *The Sleeping Beauty*," 101–102. However, note that Gail Grant defines this same movement as simply a *gargouillade*: "In the Cecchetti method and the French School, the step [*gargouillade*] resembles a pas de chat with a double rond de jambe, actually a rond de jambe and a half *with the commencing leg*. A brilliant executant will also do a double rond de jambe with the closing leg." Grant, *Technical Manual*, 58. Italics added.

Italian influence. Vazem's reference to Petipa's "coarser" style may refer to new step vocabulary that began to be part of Petipa's work as he choreographed for the Italian ballerinas who danced in St. Petersburg from the mid-1880s into the first years of the twentieth century. These artists brought with them the virtuoso technique of the Italian school, which included a more pervasive and developed use of *pointe* work.[102] (In this volume, we will encounter numerous variations originally created for Italian ballerinas and others that incorporate what we deem to be Italian influences.) Their movement vocabulary included hops on *pointe* in a variety of positions and *fouetté* turns for the women, some of whom were able to do extreme repetitions of certain steps, like the multiple *fouettés* in *Swan Lake.*[103] The men's step vocabulary included turns *à la seconde*, multiple *pirouettes* (in the double digits), and *double tours en l'air*. The arrival of Enrico Cecchetti in 1887 in St. Petersburg (where he was hired as leading dancer and second ballet master of the Imperial Ballet) helped ensure the absorption of such steps into the Russian school.[104] Too, in order to more fully master the steps of their Italian colleagues, Russian ballerinas traveled to Milan to study with the celebrated teacher Caterina Beretta, who had briefly served as *maîtresse de ballet* in St. Petersburg in 1877 and then taught in Milan from 1879.[105]

Evolution of the pas d'action. Perhaps Petipa's most significant innovation in the creation of ballets in Russia can be seen in the way he *structured* dances, most strikingly in his transformation of the free-form *pas d'action* into a clearly structured multimovement dance suite. Both types were grounded in narrative, but while the earlier type was flexible and could be shaped according to whatever the composer and choreographer chose for the given situation, Petipa's settled into a grander and neater set form that remained largely the same from ballet to ballet.[106] The five works that form the core of our study allow us to trace this process.

What do we mean by the term *pas d'action*? Most Parisian ballet-pantomimes were comprised of nearly equal amounts of pantomime and dance. In this book, we refer to a scene in which the two intersected—that is, dance that included pantomime and pantomime that included dance—as a *pas d'action* (literally, dance with action *or* dance of action, though the term was not in widespread use at the time), or *scène dansante* (danced scene), a term used in printed programs in the second half of the nineteenth century.

Notably, in the production documents (scores, manuals, etc.) that describe this type of scene, there was no stable term used to label it. Various descriptive terms were used, as

[102] Petipa had a love-hate relationship with Italian technique and style. While he professed to disapprove of the Italian style and step vocabulary, he nevertheless, in his usual manner, choreographed to the strength of his ballerinas. See Meisner, *Marius Petipa*, 171 and 292. Meisner also cites Petipa's interviews published in the *Peterburgskaya gazeta* on 2 December 1906 and 2 May 1907, in which he discussed his aesthetic views. Meisner, *Marius Petipa*, 398n75.

[103] We note that the extreme repetition of a single step—performed twelve, twenty-four, or thirty-two times—would necessarily result in reduced step vocabulary being employed in any given dance: the repeated step would fill a substantial number of measures, thus leaving less time for other enchaînements made up of a variety of steps.

[104] Enrico Cecchetti was an Italian dancer, ballet master, choreographer, and teacher. He taught at the Imperial Ballet School, St. Petersburg, 1887–1902, and later returned to Italy, teaching at La Scala in Milan.
    Alexander Shiryaev chronicled this era of Italian ballerinas in his memoirs. See Beumers et al., *Alexander Shiryaev*, 96–106. See also Meisner, *Marius Petipa*, 198–206, and Wiley, *Century*, 307 ff., especially 314–320 and 350–356.

[105] Caterina Beretta was eventually director of the Scuola di Ballo at La Scala (1905–1908). See Meisner, *Marius Petipa*, 202, and Beumers et al., *Alexander Shiryaev*, 105.

[106] For a broader discussion of structure in Petipa's ballets, see Tim Scholl, *From Petipa to Balanchine* (New York: Routledge, 1994), 4–12.

we shall see (such as "Scène de la table" or the less specific "Scène et Pas"), and the scene type was effective and well known. But like other formal structures (for example, "sonata form," in instrumental music and "solita forma" in Italian opera), it was not given a generic appellation during its heyday, doubtless because nobody deemed one necessary.

Let us now turn to some specific examples of *pas d'action*, starting with *Giselle*, in which we find scenes of dance infused with action in both acts.[107] (Ivor Guest praises Perrot for developing the *pas d'action* in the course of his career; Coralli also proved his mastery of it in *Giselle*, and we have also found numerous compelling examples of it in the works of Mazilier discussed in this volume.[108]) Here are some instances of such *pas d'action* as seen in Justamant's staging manual for *Giselle* as produced in Lyon (in the 1850s), which we believe has close ties with the Paris Opéra production. (See Chapters 2 and 3.) Note that the story advances in all of these instances:

In Act One:

- Both dancing and action/mime take place during Giselle and Loys's "date" (sometimes referred to as a *scène d'amour*), in which Giselle plucks the daisy petals
- Giselle and Loys's conversation shortly after the beginning of the waltz as Giselle invites Loys to dance
- The crowning of Giselle as queen of the vintage during the march
- Mimed exchanges between Loys, Berthe, and Giselle during the *pas de deux* at the beginnings of the entrée and the coda

In Act Two:

- Myrtha's enjoyment (both mimed and acted) of flowers and nature during the second section of her entrance dance
- During her initiation dance as a Wili, Giselle exclaims, "Now *I* will fly!"
- During Giselle's first encounter with Albert, they both dance and act (he seeks, she hides)
- During the danced bacchanale, Hilarion pleads for mercy and Myrtha refuses
- During the adagio and coda of the *pas de deux*, Giselle and Albert express their love and grief and make further pleas to Myrtha for clemency

These frequent combinations of dance and action created a medium in which the narrative developed organically, its expression moving easily between dance and mime or other forms of acting.

In the unfolding of *Paquita* and *Le Corsaire*, by Joseph Mazilier (Perrot's senior by nine years), we find a similar blending of dance and action. As in the Paris *Giselle* libretto,

---

[107] Note that Coralli choreographed *Giselle* except for two *pas* for Carlotta Grisi. See Chapter 2, note 1.

[108] Ivor Guest, *Jules Perrot: Master of the Romantic Ballet* (London: Dance Books, 1984), iii. Guest declares: "The secret of his [Perrot's] genius was to be found in his choreographic method: his skill in peopling the stage, setting the scenes in movement and breathing life into the narrative, and an ability, quite novel in his time, to weave the dances into the action. Analysis of his ballets from the choreographic viewpoint reveals that his supremacy rested on two exceptional abilities. The first was his development of the *pas d'action*, a dance scene envisaged as an integral part of the dramatic action that progressed or assisted the narrative in terms of dance. In his ballets, passages of this nature reduced the reliance on long stretches of mime, which so frequently provoked tedium, and added new depths of meaning and mood." Perrot's second ability, according to Guest, was "his mastery in composition of passages of pure dance." Guest, *Jules Perrot*, ii–iii.

the libretto for *Paquita* contains no set designation of *pas d'action* scenes, which include the following:

In Act One:

The dance rehearsal led by Inigo

Inigo's impassioned declaration of love for Paquita, during which she responds only with dance

Two men vying for Paquita's affections during the entrée of the *Pas de Mlle Carlotta Grisi*

In Act Two, Scene I:

Paquita's solo and eventual duet with Inigo as he drinks himself into a stupor

Likewise, the libretto for *Le Corsaire*, which premiered in Paris a decade after *Paquita*, contains no reference to *pas d'action* scenes. However, Justamant, in his staging manual documenting the 1857 Lyon production of *Le Corsaire*, provided titles for danced scenes that constitute *pas d'action*. These titles call attention to the combination of dance and action and distinguish these passages from action scenes that contain no dancing and dances that include no overt action:

In Act One, Scene II:

Scène de la table: love scene between Medora and Conrad during which Medora dances both alone and partnered by Conrad

In Act Two:

Scène et pas du Derviche du pacha et de Medora: comic scene in which the Pasha attempts to embarrass a traveling dervish (Conrad in disguise) with the attention of his harem women, while Conrad attempts to get close to Medora without the Pasha noticing

Act Three, Scene I, also includes a *pas d'action* which is not named as such by Justamant. In this scene, Medora uses her charms to disarm the Pasha and enable her to escape with Conrad. As with the earlier *Scène de la table*, here Medora both dances alone and is partnered by the Pasha.

The posters and programs for St. Petersburg productions of *Giselle*, *Paquita*, and *Le Corsaire* also provided titles for some (but not all) *pas d'action*. The poster for the 1858 Petersburg premiere of *Corsaire* (staged by Perrot) includes four numbers whose titles indicate (or suggest) *pas d'action*: *Ballabili d'action*, *Scène de seduction*, and two *scènes dansantes* (in the second and fourth scenes).[109] Perrot soon added a fifth *pas d'action*, titled *L'esclave, pas scenique*. The libretto for Petipa's 1881 revival of *Paquita* includes two *pas d'action* in its list of dances: a *Scène dansante* in Act One and a *Pas scènique* in Act Two.[110] By 1889, a short duet for Giselle and Loys in the first act of *Giselle* was titled *Scène*

---

[109] See Appendix E (iii).
[110] See Appendix D (iv).

dansante (we refer to this number as the *louré pas de deux*; see Chapter 3). Here the lovers flirt and blow kisses to each other as they dance.

In the ballets that he created anew (as opposed to his revivals of existing ballets), Petipa continued to mix dance and action; he also used the term *pas d'action* to refer to a distinct formal structure that combined the two. We refer to Petipa's expanded version of the *pas d'action* structure as a "multimovement dance suite" in order to convey its greater scale and the fact that it includes several distinct segments.[111] These large-scale dance structures combine (on one hand) the narrative-driving mimetic elements of earlier *pas d'action*—one or more of the movements includes mime content or acting—with (on the other hand) divertissements comprised of various numbers, such as an entrée, adagio, variations, and coda (for example, the *pas de cinq* in the opening scene of Mazilier's *Le Corsaire*; see Chapter 6).

This is not to say that Petipa was the very first to employ this structure. In fact, the four-movement *Pas de Mlle Carlotta Grisi* (or "pas des tambourins," as one newspaper critic called it) in the first act of Mazilier's *Paquita* is an example of the *pas d'action* structure (or multimovement dance suite) that was later taken up by Petipa. This *pas* comprises four distinct movements—entrée, two variations, and coda—with pantomime included in its opening movement. Although the action—according to Justamant's manual, two men nearly come to fisticuffs over Paquita—does not relate directly to the plot of the ballet, the structure of the multimovement dance suite and the inclusion of action is clearly in place in this 1846 Parisian ballet. In retrospect, one may see it as an inspiration and model for Petipa's later multimovement *pas d'action*.

Beginning with *The Pharaoh's Daughter* in 1862, Petipa regularly included such *pas d'action*, or multimovement dance suites, in his ballets, and in many cases he used the term *pas d'action* in their titles. In contrast to the intimacy of most *pas d'action* created by his predecessors, some of Petipa's *pas d'action* were extended and grandiose affairs that featured a large cast of performers. For example, the four-movement *Grand pas d'action* in the first act of *Sleeping Beauty*—which includes the famous "Rose" adagio—featured twenty-four performers, including non-dancing characters and students.[112]

Both of Petipa's original ballets that figure in our study include *pas d'action*. In *La Bayadère*, Petipa saved the *pas d'action* until the ballet's final climactic scene, the wedding of Solor and Hamsatti. The shade of Nikia appears numerous times during the various movements (entrée, adagio, variations, and coda) that make up the dance. In *Raymonda*, the second-act *Grand pas d'action* (adagio, four variations, and coda) expresses Abderrakhman's amorous pursuit of Raymonda.

Petipa also added a *pas d'action* to the opening scene of the Petersburg *Corsaire* in 1899 (see Chapter 7). Titled "Finesse d'amour" in the program (but "Pas d'action" in the choreographic notation), this relatively brief number comprises 129 bars divided into four movements and accompanies Medora as she teases the Pasha in the presence of Conrad. The formalization in this particular *pas d'action* in Petipa's 1899 *Corsaire* is typical of classicism and stands as both a departure from the organic and natural combination of dance and action found in *Giselle* and a miniature exemplar of the clarity of structure (dance, pantomime, and their combination in the *pas d'action*) that came to dominate Petipa's late multi-act ballets, such as *Raymonda*.

---

[111] See Doug Fullington, "Finding the Balance: Pantomime and Dance in Ratmansky's New/Old Sleeping Beauty," *Oxford Handbooks Online* (2017). doi: 10.1093/oxfordhb/9780199935321.013.169.

[112] See the *Sleeping Beauty* libretto, tr. in Wiley, *Century*, 362.

In sum: Petipa is often credited with being a great innovator who essentially reinvented ballet by largely remaking the French ballets that he staged in Russia and departing significantly from them in his new works by rejecting older structures and creating completely new ones. But this formulation separates him from the ballet masters who came before him to an extent that is not supported by the evidence. Rather, Petipa's work may be more accurately viewed as contributing to the ongoing evolution of ballet.

Among Petipa's important contributions to this evolution, we have identified the two discussed above: expanded step vocabulary and an expanded version of the *pas d'action* as a multimovement dance suite. First, Petipa incorporated Italian academic dance technique into his compositional style during the period in which he created new ballets (and revised older ones) for Italian ballerinas in St. Petersburg, that is, from 1887 to 1901 (from Virginia Zucchi through Pierina Legnani). In doing so (and sometimes against his better aesthetic judgment[113]), Petipa was working as his predecessors had (and as many of his successors did as well, including Balanchine); that is, he assessed the particular strengths of the ballerina for whom he was choreographing and created dances that showed her to best advantage. And in the case of dancers who had come to Russia from Italy, this included virtuoso steps on *pointe*, extreme repetition of steps, and an increase in acrobatic jumps and turns.

Second, as our close study of formal structures in these ballets has shown, Petipa can rightly be credited with the formalization of the French *pas d'action* into a lengthy multimovement dance suite that retains the narrative underpinning of its predecessor *pas d'action*, but instead of arising from and unfolding organically according to the dramatic situation, hews to a predetermined and expansive formal structure.

Now we turn to the five ballets that form our study. In the pages that follow, we will take a close look at *Giselle*, *Paquita*, *Le Corsaire*, *La Bayadère*, and *Raymonda*, in each case outlining the ballet's genesis and early performance history, offering short sketches of its characters and detailed descriptions of its music (an integral part of the work), enumerating the sources we consulted, and finally, providing a lengthy and detailed scene-by-scene description of the ballet, based on our reading of those sources. Our main intent in so doing, as scholars and lovers of ballet, is to share with our readers what we have gained from our studies: a far stronger sense than what we had heretofore known about what happened when the curtain went up on these ballets in their earliest incarnations.

---

[113] See note 102 in this chapter.

2

Giselle in Paris and Lyon

Giselle, today the most celebrated of the Romantic "Golden Age" ballets, made its debut at the Paris Opéra on 28 June 1841, the twenty-second birthday of the up-and-coming Italian ballerina who played the title character, Carlotta Grisi. The leading man, Lucien Petipa, had successfully partnered Grisi in her Opéra debut four months earlier in Donizetti's opera *La Favorite*. François Simon played the role of Hilarion. Adèle Dumilâtre, famous for her beauty, played the Wili Queen Myrtha; the cast also featured Elina Roland (as Giselle's mother Berthe), Caroline Forster (as Bathilde, Albert's noble fiancée), Eugène Coralli (as Wilfride, Albert's faithful squire), Sophie Dumilâtre and Mlle Carré (as leading Wilis), and a young, tall comic actor, Louis Petit, in the role of the Old Man (since expunged from most productions of the ballet). The choreographer was Jean Coralli; Jules Perrot contributed by devising two *pas* for Carlotta Grisi.[1] Adolphe Adam, acknowledged as the Opéra's best ballet composer, wrote the music (which was supplemented shortly before the premiere by Burgmüller's "Peasant" *pas de deux*). The ballet's libretto, collaboratively written by Théophile Gautier and Vernoy de Saint-Georges, opens like a ballet *comique* with its merry villagers, love triangle, charming

---

[1] The question of who really choreographed *Giselle* has now been answered after many years of uncertainty owed to the fact that while Coralli is the choreographer of record, whisperings in the press and Adolphe Adam's memoirs both hint that Perrot devised some of the choreography. A recently discovered letter of 1842 by Jean Coralli (written to the *Morning Post* of London to correct its misattribution of the *Giselle* choreography to Deshayes and Perrot) settles the matter. Coralli declares that "the whole choreography was created by myself, with the exception of the two pas danced by Mlle. Grisi, which were under the direction of M. Perrot." *Morning Post*, 2 April 1842, qtd. in Jennifer Thorp, "Jean Coralli and His Family in London," in Sasportes and Veroli, *Giovanni Coralli, l'autore di Giselle*, 29. See also, in the same volume, Olivesi, "Entre discretion et quête de reconnaissance," 179–184.

But before Thorp's revelation of Coralli's confirmation of his authorship, Serge Lifar—without evidence, and for reasons of his own—promulgated the notion that Perrot was responsible for most if not all of *Giselle* and denigrated Coralli by calling him "a craftsman rather than a master." Serge Lifar, *Giselle, Apothéose du ballet romantique* (Paris: Albin Michel, 1942), 138, qtd. in José Sasportes, "Giovanni Coralli coreografo europeo," in *Giovanni Coralli, l'autore di Giselle*, 11. See Patrizia Veroli, "La dernière étoile de Diaghilev dans la Russie en émigration. Serge Lifar de 1929 à 1939," *Reherches en danse* 5 (2016), https://doi.org/10.4000/danse.1419, and Patrizia Veroli, "Serge Lifar as a Dance Historian and the Myth of Russian Dance in 'Zarubezhnaia Rossiia' (Russia Abroad) 1930–1940," *Dance Research: The Journal of the Society for Dance Research* 32, no. 2 (2014): 105–143.

Lifar's disparagement of Coralli took hold and may have influenced the usually even-handed Ivor Guest, who in comparing Coralli to Perrot wrote that the latter cut a "dull" figure and lacked the international experience of Perrot. Ivor Guest, "Jean Coralli and the Influence of Eugène Scribe at the Porte Saint-Martin Theatre," in *Prima la danza! Festschrift für Sybille Dahms*, eds. Gunhild Oberzaucher-Schüller, Daniel Brandenberg, and Monika Woitas (Würzburg: Königshausen Newmann, 2004), 253, qtd. in José Sasportes, "Giovanni Coralli coreografo europeo," 10. As Sasportes countered, Coralli's international career (which took him to London, Vienna, Milan, Lisbon, and Paris) and that of Perrot were of equal importance (pp. 9–13).

Coralli was successful in the 1820s at creating ballets of several types (for such performers as the young Jules Perrot and the brilliant mime and comic dancer Charles Mazurier) at the commercially run popular Théâtre de la Porte-Saint-Martin (a place considered a forward-looking counterpart to the more rule-bound Opéra of the 1820s). The ballets he created later were held in high regard, too (including *La Tarentule*, *Le Diable boiteux*, *La Péri*). Therefore it should not be surprising that his choreography for *Giselle* prospered. See Maria Zhiltsova, "Jean Coralli au Théâtre de la Porte-Saint-Martin," 105–122, and Maria Venuso, *Giselle e il teatro musicale: nuove visioni per la storia del balletto* (Firenze: Polistampa, 2021), 39 ff.

Five Ballets from Paris and St. Petersburg. Doug Fullington and Marian Smith, Oxford University Press.
© Oxford University Press 2024. DOI: 10.1093/oso/9780190944506.003.0003

dances, and a showdown between two male rivals. But with the wholly unexpected death of its lively heroine at the end of the first act, the ballet turns into a ghost story and ends as a moving tale of transcendent love.

The genesis story of *Giselle* is well known because Gautier—the balletomane, poet, novelist, critic, staunch defender of Romanticism, and man-about-town who conceived the libretto—made a point of telling it. According to his account, he was struck by two ghost stories. One was in a poem of Victor Hugo, "Fantômes," about a beautiful young Spanish girl whose love for dancing leads to her demise. Here are excerpts from this 28-stanza poem:

> Alas! How many maidens fade and die
>   I've seen. Hard fate! yet death must have his prey.
> The grass beneath the mower's scythe must lie,
> And frolic dancers, gaily floating by,
>   Must crush the roses in their way. [. . .]
>
> Their spirits own my soul's affinity,
>   And life and death with us commingled be;
> Their steps I help, or with their wings I fly.
> Transcendent vision! now like them I die,
>   And then once more they live like me.
>
> So tranced, to all my thoughts their forms they bend;
>   I see, I see them come, I hear them call!
> Then dancing round a tomb, their figures blend,
> Then slowly fading from my sight they wend,
>   And musing, I remember all.
>
> One above all, an angel girl of Spain—
>   White hands, a breast no sighs unholy swell,
> Black eyes, where did the South's bright languor reign—
> That untold charm and halo which pertain
>   To brows which fifteen summers tell. [. . .]
>
> No, it was not of love she died! for her
>   Love as yet kindled neither joy nor woe;
> Her heart as yet thrilled with no loving care,
> And while all cried aloud that she was fair,
>   None the same whispered to her low.
>
> Balls caused her death: with eager, boundless love,
>   Balls—dazzling balls—filled her with ecstasies;
> And now her ashes thrill and gently move,
> When, in a balmy night, white clouds above
>   Dance round the crescent of the skies. [. . .]
>
> Balls her delight! too dearly loved and sought!
>   Of them, for days before, she thinks and dreams;

Women, musicians, dancers, stopt by nought,
Come in her sleep, following each girlish thought,
    And round her bed the revel streams. [. . .]

The *fête* began. She, with her sisters, laughs
    And hastes; her fan she flutters 'neath her hand;
Then, sitting down amid the silken scarfs,
Her bounding heart the joyous music quaffs,
    Poured from the vast melodious band.

She was all dance, and laughter, and delight.
    Dear child, she brightened our sad idleness;
For 'tis not at a ball all hearts are bright—
Ashes round silken tunics wing their flight,
    And pleasure yields to weariness.

But she, in the delirious waltz borne round,
    Flew by, and then returned, breathless and fleet,
Intoxicated with the flute's soft sound,
The magic *fête*, where lights and flowers abound,
    And noises of voices and of feet.

What joy to bound distracted in the crowd!
    To feel in dance the senses multiplied!
Scarce knowing if you float upon a cloud,
Or chase the flying earth, or, new endowed,
    You tread some fast-revolving tide!

Alas! she had to quit when dawn displayed
    Its light, and wait, exposed, her cloak to find.
How often thus the giddy, thoughtless maid
Feels, shivering, on her naked shoulders laid,
    The cold blast of a chilling wind!

What dismal morrows on the ball ensue!
    Farewell child-laughter, dance, and dress, and whim!
To song succeeds the cough that pierces through,
To rose and white, the fever's livid hue,
    To star-bright eyes—eyes quenched and dim.

Dead at fifteen!—loved, lovely, happy, gay,
    Leaving the ball; long, long to make us weep.
Dead! from her frenzied mother torn away
By Death's cold clutch; e'en in her ball array,
    And in a coffin put to sleep.

Decked was she ready for another ball;
    Death was so eager such a prize to have,

Roses which garlanded her brows withal,
And bloomed on her at yester festival,
  Were scarcely faded on her grave.

Poor mother! unforeseeing destiny,
  On such weak reed, such weight of love to heap;
Watching so long on her frail infancy,
So many nights have sat her cradle by,
  And kisses her darling's tears to sleep.

And all for what? If now the loved, lost maid,
  Coffined, and food for worms (ah! dismal sight!)
Within the tomb, where we her beauty laid.
Is wakened by some revel of the dead,
  On a clear moonlit winter night;

A grinning spectre tends her toilette wan
  In mother's stead, and cries, "'Tis time to haste";
An icy kiss prints her blue lips upon,
And the gaunt fingers of the skeleton
  'Mid her long floating tresses placed;

Then leads her trembling to the ghastly dance,
  Where phantoms whirl in mazes through the gloom;—
The great pale moon stares down as in a trance,
And the night rainbow, through the sky's expanse,
  Stains the gray clouds that dimly loom.

Young girls, whom balls and frolic *fêtes* allure,
  Think on this Spanish maid with pensive ruth;
With rapturous hand she hastened to procure
Harvest of all life's roses, sweet and pure—
  Affection, pleasure, beauty, youth.

From *fête* to *fête* the luckless child they took,
  As of that nosegay all the hues she tried.
Alas! this life how quickly she forsook,
And, like Ophelia, carried by the brook,
  While she was gathering flowers, died.[2]

Gautier's other literary inspiration was a passage in Heinrich Heine's *De l'Allemagne* (On Germany) about Wilis, spectral brides who rise from their graves at midnight to dance beguilingly in the moonlight:

[2] Victor Hugo, "Fantômes," a 28-stanza poem from *Les Orientales* (Paris: Charles Gosselin, 1829), critical edition, ed. Élisabeth Barineau, vol. 2, 134–137 (Paris: Librairier Marcel Didier, 1968); translated into English by Henry Carrington in *Translations from the Poems of Victor Hugo* (London: Walter Scott, 1887), 61–65.

In parts of Austria there exists a tradition ... of Slavic origin: the tradition of the night-dancer, who is known, in Slavic countries, under the name Wili. Wilis are young brides-to-be who die before their wedding day. The poor young creatures cannot rest peacefully in their graves. In their stilled hearts and lifeless feet, there remains a love for dancing which they were unable to satisfy during their lifetimes. At midnight they rise out of their graves, gather together in troops on the roadside and woe be unto the young man who comes across them! He is forced to dance with them; they unleash their wild passion, and he dances with them until he falls dead. Dressed in their wedding gowns, with wreaths of flowers on their heads and glittering rings on their fingers, the Wilis dance in the moonlight like elves. Their faces, though white as snow, have the beauty of youth. They laugh with a joy so hideous, they call you so seductively, they have an air of such sweet promise, that these dead *bacchantes* are irresistible.[3]

Gautier responded to Heine's words by saying aloud, "What a pretty ballet this would make!" Then, as he recalls:

In a burst of enthusiasm, I ... took up a large sheet of fine white paper and wrote at the top, in superb rounded characters, "*Les Wilis*, a ballet." But then I began to laugh, and I threw the sheet aside without giving it a further thought, saying to myself, with the benefit of my journalistic experience, that it was quite impossible to transpose onto the stage that misty, nocturnal poetry, that phantasmagoria that is so voluptuously sinister, all those makings of legend and ballad that have so little relevance to our present way of life. That same evening I was wandering backstage at the Opéra with my mind still full of [Heine's] ideas, when I met that amusing man [Vernoy de Saint-Georges, who had written the stories for successful ballets]. ... I related the tradition of the Wilis, and three days later the ballet of *Giselle* was written and accepted. In another week Adolphe Adam had sketched out the music, the scenery was nearly ready, and the rehearsals were in full swing.[4]

Gautier might be overstating the brevity of the timetable here. For instance—to be precise about it—Adam took fifty-nine days to compose the score.[5] But a rehearsal for the first act did take place on 12 May 1841, even as Adam was still composing the second act.[6] And it is true that the Opéra's director Léon Pillet did push the project along with unusual urgency, hoping to capitalize quickly on the popularity of Carlotta Grisi, whose

[3] Théophile Gautier, *Histoire de l'art dramatique*, vol. 2, 133–134 (Paris: Édition Hetzel, 1858), tr. in Gautier, *Gautier on Dance*, 94–95. As Edwin Binney III notes, the original passage by Heine is 194 words long, and Gautier's version is reduced to 162 words. Gautier alters Heine's text as well, as Binney points out: "Joie si effroyable" becomes "joie si perfide." "Dans leur tombeau" and "anneaux étincelans" in Heine become "sous leurs tombeaux" and "anneaux brillants" in Gautier. And Heine's sentence: "Elles l'enlacent avec désir effréné, et il danse evec elles jusqu'à ce qu'il tombe mort" is shortened by Gautier to: "Il faut qu'il danse avec elles jusqu'à ce qu'il tombe mort." Edwin Binney 3rd, *Les ballets de Théophile Gautier* (Paris: Librairie Nizet, 1965), 91. See the translation of Gautier's shortened version in the libretto, Appendix C (i).

[4] Gautier, *Histoire de l'art dramatique*, vol. 2, 137–138, tr. in Gautier, *Gautier on Dance*, 94–95. According to Arthur Pougin, as Vannina Olivesi points out, the project was initiated by Gautier, Perrot, and Adolphe Adam, who joined forces with Saint-Georges. And for Gautier, continues Olivesi, it was crucial to work with Perrot because of his proximity to Carlotti Grisi. Olevesi, "Entre discretion et quête de reconnaissance: Jean Coralli à l'Opéra," 180–181; Arthur Pougin, *Adolphe Adam, sa vie, sa carrière, ses mémoires artistiques* (Paris: G. Charpentier, 1877), 162.

[5] Adam composed the first act in seventeen days (11 April–28 April), and completed the entire ballet on 8 June. He dated each portion of the score as he composed it.

[6] *Le Moniteur des théâtres*, 12 May 1841, tr. in Guest, *Romantic Ballet in Paris*, 359.

recent debut at the Opéra had caused a sensation. Too, Vernoy de Saint-Georges, an experienced librettist, did indeed help build a strong plot around a young woman who loves to dance and who dies before her wedding day to return as a ghostly Wili.

Gautier's original conception was long on atmosphere but short on character development and plot. The first act was to be set "in the ballroom of some prince."

> The chandeliers would have been lit, the flowers placed in vases, buffets laden with food, but the guests would not have arrived yet. The Wilis would be shown for an instant, attracted by the idea of dancing in a room sparkling with crystals and gilt, and the hope of ensnaring some new companions. The Queen of the Wilis would touch the floor and with her magic branch give the feet of the dancing ladies an insatiable desire for contredanses, waltzes, galops, and mazurkas. The arrival of the lords and ladies makes them fly away like airy shadows. Giselle, after having danced all night, spurred on by the dance floor and the desire to keep her lover from dancing with other women, would be surprised by the morning chill like the young Spanish girl [of Hugo's poem], and the pale Queen of the Wilis, invisible to everyone, would put her icy hand on Giselle's heart.[7]

Act Two was to be set in a "forest glade," and much of Gautier's conception centers around ghostly character-Wilis from Spain, Hungary, and India. His description exemplifies his talent for describing the sensuous, his unabashed admiration of beautiful women, and his fascination with the exotic. The action—such as it is—takes place at "a certain time of year" when

> the Wilis gather in a forest glade by the shore of a lake, where large water lilies spread their disc-like leaves on the viscous water which closes in on the drowned dancers. Moonbeams glitter between those black, carved-up hearts that seem to float like loves that are dead. Midnight chimes, and from every point of the horizon, led by will-o'-the-wisps, come the shades of girls who died at the ball or on account of dancing: first, with a purring of castanets and a swarming of white butterflies, with a large comb cut out like the interior of a Gothic cathedral, and silhouetted against the moon, comes a cachucha dancer from Seville, a gitana, twisting her hips and wearing finery with cabalistic signs on her skirts—then a Hungarian dancer in a fur bonnet, making the spurs on her boots chatter, as teeth do with cold—then a *bibiaderi* [bayadère] in a costume like Amani's, a bodice with a sandal-wood satchel, gold lamé trousers, belt and necklace of mirror-bright mail, bizarre jewellery, rings through her nostrils, bells on her ankles—and then, lastly, timidly presenting herself, a *petit rat* of the Opéra in practice dress, with a kerchief round her neck and her hands thrust into a little muff. All these costumes, exotic and commonplace, are discoloured and take on a sort of spectral uniformity. The solemn assembly takes place and ends with the scene when the dead girl leaves her tomb and seems to come to life again in the passionate embrace of her lover who believes he can feel her heart beating alongside his.[8]

---

[7] Gautier, *Histoire de l'art dramatique*, 137–138, tr. in Gautier, *Gautier on Dance*, 94–95.

[8] Preface to *Giselle*, published in Théophile Gautier, *Théâtre: mystère, comédies et ballets* (Paris: Charpentier, 1872), 366, tr. in Guest, *Romantic Ballet in Paris*, 2nd ed., 205.

As Gautier later admitted, he was ignorant "of theatrical devices and the demands of the stage" when he first conceived of the ballet.[9] But, in collaboration with Saint-Georges, he devised a story with compelling characters and several conflicts—between Duke Albert and his squire, between Giselle and her mother, and of course among the characters in the two love triangles, for the attractive Giselle has two suitors, and her lover, as it turns out, has two girlfriends.

Act One. As the curtain rises on a picturesque scene in a small German village, vine-gatherers depart for the harvest. Hilarion the gamekeeper arrives, hoping to see the lovely Giselle. He hides when his rival Albert—really a Duke disguised as a peasant named Loys—emerges from his cottage with his squire Wilfride. Wilfride begs his master not to pursue Giselle, but Albert ignores this advice and sends Wilfride away. Albert knocks on Giselle's door; she comes out of her cottage and the two of them delightedly talk and dance together. As they embrace, Hilarion, unable to restrain himself any longer, runs up to Giselle and reproaches her conduct. Giselle reacts disdainfully, and Albert warns him to cease his amorous pursuit of Giselle. Angrily, Hilarion departs.

A troupe of young vinegatherers comes to fetch Giselle, for duty calls—the grapes must be harvested. Giselle, passionately fond of dancing and diversion, talks them into postponing work and dancing instead. Everyone joins together in a merry German waltz. The carefree scene is interrupted by Giselle's mother Berthe, who comes out of her cottage to upbraid her daughter: "You are always dancing instead of working! What's more, Berthe says, your health is fragile, and if you dance too much, you could die." As the village girls gather around, Berthe tells the frightening tale of the Wilis—ghosts of dead brides-to-be who never reached their wedding day—who rise from their graves at night to kill any men who happen by. The village girls are terrified by this story; Giselle alone is unfazed and laughs it off.

The fanfares of the hunt are heard in the distance. Albert is worried by this sound, and he quickly hurries the peasant girls away and departs the scene himself. Hilarion, now alone, furtively gains entry to Albert's cottage in an attempt to find out his rival's true identity. Soon the noble hunting party, including the magnificently dressed Prince and his daughter Bathilde, arrive in the village, hoping to find a favorable spot for repose and refreshments during the heat of the day. Berthe and Giselle happily oblige. Bathilde finds Giselle charming and engages her in conversation, inquiring about her work and her pastimes, and asking if she has a sweetheart.

The Prince sends his retinue back to the hunt, informing them that he will summon them with his horn later. After all is quiet, Hilarion emerges from his rival's cottage holding a nobleman's sword: he has figured out that his rival is a great lord; a seducer in disguise! He hides the sword, waiting for the right moment to expose the truth about Albert.

Now it is time for the harvest festival. A wagon decorated with flowers comes into view and a little Bacchus is carried triumphally astride a cask in keeping with an old country tradition. Giselle dances with Albert, surrounded by the entire village. The happy scene ends with a kiss that Albert bestows on Giselle.

At this sight, the fury of the jealous Hilarion knows no bounds. He throws himself into the middle of the crowd and declares Albert to be a nobleman in disguise. Giselle responds with disbelief. But Hilarion produces Albert's sword for all to see. He then

[9] *La Presse*, 5 July 1841, tr. in Gautier, *Gautier on Dance*, 98.

seizes the horn and blows it forcefully, summoning the entire hunting party, which comes rushing in. The nobles recognize Duke Albert and overwhelm him with salutations and deference.

Giselle can no longer doubt Albert's deception. She is devastated and goes mad. She recalls her happy times with Albert, seizes his sword, and nearly kills herself before he grabs it away. Life seems to abandon her; her mother takes her in her arms, and moments later, Giselle dies. Albert tries to revive her but determines that her heart has ceased to beat. He is consumed with despair as the peasants and noblemen gather sorrowfully around Giselle's lifeless body.

Act Two. The curtain opens in a dark and gloomy forest on the banks of a pond. Giselle's tombstone can be seen at the left; the bluish gleam of the moon gives a cold and misty appearance to the scene. Several gamekeepers arrive, cheerfully greeting one another and hoping to set up an observation post. But Hilarion warns them away: this is the place where the Wilis gather at night, attacking any men who stray into their territory, drowning them or forcing them to dance themselves to death. Distant chimes strike midnight—the hour when the Wilis appear—and the men flee in terror as will-o'-the-wisps flash threateningly around them.

Myrtha, the queen of the Wilis, arrives on the scene, mysteriously radiant and piercing the shadows of the night. She summons the other Wilis to join her in a fantastic ball. The Wilis, including Moyna and Zulmé, present themselves to their sovereign, and soon all of the Wilis are waltzing with abandon, gratifying their love for dancing which they were unable to fulfill in life. Before long, at a sign from the queen, the dance comes to an end, and Myrtha announces the arrival of a new Wili.

Giselle appears, rising from her grave, wrapped in a shroud. When Myrtha touches her with her rosemary branch, the shroud falls off and Giselle is transformed into a Wili. She dances with fervor until a sound is heard in the distance. The Wilis disperse and hide themselves.

Some youths are returning from a festival in a neighboring village. The Wilis detain them and try to force them to dance. However, an old man throws himself in the villagers' midst and warns them of the danger; they barely escape, with the Wilis in hot pursuit.

The grief-stricken Albert appears with his faithful squire, Wilfride. Though Wilfride begs his master not to linger near the fatal tomb, Albert sends him away. Soon thereafter, Albert, in his state of sorrow, believes he sees the ghost of Giselle. He tries to embrace her, but he cannot. She looks at him lovingly and throws him some roses. She disappears back into her tomb. Albert is about to depart the scene when he sees Hilarion.

Hiding behind a tree, Albert watches as the poor, hapless gamekeeper, frightened nearly to death and begging for pity from the Wilis, is forced to dance himself to exhaustion. The cruel Wilis throw him into the pond and then begin dancing among themselves.

Then, to Albert's horror, Myrtha spots him in his hiding place: a fresh victim! Desperately, he tries to escape, for he knows what cruel fate awaits him. But Giselle reappears miraculously, takes him by the hand, and leads him to her tombstone, a marble cross, which holds a power even stronger than that of the Wilis. Consequently, just as Myrtha is about to touch him with her scepter, it breaks in her hands. Myrtha is furious at her loss of power; the Wilis try to attack Albert, but they are prevented from doing so by a power greater than themselves. (This attack scene is accompanied by a fugue.)

As a last resort after watching the Wilis' fruitless attempts to assail Albert and seeking revenge on the Wili who robbed her of her prey, Myrtha extends her hand toward Giselle and casts a spell on her. Giselle begins a slow, graceful dance, as though transported by an involuntary delirium. Just as Myrtha had hoped, Albert is unable to resist Giselle and he leaves the cross—the only thing that could protect him—and begins dancing ardently with her. Giselle has no choice but to keep dancing, for she is under Myrtha's spell. Albert becomes exhausted.

Just as it seems Albert will dance himself to death, the first rays of the sun appear. It is morning! The chimes strike four. Albert's life is saved. Because the Wilis lose their power in daylight, they must withdraw. Giselle, too, must return to her grave. Albert kneels by her and gives her a kiss, as if to restore her to life, but Giselle seems to say that she must obey her fate and leave him forever. Suddenly, loud fanfares are heard; Wilfride, the faithful squire, arrives on the scene with the Prince and Bathilde, whose efforts, he hopes, will be more effective than his own in persuading Albert to leave this place of sadness. Giselle points Albert toward Bathilde, as if to tell him it is her last wish that he marry the young noblewoman. Albert is heartbroken, but the Wili's command to him seems sacred. With sorrow, Albert gathers up the flowers on her grave and lovingly presses them to his lips and to his heart. As he falls into the arms of those who surround him, he reaches out his hand to Bathilde.

Characters, in order of appearance

As the head gamekeeper, **Hilarion** holds a position of prestige and authority in the village. He answers to the Prince, protects the forest, and keeps poachers away from the game. He lacks the refined manners of an aristocrat, but he is strong and skilled. He is also a man of powerful feelings who is in love with Giselle and envious of Loys, and is frustrated and angry at being the odd man out in a love triangle. His love for Giselle never wavers in either the first or second act.

Crucially, Hilarion also acts as a narrator of sorts in his three first-act solo scenes, starting by directly pointing to the cottages of Giselle and Albert and explaining to the audience the two lovers' mutual affection and his own vexation. Thus, the character must exude energy as a man with a personal story to tell—a story of love for Giselle, rancor toward Albert, and confusion followed by a sense of triumph when he finally figures out the mystery of his rival's identity and then exposes it to the entire village.

Albert, who taken the false name "Loys" and pretends to be a peasant, is really a nobleman. Despite his engagement to Bathilde, the daughter of the Prince of Courlande, he enjoys escaping to the little village near his castle to see Giselle. He is youthful, stubborn, and accustomed to having his way. He does not seem to have considered the consequences of his Act One ruse, which of course prove to be dire.

In the second act, Albert is heartbroken and humbled. In the end, though Giselle has given him the gift of her love, death makes it impossible for Albert to abide with her forever. He must return to his mortal life and to Bathilde, whose forgiving hand he gratefully accepts.

A note: In this book, following the original libretto and other early sources, we use the name "Albert." The Germanic variant "Albrecht," as Ivor Guest has pointed out, came into use in England in the twentieth century, "being justified by Gautier's use of it in the article on *Giselle* in *Les beautés de l'Opéra*."[10]

---

[10] Guest, *Jules Perrot*, 69.

The squire **Wilfride**, probably of noble birth and about the same age as his young master Albert, is sensible and discreet. He makes his first entrance early in the ballet alongside his master as the two argue about the wisdom of Albert's plan to woo Giselle. Wilfride does his best to keep Albert away from Giselle in Act One and from her grave in Act Two.

Wilfride is steadfast, loyal, and utterly devoted to Albert's welfare, even in the worst of circumstances. He is wiser than his master, but must also show restraint, and is obliged to obey his master's orders. His approach is to offer advice—sometimes emphatically—and then do Albert's bidding.

Giselle. The title character is one of the most compelling of the nineteenth-century stage: the pretty and vivacious young villager, who falls in love with a disguised nobleman, dies of a broken heart when he betrays her, and then returns in ghostly form and ultimately saves him from the murderous attacks of her sister Wilis. Giselle's radical transformation from vibrant village girl to bloodless ghost offers special challenges and rewards to the performer and has enthralled audiences for many generations.

As the nineteenth-century sources tell us, Giselle is high-spirited to the point of being a bit rebellious: she breaks the rules by leading the other girls in a merry waltz when they are supposed to be harvesting grapes. Yes, she is a vivacious and popular girl whose mother believes that "fatigue and excitement could be fatal to her," but this worry in no way decreases Giselle's vibrancy nor her feistiness.[11] (Berthe's concern for her daughter's physical health is a leftover—never fully explained in the *Giselle* libretto—from Hugo's poem in which the dance-loving Spanish girl, once a frail infant, dies as a teenager after taking a chill late in the evening at a ball.) In Act One, Giselle is the most popular girl in the village, esteemed by her female friends and pursued by two prospective suitors. She is the one whom all the girls want to greet as the workday begins and the one who is crowned Queen of the Vintage at the harvest festival. (We note that Giselle, in the nineteenth-century sources we have examined, does not suffer a bout of fatigue during the Act One waltz.)

More than a few dancers playing this role, however, have made Giselle a fragile, psychologically vulnerable character throughout the first act—quivering lips, eyes darting, weak smile, cowering, simpering, and in some cases, so painfully shy that she can scarcely summon the courage to meet Loys's eyes with her own in the first-act *scène d'amour* (the daisy-petal scene).[12]

A weak and simpering Giselle, however, is quite at odds with the self-confident, cheery Giselle called for in the original sources. For Giselle is unafraid to speak her mind and quite ready to defy anyone with whom she disagrees.

First, we see her becoming annoyed with Loys, who is late for a "date" in their first scene together. (He is playfully hiding from her.) Giselle spunkily says, "He will pay for this!" and is leaving the stage when Loys finally does appear. And then she confidently plays "hard to get" for much of the scene.

Next, we see her standing up to Hilarion, who has interrupted her flirtatious cavortings with Albert and chided her for kissing Loys. After crossing her arms in front of her

---

[11] In Scene VI of the libretto, Berthe tells Loys that "fatigue and excitement could be fatal to her, the doctor has told her; it could do her harm." See Appendix C (i).

[12] The term *scène d'amour*, which does not appear in the early *Giselle* sources (autograph score, orchestra parts, copied orchestra score), was used possibly for the first time in Adam, *Giselle*, reduction by V. Cornette (Paris: Meissonier, n.d. [1841?]), 9.

chest and forcing Hilarion to walk backward as she advances on him, she says, "If I gave Loys a kiss, it is because I love him." And when Hilarion asks "and me?" she responds with a laugh, says, "I don't care," and runs happily to the other side of the stage.[13]

Next, we see Giselle standing up to her mother, Berthe, who is displeased that the village girls have thrown aside their grape-harvesting tools and are waltzing instead of working.

Thus has Giselle defied her three main interlocutors in Act One—Loys, then Hilarion, then Berthe—displaying a good bit of verve and even chutzpah. Therefore, in the final scene of Act One, Giselle's sudden descent into madness should come as a shock to the audience. To see a strong and lively young woman go mad is a far more potent theatrical experience than seeing a simpering, weak one do so, for she is travelling a much greater psychological distance.

More important, Giselle's strong will and sparkling personality in the first act turn into a quiet, steely strength in the second act: she is the only one of all the characters on stage who defies Myrtha, the fiercest character in the ballet. Even though Giselle is now a ghost, her fundamental strength and natural defiance remain in place. We see this plainly when she bursts through a perfectly placed line of Wilis to save Albert when he finds himself face to face with Myrtha. Much to Myrtha's dismay, Giselle leads Albert to the cross (because the power of Wilis—like that of vampires—is nullified by the cross). As long as Albert stands by it, the Wilis cannot harm him. Myrtha's strategy is to force Giselle to dance so beguilingly that Albert cannot help but leave the safety of the cross to get closer to his beloved Giselle. As the libretto says,

> Soon [Giselle's] graces and ravishing poses attract him despite himself; this is what the queen wanted: he leaves the holy cross that protects him from death, and approaches Giselle.

Still, Giselle has already stalled for time by bringing him to the cross (if only for a short time), and she does manage to keep him alive until dawn, when the power of the rising sun forces the Wilis to return once again to their graves. Giselle's goodness and love has triumphed over Myrtha's cruelty and saved the life of the man Giselle loves.

Giselle's mother, **Berthe**, is a wise woman of strong convictions who loves her daughter deeply. She appears several times in the first act; her celebrated mime monologue, in which she explains to the village girls who the Wilis are, is one of the best in the nineteenth-century ballet repertory. Like her daughter, Berthe is a woman of fortitude and a force to be reckoned with. Indeed, until the first-act finale, the mom-and-teenager relationship between them might be recognizable today: a mother fearing for the safety of a daughter who prefers to throw caution to the wind. Finally: Berthe is *not* dotty or confused (see below).

The **Prince of Courlande** is a magnificently wealthy landowner of proud bearing and great authority. The highest-ranking person in the ballet, he enjoys hunting as a pastime. Comfortable being served by the lowly villagers who live on his land, the Prince is also quite at ease when he speaks with his gamekeeper Hilarion, whom he approaches in the final scene of Act One. The Prince is respected, and a bit feared, by his prospective son-in-law Albert.

---

[13] These quoted lines are from Henri Justamant's staging manual for *Giselle* (pp. 14 and 25), which will be discussed at length later in this chapter.

Bathilde, the daughter of the Prince of Courlande, is a dignified, elegant young woman who is happily engaged to Albert. She is "kind and generous" as Gautier says; she steps across social boundaries to chat amiably with Giselle, and when Giselle dies, Bathilde "melts in tears." Moreover, at the end of Act Two, she kindly returns to take Albert back after his near-death ordeal. (Soviet-era productions of *Giselle* depicting Bathilde as a heartless aristocrat do not reflect what is described in the performance sources discussed in this volume.)

Myrtha, Queen of the Wilis, is much more than an icy, cruel female bent on hurting any mortal men who happen across her path. Though many latter-day Myrthas are simply cruel, her actions (as stipulated in the sources) and her music actually reveal her to be a more complex and interesting character—specifically, one with a soft, nature-loving side.

In her opening solo scene, consisting of three consecutive variations, we see her enjoying herself thoroughly in a lush, humid, and inviting night setting (in a "burning sensuous atmosphere," as Gautier said).[14]

Next, her queenly authority comes to the fore: she summons the Wilis from their graves and exerts full control over them—supervising their dancing at the "bal fantastique" and then, Svengali-like, dictating Giselle's movements right after she has emerged from her fresh grave. Finally, once Myrtha has allowed her cruel side to emerge fully, she heartlessly orders the Wilis to kill first Hilarion and then Albert. She is a sort of emcee of death in the lengthy scene in which she compels Giselle to inveigle Albert away from the safety of the cross. Here, her cruelty and bitterness are on full display, and she wants nothing more than for Albert to die as Hilarion has.

The Wilis, ghosts of young brides-to-be who died before their wedding days, like their Queen first appear to be harmless. Beautiful and ethereal, they gather every night on the banks of a pond by a forest to dance together, enjoying their sisterhood and the lushly vegetated scenery around them (which includes, according to the libretto, rushes, reeds, clumps of wildflowers, aquatic plants, birch trees, aspens and weeping willows). Some of their actions in their opening ensemble number, a *bal fantastique*, even suggest bathing in a pool or lake according to Justamant's account of it: he shows seven of them, backs to the audience, kneeling on one knee, "lower[ing] themselves forward and then raising their arms *en couronne*" three times, framed by four pairs of Wilis on each side, shifting positions between standing and kneeling.[15] All of this is done to pleasantly flowing, feminine-sounding music (flutes, trills, harp, major key). The Wilis keep up their sensuous ways when, a couple of scenes later, they strike "voluptuous" poses in an attempt to attract some village youths who are passing through the woods.

It is not until later in the act that the vampire-ish side of their nature is revealed when they follow their Queen's orders and attack Hilarion, ensuring his death. The Wilis continue in this vein until the sunrise dissipates their powers and they totter weakly back to their graves.

A contextual note: As noted in Chapter 1, the "females at play" scene was a favorite scene type at the Opéra in both ballets and operas during the period *Giselle* was created. But the usual practice was for such females at play to dance or sing, or both, in a pleasing manner—not to hector anyone, much less turn out to be murderous vampires. *Giselle's* dramatically effective genre-bending surely contributed to the ballet's appeal to its early audience, who would have understood the irony of it.[16]

---

[14] Gautier, *Histoire de l'art dramatique*, vol. 2, 133–142, tr. in Gautier, *Gautier on Dance*, 98–99.

[15] Justamant, *Giselle*, 144.

[16] The Wilis may also be generically related to indigenous Americans depicted in another ballet, which is discussed in Spencer et al., "Justamant's *Le Bossu*."

The Music

Adolphe Adam, acclaimed as the finest ballet composer of his era, was deluged with praise for his *Giselle* score at the time of the ballet's premiere. One critic lauded him for the appropriately German tone; for the "elegance, freshness, and variety of the melodies," the "new and daring harmonic combinations."[17] Another called his score "a gift to which ballet-pantomime is not generally accustomed,"[18] a nod to the belief that theater composers seldom saved their best ideas for ballet, expending them instead on opera, in 1841 a more musically prestigious genre.

Before examining the music of *Giselle*, we shall list the sources that preserve it in its earliest forms. First is Adam's autograph score for *Giselle* (that is, the score in his own hand), now bound in a single volume and comprising 131 folios, and housed at the Bibliothèque Nationale de France, Département de la Musique.[19] As noted above, Adam composed the score between 11 April and 8 June 1841, signing and dating each new section as he worked. In black ink, the composer also wrote annotations from the libretto into the score (some of them verbatim quotations), indicating what action he intended to portray musically at various junctures in the score (for instance, "Entrance of Hilarion"; "you will be turned into a Wili"; "Loys, worried, leads everyone off the stage"; "Satanic laughter").

The autograph score, unsurprisingly, includes a number of passages that never made it into the final version of the ballet. (For instance, music apparently intended as the soundtrack for Giselle imagining her wedding to Loys in Act One is struck through.)

[17] Escudier, *La France musicale*, 4 July 1841. See the letter of Adam to Saint-Georges, published by Serge Lifar in *La danse: les grands courants de la danse académique* (Paris: Denoël, 1938), 281–284. As Lifar points out, Adam's comments bear striking similarities to remarks made by Escudier in this review of *Giselle*. Adam: "They noticed especially a waltz danced by Petipa and Carlotta, which had, I believe, all the German color indicated by the locality." Escudier: "A ravishing waltz, with the German color of the subject . . . will have the popularity of Strauss's most beautiful waltzes." Adam: "[In] the march of the vine-gatherers, the rhythm is original." Escudier: "The divertissements begun by the vinegatherer's march are of striking and original rhythm." Adam: "The *pas de deux* of Carlotta and Petipa of which the last motif [is] in the genre villageois, is pleasing." Escudier: "The *pas de deux* between Giselle and Loys ends with a *louré* movement, which affords great pleasure." Adam: "The galop, except for the reprise in the middle, is mediocre and a little common." Escudier: "The galop which ends the divertissement is less distinguished than the pieces which preceded it, but the rhythm is fetching, and that is all one needs for a galop." Adam: "That which is the best as music is the finale, where the mad scene is found; it is treated like the finale of an opera. It had much effect." Escudier: "The final of the first act, where one finds the mad scene, is a complete piece with all its developments, and we don't know if there exists a better finale in all of the operas of the composer." Adam: "At the appearance of Mlle. Dumilâtre [Myrtha] there was a very novel effect—it is the quartet of muted violins in the high range, accompanied by four harps." Escudier: "We must cite . . . the novel effect of the orchestra which accompanies the appearance of the queen of the Wilis; on the arpeggios of the harp, four first violins, with mutes, execute in the high strings a melody in four parts, of which the effect is truly magical. Really, one feels suddenly transported to the domain of the fairies. This combination of instruments is entirely new, and the effect is excellent." Adam: "There is also something new in the connection of the application of the dance to the music in the effect of the fugue where all the dancers follow the entrances of the subject of the fugue." Escudier: "There are those who will tell you of a heavy . . . music in this score: it's the learned music. . . . It's a very original idea. Four entries of the subject reproduced by four entries of corps members. Is a fugue a good thing in a dance? It's a new problem which M. Coralli has just victoriously resolved. However, we suspect strongly that M. Adam, who is not a [choreographer] . . . had a bit of a say in the setting of this segment." Adam: "The last *pas* danced by Carlotta is a viola solo admirably played by Urhan. The use of a [viola] soloist is very rare; I only know of two examples: the accompaniment of a simple, naïve and pretty air in *La fête du village voisin* of Boieldieu and that of an air of *Freischütz*, sung by Mlle Nau." Escudier: "Nothing is more sweet or melancholy than this instrument, so rarely used as a *récitant*."

[18] *Le Constitutionnel*, 1 July 1841.

[19] Paris, Bibliothèque Nationale de France, Département de la Musique, MS-2644.

The musical examples in this chapter are drawn from the autograph score unless otherwise noted. We employ Adam's numbering for Act One and, in the absence of the composer's scene numbering in Act Two, we use the numbering found in the Titus *répétiteur* (a rehearsal score created shortly after the premiere of *Giselle*; see later in this chapter).

Another important source for *Giselle* is the orchestra score, likely copied by the Opéra's scribes from the autograph and comprising three volumes.[20] It is not dated but may also have been created as early as 1841.[21] Today housed at the Bibliothèque-Musée de l'Opéra, this score includes some copying errors and many post-1841 annotations and revisions. In the same archive one may find a set of extant parts and short scores comprising fifty-three items. Most of these appear to have been in use from 1841 through 1868, the years of Giselle's initial twenty-seven-year run in the Opéra's repertory.[22]

Finally, let us note the so-called *Pas des paysans*, or Peasant *pas de deux*, a multi-movement divertissement for the dancers Nathalie Fitzjames and Auguste Mabille added to the harvest festival scene in time for the premiere of *Giselle*.[23] (It was placed directly after Giselle and Albert's *pas de deux*, according to the copied orchestra score.) The six-movement suite was composed by Johann Friedrich Franz Burgmüller, its final waltz having already been published as *Souvenir de Ratisbonne*, op. 67 (Ratisbonne, or Regensberg, being Burgmüller's birthplace.)[24] We do not know if Burgmüller composed the other five numbers in this suite expressly for *Giselle* or if he had already composed them. It does not appear, of course, in Adam's autograph score, but may be found in the parts and the copied orchestra score.

Now we shall point out salient features of the *Giselle* score.

Recurring motifs

Let us begin with an accounting of the recurring melodies that are heard in *Giselle*. There are many of them, though neither Adam nor the critics made mention of them in their commentaries—perhaps because ballet audiences were accustomed to such motifs, for they were common in Parisian ballet scores of the period. They are well worth noting, for they accomplish a great deal of dramatic work: enhancing characterization, supplying information, helping the audience follow the action, providing the depth afforded by recollection, and bringing cohesiveness to the drama.

One motif each is allotted to particular characters or groups of characters: Hilarion, Berthe, the hunting party of nobles, the vinegatherers, and the Wilis (when they are in

[20] Paris, Bibliotheque Nationale de France, Bibliothèque-Musée de l'Opéra, A-533 (A 1–3).

[21] Its pages bear the mark of an inventory made in 1854.

[22] Paris, Bibliothèque Nationale de France, Bibliothèque-Musée de l'Opéra, MAT-332 (1–53).

[23] This addition was likely made at the behest of the banker Alexandre Aguado. Concerning the interpolation of the Burgmüller *pas de deux*, see Horst Koegler, "Wenn die Musik die gehorsame Tochter des Tanzes zu sein hat" [When music must be the obedient daughter of dance], in *Prima la danza. Festschrift für Sibylle Dahms*, eds. Gunhild Oberzaucher-Schüller, Daniel Brandenburg, and Monika Woitas (Würzburg: Königshausen und Neumann, 2004), 374.

[24] See Guest, *Romantic Ballet in Paris*, 2nd ed., 211. *Souvenir de Ratisbonne* is dedicated to the Duchess of Kent (1786–1861), Queen Victoria's mother. *Souvenir de Ratisbonne, grande valse brillante pour le piano*, op. 67 (Paris: Colombier, n.d.). Incidentally, Queen Victoria attended two performances of *Giselle* in London in 1842 and ordered an arrangement of dances based on Adam's score to be played at a ball in Buckingham Palace in April of the same year.

Ex. 2.1a Vinegatherers' motif; Act One, No. 1, bars 1–10

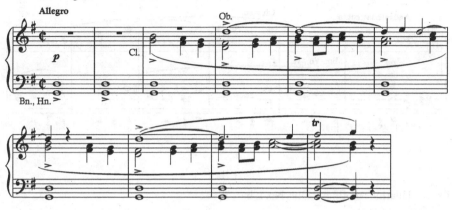

Ex. 2.1b Act One, No. 5, bars 249–263 (text from Titus *répétiteur*)

attack mode). The first of these is the *vinegatherers' motif*, sounded at curtain-up as the vinegatherers appear: it is country music, plain and simple, with a drone in the lower register accompanying a sweet stepwise tune played by wind instruments (Ex. 2.1a). It returns later in Act One as Giselle is describing her daily activities to Bathilde: "in the morning I work." (Ex. 2.1b). And it comes back again—wistfully—before curtain-up in Act Two (Ex. 2.1c), this time answered by a mournful-sounding oboe.

Hilarion's motif, which hints at his furtiveness (Ex. 2.2), is heard as he arrives on stage for the first time and again for two of his later entries in Act One.

Berthe's motif reflects the fact that she is talking when she arrives on stage (indeed, Berthe as a character has plenty to say): it is syncopated, following one of the techniques typical of "talking music" in Parisian ballet in the 1830s and 1840s (Ex. 2.3a).[25] One fragment from Berthe's motif, the neighbor-note figure *do-re-do*, is incorporated meaningfully into later conversations as Berthe speaks her mind—first admonishing her

[25] For a discussion of "talking music" in ballet, see Smith, *Ballet and Opera*, 101–114.

Ex. 2.1c Act Two, No. 1, bars 13–18

Ex. 2.2 Hilarion's motif; Act One, No. 1, bars 35–42

daughter and the village girls to "listen well" as she warns them of the danger of the Wilis (Ex. 2.3b), and again as Berthe tells Bathilde that Giselle's dancing is foolish. In both cases, says Berthe, Giselle's well-being is at stake.

The *hunting party's motif* is, unsurprisingly, a horn call (Ex. 2.4), which sounds in the distance as Giselle and her mother return to their cottage after Berthe has unsettled the village girls by telling them about Wilis. It is heard again not long afterward as the hunting party, still in the woods, gets a little closer and Hilarion approaches Loys's empty house curiously. And it is heard again, even louder, as the hunting party arrives on the stage. After the aristocrats' sojourn in the village, we hear the motif again as they return to the hunt. The horn call is always diegetic (heard by the characters).

Finally, the *Wilis' attack motif*: this ferocious bit of music is first heard when the Wilis start chasing Hilarion, again as they assail him, a third time as they turn their fury on Albert, and yet again as they try to kill him (Ex. 2.5). It communicates their relentlessness.

The waltz. Giselle leads her friends in an animated waltz in Act One (Ex. 2.6a), and its main theme is quoted later in the act to refer generally to Giselle's love for dancing: first as mother and daughter argue about it; next when Giselle begins to dance after Bathilde asks her what her pleasures are (Exx. 2.6b and 2.6c). Both times, Berthe (to the sound of the neighbor-note figure from her motif) voices firm objections.

Giselle's sad recollections in the mad scene. After Giselle finds out that Albert has betrayed her, she loses her mind and—wandering the stage forlornly in a daze—recalls happy events that had transpired earlier in the act, both of them accompanied by melodies using the pitch configuration *mi-fa-re.* The first is the flirtatious

Ex. 2.3a Berthe's motif; Act One, No. 4, bars 204–211

Ex. 2.3b Berthe says, "Listen well" (*bien écoute*); she is about to warn Giselle and the village girls about the Wilis; Act One, No. 4, bars 253–254 (text from Titus *répétiteur*)

Ex. 2.4 Hunting party's motif; Act One, No. 5, bars 1–4

Ex. 2.5 Wilis' attack motif; Act Two, No. 13, *Allegro feroce*, bars 1–6

encounter in the daisy-petal scene (known more commonly as the *scène d'amour*[26]) in which Giselle playfully plucks petals from a daisy to find out if Albert really loves her (Ex 2.7a).[27]

---

[26] See note 12, earlier in this chapter.
[27] This scene is not always performed as a playful one today.

Ex. 2.6a Waltz; Act One, No. 4, bars 54–63

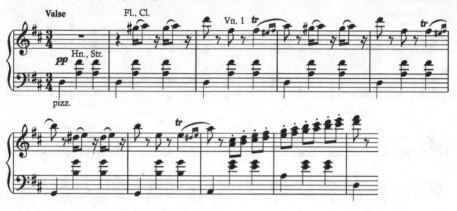

Ex. 2.6b Act One, No. 4, bars 229–238: Mother and daughter argue, bars 229–236; Berthe warns her daughter, bars 237–238 (text from Titus *répétiteur*)

The daisy-petal music returns in the mad scene immediately after Giselle has turned Albert around and said, "It is not him" (Ex. 2.7b); soon she will re-enact the memory of plucking the petals from the daisy.[28]

The second of Giselle's sad recollections in the mad scene is of the *louré* the couple so affectionately danced at the harvest festival (Ex. 2.8a). The accompaniment drops out at the neighbor-note figure (Ex. 2.9b, bars 232 and 236–237) as Giselle's mind drifts. This broken-off neighbor-note fragment is then is played *forte* in bar 238, followed by a downward scale in the high register as Giselle runs down to the footlights to the left, and then *pianissimo* in bar 240 followed by an upward scale in the high register as she goes to the

---

[28] Titus *répétiteur*, 79. See note 78, later in this chapter.

Ex. 2.6c Act One, No. 5, bars 268–282: Giselle tells Bathilde that she dances in the evenings, bars 271–278; Berthe expresses her objections, bars 279–282 (text from Titus *répétiteur*)

Ex. 2.7a Daisy-petal music; Act One, No. 3, bars 66–74

right—an effective portrayal of Giselle's derangement. The fragment is also reminiscent of Berthe's motif, ensuring that Berthe's warning resounds during this crisis.

When Hilarion and the gardes-chasses first spot Giselle's grave, we hear the *louré* again, this time chromatically and wistfully reharmonized (Ex. 2.8c).

Ex. 2.7b The daisy-petal music in the mad scene; Act One, Finale (*Scène de folie*), bars 189–195

Ex. 2.8a *Louré*; Act One, No. 8 (*Pas de deux*), bars 120–131

Later in the act, as the Wili Giselle emerges from her grave, Adam brings back once again the three-note *mi-fa-re* figure from the beginning of the *Louré*, this time unmoored from its gently rocking accompaniment (Ex. 2.8d).[29] The strings play the figure and the flute echoes it with an up-a-third-down-a-second response on pitches *fi-la-sol*. We hear the echo again at the moment when Albert, much to his surprise, first sees the Wili Giselle (Ex. 2.8e). Here, all that is left of the *louré* is this flute echo, which remains as a fleeting

---

[29] This three-note figure may, at the same time, refer to the daisy-petal theme (which also uses the pitches *mi-fa-re*), though to our ears the equal duration of the three pitches more strongly suggests the *louré* theme.

Ex. 2.8b The *louré* returns in the mad scene; Act One, Finale (*Scène de folie*), bars 228–241

Ex. 2.8c The *gardes-chasses* see Giselle's grave; Act Two, No. 3, bars 1–10

symbol of the couple's one-time happiness. At the same time, it can be read as an almost playful greeting from the Wili Giselle to Albert. (For, as we shall point out below, this Act Two scene mirrors the Act One scene in which Albert playfully hid from Giselle.)

Berthe's description of the Wilis is a twenty-two-bar passage in which she explains to the village girls who the Wilis are ("the earth opens up and shroud-covered phantoms come out"; Ex. 2.9).[30] It recurs nearly note-for-note in Act Two as Berthe's words come to

---

[30] Titus *répétiteur*, 26.

Ex. 2.8d Act Two, No. 10, bars 19–25; note that the music in this passage has modulated to D major

Ex. 2.8e Albert sees the Wili Giselle for the first time; Act Two, No. 13, *Andante moderato*, bars 1–6

life with the emergence of the will o' the wisps, the first supernatural life-form to be seen in the ballet.

The rising arpeggio that characterizes this passage belongs to the category of the "ombra topic," as Helena Kopchick Spencer has pointed out—a topic representing "ghosts, gods, moral values, or punishments"[31] in eighteenth-century music, and in the nineteenth century one that "continued to prove effective for scenes of supernatural

---

[31] Leonard Ratner, *Classic Music: Expression, Form, and Style* (New York: Schirmer, 1980), 24. See Spencer, "*Jardin des femmes*," 320.

Ex. 2.9 Berthe tells the village girls about the Wilis; Act One, No. 4, bars 256–270

apparitions: indeed, its rising scalar or arpeggio figures were still a potent metaphor for spirits rising from the dead."[32]

Borrowed music

One critic pointed out that Adam's score was "entirely new" (or nearly so), for indeed, Adam made little use of borrowed music in *Giselle*, mostly eschewing the longtime

[32] Spencer, "*Jardin des femmes*," 320. As she writes, "Ratner has identified examples of the ombra topic in nineteenth-century works such as Verdi's *Macbeth* (namely, Macbeth's vision of the ghosts of eight kings in Act III)." Spencer, "*Jardin des femmes*," 320n480. See Leonard Ratner, *Romantic Music: Sound and Syntax* (New York: Schirmer, 1992), 70.

practice of relying on pre-existing music—and its contextual implications—to help explain the action.[33] (The practice was on the wane anyway by 1841.) However, he did make two such referential borrowings in *Giselle*. In the first, heard shortly before Giselle unknowingly meets her rival in love, Bathilde, Adam alludes to the eventual sad outcome of Giselle's liaison with Albert by using the main melody from a popular song of the day, "Mes rêves de jeune fille," about a young girl who, like Giselle, loves to dance and whose dreams of marrying go sadly unfulfilled (Exx. 2.10a–b).

Loïsa Puget (music) and Gustave Lemoine (text) "Mes rêves de jeune fille" [1840?][34]

[Avec grace.]
Jeune fille de quatorze ans,
je rêvais de fleurs, de rubans;
toujours les robes les plus belles
et les modes les plus nouvelles.
la nuit, sur mes doigts je comptais
les *galop*s que je danserais
[Doux.] et puis, je m'invitais d'avance
en me fesant la révèrence
    [Doux et un peu moins vite.]
    mon Dieu, mon Dieu!
    que je rêvais de belles choses!
    [Très doux.] dans l'avenir, je ne voyais
    que fleurs et roses!

[Gracefully]
Young girl of fourteen,
I dreamed of flowers, of ribbons;
always the most beautiful dresses
and the newest fashions.
At night, I counted on my fingers
the *galop*s that I would do
[Softly] and then, I invited myself to dance
by doing a little bow to myself
    [Softly and a little more slowly]
    My god, my god!
    how I dreamed of beautiful things
    [Very softly] in the future, I saw
    nothing but flowers and roses!

2ᵉ Couplet.
Jeune fille de quatorze ans,
je rêvais de maris *[Bas.]* galans
de mien était un beau jeune homme,
qui venait d'Espagne ou de Rome
son cœur était un vrai trésor;
il avait des éperons d'or;
j'étais fière d'être sa femme
et l'on disait place à madame
    [Très doux, moins vite.]
    mon Dieu, mon Dieu!
    que je rêvais de belles choses!
    [Très doux.] dans l'avenir, je ne voyais
    que fleurs et roses!

2ⁿᵈ Couplet.
Young girl of fourteen,
I dreamed of *[softly]* gallant husbands
Mine was a handsome young man
who came from Spain or Rome;
his heart was a real treasure;
he had spurs of gold;
I was proud to be his wife
and people said "make way for madame"
    [Very soft and slower]
    My God, my God!
    how I dreamed of beautiful things!
    [Very softly] in the future, I saw
    nothing but flowers and roses!

---

[33] *La France musicale*, 4 July 1841. See Smith, *Ballet and Opera*, Ch. 4: "Ballet-Pantomime and Silent Language," 97–123.

[34] This is probably the song by Puget referred to in Escudier's review of the *Giselle* score. See Guest, *Romantic Ballet in Paris*, 2nd ed., 213. The song may be seen online at https://babel.hathitrust.org/cgi/pt?id=mdp.390 15080939021&view=1up&seq=1.

3ᵉ Couplet.	3rd Couplet.
Jeune fille de quatorze ans,	Young girl of fourteen,
je rêvais de fleurs et diamans;	I dreamed of flowers and diamonds;
un jour, j'étais une duchesse,	one day, I was a duchess,
le lendemain, j'étais princesse;	the next day, I was a princess;
je m'éveillais reine un beau jour	I woke up as a queen one fine day;
à mes pieds j'avais une cour!	I held court!
on me bénissait à la ronde	I was admired all around
[gaiement] et je mariais tout	*[gaily]* and I married
le monde.	everyone.
[Tristement]	*[Sadly]*
mais las! après avoir rêvé	But alas! after dreaming
si belles choses dans l'avenir	such beautiful things in the future
je n'ai trouvé *[a volonté]* ni fleurs, ni	I did not find *[ad lib.]* either flowers,
roses!	or roses!

Ex. 2.10a Puget/Lemoine, "Mes rêves de jeune fille," bars 9–12

Ex. 2.10b Berthe welcomes Bathilde and the rest of the hunting party; Giselle meets Bathilde shortly thereafter; Act One, No. 5, bars 170–177; the tune is borrowed from "Mes rêves de jeune fille" and recast in $\frac{2}{4}$

Adam borrows from another outside source in the opening number of Act Two as the gardes-chasses convivially greet one another in the forest glade. The quotation this time is from the hunters' chorus, "Die Tale dampfen, die Höhen glüh'n," in Act Three of Weber's *Euryanthe* (1823), in which a group of happy hunters arrives in a remote place (in their case, a gorge), not realizing its dangers (Ex. 2.11a).

Weber's hunters are singing about the joy of the hunt; their mood, and perhaps even their words, would likely been recalled to the minds of any spectators familiar with Weber's opera. (The satirist author of "La Musée Philipon" certainly recognized it: "Some gamekeepers arrive and mime the chorus of *Euryanthe*. Even though it is mime, this chorus is perfectly recognizable. Decidedly, pantomime is a very expressive language!"[35])

[35] Lorentz, "Parodie de Giselle ou les Willis, ballet en deux actes," *Musée Philipon* (Paris: Chez Auber et Cie 1842–1843), 65–70.

Ex. 2.11a End of the hunters' chorus "Die Thale dampfen," *Euryanthe*, Act Three (Weber, text by Helmina von Chézy: "Let the horns blare with the Choir, you princes of the forest"); this chorus included four horns and bass trombone on the stage

Adam draws from the last four bars of Weber's chorus, using both its rhythm pattern and the distinctive sequence of harmonies, I–I$^{5/7}$–II$^{5/7}$–V$^{5/7}$–I$^{5/7}$–I, to spin out the forty-nine bars for the gathering of gardes-chasses in the forest glade (Ex. 2.11b shows the last twelve of them).

Adam also borrowed several excerpts from a work that he himself had composed: *Faust* (London, 1833), a ballet little known in Paris.[36] But he clearly did not select them for their intertextual referential value. Indeed, they went unmentioned in critical reviews, and were unlikely recognized by audiences at all. Adam, who never lacked for invention, surely reused them because he found them effective and knew they would otherwise lie fallow.[37]

The first of these is the "Marche Diabolique" in D major, which is played in Act One as an army of demons from hell files past Faust after being ordered to do so by Mephistopheles (Ex. 2.12a). (It comes back in Act Three, first in G major, then D major as the demons come on stage again.[38])

Adam gives this march to the villagers in *Giselle* as they arrive in a merry mood to celebrate at the harvest festival. That is, a *marche diabolique* has become a *marche champêtre*. The main difference is in the mood set by the introduction: In *Faust*, the march is preceded by Mephistopheles's severe, brass-dominated, martial-sounding exhortation to

---

[36] Guest, *Romantic Ballet in Paris*, 2nd ed., 156.

[37] Similarly, Adam used passages from *Faust* in his comic opera *Le Chalet*. Ivor Guest writes "[In 1833 Adam's] important work still lay in the future, but he had already shown an aptitude for writing ballet music when his brother-in-law, Pierre Laporte, manager of the King's Theatre in London, had asked him to compose the score for Deshayes' ballet *Faust* in 1833: this early work has now apparently disappeared, but Adam later incorporated several passages from it in *Giselle* and his comic opera, *Le Chalet*." Guest, *Romantic Ballet in Paris*, 2nd ed., 156. Guest did not have the opportunity to examine Adam's music for *Faust*. Fortunately, Adam's autograph score for *Faust* is now available at the Bibliothèque Nationale de France, Département de la Musique, MS 2654. For a discussion of this score and other *Faust* ballets, see Kristin Rygg, "Faust Goes Dancing," in *The Oxford Handbook of Faust in Music*, eds. Lorna Fitzsimmons and Charles McKnight (New York: Oxford University Press, 2019), doi: 10.1093/oxfordhb/9780199935185.013.24.

[38] It also appears in Act One, No. 5, fol. 65^r ff. No action is specified, and it is struck through.

Ex. 2.11b Spinning off from Weber's chorus "Die Thale dampfen"; Act Two, No. 2, bars 48–59

the demons to file past Faust (Ex. 2.12b). But in *Giselle*, it is introduced by a friendly call-and-response *allegro marcato* that evokes the feeling of villagers greeting each other as they happily make their way to the festival (Ex. 2.12c).

Adam's second borrowing from *Faust* is taken from a scene in which the title character dances with Marguerite (Ex. 2.13).[39] Adam reused this music in *Giselle* for a loving *pas de deux* between Albert and the Wili Giselle in Act Two). It is only slightly different from the version in *Faust*: it is slower (*larghetto* instead of *andantino*); the flute and violin play the melody in octaves (instead of the violins and clarinet in unison), and the accompaniment is lighter, requiring no bassoons or horns.

Adam's third borrowing from *Faust* is a sweet and tender melody that was allocated to Marguerite as she approached the chapel in Act Two (Ex. 2.14a).[40] In *Giselle*, it is used for the heartbreaking scene late in the ballet when Albert begins to move Giselle from her own grave to a bank of flowers (Ex. 2.14b). It is heard again a few moments later as she sinks into her new grave.[41]

[39] This action may be deduced from the annotation in the *Faust* autograph score on fol. 159ʳ at the next iteration of this music: here, in Act Three, Faust reminds Marguerite that they danced together. The music comes back in its original key, D major.

[40] The same melody is played by clarinet in F major in *Faust*, Act One, No. 1, *Andante non troppo*, bars 39–46. No action is specified in the score.

[41] The movements of the characters are given in the Titus *répétiteur*.

Ex. 2.12a *Faust*, Act One, No. 3, "Marche Diabolique," bars 1–11

Ex. 2.12b Introduction to the "Marche Diabolique" from *Faust*, Act One, No. 2, bars 25–31: Mephistopheles exhorts the demons to file past Faust

Ex. 2.12c Introduction to march of the villagers in *Giselle*, Act One, No. 7, bars 1–9

Ex. 2.13 *Faust*, Act Two, allemande section of *Grand pas de quatre*, bars 7–12: Faust and Marguerite dance together

Ex. 2.14a *Faust*, Act Two, No. 8, bars 21–28: Marguerite approaches the chapel ("Marguerite s'approche de la chapelle")

Sound worlds

Recurring themes were not remarked upon by newspaper critics of *Giselle* in 1841, perhaps because theatergoers were so accustomed to ballet composers making use of the device. But critics did take special notice of Adam's treatment of the supernatural world of the second act.

It is the first time that we have seen the fantastic treated with a due regard to grace and charm, and perhaps this will never be more happily achieved.[42]

[42] *La France musicale*, 4 July 1841, tr. in Guest, *Romantic Ballet in Paris*, 2nd ed., 214.

Ex. 2.14b Giselle and Albert: he begins to move her to a bank of flowers; Act Two, *Après le pas de deux*, bars 72–79

Adolphe Adam has composed for the world of supernatural dance airs full of charm, of elegance, of grace and of melancholy; it is a novel and distinguished score.[43]

Indeed, Adam did his part in conveying the ballet's dualism by creating two very different sound worlds, one for each act. The "tint" of the first act—until the finale—is mostly bright. (The only musical hint in Act One of the forbidding spirit world is heard when Berthe momentarily raises worrisome thoughts in her mime solo; Ex. 2.9). In the second act, however, Adam creates an appropriately dark and mysterious sound world by deploying many more flat-side keys and unstable harmonies than he did in the first act, more minor-mode passages, special string techniques (included muted strings and tremolo), and other effects. These include, for example, his "quartet of muted [divisi] violins in the high range, accompanied by four harps," which made for "a very novel effect at the appearance of Mlle Dumilâtre," who portrayed Myrtha, the queen of the Wilis.[44] Adam had saved the harps, which remain silent in all of the dramatic scenes in the first act and the opening scenes of the second, for this all-important moment. And their effect, in the nine-bar introduction, is striking. But the sound of the muted divisi violins that enter two bars later is even more surprising. The ethereal, other-worldly quality of this music, most of which is played on the violin quartet's E strings, provides effective contrast to the preceding passage, which reflected the fear of the worldly gamekeepers in its busy sixteenth notes in the low strings. Indeed, it is starkly different from *all* the preceding music in this ballet, which is conventionally scored and only one short segment

[43] *Le Constitutionnel*, 1 July 1841.
[44] These are Adam's words. See note 17, in this chapter.

Ex. 2.15 Act Two, No. 5, bars 10–17

Ex. 2.16 Act Two, No. 8, bars 5–20

of which (the G major *andante* in the mad scene) called for muted strings. Together with the dimly lit set and the first sight of Myrtha in her veil, rising up on a trap—an unconventional sight that imparts something of the bizarre nature of the Wilis—this strange quartet is very effective (Ex. 2.15).

Further, the composer was pleased with the magical evocation in A-flat major, scored for two English horns and two bassoons (Ex. 2.16). Played as Myrtha calls the Wilis forth with her wand, the evocation provides in its reedy glory a suitable aural complement

Ex. 2.17a Wilis' "Satanic laughter" (*rire Satanique*); Act Two, No. 13, *Allegro feroce*, bars 151–154

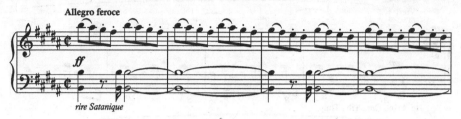

Ex. 2.17b The Wilis spot Albert, "rires Sataniques des Willis"; Act Two, No. 13, *Allegro feroce*, bars 195–201

to the natural woodland setting and implies that Wilis are related to the trees around them—born from nature. A fuller woodwind choir, replete with arpeggio outbursts, enhances the effect a few moments later.

Also effective is the "Satanic laughter" that Adam writes for the Wilis immediately after Hilarion falls, his death imminent (Ex. 2.17a).

Shortly thereafter, the Wilis spot Albert, and they laugh again, here assisted by booming trombones and ophicleides (Ex. 2.17b).[45]

Musical genres

Waltzes. In keeping with the German setting, Adam wrote four waltzes, including one for Giselle's entrance (Ex. 2.24) and another for her merry dance with the vinegatherers (the one Berthe disapproves of; Ex. 2.6a). As noted above, a waltz by Burgmüller, "Souvenir of Regensburg" or *Souvenir de Ratisbonne*, is among the set of dances added shortly before the premiere to accommodate the last-minute addition of the Peasant *pas de deux* (Ex. 3.6a–f).

---

[45] On Adam's allusions to the Turkish in this terrifying bacchanale, see Spencer, "*Jardin des femmes*," 327–329.

Ex. 2.18 Act Two, No. 7, bars 1–6

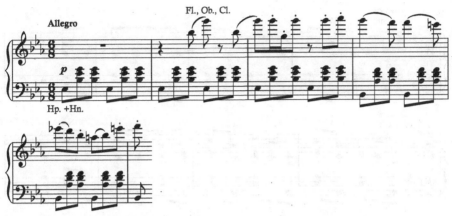

There are more waltzes, of course, in the second act. Right after the above-described ethereal entrance number, Myrtha dances to two consecutive waltzes, the first in A-flat major, the second in E-flat major. The second of these, with its hemiola, syncopations, and opening five-measure phrase, is unlike the straightforward and beguilingly simple melodies of Giselle's waltzes in Act One, and the odd alternation between low notes and high in its first phrase further suggest that something may be off kilter (Ex. 2.18). Yet another waltz, a now-standard number for Giselle, was added some years later as a variation in the *pas de deux* in Act Two (this will be discussed in Chapter 3). Cleverly, it makes use of the daisy-petal theme (Ex. 3.3).

Louré. A *louré*, a slowish dance in which the emphasis falls on the first beat of every measure, is danced by Loys and Giselle in Act One (Ex. 2.8a).[46] Adam noted in a letter that it is in the "genre villageois"; with the exception of a sixteen-bar passage in F minor, he also called for it to be played very softly until the last twenty bars.[47]

Galop. A rousing and lively galop (recognizable by its booming can-can-style backbeat) ends the divertissement, just as the galop typically came last in the set of social dances played by the musicians in the real-life ballroom (Ex. 2.19).

Character dances. The waltz, as a German character dance, is the prevailing character-dance type of this ballet. For apparently the idea of incorporating other types of character dances in *Giselle* was scrapped before the ballet's premiere, though Adam had woven bits of appropriate character music into the waltz of the *bal fantastique* to accommodate the dancing of the "foreign" character Wilis the librettists called for.

[46] The best-known *lourés* in today's classical-music world are those composed for dance suites, by, for example, J.S. Bach and G.F. Telemann. These are usually in $\frac{3}{4}$ or $\frac{6}{8}$. The best documented *lourés* known to dance historians, on the other hand, are those performed in the theater or in the court in the seventeenth and eighteenth centuries. See Wendy Hilton, "Loure," in *International Encyclopedia of Dance*, vol. 4, 231–232. The *louré* is also a bowstroke in which several notes are played in one stroke, rather gently and giving the impression of legato but with slight breaks between the notes. According to Jean-Jacques Rousseau: "Lourer: It is to nourish the sounds with sweetness [or softness], & to mark the first note of each bar more noticeably than the second, although of the same value." Jean-Jacques Rousseau, *Dictionnaire de musique* (Paris: Chez le Veuve Duchesne, 1785), 267. Among *lourés* in $\frac{4}{4}$ is one by Carl Bohm in *Hausmusik*, no. 2 (Berlin: N. Simrock, 1894).

[47] Adolphe Adam, letter to Saint-Georges, published by Serge Lifar in *La Danse*, 281–284.

Ex. 2.19   Act One, Galop, bars 19–26

Several Wilis present themselves, in turn, before their sovereign. First there is Moyna, the Odalisque, executing an oriental dance-step; then Zulmé, the Bayadere, who displays her Indian poses, then two French women, dancing a sort of bizarre minuet; then the German women, waltzing amongst themselves.[48]

This includes eight bars of a bolero (Ex. 2.20a) and eight bars of generically Middle Eastern-sounding music (played by oboe; Ex. 2.20b).[49] The "national" music remained in place, even though the Wilis were not wearing character costumes as Gautier had once imagined they should, and the choreography—except for that of the Spanish Wili (one could argue)—is classical without any hints of "national" dance.[50]

Marches. Two processions are called for in *Giselle*. One takes place during the harvest festival in the village: a little Bacchus, astride a barrel, is carried in by four *vignerons* ("four vigorous Germans," as one observer put it[51]) and followed by "peasants and children."[52] This little procession is not given its own music, but rather, occupies a few measures of the very long march (described above, and originally from *Faust*) that serves as the soundtrack for the entire festival scene—a scene that opens, according to Justamant, with the entrance of the merrymakers *en sautant* and includes a choreography for village dancers who make way for the procession of the little Bacchus (see Ex. 2.12a).[53]

The other march Adam composed for *Giselle*, for "la chasse" (the hunt), represents another class of people entirely.[54] Played by the brass and exuding grandeur, it signifies the presence of the noble hunting party. But before the march begins and before the

[48] Recall Gautier's original sketch (see p. 56), in which he called for a Gitana, a Hungarian dancer, and a bayadère.

[49] For more details, see Smith, *Ballet and Opera*, 192–193. Smith notes argues that the *bal fantastique* music also alludes to the French and German dancers mentioned in the libretto.

[50] See Smith, *Ballet and Opera*, 194. An eight-bar section on page 155 of Justamant's *Giselle* staging manual includes a turn "sur l'orteil" followed by a pose on a flat foot. The accompanying drawing shows the dancer with arms raised in fourth position. This is performed four times. The flat-footed pose may have been intended to reflect a Spanish dance pose; we find similar poses in Petipa's choreography for the *Grand pas* in *Paquita* (see Chapter 5).

[51] Published *Giselle* Argument, anonymous, Bibliothèque Nationale de France, Département de Musique.

[52] Justamant, *Giselle*, 60.

[53] The title "Marche des vignerons" is used in Adam, *Giselle* (Cornette), 32.

[54] "La chasse" is the name given this march in Adam, *Giselle* (Cornette), 22.

Ex. **2.20a** Spanish Wili; Act Two, No. 9, bars 74–81

Ex. **2.20b** Middle Eastern Wili; Act Two, No. 9, bars 82–89

hunting party arrives, we hear forty measures of distant horn calls that grow ever louder, signaling that these worthies and their *sonneurs* are approaching somewhere nearby in the woods and soon to appear (Ex. 2.4). The sound of these horn calls causes the hapless and deflated Hilarion, who is alone on stage, to be struck by an epiphany: Loys must be affiliated with these nobles!

Freshly energized, Hilarion quickly resolves to break into his rival's cottage to seek proof for this newly formed hypothesis, even though the increasingly louder horns are making it clear to him, and the audience too, that the hunting party is close by. Indeed, just before Hilarion disappears through the door into the cottage (according to the Titus *répétiteur*), the *sonneurs* playing *trompes de chasse* (hunting horns) arrive on stage, which makes for a louder, brighter, and more thrilling sound than it would from the orchestra pit. Soon thereafter, the horn calls give way to the splendid march itself, and the whole hunting party begins to arrive on stage (Ex. 2.21).

Now, for fifty-one measures (according to the Titus *répétiteur*), or approximately sixty seconds—a long time!—the hunting party enters (presumably in procession), surely impressing audiences with the magnificent costumes of the nobles, the sound of *trompes de chasse* being played on stage, and the variety of character groups. At the Opéra in

Ex. 2.21 "La Chasse"; Act One, No. 5, bars 97–104; the *trompes de chasse* are given parts independent of the full brass section in the orchestra pit

the original production, the Prince and Bathilde even entered on horseback (the Titus *répétiteur* stipulates the place in the score where they dismount, Bathilde assisted by Wilfride).[55]

Fugue. For the scene in which the Wilis attack Albert as he stands at Giselle's tomb—protected by the cross—Adam composed a four-part fugue in G major (Ex. 2.22). The severity and seeming relentlessness of the fugue, perhaps, made it appropriate for ushering in hordes of dangerous characters. Jean-Madeleine Schneitzhoeffer had similarly provided a fugue for a scene in *La Sylphide* in which witches come on stage in groups (each group in that ballet, as in *Giselle*, arriving with a statement of the fugue theme).[56] And as we shall see in Chapter 6, Adam also composed a fugue in *Le Corsaire* for the entrance of the pirates and their prisoners.

Conventions

Humor. As noted above, the first act of *Giselle*, in the manner of a comic opera, is mostly light-hearted and laced with humorous bits (like Albert making kissing sounds as he hides behind the door to Giselle's cottage). The second act, too, features whiffs of comedy, including the gardes-chasses' fearful reaction to the chiming of midnight (in the time-honored manner of easily spooked rustics) and their ensuing initial encounter with the will o' the wisps. Another light-hearted scene (long since eliminated), shows reveling villagers' brief nocturnal encounter with the Wilis, brought to a swift end by an Old Man played by the comic actor Louis Petit, whom Gautier described later as "quite the tallest

---

[55] In the Titus *répétiteur*, the instructions are "la chasse entre," "les seigneurs arrivent" (bar 113), "ils arrivent" (bar 124), and "Entrée de Wilfride de Bathilde et du Prince" (bar 138). From this we presume that they were entering in procession. Nowadays, tradition dictates that they file in from upstage left, but Titus is silent on the matter.

[56] Schneizhoeffer, *La Sylphide*, Bibliothèque Nationale de France, Bibliothèque-Musée de l'Opéra, A-50¹. Schneitzhoeffer borrowed a fugue for the occasion: J.S. Bach's Fugue in F major from Book II of the *Wohltemperierte Klavier*.

Ex. 2.22 Act Two, Fugue, No. 14, bars 1–12

mortal in existence." Though no descriptions of his performance in *Giselle* seem to exist, one can at least picture his comic acting by reading Gautier's descriptions of his portrayals of other characters: he "played his role of a grotesque buccaneer [in *Jovita*] with movements of a semaphore gone mad," and in *La Fille mal gardée* played the simpleton "who is carried into the sky by his umbrella like the drollest cardboard puppet. Every joint seemed held in place with a mere knot of thread, so incredible were the antics of which he delivered himself."[57]

Violence (or threat of violence). Passions run strong in this ballet and lead to threats of violence between Albert and Hilarion, Giselle's seeming intention to run a sword through her own breast, the Wilis' murder of Hilarion, and their intended murder of Albert.

Presence of children; large cast size. Along with the fifty-six villagers (adults and children) in *Giselle* noted above, eight lords, eight ladies, four musicians, four pages, and an unnamed number of *chasseurs*, *piqueurs*, and valets partook in the action of the first act, according to the 1841 libretto. (This is not counting the main characters or soloists and eight coryphées of the divertissement.) Today, by contrast, one often sees first-act casts of thirty or forty such minor characters instead of the eighty-odd of the original *Giselle*.

The same downsizing holds true for the second act, which in the ballet's first production required thirty Wilis (aside from Myrtha, Moyna, and Zulmé), and villagers and nobles of unspecified number from the first act. The Wili population in many latter-day productions has been reduced to twenty-four and is sometimes lower. And the villagers and nobles do not always appear in the second act—in fact, they rarely do.

[57] Review of *Jovita* in *La Presse*, 11 November 1853, tr. in Gautier, *Gautier on Dance*, 264; review of *La Fille mal gardée* in *La Presse*, 25 April 1853, tr. in Gautier, *Gautier on Dance*, 246.

Spectacle; special effects; horses. One may count three spectacular scenes in this ballet: the merry harvest festival with its procession of villagers carrying a child Bacchus on his wine cask, the magnificent procession of the noble hunting party (with hunting horns blasting and horses), and the entrance of Myrtha in all of her weird, glamorous glory in an enticing woodland setting in Act Two. Special effects, all in the second act of course, include the rising of Myrtha from her grave (on a trap), Myrtha's glide across the lake (on a *chariot*[58]), Giselle's soaring overhead flight (using a *lit de fer*[59]), her supernatural leap up in the tree to pick a flower (using a swing or a seesaw[60]), and her sinking into her flowery grave (on a trap) at the end.

Props: specifically, flowers. Flowers carry particular meaning in this ballet as symbols of the love between Giselle and Albert: first, the daisies that she de-petals in the *scene d'amour*. Flowers then connect the two lovers in Act Two when Giselle, a ghost who cannot be grasped by Albert, throws flowers to him (including roses); he is able to pick them up from the earth.[61] And the new grave to which Albert carries the dying Giselle in Act Two is "a ground of grass and flowers," according to Justamant.[62]

Flowers are also favored by Myrtha, whose very name is taken from the myrtle flower, a symbol of Venus, the goddess of love (according to a nineteenth-century French dictionary of flower symbolism[63]). Myrtha emerges from flowers in her first appearance, delights in picking pretty flowers out of a tree, dances and plays with them, and (says Justamant) throws them onto Giselle's grave. She also fashions a wand out of rosemary branches (rosemary meaning "your presence revives me," according to the same dictionary—appropriate because Myrtha uses the wand to raise the Wilis from their graves). And she places on Giselle's head the "magic crown of verbena and asphodel," flowers said to symbolize, respectively, enchantment and regret (as the dictionary puts it, "my regrets follow you to the tomb"[64]).

Reception

Giselle, by all accounts a great attraction to audiences from the beginning, was hailed two days after its premiere as the most successful ballet at the Opéra since "*La Sylphide* [1832] of glorious and triumphant memory."[65] A series of playful comments made in the *Courrier des théâtres* during the first month of performances convey the tumult with which audiences greeted the new ballet. "There is a fire at the box office ... not even all the firemen in the world would be able to do anything about it; the conflagration can only be put out little by little up to the eighty performances predicted. But it remains to be seen if there are even more" (4 July; in fact, the ballet was performed 133 times at the Opéra in the nineteenth century)[66]; "The *grande affaire* of today, the only thing

---

[58] Justamant, *Giselle*, 136.
[59] Titus *répétiteur*, 122.
[60] Justamant, *Giselle*, 138.
[61] The roses are mentioned in the Titus *répétiteur*, 126.
[62] Justamant, *Giselle*, 219.
[63] Charlotte de la Tour, *Le Langage des Fleurs*, 7th ed., augmented (Paris: Garnier, 1858), 303.
[64] de la Tour, *Le Langage des Fleurs*, 293–305.
[65] *Le Moniteur universel*, 30 June 1841, tr. in Cyril Beaumont, *The Ballet called Giselle*, 2nd rev. ed. (London: Beaumont, 1945; London: Dance Books, 1996), 27. Citations refer to the Dance Books edition.
[66] Remarkably, this prediction came true: in its first run (1841–1853), *Giselle* was performed exactly eighty times, according to the *Chronopéra* database, http://chronopera.free.fr/. It was performed forty-nine more

one can occupy oneself with after sunset, is the performance of the new ballet at the Opéra, *Giselle*, for which Paris has unanimously declared its [enthusiasm]. Any other activity is only a pretext, carried out while patiently awaiting the hour of eight o'clock in the evening" (7 July); "[Not one person more] would have found a seat last night at the Opéra. The vogue of *la Carlotta-Giselle* is complete; it is delirium" (8 July); "the century has returned to mythology and resuscitated Terpsichore" (10 July); "*Giselle*, tomorrow at the Opéra/ at the Opéra tomorrow, a full house/ Tomorrow success at the Opéra, shows and actors/ And, to conclude, giant receipts" (13 July); "It has only been five days since *Giselle* was last performed at the Opéra, and it seemed to the public last night that it was five months" (20 July); "Giselle! Giselle! is the cry from all sides" (27 July).

Critics were especially taken with the second act: one called the ballet "a delight," but with the qualification that its "originality and poetic effects largely compensate for the old-fashioned rusticity of the first act."[67] Another critic called the first act a prologue that is "graceful but a bit long" but declared that "the second act draws the eye from seduction to seduction; from enticement to enticement."[68] Escudier found the whole ballet to be "a touching and delicious fantasy,"[69] and Jules Janin, one of the best known critics in Paris, wrote admiringly that

> nothing is lacking in this charming work: neither invention, nor poetry, nor music, nor the arrangements of new *pas*, nor the number of beautiful dancers, nor the harmoniousness filled with of life, grace and energy, nor Adèle Dumilâtre, nor above all la Carlotta Grisi. Thank goodness, here is what they call a ballet![70]

Of the many encomiums bestowed on Grisi for her performance in this ballet, few were more vivid, as Ivor Guest has pointed out, than this by J. Chaudes-Aigues:

> But the real Queen of the festival was, beyond comparison, Carlotta Grisi. What a charming creature! And how she dances! We already knew, from the *pas* she has danced from time to time since her arrival at the Opéra, that she was graceful, light, supple and charming, but what we did not guess was the strength she displayed in this new ballet. So slender, so fragile, and yet so indefatigable! It is truly incredible. Just remember that from one end of *Giselle* to the other the poor child is perpetually in the air or on her *pointes*. In the first act she runs, flies and bounds across the stage like a gazelle in love, so much so that the peace of the tomb does not seem too profound for such racing and expenditure of effort. And yet this is nothing compared to what is in store for her in the second act. Here she must not dance as she did just before, but must be a thousand times lighter and more intangible, for now she is a shade. No longer is the earth beneath her feet, no longer has she any support! She cleaves the air like a swallow; she balances on rushes, she leans from the treetops—this is an actual fact—to throw flowers to her lover . . . Decidedly Mlle Taglioni has found a successor.[71]

times between 1863 and 1868, and then again, of course, countless times in the twentieth century and beyond at various houses.

[67] *Le Constitutionnel*, 1 July 1841, tr. in Guest, *Romantic Ballet in Paris*, 3rd ed., 351.
[68] *La Revue et gazette musicale*, 4 July 1841.
[69] *La France musicale*, 4 July 1841.
[70] *Le Journal des débats*, 30 June 1841.
[71] J. Chaudes-Aigues, *Le Moniteur des théâtres*, 30 June 1841, tr. in Guest, *Romantic Ballet in Paris*, 2nd ed., 210–211.

One cannot underestimate the part Grisi played in the success of *Giselle* in its initial run, and, remarkably, other than two performances by Elisa Bellon in September 1842, she danced Giselle at every single performance of the ballet for eight years until she left the Opéra in 1849—for much of that time dancing other major parts at the Opéra as well (see Chapter 4).[72]

After Grisi's departure, the ballet was put on hiatus, and her role taken over by Regina Forli when *Giselle* returned to the stage on 11 August 1852.

A note on the manner of Giselle's death and burial. In recent years, questions have arisen about whether Giselle died of a broken heart or by her own hand. Gautier himself is to be blamed for the confusion: he wrote more than one account of the story.[73] Let us consider his varying versions (emphases added):

Libretto (1841)

> She takes Albert's hand, places it on her heart, and then quickly pushes it away with fear. She seizes Loys's sword, resting on the ground, first of all playing mechanically with this weapon, *and is about to let herself fall on its sharp point when her mother hurries toward her and grabs it away.* The love of dance returns to the poor girl's memory: she believes she hears the music of her dance with Albert.... She lunges forward and begins to dance with ardor, with passion.

Letter to Heine in *La Presse* (1841)

> Her strength is soon exhausted, she falters, and bending down, picks up the fatal sword that Hilarion has brought and would have fallen on its point if Albrecht had not snatched the weapon away in a movement of desperate rapidity. *Alas, his action is of no avail, for its point has already found its mark. It has pierced Giselle's heart, and she dies,* comforted at least by the profound sorrow of her lover and the tender pity of Bathilde.[74]

Les beautés de l'Opéra (1844)

> Then, as a glimpse of reason darting through her brain reminded her of the sad truth, and her eye fell on the glittering insignia of Count Albrecht's rank and her own desolation, *she seized the sword, and sought to plunge it in her side. The rapid hand of Loys has held the weapon aside, but not before a deep and fatal wound had pierced the young and innocent maiden's breast.* Even in the last mortal agonies, poor Giselle sought to find relief in dancing.[75]

It is perhaps unreasonable to think that Gautier's latter two accounts of the story are meant to describe actual stagings. As John V. Chapman has said of some of Jules Janin's writings on ballet, "He writes as a poet does, from his imagination."[76] In any case, none

---

[72] Guest, *Romantic Ballet in Paris*, 2nd ed., 215.

[73] On this and other matters, see Alastair Macaulay, Doug Fullington, Maina Gielgud, Jane Pritchard, Alexei Ratmansky, and Marian Smith, "Giselle: Questions and Answers," *Alastair Macaulay* (blog), 10 October 2020, https://www.alastairmacaulay.com/all-essays/giselle-questions-answers.

[74] La Presse, 5 July 1841, tr. in Gautier, *Gautier on Dance*, 97–98.

[75] Théophile Gautier, Jules Janin, Jean-Baptiste Giraldon, and Philarète Chasles, *Les beautés de l'Opéra* (Paris: Soulié, 1844), published in English as *Beauties of the Opera and Ballet*, ed. Charles Heath (London: David Bogue, 1845), "*La Giselle*," 8. Citation refers to the English edition.

[76] Here, we are paraphrasing Chapman, who writes of Jules Janin: "Janin entered the enchanted realms of ballet through the door of his imagination. He closed his eyes to the world at large and stepped into a dream world, a place of poetic fantasy which was created as much in his own mind as on stage. The most poetic of Janin's reviews was devoted to *Giselle* (1841). In his description of the second act there is no indication that his

of the early productions of *Giselle* we have studied for this volume reflect Gautier's post-premiere revisionist retelling of the heroine's demise. That is, *Giselle* dies of a broken heart in all of them (in Paris, Lyon, and St. Petersburg) and not by a wound of the flesh.

Incidentally, one of the eyewitnesses to the first production, a rather sardonic critic, affirms that Giselle died of a broken heart but also ridicules the idea that excessive dancing had killed her (a concept from Victor Hugo's *Fantômes* that Gautier carried over into *Giselle*):

> Giselle dances like the bird sings, when she is happy or sad, when she is alone or with her friends, when she is waiting for Loys or when she is near him. No matter how much her mother scolds her [about excessive dancing], Giselle ignores her, and yet you cannot say of Giselle, like Victor Hugo said of his Spanish girl in *Les Fantômes*:
>
> *She loved dancing too much, that's what killed her.*
>
> Giselle dies for something other than having danced too much: what kills her is the sorrow upon suddenly finding out that Loys is a prince in disguise, and that the person she believed her equal is Duke Albert de Silesia! Didn't Giselle know that we have seen kings marry shepherdesses? How can you bring up children so badly and give them such an incomplete education?[77]

This is not to say that directors of latter-day stagings are obliged to adhere to the broken-heart approach, but simply that a suicide was not staged in the early productions we have examined.

Some have wondered, too, why Giselle was not buried in a churchyard, and even surmised that the placement of her grave in unconsecrated ground was owed to her purported suicide. Again, there is nothing in the sources to suggest that this was so. We believe that, simply as a practical matter, Giselle was buried in the optimal locale for the Wilis' scene—a lush, verdant, somewhat remote area next to a body of water into which the Wilis could toss their exhausted victims. This approach left plenty of room for dancing in the middle of the stage. Further, it repeated a striking visual motif from the opera *Robert le diable*, in which a large lone cross prop was used to great effect: the title character clutched it at a crucial moment in the action, just as Albert did in *Giselle*.

Scene-by-scene description of *Giselle*, as recorded in the Titus *répétiteur*

Now let us look at the earliest well recorded production of *Giselle*, going scene by scene through the Titus *répétiteur*, which was likely annotated in 1841.

First, what is the Titus *répétiteur*, and why was it created?[78] It is a 156-page musical score of the entire ballet, used for rehearsal. Written for two stringed instruments, it

---

subject is stage-bound; he writes as if he was actually witnessing the awakening of enchanted forest spirits. He writes as a poet does, from his imagination." John V. Chapman, "Jules Janin and the Ballet," *Dance Research* 7, no. 1 (Spring, 1989): 69.

[77] *La Revue et gazette musicale*, 4 July 1841.
[78] St. Petersburg State Museum of Theatre and Music (GMTMI), GIK 7114/8a. The title "Titus *répétiteur*" was given to this manuscript before it was added to the collection of the St. Petersburg State Museum of Theatre and Music. For an earlier discussion of this score, see Marian Smith, "The Earliest *Giselle*? A Preliminary Report on a St. Petersburg Manuscript," *Dance Chronicle* 23, no. 1 (2000): 29–48.

is abundantly annotated in red ink—between the staff lines and in the margins—with descriptions of the action. (Alas, descriptions of the dancing were written into a separate document that is likely no longer extant.[79]) According to the records at the State Museum of Theatre and Music in St. Petersburg (where the Titus *répétiteur* is housed), the annotator was Antoine Titus Dauchy, known as Antoine Titus, ballet master of the Imperial Theater, St. Petersburg from 1832 to 1849. He (with the help of at least one other person) likely annotated the manuscript in 1841 (the year Titus was dispatched to Paris to view potential new repertory) and then used it when he staged *Giselle* in St. Petersburg, where the ballet premiered on 18 December 1842 (for further discussion, see Chapter 3).

This document is a treasure trove of information, for it provides the earliest known details about how *Giselle* was performed, including when characters entered and exited, where they went on stage, what lines of dialogue they mimed, and how their movements and interactions were coordinated to the music (to the extent that the music in a few cases matches notes to syllables of French words that were being "spoken").

Let us now proceed to the scene-by-scene description of *Giselle* as described in the Titus *répétiteur*, which we will freely paraphrase from and quote.

Act One

Introduction. Adam's brief orchestral introduction begins "with fire" (*allegro con fuoco*), tonicizing G major in a series of furious arpeggios (Ex. 2.23a), and after twenty measures, turning to a sweet, lilting E-flat major *andante* in $\frac{6}{8}$ (Ex. 2.23b). Thus does Adam start by giving a jolt to the audience, prefiguring first the fury to come, and then, by contrast, evoking the dreamy and peaceful mood of the countryside—or perhaps the afterlife.[80]

The setting, as the libretto tells us, "represents a pleasant valley in Germany. In the distance, vine-covered hills, across which runs a road leading into the valley." And the curtain rises on "a tableau of grape-harvesting on the Thuringian slopes in the early morning" in which "vinegatherers depart to continue the harvest."

No. 1. To the accompaniment of cheery country music (Ex. 2.1a), vinegatherers cross the *montagne* (a raised platform-like structure upstage that is incorporated into the scenic design) from left to right. At the same time, lords and ladies cross the stage from right to left and go up the *montagne*. Because it makes no sense dramatically for aristocrats to be tromping around in the village at such an early hour, we believe that bringing out lords and ladies along with the humble vinegatherers at the very outset of the ballet was intended to introduce—in abstract, non-realistic fashion—the two

---

[79] One may find the phrase "voir mon livre" [see my book] in some dance numbers in the Titus *répétiteur*. For example: in the music for the March in Act One (No. 8): "see my book, no. 1"; "see my book no. 2," and so forth up to no. 16.

A scant few references to choreography may be found in the Titus *répétiteur*. For instance, in the harvest festival march (No. 8): "Les Enfants" [The Children] followed by "tout le monde arrive" [everyone is coming], "on commence les jetés" [we begin the *jetés*] and "les hommes traversent les lignes des femmes" [the men cross the lines of women].

[80] Adam had originally composed this dream music for a scene (in No. 3) in which Giselle tells Albert of her dream about his being engaged to a noblewoman. That scene was likely omitted from No. 3 before the ballet's premiere.

Ex. 2.23a Introduction, bars 1–4

Ex. 2.23b Introduction, bars 32–36

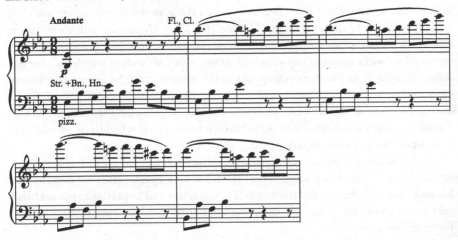

contrasting social classes whose interplay fuels the action in the first act. Soon, everyone has departed, and Hilarion appears as his furtive musical theme is sounded (Ex. 2.2).

Hilarion: "Nobody sees me." He looks around on all sides and says again, "Nobody sees me." Designating the house of Giselle, he says, "Here lives the one I love" (soft, sweet music), and making a menacing gesture (harsh music), he approaches Loys's house, and he listens. "Here is a young man, you and she, you love each other, and you plan to marry. But no, I swear that this will not happen. She will be mine." He approaches the house of the young man and listens: "But someone is coming. I am leaving." He exits, going by the side of Loys's house.

No. 2. Loys and Wilfride enter, and the music tells us they are arguing.

Wilfride: (to Loys) "Here with this costume, what are you planning to do?" *Loys* (pointing at the house as the music becomes slower and softer): "She is so pretty that

I love her like a fool." Wilfride entreats Loys to come with him as the music returns to its original tempo.

Loys: (resisting) "No, I want to stay."

Wilfride: (with an air of surprise) "How can a *Grand seigneur* like you love a simple *paysanne*?"

Loys: "Yes, a *Grand seigneur* like me loves this *jeune fille*." He orders Wilfride to depart. Wilfride resists; Loys again orders him to depart. Wilfride salutes and departs.

Loys: "Finally, he is gone." Four notes in the music match the four syllables of his text, "*Il est parti.*"

Hilarion, meanwhile, has been watching from a hiding place: just as Loys said, "Yes, a *Grand seigneur* like me loves this *jeune fille*," Hilarion appeared, unnoticed. He observed the interactions between the two men, then showed his surprise when Wilfride saluted "a peasant" (Loys). An annotation tells us, "It gives him doubts about Loys." At that point Hilarion hides, "so as not to be seen," and then exits.

No. 3. Loys: (alone) "He [Wilfride] has left."

He looks around to make sure nobody is there. He approaches Giselle's house. He knocks, and knocks again, and then hides when she appears. Giselle enters, dancing, and says that she heard a knock on the door (Ex. 2.24). (Justamant tells us at that, as Giselle comes out of her cottage, it is *en sautant naturellement avec grace et un peu de laisser aller*: "while jumping naturally with grace, with a little bit of letting go." The *ballonnés* familiar to us today do not appear in the sources until the Stepanov notations circa 1903.)

Giselle: "There is nobody here." She looks around; keeps looking around; she dances. She listens. "Loys was supposed to come but he is not here. He is bad [*Il est un méchant*]. I will leave." She begins to depart, dancing. She sees Loys.

Giselle: (while turning her back) "Finally, here he is. He will pay for this" (Ex. 2.7a).

Giselle: "No," and she runs again. Loys holds her back again, places her hand around his neck, and pulls her toward the bench. They sit down and Loys tries to put his hands on Giselle's waist. She resists. He stops and links arms with her three times. The third time she runs away.

He follows her, and they walk downstage.

Loys: "What's up? [*qu'as tu*] Are you crazy? Me, who loves you so."

Giselle: "You love me—ha!" Loys takes her hand, has her turn to the other side, and takes her arm again. They go to pick some daisies and return to sit on the bench.

Giselle plucks the petals from the daisy: "This one says you do not love me." In response (to ensure a more felicitous outcome), Loys jumps over the bench, picks a

Ex. 2.24 *Entrée de Giselle*; Act One, No. 3, bars 26–30

daisy, and plucks its petals: "This one says that I love you." Loys mimes this scene on his knees.

They dance (see Ex. 2.24).

Loys: (pulling Giselle toward him) "Give me a kiss."

Giselle: "On the shoulder."

Loys: "I would like it very much." Giselle dances away from him.

Giselle and Loys dance. (At the same time, Hilarion crosses the stage sadly and hides behind Giselle's door.) Giselle keeps refusing Loys's kisses. He finally says, "I am leaving," but Giselle stops him. Loys kneels and Giselle puts her hand on his forehead (likely having kissed her finger). Giselle and Loys get to the door. Hilarion closes the door, presenting himself to them. Giselle and Loys pull back when they see him.

Hilarion: (no longer able to contain himself) "Well, do not be shy. This is all very good, you lowlife [*malheureuse*]." He walks toward Giselle. Silence. (Then the music starts up again, angrily.) He presses her toward the middle of the stage: "I saw you here, with Loys, making love, and saw you giving him kisses, you lowlife. What have you done? I don't know what's even holding me back [*Je ne sais que me retient*]."

Giselle: "I do not love you." He menaces her, his arms raised. She hunkers down but then rises up. (Here, Justamant shows her crossing her arms defiantly and intimidating Hilarion.)

Hilarion: (drawing back) "It is all the same to me. I do not care."

Loys: (getting in front of Hilarion) "Go away, go away." Here, the music matches the syllables and the angry sound of Loys's voice saying, "*Va-t'en, va-t'en*" (see Ex. 2.25, in which we show how the words can be fitted to the music).

Hilarion: "That is too strong." He runs toward Giselle.

Loys: (approaching Hilarion) "Leave."

Hilarion: "And why?"

Loys: "Leave."

Hilarion: (turning back to Giselle) "You, I love."

Loys: "Go."

Hilarion: "I will return. You will pay me back for this."

Loys chases him and forces him to leave, going with him to the back of the stage.

Before proceeding to the next scene, let us pause to discuss the genesis of the scene just described—for it is an important one which establishes the tone of the lead couple's relationship and demonstrates Hilarion's jealousy. The first version of the scene, which followed the libretto closely, included a lengthy passage of music for Giselle's recounting

Ex. 2.25 "Va-t'en, va-t'en"; Act One, No. 3, bars 173–177; these words are written in the margin of the Titus *répétiteur* next to bar 175

of her sad dream (in which Albert betrays her), and Albert's reassurances.[81] The second version was considerably longer, for Adam added some new music (which we now know as the "daisy-petal" music; Ex. 2.7a), before and after the dream music, perhaps to accommodate two separate conversations between the lovers.[82] He also repeated Giselle's entrance music toward the end, rounding out the lovers' interactions before their confrontation with Hilarion.

These alterations, apparently, were not considered satisfactory. In the next, and final version, this scene was made shorter and lighter in mood by the halving of the newly written daisy-petal passage and excising altogether Giselle's slow and lengthy recounting of her disturbing dream.

No. 4. Paysannes come and greet Giselle (see Ex. 2.1a). One of them gives Giselle her hand and has her pass. Going upstage, Giselle calls out to her companions. They all arrive. A *paysanne* asks Giselle to come cut grapes; the *paysannes* dance for several bars.

Giselle says to the *paysannes* that working is tiring; she prefers to dance. The *paysannes* stay with Giselle (instead of returning to the harvest). During this scene, Loys has gone upstage to see if Hilarion has reappeared.

Waltz. Giselle begins dancing alone in the middle of the circle of women and then invites Loys to join her (Ex. 2.6a). The lovers each dance with various group of the corps then pass through the lines of women (a sequence we will find again in Justamant). Toward the end of the waltz, annotations in the margin refer to "mon livre," suggesting further detail about the choreography was recorded elsewhere (as mentioned above). Albert takes Giselle's hand and kisses it just before Berthe appears.

Suddenly, Berthe emerges from her cottage, puts an end to the waltzing, and starts speaking (Ex. 2.3a).

Berthe: (to Giselle) "What are you doing there, you over there; are you going to cut the grapes? (to all): *Mesdemoiselles*, what are you doing there? The staff [*la hatte*], you have thrown it there?"

Vinegatherers: (while dancing) "It is Giselle."

Berthe goes to her daughter and with her apron wipes her daughter's forehead and touches Giselle's heart: "You poor thing; you will exhaust yourself."

Berthe: (as eight bars of Giselle's waltz are played) "You, with this dancing, you're not thinking that this way you could die" (Ex. 2.6b).

Giselle: (as the bars are repeated) "I am happy. My dancing, and him, and you; that's all that I love." Loys kisses her hand.

The mood of the music darkens as Berthe's theme recurs, newly cast in minor mode.

Berthe: (to Giselle) "On your back, there will grow wings."

Giselle: "The wings I will not notice."

Berthe: "Yes, you won't notice them." The music becomes emphatic as she says, "Listen well" (Ex. 2.3b). As she prepares to explain who the Wilis are, Berthe gathers the girls around her.

---

[81] This version can be pieced together only by examining the Paris orchestra parts, which reveal the various changes made to the music of this scene.

[82] This new music was written on a differently formatted folio that was added to the autograph score.

Ex. 2.26 Act One, No. 4, bars 277–279 (text from Titus *répétiteur*)

Berthe: "Over there in the dark night, young girls like you and like you"—she points to the left, the right, and the middle—"the earth will open up and phantoms will come out, covered in shrouds. On their backs they have wings. They surround those they en-counter and force them to dance till they die" (Ex. 2.9).

Now Berthe's monologue is finished, but the music becomes jaunty, telling us that Giselle remains unfazed (Ex. 2.26).

Giselle: "I do not believe all that." She crosses the stage, dancing. Berthe expresses her fears for Giselle's health; Loys reassures her. He and Giselle go upstage, saying that they will be back later.

Berthe: (to Giselle) "Come with me."

Giselle: "No, no."

No. 5. Fanfares are heard in the distance (Ex. 2.4). Giselle and Berthe go back into their house. Loys, worried, leads everybody off the stage. The vinegatherers depart upstage of the *montagne*, stage right.

Hilarion appears, looks to see if anyone can see him (see Ex. 2.2). He is thinking. He makes a gesture of vengeance. He walks toward Giselle's house. As the music becomes wistful, he sighs.

Hilarion: "Under this roof is the one I love. But she rejects me. Oh, but I am so un-lucky, so miserable. What will I do? What will happen?" He remains absorbed in his reflections. He turns and looks at Loys's house and approaches it. He listens.

The fanfares are getting louder; Hilarion runs up on the *montagne* and expresses that they are still far away. Far enough away.

Now the music becomes very lively as Hilarion is suddenly energized.

Hilarion: "I know that here is where I saw a lord who saluted him. He sent him away; he bowed while saluting him." Now he has figured out who Loys is. "Ah! I know!" He slaps his forehead. "He is a great lord! Let's get to the bottom of this mystery. I'm going into the house and if someone comes and sees me, I do not care." He runs toward the door of the house, which he tries to open. It is locked. "What should I do? This window.

I will force it." He takes his hunting knife. He says, "Nobody sees me," and enters through the window.

One can hear the hunting party.

To add greater pomp and excitement to the entrance of the Prince of Courlande's hunting party, Adam (as noted above) includes music for four "trompes de chasseurs sur le théâtre" (hunting horns on the stage), presumably performed on stage by musicians of the Prince's court.

The hunting party arrives (Ex. 2.21). The lords arrive. The hunting party continues to arrive; Wilfride, Bathilde, and the Prince enter, followed by gardes-chasses. (Note that the Prince and Bathilde are on horseback.[83])

The Prince dismounts and says, "Shall we stop here?" Wilfride helps Bathilde dismount. The Prince talks to Wilfride, indicates Berthe's house, and asks to see the mistress. Wilfride knocks on the door four times.

Berthe appears and is surprised to see so many people (Ex. 2.10b). She greets them and calls for Giselle. Giselle comes out of the house and wants to go back in. Her mother holds her back and bids her give a greeting. Giselle approaches Wilfride and gives a greeting.

Berthe (to Giselle): "You are wrong; it is the Lord and this Lady that should be greeted." Bathilde says they want something.

Giselle, hurrying, goes into the house.

Wilfride follows her. They come back out with a table and chairs.

Giselle and *Berthe*: "Here are some refreshments."

Bathilde: (to the Prince) "This girl is pretty."

Berthe invites Bathilde into the house. Bathilde prefers to take her rest in the shade. The Prince gives his hand to his daughter, and they go sit at the table—Bathilde to the left of the Prince in the middle, Wilfride to the right, standing.

Berthe gives drinks to the Prince and his suite. Bathilde sits in the chair for a moment; Giselle is standing up until the second reprise of the music.

Bathilde offers her a necklace. Giselle wants to refuse, but the princess insists. Giselle is happy.

(Bathilde's question about Giselle's work and pleasures do not appear in the Titus *répétiteur*, though Giselle's answers do appear.)

Giselle says that in the daytime she works; she likes to dance (Ex. 2.1b). As the music of the waltz is played for several measures, she begins to dance (Ex. 2.6c).

Berthe: (to the music of her own theme, in its minor-key form) "Yes, it is madness. She is dancing always, always."

The music returns to a major key, and Bathilde smiles and asks Giselle if she has someone.

Giselle: "Yes, and we love each other. He is as handsome as the day. He will be my husband." She runs to say to her mother. "Is that not right, that we will marry?"

Berthe: "Yes."

---

[83] According to the Justamant manual, the hunting party consisted of (in order) eight *sonneurs*, ten lords and ten ladies, six pages (with falcons), the Prince and Bathilde, followed by Wilfride, and finally, eight *gardes chasses*. Justamant, *Giselle*, 61. When they depart to resume the hunt, they go in this order: (1) *les gardes chasses*, (2) *les sonneurs*, (3) *les pages*, (4) *les seigneurs*. The Prince goes back into the house; Wilfride does, too, after hanging the horn up at stage right. Bathilde is already inside. Justamant, *Giselle*, 58. Presumably, their rest was not disturbed by the harvest festival that took place outside the window.

Bathilde: "She is charming." She beckons Giselle and tells her that she, too, is to be married, to a Grand Seigneur. She asks Giselle if she would like to come to the wedding. Giselle affirms her joy to be able to dance and kisses Bathilde's hand. Bathilde goes into the house.

The Prince gets up from the table and invites the suite to continue the hunt. He crosses and says to the *piqueurs* to the left and to the right that he will sound the horn when he wishes to summon them. The Prince takes the horn from a *piqueur's* hands and blows it. He crosses the stage and places himself before Giselle's cottage and puts the horn on the table.

The lengthy *cortège* files past the Prince for thirty-one bars. (Everyone leaves the stage; the Prince goes into Giselle's cottage.)

No. 6. Hilarion appears at the window of Loys's cottage (see Ex. 2.2). He withdraws (from the window) quickly and comes out of the house cautiously, very pleased with what he has just found. He knows vengeance is at hand.

Hilarion: "I *said* he was a Great Lord. Now I have the evidence. You, Loys, and you, Giselle, you are planning to love one another; that will never be." He indicates the sword and the *collier* (ruff or necklace) that he has just stolen. "I will have my vengeance." He hears a noise and looks around for a place to hide the Prince's insignia. "Ah! Under this bush." He runs to the bush, presumably hides the objects, then exits stage left.

Next comes the harvest festival, a long, danced divertissement that takes place while the action is suspended. It consists of four numbers, all light-hearted: first, a march in which the villagers, in a merry mood, come on stage and then dance; second, a four-movement *pas de deux* for Giselle and Albert; third, the Peasant *pas de deux* with music by Burgmüller, and finally, the galop, a large ensemble dance. (Notably, galops were popular in the ballroom as the rousing last dance in a set.)

March. After a brief and rousing introduction (Ex. 2.12c), the march itself begins (Ex. 2.12a).[84] As the annotations tell us, children are seen first; they are followed shortly by the rest of the village. Few annotations are given for the actual choreography (see note 79, earlier in this chapter). This scene is described in the libretto thus:

> A march commences. The harvest is finished. A wagon, decorated with grape leaves and flowers, slowly comes into view, followed by all the peasants of the valley, their baskets full of grapes. A little Bacchus is carried triumphally on horseback astride a cask, in keeping with an old country tradition.

Pas de deux of Giselle and Loys. This dance is comprised of four movements (Exx. 3.5a, 3.1e, 3.5b, and 2.8a). Three of them are connected by transitional musical passages, in keeping with a practice sometimes followed in mid-century French multimovement dances.[85] The *louré* (discussed earlier in this chapter) is the last movement, or coda (Ex. 2.8a). This *pas de deux* will be discussed further in Chapter 3.

---

[84] Note that thirty-two bars of the march are struck through in Titus, a change not made in the autograph or any of the Paris sources we have examined; this cut may have been made at a later point in St. Petersburg, for the Titus *répétiteur* appears to have been used for several decades in St. Petersburg.

[85] We will see this feature in the *pas de trois* of the St. Petersburg *Paquita* and also find it in the Act One *pas de deux* of Tchaikovsky's 1877 *Swan Lake*.

Peasant pas de deux. Although this *pas*, with music by Burgmüller, it is not included in the Titus *répétiteur*, we do know that it was performed in the St. Petersburg production (because it is included in the list of dances on the 1842 poster).[86]

Galop. Next comes the galop, which is titled "No. 5 du Divertissement" in the autograph and similarly in the Titus *répétiteur*, suggesting the four movements of the preceding *pas de deux* for Giselle and Loys constituted numbers 1–4 (recall that the Peasant *pas de deux* was a late addition to the score). The Titus *répétiteur* gives us a few hints about the choreography by referring to circles (*ronds*) and a *moulinet* as well as to the galop step itself (Ex. 2.19).

Finale. Hilarion throws himself into the middle of the crowd.

Hilarion: (to Loys, with irony) "You chased me away." (to Giselle): "You, too. You, and him, you plan to marry. That will never be."

Loys: "And why?"

Hilarion: "For the reason that you are a Grand Seigneur. I will give you the proof." While he goes to look for the insignias, the two lovers remain on the stage.

Hilarion leaves; he comes back with the *tocque*, a cap of a type worn by noblemen, and the sword. (Earlier in the Titus manuscript, the telltale possessions were a *collier* and a sword.)

Hilarion: "These are yours; I swear it." (At this point the music builds to *fortissimo* and the musical sentence ends with a bang.) There is general stupefaction amongst the crowd. Loys tries to throw himself upon Hilarion.

Loys: "He is lying."

Hilarion: "Ah, I am lying. Well, I swear again that this sword is his."

Giselle is thunderstruck with surprise; she staggers, nearly falling.

Albert tries to reassure Giselle. (Note that his name in the Titus *répétiteur* switches from Loys to Albert as his ruse is exposed.[87])

Hilarion: "Ah, that's not true" (meaning the reassurance). In a fury, Albert lunges at him; Hilarion steps back as he holds the sword in front of him and protests that it belongs to Albert (Ex. 2.27). Albert takes it from him, intending to thrust it through him.

Wilfride throws himself before Albert.

Everyone crosses the stage in a "mouvement analogue" as the orchestra plays a series of unison Bs, *fortissimo*. Hilarion falls on the table and under his hand finds the Prince's

---

[86] As for the placement of the Peasant *pas de deux* (which was added shortly before the premiere of the ballet in Paris), the list of danced numbers in the 1841 libretto suggests the Peasant *pas de deux* was danced before the *pas de deux* of Giselle and Loys at the festival. But the orchestra parts, copied full score, and even the satirical cartoon in *Musée Philipon* (p. 67) confirm that the *pas* followed the *pas de deux* of Giselle and Loys. The Peasant *pas de deux* was also performed after the *pas de deux* of Giselle and Loys in St. Petersburg in 1842, according to the performance poster. See Appendix C (iii).

[87] The first use of "Albert" comes in the annotation "Albert cherche à la rassurer" (Albert tries to reassure her) after Hilarion has accused "Loys" of deceiving Giselle. The last use of "Loys" comes a few moments later in the action in the annotation "Loys lui recommande le silence": after the Prince has asked "Loys" about his disguise, Loys tells him to be quiet.

Ex. 2.27 Albert lunges at Hilarion; Act One, *Finale*, bars 29–36

Ex. 2.28 Hilarion sounds the horn, summoning the Prince et alia; Act One, *Finale*, bars 73–76

hunting horn. Then, there is silence from the orchestra pit. The orchestra waits to play until Hilarion lifts the horn to his lips. Hilarion sounds the horn (Ex. 2.28).

The *cortège* (the hunting party, presumably in procession) starts to file in (this takes seven bars). They take up their positions as before. Wilfride is holding Albert back and wants to make him flee by going around to the left.

The Prince appears and finds himself face to face with Hilarion. Everyone in the Prince's suite bows. (A silence of three and a half beats follows, to emphasize the impact of the moment.)

The Prince asks what is going on. Hilarion points out Albert to him.

The Prince recognizes Albert. Hilarion is satisfied.

Albert removes his hat.

Everyone (presumably, those in the hunting party) salutes him.[88]

---

[88] At this juncture in the Titus *répétiteur*, following page 72, a seventy-seven-bar *allegro mosso* in E minor is pasted in, replacing what appears to be forty-two measure of Adam's original score. Its mood is one of worry and consternation (which is appropriate for the action); its melody features syncopation, which is characteristic of "talking music" in ballet. We have not identified the composer of this interpolation.

Note further that the pages of this *répétiteur* were numbered after this *allegro mosso* was pasted in. The added music is notated on pages 74 and 75 of an added folio that is numbered pages 73–76. Pages 73 and 76 are blank.

The Prince bids Albert come forward and asks him for an explanation of his disguise (angry music is played). Loys asks him to be quiet.

Bathilde enters, as the music bursts into a loud and stressful-sounding passage.

Hilarion says to Giselle, "I told you he is a Prince; a Grand Seigneur." As the same music continues, Bathilde says: "But he is my fiancé."

Giselle: "YOUR fiancé?"

Bathilde: "Yes, mine."

Albert tries in vain to keep Bathilde from talking. Giselle separates Albert and Bathilde and curses them. Albert asks for forgiveness from Bathilde; she rejects him and runs to Giselle. Giselle falls into her mother's arms.

A note in the margin, directly before the mad scene, says: "General movement of everyone in a semicircle" (*en chartron*). The villagers keep to stage left, the nobles to stage right. As for the principals in front: Hilarion is at the right, then Berthe with Giselle in her arms. Albert, the Prince and Wilfride are on the same line. "The sword remains on the floor. [. . .]"

Mad scene. Giselle becomes crazy. She turns Albert around, saying that he is not Albert.

She goes to upstage center and calls out "I need my beloved. He broke my heart."

Everyone is listening.

She goes toward her mother then comes back to midstage. She falls to her knees and plucks petals from the daisies and holds them up to her heart (Ex. 2.7b).

Now she picks up the sword and plays with it. She wants to throw herself on the sword but Albert rushes in front of her.

As this happens, there is a general movement of fear (among the onlookers). Hilarion, pained, comes from the back of the stage near Wilfride. In front of the Prince, he blames himself for Giselle's madness. The actors (presumably village onlookers) slowly fill up the stage.

Now Berthe and Bathilde come up to Giselle, who pulls away from them, laughing. (The music imitates the sound of deranged laughter.)

"Leave me alone," says Giselle. She runs to the left, down to the footlights. Then she runs to the right. (A flute plays a downward scale as she runs to the footlights, and an upward scale as she runs to the right.)

She dances (the *louré* music is played; Ex. 2.8b). It seems that she is going to die dancing.

The orchestra must slow down *ad libitum*, following the action.

Her reason returns; she recalls everything that has just happened. She is suffering (loud and anguished music is playing.) She is still suffering. She appeals to everyone around her. She continues to appeal to them.

Note to the orchestra: "Follow Giselle's movements." She is still calling out to those around her.

She dies in her mother's arms. When Giselle dies, Albert throws himself onto her lifeless body, takes her hand, touches her heart, and says "it beats no more."

As anguished music plays, Hilarion falls to his knees in the middle of the stage. Albert takes Hilarion by the arm, leads him to Giselle, and blames Albert for Giselle's death.

Hilarion then steps back, afraid. He bares his breast and says to Albert, "Kill me. I have earned my fate."

Albert reaches for his dagger and runs toward Hilarion. Wilfride holds him back and drags him almost to the middle of the stage. Albert pulls away from his squire and comes back to throw himself again on Giselle's lifeless body.

Wilfride takes him and drags him to the back of the stage, summoning the piqueurs to come rescue them.

During Albert's despair, Hilarion is still looking at Giselle, expressing his deep sorrow. Then he approaches her and falls at her feet.

General tableau. Everyone falls on their knees in different groups.

Act Two

The setting, according to the libretto, "represents a forest on the banks of a small lake. A damp and chilly spot where rushes, reeds, clumps of wildflowers, and aquatic plants grow. Birch trees, aspens and weeping willows droop their pale foliage to the ground. To the left, beneath a cypress, stands a white marble cross on which Giselle's name is engraved. The tomb is overgrown with the thick vegetation of grasses and wildflowers. The bluish gleam of a very bright moon gives a cold and misty appearance to the scene."

No. 1. The second-act orchestral introduction opens with a severe-sounding *fortissimo* brass blast on B, reminding the audience of the distress with which Act One ended. A lugubrious pall is cast by the fateful sound of funeral-march rhythm (ta ta—t'TA) and funeral-march plagal cadences. Then, the vinegatherer's music from the opening scene of Act One returns for a few moments, this time with a somber feel and a plaintive oboe solo in the upper register (Ex. 2.1c).

No. 2. Shortly after the curtain rises, however, the mood becomes lighter and livelier; a *chasseur* is seen, on the lookout, stage right (on a *petite montagne*); he sounds his horn (playing the hunting call from Act One; see Ex. 2.4), and then listens. Another hunter appears and sounds the same horn call from the *montagne* at stage left. The first hunter now sees his mate. The music increases in jollity: various instrument groups play a happy little melody fragment (the one borrowed from Weber's *Euryanthe*, Ex. 2.11a) as the hunters gather together. The first one signals to the other hunters, and then comes downstage to greet a third hunter (Ex. 2.11b). *Chasseurs* arrive little by little and soon are all assembled, the happy melody marking the sense of conviviality with a *fortissimo*. The men take their place at stage left, toward the front, drinking all the way up to Hilarion's entrance (that is, for five measures at least). As Hilarion arrives, the music becomes suddenly reverts to *pianissimo*. Hilarion heads toward them and asks what they are doing.

Hunters: "As you can see, we are drinking. We are lost."

Hilarion: "We will not stay here." He turns around and is devastated. (The music suddenly sounds threatening.) Hilarion recognizes the place with fright as the forest frequented by the Wilis. He returns to his comrades.

Hilarion: "Let's not stay here."

Hunters: "But why?"

Hilarion points, with his finger, to Giselle's tomb (as the orchestra plays a hymn-like passage).

No. 3. Now the key changes to A-flat major, the key of the happy Act One *louré*, with a flute solo playing the melody line more slowly that it had been played before (Ex. 2.8c).

Hilarion: "This tomb here; under this tomb lies the one I loved so much." The music has slowed down, but it returns to its first tempo as Hilarion recoils in fright, and says, "My friends, let's get out of here, because"—he designates on all sides—"phantoms will come out, and they will seize us and make us dance until we die" (see Ex. 2.9).

Now the clock strikes midnight; groups of hunters do something at each strike of the clock up till the last strike (though there is a word missing from the Titus *répétiteur* at this point; likely they count the strikes, as they do in the Justamant manuscript). Adam calls for the striking of midnight by a "cloche sur le théâtre" (a chime on the stage), which brings realism to the scene and heightens the sense of danger.

No. 4. The will o' the wisps (*feux follets*) appear; the men step back, terrified by this sight. They run away in a disorderly fashion. Hilarion alone remains, running to all sides with fright. Believing himself to be pursued by will o' the wisps, he prostrates himself at the foot of Giselle's tomb. Then he exits, losing his reason (Ex. 2.29).

No. 5 (Andante). Myrtha arises from the flowers. She removes her veil. The muted string quartet begins to play; she dances (Ex. 2.15). She is at stage left. She goes onto the *montagne*, and glides on the lake.

No. 6 (Andante). Myrtha balances, dancing, in front of a tree (Ex. 2.30). She plucks some flowers. Perceiving a pretty one on a branch, she climbs up and balances. She

Ex. 2.29 Act Two, No. 4, bars 182–185

Ex. 2.30 Act Two, No. 6, bars 52–57

comes back down. She goes upstage, still dancing, and plays with the flowers. She puts the flowers down; this is followed by a pose, *sauté* to the right, then *sauté* on the bank to the left. (These movements match music that sounds like echoes in the woods.) Then she places herself for her variation.

No. 7 (*Allegro*). Myrtha next dances an *allegro* waltz (Ex. 2.18).

No. 8. After the waltz, Myrtha plucks a branch of rosemary at stage right. She touches the tombs, to the left and right. She makes a magic evocation and turns several times around the graves (Ex. 2.16). The Wilis come out of their graves. They take off their veils. They come downstage as muted violins play. Poses and ensembles; groups and poses. As woodwinds play, a second group is formed.

No. 9. The Wilis' dances feature a number of short solos, duos, and trios with a passage for the corps de ballet midway through and again at the end. Annotations suggest groupings of the corps that may have framed the dancing space inhabited by the soloists.

> *Andante*, B-flat major, $\frac{3}{4}$
> > "Pas de trois" (40 bars), includes "4th general group on the knee"
> > and "5th general group"

> *Allegro non troppo*, E-flat major, $\frac{6}{8}$
> > "Pas des echos"
> > "Myrtha places herself" (7 bars)
> > "6th group | Myrtha alone | She dances" (25 bars)
> > "Zulmé and Moyna dance" (16 bars, Exx. 2.20a–b)

> *Allegro con moto*, B-flat major, $\frac{3}{8}$
> > "Zulmé and Moyna dance" (17 bars)
> > "Moyna dances alone" (19 bars)
> > "The corps de ballet dances" with Moyna (16 bars)

> *Tempo 1*, E-flat major, $\frac{6}{8}$
> > "Zulmé places herself" (7 bars)
> > "Zulmé dances" (8 bars)
> > "Moyna dances" (8 bars)
> > "the 2nd time it is Myrtha who dances" (8 bars are repeated)
> > "Zulmé" (8 bars)
> > "the 2nd time Moyna and Zulmé" (8 bars are repeated)
> > "Myrtha alone" (11 bars)
> > "the corps de ballet | Final" (31 bars)

During the *pianissimo* passage that follows the dance, Myrtha goes up on the grassy bank holding the branch in her hand. The dancers arrange themselves in a "Groupe Final."

No. 10 (*Andantino moderato*). Myrtha summons the Wilis. They arrive.

Myrtha: "From this tomb, a Wili will come out. Like you and like me." Here, Myrtha echoes the language of Giselle's mother Berthe, who in the first act said that "young girls like you and like you . . . the earth will open up and phantoms will come out."

Giselle comes out of her tomb, the Wilis kneel; Myrtha touches her with her branch; Giselle's veil disappears; immediately Giselle comes down and kneels. Myrtha takes the crown and puts it on Giselle's head (Ex. 2.8d).

No. 11. The second time, Myrtha touches Giselle's wings with her branch. Her wings open; Giselle dances (Ex. 2.31) to music that is loud and aggressive. (The dancing of the Wili Giselle is virtuosic from the beginning, in contrast to that of Myrtha and the other Wilis, who began dancing slowly and then progressively moved faster and more aggressively over time.) Giselle's solo ends with a "general group" rather than a solo. (This is notable, for at the same moment in the Justamant manuscript, the Wilis form a large cross—a "general group" at the end of Giselle's entrance solo. The effect is stunning, and quite unlike what one usually sees in most of today's productions of the ballet. Because a grouping of some sort is made at this juncture, according to Titus, one may imagine that it was a cross, which would mean that it might have had its origins in the Paris production.)

This number was likely shortened owing to Carlotta Grisi's wishes. Giselle's first danced appearance in Act Two was intended to be longer, as we can see from Adam's autograph score. But twenty consecutive bars of it were cut before the premiere of the ballet, likely in response to a complaint from Grisi about the amount of dancing she was required to do. Ivor Guest writes, "A few cuts were made in the part of Giselle to spare Carlotta," who had been indisposed during the rehearsal process.[89] Other cuts were made in later numbers involving Giselle, likely for the same reason.

The Wilis hear a noise. Myrtha summons them. They hide so they can watch. The peasants enter. (These are villagers returning from a festival in a neighboring hamlet.) To the sound of harps, Wilis appear. The peasants are surprised. The Wilis try to persuade the peasants to waltz with them.

No. 12. As the strings play frantic, busy music, the Old Man warns the villagers of danger. The peasants run away, pursued by Wilis (see an earlier example of the running-away music, Ex. 2.29).

Half-night (lighting cue). Albert and Wilfride appear; they walk very slowly (Ex. 2.32). They reappear at the base of the *montagne.*

Albert: "It is here that the one I love reposes." He falls to his knees at the grave.

Wilfride: "It crushes my heart; I cannot leave him here alone." He has Albert pass to the other side, telling him that "she is dead; do not think of her anymore."

No. 13. The music becomes frantic, and Wilfride begs Albert to leave this place. Albert crosses in front of Wilfride and comes back to Giselle's tomb.

Albert: "How can you wish me to leave this place? Never. I am going to die near her. Go away. Go away." Wilfride steps back and goes away to find Bathilde. He goes out by way of the *montagne.*

Albert takes the flowers and tosses them onto Giselle's tomb.

Day (lighting cue). Giselle appears. *Full daylight* (lighting cue). Albert sees her (Ex. 2.8e). She disappears. Albert looks for her. (Here, in the Justamant manuscript, we see that Giselle is hiding behind some reeds; she parts them to the sound of rustling music and peeks out at Albert.)

Albert: "She is dead." He comes back; he sees her at the cross (her grave); he runs to catch her at the grave. He cries, sees her again, and pursues her again. (Note below the staves: Giselle crosses and goes into the wings to get into the *lit de fer,* a device that makes

---

[89] Guest, *Romantic Ballet in Paris,* 2nd ed., 207. The cut material is not included in the Titus *répétiteur.*

Ex. 2.31 Act Two, No. 11, bars 28–36

Ex. 2.32 Oboe aria; Act Two, No. 12, *Andante*, bars 2–9

possible her upcoming flight.) Albert leaves and reappears on the stage, alone. He sees Giselle, who crosses on the *lit de fer*.

Albert follows her and calls out to her two times. "It is nothing more than a spirit," he says. He looks for her and goes upstage to the left. On a piece of stage machinery, Giselle goes up stage, where he tries to grasp her. She disappears; he falls to his knees.

Lento (*Larghetto* in Adam's autograph). Giselle appears; she dances around him (Ex. 2.13). Albert gets up; Giselle sends him a kiss (a reversal of their first scene in Act One; see below). Albert sees her and says, "It is me." He tries to take hold of her; he takes a step. He holds her wings. She draws back two times. He has her jump. He watches her as she dances; he wants to grasp her. *Glissade* and *jeté en tournant*. Then, the manual states, "gestures finish here."

Allegro. She goes upstage and into the last wing, stage left. Albert goes upstage looking for her. He finishes searching. She returns to the stage; she throws flowers to him. They dance together. Giselle exits to the right. Albert remains, overwhelmed.

He sees her. She leans over a branch and throws roses to him. He picks them up and lays them on the tomb. He goes back and prays. She goes back to the cross and disappears. Albert reaches for her but only the cross remains in his arms.[90]

To a sorrowful oboe solo, Albert says, "I do not want to stay here." He goes toward the left to make his exit.

He sees Hilarion. Albert walks away.[91] The music changes to the Wilis' attack motif; Hilarion is running, terrified, pursued by the Wilis, who are led by Myrtha (Ex. 2.5).

Bacchanale. They force Hilarion to dance. A Wili leads him to the back of the stage to the base of a tree. Myrtha orders a Wili to bring Hilarion downstage. He kneels, and Myrtha touches him with her branch (the rosemary scepter). He begs her for clemency; she refuses. Again he begs; again she refuses: "You must dance."

Hilarion begins to dance. Again, he supplicates the Queen. She responds, "No, no." The Wilis form a circle around him; he turns with the Wilis. Satanic laughter (Ex. 2.17a). He goes upstage, whirling up to the top of the *montagne*. The Wilis throw him into the lake.

After the bacchanale, Myrtha calls to the Wilis. She dances alone, followed by Moyna and Zulmé; then all the Wilis dance. The break into Satanic laughter once again as they spy Albert (Ex. 2.17b).[92]

Albert is frightened as the furious Wilis try to make him dance. He runs away.

Giselle: "Flee, or you die like Hilarion." The Wilis chase them. A device glides toward the cross (presumably with Giselle and Albert on board). Myrtha pursues them. She wants to strike Albert. Her scepter breaks; she is furious. Myrtha orders them to dance. Myrtha starts; then Zulmé and Moyna and the corps de ballet.

No. 14 (Fugue). The Wilis, furious, and circling around Albert, are repelled by a superior power (Ex. 2.22). Myrtha seeks out the lovers and tells Giselle to dance. Giselle is one foot from the cross, near Albert.

This fugue scene, in which the Wilis fail miserably at attacking Albert, is a perfect set-up for the subsequent *pas de deux*, which is Myrtha's diabolical response to Giselle's thwarting of her plans. For by placing Albert in such close proximity to the cross, Giselle has prevented the Wilis from attacking him: the Wilis are a species of vampire whose evil powers are outmatched by a cross. Giselle's strategem worked so well that the powers of Good actually broke Myrtha's wand. But now, a freshly infuriated Myrtha orders Giselle to dance so beguilingly that Albert, unable to resist temptation, will leave the cross so he can be near her.

Note, further, that the fugue remained intact in the Paris orchestra parts, suggesting it remained part of the Paris performance score through 1868. Ultimately, it was cut from the St. Petersburg production, and it is rarely seen today. At some point after it was cut, the music just ahead of the cut was revised to effect a direct transition to the subsequent *pas de deux*.

A further note: Eighty-four bars of heretofore unknown music, in $\frac{6}{8}$ meter and presumably for tutti orchestra, are found directly after the fugue in the Paris orchestra parts.

---

[90] As indicated in the autograph, a total of thirty-two bars are cut from the dancing passages of this number. As suggested above, these bars may have been omitted to reduce the amount of dancing required of Grisi.

[91] According to the libretto, he remains and witnesses Hilarion's demise. See Appendix C (i).

[92] The pages for this passage in the Titus *répétiteur* were out of order at the time they were collated and bound.

This music does not appear in the autograph score or copied full score, and no further reference to it has yet been found. It is cut from the parts, either struck through or with folios sewn shut or removed. The character of the music, marked *Allegro marcato*, suggests dance rather than action.

Pas de deux. During the solo viola introduction, Myrtha orders Giselle to dance; Giselle begs her to relent.

Myrtha: "You must dance."

Larghetto. After Giselle begins to dance (to a seductive viola solo melody), Albert leaves the cross (Ex. 2.33a). Giselle begs Myrtha for mercy during the B section of the music, shortly before the reprise of the main melody. Myrtha refuses.

During the two bars of music that come after the adagio, Myrtha touches Giselle's hand to make her dance even more.

Andantino. The solo viola continues. We presume the choreography of this number was likely, as it remains today, a combination of solos and a duo section (Ex. 2.33b.)

Andante. Myrtha touches Albert with her hand, forcing him to dance (Ex. 2.33c).

In Adam's autograph score one may find, after Albert's variation, a short transitional passage that led to a fifteen-bar reprise of the *andantino* (Ex. 2.33b), a reprise that may have been intended for Grisi to dance. But both the transitional passage and the *andantino* reprise were cut in the autograph and in the Paris orchestra parts, and the music does not appear in the Titus *répétiteur*.[93]

Allegro moderato. The first sixteen bars of the coda are given over to mime (Ex. 2.33d). Giselle begs Myrtha to save Albert.

Myrtha: "No, he must die." Giselle throws herself into Albert's arms. Myrtha tears her away from Albert and forces her to dance.

No. 15 (Finale).[94] Albert falls exhausted. Myrtha exults (Ex. 2.34). Giselle holds Albert up. Myrtha pushes Giselle away and orders the Wilis to make him dance until he dies. The Wilis force him to dance. Albert falls; Myrtha and Giselle encircle him. (The clock strikes four times; Adam calls for the striking of four in the morning by the same "cloche sur le théâtre" that struck midnight.) Sunrise. The Wilis seem to lose their powers and vanish like shadows.

Myrtha: "The sun is rising; we must go back into our graves" (Ex. 2.35). Myrtha goes slowly backward toward her tomb, totters, and disappears (Ex. 2.14b).

At the same time Giselle tells Albert to flee she approaches her tomb. He wants to take her out (of her tomb). He places her on a bank of flowers. Giselle says, "*adieu*."

A fanfare sounds in the distance.

Albert: "No, no, you will not die."

Giselle: "Flee, marry Bathilde."

Wilfride appears at the back of the stage.

Albert: "No, no, I love only you." He hears a noise, sees Wilfride, and returns to the place where Giselle has just disappeared. Giselle sinks little by little.

Wilfride: "Let us flee, let us flee; leave this place!"

---

[93] The idea that this music was meant as a brief solo for Giselle is strengthened by the subsequent interpolation in the 1860s of two variations (to be discussed in Chapter 3), at least one of which was intended for Giselle, and may have served as a replacement for the jettisoned reprise of the *Andantino*.

[94] Eighty-four bars of the 170 originally composed for the finale were cut out, likely to streamline the action and drive it forward. (The cuts begin in the segment of the finale beginning at sunrise.) These significant revisions are unlike the revisions made in the Act One *scène d'amour* (No. 3) which made for an expansion of the scene as originally conceived.

Ex. 2.33a Act Two, *Pas de deux*, bars 7–14

Ex. 2.33b Act Two, *Pas de deux*, bars 44–52

Wilfride wants to lead Albert away. Albert extricates himself with difficulty and rejects Wilfride. He runs to Giselle, who disappears entirely.

At the same time, Wilfride goes up on the *montagne* and summons everybody. Albert is in despair. He lets himself fall on the grave. (*Il se laisse tomber sur le tombeau.*)

Ex. 2.33c Act Two, *Pas de deux*, bars 107–112

Ex. 2.33d Act Two, *Pas de deux*, bars 125–133

Wilfride leads Bathilde in; he goes to get Albert, who, upon seeing Wilfride, goes back to where Giselle disappeared. He pulls up a flower and kisses it transportedly. Wilfride goes to get him and leads him to the Princess. After the final measure: "Tableau pathétique."

Thus we have seen in the Titus manuscript an account of the action that makes it possible to draw some conclusions about the ballet's general values. First, it is a drama with dancing, one in which the mime and action scenes take nearly as much of the running time of the ballet as the dancing, and in which—even in the dance numbers—acting and narrative elements play a part. And it features several characters whose actions are important to the story but who do not dance at all. (Indeed, of the eleven named characters in the ballet, only six dance—and one of those, Hilarion, does so only briefly and against his will.) We learn from this manuscript, for instance, much more about the characteristics of Berthe and Bathilde, and see how the actions of Wilfride and Bathilde at the very end of the ballet bring the story full circle.

Second, the characters speak often, and have a lot to say. Their "utterances," laid out carefully by the annotator, are sometimes quite extensive and reveal aspects of their personalities that would otherwise be unknown.

Ex. 2.34 Act Two, *Après le pas de deux*, bars 1–16

And third, Adolphe Adam's music is so tightly coordinated to the action that it serves the drama in multiple ways that we would not have recognized without seeing the annotations. It is no surprise, of course, that Adam projects the various moods of the characters as appropriate (happy, frightened, angry). But from the Titus manuscript we learned that he also, on occasion, reflected their bodily motions: for instance, when the mad Giselle is running down to the footlights and then across the stage, he gives her first a descending flute scale and then an ascending one. And he provides an ever-rolling soundscape that not only provides ambient sounds (the clock chiming, the hunting horns blowing) but the sounds of the characters' voices (as in the case of Albert's angry "go away, go away" in Act One, Giselle's crazed giggle in the mad scene, and the satanic laughter of the Wilis in Act Two).[95] This makes the story more vivid and the characters more palpable as real human beings (even the ghostly ones), strengthening the narrative even more.

Justamant's manual for *Giselle*

About sixteen years after the Titus *répétiteur* was created, Henri Justamant made another manuscript—a 236-page staging manual—that recorded the action of *Giselle* and the choreography, too, in meticulous detail.[96] Justamant's manual is not written into a musical score, as Titus's is, and therefore offers less information than the earlier manuscript about how the music fits the action. Justamant does, however, inform the reader in most cases when a new musical number starts, and sometimes says how many measures are needed for particular passages of mime and choreography.

[95] These musical voices are discussed by Smith in *Ballet and Opera*, 101–114.
[96] Deutsches Tanzarchiv Köln, Item Number 52915. See Introduction, note 19.

Ex. 2.35 Act Two, *Après le pas de deux*, bars 56–63

As one can see from the few mentions of the Justamant manual above, it provides an even greater wealth of details than Titus does. For he includes drawings—hundreds of them—showing the placement of the actors on the stage, blocking, and choreography. He also writes down, in the manner of a play or libretto, the lines of text "uttered" by the characters. And, crucially, he supplies written-out prose descriptions of the choreography, using the names of particular steps and movements.

A close comparison of Titus's and Justamant's accounts of *Giselle* shows that the two are very similar in content, and—we believe—based fundamentally on the same production: the one that premiered at the Paris Opéra in 1841.

Yet, as Sergey Konaev has shown, Justamant's manual likely represents a revival of *Giselle* staged by Justamant not in Paris but at the Grand Theatre de Lyon, in October 1858. (This production starred the dancer Carlotta de Vecchi, who is mentioned in the manuscript.[97] It also features a smaller corps de ballet than the one listed in the Paris Opéra's libretto.) Justamant had first staged *Giselle* in Lyon no later than 1850, as Helena Kopchick Spencer has ascertained, and it is easy to imagine that he attended performances or rehearsals of the Paris Opéra's production to gather information about the ballet (just as he did in the case of *Le Corsaire*, as we shall see) before he staged it in Lyon. He would have done so before the ballet went out of the Opéra repertory for a decade in 1853.[98]

Justamant's staging manual for *Giselle* describes a ballet that is not only strikingly similar to Titus's *Giselle*, but also one that holds much in common with the *Giselle*

---

[97] Sergey Konaev, "Khronika osnovnykh postanovok s vstavnymi variatsiami" [Chronicle of main productions with inserted variations] in *Giselle* program book (Moscow: Bolshoi Theater, 2019), 86.

[98] A "reprise" of *Giselle* at the Grand Théâtre with Mlle Delechaux in the title role is reviewed (favorably) in *L'Argus*, 6 October 1850, which was during Justamant's 1849–1861 tenure there as ballet master. The same newspaper on 2 October 1853 noted that Mlle Delechaux again danced Giselle, this time with a Monsieur Tilly. We thank Helena Kopchick Spencer for pointing this out to us.

detailed by Nikolai Sergeyev in Russia at the turn of the twentieth century. So it stands as one of three descriptions, all emanating from the original Paris Opéra production, and all bearing bear crucial similarities to one another: proof of the general stability of the ballet as it existed in Paris, Lyon and St. Petersburg, a matter that will be taken up in Chapter 3.

Weak/strong sides of the stage

Now, let us consider the matter of power-weighted sides of the stage, which we noted in Chapter 1. For we can see in Justamant's manual for *Giselle* that stage left is the side of greater political power, in keeping with the precedent suggested by Antonia Banducci. The village is on the "weak" side, stage right; the castle (whether visible to the spectators or not) is on the "strong" side, stage left. Accordingly, the villagers tend to enter and exit stage right and the nobles, stage left. Too, Giselle's cottage is at stage right in Act One; Albert's is at stage left. In Act Two, Giselle's grave is at stage right; Albert and Wilfride approach the grave from stage left. Giselle appears amongst the reeds at stage right when she tantalizes Albert in Act Two. And, as we show below, power struggles involving push-pull action consistently take the form of right-left movement in which Wilfride, wishing to end Albert's entanglements with Giselle (dead or living), tries to draw his master toward stage left. When Albert wants to flirt with Giselle on the bench in Act One and bury her in a flower-lined grave in Act Two, he physically conveys her to his own side of the stage, stage left.

Further, nearly all of Giselle's and Albert's entrances and exits follow this power-side rule. The only exceptions for Giselle come in Act Two shortly after she makes her first ghostly appearance to Albert. He has made his mournful entrance stage left as one would expect, and she has, after several minutes, turned up (behind a clump of bullrushes) at stage right as one would expect. But now the usual order is scrambled: twice during the ensuing scene Giselle briefly exits stage left and re-enters whence she departed. One of these re-entries is on an overhead device that allows her to soar over the startled Albert; the other is a brief departure, after which she re-enters with flowers, which she throws to him. Giselle is momentarily more powerful than the bewildered Albert, and her entrances and exits demonstrate the topsy-turvy nature of the scene.

Albert, too, breaks from the usual rule during his encounters with Wilis: he exits stage right while chasing the Wili Giselle, and then enters stage right a few moments later at the beginning of the crucial scene in which he is literally in the clutches of the Wilis (and apparently on the verge of being murdered by them). This is the exception that proves the rule, for he is clearly out of his usual power zone and his entrance from stage right makes this abundantly clear.

There are also a few instances of stage action in which two interlocutors, each wishing to gain the upper hand, switch positions. For example, after scoffing at Berthe's warning to the village girls about the Wilis, Giselle crosses in front of her mother to move to the more powerful position, and then her mother bodily moves her back to the weaker one. (One might argue that these movements are owed simply to the fact that Berthe is trying to shoo her daughter back to their cottage, which happens to be positioned at stage right. But the frequent instances of position-switching in later ballets, as we shall see, suggests that it was done to communicate one-upsmanship to the audience.)

An examination of five scenes

Simply put, the Justamant manual shows that the story of this ballet was conveyed to the audience moment by moment, detail by detail, with small actions and interactions carefully wrought and strategically placed in the action so as to demonstrate the characters' personalities and emotions as the story unfolds. (Justamant tells us, for instance, that the ghostly Giselle declares, "Now *I* am going to fly," before she does so; Myrtha "triumphs" as Albert falls exhausted and nearly dead.) Such details allow personalities and emotions to emerge in their fullness and bring forth nuances in interactions between characters that strengthen and bring more interest to the drama.

So let us now consider five instances of how the small details in the Justamant manuscript accomplish larger dramatic goals, beginning with excerpts from Giselle's first few scenes. (Some of the action discussed in the remainder of this chapter will be familiar to the reader, for it was described in the Titus manuscript as well.)

(i) In a sequence of events that transpires after Giselle makes her first appearance, we can see her love for dance, and her strength, self-confidence, and liveliness. These events also show the happy and playful nature of the relationship between the two lead characters. (Libretto, Act One, Scene IV; autograph score, No. 3. All quotations are from the Justamant manual, pages 13–27, unless otherwise indicated.)

As Giselle emerges from her cottage in her first appearance in the ballet, she is happily anticipating a visit from Loys, who has just knocked on her door (Ex. 2.24). But Loys, in a bit of flirtatious trickery, has hidden himself from her view. She searches for him and decides to dance for a while since "he's not here yet." Then Loys steps out momentarily from his hiding place and makes a kissing sound.

As the Justamant manuscript describes it, Giselle then says,

"I just heard the sound of a kiss," and runs upstage. She looks, then takes a few steps to the other side, and looks again. "I do not see anything." Coming downstage, "I am here—oh, when he (she indicates Loys's house) gets here, *he will pay for this.*" [Emphasis added.]

She continues in this light-heartedly annoyed frame of mind:

Imagining that he is in front of her, she says to him while walking backward. "If you misbehave, I will not pardon you, no no."

Without seeing him, she bumps into him, turns her head halfway to the right [toward the audience] and seeing who it is, turns her face back to the left with a joyous look, then, with her head: "Ah, let us see!"

Thus, she has taken the audience into her confidence and expressed her feelings but made sure to hide them from Loys for the moment.

Now the tug-of-war continues with Giselle playing hard-to-get (Ex. 2.7a):

Loys tries to read her face and appears to say to himself that she is angry. He touches her arm and says, "Hello, Giselle." Giselle doesn't answer. He offers his hand. She greets him and turning away to her left she runs toward her house. He runs after her.

This back-and-forth between the two principals continues (and includes the daisy-petal scene); the scene ends with more of the same:

Loys says, "Well, goodbye," and he goes upstage.

Giselle: "Well, hello!" but sees that he is going. In a serious manner, she claps her hands to call him back.

Loys turns around immediately.

Giselle: "Come here, quickly," She designates near her.

Loys runs fast to her and kneels.

Placed *en arabesque* on the left foot, she kisses the fingers of her right hand and puts them to Loys's forehead then turns sharply away (he stands up) and runs away to her house.

Giselle's next interaction is with Hilarion, who has witnessed much of the flirtatious encounter between Giselle and Loys and has hidden inside Giselle's cottage to wait for her. This interaction further demonstrates Giselle's feistiness. Note, too, that Loys is amused by it; his attitude helps to keep the mood light.

She opens the door and finds herself facing Hilarion. Surprised and confused, she lowers her head and walks backward [as he advances on her], nearly running.

Hilarion, his arms crossed on his chest and with a furious manner, is advancing on her.

Loys is surprised, not knowing what to do, and observes what is going to happen.

Hilarion: "That's very nice. I was there," he indicates the house, "I saw you kiss this man," he points to Loys, "and I, who love you so much, you reject me. Oh, I will have vengeance."

Giselle, fearful, hunkers down quickly, but then immediately straightens back up, crossing her arms on her chest with a fierce look, standing right in front of Hilarion, advancing on him and forcing him to walk backward, then after some steps, she opens her arms as if to say, "Well, so what?"

Loys is amused by this scene.

Hilarion, very surprised, steps backward, not knowing what to say.

Giselle: "If I kissed Loys, that is what I wanted to do."

Hilarion: "And me?"

Giselle: (laughing) "You, I don't care about." She runs to stage left, joyously.

Hilarion, furious, goes toward her.

Loys comes downstage quickly to bar his passage and says to him, "What do you want?"

Hilarion: "That does not concern you."

Loys: "Get out of here immediately" [Ex. 2.25].

Hilarion: (with a bit of fear) "But, of course, I will." He goes upstage a little, as though he is leaving, but he runs toward Giselle (seeing that Loys's back is turned). He threatens her with revenge.

Giselle laughs down her nose at him.

Loys turns around, and seeing him near Giselle, goes toward him, puts his right hand on him, pushes him toward upstage, and turns him around.

Hilarion: (to Loys) "You, too, you will pay me for this."

Loys: "Go away, or beware." He advances toward him.

Hilarion draws back, defying him, and being a bully.

Giselle tries to calm her sweetheart.

Loys makes a gesture of striking him.

Giselle stops his arm.

Hilarion quickly exits.

Finally, as the scene comes to a close, the actions of the two principals are revealing. Giselle expresses her affection for Loys. And the amiable and comfortable nature of their relationship is demonstrated in her ability to calm him down, and in their simple act of chatting as they come downstage.

These actions also constitute an effective link between the Hilarion-versus-Albert scene and the waltz scene to come.

Giselle has Loys come downstage with her and tells him, "Calm down and let it go."

Loys: "You're right." He hears the sound of young girls who are approaching.

They both look and come downstage, talking.

(ii) Small details in Berthe's scene demonstrate see her strength, her wisdom, the push-pull nature of her relationship with her daughter, and—always—Giselle's spirited resistance. (Libretto, Act One, Scene VI; autograph score, No. 4 and opening of No. 5. All quotations are from the Justamant manual, pages 39–46, unless otherwise indicated.)

The focal point of this scene, of course, is Berthe's telling the village girls about Wilis—who they are, what they do, and the grave danger they pose. But it also displays the nature of Giselle's relationship with her mother (Berthe, stern; Giselle a teenager who chafes at her mother's strictures). It shows that Loys and Giselle would far rather continue their frolicking than part company and shows Giselle's willingness to defy her mother. Finally, in a short series of events toward the end of the scene that deftly provides a smooth elision into the ensuing action, it demonstrates Loys's sudden uneasiness upon hearing the sound of the approaching hunters and his solution to the problem: he sends the village girls back to the vineyard and away from the sound of the hunting horns.

The scene begins when Berthe emerges from her house to bring the young people's merry waltzing to an abrupt end, reflected in the music's sudden stop on an unexpected dissonant chord, which is followed by the sound of Berthe's theme.[99]

Berthe comes out of her house and goes toward center [Ex. 2.3a].

Giselle, seeing her mother, hastens to the other side bringing Loys with her.

Berthe, surprised to see the vinegatherers dancing, says to them, "Why are you here instead of going to cut the grapes?"

The young girls: "It is Giselle who wanted it." They point to Giselle.

Berthe goes toward her daughter.

Giselle, who was trying to remain unseen, now goes in front of her mother.

Giselle: "Here I am, Mother."

Berthe: [the music of the waltz is played; Ex. 2.6b] "Ah, what a state you are in." She takes her apron and wipes her [Giselle's] forehead. "You dance, you will become sick, and you will die."

Giselle: [the music of the waltz is played again] "Oh no, when I dance," she waltzes, "and Loys and"—to him she reaches out her hand which he is quick to take—she takes her mother's hand and puts them both on her heart and says with expression, "I am happy."

Berthe: [frantic version of Berthe's theme] "You will become a wili."

Giselle: "A wili—what is that?"

Berthe: [dark, lugubrious music; Ex. 2.9] "Well, I will tell you." She goes upstage a little and calls the young girls to come around her.

"Down there, in the distance, are wilis: young girls who died from dancing.

And at night and a certain hour, they come out of the ground where they rest and start dancing; when they see men, they grab them and force them to dance with them until they fall dead."

Giselle, holding Loys by the arm, experiences a kind of fright while listening to the story of her mother and asks Loys if it can be so.

He answers, "No."

The young girls also feel the sentiment of fear after hearing the story and chat among themselves about it.

Giselle [jaunty minor-key music; Ex. 2.26], smiling, puts her finger on her mother's forehead and says, "All this is imagination: I do not believe it at all, and I will always dance." She goes to the other side [down right, passing in front of her mother] doing

---

[99] This diminished seventh chord is still used at the close of the waltz, though the waltz no longer precedes Berthe's entrance in most productions because of a brief *pas de deux* for Giselle and Loys that was inserted later (see Chapter 3). Unless Berthe interrupts the waltz, there is no reason to finish it on a dissonant chord.

three times in a row and starting on the left foot, *temps de cuisse, brisé en avant, pas marché en avant.*

Berthe follows her, saying, "Oh my god, she does not want to believe anything." "Please believe me, my dear child."

Giselle: "What you are telling me does not exist."

Loys comes to join them.

Berthe: "I assure you it is true and misfortune will happen to you."

Giselle: "No, no. Instead, let me go with Loys."

Berthe: "No, that's enough dancing."

Giselle suddenly passes in front of her mother to rejoin Loys. [Berthe is now a position weaker than her daughter.]

With her left arm she takes his right arm and leads him [upstage left].

Berthe runs after her daughter, seizes her by the hand, and has her pass in front of her, with an attitude of scolding. Berthe has Giselle pass to Berthe's right. ([Now Giselle is in the weaker position.]

The young girls: (during this scene, they have retrieved their baskets)

Giselle goes downstage toward stage right, sulking.

Berthe: "I want you go back."

Loys follows them and says to Berthe, "I beg of you, stay here another moment?"

Berthe: "No, no. Time to go."

The sound of the horns of the chasse are heard [Ex. 2.4].

The young girls are stage right; they run to the other side to see.

Giselle: (to her mother) "Listen."

Loys seems surprised and says, "I will see what it is." He goes upstage and goes toward the *montagne.*

Giselle wants to follow, but her mother holds her back.

Loys recognizes the prince's hunting party. He soon comes downstage, worried. He doesn't know what to do.

All of a sudden, an idea comes to him. He runs to his door and gets out his key, which he puts [in his costume].

Then he goes toward Giselle and says, "It is a hunting party which comes this way, and after you go back, I will lead the young girls to work."

Berthe is satisfied with this.

Giselle gives Loys her hand.

Loys takes her hand and kisses it and says to her, "See you later."

Giselle, forced by her mother to come back, says to goodbye to him with her hand on the door.

Berthe: "Let us go. Let us go inside."

Loys says to the young girls, "You follow me." He goes up on the *montagne* and departs stage left.

The young girls follow Loys, running.

(iii) *Until he retrieved Albert's insignia from the cottage, Hilarion was angry, frustrated, depressed, confounded. Now, in the first portion of the Act One finale, before the mad scene, we see what Hilarion is like when he is on the verge of triumph. He has at last discovered the identity of his rival and is more than eager to share it with everyone and bring an end to Loys's involvement with Giselle. (Libretto, Act One, Scenes XI, XII, and XIII; autograph score, Act One, Finale. All quotations are from the Justamant manual, pages 101–112, unless otherwise indicated.)*

Here, we have Hilarion's long-awaited and triumphant unmasking of Loys as a deceiver in a complex scene wherein events unfold quickly and principal characters and onlookers act and react with varying degrees of surprise, confusion, and distress.

Indeed, aside from notating the blocking and the words "spoken" by the characters, Justamant takes particular care to name the emotions and reactions of several key characters at various times in the flow of events: Loys and Giselle are "shocked by Hilarion's audacity" when he violently pushes them apart; Hilarion speaks "angrily" to them. Loys is at first anxious when Hilarion tells Giselle of the ruse (he says to himself "great God"), but then "recover[s]," and accuses his rival of being crazy. But when Hilarion retrieves the sword from its hiding place, Loys is "thunderstruck"; Giselle is "stupefied, shocked"; the peasants are "surprised." Hilarion is "defiant" when Loys appears ready to stab him with a dagger. When Loys, "at the height of fury," goes so far as to seize Hilarion's sword and prepares to strike his rival, Wilfride comes out of Giselle's house to stop him, and Giselle is "surprised." When Wilfride tells Loys that the Prince is nearby (pointing toward Giselle's house), Giselle "begins to see the truth and despairs." When Hilarion seizes the horn and blows it to summon the hunting party, Giselle "wonders what this may bring." Hilarion, upon seeing the Prince confront Albert (Loys), "appears to be happy about what has happened." Later, when Giselle tells her mother that Loys is a Lord, Bathilde is "amazed."

Now, let us note Hilarion's four important actions in the opening sequence of the Act One finale as Justamant records it. Hilarion is busy in this scene, acting as a sort of emcee and instigator, and making sure that Loys's unmasking takes place satisfactorily.

Hilarion starts it all by coming downstage and "violently push[ing]" Giselle and Loys apart as they stand close together in the final pose of the preceding dance number. Loys denies Hilarion's claims and threatens him first with a dagger and then a sword. (Notably, Wilfride dashes out of Giselle's cottage just in time to seize the sword. Giselle is surprised by this as Justamant says—she is probably wondering why this squire with whom she had recently served refreshments is interacting with her peasant boyfriend.)

Second, he sounds the horn to summon the hunting party.

Third, as the peasants begin to arrive, Hilarion instructs them to "'keep [Loys] in your view,' and he goes into Giselle's house" (presumably to summon the Prince, who is still resting inside). After the hunting party has arrived and the Prince has emerged from Giselle's cottage and asked Albert (Loys) to explain why he is wearing a "disguise," Hilarion "appears to be happy with what is happening." As Berthe comforts her daughter downstage and Bathilde (nearby) learns with astonishment that Giselle is engaged to Loys (Albert), the Prince asks Hilarion a question as the two stand at upstage center.

Hilarion, in his fourth action before the mad scene, is more than happy to break the news:

Prince: (to Hilarion) "You. Tell me what you know."

Hilarion: "He lived in this house and was making love to this young girl to seduce her."

Thus, Hilarion—having gained some control at last and reveling in his new power—does his best to make sure everyone on the stage learns of Loys's deception, and quickly.

In sum, Hilarion's actions during this scene demonstrate his determination to settle a score and expose the deceptions that have troubled him deeply since before curtain-up. Also, his own eagerness to see the impending blow-up also helps build anticipation in the audience for the confrontation scene and, as it turns out, the mad scene to follow—something Hilarion was not expecting at all.

(iv) The opening scene of Act Two is light-hearted, even comical, and it constitutes one of the first steps in bringing the audience into the supernatural world by showing the surprised reaction of the hunters to the feux follets (will o' the wisps)—a scene surely meant to give the viewer a shivering ghost-story pleasure and a smile before things turned serious. (Libretto, Act Two, Scenes I and II; autograph score, Act Two, Opening. All quotations are from the Justamant manual 127–134 unless otherwise indicated.)

After a scary and lugubrious musical introduction (*entr'acte*)—a powerful musical indication that we have left the sunny village behind for a much darker place (Ex. 2.1c)—the curtain opens on a night-time scene by a pond, with Giselle's grave at stage right. A lone *garde-chasse* at center stage blows his horn; soon others arrive, greeting each other in a friendly manner. The music gets louder and more jolly, mirroring the mood of the men.

The first garde-chasse says, "We must wait for our boss [Hilarion], but while we're waiting we can drink a bit; and what do you say?" After all of the other gamekeepers agree, he detaches his gourd, goes downstage left, followed by his comrades, and they drink.

But before long, Hilarion appears at stage right on the *montagne*, sees his companions, comes down to them, and asks them what they're doing. "We're drinking. At your service," they answer (Ex. 2.11b). But Hilarion gives them a warning: "No, no, quickly, listen to me. You can't stay here; there is a danger." He then explains:

Hilarion: "It appears that at the striking of midnight, out of the earth come ghosts which—when they perceive men—seize them and torment them until they fall dead" [Ex. 2.9].

The gamekeepers: "That is not possible."

Hilarion: "But it is true. Let us get out of here." He goes toward stage right.

The gamekeepers go upstage, talking among themselves.

Hilarion: (to the gamekeepers) "Where are you going? It is this way."

The gamekeepers: "But no, here, let us go this way."

Hilarion: (walking, nearly recoiling) "I am telling you, it is this way. Come."

The gamekeepers keep going upstage, talking among themselves.

Hilarion bumps against the tomb of Giselle. Perceiving the cross and the name of Giselle, he leaves with terror.

The gamekeepers run toward Hilarion and say, "What has happened to you?"

Hilarion: (with emotion) [the jolly music disappears and sad music is heard] "Ah, my friends, you remember the young girl Giselle whom I loved and also who died so sadly?"

The gamekeepers: "Yes, and?"

Hilarion: "Well, here is where she reposes." He points to her tomb. [A sad version of the *louré* is played; Ex. 2.8c.] "Come look."

They all come to the tomb.

When they get there, they remove their hats [to show respect] and look at the inscription.

Hilarion: "You see it is really her. Let us not stay here. Let us get out of here. Let us leave her in peace." He goes upstage slowly, talking with the guards.

Now, the mood shifts again as the clock strikes. Could it be midnight, the hour Hilarion warned them about? The once-casual *gardes-chasses*, now gathered in a tight clump at center, count the chimes on their fingers, the music shifting keys at each chime to create a spooky, unmoored feeling.

Midnight sounds.

All stop, hearing the chimes, and count them on the fingers and at the twelfth strike, fright overtakes them, and they dash to stage left.

Next come the first supernaturals of the ballet—will o' the wisps—who stop the moving clump of men from escaping stage left, then stop them from escaping stage right, and then surround them on all sides, holding them in the middle.[100] (These will o' the wisps, or *feux follets*, are drawn in red ink in the manuscript, indicating that they are female.)

The will o' the wisps appear to them.

The men freeze with fear and then dash to stage right.

The others [will o' the wisps] hold them back, still appearing before them

the men go upstage toward the back, running.

---

[100] *Feux follets* are spirits (manifested in the form of small flashes of phosphorescent light) that behave menacingly.

The will o' the wisps appear on all sides.

The men dare not move.

Hilarion, facing the audience, comes down a little. His legs are trembling.

The gamekeepers, backs to the audience, draw back with fright and go one after the other, bumping into Hilarion, who at each movement feels a shiver.

They come downstage, pressing each other close, to get away from the will o' the wisps.

All the gamekeepers: (getting their courage back) "Oh! we must flee. Everyone who can, save yourself."

They disband, then escape on all sides, getting away from the will o' the wisps [Ex. 2.29].

Shortly after the gamekeepers get away from the malevolent will o' the wisps, Hilarion too escapes, terrified.

Thus, during the course of the above-described sequence of events, the mood has shifted from jolly to nervous to downright frightened. Moreover, the audience and on-stage mortals alike have now seen evidence of supernatural life in the Wilis' territory.

(v) The advent of Myrtha. Here we find details not only of Myrtha's choreography but of her other actions and her moods in the scene of her first appearance, before she brings her Wili subjects to life. These details expose distinct and intriguing—even attractive— characteristics that are not always associated with this character today. Note how many flowers are seen here; it seems that Myrtha was practically surrounded by them, and had plenty to choose from. (Libretto, Act Two, Scene III; autograph score, Act Two, "Apparition et scène de Myrtha." All quotations are from the Justamant manual, pages 135–143, unless otherwise indicated.)

After the will o' the wisps have scared away the gardes-chasses, the dramatic space is opened up for the advent of Myrtha, the Queen of the Wilis. Her music is overtly weird: a quartet of muted violins playing slowly in a high register in E-flat major accompanied by a harp (Ex. 2.15). (As noted above, Adam called this sound "novel.") Complementing the aural strangeness is an equally strange sight: Myrtha slowly rising on a trap, covered in a veil. When she arrives at stage-level the veil disappears below and she steps forth, pro-ceeding to stage right and then making a turn back to center stage while lifting her right arm gradually, performing *pas de bourée sur les orteils* the entire time. After she finishes the scene by gliding languorously across the lake (presumably for ten bars) on a "chariot," she then makes a quick run downstage to look all around her, drinking in the scenery.

If this first number has established that Myrtha is supernatural—and the kind of ghost who enjoys gliding across a lake—the next number demonstrates her playfulness and continues the theme of her pleasure in nature. (It might be called a "charm song" in today's musical-theater parlance.) The music, switching from the ethereal, muted timbre of the first number to bright and friendly sounding waltz music, is in a new key, A-flat major (Ex. 2.30). Myrtha is basking in her surroundings. She listens to a forest echo—first to the right, and then to the left, and the music pauses as she listens on each side. Then she gathers flowers at stage right, at the first wing and then at stage left, at the second wing. Then, spotting some flowers up in a little tree near the banks of the lake, she exclaims "Oh! They are pretty!!" Then,

She puts her foot on the swing and, while swinging on it, the 3rd time catches the flowers with her left hand. She comes down then goes to place herself while she makes a bouquet by putting the flowers together.

Next—presumably, while still holding the flowers—she crosses to downstage left in a repeating sequence of steps (for a total of four times in four bars) that is fleet and smooth: *chassé glissé croisé, cabriole battu en arrière place en fuite, pas de bourrée dessous dessus en face*. Then, she *bourrées* to center, raises her left leg *à la seconde* as she leans her body to the right, and runs toward Giselle's tomb. She places herself in *arabesque*, letting the flowers fall to the ground, then turns and goes to stage left. There, she lets more flowers fall to the ground, also while posed in *arabesque*.

This scene is described by Gautier:

The reeds part and there come into view, first, a little twinkling star, then a crown of flowers, then two beautiful blue eyes, looking gently startled and set in an oval of alabaster, and then finally the whole of that lovely form—slender, chaste, graceful, and worthy of Diana of old—that we know as Adèle Dumilâtre. It is the Queen of the Wilis. With that melancholy grace that is characteristic of her, she frolics in the pale starlight, skimming across the water like a white mist, poising on the bending branches, stepping on the stalks of flowers like Virgil's Camilla, who walked on the corn without bending it, and with a wave of her magic wand summons her subjects, the other wilis, who emerge in veils of moonlight from tufts of reeds, clusters of shrubbery and blooms of flowers to take part in the dance.[101]

Echoes of Act One in Act Two

The Justamant manual discloses that certain actions in Act One were repeated in Act Two. Latter-day alterations to the ballet have had the effect of making these echoes disappear. But once rediscovered, their dramatic significance is easy to appreciate, for they help convey the reversal that lies at the heart of this ballet. In each case cited below, the first instance is a mundane action without portentous significance; the echo is its sad re-enactment in the shadow of death.

Wilfride tries to get Albert to leave Giselle's house at stage right (p. 9ff)	Wilfride tries to get Albert to leave Giselle's grave at stage right (p. 167ff)
Giselle looks for Albert; he is hiding behind the door and he makes a kissing noise, stage right; she goes there but he has hidden again. (p.14ff)	Albert is near the gravesite mourning Giselle; for a moment she peeks at him through the bullrushes, which makes a sound, stage right; he goes there but she has hidden again (p. 169ff)
Albert leads Giselle (his arm around her waist, hers around his shoulder) from far stage right to the bench at stage left. (p. 17)	Albert leads Giselle (his arm around her waist, his around her shoulder) from far stage right to her new flowery grave at stage left. (p. 219)

[101] Gautier, *La Presse*, 5 July 1841, tr. in Gautier, *Gautier on Dance*, 99.

First: *Giselle and Albert, Hide and Seek.* Early in Act One, in a light-hearted scene—the two lovers' first joint scene of the ballet—Albert teases Giselle by first knocking on her door at stage right and then hiding before she emerges from her cottage. He teases her again (after she has searched fruitlessly for him) by stepping out momentarily from his hiding place to make a kissing noise. ("I just heard the sound of a kiss," she says, and she runs upstage to investigate, but finds nothing.) After awhile, Albert finally comes out of his hiding place; the audience can see him, but Giselle cannot because she is facing stage left. Eventually, Giselle and Albert make contact at midstage when she bumps into him while facing the other way. Thus is the stage set for a flirtatious scene between the two of them in which Giselle throws a daisy angrily to the ground and Albert picks it up. Here—after Albert alters the game—the flower affirms Albert's love for Giselle. Instead of "loves me, loves me not," he says, the flower petals mean "I love you very much, I love you passionately, I love you like crazy."

Giselle and Albert's first joint scene of Act Two echoes this hiding and seeking, but the mood is entirely different; moreover, the roles are reversed, and the dead Giselle is now in control; Albert is distraught and desperate. She seems to have retained her playful wit; he is in despair. As he stands at center, Giselle—concealed behind a clump of reeds near her grave at stage right—parts the reeds (which make a rustling sound) and peeks out (Ex. 2.8e). "At the sound of rustling reeds [Albert] turns his head to the right and, seeing Giselle, runs toward her." But he finds nothing. Soon thereafter, she tantalizingly peeks out again from another clump of reeds nearby—Justamant's drawings show that reeds are placed on the stage for her to peek through—but then "closes the reeds" before he can get there. She then appears to him a third time—in spectacular fashion—flying overhead on a piece of stage machinery from stage left to stage right. He runs to find her, futilely. Finally, Giselle appears from behind the second clump of reeds again, and by now Albert is at his wit's end. Instead of running toward Giselle this time, he stays in place and simply puts his left hand on his head ("I am losing my mind") and his right hand on his heart ("it's my heart that suffers. Oh, my God, have mercy on me"). Going down on one knee, he puts his head in his hands. Thus the stage is set for a tender *pas de deux* in which Giselle lovingly throws flowers to Albert and he gratefully picks them up. Here, the flowers affirm Giselle's love for Albert.

Wilfride vs. Albert. One of the ever-sensible Wilfride's main tasks is to keep his master away from Giselle, and his first appearance in both acts shows him doing his best: first, to dissuade his master from pursuing her at all, and in the second act to keep him away from her grave because it is a place of danger. The general thrust of the action in both cases is along a diagonal axis between upstage left and downstage right, Albert pulling one way and Wilfride the other.

The action of the scene plays out as follows in Act One: the two men emerge from Loys's cottage at stage left, Wilfride behind his annoyed-looking master. They are clearly having a disagreement; the music matches the varying moods of the two men. Wilfride asks Albert why he keeps coming here; the answer is "because there [in this house] lives a young and pretty girl whom I love like a fool." Wilfride tries to persuade him to give up his quest, reminding him of Bathilde. Albert refuses to leave, saying "I am staying here" and "go away—get out of here." Wilfride bows and departs.

In Act Two the two men, as before, make their way from stage left toward stage right where Giselle's grave may be seen, but this time Albert is weak, leaning on the ever-supportive Wilfride as they walk slowly, side by side. Albert's music is a soft and mournful oboe aria (Ex. 2.32) instead of the impetuous musical outburst that he required in the parallel scene in the first act. As before, Wilfride asks his master why he has come here; the answer is a heartbreaking variant of what Albert said the first time: "Because here lies the one I weep for." As before, Wilfride tries to persuade him to leave (Wilfride's music is a frantic-sounding *fortissimo allegro* played by full orchestra). As before, Wilfride does his best. (This time he pulls his master up from his kneeling position by the grave and firmly leads him back upstage left before Albert breaks free and runs back to the grave.) As before, Albert refuses to leave, and orders his servant away, saying, "Go away; I am staying here." As before, Wilfride bows and departs.

   Albert leads Giselle to stage left. One of Albert's first actions in the ballet is to persuade Giselle to come to stage left and sit on a bench with him. Her first response: "Me—go sit with you? Oh, certainly not," and she takes two steps away (toward stage right). He stops her; he invites her again. Giselle seems to hesitate and does not respond. He puts her arm around his shoulder, places his own arm at her waist, and the two of them performing *glissades* to the bench. She sits but is a bit sulky about it. (By the end of this scene, though, they are very happy.)

   Toward the end of Act Two, Albert succeeds again at getting Giselle to move from stage right to stage left, only this time his purpose is to keep Giselle from sinking into her own tomb as the other Wilis sink into theirs. Ever weakening, she has fallen at the foot of her tomb at far stage right; Albert runs to her and hastens to lift her up. Then, as he did in Act One, he puts her arm around his shoulder, puts his hand on her waist, and leads her all the way across the stage. This time, his goal is not a bench, but a "terrain" of grass bordered with flowers at stage left. She can scarcely sustain herself and appears to be dying. He "passes her gently in front of himself" and lays her in repose in the terrain.[102] Shortly thereafter (but not until Wilfride has interrupted the two lovers' last conversation by coming to retrieve his master), Giselle tells Albert, "Forget me, and go to the one whom you must marry; goodbye." She disappears into the earth, and the flowers that border the terrain begin to bend toward her, and to cover her.

Justamant's manual reveals a *Giselle* in which many details of the action and staging—an astonishing number of them, painstakingly recorded—are dedicated to the service of story and character. First, the gendering of the sides of the stage (following an Ancien regime practice) helps to convey to the audience, subtly and simply, the opposition and attraction of the two principal characters and the power differential between them. Second, conversations and interactions (of which five are described above) reveal to the audience the personalities of the characters and their states of mind at various junctures in the action. Third, the ironic echoes of Act One in Act Two offer the viewer a chance to reflect on the overall arc of Giselle and Albert's story from its beginning in a sunny valley to its end at a moonlit grave—and to feel more keenly the heartbreak of the final outcome.

   By the time Justamant staged *Giselle* in Lyon in the 1850s, the ballet had been on the St. Petersburg stage for several years, its productions there guided by the Titus *répétiteur*

---

[102] He does so, presumably, because (as the libretto tells us) "conscious of the doom that threatens Giselle, [Albert] carries her in his arms far from her tomb and puts her down on a knoll, amidst a clump of flowers" so that she can find eternal rest.

(which, as we can tell from various annotations therein, continued to be used into the 1870s, perhaps superseded by a new *répétiteur* only when Petipa revived the ballet in 1884). Let us now turn our attention to that Russian city and trace the path of *Giselle* as it was performed there from 1842 until it was notated in the early years of the twentieth century.

3

Giselle: From Paris to St. Petersburg
and Back Again

In *Giselle* we see by far the strongest throughline in the performance trajectory of the five ballets under discussion in this volume, for the St. Petersburg version of this ballet followed its Parisian model faithfully and then endured. Unlike *Paquita*, whose dance content we will see was significantly changed in its first Petersburg production, and *Le Corsaire*, which underwent many alterations over time, *Giselle* started its life in Russia as a sort of close replicate of the Paris production and then remained relatively stable in St. Petersburg after *Giselle* left the Paris Opéra's repertory in 1868—and indeed, all the way into the twentieth century.

By "relatively stable" we do not mean that *Giselle* stood untouched during all those years in the repertory of the Opéra and then in St. Petersburg. As we shall show in this chapter, several changes were made along the way: the fugue scene was dropped and so was the scene with the Old Man. The lead couple's *louré*, danced at the harvest festival, was moved to an earlier place in the act and shortened. New variations for the title character in both acts came and went as ballerinas arrived and departed. (Two such numbers became canonical parts of the ballet.) Some characters' names changed for a while (Bathilde became Matilda) or permanently (Hilarion became Hans in Russia). To keep up with changing tastes and new ballerinas, the ballet had to evolve, and it did. But the general structure of *Giselle* and the slots assigned to its danced segments remained in place, and the ballet's characters and main plot stayed the same.

Even some floor patterns and choreographic details survived as the years went by, a surprising fact, perhaps, for those of us accustomed to the oft-repeated assertion that Marius Petipa wrought major changes to the ballet in 1884, distancing *Giselle* from its French roots and remaking the second act in a new vein that dispatched much of the old choreographic structure and introduced significantly larger patterns unseen before.[1] But there can be no doubt that the ballet as notated by Nikolai Sergeyev during the years around the turn of the twentieth century in St. Petersburg is quite similar in many respects to the version recorded by Justamant in his staging manual more than forty years earlier in France. The diagonal line of Wilis was already there; the structure of the first act's *scène d'amour*; the choreography for Giselle's initiation dance as a new Wili—none of these were the inventions of Petipa; they were all in place in the 1850s (and, likely, earlier), before Petipa made any of his own contributions to the ballet. This

---

[1] For example, Natalia Roslavleva offers no citation for the following assertion: "In 1850 Petipa produced *Giselle* for Carlotta Grisi after Perrot's indications, but introducing many of his own independent touches in the dances of the wilis (act 2). (Later, in a production of 1884, he expanded these into the famous 'Grand Pas des Wilis.')" Roslavleva, *Era of Russian Ballet*, 88. Likely relying on Roslavleva, Susan Au wrote, "His [Petipa's] 1884 revision is usually cited as the most influential. One of his major changes was the expansion of the wilis' dances into a *grand pas des wilis*." Susan Au, "Giselle" in *International Encyclopedia of Dance*, vol. 3, 181.

Five Ballets from Paris and St. Petersburg. Doug Fullington and Marian Smith, Oxford University Press.
© Oxford University Press 2024. DOI: 10.1093/oso/9780190944506.003.0004

affirms the durability of the French *Giselle* in St. Petersburg. It also backs up Nikolai Legat's striking claim, in 1905, that Petipa had retained elements of the original ballet in his own production in St. Petersburg. Sergey Konaev quotes the key passage:

> Petipa told me that the Wilis' *mise-en-scène* belonged to Perrot. While working on *Giselle*, Petipa kept many of the dances that seemed to him magnificent. Making some additions to the performance, he left many of Coralli-Perrot's masterpieces untouched.[2]

Thus, as one can see, the story of *Giselle*'s journey through nineteenth-century St. Petersburg is one of both change and continuity. In this chapter we trace that history, chronicling some of the comings and goings of dancers and ballet masters, as well as scenes, *pas de deux*, and solo variations. Then, we offer a detailed scene-by-scene description of the St. Petersburg *Giselle* as it was eventually notated by Sergeyev. (Here, we make occasional comparisons of the production he recorded with Justamant's mid-century version in order to demonstrate the similarities and differences between them.) Finally, we describe how the St. Petersburg production came back to Paris and the West in the early twentieth century.

Let us begin with the 1842 premiere of *Giselle* in St. Petersburg, but not before noting the close institutional connection between the Paris Opéra and Imperial Ballet. Ballets from Paris were frequently taken up in St. Petersburg, and a close consanguinity was assured by the constant presence in Russia of French ballet masters and dancers. In the case of *Giselle*, the two companies engaged in a particularly high degree of interchange. For example, they shared a ballet master, Jules Perrot, who choreographed numbers for the original ballet in Paris in 1841, staged the St. Petersburg production in 1850, and coached the title role for the 1863 Paris revival. They shared several ballerinas who performed the role of Giselle in both cities (these included Carlotta Grisi, Marfa Muravieva, and Adèle Grantzow) as well as the ballet master Arthur Saint-Leon, who coached Muravieva (in addition to the tuition she received in Paris from Perrot) and Grantzow for their Paris and St. Petersburg (and Moscow) debuts in the title role. The two companies also held in common some of the interpolations, cuts, and other revisions made to the score of *Giselle*, showing that the two versions of the ballet evolved roughly in parallel up till 1868, the year *Giselle* left the repertory of the Paris Opéra.

Giselle in St. Petersburg

Giselle was first performed in St. Petersburg on 18 December 1842 at the Bolshoi Theater. The staging was by the ballet master Antoine Titus, who was aided by an annotated *répétiteur* based on the Paris Opéra production (see Chapter 2).[3] (As noted earlier, Titus was dispatched to Paris by the Imperial Theaters in St. Petersburg to gather information

---

[2] Konaev quotes from Fedor Lopukhov's 1972 *Choreographic Revelations*, in which the author recounts this 1905 conversation with Nikolai Legat. Konaev, "Khronika osnovnykh postanovok," 90. Note that Perrot, as first ballet master in St. Petersburg, had supervised the Imperial Ballet's 1850 production, which would account for Petipa's attribution of the Wilis' *mise en scène* to Perrot.

[3] Irina Boglacheva, ed., *Peterburgskiy balet. Tri veka: khronika. Tom II. 1801–1850* [The Petersburg ballet. Three centuries: A chronicle. Volume II. 1801–1850] (St. Petersburg: Academy of Russian Ballet named after A.Y. Vaganova, 2014) [hereafter: *Khronika II*], 279–280.

about the Opéra's production. The poster for that premiere attributes the ballet to both Jean Coralli and Théophile Gautier and the staging to Titus; see Appendix C (iii).) The performance, a benefit for Titus, featured the Russian ballerina Elena Andreanova in the role of Giselle, with Irakly Nikitin as Albert and Tatiana Smirnova as Myrtha. Fleury (whose real name was Bernard Nonet) performed the role of Hans, as Hilarion was renamed, and Pierre Frédéric Malavergne (known simply as Frédéric) was the Prince of Courlande, or "German sovereign Prince," as the role is listed on the poster. Olga Shlefokht and Emile Gredelue danced a *pas de deux* in the first act that we assume was the Peasant *pas de deux*.

The production featured plenty of Russian talent in the female roles and was a boost for the St. Petersburg Imperial Ballet, which was still mourning the departure earlier that year of Marie Taglioni.[4] The dancers, particularly Andreanova, were praised by the critic Rafail Zotov in *Sevenaya pchela*, who drew particular attention to the production's many special effects:

> But above all in this ballet are the scenic effects, and for these, the honor belongs completely [to the machinist] M. Roller. Completely new on our stage, in the second act, was the horizontal flight of Mlle Andreanova. It is so lovely that everyone was delighted. Only painting or poetry could give us such a picture. Therefore, the flights of Mlle Smirnova and the swinging on the tree of Mlle Andreanova, who throws flowers from there to Albert, are truly beautiful. The appearance of Giselle from the tomb is also very charming, but her disappearance is even more charming. This is a silent love poem.[5]

In the ensuing seasons, visiting artists chose *Giselle* for their Petersburg debuts, and over time changes were made to the production. The famed Danish ballerina Lucile Grahn scored success in *Giselle* on 30 January 1843, partnered by Christian Johanson as Albert.[6] The Austrian ballerina Fanny Elssler danced the title role on 1 October 1848, again with Johanson.[7] According to the poster, the production included a *pas de trois* for Elssler and two women in Act One. Ivor Guest noted that the scene with the peasants in Act Two was cut. Indeed, the role of the Old Man, included on the poster for the 1842 premiere, is absent from the poster for Elssler's Petersburg debut.[8] With this performance, we see additional character names changed: the Prince was renamed "Herzog" (Duke) and Albert became a "Count."[9]

1850 saw the first St. Petersburg production of *Giselle* supervised by Jules Perrot, who served as ballet master there from the end of 1848 until 1859, when he was succeeded by Arthur Saint-Léon, who remained in the post until 1870.[10] For this performance, on 8 October, Carlotta Grisi reprised the title role in her Petersburg debut, partnered by Johanson.[11] The poster again attributes the ballet to Coralli and Gautier (with no

---

[4] About Taglioni's time in St. Petersburg, see Wiley, *Century*, 81–89.

[5] Rafail Zotov, *Sevenaya pchela*, 29 December 1842, qtd. in *Khronika II*, 279–280.

[6] *Khronika II*, 281.

[7] *Khronika II*, 301–304. See also Guest, *Elssler*, 239–243.

[8] See Guest, *Jules Perrot*, 252–253. Elssler had made her *Giselle* debut in London on 30 March 1843, where she made a great impression with her dramatic interpretation. See Ivor Guest, *The Romantic Ballet in England*, rev. ed., 1972 (Reprint, Hampshire, UK: Dance Books, 2014), 97–100. Elssler danced *Giselle* in many European cities, but never in Paris.

[9] Wilfride is listed as "Silfride," which may be a typographical error.

[10] Without further elaboration, Ivor Guest remarked, "In the light of its later acceptance as a classic, *Giselle* was surprisingly ignored by Jules [Perrot] during his years in Russia." See Guest, *Jules Perrot*, 282–283.

[11] *Khronika II*, 316.

mention of Titus), but Perrot is listed as choreographer of a *pas de cinq*, with music by Cesare Pugni, inserted into Act One for Giselle, Albert, and three women.[12]

The Russian ballerina Nadezhda Bogdanova made her St. Petersburg debut in *Giselle* in the Perrot production on 2 February 1856, with Johanson as her Albert.[13] Gautier is no longer listed on the poster, but "mise-en-scène par Mr Jules Perrot" finally acknowledges Perrot's contribution as stager. "Loys" is no longer listed as an alias for Albert on the poster, and the order of dances suggests the Act One *pas de deux* for Giselle and Albert was danced after the Peasant *pas de deux*, rather than preceding it, as in earlier performances.[14] (This order would remain at least through Adèle Grantzow's debut in 1866.) Later that year, on 13 November, Bogdanova danced a single performance of the first act of *Giselle* at the Paris Opéra, where she had been a student and a member of the corps de ballet.[15]

The Russian ballerina Marfa Muravieva made her St. Petersburg debut in *Giselle* on 8 November 1862 in a production likely supervised by Saint-Léon (who was currently first ballet master), though the staging remained attributed to Perrot on the poster.[16] Johanson once again took the role of Albert, with Frédéric as Hans, and Elizaveta Nikitina as Myrtha. According to the poster, Bathilde became "Matilda," and Wilfride lost his name and was simply called "Squire of Count Albert." The character names listed on this particular poster, incorporating the changes we have thus far noted, endured well into the twentieth century, at least into the early 1920s.

The 1863 Paris revival

Accompanied to the French capital by her champion Saint-Léon, Muravieva made her Paris Opéra debut the following year on 8 May 1863 in a lavish and successful revival of *Giselle* supervised by Lucien Petipa, ballet master at the Opéra from 1860 to 1868.[17] Acclaimed for her brilliant technique rather than her adequate mime skills, Muravieva was partnered by Louis Mérante and coached in the role by Perrot, who had returned to Paris from St. Petersburg in 1861 after being terminated by the Imperial Theaters the previous December.[18] *Giselle* had not been performed in Paris since 1853. Muravieva, worried *Giselle* was not current enough to effectively demonstrate her skills, had hoped to make her debut in a new ballet.[19] Her concern may have precipitated the addition of new dances in *Giselle* in order to distinguish Muravieva from the other stars who had danced the role, to highlight her gifts, and refresh the ballet. As noted above, such new dances were commonly created for revivals and debuts of existing ballets, and we shall see more instances of them as our study continues.

[12] See Guest, *Jules Perrot*, 253. See also *Khronika II*, 316.
[13] See Irina Boglacheva, ed., *Peterburgskiy balet. Tri veka: khronika. Tom III. 1851-1900* [The Petersburg ballet. Three centuries: A chronicle. Volume III. 1851-1900] (St. Petersburg: Academy of Russian Ballet named after A.Y. Vaganova, 2015) [hereafter: *Khronika III*], 47. See also Guest, *Jules Perrot*, 295.
[14] Other changes may have been made to character names, but the extant poster held by the St. Petersburg State Museum of Theatre and Music is bound so tightly that some of the names cannot be seen in their entirety.
[15] See Ivor Guest, *Ballet of the Second Empire 1858-1870* (London: Adam and Charles Black, 1953), 63.
[16] See Guest, *Jules Perrot*, 327. The poster states, "mise en scène par Mr. Jules Perrot"; no mention is made of Saint-Léon. See also *Khronika III*, 96–97, wherein the production is credited to Titus.
[17] The revival featured new designs, the originals having burnt in 1861, and a large cast: ninety peasants, a hunting party of forty courtiers, and fifty Wilis. See Guest, *Second Empire 1858–1870*, 60–64.
[18] See Guest, *Second Empire 1858-1870*, 59–62, and Guest, *Jules Perrot*, 316–319 and 326–327.
[19] See Guest, *Second Empire 1858-1870*, 60.

Ex. 3.1a *Pas dit de l'Hôtel de Ville*, bars 1–8

Casting notices for Muravieva's Paris performances indicate the addition of six women to Giselle and Loys's Act One *pas de deux*, suggesting a new dance supplanted the original.[20] This is borne out in the Paris orchestra parts and conductor's short score wherein the Act One *pas de deux* is replaced with the so-called *Pas dit de l'Hôtel de Ville*.[21] No composer is credited, but one of the movements is retained from Adam's original *pas de deux*. The *pas* comprises six sections, with a short transition before the final galop:

Allegretto, E major, $\frac{6}{8}$	22 bars
Adagio, E major, $\frac{4}{4}$	27 bars
Moderato, E major, $\frac{3}{4}$	33 bars
Moderato, A major, $\frac{4}{4}$	28 bars
Moderato, E major, $\frac{4}{4}$	36 bars
Tempo di Gallopo, D major, $\frac{4}{4}$	154 bars

The casting of each section is not indicated in the musical sources, but the nature of the various numbers suggests an augmented *pas de deux* structure, with the opening number serving as an entrée (Ex. 3.1a) followed by a slower adagio (Ex. 3.1b). The third movement is a piquant *scherzando* scored for full orchestra, suggesting it may have been a group number (Ex. 3.1c); number 4, titled *1er Echo*, is a flute solo and therefore, because of its light scoring, may have been a variation for Giselle (Ex. 3.1d);[22] number 5,

---

[20] *L'Orchestre*, 9 May 1863.

[21] Paris, Bibliotheque Nationale de France, Bibliothèque-Musée de l'Opéra, MAT-332 (1–53). The original *pas de deux* has been removed from some orchestra parts, the folios sewn together in others, and parts struck through in others.

[22] Ivor Guest explained the meaning of the term "echo": "*Echo*, or sometimes *écot*, was a term then in use to denote a short variation included in a pas." Gautier, *Gautier on Dance*, 172n3. Alternatively, Knud Arne Jürgensen has explained that the term "echo, when used in the title of a solo dance, can mean "the

Ex. 3.1b *Pas dit de l'Hôtel de Ville*, bars 24–31

Ex. 3.1c *Pas dit de l'Hôtel de Ville*, bars 52–55

titled *2me Echo*, is the section retained from Adam's original *pas* and may have been a variation for Albert (Ex. 3.1e). The number is transposed up a semitone and has a revised ending. The lengthy galop is labeled "Coda" (Ex. 3.1f). Although no choreographer is credited, the likely possibilities include Lucien Petipa, Saint-Léon, or Perrot.

Whether the *Pas dit de l'Hôtel de Ville* was originally interpolated in Paris or brought there by Muravieva is difficult to determine from Parisian sources alone. The music for the *1er Echo* also appears in a Moscow Bolshoi Theater catalog of interpolated variations.[23] Whatever the case, the *pas* appears to have achieved the desired effect, as described by Ivor Guest:

reappearance on stage." Knud Arne Jürgensen, *The Verdi Ballets* (Parma: Instituto nazionale di studi verdiani, 1995), 62.

[23] See Konaev, "Khronika osnovnykh postanovok," 88. Page 75 of the same publication includes an image from a Moscow Bolshoi Theater document, dated "1900s" by Konaev and listing the musical incipits of interpolated numbers, that includes this variation as entry "N 102." See also a detail of this same image on page 87.

Ex. 3.1d *Pas dit de l'Hôtel de Ville, 1er Echo*, bars 101–105

Ex. 3.1e *Pas dit de l'Hôtel de Ville, 2me Echo* (Adam), bars 129–137

In the first act [Muravieva] was loudly applauded at the end of her *pas de deux* with Mérante, which had included an exciting moment when the fury of her dancing suddenly calmed, and, in the words of Jouvin, "she broke measure with the *rallentando* such as singers use at the end of an aria."[24]

An interpolated flute solo titled *Echo de Mme Zina* (Ex. 3.1g) precedes the flute solo *1er Echo* in the orchestra parts. The variation is notated in a hand unlike the others in the manuscripts and taped at the binding in each part, suggesting it was inserted into the scores after the rest of the *pas de deux* was compiled. The title and score situation suggest the number was added for Zina Richard, who took over the role of Giselle from Muravieva on 30 September 1863, and it likely replaced Muravieva's probable solo danced to *1er Echo*.[25] The performance was Richard's debut

---

[24] Guest, *Second Empire 1858–1870*, 61–62.

[25] The *1er Echo*, *2me Echo*, and *Echo de Mme Zina* are variously pinned shut or folded in the Paris orchestra parts, suggesting that sections of the *pas de deux* were included or omitted in a given performance over time. About Richard's debut, see Guest, *Second Empire 1858–1870*, 63.

Ex. 3.1f *Pas dit de l'Hôtel de Ville*, Coda, bars 171–186

Ex. 3.1g *Pas dit de l'Hôtel de Ville*, *Echo de Mme Zina*, bars 84–87

in the complete ballet; she had already performed the second act in St. Peterburg in 1855.[26]

The Act One dances are listed in casting notices in the 9 May and 1 June 1863 editions of *L'Orchestre*:

---

[26] For example, on 1 December 1855. See *Khronika III*, 45.

Pas des Vendanges,
Mlle Mourawief, M. Mérante.
Valse,
Mme. Zina, M. Chapuy.
Pas de deux,
Mlle Mourawief, M. Mérante,
Mlles Schlosser, Pilvois, Mercier,
Stoïkoff, Fiocre et Baratte.
Galop final.

The *Pas des Vendanges* for Giselle and Albert may refer to an excerpt from the final *louré* section of the original Act One *pas de deux* (Ex. 2.8a). The redaction exists among the Paris matériel, wherein it is preserved on paper dating from the 1860s in the conductor's short score and several orchestra parts—in some parts it is a loose folio; in others it is bound following the Act One waltz, which has since become its canonical position in the ballet.[27]

Why was the *louré* retained in *Giselle* once another *pas de deux* had taken its place? The answer surely lies in its melodic theme, which returns (as noted in Chapter 2) during the mad scene, during Giselle's recollection of happier times with Loys, as well as during the opening of Act Two, when Hilarion and the hunters happen upon Giselle's grave in the woods. Eliminating the initial statement of the melody would render its return meaningless. The solution of shortening the number allowed its inclusion without adding much time to the first act. Placing it after the waltz took advantage of that number's interrupted ending, a diminished chord built on G-sharp. That dissonant chord, intended to accompany Berthe's abrupt entrance, now served as a segue to the shortened *louré*, which was transposed up a semitone—from A-flat major to A major—providing a smooth resolution of the diminished chord. The dance remained a *pas de deux* for Giselle and Albert. We will see in our exploration of the Stepanov notation of *Giselle* that the St. Petersburg choreography retained elements of the longer version of the dance preserved in the Justamant manual. Perhaps the Paris production in the 1860s did as well.

When was the *louré* shortened and moved to a new position in the score? The answer for the Paris production appears to be 1863. Whether this solution for retaining the *louré* originated in Paris or was brought with Muravieva or others from St. Petersburg or elsewhere, the sources do not reveal. Nevertheless, we can confirm that the shortening of the *louré* in the Paris production of 1863—rendering a brief version that is retained in many productions today—was the result of replacing the original *pas de deux* for Giselle and Loys with the *Pas dit de l'Hôtel de Ville*.

Returning to the 1863 Parisian list of Act One dances: "Valse" surely refers to the Peasant *pas de deux*, whose extended final number, *Souvenir de Ratisbonne*, is a waltz. (Ivor Guest confirmed that Zina Richard and Alfred Chapuy first danced the Peasant *pas de deux* on 8 May 1863.[28]) Because the dance is listed as *Valse* rather than *Pas de deux*, it is possible that only the final waltz of the Peasant *pas de deux* was danced, although the Paris orchestra parts show no evidence that the earlier movements of the *pas de deux* were cut. Perhaps *Valse* was the term used to refer to the entire *pas de deux*. Several years later, in 1866, Gautier used the same term in his review of Grantzow's debut performance: "Mlle [Angelina] Fioretti danced the *valse* in the first act very well, but perhaps a

[27] MAT-332 (17, 25, 41, 48).
[28] Guest, *Romantic Ballet in Paris*, 2nd ed., 297–298n88.

Ex. 3.2   Act Two interpolated variation, bars 3–10

little coldly."[29] (Guest confirmed that Fioretti made her debut in the Peasant *pas de deux*, or possibly only the waltz, on 11 May 1866.[30])

The subsequent *pas de deux* would then refer to the new *Pas dit de l'Hôtel de Ville*, performed by Giselle, Albert, and six women. The number of ensemble women seems to have held when Richard took over the role of Giselle at the Opéra, but by the time Adèle Grantzow was performing the *pas* there in 1866, the number of women appears to have been reduced to four.[31] This change may have been made earlier: the Act One *pas de deux* appeared on a gala program performed at Versailles on 21 August 1864 in honor of the King of Spain. The cast featured Muravieva, Mérante, and four women.[32]

A second interpolated number, an anonymous thirty-eight-bar variation for solo violin and strings, is preserved in the Paris orchestra parts in the Act Two *pas de deux* following Albert's variation (Ex. 3.2). We assume this number served as a solo for Giselle that was likely danced by Muravieva or Richard or by both ballerinas before it was replaced by the waltz variation added for Grantzow in 1866 (see next section).[33] The provenance of the number is unknown to us.

Variation pour Mlle Granzow

Adèle Grantzow, a German ballerina and protégée of Saint-Léon who was an expressive mime as well as an exceptionally accomplished technician, danced *Giselle* in three major cities in 1866. She first danced the role in Moscow on 28 January, made her Paris Opéra debut in the role on 11 May, and ended the year in St. Petersburg, where she made her debut in the role on 13 December, partnered by Johanson. Saint-Léon rehearsed Grantzow on each occasion.[34]

---

[29] Gautier, *Le Moniteur universel*, 14 May 1866, tr. in Gautier, *Gautier on Dance*, 318.
[30] Guest, *Romantic Ballet in Paris*, 2nd ed., 297–298n88.
[31] See casting notices in *L'Orchestre* on 1 October 1863 and 12 May 1866, respectively.
[32] *Le Ménestrel*, 28 August 1864, 307.
[33] We make this assumption because the parts are notated on paper dating from the 1860s (when Muravieva and Richard danced the role of Giselle in Paris) but were apparently supplanted in 1866 by the waltz variation.
[34] Arthur Saint-Léon, *Letters from a Ballet Master: The Correspondence of Arthur Saint-Léon*, ed. Ivor Guest (London: Dance Books, 1981) 131, Letter 31, note 5; and Guest, *Second Empire 1858-1870*, 92. The St. Petersburg poster credits only Coralli and neither Perrot nor Saint-Léon. See also *Khronika III*, 122.

Ex. 3.3 *Variation pour Mlle Granzow* (Minkus), bars 10–17

A waltz, attributed to Ludwig Minkus, was inserted for Grantzow in the *pas de deux* of the second act (Ex. 3.3). At what point the interpolation was first made has not, to our knowledge, been determined. Olga Fedorchenko has confirmed that Moscow audiences did not see the variation until 28 October 1866, which suggests Paris may be the city of origin, although it is possible the variation was added to the Paris production after Grantzow danced the role in St. Petersburg.[35] Whatever the case may be, the waltz was added to *Giselle* scores in three cities: it is found in the same Moscow catalog of interpolated variations mentioned above, in the Paris orchestra parts—wherein it is titled *Variation pour Mlle Granzow* and replaces the anonymous violin solo (Ex. 3.2)—and in the St. Petersburg sources held at Harvard Library (see later in this chapter).[36] Both Guest and Fedorchenko suggest Saint-Léon was the original choreographer of the variation.[37]

The music for this interpolated waltz is notable for its clever adaptation of the "daisy-petal" theme, the primary melody of the Act One *scène dansante* (see Ex. 2.7a). Moreover, its lengthy duple-meter introduction, which modulates from A-flat major to E-flat major by way of C-flat major, is also based on the daisy-petal theme. Although we do not know whether the idea for using this motif belonged to Minkus himself or to Saint-Léon, this ingenious variation, which serves to strengthen the musical connection between the two acts of the ballet, has become a canonical part of the *Giselle* performance score, as noted earlier.

While the Paris orchestra parts and casting notices suggest the *Pas dit de l'Hôtel de Ville* was performed in the first act of *Giselle* from 1863 until the ballet went out of repertory in 1868, a

---

[35] Describing Grantzow's performance as Giselle on 28 October 1866 at the Bolshoi Theater, Moscow, the reviewer for *Golos* wrote: "Toward the end of the ballet, the artist danced a new variation, which we have not yet seen here," referring to it as "a wonderful solo by Mr. Minkus." Qtd. in Olga Fedorchenko, "Balerina Adel' Grantsova: 'Zakonnaya naslednitsa' talanta Tal'oni" [Ballerina Adèle Grantzow: "Rightful Heiress" of Taglioni's Talent], *Muzykal'nyy teatr: spektakl', rol', obraz* [Musical theater: performance, role, image], 1 (St. Petersburg: Asterion, 2019): 104–105.

[36] See the image reproduced on page 139 of Konaev, "Khronika osnovnykh postanovok," that includes the variation as entry "N 197." Grantzow's name is spelled both Grantzow and Granzow in sources.

[37] Neither author provides a supporting citation. See Guest, *Jules Perrot*, 350, and Fedorchenko, "Balerina Adel' Grantsova," 104. Saint-Léon served intermittently as guest choreographer at the Paris Opéra and was also active in Moscow during his years as ballet master in St. Petersburg. See Saint-Léon, *Letters from a Ballet Master*, 26.

notice in St. Petersburg suggests Grantzow danced a different first-act *pas* when performing *Giselle* in the Russian capital during this period. A review in *Golos* of a benefit performance for Christian Johanson, given at the Bolshoi Theater on 14 January 1868, reported that the ballerina Ekaterina Vazem "danced a big and difficult adagio from *Jovita*, the same *pas* that Mlle Grantzow performed with such success in the ballet *Giselle* last season."[38] This once again illustrates the malleability of both the score and the choreography of repertory ballets.

Pavel Gerdt, an important *premier danseur* who will figure prominently in all five of the ballets in the present study, made his debut as Albert on 8 October 1870 at the Bolshoi Theater, St. Petersburg, partnering Grantzow in *Giselle*,[39] and continued to dance the role for the next two decades. A review of his premiere performance in *Golos* states that yet more new material was performed by Grantzow: "The adagio and variation in the large *pas* of the first act, performed for the first time, caused thunderous applause."[40]

Giselle continued to serve as a vehicle for ballerinas in the St. Petersburg Imperial Ballet. The Russian ballerina Ekaterina Vazem debuted as Giselle at her benefit performance on 12 February 1878, partnered by Gerdt. Critics noted she was less suited to the role than others (Vazem's younger colleague Maria Gorshenkova was named) because she lacked both dramatic interpretation and a light, aerial quality.[41] (However, we will find Vazem enjoyed greater success in other ballets in our study, particularly in *Paquita* and *La Bayadère*.)

Giselle in St. Petersburg under Marius Petipa

The first production of *Giselle* supervised by Marius Petipa was a revival given on 5 February 1884 at the Bolshoi Theater, St. Petersburg.[42] The poster states that the ballet was "restaged [*vnov' postavlennyy*] by balletmaster M. Petipa." The performance featured Gorshenkova, a dancer known for her lightness and jumping ability who had already essayed the title role while she was a student.[43] She was partnered by Gerdt (Albert) in a cast that included Felix Kshesinsky (Hans), Sofia Petrova (Myrtha), Alfred Bekefi (*Herzog*) Marie Petipa (Matilda), Maria Legat (Berthe), and Alexander Chistyakov (Squire).

The poster offers less information about the dances performed in this revival than earlier posters had done. It does tell us that the first act featured a *Valse* danced by Gorshenkova, Gerdt, and sixteen women, and a *Pas-de-deux* (likely the Peasant *pas de deux*) featuring Evgenia Voronova and Platon Karsavin. Dances in the second act included a *Solo* danced by Petrova; the *Pas des wilis* performed by Petrova, Anna-Natalia Gruzdovskaya, Elizaveta Kruger (the latter two likely dancing the roles of Moyna and Zulmé), and twenty-four women; and a *Pas-de-deux* featuring Gorshenkova and Gerdt.

By this time, Petipa's experience with *Giselle* dated back more than forty years. On 13 May 1843, he made his debut as *premier danseur en tous genres* at the Grand-Théâtre, Bordeaux, dancing the role of Albert opposite Elisa Bellon.[44] A year later, on 24 June 1844,

---

[38] *Golos*, 16 January 1868, qtd. in *Khronika III*, 133.

[39] *Khronika III*, 151.

[40] *Golos*, 10 October 1870, qtd. in *Khronika III*, 151.

[41] *Khronika III*, 194. For Vazem's own assessment of her performance in *Giselle*, see Ekaterina Vazem, "Memoirs of a Ballerina of the St. Petersburg Bolshoi Theatre: Part 4," tr. Nina Dimitrievich, *Dance Research* 6, no. 2 (Autumn 1988), 36.

[42] *Khronika III*, 229–230.

[43] Gorshenkova performed the title role in the second act of *Giselle*, partnered by Gerdt, as part of a benefit program for Alexandra Kemmerer on 14 December 1875. See *Khronika III*, 182.

[44] Meisner, *Marius Petipa*, 46.

he partnered Marie Guy-Stéphan in *Giselle* for his first performance at the Teatro del Circo in Madrid.[45] Shortly after he arrived in St. Petersburg, he appeared opposite Elena Andreanova in *Giselle* on 23 November 1847.[46] But the role of Albert in St. Petersburg in the years following Petipa's arrival was effectively the province of Christian Johanson, who danced it for more than two decades before relinquishing it to Gerdt. Both of these artists excelled in classical dancing, whereas Petipa's strengths lay in mime and character dance.[47]

As to the matter of Petipa's choreographing anything for *Giselle* or making revisions before 1884: the sources available to us are silent regarding what involvement, if any, he had in the Petersburg productions of *Giselle* supervised by his predecessors Perrot and Saint-Léon prior to Petipa's accession in 1870 to first ballet master upon Saint-Léon's death.[48] Likewise, any changes he may have introduced in the 1884 production are not made clear by the list of dances or casting included on the poster. By far the best information about Petipa's staging of *Giselle* comes from a document created nearly two decades after Petipa made his first staging of this ballet: the choreographic notation of *Giselle* made by Nikolai Sergeyev. This will serve as the basis of our step-by-step description of *Giselle* in St. Petersburg at the turn of the century, below. In the meantime, let us look at several more performances of interest along the way.

Petipa's next revival of *Giselle* on 12 April 1887 marked the St. Petersburg debut of the Italian ballerina Emma Bessone. Gerdt was Bessone's Albert, with Kshesinsky as Hans and Anna Johanson as Myrtha. The *Peterburgskaya gazeta* noted Bessone's second act variation was staged by the ballerina herself.[49]

Variation pour Mlle Cornalba

The next Italian dancer to debut in *Giselle* was Elena Cornalba on 18 December 1888, partnered by Gerdt.[50] Cornalba's name is attached to the second variation added to *Giselle* that has since become canonical (the first being the "daisy-petal" waltz added to Act Two). This variation, likely composed by Riccardo Drigo, was not initially created expressly for *Giselle* but was first interpolated by Petipa into the ballet *Fiammetta* on the occasion of its revival in St. Petersburg on 6 December 1887.[51] *Fiammetta*, with music by Ludwig Minkus and choreography by Arthur Saint-Léon, had first been performed in Moscow on 12 November 1863. The following year, the ballet was presented in St. Petersburg and then in Paris, the production in the latter city being a shortened version titled *Néméa*. Both productions featured Marfa Muravieva.

Petipa revived *Fiammetta*, with additional music by Drigo, for Cornalba's St. Petersburg debut. The music for this variation is not included in Minkus's Paris score for *Néméa*, a fact that strengthens the possibility that it was composed by Drigo, although

[45] Ibid., 48. See also Laura Hormigón, *Marius Petipa en España, 1844–1847: Memorias y otros materiales* (Madrid: Danzarte Ballet, 2010), 211, 234.

[46] *Khronika II*, 296.

[47] For a survey of Petipa's Russian performing career, see Meisner, *Marius Petipa*, 66–70.

[48] See Meisner, *Marius Petipa*, 157.

[49] *Peterburgskaya gazeta*, 14 April 1887, qtd. in *Khronika III*, 257–258. Konaev cites and provides a manuscript example of a variation composed for Bessone in *Giselle* that is preserved in the Bolshoi Theater Music Library, Moscow. Konaev, "Khronika osnovnykh postanovok," 91.

[50] *Khronika III*, 272.

[51] See Konaev "Khronika osnovnykh postanovok," 92–93. See also, *Khronika III*, 266-267.

Ex. 3.4 *Variation pour Mlle Cornalba* (Drigo), bars 10–17

definitive confirmation, to our knowledge, has yet to be produced. That the variation was danced by Cornalba is confirmed by sources in St. Petersburg and Moscow and at Harvard, where musical scores indicate that the variation was for her (for instance, the appellation "Variation pour Mlle Cornalba").[52]

The variation is a violin solo in three parts with introduction, not unlike the form of the variation composed by Minkus for Nikia in the Kingdom of the Shades scene from *La Bayadère* (see Chapter 9). The opening melody in $\frac{6}{8}$ meter will be familiar from nearly all modern productions of *Giselle* (Ex. 3.4).

The variation was subsequently interpolated into Act One of the St. Petersburg *Giselle* as a solo for the titular ballerina, and though we do not know exactly when, it is clear that it had become part of the ballet by at least 1903. The poster for the 1 January 1889 St. Petersburg performance of *Giselle* featuring Cornalba includes a *Solo* among the dances in Act One. Let us review the various dances listed for Act One on this poster, noting that, as in 1884, no *pas de deux* for Giselle and Albert is listed.

1. Entrée—Cornalba (Giselle's first entrance)
2. Valse—Cornalba, Gerdt, and 16 women
3. *Scène dansante*—Cornalba, Gerdt (this is likely the shortened *louré* movement of the original *pas de deux*, discussed above)
4. Fête des vendanges—40 women plus an undesignated number of male dancers (*tantsovshchiki*) (likely the first part of the March)
5. Solo—Cornalba
6. Final—all participants (likely the end of the March)
7. *Pas de deux*—(Varvara) Nikitina and (Platon) Karsavin 2 (likely the Peasant *pas de deux*)
8. Galop—all participants

---

[52] No fewer than four copies of the variation are preserved among the Harvard sources—MS Thr 245 (5, 7, 8) and MS Thr 465 (205). The variation's incipit is included in the Bolshoi catalog of interpolated variations, entry No. 198, wherein the number is identified as "Ballet Fiametta [sic] | Variation Cornalba." See Konaev "Khronika osnovnykh postanovok," 139; a detail of the image can be found on p. 92. The number is designated *Variation Mlle Cornalba* in the manuscript full score of *Giselle* preserved in the Central Music Library of the St. Petersburg State Academic Mariinsky Theater, vol. 1, 142–148 (shelf number unavailable). Natalia Zozulina has confirmed by personal correspondence that the variation is also included in a *répétiteur* of *Giselle* held by the Central Music Library (citation unavailable), wherein it is labelled as Cornalba's variation from *Fiammetta*.

This list suggests the *Solo* was interpolated within the March (*Fête des vendanges*), the same position the *Fiammetta* variation holds in the Harvard sources. However, whether the *Solo* here represents the interpolated variation from *Fiammetta* or another number cannot be confirmed with the sources at hand.[53] We can confirm, however, that the Cornalba variation was added to the St. Petersburg *Giselle* at least by 1903, when Anna Pavlova made her debut in the title role. The Stepanov notation of the variation, which we will discuss shortly, bears her name.

After a decade out of repertory, *Giselle* was revived for the St. Petersburg debut of Italian ballerina Enrichetta Grimaldi on 5 September 1899. Grimaldi was partnered by Nikolai Legat (Albert), with Pavel Gerdt taking the role of Hans and Olga Preobrazhenskaya as Myrtha.[54] The performance program includes the same resumé of dances that had been listed on the poster ten years earlier for Cornalba. In his *Giselle* chronology, Konaev cites Petipa's letter to Prince Sergei Volkonsky, then director of the Imperial Theaters, in which the balletmaster notes the care he took in preparing Grimaldi in the role: "Monsieur Prince, I can assure you, my Prince, that I will exert all my zeal for Mademoiselle Grimaldi's debut in *Giselle*."[55] Grimaldi indeed achieved success in the revival.

Three months later, on 28 December 1899, Preobrazhenskaya made her debut as Giselle, partnered by Georgi Kyaksht, and nearly two years later, another Italian ballerina, Carlotta Zambelli, took over the role on 28 October 1901, partnered by Nikolai Legat.[56] Valerian Svetlov recorded details about Zambelli's Act One variation:

> The solo in the 1st act (a variation from the opera Hamlet, [by Ambroise] Thomas: "La fête du printemps") she had to encore at the request of the audience; they also warmly greeted her solo and variations in the *pas de deux* of the 2nd act.[57]

On 30 April 1903, Russian ballerina Anna Pavlova made her debut as Giselle to great acclaim. Her performance of the first-act *Variation pour Mlle Cornalba* was encored. Pavlova was joined by Nikolai Legat as Albert and Julia Sedova as Myrtha, with Tamara Karsavina and Mikhail Fokine making their debuts in the Peasant *pas de deux*.[58]

The revival was prepared by assistant ballet master Alexander Shiryaev, who claimed in his memoirs, written in the early 1940s, to have staged the ballet solely from memory:

> Shortly before the end of [the 1902–1903] season I revived *Giselle* entirely from memory. The work on this ballet gave me a double pleasure. First of all, I loved *Giselle*

---

[53] Yury Burlaka has asserted that a different variation composed by Drigo was interpolated into *Giselle* for Cornalba in 1888. That variation subsequently became part of the Peasant *pas de deux* in Soviet-era productions of *Giselle*. See Yury Burlaka, ed., *Classical Repertoire for Ballet Competitions: Pas de Deux and Duets*, vol. 5 (St. Petersburg: Compozitor, 2017), 50–51. See also Rodney Edgecombe, "A Ragbag of Ballet Oddments," *Brolga* 23 (1 December 2005): 12–21, available online at https://ausdance.org/au/articles/details/a-ragbag-of-ballet-music-oddments.

[54] *Khronika III*, 360.

[55] Konaev, "Khronika osnovnykh postanovok," 93.

[56] About Preobrazhenskaya's debut, see *Khronika III*, 365–366. About Zambelli's debut, see Natalia Zozulina and V.M. Muronova, eds., *Peterburgskiy balet. Tri veka: khronika. Tom IV. 1901–1950* [The Petersburg ballet. Three centuries: A chronicle. Volume IV. 1901–1950] (St. Petersburg: Academy of Russian Ballet named after A.Y. Vaganova, 2015) [hereafter: *Khronika IV*], 25.

[57] Valerian Svetlov, *Terpsikhora: Stat'i ocherki i zametk* [Terpsichore: Articles, essays, and notes] (St. Petersburg: 1906), 246. Thanks to Sergey Belenky for providing this citation.

[58] *Khronika IV*, 47.

as a fine and unsurpassed example of Romantic Ballet. Everything was pleasant here: the poetic plot based on an old German legend about Wilis, the melodious music by Adolphe Adam, and the excellent dance compositions. But, above all, Anna Pavlova was to take the lead, and her great choreographic talent was still only beginning to unfold. *Giselle* was Pavlova's first major ballet, and subsequently it became the "star turn" of her repertoire. Anna Pavlova's leaps have stayed in my memory. The duration of her flights remains unsurpassed. The production was a huge success with the public. My production of *Giselle* has survived on the Leningrad ballet stage without any major changes until the present day.[59]

Though Shiryaev staged Petipa's production, Petipa was nonetheless involved: Pavlova sought out the master's tuition. In his diary, Petipa first notes rehearsing Pavlova at the Theater School on 29 March, a month before her debut. On 15 April, he wrote, "I showed the first act of *Giselle* to Mlle Pavlova II," and on 28 April, "Mlle Pavlova came to ask me to go tomorrow to see her rehearse *Giselle*." He attended her debut the following day.[60] As she did with other ballets in our study, Pavlova gave *Giselle* a new lease on life through her acclaimed performances.[61] Critics wrote of "frail, exquisite Pavlova, who brought back the almost forgotten fragrance of *Giselle*."[62]

With Pavlova's acquisition of the title role, we reach the period when *Giselle* was documented by Nikolai Sergeyev using the Stepanov notation system. Whether or not it was intended to do so, this project served to codify the ballet in the form in which it would be transmitted back to the West: the notation was used by Sergeyev to stage *Giselle* in France and England on no fewer than five separate occasions through the 1940s.

Sources

We turn now to a discussion of the sources that enable us to describe the St. Petersburg production of *Giselle* in the form it had taken by the turn of the twentieth century.

Libretto. The 1889 *Giselle* libretto (Appendix C [ii]) is a reprint of the 1842 libretto despite the various changes made in the intervening years to characters' names on posters and in programs and the eventual omission of the peasants' second-act encounter with the Wilis and the fugue.[63]

Mariinsky Theater production documents. Two sources preserved in Russia lend rich detail to our knowledge of the Petersburg *Giselle*. Four pages documenting the stage settings and listing props and other elements of the Mariinsky Theater production of *Giselle* are part of a larger bound manuscript, dated 1893–1905 and held by the St. Petersburg State Museum of Theatre and Music.[64] This volume contains similar information for many of the ballets in the St. Petersburg Imperial Ballet repertory. Notes regarding

[59] Beumers et al., *Alexander Shiryaev*, 116. Shiryaev's memoirs are included in this publication in an English translation by Birgit Beumers, 81–128.

[60] Lynn Garafola, ed. and trans., *The Diaries of Marius Petipa*, Studies in Dance History, vol. 3, no. 1 (Spring 1992), 12, 14–15.

[61] About Pavlova's performance in *Giselle*, see John and Roberta Lazzarini, *Pavlova: Repertoire of a Legend* (Schirmer Books: New York, 1980), 62.

[62] Qtd. in Andrew Foster, *Tamara Karsavina: Diaghilev's Ballerina* (London: Andrew Foster, 2010), 93.

[63] Yury Burlaka and Anna Grutsynova, eds., *Libretto baletov Mariusa Petipa* [Librettos of ballets by Marius Petipa] (St. Petersburg: Compozitor, 2018), 5.

[64] St. Petersburg State Museum of Theatre and Music (GMTMI), GIK 16917.

properties, costumes, and the like were made initially in black ink and, by virtue of many annotations and strikethroughs in various inks and pencil, appear to have been revised a number of times over a period of years. Some of the annotations are dated with the year they were made—a number of them post-date the compilation period of the manuscript. The pages dedicated to *Giselle* were likely first recorded circa 1889—the cast list includes Gorshenkova as Giselle and Stanislav Gillert as Albert.[65] Gillert made his debut in the role, partnering Gorshenkova, on 22 October 1889.[66]

Drawings by Pavel Gerdt. The other source preserved in Russia is a set of drawings by Pavel Gerdt, preserved in the Gerdt archive at the A. A. Bakhrushin State Central Theatre Museum in Moscow, which documents *pas de deux* choreography for several ballets, including *Giselle*—two pages include excerpts from the Act Two *pas de deux*.[67]

Materials from the Sergeyev Collection. For additional contemporaneous production details, we turn to American shores. The variety of *Giselle* sources held in Harvard Library's Sergeyev Collection includes a heavily annotated printed piano reduction with manuscript interpolations, *répétiteurs* of interpolated numbers, a manuscript orchestra score and parts with musical annotations, a choreographic notation made in the Stepanov method, a manuscript mime script of Act One, and a printed program of a Mariinsky Theater performance on 15 October 1903.[68]

Annotated printed piano reduction. The printed piano reduction shows decades of use and includes many penciled annotations in English that likely date from Sergeyev's years staging the ballet in England (see below).[69] Musical numbers have been inserted, and the reduction has otherwise been altered to bring the score into agreement with the notated version of the ballet. *Répétiteurs* of the Peasant *pas de deux* and Cornalba variation are filed as separate items.[70]

Manuscript orchestra score. The undated and unsigned manuscript orchestra score appears to have been created in Riga in the 1920s during Sergeyev's years at the Latvian National Ballet.[71] The instrumentation is neither Adam's original nor is it likely the

---

[65] Ibid., fols. 75v–77r.

[66] *Khronika III*, 282–283.

[67] Pavel Andreevich Gerdt, Drawings: the dance schemes for A. Adam's ballet "Giselle" [1894], A.A. Bakhrushin State Central Theatre Museum (GTsTM), KP 168405 | *fond* 336. The top and bottom halves of the first page of sketches are taped together; close inspection reveals the drawings found on the second page are a continuation of the material on the top half of the first page. The bottom half of the first page follows the material on the second page. The first page is reproduced in the Bolshoi Theater *Giselle* program book (2019), 141.

[68] The printed program is housed as part of item MS Thr 245 (247), Harvard Theatre Collection, Houghton Library, Harvard University.

[69] The printed piano score, MS Thr 245 (5), is the Cornette reduction. The score shows heavy use over time, with many pages torn and frayed; it is heavily annotated in pencil in English and also heavily marked in red and blue pencil in the same hand as the orchestra score (see later in this chapter). An interpolated manuscript page including a piano reduction of part of the Act One waltz follows page 18 and is numbered in pencil as page 19, with the verso side numbered page 20; a manuscript piano reduction page of the shortened *louré pas de deux* follows, marked with red dynamics; the verso side is blank; an interpolated manuscript *répétiteur* of the same *pas de deux* is cut off at the bottom of the page; the verso side has page 20 of the printed piano reduction pasted to it and is renumbered page 24 in pencil; a manuscript piano reduction of the Cornalba variation is interpolated after page 34 and bears the same red and blue markings. This is followed by a manuscript piano reduction of the Peasant *pas de deux*, with similar markings; a manuscript *répétiteur* of the Grantzow variation is interpolated after page 98; the verso side of the third page is blank.

[70] The manuscript *répétiteurs* include MS Thr 245 (7), the Cornalba variation and Peasant *pas de deux*, comprising five folios bound together, and MS Thr 245 (8), another manuscript *répétiteur* of the Cornalba variation, in a different hand and titled *Musette*, comprising three folios that are stitch-bound and taped at center.

[71] The manuscript orchestra score, MS Thr 245 (6), is in two bound volumes, 304 pages, with a Russian-language stamp in the first volume on the second inside page, lower right corner of the recto side; the score is written in black ink with red and blue ink annotations and dynamic markings, and pencil annotations, some in English; orchestra parts are preserved as MS Thr 245 (9), with the Peasant *pas de deux* parts held as MS Thr

instrumentation used in St. Petersburg. But it corresponds closely with the choreographic notation created in Petersburg, and therefore may be considered a crucial document for understanding the Petersburg production.[72] It also offers a stark view of how much the score had been cut in St. Petersburg during the years between *Giselle*'s 1842 premiere and the early twentieth century: the Riga score omits 461 of the roughly 2,307 bars that appear to have comprised the Paris first act and 218 bars of the second act's 1,637 bars. Taking interpolations into account, total cuts in the Riga score amount to approximately 17 percent of the Paris score.

In the first act, we find cuts and alterations in just over half of the numbers. With the exception of its final eight bars, the music for Hilarion's first entrance is omitted, thereby significantly reducing the gamekeeper's function as narrator. Eliminating his scene-setting opening monologue requires an audience to deduce the nature of Giselle and Albert's relationship based on their initial encounter. The reprise of the main theme and the coda of the march (which precedes the Cornalba variation) are omitted. Giselle and Loys's Act One *pas de deux* is also omitted except for the shortened *louré*, which is placed immediately following the waltz. Thus Act One lacks a formal multimovement *pas de deux* for the lovers. Both of the man's variations in the Peasant *pas de deux* have bars omitted from their final sections.

In Act Two, six of nine numbers have cuts or revisions. In the scene of the peasants and Wilis, all but the first fourteen bars are omitted; the last four of these are revised to facilitate a transition directly to the following number, Albert's entrance. In the bacchanale, two ten-bar passages are omitted, as is the fugue at the end of the number; the bars just prior to the fugue are revised to facilitate a transition to the subsequent *pas de deux*. The Grantzow variation is interpolated after Albert's variation, providing Giselle with a solo immediately preceding the coda.

Choreographic notation. The centerpiece of the Sergeyev Collection's *Giselle* materials is the 110-page choreographic notation (CN) in Nikolai Sergeyev's hand.[73] Like most extant examples of Stepanov notation, this document is made in pencil on oblong-format paper and is not a complete, finished record of the ballet in the way the Justamant manuals are. Rather, it is a rather spare account of both acts with the level of detail varying throughout. (The manuscript mime script of Act One, which also appears to be in Sergeyev's hand and is housed as a separate item in the collection, is a compilation of the action and mime annotations found in the CN, though we do not rule out the possibility that the mime script was created before the CN.[74] We surmise that Sergeyev may have created this mime script for use in rehearsals.)

The CN provides a description of physical movement—steps, actions, entrances, and exits. Dance movements for legs and feet are either notated or described in prose

245 (10). Wiley has identified the score thus: "The score of *Giselle*, which bears neither date nor place, seems also, on the basis of format and hand, to be part of this series [of scores copied in Riga]." See Wiley, "Dances from Russia," 99n15; see also 100 and 109–110.

[72] The Riga *Giselle* orchestra score from the 1920s employs its own numbering system, but this does not prevent it from lining up well with the choreographic notation made by Sergeyev in St. Petersburg.

[73] Choreographic notations of *Giselle* comprise three items in the collection: MS Thr 245 (2), the complete ballet, with the exception of the Peasant *pas de deux*, 110 pages plus interpolated sheets; MS Thr 245 (4), the Peasant *pas de deux*, fourteen pages plus a manuscript piano reduction; and MS Thr 245 (227), a second notation of the Peasant *pas de deux* woman's variation.

[74] MS Thr 245 (3). We note that the scribal hand (Sergeyev's) is the same as that for extant mime scripts for *Paquita*, MS Thr 245 (29), see Chapter 5; *Le Corsaire*, MS Thr 245 (1), see Chapter 7; and *La Bayadère*, Museum of the State Academic Bolshoi Theatre (GABT), KP 3949 | *fond* 1, *op.* 1, item 78, see Chapter 9.

(movements for head and upper body are rarely recorded). An outline of the action is provided by ground plans that show the path of the artists on stage and annotations containing key statements of mime conversations. These are recorded in terse prose and often in the order gestures would have been made by the performers—for example, Berthe's blunt declaration to Giselle, "If you dance, you will die." (We will find greater choreographic detail in the notations of *La Bayadère* and parts of *Le Corsaire*—specifically, *Le jardin animé*—and far more mime and action recorded for much of *Paquita*.)

Performers listed in Act One of the CN include Anna Pavlova (Giselle), Nikolai Legat (Albert), Pavel Gerdt (Hans, called "Forester"), Ivan Kusov (Squire), Giuseppina Cecchetti (Berthe, called "Mother"), and Stanislav Gillert ("Herzog," though more often called "Duke"). Matilda is referred to as "Duchess."

With a single exception, the record of Act One represents the cast that performed at the Mariinsky Theater on 30 April 1903, Pavlova's debut. Antonina Yakovleva took over the role of Berthe from Giuseppina Cecchetti at this performance. The appearance of Cecchetti's name in the notation therefore suggests that the process of notating Act One began prior to this date—Cecchetti performed the role of Berthe in all eight performances given between 1899 and 1901. Just as Cecchetti and Pavlova seem not to have performed the roles of Berthe and Giselle in the same performance, neither do their names appear together in the CN. Rather, "Giselle" is the identifier used in the CN for the titular role in scenes that mention Cecchetti, and "Mother" refers to Berthe in scenes that mention Pavlova.

The notation of Act Two presents greater challenges for dating the manuscript. The earliest date of notation is likely 1899; Pavlova is listed throughout the act as Zulmé, a role she first danced on 26 September 1899, replacing Lubov Petipa, who took over the role of Myrtha from Olga Preobrazhenskaya. Two different dancers, however, are listed in the role of Myrtha, and in at least one instance both are listed on the same page. The first and most frequent is Varvara Rykhlyakova, who danced the role only twice—on 6 October 1904 and 15 March 1907—both performances post-dating Pavlova's acquisition of the title role.[75] The second is Julia Sedova, who first performed the role of Myrtha on 28 October 1901. Thus the process of notating Act Two may have begun as early as 1899 and continued as late as 1907, though 1904 seems more likely as it is closer in time to the period during which the rest of the CN was made. Annotations appear to have been added to the CN over a period of time.

Other artists' names in the second act include Nikolai Legat as Albert (also referred to as "Prince" in this act) and Gerdt as Hans (again also listed as "Forester"). No artist's name is given for the role of Giselle in this act. Incidentally, the name "Myrtha" is never used in the CN. She is sometimes called "Vilis" or "Lady of the Wilis"; otherwise, a performer's name is given.

Scene-by-scene description of the St. Petersburg *Giselle* at the turn of the twentieth century

Our description of the St. Petersburg *Giselle* will be based on the CN with occasional detours to the Justamant staging manual for comparison of choreography and other

---

[75] Lydia Kyaksht replaced Pavlova in the role of Zulmé on 30 April 1903.

elements in order to reveal similarities that connect the two accounts as well as their differences. To help the reader keep track of the music that accompanies the action and dance, we will not only provide musical examples in our description below but will also reference musical examples already provided in this chapter as well as in Chapter 2.

The CN is in many ways similar in content to the more thorough and detailed Justamant staging manual even though its prose is often terse. (In this regard, as mentioned earlier, readers will notice that word order in the CN's mime phrases often represents the order in which gestures were performed by the artists instead of reflecting speech syntax.) We find strong similarities in many (though not all) details of the action. The placement of dances is also mostly consistent between the two accounts, though with some notable differences, the most obvious of which are the two now-canonical interpolated variations for Giselle in the CN. The forty-plus years that separate the two records are also represented by their difference in step vocabulary—for instance, the Cornalba variation, as danced by Pavlova, features sustained *pointe* work of a kind not found in Justamant. Nevertheless, the general structure of dances, particularly solos—with their diagonal orientation and repeated enchaînements—remains.

The scene numbering in the first act of the CN corresponds to both Adam's autograph and the Titus *répétiteur*.[76] While the autograph omits numbering in Act Two, the Titus *répétiteur* and CN divide their scenes and dances into fifteen numbers, although Nos. 1 and 3 are not noted in the CN. The two sources otherwise match in their assignment of numbers through No. 10 then diverge until the finale, which is No. 15 in both sources. We include the numbering given in the CN.

Although his alias is not used in the CN, we will refer to Loys, rather than Albert, until the point at which his duplicity is exposed.

Act One

The stage setting for Act One preserved in the Mariinsky Theater production book features two rather ornate buildings at each side of the stage: a double-story house at stage right belongs to Berthe, Giselle's mother, and a single-story dwelling at stage left is the home of Loys. Two benches are positioned on stage left, and a table and two chairs are placed at either side. A rough sketch of hills can be seen in the distance, and the whole of the scene is framed from above with leafy branches.

No. 1. Following the Introduction (Exx. 2.23a and 2.23b), peasant men and women walk to work in groups, crossing upstage from left to right (Ex. 2.1a).

No. 2. Loys comes out of his house and "looks tenderly" toward Giselle's home at stage right. He walks to center, circles upstage, then continues toward the door. His squire enters, presumably also from Loys's abode, and walks toward his master.

Squire: "You, from there leave, before your fiancée sees you in such dress."

Loys: "I love this peasant girl so, and will not leave this place."

The squire implores Loys to listen to him, but Loys refuses and commands the squire to leave. He exits upstage left. Loys follows behind to ensure his departure.

---

[76] The printed piano reduction, like the Riga score, employs a different numbering system.

No. 3. When he is certain he is alone, Loys approaches Giselle's door and knocks. The door opens and Giselle enters. Loys first hides behind the door, which remains open, then runs behind a tree upstage right. Giselle traces the familiar counterclockwise circle around the stage, performing *tombé, glissade, ballonné* seven times; the working leg in the *ballonné* makes a *rond de jambe* through *à la seconde* to *cou-de-pied devant* (Ex. 2.24). (Justamant offers something simpler and arguably more carefree: "[Giselle] *sautant naturellement* with grace and letting go a little [with abandon].") Reaching center, Giselle runs in one direction and then the other.

Giselle: "Nobody is here." Dancing again, she performs two *ballottés, ballonné, grand jeté en avant* twice. "To me, there, somebody knocked."

Loys sends audible air kisses to Giselle from his hiding place behind the tree. Giselle listens and wonders who could be sending her kisses. Loys sneaks up on her. Stepping backward, Giselle bumps into him at center stage. She is disconcerted (Ex. 2.7a). Loys flirtatiously touches her hand.

Giselle runs away toward her house. Loys follows, takes her hand, and stops her. The couple takes "2 steps in place (step forward and step back)." Linking arms, they return to center.

Loys: "I beg you, do not go."

Giselle: "No." She ducks under Loys's arm, playfully does three *demi-emboîtés derrière* as she dodges him and runs away to the house. Loys follows. Arriving ahead of Giselle, he stands on the doorstep and blocks her entrance.

Loys takes her by the waist. She places her left hand on his shoulder, and he leads her in a series of *glissades changée* as they travel to the bench at stage left. Giselle sits down.

Loys sits next to her and attempts to move closer. Giselle gets up suddenly and runs again toward her house with Loys in pursuit.

Again he takes her hand. In a near repeat of their previous movements, they take steps forward and back before Loys turns Giselle around, takes her by the arm, and leads her to center where he confesses his ardor.

Loys: "I love you, I swear."

Giselle: "Wait! Come here." She walks stage right and picks a few white daisies.

They return to the bench, again performing *glissades* across the stage. This time Giselle leads Loys; an annotation notes that she "lures him."

Giselle sits as Loys stands beside her, watching, his left foot on the edge of the bench. She begins to "divine": "Loves me, loves me not, loves me . . ." The last petal is "loves me not." Giselle drops the flower and cries. Loys consoles her and says, "Look," taking another flower and performing the "divination" until the last petal is "loves me." Giselle is delighted. She runs away upstage center.

The couple dances together, repeating Giselle's earlier steps: two *ballottés, ballonné, grand jeté en avant*.

Loys: "I beg for one kiss."

Giselle: "I will not kiss you."

Loys tries to catch Giselle, but she escapes under his arm, running left as he goes right. They meet at center and continue dancing: *glissade, grand jeté en avant* six times as they travel around the stage in a counterclockwise *manège*.

Dropping to his knee, Loys again entreats Giselle: "I beg you, just one kiss." She runs up to him, kisses her finger, and puts it to Loys's forehead. She turns to run inside but instead collides with Hans, who has entered upstage right. Giselle blushes. Hans moves to stand between Giselle and Loys. He confronts Giselle.

Hans: "Well, you are kissing him, and he kisses your hands."

In a "jealous rage," he attacks Giselle "with his fists. She is scared but gets up immediately, folds her arms, and attacks him in return." Hans steps back.

Hans: "Listen. I love you."

Giselle: "You disgust me. I despise you."

Loys grabs Hans by the shoulder, turns him away from Giselle, and orders him to leave (Ex. 2.25). Hans moves around Loys to get back to Giselle and begs her to listen to him. Loys turns him again and sends him away. Hans exits angrily upstage left, "sending threats."

We pause here to mention two sheets of plain, unlined paper inserted into the CN in the middle of the previous scene. The pages are divided, grid-like, into numerous small boxes. These contain, in Sergeyev's hand, the ground plans and prose descriptions of the action of the so-called *scene d'amour*, the confrontation with Hilarion, and the subsequent entrance of Berthe, omitting the intervening waltz. The ground plans are drawn from the stage perspective, different from the main CN, wherein ground plans are usually drawn from the audience perspective. In effect, the two pages constitute a composite version of these portions of the CN. Perhaps they were used in rehearsal, where having fewer and smaller sheets of paper to hold would be a convenience for Sergeyev.

No. 4. The female corps de ballet enters with baskets upstage right. Giselle and Loys "greet the girlfriends." The women form a semicircle around Giselle as Loys runs downstage left.

Giselle: "You and you, what are you doing?"

Girlfriends: "We gathered grapes there."

Giselle: "Take your baskets off [your arms] and we will dance here."

Girlfriends: "All right."

The women set down their baskets and the waltz begins.

Waltz. The corps de ballet choreography for the waltz and subsequent *louré pas de deux* is notated separately from that for Giselle and Loys. (The structure of the waltz and much of its ground plan are substantially similar to that recorded by Justamant, but the steps for the most part are different.)

Giselle begins upstage center, performing three *précipités* and *pas de basque* on the diagonal (Ex. 2.6a). She repeats the same to the other side, followed by *balancés en face* as she returns upstage. The corps performs *balancés* and *soutenu*. These opening enchaînements are repeated. Giselle travels downstage a third time with *piqué grand rond de jambe en l'air* on alternating legs followed by four *piqués ronds de jambe en l'air* as she turns in place to the left. The *grands ronds de jambe* are repeated. The corps, meanwhile, performs a series of *temps levés, balancés, piqués degagés*. Giselle runs to Loys.

Giselle: "You with me, dance."

Loys: "All right."

She takes Loys by the hand and together they make a clockwise circle around the stage, Giselle performing three *ballonnés derrière* and *pas de basque en arrière* as she travels backward and Loys performing the same steps in the reverse as he moves forward. The corps, having come together in groups of four to form small semicircles on either side of the stage, performs *pas de basque* as the women turn in place, followed by *balancés*.

Arm in arm, from upstage center, Giselle and Loys travel downstage in a zigzag pattern performing *ballonnés* and *pas de basque*. The corps repeats its *pas de basque* circles, then moves downstage with more *pas de basque* to form two rows behind Giselle and Loys. Loys lifts Giselle by the waist. After he lowers her, she rises with *sous-sus* and leans her body to the left into Loys's arm. They move away from each other with *ballonnés*—the corps, still in groups of four, also moves apart, performing multiple *glissades* that end in a step to *tendu croisé devant fondu*—then run back to center and repeat the lift to the other side. They move apart again and join the corps, who "turn in pairs and hold hands" as they perform *balancés*. Giselle and Loys each join four different pairs as they turn a circle, the direction of the turn changing with each repetition.

The women move to form a diagonal line upstage right, performing *pas de basque*. Giselle, now downstage right, says, "I will dance here." Traveling upstage along the diagonal, she performs a *piqué tour en dedans* with *double rond de jambe en l'air* to the left eight times. She meets Loys upstage and together they return, arm in arm, performing the *ballonné, pas de basque* enchaînement four times. The corps performs *balancés* and *soutenu* twice before moving into two parallel lines on the same diagonal.

After an enchaînement of *temps levé en développé devant, balancé, assemblé en tournant*, and a spring to fifth position on *pointe* three times, the corps forms pairs (made up of a dancer from each line) that join right hands, switch places, and return as the dancers perform *balancés*. Giselle and Loys, standing together downstage right, "admire the dances" and "watch the dancing pleasantly." (This is the moment in many modern productions when Giselle appears to experience heart palpitations.)

The corps comes forward with *pas de basque* and forms a single row across the stage, those on the right facing upstage and those on the left facing downstage. Giselle and Loys join at either end as the line rotates in a clockwise direction, its axis remaining at center, like the spokes of a wheel. The dancers perform *pas de basque* as they travel, the line making a quarter turn with each set of three *pas de basque* and *assemblé devant*.

Continuing with *pas de basque*, the corps splits at center, travels downstage in two lines (likely flanking Giselle and Loys at center), circles back upstage, comes down again, and finally returns to its initial semicircular formation.

Giselle performs *chaînés* on *demi-pointe*, traveling in front of Loys. He lifts her as the corps resumes its *temps levés en développé devant*. All of this is repeated and leads to the conclusion of the waltz. No final pose is given for Giselle, Loys, or the corps de ballet.

A more spectacular final sequence for Giselle and Loys is recorded by Justamant: traveling on the diagonal from upstage left, Loys supports Giselle in four overhead lifts as she performs *grands jetés ordinaire*.

Louré. The shortened *louré* movement from Giselle and Loys's original Act One *pas de deux* (discussed above; see Ex. 2.8a) is labeled "Dance | Legat together with Giselle."

Traveling away from Giselle on a diagonal toward upstage left, Loys performs *petit sissonne, tombé en arrière, tendu effacé devant fondu* three times before returning to Giselle.

Taking her by the hand, he leads her in *temps levés en arabesque* traveling backward on the diagonal. They change direction and repeat the phrase.

Arm in arm, the lovers trace a zigzag pattern as they travel downstage, performing *ballonné, jeté en avant* four times. Separating, each makes a spiral pattern as they move upstage with *glissade, piqué en demi-arabesque* eight times on alternating legs, making a full turn with each pair of steps.

Reuniting upstage right, they travel down the diagonal, flirtatiously reaching out a hand to each other in alternation. Loys travels backward and performs the same *glissade, piqué en arabesque* as Giselle performs *piqué en arabesque* followed by two *demi-emboîtés devant*.

Arriving downstage right, Giselle begins a series of *piqué tours en dedans* that will take her upstage left as Loys "walks over to the other side," upstage of Giselle. Giselle switches to *chaînés* on *demi-pointe* that bring her downstage right, opposite Loys at center.

As the corps begins to dance in place, Giselle and Loys perform *entrechat cinq, pas de bourrée en tournant*, exchanging places, and *piqué en demi-arabesque* four times. They travel downstage to finish the dance—Giselle *bourrées*, Loys walks. He lifts Giselle by the waist, kneels, and places her on his knee.

This choreography for the shortened adaptation of the *louré* incorporates elements found in the longer version recorded by Justamant (which we will describe later in this chapter).

Berthe enters from the house (Ex. 2.3a). Encountering the girlfriends first, she greets them and asks, "Where is my daughter?" They point out Giselle. Berthe kisses her and wipes her face with a handkerchief.

Berthe: "Tell me, what were you doing here?"

Giselle: "I am dancing here with my fiancé" (Ex. 2.6b).

Berthe: "If you dance, you will die."

The "Mother's storytelling" begins as Berthe says to the girlfriends, "Listen to what I have to say. When the sun goes down and night comes, one who is beautiful and who is in love will die. She will rise from her grave and when one visits [the grave], he will be captured and tortured until he dies" (Ex. 2.9). The girlfriends laugh and call Berthe's tale nonsense. She replies, "It is true. Take your baskets and leave."

No. 5. The girlfriends depart. Berthe takes Giselle's hand and leads her into the house. Loys runs off, exiting upstage left (Ex. 2.4).

Hans enters the empty stage from upstage left and moves downstage center to deliver his monologue.

Hans: "Some power takes me here. I love her. She refuses to talk to me. She loves another, abandoned me, but I will try to talk with her, and I will beg her for love."

He goes to Giselle's door but hears the sound of a "trumpet." Running up the *montagne*, he observes the Duke's hunting party. He runs to Loys's house, opens the window, and climbs in.

The squire appears upstage right and invites all who are behind him to enter. The Duke and Matilda, walking arm in arm, are preceded by twelve men who form a diagonal line at stage left and four men and four women who congregate at stage right, the men behind the women (Ex. 2.21). (These are surely the court ladies, gentlemen, and pages who are mentioned in the various printed cast lists without further detail.)

Duke: "It is lovely here. I am tired." He calls for the squire to knock on the door of Berthe's house and ask for food.

Squire: "All right." He goes to the house and knocks three times.

Berthe emerges, bows, and asks, "What do you need?" (Ex. 2.10b). A servant (the squire?) asks Berthe to prepare a table for supper. She agrees and returns to the house, calling for Giselle. She returns with her daughter, bringing Giselle out "against her will," and tells her to greet their guests, something Giselle does not want to do. She balks, but her mother holds her and commands, "You greet them." Giselle addresses the servants rather than the nobles, whom Berthe then points out. Giselle welcomes the Duke and Matilda and invites them to the table. They thank her.

Giselle is astonished by the luxury of Matilda's clothing. She runs to her mother, points to Matilda, then "quietly tiptoes" to Matilda's train and examines it.

Meanwhile, the Duke and Matilda have sat at the table. The squire pours wine.

Matilda: (to the Duke) "How beautiful Giselle is." She notices Giselle examining her dress and asks her if she likes it.

Giselle: "Very much."

Matilda affectionately takes Giselle by the waist and brings her downstage.

The following conversation, given in the CN, is a telescoped version of the more extended interactions documented in the Titus *répétiteur* and Justamant manual:

Matilda: "Tell me what your heart says."

Giselle: "I weave. I love one. And when evening comes, I dance."

Tracing a circular pattern, Giselle performs an enchaînement of two *précipités*, *pas de basque* four times to the strains of the earlier waltz (Ex. 2.6c).

Berthe: (interrupting) "If she dances, she could die."

Giselle: "He will marry me, will he not?"

Berthe: "Yes, he will."

Matilda: (turning to the Duke) "She is unaffected. I will give her a necklace."

Duke: "Wonderful."

Matilda calls Giselle, who comes to her. Matilda puts the chain on her neck.

Blushing, Giselle thanks Matilda and kisses her hand. She runs to show Berthe her gift.

Mother and daughter are in awe of the necklace. Berthe tells Giselle to thank Matilda (the CN is redundant here) and invite her, with the Duke, into the house.

The Duke accepts and crosses the stage.

Duke: (to the squire) "Take care of everyone's rest." The squire agrees. "I am going to rest. But in case something amiss happens, blow the horn three times. Farewell." He gives the horn to the squire, who hangs it on the fence.

The Duke escorts Matilda into the house. Everyone gradually leaves and the stage is once again empty.

No. 6. Hans appears holding a chain and sword in his hands.

Hans: "He is a count, and this is his sword and chain. He wants to deceive her." He laughs gloatingly. "He will abandon her and never marry her." Hans runs behind the house threateningly.

The CN's fairly brief description of the hunt scene can be augmented by a unique and valuable account penned half a century later by Tamara Karsavina as part of her "Lost Steps" series published in *The Dancing Times*.[77] Lamenting that in current productions of *Giselle* "some passages of outstanding merit are not there anymore," Karsavina describes several passages of the hunt scene that contribute to the illumination of Giselle's character. Her

[77] See note 120 in this chapter.

description of this scene is worth quoting in full and includes elements found in the CN and the Justamant accounts:

> The omitted passage is a scene which shows the charming rusticity of Giselle, her innocent gaiety of heart. When the hunt halts at the cottage, Giselle runs in, unaware of the noble visitors. On seeing them her first impulse is to run away, but prompted by her mother she conquers her shyness and, twisting her apron, adorably gawky, demurely drops a deep curtsey to a servant (and what a touching picture Pavlova made of this). One can feel a suppressed titter going among the court-trained servants. "There is the Princess," points out the huntsman. Giselle's sentence, "The one over there?" stands in amusing contrast to the polished manner of the servant. She questioningly pokes her finger at the majestic figure of Bathilde, ahead of her, to make quite sure this time. Then, visibly awed, she advances and respectfully begs the princess to partake of some refreshment. As Bathilde, with a gracious nod, passes in front, Giselle swiftly runs behind her to dust the chair with her apron. Deeply impressed by so much splendour and beauty, the naïve child makes so bold as to kneel by the chair and lean her cheek against the velvet of Bathilde's robe. Not enough is made today of this latter episode. In the original version Giselle shyly advanced and, on Bathilde's slightly turning her head, retreated. This manoeuvre repeated itself, leaving the spectator in no doubt that Giselle's heart beat fast.
>
> The following dialogue is designed to give a human touch to the otherwise purely functional part of Bathilde; the part that the French would call *utilité*. When, delighted by the charming peasant, Bathilde asks her whether she loves anyone, she does not do so as a princess, for the emphasis of this passage is in the sudden sympathy and understanding born between two girls, each one in love. This is how it was set; Bathilde put her arm round Giselle and led her apart, whispering in her ear, "Does your heart say anything?" In her confusion, her cheeks aflame (it can be conveyed) Giselle turns her head away. The princess gently turns Giselle's head towards her, looks into her eyes, and the barrier between their ranks is no more; in a sudden gush of happiness and pride, Giselle tells the princess that she is going to be married to her beloved. This interpretation was not only a very beautiful moment, but it also made the tragedy of Giselle's betrayal all the more poignant.[78]

Giselle's greeting of the nobility, as described by Karsavina, follows a similar narrative in Justamant; however, in that manuscript her behavior is characterized as "contrary" rather than shy:

> Berthe comes back, leading Giselle, who is acting contrary. She makes her [Giselle] pass in front of her.
>
> Then she pulls on her dress by the back and says, "Greet them."
>
> Giselle goes toward Wilfride and salutes him.
>
> Berthe pulls her by her dress, shakes her head "no" and shows her the prince.
>
> Wilfride laughs and shows her Mathilde.

---

[78] Tamara Karsavina, "Lost Steps (III): Giselle's Character," *Dancing Times* New Series, no. 519 (December 1953): 139. See also note 120 in this chapter.

Giselle says to her mother, "Oh, I did not know"; she goes toward Mathilde and greets her respectfully: "What would you like, madame?"

Mathilde: "I am tired, I would like some milk and then rest."

Giselle: (with verve) "I will first serve you here," and she goes back in the house with her mother.[79]

In discussing the personal interaction between Giselle and Bathilde/Matilda, Karsavina uses nearly the exact words that we find in the CN: "Does your heart say anything?" This brief dissolution of the class barrier between the young women is an important detail that Justamant initiates already when Mathilde gives her necklace to Giselle:

Mathilde: (to Giselle) "Why are you looking at my dress?"

Giselle: "Oh madame, it is so pretty, and it fits you so well."

Mathilde: "But you, too, look so charming in your dress."

Giselle: "Oh, it is not the same thing."

Mathilde takes off a gold necklace she is wearing and puts it on Giselle. "Here you are, like me. I am giving this to you."

Giselle looks at it with joy and astonishment. "Oh, you are so kind." (aside) "What happiness!"[80]

Finally, Karsavina includes a detail that is barely mentioned in the CN but presented thoroughly in the Justamant manual: Giselle, overcoming her reticence in response to Bathilde's gentleness and meeting the princess's gaze with her own, reveals she is engaged to be married. Justamant preserves this exchange with characteristic assiduousness:

Mathilde takes Giselle aside and says to her, "Tell me, and your heart," she puts her hand on Giselle's heart, "has it spoken?"

Giselle lowers her head and dares not respond.

Mathilde: "Let us go—let us talk about it."

Giselle leans toward Mathilde's ear and says with her head, "Well yes, yes." She goes upstage a bit and designates Loys's house. "Here is a handsome young man whom I love"—she comes downstage—"and who will marry me."

She comes downstage a little more than Mathilde to talk to her mother.

Berthe is following the scene without paying attention.

Giselle [to Berthe]: "Isn't it true that Loys and I will be married?"

---

[79] Justamant, *Giselle*, 50–51.
[80] Ibid., 53.

Mathilde: "My congratulations, Giselle, and me, too. I am going to be married to a great lord, but also a handsome young man." She goes upstage a little. "And in my palace you will come to my wedding." She comes downstage.

Giselle jumps for joy.[81]

No. 7: March. Returning to the CN, the "Dance of the Peasants" is described as a "grape harvest festival" (see Ex. 2.12a). The corps of "grape gatherers" enters upstage left in four rows of three male-female couples. The first row begins to dance. Traveling downstage, they perform *glissade, jeté* to *demi-attitude devant* four times on alternating legs followed by eight *temps levés en cou-de-pied* (essentially a skipping movement) during which the dancers join hands, form a circle, and make a single clockwise turn. The second row takes up the enchaînement in the same manner while the first group repeats it and travels across the downstage from left to right. The groups continue moving around the stage as the third row follows and, finally, the fourth. After the last turn has been completed, the ensemble forms four rows of six dancers.

Splitting at center, they travel toward the wings with three *jetés en avant* and a *jeté ordinaire* to change direction. They return to center in the same way. The first half of the enchaînement is repeated, after which all the dancers travel *en masse* upstage left with eight *jetés en avant*. Arriving, they assemble in two rows of men behind two rows of women.

As the trio section of the march begins, eight coryphées enter upstage right in a line, performing eight *temps levés en demi-arabesque* as they circle the stage in a clockwise *manège*. They assemble in a row downstage of the corps and dance in place, performing a step to *cou-de-pied devant* on the left leg followed by two *temps levés* on the left leg as the right leg is gradually raised in *attitude devant*. They continue with *glissade* and two *jetés*, making a turn to the left. This enchaînement is repeated followed by further *glissades, jetés*, and *demi-emboîtés derrière*.

The dancing pauses at the end of the trio. We note here the inclusion in Justamant of six coryphées—"jeunes filles coryphées," later referred to as "friends" (*les amies*). They arrive ahead of the revelers and enter Berthe's house to look for Giselle. They re-emerge with her, and four of the six dance the end of the march with the ensemble. The Justamant march is not part of the divertissement proper but instead functions as a sort of *pas d'action* as the trio begins:

Loys arrives followed by little Bacchus sitting on a small wine barrel, carried on a litter by four vinegatherers that is followed by peasants and children.

They come to place in the middle of the dance [having walked through a double column of vinegatherers that reassembles into two rows across the stage], facing Giselle's house, where they place the litter on the ground. Bacchus gets off and raises his wine barrel. . . .

Loys is called by Giselle at her door.

Giselle, having on her head a crown of vine branches, comes out of her house followed by her friends and her mother.

[81] Ibid., 55–56.

Loys takes her hand and leads her to the litter, which she gets on, taking the place of Bacchus.

The friends mingle in the following figure by putting themselves in the middle of the women.

Returning to the CN (wherein we note Loys is unaccounted for until the end of the galop), we find a streamlined account of the proceedings, with few details: The entire group approaches Berthe, who has emerged from the house.

Berthe: "What is it?"

Everyone: "We want to see Giselle."

Berthe goes to fetch her daughter and brings her outside. Everyone greets Giselle and asks her to dance.

Berthe: "Oh! She keeps dancing. How terrible. But all right, this is the last time."

Whether Giselle is crowned Queen of the Vintage is not mentioned in the CN. Two subsequent dances are listed at this point—"1) Variation Giselle" and "2) *Pas de deux*." However, the CN continues with two pages of ensemble choreography set to the final section of the march. These pages are struck through. As discussed above, the recapitulation and end of the march, listed as *Final* in printed programs, followed Giselle's solo.

Arrows in the ground plan direct "everyone" to form five rows across the stage "in three chords"—a reference to the three *pianissimo* chords signaling the return of the opening march theme. The coryphées likely form the first row, with the corps women comprising the second and fourth rows, and the men the third and fifth. All perform *piqué ballonné* on each foot, two *soubresauts*, *changement* twice. Moving downstage to the right then left, they continue with *jeté en avant*, *pas de bourrée en avant*, *glissade*, *jeté* to each side.

Arriving downstage, the group continues with combinations of *demi-emboîtés derrière*, *assemblés*, *changements*, *temps levés en demi-attitude derrière*, and *temps levés en cou-de-pied devant*. At one point, they alternate a pose in fifth position on *pointe* with a lunge position. Approaching the end of the march, step notation in the CN is mostly replaced by prose descriptions, including "*glissade jeté* all in a circle" traveling upstage, "*glissade jeté* 4 times" returning downstage, and a final "circle on *pointe* [here, the symbol indicating *pointe* is used] and on the knee."

The end of the march seems to have been expunged from the ballet by at least 26 September 1910, when Tamara Karsavina made her St. Petersburg debut as Giselle (having already danced the ballet abroad).[82] For this performance, the designation *Final*, previously used in printed programs to indicate the end of the march, now comes after *Pas de deux*, where it surely must refer to the galop at the end of the divertissement. The omission of the end of the march accounts for the strikethrough of its choreography in the CN.

Justamant also includes the end of the march. After the ensemble, assembled in a pinwheel formation, dances around Giselle, who is lifted high on the litter, the dancers assemble in pairs in a block formation with the four coryphées downstage of the main group. They split at center and travel to the wings and back, then move upstage and down, their steps including *glissades*, *jetés*, and *pas de basque*. At the end, the women run

---

[82] See *Khronika IV*, 134–135, and Foster, *Karsavina*, 99.

a circle around their partners as the men strike the tambourines they have carried since the beginning of the dance.

Giselle's variation. The following variation, which bears Pavlova's name in the CN, closely resembles the version danced today that is set to the music titled *Variation pour Mlle Cornalba*, discussed above (Ex. 3.4). Only movements for feet and legs are recorded.

Beginning presumably at center, Giselle poses in *tendu effacé devant*. After *tombé, glissade*, she performs *piqué en arabesque, fondu, coupé dessous, jeté* to *tendu effacé devant fondu, relevé double rond de jambe en l'air*. She walks forward with *piqués petits battements* then performs *relevé renversé, pas de bourrée en tournant* on *pointe*. The annotation "1½ times" suggests that she repeats the opening *piqué en arabesque* and *relevé rond de jambe*, and then she *bourrées* downstage left. Giselle continues with *piqué en arabesque en tournant, relevé battement devant, passé développé* to *arabesque* three times (although we note that the music appears to allow for only two iterations), traveling upstage on the diagonal. The opening section concludes with *glissade, piqué double pirouette* to fifth position to each side and a run upstage left.

The second part of the variation comprises thirty *temps levés sur la pointe* on the left foot, traveling on the diagonal, the working right leg making a single *rond de jambe en l'air* with each *temps levé*. Reaching downstage right, Giselle runs upstage left for a final diagonal enchaînement set to the third section, marked *allegro vivo: relevé petit passé* on each leg—making a half turn with each *relevé*—single *pirouette* from fifth position, *double pirouette* from fifth position three times. She concludes with four *chaînés* on *demi-pointe* to finish *en face* in *attitude à terre*.

A "variant" final enchaînement is also provided: *piqué double pirouette* on the right foot to *piqué* single *pirouette* on the left foot, six *piqué tours en dehors, piqué double pirouette* to *piqué* single *pirouette*, and *chaînés* on *pointe* to finish. No final pose is given.

With this variation, created for Elena Cornalba (we will assume for purposes of our discussion that the CN represents a version at least similar to the one she danced), we encounter for the first time in our study the pervasive *pointe* work associated with the technique of the Italian school.[83] In particular, the thirty consecutive *temps levés sur la pointe* represent a choreographic feature found neither in Justamant nor in most other dances we will examine in the CN. A similar passage can be found in the first-act variation for Aurora in *Sleeping Beauty*, created by Petipa for Carlotta Brianza in 1890.[84] And we will encounter this sort of step repetition again in *Raymonda* (see Chapter 10), which was originally choreographed by Petipa for Pierina Legnani in 1898.

As discussed, the addition of Giselle's variation and inclusion of the redacted *louré* movement appear to have been precipitated by the removal of the original *pas de deux* for Giselle and Loys that came at this point in the first act. This *pas*, comprised of four discrete movements, and the subsequent galop made up the five original numbers of the Act One divertissement. The addition of the Burgmüller Peasant *pas de deux* significantly expanded the harvest festival.

---

[83] As discussed in Chapter 1, from the mid-1880s into the early years of the twentieth century, the St. Petersburg Imperial Ballet welcomed numerous Italian ballerinas as guest artists. Most of them possessed strong *pointe* technique and contributed significantly to the development of the same in the Russian school.

[84] See Gorsky, *Two Essays on Stepanov Dance Notation*, 65–68.

Let us depart briefly from our description of the St. Petersburg *Giselle* to consider the version of the "Pas de Deux, de Loys et Giselle" recorded by Justamant in order to gain a more complete picture of the once-substantial Act One divertissement.

Giselle and Loys's pas de deux as recorded by Justamant. During the four-bar introduction Loys asks Berthe if Giselle may have permission to dance with him. Berthe looks at her daughter and at Loys and replies, "If she would like to." Giselle responds, "Yes, with pleasure."

She gets up and dances to center as the slow, waltz-like entrée begins (Ex. 3.5a). As she concludes her phrase with a *pirouette*, Loys joins her. They dance in unison, their steps including *pas de bourrée*, a run forward, and *entrechat trois* to each side. After Giselle makes a series of *piqué tours en dehors*, each of which ends in a supported *arabesque*, she travels down the diagonal with *chassé contre chassé*, *assemblé*, *sous-sus*, and a pose in *plié*. Loys follows behind Giselle, performing the same steps and posing *en attitude*. They repeat the enchaînement then travel together across the stage with *glissades*, raising opposite arms with each repetition.

Next, traveling upstage, Giselle does *glissade failli*, *jeté*, and *relevé développé devant* as Loys, kneeling, supports her three times. Arm in arm, they return downstage with *pas de bourrée couru*, *entrechat trois* and repeat the enchaînement traveling upstage. Their final diagonal includes a series of *glissades* and poses *en arabesque* to alternate sides. Facing Loys and holding him around the neck with her right hand, Giselle makes a *relevé* on the right foot, extends her left leg forward, and leans back. Loys, holding Giselle by the waist with both hands, makes a *tour de promenade* to the left. For the final pose, Giselle holds both arms overhead.

The second number begins with an eight-bar solo for Giselle (Ex. 3.1e, above, but here in E-flat major). Tracing a zigzag downstage, she performs *entrechat trois*, *jeté*, *relevé développé devant*, *grand assemblé* three times followed by three turns, traveling downstage right. A blank page follows in the staging manual. Though no description or annotation is given, the remaining twenty-seven bars of the number may have been danced by Loys.

Giselle's variation, a florid flute solo, is labeled "that of Mlle Carlotta," a likely reference to Carlotta de Vecchi, for whom Justamant revived *Giselle* in Lyon in 1858 (Ex. 3.5b).[85] The choreography consists of a battery of small jumps—*rond de jambe sauté*, *jeté*, *brisé*, *assemblé*, *entrechat quatre*—as well as steps performed on *pointe* ("sur l'orteil"). A final diagonal begins with a series of *pas de bourrée en tournant*, *assemblé*, two *échappés* "sur les orteils," a turn on the left toe, *jeté* three times. Giselle finishes the variation with what are likely *chaînés*: "finir par des pas marcher en tournant, et terminer en position." The final pose is not described.

The substantial *louré* coda begins with a brief mimed exchange (Ex. 2.8a):

Loys: (to Berthe) "I beg you, please let Giselle dance with me."

Berthe: "No, no, she is too tired, and she is too hot."

Giselle begs her mother to let her join Loys.

To entice Giselle, Loys begins to dance. In much the same way as he begins the shortened version of the *louré* in modern productions, Loys travels backward across the stage, facing Giselle. His steps recorded by Justamant include *fouetté sauté*, *glissade*, *jeté* three times.

[85] See Konaev, "Khronika osnovnykh postanovok," 86.

His ploy achieves the desired effect: "Giselle, who cannot contain herself while Loys dances, is held back by her mother, and while begging her mother, passes to the other side and runs to the middle. Loys, seeing her, comes running toward her."

Giselle and Loys move away from and toward each other with a series of *temps levés en arabesque*, Shortly after, they perform the well-known zigzag downstage, arm in arm. Their enchaînement includes *ballonné, brisé*, and *jeté en avant*. Their dance continues with more unison choreography and eventually some lifts: at one point the couple performs "trois temps sauté naturellement," after which Giselle does a *"grand jeté en avant* on the right foot" as Loys "lifts her, holding her by the waist." This enchaînement is performed four times to alternate sides.

Near the end of the coda, Giselle and Loys cross paths twice at downstage center, performing four *jetés en tournant* each time. After a unison single *pirouette*, Giselle goes toward Loys. Putting her arms around his neck, she steps "sur les orteils en 5me" for their final pose.

The mimed conversations that introduce the entrée and coda link the action with the dance by reinforcing Giselle's love of dance and of Loys, Berthe's concern that

Ex. 3.5a Act One, *Pas de deux*, bars 5–10

Ex. 3.5b Act One, *Pas de deux*, bars 84–87

Ex. 3.6a Peasant *pas de deux* (Burgmüller), bars 1–4

Giselle will overexert herself, and Loys's ardent love for Giselle as well as his deference for Berthe.

Peasant pas de deux. Returning to the Harvard materials, we find that the Peasant *pas de deux* that follows Giselle's interpolated variation is preserved separately from the main CN. Twelve pages of choreographic notation document the performance of Agrippina Vaganova and Mikhail Obukhov, who performed the *pas* together on 9 November 1905 and possibly during the previous season.[86]

The six-movement *pas* by Friedrich Burgmüller opens with a brief 26-bar *polacca* (Ex. 3.6a). The couple begins their entrée upstage left. The "cavalier holds the lady by the arm" as they perform *temp levé en demi-arabesque, demi-emboîté derrière* three times followed by *demi-emboîtés devant* and *grand jeté en avant.* This enchaînement is repeated, then the couple travels back up the diagonal with *glissade, relevé développé devant, tombé, chassé en tournant, cabriole derrière, demi-emboîté derrière* three times. They continue, traveling across the stage arm in arm, with a run on *demi-pointe* and *pas de basque* twice, after which the man lifts the woman in a *tour jeté.* After repeating the same to the other side, the woman travels toward center with four turns on either *pointe* or *demi-pointe* (both symbols are drawn on the ground plan). The man walks beside her. Reaching center, they begin the adagio.

As short as the *polacca*, the twenty-bar *andante* is choreographed as a series of partnered movements for the ballerina (Ex. 3.6b). She begins with a supported *double pirouette développé devant, grand rond de jambe en l'air* with a *tour de promenade, fondu, passé, piqué en arabesque* into another *tour de promenade.* After this is repeated, the couple separates and walks upstage left. Traveling on the diagonal, the woman *bourrées* downstage then performs a *piqué tour en demi-attitude devant* to *demi-arabesque* as the cavalier "turns her around and [while she holds the *arabesque*] himself turns in place." More supported turns follow, and the entire enchaînement is repeated. Facing the man, the woman performs *piqué en arabesque.* Holding both hands, they make a *tour de promenade* to the right, and she finishes with a single *pirouette.* A final diagonal features *bourrées* punctuated by *double pirouettes.* The couple separates, turning away from each other, and reunites for a final supported *double pirouette.*

Solo variations follow, and here we encounter two of the Sergeyev Collection's handful of notated male solos. The first is in $\frac{2}{4}$ meter with a dotted-rhythm melody (Ex. 3.6c).

---

[86] Thanks to Andrew Foster for providing this casting information.

Ex. 3.6b Peasant *pas de deux* (Burgmüller), bars 27–31

Only the second of three ground plans includes notated steps. The man begins traveling on the diagonal from upstage left. He makes a complete turn to the right before reversing his diagonal and traveling right to left. He runs upstage left to begin the notated enchaînement, also on the diagonal: *brisé, ballonné battu, temps levé en tournant en cou-de-pied derrière, demi-cabriole devant, pas de bourrée, tombé, demi-emboîté derrière, assemblé*, single *tour* to the left, single *tour* to the right twice. The ground plan next indicates travel across the stage from right to left. The use of two consecutive arrows suggests an enchaînement that is repeated. The variation concludes with four *pirouettes*.

Justamant documents a different structure for this number. Titled "ensembles," it begins with the couple traveling on the diagonal from left to right with *ballonné, brisé, jeté en avant, assemblé*. The woman steps forward *en attitude* and the man lifts her overhead. As soon as she is lowered, she performs a *relevé* and turns quickly ("vivement") to her left in *arabesque*, the man supporting her by the waist. They repeat the entire enchaînement to the other side. The woman continues alone ("la danseuse seule") with *pas de bourrée, glissade, assemblé*, and two *échappés* "sur les orteils" twice and finishes with a *pirouette*. The man dances the remaining twenty bars alone ("le danseur seul continue jusqu'a la fin de l'allegro"), but his steps are not recorded. By listing the number of bars allotted for each section, Justamant makes clear that the thirty-seven-bar number was performed in its entirety. In contrast, the piano reduction included with the CN replaces the final thirteen bars with a single bar comprised of two chords.

The woman's variation notated in the CN features three enchaînements, each highlighting a different skill: *pointe* work, small jumps, and turns. She begins upstage center and travels in a zigzag pattern with *bourrées*, a *relevé en cou-de-pied derrière* on the left foot, and a *relevé petit passé* on the right foot three times to alternate sides. The jumping sequence, performed on the diagonal from upstage right, includes three *brisés volés*, each separated by two *brisés*, followed by a final *brisé* and two *pas de chat*. After a run upstage left, she begins the turning combination: a *ballonné* on one foot then the other, each performed while making a half turn to the right, *pas de basque*, and a single *tour* to the right,

Ex. 3.6c Peasant *pas de deux* (Burgmüller), bars 47–51

landing in *demi-arabesque fondu*. This enchaînement is performed three times followed by turns on *demi-pointe*. No final pose is given.

This variation comprises twenty-four bars preceded by a two-bar introduction as it was performed in the St. Petersburg production (Ex. 36d). Turning to Justamant, we find that the woman's variation fills forty bars (achieved by the repetition of two eight-bar phrases not repeated in the CN version) plus introduction. It is labeled "variation de La Dame," and Justamant also included the name "Mlle Girod" in parenthesis, which may refer to Rose Marie Girod, a French dancer who performed briefly in St. Petersburg in the 1850s.[87] The step vocabulary includes a variety of small jumps as well as *piqués* and *relevés* on *pointe*. (While Justamant does not indicate a repeat of the opening enchaînement in prose, the ground plan features two diagonals and thus suggests it. We have found the ground plan can sometimes clarify confusing or omitted elements in Justamant's prose descriptions.) The variation ends with a choice of *saut de basque* or *gargouillade*.

As he did with the man's earlier solo, Justamant omits the man's second variation, writing only "Suit la variation du Danseur" (the variation of the *Danseur* follows). The entire variation is preserved in the CN, however: dancing to a buoyant $^6_8$, the man begins at center with *grande cabriole fouetté*, *grand jeté en avant*, and a *ballonné battu* on each leg (Ex. 3.6e). The enchaînement is repeated to the other side followed by a zigzag backward upstage: four *sissonnes fermé* to alternate sides and two *pas de bourrée*, *échappé battu*, the first landing in *cou-de-pied*, the second in fifth position. This enchaînement is also repeated, setting up a final diagonal from upstage left. Facing the upstage corner, the man performs *chassé*, *jeté battu en tournant* twice. He then changes direction and travels across the stage from right to left. The steps are not notated a second time, nor is a repeat sign drawn, but the ground plan suggests a repeat of the enchaînement on the other leg. No additional steps or final position are given.

The concluding waltz, Burgmüller's *Souvenir de Ratisbonne*, serves as both a second variation for the woman and a coda for both dancers (Ex. 3.6f). As with earlier

---

[87] About Girod, see Konaev, "Khronika osnovnykh postanovok," 86.

Ex. 3.6d Peasant *pas de deux* (Burgmüller), bars 86–89

Ex. 3.6e Peasant *pas de deux* (Burgmüller), bars 110–115

numbers, the version in Justamant accounts for all of the music included in Parisian sources, while the CN represents a shortened version. In the latter, the woman begins upstage left and travels down the diagonal with eight *pas de valse*, performed without turning. She retraces her path, moving backward with *entrechat cinq* and a step back into *tendu effacé devant fondu* three times. She returns down the diagonal with *pas de valse*, this time *en tournant*. She moves across the stage from right to left with *entrechat trois*, a step back turning around to the right, and a *piqué en arabesque*, facing downstage left, three times. After traveling upstage on *demi-pointe*, she is joined by her partner.

In a similar final section as the one danced by Giselle and Loys in the *louré pas*, the couple performs unison steps opposite one another, crossing the stage four times, passing at center. Their enchaînement consists of two *sauts de basque* and *cabriole devant*. They conclude with four *balancés* traveling backward upstage and a run downstage for a supported *double pirouette*, the women finishing *à la seconde*, likely leaning to the side, arms overhead.

Justamant follows a similar format for the final number, although the ballerina performs *pas de valse en tournant* right away. She circles upstage with *pas d'almande*—that is, *pas allemande*, a traveling step likely similar to *pas de bourrée*—and begins a zigzag downstage performing a repeated enchaînement of *brisé* "sur l'orteil," a quick turn, and *jeté de côte*. Returning upstage with a series of *glissade, jeté*, and *relevé* "sur l'orteil," she is met by her partner. They travel downstage together performing waltz steps naturally (*valse naturellement*). She continues the step, circling her partner and holding his

Ex. 3.6f Peasant *pas de deux* (Burgmüller, *Souvenir de Ratisbonne*), bars 149–156

hand. They separate and traverse the stage twice from opposite sides with two *grands jetés en tournant* and a combination of small jumps, crossing paths each time at center. Continuing separately, they next travel upstage with a series of *brisés* followed by alternating single *tours en l'air*: first the woman, followed by the man, then the woman to the other side, again followed by her partner. They traverse the stage separately four more times, crossing twice with *petits jetés en tournant* and twice again, as before, with *grands jetés en tournant* and small jumps. They travel upstage, turning in *arabesque*, and join at center for a final circular pass around the stage. They conclude the *pas* with a single unison *pirouette* "et groupe à volonté" (a group at will, that is, of their choosing).

We mention only briefly a further source for this *pas de deux*: a choreographic notation of the entrée, adagio, and coda made in Saint-Léon's *Sténochorégraphie* method.[88] As in Justamant, the couple waits for eight bars before beginning the entrée. (In the CN, they begin in the first bar.) In agreement again with Justamant, no cuts are made in the final waltz, whereas in the CN this movement is cut significantly. In all three sources, the woman begins the final waltz as a solo and her partner joins her midway through the dance.

Galop. The St. Petersburg galop (Ex. 2.19) begins with the eight coryphées in a single row performing an array of *petit allegro* steps and steps on *pointe*, including *bourrées*, *piqués sur les pointes*, *piqués en cou-de-pied devant*, *demi-gargouillades*, *piqués ballonnés*, *entrechats quatre*, and *échappés*. The row splits at center and two opposing rows of four traverse the stage in a series of *temps levés en demi-arabesque* while the corps enters and forms four rows across the stage: rows of women alternating with rows of men. In this block formation, they perform *entrechats quatre* and *bourrées*, circling in place, followed by rocking *temps levés en demi-arabesque* and *temps levés en cou-de-pied devant*.[89]

[88] Paris, Bibliotheque Nationale de France, Bibliothèque-Musée de l'Opéra, RES-234. See Arthur Saint-Léon, *La sténochorégraphie, ou L'art d'écrire promptement la danse* (Paris, 1852). About *Sténochorégraphie*, see Ann Hutchinson Guest, *Choreo-Graphics: A Comparison of Dance Notation Systems from the Fifteenth Century to the Present* (New York: Gordon and Breach, 1989), and Sandra Noll Hammond, "La Sténochorégraphie by Saint-Léon: A Link in Ballet's Technical History," Proceedings, *Society of Dance History Scholars* (1982), 148–154.

[89] The third and fourth pages of the galop in the CN include ground plans and steps for an ensemble of twelve women (no men). These may represent a later arrangement of the mixed ensemble passages of the dance for use in a staging with reduced forces. Cyril Beaumont's "simplified choreographic script" of *Giselle* describes the galop as danced by an ensemble of women. His description is based on a version performed by the Markova-Dolin Ballet, for which Nikolai Sergeyev staged the *Giselle* in 1935. See Beaumont, *Ballet called "Giselle,"* 99.

The middle section features *pas de valse* (without turns), the corps traveling to the wings. The coryphées return, traversing the stage again in two opposing rows with steps on *pointe*. Re-assembling into a single row downstage center, the women continue with *ballonné sauté devant* on each leg, *piqué en cou-de-pied devant*, *soutenu* twice. After traveling upstage with *ballotté, chassé en tournant, demi-cabriole derrière* three times, the coryphées run forward and to the sides as the corps returns to its block formation and performs *soubresaut, changement, soutenu* twice.

At the reprise of the main theme, the corps joins the coryphées performing *temps levés* across the stage in opposing rows that cross at center. The ensemble next assembles in a block formation: the coryphées travel downstage with *jeté en avant, pas de bourrée, glissade, assemblé* to alternate sides while the corps resumes their rocking *temps levés*. In the last bars, all perform the galop step in pairs, circling the stage then moving to the sides as Giselle and Loys run to center from downstage right.

Before continuing to the Act One finale, the Justamant galop deserves mention. While the St. Petersburg version features primarily ballet step vocabulary, the Justamant galop is a couples' social dance. His drawings indicate a variety of dance "holds" that the couples assume as they perform the various steps, which include the galop (traveling laterally and not forward as in the CN), *pas d'almande*, and *pas de valse en tournant*. At one point, the couples assemble upstage left in block formation. All face left, extend their arms to the sides, and hold their neighbors by the shoulders. Traveling laterally, the entire block galops until the dancers reach the edge of the stage. Making a quarter turn to the right and taking the shoulders of their new neighbors, the dancers cross the stage to the opposite wing. The pattern continues until the block has covered the full expanse of the stage. At the end of the dance, groups of two couples form circles, take each other by the shoulders, and turn as they perform multiple *glissades*. Giselle and Loys galop downstage at center and finish with a "passé ordinaire."

In both the CN and the Justamant versions of the galop, Giselle and Loys are downstage center as the finale begins.

Returning now to the CN, Hans runs down center and pushes the couple apart.

Hans: "You think he loves you?"

Giselle: "Yes."

Hans: "You believe he will marry you?" He laughs.

Giselle: "Yes."

Hans: "Never. He is a nobleman, and I will prove it to you." Running to retrieve the chain and sword, he brings them out and shows them to Giselle. "These belong to him." Giselle runs up to Loys and asks if this is true.

Loys: "I will kill him." He grabs the sword from Hans and tries to stab him (Ex. 2.27). The squire intervenes, and Loys drops the sword.

Hans blows the horn three times (Ex. 2.28). Everyone (presumably this refers to the hunting party) gradually enters the stage. The Duke (Gillert) enters from Berthe's house.

Duke: "What has happened?" He sees Albert and approaches him. "Your costume is magnificent." (This is likely a sarcastic statement referring to Albert's peasant clothing. Sergeyev's choice of words here reflects the nature of the CN as an eyewitness account of the ballet.) "And your fiancée is going to see you in it. She is here. Look."

Albert greets Matilda, who also has come out of the house. He kisses her hand.

Matilda: "What is the matter with you? You look so odd."

Albert: "Oh, it is nothing."

At this moment, Giselle runs up and pushes them apart.

Giselle: (to Matilda) "Are you his fiancée?"

Matilda: "Yes."

Giselle: "You are marrying him?"

Matilda: "Yes!"

Giselle: "Never! Never!"

Giselle walks backward in terror and curses. She rips off the necklace and throws it at Matilda, cursing her. She steps back and continues to curse the fiancée. Giselle falls into her mother's arms in exhaustion. Terrified, Berthe embraces Giselle and tries to calm her down. She loosens Giselle's hair.

"*Scene of madness*." Acting "as though in a fit of insanity," Giselle gets up slowly, laughs twice, and falls down again.

Albert steps away unnoticed, another departure from earlier sources in which Albert remains fully engaged throughout the following *scène de folie*.

Giselle "walks in circles around the stage, staring somewhere, and begins to recollect something with the left hand as if wiping a knife, standing in place, doing everything very vaguely and frighteningly sluggishly." Sergeyev's account of Pavlova's movements is an excellent example of the literal descriptions of action that he documented in the notations he created.

Giselle: "I remember the wedding." Again, she curses Matilda. She picks a flower and begins divining: "He loves me, he loves me not," etc. (Ex. 2.7b).

Circling around to center, she steps on the sword and picks it up in terror. She holds it by the blade's edge and swings it a little in place. She walks, dragging the sword behind her. Stopping, she looks at the sword. Albert runs up and grabs it from Giselle, who runs forward. As Albert walks away, upstage and across to the left, Giselle runs first to her mother's embrace. Next, she runs backward, sees Matilda (presumably with her father, who is embracing her), stops "in a pose," sees her mother, smiles happily, then runs again to her mother's arms, falling on her chest. Berthe hugs and consoles her, but "does not know how to help her."

Giselle: (moving upstage with Berthe) "I remember [my] fiancé." Seeing something, she "runs [stage left], pointing somewhere. Stops for a moment. Looks the other way into nowhere. Runs [stage right], pointing somewhere. Stops for a moment. (Ex. 2.8b)

At the return of the *louré* melody, Giselle dances, traveling backward with a series of *temps levés en demi-arabesque*. She crosses the stage twice then travels forward in a zigzag with *ballonné, pas marché, jeté en avant* four times.

She "grabs her heart in exhaustion," experiences "fits of suffocation," and "suffers terribly." Walking, she circles the stage, asking for help.

She runs to Berthe, who comes forward to meet her. Berthe "hugs her, kisses her, and does not know how to help."

Giselle calls Albert, who runs up to her and takes her hand.

Giselle: "I bless you."

She experiences "weakness, and she dies. [She] falls."

Berthe and Albert try to revive her. Berthe sobs, not knowing what to do.

Albert runs to Hans, who is kneeling and praying.

Albert: "Admire your victim."

Albert grabs Hans by the arm and drags him to Giselle's body. Hans begs Albert to let him go. Albert grabs the sword from a grandee and attacks Hans. He wants to stab him, but the squire stops him again and takes the sword away.

Albert runs to Giselle's body and sobs. Hans drops to his knees and prays to God for mercy.

Thus ends Act One in the CN.

Act Two

The Mariinsky production manuscript includes a sketch of the Act Two stage setting that features a wooded clearing. Giselle's grave, marked by a large cross, is downstage left. It is accessed by a small staircase that is hidden from audience view by a low panel. At stage right, what appears to be the flower bed onto which Albert will ultimately lay the fading body of Giselle is similarly decorated with a front-facing panel.

The opening scene as recorded in the CN suggests a different order of events from those found in our earlier sources. No. 1 is omitted (as is No. 3), so we will assume that number comprised the music played before the curtain rises (Ex. 2.1c).

No. 2. Twelve hunters enter the stage, one by one, from various wings. They congregate downstage left and eventually form a semicircle.

Hans enters upstage center, searching for Giselle's grave. Finding it, he kneels and cries.

Hans: "I loved her, and I killed her." He falls on the grave, crying.

No. 4. As everyone listens, chimes strike midnight. The hunters make to leave, but seeing Hans, they wake him. Hans—who apparently had fallen asleep—is frightened and asks them why they are here.

Hunters: "We were drinking wine here."

Hans: "This is not a place to drink. Dead people come out here from their graves and they are covered by veils. They will catch you and you will die. Save yourselves. See these lights?"

Everyone runs away, scared, as will-o'-the-wisps appear—an effect the CN suggests was achieved by lighting (Ex. 2.29).

Myrtha. We encounter similar details of Myrtha's initial trio of dances in all our sources. During the slow, quiet opening section, she makes her appearance, dances briefly, and glides across the lake. The second section, a triple-meter *andante*, functions as a *pas d'action* in which Myrtha gathers flowers, balances in trees, and otherwise enjoys her natural surroundings. The final *allegro* waltz features bravura dancing.

No. 5. According to both the CN (as well as Justamant), Myrtha rises out of a trap in the stage floor at center, the CN noting this is done "quietly with [the] motif," an apparent reference to the music (Ex. 2.15).

Beginning at center and traveling left, Myrtha performs *glissade, tour de promenade en dehors en arabesque* (a step also found in Justamant), *tendu effacé devant fondu*, leaning forward then raising the body, arching the back, and straightening the standing leg. This is repeated to the other side and followed by a *bourrée* around the stage in a counterclockwise circle. Arriving at center, Myrtha runs into the wings upstage right and reappears as she traverses the stage—"gliding on the lake," as Titus noted—on a piece of stage machinery. According to the CN, she "rides by on a cart," while Justamant refers to a "chariot" and provides an elaborate drawing of Myrtha flying along the water with the following description: "posing in *arabesque* on the left foot, she traverses the stage." Both of these sources are in agreement with the Titus *répétiteur*. Myrtha re-enters upstage left to begin the second part of her dance.

No. 6. She performs a series of *temps levés en arabesque* and *pas de bourrée* (Ex. 2.30). At the echo motif in the music, she does *pas de bourrée* on *pointe* and *piqué en arabesque* to each side, her steps matching the rhythm of the melody. She "listens" (in Justamant the listening, rather than steps, coincides with the "echo" motif in the music) then runs upstage left and "picks up flowers by the tree 2 times." Holding the flowers and traveling downstage in a zigzag pattern, she performs *glissade, fouetté sauté, pas de bourrée* on *pointe* three times to alternate sides followed by a repeat of the *piqués en arabesque* at the echo motif. Her dance concludes with a spiraling *bourrée* and a kneeling pose at center. This account in the CN omits Myrtha's balance on the tree branches, a feature included in both Titus and Justamant.

During the musical transition to the third section of the dance, in agreement with Justamant, Myrtha "throws the flowers toward one side and the other."

No. 7. The final part of her entrance dance, set to a waltz in $\frac{6}{8}$ meter (Ex. 2.18), features her most virtuosic choreography yet. Traveling downstage in a zigzag pattern, Myrtha performs *assemblé, sissonne double rond de jambe en l'air, grand jeté en avant* four times to alternate sides. Returning upstage, she continues with a series of six *pas de bourrée* on *pointe, relevé développé à la seconde* to alternate sides. She *bourrées* upstage left where she begins a diagonal of eight *pas de bourrée en tournant, jeté en avant*. Turning to travel left, she repeats the same steps another eight times before turning again abruptly to the right for a *bourrée* across the downstage and a final pose in *attitude à terre*.

Justamant documents equally virtuosic albeit different enchaînements whose step vocabulary includes *grand assemblé, grand jeté en avant, grand fouetté*, and *fouetté sauté*. Myrtha's final combination is also a turning sequence: a series of *pas de bourrée en tournant, grand jeté en avant en attitude*.

No. 8. At the scene of invocation, the CN instructs, "The Lady of the Wilis [here, Rykhlyakova] walks to the grave and takes a myrtle branch. She goes to center stage and calls from 2 sides the Wilis" (Ex. 2.16). In addition to Giselle's grave at stage right, the ground plan indicates a second "grave" at stage left (the same onto which Albert will lay Giselle during the ballet's finale) next to which is written, "takes a myrtle branch off the grave." (In the Paris production, this feature at stage left was a mound of flowers.)

The corps of veiled Wilis enters, walking, from each side. Their slow, deliberate steps are notated with the annotation, "arms on chest crossed everyone." Myrtha orders the Wilis to remove their veils. They walk into the wings, where the veils are discarded, and return, forming three rows of four dancers on each side of the stage, positioned on a slight diagonal. The ensemble begins to dance, stepping gently from side to side. They stop and pose as Egorova (Moyna) runs in from downstage right, followed by Pavlova (Zulmé) from downstage left.

Justamant's "magical evocation" follows a similar plan. As Myrtha summons the Wilis, she says, "You all who sleep in this earth and who like me died from love—I, your queen, want you, at my voice, to come out of your tombs." After the Wilis enter from each side, most arrange themselves in a large semicircle upstage facing a smaller row of downstage Wilis who have their backs to the audience. Holding each other by the waist, the Wilis "bend their heads to the right, then to the left, and one time again to each side." This tender movement reminds us of the opening of the "Russian dance" in George Balanchine's *Serenade*, in which five women, also holding each other by the waist and facing away from the audience, tilt their heads to one side and then the other.

Pas des Wilis. As noted earlier, the oft-repeated notion that Petipa greatly expanded the *Pas des Wilis* is not borne out in our sources.[90] Let us consider cast size and the amount of music used for this number. The 1841 Paris *Giselle* featured a cast of thirty Wilis that was expanded to fifty Wilis in 1863.[91] While not all of the St. Petersburg posters and programs make clear the total number of corps Wilis—Grantzow's 1866 debut featured nineteen plus "other dancers," Petipa's 1884 revival featured twenty-four, and Cornalba's performance on 1 January 1889 included twenty-four plus students—the St. Petersburg production does not appear to have utilized a greater number of Wilis than the Paris productions. In fact, by the turn of the century, fewer Wilis were cast: from 1899 onward, the number of corps Wilis listed in the program is twenty-four, the same number as recorded in the CN. As for the music used, nothing in the sources we have consulted suggests changes to the score of the *Pas de Wilis* as Adam first composed it, beyond an added repeat of the eight bars of "Spanish" music (Ex. 2.20a).[92]

The Titus *répétiteur*, Justamant, and CN all call for ensemble dancing at the beginning and end of the *Pas des Wilis*. The order of solos, duos, and so forth differs in each source. The CN also differs from Titus and Justamant in the two brief passages danced by the corps between solo sections, one of which is simply a series of *pas de bourrée* performed in place.

No. 9. According to the CN, the Wilis form three rows of eight across the stage with Moyna and Zulmé downstage center. Dancing in pairs, they join right hands and "turn in place" (*Andante*, B-flat major, $\frac{3}{4}$). Their movements comprise three *piqués petits battements* and a *soutenu*, which are first performed as they turn to the right and again as they turn to the left. Next, the partners exchange places by stepping forward into *arabesque*. Changing direction with a *soutenu*, they perform the enchaînement three more times.

The ensemble *bourrées* toward the middle of the stage and assembles in a star formation. Kneeling toward center, the Wilis alternate bending forward with their arms crossed on their chests and raising up, arms overhead, backs arched. (In Justamant, this ritualistic activity occurs before the dancing begins.) Standing, the Wilis return to three rows on either side of the stage with a series of *tendus de côté, fondus degagés, pas de bourrée*.

---

[90] *Pas des Wilis* is a title used on posters, and later in programs, as early as Bogdanova's 1856 St. Petersburg debut.

[91] Guest, *Second Empire 1858–1870*, 61.

[92] This repeat was added to the Titus *répétiteur* and also is in the Riga score. It was added and then erased in the Harvard printed piano reduction.

During the musical transition, the corps performs four *pas de bourrée* in place, stepping in time with the melody.

Moyna's variation (*Allegro non troppo*, E-flat major, $\frac{6}{8}$) is built on short phrases performed to alternate sides in a zigzag pattern. Traveling upstage, she performs multiple *relevés en arabesque, pas de bourrée*. She *bourrées* upstage right and begins a series of *glissade, entrechat cinq de volée, relevé en cou-de-pied devant, relevé en demi-arabesque* three times, traveling downstage. She finishes with *chaînés* on *demi-pointe*, traveling right and ending *en face*.

Zulmé's variation follows (Ex. 2.20a). She travels directly downstage with multiple *pas de bourrée* on *pointe, relevé en arabesque* to alternate sides. She returns upstage in a zigzag pattern with a series of *demi-cabriole derrière, chassé*. She moves upstage right and begins a final diagonal of *pas de bourrée en tournant, grand rond de jambe en l'air sauté, pas de bourrée en tournant, relevé en demi-arabesque* three times followed by *chaînés* on *demi-pointe* to the downstage left corner, also finishing *en face*.

The corps takes over with a simple passage of *temps levés en demi-arabesque, chassé* on each leg followed by a *bourrée* upstage, more *temps levés*, and a *bourrée* returning downstage (Ex. 2.20b).

At the change to $\frac{3}{8}$ meter (*allegro con moto*, B-flat major), Myrtha begins a solo upstage center. Traveling downstage in a zigzag pattern, she performs *grand jeté en avant, entrechat six* four times to alternate sides. She moves back up the zigzag with *pas de cheval devant, fouetté passé développé sauté, chassé, fouetté grand rond de jambe en l'air sauté* three times before she *bourrées* upstage left in anticipation of a final diagonal: *sissonne doublée* eight times and then *chaînés* on *demi-pointe* across the stage, right to left.

The Wilis corps repeats its *pas de bourrée* in place during the musical transition that leads to a duo for Egorova and Pavlova (a return to the *allegro non troppo*, E-flat major, $\frac{6}{8}$). Traveling side by side down center, the pair performs *glissade, relevé rond de jambe en l'air* four times on alternate legs, *cabriole derrière, assemblé*. They repeat the *relevés ronds de jambe* before traveling to opposite downstage corners with *chaînés* on *demi-pointe*.

The coda begins with a series of *demi-arabesques voyagé* performed by the upstage row of Wilis (marked as "I" on the ground plan) who travel to center from either side. They meet and perform *ballotté* then *saut de basque* as they travel away from center to begin again. They are next joined in repetitions of this enchaînement by the middle row ("II") then the front row ("III") and finally the solo Wilis ("IV," also referred to in prose as "two," that is, the two solo Wilis). After this, the *voyagé* step performed in full, ninety-degree *arabesque* as the rows of dancers traverse the entire stage, crossing at center. They continue with *ballotté* then *ballonné de côté* to change direction. The CN explains the enchaînement: "Switch to [full] *arabesque* and[,] in place[,] the foot forward and back"—this refers to the *cou-de-pied devant* and *derrière* positions of the foot in the *ballonné*. The Wilis cross the stage again before all move to the sides with *temps levés en demi-arabesque*.

Myrtha begins a final solo, crossing the stage twice on diagonal trajectories with three *grands jetés en avant, assemblé, entrechat six*. She continues with a manège of *glissade, saut de basque* eight times. Arriving upstage left, she breaks into *piqué tours en dehors*, traveling downstage right. She turns to the left and *bourrées* in a wide circle that brings her to center. As she turns in place, the entire ensemble, performing *temps levés en demi-arabesque*, rushes from their places along the wings to form three lines upstage of Myrtha, the solo Wilis flanking their queen.

Together, all perform rocking *pas de bourrée* and *fouettés sautés* to *demi-arabesque* that culminate in five consecutive *fouettés sautés* to full *arabesque*. The Wilis finish their dance with *sous-sus*, arms overhead.

Justamant provides a simpler structure for the internal solos, though it is difficult to determine this structure in detail because the pages in the manuscript are mis-collated, making the assignment of choreography to music challenging. Following the order of pages in the staging manual, a lengthy solo for Myrtha, comprising forty bars, is followed by an "Entrée d'une deuxieme danseuse" (eight bars), an "Entrée et variation d'une deux-ieme danseuse" (twenty-five bars), and a "variation de la reine" (eight bars). The two eight-bar solos surely correspond to the "Spanish" and "Eastern" passages (Exx. 2.20a–b). The twenty-five-bar solo likely corresponds to the passage of the same length that precedes these two shorter sections. This leaves the forty-bar solo for Myrtha, which can, with some effort, be fitted to the remaining music that precedes the coda. The coda itself begins with two pairs of Wilis who traverse the stage on diagonals, followed by Myrtha, and continues with a passage for the entire ensemble.

Returning to the CN, we see that the Wilis, having completed their energetic finale, turn to face upstage as a quiet postlude begins. Kneeling again, arms crossed on their chests, they bend forward then raise up, arms overhead. They stand and walk to form the familiar single diagonal line at stage left. Pavlova and Egorova are placed at the down-stage end of the line.

No. 10: Giselle's invocation. The ensemble stands in *arabesque*, facing Giselle's grave. Myrtha (Rykhlyakova is named on the ground plan) walks across the stage to the tomb. Annotations describe the rest of the action: "Giselle is lifted from the trap door [that is, she rises up from below stage], and Sedova [named in the annotations as Myrtha on the same ground plan that lists Rykhlyakova] calls her and touches her and pulls away her veil" (Ex. 2.8d).[93] The action continues: "*Vilis* [Myrtha] touches Giselle with a branch. Giselle opens her wings and turns." She makes "4 circles" in place, hop-ping in *arabesque* (Ex. 2.31). Traveling upstage in a zigzag pattern, she continues with three sets of two *sissonnes doublée*. She turns and runs upstage left then travels down the diagonal with *pas de bourrée en tournant*, *jeté en avant* twice and *chaînés*. She fin-ishes in *arabesque à plat*. During this final diagonal, the corps stands in *arabesque* (the CN does not indicate if the *arabesque* has been held throughout the entrée until this point), then the Wilis briefly "put down" their legs before resuming the *arabesque* at the end of Giselle's entrée.

The dance performed by Justamant's Giselle is closely related to that of her Stepanov sister but also features non-dancing elements: Giselle turns in place *en arabesque*, makes a *relevé*, then poses *à plat*. From a lowered position *en face*, she says, "Now I am going to fly," before running upstage right. She crosses the stage with *grand sissonne doublée*, *grand rond de jambe en l'air en dehors*, *assemblé* three times to alternate sides. She con-tinues with *chassé contre chassé*, *assemblé* to reach center, where she performs a *grand pirouette à la seconde* and *pirouette en cou-de-pied*, finishing in fifth position on *pointe*. In a stunning conclusion, timed to coincide with Giselle's final rise onto *pointe*, the entire

---

[93] As mentioned earlier, the two dancers are simultaneously listed in the role of Myrtha, which suggests the ground plan and accompanying annotation were written at different times.

band of Wilis rushes toward Giselle and forms a cross with the newly inducted Wili at its axis.

No. 11. Returning to the CN, Sergeyev notes that everyone "flies" away, and the ensemble runs into the wings. As in Justamant—in which Myrtha, hearing a noise, commands, "You and you, fly away"—the subsequent scene with the peasants and Wilis is omitted in the CN.

No. 12. The "Entrance of Albert and his Squire" is documented only briefly in the CN. The pair enters upstage left and walks directly toward Giselle's grave (Ex. 2.32). "Having found the grave, Legat orders [the squire] to leave."

As she does in Justamant, Giselle appears amid foliage upstage right. (Justamant refers to "reeds"; the CN refers to "a bush"; Ex. 2.8e). Albert runs and tries to embrace her, but she disappears. Appearing again, Giselle poses briefly, passes Albert with a *tour jeté*, and runs across the stage, exiting into the wings. She appears a third time, flying across the stage on a mechanism from left to right. (Justamant describes the action: "Giselle, lying on a *char* [*chariot*?]", crosses the stage and disappears into the wings.")

Albert: (alone on stage) "She flies here, but this is my fantasy. I will pray to God."

Appearing again as the music changes to $\frac{2}{4}$ meter, Giselle runs on, circles Albert, who is kneeling, and poses next to him in *arabesque à plat* (Ex. 2.13). Albert cries and calls out, "Giselle." She circles him, performing *pas de basque, fouetté sauté en tournant* four times. (In Justamant, Giselle crosses in front of Albert and back, performing *balancé en avant, balancé en arrière, glissade, grand jeté ordinaire en tournant* to each side.) She touches Albert's shoulder and runs away.

Albert: "I beg you, do not go." He wants to catch her, but she runs past him and poses. The "Prince" again wants to embrace her. Giselle runs under his arms, but this time he catches her by the wings. "I ask you, do not leave here."

As Albert holds her wings—an unusual partnering feature mentioned not only in the CN but also in the Titus *répétiteur* ("il lui prend les ailes") and Justamant—Giselle performs three *piqués en demi-arabesque.* Justamant provides a lovely description of the same moment (with slightly different choreography), in which Giselle, "giving in to the movement," leans her body back toward Albert as she raises her right leg to the front; as she next falls forward, Albert "follows the movement by raising his left leg"; this is done three times.

Returning to the CN, Giselle breaks away and circles Albert again, performing *pas de basque, tour jeté* twice, with Albert lifting her for each jump. In Justamant, as before, Giselle passes in front of Albert and back, lifted each time in a *grand jeté ordinaire.*

Next the lovers dance opposite each other in unison, rising with a *sous-sus*, running and crossing at center, and finishing the phrase with what is notated as a *sissonne fermé*, although the step traditionally is performed as an *assemblé.* (Justamant calls for *grand assemblé derrière.*) They repeat the enchaînement, then Giselle exits into the stage left wings. She returns, running upstage to "pick flowers from a bush." The lovers dance again, mirroring each other and crossing at center as they perform *pas de bourrée, ballonné, petit tour jeté* four times. Giselle circles Albert with two *relevés en arabesque* and runs upstage left. With Albert in pursuit, she crosses the stage on the diagonal with a *grand jeté en avant*, throwing a flower back over her head. She circles upstage with *relevés en arabesque* and repeats the *grand jeté*, throwing a second flower. (In Justamant, Giselle performs *glissade, jeté ordinaire* as she throws the flowers.)

Giselle runs into the wings at stage right as Albert picks up the blooms, kisses them, and says, "She gave me flowers."

Giselle next appears on the branch of a tree, swung out over the stage. She drops more flowers for Albert, who gathers and admires them. Writing about stagecraft in 1954, Karsavina described the mechanics of this magical moment:

> Take for example, the apparition of Giselle when in the second act, swaying on a tree branch, she becomes visible to her lover. The audience see, or should see, the wraith of Giselle, light as air, above, and down below Albrecht kneeling, stretching his arms towards the unattainable form. Yet this moment of exquisite pathos is omitted from present productions. But come behind the scenes into the last wing and you shall see a couple of sturdy stage-hands, to all appearances playing see-saw. The contraption is simple: one of the lower branches of the tree has a slender piece of wood on hinges—the whole concealed by the foliage. A small platform to place the foot on enables the dancer to appear first as if standing on the branch. Leaning sideways against the plank as it tilted down, the dancer can unfold a beautiful *arabesque penchée*.[94]

Giselle disappears and Albert cries, "She flew away." He searches for her.

Giselle enters and mounts the steps to her grave. Seeing her, Albert runs to the grave and attempts to embrace her a final time, but she disappears through the same trap by which she first appeared. Albert falls on the grave and cries.

Albert: (hearing a noise) "Someone is coming." He gets up and runs away.

We note that some pages of the Justamant manuscript that document the foregoing action and dance are bound out of order, as they were in the Wilis' dance. Too, the action occurring after Giselle first throws flowers and leaves the stage (comprising fifty bars of music) is omitted or missing. So, unfortunately, we cannot fully compare the earlier to the later version of this bittersweet and even flirtatious *pas de deux* between the two lovers. (The Justamant manual continues with the subsequent bacchanale.)

No. 13. Hans enters running at the beginning of the bacchanale (Ex. 2.5). The ground plan indicates his path—a broad zigzag downstage that is blocked successively by groups of four Wilis at every turn. He arrives downstage left, face to face with Myrtha (Sedova).

Hans: "What do you want from me?"

Myrtha: "You must die here."

The Wilis begin to dance, performing multiple *temps levés en demi-arabesque* to alternate sides. Terrified, Hans runs from Myrtha but is surrounded by four Wilis downstage right who form a circle and run around him, holding hands. Then, as the Wilis stand in place, Hans makes two turns as he moves toward stage right (whether he is performing

---

[94] Tamara Karsavina, "Lost Steps (V): Stage Illusions," *Dancing Times* New Series, no. 521 (February 1954), 282.

dance steps is not indicated). The next ground plan shows Hans moving from one side of the stage to the other and back again: "Gerdt begs all for mercy."

Wilis: "No! No!" The entire group forms a circle, surrounding Hans. Holding hands, they run in a clockwise direction then return to their lines by the wings. They grab Hans and throw him from one side of the stage to the other. Dancing in place, they perform *fouetté rond de jambe en l'air sauté* on alternate legs. They re-form their running circle around Hans then move to their fateful single diagonal line with Myrtha placed downstage left. Hans falls at the queen's feet.

Myrtha: "You will die here."

The gamekeeper lies on the ground and suffers. He stands up and is caught by the Wilis. One by one, they push him up the line. Exhausted, he returns, performing *jetés en avant*. Again the Wilis push Hans up the line, turning him as he goes. When he reaches the end, four Wilis "push the forester into the water and he dies. All the Wilis laugh" (Ex. 2.17a).

The CN's account of Hans's death fills a mere three pages. Following a detailed description of his initial entrance and how his paths of escape are cut off by the Wilis, the action is documented with hastily drawn ground plans accompanied by brief annotations and few step notations.

In contrast, the Justamant account, a full fourteen pages, is rich in detail describing the constant movements of players in this scene. An initial four Wilis *en scène* "call their companions" to aid in trapping Hilarion. When he asks Myrtha, "What do you want of me?" she replies, "We want you to dance with us," and orders Moyna and Zulmé to "seize him." The Wilis form a large semicircle that frames the stage and bars Hilarion's escape. When Moyna and Zulmé bring him upstage, they reposition themselves and block the wings. At one point, the Wilis form three circles into which Myrtha commands he be thrust, one after the other. The queen herself "takes Hilarion by the hands and . . . makes him go and half-fall to the right and to the left. . . . [she] picks him up, then pushes him forcefully toward the first of the Wilis." The scene ends in the same manner described in the CN: the Wilis form a single diagonal line along which they push Hilarion toward his fate at upstage right.

Justamant carefully traces Hilarion's physical and psychological decline throughout the bacchanale. At first, "weakening, he falls between [the Wilis], his legs bending." Soon, "he no longer knows where he is," "can scarcely hold himself up," "is like a lifeless body and lets go," and "has totally lost his mind." Finally, he "falls in the lake and disappears."

With Myrtha in the lead (Rykhlyakova again, here called "Lady of the Wilis"), followed by Moyna and Zulmé and then successive groups of four Wilis, the ensemble travels from downstage left to their exit upstage right with two sets of *glissade*, *jeté* and two *grands jetés en avant* twice.

All of the Wilis immediately return, running, and re-form their diagonal line. Albert appears upstage right and approaches Myrtha (Ex. 2.17b).

Albert: "What do you want from me?"

Myrtha: "You are going to dance here."

Albert: "I beg you, beg you."

Myrtha: "No! No!"

Entering downstage right, Giselle runs toward Albert and, striking a pose, seeks to protect him from Myrtha. They run toward the grave, pursued by the queen, who carries a myrtle branch in her right hand. The other Wilis also pursue them before circling up-stage to form two rows of eight at center, as the remaining eight re-form their diagonal line at stage left. Myrtha signals with her hand for the lovers to stop. The myrtle branch breaks. Myrtha throws it in terror. The subsequent fugue is omitted, and the CN contin-ues with the *pas de deux*.

As he did for the bacchanale, Justamant documents broadly similar action for this scene but with a vivid richness of detail. The Wili band, having regrouped stage right after Hilarion's death, dances in a counterclockwise circle around the whole of the stage. They spy Albert offstage before they make their exit. They "make a sign of joy" and Myrtha retrieves him from the wings, "happy with her catch." The Wilis form a semicircular blockade through which Giselle bursts dramatically at upstage center, entreating Albert, "Get away from the queen.... You cannot stay, because it is death. Flee!" The lovers run up-stage, around the Wilis' line. A furious Myrtha orders her troupe to follow them. Creating a bit of stage magic, Albert and Giselle "place themselves on the gliding trap which soon conveys them to the cross": Giselle poses in *arabesque*, arms overhead, as Albert, kneeling and facing her, holds her by the waist.[95] Myrtha and the Wilis "are stupefied and raise their arms." As the lovers cling to the cross, Myrtha "runs toward them and goes to touch Albert with the branch, which breaks in her hand. She draws back, frightened, and then furious. She goes toward Giselle, touches her hand on Giselle's shoulder and [with] the other hand she forces her to leave the tomb.... 'You go dance, I wish it.'"

No. 14: Pas de deux. As recorded in the CN, the adagio begins with Giselle at center and Albert at the cross. Unassisted, Giselle performs *développé à la seconde* with the right leg, which then passes through fifth position to *arabesque*, *tour de promenade* to the right, *assemblé, entrechat six, petit développé* to right foot *tendu effacé devant fondu, degagé, grand rond de jambe en l'air fouetté*. "Quietly" is written above the notated phrase (Ex. 2.33a). Albert leaves the cross and approaches Giselle. Separately, the lovers trav-erse the stage several times, entreating the Wilis ("walk and ask"). All the Wilis refuse, replying "No!"

At center, Albert partners Giselle by the waist. Beginning with *sous-sus croisé*, she does *développé croisé devant* with the right leg, *grand rond de jambe en l'air, tour de prom-enade en arabesque* to *à la seconde en face*. Giselle "walks a little ahead" downstage right and continues with *tombé* on the right foot, *chassé, tour jeté*. She returns downstage right with *glissade, jeté, relevé développé croisé devant* twice. Two Wilis from each side run toward the lovers. Taking them by the shoulder and hand, "they walk away a few steps backward" before Giselle and Albert escape their grasp and return to center.

The lovers face each other, Giselle oriented toward upstage left, Albert holding her right hand in his. From fifth position on *pointe*, Giselle performs *développé devant* with the right leg, *fouetté arabesque*. After a *tour de promenade* to the right, Albert lifts Giselle: "carries on the chest and slowly puts her down on the floor." Traveling right, Giselle performs three *relevés en arabesque*. Albert then lifts her in *arabesque*. This is re-peated to the other side, then Giselle *bourrées* around Albert, "he goes down on his knee," and she poses next to him in *attitude à terre*.

---

[95] According to Ivor Guest, use of a similar mechanism was at least explored in Paris in 1863: "Another de-vice invented for this revival of *Giselle* was a sliding trap, on which Giselle and Albrecht were to glide towards the tomb at the end of Act II, but difficulty was experienced during rehearsals in keeping the mechanism greased, and the projected group may have been abandoned before the first performance." See Guest, *Second Empire 1858–1870*, 63.

The two pages of sketches by Pavel Gerdt, mentioned above, document the first part of the adagio, from its beginning through the supported *développé devant* that follows the moment when the Wilis pull the lovers apart. The detailed drawings both confirm and augment the choreography recorded in the CN, with only minor differences. Nine full-body drawings of Giselle document her opening solo movements. Albert, from the safety of the cross, reaches toward Giselle. After Giselle and Albert plead with each line of Wilis, they come together for the supported *tour de promenade en arabesque*, Giselle's raised arms creating a parallel line with her raised left leg. The next set of images documents Giselle's position in the air during her *tour jeté* traveling away from Albert as he reaches toward her with both arms. The following drawings depict the lovers' return downstage and the two supported *relevés développés*, shown to be performed *en effacé* with Giselle turned toward Albert as he holds her left wrist with his right hand. Next, as pairs of Wilis pull them toward the wings—each taking the lovers by the hand and shoulder, as described in the CN—Giselle and Albert look back at their captors. Gerdt then pleads with Myrtha. The Wili queen's head is turned away from Albert as she stands in what appears to be *tendu de côté fondu*, her right leg extended toward him, her torso leaning away, arms open to the side. In the final set of drawings, the lovers embrace. Still facing each other, Albert then supports Giselle in *développé devant*, holding her right hand with his. She is leaning far back with her left arm raised overhead. Albert stands in an open fourth position *fondu*, his left arm extended to the side.

Turning now to Justamant, we find a greater focus on dramatic action in the *pas de deux* as well as choreography that is both similar to and different from the CN. Strikingly, Giselle's opening solo adagio seems to encapsulate her dual nature as lover and Wili (a characteristic about which the CN is silent). Twice she performs *sous-sus, entrechat six, tombé plié, tour de promenade en arabesque*. After the first time, she runs toward Albert, "bringing a finger of her right hand to her mouth as if to recommend to him silence." After the second time, however, she remains in *arabesque* and reaches out with both of her arms, entreating him. Her lover cannot resist: "Albert, eyes staring at her, believes she calls him to leave the cross, and he goes to her." Myrtha "immediately mounts the grave with joy" as Albert leaves its protection. Giselle, having risen on the right *pointe* and extended her left leg forward, falls back. Albert "receives her in his right arm, looking at her with love," and the supported adagio begins. The lovers soon separate to beseech the Wilis at either side of the stage, and later Giselle entreats Myrtha again. However, they are not pulled apart by pairs of Wilis as in the CN and Gerdt's drawings. At the end of the *pas*, Giselle and Albert face each other, their arms overhead. Giselle inclines toward Albert, opening her arms, as he leans forward and kisses her forehead. Turning to the side, Giselle allows her face to fall into her hands, as though weeping.

Solos and duo. Both Justamant and the CN retain the series of short solos and duos that comprise the next number, though their recorded steps are largely different. During the musical transition following the adagio, Myrtha commands Giselle to dance, and she begins with an eight-bar solo. According to the CN, she travels upstage left from downstage center performing four *sissonnes double ronds de jambe en l'air* to alternate sides with a step back after each jump (Ex. 2.33b). She returns down the diagonal with a series of *sissonnes soubresauts*, her knees bent as in *temps de l'ange*. The last jump ends in *arabesque fondu* followed by *pas de bourrée* on *demi-pointe* to *attitude croisé à terre*. Justamant records equally vigorous choreography: alternating *sous-sus* and *temps de cuisse* are followed by three *entrechat six*, *entrechat sept*, another *temps de cuisse*, three *brisés, grand jeté en avant*.

Albert takes over from Giselle (his steps are not recorded in Justamant), traveling down the diagonal from upstage left with *pas de basque, temps levé en demi-arabesque, assemblé, sissonne ouverte battu* to *arabesque fondu, assemblé*, and three *entrechat six* twice. He traverses the downstage, right to left, with *glissade, sissonne ouverte* to *arabesque fondu* (the legs bent in the air), *assemblé* twice. He continues with *relevé à la seconde, passé développé* to *tendu croisé derrière fondu, grand port de bras, relevé tour en arabesque, plié, double pirouette* opening *à la seconde, fouetté arabesque à plat fondu*.

Albert runs to Giselle, now downstage left. He lifts her by the waist in successive *développés devant*, each separated by an *assemblé*. Each lift is higher than the previous one, the CN noting, "Giselle and Prince rise gradually, but higher and higher 4 times." A series of *sissonnes fermé* follows, then Giselle runs forward at center and finishes the number on her own. She performs *entrechats quatre* and *relevés petits passés*, traveling backward toward upstage right. Changing direction, she continues upstage with sixteen *entrechats quatre*. Next, she traverses the stage with a spring to *arabesque* on *pointe* three times, and *fouetté sauté* to change direction. She repeats the enchaînement, crossing right to left, and concludes with a diagonal of *emboîtés en tournant*.

Giselle's solo recorded in Justamant likewise is filled with continuous small jumps. Though none is repeated sixteen times, as we find in the CN, their variety is impressive and includes *brisé, sissonne en tournant, ballonné, jeté, fouetté sauté, assemblé, royale, entrechat sept*, and *glissades tacqueté*. The succession of three *arabesques* found in the CN are here performed as *piqués en arabesque* with a *pas de bourrée* and *grand assemblé* to change direction. Giselle finishes with a series of *pas de bourrée en tournant* and *échappés* followed by a *pirouette* to the knee.

Albert's variation. The CN's ground plan for the first enchaînement of Albert's variation reminds us that the Wilis continue to flank either side of the stage in lines of twelve. From a starting pose of *tendu croisé derrière* at upstage left, Albert travels down the diagonal with *glissade, cabriole devant*, two *demi-emboîtés derrière, assemblé*, three *entrechats six* twice (Ex. 2.33c). He returns up the diagonal with a *ballotté* and two *grands jetés en tournant* twice. After beseeching the Wilis, who respond "No!" he begins a final diagonal: two *cabrioles derrière* (without a step between), *jeté* twice, followed by *glissade, entrechat cinq de volée*, and four *pirouettes* to the knee—Albert "falls in exhaustion on Giselle's grave."

Like his earlier solo, Albert's variation is not documented in Justamant, which states merely, "Suit la variation d'Albert" (Albert's variation follows).

Giselle's interpolated waltz variation. While Justamant moves straight to the coda, the CN includes the interpolated waltz variation first performed in 1866 by Adèle Grantzow (see above; Ex 3.3). During the introduction, Giselle runs across the stage to meet Albert and says, "You remember I loved one there and danced." She runs away upstage left.

Tracing a wide zigzag, Giselle performs a series of *fouettés sautés* and *grands fouettés en tournant*, followed by *cabriole devant, pas de bourrée* twice. Arriving downstage right, she dances in place—a series of *entrechats quatre* alternating with *relevés double ronds de jambe en l'air* followed by *relevés en demi-attitude devant*, the body leaning forward then raising up, progressively higher with each *relevé*, the extended leg finally fully stretched. She repeats the *entrechats quatre* and *relevés ronds de jambe en l'air* then runs across the stage to Albert.

Giselle: "You come with me." She travels away from Albert with *piqués de côté en cou-de-pied devant* as she "lures him" (we remember the same annotation in the Act One *scène d'amour*). The ground plan suggests Albert does not follow Giselle but instead remains by her grave. She returns down the diagonal with *jetés en avant* "6 or 8 times??"—Sergeyev seems uncertain as to the number of repetitions. Giselle concludes with a pose in *arabesque à plat* and "runs away into the wings."

Coda. As in the Titus *répétiteur*, the coda in Justamant begins with a brief mime scene:

Albert feels himself weakening and cannot get a clear sense of what he is experiencing.

Giselle, who cannot quit looking at him, sees that he is suffering. She goes toward him with fear and urgency and asks, "What do you feel?"

Albert: "I do not know. My forces are abandoning me." Giselle takes him in her arms.

Myrtha, who fears her prey is escaping, goes toward Giselle to separate her from Albert. Giselle, seeing her coming, passes quickly to the other side of Albert without leaving him. Albert extends his arms as though to prevent Myrtha's advance.

The queen makes a sign to the two Wilis to seize Giselle. They immediately take hold of her and lead her upstage.

Albert: "Mercy for her."

Myrtha: (also going upstage) "No." (to Giselle) "And you, dance, again."

Albert goes upstage, overwhelmed.

Turning to the CN, we find this 24-bar scene is replaced with a dancing passage for the corps of Wilis. Remaining in their lines along the wings, they perform *temps levé, ballotté, saut de basque, pas de chat* four times. They *bourrée* upstage for four bars and back for four more.

Continuing with the CN, Albert dances next, traveling down the diagonal toward Myrtha (now Egorova) at downstage left. Facing upstage, he performs *chassé* (turning to his left), *tour jeté battu, glissade, entrechat cinq*, facing upstage again as he lands, three times. He begs Myrtha for mercy, but she replies, "No."

Circling the stage, he continues with a series of *temps de flèche derrière* and meets Giselle upstage left. The lovers traverse the stage, Giselle nearly gliding on its surface as she performs a series of four *temps levés en arabesque, assemblé, soubresaut*, her legs bent as in *temps de l'ange*, as Albert holds her by the waist throughout. They cross the stage three times then separate and circle upstage with four *temps levés en demi-arabesque*. Meeting at center, they exchange places twice in a fleuret pattern, performing *pas de bourrée, ballonné, temps de flèche devant* four times. The Wilis join in, repeating their *temps levé, ballotté, saut de basque, pas de chat* enchaînement twice. Side by side, Giselle and Albert travel forward with four *grands fouettés sautés*. Their steps are mirrored by the Wilis, who perform *ballonnés de côté* three times to alternate sides (followed by *bourrées* as they turn a circle in place). Albert falls in exhaustion. Giselle helps him to get up.

The CN offers more dancing for Albert in the coda than does Justamant, whose coda comprises a 16-bar solo for Giselle, an eight-bar solo for Albert (the only notated solo choreography for him in the production manual—the steps include a series of *brisé fouetté, jeté ordinaire,* and *temps de cuisse,* concluding with *chassé* and two *soubresauts*)—and a duo that resembles much of what is recorded in the CN.

No. 15. The finale preserved in the CN begins with a brief mimed exchange. Myrtha stands at center between the lovers.

Myrtha: (to Albert) "You must die here."

Giselle: "I beg you, I beg you."

Myrtha: "No!"

Giselle and Albert together ask for mercy, but Myrtha is resolute.

Alone, from upstage center, Albert performs a series of *sissonnes doublée.* The Wilis continue their incessant dance, performing *temps levés* followed by *bourrées* upstage and back. Albert falls again as four o'clock strikes: "Everyone listens to the sound of the tower clock" (a reference to a nearby church or other building). Dawn is approaching.

Giselle again begs Myrtha to save Albert. The queen "remains inexorable," claiming Albert will surely die.

The Wilis walk to center and form three rows, facing upstage. Myrtha remains downstage of her subjects, flanked by Moyna and Zulmé. Kneeling and bending far forward, their arms crossed on their chests, they next raise up, arms opening to first position, and "look at the sun." Rising onto *pointe,* the Willis *bourrée* into the wings, Myrtha and her lieutenants exiting downstage left.

Albert, exhausted, is barely able to get up. Giselle *bourrées* backward, away from Albert and toward her grave. Following her, he "picks up Giselle and carries her to another grave [the mound of flowers at stage left], thinking she will not leave this way. Albert runs and calls for someone to come. He returns to Giselle. She is on her grave, and he does not know what to do to keep her from disappearing again."

Giselle: "Farewell! Farewell!" Slowly, she goes down on her back and is gradually enclosed in her floral grave.

"Albert calls a second time for someone to help. His strength is fading, and he falls dead." Five "grandees" run on from upstage left. They surround Albert and find him dead as the ballet comes to an end.

That Albert dies rather than lives would seem to render meaningless much of the drama and suspense of the second act. In particular, Giselle's efforts to save him would be for naught. The 1889 reprinted libretto, based as it was on the 1841 Paris original, makes no mention of Albert's death. However, a 1910 synopsis of the ballet that accompanied New York performances of *Giselle* by The Imperial Russian Ballet and Orchestra, Anna Pavlova's touring company, closely matches the description in the CN:

> Albert, in his emotion, calls for help, but Giselle vanishes.
>
> Servants, responding to Albert's feeble call, find the broken-hearted nobleman prone upon the ground—dead.[96]

---

[96] Program book for New York performances of The Imperial Russian Ballet and Orchestra, 1910, unpaginated. The program listing states, "GISELLE, in two acts, Poem by Theophile Gautier, Music by Adolphe Adam, revived and rearranged by Mikhail Mordkin." The lengthy synopsis, which features a subtitle, "The Fairies of the Forest," restores the character names Loys, Wilfried (sic), and Bathilde. Hilarion remains Hans.

The Justamant finale remains closer in detail to the original libretto. As Giselle's spirit is waning with the rising sun, Wilfride comes to warn Albert of the imminent arrival of the Prince and Mathilde. After Giselle disappears, they enter with eight gamekeepers:

Albert with despair, gathers up some flowers from the tomb where Giselle has just disappeared and embraces them transportedly.

The Prince and Mathilde, seeing Albert, go toward him.

Albert sees them and, overwhelmed with sadness, falls into the arms of the Prince, reaching one hand to Mathilde.

As this account of the CN has shown, by the turn of the twentieth century the St. Petersburg *Giselle* had forgone its Act One *pas de deux*, a loss mitigated by the inclusion of the short *louré pas de deux* (also utilized in Paris) and the Cornalba variation. The production had also expunged Hilarion's introductory monologue, which set the tone of the ballet in the original production by providing the audience with important details of the plot. In Act Two, Albert's variation was followed by the inserted waltz variation for Giselle (again, the same solution incorporated in the Paris production nearly forty years prior), and the scene with the peasants and the Wilis' fugue were omitted.

In addition, just as we found that similarities between the Titus *répétiteur* and Justamant staging manual suggest a common origin, so too do the many similarities between the CN and the Justamant manual (structural, narrative, and choreographic) point to this same source—the 1841 Paris production—and confirm a high level of fidelity to the ballet's origins given the many years *Giselle* held the stage in the Russian capital. The changes in characterization that are familiar to audiences today (see the discussion of characters in Chapter 2), as well as the further shortening of the ballet, were yet to come.

Giselle's return to the West

In the new century, as Russian dancers increasingly organized and participated in international tours, *Giselle* became an attractive programming option for several reasons. It enjoyed a modicum of cachet as the foremost ballet of the bygone Romantic era, it could be performed with just three leading dancers (Giselle, Albert, and Myrtha), and it was short, and easily made even shorter, thereby allowing it to be paired on the same program with another work or a selection of divertissements. Act Two had already been somewhat streamlined with the elimination of the peasant scene and the Wilis' fugue, and now Act One received similar treatment in many touring productions with the omission of the Peasant *pas de deux* and the shortening of narrative passages.

As we briefly discuss *Giselle*'s re-entry into the Western ballet repertory during the first decades of the twentieth century, we will find three Russian ballerinas and one *régisseur* figuring prominently in the Russian diaspora: Anna Pavlova, Tamara Karsavina, Olga Spesivtseva, and, of course, Nikolai Sergeyev, who staged *Giselle* more than any other ballet after his emigration.

Anna Pavlova's international tours

Giselle was a staple of Pavlova's international touring repertory over the course of more than twenty years.[97] In 1908 and 1909, she performed *Giselle* with colleagues from the Imperial Ballet on European tours organized by the impresario Edvard Fazer.[98] From 1910, she toured a production credited to both Alexander Gorsky and her dancing partner Mikhail Mordkin.[99] And in 1913, Ivan Clustine restaged *Giselle* for Pavlova in a version she would continue to perform until 1930.[100]

A review by Carl Van Vechten of a matinee performance of *Giselle* given on 15 October 1910 at the Metropolitan Opera House in New York gives some sense of the drastic cuts that had been made in the ballet, in part, surely, because it was just one of several numbers on the program. His description notes various features of the truncated production and also expresses an ambivalence about Adam's score (an ambivalence that was shared by others in the West who assessed the score later in the twentieth century).[101] Van Vechten's assessment of the score likely had as much to do with a lack of understanding of the function of the music (to closely support the narrative) as it did with changing tastes:

> The music is gently fragrant, a little faded here and there, but a pretty score, and one of Adam's best. Cuts were made freely. In fact, almost one-half of the music had been taken out, and this was probably for the best, as far as present-day audiences are concerned. There was one interpolation. In the first act a waltz from Glazounov's *Raymonda* was introduced, which was very much as if some conductor had performed *Also Sprach Zarathustra* somewhere in *Fra Diavolo*.
>
> Mlle. Pavlova yesterday revivified this honeyfied and sentimental score of Adam's, full of the sad, gray splendor of the time of Louis Philippe [that is, 1830–1848]. Grisi is said to have been gently melancholy in it, but Pavlova was probably more than that. Her poetic conception of the betrothed girl's madness when she finds that her lover has deceived her, and her death, came very close to being tragic. It is almost impossible to describe the poetry of her dancing in the second act, where as one of the Wilis she engages in the wildest sort of measures under the forest trees.
>
> Mr. Mordkin has no dancing to do in this ballet, but in appearance and action he was superb.[102]

The 1910 Ballets Russes performances in Paris

After a hiatus of more than forty years, *Giselle* returned to the Paris Opéra stage on 18 June 1910 in a performance by Serge Diaghilev's Ballets Russes.[103] Tamara Karsavina led

---

[97] About Pavlova, see Lazzarini, *Pavlova*, and Jane Pritchard with Caroline Hamilton, *Anna Pavlova: Twentieth Century Ballerina*, rev. and extended ed. (UK: Booth-Clibborn, 2013).

[98] See Pritchard, *Pavlova*, 23–25, and Lazzarini, *Pavlova*, 13, 96.

[99] See Lazzarini, *Pavlova*, 219.

[100] Lazzarini, *Pavlova*, 168, 219.

[101] For instance, Roger Fiske described the score with similarly mixed sentiments as had Van Vechten: "The music, though far from great, is wonderfully effective in its place, and decidedly better than most ballet music of its day." Roger Fiske, *Ballet Music* (London: George G. Harrap, 1958), 15.

[102] "Russian Dancers Again Triumph Here," *New York Times*, 16 October 1910, 13.

[103] About the production, see S[erge] L[eonidovich] Grigoriev, *The Diaghilev Ballet: 1909–1929*, ed. and tr. Vera Bowen (UK: Penguin Books, 1960).

the cast, partnered by Vaslav Nijinsky as Albert, called Loys and then Prince of Thuringia in this production.[104] The particulars of the staging were credited as follows:

Danses et mise en scène d'après Marius PETIPA,
Fugue et variation de Mlle LOPOUKHOVA et M. NIJINSKY,
composées et réglées par M. FOKINE.[105]

Mikhail Fokine, then choreographic director of the Ballets Russes, supervised the production, which was based on the St. Petersburg staging. In addition to the usual characters (Hilarion and Bathilde were given their original names, but Berthe was simply "La mère de Giselle"), the cast featured a "valet d'armes" (perhaps the Wilfride role), a "page de Bathilde," and a "bouffon." Lydia Lopokova performed the role of "une paysanne." The action was set near Heidelberg, the second act in "Le Cimetière des Willis." As in the CN, Albert ultimately dies: "The Wilis disappear. The Prince leads Giselle back to her grave: he exchanges a final kiss with her. Then, overwhelmed by pain, he falls, and is united in death with the one he loves."

Two heavily marked piano reductions used in conjunction with the Ballets Russes production of *Giselle* are preserved in the Harvard Theatre Collection.[106] Of interest is the inclusion of the Cornalba variation (as a single-violin *répétiteur*) as well as a variation from Lev Ivanov's ballet *The Haarlem Tulip* (a two-violin *répétiteur*, no composer credited) with "La variation d'homme pour Giselle 1er acte" written in pencil on the title page (Ex. 3.7).[107] (*The Haarlem Tulip*, with a score by Boris Fitinhof-Schell, was created in 1887 for the Italian ballerina Emma Bessone and revived in 1903.)

An annotation at the end of the shortened *louré* suggests these variations followed it in what seems to have been an attempt to fashion something of a traditional *pas de deux* from several disparate numbers: "Variations de la danseuse et du danseur puis Suite p. 32" (page thirty-two being the first page of the heavily cut march of the vinegatherers).[108] Taking these numbers together with information from additional annotations in the scores, we find the danced numbers in the first act were grouped together in one unit, beginning with the waltz, which was performed in its usual place. The order appears to have been:

Waltz
Flute solo from Giselle and Loys's Act One *pas de deux* (Ex. 3.11b)
> An annotation in item 205 states, "Variation of one of the peasant girls, to be danced by Lopokhova or [Elena] Poliakova." Six bars are struck through in item 205, and the entire variation is struck through in item 206.

[104] Our reference is the published scenario included in a program for a 10 April 1911 performance in Monte Carlo courtesy of Andrew Foster. About Karsavina, see Foster, *Karsavina*, especially 90–101, and Karsavina, *Theatre Street*.

[105] Printed program for the 1910 Ballets Russes Paris season courtesy of Andrew Foster.

[106] S[erge] L[eonidovich] Grigoriev papers, MS Thr 465 (205 and 206), Harvard Theatre Collection, Houghton Library, Harvard University. Both copies are the Cornette reduction and are heavily annotated with cuts, information about interpolations, and stage directions. Item 205 includes manuscript interpolated music. A note in Russian on the back cover of item 206 reads: "Score with notes by S.P. Diagilev [sic] and M.M. Fokin [sic]."

[107] Another annotation, at the top of the title page, reads "for the ballet *Vain precautions* [*La Fille mal gardée*] | man's variation in 'Pas de deux.'"

[108] This annotation is found in item 205.

Ex. 3.7 Variation from *The Haarlem Tulip* (Fitinhof-Schell?), bars 1–9 (source: MS Thr 465 [205])

Louré (shortened and marked "Pas de deux")
The Haarlem Tulip variation
Cornalba variation

> Various annotations disagree as to the order of these two variations, with most suggesting the *Haarlem Tulip* variation preceded the Cornalba. The manuscript scores are bound in item 205 in this order.

March

The galop is struck through. Berthe's entrance follows the march, and the subsequent hunt scene proceeded directly to the finale and mad scene. In Act Two, the Grantzow variation (a single-violin *répétiteur*) is inserted after Albert's variation.[109]

Our description here is based on a preliminary assessment of these heavily annotated scores. Further study will undoubtedly yield more precise details. Ballet Russes *régisseur* Serge Grigoriev attributed the cuts, revisions, and interpolations directly to Diaghilev, noting the Act Two fugue was reinstated for the production.[110] The choreography attributed to Fokine appears to include the fugue, the flute solo for Lopokova, and a variation for Nijinsky, possibly that from *The Haarlem Tulip*.[111]

---

[109] Like the other manuscript interpolations, this one is included in item 205.
[110] Grigoriev, *Diaghilev Ballet*, 43. The fugue is struck through in item 205.
[111] The flute solo danced by Lopokova and the fugue were mentioned in a press notice in *Le Figaro*, 20 June 1910, 5, and in a review by Adolphe Jullien in *Journal des Débats*, 26 June 1910, 1.

Grigoriev summed up the audience response and also indicated the attitude toward *Giselle* behind the scenes:

> To lovers of pure classical dancing the performances of Karsavina and Nijinsky were a delight; while the charming settings by [Alexandre] Benois and the perfection of the *ensembles* produced an excellent impression. On the whole, however, the ballet failed to win the success hoped for by Benois and the rest of us. Diaghilev was proved right in predicting as he had at St Petersburg that it was not what the Paris public would wish to see danced by Russians. They in fact found *Giselle* old-fashioned and lacking in excitement. But its comparative failure had no adverse effect on our season as a whole. The theatre continued to be packed as before; and no one except Diaghilev really minded about *Giselle*.[112]

Giselle remained in the Ballets Russes repertory until 1914, with Karsavina dancing every performance except for two featuring Pavlova.[113] After Enrico Cecchetti joined the company in 1911, he performed the role of Giselle's mother, as did Nikolai Kremnev in later performances.[114] (The role was performed by Raisa Matskevich in the 1910 Paris premiere.)

Karsavina had first essayed the role of Giselle in Prague on 24 April 1909 in a production by Achille Viscusi, who also partnered her as Albert.[115] In 1910, she danced thirty-six performances of the second act of *Giselle* (titled *Gisela*) with Fedor Kozlov at the London Coliseum just ahead of the Paris season of the Ballet Russes.[116] Her St. Petersburg debut as Giselle, in which she was partnered by Samuil Andrianov, followed later that year on 26 September.[117] On 23 January 1911, Karsavina led the notorious performance in which her partner Vaslav Nijinsky's costume caused a scandal that led to his dismissal from the Imperial Ballet.[118] Her last *Giselle* at the Mariinsky was given on 15 May 1918, with Petr Vladimirov as her Albert.[119] As noted earlier, Karsavina's illuminating writings on *Giselle* (some of which have been quoted in this chapter) are preserved in part in her *Lost Steps* series published in *The Dancing Times* in the 1950s. Over the course of several installments, she discusses step execution, stagecraft, and the character of Giselle, all in relation to the St. Petersburg production.[120]

---

[112] Grigoriev, *Diaghilev Ballet*, 47.

[113] Pavlova's performances were given on 28 October and 6 November 1911. See Foster, *Karsavina*, 98–99.

[114] See printed programs included in MS Thr 465 (242). See also Richard Buckle, *Diaghilev* (London: Weidenfeld and Nicolson, 1979), 209 and 211.

[115] Foster, *Karsavina*, 93–96.

[116] Ibid., 98.

[117] Ibid., 99. See also *Khronika IV*, 134–135, in which the editors list Gerdt in the role of Albert and Andrianov as the "Sovereign prince"; the printed program confirms Andrianov danced the role of Albert and Gerdt performed as the Duke (*Herzog*).

[118] Andrew Foster has asserted that Matilda Kshesinskaya was responsible for sabotaging Nijinsky in an attempt to thwart Karsavina, her primary competition. See Andrew Foster, "Kschessinska versus Nijinsky" [part one], *Dancing Times* 111, no. 1324 (December 2020), 24–27; [part two] *Dancing Times* 111, no. 1325 (January 2021), 20–23; and *Khronika IV*, 139. See also Foster, *Karsavina*, 133.

[119] Foster, *Karsavina*, 100 and 233.

[120] "Lost Steps (I): 'Giselle'," *Dancing Times* New Series, no. 517 (October 1953): 9–10; "Lost Steps (II): Second Act Of Giselle," *Dancing Times* New Series, no. 518 (November 1953): 75; "Lost Steps (III): Giselle's Character," *Dancing Times* New Series, no. 519 (December 1953): 139; "Lost Steps (V): Stage Illusions," *Dancing Times* New Series, no. 512 (February 1954): 281–282.

The 1924 Paris Opéra revival

A third ballerina associated with the return of *Giselle* to the West was Olga Spesivtseva, who had made her *Giselle* debut in Petrograd on 30 March 1919. Her ethereal quality in the second act was regarded as an ideal embodiment of the Romantic era.[121]

The Paris Opéra revival on 26 November 1924 marked the return of *Giselle* to the Opéra repertory after an absence of fifty-six years. Spesivtseva danced the title role partnered by *étoile* Albert Aveline. The production was staged by Nikolai Sergeyev using the Stepanov notations of the ballet. (Incidentally, the program mistakenly credited Sergeyev as choreographer rather than stager.) According to Ivor Guest, Jacques Rouché, director of the Opéra from 1914 to 1945, "had originally thought of inviting [Olga] Preobrazhenskaya to stage [*Giselle*], but in the end he entrusted the task to Nicolai Sergueyev. . . . The shy, dedicated young ballerina [Spesivtseva] was happy to be working with a compatriot."[122] Indeed, as Sergey Konaev has revealed, Spesivtseva valued Sergeyev and advocated for his return to Petrograd from Riga, where he established and led the ballet of the Latvian National Opera from 1922 to 1925. At her request, "Sergeyev was invited to the Paris Opéra for the landmark revival of Giselle."[123] As Konaev notes, "The ballerina would agree more easily to an engagement abroad if she knew Sergeyev would stage it."[124]

Sergeyev was sought after as a stager. Konaev explains how he had the upper hand over other Russian emigrés:

> Despite the large number of Russian ballet troupes that toured the West and sometimes staged adapted versions of the classics, Sergeev was indeed almost the only balletmaster in exile who knew the Mariinsky Theater performances "in detail." His credibility was reinforced by his professional experience, choreographic notation, and *régisseur*'s music library.[125]

As the printed program for the revival shows, Sergeyev staged a reduced version of what he had known in St. Petersburg and what his notations prescribed. The corps de ballet numbered just eighteen women and five men. The Peasant *pas de deux* is not mentioned. The credits and main roles were listed thus:

Giselle ou Les Wilis

Ballet-Pantomime en 2 actes, de Saint-Georges,
Théophile Gautier et Coraly

Musique de Adolphe Adam
Chorégraphie de M. Nicolas Serguéev
Décors et costumes d'après les maquettes de M. Alexandre Benois
Décors executes par M. Nicolas Benois
Costumes de la Maison Muelle

---

[121] *Khronika IV*, 230–231. Spesivtseva was partnered by Petr Vladimirov.
[122] Ivor Guest, *The Paris Opéra Ballet* (Alton, UK: Dance Books, 2006), 78.
[123] Konaev, "My vse visim v vozdukhe," 561.
[124] Ibid.
[125] Ibid., 559.

Sous la direction de M. Henri Büsser

Giselle	Mlles	Spessivtzeva
La Reine des Wilis		de Crappone
Comtesse Bathilde		Soutzo
2 Wilis		Rousseau
		Damazio
La Mère		B. Kerval
Albert	MM.	A. Aveline
Hilarion		P. Raymond
Le Duc		Ryaux
L'Ecuyer		Peretti

The conductor Henri Busser was credited with restoring Adam's orchestration. André Rigaud announced details in *Comoedia*: "Henri Busser, who will conduct the orchestra, has restored Adolphe Adam's music to its romantic character, with the harp, flute and viola solos of yesteryear."[126] Busser published a piano reduction of his "révision et arrangement" in 1943.[127] Described as "Version du Théâtre National de l'Opéra de Paris," the score is severely cut, mostly within narrative numbers, though it does include both the Cornalba and Grantzow interpolated variations. Whether the published score represents that used in 1924, we have not confirmed.[128] Moreover, we note that while the orchestra parts in use at the Opéra through 1868 include cuts and interpolated numbers as discussed in this chapter, they do not show signs of reorchestration of Adam's score.

André Levinson gave the performance a mixed review:

The program, which, moreover, abounds in errors, attributes by an inconceivable misunderstanding the choreography of the piece to M. Nicolas Sergueev. The latter who, having completed his studies at the imperial school, was for many years regisseur at the Mariinsky Theatre, applied himself with rare patience to "notate" according to the Stepanoff method the principal ballets of the repertoire. His precious notebooks allow him today to reconstruct *Giselle* exactly according to Petipa. He has never, as far as I know, composed by himself. This conscientious and faithful man swears only *in verba magistri*. He attaches himself with the same obstinacy to the imperishable beauties of the work as to certain secondary and out-of-date details of staging. His *Giselle* has the truth of a meticulous copy. This is not the whole truth.

It lacks the supreme virtue of a work: the real presence of a creator, the breath of inspiration.[129]

---

[126] *Comoedia*, 26 November 1924, 1. André Schakevich provides further detail about Busser's work on the score: "There came, first of all, a revision of the score which has been not a little mutilated since its first performance. The conductor Henri Busser, who was to be in charge of the first performance, consulted the Opéra's library and adopted the orchestration as found in Adolphe Adam's manuscript." Schaikevich, *Olga Spessivtseva, magicienne envoutée* (Libraire Les Lettres: Paris, 1954), [page number not given], tr. in Crisp, "*Giselle* Revived," 56.

[127] Adolphe Adam, *Giselle, ou, Les wilis: Ballet-pantomime en deux actes de Théophile Gautier et Saint-Georges. Revision et arrangement de Henri Busser* (Paris: Editions Max Eschig, 1943).

[128] The extant orchestra parts do not appear to have been used in the performances of the revival. Rather, annotations in the copied orchestra score, A-533 (A 1–3), suggest that it may have served as a source for the 1924 score.

[129] *Comoedia*, 28 November 1924, 1.

Levinson went on to complain further that, despite "complete fidelity to the best choreographic tradition," the production did not completely succeed due to an "absolute lack of theatrical sense" on the part of Sergeyev. The first act was compared unfavorably to a recent Paris production of *Giselle* staged by former Mariinsky dancer and choreographer Boris Romanov and presented by Ballet Romantiques Russes at the Théatre des Champs-Élysées: "We were far from the wonderful animation, from the powerful rhythm achieved by Boris Romanoff in his memorable version of the first act."[130]

Levinson's objections notwithstanding, he praised Spesivtseva, concluding, in heady terms, "All these significant reservations do not in any way effect the very great success of a performance in which we have seen the character of a beautiful dancer strive victoriously for a work of the noblest inspiration."[131]

Giselle remains in the repertory of the Paris Opéra to this day.

Sergeyev's subsequent stagings

Eight years after the Paris revival, Sergeyev staged *Giselle* for London's Camargo Society. The production premiered at the Savoy Theatre on 20 June 1932 and featured Spesivtseva as Giselle partnered by Anton Dolin in his debut as Albrecht, as the character was named, with Frederick Ashton as Hilarion. The costumes were borrowed from the Anna Pavlova Company, and Spesivtseva wore her costumes (designed by Benois) from the Paris revival.[132] The Savoy season also included Sergeyev's staging of the second scene of *Swan Lake* (called *Le Lac des cygnes Act II*).[133] Kathrine Sorley Walker noted that these two ballets represented "the first large-scale productions by a British company of authentic Russian versions."[134] Brief performance footage of Spesivtseva as Giselle in Act One reveals what seems to be a robust characterization in the mold of the nineteenth-century Giselles revealed in our sources.[135]

Sergeyev next staged *Giselle* for the Vic-Wells Ballet in 1934, having already staged the first two acts of *Coppélia* for the company the year before. The premiere was given on 1 January at the Old Vic, with Alicia Markova making her debut in what would become her most celebrated role. Stanley Judson replaced an indisposed Dolin as Albrecht, and Robert Helpmann "managed to make quite a lot of the subsidiary part of Hilarion," according to Mary Clarke, a comment reminding us how much the role had already lost over time.[136] Margot Fonteyn made her debut in the title role on 19 January 1937, partnered by Helpmann. Footage of the pair shows them dancing part of the *louré pas de deux* in a performance at Sadler's Wells Theatre that same year.[137]

---

[130] The Ballet Romantiques Russes production, described as a "paraphrase chorégraphique de Boris Romanoff," opened on 16 April 1924 and featured Mariinsky dancers Elena Smirnova and Anatole Obukhov in the leading roles. The program book for the season is preserved as *Recueil factice de programmes et articles de presse concernant Boris Romanoff et les ballets romantiques russes, avril 1924*, Paris, Bibliothèque Nationale de France, Département des Arts du Spectacle, 4-RO-12786.

[131] *Comoedia*, 28 November 1924, 1.

[132] Angela Kane and Jane Pritchard, "The Camargo Society Part I," *Dance Research* 12, no. 2 (Autumn 1994): 52–53.

[133] Kathrine Sorley Walker, "The Camargo Society," *Dance Chronicle* 18, no. 1 (1995): 43–45.

[134] Ibid., 43.

[135] Huntley Film Archives, film 1015266, https://www.youtube.com/watch?v=E6stekrYaWk.

[136] Mary Clarke, *The Sadler's Wells Ballet: A History and an Appreciation* (New York: Da Capo Press, 1977), 93.

[137] The footage is available online at https://www.youtube.com/watch?v=6Sc3ZLBESTU.

Sergeyev's staging for the short-lived Markova-Dolin Ballet, which premiered in 1935, is particularly significant because it served as the basis for Cyril Beaumont's detailed analysis and description of the ballet included in his important monograph, *The Ballet Called Giselle*, first published in 1944.[138] (A brief material reminder of Sergeyev's work with Dolin is preserved on an inside cover page of the CN, where a penciled annotation reads, "on Wednesday 11 [September 1935] in the morning Dolin.")

The International Ballet production of *Giselle*, Sergeyev's fourth staging of the ballet in England, was first performed on 15 September 1942 at His Majesty's Theatre, London, with the company's director Mona Inglesby and Harold Turner in the leading roles.[139] Sergeyev's work with International Ballet was possibly that in which he enjoyed the most freedom due to the willingness of Inglesby to grant him maximum authority over the productions he staged.

In 1947, the Peasant *pas de deux* was added to International Ballet's production of *Giselle*. A note accompanying a listing of the company's repertory in the 1948 *Ballet Annual* states: "In 1947 Serguéeff reintroduced the peasant *pas de deux* into Act I. It is believed that no other company includes this dance."[140]

Finally, crossing the Atlantic, we note one last staging that involved, perhaps surprisingly, George Balanchine. On 15 October 1946 at the Broadway Theater in New York, Ballet Theatre premiered a production of *Giselle* credited to Dimitri Romanoff, "with contributions by George Balanchine and Antony Tudor."[141] The Cuban ballerina Alicia Alonso danced the title role, partnered by Igor Youskevitch. As described in the catalog of his works, "Balanchine arranged the traditional Maryinsky staging of Giselle's grave scene in Act II: Albrecht prevents Giselle from disappearing into her grave and lays her on a bed of flowers; but Giselle sinks away and only the flowers remain."[142] Youskevitch recalled the moment as well as Balanchine's approach:

In his own works Balanchine was contemporary and forward-looking in his invention. In regard to classical ballet, he was just the opposite. He was at American Ballet Theatre when Lucia Chase decided to stage *Giselle*. . . . Balanchine advised us on certain scenes. One change he insisted on was to do the old Russian version of the ending of the second act. Instead of Giselle returning to her original grave, Albrecht would pick her up and bring her across the stage and deposit her in another grave. This grave was mechanical. When she was placed on it she would go down, grass would grow on top, and she would disappear. Dramatically, it didn't work at all. People laughed. I was looking for Giselle in the grass! It lasted, I think, one performance.[143]

The original ending may not have survived in the Ballet Theatre production, but Balanchine's allegiance to the traditions of his years in St. Petersburg/Petrograd is both a reminder of the enduring lineage of *Giselle* and a connection all the way back to Adam, who first had the idea for such an elegiac ending:

---

[138] Beaumont's analysis and description are found on pp. 85–125.
[139] Inglesby, *Ballet in the Blitz*, 49.
[140] *The Ballet Annual*, Second Issue, Arnold L. Haskell, ed. (London: A. & C. Black, 1948), 161.
[141] American Ballet Theatre, *Giselle* press kit, 2001–2002.
[142] Leslie George Katz, Nancy Lassalle, and Harvey Simmonds, eds. *Choreography by George Balanchine: A Catalog of Works* (Viking: New York, 1984), 173–174.
[143] Francis Mason, *I Remember Balanchine* (New York: Doubleday, 1991), 301.

I composed this music with happiness. I was in a hurry, which always fires my imagination. I was very close with Perrot, with Carlotta; the work was set up, so to speak, in my living room. At the dress rehearsal, I made a change that was approved by my collaborators, by Saint-Georges and Théophile Gautier. Giselle, at the first rays of day, returned to her tomb. I did not find this ending poetic enough. I had the idea for her to be carried by her lover to a bush of flowers, and to make her disappear little by little. This dénouement better ended this legend full of poetry and had all the success I expected.[144]

---

[144] Qtd. in Arthur Pougin, *Adolphe Adam: Sa vie, sa carrière, ses mémoires artistiques* (Paris, 1877), 162. Available online at https://gallica.bnf.fr/ark:/12148/bpt6k64572131/f7.item.texteImage.

4

Paquita in Paris and Lyon

Carlotta Grisi's spectacular success in *Giselle* led to a series of new starring roles for her at the Opéra. First came Beatrix, a Flemish goldsmith's daughter who makes a daring trip to Venice in *La Jolie fille de Gand* (1842). Next was the Persian fairy who appeared in an opium dream to an Egyptian man in *La Péri* (1843). Then came Mazourka in the comedic romp *Le Diable à quatre* (1845), which required Grisi, as a rebellious Polish housewife, to inhabit the body of a snooty Countess.

In the spring of 1846, audiences eagerly awaited their next chance to see the versatile Grisi in a new role, this time in a yet-to-be-named "ballet-impérial," as the newspaper columnists referred to it, for it was set in the period of the Napoleonic empire—specifically, in the year 1810—in French-occupied Spain. Though Napoleon had been dead for more than twenty years at the time of *Paquita*'s premiere, his memory in France remained alive and his admirers ever fervent. Bonapartists had been forced to keep their true loyalties (and their Napoleon-themed merchandise) under wraps during the Restoration of the Bourbons (1815–1830). But the new regime that rose to power in 1830 under King Louis-Phillipe loosened official suppression of Bonapartist enthusiasm.[1] And in December 1840, despite the protests of his detractors, Napoleon's mortal remains were returned with great fanfare to Paris from the island of St. Helena. After arriving at Neuilly, the Emperor's coffin was conveyed in a magnificent procession to Paris and around the city to the strains of specially commissioned funeral marches composed by Adolphe Adam and Daniel Auber. Followed by thousands of Parisians the procession made its way to the Invalides, where Mozart's Requiem was sung by the city's top opera stars.[2] The

---

[1] Sudhir Hazareesingh argues that during the 1830s, Napoleon was "officially incorporated into the memory of the French state" with the placement of a statue of Napoleon on the Vendome column, the completion of the Arc de Triomphe, and the return of Napoleon's remains to the Invalides in 1840. Sudhir Hazareesingh, "Napoleonic Memory in Nineteenth-Century France: The Making of a Liberal Legend," *Modern Language Notes* 120, no. 4 (September 2005), 761–762. See also Sudhir Hazareesingh, *The Legend of Napoleon* (London: Granta UK, 2005), in which he describes the brisk trade in Napoleon souvenirs (63–98) and the subversive displays of loyalty to Napoleon (122–150), and Jean Tulard, "Le retour des cendres," in Pierra Nora (ed.), *Les lieux de mémoire* (Paris: Gallimard, 1986), vol. 2 (2), 81–110.

[2] "Mmes Grisi, Damoreau, Persiani and Dorus, sopranos; Pauline Garcia, Eugénia Garcia, Albertazzi and Stolz, contraltos; Rubini, Duprez, Ponchard, Alexis Dupont and Nasset, tenors; and Lablache, Tamburini, Levasseur, Baroilhet and Alizard, basses." J[acques]-G[abriel] Prod'homme, "Napoleon, Music and Musicians," tr. Frederick H. Martens, *Musical Quarterly* 7, no. 4 (October 1921), 604. Of their performance, and of the specially commissioned funeral marches, Adolphe Adam wrote in a letter to a friend: "Never has this master-piece by Mozart been sung with such brilliance. The dress rehearsal was held at the Opéra, before an immense assembly of people and caused a tremendous sensation. After the mass the three funeral marches composed by Auber, Halévy and myself were played, and on this occasion I had the pleasure of triumphing over my two illustrious rivals. Auber's march made no impression whatever; that of Halévy was judged to be a fine symphonic composition, lacking the character demanded by the occasion. My own was more fortunate: I had written it in two sections, one funereal, and the other triumphant; and this contrast was perfectly grasped by the public, which understood as well as I did, that this funeral, taking place twenty years after the hero's death, should be a triumph.

"The day of the ceremony, together with my two hundred musicians, I went to Neuilly, where Napoleon's casket was to be disembarked, to conduct these marches. Unfortunately, the cold was so excessive that the artists

day's events were evocatively described by Victor Hugo and soon published as "Funérailles de l'empereur Napoléon."[3]

All of this is to say that the "ballet-impérial" *Paquita*'s setting during Napoléon's heyday may reasonably have been expected by the Opéra's directors to have been welcomed by ballet-goers in 1846. Playing to the audience's nostalgia, and perhaps to its pride in the days of France's rule over most of Spain, the new ballet offered a plot that depicted its French characters more favorably than its Spanish ones and featured splendidly reproduced uniforms of Napoleon's army.[4]

Further, Bonapartism aside, the new ballet's location in a craggy setting in the Valley of the Bulls near Saragossa was another likely draw, for it held exotic appeal and allowed for the inclusion of plenty of Spanish character dance, which French audiences particularly favored.

Of the five ballets we examine in this volume, the original French version of *Paquita* is the least known today. First performed on 1 April 1846, the ballet (with libretto by Paul Foucher, music by Édouard Deldevez, and choreography by Joseph Mazilier) found success in Paris and remained in the Opéra's repertory for five years. When *Paquita* went to Russia in 1847, its divertissements were altered and supplemented with new dances by Pierre Frédéric Malavergne and Marius Petipa. More than thirty years later, in 1881, Petipa again made changes to the ballroom scene in the Russian production (using music by Minkus and others), the most significant being the additions of the children's mazurka and the *Grand pas*.

Paquita, as most audiences know it today, is this justly famous and highly popular *Grand pas*, which includes variations that have been interpolated over the years since 1881. The cloak-and-dagger comedy-drama that led up to the final ballroom scene was scuttled early in the twentieth century, and the *Grand pas*—occasionally bearing some resemblance to the one created in 1881—was usually danced on its own. However, several complete productions have been presented since 2001, when Pierre Lacotte staged a full *Paquita* for the Paris Opéra Ballet.

In this chapter, we shall describe in some detail the original *Paquita*, showing that it was a melodramatic ballet in which mime and action scenes predominated until the climactic ball that ends the ballet, and that its score was attentive to the widely varying needs of the ballet, which included skullduggery, a love story, the presence of three distinct ethnic groups, and dances of several types.

Spanish dance. Before proceeding further, let us pause to consider Spanish character dance. Parisian audiences' long-time fondness for character dance in general burst into a full-blown mania in the 1830s, and by 1840 one eulogist of the recently deceased Pierre

---

and their instruments were frozen, and the performance was a very defective one. During the entire progress of the procession, my musicians played my march and that of Auber. Halévy's march could not be played, because his symphony was too difficult to execute, and not sufficiently rhythmic to allow it to be marched to."

[3] Victor Hugo, "Funérailles de l'empereur Napoléon: détails circonstanciés des actes qui ont signalé la journée du 15 décember, 1840" (Genève: imprimerie de Vaney, 1840). Later editions include "15 décembre 1840. Funérailles de l'Empereur. Notes prises sur place." *Choses vues*—in *Œuvres complètes, histoire* (Paris: Robert Laffont, 1987), 808–809, 815. Hugo's description is available online at https://fr.wikisource.org/wiki/Choses_vues/1840/Funérailles_de_Napoléon.

[4] See https://library.brown.edu/info/collections/askb/veterans/ for photographs of members of Napoleon's army probably taken 5 May 1858 on the thirty-fifth anniversary of Napoleon's death. The uniformed men depicted are in their seventies and eighties.

Gardel could lament that "the dance [at the Opéra is now] composed of only so-called *pas de caractère*."[5] Such *pas* covered a wide geographical range: from Naples, the tarantella; from Sicily, the sicilienne; from Poland, the redowa, varsovienne, krakowiak, mazurka; from Spain, the bolero, cachucha, and Jaleo de Xeres; the Tyrol, Styria, Russia, Scotland, Lithuania, and many other places were represented as well.

The new wave of popularity of Spanish dance in particular at the Opéra may be traced back to the sensational appearance there in January 1834 of four Spanish dancers—including Dolores Serral and Mariano Camprubì—who danced both in the Opéra's Carnival balls and in the Spanish dance scene in *La Muette de Portici*.[6] Reviews of this couple tell us of their dancing's passionate, fiery and voluptuous quality, and of their twisting torsos and arched backs. Théophile Gautier even recommended that the Opéra hire them on a permanent basis. His descriptions are particularly vivid, including this one:

> They dance with their whole body, they arch their backs, bend sideways, and twist their torsos with the suppleness of an almeh or a grass snake. In poses renversées the dancer's shoulders almost touch the ground; her arms, dreamy and passive, have a flexibility and a limpness like that of a loosened scarf. . . . [T]his voluptuous languor is succeeded by leaps of a young jaguar. . . . Spanish male dancers . . . always appear to be passionately in love. . . . [Insolently holding their bodies back], they possess a certain ferocious grace, a particular allure . . . which is theirs alone.[7]

Nor did Gautier shrink from making damning comparisons between these Spanish dancers and classically trained ballet dancers at the Opéra, comparisons that articulate the prevailing essentialist point of view as well as Gautier's personal yearning for more variety of style in dance in ballet. His comparisons also offer useful specific details about Serral and Camprubí's movements and style:

> Dolores and Camprubí have nothing in common with our own dancers. They have a passion, a vitality and an attack of which you can have no idea. . . . There is nothing mechanical in their dancing, nothing that appears copied or smacks of the classroom. Their dancing is an expression of temperament rather than a conforming to a set of principles; every gesture is redolent of the fiery Southern blood. Such dancing as this with blonde hair would be a complete contradiction.[8]

> The lady is young, light, free in her poses, forming her attitudes with admirable clarity, producing her sparkling smile only when the moment is opportune, barely raising the sequined folds of her basquine above the knee, and never indulging in those awful *écarts* of the leg that make a woman look like an open compass.[9]

[5] *Le Courrier des théâtres*, 10 and 14 November 1840, tr. in Guest, *Romantic Ballet in Paris*, 2nd ed., 94.

[6] The Opéra held carnival-season balls for the public, and entertainers customarily appeared at some point during the evening and performed in a space cleared for them on the dance floor while the ball attendees stood by and watched. The Opéra also hired guests, or its own dancers, to lead some of the dances for the attendees. See Arkin and Smith, "National Dance," 18–19.

[7] Gautier, *Voyage en Espagne* (Paris: Charpentier, 1845), ch. 12, tr. in Ivor Guest, "Théophile Gautier on Spanish Dancing," *Dance Chronicle* 10, no. 1 (1987): 7.

[8] *La charte de 1830*, 18 April 1837, tr. in Gautier, *Gautier on Dance*, 8.

[9] Ibid., 7–8.

The January 1834 triumph of Serral and Camprubì led directly to a plan, in the succeeding Opéra carnival season (winter 1834–1835), to present principal ballet dancers—not dancers from outside the ballet world—performing a variety of character dances as ballroom entertainment. As *Vert-Vert* reported it,

> The great success obtained at the last Carnival gave rise to the idea of seeking a new success with an array of national dances of the different peoples of Europe and in some local dances from our southern provinces. Thus we will see the execution in turn by the leading principal ballet dancers of the Opéra, with Mlles. Taglioni and Elssler leading, of the *pas styrien*, the mazurka, boleros and fandangos from Andalusia, the tarantellas of Naples, and dances of the Languedoc region—*las Treias* and *lo Chibalet*.[10]

Thereafter, principal ballet dancers (including blond ones) expanded their repertories to include character dance of all sorts and began performing it regularly on the stage of the Paris Opéra. One of the first was Fanny Elssler, who in 1836 at the Opéra, in the role of a Spanish dancer named "Florinda" in a new ballet called in *Le Diable boiteux*, stunned the audience with her performance of the cachucha (a dance first introduced to Paris by Dolores Serral).[11] Of the cachucha—a solo dance in triple meter, performed with castanets—Gautier wrote:

> [It] is a national dance of a primitive character. . . . It is a charming poem written in the twisting of the hips, sidelong expressions, a foot advanced and then withdrawn, all joyfully accompanied by the chatter of castanets and having more to say on its own than volumes of erotic verse.[12]

A quick glance at few reviews can offer a sense of the highly favorable reception with which the cachucha was received in Paris and beyond when danced by Elssler and others:

> Those swayings of the hips . . . those provocative gestures . . . and, above all, Elssler's sensuous grace, lascivious abandon, and plastic beauty were all greatly appreciated by the opera-glasses of the stalls and boxes.[13] (Paris, 1836)

> Never in our remembrance is there a pas de caractère so beautiful as the *Double Cachucha* danced by her [Fanny Cerrito] and [Jules] Perrot. . . . [W]hen the cachucha really does begin, it is an inspiration; she is a creature of fire. It is in the Spanish spirit

[10] *Vert-Vert*, 24 December 1834.

[11] So says Gautier in *La Presse*, 2 October 1837, tr. in Gautier, *Gautier on Dance*, 18. Dolores Serral, he writes, "was the first to import the *Cachucha* to Paris and has been imitated, first by Fanny Elssler and now by Mlle Noblet. In spite of the great reputation and higher standing of her rivals, Dolores Serral is still to the best of our knowledge the leading exponent of the *cachucha* and the *bolero*."

[12] Gautier wrote this description after seeing Dolores Serral. Gautier, *La chart de 1830*, 18 April 1837, tr. in Gautier, *Gautier on Dance*, 8. The cachucha, as notated by Friedrich Zorn in 1887, has been translated into Labanotation by Ann Hutchinson Guest in *Fanny Essler's "Cachucha"* (London: Dance Books, 1981). Zorn's notation may be found in *Grammatik der Tanzkunst. Theoretischer und praktischer Unterricht in der Tanzkunst und Tanzschreibkunst oder Choreographie nebst Atlas mit Zeichnungen und musikalischen Übungs-Beispielen mit choreographischer Bezeichnung und einem besonderen Notenheft für den Musiker* (Leipzig: J. J. Weber, 1887; Hildesheim: OLMS, 1982). An English edition was edited by Alfonso Josephs Sheafe as *Grammar of the Art of Dancing: Theoretical and Practical: Lessons in the Arts of Dancing and Dance Writing (Choregraphy) with Drawings, Musical Examples, Choreographic Symbols and Special Music Scores* (Boston: Heintzemann Press, 1905; Whitefish, MT: Kessinger, 2009).

[13] Charles de Boigne, *Petits Mémoires de l'Opéra* (Paris: Librairie Nouvelle, 1857), 132, tr. in Beaumont, *Complete Book*, 121.

of defiance that she and Perrot dance *at* each other. The fury, as it were, of this part of the dance is beautifully relieved by those exquisite attitudes, where Cerrito falls upon one knee with languishing expression, while Perrot stands over her.[14] (London, 1842)

In eight performances, Fanny danced the *Cachucha* twenty-two times, yet who can boast that he knows this dance completely or can say that the twenty-second performance was not just as interesting as the first. That this should be so is the finest victory of natural grace over art, just as a rose, though seen a thousand times, is still a rose and the queen of flowers. I have been present at many a stormy evening in the theatre, but I have never witnessed such general and unrestrained excitement as at the last appearance, and particularly after the *Cachucha* had been performed a third time.[15] (Vienna, 1837)

After the galvanizing success of *Le Diable boiteux*, Spanish dance soon figured prominently among the many types of character dance that came to thrive in both operas and ballets at the Opéra, and across Europe, including St. Petersburg, and memorably in the works of Marius Petipa. *Don Quixote, The Nutcracker, Swan Lake,* and *Raymonda* are but a few of the ballets in which Petipa included Spanish dance. And he made sure to imbue the above-mentioned *Grand pas* for *Paquita* with a Spanish flavor.

Sources for Spanish dance. Fortunately, some descriptions of nineteenth-century character dances (for amateurs and professionals, the ballroom and the stage) are available today. Published books of instruction on social dancing (which could include character dance) are rather useful: for example, Henri Cellarius, *La danse des salons* (Paris, 1847), translated into English and published in London in 1847 as *Fashionable Dancing*,[16] and *Read's Characteristic National Dances* (London 1853).[17]

Carlo Blasis, the ballet master and well-published theoretician, paid more and more attention to character dance in his various treatises over time as national dance grew in popularity and diversity.[18] For instance, in his *Notes Upon Dancing* (London, 1847), he devoted thirty-two pages to a discussion of the history, style, expressive qualities, music and steps of more than fifteen national dances, with an emphasis on Spanish ones. He greatly expanded his scope in a later treatise (*Tantsy voobschche, baletnye znamenitosti i natsional'nye tantsy* [*Dances in General, Ballet Celebrities, and National Dances*]) (Moscow, 1864), discussing fifty-two national dances and devoting seventy pages to the subject. Friedrich Albert Zorn's extensive dance manual also includes descriptions of character dance steps.[19]

Justamant, in his painstakingly notated staging manuals, offers some of the most useful information of all on how to perform theatrical character dance, including that of the Spanish type, for instance in *Les Conscrits espagnols ou le recrutement forcé* (Lyon

---

[14] Original emphasis. *The Times*, qtd. in Ivor Guest, *Fanny Cerrito: The Life of a Romantic Ballerina*, 2nd ed. rev. (London: Dance Books, 1974), 44–45.

[15] Heinrich Adami in his résumé of Elssler's eight-performance season in Vienna in the summer of 1837. Qtd. in Guest, *Fanny Elssler*, 80–81.

[16] Cellarius lists many patterns and figures, and many are made as the dancers use polka and mazurka steps. These patterns and figures include "le Corbeille" (the Basket), which sometimes appears on the stage in ballets as well. Henri Cellarius, *La danse des salons*, 2nd ed. (Paris: [Chez l'Auteur], 1847), translated into English and published as *Fashionable Dancing* (London: David Bogue, 1847).

[17] *Read's Characteristic National Dances; a Series of Popular Tales* (London: Read and Company, 1853). See Arkin and Smith, "National Dance," 27, 62n74.

[18] See Arkin and Smith, "National Dance," 30–34.

[19] See note 12, earlier in this chapter.

1850/51), *Paquita* (Lyon, 1854), *Quasimodo, ou La bohémienne* (1859), and *Les Folies espagnoles* (Paris 1885).[20]

The composer Édouard Deldevez, in his later years looking back to the 1840s, recalled with pleasure being "entrusted [by the Opéra director Léon Pillet] with an important new libretto for which he held high hopes: *Paquita*." Written by the young playwright Paul Foucher, the ballet centers upon a lively young woman whose path to happiness is impeded by a cunning, remorseless Spanish general and a mercurial Roma (Gypsy) dance-troupe leader. Neither of these evildoers, however, is a match for the heroine, who by her powers of intellect and sheer chutzpah has by the end of the ballet has not only discovered her French heritage and her long-lost family but also found true love.

   Act One: The Valley of the Bulls near Saragossa, in the days of the French occupation of Spain. A French General, the Comte d'Hervilly together with his mother and his son, the young officer Lucien, convene with the Spanish Governor Don Lopez de Mendoza and his sister, Dona Seraphina. The Governor—whose territory has been conquered by Napoleon's army—shows his displeasure as d'Hervilly proposes that his son Lucien marry Dona Seraphina.

   Lucien's attentions, however, are soon captured by the beautiful young Paquita, who arrives with a troupe of Roma. She has long been subjected to the whims of Inigo, the leader of the troupe, who declares his passionate love for her but also berates her and threatens her with violence. Paquita, disdainful of Inigo, in quiet moments draws comfort from a miniature portrait of a man she presumes to be her father, who was killed by bandits many years ago.

   Even though Lucien has fallen in love with Paquita, Governor Mendoza, intent on preventing the proposed marriage of Lucien and Dona Seraphina from taking place, secretly hires Inigo to kill the prospective bridegroom. Governor Mendoza then tricks Lucien into believing Paquita has invited him to her dwelling place up in the hills. As Lucien elatedly departs for Paquita's house, he tells his father that he will return in time for the grand ball to be given at the French Commander's palace in Saragossa the following night in honor of his upcoming marriage to Dona Seraphina.

   Act Two, Scene I: The interior of a dwelling place. Paquita enters alone, daydreaming wistfully of Lucien. But she quickly hides upon seeing (through the window) a masked man in a cape coming toward her abode. It is Governor Mendoza, accompanied by Inigo. The men come into the house, thinking they are alone. In horror, she listens as they plot a murder: Inigo will drug the victim, and then stab him ("Strike him without mercy," says Mendoza before he pays Inigo and departs). Paquita, in the ensuing comic scene, while trying to sneak out of the house to warn the intended victim (whoever he may be), accidently trips over a chair, thus making her presence known. She assures Inigo that she had just arrived home and overheard nothing. Soon thereafter, the lovestruck and naïve Lucien arrives at the door. Inigo welcomes him with grandiose offers of hospitality, inviting him to stay the night. Paquita does everything in her power to warn her beloved that his life is in danger, but he fails to understand. After much ado, Paquita manages to switch the two men's wine glasses at dinner so that Inigo drinks the drugged wine. He

[20] The Justamant manuals for these ballets featuring Spanish dance (except for his *Paquita* manual) are mentioned in Jeschke et al., *Les choses espagnoles*. On Justamant's *Esmeralda*, see Jeschke, Gabi Vettermann, and Isa Wortelkamp, "Arabesken. Modelle 'fremder' Köperlichkeit in Tanztheorie und inszenierung," in Claudia Jeschke and Helmut Zedelmaier, eds., *Fremde Körper, andere Bewegungen*, 169–210 (Münster: Lit, 2005), and Jeschke, "Choreo-graphing Spectacularity," *de-archiving movement #3*, ed. Rose Breuss and Claudia Jeschke (Munich: epodium, 2017): 28–40, https://www.epodium.de/e-zine.

falls unconscious, and Paquita engineers a clever escape through a rotating fireplace with Lucien only seconds before Inigo's team of assassins arrives on the scene. Astonished to discover Inigo asleep, the assassins wake him up. He explodes with anger when he sees through the window his would-be victim and Paquita outdoors, fleeing the house.

Act Two, Scene II: A magnificent ballroom in Saragossa at the residence of the French commander. The curtain opens on a ballroom full of guests wearing splendid military uniforms and gowns of the Empire period. Suddenly the dancing stops and the crowd parts in astonishment: Lucien has just arrived, disheveled, followed by Paquita. Lucien tells the assembled ball-goers that he was held captive at an isolated house but was saved by the love and courage of Paquita, whom he loves. Paquita refuses Lucien's public marriage proposal, mindful of her lowly station, and tries to depart the scene. But suddenly her gaze falls on the Governor Don Lopez Mendoza, whom she had not noticed at first. Pointing at him, tells the crowd that he had ordered and paid for the murder of Lucien. The Governor's sword is taken away from him, and he is led away, followed by his daughter. Paquita, making another move to leave the premises, now finds herself in face to face with a portrait placed in the front of the stage. She hurriedly draws the miniature from her bosom. There can be no more doubt: the image in her locket matches the portrait displayed in the ballroom, which depicts d'Hervilly's brother. She realizes that she was kidnapped as a child and then raised by Inigo. So her blood heritage is French: she is the Count d'Hervilly's niece! The Count kisses Paquita, lovingly welcoming her to the family, and orders the ball to resume. Paquita and Lucien joyfully celebrate their engagement. Divertissement.

The choreographer charged with putting this story in motion was Joseph Mazilier, and Deldevez enjoyed a "intelligent and most pleasant" collaboration with him.[21] ("He did nothing," recalled the composer approvingly "until after hearing and pondering the music for a long time and profiting from [my] intentions for the stage, which he knew how to bring to light."[22]) Further, Deldevez notes with pride that Pillet "put at my disposal the *premier sujets* [performers of the top rank] Carlotta Grisi, Adèle Dumilâtre, Plunkett, Petipa, Elie, etc." Does he mean that, as in the creation of *Giselle*, a collaborative effort among dancers, composer, and choreographer took place?[23] In any case, the cast list of *Paquita* reminds us that the Paris Opéra ballet was a repertory company.[24] Though some of its principals came and went as international stars, the Opéra kept a stable of top-ranking performers whom the audience expected to see regularly in various dramatic roles fitting their types. The familiar set of cast members, thus, were accustomed to working together. In *Paquita*, Lucien Petipa, admired "for his handsome looks, elegant bearing, and talent for mime,"[25] had appeared with Grisi before in ballets at the Opéra, playing opposite her in all of them.[26] Georges Elie, a specialist in character roles and a highly praised comic actor, had played alongside Grisi and Petipa in *La Jolie fille*

---

[21] On Mazilier, see John Chapman, "Joseph Mazilier," in *International Dictionary of Ballet*, vol. 2, 934–937 (includes detailed timeline), and Susan Au, "Joseph Mazilier," in *International Encyclopedia of Dance*, vol. 4, 339–343.

[22] Deldevez liked this approach because it avoided "changes, cuts, retouching, deletions, etc." in the music. Edouard Marie Ernest Deldevez, *Mes mémoires* (Le Puy: Marchessou Fils, 1890), 34.

[23] Adolphe Adam said of that parts of *Giselle* were created in his own living room with Grisi and Perrot. Pougin, *Adolphe Adam*, 162. Unfortunately, Deldevez offers no further details about what he did with the performers who were "at his disposal."

[24] Its casts did not rotate (though substitutions were made sometimes for a performance or two), and the availability of performers in a given season could affect both the creation of the ballet and its ability to remain on the stage.

[25] Monique Babsky, "Lucien Petipa," in *International Encyclopedia of Dance*, vol. 5, 148–149.

[26] *Giselle*, 1841; *La Jolie fille de Gand*, 1842; *La Péri*, 1843; *Le Diable à quatre*, 1845.

de Gand. (Gautier's beguiling eyewitness descriptions of Elie's performances in various ballets are well worth reading.[27])

Too, highly regarded dancers regularly brought additional luster to the Opéra's ballets in stand-alone set pieces that transpired during respites from the action. In *Paquita* these stars were Adèle Dumilâtre and Adeline Plunkett, who danced a substantial multimovement *pas de deux* in the ballroom scene.[28]

Reception

A warm and enthusiastic welcome greeted *Paquita* at its premiere on 1 April 1846 at the Opéra, the audience calling back the principals and according the same honor to Mazilier, "who can turn any metal into gold!!"[29] Deldevez, who (much to his surprise) was invited at the last minute by the choreographer to sound the midnight chimes in the first scene of Act Two, was pleased after playing a part in the performance and exhilarated by the success of the evening.

Here is his happy recollection of the ballet's merits as he recalled them when he wrote his memoir many years later:

> The work was completely successful. The pantomime [was] . . . brought to life with voluptuous poses, elegant steps, graceful attitudes which combined charm with action, in a sort of dialogue with the music—for example. . . . the turning of the fireplace; the Gypsy girl [Paquita] turning round and disappearing on sight without the brigand being able to accomplish his sinister design.[30]

His score was fairly well received by most of the critics, though not showered with unanimous praise. One critic called it the work of a "talented composer" which, however, lacked color and made too much use of wind instruments.[31] Another implied that Deldevez's music had gone into too much detail, but appreciated his inclusion of the well-known "Queen of Prussia" waltz in the ballroom scene.[32] Gautier, in anodyne remarks, called it "rhythmical, not too noisy, and abundant in melodies, bearing witness to a fresh and graceful talent" and declared that "[i]t made its own contribution to the success of the work."[33] The critic for *La France musicale* (perhaps with a mind to sheet music sales for the publishing company that owned the newspaper) did praise Deldevez's music unequivocally:

> As for the music, it has, from the first day, obtained the votes of connoisseurs. . . . A ballet in which there are at least ten delicious pieces, such as the waltz, the bohèmienne, the

[27] See, for instance, his descriptions of Elie in *Nathalie*, *Les Mohicans*, and *Les Noces de Gamache*, as well as his description of Jean-Baptiste Barrez in *Manon Lescaut*, all in *La Presse*, tr. in Gautier, *Gautier on Dance*. These are quoted in Smith, "The Disappearing Danseur."

[28] Deldevez wrongly implies that Plunkett was planned for the cast from the start. According to Ivor Guest, the *pas de deux* (inserted to celebrate Dumilâtre's return from Milan, where she had been performing at La Scala) was meant for Dumilâtre and Grisi. Plunkett was later cast instead because Grisi "felt she might find herself at a disadvantage being exhausted by the exigencies of an important role while Dumilâtre would be quite fresh." Guest, *Romantic Ballet in Paris*, 2nd ed., 253–254.

[29] *La France théâtrale*, 5 April 1846. It is Deldevez who wrote that all of the principals were called back for ovations. Deldevez, *Mes Mémoires*, 35.

[30] Deldevez, *Mes Mémoires*, 34–35.

[31] *La France théâtrale*, 5 April 1846.

[32] *L'Album de Sainte-Cécile, revue des théâtres lyriques*, 20 April 1846.

[33] *La Presse*, 6 April 1846, tr. in Gautier, *Gautier on Dance*, 170.

allemande, the *pas des manteaux*, the bolero by Carlotta Grisi and the final galop in the first act; the cachucha, the *jaleo de jerez*, the waltz of Carlotta and Petipa, the jaleo of Carlotta, in the second act, can be placed among the best ever composed for the Opéra. Paquita's music will soon be in everyone's ears and on all pianos.[34]

The libretto fared less well among the journalists in attendance, however. One critic called it implausible and naïve; another chided Foucher for drawing too much inspiration from pre-existing works: "*La Gipsy, Minuit* [. . .], *Alibaba, Le Tyran peu Délicat*— each sent a contingent." But "luckily," he continues:

> M. Mazillier was there to rejuvenate all these old ideas, and the administration mounted M. Paul Foucher's ballet with great luxury and care: beautiful sets, brilliant costumes, charming dances perfectly regulated by the skillful choreographer, and above all the talent of CARLOTTA GRISI, ensured the success of *Paquita*.[35]

The sourest critique of them all, by Hippolyte de Villemessant, disdained the lavish ballroom set for its inauthenticity, though it had pleased many in the audience:

> There is nothing of the Moorish style, nothing of the imperial period in this rather poorly painted canvas, which nonetheless dazzles the crowd with the brilliance of its lights and by a prospect which is actually very common and very banal. It is a jumble of all styles, and the statues that carry the candelabra seem to be twisting in the anguish of a terrible colic.[36]

He also railed about the "dreadful imperial uniforms and these unsightly women's costumes, [. . . with a high] waist below the arms." (Jules Janin, on the other hand, said that "This Empire in silk, satin and velvet, and the glitter of helmets and breastplates [are] . . . not so ridiculous as some make out."[37]) But even de Villemessant greatly admired the dancing:

> The choreographic part is the best; the *pas des manteaux*, and the *pas de trois*, in the first act, are charming and full of originality; as for the second act, it is summed up almost entirely in Carlotta; never had the pretty dancer been lighter, more lively, than in the role of Paquita; in the second act, she does wonders. She crosses the stage on the same point and without putting the other foot or the heel on the ground, it seems that she has wings which support her in the air.

So, of course, did Gautier, whose personal friendship with Grisi kept him from being an unbiased reporter but whose account here is nonetheless informative:

> The richness and originality of the Empire costumes, the beautiful scenery, and above all the perfection of Carlotta's dancing carried off the honours. Her last *pas* was daring and difficult beyond belief. There were some hops on the tip of the toe combined with a dazzlingly vivacious spin that caused both alarm and delight, for they seemed

---

[34] *La France musicale*, 1846, written after the third performance. It is possible that the writer of this critique had consulted with Deldevez. See note 52, below.

[35] *La France théâtrale*, 5 April 1846.

[36] Hippolyte de Villemessant, *La Sylphide*, April 1846.

[37] *Le Journal des débats*, 6 April 1846, tr. in Guest, *Romantic Ballet in Paris*, 3rd ed., 421.

impossible to perform, even though repeated eight or ten times. The ballerina was greeted with thunderous applause and twice recalled after the curtain had fallen.[38]

This *pas* similarly dazzled P. A. Fiorentino, who declared it "worth all of the rest of the ballet put together. It is but a variation lasting at most ten minutes, but we have never seen anything more aerial, more vaporous or more rapid. It is a jumble of *ronds de jambe* and *emboîtés sur la pointe* which even the most experienced eye could not follow without becoming dazzled and dizzy."[39] (It is no wonder that Grisi was heard to say backstage to Mazilier, "Oh, Master, how sore my toes are!"[40])

Grisi was without doubt the hit of the evening. But critics also lauded Mme. Robert, who shone in her appearance in the festival in Act One, and Dumilâtre and Plunkett, who drew warm applause for their performance of the *pas de deux* in Act Two. Also causing a stir was the *Pas des manteaux*, a prop dance performed in the first-act festival by an all-female ensemble of twenty corps de ballet dancers, half of them dressed as males and whipping enormous capes in the air to create shapes and patterns. Fiorentino called the *pas des manteaux* the best choreographed number in the ballet and admired it for its grace, color, and ensemble.[41]

Paquita remained in the Opéra's repertory for five years, appearing there forty times. Like other successful ballets, it was given the compliment of a parody vaudeville version in Paris[42] and was also produced in various other cities, including London (1846, with Grisi), St. Petersburg (1847, with the involvement of Marius Petipa, who danced the part of Lucien), Naples (1848, in a three-act version with Nathalie Fitzjames, which appears to have been a revised version of the St. Peterburg production[43]), and Milan (1852, a three-act version with Amalia Ferrari[44]). In stagings by Luigi Brétin featuring his wife Flora Fabbri, *Paquita* also appeared in Madrid (1852) and in two Andalusian cities, Sevilla and Cádiz (both in 1853).[45]

---

[38] *La Presse*, 6 April 1846, tr. in Gautier, *Gautier on Dance*, 169.

[39] *Le Constitutionnel*, 7 April 1846, tr. in Guest, *Romantic Ballet in Paris*, 2nd ed., 254.

[40] Deldevez, *Mes Mémoires*, 35.

[41] Here is an evocative description of the *pas des manteaux* written by a critic in London in 1846 after seeing *Paquita* there (with Grisi in the title role): "Among the *pas d'ensemble* may be mentioned a very clever one called the *Pas des manteaux*, danced by the peasants. One would think that all groups depending upon the arrangement of scarves, and other spreading articles of attire, had been exhausted, but the thick red mantle now folded round the figure, now extended wide is a new material, and is turned to account." *Times* of London, 4 June 1846, qtd. in Beaumont, *Complete Book*, 190.

[42] *Paquita, ballet-vaudeville en trois actes, imité du ballet de M. Paul Foucher*, par MM. Paul et Paul de Faulquemont. Musique de Bariller, Danses réglées par M. Scio, Mis en scene de M. Oscar. Performed at the Théâtre Beaumarchais (Paris: Michel Lévy, Frères, 1847). M. Scio, the choreographer, was likely the same M. Scio who had been a longtime member of the corps de ballet at the Opéra. See Smith, "The Disappearing Danseur," 51, 54.

[43] Deldevez's score was supplemented or supplanted with music by Nicolò Gabrielli, and a *pas de trois* in the third act was choreographed by Francesco Mérante. Title and publisher given in the inside cover of the libretto: "Paquita, ballo di mezzo carattere in tre atti, composto dal Signor Patipá, da rappresentarsi nel Real Teatro S. Carlo. Napoli, Tipografia Flautina, 1848." A copy is held at the New York Public Library for the Performing Arts in the Cia Fornaroli Collection, *MGTY 80-3267.

[44] Title and publisher given in the inside cover of the libretto: "Paquita; ballo di mezzo carattere in tre atti di Giovanni Galzerani da rappresentarsi nell'i. r. Teatro alla Canobbiana, l'autunno 1852. Milano, Coi tipi di Luigi di Giacomo Pirola." A copy is held at the New York Public Library for the Performing Arts in the Cia Fornaroli Collection, *MGTY-Res.

[45] Many thanks to Laura Hormigón for sharing this information with us, along with these details: in January 1852, Gilbert and Denisse danced only the *pas de deux* of *Paquita* at the Teatro Principal de Barcelona. In October 1852, the complete ballet was staged by Luigi Brétin in Madrid's Royal Theater (Teatro Real), starring Flora Fabbri and Ernest Gontié; scenery by Eusebio Lucini; the Deldevez score was supplemented with music by Johann Daniel Skoczdopole. (The setting and time period of the ballet were also changed.) In 1853, Fabbri and Gontié danced the *pas de deux* in some "Galas" in other theaters in Madrid. *Paquita* was also performed

It is to Petipa, however, that we owe the ballet's longevity. For before *Paquita* finished its run at the Paris Opéra in 1851, the ballet had already been transplanted to St. Petersburg, where Petipa retained it the repertory into the twentieth century.

Characters, in order of appearance

A French general, the Count of Hervilly. The General, a quietly dignified and sympathetic man who loves his family, is determined to honor the memory of his brother, who was murdered by bandits in 1795 in the wild landscape of the Valley of the Bulls, near Saragossa. (The action of the ballet takes place fifteen years later, in 1810.[46]) As commander of the occupying French forces in Spain, the General is the most politically powerful character in the ballet, and therefore is often accompanied by an entourage. Even more important, however, is that he is the head of his family, which means that his entourage often includes his son, his mother, and his daughter-in-law-to-be, Dona Seraphina. His closeness to his family helps make him a sympathetic character. Unlike the head villain (the Governor), the Count has tender emotions and is willing to express them.

The Countess. The Countess is the General's mother and Lucien's grandmother. And though her actions and "spoken" lines are few, her very presence underscores the family ties that bind the Hervilly family—a loving group that will take Paquita into its fold by the end of the story. The Countess is particularly perceptive when it comes to her grandson: she is the first to notice his lukewarm regard for his Spanish fiancée, and the first in the ballroom scene to sense the danger behind his unexplained absence. Her steadiness and perceptiveness provide gravity and a fitting counterweight to the unpredictable actions of the ballet's evildoers.

Governor [of the territory] Don Lopez de Mendoza, the main villain of this ballet, can appear to be cordial. But he is a duplicitous schemer who resents the French occupation of his homeland. Worst of all is his ruthless planning of Lucien's murder even as he "plays nice" with the Hervilly family, agreeing to his sister's engagement to Lucien and entertaining them ceremoniously at the festival. Mendoza's cunning treacherousness, hidden beneath a faux-gracious veneer, makes him the most dangerous character in the ballet.

Inigo, chief of a band of Romani dancers, is a rough-hewn and unsubtle man with a big personality who doesn't keep his anger in check. There are two sides to him: On one hand, he threatens Paquita with violence and willingly agrees to kill Lucien for hire. On the other, he has tender feelings for Paquita (when he is not threatening her) and engages in humorous interactions with her as though they were a husband/wife comedy team. The original Inigo was played by Georges Élie, who was acclaimed for his comic acting—and indeed this was a part that would have been considered largely comical, for violent behavior was by no means reserved strictly for serious characters. But he was "equally suited to serious parts," as Gautier wrote after seeing him as Bustamente in *La Jolie fille de Gand.*[47] Inigo is one of the three leadings actors in the ballet, and his part calls for one

in 1853 in Sevilla and Cádiz (both Andalusian cities) by the ballet company created by the couple Fabbri/Brétin after finishing their contract with the Royal Theater of Madrid. Both productions were modest and the one in Sevilla had no scenery.

[46] This date is given in a document indicating the place, and sometimes the date, of the action of various ballets and operas at the Opéra. Archives nationales, AJ[13] 215. See Smith, *Ballet and Opera,* 22–25.

[47] Gautier, *La Presse,* 2 July 1842, tr. in Gautier, *Gautier on Dance,* 111.

foray into dance (of the comic type): in the dinner scene he cachuchas with Paquita as he falls into a drug-induced stupor. We will see in Chapter 5 that Mazilier and Perrot both performed the role of Inigo in St. Petersburg.

Paquita, the heroine of the ballet and by far the smartest of all of the characters, demonstrates five of her signal traits early in the action. First, she shows her independence by lagging behind the rest of Inigo's troupe of Romani dancers to pick flowers along the path, and then, her friendliness to her peers, by handing the flowers out to them. Shortly thereafter (despite at first being afraid of Inigo's threats), she shows her feistiness by standing up to him. And he when declares his love for her—and even his desire "to be her slave"—she actually mocks him, demonstrating her audacity. Next, alone on stage, she shows her tenderness when she pulls out a miniature portrait she always keeps with her and looks with "an indescribable sweetness at the features of the man who surely is her father, and dreams of the joys of a family life."

As the action unfolds, of course, we also see Paquita's resourcefulness—and the comedic skill of the actress playing the role—for instance, as she maneuvers her way through the dinner scene, in which she outplays Inigo to avert disaster, all the while leading the way for the naïve Lucien (who quite lacks the keen perceptiveness that Paquita possesses in abundance). The actress playing this role must, of course, not only demonstrate all of these qualities, but also perform virtuosically both Spanish character dance and classical dance. Her magnetism as a character and dancer must carry the action and shine brightly whenever she dances and bring special charisma during her final celebratory *pas de deux* with Lucien at the end.

Lucien d'Hervilly, son of the General, is a good-hearted young nobleman who is willing to enter his arranged marriage with Dona Seraphina until the moment he encounters the beguiling Paquita, who instantly steals his heart. So ardent is Lucien's passion for Paquita that he does everything in his power to woo her, defending her against Inigo's physical threats, extending offers of money, asking her to give him the posy she is wearing, showing genuine sympathy for her reticence, and rushing off to her dwelling place the moment he finds out where it is. In short, once smitten, he never wavers in his enthusiasm for Paquita. And in the final series of celebratory dances, he dances (in keeping with his upper-class status) in the classical style, though with character-dance allusions to the Spanish locale.

Dona Seraphina, sister of the Governor, is a young ruling-class woman whom, we can imagine, is pleased to be engaged to the handsome Lucien and disappointed to be led away with her father during the ball scene after his evildoing is exposed. She has very few "spoken lines" but can project the well-bred demeanor of someone of her social prestige and the fresh hopes of a young bride-to-be.

The Bandits. The shady characters hired by Inigo and the Governor to assassinate Lucien are—as the music tells us—on the comic side of the character spectrum.

Anti-Roma stereotypes. The libretto for this ballet endows the main Roma character, Inigo, with many of the qualities that Romani people were (and still are) held to have: a talent for music and dance, a disposition for living life on the road, rough manners, dishonesty, a willingness to commit bad deeds, and a tendency to kidnap children. By contrast, Paquita is virtuous, white-skinned (as the characters point out), and possessed of "native nobility" (as the libretto tells us)—qualities that make her superior to the people she has lived with for most of her life.[48] Gautier poked fun at the stereotyping:

---

[48] See the classic study by a Romani activist on anti-Roma discrimination: Ian Hancock, *The Pariah Syndrome: An Account of Gypsy Slavery and Persecution* (Open Library: Karoma, 1987),

But who is this pretty creature with the delicate complexion, azure blue eyes and golden hair—a white rose set in a bouquet of red roses? Moorish blood cannot possibly flow in those thin blue veins. There must be some secret story of a child lost or believed dead. For she cannot be a daughter of that tribe with copper-coloured skin, hooked noses and slanting eyes, and as you know, gypsies are great stealers of children, particularly on the stage.[49]

In this chapter, we are using the terms "Roma" and "Romani" instead of "Gypsy" because most scholars and activists who are Roma reject the use of the latter term, finding it insulting. Though the matter is complicated we, as non-Romani scholars, choose to err on the side of caution and respect.

The Music

The musical sources for *Paquita*, like those for *Giselle* and so many other nineteenth century ballets originating at the Opéra, have been preserved carefully at two component institutions of Bibliothèque Nationale de France: the Département de la Musique, where one may find Deldevez's autograph score, and the Bibliothèque-Musée de l'Opéra, where one may find the copied orchestra score (736 pages bound in two volumes), a short score, a *répétiteur* (Rep) with a few annotations, and orchestra parts.[50] Our musical examples are drawn from the copied orchestra score, and we employ Deldevez's numbering system unless otherwise noted:

Varying demands of the action

Eduoard Deldevez's music for *Paquita* meets the varying demands of the action, which (melodrama that it is) calls for sweet sentiment, scariness and nefarious action, violence, and suspense. Here, we offer brief examples of each of these in turn.

Sweet sentiment. Lucien's sudden and strongly felt declaration of love to Paquita comes in an impassioned melody in the manner of a tenor aria (Ex. 4.1), its short agitato introduction demonstrating that the young Frenchman can barely contain himself.

Another example may be found in the melody reserved for Paquita in the ballet's two plot-turning recognition scenes (Ex. 4.2). The soaring melody of this "recognition" motif is heard first in Act One as a beleaguered Paquita suddenly finds herself in the terrain of the place where she had been kidnapped as a young child; it recurs at the climactic

---

http://www.oocities.org/~patrin/pariah-contents.htm. See also the more recent work, Aidan McGarry, *Romaphobia: The Last Acceptable form of Racism* (London: Zed Books, 2017), and the blog post by Margareta Matache, "The Legacy of Gypsy Studies in Modern Romani Scholarship," *FXB Center for Health & Human Rights at Harvard University* (blog), 14 November 2016, https://fxb.harvard.edu/2016/11/14/the-legacy-of-gypsy-studies-in-modern-romani-scholarship/.

[49] *La Presse*, 6 April 1846, tr. in Gautier, *Gautier on Dance*, 167.

[50] The autograph score (bound in two volumes, shelf mark MS-7166, and lacking annotations regarding stage actions) is available online at http://gallica.bnf.fr/ark:/12148/btv1b52513997z. The copied orchestra score (shelf mark A-550 (A 1–2)) is available online at gallica.bnf.fr. In addition to orchestra parts, the *matériel*, MAT-355 (1–64), includes a *répétiteur* (23–24) and a short score (25–26).

Ex. 4.1 Lucien's declaration of love; Act One, No. 11, bars 54–60

Ex. 4.2 Recognition motif; Act One, No. 7, bars 1–8

moment in the ballroom scene when she sees a portrait of her long-dead father that matches the miniature in her locket, solving once and for all the mystery of her true origins.

For *scariness and nefarious action*, Deldevez always turns to the minor mode, as when the Governor arrives on the scene to finalize the plans for Lucien's demise (Ex. 4.3).

Deldevez also deploys as needed the ever-useful tools of tremolo, chromatic scales, and key-center instability, as when Inigo and Governor Lopez first hatch their evil scheme (Ex. 4.4).

Violence. To depict Inigo's threats to Paquita of violence and his ensuing scuffle with those defending her, Deldevez makes use of accents and insistent dotted-eighth rhythms (Ex. 4.5). This is repetitive "wallpaper music" that does not follow details of the action, like Inigo raising his hand to strike Paquita or his shoving away of a bystander. Instead, it expresses the prevailing mood of anger and contentiousness.

Ex. 4.3 The Governor plots Lucien's demise; Act Two, No. 2, bars 1–7

Ex. 4.4 The Governor and Inigo hatch their scheme; Act One, No. 11, bars 114–125

Suspense. As Paquita and Lucien seek desperately to escape before the assassins' imminent arrival, Deldevez's music enhances the suspense of the situation by repeating the same "hurry" motif multiple times as it modulates. Again, this is "wallpaper" music that keeps repeating and expresses the prevailing anxiety instead of the characters' particular actions (the throwing down of the pistols, the search for the sword, etc.; Ex. 4.6).

Ex. 4.5 Anger and contentiousness; Act One, No. 5, bars 1–8

Musical genres

Waltzes. There is a "valse de scène" in Act One that is performed by Paquita—first as she is choreographing it in No. 6 (to Inigo's frustration), and then again as she is performing it for the entertainment of a crowd (including Lucien; Ex. 4.7).[51]

There are also two waltzes in the ballroom scene during the grand celebration that closes the ballet. The first is a *Valse des hussards* (Exx. 4.8a–b). The hussards return for another waltz, the "Queen of Prussia," in the finale (Ex. 4.26, below).

Bolero. Deldevez also included national dances in the *Paquita* score. He composed several dances of the bolero type—that is, they are in triple meter and make use of repeating rhythmic patterns. They are all used for dances meant to project Spanish identity:

The *Pas des manteaux* in Act One, an ensemble prop dance performed at the festival (Ex. 4.16, below)

The "*bolero* de Carlotta Grisi," as Escudier called it in *La France musicale* (called *Pas de Paquita* by Justamant, "pas des tambourins" by the critic Fiorentino, and *Pas de Mlle Carlotta Grisi* in the musical scores), in which Paquita dances for a crowd of bystanders and then is asked by Inigo to collect money from them. It included two couples as supporting dancers in Lyon and apparently in Paris, too (Act One; Exx. 4.17a–b, below).

The cachucha that Paquita performs during the dinner scene in Act Two (along with Inigo, according to Justamant; Ex. 4.18, below).

The jaleo performed by Paquita and Lucien in the finale (Act Two; Ex. 4.21, below).

Allemande. The opening number of the *pas de trois* performed in Act One at the festival was referred to by some observers as an "allemande," likely for the noodling and occasional references to yodeling style in the music (Ex. 4.9).[52]

---

[51] *La France musicale*, April 1846.

[52] It was probably Deldevez himself who wrote the words "divertissement pas tyrolien" in a blank space on the page before the beginning of the *Pas de trois*. The word "Styrien," perhaps in a later hand, is written in pencil below the word "tyrolien." (The musical styles of Styria and the Tyrol, today both Austrian states,

Ex. 4.6 Suspense; Act Two, No. 9, bars 12–23

Ex. 4.7 Paquita creates a dance; Act One, No. 6, bars 47–54

may have been considered the same by the pencil-wielding notator.) Bibliothèque Nationale de France, Département de la Musique, MS 7166. The reviewer for *La France musicale* (probably one of the Escudier brothers), referred to an allemande in a review praising Deldevez's music in *Paquita* (see p. 198 earlier in this chapter). Perhaps Escudier had consulted with the composer before writing the review, as he likely did in the case of *Giselle*, and he simply used the term "allemande" to refer to the piece Deldevez called the "pas tyrolien."

Ex. 4.8a *Valse des hussards* (A section); Act Two, *Valse*, bars 7–15

Ex. 4.8b *Valse des hussards* (B section); Act Two, *Valse*, bars 89–96

Music for three distinct cultural groups

Deldevez offers music here and there to reflect the three distinct groups of characters: French, Spanish, and Roma.

French music. The most pointed reference to France comes is a minor-key rendition of the popular French song "Malbrouck s'en va-t-en guerre" (Malborough goes to war), played shortly after Paquita makes her entrance, slyly conveying her true heritage to the audience (even though she is yet unaware of it herself; Ex. 4.10).[53] Fiorentino describes this entrance thus: "See her skimming, like a bird in flight, over the enormous rock in the middle of the stage, and alighting, proud and breathless, in the midst of her

---

[53] For further information, see C.D. Brenner, "The Eighteenth-Century Vogue of 'Malbrough' and Marlborough," *Modern Language Review* 45, no. 2 (April 1950): 177–180. Recall, too, that this song had been used by Beethoven to represent the French in his 1813 *Wellington's Victory*, op. 91.

Ex. 4.9 Allemande; Act One, *Pas de trois*, bars 8–16

Ex. 4.10 "Malbrouck s'en va-t-en guerre"; Act One, No. 4, bars 153–160

companions."[54] (That is, she first appears at the top of the Valley of the Bulls, up above the big scenic rock façade that frames the stage, before descending quickly into the valley.)

Conspicuously French music also opens the ballroom scene, which is steeped in Frenchness: it is set the French commander's palace in which many of the guests are wearing the uniforms of Napoleon's army and in which ballgoers are performing typically French dances of the Empire period (Exx. 4.17a–b, below). Moreover, the scoring is reduced to the smaller forces one might find in contredanse orchestras of the period, which often featured strings and two or three wind instruments (French horn, oboes, flutes, clarinets, for instance).

As the curtain goes up on the ballet's final scene, the guests are performing a contredanse (Exx. 4.11a–b).

---

[54] *Le Constitutionnel*, 7 April 1846, tr. in Guest, *Romantic Ballet in Paris*, 2nd ed., 254.

Ex. 4.11a Act Two, *Contredanse française* (Section A), bars 1–8

Ex. 4.11b Act Two, *Contredanse française* (Section B), bars 40–44

Ex. 4.12 Gavotte de Vestris; Act Two, Gavotte, bars 1–16

After the contredanse is finished, two male-female couples begin a gavotte to the music of the "Gavotte de Vestris."[55] The exact steps of the gavotte performed by Vestris

[55] Through much of the nineteenth century, as Carol Marsh points out, "the term *gavotte* seems to have been synonymous with the 'Gavotte de Vestris,' a theatrical duet by the famed dancer Gaetano Vestris first performed in the 1760s or 1770s." Carol G. Marsh, "Gavotte," in *International Encyclopedia of Dance*, vol. 3, 123–125. See also Sandra Noll Hammond, "The 'Gavotte de Vestris': A Dance of Three Centuries," in *Proceedings*, Society of Dance History Scholars (1984), 202–208, and Meredith Ellis Little, rev. Matthew Werley, "Gavotte," *Oxford Music Online*, https://doi.org/10.1093/gmo/9781561592630.article.10774. However, Edmund Fairfax

have not been preserved, but this particular piece of music was well known and widely danced. In this case it is scored for flute, oboe, bassoon, and strings.

Such "classical" dances as gavottes, minuets, and contredanses automatically conveyed Frenchness to ballet audiences in France for most of the nineteenth century. When a French character was featured in a character-variety divertissement, she might perform one such classical dance. (In *La Péri*, for example, when four European women are introduced into a harem in Cairo, the Scot dances a jig, the German a waltz, the Frenchwoman a minuet, and the Spaniard a bolero.[56]) Thus, seeing and hearing these dances performed in a ballroom by many guests would certainly have made the setting recognizable as French, even though the action was situated in Spain.

Roma music. Here, we shall identify several examples of music created by Deldevez to mark the appearance of Romani characters. In general, he reserves pastoral music for the Romani, giving them a distinctive outdoorsy sound. (This pastoral music would not be automatically associated with Roma people by today's listeners, for it is not in the Hungarian-Roma style that one finds in, for instance, the *Rondo alla Zingarese* movement of Brahms's Piano quartet no. 1, op. 25.[57]) He signals the first appearance of Inigo and the band of Romani with a few bars of melodic fourths and fifths (Ex. 4.13, bars 1–4) which then prove to be related to a drone that, in turn, soon comes to underlie a pleasant and inviting melody (Ex. 4.13, bars 5–14). The occasional tambourine shakes in this pastorale denote the presence of Romani.

Another melody with the simplicity of a country dance is sounded as the Romani rehearse their show, and again shortly after Paquita has danced to "Malbrouck" (Ex. 4.14).

When the Roma dance troupe reappears shortly before their festival performance takes place, Deldevez does give them music that hints at the full-octave violin glissando that is associated with the Hungarian-Roma style of violin playing: a fortissimo A-minor melody begins with an ascending octave played by the upper strings; the upper note is preceded by an ascending grace-note flourish. The grace-note flourish leading to E is also played by flute, piccolo, clarinet, supplemented with E's in various registers by nearly every other instrument in the orchestra, and supported by cymbals, bass drum, timpani, and glockenspiel. The short attention-getting opening soon gives way a tuneful country-dance melody in A-major (see bars in 11ff. in Ex. 4.15). Of this music, Gautier wrote: "Here are the tambourines, the traditional *panaderos* with their copper discs which thrill and peal under the gypsies' thumbs; the castanets rattle and chatter, the festival commences. . . . Begone dull care!"[58] Deldevez, making use of a common framing strategy, brings this music back a bit later as the troupe leaves the stage at festival's end.

Another exception to the Deldevez's rule of composing pastoral music for Romani characters is the little E-minor melody played by the first violins (and soon joined by flutes) as Paquita asserts her control over Inigo in No. 6. The violins' spiccato bow strokes,

---

has recently suggested that the "Gavotte de Vestris" originated not with Gaetano Vestris but with his son, Auguste Vestris, and was likely created in the winter of 1799–1800. Edmund Fairfax, "The famous nineteenth-century ballroom dance the 'Gavotte de Vestris,'" Facebook, 3 November 2022, https://www.facebook.com/profile.php?id=100013492210728.

[56] *La Péri* libretto (Paris, 1843).

[57] See Ralph Locke's thoughtful discussion of Roma music and its influences on non-Roma composers in the nineteenth century in Locke, *Musical Exoticism*, 135–149.

[58] See Théophile Gautier, *The Romantic Ballet as seen by Théophile Gautier*, tr. Cyril W. Beaumont, rev. ed. (London: C.W Beaumont, 1947), 77.

Ex. 4.13 First appearance of Inigo and his troupe; Act One, No. 4, bars 1–14

Ex. 4.14 Simple country music for the Romani; Act One, No. 4, bars 71–80

minor key, and the series of half-step sixteenth-note figures seem to hint at Hungarian-Roma-style violin playing (see Ex. 4.28, below).[59]

[59] See Jonathan Bellman, *The Style Hongrois in the Music of Western Europe* (Boston: Northeastern University Press, 1993), especially chapter 5.

Ex. 4.15 Beginning of the festival performance; Act One, No. 8, bars 1–20

Spanish music. Deldevez reserves most of his Spanish-style music for particular dance numbers. We first encounter it in Act One in the *Pas des manteaux* performed at the festival, a bolero with a heavy emphasis on the downbeat of every measure and with a grace note sometimes preceding the second eighth-note (and infrequently the first or third eighth note; Ex. 4.16).

We encounter another bolero in the final section of the dance that Paquita performs for the public at Inigo's request (called variously the "Pas de Paquita," and the "pas des tambourins," among other titles) as noted above; Ex. 4.17a).[60] This sensational dance was performed (according to Justamant) with two majo/maja couples plus Paquita, so it is effectively a *pas de cinq*. And another bolero is to be found in the finale of the dance (Ex. 4.17b).

---

[60] *Le Constitutionnel,* 7 April 1846, tr. in Guest *Romantic Ballet in Paris,* 2nd ed., 254. See p. 205 in this chapter.

Ex. 4.16 Act One, *Pas des manteaux*, bars 25–33

Ex. 4.17a Act One, *Pas de Mlle Carlotta Grisi*, bars 199–202

Ex. 4.17b Act One, *Pas de Mlle Carlotta Grisi*, Coda, bars 251–258

Another Spanish dance is the cachucha Paquita performs tableside at Inigo's request during the dinner and drink-switching scene in Act Two, Scene II, No. 8 (Ex. 4.18).

Rising from his seat, Inigo joins Paquita (according to Justamant) to perform a cachucha *à deux* (Ex. 4.19) for which Deldevez supplies yet another bolero. Their performance together is comical, and the music, with its grace notes and wallpaper approach, supplies a madcap feel.

The next number follows up with the same rhythmic motif, but the music now *alla breve* and in a minor key (Ex. 4.20). The cachucha dancing is over, Inigo is on the floor in a stupor, and Lucien and Paquita are now turning their attention to escaping.

Returning to the boleros composed by Deldevez: In the ballroom scene in Act Two, after the joyful resolution has been reached, a series of celebratory dances are performed. Though most of them are not in the Spanish style, Deldevez does provide more bolero music in a festive "Jaleo" (Ex. 4.21).

Ex. 4.18 Cachucha in dinner scene; Act Two, No. 8, bars 5–12

Ex. 4.19 Inigo joins Paquita in dancing; Act Two, No. 8, bars 74–81

Ex. 4.20 Lucien and Paquita's attention turns to their escape; Act Two, No. 9, bars 1–5

Ex. 4.21 Act Two, *Fin du 2° acte* (Jaleo), bars 13–20

Recurring motifs

Deldevez, in keeping with custom, used motifs to represent particular characters and ideas. (We count them as "recurring" if they are used in more than one scene.) There are four such melodies in *Paquita*: one for Inigo, one for the Romani (as a group), one for Paquita's recognition of clues to the mystery of her long-lost family, and one for the love between Lucien and Paquita.

Inigo's motif is a bare and simple succession of rising and falling fourths and fifths, played in unison (Ex. 4.13, bars 1–4), and it is associated with him the four times it is played. We hear it first upon the arrival of Inigo and his troupe (in Act One, No. 4). It comes back again briefly toward the end of No. 10 as Inigo takes Paquita brusquely by the hand and leads her back into the tent. (In this case, the Inigo theme is mixed with the Romani theme; see Ex. 4.22). Shortly thereafter, immediately before the end of No. 10, the motif comes back softly as Inigo emerges from his tent in a dreamy mood. And it recurs again in Act One, No. 11 as (according to Justamant) Inigo and the Governor finish their secret evil-intentioned meeting and part ways.

The *Romani motif* is first played immediately after the Inigo melody as a pleasant and inviting element of their arrival on the scene (Ex. 4.13, bars 5–14). It recurs in No. 4 as the latecomer, Paquita, arrives (this time played sweetly by the flute with soft string accompaniment, indicating her presence). And it is heard again in No. 10 as Paquita and Lucien look at each other as the stage is clearing and they depart in (thanks to Inigo) separate directions (Ex. 4.22).

The *Recognition motif.* Early in Act One, Paquita, during a rare moment alone, looks around and suddenly realizes that she is standing very near the site of her long-ago kidnapping (Ex. 4.2). The realization, of course, constitutes a key development in the action.

The Recognition motif returns toward the end of Act Two, Scene II, as Paquita discovers the portrait in her medallion matches exactly the painted portrait in the Commander's palace. This brings her great happiness, for it shows that she is a member of the Hervilly family.

The *Lucien and Paquita love motif,* an oboe solo in the manner of a tenor love aria (marked *canto espressivo* in the Rep) is heard in Act One, No. 11 as Lucien first makes

Ex. 4.22 Inigo motif alternating with Romani motif; Act One, No. 10, bars 62–71

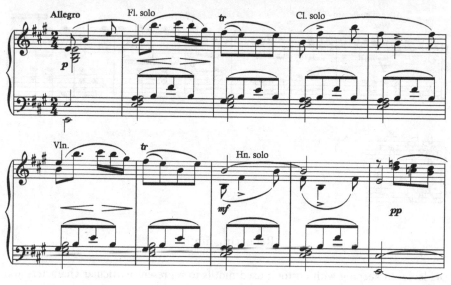

known his affection for Paquita. It recurs as a recollection toward the beginning of Act Two as Paquita, all alone at Inigo's dwelling place, thinks longingly of Lucien ("She sighs," according to the Rep, "dreaming of the handsome officer whom she will never see again"). This time, the music is played softly by the first violins, who are then joined in the second phrase by flutes, oboes, and clarinets.

Borrowed music

Musical borrowings in this score range from short quotations woven into the action to full pre-existing pieces used as dance numbers. One of the former type is the opening line of the song "Malbrouck s'en v-a-t'en guerre" (as noted above), intended to denote Paquita's French heritage. Another, from the opera-ballet *Le Dieu et la Bayadère* (1830), is a phrase sung with disappointment by a powerful male after a low-status female has rejected his offer of money.

Sa recompense est dans son coeur	Her reward is in her heart,
Et ce n'est qu'une bayadère	and she is only a bayadère,
Ah! quel dommage! ah! quel malheur!	oh, what a shame, oh, how unfortunate!

(*Le Dieu et la Bayadère*, Act One, scene IV, text by Eugène Scribe)

This snippet interrupts Lucien's ardent love song and refers to Paquita's refusal of his attentions, underpinning his disappointment (Ex. 4.24, bars 25–29).

Deldevez places this musical quotation at the point in the action when Lucien offers money to Paquita, and she refuses, knowing "the distance separating a poor *gitana* and

Ex. 4.23 Lucien and Paquita love motif; Act One, No. 11, bars 8–16

Ex. 4.24 "Et ce n'est q'une bayadère," from *Le Dieu et la Bayadère* (Auber), quoted in *Paquita* Act One, No. 11, bars 21–29 (source: Rep)
In *Le Dieu et la Bayadère*, the powerful male, L'inconnu, was played by the tenor Adolphe Nourrit; the bayadère, Zoloé, was played by Marie Taglioni.

an officer."[61] (Thus does the musical quotation qualify as a classic *air parlant*; a tune associated with words that, when played by instruments alone can bring its words and their original context to the mind of the hearer.[62])

Three lengthier borrowings are also cleverly placed by Deldevez in his score: First, the *Folie d'Espagne* forms the basis of the Introduction (Overture), its antique-sounding repeating melody invoking the past and its name pointing to Spain (Exx. 4.25a–b).

Second, the music associated with the "Gavotte de Vestris," well-known to social dancers in eighteenth-century and Empire France, is played as the guests dance in the Commander's ballroom (Ex. 4.12). (The contredanse played at curtain-up in that scene is

---

[61] Libretto, Act One, scene VIII. See Appendix D (i).
[62] See Smith, *Ballet and Opera*, 101–114.

Ex. 4.25a *La folie d'Espagne* (from Oxford Music Online, "Folia," designated as being of the later folia type)

Ex. 4.25b *La folie d'Espagne* in the Introduction, bars 5–13

likely borrowed, too, though we have not identified the source.[63]) And third, the "Queen of Prussia" waltz brings the ballet to a close as the *pas de deux* music for the happy couple (Ex. 4.26). Deldevez's borrowing of this waltz "produced a very good effect," wrote one critic approvingly.[64]

This survey of features of the *Paquita* score shows that, like other effective ballet scores of the era, it deployed a wide variety of tools and did its work without calling so much attention to itself that it detracted from its overall purpose. Deldevez deftly creates the right mood at the right time, calls on his command of various dance genres, furnishes music appropriate to the three distinct cultural groups, uses a few recurring motifs and melodies to help identify and characterize, and makes clever use of well-placed borrowed music. Of course, the referential meaning of these borrowings (like those in *Giselle*) is mostly lost on today's listeners, because the popular tunes in question are no longer

[63] Guest suggests this. See *Romantic Ballet in Paris*, 2nd ed., 254.
[64] *L'Album de Sainte-Cécile, revue des théâtres lyriques*, 20 April 1846.

Ex. 4.26 "Queen of Prussia" waltz; Act Two, *Fin du 2° acte*, bars 166–173

recognizeable as such. One of them is still effective today anyway: the *Folie d'Espagne*, which opens the ballet with a flourish, its archaic-sounding melody and tambourine flourishes immediately signaling to the audience, in charming fashion, that the ballet takes in the past and is likely to involve Roma characters.

Similarly, Deldevez's pastoral approach to Roma music does not always signal the presence of Roma people to the audience today as the Hungarian-Roma style would do, for in the years since the composition of this score, this latter style has become more typical for that purpose. Yet, it is still successful. It is a score little known in its entirety today but one that served its purpose well.

Sources

Let us now turn to the other *Paquita* sources we have examined in addition to the music sources already discussed.

Libretto. First, the libretto (see Appendix D (i)), which, aside from laying out the action in detail (over the course of eleven pages), provides a full cast list and names some of the dances to be performed. The total number of characters was 183: nine characters listed as "personnages" (though some were only bit parts), and (in Act One) seventeen Roma (nine men, eight women), fifty-three Spanish villagers (thirteen men, seventeen women, nine boys, fourteen girls), three women in the *pas de trois*, two lead dancers and twenty others in the "corps de danse" (a.k.a. *Pas des manteaux*), and two mayos and two mayas who joined Paquita in her "pas des tambourins." The characters listed for Act Two include two male/female couples who dance the gavotte, fifteen French and five Spanish officers, eighteen ladies of the court, twenty-one children (all girls), twelve members of the "corps de dames dansant" (women in the ballroom scene), eight hussards (all women), and the women who dance the *pas de deux*. Of course, many performers in the corps de ballet appeared in more than one role (and so did the tall character actor Louis Petit, who played both the sculptor in Act One and a superior officer in Act Two).

(As always, one must recall that the librettos in these French ballets were finalized before the music and choreography were created, and that the details could change once the ballet was actually being rehearsed and shaped.)

Justamant staging manual. A second important source for *Paquita* is the staging manual created by Justamant.[65] Its opening pages refer to a production of *Paquita* at the Grand Theater in Lyon on 6 December 1854, with "Mise en scène et danses par Monsieur Justamant." The manual, 246 pages long, unpaginated, is bound together with a printed libretto from the Paris production. It begins with a title page and cast lists documenting three seasons of performances (1854–1857), lists that include Justamant hinself in the role of Inigo. These are followed by a notation key and list of dances. Then comes a meticulous description, with hundreds of drawings, of the ballet's three scenes. The notations for the set dances are placed toward the end of the manual: these include the *pas de trois*, *Pas de Paquita*, and *Pas des manteaux* from the first act, and the *Valse des hussards* and *Pas final* of the ballroom scene. Finally, a list of accessories describes props and additional costume items necessary for both acts. Stitched into the binding at the front of the manual, along with the libretto, are eight full-color plates by Alexandre Lacauchie featuring members of the original Paris cast and labeled "Galerie dramatique | Académie royale de musique."[66]

Whether the attribution of *mise en scène* and dances to Justamant means that he devised these elements himself or staged pre-existing material is unclear. What is certain is that cast numbers for the Act One divertissement in the Lyon production match those in the Paris cast list, and dances performed in the Lyon ballroom scene also correspond to some of the dances listed in the Paris libretto. Too, Deldevez's musical score is followed very closely with only a few exceptions, mostly in the ballet's final dances.[67]

These striking parallels suggest that the Lyon production may have been a restaging of Mazilier's Paris *Paquita*, an enticing prospect, for it would mean that we have at our fingertips a detailed account of this ballet telling us how it was performed at the Opéra. We cannot state with certainty that this manual represents the Paris production, though, in the absence of ironclad proof. However, we have chosen to describe in detail the production preserved in Justamant's manual, which gives us a clear view into a major nineteenth-century French ballet, whether it originated in Paris or Lyon.

One final note: In the Paris *répétiteur*, Lucien is called Ernest.

Paquita in Paris and Lyon: A scene-by-scene description

For our scene-by-scene description (which combines literal translations as well as paraphrases from the Justamant manual), we follow Justamant's numbering and provide a guiding phrase before each section to summarize its action. We also, from time to time, as noted, draw information from the Paris libretto and musical sources, as well as various published reviews, to create a fuller picture of the ballet.

Introduction: Deldevez's introduction begins with a rendition of the *Folie d'Espagne* (perhaps to draw the audience into the Spanish past; Ex. 4.25b), which he soon

---

[65] Theaterwissenschàftliche Sammlung der Universität Köln, Schloß Wahn, Inventory Number 70-479.

[66] These are from the collection *Petite galerie dramatique ou Recueil de différents costumes d'acteurs des théâtres de la capitale* (Paris: Martinet, 1796–1843), an extensive series of plates representing actors. These plates were hand-painted.

[67] There is no opening jaleo in the final dances of the ballroom scene in the Justamant manual, and there is a long solo for Paquita that has no corresponding music—according to the order Justamant presents the dances—in the Paris score. (Alterations to a series of dances in a divertissement are commonplace, as one can see throughout this book.)

embellishes with a few shakes of a tambourine to give the audience a sense of locale and the presence of Roma people.[68] This is followed by a tonic-destabilizing excursion into some threatening territory to hint at the skullduggery to come. Ultimately, the Introduction gives way to a charming pastoral-sounding theme (in $\frac{3}{4}$, with emphasis on the first beat, and thus sounding like a polonaise).

Act One

No. 1: A sculptor engraves a memorial tablet; Spanish peasants relax in the sun; the Governor and the General arrive. According to the libretto, the scene is situated in a valley is surrounded by rocky cliff walls; a natural staircase is carved into the stone. On the audience's right, a tent is prepared for the Romani. To the left, a marble tablet. (The dancers will first appear at the top of the cliff wall and then make their way down into the valley.)

As the curtain rises on the Valley of the Bulls, near Saragossa, the music (still in $\frac{3}{4}$ with emphasis on the first beat), blossoms into a certain magnificence. A sculptor is busy engraving an inscription on a marble tablet; Spanish peasants are stretched out or grouped nonchalantly in the sun, smoking cigarettes. The sculptor asks one of them for tobacco and receives it. The Governor enters, soon followed by the General and his family; a timpani roll in the preceding measure indicates their high station. They stroll in slowly. The General, after a brief chat with the sculptor, reads a paper with the inscription on it, looks at the marble tablet, sighs. His head falls into his hands.

No. 2: The General tells his sad story. The music, marked "*express[ivo]*" in the Rep, offers a sweet and plaintive oboe melody sometimes joined by flutes and violins. Lucien asks his father what is the matter. His father replies, "My brother, my beloved wife, my little girl, were felled here, murdered. . . . I wanted to put up this stone (he points to it) in remembrance of those I loved and who are now in heaven." As Lucien and his grandmother share in the Governor's emotion, the General shows a bit of impatience.

No. 3: The marriage between Lucien and Dona Seraphina is arranged. Lucien, sad and pensive, seems preoccupied, as the Rep notes in bar 4. Lucien becomes worried when his father tells him that a marriage of the "young people" is in order. Soon thereafter, the General joins the hands of Lucien and Dona Seraphina, and the Spanish governor, in an aside, says that "this is a political marriage that is involuntary" (Rep). The Governor then returns to his normal "voice" and invites the visitors to go on a stroll, to be followed by attending the festival at which the *baladins* (traveling entertainers) will perform (he points to the tent). Then, as the General, the Governor, and Dona Seraphina chat upstage, the grandmother asks Lucien if he truly loves his fiancée.

Lucien: "No."

Grandmother: "That time will come."

Lucien: "I don't think so."

Grandmother: "She is pretty, though."

Lucien: "But my heart feels nothing for her."

---

[68] The Introduction is omitted in the Rep, surely because it did not call for the presence of the dancers.

Now it is time to depart; everyone, including the sculptor and the peasants, leaves.[69]

No. 4: The Roma arrive and rehearse for the festival. "From the top of the [rocky cliff] at the back of the stage, we see a crowd of villagers and gypsies coming down to a festival," as the critic de Villemessant describes the opening of this scene.[70] Here, Deldevez supplies happy and decidedly "country" music, with a drone, and—eventually—tambourines (Ex. 4.13). Inigo is first seen at the top of the cliff, looking around to all sides and summoning his companions. Men come down first; then women. Four Roma men arrive at stage level, pulling a wagon filled with the objects and instruments of their livelihood; Inigo encourages them to move faster. Once everyone has arrived, Inigo looks around: "Ah, let's see where we are!"

As the music livens to a *più animato* in $\frac{6}{8}$, everyone goes to the front of the stage (Rep). Inigo spots the tent the Governor has set up and says, "Ah, this is where the Governor is giving the party he wanted us to come to. Let's see if you remember the dance you are going to perform." What follows is a brief rehearsal of the upcoming divertissement. To an eight-bar phrase of music, repeated, four groups perform a passage from their dance (Ex. 4.14). First, three male-female couples perform a combination of *chassé soubresaut* twice on each leg as each couple traces a square pattern.

Inigo: "That's going well. Let's see the others."

He designates another group of three couples to come to center. Each couple holding hands, the second group begins with *pas tombé*, the men passing behind the women as they let go of hands. Justamant's drawing suggests the men take the women by the waist with their left hand, and both turn a circle to the right with three *temps levé*, right arms lifted overhead, the women's arms framing their partner's heads.

Inigo: "That's good."

He next calls two women, who cross at center performing a combination of *pas de bourrée couru, soubresaut, coupé dessous, brisé en arrière* three times. Having crossed, they turn in places with three *glissades* and a *coupé*.

Inigo: "Very good. Now I want to see my children. Come forward, kids (*moutards*)!"

Eight boys run to form a line across the stage.

Inigo: "Attention. Let's go."

He beats time with his hands as the boys travel downstage and upstage with multiple *sauts de basque*, finishing with two *appels* (stamps of the foot) on the right foot.

---

[69] Here, a "No. 3 bis" has been added to the Rep following two other versions of No. 3 (the first of which is struck through). This new version consists of fifty-two bars of *Moderato*, $\frac{4}{4}$, D major. This same music has been added to the copied orchestra score on paper different from the rest of the score; it appears to have been inserted as a replacement for the original No. 3. Justamant's No. 3, however, corresponds to the second version in the Rep—*Allegro non troppo*, $\frac{3}{8}$, A major.

[70] H. de Villemessant, *La Sylphide*, April 1846. There are seven Roma men followed by six Roma women descending the rock staircase in the drawings of this scene in Justamant, and many more merrymakers joining in from stage level.

Smiling and satisfied with the rehearsal, Inigo sends the boys running into the tent, while those with the wagon take it into the wings.

Paquita arrives late. Next, the key and meter change (D minor, common time) as "Inigo sees that one of his danseuses is missing—the prettiest one" (Rep). Inigo searches for her among the group, and then dispatches them to look for her—they go upstage, each following a different trajectory. Inigo leaves the stage, saying "She will pay me back for this" (recall that Giselle had said "he will pay me back for this" when Loys has stood her up for their date early in Act One).

Then, as the music switches to the Romani motif we had heard at the beginning of this number (Ex. 4.14), Paquita appears at the top of the rocky cliffs (Rep). She is in a reverie, carefully arranging the flowers in her hands into a bouquet. Her companions below all lift their arms up toward her and call out to her. After she descends the steps in the rock, her friends surround her in a semicircle behind her (men in the back). Paquita explains that she had been gathering flowers for them, and she hands a flower to each friend, starting at her right, and then tucking the last flower into her belt. Her friends then warn her that Inigo is angry. When Paquita asks where he is, all of them indicate stage right (using both arms, at shoulder height). She says, "I'll go to him," and, going toward stage right, is surprised to find herself face to face with him.

No. 5: An angry Inigo threatens Paquita. To suddenly agitated music, Inigo, with arms crossed in front of his chest, advances angrily toward a fearful Paquita, forcing her to back up many steps—about halfway across the stage (Ex. 4.5). (This same sequence of events occurs in *Giselle* as she suddenly is confronted by an angry Hilarion, who, arms crossed, backs her up across the stage; moments later Giselle—now angry and with arms crossed—backs *him* across the stage.)

> *Inigo*: (still advancing [on Paquita]) "Where were you? Speak, speak."
>
> *Paquita*: "I don't dare."
>
> *Inigo*: "I'll *make* you dare."

He threatens her, and several of the Roma men step in to prevent him from hitting her. Inigo shakes them off.

> *Inigo*: (to Paquita) "Come here."
>
> *Paquita*: "Not right now."

She flees the furious Inigo, and after some pushing and shoving with him, the men go into the tent, followed by all of the women except Paquita, who, at far stage right, says "Oh, my god, what will happen to me?"

No. 6: Scène dansante, in which Paquita shows her mettle. In this scene Paquita (far from feeling fearful as she did in the preceding scene) openly mocks Inigo, disobeys his directives, ignores his pleas, and dances blithely away as he tries to engage her in conversation. This is a *scène dansante*, and like the one in *Giselle*, it is placed early in the action of the ballet and similarly serves to demonstrate the personalities of two of the ballet's main characters and the relationship between them. In this case, it shows both that Inigo is an impetuous man, and that he at once desires and seeks to oppress Paquita. And Paquita, for her part, shows herself to be plucky, insouciant, and capable of being a smart aleck. In this scene, she is both flirtatious with Inigo and openly disdainful of him.

Ex. 4.27 Inigo expresses his ardor for Paquita; Act One, No. 6, bars 3–6

And she is in control, a state of affairs reflected in the fact that Deldevez grants the lion's share of the music of this scene to her, Inigo being allotted—apart from his initial expression of ardor rendered in the manner of "expressive singing" (*canto espressivo*)—only bits of "outburst" music here and there. The contrast between his unsubtle anger and her blithe non-responses creates a comic effect.

As the scene opens, the audience hears Inigo's *canto espressivo*, which is in a much sweeter, milder vein than the *allegro agitato* of the preceding scene: a gently rocking eighteen-bar 𝟞/𝟠 *andante* in G major (Ex. 4.27). Paquita is at far stage right, facing away from Inigo, who stands at stage left, his arms crossed.

> *Inigo* (to himself as her looks at Paquita from a distance): "I am alone with her. She is so pretty! I love her so! How I suffer—she doesn't even want to look at me." (more abruptly) "Well, I will go over there."
>
> Paquita sees out of the corner of her eye that he is coming.
>
> *Paquita* (to herself): "There he is—we shall see."

Inigo, approaching her (though her back is still turned), declares his love:

> *Inigo*: "Paquita, you are angry with me. If only you knew how I suffer; it's because I love you like a fool."

Smiling, her back still turned, she says to herself, "Yes, I know it very well." He continues, "Ah, if you like, instead of ordering you around as a master, I would always be a slave," and he falls to his knees.

The ensuing developments are summarized by Fiorentino as follows: "See [Paquita] happily casting aside her striped mantilla and replying to Inigo's volcanic sighs with leaps and bounds, frantic pirouettes and disdainful entrechats."[71] First, instead of responding to Inigo, who had just offered to become her slave, she begins dancing in place to a staccato *allegretto*, a passage marked "Paquita mocks Inigo" in the Rep (Ex. 4.28).

> She does *coupé dessous*, the left foot, *des petits ronds de jambe en dehors*, and *fouetté dessous*; the same on the other leg; *coupé dessous*, the left foot, *glissade failli dessus*; the same on the other leg; and again one time on each leg; the same *pas* in its entirety.

Inigo cannot countenance this indifference. He gets up, concentrating his anger, but Paquita continues to dance.

---

[71] *Le Constitutionnel*, 7 April 1846, tr. in Guest, *Romantic Ballet in Paris*, 2nd ed., 254.

Ex. 4.28 Paquita mocks Inigo; Act One, No. 6, bars 19–22 (source: Rep)

Coming downstage, she does, starting on the right foot, *pas de bourrée couru*, the right foot, finishing in 4th position on 2 feet, *jeté dessus*, 2 *petits jetés ordinaire*; these movements are done two times on each foot.

Then . . . she does *jeté ordinaire*, *relevé sur l'orteil*, *en degagent* the leg *à la demi-seconde*; these movements are done 2 times on each foot; then, going upstage a little, she does 4 *emboîtés* and a *pirouette*.

Inigo beseeches Paquita.

Inigo: "How [can] you see me at your knees beseeching you, and instead of answering me, you dance. Come on—speak to me."

Paquita dances and ignores Inigo's pleas. Paquita, instead of answering, poses on one leg, smiles at him and runs away. (Here, according to the Rep, Paquita says, "Don't interrupt me, because I'm creating a new dance to do at the festival.")

Inigo runs after her, grabs her by the hand, makes her come back suddenly, takes two steps forward, saying to her, "But *Sacre bleu*, speak."

Paquita does not respond and dances again (Ex. 4.7).

Starting on the right foot, she does a *pas marché en avant*, *relevé sur l'orteil*, *en passant*, the left leg *en temps de cuisse en avant*, *pas marché en* the left foot *en avant*, *relevé sur l'orteil* turning to the right, with the right leg in *demi-seconde*; these movements fill 2 measures and she does them 4 times in a row.

Inigo looks at her angrily, saying that she finished it badly. He goes toward her at the end of eight measures.

Paquita does the same *pas* going to the other side and on the other foot.

Inigo stays in place, his anger gnawing at him.

She goes back, doing *sissonne*, the foot in back, *brisé en avant en tournant*, and *fouetté en dedans*, at hip height being on *relevé sur l'orteil*, arriving quickly, and *assemblé derrière*; these movements she does 2 times on each leg; the leg that is behind, *pas de bourrée dessus dessous taqueté* in place, one time on each foot, and *coupé dessous*, *fouetté sauté dessous*, *pas marché en arrière sur l'orteil*, a turn in *attitude*; again one time the same *pas*.

Inigo has been moving toward her. He stamps his foot furiously. Paquita advances with both hands extended, as if to say, "Oh!" Then she starts dancing again.

Ex. 4.29 "I'm talking to you. You don't answer me." Act One, No. 6, bars 71–78

She does, beginning on the right foot, *pas marché en avant sur l'orteil*, placed in arabesque; *pas marché en avant croisé sur l'orteil*, turning to the right *en dehors* and placed in *attitude* with *demi bras*, the right shoulder to the public; that fills 2 measures; she does these movements again 2 times.

Inigo reflects for a moment, then suddenly says to himself, "She must be mine." He runs and takes her violently in his arms. Paquita, defending herself, manages to get out of Inigo's arms by jumping to the side with a *saut de basque*. Inigo is stunned by her strength.

Inigo: (at the height of fury) "Oh yes, I'm talking to you. You don't answer me. I'm on my knees, and you're dancing. I tell you that I love you, do you hear—and you don't love me." [Ex. 4.29].

Paquita: (with a little movement of her head) "Oh, no."

Inigo: (having seen it) "Well, I wish it, and I am your master."

Paquita: "Oh, no."

Inigo: "You will see." He lifts his arm to strike her. Paquita proudly raises her head with a terrible look of firmness, then suddenly starts to smile, raising her shoulders a little.

She rests her left arm on Inigo's right shoulder, looks at him with a smile, and strokes his cheek with her right hand. (The Queen in *Sleeping Beauty* uses the same sort of sweet persuasion to calm her husband's anger.[72])

Inigo remains stunned and his anger subsides as he takes in this graciousness (Ex. 4:30).

Paquita then does *sissonne derrière*, the right foot (and turning behind Inigo), 2 *glissades dessus* and *jeté en avant*; having changed places, she does the same *scène* and the same *pas*; she traverses the stage, passing in front of him, and starting on the right foot, she does *chassé* on two feet, *cabriole battu en arrière*; again one time; *coupé dessous soubresaut*, the right foot doing *temps de cuisse en dedans*, the left leg and shoulder to him; the same on the other leg; again one time the entire *pas*, but after the 1st *temps de cuisse*,

---

[72] Marian Smith, "New Life for Character and Story in *Sleeping Beauty*," Oxford Handbooks Online (March 2017), doi: 10.1093/oxfordhb/9780199935321.013.172.

Ex. 4.30 Paquita smiles, strokes his cheek, and then dances; Act One, No. 6, bars 91–98

do a *soubresaut*; she goes upstage doing 4 times, on the same foot, *glissade en arrière*, *jeté ordinaire*, *coupé dessous*, *temps de cuisse en arrière*.

Inigo, meanwhile, appears to be thinking, and suffering.

Having the left foot behind, she does *pas de bourrée dessous*, *assemblé* to the side on 2 feet, turn to the right on the left toe; these movements she does 4 times in a row; then, 4 times in a row, step over [crossing] on the left toe and a turn to the right, and *saut de basque*.

Inigo, impatient and desperate, goes back into the tent.

No. 7: Recognition scene.

Paquita [going toward the tent at stage left]: "Finally, he is gone." [Recall that Loys said the same after Wilfride had left the scene early in Act One.] "He is leaving me alone here, and I can give myself up to my thoughts." Walking around, she pulls up the medallion that is suspended from her belt, contemplates it, and kisses it [Recognition motif, Ex. 4.2]. "I've had it ever since I was very young."

She feels "an indescribable sweetness at the features of the man who surely is her father, and dreams of the joys of a family life."

Paquita: "Ah" [thinking of the man depicted in her medallion], "what a joy to be near him instead of being there with this miserable man" (she goes toward the tent) "who hits me, and talks about love, and who horrifies me" (she recoils). "When I think I shall be married to someone I love; that I will have little children that I will rock. Alas, God did not wish it." She is overwhelmed. She walks mechanically toward the tent.

Now, Paquita lifts her eyes and looks at the terrain around her; she suddenly believes she recognizes it. She walks around, taking a good look, and finds herself right in front of the memorial tablet.

She reads the inscription, and putting her hand to her head (and stepping forward a little), [says,] "Yes, I remember coming here as a child, being carried by an officer" (she then moves away from the tablet and faces forward toward the audience, and continues her recollection) "and that men wrapped in cloaks struck him in the heart, that he fell dead, there" (she points at the tablet) "and that I was taken far away."

She comes downstage and falls to her knees [facing the audience], and raises both hands, holding the medallion.

Paquita: "Oh, God, make it so you find my father or my family." She looks at her medallion.[73]

No. 8: *The festival takes place*. According to the Rep, "Here, soon it will be time for the festival. The stage fills up." Paquita hears noise, she remembers her unhappy state; she puts the medallion back on her belt, suspending it on the left side, and goes back into the tent.

The stage fills with people: On the top of the rocky cliff, Spanish peasants; from all sides, others arrive (Ex. 4.15). French soldiers come to place themselves at the top of the rocky cliff, too. (Justamant's drawing shows both men and women sitting on the rocky steps as well.) The mood is festive, as Gautier reports in his review.[74]

The Governor's male servants come from stage left to stage right, where they arrange a long line of armchairs and chairs extending from downstage to upstage. As soon as they are finished, they take their places, standing in a line at the bottom of the rocky staircase, in front of the gathered crowd.

The General, the Governor and their parties return from their promenade. At the Governor's invitation, they fill the seats that have just been set out for them, while the Governor remains standing. Inigo emerges from the tent; the Governor tells Inigo to summon his troupe. With a bow, Inigo does so. Standing in front of the tent, he begins stepping forward toward stage right and is followed by his troupe of twenty dancers, emerging from the tent (now wearing the performance costumes) in a neat formation of pairs, women on the left. At Inigo's command, the first five women swing off their line to form a new line directly in front of the Governor, greet him and then, in a procession (led by the dancer at the upstage end of the line), return to stage left. In groups of five, the dancers, group by group, do the same.

The music changes to a march (D major, common time), and Inigo (his back to the audience) gives another command to his dancers, who now form two semicircular rows across the stage, men behind women, each line holding hands. Next, Paquita and the three women who will dance the *pas de trois* enter and come to center stage in front of their colleagues, the three women standing upstage of Paquita, whose placement signifies she is the lead *danseuse* of the divertissement.

In a recitative (with a short ad-lib *lento* section) that interrupts the march, the Governor asks the General if he would like the entertainment to begin, and the General responds, "I would like it very much." The Governor tells Inigo to start the fête, and then sits down. Inigo announces the fête is starting; the dancers all take their places. (During the ensuing performance of the *Pas des manteaux*, the servants exit stage left.)

---

[73] In the Rep, there is a little march at the end of this scene, followed by a short variation on the Recognition motif (*Allegro molto*, ⁶⁄₈, E-flat major, 24 bars). Neither of these pieces of music is indicated by Justamant, though it is possible that he used them.

[74] *La Presse*, 30 July 1846, in Gautier, *Gautier on Dance*, 167.

Ex. **4.31a**   Act One, *Pas de trois*, Variation 1, bars 68–72

Ex. **4.31b**   Act One, *Pas de trois*, Variation 2, bars 100–108

The Act One divertissement comprises three numbers: the *pas de trois*, *Pas des manteaux*, and *Pas de Mlle Carlotta Grisi*, as the final dance is titled in the Paris scores. A brief scene, No. 9, separates the *Pas des manteaux* and *Pas de Mlle Carlotta Grisi*, and therefore the first two numbers make up a "1er Divertissement," while the third is a "2e Divertissement," according to the orchestra score and short score.

Justamant reverses the *Pas des manteaux* and the *Pas de Paquita*, as he calls it, and places the scene (No. 9) immediately following the *pas de trois*. Our description, based on the Justamant manual, will follow his order.

Pas de trois. The Justamant *pas de trois* for three women is a suite of classical dances comprising an entrée, three variations, and coda. Justamant's "jeune gitana[s]," as they are called in his list of roles, include "une première danseuse et deux 2me danseuses."

The pair of lower-ranked dancers begins the entrée, a bright $\frac{2}{4}$ in D major, performing in unison for sixteen bars (Ex. 4.9). A drone in the introduction evokes a country sound, in keeping with Deldevez's approach to Roma music. The lead *danseuse* takes over alone before she is joined by her companions. Together, they traverse the stage in a series of *piqués en arabesque* "sur l'orteil." The second *danseuses* finish the entrée with a series of unison steps performed as a tight pair and finally break away to opposite wings to finish "poser en arabesque allongée."

Three variations follow. The first, a buoyant $\frac{6}{8}$ in F major (Ex. 4.31a) notated for "Mlle Camille," features steps of elevation: *assemblé, battu en cabriole, brisé, grand jeté en tournant*, and *fouetté battu*. The final step is a common ending for Justamant: *pirouette sur le cou-de-pied*.

The second variation is a sprightly $\frac{2}{4}$ in A major (Ex. 4.31b) for "Mlle Deleau" (the *première danseuse*). Here, steps of lesser elevation (*jeté ordinaire, petit cabriole de côté*)

Ex. 4.31c Act One, *Pas de trois*, Variation 3, bars 147–151

Ex. 4.31d Act One, *Pas de trois*, Coda, bars 195–203

combine with *pointe* work ("pas de bourrée dessous dessus taqueté," "temps piqué sur les deux pointes," "un tour par la droite sur l'orteil gauche"). The final step is likewise a *pirouette*, but this time "au goût de la danseuse" (to the dancer's taste).

Variation three, a rhythmic $\frac{6}{8}$ in B-flat major (Ex. 4.31c) for "Mlle Saliné," features even more complex steps of elevation: *grande cabriole de côté battu, rond de jambe fouetté en dehors, cabriole en arrière battu placée en arabesque,* and *sissonne fondu.* Steps "sur l'orteil" as well as extensions of the leg are introduced midway through. Traveling downstage, the dancer performs "un grand rond de jambe à hauteur de hanche de la 4er derriere à la 4er devant."

The coda begins with Mlle Duleau traveling downstage performing "entrechat quatre échappé sur les pointes" (Ex. 4.31d). Mlles Saliné and Camille next dance together, repeating Duleau's steps as they travel from opposite upstage corners to meet at downstage center. All three dancers join for the ending—traveling away from center and back again, the *première danseuse* pairing briefly with each of her lower-ranked sisters, all three traveling together downstage—and share a final pose at center, Duleau standing "sur les pointes," the others standing on either side of her, supporting her by the waist, as they lean back and away, side arms open.

A note in Justamant's manual at the end of the entrée reads, "See the new variations at the end of the *pas.*" Sure enough, following the coda, Justamant includes three variations (for Mlles Leblond, Bertin, and Navare, respectively), perhaps choreographed by himself. Bearing neither time nor key signature, the bars listed following each combination nevertheless add up to match the score. Notably, the second solo begins with Duleau's first two combinations from her earlier variation before continuing with new material.

No. 9: Paquita reluctantly collects money from the crowd; Lucien becomes curious about her ethnic heritage. At the end of the *pas de trois*, Paquita and Inigo, who is holding a tambourine, are standing near the tent; he instructs her to collect money from the crowd. With pride and dignity, she refuses. But taking her by the hand, he brusquely passes her to his right, gives her the tambourine, and orders her to obey. With a sigh of resignation, she begins the collection by the side of the tent, stage left, holding out the tambourine in front of her, making her way in a half-circle to stage right, thanking those who put money into the tambourine. When she gets to Lucien, who is still seated at stage right, she feels an emotion, in spite of herself. Lucien, struck by her beauty, throws his entire coin-pouch into the tambourine. She thanks him, though she is a bit confused.

Inigo has been watching from stage left, and now crosses the stage, takes her by the hand, and tells her to hurry up. He counts the receipts as she crosses behind him, now taking a position to his left (that is, the power position). Inigo, unhappy with the take, tells Paquita she must dance again.

She refuses, saying she is too tired. Lucien, observing their conversation, rises from his seat without delay, rushes over, and grabs Inigo's arm just as he raises it to strike Paquita. Then Lucien pushes Inigo away, strongly, to Lucien's right (the weak position). At first Inigo does not know who pushed him away, and he goes to attack Lucien—but he quickly backs away and makes excuses when he sees Lucien giving him a severe look. Lucien orders him to get away, and Inigo answers, "Yes, yes, right away."

An eyewitness to the scene described it thus:

Breathless but smiling, she obeys Inigo's order to solicit the generosity of her admiring audience, holding out her little tambourine. . . . Paquita cannot look at Lucien without her heart fluttering with an emotion that is as gentle as it is violent. For his part, the young officer is greatly taken with the gypsy girl's grace. He rises to his feet, following her with his eyes and gestures, and when the brutal Inigo, discontented with the collection, attempts to strike the trembling girl, he separates them and, with an imperious gesture, grasps the arm that was about to strike her.[75]

Now Lucien takes Paquita by the hand, leads her to his father (the General), who is still seated at stage right with his mother and Seraphina.

Lucien: "My father, see how this *jeune fille* is beautiful, and how her whiteness doesn't look anything like these people here"—he points to Inigo.

The General (and his family) [agree]: "Yes, she's very pretty."

Lucien asks Inigo who she is. Inigo replies they are family.

Lucien: "You lie."

Inigo steals Paquita's medallion; Inigo tries to keep Paquita from dancing but Lucien intervenes. Lucien asks Paquita who she is. "Alas," comes her answer, "I don't know anything. All I have is this portrait." But at the same time, Inigo has come up behind Paquita and surreptitiously taken the medallion from her. Now, she looks for it—but

---

[75] *La France musicale*, 5 April 1846, tr. in Guest, *Romantic Ballet in Paris*, 3rd ed., 421. The article is signed with the initials O.P.R.A.

cannot find it in its usual place on her belt. She looks on the ground, in vain, and then accuses Inigo of stealing it. The Governor steps in between Inigo and Paquita, telling her to back off.

Lucien (concentrating his spite) tells the Governor to leave the girl here.

Governor: (taking on a phonily accommodating mien) "As you wish—I was only asking her to stay and dance."

Lucien: "Very well, you are welcome."

Paquita: (with joy) "Yes, with pleasure."

Inigo has noticed Lucien gazing at Paquita, so he comes up to her and instructs her not to dance.

Paquita: "Now I *want* to."

Governor: [intervening] "Be quiet and let her dance."

Inigo resigns himself to it and appears to accept it with good grace.

Lucien and the Governor sit down.

Paquita places herself for dancing.

Pas de Paquita. Justamant's notation of the *Pas de Paquita* (*pas des tambourins*) is a rousing *pas de cinq* for Paquita and two male/female couples, comprising an entrée, two variations, and a two-part coda. The dance and action of this *pas de cinq* are infused with amorous and good-humored flirtation, and Paquita's part calls for dazzling, virtuosic dancing. Justamant provides some commentary letting us know the narrative significance of the dance, during which "Lucien is transported with joy over Paquita."

The entrée, a pleasant and moderate $\frac{3}{4}$ in G major with chromatic inflections (see Ex. 4.7), begins with the two couples, each woman having her arms on her partner's shoulder and the men with their arms crossed. The description of the first combination is preceded by a parenthetical "en temps de cachucha." The pairs perform identical steps in

Ex. 4.32a Act One, *Pas de Mlle Carlotta Grisi*, Entrée, bars 45–52

Ex. 4.32b Act One, *Pas de Mlle Carlotta Grisi*, Variation, bars 117–121

opposition, traveling to center and back out to the wings with a series of small jumps punctuated by poses in which the dancers lean toward or away from each other.

With the couples finishing at the sides, Paquita begins a brief solo highlighted by three *grands ronds de jambe à la seconde* and "relever sur les deux pointes, les bras en couronnes" (Ex. 4.32a).

The men approach Paquita at center, and a vignette plays out in which they fight for her affections:

The man on stage right takes Paquita's hand and kisses it. The other sees this and comes a little in front of Paquita, pushes the kisser's head back, then pokes him.

[*Second man*]: "Why did you kiss her hand? I did not do so."

[*First man*]: "Ah, it doesn't concern you."

[*Second man*]: (in anger) "We'll see about that."

[*First man*]: "Well, yes."

They run toward each other and begin a fist fight.

Paquita: (separating them) "Calm down. I'll *make* you agree by giving you my two hands."

The men each grab a hand and kiss it. They take Paquita by the waist and assist her in various steps, moving her upstage and down as she performs *jetés en arrière* and *en avant*, *attitudes en pointe*, and an *entrechat six* as they lift her. Finally, all three perform a *pirouette sur le cou-de-pied*, Paquita finishing "sur les pointes" as the men support her by the waist.

[*The two women*]: (coming up to their partners and striking them on the shoulder) "Well, we are here."

The men: "Ah! It's as it should be!"

The couples continue the dance as it had begun, eventually finishing with each woman holding her partner's shoulder with one hand and performing an *appel* (a stamp of the foot) while leaning back, the other arm raised in the air.

The following variation is cut in Justamant ("une variation coupé"), although it is not struck through in the Rep (Ex. 4.32b).

Paquita's variation, a quick, light G-major flute solo in $\frac{2}{4}$ (Ex. 4.32c), begins with multiple *grands sauts de basque* and continues with *piqués en arabesque* and *piqués degagés*. At one point, following four *sauts de chat*, she performs "six petits changements de pieds sur les orteils." The variation concludes with the obligatory *pirouette sur le cou-de-pied*.

Ex. 4.32c Act One, *Pas de Mlle Carlotta Grisi*, Paquita's variation, bars 153–157

The coda is begun by the two couples, each of the dancers holding a tambourine which they repeatedly strike and also hold overhead with both hands (Ex. 4.17a). Next, Paquita performs a final entrée filled with jumps, including *cabriole de côté battu*, *fouetté sauté*, *brisé*, *assemblé*, *saut de basque*, and *sissonne en tournant*, finishing with a "pirouette sur le cou-de-pied et la jambe croisé derrière."

The other dancers run from either side as the music changes to a $\frac{3}{8}$ "mouvement de valse" (Ex. 4.17b). Paquita, "sur les pointes," strikes the tambourines of her fellow dancers, the women first, who then change places with the men. Then she performs eight *sauts de basque* as she travels down a diagonal line formed by the couples at stage left. With each *saut de basque*, she strikes a tambourine held in her path. As soon as a tambourine is struck, that dancer runs downstage to rejoin the line and continue the pattern.

Paquita moves to center while making two turns to the right, and the other dancers surround her in a square formation, the women in front, posing and raising their tambourines overhead. Paquita continues to strike the tambourines, moving downstage from the men to the women. Similar patterns and combinations continue, the men at one point lifting Paquita together by the waist. Finally, all five dancers form a row across the stage and travel down performing *glissade dessous*, *coupé dessous*, *petits sauts de basque en face* three times on each leg, with the right arm held overhead. A single *pirouette* for all precedes a final series of poses, and the number ends with the dancers surrounding Paquita, who on the final two chords strikes the tambourines of the men and then the women. As one critic wrote, "In the *pas des tambourins*, Mlle. Grisi performed prodigies of lightness, elevation and *parcours*; in her last *écot* especially, she performs *temps de pointe* which bring forth thunders of applause."[76]

Pas des manteaux. We will describe in detail the choreography for the *Pas des manteaux* (Dance of the capes), an elaborate group dance featuring a lead couple and an ensemble of couples. The number as it was performed in Paris caused quite a sensation, in part because it was inspired by the popular touring group of children, the Danseuses Viennoises, who had fascinated Opéra audiences the year before with their precisely executed performances of ensemble character dance choreographies.[77]

The male roles in Paris were danced by females *en travestie*—just as the male roles of the dances performed by the Danseuses Viennoises were danced by girls—however,

[76] *Le Constitutionnel*, 7 April 1846, tr. in Guest, *Romantic Ballet in Paris*, 2nd ed., 254.

[77] Founded by a Frau Josephine Weiss, the troupe of thirty-six girls and one boy (Frau Weiss's son) performed twenty-nine times at the Opéra in January, February, and March of 1845 (assuming they performed at their own benefit on 15 February). Immensely popular, they were lauded for their astonishing precision; the critic for *La Revue musicale* compared them favorably to the Opéra's corps de ballet and expressed astonishment at the troupe's *pas de miroir* (mirror dance). ("Two troops of children placed on either side of a gauze scrim—with one depicting the people and the other reflecting them—is something miraculous.") *La Revue musicale* (1845), 277. Guest, *Romantic Ballet in Paris*, 2nd ed., 253; *La Revue de Paris* (1845), 321; and the Théâtre de l'Opéra—Journal, Bibliothèque-Musée de l'Opéra, reference collection. The troupe (numbering forty-eight) toured in eastern Canada in 1847. James H. Marsh, *The Canadian Encyclopedia* (Toronto: McClelland & Stewart, 1999), 626.

Justamant refers to them as men (and draws them in black ink instead of the usual red ink used for women). Because the male lead in Justamant's staging was danced by an actual man (Mr. Bertolo, who also performed as part of the lead couple in the final scene's *Valse des hussards*), it seems likely that the male ensemble roles were also danced by men in Lyon. Whatever the case, the "men" hold red capes, as though they are bullfighters.[78] The music is a lively $\frac{3}{8}$ in G major, and Guest refers to the dance as "a sort of cachucha."[79] The step vocabulary includes primarily *pas marché*, *coupé dessous* with a drag of the foot ("en trainant la jambe"), *brisé*, *jeté*, *soubresaut*, *saut de basque*, *valse*, and *pas allemande* in a variety of combinations. Our description of Justamant's twenty figures (each a series of enchaînements) will focus primarily on the patterns created by the ensemble and the logistics of working the capes, explained in detail by Justamant, who also points out that during the dance the Governor "has not lost sight of Lucien and understands his love" for Paquita.

No. 1: After seven bars of the lengthy twenty-three-bar introduction, five couples begin upstage right. The men, with capes attached at their shoulders, have their left hand on their waist and their right hand extended to the side, holding the cape. The women have their right hand on the men's left shoulder and their left hand on their hip. Traveling downstage on the diagonal with *brisé croisé*, *soubresaut*, *pas marché en avant*, and *coupé dessous*, the men bring the cape in front of their chest and the women raise their right arm, "bien jouer les hanches" (four bars). Repeating this step combination, the men open the cape and the women rest their right hand on the men's shoulder (four bars). The dance is repeated from the beginning but the ensemble stops short of completing the full enchaînement (six bars, followed by a bar of fermata and two bars of vamp).

No. 2: At the introduction of the main musical theme (Ex. 4.16), a second group of five couples begins from upstage left and repeats No. 1, traveling downstage on the diagonal (16 bars). Justamant writes, "tout le pas doit etre danser dans le styl espagnol" (The entire *pas* must be danced in the Spanish style).

No. 3: From opposite sides where they line the wings, the groups travel toward center, the women keeping their hand on the men's shoulder, the men again bringing the cape across their chest (six bars). Reaching center, the men open the capes, framing the women, who pass to the other side of their partner, making a full inside turn (two bars). The women cross in front of the men again and together they travel toward the wings making two turns, the men continuing to frame their partner with their cape (eight bars? no number of bars is given). No. 3 is repeated, the women finishing inside of the men, who put one end of the cape into their belt to free their arm (sixteen bars).

No. 4: The lead couple begins from upstage left, left arms on the waist, his right arm extended and holding his cape open, her right arm on his left shoulder. They perform an enchaînement similar to No. 1, followed by a series of *jetés*. Circling the stage in counterclockwise direction, they arrive downstage center. Meanwhile, the ensemble women make a *port de bras*, leaning forward, while the men perform a *soubresaut*, swinging forward and back; these movements are performed four times (sixteen bars).

No. 5: The lead couple repeats part of No. 3 as the ensemble travels upstage. Once there, the men place an arm around the women's shoulders so both dancers are wrapped in the cape (eight bars).

---

[78] The 1846 Paris libretto (see Appendix D(i)), presumably in the spirit of *travestie*, lists the female dancers in this numbers as "MM." (*messieurs*), though most of the same names appear as females in the libretto for *Le Diable à quatre* (1845), wherein they were cast as children and "nymphes." This suggests that the cast of the *Pas des manteaux* in *Paquita* in Paris was made up of young dancers.

[79] Guest, *Romantic Ballet in Paris*, 2nd ed., 253.

Ex. 4.33 Act One, *Pas des manteaux*, bars 90–97

No. 6: The entire group travels downstage, the lead couple making a turn to the right (seven bars), then the men remove the capes from around the women (one bar).

No. 7: The women travel backward, wrists on their swaying hips, while the men throw the cape above their partner's head in a circular motion (two bars) then collect it behind their back (2 bars). The lead woman's steps include "valse russe." After four throws, the men place the capes on the women's shoulders (twelve bars).

No. 8: As the music modulates briefly to C major (Ex. 4.33), each woman raises her arm to hide her face from her partner, lowers her head, and mimes "no no no" using the other hand. The men, behind the cape-wielding arms of the women, try to catch a glimpse of their faces. As the women continue with an *appel*, the men pass behind them to the other side (two bars). This figure is repeated three times (six bars).

No. 9: The women, still wearing the capes, open their arms to the side, and the men, now behind them, place their hands on the women's shoulders (one bar). The women put their hands on their hips and the men raise their arms *en couronne* (one bar). This sequence is repeated two times (four bars), after which the men retrieve their capes from the women's shoulders and throw them over their arm. The women drop to their knee as the men pose over them with the caped arm outstretched (two bars).

No. 10: The music returns to G major for a transitional passage heading back to the main theme. The lead couple and ensemble men form a row across the upstage with their capes held open in front of them at collar height (four bars). The ensemble women run to follow then and place themselves (likely kneeling) behind the men at the point where each cape meets the next (with two women at the center "joint") (four bars).

No. 11: The women open and close the capes four times, making a peek-a-boo appearance with each opening (eight bars).

No. 12: Traveling along the diagonal from upstage left, the lead woman performs *glissade, tombé plié*, her partner following behind, holding his cape open in front of him (two bars?). He passes the cape in front of her, hiding her from view. She stands, placed between the man and his cape, and makes a turn to the right (two bars). During these first four bars, the ensemble forms a semicircle across the stage. The women take one end of their partner's cape with one hand and turning to face upstage, back to back with the men. Taking the other end of the cape with their free hand, the women complete their turn, posing in front of the men on one knee (four bars). They hold the cape open behind them with the collar of the cape held at waist height. The men perform *pas marché soubresaut en avant* and then, putting a hand on their partner's shoulder, repeat the step *en arrière*, one arm held high, as they swing forward and backward (six bars). After two bars, the women drop the capes, covering themselves from the waist down, and hold their arms *en couronne*. The men take the capes, putting them over their left arm, while the women pass in front of them to stand by the wings. The couples on stage left turn their backs to the public and the lead couple turns toward stage left, the woman taking the right arm of her partner (two bars).

No. 13: Justamant skips the number 13.

No. 14: At the return of the main theme, the ensemble men give their right arm to the women, and the principal couple leads everyone in a promenade around the stage (eight bars), performing the enchaînement from No. 1, the ensemble arriving upstage facing the public, the lead couple at center front (sixteen bars).

No. 15: During this transition, the ensemble moves out to the wings as the leads perform four mazurka steps *en tournant* (four bars). The men open their capes in front of themselves while the women perform *balancé* in place (two bars).

No. 16: Traveling toward center while the lead couple moves farther downstage, all perform the first two bars of No. 12. When the women come between the men and the capes, all perform four *balancés*, during the fourth of which the women take the capes and return them to them men as in No. 12 (eight bars). All of this is repeated one time (eight bars).

No. 17: No number of bars is given for No. 17, so we must deduce them based on the description of the movements. These include a *tombé* and *balancé* as the men carry the open capes to the side. The women do the same step and raise their arms *en couronne*, holding their position for one bar (two bars?). This step is repeated as the men and women change places, the men flipping the capes and the women posing with hands on hips (two bars?). Justamant notes that the principal couple does the same combination of steps four times on each side, followed by the clarification that the lead man performs the combination only seven times, after which he wraps the cape around his partner, who places herself under his outstretched right arm (sixteen bars total for No. 17?).

No. 18: During this transition, the lead couple makes two mazurka steps *en tournant* as the ensemble moves upstage to form a semicircle (three bars).

No. 19: The ensemble repeats No. 11 for four bars. The women dance a circle around their partners, who remain in place and pass their capes behind their backs, with arms overhead, and back to the front. Meanwhile, the first dancers, both under the cape and each holding one side, travel downstage with *pas marché, coup de talon à terre, pas marché, jeté dessus, soubresaut* three times in a row, followed by *pas marché, coupé dessous, assemblé derrière* (eight bars). No. 19 is repeated, but this time the women make a complete circle around the men then stand under their raised arms, which adds one more measure to the enchaînement (nine bars).

No. 20: All repeat the second part of No. 3, making two turns, the women finishing in front of the men (six bars). The women kneel and take the ends of their partners' capes with both hands as the men stand between the capes and the women (two bars). All have arms outstretched.[80]

No. 10: The Governor breaks away from his guests and surreptitiously asks Inigo to murder Lucien. The Governor's servants come from stage right and wait in the back. They salute the Governor, who gets up and says to his guest: "General, now the table is served and it awaits us." The General and all of his entourage say, "Governor, we are at your service." The Governor then politely excuses himself, explaining that he must go take care of some business. Inigo returns all of his troops to the tent.

---

[80] With our guesses added in and assuming seven free bars at the beginning, Justamant accounts for 255 of 264 total bars of music.

The General, with his mother and Serafina on his arms, followed by his entourage, departs upstage right. Lucien remains in the back, going away and looking at Paquita.

The Governor, going back upstage right, watches as everyone is leaving. Inigo perceives that Paquita is looking at Lucien and brusquely takes her by the hand and leads her with him into the tent. Lucien disappears.

Governor: "Finally they have all left."

Inigo, in a dreamy state of mind, comes out of the tent.

The Governor sees him and stamps his foot.

Inigo turns his head.

Governor: "Stay there—I want to talk to you." He comes downstage and looks all around. "You are furious with that young officer." [Inigo agrees.]

Governor: "Do you want revenge?"

Inigo: "Yes."

Governor: "Then you must kill him with a swift stab of a dagger."

Inigo: "But kill your brother-in-law?"

Governor: "Precisely—I don't want this marriage to take place."

Inigo: (trying to read the Governor's face) "But why?"

Governor: "It's my idea, and I'll answer for everything."

Inigo: "Well, we shall see."

No. 11: Lucien declares his devotion to Paquita and offers her money. The two conspirators hear noise, quickly end their conversation, and part, Inigo bowing to "his excellency." The Governor goes toward his guests. To a canto espressivo, Paquita appears, in dreamy mood (Ex. 4.23). When Inigo asks what she is thinking about, she replies, "Oh, nothing."

Inigo: "In a little while we will leave; I'm going to give the order. Go get your mantilla."

Paquita agrees to do so. Inigo goes into the tent; she falls back into her reverie and crosses to downstage right. Lucien appears upstage left; there is joy on his face when he sees Paquita.

Lucien: "She's alone."

Paquita sees him and visibly shows emotion. Lucien approaches her, looking around on all sides.

Lucien: "Mademoiselle, permit me to compliment you on your dance and on your beauty."

Paquita: "Oh, Monsieur, you are too indulgent."

Lucien: "But you appear to be sad and downtrodden; is it because of the brutality of that man?" He points toward the tent.

Paquita: "Oh, no—I'm accustomed to it."

Lucien: "You could be much happier."

Paquita: "And how so?"

Lucien: "By coming with me to a palace, where you could have beautiful clothes, unlike that sad little dress you are wearing now."

Paquita lets out a big sigh, putting her hand on her heart.

Lucien: "If you have any doubts"—he holds out his money-purse, offering it to her.

Paquita, a bit hurt, declines his offer, and goes upstage a little, to her right.

Inigo eavesdrops on Paquita and conspires with the Governor. The music is now agitated (Ex. 4.1). Lucien takes Paquita's hand and brings her back a little.

Lucien: "Oh, please do not leave. Let's please sit down together."

Paquita: "I would like that."

He offers her a chair and sits down near to her. She is facing stage left; he is facing the audience.

Lucien: (passionately) "Paquita, I love you."

Paquita: "You, a nobleman, love me, but I am nothing; practically a beggar. Oh, it's impossible."

Lucien: "I swear it to you. Please come with me."

Paquita: "Never, never." She gets up and turns toward the tent so she can flee Lucien.

He goes to her (to her right) and begs her to stay. Paquita stops. He asks if he may come see her at her house. As he asks that question, the Governor enters from stage left and starts going upstage. At the same time, Inigo is coming out of his tent. The two of them make a sign of mutual understanding. The Governor continues to walk.

Paquita: [to Lucien] "At my house—that's impossible."

Lucien: "Well, then give me the flowers you are carrying." Paquita hesitates.

Paquita: (with chagrin) "I cannot."

Lucien: "There's nothing more for me to do than to leave." He goes upstage and finds himself nearly face to face with the Governor, who steps backward and salutes him courteously. Lucien gives him a cold, fierce military salute, and departs.

Paquita, regretting that she refused to give Lucien the flowers, now takes them out of her belt and runs to call out to Lucien, but instead finds herself face to face with Inigo. He looks at her with a taunting and snide smile.

Paquita: (coming downstage) "I'm so glad I didn't give [Lucien] the flowers."

Inigo: "Paquita, go get your mantilla."

She goes into the tent. Now, to twelve bars of skullduggery music, the Governor comes to find Inigo (Ex. 4.4).[81]

Governor: "Well, now you have seen what you will do."

Inigo: "I will kill that officer."

Governor: "Good." He takes his leave in silence, going upstage toward his guests; Inigo goes back into the tent.

No. 12: The Roma depart; the General and his party prepare to depart; the Governor tricks Lucien into going to Paquita's house. The General enters followed by his suite (which is comprised of ten people). The Governor goes before them, and they come downstage, chatting. The Roma come out of their tent in no particular order and are still getting dressed. Inigo comes with Paquita, who is wearing a mantilla around her shoulders. Lucien is looking for his family; paysans come in from all sides.

Once everyone is in place, the Governor announces that all of the *jeunes filles* are to bring their bouquets and put them into a big basket. The basket is held by a *jeune fille*. (The ruse is that the basket of flowers will be presented to the General as a gift; this will allow the Governor access to Paquita's bouquet, which he needs for his evil scheme.)

Paquita is the first to put in her bouquet; then she returns to Inigo's side. The Governor is watching closely; he approaches the basket and removes the bouquet Paquita had deposited, just as another *jeune fille* is putting hers in. The Governor takes the *jeune fille* by the hand; they walk downstage a bit, and he points out Lucien to her, telling her to give Lucien Paquita's bouquet on Paquita's behalf. She does so, telling Lucien that the bouquet is from Paquita, and pointing her out to Lucien.

Lucien is delighted; he kisses the bouquet and asks the girl to tell him where Paquita lives. She says that Paquita lives up high on the mountain.

Lucien: "Thank you, my child."

She goes back to her place.

As soon as the Governor made his announcement about the basket, all of the *jeunes filles* have been throwing their bouquets into it and saluting the General. The General has been circulating around with his mother and Dona Seraphina, thanking everyone.

The peasants leave, climbing up steps in the rocks. Then the Roma leave and are the last to disappear.

The General, accompanied by the Governor and his suite, leave, at the foot of the mountain, stage left. Lucien is looking all around for Paquita. He calls for his servant, who arrives, carrying a cape, which he puts on Lucien's shoulders. Lucien tells the servant to withdraw, and then begins to climb the steps of the mountain, while enveloping himself in his cape.

The Governor appears at the bottom of the mountain, also in a cape and holding a mask in his hand. As soon as Lucien is at the top of the mountain, he says "I will get my vengeance," makes a threatening gesture, puts his mask on his face, envelops himself in his cape, and starts up the mountain steps himself.

---

[81] Justamant does not refer to this music, perhaps because it is not in a new meter—that is, it is in $\frac{4}{4}$, which is the meter of the previous number.

Act Two, Scene I

Entr'acte. At bar 8 of the *entr'acte* (a medley), the curtain opens on a scene depicting the interior of a small dwelling-place of Romani people. The libretto describes it thus: "At the back, a fireplace. A little to the left, an armoire; between the armoire and the fireplace, a window with shutters. Table and chairs to the right at the front of the stage. A door to the side, at the right; a rustic clock, chair, etc." Justamant's drawing of the stage setting matches every element of this description.

No. 1: Paquita arrives at the house. Paquita comes in; she is agitated. She looks all around and establishes that nobody is there, and then goes back upstage to lock the door. Coming back downstage to stage right, she reflects.

Paquita: (to herself) "Despite myself, I am dreaming of that nice officer, who had such a noble air, and who said he loved me." She sighs. "Alas, I might never see him again."

Paquita sees the bandits arriving; she hides. Paquita hears a noise under the window; she opens the shutters and draws back upon seeing a masked man outside the window.

Paquita: "A masked man in a cape—what can this mean?" She goes quickly to close the shutter.

Then she hears another noise at the door (and leans in the direction of the door, putting her left hand to her ear). "They're coming here! I must hide." She looks around the room. (pointing to the armoire) "There!" She hides behind it.

No. 2: Inigo conspires with the Governor.

Inigo comes in, looks around on all sides, and tells the Governor to enter.

The Governor comes in . . . takes off his mask, and opens his cloak.

Governor: "We are alone."

Inigo: "Yes. You may speak freely."

Governor: "Just how are you planning to kill the officer?"

Inigo: (smiling, with a fine air) "I'll show you." He goes to the armoire, pulls out a bottle, and shows it to the Governor.

Governor: "Yes, and . . . ?"

Inigo: "Well, when he drinks what is in this bottle, he will fall sleep right away."

Governor: "Ah! I understand!"

Inigo puts the bottle back in the armoire.

Inigo explains, and acts out, what he will do: when the officer arrives, Inigo will welcome him, give him dinner, and Lucien will drink the wine, and go to sleep at the table. Then, explains Inigo, drawing his dagger and going to the table, "I will creep up behind him quietly and stab him, like this." He sticks the dagger forcefully into the table. Both men hear a slight noise—it is Paquita, who has been following the conversation, and has stuck her head out in order to see better. When Inigo jabs the dagger into the table, she gasps and sticks her head back in.

Inigo leans toward the armoire and puts his hand to his ear; he then goes to the door to check; the General puts his mask back on. But, coming back downstage, Inigo says, "It's nothing." The Governor is relieved, says he is satisfied, and puts on his cape, preparing to depart. Inigo curses, "*Le diable*"—catches up with him and pulls him by his cape. With his eyes, the Governor asks what he wants. Angrily, Inigo responds, "You forgot to pay me." The Governor opens his cape, takes out his money-pouch, and throws it to Inigo, who catches it. The Governor departs, draping himself in his cape. Inigo puts the money-pouch in his pocket, and goes toward the table, where the knife is still sticking up.

No. 3: The bandits arrive; Paquita is caught as she tries to sneak away. The Rep tells us that Inigo goes to the window and whistles. Soon, four men appear.

Justamant provides a slightly different account: Inigo pulls the knife back out of the table, and goes to the window, as he reflects. He opens the shutters and calls out. Then he goes to the door, opens it, and calls out again.

Two bandits appear at the window; Inigo signals them to enter; they come in, as do the two bandits at the door. They gather around their chief, who asks them if they want to be in on the action that will take place (he points to the clock) at midnight. The bandits ask if they will be paid.

Inigo: "I don't know anything about that."

Bandits: (heading for the door) "No money—then, goodbye."

Inigo: (cursing) "*Le diable*." (calling out to the bandits) "Don't be in such a hurry."

They come back downstage and Inigo takes out the money-pouch and gives money to the two on the right, while the two on the left say, "Aha—he *does* have money."

Inigo then takes the two bandits on the right by the hand and leads them to the fire-place. He places them there, backs to the fireplace, and then makes the fireplace revolve so the two bandits disappear.

Next, he approaches the other two bandits and pays them, too.

Meanwhile Paquita has been sneaking across the floor stealthily, watching them. Now she accidentally runs into a chair.

Inigo and the two bandits look at her, frightened at first but then relieved when they see her. Inigo goes upstage, takes her by the hand, and makes her come downstage with him. The two bandits profit from the situation by leaving. Paquita is pretending to limp as she walks. Inigo asks her what she is doing, and she explains that she wasn't looking where she was going and hurt herself by running into a chair. He gives her a snide look and accuses her of coming there to spy on him. She denies it; he says he is sure she is lying. He goes to the window and looks out; she says to herself, "When I think of this poor man who is coming here and might be assassinated—it's terrible."

No. 4: Lucien arrives; Paquita tries to warn him away. There is a knock at the door. Inigo (from near the window) and Paquita (from downstage) both run toward the door. Inigo leads her downstage by the hand and says, "If you say anything, I will kill you." She looks at him with a proud disdain. She follows him to the door, and in order to see over Inigo's head, she goes up on pointe. All of a sudden, she cries out, "Great god, it's him," and she runs downstage in terror. Inigo invites the officer in.

Lucien: (coming in) "Ah! It's her!"

As he opens his cape, Lucien asks Inigo for hospitality for the night and supper.

Inigo: "Certainly," [. . .] but to himself, "He'll never get out of here alive."

At the same time, Paquita asks Lucien why he has come. Lucien tells her it is because of the bouquet she arranged to give him. She answers in a lively manner: "But no, but no, it wasn't me!" Lucien is very surprised.

Now Inigo comes back, cutting off their conversation, and invites Lucien to the table. Lucien takes off his cape and his sword. Inigo grabs the sword and says to himself, "I must hide it—but where?" Lucien puts his kolbak (big, tall hat) on the table. Inigo has his back to the others as he looks for a place to hide the saber.

Inigo: (to himself) "Of course! In the armoire!" He puts the saber in the armoire and carefully closes it.

During this time, Lucien is trying to kiss Paquita's hands and her neck.

Paquita, frightened, resists, and tells him that he is in danger of being killed. Lucien does not understand and keeps trying to kiss her.

Inigo: (facing the armoire and backing up toward the middle of the room) "They'll never find it there."

Paquita has a sudden inspiration and throws the cape over Inigo's head. Lucien laughs at this seeming joke. Paquita leads him to the door while Inigo struggles with the cape. Lucien, uncomprehending, resists a bit. As soon as Inigo manages to throw off the cape and throw it onto the floor, Paquita stops speaking and gesturing to Lucien, and pretends to be indifferent.

Inigo takes her by the hand and throws her nearly all the way across the stage (to stage right) to his right.

Inigo: (coming toward Paquita to strike her) "You threw that cape over my head."

Lucien runs to place himself between the two of them.

Lucien: (to Inigo) "It was just a joke!"

Inigo gives Paquita a fierce look. Lucien asks about supper. Inigo hangs the cape up on the wall. Lucien goes to the table and puts his *kolbak* on it (Justamant's drawings show

Ex. 4.34 "Tenor aria" as Lucien finds himself alone; Act Two, No. 5, bars 7–14

that he had placed it on his head again as Paquita led him to the door). During this time, Paquita says to herself "Ah! I know how to play this."

She makes a very small gesture to Lucien, warning him to be careful. She points toward Inigo, and then stops suddenly. Inigo thinks he saw her gesturing. He crosses downstage diagonally to the couple, taking Paquita by the hand and putting her to his right (the weak position).

Inigo: (to Paquita) "Come with me, so we can get the officer's supper."

Lucien sits down. Inigo tells him they'll be back soon. As he goes to the door, Paquita takes a side trip going by Lucien and tells him to try to flee. He understands nothing of what she says but finds her funny and attractive.

Noting that Paquita is not behind him, Inigo comes back, grabs her by the waist, and walks her ahead of him to the door. Paquita takes a last look at Lucien as she and Inigo go through the door (to the kitchen).

No. 5: Despite Paquita's frantic gestured warnings to Lucien in the preceding scene, Lucien now only slowly figures out that he is a captive in Inigo's dwelling. The music is sweet and sounds like a tenor love song (Ex. 4.34).

Lucien, now alone, doesn't know what the devil to think. All of those signs she was giving him—"Telling me yes, no, go away—my goodness, it's strange."

He walks around the room, looking about on all sides. "Let's see where we are."

He goes to the window and finds it is locked. He is surprised to discover that, even when he pushes on it, it won't open. [He goes to the door—same result.]

"This time," he says, "it makes me suspicious." He puts his hand on his belt. "Bah, I am armed." Then he is surprised: "I don't have my saber anymore. Where is it?"

He looks all over for it. "I hear a noise; someone is coming. Well, bad luck to whoever it is."

He runs and picks up a chair, which he holds to his side with his right hand, ready to defend himself, his eyes fixed on the door.

Ex. 4.35   Paquita enters with plates; Act Two, No. 6, bars 1–8

Deldevez chose not to follow Lucien's motion around the stage or his observations and his reactions to them, but, rather, to offer a single unified tune, in ABA form. The sweetness of the melody is appropriate for the affectionate, naïve Lucien.

No. 6: The dinner scene begins. The music changes to a sprightly $\frac{6}{8}$ with a comic feel that serves as wallpaper (Ex. 4.35).

Paquita enters the room with a plate in her hands—she runs toward Lucien to give him a sign. Lucien sees her and smiles over the idea he had had. He goes toward her, wanting to speak with her. But at that moment, Inigo comes in (plate in hand) and runs to where they are standing, taking a position between them. He looks at each of them sharply to make sure they are not saying anything. Then he goes toward the table, shaking his head "no." Inigo puts the plate on the table, picks up the *kolbak*, and says to Paquita: "*Alors, voyons*, put your plate on the table and put the lid on it." He goes toward the buffet and puts the kolbak on a chair. Paquita goes to put the plates on the table. Lucien goes over to the table and tries to take Paquita's hand. Seeing Inigo, Paquita runs over to the armoire to look for something in it.

Carrying a bottle and some drinking glasses, Inigo puts them on the table and returns to the buffet. Carrying plates, Paquita crosses paths with Inigo and goes to the table. Lucien wants to take her by the waist. Paquita fends him off and tries to make signs to Lucien to be on guard.

Lucien: (turning his head to look at Inigo) "Bah! He's busy." He tries to kiss Paquita, who keeps rebuffing him.

Meanwhile, Inigo is expressing his satisfaction with the proceedings.

Inigo: "He is going to eat, then he's going to fall asleep, and then I will kill him with the dagger." He rubs his hands together. "I am content." He looks at the table that is set, and he calls out to Paquita.

Paquita: (coming to center) "I'm here."

Inigo tells her that they should leave the officer to eat in peace, and he turns away a bit and says to himself, "It's more certain that way."

Paquita takes advantage of the moment to make a small gesture, telling Lucien to "keep me here."

Lucien: [to Paquita] "Sure." (to Inigo) "Let's see—I love a good time. Please come eat with me."

Inigo: (surprised and embarrassed) "Me, with you? You do me too much honor."

Lucien: "Not at all. It's what I'd like!"

Inigo: (empowered) "If you wish, then I accept." The men go toward the table, and Paquita goes to get another glass.

The two men sit down opposite each other (Inigo's back to stage left); Paquita says she will serve them. She pours them a drink and Lucien drinks to her health. Paquita thanks him graciously.

Lucien: (to Inigo) "We toast."

Paquita passes to Inigo's left as the two men drink.

Inigo: (to Lucien) "How do you like the wine?"

Lucien: "Just fine."

Inigo: "Then let's drink some more."

They pour out another glass. Paquita takes advantage of this moment to crouch down by Inigo and remove his pistol from his belt. The men continue to chat. Paquita quickly opens the chamber of the pistol, blows the powder out, closes the chamber back up, and puts the pistol on the floor.

Inigo hears a noise, turns around, and asks Paquita what she is doing.

Paquita: "Oh, I put the pistols on the floor so they wouldn't bother you."

Inigo: (indifferently) "Ah, that's good." He picks up the bottle and pours out another glass.

Paquita then pulls his second pistol out of his belt and does the same thing.

Lucien and Inigo continue to drink.

Inigo: (to Paquita) "You will dance—that will brighten up the meal." (to Lucien) "Would you like to see that, my guest?"

Lucien: "Yes, with pleasure."

Inigo gets up to fetch the castanets, which are hanging on the wall in the back.

Profiting from this moment, Paquita says to Lucien, "Beware of him. He wants to kill you!"

Lucien: "Oh, I understand now."

No. 7: The dinner scene continues; Paquita switches the wine glasses. Inigo gives the castanets to Paquita, and then slaps his forehead, saying he is thinking of getting a bottle of delicious wine out of the armoire (he points to the armoire). Inigo goes to the armoire.

Paquita: [to Lucien] "You must not drink that wine. It will make you go to sleep."

Lucien: (making a movement of indignation) "Ah, thank you, my child."

Inigo comes downstage right holding the bottle up with this left hand.

Paquita goes toward the center of the stage.

Lucien is watching the movements of Inigo and Paquita carefully.

Inigo: "If he drinks this, he will go to sleep quickly, and then"—poking the handle of his dagger—"I am confident I will be able to deliver the fatal blow."

Paquita: (watching Inigo's movements) "Oh, no, not again."

Inigo: (turning around) What are you doing?

Paquita: "Arranging my blouse."

Inigo goes to the table, puts the bottle down, and takes his seat.

Paquita follows, taking a seat at the end of the table [with Inigo on her left, and Lucien on her right], putting her elbows on the table and her face between her two hands.

Inigo: (uncorking the bottle, to Lucien) "It is famous, you will see." He pours him a drink.

Lucien: (making a gesture of anger) "But you're not pouring one for yourself."

Inigo: "Ah, that's because I already had my fill of the other wine. Let's drink to your amours."

Inigo picks up his glass to toast.

Paquita, to keep them from drinking, drops a stack of plates on the floor, behind Inigo.

Inigo turns to look down at the floor where the broken pieces are.

Paquita, quickly profiting from this moment, stands up and exchanges the Lucien's and Inigo's glasses, and then with haste sits down again and puts her elbows back on the table.

Lucien understands what she is up to and laughs at the ingenuity of her idea. Inigo gets up and looks angrily at Paquita.

Paquita (pretending to be afraid) "Oh my goodness—I didn't mean to do that."

Inigo: "It's one of your tricks. You stay there and pick up the pieces."

Paquita, afraid, goes to stage right [the other side of the stage].

Inigo, furious, chases her.

Lucien stands up.

Inigo is ready to strike Paquita.

Lucien stops him. (to Inigo) "Calm down; don't hit her. It was only a harmless joke. Let's go back to the table." He leads Inigo back to the table.

Inigo [as he is being led away—he is to Lucien's right] looks at Paquita with ferocious eyes.

Lucien and Inigo take their places at the table (but they remain standing).

Paquita comes to center and looks at Lucien [she is behind him].

Lucien: (to Inigo) "Let's drink your good wine."

Inigo: "You're right. Let's drink." They toast.

Lucien: (turning toward Paquita) "Drink."

Paquita (with her eyes) says "yes" to Lucien.

Inigo pretends to drink; he watches Lucien drink. (to himself) "Good. Lucien has drunk." (with an devilish smile) "He has drunk. I can drink."

Lucien (in turn) watches Inigo drink, and says, with a smile, to Paquita, "He's drinking it."

Inigo now passes in front of the table and hands the castanets to Paquita, and then comes back and sits down. Lucien has turned his chair around, toward the center of the room, so he can watch Paquita dance.

Inigo: (to Paquita) "Let's go! Dance."

No. 8: Paquita dances tableside at Inigo's behest. To the music of a bolero (Ex. 4.18), starting on the right foot, Paquita does the first step of the cachucha ("le premiere temps de la cachucha") and then steps to the side on her left foot,

jeté dessus en tournant, and an *appel devant*, the left foot, carrying the body back, the right arm in the air, the left [arm] under [the right arm]. Same *pas* starting on the left foot. Again one time on each foot.

Starting on the left foot, a step to the side, twisting [*tortiller*] the right foot *à terre*, *brisé croisé*, *soubresaut*, on the left foot, *pas marché en avant*, *croisé* the right foot, *soubresaut*, then *tombé* to the left side, the right foot *croisé derriere*, *en balançant* carrying the arms *de la couronne*, the hands on the hips.

Inigo, seeing that Lucien is occupied looking at Paquita, goes to the door to see if the men have arrived. Paquita takes advantage of this situation and jumps up onto the chair. (Then she attempts to warn Lucien about what is going to happen.) She counts, on her fingers, the twelve strikes of the clock.

Paquita: (to Lucien as she jumps back down to the floor) "They're coming here."

Lucien: "Good to know."

Inigo comes back. Paquita does one *saut de basque en tournant* and another *en face*. Inigo arrives right next to her just as she finishes. Lucien sits back down.

Inigo and Paquita dance. Starting on her right foot, Paquita, turning her back to the audience, does *pas marché de côté* on her right foot, bringing back the left leg "derrière en la trainant" (Ex. 4.19). She does this four times. Inigo does the same steps, *en face* to the audience. (They are several feet apart; they have made a circle, opposite one another, and finish with Paquita directly in front of the seated Lucien, who tries to put his hands on her waist.) She now dances back to her starting point, doing *saut de basque en face* and *saut de basque en arrière* one more time. Inigo does the same steps, continuing his circle.

They next repeat the same *pas* and entire combination, but this time, Inigo's head is heavy as he does the *sauts de basque*. She starts on the right foot, and does two *sauts de basque* advancing, arriving face to face, right shoulder to right shoulder with Inigo. She does *pas marché en avant* on the right foot and "jeté ordinaire en tournant, frapper du pied droit à terre," with her back to the audience. Inigo does the same *pas*.

Inigo's legs start giving way. (to himself) "My chest is burning, I am suffering, my vision is fuzzy—what is going on? Oh, it's nothing. I am fine."

During this time, Lucien is kissing Paquita.

Paquita: Pretend to fall asleep, while I keep an eye on Inigo.

Paquita continues to dance. Lucien feigns sleep, seated at the table, his head resting on his arm.

Inigo, at the moment when he was going to start dancing, sees Lucien [apparently] sleeping.

Inigo: "Oh, finally, he is falling asleep. But I am suffocating; my head is about to burst." He pulls his handkerchief out of his pockets—the medallion falls out and lands on the floor.

Ex. 4.36 The clock begins to strike midnight; Act Two, No. 9, bars 79–82

Paquita sees it and runs to pick it up. (to herself) "Ah, I knew very well that you were the one who stole it." She attaches it to her belt.

Inigo wipes his brow; his legs bend; his head falls forward; he is falling asleep. He lifts his head, as though he is lost. He sees Lucien. (to himself) "Let's go—I am supposed to kill him."

Inigo advances toward Lucien.

In a broadly comical sequence, Paquita quickly comes over to stop him, placing her hands on Inigo's left shoulder. She does *pas marché* on her right foot, and a *jété ordinaire en tournant* while passing in front of him, and puts her hands on his neck while doing the same step in reverse (*en revenant*).

Inigo tells her to leave him alone. She leads him in some more dancing—his head is bowing over, despite himself. She makes a lively turn and continues to lead him, dancing.

Inigo: ([to Paquita], enraged) "...I am my own boss..."

He takes Paquita's hand and brings her back roughly, to his right [a bold move intended to take his power back].

He goes toward Lucien, dagger drawn, walking unsteadily.

Paquita pleads with him.

Inigo raises his arm so he can stab Lucien. The dagger falls from his hand and he collapses on himself, his head on his chest.

Paquita, a few feet behind him, falls to her knees and raises her hands prayerfully, invoking the heavens.

Inigo tries to get up on his feet, and mustering all the strength that he can, he reaches down to pick up the dagger. He passes his hands over his eyes to see the dagger more clearly. Just at the moment when he is rallying, he falls to his knees, puts his hand to his throat, and turns around. He falls backward, apparently dead. [His head is pointing downstage left.]

Paquita throws her arms up in the air and cries out joyfully.

No. 9: Paquita and Lucien escape; the murder plot is foiled; Inigo dies.

Lucien gets up and lets out a cry, "Ah!" [Ex. 4.20]

Paquita thanks heaven.

Lucien goes to Inigo, looks at him, puts his hand on his heart, and says to Paquita, "He's sleeping." (approaching Paquita) "Now come with me, let's flee."

Paquita: (pointing to Inigo) "Impossible."

Lucien: "Eh, why?"

Paquita goes to the window, then to the fireplace, and then to the door, and then comes back downstage, explaining to Lucien that four men are posted in these places, ready to assassinate him.

Lucien: (looking at Inigo) "What a miserable jerk!" He sees the pistols on the floor and runs to pick them up. "Ah—pistols!"

But Paquita shows him that the ammunition has been removed. Lucien throws the pistols to the floor in a rage.

Lucien: "I will die, assassinated." He puts his hands to his head. "No weapons. But—my sword. My sword! Where is it?"

Paquita, in despair, has gone to the other side of the stage [to stage right]. Lucien makes a circle, starting in the center toward stage left, toward the back, and all the way to stage right, finally facing the armoire.
The armoire is open, and Lucien sees his sword inside. He picks it up, pitches the scabbard away from himself, comes downstage.

Lucien: "At least my death won't come cheap!" (to Paquita) "Come with me, let's get out of here."

He takes her by the left hand and leads her to the door. [His right hand is raised, holding the sword.]

At this moment, midnight sounds [Ex. 4.36)].

Lucien and Paquita stop in their tracks, then turn around, facing the room, his right hand still raised and holding the sword.
While the clock is striking, Paquita notices that the back of the chimney is moving slightly. She is struck with an idea. She goes to the table and blows out the candles. Then she puts her arm around Lucien's waist and leads him to the fireplace. The fireplace is rotating. Paquita and Lucien place themselves, their backs to the fireplace.
The room is dark. The bandits start to appear—one at the window, one at the door, two coming in on the rotating fireplace. By the twelfth chime of the clock, Lucien and Paquita have entirely disappeared, and all of the bandits have entered.
The newcomers creep in stealthily, and after arriving at center, recognize each other thanks to the lantern carried by the bandit entering through the door. Following him in a row as he shines the lantern light, they all see a man lying down. They point him out to

each other and advance toward him as they draw their daggers, all lined up to one side of the prone figure. They are all about to start stabbing him when they recognize that it is Inigo. They pull him up and shake him a bit.

Inigo comes to, but is tottering and half asleep.

Inigo: (recognizing his companions) "The officer. Where is he?"

Bandits: "We haven't seen anyone."

Inigo: "Look, look for them."

The bandit with the lantern searches briskly, making a turn around the room, until he gets to the window.

All of a sudden, outside the window, he sees Lucien and Paquita fleeing. [Lucien's sword is still drawn, and he is still holding it up in his right hand.]

[*Bandit*:] "There they are! There they are!"

Inigo starts going upstage to look, but after two steps his knees buckle and he collapses.

The bandits help him up at first and then let him down onto the floor. One of them puts his hand on Inigo's heart.

Bandit: (to the others) "He is dead."

The curtain falls.

Act Two, Scene II

A note on historical dance in the ballroom scene. The final scene of the ballet opens with a brief French contredanse for a large number of male-female couples, followed by an even shorter version of the celebrated "Gavotte de Vestris" for two male-female couples. Both of these dances were immensely popular in Empire-period France, and seeing them executed, even briefly, on stage three decades after their heyday would surely have evoked memories for older members of the audience. Indeed, the careful attention paid to this social-dance choreography and its music, as well as the costumes, would have given spectators of any age a full dose of Empire-period style (like it or not—and some critics did not). For the contredanses (as noted above), the music was either borrowed from the past or newly created to sound old, and the music for the "Gavotte de Vestris" was the real thing. The execution of social dances, too, as we shall see, were meant to be "of the era."

The ballet's third and final scene is set in a magnificently decorated ballroom at the house of the French commander in Saragossa. The libretto describes it thus:

Moorish architecture decorated in the style of the Empire period.—A large portrait of an officer is in the foreground of the room.—Tableau of a period ball. Soldiers of all ranks, old generals, young hussars, dragoons, soldiers of the light brigade, etc.; in sum, all the magnificent uniforms of the Empire. Among these brilliant representatives of Napoleon's army, Frenchwomen attired in the grand court costume of the ladies of the Empire.—The Spanish nobility, in national costume, also figure in this ball. When the curtain rises, French contredanse and the *gavotte Classique*.

When the curtain rises the ball is already in full swing: a contredanse is being performed and the back and sides of the stage are filled with ball-goers watching the dance floor.

No. 10: Contredanse française. The dancers are in motion (Exx. 4.11a–b). "The tableau should be animated," Justamant writes. His drawing shows twenty couples arranged in five quadrilles (squares made up of four couples each). But for the dancing itself, instead of providing the usual drawings with details written in prose, Justamant simply provides this list of instructions, each item preceded by a freestanding tilde:[82]

~ *tous les quadrilles, chassé croisé huit, tour de main avec sa dame (8 mesures)*

All the quadrilles: First change places with your partner, the lady passing in front of the man using chassé steps (all eight people participate in this "chassé croisé"). Then, the man turns his partner with either one hand or both.

~ *avant deux, exat [sic], comme à l'époque mais, les quatres personnes de face (16 measures)*

Two of the facing couples—the "heads"—go forward, then back, "exactly as during the era, but the four people are facing each other."

~ *chassé huit (8 mesures)*

Chassé steps, probably going around the circle and back

~ *avant deux pour les autres (16 mesures)*

The other two facing couples go forward, then back.

~ *chassé huit (8 mesures)*

Chassé steps, possibly going around the circle in the other direction and back

The quadrille finished, each cavalier thanks his lady and leads her to her place or goes for a walk. Justamant also writes, "N. B. In the quadrille, steps from the era must be used, such as the *pas d'été, flic flac, glissades, coupés, temps de cuisse.*"[83]

Après la quadrille. The subsequent brief scene (titled *Entrée du General* in the Paris musical sources) likewise has reduced scoring in keeping with the Empire-era ballroom sound world.

The General, giving his hand to Seraphina (his prospective daughter-in-law), is following the Governor, who gives his hand to the Countess (his prospective grandmother-in-law). They all enter from stage left and go to the center.

---

[82] Many thanks to Carol Marsh for providing explanations of what Justamant's abbreviated instructions mean.

[83] These instructions are from Justamant, *Paquita*, 102. Page 103 is mis-numbered as 104; the correct page 104 follows what should be page 103.

Everyone rises [in their honor].

The General and his mother are looking everywhere to see if Lucien is present.

The officers salute their general [Justamant's drawing shows they are bowing].

The General welcomes the officers and invites them to enjoy the ball. As they go to invite women to dance with them, the grandmother is worrying.

Countess: "I don't see my grandson here at the ball."

Seraphina: "Oh, don't worry. He will be here soon."

Governor: "Yes, I assure you, he is coming."

[During this conversation,] the officers make their invitations to the women.

[. . .]

General: (going to get Seraphina) "And you my child, don't you want to dance?"

Seraphina: "Dance, oh no!"

General: "Then let's go sit down."

The General and the Governor give their hands to the ladies and go sit down on the *fauteuils* downstage right.

[During this time,] the officers who dance the gavotte place themselves.

Gavotte. The next dance (as noted above) is an abbreviated version of the "Gavotte de Vestris."

Gavotte
Two officers and two ladies

[The two couples stand next to each other, each lady to the right of her partner, and travel downstage.]

The men have the right foot front.
The ladies have the left foot [front].

They do *pas marché en avant* on the front foot *en dégegant* [as they *degagé*] *à la demi seconde* the back foot, *sissonne* the back foot, three *jeté ordinaire en reculant* [going backward] and *assemblé derrière* (4 bars).

The same steps from the other leg (4 bars).

[The couples continue traveling downstage, now in a zigzag pattern.]

From the back foot, and coming downstage, *coupé dessous*, *jeté en avant*, *temps de cuisse*, and *jeté en avant*. The same steps from the other leg. In all, two times each [leg].

At the 4th *temps de cuisse*, the ladies turn and stay with their backs to the public [and slightly downstage of the men] (8 bars).

[The couples next travel away from each other on the diagonal, the men moving upstage, the women moving downstage.]

All going backward and from the foot, this is *en l'air*, they do 4 *jeté ordinaire*, *coupé dessous*, *assemblé devant*, and *changement de pied* (4 bars).

[The couples move toward each other in a zigzag pattern.]

The ladies having their back to the public and being almost opposite the men [they are slightly stage right of the men], coming toward each other on a zigzag, and the left foot back, they [all] do *coupé*, *jeté*, *temps de cuisse* 4 times, but at the 4th time, the ladies turn to face the public (8 bars).

[The couples are next to each other again, the women only slightly downstage of the men.]

From the leg that is *en l'air*, going backward, they do four *jeté*, *coupé dessous* and *assemblé*, *changement de pied* (4 bars).

Recognition scene. The dance is interrupted by a noise and the arrival of Lucien and Paquita. All heads turn to see where the noise is coming from. (Now, Deldevez returns to the much fuller instrumentation of an 1846 orchestra.)

Lucien, holding Paquita and his saber, arrives, rushing in.

Everyone stands up.

The General and his family, who are very surprised, go to him.

Lucien hands his saber to the doorman. Everyone comes downstage to listen to Lucien.

The Governor, recognizing Lucien, passes to the other side and surreptitiously looks at Paquita.

General: (to his son) "What has happened to you?"

Lucien: "In the night, after getting lost on the mountains, I asked for hospitality for one night, then I was locked up and almost murdered by several men. I owe my life to this *jeune fille*, who saved me, and with whom I was able to flee and come here."

During this time, Paquita, looking around on all sides, finds herself very close to the Governor. She recognizes him and makes a gesture of terrible fright.

The Governor recognizes her but acts like he is not paying attention.

Lucien takes her by the hand and leads her over to his family.

The General and the rest of the family thank her happily.

Paquita is confused by all of this kindness.

General: "My child, please tell us what took place."

Paquita: "With pleasure. It was nighttime when a man covered with a cape and mask came to my master's house. He gave him money to kill Lucien, but I saw it because I was hidden."

General: "And you could see this man's face?"

Paquita: "Oh, yes."

General: "And you know who he is?"

Paquita: (throwing a quick look at the Governor) "Yes."

General: "And where is he?"

The Governor doesn't know what demeanor to assume.

Paquita: (resolutely and going toward the Governor) "Him. That's him."

Everyone: "Good lord. What infamy!"

Governor: (stupefied at first but quickly regaining his aplomb) "Monsieur, this girl is crazy, and I hope that you don't believe what she said. I am a man of honor."

Seraphina: (who has rejoined her brother and heard him) "I know very well that he is not guilty."

Paquita: (going upstage a little) "But Messieurs, I swear before God that he's the one I saw."

The Governor, raising his shoulders, reassures his sister.

General: (going to the Governor and looking at him with contempt) "You are a coward." He calls two officers. "Arrest this man and take him away from here." He returns to his son.

Officers: (to the Governor) "Your sword."

The Governor, impudently, hands it over.

General: "Lead him away."

The officers compel the Governor to leave, his sister with him.

Everyone follows their movements; the General comes downstage a little to avoid seeing them.

During this scene with the Governor, the Countess and Lucien never cease to lavish caresses on Paquita.

General: (to Paquita) "And you, my child, you have saved my son, what may I do for you?"

Paquita: "For me, nothing."

Lucien: (to his father, with passion) "My father, I love Paquita. Please give your consent for me to marry her."

Paquita: (in a lively manner) "But no, your spouse, oh, that is impossible."

Lucien: "But why?"

Paquita: "Because you are grand and noble, and I am lowly—no, let me go, and think of me sometimes. Adieu, adieu." She keeps going upstage little by little.

Lucien and his father supplicate her to stay (while following her movement).

Paquita, as a last effort, starts running. All of a sudden, she perceives with surprise the portrait of the General's brother. She looks at it closely, and from her bosom pulls out her medallion and compares it to the portrait. She lets out a cry.

Everyone: "What is going on?"

Paquita takes Lucien's hand, leading him to the back of stage and giving him the medallion, and says, "Look."

Lucien recognizes a portrait of his uncle, and he gives it to his father and grandmother.

General: (seeing the medallion) "Great Lord—it is my brother who was assassinated." He points to the two portraits. "This is certainly the same face."

Countess: "Yes, yes, that's my son."

General: "So this *jeune fille* is his daughter."

Paquita: (with joy) "Great Lord—what happiness."

General: (to Paquita, with transport) "Come into my arms."

Paquita runs and throws herself into his arms with happiness. The Countess kisses her effusively.

Lucien: "This joy has reached its height."

General: (to Lucien) "Here is your wife."

Lucien and Paquita throw themselves into each other's arms.

Countess: "My child, come with me, so that you can change into a new gown." She leads Paquita, followed by Lucien who gives her his hand, stage right.

General: (to everyone) "Now, Messieurs, let us forget this family and resume the dancing." He goes to sit down.

Those who do not dance also take their seats, and the dancers place themselves for the waltz.

During the waltz, Lucien comes back holding the hands of his grandmother and Paquita. They take their seats.

Valse des hussards. The ballroom divertissement begins with the *Valse des hussards*, a light but sweeping waltz in E-flat major with a middle section in B-flat major (Exx 4.8a–b).[84]

Justamant's *Valse des hussards* features a lead couple (designated as 3rd *danseuses*) and six male-female ensemble couples, though the cast list in the front of Justamant's manual suggests four women may have danced male roles *en travestie*. (All eight of the hussards in the Paris production were danced by women.) The choreography has the look and feel of a social dance; "le pas d'almande" (*allemande*, that is, German step) is called for frequently later in the dance as well as *valse* steps that feature what appears in Justamant's drawings to be a traditional waltz hold.

---

[84] More than half of the B section bars are struck through in the Rep (31 of 61), as well as most of the return of the A section (46 of 51 bars, although eleven bars are marked "bon," meaning they should be kept). Justamant, however, accounts for the entire number (206 of 209 bars, not including seven bars of introduction).

Ex. 4.37a Act Two, *Pas de deux*, bars 7–14

Justamant records the dance in twenty-one figures, of which the lead couple dances the first two. After the cavalier presents the woman, taking her by the hand as she crosses in front of him with a turn, the couple faces each other, holding downstage hands and taking their partner's waist with the upstage hand. They perform *pas marché en avant*, and two *soubresauts*, the first leaning forward, the second leaning back. They repeat this two times and continue, now facing the audience, by coming downstage, holding inside hands, crossing (the woman in front of the man), and turning to the inside with a *valse* step (Ex 4.8a).

The ensemble (three couples at each side) joins the lead couple, and performs figure No. 1 four times before traveling to center to form a column. The lead couple, starting upstage, begins a sequence in which they move toward opposite wings with a turn and then go downstage past the uppermost couple in the column. As they do this, the ensemble couples cross each other with *valse en tournant*. Turning again, they cross in front of the upstage couple to join in the center of the column and move downstage past the second couple before traveling out again with a turn. They continue moving in and out of the column, progressing downstage, until they reach the head of the column. Meanwhile the ensemble couples alternate crossing each other with a *valse en tournant* and performing *balancé* in place, the latter with arms crossed as shown in Justamant's drawing.

The column moves as one toward stage right and left two times, the men partnering the women, before alternating couples separate from the column and travel toward each wing. The ensemble regroups in a row upstage, the lead couple at center in front, as the music transitions to the B section (Ex. 4.8b).

All dance in unison until figure No. 12, at which point the lead couple dances alone, waltzing a counterclockwise circle around the stage. They retrace their steps with a repetition of figure No. 7, which included *chassé glissé*, *soubresaut*, *coupé dessous*, and (for the woman) *saut de basque en tournant*. The ensemble moves to a diagonal formation from upstage left to downstage right, the leads again placed in front of them, in preparation for the return to the A section. All perform in unison until breaking away to form three circles, two couples in each upstage corner and three couples, include the leads, at downstage center. With dancers holding hands and facing inward, the circles rotate to the left.

Ex. 4.37b Act Two, *Pas de deux*, bars 44–51

Ex. 4.37c Act Two, *Pas de deux*, bars 77–85

Ex. 4.37d Act Two, *Pas de deux*, bars 117–124

Ex. 4.37e   Act Two, *Pas de deux*, bars 151–153

Ex. 4.38a   *Fin du 2° acte*, bars 116–120

Forming a row across the stage once again, the ensemble backs the lead couple, men partnering women in *saut de basque en tournant* and *en face*. At the end, the women fall back to the left and each cavalier catches his partner in his arm.

Pas d'éventails. A *Pas d'éventails* (Dance of the fans)—a dance for two women, performed in Lyon by "Mlles Duleau et Saliné"—is included in Justamant's list of dances, but pages cut from the manual following the *Valse des hussards* suggest this number was removed at some point. The Paris production also included a *pas des éventails*, as reported by the critic Fiorentino, who noted that the dance featured dancers who held a fan in one hand and played castanets with the other.[85] However, a review in *L'Album de Sainte-Cécile* confirms that this fan dance was performed by the corps de ballet and therefore was not the same dance as the second-act *pas de deux* performed by Dumilâtre and Plunkett.[86]

We believe we have found a notation for the *pas de deux* in another Justamant manuscript—a compilation of dances (eight *pas de deux* and one *pas de cinq*)—which includes a "Pas de deux | (musique de *Paquita*) | dansé par Mlles Navare et Leblond."[87] Although the notation is mostly unfinished, the information provided by Justamant can nevertheless be matched to the score of the *Paquita pas de deux*.

Here is a description of the musical structure of this *pas de deux* as given in the Paris musical scores, with our comments explaining where Justamant provides choreography or other information.

[85] *Le Constutionnel*, 7 April 1846. See also Guest, *Romantic Ballet in Paris*, 2nd ed., 253.
[86] *L'Album de Sainte-Cécile*, 20 April 1846, 4.
[87] Bibliothèque Nationale de France, Bibliothèque-Musée de l'Opéra, B-217 (1), 157–165, available online at https://catalogue.bnf.fr/ark:/12148/cb44451007d. The 165-page manuscript is bound in a notebook titled *Pas Noble avec adagio* on the cover and *Divers Pas Nobles Composée par Mr H Justamant* on page 1, where the contents are listed. See Appendix B.

Ex. 4.38b *Fin du 2° acte*, bars 213–220

Ex. 4.38c *Fin du 2° acte*, bars 265–272

Allegro moderato, $\frac{2}{4}$, A major (Ex. 4.37a)

6 bars (introduction) plus 35 bars

Justamant records 35 bars of choreography for two women.

Transition

2 bars in $\frac{6}{8}$ meter

Andante, $\frac{6}{8}$, B-flat major (Ex. 4.37b)

31 bars

Omitted in Justamant, which includes the annotation, "L'andante e[s]t Passée."

Transition

4 bars in $\frac{3}{8}$ meter (these are struck through in the Rep)

2 bars in $\frac{6}{8}$ meter, A major

Omitted in Justamant, which includes the annotation, "l'introduction e[s]t Passée."

Allegretto, $\frac{2}{4}$, A major (Ex. 4.37c)
 39 bars (plus an eight-bar repeat)
 Omitted in Justamant.

(No tempo given), $\frac{2}{4}$, D major (Ex. 4.37d)
 1 bar (introduction)
 34 bars (plus repeats of 24 bars)
 Justamant records a "1re variation Mlle Leblond" with music marked "sans
  reprises." The notated dance accounts for thirty-two bars.

Moderato, $\frac{4}{4}$, D major (Ex. 4.37e)
 25 bars (bars 1–5 are struck through in the Rep; the following three staves are covered by a paste-over of bars 1–13)
 Justamant records eight bars of a "Variation de Mlle Navare" that fill the top half of
  a page and correspond to this number. Three blank pages follow.

Allegro moderato, $\frac{2}{4}$, A major (see Ex. 4.37a)
 This number is a near repeat of the opening section of the pas.
 4 bars (introduction)
 52 bars (plus repeats of 20 bars; one bar is struck through in the Rep)
 Justamant records eight bars for "Mlle Leblond seule," but as with earlier numbers he
  abandons the rest of the dance, leaving nine subsequent pages tantalizingly empty.

Pas final. The Pas final serves as a coda for the divertissement and features groups of
women dancers, an extended entrée for Paquita, the return of the hussard couples—dancing
again to a waltz—an entrée for Paquita and Lucien, a pas de six for four women and two
men, and a closing passage for the entire cast. (The title for this closing passage in the Rep is
"Ensemble et pas de deux de Carlotta et Petipa.")
  Justamant does not appear to have notated the jaleo (as the passage is called in the
Rep) that makes up the first 113 bars of the score (Ex. 4.21). But he does notate the next
number, which perhaps was the first number in his finale, a G major allegro moderato in
$\frac{2}{4}$ (Ex. 4.38a). Here, four coryphées dance in unison, the two on stage left mirroring the
movements of the two on stage right, for twenty-five bars. "Deux premiere danseuses"
take over, also mirroring each other's steps as they dance side by side, for another twenty-
three bars.
  A substantial variation for Paquita marked "(2e pas)" follows, the first two pages of
which appear to be pasted over existing pages in the manuscript, suggesting an interpolation. No musical indications are provided beyond an allocation of at least 52 measures
(at least one movement passage does not seem to have numbers of bars allocated to it)
among six choreographic figures.[88] Accompanied by drawings often depicting Paquita
flying through the air, the description of steps include sissonne, piqué rond de jambe, brisé
de coté, relevé sur l'orteil en tournant un tour en dedans, rond de jambe fouetté, fouetté
brisé battu, and various piqué arabesques and attitudes. The final figure begins with a diagonal of eight pas de bourrée en tournant, followed by grand fouetté sauté en arabesque,

[88] Four glissades performed over the course of two bars suggest duple or compound duple meter.

then "relevé sur l'orteil" on the left foot and *rond de jambe fouetté* with the right, performed twice, before finishing with a *pirouette sur le cou-de-pied*.

We return to the score, as written, with the waltz in D major (the "Queen of Prussia" waltz, Ex. 4.26) and the return of the six hussard couples. After twenty-six bars, they relinquish the stage to the lead hussard couple ("rentrée du 3m et la 3m danseuse"), who repeat a short phrase of partnered *jetés dessus en tournant*, two *sauts de basque*, and *chassé glissé de coté soubresaut* four times.

Next comes a 40-bar passage in E major, $\frac{2}{4}$ (Ex. 4.38b). Justamant does not mention this music, but he likely did use it, for his notation of the subsequent choreography for the return of "deux 1er danseuses" followed by Lucien and Paquita fills forty bars.[89]

Like the groups of women before them, the two danseuses perform sixteen bars of mirrored choreography, finishing with three turns "sur l'orteil" and a *saut de basque* "au public." Lucien and Paquita follow with a terrific entrance, coming down the diagonal as he lifts her in three *grands jetés*, each separated by a *pas de bourrée en tournant* for Paquita as Lucien passes in front of her, all the while his hands on her waist and her hands on his shoulders. Separating, they travel back up the diagonal, beginning with a *pas tombé croisé*, followed by a quick turn to the right for Paquita and an *arabesque allongée*, supported at the waist by Lucien. This sequence is repeated twice before the entire entrance is danced again from the *grand jeté* lifts. Paquita finishes with a pirouette, after which she takes Lucien's hand and shoulder as she poses *en arabesque*.

The final section of the score is a $\frac{3}{8}$ in A major, marked "très vite" (Ex. 4.38c).[90] During the four-bar introduction, Paquita goes upstage to retrieve the other women. The four women resume dancing with vigor, arms held to one side, then *en couronne* during *emboîtés* "sur les orteils," and finally on hands their hips as they perform "pas tombé le pied croisé, en balançant." Lucien and a "2me danseur" join them in a *pas de six*, the men partnering the women in *arabesques* and *sissonne* lifts. The group next forms three couples, the two male-female couples at the sides, a female-female couple at center.

Finally, the six are joined by all: hussards, officers, and all the ladies. (Justamant accounts for twelve couples plus the six dancers from the previous section. Strangely, Paquita is unaccounted for in this last section of the *Pas final*.) Together, they perform a series of *soubresauts* and waltz steps and conclude the ballet in a pose, the women leaning back into the men's arms.

Thus ends our step-by-step description of *Paquita* as drawn from the Justamant manuscript (with bits of added information from the Rep and a few other sources). What these sources reveal is a largely comedic melodrama in which the plot is utterly dependent on the lively, resourceful, even wily, Paquita, who must use a variety of strategems to extricate herself from her terrible predicament, and who, along the way, saves Lucien and exposes the corruption of the main villain, Don Lopez de Mendoza. It features an exotic Spanish setting, domestic comedy and strife, Roma people whose leader embodies negative Roma stereotypes of the sort still alive today, French blue-bloods, children, dance numbers of several types, and the spectacular dancing of the leading ballerina. The first two scenes of the ballet, consisting largely of mime and action, are laced with full-on dance numbers including the festival performance and, later, Paquita's *pas des*

---

[89] Following the annotations in the Rep—indicating a repeat taken, a repeat omitted, an added bar, and one revised bar—the total number of bars left for dance equals exactly forty.

[90] Taking into account six bars that are struck through in the Rep, Justamant accounts for all of the music.

tambourines. They also include *pas d'action* (scenes mixing dance and action) that offer the audience a good deal of diversion and variety—for instance Paquita's choreographing of her own dance for the festival as Inigo tries to declare his love for her, and the Roma company's dance rehearsal. But it is only in the final scene (after a short mime scene in which all of the plot's problems are resolved) that the dancing is unleashed full-scale. The act becomes a lengthy dance party featuring several numbers and culminating in a joyous waltz for the ensemble.

The popularity of this ballet in Paris, which remained in the repertory of the Opéra for five years, reminds us of the broad reach of audiences' tastes for Romantic ballet and the considerable skill set of the Opéra's ensemble company, which could handle the ethereal *Giselle* and the earthbound *Paquita* at the same time.

One year into *Paquita*'s run at the Opéra, the ballet also started a new life in Russia. Let us now return to St. Petersburg to see how that story unfolded.

5

Paquita in St. Petersburg

As *Giselle* had appeared in St. Petersburg the year after its premiere, so *Paquita* arrived in the Russian capital in 1847, one year following its first Paris performance. The ballet was given a warm welcome, and—together with Mazilier's *Satanilla*, staged in 1848—was hailed for rejuvenating the somewhat stale repertory of the Imperial Ballet. The resignation of ballet master Charles Didelot in 1829 (his successors Alexis Blache and Antoine Titus were far less successful in the job) and the more recent departure in 1842 of Marie Taglioni (who had brought with her fresh repertory) had left the troupe without strong artistic leadership and without stars.[1]

Marius Petipa was associated with *Paquita* in Russia from the outset. He staged the Petersburg premiere jointly with Pierre Frédéric Malavergne (Frédéric) and danced the role of Lucien. The ballet marked a new beginning for him as much as it did for the Imperial Ballet. *Paquita* was the first work he staged and performed in Russia, and one of the last he rehearsed while still active as ballet master.

Petipa's interest in Spanish dance. Paquita's Saragossa setting and its opportunities for Spanish dance must have held special attraction for Petipa. His years in Spain (1844–1847) immediately preceding his appointment as *premier danseur* in St. Petersburg afforded him an apprenticeship in Spanish dance that served him well throughout his career.[2] Spanish-inflected choreography no doubt filled his numerous ballets set in Iberian locales, including the early divertissement titled *The Star of Granada* (1855), the one-act episode *The Traveling Dancer* (1865), which Petipa planned to revive as late as 1904, and the multi-act ballets *Don Quixote* (1869), *Zoraiya, the Moorish Girl in Spain* (1881), and *The King's Command* (1886).[3] Petipa also included Spanish dances in ballets set in other regions, for example, *Raymonda* (1898, see Chapter 10), or fairytale lands, such as *The Nutcracker* (1892). In 1878, he staged the dances for the St. Petersburg premiere of Bizet's *Carmen*.[4]

Petipa became a master of synthesis, incorporating Spanish dance vocabulary into the *danse d'école*. Ekaterina Vazem, whose suggestion of a new ballet set in Spain provided the impetus for *Zoraiya* (in which she created the title role), remembered Petipa's enjoyment of the Spanish idiom: "Petipa worked on *Zoraiya* with much pleasure. The ballet gave him a great opportunity to use his knowledge of Spain, where he spent some of his early years. His composition was most successful, skillfully combining Spanish and [in the case of *Zoraiya*] exotic, oriental choreography."[5]

---

[1] See Wiley, *Century*, 81–89.
[2] On Petipa's years in Spain, see Hormigón, *Marius Petipa en España*. See also Laura Hormigón, "Petipa in Spain," *Ballet Review* 47, nos. 3–4 (Fall–Winter 2019): 69–72, and Meisner, *Marius Petipa*, 48–54.
[3] The revival of *The Traveling Dancer* was to be on the same program as Petipa's new ballet, *The Romance of the Rosebud and the Butterfly*, slated for performance in January 2004 at the Hermitage Theater in St. Petersburg, but ultimately canceled. For one account, see Meisner, *Marius Petipa*, 278–280.
[4] See *Khronika III*, 194–195.
[5] Vazem, "Memoirs: Part 4," 38.

Five Ballets from Paris and St. Petersburg. Doug Fullington and Marian Smith, Oxford University Press.
© Oxford University Press 2024. DOI: 10.1093/oso/9780190944506.003.0006

Mazilier's influence on Petipa. In addition to providing an opportunity to indulge his love of Spanish dance, *Paquita* brought Petipa into greater contact with the work of Joseph Mazilier, a choreographer whose particular strengths would influence the younger artist's work.[6] The intensity of Mazilier's dramatic scenes surely appealed to Petipa, whose gifts as a mime and commitment to passionate performance were cele- brated.[7] Mazilier also demonstrated a well-honed skill in creating multimovement dance suites (such as the *Pas de Mlle Carlotta Grisi* in *Paquita* and the Act One *pas de cinq* in *Le Corsaire*) and a deftness in deploying both soloists and ensemble in large-scale, culmi- nating dances, such as a coda or finale (the finale of *Paquita* being an excellent example, if indeed Justamant's staging manual is representative of Mazilier's work)—both widely admired elements of Petipa's ballets.

Paquita was not, of course, the only Mazilier ballet produced by Petipa. The reper- tory of the older master's ballets that Petipa restaged demonstrates an ongoing engage- ment with Mazilier's work. In 1848, Petipa staged the Petersburg premiere of Mazilier's *Satanilla, or Love and Hell* (originally, *Le Diable amoureux*)—collaborating with his fa- ther, Jean Antoine Petipa—and danced the role of Count Fabio. Petipa also knew and worked with Mazilier, performing in the choreographer's 1851 St. Petersburg revival of *Le Diable à quatre* (under the title *The Willful Wife*) during the single year that Mazilier was contracted as a choreographer and performer by the Imperial Theaters.[8] (Perrot had revived the ballet the year before, and Petipa revived it as well in 1885.) Petipa was the first Russian Conrad in Perrot's 1858 staging of Mazilier's *Le Corsaire*, and, over the course of the next forty-plus years, went on to revive *Corsaire* multiple times, adding new dances and making revisions to existing material to such an extent that he significantly altered the content of the ballet (see Chapters 7 and 8).[9]

Among the ballets explored in this volume, we find abundant examples of Petipa's original choreography that demonstrate Mazilier's influence. The 1881 Petersburg *Paquita* closes with a multimovement *Grand pas* for the heroine, Lucien, soloists, and coryphées whose coda additionally incorporates a large corps de ballet and an ensemble of children who performed earlier in the scene. Petipa's 1877 *La Bayadère* is predicated on high drama and features an entire scene centered around the physical and emo- tional confrontation between the ballet's leading women, Nikia and Hamsatti. Later, the Kingdom of the Shades scene comprises entrées, ensembles, *pas de deux*, variations, and a coda over the course of nine danced numbers. The ballet's final *pas d'action* is an- other multi-movement dance suite for leading dancers and soloists whose dramatic content drives the narrative forward to its tumultuous conclusion. Finally, Petipa's 1898 *Raymonda* includes no fewer than four multimovement dance suites, including a central *pas d'action*. The codas of each of these dances feature multiple constituencies—soloists, coryphées, corps de ballet, children—assembled into a coherent framework of entrées. And though not an overly dramatic work—indeed, the ballet showcased the gifts of a

---

[6] Petipa had performed the role of Federico in Mazilier's *Le Diable amoureux* at the Teatro del Circo in Madrid in 1845 (where the ballet was titled *El Diablo enamorado*). See Hormigón, "Petipa in Spain," 69, and *Marius Petipa en España*, 199–201.

[7] For Vazem's assessment of Petipa's acting abilities, see Vazem, "Memoirs of a Ballerina of the St. Petersburg Bolshoi Theatre: Part 2," tr. Nina Dimitrievitch, *Dance Research* 4, no. 1 (1986): 17–19, and Meisner, *Marius Petipa*, 66–70.

[8] See Meisner, *Marius Petipa*, 56–57.

[9] In addition to these ballets, Mazilier himself staged Albert's *La Jolie fille de Gand* (under the title *The Flemish Beauty*) and his own *Vert-Vert* while working in the Russian capital. See *Khronika II*, 19–20 and 21–22, respectively.

brilliant technician rather than an expressive mime—*Raymonda* nevertheless features an exciting *scène dramatique* for the ballerina and the antagonist Abderrakhman. Even as he approached the age of eighty, Petipa continued to deploy and refine skills and forms he had learned from his predecessors.

Let us now consider select *Paquita* performances in St. Petersburg. This chronology will demonstrate *Paquita*'s active place in the repertory for decades and reveal that early performances of the ballet brought Petipa, Mazilier, and Perrot together with the leading dancers of their day—both resident and guest—for debuts, benefits, retirements, and intrigues. Through the years, roles were taken by reigning stars and emerging ballerinas, and by character artists, choreographers, and ballet masters—and at times, the ballet was featured in the Theater School repertory as well. Thus the Imperial-era *Paquita* ably held its own on the Petersburg stage for the better part of seventy-five years.

The 1847 St. Petersburg premiere

The St. Petersburg premiere of *Paquita* was given on 26 September 1847 at the Bolshoi Theater.[10] Elena Andreanova, the first Russian Giselle, danced the title role alongside Petipa as Lucien. The performance was a benefit for Frédéric, who staged the ballet together with Petipa and also played the role of Inigo.[11] Konstantin Lyadov was the conductor and orchestrator of the Deldevez score as well as the composer of a galop that was added at the end of the ballet.

The poster and the list of dances included in the libretto confirm that, unlike Titus's staging of *Giselle* five years earlier, the Petersburg production of *Paquita* was not intended to be an exact or even close restaging of Mazilier's Paris original. The ballet was presented in three acts instead of two acts and three scenes. Danced numbers retained from the Deldevez score were recast and, therefore, likely newly choreographed. The Act One divertissement included the same dances as in Paris, but the *pas de trois* was danced by two women and a man (Tatiana Smirnova, Anastasia Yakovleva, and Christian Johanson) rather than by three women. The cast list in the libretto for the *Pas des manteaux*, which includes sixteen women "in men's costumes" and sixteen women "in women's costumes," confirms that this number was performed with half of its dancers in travesty, but the dance appears to have lacked the lead couple of the Paris production.[12] The *Pas de Mlle Carlotta Grisi* that had brought forth "thunders of applause" in Paris was performed as a *pas de neuf* for Andreanova, six women, and two men.[13]

Act Three saw the most change in the production. Following the *Contredanse française* (for which two women, one a senior student, are listed as participants on the poster) and gavotte (for two male-female couples), thirty-two students performed a *Pas de fleurs*. Also included in the production was a *Valse pas de folie* danced by Petipa and Andreanova; five women (four of them senior students) followed in a *pas de cinq*, and Petipa and Andreanova returned for *El haleo de Cadix*. Finally, the leading performers

---

[10] *Khronika II*, 293–295.

[11] On Frédéric and Petipa's possible roles in producing *Paquita* for the St. Petersburg stage, see Meisner, *Marius Petipa*, 55–58.

[12] The St. Petersburg librettos, posters, and programs consistently spell the title of the dance *Pas de manteaux* rather than *Pas des manteaux*. We use the latter (grammatically correct) spelling, which is also used in the Harvard *répétiteur*.

[13] *Le constititionnel*, 7 April 1846, tr. in Guest, *Romantic Ballet in Paris*, 3rd ed., 424.

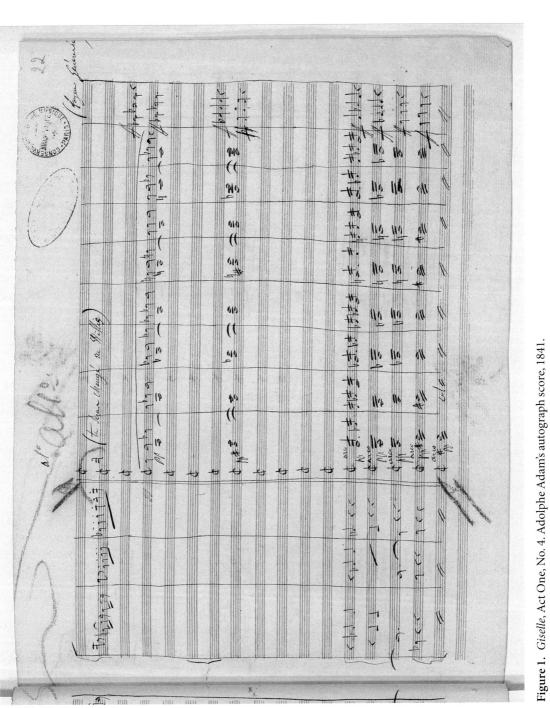

Figure 1. *Giselle*, Act One, No. 4. Adolphe Adam's autograph score, 1841.
"tu seras changé en Willi" | "frayeur Générale" [you will be changed into a Wili | general fear]

Figures 2–5. (top left) Carlotta Grisi as Giselle, Act One. Etching published by Hautecoeur-Martinet, Paris, 1841. (top right) Sketch attributed to Paul Lormier of Giselle's Act Two costume, 1841. Text on left side: "very diaphanous wings" | "edges [indistinct]" | "all the trim will be verbena [indistinct] little flowers". Text on right side: "reeds and verbena" | "green ribbon" | "belt [indistinct], three skirts standing out two finger widths, which will give the wearer the air of a light vapor." (bottom left and right) Costume drawings by Paul Lormier of Duke Albert, Acts One and Two, 1841. Pencil, pen, watercolor.

Figures 6–9. Drawings from "Grise-Aile" (satirical parody of *Giselle* by Lorentz), *Musée Philipon*, Paris, 1843. (top left) Myrtha traverses the stage while posing on a rolling device. (top right) Giselle and Albert in the Act Two *pas de deux*; note that their costumes match those in Lormier's drawings from the final scene, Figures 3 and 5. (bottom left) Albert's final farewell with Giselle, who sinks into a bed of flowers; note Albert's costume. (bottom right) Arrival of Bathilde on horseback (she is riding side saddle); Albert, with Wilfride or the Prince of Courlande, is holding a flower that he saved from the gravesite.

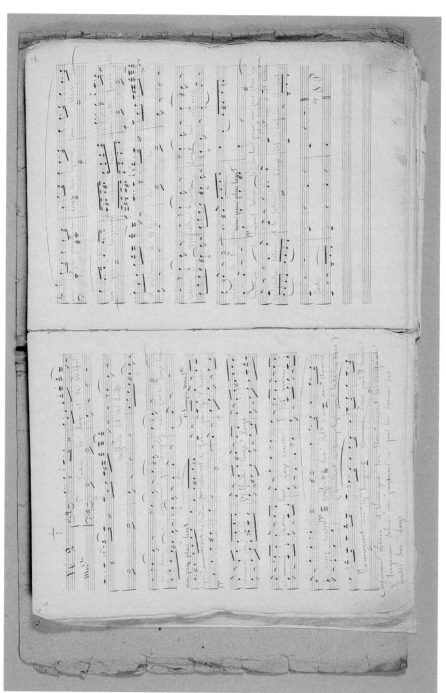

Figure 10. *Giselle*, Act One, No. 2, Titus *répétiteur*, 1841/1842.

Figures 11–12. Costume drawings by Alfred Albert of Bathilde (left) and a page in travesty (right), 1863. Crayon, watercolor.

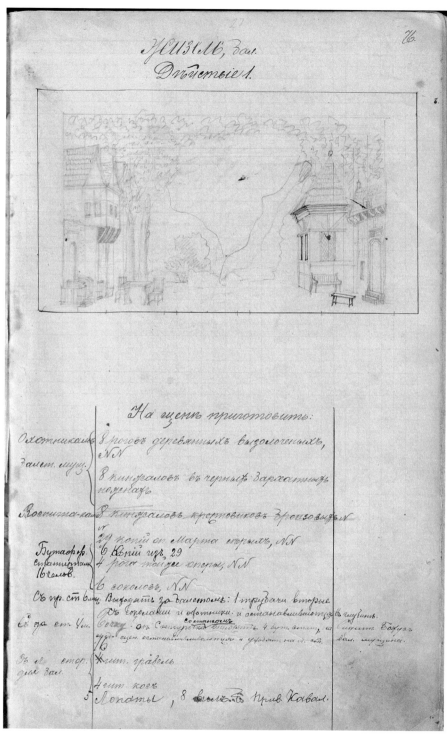

Figure 13. Page from the Mariinsky Theater manuscript volume of production documents describing the stage setting and properties for *Giselle*, Act One, 1889.

Figure 14. *Giselle*, Act Two, Nikolai Legat partnering Anna Pavlova by the wings.
Photograph by Ernst Schneider, Berlin, 1909.

Figure 15–18. (top left and right) Costume drawings by Henri d'Orschwiller depicting Georges Elie as Inigo and Carlotta Grisi as Paquita, Act One. Pencil, watercolor. (bottom left) Caroline Lassia in the *Pas des manteaux* from *Paquita*. Lithograph published by Martinet, Galerie Dramatique, 1846. (bottom right) Costume drawing (unsigned) depicting Hussards (of seven regiments), 1846. Pencil, watercolor.

(Théâtre de l'Opéra. — *Paquita*, ballet-pantomime; deuxième acte. — Jarigo, M. Élie; —Saint-Vallier, M. Peti, a; — Paquita, mademoiselle C. Grisi.)

Figure 19. Press illustration by H[enry Augustin] Valentin depicting action from *Paquita*, Act Two, Scene I, 1846.

Figures 20–25. Six drawings from Henri Justamant's staging manual for *Paquita*, circa 1854. Act One, No. 6: Inigo declares his love for Paquita; she ignores him as she creates a dance for the festival.

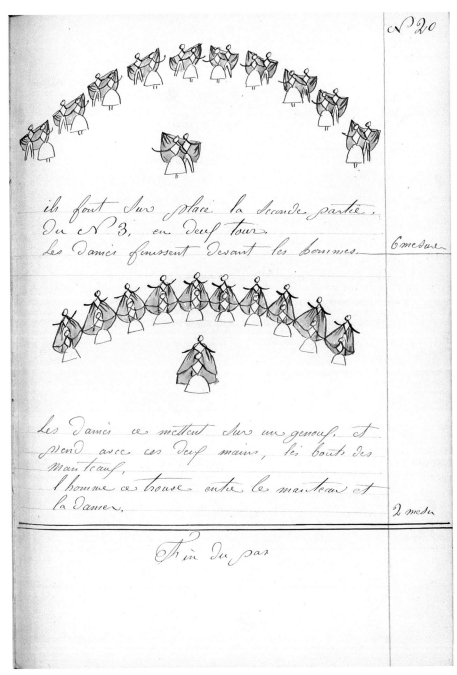

ils font Sur place la Seconde partie
Du N 3, en deuf tour.
Les Dames finissent Devant les hommes.

6 mesure

Les Dames ce mettent Sur un genouf, et
prend avec ces deuf mains, les bouts des
Manteauf,
l'homme ce trouve entre le manteau et
la Dame.

2 mesu

Fin Du pas

Figure 26. Final figure of the *Pas des manteaux*, Justamant staging manual for *Paquita*, circa 1854.

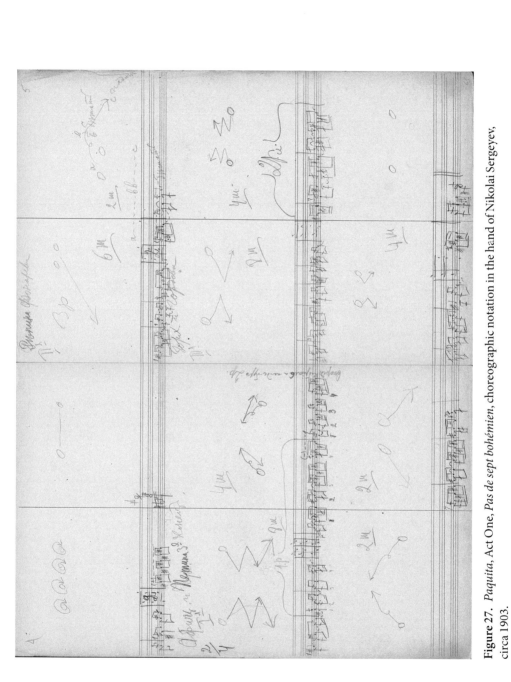

Figure 27. *Paquita*, Act One, *Pas de sept bohémien*, choreographic notation in the hand of Nikolai Sergeyev, circa 1903.

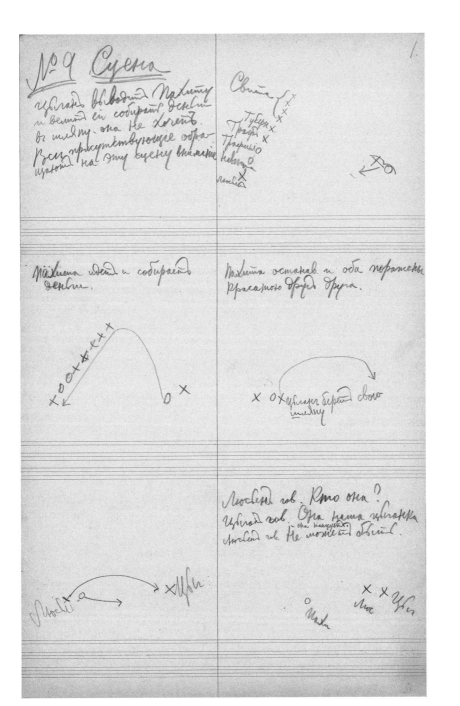

Figure 28. *Paquita*, Act One, No. 9, choreographic notation in the hand of Nikolai Sergeyev, circa 1903.

Figure 29. *Paquita*, Act Three, end of children's mazurka and beginning of *Grand pas, répétiteur* (undated).

Figure 30. *Paquita*, drawings by Pavel Gerdt (dated 1894) showing the opening of the adagio of the *Grand pas*.

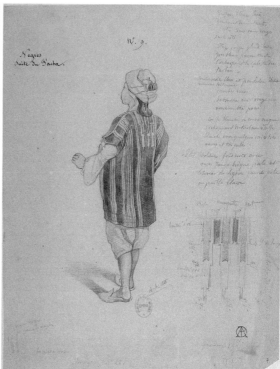

Figures 31–34. Costume drawings by Alfred Albert for *Le Corsaire*, 1855 (for 1856 Paris production): (top left) "Pasha"; (top right) "Black people in the service of the Pasha" (a child); (bottom left) "Algerienne"; and (bottom right) "Persian dancer." Pencil, watercolor.

(including Frédéric) joined the ensemble for Lyadov's *galop général*. Whether any of the dances that appear to have been new to this final act were performed to music by Deldevez is a question additional source material may answer. The *pas de folie* and jaleo were character dances, the former making a particularly favorable impression, according to Rafail Zotov, who praised many of the performers in his extensive critique of the premiere published in *Severnaya pchela*. He concluded his review with an assessment of the new *premier danseur*:

> What can I say now about the debutant? He danced in the *pas de folie* and *El Haleo*, hence in two characteristic dances. The lightness and strength in him are amazing, but we will wait for his future debuts in dances of a noble and serious kind and then we will give a detailed account of him. For now, one saw only that it [*Paquita*] was a wonderful acquisition for our troupe, because with their great talent, everyone looks good [in the production].[14]

The success of the production was felt to reinvigorate the Petersburg ballet and its audience: *Paquita* was performed eighteen times during the 1847–1848 season—more than the eight performances of *La Péri* and four of *Giselle* combined. The ballet underwent some revision, no doubt under the watchful eyes of Petipa and Frédéric.[15] The poster for the third performance on 1 October 1847 lists what was formerly a *pas de neuf* as a *pas de sept*: Andreanova and six women are listed, but the men's names are omitted. (If the choreography remained the same despite the title change, the omission of the men's names may suggest they had filled a non-dancing function in the number.) The poster also lists the gavotte before the contredanse, and the jaleo is no longer included.

The following season, Petipa and Andreanova performed the leading roles in a Moscow production of *Paquita*, staged by Petipa and his father Jean Antoine, that premiered at the Bolshoi Theater on 23 November 1848.[16] Less than two weeks after the premiere, on 5 December, during the first act, a dead cat was thrown onto the stage with a note attached to its tail bearing the inscription, "To the *première danseuse étoile*." The cat struck Frédéric Montessu, Andreanova's saltarello partner, in the head. The ballerina was so shaken she could not continue, but the audience, outraged by this cruel act of a rival faction, thundered its approval of her artistry, and Andreanova eventually returned to finish the performance.[17]

The 1851–1852 season saw Mazilier spend a year in St. Petersburg as choreographer and performer, during which time he staged *Paquita* as a benefit for Marius Petipa on 27 November 1851.[18] The all-star cast included Carlotta Grisi (Paquita), Petipa (Lucien), and Mazilier (Inigo). Over the next several seasons, performances of *Paquita*

---

[14] *Severnaya pchela*, 6 October 1847, qtd. in *Khronika II*, 293–295.

[15] See Wiley, *Century*, 174–175.

[16] See Meisner, *Marius Petipa*, 29, 300.

[17] *Khronika II*, 297. This sensational occurrence has been referenced in many publications. See Meisner, *Marius Petipa*, 61–62, for an account.

[18] *Khronika III*, 20. Mazilier was engaged at a time when it was uncertain whether Perrot would be available for the 1851–1852 Petersburg season. See Guest, *Perrot*, 261, and Alexander Pleshcheyev, *Nash Balet (1673–1899)* [Our Ballet (1673–1899)], 2nd, supplemented ed. (St. Petersburg: Th. A. Pereyaslavtsev and A.A. Pleshcheyev, 1899; St. Petersburg: Music Planet, 2009), 217–218. Citations refer to the Music Planet edition. For details about Mazilier's appointment in St. Petersburg, see Olga Fedorchenko, "Zhozef Mazil'ye v Peterburge (1851–1852): novyye dokumenty i fakty" [Joseph Mazilier in St. Petersburg (1851–1852): new documents and facts], *Vestnik Akademii Russkogo baleta imeni A. Ya. Vaganovoy* [Bulletin of the Academy of Russian Ballet named after A. Ya. Vaganova], 5 (2020): 36–45.

continued to feature luminaries and saw several debuts as well. A benefit performance on 13 December 1853 for the dance teacher Eugène Huegé, for example, featured Rose Marie Girod (Paquita), Petipa (Lucien), and Perrot (Inigo).[19] A St. Petersburg Theater School performance of the first act on 26 March 1854 featured Maria Surovshchikova, who only months later married Petipa.[20] And a revival of *Paquita* on 10 January 1856, a benefit performance for Christian Johanson, marked the debut of Anna Prikhunova in the title role, joined by Petipa (Lucien) and Frédéric (Inigo).

We see from this select performance history that not only did the leading French choreographers of the period not only knew each other, but they worked together, staged each other's ballets, and even performed together. Moreover, this slice of history confirms an accepted practice we encountered with *Giselle*—regular revision, which was surely regarded as necessary for the longevity of a ballet in repertory. Petipa's subsequent revival of *Paquita* would once again prove this point.

The 1881 St. Petersburg revival

Following the creation of two original ballets on Spanish themes in the 1860s and 1870s—*Don Quixote* and *Zoraiya*—Petipa returned to *Paquita* in 1881 after the ballet had been out of repertory for a period of some fifteen years. He revived it as a vehicle for Ekaterina Vazem, refreshing it with new dances set to music by Ludwig Minkus. With these now-celebrated additions, *Paquita* remained in the St. Petersburg repertory until shortly after the 1917 Revolution.

The revival premiered at the Bolshoi Theater on 27 December 1881 and featured not only new dances by Minkus but a new overture by Ludwig Maurer.[21] Vazem, who had created the role of Zoraiya as well as the role of Nikia in *La Bayadère* (see Chapter 9), achieved a great success as Paquita. She was partnered by Pavel Gerdt as Lucien, with Felix Kshesinsky as Inigo and Lev Ivanov as Don Lopez de Mendoza. With this production Dona Seraphina (Maria Zest) became the niece, rather than the sister, of Mendoza. The Countess (Maria Legat) appears in the cast list as Lucien's mother, but this appears to be an error—she remains his grandmother in the libretto (which recounts essentially the same story as in 1847 but with new prose; see Appendix D (iv)).

In her memoirs, Vazem recalled the circumstances surrounding the revival:

> In the following season, at the end of 1881, for my benefit performance, Petipa revived Mazilier's *Paquita*, an old ballet which had not been performed for a long time on our stage. This work, dating from the 1840s with its naïve, melodramatic story, with its sharply drawn 'villains' and 'virtuous' characters, was rather modest in its choreographic content and appeared very dated. But Petipa was anxious to revive it and he wrote to me in the summer, while I was still abroad, trying to persuade me to take it for my benefit performance, tempting me with the promise to compose for it some new and interesting dances.[22]

---

[19] *Khronika III*, 30.
[20] Ibid., 35.
[21] Ibid., 215–216.
[22] Vazem, "Memoirs: Part 4," 39.

The Act One divertissement comprised the usual three numbers—*pas de trois*, *Pas des manteaux*, and the newly named *Pas de sept bohémien*. The *pas de trois*, which featured a newly composed coda by Minkus (see below), was performed by Anna Johanson, Sofia Petrova, and Platon Karsavin. The *Pas des manteaux* was danced by twelve (rather than sixteen) all-female couples, with half of the women performing in travesty as in the 1847 production. The *Pas de sept bohémien* featured Vazem and six women. Kshesinsky (Inigo) and Lukyanov (one of four Romani) are also listed as participants in this dance, bringing the total number of performers to nine—the same number listed for the initial 1847 *pas de neuf*.

The execution of the dance numbers in the first act disappointed Konstantin Skalkovsky (writing for *Novoe vremya*), who found the preparation of the dancers lacking:

> The first act of *Paquita* did not meet expectations. Neither the *pas de trois*, the only one staged as it was performed in 1847, nor the *pas de manteaux*, which delighted our fathers, nor the other dances of this act had much success. Much was to be expected from the *pas de manteaux*, performed by twenty-four dancers at once, but probably because thirty-five years ago it was danced by the best soloists: Smirnova, Yakovleva, Prikhunova, Sokolova, Panova, etc., but now it went to the second dancers who did not take the trouble to rehearse the dance as attentively, and so there was not such an effect.[23]

But the third act was a roaring success. Just as Frédéric and Petipa had added new dances to the ballroom scene in the 1847 production, so did Petipa revamp it once again. His first new addition was a still-celebrated mazurka for twenty-four students of the Theater School, among whom were Vladimir Stepanov and Alexander Shiryaev, both in their early teens.[24] The *Valse pas de folie*, now *Valse de la folie*, remained part of the divertissement, but instead of featuring Paquita and Lucien, it was performed by revelers from the crowd, Maria Gorshenkova and Nikolai Manokhin.[25]

The *pièce de résistance* of the final act was the freshly minted *Grand pas* for Vazem, Gerdt, and an ensemble of soloists and coryphées, performed in the ballet's final act. Vazem confirmed the triumph of Petipa's new creation:

> His great success and the climax of the ballet was the newly created *Grand pas* to music by Minkus, which was most effective in its varied dance numbers. Taking part were the ballerina and her partner, with several female soloists and dancers of the second rank.

[23] Konstantin Skalkovsky, *Novoe vremya*, 29 December 1881, qtd. in *Khronika III*, 215–216. According to the poster for the 1847 premiere, Smirnova and Yakovleva danced the *pas de trois*, rather than the *Pas des manteaux* (unless they performed both and were not named as dancers in the latter), and Prikhunova, Sokolova, and Panova were at the time senior students. It is possible this writer was basing his information on an entry that stated these dancers performed the *Pas des manteaux* in A. Volf, *Khronika peterburgskikh teatrov s kontsa 1826 do nachala 1881* [Chronicle of the Petersburg Theaters from the End of 1816 to the Beginning of 1881], 3 vols. (St. Petersburg, 1877–1884), qtd. in *Khronika II*, 295.

[24] All of the students are listed by name in the published libretto.

[25] The popular *Valse de la folie* had something of a life of its own—Lev Ivanov included it on a 28 July 1889 program during the annual summer season at the theater in the village of Krasnoe Selo. See Wiley, *Lev Ivanov*, 57. The waltz was eventually removed from *Paquita* altogether but not forgotten, as evidenced by this report in *Teatr i Iskusstvo*: "Meanwhile, now that the gitano Inigo is performed by Mr. [Felix] Kshesinsky 1, this act [Act Two] makes one forget not only about the dance *pas de folie* that was removed from the program, but perhaps even about the *pas de manteaux* itself." *Teatr i Iskusstvo* 41 (1897), qtd. in *Khronika III*, 317–318.

This *Grand pas* had an exceptional success with the public. Indeed, it was one of Petipa's masterpieces; it began with an imposing entrance for all the participants, followed by a beautiful adagio, performed by all the dancers placed diagonally on the stage from the first wing to the right of the audience to the last wing on its left, and concluding with a series of variations for the soloists. I always danced the *Grand pas* with the greatest pleasure, as did my principal partners, Johansson, Nikitina, Shaposhnikova, and others.[26]

So popular were the third-act dances that they were performed on their own at a benefit performance for Petipa on 17 January 1882—just three weeks after the revival premiere. As soon as the mazurka came to an end, the audience called the choreographer to the stage, where he was surrounded by the student performers.[27] And on 2 May 1883, the St. Petersburg Imperial Ballet brought *Paquita* to Moscow with Vazem in the title role. The children's mazurka made a strong impression, as it had in St. Petersburg, and was encored.[28] Vazem performed *Paquita* for the last time on 12 February 1884:

My farewell performance [which the ballerina had programmed herself] concluded with the second and third acts from *Paquita*, where, in the *Grand pas*, I said my final goodbye to the public.

The warmth of the reception given me by my colleagues and the audience exceeded all my expectations.[29]

On 23 September 1884, Maria Gorshenkova made her debut in the role of Paquita. A mishap reported in the press, involving a supported *double pirouette* in the Act Two *pas scénique*, gives us the briefest idea of the choreography for a dance about which we know little in Petipa's version. The *Grand pas* elicited "endless applause."[30]

Although a number of ballerinas would assume the title role over the next decades, Gerdt and Kshesinsky steadfastly remained in theirs—that is, in the roles of Lucien and Inigo, respectively—until the early years of the twentieth century. When Kshesinsky was fêted with a benefit performance on 31 January 1888 in celebration of his fifty years on stage, the program included the first and second acts of *Paquita*, featuring the honoree as Inigo.[31]

The Italian ballerina Virginia Zucchi made her debut as Paquita on 2 November 1886. The reviewer in *Minuta* reported that a *pas de voile* danced by Zucchi and Gerdt received an ovation.[32] Zucchi's is a unique situation: she managed the role mostly by interpolating numbers she already knew. Ivor Guest provides further details:

Virginia had not had time to absorb the part [of Paquita] fully; although she had mastered the mime passages, the only dance she was able to learn thoroughly was the *cachucha*, which she performed in the second act with Kshesinski and Gerdt. In her interpretation this acquired a dramatic significance it had lacked before. For her other

---

26 Vazem, "Memoirs: Part 4," 39.
27 *Khronika III*, 217.
28 *Khronika III*, 223. See also Vazem, "Memoirs: Part 4," 40–41.
29 Vazem, "Memoirs: Part 4," 45. See also *Khronika III*, 230.
30 *Peterburgskaya gazeta*, 28 September 1884, qtd. in *Khronika III*, 233.
31 *Khronika III*, 268.
32 *Minuta*, 4 November 1886, qtd. in *Khronika III*, 254.

variations, she inserted dances that had been seen before: in the first act, a variation to a Strauss waltz that she had performed in *Les pommes d'or* at Kin Grust and, in the ballroom scene in Act III, the *pas de voile* from *Brahma*. This latter dance now included a striking effect that Adelina Sozo had introduced at the Zoological Gardens in the summer—a *pas de bourrée* performed on a moving strip of material.[33]

Zucchi danced the role again on 9 November 1886 in the farewell benefit performance for Ludwig Minkus on the occasion of his release from the post of ballet music composer (a position that was then abolished).[34]

Zucchi was the first in a line of Italian guest artists in St. Petersburg who essayed the role of Paquita with Gerdt and Kshesinsky. The two stalwarts partnered guest Italians Emma Bessone in 1887, Palmira Pollini in 1893, and Carlotta Zambelli in 1901.[35]

Matilda Kshesinskaya's successful debut as Paquita on 20 February 1894—also with Gerdt and Kshesinsky—marked the emergence of a new generation of Russian dancers to assume the ballet's leading roles.[36] Kshesinskaya's brother Iosif followed in his father's footsteps with a celebrated debut as Inigo on 10 October 1899.[37]

As we saw with Zucchi's performance, danced numbers were periodically interpolated into the ballet on special occasions or to feature particular dancers. A *pas de quatre*, set to music by Ernesto Köhler and choreographed by Enrico Cecchetti, was interpolated into a performance of *Paquita* on 26 April 1898 and performed by senior students—Julia Sedova, Lubov Egorova, Mikhail Obukhov, and Mikhail Fokine—all of whom went on to have major careers.[38] A benefit performance for Alfred Bekefi, in observance of twenty-five years of service, was given on 21 November 1901 and featured not only Zambelli in her debut as Paquita but also the benefit artist performing a '*Fandango*,' *pas Espagnole*, which preceded the mazurka, with Matilda Kshesinskaya.[39]

Petipa remained involved in the ongoing evolution of *Paquita* well into his middle eighties. On 5 March 1904, he rehearsed Anna Pavlova for her debut in the title role and subsequently noted the same in his diary: "I went to mount the role on her; composed a new variation to new music by Mons. Drigo." (The question of which variation this may have been will be discussed below.) Petipa rehearsed Pavlova again on both 11 and 17 March. On 21 April, he rehearsed Olga Preobrazhenskaya, who also was preparing for her debut in *Paquita*, and he rehearsed at least twice more after that.[40] Preobrazhenskaya performed on 25 April 1904, partnered by Sergei Legat as Lucien and Iosif Kshesinsky as Inigo.[41] "Great success for Mlle. Preobrajenska," Petipa wrote in his diary. The *pas de trois*

---

[33] Ivor Guest, *The Divine Virginia: A Biography of Virginia Zucchi* (New York: Marcel Dekker, 1977), 97–98.

[34] *Khronika III*, 254.

[35] The 22 November 1887 benefit performance for Emma Bessone included the third act of *Paquita*, in which she danced the *pas de deux* and finale with Pavel Gerdt. *Khronika III*, 265. Palmira Pollini made her debut in *Paquita* on 17 October 1893. The reviewer for the *Peterburgskaya gazeta* deemed she was successful only in an interpolated Spanish dance. *Peterburgskaya gazeta*, 18 October 1893, qtd. in *Khronika III*, 312. According to Valerian Svetlov, Carlotta Zambelli danced with "extraordinary lightness, grace, and beauty" in her performance as Paquita as 21 November 1901. Valerian Svetlov, *Terpsikhora* (St. Petersburg, 1906), qtd. in *Khronika IV*, 25–26.

[36] *Khronika III*, 317–318.

[37] Ibid., 363.

[38] Ibid., 348–349.

[39] *Khronika IV*, 25–26.

[40] Garafola, ed., *Diaries*, 47–51.

[41] *Khronika IV*, 57.

was danced by Pavlova, Sedova, and Nikolai Legat, and Petipa's daughter Vera performed in the Act One *pas de sept*.[42]

Pavlova and Fokine made their debuts as Paquita and Lucien on 2 May 1904, with Iosif Kshesinsky as Inigo and Gerdt as Don Lopez. Fokine had been promoted to first dancer the day before. The writer and dance historian Alexander Pleshcheyev praised Pavlova and also reported that Vera Trefilova distinguished herself so highly in her variation that the audience obliged her to perform it three times. He also remarked on the "stylish" performances of Sedova, Agrippina Vaganova, and Nikolai Legat in the *pas de trois*.[43]

As she had done in *Giselle*, Pavlova achieved great success in *Paquita*, certainly due in no small part to the ballet master's coaching and the personalized interpolations he made for her. She delivered dress circle box tickets to Petipa the day before the premiere and three days later visited him at home to thank him for *Paquita*.[44] Writing about a performance of *Paquita* that closed the season on 27 April 1905, Valerian Svetlov, a passionate champion of Pavlova, described her performance in the third act:

> Mlle Pavlova 2 appeared in the 3rd act of *Paquita*, in the famous *grand pas*. . . . No analysis, not even the most detailed, will give an accurate idea of the perfection of her choreographic masterwork. This is why all stars and starlets, surrounding her in the *grand pas*, paled as soon as Mlle Pavlova entered the stage. Her talent is absolutely exceptional.[45]

Despite these notable early twentieth-century triumphs, *Paquita* became a periodic focus of Petipa's ire, likely the result of singular authority over casting being wrested from his control in 1903.[46] On 30 September 1904, he complained in his diary about what he regarded as poor casting in the *Grand pas*, made by the theater's ballet committee. He did not attend the rehearsal that day. He complained again on 24 October about the performance of *Paquita* that evening:

> First performance of the season of Mlle. Pavlova, in the *grand pas* of the last act. Variations—[Olga] Chumakova, [Elena] Makarova, and [Ekaterina] Ofitserova, who were all a great fiasco; next time they will be danced by [Varvara] Rykhlyakova, [Lubov] Egorova, [Elizaveta] Vill', [Lydia] Kyaksht, and [Anna] Pavlova II.[47]

Practical information may be gleaned from such entries, including what appears to be confirmation that five female variations were currently danced in the *Grand pas*. Published programs provide further detail about the ongoing presentation of the ballet: for instance, the program for the 24 October 1904 performance (and seemingly from thereon) consolidates Paquita's Act Two *solo* and the subsequent *pas scènique* into a single *scène mimique* performed by Paquita, Lucien, Inigo, Don Lopez, and the four Romani bandits, a list that comprises all of the participants in Act Two.

[42] Garafola, ed., *Diaries*, 50–51.

[43] Alexander Pleshcheyev, *Peterburgskiy dnevnik teatrala*, 1904, no. 19, qtd. in *Khronika IV*, 58. Tamara Karsavina is listed as performing the *pas de trois* in the program, but Sedova danced instead.

[44] Garafola, ed., *Diaries*, 51.

[45] *Birzhevyie vedomosti*, 29 April 1905, qtd. in *Khronika IV*, 72.

[46] See Meisner, *Marius Petipa*, 277–278.

[47] Garafola, ed., *Diaries*, 56–57.

After Petipa's death in 1910, *Paquita* remained in the repertory and important role debuts continued. On 23 December 1912 Tamara Karsavina made her debut as Paquita with Samuil Andrianov as Lucien and Alexander Monakhov as Inigo. The *pas de trois* was danced by Vaganova, Ludmilla Schollar, and Petr Vladimirov.[48] Elena Smirnova made her debut on 30 November 1914, partnered by Andrianov, with Iosif Kshesinsky as Inigo.[49]

But *Paquita*'s time in the repertory was growing short. At a meeting of the Mariinsky Theater directors on 14 May 1919, a number of ballets were removed from the repertory of the State Ballet Company (as the former Imperial Ballet was then called). In addition to *Paquita*, these included *Bluebeard*, *The Caprice of the Butterfly*, *The Enchanted Forest*, *Fiammetta*, *The Awakening of Flora*, *Graziella*, *The Halt of the Cavalry*, *The Magic Flute*, and *The Romance of the Rosebud and the Butterfly*.[50] Although the ballet that had introduced Marius Petipa to Russia was officially eliminated from the company repertory, *Paquita* was featured in summer performances, and excerpts, especially the *Grand pas*, continued to be performed by the Theater School (as well as a complete performance staged by Alexander Shiryaev in 1922).[51] Eventually, these celebrated divertissements would find a permanent home in the Soviet repertory.

Sources

Materials from the Harvard Theatre Collection. We will again use the documents of the Sergeyev Collection—primarily choreographic notations and a violin *répétiteur*—as our primary sources for a scene-by-scene description of the St. Petersburg *Paquita* at the turn of the twentieth century, supplemented with additional sources to fill in gaps and provide further detail.

Choreographic notation. *Paquita* is well-represented in the Sergeyev Collection. Sources include a 155-page choreographic notation (CN) in the Stepanov method, which, like the Stepanov notation of *Giselle*, is written on portrait-format paper in Sergeyev's hand.[52] (A second scribe, Rakhmanov, is represented by a second notation of the student mazurka, written on oblong-format paper.) One of the CN's title pages is dated 1905 and the Act One *Pas de sept bohémien* is dated 1904. The document is rich in details of action and pantomime for Acts One and Two, but only dances are notated for Act Three. Additional notations of select variations and passages of small ensemble dances, in yet another scribal hand, are included in the collection's miscellaneous folders.[53] These give us an idea of the choreographic variants that existed between versions of solos danced by multiple artists, a phenomenon we will encounter elsewhere, such as in the Justamant staging manual for *Le Corsaire*.

[48] *Khronika IV*, 158–159.
[49] Ibid., 176.
[50] Ibid., 232–233.
[51] Preobrazhenskaya performed the title role in performances during the summer of 1920. *Khronika IV*, 248. The school performance was given at the Maly Opera House on 12 February 1922 and featured students Olga Mungalova and Petr Gusev as Paquita and Lucien, with Shiryaev as Inigo. *Khronika IV*, 263.
[52] MS Thr 245 (28), Harvard Theatre Collection, Houghton Library, Harvard University. The CN folders include numerous slips of white paper containing English translations of much of the CN prose in Mona Inglesby's hand.
[53] MS Thr 245 (227–228).

We find only a few dancer names listed in the action scenes documented in the CN, but many more are included in the notated dances. Anna Pavlova's name appears as Paquita throughout the action of Acts One and Two. Iosef Kshesinsky is named as Inigo, although this character is more often referred to as "Tzigane" (*Tsygan*), a French term for a Romani person. (We will translate this as "gitano" but will otherwise continue to use the terms "Roma" and "Romani" in this chapter.) Ivan Kusov is also named in Act One; he performed the role of a Romani.[54]

Don Lopez de Mendoza is called "Governor," Lucien's father (the General in Justamant's manual) is "Count," Dona Serafina is "Niece," and Lucien's grandmother is "Countess." Lucien is always "Lucien"; this character's name is not replaced with a dancer's name or any other identifier. The action in the CN rarely includes mention of the larger onstage ensemble beyond general entrances and exits.

Whether the bulk of the choreography documented in the CN is the same as that made by Petipa for the 1881 production, we cannot be certain. *Paquita* was regularly in repertory during the intervening years, so revisions were possible and even likely.

Mime script, synopsis, and printed materials. Complementing the CN is a manuscript mime script in ink (with pencil annotations) of Acts One and Two, dated 10 December 1922, the period during which Sergeyev was directing the Latvian National Ballet.[55] The document is in Sergeyev's hand and is a near-verbatim copy of the CN's prose annotations relating to action and pantomime. A particular benefit of the mime script is its clarification of the placement in Act Two of Nos. 4 through 9, information that is not included in the CN. Other related materials include a brief manuscript synopsis in ink in an unidentified hand (a pencil draft in the same hand is filed with the ink copy)[56] and a program for a performance of *Paquita* at the Mariinsky Theater on 24 October 1904.[57] Finally, the Harvard Theatre Collection also holds two bound volumes of librettos of St. Petersburg Imperial Theater productions, one of which includes a libretto for *Paquita*, dated 19 November 1901.[58] The text is the same as that in the 1881 libretto.

Répétiteur. The music sources for *Paquita* in the Sergeyev Collection include a two-violin *répétiteur* (Rep), lightly annotated, that includes names of Imperial Ballet dancers dating back to the 1881 revival and surely comes from St. Petersburg.[59] The bound document consists of 183 pages with various cuts marked mostly in pencil. A comparison of the Rep with the *répétiteurs* from Paris confirms that all of the action numbers were retained in the St. Petersburg production (at least at the time the Rep was created and in

[54] Both Iosef Kshesinsky and Ivan Kusov performed with Pavlova in her debut performance on 2 May 1904.

[55] MS Thr 245 (29).

[56] MS Thr 245 (30).

[57] MS Thr 245 (247). An English translation of the program's contents in Mona Inglesby's hand is included with this item.

[58] Petipa, M., Ivanov, L., *Imperatorskiy Sankt-Peterburgskiy Bol'shoy teatr, Mariinskiy teatr*, & John Milton and Ruth Neils Ward Collection. (1875). *Collection of 36 ballet scenarios, chiefly from the St. Petersburg Imperial Ballet, in the collection of J.M. Ward, [1875–1907]*, GEN TS 5000.10, Harvard Theatre Collection, Houghton Library, Harvard University. Typewritten English translations of the librettos by Roland John Wiley are included with this item.

[59] MS Thr 245 (38).

use) with only minor deviations.[60] Our musical examples in this chapter will be drawn from the Rep unless otherwise noted.

Manuscript orchestra score. A 372-page manuscript orchestra score, dated 10 October 1922, appears (as in the case of *Giselle*) to have been copied and likely orchestrated in connection with Sergeyev's Riga production (more on this below).[61] Indeed, musical details contained in the *Paquita* Rep—tempo markings, annotations regarding instrumentation, penciled cuts—are observed in the orchestra score, suggesting the St. Petersburg Rep in Sergeyev's possession was used as the guide for orchestration. Corresponding instrumental parts are also preserved along with additional items— piano reductions and orchestra parts—for individual numbers.[62] A lightly annotated manuscript piano reduction of the complete ballet in ink (with a pencil draft) is also likely of Riga provenance.[63]

Additional sources. Other select sources we will use for our description include Mariinsky Theater production documents,[64] drawings made by Pavel Gerdt of the adagio from the *Grand pas*,[65] memoirs and reviews, and even film footage from the later twentieth century.

The St. Petersburg *Paquita* at the turn of the twentieth century: A scene-by-scene description

Note that the St. Petersburg *Paquita* was significantly different from the production documented by Justamant, not only in the dances but in certain details of the action, particularly the tense and loaded encounters between Paquita and Inigo. This suggests, as mentioned earlier, that the St. Petersburg version of *Paquita* does not draw nearly as closely from its Parisian model as *Giselle* did. Therefore, we do not make a close, direct comparison between the two versions of the ballet, as we did with the Paris and St.

---

[60] The following is a list of the most significant differences found in the St. Petersburg *répétiteur* held at Harvard, MS Thr 245 (38), compared to the Paris *répétiteur*, MAT-355 (23–24):

Act One, No. 1 is divided into an "Introduction" and No. 1.

Act One, No. 3 matches the longer of the two Paris versions of No. 3, minus ten bars; a further forty-six bars are struck through in pencil.

Act One, No. 6 is longer by several bars owing to some repeats, notwithstanding a strike-through of sixteen bars.

Act One, No. 8 is thirty-six bars shorter (not accounting for thirty bars struck through in the Paris *répétiteur*).

Act One, No. 11, titled "Finale," comprises the Paris Act One, No. 11 and "Final"; the number is twenty-five bars shorter than in the Paris *répétiteur*, and thirty-three bars near the beginning of the number are struck through.

Act Two, No. 8 is shorter by ten bars (not accounting for eight bars struck through in the Paris *répétiteur*).

Twenty-nine bars are struck through in the scene following the Act Three gavotte.

[61] MS Thr 245 (39). The score calls for triple flutes (one doubling piccolo); double oboes, clarinets, and bassoons; four horns; two trumpets; three trombones; tuba; percussion (including tambourine and tamburo); harp; and strings. Metronome marks are given for much of the *Grand pas*. While these markings do not represent St. Petersburg performances, they nevertheless tell us the tempi set by Sergeyev in his staging of the dances. See Wiley, "Dances from Russia," 99–100, 108–110.

[62] MS Thr 245 (31–35).

[63] MS Thr 245 (36–37). Annotations made in pencil and red and blue crayon concern both music and action. Page 106 indicates the use of "chimes" for the strikes of midnight.

[64] St. Petersburg State Museum of Theatre and Music (GMTMI), GIK 16917, fols. 77v–77r.

[65] A. A. Bakhrushin State Central Theatre Museum (GTsTM), KP 168404 | *fond* 336, *op.* 1, *ed. khr.* 1.

Petersburg productions of *Giselle*. For in the case of *Giselle*, we were asserting that the French and Russian productions derived from a common source, an argument we are not making in the case of *Paquita*.

Act One

The stage plan for the opening locale of the turn-of-the-century Petersburg *Paquita* corresponds fairly closely to that described in the 1847 Petersburg libretto:

> The Valley of the Bulls near Saragossa. Large, roughly crafted stone bulls are seen sculpted in the distant hills. At the right, still at a distance, huge cliffs rise up, with a natural staircase cut into the stone. Also at the right, a tent for the gitanos.

The later version, as shown in the Mariinsky's volume of production documents, shows a pathway winding down into the valley at upstage center that fills the entire sixth wing and most of the fifth. Two tents, one on each side of the stage, fill the fourth wing. The tent at stage left is struck through in pencil and a third tent is penciled in the third wing at stage left. The stone monument is in the second wing at stage right. In front of it are two benches and three chairs for the guests of the Governor.

Introduction. The Rep includes neither the Paris introduction nor the Maurer overture from 1881.[66] Instead, the first forty-seven bars of No. 1, the polonaise-like pastoral theme in D major, function as an introduction. An annotation in the Rep indicates the curtain goes up at bar 25. The sculptor is working on the monument.

No. 1. The Governor comes to inspect the results. He pays the sculptor and announces that all are coming. An annotation in the Rep at bar 1 states, "A crowd is entering." The Governor's suite arrives, including the Count, Countess, Lucien, and Niece.

Moving to center, the Governor explains to the Count, "This is the place where your brother was killed."

No. 2. The men take off their hats and all bow their heads in prayer. The Niece crosses the stage toward the monument.

No. 3. "Do not cry," says the Governor. "Think about the young ones, if Lucien will marry my niece."

The Count goes to the Niece and the Countess to Lucien.

Countess: "Do you like her?"

Lucien: "Yes."

Countess: "Do you want to marry her?"

Lucien: "I don't have anything against it."

Countess: "Then ask her."

Lucien walks across the stage and offers his hand to the Niece. Together, they exit upstage left with the others.

No. 4. Peasants and Romani (Rep: "Tsyganskiy") begin to fill the stage to the sounds of a pastoral melody (Ex. 4.13). One of the Romani (Kusov) calls for Inigo, who enters from the mountain path after a crescendo in the music that builds over fourteen bars. The

---

[66] Because the Introduction is also omitted from the Paris *Paquita répétiteur*, it is possible that it was also missing from the musical source used by Konstantin Lyadov when scoring the ballet for the 1847 St. Petersburg premiere, particularly if that source was also a *répétiteur*. The lack of a musical introduction in the Petersburg *Paquita* performance tradition is likely the reason for the addition of the overture by Maurer in 1881.

Rep announces, "Main Gitano enters" (Ex. 4.14). A conversation between the Roma man and Inigo appears to replace the Romani rehearsal described by Justamant. Inigo shakes hands with the Roma, takes off his coat, and puts it on his arm.

Inigo: "You prepare everything." They walk, switching places (so that Inigo is now stage left) and looking around.

Inigo: "Here there is not one beauty" (that is, Paquita is not here). He claps his hands and calls for the Roma.

Inigo: "Did you see the beauty?"

Roma: "No."

Inigo: "Bring her here." Then, moving aside, he addresses the audience again: "I love her and will marry her. Her dancing will bring me lots of money."

"Everyone is hiding," written at this point in the CN, suggests that the company of Romani leaves the stage in advance of Paquita's entrance.

Roma: "She is coming here."

Inigo: "Hide these and these." (The items or characters being hidden are not identified in the CN.)

Roma: "Okay." He exits stage left.

Inigo: "She is coming. I will talk to her." He hides in the tent at stage right.

At the reprise of the pastoral tune, Paquita (Pavlova) makes her way down the mountain path, gathering flowers. According to the librettos (the Paris and both the 1847 and 1881 St. Petersburg versions) and Justamant, Paquita distributes flowers to the crowd of Romani, but according to the CN she dances instead (Ex. 4.10). Her entrance choreography is similar to that for Giselle's first appearance in the St. Petersburg production. Alone on stage, she traces a large circle in small jumps—*tombé, glissade, ballonné* eight times. (The working leg in the *ballonné* makes a *rond de jambe* through *demi-seconde* to *demi-attitude devant*.) She continues with an enchaînement of *glissade, cabriole derrière, assemblé, piqué de côté en cou-de-pied devant, piqué tour en demi-arabesque*, two *demi-emboîtés derrière* three times. Three *demi-cabrioles derrière* are followed by a *bourrée* across the stage and *chaînés* on *demi-pointe*. Her dance ends as she is abruptly stopped by Inigo, who has re-emerged downstage left.

No. 5. Moving to center, Inigo accosts Paquita (Ex. 4.5). Their confrontation is played out in private, contrasting with the scene in Justamant that occurs in the presence of all the Romani. An annotation in the Rep at the beginning of this number identifies the episode as "Love scene | Gitano and Paquita (negative feelings of Paquita and Gitano)."

Inigo: "What were you doing there?"

Paquita: "I was gathering flowers." She shows him her bouquet, which Inigo grabs from her and throws down.

Inigo: "You think about it. I am first here. I love you and will marry you." He threatens her, raising his hand "at the chord"—a musical cue that may refer to the climax followed by a *fermata* in the Rep at bar 31. Paquita crosses her arms on her chest and proudly poses in defiance. Inigo is ashamed and returns to the tent.

No. 6. "She dreams," written in the CN, refers to Paquita's reverie. Her mime prose is written in two parts that are numbered using Roman numerals:

I: "He tortured me," and [she] cries. "He sends me to beg. He wants to marry me and send me to beg."

II: "My parents were killed, and I was stolen. I remember, I will look at my medallion." The Gitano [Inigo] calls her from the tent.

Following a two-bar introduction, the first mime statement (I) was likely accompanied by the first two four-bar phrases of No. 6 (Ex. 4.27). (The next eight bars are struck through in the Rep.) Though the sources offer no information about the exact musical placement of these mime statements, the second part (II) seems to belong at the beginning of No. 7, set to Paquita's Recognition motif (Ex. 4.2).

Next, accompanied by cascading triplets, Paquita makes a counterclockwise circle around the stage, demonstrating, perhaps with sarcasm, how she is forced to collect money (Ex. 4.28).

Inigo interrupts Paquita, calling her twice from the tent. She runs to him upstage left and the *scène dansante* begins. This is confirmed by the Rep annotation, "Paquita's dance with the Gitano (classical)." Here, as we have seen in Justamant, dance and pantomime are interwoven as Inigo expresses his unrequited love for Paquita.

As in *Giselle*, the *scène dansante* in *Paquita* is placed early in the first act, but here it involves the heroine and the antagonist rather than two lovers. Inigo, the Romani chief and Paquita's guardian, both desires and oppresses her. Using the Rep together with the CN, we can identify the mime and dance passages in Petipa's production. However, although the CN is elsewhere unusually rich in mimetic content, here it offers few details beyond the notation of the choreography. Nevertheless, the sources confirm that the *scène dansante* here is similar to the Paris original: Inigo tries to woo Paquita, but she ignores every entreaty by responding only with dance.

Accompanied by a pleasant *allegretto* (G major, $\frac{3}{4}$), Inigo follows Paquita as she dances (Ex. 4.7). She begins with a diagonal of *emboîtés* and a *relevé développé croisé devant* four times. Next, she circles the stage with three *précipités*, *piqué en demi-arabesque* three times followed by a run downstage left and *grand jeté en avant* to *arabesque fondu*. Inigo, who has run ahead of her, "goes on his knee and begs her," but she backs away from him with *temps levés en arabesque* (separated by a step back). She teases by approaching him with *emboîtés* and a *grand jeté en avant* then backing away. She travels stage left with repeated *assemblés* into *sous-sus* followed by *piqué tours en dedans*, but she is cut off by Inigo, whose arrival to block her path coincides with a fermata that interrupts the melody (Rep: "Wait"—an annotation for the rehearsal violinists). Unfazed, Paquita backs away with more *temps levés en arabesque* (again separated by a step back) then approaches Inigo with *emboîtés* and a *piqué en arabesque*.

After another repetition of this back-and-forth, Inigo can no longer contain himself (Rep: "The Gitano comes up for the love scene"; Ex. 4.29). Grabbing Paquita by the waist, he tries to kiss her. She frees herself and runs upstage left. The Rep indicates she strikes a pose at the culmination of this section (a diminished chord marked *forte*), but the CN offers no further details.

The final section of the *scène dansante*, the lilting *moderato* (G major, $\frac{6}{8}$), begins with a diagonal of *bourrée, glissade, piqué développé croisé devant* three times as Inigo walks alongside Paquita (Ex. 4.30). She breaks away from him, running stage left to begin a diagonal upstage of *chassé, tour jeté, relevé effacé devant* four times. She circles the stage with *temps levés en demi-arabesque* on alternating legs then travels directly down center with *pas de bourrée taqueté*. She runs upstage left for a final diagonal of *piqué tours en dedans* followed by *chaînés* on *demi-pointe*.

No. 7. As mentioned above, No. 7 likely begins with Paquita's examination of the portrait in her medallion, which elicits her vague memories of the event that changed her destiny (Ex. 4.2). The 1881 libretto provides greater detail:

Alone, Paquita takes from her bodice the portrait which she has kept from child-hood, and which she has managed to keep. The portrait does not give the country of origin of the person it depicts; with boundless anguish she studies the features of him for whom she is surely obliged for her existence, and dreams of the joys of family life. . . . Looking out at the surrounding landscape, she recognizes the place where a horrible scene occurred, a scene of which her memory preserves to this day only trou-bled recollections.

Yes, it is here, here that she watched the officer fall dying, who had taken her into his arms and from whose arms someone's foreign, unfamiliar hands wrested her.

The CN continues as Inigo approaches Paquita, meeting her at center.

Inigo: "The nobles are coming, so you will dance and collect money."

Paquita: "No, I will not."

Inigo: (insisting) "I will make you," but Paquita walks away toward the tent.

While nearly half of this number is cut in the Rep (twenty-five of fifty-six bars), Paquita's Recognition motif, intended for her reverie, remains plus an additional six bars of agitated music to accompany her exchange with Inigo.

No. 8. Bright, annunciatory music reintroduces the peasants who enter down the mountain path (Ex. 4.15). Romani enter from both sides. The Governor follows, bring-ing his entourage with him from upstage left.

Governor: (addressing his party and pointing at the chairs) "Sit down. The gitanos are going to dance." He calls Inigo, who enters from the tent, bows, and asks what they want.

Governor: "What will you show us?"

Inigo: "Wait."

No. 8½. Accompanied by a fanfare, Inigo claps his hands, and six women appear (per-haps the *pas de sept* ensemble). "They will dance," he says. "Good," replies the Governor, and he sits down to watch.

Inigo presents his suite of dances to the assembled aristocracy. Following the order of the Paris production, the divertissement begins with the *pas de trois* followed by the *Pas des manteaux*. After a short scene, the dances conclude with the *Pas de sept bohémien* for Paquita and six Romani women.

Pas de trois. The *pas de trois* was highly regarded by Petipa. Nikolai Legat recalled the choreographer's fondness for the dance in his memoirs:

> One of [Petipa's] favourite compositions was a *pas de trois* in the ballet *Paquita*, which was danced by [Matilda] Kshesinskaya, Anna Johanssen and myself. Petipa used to call this his 'golden *pas de trois*.' 'Imposs better tance!' he used to say in broken Russian.[67]

Let us consider, briefly, what information is available about the history of the Petersburg *pas de trois*. We know that, beginning with the 1847 production, the dance was per-formed by two women and a man rather than by three women, as it had been in Paris. We also know that the music preserved in the Rep is a varied assortment of numbers

---

[67] Nicolas Legat, *Ballet Russe: Memoirs of Nicolas Legat*, tr. Sir Paul Dukes (London: Methuen, 1939), 19. Legat's memoirs have been republished in *The Legat Legacy*, ed. Mindy Aloff (Gainesville: University of Florida Press, 2020).

by Deldevez, Cesare Pugni, Adam, and, presumably, Minkus. Because all of this music, with the exception of Minkus's contribution, was composed prior to the ballet's 1847 St. Petersburg premiere, the possibility exists that its score was assembled expressly in that year to form the Petersburg *pas de trois* and then continued to be used in the 1881 production. Is it possible that the choreography, too, may have remained in place since 1847? One eyewitness, Skalkovsky, writing in *Novoe vremya* in 1881 (quoted above), went so far as to assert that the *pas de trois* in Petipa's current revival was the only dance in the ballet performed as it had been in that first St. Petersburg production staged in 1847 by Petipa and Frédéric. But whether he was referring to the consistent casting of two women and a man, the musical numbers (save for the Minkus coda), or the choreography is a question that is not answered by our sources.

Other clues, however, suggest that the *pas de trois* choreography was not altogether new to the 1881 production. For instance, when Petipa later defended his authorship of his 1881 contributions to *Paquita* in an undated letter to the publisher of *Novoe vremya*, he mentioned the children's mazurka and *Grand pas*, but not the *pas de trois*, strengthening the possibility that it was already in place before the 1881 revival:

> In 1847, in St. Petersburg, I staged and made my debut in the ballet *Paquita*. In the last act there was only a quadrille, a gavotte, and a *pas de deux*. When I restaged this ballet [in 1881] under the management of His Excellency Mons. I[van] Vsevolojsky, I composed a mazurka for the pupils of the school and a new *grand pas*. I left the quadrille and gavotte.[68]

The CN documents, at least in part, the performances of Tamara Karsavina, Agrippina Vaganova, and Nikolai Legat, the intended cast for Pavlova's debut on 2 May 1904. (Julia Sedova ultimately replaced Karsavina, likely due to the latter's ill health at the time.[69]) Their names are listed only once in the CN—separately, in connection with particular solos. The notated choreography may represent revisions made for these dancers or for dancers that recently preceded them in their roles. Alternatively, at least some of the choreography may represent the steps performed by the 1881 cast or even some steps that reach all the way back to 1847.

In addition to the main CN, a second, partial notation of the *pas de trois*, in a different hand, is preserved in one of the collection's miscellaneous files.[70] Here, the dance is notated on oblong-format paper that includes staves only (ground plans, written on the staves, are drawn from the stage perspective rather than the audience perspective). This second notation includes the entrée, both short solos, second variation (labeled "Variation No. 1"), and coda. The most important feature of this additional notation is the inclusion of positions of the arms and occasionally the positions of the torso and head, although the latter are notated mostly in a default, upright position.

Finally, we observe that the notated choreography, as in Justamant, represents the *danse d'école* and does not include any apparent Spanish character dance steps. However, this does not preclude the possibility of upper body movements that may have had a Spanish character.

---

[68] Tr. in Garafola, ed., *Diaries*, xiii.
[69] Thanks to Andrew Foster for this information about Karsavina.
[70] MS Thr 245 (228), 19–23.

Entrée. The entrée is set to the good-natured music Deldevez composed for the opening of the Act Two *pas de deux* of the Paris *Paquita* (see Ex. 4.37a). The trio begins upstage left in *tendu croisé derrière*, the man between the two women. He holds their outside hands, and their inside hands are placed on his shoulders. They traverse the stage diagonally with a series of small *temps levés* and *pas de bourrée*. Reaching the opposite downstage corner, they continue with *chassé*, *tour jeté*, *assemblé* and run upstage right to repeat all of these steps to the other side, finishing at center. After a series of *temps levés*—during which the dancers rock forward and back in place—punctuated by a *sissonne*, the woman on the left travels toward the stage left wings with turns on *pointe*. She will return for the first short solo following the entrée. The remaining pair travels upstage with *tombé*, *chasse en tournant*, *temps levé*, *jeté en tournant* and returns with *temps levé* and two *grands jetés en avant*. After repeating this to the other side, they finish with an *assemblé* and a pose facing downstage right—the woman in *arabesque* on the right *pointe*, the man supporting her by the waist.[71]

The entrée is followed in the Rep by a nine-bar passage—*Allegro*, $\frac{4}{4}$, A major—that is struck through in pencil. This may at one time have served as a transitional passage or accompanied a brief dance. We have not identified the composer. Such short transitional passages are a feature of mid-century multimovement dances (examples are found in the scores of both *Giselle* and Deldevez's *Paquita*).[72] Their existence in the score of the *pas de trois* therefore strengthens the possibility that the dance was initially assembled in 1847.

Short solos. Next, forty bars of lilting music from Pugni's ballet *Ondine* serve as accompaniment for two sixteen-bar solos (eight additional bars are struck through in the Rep), the first for the woman who left the entrée early, the second for the man (Exx. 5.1a and 5.1b).[73]

Here the CN includes the names of Vaganova and Nikolai Legat as the performers of the short solos. Vaganova begins at center in *tendu croisé derrière*. Traveling downstage, she performs *assemblé*, *double rond de jambe en l'air sauté*, *glissade*, *piqué développé devant* three times.[74] Running around to upstage center and posing again in *tendu croisé derrière*, she next traces a zigzag pattern as she travels downstage with a variant of her first enchaînement: *glissade*, *assemblé*, *glissade*, *piqué développé devant*, finishing in fifth position on *pointe* after the third time. She completes her solo with turns on *demi-pointe*. No final pose is given.[75] Legat is next: beginning right of center in fifth position, he performs alternating *entrechats quatre* and *entrechats six* followed by *sissonne simple*, *chassé*, *tour jeté*, crossing center. He repeats the enchaînement to the other side.[76] Next, traveling in a counterclockwise direction around the stage, he performs a series of *sissonnes doublée battu*. Arriving at center, he finishes with four *pirouettes* to *attitude à terre.*

[71] The additional CN records the woman's position as *demi-arabesque* with arms in fourth position.

[72] Examples in *Giselle* include the Act One *pas de deux* for Giselle and Albert and the Act Two dances of the Wilis and *pas de deux*; examples in *Paquita* include the Act One *pas de trois* and *Pas de Mlle Carlotta* and the Act Two *pas de deux*.

[73] The Pugni music used in the *Paquita pas de trois* is taken from the first variation (*Allegretto*, $\frac{6}{8}$, B-flat major) of a *pas de quatre* in the opening scene of the ballet *Ondine*, preserved in a manuscript two-violin *répétiteur* available at https://imslp.org/wiki/Ondine_(Pugni%2C_Cesare), pp. 12–13; the music returns at a *forte* dynamic level for a passage marked "Ondine et Beppo" on page 14.

[74] The additional CN records a single *rond de jambe en l'air sauté*.

[75] The additional CN records two *piqué tours en dehors* followed by two *chaînés* on *demi-pointe*.

[76] The additional CN records three *entrechats six* and an *entrechat cinq* moving directly into the *chassé* and *tour jeté*.

Ex. 5.1a Act One, *Pas de trois*, short solo (woman), from *Ondine* (Pugni), bars 1–9

Ex. 5.1b Act One, *Pas de trois*, short solo (man), from *Ondine* (Pugni), bars 18–21

Variation 1. The first variation is set to music by Deldevez, the coloratura flute solo from the Act Two *pas de deux* of the Paris *Paquita* (see Ex. 4.37e). The CN documents the performance of Karsavina.[77]

She begins with a *bourrée* across the stage followed by *piqué rond de jambe en l'air, relevé développé croisé devant* three times to alternate sides. After *entrechat quatre, changement* twice, Karsavina runs upstage. Next, traveling downstage in a zigzag pattern, she performs *brisé volé, pas de chat, pas de bourrée* on *demi-pointe* four times to alternate sides. She moves upstage left on the diagonal with a series of *piqué* steps on the left *pointe* followed by a backward zigzag of *pas de bourrée de côté, échappé battu* three times. Her final diagonal features six *piqué tours en dehors* and finishes downstage right with *glissade, piqué en demi-arabesque.*

A subsequent seventeen-bar reprise of the *Ondine* music in the Rep, possibly once another solo dance passage, is struck through in pencil.

Variation 2. The second variation is also set to music by Deldevez, the final variation of the Paris *Paquita* Act One *pas de trois* (see Ex. 4.31c). No dancer name is given for this female solo in the CN.

The opening movements match the strong rhythmic pulse of the music. At center, the dancer begins with *sous-sus, entrechat six, pas de cheval* to *relevé en demi-attitude effacé*

---

[77] Although Karsavina did not perform the *pas de trois* on 2 May 1904, she surely rehearsed it during the prior weeks, at which time the CN may have been recorded. According to Andrew Foster, Karsavina performed the *pas de trois* no earlier than 15 December 1904. Personal correspondence.

devant twice to alternate sides.[78] Then, as the music winds its way back to a repetition of the opening, the dancer travels gently upstage with multiple *ballonnés battu, pas de bour-rée* before running forward to repeat the dance from the beginning.[79] She follows this with a run upstage left and a diagonal of *glissade, cabriole devant, piqué tour en dehors* three times.[80] The next diagonal, from upstage right, is even more virtuosic, featuring a single *tour, temps levé,* and two *grands jetés en avant en tournant.* This enchaînement is performed two and a half times; the initial *tour* is replaced by a *jeté en tournant* for the repetitions. A final run upstage left is followed by a diagonal of *piqué tours en dedans.*[81] The dancer finishes with a *relevé en arabesque* on the left leg, right arm overhead, left arm side, head turned left toward the audience.[82]

Variation 3. The music for the man's variation is from Act One of Adam's *Le diablé à quatre,* which was presented as *The Willful Wife* (*La Femme capricieuse*) in St. Petersburg (Ex. 5.2).

The martial quality of the music is complemented by bravura steps. Beginning upstage left in *tendu croisé devant,* the man performs *glissade, cabriole devant,* two *emboîtés der-rière* three times before a run upstage right and a repetition of the enchaînement to the other side. A run around to the left brings him to center, where he dances in place: *sous-sus, entrechat six, sou-sus, double tour en l'air* to the left. After repeating the enchaîne-ment plus the first *sous-sus* of what would appear to be another repetition, Sergeyev has written "etc." No further steps are given.

Coda. The women begin the coda, the music of which shares the same sunny disposi-tion as the entrée and is presumably composed by Minkus (Ex. 5.3).

After four bars of a simple fanfare and two bars of vamp, the dancers travel toward each other from opposite sides of the stage with five *temps levés en arabesque* (crossing at center) and a *grand fouetté* to change direction. They perform this three times to al-ternate sides then run upstage left. Traveling side by side as they trace a zigzag pattern, they continue with *ballonné, saut de basque,* and two *jetés en avant* three times to alter-nate sides. After another run upstage left, they are joined by the man for a variant of the opening enchaînement: *glissade,* four *temps levés en arabesque, assemblé, soutenu* three times to alternate sides.[83] Then the dancers travel backward toward center with *glissade, jeté* three times.

At the return of the opening melody, the trio begins a series of lifts and poses. As depicted in the ground plan and described in brief prose in the CN, the man turns to the woman on his right, lifts her by the waist as she faces him, and carries her around to his left side, where he sets her down. The additional CN indicates that the woman performs a *tour jeté* as she is lifted. At the same time, the woman on the left steps in front of the man and poses briefly while he lifts the first woman. The additional CN provides two positions for this posing dancer: in the first, she stands with her left foot *tendu devant,*

[78] The additional CN records *sous-sus, entrechat quatre, pas de cheval, relevé retiré* as the opening enchaîne-ment. The repeat of the enchaînement is omitted.
[79] This second enchaînement is recorded in the additional CN as *pas de bourrée, fouetté sauté* three times to alternate sides.
[80] The additional CN calls for *double piqué tours en dehors.*
[81] Instead of a run upstage, the additional CN calls for *temps levé, pas de bourrée* four times to alternate sides as the dancer travels upstage.
[82] In the additional CN, the left arm is bent ninety degrees and the wrist is twisted inward. This position suggests that the wrist or hand may be on the waist. If the dancer was holding castanets, she would likely have had her wrist, rather than her hand, on her waist.
[83] In the additional CN, the *temps levés* are notated with the leg raised to the front at ninety degrees, which we assume is an error.

Ex. 5.2 Act One, *Pas de trois*, Variation 3, from *Le Diable à quatre* (Adam), bars 1–9

Ex. 5.3 Act One, *Pas de trois*, Coda (Minkus), bars 1–14

arms in second position; in the second, she poses with her left foot in *tendu derrière fondu* as she holds her arms in first position, wrists flexed and turned in, torso leaned forward, back arched. Both women then run behind the man to return to their initial places. This series is performed three times, then the dancers move upstage with *glissade*, *jeté* twice.

As the final section begins, the trio travels downstage with three *ballonnés, jeté en avant* and upstage with two *sauts de basque*. After repeating this to the other side, they run toward the footlights and take their final pose. The CN includes only a ground plan, which indicates that the man stands behind one of the women—the additional CN indicates that she poses in first arabesque on *pointe*—holding her by the waist. The other woman is on his right, her left hand on his shoulder—the additional CN indicates that she poses in fifth position on *pointe*, left arm overhead.

The combination of Petipa's buoyant choreography and a varied and balanced suite of musical selections, made all the more interesting by the inclusion of short solos following the entrée, resulted in a *pas de trois* that retained its popularity throughout the years *Paquita* was in the Imperial Ballet repertory. Tracing its casting, we find that numerous dancers who went on to have careers as leading artists at one point counted the *pas de trois* among their roles.

Pas des manteaux. From the 1847 premiere onward, the St. Petersburg *Pas des manteaux* featured ensemble couples, the male roles of which were danced by women in travesty, but lacked the principal couple of the Paris production. The dance was popular and in early performances was encored.[84] The *Yearbook of the Imperial Theaters* for the 1892–1893 season paid tribute to *Paquita's* many years in the repertory and, in particular, the longevity of the *Pas des manteaux*, which was "especially liked by the public" and "has been preserved in the ballet *Paquita* up to the present time, in spite of the fact that many dances were changed during subsequent revivals."[85]

With the *Pas des manteaux*, we begin to encounter Petipa's incorporation of Spanish character dance steps into his choreography for *Paquita*. Some of this movement vocabulary is described in *The Fundamentals of Character Dance* (FCD) including stylized versions of ballet-based vocabulary, such as *balancé, glissade, pas de basque*, and *sissonne* that can be performed "in the Spanish manner," as Justamant might say.[86] For example, the Spanish character *glissade* described in the FCD consists of a step backward into *fondu*, the extension of the front foot in *tendu*, and the gliding of the front foot to meet the back foot.[87]

Spanish-inflected choreography in the *Paquita* CN is notated like other movements, without use of particular character step names of the kind we will find in the notation of the Hungarian-flavored choreography in the *Raymonda* notation (see Chapter 10). Reference to descriptions in the FCD can assist in identifying the stylized character steps notated in the CN. Another source documenting this step vocabulary is preserved in the Sergeyev Collection—several pages of manuscript Spanish dance exercises written using Stepanov notation are among the holdings.[88] (We note that the general lack of notated upper body movement may prevent us from identifying further Spanish-inflected choreography among the dances in *Paquita*.)

The *Pas des manteaux* as recorded in the CN is similar in its level of detail to other ensemble dances notated by Sergeyev, for example, the *Danse des Corsaires* from *Le Corsaire*

---

[84] For a description of the 30 October 1847 performance, at which the *Pas des manteaux* "was repeated as always," see *Khronika* II, 96.

[85] *Ezhegodnik Imperatorskikh Teatrov* [Yearbook of the Imperial Theaters] (1892–1893), 223.

[86] See especially chapter 5, "Studies in Spanish Dance," in Lopukhov et al., *Character Dance*, 108–121.

[87] Lopukhov et al., *Character Dance*, 114.

[88] MS Thr 245 (229).

(see Chapter 7). The notations of such dances include ground plans and steps that are written out in prose as often as they are notated. An enchaînement is rarely notated twice. Rather, Sergeyev often accompanied an initial notated enchaînement with a symbol (a Roman numeral I with an "X" through the stem) that he subsequently used to identify a particular set of steps in lieu of writing it again. In documenting the *Pas des manteaux*, Sergeyev used this procedure only for the opening enchaînement. Additionally, in a number of ground plans, he indicated the required number of musical bars that accompanied a given passage of choreography.

The opening ground plan of the *Pas des manteaux* is similar to what we found in Justamant—half of the couples enter along a diagonal from upstage left followed by the other half from upstage right. The allocation of bars to the movements of each group, however, suggests the dancing here begins later than it does in Justamant—likely after the entire musical introduction of twenty-three bars. The steps in the CN differ from Justamant as well. Here, the couples step forward with *temps levé battement degagé devant* followed by a *balancé* and three steps forward to first position (Ex. 4.16). They continue their advance toward the opposite corner, performing the enchaînement four times over a total of sixteen bars. The second group of couples repeats the same to the other side. Next, lining each side of the stage, the couples perform a variety of steps—*pas de bourrée, sissonne, pas de basque, glissade*—that brings them to center and back to the wings several times over a period of thirty-two bars.

This somewhat unvarying arrangement is interrupted when the ensemble travels upstage and back for sixteen bars, although they maintain their linear formation and perform a similar vocabulary of steps. The dance continues in this manner, the couples briefly forming a circle for twelve bars, a square for fourteen bars, and two rows across the stage during the brief section in C major (Ex. 4.33). At one point, they split the stage by forming two wide columns on each side, the women on the inside and the "men" by the wings. They coalesce into two rows upstage and advance toward the audience with *pas de basque*. At the final statement of the main theme, the couples again line the wings for sixteen bars before forming a block of four rows at center.

The fairly static ground plan is presumably enlivened by cape work, which is described only occasionally in prose: "Everyone runs with their capes raised up," "Cavaliers wave their capes," "Cavaliers turn their capes," and so on. At the end, the women are instructed to "embrace the cavaliers. At the same time, they [the cavaliers] turn their capes over their heads." For the final grouping, "ladies on their knees and cavaliers behind them in a pose."

The lack of choreographic excitement suggested by the CN appears to have at times been reflected in the performance of the dancers. After the revival premiere in 1881, Skalkovsky (quoted above) lamented the casting of lower-ranked dancers in the *Pas des manteaux*, a change from past practice of casting soloists that resulted in a disappointing performance. Whether the blame for this perceived weakness in the St. Petersburg production lay with the casting or the choreography itself, we cannot say, but certainly the dance documented by Justamant includes a greater variety of movement, cape work, and overall detail. In Petipa's production, the empty space at center stage created by the frequent placement of the dancers near the wings makes conspicuous the absence of a lead couple.

No. 9. After the dance, Inigo brings Paquita forward and orders her to collect money. She refuses, but Inigo forces her. Everyone is watching them. The aristocrats are lined up along stage right, where they have been enjoying the divertissement.

Beginning upstage, Paquita walks down the row, collecting money, and stops opposite Lucien downstage right. The CN records their first impressions: "They both are amazed at each other's beauty."

Lucien: (to Inigo) "Who is she?"

Inigo: "She is our Gitana, and she dances."

Lucien: "I do not believe you." Turning to the Countess, he says, referring to the light tone of her skin, "Look at her face, hands, legs. She does not belong here."

The Countess gently takes Paquita's hand and asks who she is. Lucien then takes Paquita by the hand and leads her to center.

Governor: (privately to Inigo) "Do you see she has a medallion? Steal it."

Inigo: "I will."

Lucien: (to Paquita) "Can you remember your childhood? Tell us about it."

Paquita: "I will tell you everything. I grew up remembering that someone was killed. I have a medallion I will show you." Paquita reaches for her medallion, but it has disappeared. Everyone begins looking for it, thinking she simply lost it.

Lucien: "What are you looking for?"

Paquita: "Someone stole my medallion."

Lucien: "Who?"

Paquita: (pointing at Inigo) "Him."

Lucien: (approaching Inigo) "Return the medallion."

Inigo: "I have not seen it. Maybe she lost it there."

Lucien: (returning to Paquita) "Do not cry. Please dance for me."

Inigo separates Paquita and Lucien with displeasure. Inigo and Lucien move to opposite sides of the stage. Inigo sits.[89]

Pas de sept bohémien. The St. Petersburg *pas de neuf* (which shortly after the 1847 premiere was designated a *pas de sept*) was renamed *Pas de sept bohémien* in 1881, although it retained a variant of the number's Parisian title in the Rep, where it is called *Pas de Carlotte* [sic]. Petipa utilized all four sections of the multimovement dance, including the second section that is omitted in Justamant. In addition, by the time the *pas de sept* came to be notated in 1904 (the date on the CN's title page for the dance), a second option for Paquita's solo variation was included. The choreography is primarily drawn from the *danse d'école*—the women dance on *pointe*—but nevertheless incorporates elements of both Spanish character dance and more generic step vocabulary that we will continually find Petipa using in character-inflected numbers (for instance, consecutive *demi-valse*, employed as a traveling step).

Remarkably, the CN represents the performances (at least in part) of no fewer than three esteemed ballerinas who played the role of Paquita: Kshesinskaya, Pavlova, and Preobrazhenskaya. All three dancers performed the ballet within a span of four months during the first half of 1904: Kshesinskaya on 11 and 25 January (only the third act on the latter date), and Preobrazhenskaya and Pavlova making their respective debuts on 25

---

[89] Two pages that follow in the CN disrupt the order of the documented action. The first page repeats the beginning of No. 9 and includes the following prose: "Kshesinsky brings Pavlova [to the Governor's guests] and she does not want to go," and "Pavlova collects money." The second page contains the beginning of Countess Sybille's story from Act One of *Raymonda* (see Chapter 10), written in pencil then erased: "The story | Listen to me. When night comes, a lady comes down here and looks at what is going on. If she sees that, she is not happy," etc.

April and 2 May. Additional notations of ensemble passages and Paquita's interpolated variation provide further detail and variants.

Entrée. The entrée documents the performance of "Kshesinskaya and 6 lady coryphées | tambourines in their hands." Beginning upstage left, the coryphées travel in single row throughout the opening thirty-two bars (see Ex. 4.7). Advancing downstage in a zigzag pattern, they perform two *ballonnés, jeté en avant, piqué en demi-arabesque,* two more *ballonnés, piqué en demi-arabesque, entrechat cinq* four times to alternate sides. Traveling backward from downstage left on the diagonal, they continue with two *temps levés en arabesque, relevé passé* to *attitude devant,* two *emboîtés derrière* three times. An exciting dash downstage with five *emboîtés devant* culminates in *grand jeté en avant.* The dancers repeat the last two enchaînements to the other side, traveling upstage and back, and finish in a diagonal line right of center.

Kshesinskaya enters down this diagonal from upstage left, performing five *emboîtés devant* and *grand jeté en avant* before returning upstage backward with a series of *temps levés en arabesque* on the right foot (Ex. 4.32a). No number of repetitions is given but based on the simultaneous choreography performed by the coryphées this enchaînement should be performed three and a half times (finishing in fifth position on *pointe*), after which Kshesinskaya continues downstage right with turns on *demi-pointe.* The coryphées, in their line, perform six *temps levés en attitude devant* on the right foot, turning a half circle to the left—left arm overhead, right arm side, head turned left then changing to the right. Now facing upstage left, they perform five *temps levés en arabesque* on the left foot—torso pitched forward, left arm forward, right arm side. With a *coupé dessous,* the dancers make a half turn to the right. After performing this enchaînement three and a half times, they run to form a row across center stage as Kshesinskaya finishes her entrance. From here they travel backward upstage, executing fast footwork: *entrechat quatre* alternating with *relevé petit passé* followed by *piqués petits passés.* Splitting at center, they rush forward with multiple *précipités* and run to form lines of three at each side.[90]

Kshesinskaya follows with her second entrance, tracing a zigzag pattern down center in four segments. The CN provides only prose descriptions of her dance: "4 chosse" [*chassé*] and "p-d-bure" [*pas de bourrée*] are written alongside each segment of the zigzag.[91] Assigning sixteen bars of music to this passage results in each segment comprising four bars—four *chassés* to advance and a *pas de bourrée* to change direction for the next segment. At the edge of the notation box, above a lone notation of a fifth position on *pointe,* Sergeyev has written: "In place movements of torso and hands | Wait 12 and movement of hands." This notation and annotation may be intended for the coryphées. The next box, in which Paquita is placed at center, offers merely, "in place *pas* 4 times," without notation. The subsequent box includes a single annotation: "turns on [*demi-pointe* symbol]."

Greater detail resumes in the next notation box, in which Kshesinskaya and the coryphées move upstage with *chassé, tour jeté* twice and back downstage with multiple *précipités.* The accompanying annotation instructs, "Everyone does this *pas.*" Kshesinskaya disappears from the next three ground plans.

---

[90] *Précipité* is the notated step, but "baloné" [*ballonné*] is written on the ground plan.

[91] Sergeyev sometimes wrote the names of dance steps phonetically in Cyrillic. We provide these spellings from time to time when quoting directly from the CN but usually give the French spelling instead.

Four coryphées continue, two on each side. (The two others, presumably those who will begin the subsequent variation, have left the stage.) Moving in unison, they travel left, twice repeating an earlier enchaînement of two *temps levés*, *relevé*, and *emboîtés*. They travel upstage with *pas de cheval*, *jeté*, *assemblé en tournant* three times and form a single row. After two *balancés* in place, they advance downstage behind Kshesinskaya, who appears again in the ground plan. They perform "*fote [fouetté] 4 times*"—an additional CN confirms the step is a *grand fouetté*.[92] After *emboîtés* alternating *tendu devant* and *cou de pied devant* three times, all turn in place on *pointe* and strike a final pose: left foot extended forward in *attitude à terre croisé devant*, right hand (or wrist) on the waist, left arm overhead, back arched, head turned to the left.[93]

Variation. The second section, a lilting *allegretto* in $\frac{2}{4}$, D major (Ex. 4.32b), features the six coryphées in pairs. The names of these women, given in the CN, correspond to the cast that performed with Pavlova on 2 May 1904. The first pair listed is "[Ekaterina] Ofitserova and [Lubov] Petipa 3." The dancers mirror each other's movements as they travel downstage in opposing zigzags with a series of *glissade*, *piqué en demi-arabesque*, *glissade*, *assemblé* three times to alternate sides. They continue with "forward *cabriole* and *pas de bourrée* 2 times," then travel upstage with *chassé en tournant*, *demi-cabriole derrière*, and two *pas de chat* twice. A final series of *pas de bourrée*, *demi-cabriole devant*, *pas de bourrée*, *pas de chat* takes the pair to opposite downstage corners.

Next, "[Sofia] Repina [and Alexandra] Fonareva" take over from upstage left, dancing in unison: *grand jeté en avant*, two *emboîtés derrière* three times followed by *chassé en tournant*, *temps levé* traveling backward upstage toward center. A run downstage left ends with "padicha" [*pas de chat*].

Finally, "[Luisa] Borkhardt and [Apollinaria] Gordova" begin, like the first pair, from opposite upstage corners. They perform *glissade*, *assemblé*, *glissade*, *piqué en demi-arabesque*, and two sets of *entrechats quatre* alternating with *relevés petits passés*, all repeated to the other side. They return upstage with a series of *relevés en arabesque*, *chassé* then return downstage, repeating their first enchaînement. They finish the variation with *pas de bourrée* on *pointe* and *pas de chat*.

Paquita's variation. "Variation Kshesinskaya | $\frac{2}{4}$" and a ground plan is all that the CN preserves of what seems to have been the variation danced to the original Deldevez solo for Paquita (Ex. 4.32c). The music is struck through in pencil in the Rep. An ink annotation following the entrée directs the rehearsal violinists to the interpolated variation that follows the Deldevez variation: "Segue Variation: R[iccardo] Drigo."

[92] See Ms Thr 245 (228), 1–2.

[93] Four pages of notation, filed at the end of the *pas de sept*, document Paquita's entrée steps as performed by Olga Preobrazhenskaya, who made her debut in the role just a week before Pavlova (see above). Consisting mostly of ground plans, this version suggests Paquita's opening diagonal and return upstage was performed by Preobrazhenskaya to alternate sides; thus she would travel downstage on alternate diagonals despite the line of coryphées at stage right (which are not included in Preobrazhenskaya's ground plan).

The scant notation of Preobrazhenskaya's second entrance, from upstage center, includes a ground plan that describes travel directly downstage in four segments followed by "in place *pas*" and turns on *demi-pointe* traveling downstage right.

In a third segment, Preobrazhenskaya travels down the diagonal from upstage left in a zigzag pattern, runs downstage left, then travels up the diagonal with a series of "*balancé* 3 times." This is followed by "fote [*fouetté*] 3½ times," which surely corresponds to the coryphées' *fouetté* passage. After advancing downstage, Preobrazhenskaya turns a circle on *pointe*, again corresponding to the coryphées' movements. Her final pose involves moving from *plié tendu derrière*, torso inclined forward, to a pose opposite that of the coryphées: right leg forward, slightly bent and on *demi-pointe*, head turned right. No arms are given.

Interpolated variation. The interpolated variation is identified in the Rep as "Variation | Music R[iccardo] Drigo | from the ballet *The Pharaoh's Daughter* | for Mlle Pavlova."[94] This number boasts a vigorous polonaise rhythm: bar 1 of the Rep is marked "marcato" and bar 3 "bien ritme" (Ex. 5.4).

The interpolated "Variation 1st Act *Paquita* | $\frac{3}{4}$" in the CN does not bear Pavlova's name, but the additional CN is titled "Variation Pavlova 1st act ballet *Paquita*."[95] The dance starts with a bang: *sissonne fermé, relevé développé devant*, single *demi-gargouillade*, and a series of five *relevés petits passés* as Pavlova turns a clockwise circle in place. This opening enchaînement is repeated to the other side.[96] Pavlova continues with *bourrées* back and forth across the stage punctuated by *entrechats cinq* and followed by another circle of *relevés petits passés* in place. The *bourrées* are repeated followed by a run downstage right.[97]

Traveling backward up the diagonal as the main melody returns, Pavlova drops to her left knee, the front foot raised on *demi-pointe*, her torso and head bent forward. She springs up to *relevé développé devant* on the left *pointe*, followed by *tombé, chassé en tournant, cabriole derrière*, and an *emboîté derrière* to bring her back to the kneeling position and begin again for two more repetitions of the enchaînement.[98] Pavlova runs upstage right for her final diagonal. She makes a *bourrée en tournant*, single *tour* three times then completes the variation with a *double piqué tour en dehors* and final pose in *tendu devant fondu*.[99]

With its strong polonaise rhythm, the interpolated variation presents an energetic and fiery portrait of Paquita, complementing her personality as demonstrated in the ballet's action scenes, in contrast with the lightness of the Deldevez flute solo.

Coda. The coda is a significantly shortened version of the Deldevez original: seventy-six bars out of an original 125 (not including some brief repeats) are omitted from the Rep. After a single bar of introduction, the opening bolero (Ex. 4.17b) is given to the ensemble. The dancers begin in lines of three from opposite upstage corners, traveling on the diagonal and crossing at center, with *entrechat trois, saut de basque*, four *petits emboîtés, assemblé* three times.[100] All run to meet at center before moving away toward the wings with *ballotté, saut de basque, pas de chat*.[101] They run back to center and

[94] Petipa's *The Pharoah's Daughter* had most recently been revived in St. Petersburg on 21 October 1898, featuring Matilda Kshesinskaya in her debut as Aspicia. See *Khronika III*, 253–254. Pavlova did not dance the role of Aspicia until 29 January 1906 (see *Khronika IV*, 81–82), but she made her debut in the role of Ramzea on 23 November 1903. Whether the variation interpolated into the *Paquita pas de sept* was added for Pavlova in *The Pharoah's Daughter* at that time has not, to our knowledge, been confirmed. The variation is not included in the *répétiteur* of *The Pharoah's Daughter* that is part of the Sergeyev Collection, MS Thr 245 (155).

[95] MS Thr 245 (228), 43.

[96] The additional CN offers a variant: *sissonne ouverte* to *arabesque, coupé dessous, piqué retiré, tombé*, two more *piqués retirés*, closing to fifth position *plié*; this is repeated three times with no *relevé* circle.

[97] The additional CN again provides a variant: the *bourrée, entrechat cinq* sequence is performed four times followed by a diagonal of seven *sissonnes fermé* and a characteristic pose. Here, Pavlova steps forward with the left foot to narrow fourth position *plié croisé*, the right arm overhead, the left arm extended forward from the shoulder, abducted thirty degrees to the side, and bent ninety degrees at the elbow (the hand or wrist may be on the waist with the elbow pushed forward), the back arched, and the torso leaning to the right.

[98] The additional CN prescribes kneeling on the right knee followed by *relevé en arabesque* on the right *pointe, plié, chassé, tour jeté, relevé en arabesque* four times.

[99] The additional CN offers the following final enchaînement: *bourrée*, making a complete turn to the right, followed by a step to *demi-arabesque fondu* three times. The variation concludes with three *chaînés* on *demi-pointe*, finishing in fifth position *plié*, arms extended forty-five degrees to the side.

[100] An additional CN of this opening passage calls for *assemblé* and four *piqués taqueté* after the *saut de basque*. See MS Thr 245 (228), 3.

[101] The additional CN includes a *pique en demi-arabesque* before the *ballotté*.

Ex. 5.4 Act One, *Pas de sept bohémien*, Interpolated variation, from *The Pharaoh's Daughter* (Drigo), bars 1–14

perform the enchaînement three more times before returning to the wings with turns on *demi-pointe*.[102]

As the music shifts to $\frac{3}{8}$ meter, propelling the energy forward with greater speed, Paquita enters upstage center (Ex. 4.17a). Here we must turn to the pages documenting Preobrazhenskaya's steps, which reveal a breathless, exuberant final entrance. She travels down center with a series of *piqués double ronds de jambe en l'air* alternating with four *emboîtés devant*. Circling around to upstage right with *pas de basque*, she continues with a shallow diagonal of *temps levé battement degagé devant*, *balancé* then returns upstage with a *saut de basque* and *emboîtés*. After repeating this to the other side, she whirls downstage in *chaînés* on *demi-pointe* then retraces her steps with Spanish *glissades* four times. After a ground plan that is struck through, a subsequent annotation—"Two last plans repeat 2 times"—is difficult to assess. Preobrazhenskaya continues by turning a circle to the right, which may correspond to the ensemble's circles of *emboîtés* (see below). A final run downstage is the last indication of Preobrazhenskaya's movements.

---

[102] In the additional CN, the run back to center is omitted and the enchaînement is performed only two and a half times. The turns on *demi-pointe* are here confirmed to be two *chaînés*; these are followed by a lunging pose in fourth position.

Meanwhile, the ensemble at each side performs eight *balancés* in place then continues with more *balancés, temps levés,* Spanish *glissades, sissonnes* with *pas de bourrée,* and
emboîtés en tournant.[103] Forming a single row as they head toward the finish, the women
perform *rond de jambe en l'air* into a lunging fourth position followed by a circle of *emboîtés
devant.* After another *rond de jambe en l'air* and two *balancés,* they "run" forward with
emboîtés devant to form a half circle around Paquita. Details of their final pose are not given.

No. 10. The Governor offers his thanks for the dances and throws Inigo a wallet. He
addresses the guests and offers to provide a breakfast (*pozavtrakat'*). Everyone gets up
and exits in pairs.
   Governor: (to Inigo) "Stay here and I will talk to you." He leaves after everyone else.
Inigo sends Paquita to the tent and he is alone on stage.
   Inigo: "I am to stay here in order to discuss something." The Governor enters and
approaches Inigo at center.
   Governor: "Do you see this officer?" The CN is silent as to how the Governor indicates
Lucien, who is presumably offstage.
   Inigo: "Yes."
   Governor: "Kill him."
   Inigo: "Kill him? But he is to marry your niece."
   Governor: "He will not," and he whispers to Inigo, who reacts with a look of amaze-
ment. "You will kill him." He leaves.
   This conversation differs from the Paris and 1881 St. Petersburg librettos: here, the
Governor directly commands Inigo to kill Lucien rather than suggesting that he will
pardon Inigo should he kill the man he hates. (In the 1847 Petersburg libretto, Mendoza
more explicitly encourages Inigo to kill Lucien.)
   No. 11. Paquita enters, dreaming of Lucien: "Ah! He is so handsome" (Ex. 4.23).
   Inigo calls her as he goes into the tent, but she replies that she is going to dream. Lucien
enters upstage right—"Ah! She is here!"—and quietly steals up to Paquita and takes her
by the waist. Startled, she steps back.
   Lucien: "Do not be afraid of me. I will take care of you" (Ex. 4.1). He hands Paquita a
wallet, but the gesture upsets her, and she refuses the money.
   Lucien: "I think I haven't done it right." He apologizes. "I beg you, leave this company
and go with me."
   Paquita: "I will not go."
   Lucien: "Why not?"
   Paquita: "You are noble. I am so poor. You will leave me and marry her [that is, the
Niece]."
   Lucien: "I will never marry her. I love you." He sees a corsage on her dress and asks her
for it.
   Paquita: "Why?"
   Lucien: "If you give it to me, I will visit you at night and tell you about my love."
   Paquita is about to give Lucien her corsage, but Inigo appears and leads her away.
   Disappointed, Lucien makes to leave. He passes the Governor and salutes him as he
departs. The Governor stops Inigo and asks what Lucien was saying (Ex. 4.4).
   Inigo: "First, he talked of love. Second, he asked for her corsage and said he would
come to her at night."

---

[103] For a description of *sissonnes* with *pas de bourrée,* see Lopukhov et al.; *Character Dance,* 114–115.

Governor: "What a thought [that is, I have an idea]."

Everyone enters again. The St. Petersburg librettos confirm that the ensemble includes the Governor's party as well as the local peasants and Romani.

Governor: (to his guests) "Everyone will be given a corsage." This explains the Governor's plan to ask the peasant and Roma women to collect bouquets to give to his guests as a sign of esteem.

The women put their bouquets into baskets. Paquita puts in her special corsage as well. The Governor takes it out and calls a woman to him. He asks her to give the corsage to Lucien and tell him it is from Paquita. The woman gives the bouquet to Lucien, who asks, "From whom?" She points to Paquita, and he is happy that he will see her. Paquita approaches Lucien, but Inigo separates them and takes her away.

Night is falling and the crowd begins to disperse. Lucien says he wants to stay alone, but the Count warns him he could be killed. Lucien replies, saying he is armed and has his sword. He puts on his coat and follows Paquita at a distance. Unnoticed by Inigo, she blows him a kiss, and the act comes to an end.

Here we mention two additional pages in the CN that document steps for ensemble couples. Because these pages are filed immediately following the *Pas des manteaux*, we assume they include choreography performed by those dancers. The passage bears the heading "Coda ballet Paquita 1st Act." "Coda" in this usage may refer to the finale of Act One, when the full ensemble returns to the stage, beginning at bar 125 of No. 11. The music that follows, a fast $\frac{6}{8}$, can be counted in two beats per bar. Applying this meter to the notated steps, the dancing would fill around thirty-six bars of music. The exact placement of the dance within the number is more difficult to determine.

The return of the ensemble for the collection of bouquets provides an opportunity for the *Pas des manteaux* couples to flank the stage and perform these steps, a wonderful example of Petipa incorporating ensemble dancing within an action scene in order to boost the level of excitement heading toward the end of an act or scene. We suggest the dancing may start as early as bar 135, which marks the beginning of several eight-bar periods (Ex. 5.5).[104]

The couples are positioned as they most often were in the cape dance—in two lines at either side of the stage along the wings, the women inside of the men. Steps include *balancés*, Spanish *glissades* (the couples exchange places as they perform these), a walking step in which the dancers perform *battement degagé demi-attitude devant* as they step forward (the couples trace a circle around each other as they perform this step), and an enchaînement consisting of a *temps levé battement degagé devant* and *petits emboîtés*. With this last enchaînement, the dancers travel upstage, where their lines partly intersect to form semicircles before they return to their original positions downstage.

Act Two

As in the Paris production of Act Two, Scene I, the St. Petersburg Act Two is a pantomime scene with minimal dancing. Mime conversations and action in the CN are documented in detail, while only a ground plan outlining Paquita's dance is provided for No. 8.

---

[104] No. 11, bar 135 in the Rep corresponds to "Final," bar 11, in the Paris score.

Ex. 5.5 Act One, No. 11, bars 135–138

The spare stage plans for Act Two preserved in the Mariinsky production documents—both overhead and front perspectives—reveal that the scene was presented in the downstage half of the stage. The upstage was cut off by the back wall of the room, creating a shallow area in front of it that kept the action near the footlights. The set featured a window upstage right, a door stage left, and a large opening at center which would seem to be the revolving fireplace. Tables (one at stage right is struck through), chairs (on both sides), and a hutch on stage right are also part of the stage plan. This layout matches the stage arrangement Sergeyev drew in the CN on the first page of Act Two.

No. 1. The CN provides a generic description of the setting: "2nd Scene | Room." The curtain rises at bar 9.

Paquita: (providing a recap of the first act's narrative to the audience) "Nobody is here. There is one officer [that is, Lucien] with a sword and moustache. He told me about love. He takes care of me, and I am crazy about him." She hears footsteps. "What is this?" She runs to the window and sees Inigo with a man in a coat and mask.

Paquita: "Where are they going?" She runs to the door and listens. "They are coming here. I will hide behind the wardrobe."

No. 2. Inigo enters, carrying a bottle. He puts his hat and coat on a chair. Locking the door, he says, "Nobody is here" (Ex. 4.3).

Governor: (who also has entered) "No one is here?"

Inigo: "You are here with me, and no one will hear us. Speak." The Governor takes off his coat and mask.

Governor: "Listen. One [that is, Lucien] will come from there [that is, the door]. He will have an epaulet and sword. You will kill him with a dagger."

Inigo: "Wait. I will come up with a plan." Inigo shows him the bottle.

Governor: "What is this for?"

Inigo: "I will pour for him from it, and he will fall asleep" (that is, the wine is drugged). He goes to the table and shows the Governor how Lucien will be asleep. "I will kill him here."

The Governor approves the plan and makes to leave. Inigo stashes the bottle in the wardrobe.

Governor: "You do not forget."

Inigo: "Give me the money." The Governor throws him a wallet. Inigo weighs it, says, "Not enough," and the Governor throws him another one.

Governor: "You will kill him here."

Inigo: "Do not worry."

The Governor puts on his mask and coat. "Kill him," he commands again, making threatening gestures with his finger as he exits. Inigo closes the door.

No. 3. Inigo rubs his hands together and says, "Now I will call them." Going to the window and opening it, he calls the bandits. Four bandits enter through the window. They sneak into the room.

Inigo: "Listen to me."

Bandits: "What?"

Inigo: "One military man will come here. When the clock strikes twelve, come in and kill him."

Bandits: "Give us money now." Inigo throws a wallet to the right and another to the left.

He takes two of bandits to the window ("window" is struck through and "fireplace" is written over it) and they leave. Closing the window, Inigo puts his arms around the other two as they walk upstage toward the fireplace.

Inigo: "I have decided to hide you in the fireplace, and you will kill him from there."

At that moment, Paquita, who is sneaking stealthily across the room, accidentally knocks over a chair. The men are startled. Paquita rubs her right knee. Inigo pulls her downstage ("avanscene") by the hand.

Inigo: "How did you get here and what do you want?"

Paquita: "I came from there [that is, the door] and hit the chair and hurt my knee."

Inigo: "Did you hear our conversation?"

Paquita: "No! No! I heard nothing."

Inigo: "No! No! You heard and are lying."

Paquita: "No! No! I did not hear anything."

Satisfied that Paquita did not hear anything, Inigo hides the bandits in the fireplace and makes it revolve. Thus the remaining bandits exit the room.

No. 4. Paquita hears knocking at the door and knows it is Lucien. She runs to keep him from entering, but Inigo grabs her by the hands and moves her so that he is standing between Paquita and the door.

Inigo: "Do not dare to move from here and to speak." He goes to the door and lifts the chain. Opening the door, he invites Lucien inside.

Lucien: (to the audience) "He is here. What a pity." Then, seeing Paquita, "But *she* is here." He shakes off his coat. "The rain got me. Lightning, horrible lightning. Would you let me come in here?"

Inigo: "You will be safe here with us. Come in. We ask you to stay here." He takes Lucien's chapeau and makes Paquita take his coat.

As Inigo puts the chapeau on a chair, Paquita throws the coat over his head and asks Lucien what he is doing there. Lucien shows her the corsage he was given. Paquita is confused as to how he got it. Inigo, having freed himself from the coat, runs to separate them.

Inigo: (to Lucien) "Take off your sword." Lucien takes his sword off and gives it to Inigo, who hides it behind the wardrobe.

Paquita: (to Lucien, while Inigo is hiding the sword) "Why are you here?"

Lucien: "I came here to tell you that I love you."

Inigo returns and separates them again.

Inigo: (to Lucien) "She and I will set the table right here. You will dine and drink with us."

Lucien: "Good!"

Inigo makes Paquita follow him.

Paquita: (to Lucien as she leaves) "You will be killed! You will be killed!"

Inigo: (to Lucien) "Stay here. We will set up the table." Inigo exits with Paquita, shutting the door in Lucien's face.

No. 5. Lucien is alone and astonished.

Lucien: "She gave me her corsage" (Ex. 4.34). "This clearly meant I must come here. She says someone wants to kill me." He hides the corsage in his belt. "I have to be careful. I will go and take a look." Walking to the window, he finds it locked. Checking the door, he also finds it locked.

Lucien: "Terrible, the door is locked. What is the meaning of that? Perhaps I will be killed." He runs to the door and knocks, but no one answers.

Lucien: "No! No! I will defend myself with my sword. But where is it?" He looks but cannot find it. "Someone is coming. I will use this chair." He runs to the chair, picks it up, and prepares to strike.

No. 6. Paquita enters carrying a basket (Ex. 4.35). She sets it on a chair and takes out napkins and plates, which she puts on the table. Lucien runs to her, takes her by the waist, and turns her.

Lucien: "You played a joke on me. I will kiss you for that." But Inigo comes in, carrying a bottle, and separates them.

Inigo: (showing Lucien the bottle) "We will drink it."

Paquita picks up the basket and goes upstage. She takes cake out of the basket and sets it on the table. Inigo sits and opens the bottle. He gets up and invites Lucien to drink.

Lucien: (to Inigo) "You drink with me." Inigo pours wine in the glasses. He lifts his glass to drink, but Lucien stops him. "We will drink to her beauty." They clink glasses and Inigo drinks, but Paquita stops Lucien from drinking, checking to see that Inigo has taken a drink. She sees him do this and says to Lucien, "You drink, too." They drink another glass.

Paquita sees the pistols and walks to Inigo, pretending to be nice to him. Paquita takes one of the pistols and blows off the gunpowder. She does the same with the other pistol. Lucien notices and pours more wine. He gets up, takes Inigo by the hand, and leads him forward.

Lucien: "What are we going to do here?"

Inigo: "I know. She will dance." He goes to the wardrobe to get castanets.

Paquita: (to Lucien) "Look, there are pistols under the chair."

No. 7. Inigo takes the castanets and gives them to Paquita, ordering her to dance. He pours wine in his own glass and shows Lucien the empty bottle.

Lucien: "You go and bring the whole basket."

Inigo: "No need. I have another one in the wardrobe." He goes to get it. Paquita runs to Lucien and says he should not drink from the new bottle. Inigo shows the bottle to Lucien.

Inigo: "Here is the wine."

Lucien: "What is this bottle?"

Inigo: "It is a wonderful thing."

Lucien: "You will drink this wine."

Inigo: "Of course." Inigo pours wine for Lucien and puts the bottle on the table.

Paquita breaks a plate and, during the commotion, switches the men's glasses. Angry, Inigo runs after Paquita and pinches her. Lucien stops him and says, "I will pay for the plate. Relax and let us drink." Paquita tells Lucien it is okay to drink. They drink.

No. 8. This number comprises the *Solo* and *Pas scènique* from the 1881 list of dances. The CN offers little information for this number, while the 1881 libretto tells us that

Paquita dances a "national dance," joined by Inigo. (The 1847 libretto calls this a "native *tzigane* [*tsyganskuyu*] dance".) The dance is not notated, and a ground plan is provided only for the opening enchaînements.

After given the signal to dance from Inigo, Paquita begins with turns on the diagonal from upstage right (Ex. 4.18). She then traverses the stage four times, each crossing bringing her farther downstage. At one point, Lucien and Paquita approach each other at center while Inigo sits at stage right.

In the middle of the dance, Lucien kicks Inigo off his chair and takes his place.

Paquita: (to Lucien during the dance) "Four men want to kill you there."

Toward the end, everyone is dancing (Ex. 4.19), and at the conclusion Inigo drops the medallion and falls asleep in a chair. Paquita picks up the medallion, kisses it, and hides it in her corset.

No. 9. Lucien gets up, takes the bottle, and wants to hit Inigo with it, but Paquita stops him (Ex. 4.20). With Lucien's assistance, she puts Lucien's coat over Inigo's head. Lucien takes Paquita's hand, leads her to center, and asks, "What's going on?" (Ex. 4.6).

Paquita: "Why did you come here?"

Lucien: "You invited me by giving me this corsage."

Paquita: "I did not."

Lucien: "Then who?"

Paquita: (pointing at Inigo) "It was him."

Lucien takes the corsage and then takes the pistol that is under the chair. Paquita tells him she blew off the gunpowder. Lucien drops the pistol and looks for his sword.

Paquita: "At twelve o'clock, four men will kill you."

Lucien walks to the wardrobe and finds his sword behind it.

The clock strikes twelve (Ex. 4.36). Paquita and Lucien walk backward toward the fireplace. Standing close in front of it, they make their escape as it revolves and reveals the four bandits who were standing on the other side of the secret entrance.[105] As before, the CN tells us that they walk "sneakily" and look around.

One of the four comes up to the sleeping Inigo, still hidden under Lucien's coat, and stabs him with a dagger. Inigo leaps up out of the chair, grabs his chest, and falls dead.

The bandits are surprised they killed the wrong man. They gather around Inigo and express remorse for his murder as Lucien and Paquita, now safely outside, hurry past the window.

Act Three

The ballet's final scene, during which Paquita's nobility is revealed, includes two of Petipa's most significant contributions: the student mazurka and the *Grand pas*. However, the two dances preceding these, the contredanse and gavotte, are themselves significant because they demonstrate a link to Mazilier's Paris production of the ballet, although the CN does not match what is found in Justamant and its relationship to Mazilier's original is uncertain. Petipa's claim, "I left the quadrille [contredanse] and gavotte" (see above), may refer simply to his inclusion of the dances rather than choreography preserved from previous productions.

---

[105] The CN states that the bandits enter through the window rather than fireplace, which seems to be an error.

While the mazurka has no connection to the ballet's plot or locale, the interpolation of the Spanish-flavored *Grand pas* reflects Paquita's adopted heritage, as did the jaleo she danced in the final scene of the Paris production. (Recall that the 1847 Petersburg staging also included a jaleo, but it appears to have been removed from the ballet shortly after its premiere.)

No action is recorded in the CN for Act Three, though nearly all of Deldevez's music intended for action and mime remains.[106] All of the dances preserved in the Rep are included in the CN: contredanse, gavotte, mazurka, and *Grand pas*.

The 1881 libretto provides a description of the scene:

A large, magnificent hall in the home of the French commandant in Saragossa. Moorish architecture with decor of the Empire period. A large portrait of an officer in the forefront of the hall. The ball scene in the taste of the epoch.

The Mariinsky Theater stage plans for Act Three, again drawn from overhead and audience perspectives, indicate three large arches supported by columns at upstage center. Lining each side are benches and chairs for ball guests. More chairs and stools frame the upstage area. The overhead perspective is struck through in pencil and redrawn with slight differences on the adjacent page: more chairs replace the benches, and the upstage chairs and stools have disappeared.

Contredanse française. The *Contredanse française* remains the curtain-raiser for the act (Exx. 4.11a–b). Performed by the assembly of French and Spanish military leaders and nobility, the dance serves to transport the audience from the Spanish countryside of the first act into a formal ballroom—from the world Paquita has known to her new surroundings as a member of the French aristocracy.

The CN offers scant information about the dance, but what is recorded nevertheless seems to be somewhat at odds with itself. Although "quadrille" and "square dance" are written at the top of the first notation page, the placement of the dancers in the ground plans suggests a longways contredanse, a country dance formation in which each couple works its way to the head of a column of couples (men in a line on one side, women in a line on the other).[107] (The longways contredanse was immensely popular in Paris in the late-seventeenth and early-eighteenth centuries but gave way to the *contredanse à la française*, or, *cotillon*, a dance for a fixed number of couples—usually four—in the mid-eighteenth century.[108])

Despite the placement of dancers in the ground plans suggesting a longways contredanse, arrows showing movement patterns and prose movement descriptions in the CN suggest quadrille dance figures, the quadrille being a dance for four couples—a simplified *contredanse à la française*—that enjoyed widespread popularity at the end of the eighteenth century. Moreover, the annotations in the CN suggest the simplified figures that evolved in the mid-nineteenth century—figures that allowed dancers to simply walk

---

[106] As noted, twenty-nine bars in the Rep are struck through in the scene following the gavotte. See note 60 in this chapter.

[107] On the longways contredanse, see Richard Semmens, *The "Bals publics" at the Paris Opera in the Eighteenth Century* (Hillsdale, NY: Pendragon Press, 2004), 164–173.

[108] On the *contredanse à la française*, see Semmens, *"Bals publics,"* 173–178.

rather than perform the more complicated step sequences of late-eighteenth-century contredanses.[109]

Returning to the ground plans, the CN indicates two columns of couples, one on stage right and the other on stage left. The annotations call for the dancers in each column to be divided into two groups, though the particular manner in which they are divided is not clear. One possibility is that each group is made up of every other couple, that is, even-numbered couples made up one group and odd-numbered couples made up the other. The 1881 cast list for the contredanse includes fourteen couples (this number was later increased to eighteen), suggesting that an odd number of couples (seven) made up each of the two columns.

Arrows indicate that the dance begins with each participant advancing toward their partner then returning to their respective lines. This is a movement referred to in some dance manuals of the late nineteenth century as "forward and back." It also resembles the *L'Été*, the second figure of a traditional French quadrille.[110] The men and women next exchange places across their lines, indicated by arrows and the annotation "transition," which could be interpreted as "cross over," another term used in dance manuals.[111] This "cross over" resembles the *Pantalon*, the first figure of the traditional French quadrille, in which men and women exchange places. These two movements are repeated then followed by a "bow."[112] Next, the first group continues, performing an oblique "forward and back," that is, on the diagonal—men and women from different couples thereby coming together and separating. This is followed by a "cross over" and a repeat of both the oblique "forward and back" and "cross over" movements. The following annotation states, "4 last plans [that is, from the first oblique "forward and back"] repeat, but other pairs [that is, the second group] dance." After this, the first group repeats the opening set of "forward and back," "cross over," and "bow," followed by the second group, and the dance concludes.

Fitting the dance to the music as laid out in the Rep seems fairly straightforward.[113] The curtain goes out at bar 4 and the dance begins at bar 9.[114] Taking repeats into account,

---

[109] In his manual *The Drawing-Room Dances* (London: E. Churton, 1847), Henri Cellarius notes that "our young people no longer dance the quadrille but rather walk the figures with a certain nonchalance." Qtd. in Desmond F. Strobel, "Quadrille," in *International Encyclopedia of Dance* 5: 286–287.

Semmens explains that the quadrille is merely a modified *contredanse à la française*. See "*Bals publics*," 177. Further, Maribeth Clarke has written, "The popularity and omnipresence that the quadrille achieved in the mid-nineteenth century is a byproduct in part of its choreographic simplification. Around 1820 it emerged as a standardized version of the *contredanse française*, a square-set figure dance (as opposed to the longways line of the *contredanse anglaise*) that had been performed alongside the minuet and the gavotte as part of courtly entertainments during the Old Regime and under Napoleon." See Maribeth Clark, "The Quadrille as Embodied Musical Experience in 19th-Century Paris," *Journal of Musicology* 19, no. 3 (Summer 2002): 506. See also Elizabeth Aldrich, "Nineteenth Century Social Dance," [n.d.], https://www.loc.gov/collections/dance-instruction-manuals-from-1490-to-1920/articles-and-essays/western-social-dance-an-overview-of-the-collection/nineteenth-century-social-dance/. Note that Aldrich states that the simplification of the quadrille occurred after the 1830s.

[110] For an example in English, see Wm. B. De Garmo, *The Dance of Society: A Critical Analysis of All the Standard Quadrilles, Round Dances, 102 Figures of Le Cotillon ("the German"), &C., Including Dissertations Upon Time and Its Accentuation, Carriage, Style, and Other Relative Matter* (New York: W.A. Pond & Co., 1875), 64, available online at https://www.loc.gov/item/05035056/.

[111] Ibid., 64.

[112] Ibid., 62–64. The bow and curtsey, which usually precede the dance figures, are described here in detail.

[113] That being said, both the opening and second sections of the dance include the annotation, "D[al] Segno al Fine," without the provision of the *dal segno* sign. Repeating back to the beginning of each section, in lieu of a *dal segno* sign, results in what appears to be the correct number of bars in which to perform the dance as laid out in the CN.

[114] "Danse" is written in ink in the Rep at bar 8 at the anacrusis to bar 9.

forty-eight bars remain in the opening half of the number (Ex. 4.11a) plus thirty-two bars in the second half (Ex. 4.11b). If four bars of music are allotted to each set of movements ("forward and back," "cross over," etc.) and the bow is added at the end of the four-bar phrase that immediately precedes it, the eighty bars of dance divide into five sixteen-bar sections that accommodate the opening movements for both groups and the four subsequent sections in which the first and second groups alternate.

The brief scene separating the contredanse and the gavotte is not included in the CN. The 1881 libretto, at first glance, seems to suggest that both the contredanse and gavotte were performed before the action begins. However, a later mention of a quadrille—possibly a reference to the gavotte performed by two couples—brings the libretto into agreement with the Rep:

At the rise of the curtain, a French contredanse and a classical gavotte.

Count d'Hervilly appears with his future daughter-in-law and the governor. The grandmother, who accompanies them, is surprised that Lucien has taken so long to return. The father calms her and asks her not to disturb the general merriment.

The quadrille [that is, the gavotte] is taken up again. But the grandmother, not seeing her Lucien, gets more and more nervous and the count begins to share the venerable old woman's anxiety.

Gavotte. As noted in Chapter 4, the subsequent gavotte is a version of the celebrated "Gavotte de Vestris" (Ex. 4.12), a dance likely created by Auguste Vestris, who later briefly instructed the young Marius Petipa.[115]

According to the ground plan, two couples stand at center, side by side, the women on the men's right. With partners holding inside hands, they travel downstage with *sous-sus*, *chassé en avant*, *chassé relevé à la demi-seconde* on the right foot, *plié, relevé à la demi-seconde* on the left foot, *plié*, four *jetés* twice. Next, positioned in a staggered formation and traveling sideways toward opposite wings, the dancers perform *glissade, entrechat trois* three times followed by *glissade, jeté battu*. This enchaînement is also repeated, then the dancers face their partners and performs *temps levé battement degagé demi-attitude devant, tombé, coupé dessous* four times. Turning to face front, they continue with *glissade, jeté battu* to each side, *assemblé, entrechat six*. Each couple next takes right hands and turns a clockwise circle. No steps are notated, but an annotation instructs, "4 times." Finally, facing front and again holding inside hands, each couple travels downstage with an abbreviated version of the opening enchaînement that ends with *entrechat six*.

At this point, the dance is interrupted by the arrival of Lucien and Paquita. The St. Petersburg librettos continue to follow the Paris original through the concluding scene of the ballet. Once the action has been resolved and Paquita has left the stage to change costume, the divertissement commences with the children's mazurka.

Mazurka. Despite the seeming incongruency (to us) of including a mazurka in a scene that opens with French ballroom and court dances and ends with *danse d'école* choreography infused with elements of Spanish character dance, the celebrated children's mazurka added to *Paquita* by Petipa was an immediately popular showpiece, displaying the

[115] See Meisner, *Marius Petipa*, 45.

strength of the St. Petersburg dance academy by featuring its students in an ensemble number of their own. Tamara Karsavina remembered the excitement felt by the students selected to participate in the mazurka:

> The favourite ballet with us small pupils was Paquita. The acme of our ambition was to dance the mazurka in the last act. White Polish surcoat with gold braid, blue taffeta skirt with white gloves (cotton) seemed to us the last word in smartness. In fact, our costumes were exact replicas of Fanny Elssler's in Katarina. The mazurka was executed by sixteen couples of children schooled to dance it with the utmost gravity and precision. It was always encored after loud "Bravi."[116]

Although our sources indicate the dance was performed by twelve student couples, rather than sixteen, Karsavina's recollections are nevertheless vivid and evocative.[117] And clearly the vitality of Petipa's choreography—regimented patterns that filled the entire stage—and the exuberance of the youthful dancers in national dress, accompanied by the celebratory strains of Minkus's mazurka, overcame any objections of contextual incompatibility. The audience did not appear to mind!

The mazurka, which is preceded by a brief entrance polonaise, is notated twice (we will call these CN1 and CN2). Neither notation is complete, but each provides essential information about this unique dance. CN1 is notated by Sergeyev on standard portrait-orientation paper and includes ground plans drawn from the audience perspective and prose annotations. No steps are notated, and numbers of bars are not given. CN2 is notated by Rakhmanov on oblong-format paper. Ground plans, drawn from the stage perspective, precede bars of notation.

Although CN1 and CN2 closely resemble each other in terms of ground plans, they are not identical. Neither do they match in documentation of actual steps. Two recent publications—one by the Soviet-era dance instructor Elizaveta Gromova, the other by the dance historian Yury Burlaka—describe the choreography for the polonaise and mazurka and can be consulted to complement and provide supplemental detail to the information found in the CNs.[118] Although both describe later versions of the dance that include subsequent changes made to the choreography, these publications nevertheless can assist in the understanding of basic step vocabulary and suggest movements for the upper body, most of which are not documented in the CNs.

Polonaise (sixteen bars). Musically and choreographically, the sixteen-bar polonaise serves as a prelude to the mazurka, its rising melody creating a sense of anticipation as the children first appear on stage (Ex. 5.6). The couples enter in a line upstage left at bar 5, the girls standing to the right of the boys. Performing a polonaise step in unison (CN1: "walk in Polish *pas*"), they step forward on each beat of the music, with a brush

---

[116] Tamara Karsavina, *Theatre Street*, 74.

[117] Natalia Roslavleva claimed the mazurka was danced by eighty students at its premiere. See, Roslavleva, *Era of the Russian Ballet*, 88–89. The cast list, however, includes the names of all students and confirms that their number was twenty-four.

[118] Elizaveta Gromova, *Detskie tantsy iz klassicheskikh baletov s notnym prilozheniem* [Children's Dances from Classical Ballets with Musical Scores], 2nd rev. ed. (St. Petersburg: Music Planet, 2010), 252–286.

Aloysius Ludwig Minkus and Alphonse Victor Marius Petipa, *Bol'shoye klassicheskoye pa iz baleta Pakhita* [Grand Pas Classique from the Ballet "Paquita"], ed. Yury Burlaka (Moscow: Planeteum, 2000). This useful secondary source includes a foreword by Herman Pribylov and an essay, "Historical Summary and Brief Description of the Ballet *Paquita*," by Olga Rozanova as well as piano reductions and descriptions of choreography. It also includes descriptions of the *pas de trois* and *Grand pas*, including fourteen variations.

of the leg on the downbeat of each bar. Reaching upstage center, they turn sharply to the left and continue directly downstage. Once all couples have reached center, the column divides. The girls move stage right, the boys stage left, and the students form lines along each wing at the annunciatory final notes of the polonaise.

Mazurka. As laid out in the Rep, the musical form of the mazurka is AABBAA CCDDEEC AABBAA. Minkus adhered to strict periodicity: A and B are eight-bar periods comprising two-bar phrases; C is a sixteen-bar period made up of four-bar phrases; D and E are eight-bar periods comprising four-bar phrases (see Exx. 5.7a–5.7e). Although the CNs, taken together or separately, do not provide enough information to link enchaînements to musical sections throughout the mazurka without significant editorial contribution, the notated dance phrases are also four bars in length and thus mirror the musical structure.

Opening. On the downbeat of the mazurka (section A), the boys take off across the stage, performing mazurka steps as they travel toward the girls.[119] Arriving, each boy bows to his partner, and each girl performs a "reverence" (CN1) in response.

Manège. Joining hands with their partners, the couples begin a counter-clockwise circle around the stage. CN1 instructs, "Mazurka everyone," but CN2 notates mazurka steps for the boys and running steps for the girls that Gromova calls *pas couru* and both the writers of the FCD and Burlaka identify as *pas marché.*[120] Because of its reference to running, we will adopt Gromova's term, *pas couru.* According to CN2, after four bars of their opening steps, the boys and girls perform *holubetz* (a Hungarian character step that involves clicking the heels together; when performed *en l'air*, the step resembles a *cabriole de côté*) and *temps levé battement degagé devant* twice for four bars.[121] The eight-bar phrase is repeated as the students form lines of six couples along each wing.

Lines at each side. The students join hands in crisscross style and travel to center with *pas de basque* for four bars. CN2 indicates the lines meet at center, one next to the other, but according to CN1, both sides merge to form a single line at center. Each dancer turns toward his or her partner—boys facing upstage, girls facing downstage—and the couples hold hands. They perform *holubetz* as they travel back to the wings for four bars. This enchaînement of *pas de basque* to center and *holubetz* to the wings is repeated.

Rows upstage and downstage. At the return of section A, the lines along the wings split. Traveling as before, with mazurka steps and *pas couru* (CN2), half of the couples travel upstage and half downstage. Arriving, they form single rows across the stage, the boys turning toward center (facing their counterparts in the opposite row), the girls turning away (toward the audience or the back of the stage). All take hands and, moving away from the row, the girls perform *pas de basque* while the boys "stamp their feet alternately (taking turns)."

Square formation. A square is formed after the upstage girls travel with *pas de basque* to form a line along stage right and the downstage girls do the same to form a line along stage left. The boys perform *holubetz* in place (CN1: "hitting heels") as the girls move, then they travel across the stage with mazurka steps, their rows exchanging position

---

[119] Gromova and Burlaka refer to the mazurka step as *pas gala.* Gromova, *Detskie tantsy,* 261–262, and Minkus and Petipa, *Bol'shoye klassicheskoye pa,* 41.

[120] Gromova, *Detskie tantsy,* 268–269; Lopukhov et al., *Character Dance,* 93; Minkus and Petipa, *Bol'shoye klassicheskoye pa,* 41.

[121] See Lopukhov et al., *Character Dance,* 50–51, 95–98; Minkus and Petipa, *Bol'shoye klassicheskoye pa,* 42; Gromova, *Detskie tantsy,* 269.

Ex. 5.6 Polonaise, bars 1–8

Ex. 5.7a Mazurka, section A, bars 1–8

as the girls perform *holubetz* and *balancé* in place. The girls travel again with more *pas de basque*, their lines moving alongside the boys' so that each girl is reunited with her partner, while the boys perform *holubetz* and *balancé* in place.[122] (Eight additional bars of this last enchaînement are struck through in CN2.)

Shifting columns. Performing mazurka steps (CN1) or *pas de basque* (CN2), the downstage couples travel right then upstage while the upstage couples travel left then downstage. All join at center to form a single column of couples across the stage; the adjoining rows of couples face each other.[123]

Performing *holubetz*, each couple travels to their right so the column of dancers separates in the middle and then re-forms as the dancers return.[124] The boys, still facing

[122] We note here that pages 5 and 6 of CN1 appear to be misnumbered and therefore collated in reverse order: page 6 should precede page 5. This is confirmed by following the progression of the ground plans and comparing them with those in CN2.

[123] According to CN2, the dancers form a vertical column at center rather than a horizontal column across the stage.

[124] This ground plan and enchaînement are missing from CN2, which allots only thirty-two bars to the "shifting column" section.

Ex. 5.7b Mazurka, section B, bars 9–16

Ex. 5.7c Mazurka, section C, bars 25–32

Ex. 5.7d Mazurka, section D, bars 41–48

center, leave their partners and travel forward with mazurka steps, coming alongside the opposite line of girls. The girls remain in place, performing *holubetz* (CN2).[125] (We note that both CNs indicate that the girls also travel—they move in the same directions

---

[125] CN2 indicates both boys and girls perform *holubetz* as the boys travel and the girls remain in place.

Ex. 5.7e Mazurka, section E, bars 49–56

as their partners, but the lines of boys and girls interweave. However, because the arrows indicating the girls' trajectory are struck through in CN2, and CN1 includes the annotation, "to the other lady"—suggesting the boys move to new partners—it seems clear that only the boys travel at this point.) The newly formed couples take hands and travel in lines toward the nearest wing with mazurka steps. Reaching the wings, each line turns to its right and circles around to re-form a single column at center that runs from upstage to downstage.[126] As the girls again remain in place, the boys travel forward with mazurka steps and are reunited with their original partners (CN1: "Coming up, own ladies").

Circle formation. All couples walk to form a circle around the stage, with each dancer facing his or her partner. (An annotation at section E in the Rep, "Big circle," is a helpful reference at this midpoint in the dance.) According to CN2, each couple dances together for four bars. Their movements include a pose in a narrow fourth position—right arm overhead, back arched—and two *temps levés battement degagé de côté* as the boys and girls exchange places with their partners. CN1 suggests different movements: "in place *pas de bourrée tourné* with their lady." Next, the circle begins to rotate—CN 2 indicates the girls travel in a clockwise direction and the boys in a counterclockwise direction. (CN1, however, suggests that only the boys move.) All perform *pas de basque* as the dancers make their way around a quarter of the circle over the course of four bars, the lines weaving in and out of one another as students pass oncoming dancers on the right, then on the left, and so on. CN2 accounts for only a single four-bar phrase, but an annotation in CN1 describes a broader trajectory: after the boys "chain[?] through two ladies, with the 3rd [lady] a turn in place and *tourné*, and etc. up to own lady." This annotation suggests the complete enchaînement is performed four times, allowing the dancers to move around the entire circle and back to their original partners over the course of thirty-two bars.

Finale. The dancers next travel in one line of couples, performing mazurka steps (CN1) or a combination of mazurka steps for boys and *pas couru* for girls (CN2). They form a single row of twenty-four dancers across the upstage (CN2 indicates two rows of

---

[126] CN2 indicates the students form a horizontal column across the stage.

dancers, the girls in front of the boys). They travel downstage with mazurka steps (CN1) or *pas de basque* (CN2), return upstage backward with *pas de basque* (CN1) or *balancé* (CN2), then come forward again and bow. Following the lead of the leftmost couple, the students circle around to the left and exit upstage right—"behind the curtain" (CN1)—with *pas de basque* (CN2).

Petipa's mastery in creating a large-scale student dance with a limited step vocabulary is evident throughout. The mazurka begins and ends with a sweeping *manège* around the stage. Between these broad gestures, Petipa deploys the students in a variety of active formations: squares, circles, columns, chains. We note one imbalance in an otherwise symmetrical succession of enchaînements: during the repetition of what we call the "shifting columns" passage, the four-bar phrase during which the couples move away from and back to the central column with *holubetz* is missing, and we question whether this repetition was perhaps omitted from the CNs in error.

Grand pas. The subsequent *Grand pas* is a suite of dances for Paquita and Lucien, six female soloists, and eight female coryphées. The terms "soloist" and "coryphée" are used in the CN and indicate the intention of casting ranked dancers in each role. The dances include an entrée, adagio, *variation après l'adagio*, five variations for women (including Paquita, but no variation for Lucien), and a coda for not only the *Grand pas* participants but also the mazurka students and the corps de ballet (presumably those who performed the contredanse). The CN includes a sixth female variation that is not in the Rep, although an instrumental part for the variation is preserved in the Sergeyev Collection's *Paquita* music files. The collection's miscellaneous files include variant versions of the solos that are part of the main CN as well as a variation that is neither in the CN nor the Rep. Dancer names listed in the notations of ensemble dances include Kshesinskaya as Paquita, Sergei Legat as Lucien, and six soloists—Alexandra Baldina, Lubov Egorova, Tamara Karsavina, Julia Sedova, Vera Trefilova, and Olga Yakovleva (listed as Yakovleva 3).

As with the Act One *pas de sept*, we will find that Petipa employs elements of character dance in his choreography. These range from Spanish character dance steps (some of which can be identified using the FCD) to steps he used more broadly when choreographing in a partly character style (traveling steps, such as *demi-valse* and *pas de basque*, and steps performed *à plat* or *à terre*) as well as characteristic poses.

In contrast, the music—most of it attributed to Minkus, including all of the ensemble numbers—lacks overt Spanish features. The opening number is a waltz, and much of the rest is in duple time. That being said, the frequently marked rhythms, generous use of the tamburo (snare drum) in ensemble dances (in the Riga instrumentation) and, in particular, the fast tempi of the *variation après l'adagio* and coda provide the necessary brio to support the vivacious choreography.

Entrée. The entrée introduces all of the female dancers in the *Grand pas* in reverse hierarchical order: the coryphées in two groups of four, the soloists in pairs and alone, and finally Paquita.

As he did in the mazurka, Minkus follows rigorous periodicity, introducing four varied melodic ideas in waltz meter, each sixteen bars in length. The form is AA in C major, BCB in G major, and ADDBCBD in C major. A shortened version of C serves as an introduction. This consistency surely liberated Petipa, enabling him to create balanced phrases from beginning to end.

First group of four coryphées (A). Dancing to the light opening waltz theme and beginning upstage left, the first group of four coryphées travels downstage in a diagonal zigzag with two *temps levés en demi-arabesque, ballonné,* and two steps forward into a narrow fourth position *plié* (Ex. 5.8a).[127] This enchaînement is performed four times, the dancers finishing in a diagonal line downstage left.

Second group of four coryphées (A). A second group of four coryphées performs the same sequence as the first but to the opposite side, beginning upstage right and finishing in a diagonal line downstage right.

Coryphées (B). To the lilting second theme, both lines of coryphées travel upstage and back twice with two *pas de valse en tournant, cabriole devant, balancé* four times to alternate sides (Ex. 5.8b).

Soloists 1 and 2 (C). Beginning upstage right, Yakovleva and Baldina travel down the diagonal with two *grands sauts de basque, relevé en arabesque, relevé en demi-attitude devant* twice accompanied by the strongly rhythmic third theme already heard in the introduction (Ex. 5.8c). Tracing an arc as they travel across the stage, the pair continues with *entrechat trois, chassé en tournant, pas de chat* twice followed by *pas de basque* downstage right, *piqué en demi-arabesque, relevé en demi-attitude devant.*

Soloists 3 and 4 (B). With the return of the gentle second theme, Karsavina and Sedova begin by "walking backward," that is, they begin upstage right, facing upstage right, in *tendu éffacé derrière* and perform *ballonné en arrière, balancé* and, turning around to their left, *temps levé battement degagé devant.* This is done three times to alternate sides. Next, after traveling across the stage from left to right with two *sauts de basque* and two mazurka steps, they finish with *échappé en plié* and a spring to *demi-attitude devant* on *pointe.*

Soloists 5 and 6 (A). As the opening theme returns, Egorova and Trefilova zigzag from upstage left with *temps levé en arabesque, saut de basque, cabriole devant* four times to alternate sides followed by turns on *demi-pointe* and finishing in fifth position on *pointe.*

Paquita (DD). Kshesinskaya's first entrance is heralded by Minkus's fourth theme, related to the first by its chromatic steps at the end of each four-bar phrase but made unique, even powerful, by its opening note which arrives two beats ahead of the sixteen-bar period. (Ex. 5.8d).

From upstage left, Kshesinskaya makes a counterclockwise *manège* around the entire stage, performing *ballonné, grand saut de basque,* and two *piqué tours en dehors.* The CN does not indicate the number of times this enchaînement is performed, but the music allows for up to four repetitions. Again from upstage left, Kshesinskaya zigzags downstage with a series of *temps levés en demi-arabesque* and *cabrioles derrière.* Her opening enchaînement—*ballonné, grand saut de basque*—is performed two more times followed by turns on *pointe* that finish downstage right.

Soloists and Coryphées (BC). During Paquita's entrance, the soloists and coryphées regroup upstage in two rows, the soloists in front. Traveling downstage together, they perform two *piqués en demi-arabesque, pas de bourrée* on *pointe* three times to alternate sides. Annotations instruct the soloists to begin on the left foot and the coryphées on the right foot.

The ensemble continues with four *pas de basque,* the coryphées splitting and moving to either side of the stage and the soloists returning upstage. Having arrived, all travel

---

[127] The Riga score includes metronome marks of ♩. = 66 for the eight bars of introduction and ♩. = 60 for section A at bar 9.

Ex. 5.8a *Grand pas*, Entrée, section A, bars 9–16

Ex. 5.8b *Grand pas*, Entrée, section B, bars 41–48

downstage with three *cabrioles devant* on alternating legs (every other coryphée beginning on the left leg, the others on the right) and *tombé, pas de bourrée à plat*, the torso
leaned forward. Returning upstage, the soloists perform *pas de basque* against the coryphées' "*ballonné* and finish on [*pointe* symbol]." The sequence concludes with an *arabesque* on *pointe* facing left, arms overhead.

 Paquita (B). With the other dancers framing the stage, Kshesinskaya performs three
piqués en demi-arabesque, pas de bourrée three times to alternate sides as she traces a
zigzag downstage. She waltzes back to upstage center, and the ensemble dances all together for the first time.

 Paquita, Soloists, and Corypheés (D). Kshesinskaya comes downstage with steps on
pointe as the others waltz upstage for eight bars. Next, everyone travels downstage with a
series of *cabrioles* for eight bars. Arriving downstage, the entrée concludes the same way
Karsavina and Sedova finished their first entrance—*échappé en plié* and a spring onto
pointe in *demi-attitude devant*.

Adagio. Three sources offer a description of the adagio. The main CN records movements for the soloists and coryphées and some choreography for Paquita and Lucien

Ex. 5.8c *Grand pas*, Entrée, section C, bars 57–64

Ex. 5.8d *Grand pas*, Entrée, section D, bars 104–112

(Kshesinskaya and Sergei Legat). An additional CN documents choreography for a twelve-member ensemble of soloists and coryphées rather than fourteen, its primary value being indication of upper-body movement.[128] Finally, Pavel Gerdt's five pages of drawings of Paquita, Lucien, and occasionally the ensemble provide a wealth of partnering details and positions of the body.

Gerdt divides the adagio into eight figures (numbered 1–8), each made up of several "movements." His full-body drawings indicate positions of the arms, legs, head, and torso. Striking takeaways are the almost constant bend of the ballerina's torso, the cavalier's single-hand partnering holds, and the presentational stances the cavalier takes when the ballerina is dancing without his assistance: from several paces away, he faces her, posing in a lunge position, arms outstretched toward her.

The adagio features a violin solo. Annunciatory chords introduce a cadenza followed by a solemn theme in G major that is later taken up by the full orchestra (Ex. 5.9).[129]

---

[128] MS Thr 245 (227), 19.
[129] Riga score: ♩ = 80 at bar 1; ♩ = 66 at bar 4.

The soloists and coryphées dance together as a single fourteen-member ensemble. They begin in a diagonal line from upstage right to downstage left, with Paquita and Lucien at the downstage end. The women step from *tendu effacé fondu* into *arabesque*. A half-kneeling, half-lunging position is drawn for Paquita by Gerdt, who then supports her by the waist as she extends one leg forward.

The ensemble next forms a single line down center. They pose again in *arabesque*, every other dancer facing the opposite wing, as Lucien supports Paquita in turns that finish in *arabesque*. The women walk to a single row downstage and perform *développé devant* three times, the third time moving through *passé* to *tendu derrière* then "quietly to the knee." According to the CN, Kshesinskaya performs two supported *pirouettes*. Gerdt draws the same and provides a finishing pose on *pointe en cou de pied derrière*, back arched.

The ensemble forms lines along the wings and performs a series of *relevés petits battements* to *tendu effacé fondu, detourné*.[130] Gerdt provides seven drawings of Paquita and Lucien; these suggest she performs similar movements as the ensemble followed by a turn ending in *arabesque*. The women next walk to center and form a circle around Paquita as Lucien remains near the stage left wings. An annotation instructs all to be on *pointe* (the additional CN indicates arms are held to the side with backs arched), then those who are upstage remain standing as those who are downstage kneel. According to Gerdt, Paquita first kneels then stands (perhaps performing *sous-sus*). The ensemble returns to its lines along the sides. Then the women run back to center and perform *tombé, chassé, tour jeté* back to the wings, where they pose in *tendu effacé derrière* facing the wings. This enchaînement is repeated. Gerdt, meanwhile, indicates more supported movements for Paquita.

As the soloists walk to a new formation, the CN indicates Legat partners Kshesinskaya in a *tour de promenade* as she poses in *demi-arabesque* on *pointe*. They conclude the *promenade* with a supported *double pirouette* finishing *à la seconde*. The coryphées having remained in lines at each wing, the soloists have formed a diagonal line from upstage right. Paquita takes her place at the downstage end of the diagonal and everyone travels downstage on *pointe*. The ensemble poses in *arabesque à plat* as Kshesinskaya moves to center. Legat "turns a few circles holding the lady's waist with both hands." Kshesinskaya performs these *tours de promenade* on *pointe*, her left leg raised to the front, arms overhead. She finishes the adagio by moving from this position through *fondu* to *relevé fouetté arabesque*. The additional CN indicates that the ensemble continues to *bourrée* on *pointe* until the end of the adagio, when they step to *arabesque à plat* then perform *failli* to fourth position *fondu*.

Several additional moments in Gerdt's drawings warrant description. As Paquita makes her supported *tours de promenade*, during which she raises her left leg to the front, she and Gerdt hold each other by the left shoulder with their left arms, their right arms held to the side in a slightly raised position. At the end of the adagio, Paquita finishes not in *arabesque* but in a *croisé* kneeling position facing downstage left as Gerdt, lunging toward stage right, holds her around the waist with his left hand. Both dancers turn their heads to look at each other. In this way, Gerdt's drawings demonstrate immediacy between the couple amid the formality of the *danse d'école*.

Variation après l'adagio. The choreography of the ensemble dance that follows the adagio is characterized by quick movements performed by the dancers as they traverse the stage,

---

[130] The additional CN indicates *relevés ronds de jambe en l'air* instead of *relevés petits battements*.

Ex. 5.9 *Grand pas*, Adagio, bars 4–11

side to side or up and down. These create a rush of excitement that matches the spark of the music, a bright *allegro* (2/4, D major) that can be viewed as a more energetic sister to the Deldevez *allegro moderato* (also 2/4, D major) that follows the entrée of the *Pas de Mlle Carlotta Grisi* (Ex. 4.32b).[131]

The consistent periodicity of the score continues to suggest Petipa's strong preference for balance and symmetry in allocating musical passages to groups of dancers. The musical form, ABBACBBA, comprises an A section of three eight-bar phrases (abb: twenty-four bars; Ex. 5.10a), a B section of three four-bar phrases (cdd: twelve bars; Ex. 5.10b), and a C section of two eight-bar phrases (ee: sixteen bars; Ex. 5.10c). The final repetition of the B section is struck through in the Rep.

First group of four coryphées (A). Beginning in a row upstage left, four coryphées perform *pas de basque*, Spanish *glissade*, *sissonne ouverte de côté*, *jeté* twice followed by a series of *demi-emboîtés*. The dancers continue with *rond de jambe en l'air sauté*, *pas de bourrée à plat*. They rush downstage right with *demi-valse* and *pas de bourrée* on *demi-pointe* to finish.

Second group of four coryphées (BB). To the martial second theme, the next group of four coryphées, in a row at center, performs *pas de cheval effacé devant*, *relevé en demi-arabesque croisé*, *assemblé*, *entrechat quatre* twice to alternate sides. They come forward with *demi-valse*, *assemblé* and return upstage with more *demi-valse*, all performed three times. Both enchaînements are repeated, then the row travels downstage left on *pointe*.

Soloists 1 and 2 (A). At the return of the A section, Baldina and Yakovleva begin upstage left with *grand jeté en avant*, a quick characteristic pose—*coupé dessous* to fifth position *pied à demi devant*, torso leaning left and twisted left, back arched, head turned left (arms are not given)—and *demi-emboîté devant* four times. Traveling downstage

---

[131] Riga score: ♩ = 120 at bar 1.

left, they perform *demi-valse* with *battement degagé en demi-attitude devant* three times while "opening the right arm gradually." The notated movements confirm the right arm is raised overhead through first position as the left arm is raised to the side. The torso, leaned forward at first, is raised with the arms, and the dancers finish each series with an arched back and neck, the head and body twisted to the right. The next enchaînement takes the dancers from downstage left to center with *emboîtés à terre en tournant*, two sets of *sissonne ouverte* and *pas de bourrée* on *demi-pointe*, and more *emboîtés à terre en tournant*. A surprise change of direction to the left and a set of *demi-valse*, the torso leaned forward, conclude this passage.

Soloists 3 and 4 (C). Karsavina and Sedova begin upstage right, once again facing the upstage corner. Dancing to the light, tripping third theme, they perform *tendu devant fondu, relevé en demi-arabesque fouetté* (turning around to the left), *pas de chat* three times on the diagonal. *Petits emboîtés* traveling sideways bring them upstage left for a repeat of the enchaînement to the other side. The ground plan in the following box indicates travel toward downstage right, but this is struck through and no fewer than six question marks fill the box!

Soloists 5 and 6? (B). Karsavina and Sedova may have continued dancing for the next twelve bars, a return of the martial B section, but we surmise that Egorova and Trefilova may have taken over at this point, although their names are not listed in the CN. An entrance at this point for soloists 5 and 6 would mirror the order of the soloist entries in the entrée and also create a sense of momentum as each subsequent solo entry is shorter than the previous one (twenty-four bars, sixteen bars, twelve bars).

Whatever the case may be, the dancers begin downstage right, facing upstage and traveling on the diagonal with *piqué degagé écarté devant, rond de jambe en l'air, pas de bourrée en tournant* (a half turn to the left to face downstage), *sous-sus* on *demi-pointe*, and "walk away," Sergeyev's term for the notated *demi-valse en arrière*. The entire enchaînement is repeated. As the coryphées move from the sides to center and form a row across the stage, the pair of soloists returns downstage left with *piqué en demi-arabesque, pas de chat* twice, finishing in *tendu effacé derrière*.

Coryphées (A: eight bars). Dancing in place to the final return of the A section, the coryphées perform a series of *pas de cheval, ballonné*, and *emboîtés* four times before performing two sets of *emboîtés à terre* and traveling upstage with *demi-valse en arrière*.

Soloists and Coryphées (A continued: sixteen bars). The six soloists form a row in front of the coryphées and all step forward into *rond de jambe en l'air sauté* followed by two steps back, all performed three times. Both lines split and travel to the sides with *demi-valse* as though to open the stage space for the subsequent variations. No final pose is given.

Variations. Six variations for female dancers are preserved in the main CN, five of which match the five variations in the Rep. Four dancers are named in association with variations in the Rep. Vazem mentions three of them in her memoirs in connection with *Paquita*: "I always danced the *Grand pas* with the greatest pleasure, as did my principal partners, [Anna] Johanson, [Varvara] Nikitina, [Alexandra] Shaposhnikova, and others."[132] (These three dancers were part of the *Grand pas* cast of the 1881 revival premiere.) Vazem's name is absent from the Rep and no variation is provided for

---

[132] Vazem, "Memoirs: Part 4," 39.

Ex. 5.10a *Grand pas, Variation après l'adagio*, section A, bars 3–18

Ex. 5.10b *Grand pas, Variation après l'adagio*, section B, bars 27–34

Lucien. Notation of a seventh variation as well as additional notations of four of the variations included in the CN are preserved among the collection's miscellaneous folders. The scores represent a variety of musical numbers, not all composed for *Paquita* and not all by Minkus. Taken together, they form a varied and balanced suite of solo dances.

Variation 1. The first variation, a swinging *allegro* in $\frac{6}{8}$, is attributed in the Rep to the composer Alexei Barmin (Ex. 5.11). The Rep identifies "Mlle Shaposhnikova" as the dancer of this variation, while the CN records the performance of Clavdia Kulichevskaya, and an additional CN that of Lubov Egorova.[133] Whether the virtuosic choreography

---

[133] For the additional CN, see MS Thr 245 (227), 18.

Ex. 5.10c *Grand pas, Variation après l'adagio*, section C, bars 63–70

recorded for Kulichevskaya and Egorova was performed by Shaposhnikova, we cannot say. The first eight bars of the final section (the variation is in ABA form) are struck through in the Rep, suggesting the variation may have been changed over time.

Beginning upstage left and traveling on a zigzag diagonal, Kulichevskaya performs *grand jeté en avant* and a run on *demi-pointe* to *tendu effacé devant fondu*. She continues with *relevé en demi-arabesque, pirouette* opening to *développé devant, tombé, glissade, pas de chat*. This enchaînement is performed three times to alternate sides, with a *jeté en avant* substituted for the *pas de chat* the last time.[134] Kulichevskaya continues, traveling upstage right, with *chassé, tour jeté* three times.[135]

The B section of the variation mirrors the opening—a zigzag from upstage right— with *glissade, cabriole devant, cabriole derrière*, and four *relevés en arabesque*, the dancer making a complete circle to the left during the *relevés*. This enchaînement is performed three times to alternate sides.[136] Kulichevskaya moves upstage, performing *pas de bourrée de côté, échappé battu* to each side. After a *détourné*, she runs upstage left for the return of the A section and a third diagonal, this time a series *piqué tours en dehors*. The first turn of each group of four turns opens in *développé devant*.[137] After three sets of turns, Kulichevskaya changes direction, running downstage left, and finishes the variation with *glissade, pas de chat* to fourth position *plié*, arms in fourth position, head turned left.[138]

Variation 2. Annotations in the Rep indicate that the second variation is "from the ballet *Tsar Kandavl* [*Le Roi Candaule*] | for Mlle Gorshenkova." The music, a languid waltz in F major, has been attributed to Riccardo Drigo.[139] Gorshenkova did not dance

---

[134] In the additional CN, Egorova begins upstage right. The *jeté en avant* at the end of the third repetition of the enchaînement is not recorded.

[135] In the additional CN, Egorova simply runs upstage.

[136] The additional CN clarifies that the *cabriole devant* is followed by *tombé, pas de bourrée*. The *cabriole derrière* is replaced by *relevé en demi-arabesque*. Egorova makes a turn to the right, rather than the left, during the *relevés*, which are performed *en demi-arabesque*.

[137] The final turning sequence differs in the additional CN: after an initial *piqué tour en dehors* opening to the front, the enchaînement continues with two *chaînés* on *demi-pointe* followed by another *piqué tour en dehors*.

[138] In the additional CN, the final run and steps are replaced by four *chaîné* turns on *demi-pointe*, finishing in fifth position.

[139] See the edition in Minkus and Petipa, *Bol'shoye klassicheskoye pa*, 194.

Ex. 5.11 *Grand pas*, Variation 1 (Barmin), bars 5–12

in the *Grand pas* in the 1881 *Paquita* revival, in which she performed the *Valse de la folie*. She made her debut in the role of Paquita in 1884, but she did not perform the leading role of Nizia in *Le Roi Candaule* until her farewell benefit on 10 January 1893, at which time this variation was presumably added to that ballet.[140] The performance of Varvara Rykhlyakova is recorded in both the CN and an additional CN.[141]

This variation provides contrast to the first: the music is soft and lyrical—the melody is played by the cello, a lovely change from the usual placement of the melody in a high register (Ex. 5.12).[142] Although the tempo is not slow—the Rep indicates *allegro moderato*—the choreography nevertheless features smooth, controlled movements.

Beginning upstage center, Rykhlyakova travels directly downstage with *piqué à la seconde, enveloppé, tombé* six times on alternating legs.[143] This is followed by a "small stop in pose," the details of which are found in the additional CN: fifth position *effacé* on *pointe, développé devant* with the right foot, left arm overhead, right arm side, back arched. She runs downstage right (torso leaned forward in the additional CN), then crosses the stage sideways with *glissade, piqué de côté en cou-de-pied devant*—arms in fourth position, head turned right—*piqué en demi-arabesque*, performed "6 times complete."[144] Reaching downstage left, she is instructed to "twist out" (perhaps *detourné*), the ground plan indicating a turn to the left and a run upstage left.

Rykhlyakova commences the third section of the variation with a diagonal of *piqué double rond de jambe en l'air, piqué en demi-arabesque* and two *pas de bourrée* on *pointe* performed three and a half times.[145] As the melody quickens with a rising scale, Rykhlyakova changes direction and *bourrées* downstage left, where she takes her final pose: *tendu effacé derrière fondu*, right arm forward, left arm side, head turned right. An annotation instructs, "look at the foot backward over the shoulder."[146]

---

[140] See *Khronika III*, 308–309.
[141] For the additional CN, see MS Thr 245 (228), 42.
[142] Riga score: ♩ = 80 at bar 1; ♩ = 150 at bar 4.
[143] In the additional CN, the *enveloppé* closes in fifth position followed by *pas de basque*.
[144] The additional CN, which does not include *glissade*, indicates a series of *piqués en demi-arabesque* on alternating legs.
[145] In the additional CN, Rykhlyakova finishes the entire sequence with a *relevé en arabesque*.
[146] The additional CN indicates *relevé en arabesque* on the left leg as the final pose.

Ex. 5.12 *Grand pas*, Variation 2, from *Le Roi Candaule* (attr. Drigo), bars 4–13

Variation 3. The Rep includes the name of Anna Johanson with the third variation, a brief, virtuosic violin solo in D major (Ex. 5.13a). The CN records the performance of Julia Sedova and an additional CN that of Tamara Karsavina.[147]

Sedova begins upstage left with a virtuosic enchaînement: *piqué tour en dehors* opening into *développé devant*, two *piqués de côté en cou-de-pied devant*, *entrechat six*, two *entrechats quatre*, *entrechat trois*, *en cou-de-pied devant* twice.[148]

The relaxed and lyrical B section (the Rep is marked *meno* and *piano*) begins with *sous-sus* and continues with multiple *pas de bourrée* on *pointe* punctuated by *piqués en demi-arabesque* as Sedova traces a zigzag downstage. The additional CN tells us Karsavina's hands are "crossed on the chest." As the opening tempo returns, Sedova travels left with *glissade*, *pique à la seconde*, *fouetté* into *attitude effacé devant* twice,[149] followed by two poses: the first in *tendu devant fondu*—the torso leaned forward—the second in fifth position—back leg straightened, front foot on *demi-pointe*, back arched, head turned left. No arms are given for either pose.[150] Although the musical timing of the poses is not indicated, the two bars preceding the return of the opening melody include a downward arpeggio outlining a diminished chord that resolves on a *forte* chord punctuated by a fermata (Ex. 5.13b). The second pose may coincide with this chord of resolution.

At the return of the A section, the first enchaînement is repeated one and half times, followed by "2 times turns and end," the ground plan indicating two turns on *demi-pointe* as Sedova travels on a diagonal toward downstage right.[151] Two final poses are given that are nearly identical to the previous poses.

Because the first enchaînement returns after the B section, this variation offers the least choreographic variety of the five. The characteristic poses, however, distinguish it as does the use of solo violin.

---

[147] For the additional CN, see MS Thr 245 (228), 24–25.

[148] In the additional CN, the first two *piqués* are *en arrière* and the jumps are *entrechat six*, *entrechat quatre*, *changement*, *entrechat quatre* followed by a Spanish *glissade*, arms in fourth position, torso bent left.

[149] The additional CN indicates *piqué en arabesque* rather than *à la seconde*.

[150] The two poses are not given in the additional CN; instead, Karsavina runs upstage.

[151] The additional CN concludes with three *chaînés* on *demi-pointe*.

Ex. 5.13a *Grand pas*, Variation 3, bars 1–10

Variation 4. The fourth variation, a sprightly *allegro*, is also attributed to Barmin in the Rep, which includes the name of the dancer Varvara Nikitina (Ex. 5.14).[152] This variation is better known today as a solo for Cupid (*Amour*) in Petipa's *Don Quixote*. Both the CN and an additional CN document the performances of Anna Pavlova.[153]

Beginning at center, Pavlova travels directly downstage with alternating *relevés en demi-arabesque* and *relevés cou de pied devant*, the direction of the body shifting so that each step is performed *effacé*. After six sets of these steps, she continues with *emboîtés sur les pointes* and a pose on *pointe* in *demi-attitude devant* that coincides with a fermata in the score—arms in first position, wrists flexed. She then leaps forward on the diagonal with three quick *pas de chat*, finishing in fifth position *plié*, arms overhead.[154]

The middle section features travel backward on the diagonal as Pavlova alternates *échappés sautés* with *sissonnes sur la pointe*, the torso bending to the right with each *sissonne*. After twelve sets—the high number of repetitions reminds us of the enchaînements Petipa made for Italian ballerinas—Pavlova runs, circling upstage, and *bourrées* in place until the return of the opening theme. Here the steps increase in speed and demand on the performer: *pas de bourrée, tendu de côté fondu* to *relevé en demi-attitude croisé devant, pas de chat* make up this lightning-fast enchaînement performed six times. Pavlova then repeats the *emboîtés sur les pointes*, pose on *pointe*, and three *pas de chat*, finishing in fourth position *fondu.*[155]

[152] Riga score: ♩ = 144 at bar 1; ♩ = 126 at bar 19 (middle section); ♩ = 126 at the repeat of bar 3 (return of the opening theme).

[153] For the additional CN, see MS Thr 245 (227), 16–17.

[154] The additional CN provides positions for arms and head throughout.

[155] The final pose in the additional CN is fifth position *plié*, arms overhead.

Ex. 5.13b *Grand pas*, Variation 3, bars 17–18

Variation 5. The fifth and final variation is listed in the Rep as "Ballet: *Le Roi Condole* [sic] | Variation | Mlle Pavlova." The suggestion that this variation was from *Le Roi Candaule* and not newly composed for Pavlova to dance in *Paquita* is at odds with the long-held understanding that Drigo composed this variation at Petipa's request for Pavlova's debut as Paquita in 1904 (see above).[156]

The variation is notated twice in the CN. The version filed first includes no dancer name. The various headings at the top of its first page read: "Variation 3rd Act 'Paquita,'" "Solo Harp," "Mus[ic by] Drigo," and "Ballerina is dancing." The second version documents the performance of Elena Smirnova, who first performed the role of Paquita on 30 November 1914, and bears the headings "Smirnova," "b[allet] 'Paquita,'" and "Solo Harp."[157] Both notations are incomplete but, taken together, provide us with most of the choreography for the variation. The languorous waltz in AABA form opens with a harp cadenza and features the instrument throughout (Ex. 5.15).[158]

The first version contains the main enchaînements but does not include transitions (for example, a run upstage for the beginning of the next combination of steps). The Smirnova notation omits the first enchaînement altogether but provides a ground plan for the second enchaînement and notation from the third enchaînement onward.

From upstage left, traveling on the diagonal, the ballerina performs *entrechat trois*, *piqué rond de jambe en l'air*, three *piqués en demi-arabesque* on the right foot three times followed by a *bourrée* across the stage, right to left. The second enchaînement travels back across the stage, beginning with a *bourrée* that is followed by *relevé à la seconde* and *relevé en arabesque*, both on the right foot, and *piqué en arabesque* (facing the downstage left corner) on the left foot, all performed three times.

The brief, active middle section of the variation, which begins upstage and travels downstage on the diagonal, features a series of *demi-cabriole devant*, *soutenu*. The first version calls for three sets on the right foot and turns to the right. Smirnova performs the enchaînement on the left foot twice then walks upstage backward on *pointe*. She makes two poses (the positions are not notated) and then performs another *soutenu* before she "moves away" toward upstage left.

[156] Petipa revived *Le Roi Candaule* (also called *King Candaules*) for Carlotta Brianza on 24 November 1891, with Drigo conducting. See *Khronika III*, 295–296. Pavlova made her debut in the ballet's divertissement *Pas de Diane* on 24 September 1900 (the editors of *Khronika IV* give the date as 10 April 1903; see *Khronika IV*, 45). She also performed the lead role of Nizia, but not until 11 October 1909. See Lazzarini, *Pavlova*, 36.

[157] *Khronika IV*, 176.

[158] Riga score: ♩ = 136 at bar 5 plus the annotation, "regarder la danseuse"; ♩. = 60 at bar 21 (middle section); ♩ = 136 at bar 40 (penultimate bar).

Ex. 5.14 *Grand pas*, Variation 4 (Barmin), bars 3–10

The third enchaînement begins upstage left in both versions and again travels on the diagonal. The first version calls for *soutenu, degagé cou de pied derrière, double pirouette* from fifth position three times. Smirnova performs two *pas de valse en tournant*, single *pirouette* from fifth position, *double pirouette* from fifth position. After three repetitions, both continue with a *tour jeté* (traveling upstage) to the knee. The dancer in the first version concludes the variation by traveling directly downstage. No choreography or final pose is given. Smirnova performs turns as she travels downstage right and finishes with a *piqué en demi-arabesque*.

Here we note an unlikely but fascinating additional source dating from the late 1970s. In the 1980 documentary *Reflections of a Dancer*, the Russian ballerina Alexandra Danilova demonstrates the fifth variation as part of her staging of the *Paquita Grand pas* for Cincinnati Ballet.[159] Dressed in street clothes and joined by British dancer Frederic Franklin, Danilova's demonstration matches and complements the choreography found in the notations, including her positions of the head and direction of the hips in the *relevés* of the second enchaînement, the position of her arms in the *cabrioles* of the middle section, and her choice of Smirnova's single and *double pirouettes* in the final enchaînement.

Other notated variations. As mentioned, notations of two additional *Grand pas* variations are part of the Sergeyev Collection. Although these variations not included in the Rep, comparison of the notated choreography with redacted versions described by Burlaka allows us to match the notations with scores attributed to Drigo.

Variation interpolated from the ballet Camargo. Following the two notations of Variation 5, the CN includes a solo with the heading "Variation Pavlova 2." The choreography is also preserved in an additional CN documenting Pavlova's performance that includes an annotation ascribing the music to Drigo.[160] Comparison of the notated choreography with Burlaka's Variation 6 suggests that the dance is set to a solo harp composition that was interpolated into *Camargo*, an 1872 Petipa ballet made for Adèle

---

[159] See *Reflections of a Dancer: Alexandra Danilova*, directed by Anne Belle (Public Broadcasting Service, 1980).

[160] For the additional CN, see MS Thr 245 (228), 41–42.

Ex. 5.15 *Grand pas*, Variation 5, from *Le Roi Candaule* (Drigo), bars 4–11

Grantzow that was revived for Pierina Legnani with new dances by Lev Ivanov on 28 January 1901 (Ex. 5.16).[161]

The main CN consists mostly of ground plans, but the additional CN provides greater detail. Following a cadenza introduction, the variation features series of *bourrées*, at times punctuated by *entrechats six*. Near the end of the variation, at the return of the opening melody, Pavlova performs a *manège* of *pas de bourrée en tournant, cabriole derrière, plié battement devant, passé relevé* to *arabesque* (the main CN calls for *relevé passé* to *arabesque fondu*) six times followed by four *piqué tours en dedans* and four *chaînés* on *demi-pointe*. The main CN indicates a final pose of *relevé en arabesque*.

Variation interpolated from the ballet La Sylphide. The second variation lacking corresponding music in the Rep is preserved in the Sergeyev Collection's miscellaneous files and bears the name of Kshesinskaya.[162] Comparison of the notated choreography with Burlaka's Variation 3 suggests that this solo is set to music that was interpolated into *La Sylphide*, which was revived by Petipa on 19 January 1892 with supplemental music by Drigo.[163] (Varvara Nikitina performed the title role, and Kshesinskaya, with Olga Preobrazhenskaya and Varvara Rykhlyakova, danced a solo role as one of Effie's friends.) Once again, the score is attributed to Drigo and features solo harp. A manuscript harp part, titled "Ballet 'Paquita' | Variation" is preserved in the Sergeyev Collection (Ex. 5.17).[164]

The demanding choreography features nearly continuous movements on *pointe*— *bourrées*, hops, *échappés*. The virtuosic ending calls for a *double pirouette en dehors, plié, relevé rond de jambe en l'air, pas de bourrée en tournant* on *pointe*.

No solo for Lucien survives in any of our sources related to Petipa's production of *Paquita*. Neither does he participate in what is notated of the *Grand pas* coda. Although

---

[161] Minkus and Petipa, *Bol'shoye klassicheskoye pa*, 96–98 (choreography description), 178–181 (piano reduction). On the revival of *Camargo*, see *Khronika IV*, 16–17, and *Ezhegodnik* (1900–1901), 176–186. In the revival, Pavlova danced a *pas de trois* in the second scene, set to music by Vasily Wrangell, with Georgi Kyaksht and Mikhail Fokine; in the fourth scene, she performed the role of Snow. See Lazzarini, *Pavlova*, 217.

[162] See MS Thr 245 (227), 17.

[163] Minkus and Petipa, *Bol'shoye klassicheskoye pa*, 89–91 (choreography description), 169–171 (piano reduction). On the revival of *La Sylphide*, see *Khronika III*, 299.

[164] MS Thr 245 (33).

Ex. 5.16 *Grand pas*, Interpolated variation, from *Camargo* (Drigo), bars 7–11 (courtesy of Maria Babanina, Bayerisches Staatsballett)

Lucien danced in the Justamant production (and therefore, perhaps, the Paris original), and Petipa himself performed two character dances in the ballet's 1847 Petersburg premiere, by the end of the century the role appears to have been limited to acting and partnering. Fokine confirmed this, describing Lucien as a "purely pantomimic role . . . in which I was required to look well, to pose, to gesticulate, to display temperament, and assist ballerinas."[165]

Coda. The coda features not only the *Grand pas* participants but also the mazurka students and corps de ballet (presumably those who performed the contredanse). Likewise, the music features not only three new themes in galop tempo but also the return of sections of the entrée and mazurka.

As we might anticipate, the galop proceeds in sixteen- and thirty-two-bar periods that comprise a form of ABBAAC. A subsequent transition is followed by the return of entrée sections A and D, then galop sections ABC precede another transition into mazurka sections AABBA. A final Galop section C leads into an extended finale.

As is often the case with Stepanov notations of extended final numbers, the CN is incomplete and notated only as far as Paquita's second entrance, that is, up to the second transition before the mazurka.

Coryphées (A: thirty-two bars). The excitement and momentum of the *allegro con fuoco* is matched by the steps of the ensemble that showcase precision and speed (Ex. .18a).[166] All eight coryphées travel in a single row downstage: *piqué en demi-arabesque, assemblé, sissonne ouverte, pas de bourrée* on *demi-pointe* three times to alternate sides followed by eight *ballonnés* directly downstage. They return upstage with *ballotté, ballonné de côté* six times to alternate sides followed by another rush downstage with *ballonnés* as the row splits and the coryphées move to either side.

Soloist 4 (B: sixteen bars). The soloists are featured next, alone and in pairs. Although her entrance calls for steps of greater elevation, Sedova maintains the quick speed of the

---

[165] Michel Fokine, *Fokine: Memoirs of a Ballet Master*, ed. Anatole Chujoy, tr. Vitale Fokine (Boston: Little, Brown, and Company, 1961), 77.

[166] Riga score: ♩ = 128 at bar 1.

Ex. 5.17 *Grand pas*, Interpolated variation, from *La Sylphide* (attr. Drigo), bars 8–16 (source: score for harp, MS Thr 245 [33])

coryphées as she dances to the broad B-section melody (Ex. 5.18b). Working her way downstage in a wide zigzag that begins upstage right, she performs *temps levé*, *saut de basque*, *cabriole devant*, *temps de flèche derrière* three times to alternate sides followed by turns on *demi-pointe* as she travels downstage right.

Soloist 3 (B: sixteen bars). Karsavina repeats Sedova's steps to the other side, beginning and ending on stage left.

Soloists 1 and 2 (shortened AA: thirty-two bars). Dancing side by side, Baldina and Yakovleva travel downstage center performing four sets of quick *tendu de côté fondu*, *pas de bourrée* on *pointe* to each side. They continue with six sets of *demi-fouetté*, *emboîté derrière*, *pas de bourrée* on *demi-pointe* followed by *detourné*.[167] The intensity of their entrance continues with two *piqués de côté en cou-de-pied devant*, three *ballonnés*, *jeté en avant* three times to alternate sides, the dancers performing as mirror images of each other as they trace a zigzag downstage. They finish by traversing the stage with a series of *demi-valse*, traveling backward and crossing at center.

Soloists 5 and 6 (C: thirty-two bars plus thirteen-bar transition). Dancing to the sequential, building C section that will lead to a reprise of the entrée and Paquita's first coda entrance, Trefilova and Egorova begin upstage center (Ex. 5.18c).[168] Side by side, they travel downstage for sixteen bars with *demi-emboîtés devant*. Working their way backward up the diagonal toward stage left, they perform a series of *glissade*, *relevé développé devant* then change direction and repeat the enchaînement traveling upstage right. They run forward on the diagonal with *piqués taqueté* and finish their entrance by crossing the stage left to right with *demi-emboîtés devant* and *pas de chat*.

Paquita (Entrée AD: thirty-two bars). The reprise of the entrée music (the meter changes to $\frac{3}{4}$) highlights Kshesinskaya's entrance (see Exx. 5.8a and 5.8d).[169] She traces a wide zigzag from upstage left, performing "saut de basque and cabriole forward" as given in the CN. No steps are notated for this first enchaînement, but the ground plan indicates

---

[167] Although the CN notes the enchaînement should be performed "6 times," the amount of music available seems to allow for only four repetitions.

[168] Riga score: ♩ = 116 at bar 51.

[169] Riga score: ♩. = 60 at bar 96; ♩. = 72 at bar 111.

Ex. 5.18a *Grand pas*, Coda, section A, bars 3–10

Ex. 5.18b *Grand pas*, Coda, section B, bars 35–42

three turns during each segment of the zigzag. Assigning four bars of music to each segment allows the enchaînement to comprise three *sauts de basque* (one for each turn indicated on the ground plan) and a *cabriole devant*, all performed three times. Reaching
downstage right, Kshesinskaya circles around to upstage center. Dancing in place, she
extends and withdraws her right leg three times—surely a nod to Spanish dance, possibly the cachucha (recall Gautier's description of the cachucha: "a foot advanced and then
withdrawn"[170])—before performing a *piqué double rond de jambe en l'air*. This enchaînement is performed three times and concludes with turns on *pointe* as Kshesinskaya travels
downstage right.

   Coryphées (A: sixteen bars). As the music returns to the galop's section A, the coryphées dash across the stage in a line from left to right.[171] Starting with a *temps levé*, they
continue with a variant of *demi-valse* in which the front leg is raised to *demi-attitude*

170 Tr. in Gautier, *Gautier on Dance*, 7.
171 Riga score: ♩ = 144 at bar 129.

Ex. 5.18c *Grand pas*, Coda, section C, bars 67–74

between steps on *demi-pointe*. Backs are arched and heads are turned left. After perform-ing the enchaînement at least twice (and possibly four times), the coryphées "run into the 1st [wing] backstage."

Soloists (B: sixteen bars). From upstage center, the soloists zigzag downstage in a single row with *glissade, assemblé, ballotté, emboîté derrière* three times to alternate sides. They finish with a *bourrée* downstage left, where they pose in a diagonal line.

Paquita (C: sixteen bars plus thirteen-bar transition). Traveling from upstage center to downstage right, Kshesinskaya returns to perform sixteen *ballonnés relevés*. As the music builds in volume, the choreography builds in momentum: reaching the downstage corner, Kshesinskaya returns up the diagonal with rhythmic *piqués taqueté* then runs downstage for a final *pas de chat*.

Mazurka students (Mazurka AABBA, forty bars). Nothing further is notated. Minimal annotations tell us that the "Mazurka children" enter next, confirmed by the return of mazurka sections A and B (see Exx. 5.7a–b).

Corps de ballet and finale (C: thirty-two bars plus forty-one-bar finale).[172] "Corps de ballet dance" is the final annotation in the CN. As mentioned, this may refer to the ensemble that performed the contredanse at the beginning of the act. This pas-sage likely begins with the return of the galop's section C, marked "Coda" in the Rep, that leads to an extended finale passage in D major that surely featured the entire ensemble.[173]

When the third act of *Paquita* was performed as an excerpt as part of a mixed bill, the contredanse, mazurka, and *Grand pas* were included. As we discover from the Rep and CN, all three of these dances were necessary for a performance of the *Grand pas* because the dancers of the first two numbers returned to participate in the coda, which func-tioned as a finale for the entire act. Andrew Foster has observed that the one-act ballets *Sylvia* and *Nenuphar*—both choreographed by Samuil Andrianov and first presented on 24 April 1916 at the Mariinsky Theater—regularly formed a popular triple bill with the third act of *Paquita*, each of the ballets featuring Tamara Karsavina and Andrianov.[174]

---

[172] Repeat signs bracketing the thirty-two bars are struck through in the Rep.
[173] Riga score: ♩ = 160 at bar 246, final twenty-five bars (including an eight-bar repeat).
[174] Foster, *Karsavina*, 218–220, 222–223. See also *Khronika IV*, 196–197.

Another mixed bill, offered on 6 March 1918, paired the first two acts of *Coppélia* (featuring Elena Lukom) and *Paquita* Act Three (featuring Karsavina with Petr Vladimirov). The programs for both of these performances confirm the inclusion of the contredanse, mazurka, and *Grand pas*.

This description of Petipa's 1881 revival of *Paquita* as it had evolved by the early twentieth century demonstrates the ballet master's diverse choreographic prowess—from his ability to create overt national dances (such as the children's Polish mazurka) to his infusion of national dance elements into classical numbers (the Spanish-flavored *Pas de sept bohémien* and the *Grand pas*). We also see Petipa's strong preference for periodicity—balance, symmetry, and regularity—in the new music he commissioned from Minkus. At the same time, we witness in Petipa's restaging his loyalty to an existing dramatic plot in tandem with his willingness to supply a revival with new dances in order to make the production current and provide a technically and stylistically up-to-the-minute role for the ballerina. Finally, *Paquita* reminds us (as will *Le Corsaire*) that the ballets of Mazilier (in addition to the more-often-mentioned works of Perrot and, later, Saint-Léon) were an early influence on the young Petipa as he developed his dance-making skills.

Indeed, *Paquita* was the ballet with which Petipa had the longest association in Russia. *Paquita* provided him with his first role and his first staging opportunity in St. Petersburg, and it remained in the repertory of the Imperial Ballet beyond his lengthy tenure. That Petipa was fond of this old ballet-pantomime seems certain: it indulged his love of mime and character dance, the two aspects of the nineteenth-century dancer's "triple threat" (the other being classical dance) at which he excelled. Yet even his classical *pas de trois* remained a source of pride: "Imposs better tance!"

Paquita in the West

Paquita was in the repertory of a group of Mariinsky dancers, led by Anna Pavlova and organized by Adolph Bolm, who toured northern European cities in 1908.[175] The tour, which also featured *Giselle*, among other works, established Pavlova's international reputation.[176] Once she had formed her own company in 1911, Pavlova continued to perform the *Grand pas*, first in a staging by Alexander Shiryaev and Enrico Cecchetti, dating from 1912, and later in a staging by Boris Romanov, beginning in 1928.[177] The *Grand pas* was among the works Pavlova danced in the final performance of her career, given on 13 December 1930 at the Hippodrome in Golders Green, Greater London.[178]

Nikolai Sergeyev staged the complete *Paquita* for the Latvian National Ballet in Riga. The first of two performances was given on 22 May 1923 with guest artists from Petrograd: Lukom as Paquita and Boris Shavrov as Lucien, with Sergeyev as Inigo.[179] In a letter to the artist Alexander Shervashidze, dated 10 January 1923, Sergeyev reported, "We are now working on Paquita. We are staging it as in Petersburg, that is, all three

[175] See Beumers et al., *Alexander Shiryaev*, 131.
[176] Lazzarini, *Pavlova*, 13.
[177] Ibid., 219, 221.
[178] See Lazzarini, *Pavlova*, 204–205, and Pritchard, *Pavlova*, 180.
[179] Konaev, "My vse visim v vozdukhe . . .," 561. See also Georgs Stals, *Das Lettische Ballett des Rigaer Oper* (Riga: J. Kadili Verlag, 1943), 51.

acts."[180] As explained above, most of the *Paquita* musical sources preserved in the Sergeyev Collection appear to have been prepared for the Riga performances, which Sergeyev presumably staged using the CN.

Additional stagings in the West of dances from *Paquita* were made mid-century by other Imperial Ballet/GATOB alumni, including Alexandra Danilova and George Balanchine.[181] Danilova's setting of *Paquita* as a divertissement for Ballet Russe de Monte Carlo premiered at the Metropolitan Opera House in New York on 20 September 1949.[182] Jack Anderson reported, "Danilova says that her choreography consisted of the traditional steps as she remembered them from the Mariinsky, filled in at times with choreography of her own."[183] *Paquita* scores from the Ballet Russe de Monte Carlo music library, now preserved at the New York Public Library for the Performing Arts, include much of the *Grand pas* (entrée, adagio, *variation après l'adagio*, Variations 2 and 5, and the variation interpolated from *Camargo*) as well as a number from Minkus's *Don Quixote* that is designated as a *pas de trois*.[184] A piano reduction of the Act One *pas de trois* from *Paquita* is preserved elsewhere in the same collection of scores. That it includes the musical transitions that are struck through in the Rep suggests that it was copied from an Imperial-era source, perhaps the Rep itself.

As *Paquita* had been part of Petipa's early success in St. Petersburg, so too did the ballet feature in Balanchine's youthful milestones. As a young teenager, he performed the mazurka,[185] and he danced the *pas de trois* with Danilova and Lydia Ivanova in the Petrograd State Ballet School graduation performance on 5 May 1920.[186] He also included the *pas de trois* on the opening program of his Young Ballet.[187]

A year prior to Danilova's Ballet Russe de Monte Carlo staging, Balanchine set the *pas de trois* from *Paquita* for the Grand Ballet du Marquis de Cuevas. Performed by Rosella Hightower, Marjorie Tallchief, and André Eglevsky, the *Pas de trois classique*, as it was called, premiered on 9 August 1948 in London at the Royal Opera House, Covent Garden.[188] All of the music was attributed to Minkus. Nearly three years later, on 18 February 1951, New York City Ballet premiered a version of this same dance, titled simply *Pas de trois* (though often referred to as *Minkus pas de trois*), at the City Center of Music and Drama in New York.[189] As was typical of his restagings of Imperial-era ballets, Balanchine's redaction of the *Paquita pas de trois* included a mix of choreography recognizable from our sources as well as new material.

[180] Konaev, "My vse visim v vozdukhe ...," 568.

[181] GATOB is the acronym for *Gosudarstvenny Akademichesky Teatre Opery i Baleta*, or State Academic Theater for Opera and Ballet, which was the name given to the Mariinsky Theater between 1917 and 1935.

[182] Jack Anderson, *The One and Only: The Ballet Russe de Monte Carlo* (New York: Dance Horizons, 1981), 296.

[183] Anderson, *One and Only*, 144. See also John Martin, "'Paquita' premiere by Ballet Russe," *New York Times*, 21 September 1949, 37.

[184] Ballet Foundation Collection of Orchestral Scores and Parts, ca. 1938–1962, New York Public Library for the Performing Arts, Jerome Robbins Dance Division, (S) *MGZMD 52.

[185] Katz et al., eds., *Choreography by George Balanchine*, 319.

[186] Elizabeth Kendall, *Balanchine and the Lost Muse: Revolution and the Making of a Choreographer* (New York: Oxford University Press, 2013), 141. Danilova gave the year as 1919. See Danilova, *Choura*, 41.

[187] Mason, *I Remember Balanchine*, 62.

[188] Katz et al., eds., *Choreography by George Balanchine*, 183–184.

[189] Ibid., 198.

Three months later, on 23 May 1951, Nikolai Sergeyev died in Nice from the effects of surgery. Despite amassing a large amount of material to support a complete revival of *Paquita*, he was able to do so only once, for two performances in Riga, three decades prior. Though its *pas de trois*, mazurka, and *Grand pas* have endured, the complete *Paquita* is the lone work among the five ballets under discussion in this volume that did not establish itself in the latter-day classical repertory.

6

Le Corsaire in Paris and Lyon

On the night of 23 January 1856, right before *Le Corsaire*'s premiere, the Opéra's *régis-seur*, "freshly gloved as always" came on stage to announce the authors of the new ballet in his "clear and metallic voice. . . . He forgot no one; but, having arrived at M. Sacré, he put [great] . . . emphasis on the unique R in the name of the excellent machinist."[1]

It was fitting for Jean-Joseph Sacré to have been singled out thus, and for an eyewitness to have memorialized the moment, because his brilliantly conceived shipwreck scene contributed greatly to *Le Corsaire*'s overwhelming success and indeed constituted one of the most stunning achievements in the history of the *mise en scène* at the Opéra.[2]

Another eyewitness, the critic Paul de Saint-Victor, was so struck by the staging of the shipwreck that he described it in an extraordinary measure of detail:

The last tableau belongs entirely to the machinist, who has made it into a poem, an enchantment, something R splendid and powerful. A large ship stands out against the waves of an immense, moving, infinite sea. The sight of women coming and going through the laces of the ropes makes the ship look like some marvelous Bucentaur [state barge of the doges of Venice] sailing towards Cythera. Standing above the motley groups of pirates and captives is Conrad, holding Medora entwined in the attitude of a sea god kidnapping a nymph from the earth. The young Greek women perform light, floating dances around the triumphant couple to the rhythm of the swaying waves.

Soon, and in marvelously realistic transitions, the sky darkens, black clouds slowly devour the light, a dull thunder murmurs on the horizon, [the ocean] swells, bristles, is covered with foam; the ship rises and falls on the enormous waves. The crescendo of the storm accelerates, the lightning thunders, the waves rise, lightning bolts rend the darkness. And then there appears the most grandiose and dramatic spectacle that the theater has ever offered to the eyes: Night and Ocean evoked in all their horror—the storm unleashed on the stage, all the noises, all the dreadful aspects of a shipwreck realized, rendered with a poignant illusion. I know nothing so sinister as this vessel which sinks, cracks and falls apart in a dark blue chiaroscuro; the tide keeps rising, the ship sinks, it undergoes from one moment to the next frightful metamorphoses. Earlier it was a ship in distress; now it is reduced by the tempest to a shipwreck rolling in the swelling sea; soon it is only a drowned coffin, the raft of Medusa[3] bearing its

---

[1] Benoît Jouvin, *Le Figaro*, 27 January 1856. "He forgot no one; but, having arrived at M. Sacré, he imprinted such a bearing on the unique R which composes the name of the excellent machinist, that one might have thought that the peaceful regisseur was very angry."

[2] There was a shipwreck scene in *L'Africaine*, 1865 (the Scribe/Meyerbeer opera that had been in the making for nearly thirty years), known for its spectacularity, but one critic compared it unfavorably to that in *Le Corsaire*, calling *Le Corsaire*'s "famous" ship "smaller but infinitely more successful than that of *L'Africaine*." Gustave Bertrand, *Le Ménestrel*, 20 October 1867. Bertrand's review was written after the premiere of the 1867 revival of *Le Corsaire*.

[3] *The Raft of Medusa*, painted by Théodore Géricault in 1818–1819, depicted the disastrous aftermath of the wreck of the ship *Méduse* in 1816 off the coast of what is today called Mauritania.

Five Ballets from Paris and St. Petersburg. Doug Fullington and Marian Smith, Oxford University Press.
© Oxford University Press 2024. DOI: 10.1093/oso/9780190944506.003.0007

passengers of shadows and white shapes, twisting desperately. Then, the night throws its black shroud over this wave-tossed tomb.

A fantastic ray comes out, caressing the folds of night: a miraculous moon emerges in the cleared sky, and strikes with light, in a magical perspective, the group of Conrad and Medora approaching, entwined at the mast, the shore of their island.[4]

Of course, this shipwreck scene is long gone from most productions on the ballet stage today: *Le Corsaire* is now best known as the stand-alone virtuosic *pas de deux* that was devised in the decades following 1915, when a *pas d'action* choreographed by Samuil Andrianov was interpolated into the ballet's second scene (see Chapter 7). But no such *pas de deux* existed in the original *Corsaire*, which was an "action ballet": a drama punctuated with danced numbers. And in this particular action ballet, Domenico Segarelli, who portrayed the leading man, barely danced at all, instead impressing audiences with his strong skills as an actor and mime.

Segarelli, whose many successes in Italian theaters had attracted the attention of the Opéra's director, was hired by the Opéra in 1855, the same year that the *Le Corsaire* libretto was begun.[5] A description of Segarelli in *L'Europe artiste*, appearing shortly after he signed his contract with the Opéra, is informative:

> His slim waist, manly beauty, distinction, elegance, [and] expressive face already place him among the upper echelon of dramatic artists. The best composers of Italian ballet have entrusted to him the principal roles in this genre of *drame pantomime*, which [in Italy] is called *ballo serio*, and of which in France one has so little idea.[6]

The leading lady, Carolina Rosati (née Galetti), who had risen to the rank of *prima ballerina assoluta* at the Teatro Apollo in Rome in 1841, soon thereafter established herself as an international star. Celebrated both for her dancing and acting, Rosati was compared to leading actresses of the spoken theater, including Carlotta Marchionni, Amalia Bettini, and Rachel.[7] ("Her miming is clear, lively, impassioned, and always easily intelligible; she knows how to make her thoughts visible, her expression conveying at once what is passing through her mind."[8]) In 1855, she signed a contract with the Opéra, and after Fanny Cerrito's departure, Rosati reigned as the Opéra's top ballerina.[9]

Le Corsaire was surely created with Rosati and Segarelli in mind, for as we shall see, the ballet relied to a great degree on well-executed mime and action scenes. Let us now turn to the libretto.

Devised by the librettist Vernoy de Saint-Georges (who had assisted Théophile Gautier in bringing the *Giselle* plot to life), the story of *Le Corsaire* was based very loosely on Lord Byron's tale in verse, *Le Corsaire* (1814), which supplied a rich set of topics dear

[4] Paul de Saint-Victor, *La Presse*, 27 January 1856\.

[5] Willa Collins points out that Segarelli modeled his miming style and technique after the famous Gerolamo de Matti, and further, that, according to Francesco Regli's 1860 *Dizionario biografico*, that he performed in many Italian theaters, in (for example) Venice, Torino, Genova, Sinigaglia, Padova, Cremona, Verona, Bergamo, Rome, and Florence. Willa Collins, *Adolphe Adam's Ballet* Le Corsaire *at the Paris Opéra, 1856–1868: A Source Study* (PhD diss., Cornell University, 2008), 88–89.

[6] *L'Europe artiste*, 22 April 1855, tr. in Collins, *Le Corsaire*, 89.

[7] Collins, *Le Corsaire*, 83.

[8] Gautier, *La Presse*, 16 November 1853, tr. in Gautier, *Gautier on Dance*, 262–263.

[9] Collins, *Le Corsaire*, 85.

to the heart of mid-century theatergoers: harem women, pirates, Turkish potentates, and seagoing vessels, which were "adored by Parisians, who have always had a maritime obsession."[10]

The ballet, however, was cast in a lighter vein than the woeful and pensive tale that inspired it. One critic summed it up as "cheerful, colorful, dramatic and end[ing] with the most astonishing masterpiece that the art of the decorator and the stagehand has ever produced."[11] It also included a lot of comedy.

Here is a summary of the plot, with added comments (some of them sardonic) from contemporary critics.[12]

Act One, Scene I: Slave market of Adrianople.[13] The action opens in a bustling market of Adrianople ("where, by the way, the white slave trade is brazenly practiced—it is quite pretty in the production, although it is odious in terms of morality; but the Opera has its own morality"[14]). The elderly and wealthy Pasha Seyd arrives to seek an addition to his harem. Several women are put at his disposal in a *pas de cinq*: "The French girl minces, the Spanish one fans herself, the Italian lowers her eyelids, the Hungarian jingles the spurs of her scarlet boots."[15] But the Pasha has already spotted Medora, the ward of the bazaar-master Lanquedem. The Pasha buys her from Lanquedem. Horrified, she tries to chase the Pasha away, for she has no desire to be anyone's property and moreover has already begun to fall in love with Conrad, the pirate chief. After the diversion of a pirate dance, Conrad gives a sign to his men, who seize Medora and the other slave women (and Lanquedem, too), and carry them away to a palatial underground grotto.

Act One, Scene II: The pirates' grotto. We find ourselves "in . . . a cave with stalactite columns, crowded with weapons, vases, open travel trunks, unrolled fabrics, a boudoir of a sea god, harborer of the spoils of shipwrecks. Conrad, lying on his tiger skin, broods indolently on Medora, curled at his feet like a familiar gazelle."[16] The two declare their love for each other. After Medora leads the women in a dazzling fan dance, Conrad (half-intoxicated by the performance) reluctantly grants her plea to liberate her friends. His henchman Birbanto, feeling cheated of his rightful booty and leery of Medora, leads the pirates vainly in a rebellion against Conrad, and then secretly persuades Lanquedem to drug Conrad with a poisoned lotus flower. Medora and Conrad engage in a languorous loving encounter "interspersed with graceful dances and kisses that the corsair steals from Medora."[17] But then he is drugged by Lanquedem. Once Conrad falls into a stupor,

[10] Théodore de Banville, "Mouvement dramatique et littéraire," *L'Artiste* (1 March 1865): 104, tr. by Gabriela Cruz in *Grand Illusion: Phantasmagoria in Nineteenth-Century Opera* (New York: Oxford University Press, 2020), 139.

[11] Saint-Victor, *La Presse*, 27 January 1856.

[12] This plot summary is utterly reliant on Ivor Guest's account in *Ballet of the Second Empire 1847–1858* (London: Adam and Charles Black, 1955), 98–99, and includes verbatim quotations from it.

[13] Today, Adrianople is called Edirne.

[14] Gustave Bertrand, *Le Ménestrel*, 20 October 1867. On the Black slave trade in France and its colonies, see Sue Peabody, *"There Are No Slaves in France": The Political Culture of Race and Slavery in the Ancien Régime* (New York: Oxford University Press, 1997); Peabody, "French Emancipation," *Oxford Bibliographies*, DOI: 10.1093/OBO/9780199730414-0253; and Seymour Drescher, *Abolition: a History of Slavery and Antislavery* (Cambridge, UK: Cambridge University Press, 2009). See also Lawrence C. Jennings, *French Antislavery: The Movement for the Abolition of Slavery in France, 1802–1848* (New York: Cambridge University Press, 2000), and William Gervase Clarence-Smith, *Islam and the Abolition of Slavery* (London: Hurst & Company, 2006).

[15] Saint-Victor, *La Presse*, 27 January 1856.

[16] Ibid.

[17] *Journal des débats*, 28 January 1856.

the pirates seize Medora and send her away along with Lanquedem, in accordance with Birbanto's wishes.

Act Two: The garden of the Pasha's palace on the Isle of Cos. Taking place in the Pasha's palace, this scene was deemed fancifully by one critic "the seraglio of the sixth canto of [Byron's] *Don Juan* transported to the gardens of an island in the archipelago"—a place where "painted eyes languish with desire, the emerald-winged cantharide buzzes in the fiery air."[18] The action opens with a dance performed by the Pasha's harem women to entertain the imperious Sultana, Zulmea. But as the dance comes to a close, the irrepressible Gulnare refuses to bow to Zulmea. Neither the subsequent arrival of the Pasha's stodgy Eunuch nor the efforts of the Pasha himself can curb Gulnare's smark-alecky behavior, which entails dancing a flirtatious polka with the Pasha, who eventually succumbs to her charms. Lanquedem soon appears at the palace with Medora, who is introduced into the harem and quickly befriended by Gulnare. Next, Conrad and his men arrive, disguised as pilgrims, to ask for hospitality. The Pasha amuses himself by having Medora dance for the "devout" pilgrims. Afterward, Conrad throws off his disguise. But his plan to rescue Medora is foiled by the treachery of Birbanto. The Pasha's men capture Conrad, and despite the pleadings of Gulnare, the Pasha declares that Conrad shall die.

Act Three, Scene IV: A summer palace on the grounds of the Pasha's palace, overlooking the Aegean Sea. The Pasha tells Medora that he will set Conrad free if she consents to become his wife. She is about to refuse indignantly when Gulnare appears and tells her to accept the proposal. Gulnare's plan unfolds smoothly. Unknown to the Pasha, she takes Medora's place at the wedding, but it is Medora with whom the Pasha returns to the summer palace. He is overwhelmed with desire, but Medora keeps him at bay and playfully persuades him to give up his pistols and dagger, leaving him unarmed at the moment—midnight—when Conrad appears suddenly at the window. After the lovers have escaped, Gulnare approaches and reveals that it is she whom the Pasha has married. He is shocked and indignant. Meanwhile, Conrad and Medora sail away, rejoicing.

Act Three, Scene V: Aboard a ship. The seas are calm; Conrad, Medora, slave women, sailors, and pirates relax contentedly on the deck of the ship. Conrad and Medora take a stroll from stern to bow and anticipate their happy future together. The pirates propose a celebration, bring up a barrel of rum, toast their captain Conrad, and then dance, each choosing a partner. Next the women perform a scarf dance, waving lengths of fabric. "Then, suddenly, a black speck on the horizon—the whistling of the rising wind— darkness falling—the sky here and there fringed with a sinister red glow—heavy peals of thunder in the distance. Finally, the storm—nightfall—the furious sea—the silhouette of the vessel, rocking with increasing force and then foundering" with a horrible creak.[19]

"Never has a ship in the theater rolled over a truer sea, more naturally foaming, with more sulphurous lightning and a storm better imitated. How well it is swallowed up in the abyss which is closing in on it with his crew of bandits and women. . . . But Conrad and Medora emerge from the abyss, and under a ray of electric light, they are seen hanging from the point of a rock. They are saved. We could not dream of a more beautiful final tableau."[20]

Jewish characters in Le Corsaire. Two of the major characters in *Le Corsaire*, Isaac Lanquedem and Medora, are Jewish, and they fit two classic stereotypes: the corrupt

[18] Saint-Victor, *La Presse*, 27 January 1856.
[19] Benoît Jouvin, *Le Figaro*, 27 January 1856, tr. in Guest, *Second Empire 1847–1858*, 101.
[20] Gautier, *Le Moniteur universel*, 20 April 1868.

Jewish merchant and the young Jewish female beauty. Moreover, they are bound by blood or by legal ties to each other (as uncle/niece or guardian/ward—the sources are ambiguous).[21] Thereby they echo the complementary father/daughter pairs Shylock and Jessica (Shakespeare), Isaac and Rebecca (Walter Scott), and Eléazar and Rachel in the opera La Juive (1835) by Scribe and Halévy.[22]

Notably, Le Corsaire took its place in the Opéra's repertory alongside La Juive, an unsparing examination of the plight of the European Jew that ends with the horrible deaths of Eléazar and Rachel.[23] Le Corsaire, by contrast, is a comedy/drama, and the Jewish ethnicity of Lanquedem and Medora is not a matter on which the plot turns.

The antisemitic overtones of the ballet, however, are obvious: Lanquedem is a man corrupt enough to sell his own niece or ward into concubinage, and his inherent depravity is the rationale for his being harassed relentlessly by just about everyone in the ballet and subjected to comic violence of The Three Stooges type. He is always referred to in Justamant's staging manual as "The Jew."[24]

Lanquedem and Medora, as "Oriental" characters, also exemplify a nineteenth-century French artistic tendency identified by Julie Kalman as a merging of the "Jewish" into the "Oriental."[25] In Le Corsaire, indeed, the two Jewish characters are found amongst a panoply of other Others from (mostly) lands around the Mediterranean: Turks, Greeks, Black people, Armenians, Circassians, Moors, Egyptians, Russians, and Italians.[26] The imagined placement of Jews in a faraway place as Exotics counted as one of the ways in which "[p]eople in early nineteenth-century France [constructed] the Jew as a way to think through the vertiginous changes taking place around them."[27] (We would aver that this exoticization of the Jew was still at play in mid-century, when Le Corsaire was created.) Those vertiginous changes in post-Revolutionary France, of course, included the radical shifts in social, economic, and political relationships brought about by the Emancipation of Jews in 1791 (that is, the granting to them of some citizenship rights, including property and electoral rights). As Kalman writes, "We can understand expressions of ambivalence toward Jews as attempts to deny or define that which threatens to break through the borders of a tidy world."[28]

Thus, adding an unsavory Jewish slave-trader to a story already set in the "Orient" and pairing him with the appealing heroine Medora may have been the librettist Saint-Georges' way of "constructing the Jew" for audiences at a time they had a particular stake in doing so. Saint-Georges also drew from other literary depictions of Oriental Jews: a woman who is "beautiful, sensual and knowing" living in a place "unbound by limitations";[29] and a man

[21] The libretto calls Medora Lanquedem's niece; Justamant calls her Lanquedem's ward.

[22] According to Marie Lathers, Jewish female models were "ubiquitous in mid-nineteenth-century Parisian studios, valued for their exotic beauty and a supposedly inherent shamelessness (they do not know they are naked)." See Marie Lathers, "Posing the 'Belle Juive': Jewish Models in 19th-Century Paris," Woman's Art Journal 21, no. 1 (2000): 27.

[23] The two works were performed at the Opéra on the night of 17 March 1856.

[24] See Anna Kisselgoff, "'Le Corsaire': Passionate Tale Told Anew," New York Times, 24 January 1988, Section 2, 6.

[25] Victor Hugo's dream of the Orient, she points out, was "'Hebraic, Turkish, Greek, Persian [and] Arab' all at once." Julie Kalman, Rethinking Antisemitism in Nineteenth-Century France (New York: Cambridge University Press, 2010), 92, quoting Hugo's introduction to Les Orientales (Paris, 1829), 4.

[26] This according to the libretto of 1856. See Collins, Le Corsaire, 279–287, regarding the minor characters and their ethnic or national origins in the 1867 production.

[27] Kalman, Rethinking Anti-Semitism, 6.

[28] Ibid., 9. See also Aaron Manela, "Arthur Saint-Leon's The Little Humpbacked Horse in Context" (Master's thesis, University of Oregon, 2011), 55–57.

[29] Kalman, Rethinking Anti-Semitism, 91 and 93.

who (according to the antisemitic trope of the Jewish merchant) is corrupt, despicable. Saint-Georges' inclusion of Jewish characters in the ballet may also have been a response to the popularity of *La Juive*, which had proven that Opéra audiences found Jewish characters compelling.[30]

Black characters in Le Corsaire. A Black character (referred to simply as a "black woman" without a name of her own) is listed among the *personnages* at the beginning of the libretto. Played originally by a performer known for her comic abilities, Mme Aline (presumably in blackface), she is Zulmea's maidservant.[31] She appears in the Pasha's palace, engaging with other characters and bringing the handkerchief scene to a close by rejoicing in the Pasha's supposed romantic interest in her. (She is mistaken; he is horrified at the thought.) That is, she is not only a servant; she is a dull-witted one. The role is demeaning.

The other Black characters in this ballet, played by children, extras, and members of the corps de ballet, appear in subsidiary rules as servants or slaves in various capacities. Many of them partake in the market scene: eleven Black males (both men and boys), eight little "maures" (moors), and sixteen little "mauresques" (female moors).[32] Some of these may be the Pasha's "little slaves" Justamant refers to in his manual.[33] "Little slaves" (likely Black) also serve Conrad in Act Two (according to Justamant). And Black adult men appear at the Pasha's court: four of them in Act Two; nine of them in Act Three, Scene IV.

This was all in keeping with custom at the Opéra, where Black servants or slaves appeared in works set in the Middle East, the Americas and the Caribbean—not implausibly, since in those regions the enslavement of Black people was practiced legally well into the nineteenth century.[34] (The presence of Black slaves in harems held a particular interest for French painters of the period as well.[35])

In France, a white fascination with Black people in general—owed in part to their keenly felt presence in post-Revolutionary France and the decades-long debates about the abolishment of slavery in the French colonies (which did not come until 1848)—as

---

[30] On Jews and antisemitism on the lyric stage (in ballets and in operas aside from Wagner's), see, for example, Diana Hallman, *Opera, Liberalism, and Antisemitism in Nineteenth-Century France: The Politics of Halévy's* La Juive, Cambridge Studies in Opera, gen. ed. Arthur Gross (Cambridge: Cambridge University Press, 2002); Jeanne Swack, "Anti-Semitism at the Opera: The Portrayal of Jews in the 'Singspiels' of Reinhard Keiser," *Musical Quarterly* 84, no. 3 (2000): 389–416; and Manela, "*Little Humpbacked Horse.*"

[31] Mme. Aline also played Berthe in *Giselle* to great effect, beginning in 1845. See Madison U. Sowell, "Nineteenth-Century Ballet in Paris: A Tale of Two Alines," in *Toute littérature est littérature comparée: Études de littérature et de linguistique offertes à Roy Rosenstein par ses collègues, ses disciples et ses amis*, eds. Danielle Buschinger, Martine Marzloff, Patricia Gillies, and Marie-Geneviève Grossel (Amiens: Centre d'Études Médiévales de Picardie, 2021), 569–582.

[32] All this according to the libretto. See Collins's translation of the libretto (Appendix E (i)) and her valuable footnotes about the casting of these roles. According to Locke in his discussion of Mozart's *Die Zauberflöte*, "'black' could, for northerners, simply mean 'darker than us' and 'Moor' generally meant Arab." In Stravinsky's *Petrushka*, the "Moor" is a dark-skinned Muslim. Locke, *Musical Exoticism*, 116, 227.

[33] According to Sarah Gutsche-Miller, there were many "Black servants (nègres, petits nègres, and négrillons) in music-hall ballets; these were a recognized character type." Personal communication.

[34] For instance, slavery was legal in the United States until 1863; in Brazil until 1888; in Turkey until 1890 (or arguably 1933), and in the French colonies until 1848. In Egypt, the import and export of Sudanese and Ethopian slaves was banned in 1877. See Natalie Arsenault and Christopher Rose, *Africa Enslaved* (Austin: University of Texas, 2006), https://liberalarts.utexas.edu/hemispheres/curriculum/africa-enslaved.html.

[35] One example among many is Jean Léon Gérôme, *Bain maure*. See Julia Kuehn, "Exotic Harem Paintings: Gender, Documentation, and Imagination," *Frontiers: A Journal of Women Studies* 32, no. 2 (2011): 31–63; Linda Nochlin, "The Imaginary Orient," in *The Politics of Vision: Essays on Nineteenth-Century Art and Society* (London: Thames and Hudson, 1991), 33–59; and *The Image of the Black in Western Art*, 10 vols., gen eds. David Bindman and Henry Louis Gates Jr. (Cambridge: Harvard University Press, 2010–2012).

well as the reluctance in many quarters in France to accept them as citizens equal to fair-skinned people, helps account for the lively presence of Black characters on the Opéra's stage, but only in minor, subservient roles, and only in faraway settings, safely distant from France.[36]

A word on Ottoman Turks in Le Corsaire. As Willa Collins has pointed out, Conrad sought revenge on the Turks—in the first version of the libretto—because a Turkish man had stolen his sister when she was a child. Therein lay the reasons (in the ballet's libretto) for his becoming a pirate in the first place.[37] He speaks of the long-ago kidnapping after Medora asks him, "Why is death always in your heart? The dagger in your hand?"

> Conrad answers [Medora] by showing her a vast curtain. He pulls it back and shows her the portrait of a child, a little girl taken away by a Turkish soldier, and in the background the flames of a fire. On the child's arm is a bloody cross. "*This child is my sister,*" said the Corsaire to Medora; "*a child that I adored. They took her from me! It is I who marked her arm thus, to recognize her one day. I became a corsair to seek revenge on the men that I abhor.*" Medora seems to say to him that her love will make him forget this cruel loss.[38]

But this backstory was expunged by the censors. As Collins says, "the commission *supérieure . . .* may have interpreted this passage as politically hostile towards the Turks in the Ottoman Empire, who were France's allies during the Crimean War, which was taking place at the time Saint-Georges wrote the libretto." And a new, acceptable version "lacks any reference to a sister or Conrad's vengeance towards his enemies":[39]

> —*But why,* says Medora, *a state so terrible? Why is death always in your heart? The dagger in your hand? Won't you now live for the one who loves you?* Conrad responds that for her he can renounce everything, his savage glory, his riches that he augments every day.—*I would give all that,* he says to the beautiful Greek woman, *for one word from your mouth, for one look from your eyes! . . . In that case, my lips will open only to bless you,* replies Medora, *and my eyes will only look at you with tenderness and grati-tude.* Conrad leaves with Medora.

It is clear, however, that the censors considered it politically acceptable to make the Pasha a bumbler who (despite saying he would like to execute two of the characters) never commits any heinous, violent deeds, and is on the whole a comic figure.

---

[36] Major characters of mixed race did appear in stage works at other houses: for instance, the popular opéra-comique *Le Planteur* (1839) by Saint-Georges and Hippolyte Monpou, which was a hit at the Opéra-Comique and a fixture of provincial theaters. See Helena Kopchick Spencer, "Louisiana Imagined: Gender, Race and Slavery in *Le Planteur* (1839)," in Diana Hallman and César Leal, eds., *America in the French Imaginary, 1789–1914: Music, Revolution and Race* (Woodbridge, Suffolk, UK: Boydell & Brewer, 2022), 100–145. On literary and visual depictions of Black women in France, see Robin Mitchell, *Vénus Noire: Black Women and Colonial Fantasies in Nineteenth-Century France* (Athens: University of Georgia Press, 2020).

(According to some terminology, European France—including Corsica—is called the Metropole, in contrast to France's overseas departments, which as a group are called Overseas France.)

[37] Collins, *Le Corsaire*, 99.

[38] *Le Corsaire* manuscript libretto, first draft of Act One, scenes V and VI. Archives Nationales, AJ[13] 500, tr. in Collins, *Le Corsaire*, 98.

[39] Collins, *Le Corsaire*, 99.

The censors' willingness to green-light a largely comical stage work set in Ottoman Turkey may be owed to the time-honored tradition of the previous century in Paris of Turkish-themed musical comedy at the fairground theaters. There, as Larry Wolff points out, as much as 20 percent of the theatrical repertory was based on Turkish subjects.[40] And the *commedia dell'arte* figure Arlequin engaged in many an escapade in these shows. Humorous plot points from the fairgrounds resurface in *Le Corsaire* (and no doubt in many other stage shows): in *Arlequin sultane favorite* (1715), an amorous Sultan winds up with the wrong bride (in his case, a veiled Arlequin), just as the Pasha in *Le Corsaire* winds up with a veiled Gulnare instead of Medora. In *Arlequin au sérail* (1747), Arlequin and his master, Octave, grow long beards and impersonate dervishes in order to rescue their two sweethearts from the clutches of the local Pasha.[41] Likewise, Conrad and the other pirates disguise themselves as dervishes in order to penetrate the Pasha's harem and liberate Medora.

The Turkish-themed fairground comedies of the eighteenth century were themselves influenced by the highly popular musical comedy *Le Bourgeois gentilhomme* (by Molière and Jean-Baptiste Lully, 1670) in which a farcical "Turkish ceremony" is performed to trick the social-climbing French *bourgeois*, all dressed up in Turkish garb, into thinking the exalted title of "Mamamouchi" is being conferred on him.[42] Some of the pseudo-Turkish words intoned at the ceremony, "Dara, dara—Biastonara," were recalled by one reviewer of *Le Corsaire*, Paul de Saint-Victor, whose description of the Pasha in *Le Corsaire* points to a generic continuity:[43]

I much prefer this Mardi-gras Turk to the fierce Ottoman that Messrs Mazilier and Saint-Georges could have inflicted on us. He is also . . . funnier with his fox-fur-lined jacket and his Schahabaham-like manner, dazed by excessive opium-smoking and fish farming in jars. The very sight of him transports you straight to an amusing Orient illuminated by the candle-lit turbans of the mamamouchis. Dara, dara—Biastonara.[44]

Characters, in order of appearance

Conrad, the pirate chief, is a man who loves passionately. Medora is the object of his affections, and he devotes his considerable energies to rescuing her from becoming first

---

[40] Bent Holm in *The Taming of the Turk: Ottomans on the Danish Stage 1596–1896* (Vienna: Hollitzer, 2014), 123–125, cited in Larry Wolff, *The Singing Turk: Ottoman Power and Operatic Emotions on the European Stage from the Siege of Vienna to the Age of Napoleon* (Stanford, CA: Stanford University Press, 2016), 56.

[41] See Wolff, *Singing Turk*, 58–60.

[42] The chevalier Laurent d'Arvieux, "a merchant and traveler to the Ottoman empire who actually knew Turkish and Arabic and had some knowledge of Middle Eastern customs," was involved in devising this scene. Larry Wolff, *Singing Turk*, 54. See also Michèle Longino, *Orientalism in French Classical Drama* (Cambridge: Cambridge University Press, 2002), 111–115 and 138–143.

[43] According to Wolff, some of the pseudo-Turkish language used in *Le bourgeois gentilhomme* may have been meant to represent a Mediterranean pidgin language, and the pseudo Mufti (originally played by Lully himself) sang some lines "in an ungrammatical but not incomprehensible Italianate jumble." Wolff, *Singing Turk*, 53. Garritt Van Dyk, citing Longino, *Orientalism in French Classical Drama*, 145, calls Molière's pseudo-Turkish "fictional language sprinkled with a smattering of commonly recognisable Turkish words." Van Dyk, "The Embassy of Soliman Aga to Louis XIV: Diplomacy, Dress, and Diamonds," *Cosmopolitan Moments: Instances of Exchange in the Long Eighteenth Century* Special Issue 9, no. 1 (December 2017), available online at https://arthist.net/archive/16976.

[44] Saint-Victor, *La Presse*, 27 January 1856. Schahabaham was a pasha in Eugène Scribe's 1820 folie-vaudeville *L'Ours et le pacha* and the title character in the opéra-bouffe *Schahabaham II*, by de Leuven, Carré, and Eugène Gautier (1854); its title is a take-off on that of *Maometto II* (1820) by Gioachino Rossini.

the Pasha's slave and then the Pasha's wife. The powerful and sensual love-bond between Conrad and Medora, demonstrated openly in several scenes, helps drive the action, and their relationship as a dynamic couple is even lent a touch of domestic realism by his expression (to himself) of slight regret at granting his lover's wish for him to free the slave women from the pirates' grotto.

Conrad is not only passionate; he is physically powerful, as the audience sees—for example—in his encounters with the mutinous Birbanto, whom he overwhelms thus:

> After a furious Birbanto draws his dagger and leaps toward Conrad, Conrad seizes Birbanto's wrist and holds it as though it is in a vise. Medora cries out and puts her arms around Conrad's neck. He reassures her with a look and a smile, and squeezes Birbanto's wrist ever so tightly. Birbanto tries to free himself but feels such pain that he drops the dagger. His legs fold under him and he ends up, despite his best efforts, falling at his master's knees. Everyone is astonished. Conrad then releases his wrist and looks at him disdainfully. Birbanto, crestfallen, picks up the dagger and walks away. [Paraphrased and quoted from Justamant's staging manual.][45]

And the audience surely felt the thrill of Conrad's long-anticipated heroic act when he appeared at the window of the Pasha's summer palace to rescue Medora in swashbuckling fashion. So strong is Conrad, in fact, that at the ballet's end, we see that he has triumphed not only over his enemies, but over the mighty forces of nature as well.

Birbanto, a bold and canny pirate, is Conrad's loyal, trusted right-hand man until, fed up by Medora's presence in the grotto, he leads an unsuccessful revolt of the pirates against their captain. Thereafter Birbanto is driven by a desire for revenge. He achieves it first, by (in disguise) kidnapping Medora and sending her away from the grotto, and then while on a mission with Conrad to rescue Medora, committing an act of betrayal that nearly leads to Conrad's execution. He then disappears from the action, and of course he is not present on the ship in the final scene as Conrad and Medora triumphantly sail away.

Birbanto, unlike Conrad, is a pirate who dances: he leads the way in the marketplace-scene bacchanale, which, according to Justamant, includes vigorous *appels* or stamping steps and ends with the pirates kidnapping all of the harem women from the merchants who were trying to sell them.

Medora, the female lead, is beautiful, desirable, Greek, and Jewish. She kindles the flames of desire in both Conrad and the Pasha, but loves only Conrad, and it is to him that she devotes her affection, entrusts her love, discloses her fears. She is also sympathetic to the slave women from the marketplace who have been kidnapped by pirates, insisting on their release, and when she gets to the Pasha's palace, she gratefully welcomes Gulnare's friendship.

Medora is also woman of strength, unafraid to express herself. Cases in point: without shyness, she drops a "talking bouquet" (*selam*) to Conrad early in the action to communicate her love for him. She tells the Pasha that she would like to harm him physically and chases him away. She "lets herself fall down nonchalantly all over" Conrad when he is seated on a divan in the grotto[46] (though she also modestly refuses some of his advances in the same scene, in keeping with ballet convention[47]). She convinces the

---

[45] Henri Justamant, *Le Corsaire*, 139–140.

[46] Justamant, *Le Corsaire*, 154.

[47] This is the ballet convention of the woman refusing a first (and perhaps second) offer to dance with a man.

reluctant Conrad to liberate the slave women, in part by leading her "sisters" in a seductive fan dance right before making the case to her lover. She stabs Birbanto's arm when he seizes her in the grotto. And she threatens Lanquedem with a knife. It is for good reason that some critics likened her to Rosina (of *The Barber of Seville*), a beautiful young woman (subject to the whims of her guardian) who averred that she could be a viper if pushed too far.[48]

Her role calls for her to dance in each scene (more than any other major character), and the nature of these dances illustrates her personality. She enters dancing in Act One, Scene I (after her brief appearance on the balcony), in a sixteen-bar sequence that leads her to the *avant-scène* as Lanquedem follows her (according to Justamant). In Act One, Scene II, she leads the ultra-feminine *Pas des éventails* (or *Pas de Medora*[49]), a multi-movement dance suite in which she dances two variations and a brief solo. (This *pas*, with its giant waving peacock-feather fans, is enough to convince Conrad to grant her wish to release the slave women.) In Act Two, she dances in the *Pas du derviche*, a number that again calls upon her feminine attractions, for the Pasha wants to unnerve the visiting dervishes by exposing them to worldly temptations. And in Act Three, she again leads a group of women, this time in a scarf dance, on the deck of the ship.

In sum, Medora is a strong woman who is passionate both in her love for Conrad and her disgust for her male adversaries, whom she is unafraid to attack physically. She is desireable to men and knows it; she also bonds well with her female friends.

Lanquedem, the bazaar-master of the market in Adrianople is Jewish (as noted above) and values riches over all else. He is easily startled (which reads as cowardice), dishonest (he lies about the jewels he has hidden in his turban), the target of everyone's anger, and the butt of many pranks. For instance, the pirates throw him into the air, spin him around so that jewels and money purses fall out of his clothing, and push him into a pile of cushions so forcefully that he falls backward until his feet point upward. Birbanto does entrust Lanquedem with one important task: to drug Conrad with the poisoned lotus flower. But in the comic scene leading up to the poisoning, Birbanto accidentally gets the flower dangerously close to Lanquedem's nose, and the hapless Lanquedem must summon the nerve to say, "Be careful!" His role is essentially a comic one, requiring a lot of acting, athleticism, and no dancing.

The Pasha Seyd, as his music tells us, is mostly a comic character: an old, jaded, wealthy man who is ridiculously egotistical and pompous. At his disposal are a harem (including Gulnare), a fleet of eunuchs (with a Head Eunuch), many other servants, and a grumpy, possessive favorite Sultana (Zulmea). His weakness for Gulnare, whose audacity appalls him, shows that he can be cajoled out of a bad mood by an attractive young female.

The generally mild-mannered Pasha does have a cruel, despotic streak: he relentlessly pursues Medora despite her obvious distaste for him; he toys with the idea of having the Head Eunuch beheaded.

As for dance numbers: the Pasha partakes without dancing in a comic polka with Gulnare and later dances a bit in the dervish scene with Medora and the ensemble—after all, he proposed this dance number in the first place. But his part does not require strenuous dancing.

---

[48] Saint-Victor, *La Presse*, 27 January 1856.
[49] This is how Justamant refers to the *Pas des éventails* at one point after the dance.

Gulnare, a member of the Pasha's harem (and later, his wife), is high-spirited and resourceful, zesty and witty, and brassy enough to warrant a cornet solo as she comes onstage in Act Three, Scene IV, to disclose her sneaky plan to Medora and Conrad. In comic scenes, Gulnare unabashedly mocks the three authority figures of the palace: the favorite Zulmea, the Head Eunuch, and the Pasha, all of whom are angered by her. But Gulnare is well-liked by the other harem women, and when a distraught Medora arrives at the palace, Gulnare immediately befriends her. The two form a fast bond, and Gulnare hatches a scheme that enables her newfound friend to escape from the Pasha's clutches.

Gulnare is first seen in her capacity as an odalisque (harem dancer) performing for the entertainment of Zulmea and next in a flirtatious dance with the Pasha (to the strains of a polka followed by an uproarious galop coda).

Zulmea, the Pasha's favorite Sultana, is cantankerous, imperious, and jealous of her man. Surely she is weary of the Pasha's wandering eye, and is clearly angry when he displays his fondness for Gulnare and then Medora.

The Head Eunuch, who with the other eunuchs is charged with guarding the harem, moves in an awkward and mechanical fashion, is humorless, and is easily befuddled by Gulnare. Like Zulmea, he finds Gulnare's disrespectful behavior appalling and refers to her (in the libretto) as a "hot-head."

Part of the appeal of *Le Corsaire* was its array of exotic characters, some of whom were portrayed in the original version in ways we now recognize as racist. But its characters are also recognizeable as figures that fit into storylines typical of other ballets and operas—characters familiar from real life: the young couple in love (Medora and Conrad), the parental figure whose actions obstruct the young couple's plans (Lanquedem), the loyal female friend to the heroine (Gulnare), the crude villain (Birbanto), the jealous wife (Zulmea) of the husband with a wandering eye (the Pasha). In this regard, perhaps, Medora is a bit of an outlier. She stays within acceptable boundaries of decorum enough to win the sympathy of audiences but at the same time is more sensuous and more violent than Western European heroines were allowed to be.

Reception

This long-awaited ballet, the premiere of which was delayed for nearly two weeks as its creators feverishly made last-minute changes, was received with torrents of praise when it finally appeared.[50] Newspaper reviews include these encomiums:

> The Opéra has just won a magnificent victory. This Corsair ballet is a sumptuous féerie [spectacle] ending in a devastating tragedy. An admirable *danseuse*, picturesque sets, costumes that seem to be borrowed from the Queen of Sheba's closet, a final storm that could put the Ocean itself to shame—nothing is lacking in this success, which is already the talk and the event of the city.[51]

---

[50] See Collins, *Le Corsaire*, 136–139. She quotes at length Adam's fascinating and "cranky account" (published on 15 January 1856 in *L'Assemblée nationale*) of the difficulties he faced as changes were made to one of the ballet's tableaux (surely the fifth). Among other things, as Collins reports, vocal choruses composed by Adam were scrapped.

[51] Saint-Victor, *La Presse*, 27 January 1856.

The success of *Le Corsaire* is reaching colossal proportions. All of Paris wants to see this splendid staging, these magical settings that go beyond anything the imagination can dream of. The vessel engulfed in waves in the third act forms the most moving and grandiose spectacle. It is the perfectly successful imitation of a dreadful reality.[52]

All the vicissitudes of a shipwreck were rendered with complete illusion by painter and stagehand—the stage of the Opera seemed to have suddenly assumed the vast proportions of a high sea. It was better than the mirage produced by the Diorama [theater]; it was the truth in all its awe-inspiring horror. How far the art of the decorator has come since the day when little lazzaroni, fastened to sheets of painted cardboard and simulating the Red Sea, caused the dénouement of Rossini's *Moses* to be greeted by insolent laughter from the audience.[53]

Though the spectacular *mise en scène* was lavished with praise, it was Carolina Rosati who was widely credited with the ballet's success. First, she was "a unique dancer and incomparable mime," and, further,

Her rapid, expressive, and passionate performance touches and moves you, while her small dazzling feet, sculptural poses, and Italian delicacy seduce and charm you. She is a complete artist who will be difficult to replace if she is allowed to leave.[54]

Her feminine allure was alluded to by other critics as well: "She is not only an accomplished virtuoso, an intelligent and witty actress, she is a woman, in the full and charming expression of the word."[55] "Le Corsaire was a triumph for La Rosati, who showed herself therein with all her poetry, all her grace, all her seductive passion. With each step of the enchantress, the whole room burst into applause."[56]

For a detailed description of Rosati's performance in *Le Corsaire*, let us turn again to Paul de Saint-Victor. He offers a clear sense of the strength of Rosati's miming, dancing, acting, and her stage persona—and shows how compelling he found her portrayal of an "Oriental," "Greek" woman. The high value he placed on the saliency of Medora's Greekness, and Rosati's ability to embody it, shines through in these remarks.

[The] greatest part of [*Le Corsaire*'s] success goes to La Rosati, who in her odalisque costumes is as beautiful as an Oriental day. What a dancer of blood and race! Her acting is clear, eloquent, even sonorous, as her movements alone subtly express the play, the nuances, the slightest intentions of the text. She is as strong and fine as steel, sculpting herself in each pose—sculptor and sculpture all at once—with her energetic and supple body lending itself to all movements. What decisiveness in her gesturing! What strength in her resolute and voluptuous walk that rends the air filled with passion on the stage and leaves behind a trail of swiftness! She has a way of crossing the stage in three leaps that makes one think of the flight of a goddess soaring on clouds to a celestial *rendez-vous*. She has developed a provocative gait that mixes feminine grace with a hint of equine fervor; something like the gallop of a centauress resounding across the

[52] L. Chérié, *Le Mercure Parisien*, no. 22 (*Nouvelle Série*) *4e année*, January 1856.
[53] Jouvin, *Le Figaro*, 27 January 1856.
[54] Pier Angelo Fiorentino, *Le Constitutionnel*, 28 January 1856, tr. in Collins, *Le Corsaire*, 144.
[55] Jouvin, *Le Figaro*, 27 January 1856.
[56] *La France musicale*, 27 January 1856.

marble soil of Greece. As Medora, she displays in turn the fierceness of a warrior, the suave servility of an amorous slave, [and] the impishness of an Oriental Rosina ready to burst the bonds of the seraglio. Flirtatious enough to awaken the sultan from his nap while she frolics around the corsair, filled with charming and lively nostalgia in the harem gardens, she transforms in a flash into a heroine to face the attack of the pirates, or to take aim at the Pasha. Thus poised in her Greek costume and her impassive profile, she [is as] Diana the Huntress trading her mythological bow for a klepht pistol, and rising up to repel the Turk from her domain, which he has desecrated.[57]

Inevitably, at least one critic found Domenico Segarelli's acting style too Italian (Segarelli "has a beautiful, meridional [southern] head, affected poses, a melodramatic performance, and an exaggerated expression. This is the standard imperfection of mimes from his country."[58]) But, French chauvanism aside, others praised him for his "excellent mime" and his "intelligent and passionate acting."[59]

So, too, did François Édouard Dauty (Lanquedem) and Francisque-Garnier Berthier (the Pasha) receive favorable mention, as did Claudina Cucchi (spelled phonetically as "Couqui") (Gulnare), who was complimented for the "vivacity, finesse, and grace" she brought to her role.[60] Saint-Georges also received a share of the praise for his libretto: it was deemed "endearing," "one of his best," and proof that he could fulfill the challenging requirements of an action ballet, which called for a great deal of mime and—for its length—relatively little dancing, and needed a well-balanced and engaging story.[61] "The first act," wrote Escudier approvingly, "is a lively and animated exhibition, which contains strong situations, mixed with scenes of good comedy, and the whole of the work perfectly prepares the catastrophe of the denouement."[62]

The praise was not unanimous. Paul Scudo, shortly after the premiere, declared the ballet a disservice to Byron's Corsair, "one of the most beautiful conceptions of modern poetry."[63] Several months later, he called Le Corsaire "a mediocre ballet that continues to attract crowds thanks to Rosati's talents and the imitation of a shipwreck, which delights all the Parisians who have only seen a gust of wind on the lake of the Bois de Boulougne."[64] Albéric Second, for his part, called the libretto grotesque and the score unworthy of Adolphe Adam.[65]

But the general consensus was that the ballet well worthy of the great acclaim accorded it. Further proof of its success is found in its prominent place in the Opéra's repertory for nearly three years: Le Corsaire was given at least sixty-three performances between January 1856 and October 1858, featuring Rosati and Segarelli each time. It left the repertory when its two stars departed, Segarelli returning to Naples and Rosati going to Russia.[66]

---

[57] Saint-Victor, La Presse, 27 January 1856, tr. in Collins, Le Corsaire, 144–145, additional tr. Géraldine Poizat-Newcomb.

[58] G. Héquet, L'Illustration, 2 February 1856, tr. in Collins, Le Corsaire, 145–146.

[59] L. Chérié, Le Mercure Parisien, no. 23 (Nouvelle Série) 4e année, February 1856.

[60] G. Héquet, L'Illustration, 2 February 1856, tr. in Collins, Le Corsaire, 146.

[61] L. Chérié, Le Mercure Parisien, no. 22 (Nouvelle Série) 4e année, January 1856; Léon Escudier, La France musicale, 27 January 1856; on the ballet d'action, see Guest, Second Empire 1847–1858, 100–101.

[62] Jouvin, Le Figaro, 27 January 1856.

[63] Revue des deux mondes, 15 March 1856, tr. in Collins, Le Corsaire, 149.

[64] Revue des deux mondes, 1 June 1856, 672, tr. in Collins, Le Corsaire, 149.

[65] L'Artiste, 27 January 1856, tr. in Collins, Le Corsaire, 149–150.

[66] Collins, Le Corsaire, 151–152. Rosati revisited the role of Medora in 1859 in Jules Perrot's staging of Le Corsaire for the St. Petersburg Imperial Ballet. In 1862, she created the role of Aspicia in Marius Petipa's The Pharaoh's Daughter.

The Music

The music Adolphe Adam composed for this ballet was well received by critics, who called it "full of movement and verve," "lively and colorful,"[67] and "svelte, easy to follow, pleasing to hear."[68] It inspired this short, laudatory overview of Adam's ballet *oeuvre*:

> Adolphe Adam created the genre of ballet music at the Opéra. Before him, these kinds of works were hasty compositions, potpourris without artistic pretension. *Giselle*, *Le diable-à-quatre*, *Griseldis*, *Le Corsaire*, are real scores. I'm not just talking about dance tunes, which have inspiration, grace, liveliness, originality and depth; I am pointing out the merit of the symphonic part, the part we pay the least attention to, and which supplies all of the meaning to the dancer's pantomime.[69]

The same writer was sufficiently impressed by the *Corsaire* score to point out Adam's celebrated fecundity as a melodist: "What he throws out the window is enough to stock a three-act opera"[70]—a compliment reminiscent of what critics had said after the premiere of *Giselle*.

Another critic, very attentive to the music, singled out several numbers, and (as a compliment) likened it to opera:

> This is a score written and orchestrated with the greatest care. We have indicated the *pas de cinq*, which is also one of the most charming [pieces] ever composed and used for a divertissement, and which we will mention again later. M. Adam borrows from each nationality its characteristic dance; from Italy its tarantella, from Spain its bolero, a jig from England[71] [sic] and so forth. The first tableau ends with a very animated and energetic bacchanal in D major. The most salient pieces, and the ones applauded the most from the second tableau, are the fugue, which accompanies the arrival of the slaves; the grand *pas* by Mme Rosati, in which the vigorous and abrupt introduction is treated in the slightly wild manner of the modern Italian school; the entire seduction scene, where there is a pretty clarinet solo, well played by M. Leroy; the sleep scene; the entrance of the pirates, and Medora's pantomime. From the third tableau we praise above all the march of the dervishes, in the style of Félicien David [Ex. 6. 10]; a charming [piece in] six-eight for the dance of the odalisques; the *pas* for Rosati in B-flat, and the scene where she recounts to the Corsair everything that [had] transpired in the preceding act under the eyes of the spectator. The last tableau is preceded by an *entr'acte* instrumented by the master's hand and of a startling effect. The same symphonic piece is repeated on the stage by saxophones, whose vibrant and magnificent sonority is matchless. Let us not forget the corsairs' orgy, [and] a gracious women's *pas* [with] an excellent duet for two flutes, perfectly executed by MM. Dorus and Altès, and the final storm, where, after so many storms [on the stage], M. Adolphe Adam

[67] L. Chérié, *Le Mercure Parisien*, nos. 21–23, January–February 1856.
[68] Paul de Saint-Victor, *La Presse*, 27 January 1856.
[69] Jouvin, *Le Figaro*, 27 January 1856.
[70] Ibid. This is a paraphrase.
[71] As Collins points out: "The English gigue is labeled 'Ecossaise' or Scottish in the music sources. Additionally, the lithograph of Victorine Legrain, the dancer who performed this dance, is wearing a tartan costume." Collins, *Le Corsaire*, 147.

managed to do something original. This ballet is only missing some words in order to be a genuine opera.[72]

Much of this original *Corsaire* score, however, is unknown to most of today's ballet audiences because significant segments of it have been expunged to make way for added dances with music by other composers. (We find this added-in music, except for Delibes's *Pas des fleurs*, inferior in quality to Adam's; see Chapter 8.) Yet extant musical evidence of the first production of *Le Corsaire* in 1856, fortunately, is plentiful enough to allow for a reading of Adam's original score—and plentiful enough for the dauntless Richard Bonynge to have made a sound recording of it.[73] This musical evidence has also been carefully scrutinized by Willa Collins in her indispensable 2008 dissertation, *Adolphe Adam's Ballet* Le Corsaire *at the Paris Opéra, 1856–1868: A Source Study*, the only full-length study dedicated to this ballet and its music. We have relied extensively on her foundational research.[74]

The sources for the first production of *Le Corsaire* in 1856 are as follows: the composing score in Adam's own hand (the autograph), preserved at the Bibliothèque Nationale de France, Département de la Musique; and, at the Bibliothèque-Musée l'Opéra, the three-volume orchestra score created by copyists at the Opéra, as well as twenty-six of the original orchestra parts (which likely numbered fifty-four in 1856).[75]

The observations that follow are based on our reading of the Opéra's copied orchestra score, with insights gained from Collins's analysis as noted; all of the musical examples are taken from the that score, and they follow its numbering. Some large unnumbered sections (for example, in Act Three, Scenes IV and V) are identified by the tempo of the passage from which the excerpt is taken.

We shall now point out a few of the features that we have found noteworthy in this score.

---

[72] *Le Moniteur universel*, 27 January 1856, tr. in Collins, *Le Corsaire*, 147–148; translation slightly modified. We are unaware of any saxophone parts for this ballet; the orchestra score does not allude to them.

[73] The 1867 version of the score, including the additions by Delibes, was recorded in 1990 by Richard Bonynge and the English Chamber Orchestra (Decca 430 2862) and re-released by Eloquence Classics (Decca 4828605) in Australia in 2018.

[74] See note 5 in this chapter.

[75] Shelfmarks are as follows: autograph score, MS-2632; copied orchestra score, A-590 (1–3); orchestra parts, MAT-395. See Collins, *Le Corsaire*, 103–120. As she reports, some of the sources mentioned in Théodore LaJarte's highly useful catalogue of the Opéra's opera and ballet scores, *Bibliothèque Musicale du Théâtre de l'Opéra* (Paris: Librairie des bibliophiles, 1878), have gone missing since the catalogue was published nearly a century and a half ago. These include the *répétiteur*, twenty-six of the fifty-four parts listed by LaJarte, and some segments of the remaining orchestra parts. It is believed that these missing sources may be misfiled but still in the Opéra's collection. See Collins, *Le Corsaire*, 174n7.

A piano reduction of Adam's score as well as a selection of interpolated numbers added to the St. Petersburg and Moscow productions have recently been published: Adolphe Adam, *Le Corsaire*, ed. Yury Burlaka (St. Petersburg, Compozitor, 2021) [hereafter: Burlaka, ed., *Le Corsaire*]. The piano reduction is by Alexander Troitsky. In addition to the score of the 1856 Paris production, a lengthy appendix includes numbers subsequently added to the ballet in Paris, St. Petersburg, and Moscow. The volume also includes Russian and English translations of the 1856 Paris libretto, a biography of Adam in Russian and English and a brief analysis of the music in Russian ("Muzykal'naya biografiya 'Korsara'" [Musical biography of *Le Corsaire*]), both by Anna Grutsynova, and a Russian-language summary of Ivor Guests's writings on *Le Corsaire* in Paris (1856 and 1867) and St. Petersburg (1858). No source citations are provided, either for music sources or for other sources used to date the various interpolations.

Ex. 6.1a   The Pasha's first entrance; Act One, Scene I, No. 1, bars 225–232

A lightness in tone

Adam's music is crucial in establishing, early on, the lightness in mood of much of this ballet. One of the first instances is heard in the slightly humorous march for ceremonious arrival of the Pasha in Act One, Scene I (Ex. 6.1a). Adam includes in the B section of this march a bass drum and cymbal in the *fortissimo* bars and a triangle in the quiet bars, these three instruments being sure-fire indicators of Turkish identity according to conventions that Western composers had adopted in the eighteenth century (Ex. 6.1b).[76] (Mary Hunter notes that indicators of Turkishness for listeners at the time were effective, not as "an imitation of an original" but "as a translation of a [widely held] perception of Turkish music."[77])

The pirates are not ferocious either (well, hardly ever), and the music plainly tells us so as they make their first appearance on stage (Ex. 6.2). Yes, Adam gives them a minor key and masculine, military-sounding bursts of brass, but the playfully placed rests and the light-hearted B section (bars 85–92), with its flute melody, even hints at the sound of a sailor's dance. (It is one of the several horn-pipe-like tunes that contribute to the nautical feel of the ballet. See later in this chapter.)

Comedy in the ballet also receives a musical boost in two of Gulnare's episodes in Act Two. First, Gulnare, who is performing for the court in the *Pas des odalisques*, begins her solo as the haughty sultana Zulmea watches from her seated position at down-stage left (on a cushion, and with maidservant standing by, reminding the audience of Zulmea's high status as the Pasha's official favorite). But only a few bars after Gulnare has begun, Zulmea rises to her feet and walks proudly toward her as Gulnare (flanked by her corps de ballet) slyly watches her out of the corner of her eye. Here is their exchange, as recounted in the Justamant manual:

Zulmea: (to Gulnare) "You ladies, do not forget that I am the only one who commands here."

[76] As Ralph Locke writes, "the Turkish style was associated with certain percussion instruments, cymbals and large drum, both of which were commonly used by the Janissary bands, but also triangle, which perhaps was inspired by the Turkish çağana, a crescent-shaped rattle with small bells." Locke, *Musical Exoticism*, 116. A Janissary was a member of an elite military unit of the Turkish army.

[77] Mary Hunter, "The *Alla Turca* Style in the Late Eighteenth Century: Race and Gender in the Symphony and the Seraglio," in Jonathan Bellman, ed., *The Exotic in Western Music* (Boston: Northeastern University Press, 1998), 43–73, 317–323, qtd. in Locke, *Musical Exoticism*, 122.

Ex. 6.1b B section of the Pasha's march; Act One, Scene I, No. 1, bars 233–240

Ex. 6.2 Pirates' first entrance; Act One, Scene I, No. 1, bars 77–92

Gulnare: (laughing) "Ha, Milady," (she bows ironically) "yes, I certainly know that you are the mistress here."

Zulmea: "Well, then bow."

Gulnare and all the ladies laugh and bow mockingly.

The music for the obsequious bow—which sounds like it goes very low—is found in Ex. 6.3, bars 12–13.

The Eunuch's response (according to the libretto) is: "This is a complete revolt . . . but the Pasha will restore order." But when the Pasha arrives, Gulnare continues her merry

Ex. 6.3 Gulnare's solo and obsequious bow; Act Two, No. 2, bars 3–13

Ex. 6.4a Polka; Act Two, No. 2, bars 1–4

pranks: she refuses to bow to him and averts his blows when he furiously tries to strike her with his staff. Finally she improves his mood by charming him with her polka-dancing.

Her polka starts out with well-mannered music (Ex. 6.4a) but suddenly becomes brash as it turns into a *fortissimo* tutti, including cymbal crashes (Ex. 6.4b).

Thoroughly won over by Gulnare's dancing, the Pasha now throws his handkerchief to her as a sign of his favor. But, mischievously, she "picks up the precious handkerchief with a false humility, then throws it back to one of her companions, who throws it back to another," as the libretto tells us. For this sequence, Adam supplies a galop (sounding like a can-can) which ends suddenly with a comedic punch (Ex. 6.5).

Ex. 6.4b Polka brashness; Act Two, No. 2, bars 9–16

Ex. 6.5 End of the galop; Act Two, No. 2, bars 134–141

Exotic music

The setting (in the Aegean, in the Black Sea, and on Turkish soil) calls for music that sounds Eastern to Western ears, and Adam accomplishes this goal in the customary ways, though with extraordinary adeptness. One of these customary ways (as Ralph Locke has pointed out), is to use exotic markers, but use them sparingly.[78] So most of the ballet is composed without a hint of anything non-Western, but the few markers here and there suffice to remind the audience of the ballet's easterly setting.

One of these pieces of exotica is heard before the curtain even rises: the short, simple, and effective introduction (worth showing in its entirety, Ex. 6.6). It begins with a roll of the timpani, and proceeds to a set of chords prolonging the dominant pitch (F) and growing constantly louder as more and more instruments join in; finally every instrument is being played. This introduction's raucousness—owed in part to loud G-flat grace

[78] Locke, *Musical Exoticism*, 43–71.

notes—hints not only at the locale but the likelihood that something menacing will happen there.

After the curtain has risen on a bustling market scene, the action begins to unfold to the sounds of busy major-key music, including the Pasha's arrival music. But the musical mood suddenly changes when the Pasha first sees the beautiful Medora and asks the merchants about her (Ex. 6.8): we hear a pair of oscillating pitches a tritone apart, which become the accompaniment for a mysterious wind melody beginning at bar 324, played by oboe and clarinet, together imitating the sound of a shawm. The brief clash of the melodic F-sharp and the accompanimental G (Ex. 6.7, bar 325) adds to the exotic feel of this short passage.

Another instance, though subtle, is the march of the caravan of pilgrim dervishes (with a camel) on its way to Mecca in Act Two (Ex. 6.8). Simplicity, as in the Pasha's march, is the key indicator of its exotic nature. But the sedate melody of this one, beginning in a

Ex. 6.6 Introduction

Ex. 6.7 The Pasha asks about Medora; Act One, Scene I, No. 1, bars 318–335

low register, expresses the gravitas and apparent seriousness of purpose of this group (though it turns out that these dervishes are pirates in disguise).

Finally, let us consider the sweet $\frac{3}{4}$ *andante sostenuto* that accompanies (according to Justamant) the procession of the Pasha's wedding party in Act Three, Scene IV (Ex. 6.9). Here, it is the harmonic vocabulary and sonority of the melody that indicate exoticism. The A section of the melody is pentatonic (for the most part), relying on the first, second, third, fifth, and sixth scale degrees. It is played by harp, doubled by wind instruments (flute and clarinet in this case), a combination that sounds exotic (and, of course, was later used by Puccini to great effect). (The B section departs from pentatonicism and reverts to a major key.)

Conversations / talking / interactions

Vocal interactions between characters occur frequently in this ballet—which, after all, is an "action-ballet"—so Adam supplies a significant amount of appropriately talkative music in the "symphonic" portions of the score.

For instance, when Medora makes her case with Conrad to release the slave-women, Adam gives her (in the violins) a turn figure, two sighing figures, and a leap up an octave that unexpectedly emphasizes an off-beat. It sounds like pleading (Ex. 6.10a). But Birbanto opposes Medora's idea, as does his melody: when his voice comes in (as bassoon and lower strings), we hear a near-inversion of Medora's melody: the turn figure reverses directions, and the sighing figures and upward leap are converted to bombastic downward leaps (Ex. 6.10b). As Collins points out, Adam's recasting of

Ex. 6.8 March of the caravan of pilgrim dervishes; Act Two, No. 3, bars 175–194

Medora's plea giving it to lower voices suggests "the men mimicking Medora's request in anger."[79]

Another example of conversational music is found in an urgent interchange between the two lovers Conrad and Medora as they are reunited at the Pasha's palace, desperate to escape together before Conrad's death sentence is carried out. For this, Adam follows the ballet-music convention of using syncopations and repeating melodic phrases to allude to the sounds of human speech (Ex. 6.11). This passage also features clear "voices," high and low—perhaps not necessarily to be coordinated to particular mime of a woman and man, but to supply an aural facsimile of the sounds of a dialogue between such a pair.

[79] Collins identifies, names, and analyzes this "turn figure" in *Le Corsaire*, 201–203.

Ex. 6.9 Procession of the Pasha's wedding party; Act Three, Scene IV, *4ème Tableau*, *Andante sostenuto*, bars 3–10

Ex. 6.10a Medora pleads with Conrad; Act One, Scene II, *Après la danse*, bars 2–7

Ex. 6.10b Inverted turn figure as Birbanto protests; Act One, Scene II, *Après la danse*, bars 34–40

Ex. 6.11 Desperate conversation/urgent reunion between Medora and Conrad; Act Three, Scene IV, *Allegro agitato, 4ème Tableau*, bars 6–29

These examples are only two of many: as the Justamant manual shows, the ballet is rife with conversations, and Adam, responding in various ways, helped bring clarity to them as appropriate.

Recurring melodies

Adam from time to time makes use of recurring melodies in *Le Corsaire*, and for various reasons.

The Pasha's march—the main motif of which is heard five times over two scenes—always signifies his presence and sometimes help amplify it, for he is a big man and a pompous one whose music comes back more times than anyone else's (Exx. 6.1a and 6.1b). We hear it first in Act One, Scene I, as the Pasha and his entourage come grandly into the marketplace. (Here, the march is diegetic—that is, heard by the onstage characters.) Collins points out that

Adam allocates over eighty measures of music to the Pasha and his entourage of eunuchs, pages, and slave women, a large duration of music that reflects the fifty-one

Ex. 6.12 Lanquedem's music; Act One, Scene II, *Après la danse*, *Allegro con moto*, bars 1–8

member entourage, . . . [and] emphasizes [the Pasha] Seyd's position of wealth and power.[80]

The main motif of this march is heard again for a few moments in the same scene as the Pasha is leaving the stage to prepare for his return trip to the Isle of Cos (with Medora—or so he thinks). This time, the motif is sounded repeatedly and in different keys as part of the non-diegetic action music; it reflects the stress and chaos of the moment (Birbanto and Conrad are devising a scheme; the Pasha is giving Medora detailed instructions about their upcoming trip; Medora is anxious). The Pasha leaves the stage, and when he returns to claim Medora toward the very end of the act, his music comes back, too, again emphasizing his grandiloquent presence and drawing the attention of the other characters. (As Justamant says, "A sound is heard" before he arrives; the characters hear it.)

In Act Two, in the Pasha's palace, the theme comes back as the Pasha returns to the stage (just as Zulmea and the Eunuch are seeking a remedy for Gulnare's incorrigible behavior). And it is woven into the comical cymbal-clashing can-can music that ends Gulnare's dance as the Pasha is chasing after the harem women who are throwing his handkerchief around. This final recurrence of the theme may coincide with the following exchange:

Pasha: (with his back to the public, to the ladies). "Ah, you will pay for this, minxes."

All the women salute him mockingly and, as the Pasha runs to strike them, they run [away from him] in all directions.

Lanquedem's music, short in duration and slightly comical, is heard only twice: first when Lanqudem is brought into service by Birbanto to ensure that Conrad will be put to sleep by the lotus flower, and second, when Lanquedem arrives on the Isle of Cos with Medora in Act Two (Ex. 6.12).

The lotus music, long, languorous, lush, and lullaby-like, is heard three times: first in Act One, Scene II, when Birbanto cut the lotus blossom and shows Lanquedem its effects by putting the sentinel to sleep with it (Ex. 6.13); second, later in the same scene when Conrad is similarly anesthetized; and third, in Act Three, Scene IV, when Medora retells the action of that scene.

The kidnapping scene. A great deal of the action music from the Act One kidnapping scene is reiterated in Act Three as Medora recounts to Conrad (in detail!) what had

---

[80] This refers to the size of the entourage as given in the original libretto. Collins, *Le Corsaire*, 210.

Ex. 6.13 Lotus music; Act One, Scene II, *Après la danse*, *Andantino*, bars 1–9

Ex. 6.14a Control over Medora—she is sold to the Pasha; Act One, Scene I, No. 2, bars 1–4

happened since they last spoke back in the grotto: the lotus drugging (as noted above), the arrival of the veiled men (Birbanto and pirates in disguise), the back-and-forth between Birbanto and Medora, and finally, the abduction.

Enslavement/Liberation. For the Pasha's purchase of Medora in Act One, Scene I (Ex. 6.14a), Adam composed a melody in which these pitches appear in order:

do–re–do–ti–la–sol

This same configuration of pitches is used in the melody played as Medora is seized again, this time by pirates in the grotto scene (Ex. 6.14b), making a subtle reference to the first time Medora lost her freedom.

Adam had also used this same basic pitch scaffolding (sometimes using a flatted "la") when Medora pleaded with Conrad in the grotto to free the slave women (see Ex. 6.10a, bars 3–4). Thus does Adam use this motif three times when the action pertains to the freedom (or lack of it) of Medora or the slave women.

Ex. 6.14b Control over Medora—she is kidnapped by disguised pirates; Act One, Scene II, *Après la danse, Allegro,* bars 61–76

Nautical music

In this ballet, the sea is never very far away. Not only does much of its action involve sailing men, and end with the spectacular inundation of their seagoing vessel, but the sea may be seen and heard even when the sailors and the ship are not present. It is visible from the Pasha's palace. It can be heard outside the Pirate's grotto. And the ballet features many characters who are preparing to board a ship or have just disembarked from one.

Adam composes music to evoke the sea, and the presence of sailing men, in several ways. He creates the sound of swelling waves, first at the opening of Act One, Scene II, telling us that the sea is just outside the grotto, and reminding us that all those arriving therein have come by ship (Ex. 6.15).

We also sense the swelling waves in Act Three, Scene V, as Conrad, Medora, and others sail happily away from the Isle of Cos (Ex. 6.16).

He also writes plenty of pieces that sound like hornpipes (sailor dances). Even when not used for dancing in the moment, these hornpipe-like dances contribute to the overall nautical feel of the ballet. The first is heard in Act One as the curtain rises on the busy market scene, and again when Medora dances onto the stage (shortly after throwing her bouquet down to Conrad from a balcony; Ex. 6.17).

Ex. 6.15 Nautical music—the sound of swelling waves; Act One, Scene II, No. 3, bars 1–8

Ex. 6.16 Nautical music—the sound of swelling waves; Act Three, Scene V, *5me Tableau*, bars 1–18

A dreamy and lyrical echo of this music (played by oboe and violin) is heard shortly after Medora's entrance as she and Conrad have their first conversation (Ex. 6.18).

A hornpipe is also heard in the *Pas des éventails* in Act One, Scene II (Ex. 6.19). Shipboard dancing in the final scene was also done to the sounds of hornpipe-style music, including the pirates' dance (Ex. 6.20), and the women's scarf dance (Ex. 6.21).

Finally, Adam composes what can best be described as "pirate music": it features instruments playing in unison in a low register (to sound like the voices of a gang of pirates); it swings and sways (implying the hauling of sails and the movement of waves); it sometimes has grace notes leading up to a strong beat (adding to the swing

Ex. 6.17 Hornpipe during the opening market scene; Act One, Scene I, No. 1, bars 2–9

Ex. 6.18 Dreamy and lyrical echo of the hornpipe; Act One, Scene I, No. 1, bars 182–189

Ex. 6.19 Hornpipe in *Pas des éventails*; Act One, Scene II, *Pas de Mme Rosati*, bars 214–221

Ex. 6.20 Pirates' dance on board ship; Act Three, Scene V, *5me Tableau, Allegro*, bars 12–19

Note the oscillation between the minor tonic and the ♭VII major in the manner of "What shall we do with the drunken sailor?"

Ex. 6.21 Scarf dance onboard ship; Act Three, Scene V, *5me Tableau, Allegro*, bars 1–10

and sway); it is in a minor key. The first instance comes early in Act One, Scene II, as the pirates descend into their secret underground grotto along with their prisoners (Ex. 6.22). Adam begins this number in classic pirate-music fashion, but then (in a musically humorous twist) takes the first five melody notes, including the grace notes (see bar 54) and makes them the subject of a fugue (starting in bar 59)—a swinging and swaying one.[81]

The second use of pirate music comes in the last scene, Act Three, Scene V, when a "mate" approaches Conrad to ask about having a party (Ex. 6.23).

And the third instance is found in the pirate dance at the onboard party (Ex. 6.24).

[81] See Chapter 2, p. 86.

Ex. 6.22 Pirates' fugue; Act One, Scene II, No. 3, bars 52–78

Musical genres

Marches. Le Corsaire called for several marches. For it featured a Pasha who required ceremony and pomp (see Exx. 6.1a–b) for his arrivals and departures, as well as dervishes walking toward Mecca (see Ex. 6.8), and marching soldiers who guard the captive Conrad in Act Three, Scene IV. (The soldiers are given the same march that the dervishes had.) The Pasha also gets a silly march as an accompaniment to the little happy dance he executes once he thinks his wedding night with Medora is nigh.

Adam also composed marches that helped generate excitement for characters before they came onstage. (Though it is not diegetic music—music that can be heard by the characters—it conveys the sense of anticipation.) Here is one example: the march that

Ex. 6.23 A "mate" approaches Conrad; Act Three, Scene V, *5me Tableau*, Allegro, bars 1–9

Ex. 6.24 The Pirates' dance onboard ship; Act Three, Scene V, *5me Tableau*, Allegro, bars 1–7

precedes Medora's arrival in Act One, Scene I (after her initial appearance on the balcony; Ex. 6.25).

Character dances. For the *pas de cinq* in Act One, the character-variety suite, Adam composes a tarantella, mazurka, bolero, ecossaise, and "a French dance" (see Exx. 6.27a–g).

Ballroom music. As noted above, a polka and galop may be found in Act Two (see Exx. 6.4a–6.5). Adam also deploys waltzes to accompany some of the action of the ballet—for example, when Medora is tricking the Pasha into turning over his weapons in Act Three, Scene IV (see Ex. 6.36). And a waltz is also found in the seductive *Pas des éventails* (see Ex. 6.29b).

Ex. 6.25 March preceding Medora's first entrance; Act One, Scene I, No. 1, bars 154–170

Feminine Medora / Masculine Conrad

Medora, who of all the heroines in the five ballets of this volume is the one whose femininity (sexuality, really) is the most on display, gives Adam several opportunities to compose music that helps bring that aspect of her character to life. We shall point out two. The first comes when we catch our earliest gimpse of Medora, who is standing on a balcony. Here Adam adroitly deploys some of the conventional tools for instantaneously conveying the presence of a female: a solo flute playing in a flat key, a rocking meter ($\frac{6}{8}$), and a lulling accompaniment (Ex. 6.26a).

Medora's feminine appeal also sets the musical mood in Act One, Scene II, for the couple's dalliance on the divan. The parallel sixths played by oboe and flute suggests the closeness of the two lovers (Ex. 26b) .

Conrad, whose masculine strength and power are often on display, warrants the most heroic music of the ballet when in the climactic action scene of Act Three, Scene IV, he rescues Medora from the Pasha (Ex. 26c).

Adolphe Adam was called upon in *Le Corsaire*, a very long and involved ballet, to write a score with music fit for action aplenty to be carried out in various exotic settings by a panoply of characters of diverse personalities, national origins, and ethnicities. He succeeded mightily, yielding one of the best ballet scores of the era, in our estimation—a score that makes apparent Adam's mastery of a wide range of styles and genres, fine abilities as orchestrator, and perhaps most of all, his wit. Where else could one "hear," all in one score, an obsequious bow in a harem, a luscious lotus flower scent in a grotto, a fugue made out of a pirate song, a dashing rescue in a Pasha's palace, a set of sea shanties on board a ship, a cataclysmic storm? Adam made of this ambitious libretto a coherent and eminently listenable account of the story—a score that can be credited to a great extent with the ballet's success.

Ex. 6.26a First appearance of Medora (on the balcony); Act One, Scene I, No. 1, bars 123–140

Scene-by-scene description of *Le Corsaire* based on Justamant's staging manual

This description is based largely on the manual created by Henri Justamant, documenting the production in Lyon that premiered on 17 February 1857, a little over a year after *Le Corsaire*'s Paris premiere.[82]

In Justamant's detailed account, he refers several times to the Paris Opéra production, which not only confirms that he saw it, but raises the possibility that his manual actually represents that production (including Mazilier's choreography), at least in part.[83] For what Justamant wrote down matches several features of the Paris production: its list of

[82] Theaterwissenschaftliche Sammlung der Universität Köln, Schloß Wahn, Inventory Number 70-441.

[83] In this manual, Justamant names the dancer when documenting choreography that was different from what was done in Paris. This suggests that he recorded Mazilier's choreography except in cases in which he provides the name of a dancer who performed in another production (such as the Lyon production). For example, for the Scene III variation for Medora—D major $\frac{3}{8}$—he provides versions danced by Carolina Rosati in Paris, Carlotta de Vecchi in Lyon (similar to Rosati but with added steps on *pointe*), and Henriette Dor (nearly identical to de Vecchi but with a difference at the end of the variation). (Note that Justamant did not indicate where or when Dor's variation was danced.)

Ex. 6.26b Medora (with Conrad); Act One, Scene II, *Après la danse, Allegro fieramente*, bars 39–50

characters in its ensemble cast is the same, its list of dances included in the ballet is the same, and its division of acts and scenes (tableaux) is the same. Too, its list at the end of movements for maneuvering the ship, lighting instructions, costume accessories, and props comport well with what one would expect from the libretto and press descriptions of the Paris production.

It is true that corps de ballet dancers are fewer in number in Justamant's manual than those listed in the Paris libretto. But that could reasonably be expected in a ballet company outside of Paris, even one in at the Grand Théâtre de Lyon, one of the best houses for ballet production in France.[84] In sum, the ballet as described in this manual might well reflect Mazilier's *Le Corsaire*. And even if it does not, it provides a coherent view of what one French version of this ballet looked like within a year of its Paris premiere.

Now, let us proceed to the scene-by-scene description. Here, particularly in the indented passages, we have included verbatim quotations from Justamant's manual—an approach that renders the prose perhaps less smooth to read but retains the character and many details of the staging manual. Note, further, that the quotations of the characters' words are intended for mime, and therefore are often unlike spoken text. Finally, we have used Lanquedem's name instead of "The Jew," which (as noted above) is the designation used for him throughout the manual.

---

[84] Adolphe Adam, in a letter to the director of the Opéra about the fee he was to be paid for the *Corsaire* score, stated that "a ballet score is not sold like an opera score and [...] the royalties in the provinces are nil because there are only three cities in France—Lyon, Bordeaux and Marseille—where ballets can be performed." Archives nationales, AJ[13] 221.II, qtd. in Collins, *Le Corsaire*, 166.

Ex. 6.26c Heroic Conrad (with trumpets); Act Three, Scene IV, *Suite de 4eme tableau, Allegro*, bars 13–50

Act One

Scene I: A square in the city of Adrianople

The set, according to the drawings in Justamant, calls for a clear space at center, with one building at each side, upstage. Medora's balcony is part of the stage-right building. At curtain-up, the audience sees groups of women seated on carpets and cushions; merchants and buyers are wending their way through the groups of women.

The *Introduction*, only forty-one seconds in length and highly effective, begins with a roll of the timpani that gives way to a rapid series of chords, all prolonging the dominant pitch F and growing ever louder, more ominous, and more raucous (Ex. 6.6). At curtain-up, it resolves nicely into a pleasant and bright B-flat major theme that helps depict the busy market scene—a theme that occasionally gives way to new music as a new character enters, and then comes back (Ex. 6.17).

A merchant, seated on cushions at stage right and smoking a pipe, tells the women at center to move around a bit. They perform a brief dance in two lines at center. Prospective buyers come and go; one makes a purchase.

Entrance of the pirates. The pirates appear at the back of the stage, coming from stage left (Ex. 6.2). The merchants make all the women get up and have them exit on each side through the wings; they leave the cushions behind. After watching everyone disappear on both sides, the pirates come downstage a bit and prepare to welcome their leader.

Entrance of Conrad and Birbanto. Conrad, followed at a distance by Birbanto, comes downstage. The pirates salute his entrance.

Conrad: (to the pirates) "Hello, friends." Walking to each side, he recommends that they keep silent and sober. The pirates answer, "Yes, Captain."

Conrad comes downstage looking like he is searching for someone, and he comes to sit down on the cushions that are at the center; he seems to be thinking.

Birbanto signals to the pirates on stage right to come to him.

The pirates, chatting, go from stage right to stage left to join their comrades and Birbanto.

All the pirates gather and talk among themselves, not paying attention to what is about to happen. Only Birbanto is observing from the corner of his eye, with his back turned to the audience.

Conrad gets up, and looking thoughtful, walks toward Medora's door.

Medora appears on her balcony [Ex. 6.26a].

Conrad, seeing her, is struck, and says to himself, "How beautiful she is."

Medora, upon seeing Conrad, has brought her hand to her heart.

Conrad graciously salutes Medora.

Medora returns his greeting and goes back to making a bouquet, picking flowers from several vases on her balcony.

Conrad looks all around him.

Medora throws the bouquet to Conrad.

Conrad quickly picks it up, kisses it, and comes down stage. Looking at the bouquet, he says, "This flower is love. This one, silence! She has been thinking of me, oh, what happiness."

He walks back upstage. With his back to the audience, he falls to his knees in front of Medora's balcony.

Medora looks at him with love and quickly goes back inside.

Birbanto, who was going to talk to his master, when he sees him on his knees, stops short, and shrugging his shoulders a bit, walks back toward his comrades.

Now Conrad stands up, presses his bouquet against his chest, summons Birbanto, and speaks into his ear (Ex. 6.25). Birbanto nods yes and walks away. The pirates move upstage; the merchants and women all come back, resuming the positions they held at curtain-up. Conrad kneels down and quickly writes on his tablets; he gets up when Medora comes onto the stage.

Entrance of Medora. Medora, who has now left her house after making a short appearance on the balcony, enters dancing. She traverses the stage several times, traveling toward, then away, from Conrad with enchaînements that include such bravura steps as *temps de cuisse, temps de flèche,* multiple *brisés, fouetté sauté,* and *grand fouetté en tournant.* She completes her entrance by approaching Conrad with a *pas de bourrée couru* and *grand jeté en avant* twice then winds down with two *jetés en tournant, glissade, pas de basque.*

Lanquedem has followed his ward and has been talking business with one of the merchants, upstage left. Then he comes downstage a bit, and chats with one of the merchants, his back to his ward.

Medora is now near Conrad, she recognizes him, she feels some emotion and seems to think, "He looks handsome" [Ex. 6.18].

Conrad is devouring her with his eyes and seems to say, "She is so beautiful." He stands up and greets her.

Medora returns the greeting with her eyes looking down, not daring to look at him because of the people around them.

Conrad: (with a mysterious air) "I have read your bouquet," and he shows it to her.

Medora listens with pleasure.

Conrad: "It will never leave me," and pressing it against his chest, he takes his tablets and hands them to Medora.

Medora takes the tablets, reads them quickly. She feels happiness, and turning to Conrad, she thanks him with her eyes, saying, "Very well," and she keeps the tablets.

A noise is heard. It is the Pasha. The merchants compel the women to get up. [. . .]

Everyone: "It is the Pasha coming this way."

Lanquedem: "That is because he likes pretty women."

Entrance of the Pasha. He enters in a ceremonial procession, which indicates his high status. The music for this march is lighthearted and a little pompous (Exx. 6.1a–b). The Pasha's guards enter first and remain at the back; the Pasha enters, seated on a palanquin. Little slaves follow, carrying chests, and remain at the back. The Pasha gets off his palanquin.

Everyone bows except for Medora and Conrad. The Pasha comes downstage, saluting on all sides, looking cheerful and happy. He eagerly agrees when the merchants approach to ask if he would like to see the women on offer. He goes and sits on the cushions on stage left; Lanquedem follows him.

Then, in a lengthy scene, the Pasha rejects all of the women brought before him; Lanquedem in some cases is secretly signaling him to say "no," demonstrating that Lanquedem hopes to sell Medora to the Pasha. Finally, the situation escalates as all the merchants push all of the women toward the Pasha, who surround him and beseech him.

The Pasha, walking toward stage right, tells them, "It is no use, no, no." He turns his head to his left and suddenly finds himself right next to Medora. He seems surprised when he sees her, and stepping back, he says, "How beautiful she is."

Medora looks at him with dignified pride.

Lanquedem has been keeping an eye on the Pasha and says, "Good, he saw her."

Medora, looking at the Pasha, feels a sort of fear and disgust.

The music becomes mysteriously exotic (Ex. 6.7) as the Pasha asks the merchants if she is on offer for sale.

Pasha: (coming to center stage, asks the merchant on stage left) "Is she yours?"

Merchant: "No," and he goes away.

Pasha: (to the merchant on stage right) "Is she yours?"

Merchant: "No," and he goes away.

Pasha: (taking a step toward Lanquedem) "Yours, then?"

Lanquedem: (humbly and with a smile) "Yes."

Pasha: (briskly) "Good, I will buy her from you, because she is the one I want." He goes to Medora.

Conrad: (reassuring Medora) "Don't say a thing."

The Pasha takes Medora by the hand and takes her to sit with him.

Medora does not know what to do; she glances at Conrad who reassures her with a gesture.

Lanquedem rubs his hands goes toward stage left also.

Pas de cinq. Everyone makes way for the dance; Medora and the Pasha are seated together on cushions (the Pasha slightly elevated); pirates, the Pasha's entourage, women, and merchants, constitute the onstage audience.

The *pas de cinq* is danced by "une italienne, une mazourka, une française, une espagnole, une anglaise," each in her native costume. A multimovement dance suite of the character-variety type, it is called by Justamant "Pas des nations | pas de cinq." It begins with an entrée (Ex. 6.27a) in which all five dancers are introduced: first the French dancer (for four bars), then the Polish (four bars), the Italian and Spanish dancers together (four bars), and finally the English dancer (four bars). Four of the women dance together until the end (the Italian woman is likely the missing dancer—she will dance the first variation). Next comes a series of solos in which each dancer expresses her own "national" identity (Exx. 6.27b–f). The *mazourka* taps her heels on the floor; the *espagnole* swivels her hips. Of particular note is the tarantella, which as Justamant said, "must be danced almost like a tarantella" with, apparently, very little alteration for the stage.

Finally, we arrive at the brief coda (Ex. 6.27g), which begins with sixteen-bar duo for the Polish and Italian dancers. They are joined by the Spanish and French dancers and finally the English one. At the end, the quintet travels downstage in a single row, the

Ex. 6.27a *Pas de cinq*, Introduction, bars 1–10

Ex. 6.27b *Pas de cinq*, *Tarantelle* (Italian), bars 3–10

women holding each other by the waist as they perform eight *jetés ordinaire* then strike a unison pose to finish, the English dancer at the center.

As one would expect, the women of this character-variety *pas de cinq* combine academic and character-step vocabulary: they begin with and end with mostly academic steps in the introduction and the coda, and in each solo section perform mostly character steps and poses.

Après le pas. In this scene, Lanquedem sells Medora to the Pasha. The music heard during the transaction (Ex. 6.14a) will be heard again as Medora is abducted in the grotto (Ex. 6.14b).

Ex. 6.27c *Pas de cinq, Mazuetta* (Mazurka, Polish), bars 3–6

Ex. 6.27d *Pas de cinq, La française,* bars 1–9 (note the similarity between this melody and that in the scarf dance of Act Three, Scene V, Ex. 6.21)

Ex. 6.27e *Pas de cinq, Bolero* (Spanish), bars 5–10

Unimpressed by the international contingent of women in the *pas de cinq,* the Pasha abruptly and rudely asks Lanquedem how much it would cost to buy his ward, Medora. He offers a chest of treasures; Lanquedem refuses, but does accept the offer of *two* chests, and asks for a promissory note with the Pasha's signature:

The Pasha responds, "You are a rascal, but I'll have to do what you say. Give me something to write with." [...]

Lanquedem has quickly taken from his jacket a paper and a pencil that he hands to the Pasha, then he presents his back [to write on] while bending forward.

Ex. **6.27f** *Pas de cinq*, *Ecossaise* (English), bars 3–10

Ex. **6.27g** *Pas de cinq*, *Final*, bars 1–9

The Pasha puts the paper on Lanquedem's back and writes on the paper.

Conrad during that time tells Medora, "Do not worry, you will not belong to that man. I will abduct you and take you far away."

Medora feels reassured.

The Pasha is finished and returns the paper and the pencil to Lanquedem.

Lanquedem takes it, turns it over and reads it, and looks happy.

The Pasha whacks Lanquedem's behind with his cane, as if to say, "Scoundrel, you doubt me."

In a preview of the pirates' show of strength to come, the Pasha walks away and recoils upon suddenly finding himself face to face with Conrad. Conrad looks at him with assurance, making the Pasha uneasy. During that time, Lanquedem, who has opened the treasure chests he acquired in exchange for Medora, takes out the purses, the pearls and the gems; he hides them in his turban, his belt, and his shirt.

Now the Pasha departs (followed by his entourage) after telling Medora he will soon return to take her away to his palace. Conrad then starts to put his plan in place by ordering his men to distract Lanquedem (or, as the libretto says, to surround him). What follows is a lengthy scene in which Lanquedem is poked, prodded, tricked, held painfully in Birbanto's vice-like arms, pushed around, dragged, forced to twirl and dance, thrown up in the air, and tossed from one pirate to another "like a rubber ball." Intended to be amusing, this scene can be read today only as a blatant display of antisemitism, owing to the fact that Lanquedem is presented to the audience quite obviously as a Jew.

During a brief downstage conversation as the abuse is taking place, the audience is reminded once again of Conrad's plan to take Medora away.

Medora: "So you promise you will not leave me in the Pasha's hands, you will take me away with you."

Conrad: "I give you my word."

Finally, the Pasha returns, followed by his numerous party, and people come onto the stage from all sides. The pirates let go of Lanquedem and laugh at him; he comes downstage briskly and breathes a sigh of relief. The Pasha takes Medora's hand and tries to lead her upstage so they can depart.

Medora frees herself and says emphatically, "I will never go with you," and passes in front of him on her way to stage right.

The Pasha, surprised, follows her.

Lanquedem tries to challenge her.

Medora looks at him severely. He hangs his head.

Pasha: (to Medora) "Why don't you want to come with me?"

Medora: (with energy) "Because I do not love you."

Conrad, meanwhile, has made a sign to Birbanto, who comes to him immediately.

He says something into his ear.

Pasha: "But you will be the queen of my palace."

Medora: "You are old and ugly, and I do not know what keeps me from tearing your face up."

The Pasha takes a few steps back from Medora, afraid. She chases after him. Conrad, as an enticement to the "almehs" (as the libretto says), and presumably the pirates, too, throws some money-purses onto the ground; they all come forward and pick them up with joy, and then come downstage to take their places for the bacchanale.[85] Medora has stopped chasing the Pasha but is still angry. She and the Pasha sit down on cushions to watch the dancing.

Bacchanale. The energetic and vivacious *Bacchanale des corsaires* is danced "by Birbanto and two third danseuses," sixteen men and sixteen women of the corps de ballet, presumably, the pirates and slave women, or "almehs" (Ex. 6.28).[86]

[85] Here, Justamant writes, "N.B. I seem to remember that at the Opera, Conrad crosses the stage and throws the purses when the Pasha tries to take Medora away, and after that he goes stage left to talk to Birbanto."

[86] The Paris libretto calls for five soloists—Birbanto and four women—rather than the three in the Lyon production.

Ex. 6.28 *Bacchanale*, bars 3–18

Justamant lays out the choreography in nineteen sections. The general disposition of the dancers sees two lines of eight couples along each side of the stage framing Birbanto and his two partners, who dance at center with Birbanto often partnering both women simultaneously. The step vocabulary is similar to that which we found in the *Giselle* Act One march—a mix of academic ballet movements and partnered steps akin to social dances. These are punctuated by frequent *appels* (stamps of the foot), which we also saw in Justamant's *Paquita* dances. The men are sometimes shown in Justamant's drawings with their arms crossed and the women with hand on hip. (Stamps of the foot were surely appropriate both for Spanish dance and for pirates.)

At one point, the corps women form two lines at center. Holding hands, the three soloists move upstage, allowing the lines of corps women to pass beneath their raised arms. The corps couples next form a triangle—in a series of partnered movements they lean away from and then toward center—and then a circle, surrounding Birbanto and the solo women—the pirates form their own inner circle, facing away from center and joining hands as they dance. The soloists move upstage and allow the ensemble to fill the space for a series of partnered movements, some of which involve pairs of couples. The lead dancers return and the entire ensemble dances together again briefly.

The lengthy bacchanale is suddenly ended at a signal from Conrad; dancing pirates seize their helpless female partners and carry them away upstage left in a chaotic scene. More pirates join the fray, rushing in from the wings, stage right, to jostle the Pasha's troupes. The Pasha and Lanquedem stand up in surprise. Medora runs toward Conrad and throws herself into his arms. The pirates, who have now defeated the Pasha's soldiers, run immediately to seize Lanquedem. Conrad, taking Medora away, laughs at the Pasha. The pirates take Lanquedem away also.

The Pasha tries to run after Conrad, but he is detained by a pirate coming from stage right, who points a pistol to his chest; at the same time others come and aim their weapons at him. Then, the Pasha, scared, runs toward stage left in the front.

The pirates pursue him as far as the middle of the stage, then run to join their comrades.

End of the first tableau.

Here, Justamant writes, "N.B. At the Opéra, the scene change between the first and second tableaux takes place in front of the audience."

Act One

Scene II: In the grotto

The libretto tells us that we are in a "subterranean palace, a vast and magnificent dwelling, where there are piles of dazzling riches: precious armor, splendid fabrics, jewels of all kinds, and vases of gold and silver."

The set, according to the drawings in Justamant, calls for a rocky cave-like grotto with stalactites hanging down from above. A curtain opening at midstage right, near the wings, reveals a divan; at stage left, a large pillow. At the back of the stage is a *monticule* (raised platform). The characters will enter on this raised platform at stage right, cross the back of the stage on the platform, and then make an 180-degree turn onto a walkway (or staircase) that is parallel to the platform and slightly closer to the audience. The walkway leads from far stage left down to the middle of stage.

Conrad and Medora arrive in the grotto. We hear a pleasant D-major *andante* at a steady tempo, evoking the sound of swelling waves, for the sea is nearby; the characters have just disembarked. Conrad leads Medora, who is covered with a white cloak (Ex. 6.15). They first appear on the *monticule* at stage right, walk to stage left, turn onto the walkway, and walk down to the stage. Once they have arrived,

Medora examines her surroundings with curiosity, then going downstage a bit she asks her lover, "Where am I?"

Conrad: "[You are] at my place, fear not. Here you will be the queen and mistress."

He shows her the cushions and takes her toward them.

Medora sits down and looks at Conrad with love.

Conrad: "When I see you here with me, my heart jumps with joy, I feel happy."

Medora: "Remember you gave me your word, love."

Conrad: (with heat) "And I do still."

Medora: (sadly) "Yes, but . . ."

Conrad: "What is it?"

Medora: (pointing at his dagger) "Why does death have to be near you always, with such a profession?"

Conrad: "Ah, that death that you fear, and these riches here, well I will give up everything for a look from you, a word from your lips." He gets on his knees.

Medora puts her arms around her lover's neck and tells him, "Let me get away for a while and fix myself up a bit." She stands up.

Conrad takes her by the waist and takes her up stage right.

Medora: (tenderly) "See you soon, my dear."

Conrad: "Go and come back soon."

Medora exits backstage just above the divan.

Conrad looks at her go, and nonchalantly comes to stand in front of the divan.

Justamant writes, "N.B. At the end of the music, and of the scene, we can see Birbanto [standing] on the big *monticule*."

Entry of pirates and their captives. We hear the unmistakable sounds of pirate music, followed by a fugue (Ex. 6.22), which creates the proper mood of skullduggery as the pirates lead their captives—Lanquedem and the slave women—into the Grotto. Here, by calling him a "thug" and pushing, shoving, and intimidating him, the pirates keep up their cruel treatment of Lanquedem, who continues to be depicted as weak and cowardly.

The women ask Conrad for their freedom. Some of the captive women, liberated from the slave traders but now consigned to the pirates, ask for their freedom.

A captive walks straight to Conrad and makes a gesture of supplication. Conrad asks her what she wants.

Captive: "I come in the name of all my companions who are slaves here, like me, [to ask you to] give us back our freedom."

Conrad turns his head away.

The Captive falls to her knees.

All the women take two steps forward and get on their knees and supplicate Conrad.[87] [They are lined up in neat rows, six on each side of the band of pirates, reaching their arms prayerfully to Conrad, hands clasped.]

Conrad: "No, no, I cannot do that."

Meanwhile, Birbanto has rallied the pirates, saying "We do not want them to go away." The pirates intimidate the women, making them return to their original places.[88] "It is of no use," say the pirates to the women. Then, having sufficiently discouraged the women, Birbanto walks past Conrad, saying to him, "These women are crazy."

Pas des éventails (called in Adam's score Pas de Mme Rosati). The *fortissimo* introduction to this extended, multimovement dance suite accompanies a brief mime exchange.

Medora, as the music starts, enters stage right and tells her lover, "If you allow it, my companions and I will dance."

Conrad: "I do allow it," and he signals them to start.

Medora goes and places herself. The women go and get the fans and place themselves.[89] Conrad sits down on his divan.[90]

One reviewer described the ensuing *pas des éventails* (fan dance) as follows:

[Medora] gets up, beckons to her companions, and dances the *pas d'éventails* to entertain her lord and master: a bizarre and charming pas. The swaying fans resemble gigantic peacock wings or wheels; they sometimes converge around [Medora] and wrap

[87] One may also find, in staging manuals for some operas by Donizetti, the instruction for a chorus to take one or two steps forward in unison, often at a tonic cadence. See Marian Smith, "Le Disposizioni Sceniche delle Opere Francesi negli Anni Parigini di Donizetti," in *Atti del Convegno Internazionale di Studio 1992*, ed. Francesco Bellotto (Bergamo: Assessorato allo Spettacolo, 1992), 371–394.

[88] Birbanto takes the main supplicating woman by the waist and brings her back briskly to her place. (Recall that a man taking a young woman by the waist—in a mime or action scene—is personal; see Chapter 1.) At the same time, the other pirates make the other women back up to the places that they had just been.

[89] Here, Justamant begins referring to the women as "ladies" (*dames*) instead of slaves.

[90] This mime exchange is recorded on page 102 of Justamant's manual. Pages 103–106 are missing from the manuscript, and the "Pas avec les eventails" is recorded on pages 107–136. An unnumbered page is added between pages 114 and 115.

Ex. 6.29a *Pas de Mme Rosati*, bars 7–14

her from head to toe with their long, shivering blades, so that it seems that all dancers are just the plumage of her wings.[91]

The dance proceeds in six movements, the first of which is the fan dance itself, performed by Medora, two third *danseuses* (we will call them soloists), and eight women of the corps de ballet. The number opens with a gentle cornet solo that perpetuates the ambience of the sea with its rolling melody (Ex. 6.29a).

The two soloists are placed in front of a row of four corps women. In a single movement, each one raises her back leg to *demi-attitude croisé* and her right arm, holding her closed fan, overhead. Leaning their bodies to the left, they flip open their fans. They step to the right, extending the fans toward the wings, and then to the left, closing the fans.

Medora *bourrées* from stage left to center. She makes a *tour de promenade* in *arabesque allongée* as the other women bourrée to make a diagonal at stage left, holding the fans in front of themselves, partially open "at chin height." Medora performs a *pas de basque en tournant* toward the two soloists, who approach her and give her their fans. She holds them at her back like wings and she poses in *arabesque à plat*, as four more corps women enter and join the others in two rows upstage of Medora.

Medora returns the fans to the soloists. The women (soloists and corps) lay their fans on the floor at center in a circle formation and kneel around them. Medora bourrées around the fans in the space between the fans and the corps. The women retrieve the fans. Medora performs an *entrechat six* at center. As she goes up, the women kneel and open their fans by pressing them to the ground, forming a "basket," as described by Justamant. Medora performs *degagé à la seconde* and a *tour de promenade* holding that position.

[91] Saint-Victor, *La Presse*, 27 January 1856.

The women split into two groups and hide themselves by opening their fans and holding them together to form two vertical circles on either side of Medora, who makes a *grand port de bras* and *double pirouette* before moving upstage with several *chassés*. Kneeling and holding their fans behind them like wings, the women form three rows through which Medora *bourrées*. Next, the corps surround her in a semicircle, fans held behind their backs so they reach above their heads, as the soloists support Medora in a reclining *degagé devant*.

Medora dances a brief solo to woodwind accompaniment. Her steps include *fouetté sauté, assemblé,* and *jeté.* As the music broadens, the opening theme returning in the full orchestra, she performs a series of *piqué en arabesque, assemblé* to alternate sides.

Holding their fans over the heads toward the wings, the ensemble *bourrées* from the sides to center. They make a "V" formation with Medora it its downstage apex. "All of the ladies lay the tip of the fan on the hip of the lady in front of them and they open the fans together," like the blinking of an eye or the fluttering of a butterfly's wings. They split again and hold their fans together above heads to form "a basket on each side" as Medora performs a *pirouette à la seconde* followed by a *pirouette en attitude.* Finally, the group comes together, standing behind Medora in a tight group. They raise the fans at various heights to form a wall of fans behind Medora, similar to that depicted in the cartoon by Félix Rey that documents what could be this same moment in the 1867 Paris revival of *Le Corsaire.*[92]

The *Pas de Mme Rosati* continues with a waltz featuring solos for Medora and another soloist, followed by a passage for the corps de ballet and both soloists (Ex. 6.29b). The fans are retired for the rest of the *pas* except for a single brief return between the solos danced by Medora and the soloist.

Medora's first variation is a mercurial number featuring large *crescendo* (Ex. 6.29c). The dance is documented twice—first as performed by Carlotta de Vecchi, Medora in the 1857 Lyon production, and second as performed by Henriette Dor, whom we shall meet again in Chapter 7 (for she danced the role of Medora in St. Petersburg in 1868). (Born in 1844, Dor was not active professionally until the 1860s.) The pages containing Dor's choreography appear to have been added to the manuscript and are unnumbered.

A comparison of the versions for de Vecchi and Dor reveals that the two women danced identical steps for the first half of the variation: a diagonal from upstage left of nine *petits ballonnés* and a *piqué en attitude*, arms overhead, followed by a pose *à plat.* Then they returned upstage with a turning series of *glissade, jeté en avant.* De Vecchi continued with *rond de jambe en l'air sauté, grand temps de flèche*, a series of *pas de basque*, and a final quick, repeated combination of *rond de jambe, jeté, relevé en tournant à la demi-seconde, jeté.* Dor, for her part, zigzagged downstage with a series of *glissade, piqué à la seconde, fouetté, relevé en tournant,* and two *jetés.* She returned upstage with *brisé, temps de flèche en tournant, jeté, assemblé, double pirouette* on *pointe, jeté* four times to alternate side. She concluded the variation with the same final combination as de Vecchi.

The ensemble continues with a languid, rolling 6/8 (Ex. 6.29d). The soloists are featured, joined by four women of the corps de ballet.

---

[92] The document is signed "Félix Y." See Bibliothèque Nationale de France, Bibliothèque-Musée de l'Opéra, ESTAMPES SCENES Corsaire (3), "*Quelques croquis sur Le Corsaire a l'Opéra*—(1867): [estampe] / Félix Y. [sig.]"; available online at https://gallica.bnf.fr/ark:/12148/btv1b8437126n.

Ex. 6.29b *Pas de Mme Rosati,* bars 68–75

Ex. 6.29c *Pas de Mme Rosati,* bars 132–139

A second variation for Medora is notated twice: one for de Vecchi and the other for Dor, and they are nearly identical. The music is a hornpipe, featuring a solo piccolo (Ex. 6.19).

The sweeping coda begins with the soloists followed by the corps de ballet and a final solo for Medora (Ex. 6.29e). The entire ensemble dances together only briefly at the end. Following a *pirouette* performed by Medora and the soloists, a final group features all dancers in two rows.

Après le Pas de Medora. This scene opens with a discussion, begun by Medora, about freeing the slave-women, an idea Birbanto opposes (Exx. 6.10a–b).

All of the ladies go back to their places. Conrad goes to Medora, and tells her, "I compliment you, you are always lovely and I am delighted."

Medora: "Conrad, oh, my friend, I have a request for you."

Conrad: (tenderly) "And what is it?"

Medora: "That all these young women, who are captives here, be freed."

Conrad: (hesitating) "But I cannot [do that]."

Ex. 6.29d *Pas de Mme Rosati*, bars 169–177

Ex. 6.29e *Pas de Mme Rosati*, bars 259–66

Medora: "Oh, [do it] out of love for me."

Birbanto, hearing Medora, goes up to the pirates and starts rousing them, [telling them] they must not accept this.

All the women come up and supplicate Conrad on their knees.

Conrad: "Well, yes, for you, I give them all their freedom." (To the women) "Go and leave now."

Medora throws herself into her lover's arms.

In sum, as the libretto put it, "Medora [has taken] advantage of the Corsair's admiration [immediately after the *Pas des éventails*] by asking him to free the beautiful prisoners."

The pirates rebel. All the ladies go toward upstage to depart the grotto, but Birbanto and the pirates stop them with a gesture. Conrad, at midstage with Medora, passes her to his right. The drawing shows Conrad putting his hands on Medora's forearms and moving her from his left to his right. This act may convey to the audience his wish to gain power back from Medora, or his resolution to assert his power in general. Conrad then comes downstage thinking, "This is too much." The pirates and the ladies have returned to their places.

> Birbanto goes to Conrad resolutely and tells him, "But all these women you want to free are ours as much as yours, and you have no right to dismiss them. I for one want them to stay."
>
> *Pirates*: (from their places) "Yes, yes, he is right."
>
> Conrad has crossed his arms to listen, and with a withering look, says, "Be quiet."
>
> *Birbanto*: (coming down) "I will not."
>
> *Conrad*: "I'm telling you to be quiet."
>
> *Birbanto*: "No, no."
>
> *Conrad*: "Beware."

In the showdown that ensues, Conrad subdues Birbanto by holding him in a vise-like grip, forcing him to drop his dagger and fall to his knees. Afterward,

> Conrad reassures Medora and says, "Do not worry, I am fine; that is how you treat a mutineer."
>
> *Medora*: ". . . Ah, I was so afraid."

Birbanto has rallied the pirates and, thinking Conrad can't see him, rushes at him with a dagger. Conrad defeats him again with an even greater show of force: turning swiftly around, he strikes his attacker's arm violently, causing the dagger to fall to the ground. Then, seizing Birbanto by the body, he makes him turn like a top in front of him and then throws him on the ground to his right, "like a bolt of lightning." (Thus does Justamant implicitly liken Conrad to Zeus as he describes this particular instance of one character asserting power over another by physically moving him or her to his right.)

All the pirates who had come down stage to support Birbanto now fall at Conrad's feet instead. Lanquedem is afraid and falls to his knees, too. Medora, at first stunned, then raises her hands to her lover.

> Conrad remains cold and proud; he crosses his arms and looks at everyone as he passes in front of them, and he tells them, "See, try to revolt [against me] another time [and you will see what happens]."
>
> The pirates do not move.
>
> *Conrad*: (to Medora with a smile) "It is nothing, it is over." (and to the ladies) "As to you, as I promised you, you can leave, you are free."
>
> All the women, joyfully, run away from by way of the *monticule* like a flock of birds that has been released.
>
> Conrad goes back up a bit and watches them go.

Now Lanquedem asks for his freedom from Medora, who responds "Never, never." The scene ends as Conrad, taking Medora by the waist, or leaning on her shoulder, takes her to stage left. After he looks severely at the pirates one more time, they exit at the front of the stage.

Birbanto comes up with another idea. Birbanto gets up from the floor, picks up his dagger, makes a threatening gesture toward Conrad, and starts thinking. Now we hear, for the first time, a bit of mildly comic music that is associated with Lanquedem (Ex. 6.12).

Then Birbanto sees Lanquedem, who is sneaking upstage in an attempt to escape. The pirates block Lanquedem and force him downstage, where Birbanto awaits.

Birbanto: "You must take your ward back; she is causing our leader to lose his mind. You need to take her far away, and also you must buy her back from us."

Lanquedem: (in consternation) "But I can't buy her from you because she belongs to me."

Birbanto: "She is ours because we stole her from you."

Lanquedem: "But I have nothing left."

Birbanto: "You lie," and putting his hand on Lanquedem's turban, he pulls it up. Several purses filled with coins fall out. "You see, ruffian."

The pirates, surprised, leap to the purses and take them.

Lanquedem wants to get them back but he cannot get at them.

Birbanto takes off Lanquedem's belt, while other pirates make him spin; jewels and other purses fall off of him.

Lanquedem struggles as much as he can to grab the jewels; finally he manages to place his foot over one of the purses.

Birbanto wraps his belt around Lanquedem's neck and mouth to keep him from crying out and leaves to confer with the pirates.

Lanquedem immediately picks up the purse, and hides it on himself thinking, "It is always something," he turns around and makes a menacing gesture at Birbanto with his fist, while walking toward him.

Birbanto turns around, puts the turban back on Lanquedem and tells him, "We are going to return your ward to you."

Lanquedem: "How?"

Birbanto: "Watch and stay here, do not move."

Suddenly the atmosphere is saturated with the lush, dreamy music of the lotus flower (Ex. 6.13).

Birbanto goes to stage left, he picks a red lotus flower, comes back to Lanquedem, and shows it to him. With a mysterious air he then takes from his shirt a little flask and pours a few drops from it onto the flower. Then he sneaks up on the sentinel that guards Conrad's divan and passes the poisoned lotus flower under the sentinal's nose. Birbanto gestures to Lanquedem: "Come here and look."

In a bit of comic stage business, as Lanquedem bends over a bit to look, Birbanto carelessly extends his arm and with his left hand (by accident) holds the poisoned flower under the Lanquedem's nose. Lanquedem quickly moves his head back and takes the flower, saying, "Be careful"; he takes a step back holding the flower with the tips of his fingers and holds it away from his own face.

Ex. 6.30 *Scène dansante* refrain; Act One, Scene II, *Après la danse*, *Allegro fieramente*, bars 23–30

Birbanto: "So you saw how he fell asleep, well—our leader will fall the same way, do you understand?"

Lanquedem: "Alas, yes."

Scène de la table. The music for this intimate *scène dansante* takes the following form: Introduction, AABAACAD, with section A serving as a refrain (Ex. 6.30).

During the thirty-bar introduction to the scene, little slaves carry the divan and table to centerstage and remain next to each piece of furniture. (Justamant adds that at the Paris Opéra they do not wait for Conrad.)

Conrad, holding Medora by the arm, enters and walks straight behind the divan while talking with Medora. Reaching stage right, they look at the grotto and come down stage. Conrad signals to the slaves to exit. They exit stage left.

Conrad: "Ah, I feel that if I didn't have your love, if you left me, I would die" [last five bars of the introduction].

Medora quickly puts her left hand on his shoulder and with her right hand touches his forehead with one finger and tells him, laughing, "You have crazy ideas," and with the same gesture, "Do not worry, I will not leave, I love you too much for that" [section A].

Conrad: "Come with me to the table" (he shows her).

Medora: "Oh, I don't know."

Conrad: "Please."

Medora: "Well, I will serve you, then."

Conrad: "All right, come, then" [section A repeated].

He takes her by the hand and brings her to the table. He sits on the divan and takes a goblet. She pours a beverage for Conrad, who drinks, and says, "Sit here next to me" [B section, Ex. 6.26b].

Medora sits on the left side, on the edge of the divan [. . .]

Conrad hands her his cup and picks up a pitcher.

Medora lets herself fall down nonchalantly all over Conrad, while handing him her cup.

Conrad pours into the cup while lying down.

Medora rests herself completely on him while she drinks, then she sits up and puts her cup down.

Conrad starts taking her in his arms.

Medora escapes him, and places herself in front of the table, with her back to the audience [section A twice].

Conrad, still lying down, nonchalantly watches her.

Medora, placed between the audience and Conrad, dances with her back to the audience (section C). Traveling back and forth across the stage, she performs a series of *fouettés sautés*, *jetés* followed by *pas de bourrée en tournant*, *entrechat trois* in place. She runs and jumps *en attitude* onto the small table in front of the divan. Conrad "gets up briskly and seizes her by the hand; he contemplates her for a moment, and taking her by the waist, he picks her up *en attitude* and carries her over to his left" as Medora makes a *grand jeté attitude*. These last movements are performed as the refrain (section A) returns. Conrad sets Medora down on her right knee, then he "bends down over her and contemplates her."

Medora gets up, passes in front of him, picks up the cup from the table and gives it to Conrad.

Leaning both hands on his shoulder, she looks at him lovingly.

Conrad drinks, holding her by the waist.

Medora leaves him, runs downstage right.

Conrad immediately puts his cup down and runs to join her.

He supplicates her.

Medora puts her right hand on his shoulder [section A].

The key changes to E-flat major for section C, which contains choreography that survived into the twentieth century in Petipa's St. Petersburg production via Jules Perrot, as we will see in Chapter 7. (This includes what we call the "couch *cabriole*" that here Medora performs as she supports herself with her hands on the divan.)

Holding onto Conrad by the hand and shoulder, Medora travels backward upstage with a *piqué petit rond de jambe en l'air en dehors*, *jeté* ten times. Reaching the divan,

she passes quickly between the table and the divan.

Conrad remains on stage left against the divan.

Medora, with both her hands pressing on the back of the divan, does a *cabriole battu en arrière*.

Conrad quickly goes and sits on the divan.

Medora backs away immediately, shaking her head "No, no," bowing her head forward a little, and then comes back.

She does another *cabriole* and backs away immediately.

Conrad tries to catch her with his hands, extending his torso.

She repeats this sequence one more time—including the "couch *cabriole*"—and then performs a final enchaînement on the diagonal: *pas de bourrée en tournant, glissade, jeté en avant* four times, finishing with a *pas de basque* "en position." Conrad sits on the divan, admiring her. Thus ends the *Scène de la table*.

> [Passionate and tempestuous music.] Conrad gets up from the divan thinking, "Ah, she is lovely." He walks toward stage left.
>
> *Conrad*: "My head is burning, I am mad with love." He runs toward her. (heatedly) "Medora, you love me, do you not?"
>
> *Medora*: "Oh yes, I love you."
>
> *Conrad*: "Have mercy on me, come here" (he indicates the divan) "with me."
>
> *Medora*: "Me, there? Oh no, no."
>
> *Conrad*: "I beg you, come."
>
> Medora, feeling emotionally moved, does not respond.
>
> Conrad takes advantage of that, he takes her by the hand and waist and pulls her gently, showing her the sofa.
>
> Medora at first lets him lead her, then she resolutely says, "No, no," and she comes down stage.
>
> *Conrad*: "Are you running away from me? Oh I beg you, come back." He goes to her.
>
> Medora, one hand on her heart, does not know what to do.
>
> Conrad goes to seize her.
>
> Medora evades him and runs away upstage.
>
> Conrad follows her. He kneels: "Ah, I am at your feet."
>
> *Medora*: (barely speaking) "No."

Conrad gets up and goes to seize her by the waist from behind; he pulls her away, whispering to her with love. Medora resists weakly and tries to escape toward stage right. Conrad has seized her quickly and keeps pulling her away. Dizzily, she lets him take her and does not resist. Conrad, still holding her, passes between the table and the divan. He kisses her on the forehead and presses her against his heart. Medora sits down (on the divan) with her arms down, looking spent. Conrad gets on his knees, takes her hand, and kisses it passionately, keeping his lips on it, looking dazzled by his happiness.

Coming from the first wing, Lanquedem enters, leading a young woman who is holding a cushion bearing the flower that Birbanto has sprinkled with a narcotic (and we now hear the lotus music again, see Ex. 6.13). He points out Medora and Conrad to the young woman, but without being seen.

The young woman approaches Medora, who sees her, and goes toward her. Conrad sits down on the sofa; the young woman greets Medora and seems to say, "This is for you." Medora takes the flower from the young women and thanks her.

The young woman goes back to Lanquedem, who has watched the scene, hiding. The two of them leave.

Medora has come down stage right, looking at the flower. She says, "How pretty it is. I will give it to Conrad as a token of my love." She presses it to her heart and goes back up stage to Conrad. "Here, you see this flower, well I give it to you as well as my heart."

Ex. 6.31 The Pirates sneak up on Medora; Act One, Scene II, *Après la danse*, [*Modéré allegro*], bars 1–4

Conrad takes the flower, looks at it tenderly, covers it with kisses and presses it to his heart. Suddenly he feels light-headed; he brings his hands to his eyes and feels a bit better. Again he brings the flower to his lips, and falls sitting down as if stricken. He gets back up right away and seems to be blind.

Medora, surprised, says to Conrad, "What is wrong?" He comes back to his senses, but he is staggering. He smiles, saying "It is nothing, the wine and its vapors, my joy, my happiness." His head falls forward. Despite his best efforts, he cannot overcome his sleepiness. He slips into a lethargic slumber.

Medora, thinking her lover has merely gone to sleep, looks at him with tenderness, kneels down, and says, "I will keep guard over him." She takes his hand and presses it to her forehead.

Now, we hear sneaky and somewhat comical music that prefigures Arthur Sullivan (Ex. 6.31). Birbanto appears, wearing a black veil; he has watched the scene between Conrad and Medora. He makes a sign, and a man with a dagger enters. Soon, Medora realizes that several men have come in; she gets up and counts the men with her right hand—"one, two, three," and then a fourth, who comes from behind the tapestry and jumps over the divan (with the sleeping Conrad on it). She is frightened. The pirates walk slowly toward her, threatening her with the dagger.

Now the music turns threatening.

Medora: "What do you want?"

Birbanto: "I want you to leave and go far away from here."

Medora: "Me, go? Oh no."

Birbanto: "You refuse?"

Medora: "I refuse."

Birbanto: "Beware." He walks toward her.

Medora responds by running toward Conrad and trying (in vain) to wake him up. (Desperate minor-key music is heard.) The pirates are distracted by a noise and back off momentarily to look all around the stage. Medora suddenly remembers the tablets—she runs to get them and places them in Conrad's hands as he sleeps. Now the pirates come back to resume their threats to Medora.

Medora resolutely stands up and crosses her arms. Looking at the bandits with a challenging air, she walks toward them.

Birbanto backs up, as do the others, surprised by the boldness of this woman (they arrive downstage).

Medora: "Ah you want me to go away because you want to kill him, but I am watching over him, and if you come close, beware." She threatens them.

Birbanto and his men talk among themselves.

Birbanto: "Go away, I tell you."

Pirates: "Yes, she should leave."

Medora then runs to Conrad again; the pirates pursue her. Quick as lightning, she seizes Conrad's dagger, turns around and strikes a menacing pose toward the pirates.

The pirates stop short, surprised.

Medora: (not moving) "If you dare touch me, if you dare come close to him, the first one who does that will fall dead." (crossing her arms [in the "fierce defiance" pose]) "Ha! ha!" and walking upon them, "Go ahead and dare!"

The pirates at first back down.

Birbanto: (to all his men) "What, we are going to stay here, and let that woman [do what she wants]?"

Medora listens to them.

Birbanto: "Come on, no more fear, let us strike."

Medora then stabs Birbanto in the arm; he cries out in pain and holds his arm; the pirates surround him and dress his wound. (Note that she does not recognize this veiled man as Birbanto.)

Medora sees what she has done, looks at the dagger, sees it is covered with blood, and throws it away in horror (Ex. 6.14b). Then in a twist that may be another attempt at antisemitic humor (or a device to increase the number of angry outbursts in this scene), Medora sees Lanquedem and says to him, "Wretch, you are the cause of all this." Lanquedem does not know what to say.

Now, with new resolve, Birbanto orders the pirates to kill Medora—since "she doesn't want to go away"—and to kill the sleeping Conrad, too. The pirates run toward the couple, daggers drawn. Medora begs them to spare his life.

Birbanto: "Well, go away then, and he will not die."

Medora, almost dragging herself on her knees and holding onto Birbanto, begs him to let her [stay].

Birbanto: (going toward stage right) "It is useless, never, never."

Birbanto orders his men to carry her out and kill Conrad. After Medora has been taken away, the pirates run toward Conrad, daggers raised. Conrad stirs. The pirates, thinking he is waking up, run away in terror.

End of the act

The curtain falls

Act Two

Scene III: The Pasha's palace on the Isle of Cos, in the garden of the harem

In the Justamant manual, there is little indication of stage setting other than a cushion on the floor near each downstage corner.[93]

Pas des odalisques. The curtain rises on bar 9 as the fortissimo beginning gives way to a sweet and very feminine-sounding melody played by strings and accompanied by harp.[94] Eighteen odalisques (harem women) are configured in various small groups, dancing.

To a sprightly $\frac{2}{4}$ in G major, a Mlle Marie dances a first variation followed by a Mlle Ferena, who performs a second variation, an equally sprightly $\frac{2}{4}$ in B-flat major.

As the harp introduces the next dance, Zulmea, the favorite Sultana, comes in, followed by her maid. She looks at the dancers with hauteur and disdain, and tells them, "Continue your dances. I want you to dance, and I am the mistress here." She then proceeds to stage left, again followed by her maid; she sits down on a cushion while her maid remains standing.

The music that follows—renowned now as the lilting entrée of the *Pas de trois des odalisques* in the St. Petersburg production (see Chapter 7)—was the final section of the opening set of dances in the third scene (Ex. 6.32). As Zulmea looks on, four second *danseuses* begin, dancing in unison in a single row.[95] After twenty-four bars, they are joined by the sixteen women of the corps de ballet, who remain to the end of the dance. The ensemble is grouped into two triangular formations on either side of the stage: in front of an upstage row of five corps women is a second row of three corps women. A pair of second *danseuses* forms the apex of each triangle. Eventually the groupings dissolve and the ensemble fills the entire stage in rows. At the end of the dance, the corps and second *danseuses* form two lines at center, creating a column in anticipation of Gulnare's entrance.

Zulmea's maid goes toward the top of the stage; she sees Gulnare coming and runs through the column of dancers to her mistress to tell her so.

Gulnare enters from upstage center, traveling downstage within the column, performing *pas de bourrée couru, grand jeté en avant* four times (Ex. 6.3). Arriving downstage, she continues with *glissade, failli, piqué de côté, battement degagé devant* four times to alternate sides. She finishes her entrance with *pas de bourrée en tournant, glissade, pas de basque.*

As the other dancers gather around, Zulmea stands up and walks toward Gulnare, and says "You ladies, do not forget that I am the only one who gives commands here."

Gulnare bows ironically; Zulmea tells her to bow again. She complies by bowing mockingly, and her women join her in doing so (Ex. 6.3, bars 12–13). They then refuse Zulmea's orders to get back to their dancing.

The Eunuch enters slowly at the back of the stage in a stilted movement style all his own ("like an automaton"). To Zulmea's dismay, Gulnare and her group take his presence

---

[93] The original Paris libretto describes the setting thus: "The Pasha's palace in the Isle of Cos. The baths of the Pasha's women, in the middle of magnificent gardens.—The view of the baths is obscured by immense draperies." But Justamant writes: "At the Opera, the décor for the second tableau [meaning Act Two] has no fountain and no bath as the brochure [libretto] shows. It is simply a garden."

[94] We are making the assumption that the curtain rises at bar 9 because Justamant says the curtain rises "at the end of the first motif"; the first phrase is eight bars long.

[95] Justamant: "N.B. at the Opera, it is two ladies who begin, on the front—then two others join the first, and Zulmea's entrance with the maidservant follows."

Ex. 6.32 *Pas des odalisques*; Act Two, No. 1, bars 104–112

Ex. 6.33a The Eunuch enters; Act Two, No. 2, bars 27–34

as an opportunity for more open displays of rebellion against the established order of the harem. They brashly laugh at the Eunuch, who to the sounds of stodgy music makes his way downstage "very slowly and with an impassive face" (Ex. 6.33a).

Then Gulnare approaches him from behind, tapping him on the shoulder, and when he whirls in the direction of the tapping, Gulnare turns away so that he cannot see her. She does it again. Soon (to whirling music that provides an aural version of being besieged from all sides, Ex. 6.33b) all of the women in her group are surrounding him, mockingly supplicating, petting him, pinching him.

Soon thereafter, one can hear the sound of the Pasha's approaching entourage. The Eunuch, relieved, says, "Ha, ha, the master is coming, now you will see." Zulmea says, "Here he comes, and we shall see."

The Pasha enters, preceded by guards and followed by lords. Holding a staff in his right hand, he makes his way downstage, center; the Head Eunuch bows low to him, almost to the ground. Zulmea, too, bows to the Pasha, and tells him that "all these ladies," and especially Gulnare, refuse to obey her, even though she is the mistress.

The Pasha calls the ladies to him, and upbraids them, but Gulnare laughs. He asks her to bow to Zulmea; she refuses.

Pasha: (bending over to look her under the nose) "But I wish it."

Gulnare, looking him also under the nose, advances on him; he backs up, very surprised. She says, "Well I do not [want to]."

Ex. 6.33b The women tease the Eunuch; Act Two, No. 2, bars 34–41

Gulnare goes back to her place.

The Pasha, surprised at first, walks toward her, thinking to himself, "That is too much."

Gulnare quickly moves to the other side [so that he is to her right in the weak position].

Now he is angry: he takes his cane with both hands to strike her.

Gulnare delights the Pasha with her dancing. To the sounds of a piquant polka, Gulnare answers by performing *rond de jambe en dehors* (presumably *en l'air*) four times in a row and "putting her *pointe* on the ground" (Ex. 6.4a). Surprised, the Pasha looks at her, and on her fourth *rond de jambe* goes to the other side saying, "Ta, ta, ta, ta," a sound of disapproval.

Gulnare repeats the step with her other foot. Still surprised, the Pasha looks at her says, "But what?" Gulnare dances away from him. Impatient, the Pasha raises his arms (Ex. 6.4b). As Gulnare continues to dance, she forces him to step backward until they arrive at center. He strikes the ground with his cane, but Gulnare simply makes him back up some more. She moves away again, traveling upstage on the diagonal with *jeté en tournant, ballonné, piqué en arabesque croisé* three times. The Pasha follows her movements with interest. She returns to him with *pas de bourrée couru, jeté en avant* twice, moves away with *fouetté sauté, jeté* twice. The Pasha takes a step toward her, and she returns with the same steps as before.

Heading upstage left—the Pasha follows her movements more than ever, looking pleased—Gulnare begins a final diagonal of four *piqué tours en dehors* separated by *glissades* and finishes with a choice of *pirouette* or *pas de basque*. The Pasha, in the heat of the moment, starts swinging his legs as if he were dancing.

Delighted with her grace, the Pasha approaches Gulnare to compliment her: "You are charming, delicious." He looks at her sideways and—this bit is added in pencil—he offers her the head of Eunuch, which she presumably refuses.

Now Zulmea is furious; Gulnare laughs at Zulmea's anger; Zulmea throws herself upon Gulnare, saying, "I am going to strangle her," and the Pasha stops her. Gulnare, laughing, hides behind the Pasha. Zulmea says, "Go to the devil!" and exits.

The handkerchief scene. The Pasha looks at Gulnare, clearly finding her charming. He says to himself, "Well, let's do what we must do," and he takes his handkerchief and throws it to Gulnare, saying, "Here, that is for you."

Gulnare infuriates him by disdainfully refusing the handkerchief. She throws it to the next lady and runs away. Several ladies now toss it from one to the next; they all run away one by one, as the Pasha, chasing after his handkerchief, saying to each lady, "No, no, no, no."

The handkerchief gets into the hands of the maid just as the Pasha gets close to her. He makes an awful face and moves quickly away as if he had seen nothing. But the maid, thrilled by the honor, jumps for joy. She follows the Pasha wherever he goes as he tries to get away from her. He pushes her away with his cane, and she goes to stage right still jumping for joy.

Zulmea has come back onstage.

Zulmea goes to [the Pasha] and tells him, "So, how did you like this?"

The Pasha recovers and takes her hand; he leads her downstage.

Zulmea: (walking along) "That served you right."

Pasha: "Oh, do not worry, I will get back to all these little minxes, and from now on you will be the queen and mistress here."

Zulmea: (happy) "For sure?"

Pasha: "I give you my word."

Lanquedem and Medora arrive. The scene opens as a little slave approaches the Pasha, pulls at his robes (to get his attention), bows to him, and tells him that someone wants to see him. With impatience the Pasha tells him to let the visitor in; the slave boy runs away toward where he had come from.

Now Lanquedem arrives as his musical motif from Act One, Scene II, recurs (see Ex. 6.12). He is leading Medora by the hand. She is veiled and her hands are in chains; a few men are following her. They remain upstage. Lanquedem greets the Pasha, who recognizes him and raises his cane to strike him. But Lanquedem steps back and says, "Wait, wait, first look at this woman I am bringing to you." He removes the veil from Medora's face, and the Pasha cries out: "It is she!—the one they took away from me. In chains, dear God."

With emotion, he removes her chains and throws them away, falls to his knees, and says, "How on earth, by what adventure did you end up here?" He stands up. Zulmea is looking at Medora with curiosity.

Ex. 6.34 The ladies sympathize with Medora; Act Two, No. 3, bars 81–84

Medora walks in front of the Pasha to his right [a power move], quickly takes the dagger from his belt and goes to strike Lanquedem with it. The Pasha runs and stops her; Lanquedem steps back, terrified. The Pasha takes the dagger back from her.

Now Medora, "all dreamy looking," sits on the cushions and looks like she is thinking.

The music switches to a sweet, gently rocking B-flat major *andante* (the main motif of which brings to mind the second movement of Beethoven's Symphony no. 6; Ex. 6.34).[96]

Gulnare returns with all the ladies, entering from all sides, and they come downstage to have a good look at the newcomer. They ask among themselves, "Who is she? Where does she come from?" Gulnare circles Medora while looking her over; the ladies do the same, and exclaim to each other, "She is so pretty!"

Medora cannot contain herself and bursts into tears.

All: "Oh, she is crying," they go to her and take her by the hand and bring her to the center of the stage. [Perhaps the sweetness of the music is meant to reflect the sense of sweet sisterhood that arises once the women's sympathy for Medora has been aroused.]

Meanwhile, the Pasha is telling the Eunuch that Medora will be his wife (in a conversation that may take place during the B section of the *andante*).

Eunuch: "My congratulations to you."

Pasha: "I feel like showing her how handsome I am, especially my waist, because I am madly in love with her."

Eunuch: "You are right."

The Pasha hands him the cane and has the Eunuch help him take off his dolman [jacket].

The two separate conversations continue. The women ask Gulnare why she is crying; they sympathize when she tells them that she has been taken far away by force from the one she loves. Gulnare pledges to protect her and says, "We will join forces [with you]

---

[96] In the passage leading up to this pastoral-sounding *andante*, some listeners might hear momentary allusions to the first movement of Beethoven's Third Symphony (the new theme in the development) and to the second movement of his Ninth Symphony. (Listen to Bonynge, *Le Corsaire*, disc two, track four, titled "Act 2: Action.") Perhaps Adam was paying a playful, private homage to Beethoven in this part of the ballet, which he composed in the summer of 1855.

against the Pasha." Meanwhile, the Pasha continues admiring himself and talking to the Eunuch, who agrees that his master is looking very good.

Now the Pasha dispatches the Eunuch to bring in some gifts, walks toward Medora and tells the women: "Listen to me, this is the one my heart has chosen, the one who will be in command here."

Gulnare: (with irony) "Never mind; she will not love you any more than I do."

Pasha: (walking in front of Gulnare) "We'll see about that."

The Eunuch returns, followed by little slaves bringing expensive-looking boxes.

Meanwhile, we see a caravan in the background, going from stage right to stage left. Medora rejects the gifts, declares that she is giving them to the ladies, and goes back to sit at stage right. Gulnare laughs and goes to take Medora's place. Now she, too, rejects the gifts, and starts pushing the boxes away with her foot. The little slaves take the boxes away; the ladies laugh at the Pasha (the music providing the laugh track). The Pasha is furious.

The caravan arrives. Justamant's drawing shows, at the back of the stage, sixteen dervishes walking two by two, as well as "two Arab horsemen on their horses, then some slaves following the caravan." In Justamant's drawing, one may also see two camels. Of the camel in the Paris production, one critic wrote:

> This camel completes the illusion. He is the domestic animal of the Koran and of Arab tales. All the sacred and fabulous figures of the East are seated on this bizarre chimera of the sands of mirage. Wherever he appears, he evokes around him the palm tree, the tent, the well, the oasis and the vigil with the stars, asleep by the story of the storyteller, and the pewter dome of the distant mosque, greeted in the whiteness of dawn by the cries and ablutions of prostrate pilgrims. I don't know what supernumeraries can fit into the Corsair's camel, but whoever this one is, he plays it wonderfully, he is pensive, he is ascetic . . .; he carries his bump with exemplary seriousness.[97]

The head dervish has been walking with slow, measured steps, head down, hands crossed on his chest (Ex. 6.8). The Pasha goes toward him and bends over to better see his face. Soon, the Dervish falls to his knees and asks the Pasha for hospitality; his request is granted.

The Pasha notices with glee that the Dervish is unnerved by the sight of four women who curiously bend over to get a good look at him. What follows is a scene in which the Pasha amuses himself by exposing the holy men to the forbidden sight of attractive females.

After the Dervish gives Gulnare a handkerchief to place over her shoulders for the sake of modesty, Gulnare walks "like a holy woman" but with a big smile on her face. (Presumably, no such comical scene ridiculing Roman Catholic nuns or priests would have been allowed at the Opéra.) The Pasha snatches the handkerchief off her shoulders from behind, laughing. The Dervish then kneels down, facing the audience, saying "We all pray to heaven for protection."

[97] Saint-Victor, *La Presse*, 27 January 1856.

Ex. 6.35a *Pas du Derviche*; Act Two, No. 4, bars 2–6

.To further embarrass the Dervishes, the Pasha proposes a dance (the music livens at this point as Adam introduces a bright, staccato *allegro* in F major), and he takes Medora by the hand to lead her to the middle of the stage. At first she refuses to dance. But then the Dervish furtively reveals himself to be Conrad in disguise! Medora can scarcely control her urge to embrace her lover. Now, "blissfully happy," she gladly accepts the Pasha's request for her to dance.

Scene and dance of the Dervish, the Pasha, and Medora. Mazilier's ability to deftly weave dance and narrative together is no more apparent than in this skillful and humorous *pas d'action* comprising several dances (No. 4 in the Paris score; "Scène et pas du Derviche du pacha et de Medora" in Justamant's manual).

As a jaunty, quirky tune commences, the Pasha makes sure to flaunt his coziness with the women of his harem by standing at center as four second danseuses dance around him, two of them briefly posing *en attitude* as they rest on a hand on his shoulders (Ex. 6.35a).[98] Next, standing in a row, with the Pasha at its center, the dancers hold each other by the shoulder as the five of them travel downstage, the women performing a series, three times, of two *petits glissades*, *brisé*, and three *jetés*. They leave the Pasha downstage and return up the diagonal with a series of *jetés en tournant*.

The music of the subsequent "variation de Medora," well-known today as the third variation in the St. Petersburg *Pas de trois des odalisques* (see Chapter 7), is a tutti *fortissimo*—large-scale, even triumphant (Ex. 6.35b). Justamant's notations for this number feature the rare and extraordinary collection of variants mentioned above (p. 375): the first is "the one Rosati dances in Paris," the second is de Vecchi's version as danced in Lyon, and the third is for Dor (Justamant does not indicate where she performed this role). We assume the two subsequent variants on Rosati's original were made to both highlight the particular gifts of de Vecchi and Dor and to distinguish them from Rosati.

Rosati. Traveling on the diagonal from upstage left, Rosati begins with a series of *grand rond de jambe fouetté en tournant, brisé, grand temps de flèche* four times. She circles the stage with "jetés ordinaire" and comes down the opposite diagonal with *grand saut de basque, grand jeté, glissade* to the knee, the body leaned back, the arms in fourth position, four times. More *jetés ordinaire* bring Rosati upstage center where she kneels and says, "Everybody, and me, let us give ourselves up to pleasure."

De Vecchi. Both de Vecchi's and Dor's variants utilize repeats in the score and are thus slightly longer than Rosati's. De Vecchi performs the same opening diagonal as Rosati but circles the stage with *piqué en arabesque* and three *petits jetés ordinaire* four times. Her second diagonal features *temps levés sur la pointe* and *piqués en attitude*. She returns

---

[98] Justamant writes, "N.B. The dance of the dervish is danced in Paris by six ladies, two at the side of the pasha, and four in front."

Ex. 6.35b *Pas du Derviche*; Act Two, No. 4 (*variation de Medora*), bars 31–38

upstage as Rosati had, but then travels directly down center with a series of *sissonnes en tournant* and *relevés à la seconde*. She concludes the variation with three turns on *pointe*, *brisé*, *pas de basque*.

Dor. A note by Justamant is our only indication of Dor's variant, which is nearly the same as de Vecchi's. The only difference is that, in the penultimate enchaînement, after the *sissonne en tournant*, Dor adds a turn to her *relevé à la seconde*, rendering it a *relevé à la seconde en tournant*.

The extended final number of the dance suite begins with the four women dancing together in a row, set to a skittering *allegretto* $\frac{2}{4}$ in G major played by strings and flute. The women are briefly joined once again by the Pasha, who then invites Medora to approach him at center. She comes, followed by the Dervish.

In a bit of mischief, "the ladies quickly have the Pasha turn his back to the audience so he will not see the dervish." Justamant writes, "N.B. During those movements, the Dervish and Medora have been making signs to each other, while also keeping an eye on the Pasha." After some stepping from side to side and jockeying for position—the women trying to keep the Pasha from seeing the Dervish and Medora, who are purposely staying out of step with the Pasha—"the Dervish leans over and says a couple of words to Medora, who listens." As the music abruptly stops, following three *fortissimo* chords,

> The Pasha immediately leaves the ladies, turns around, takes the Dervish by the waist and places him to his right [the weaker position], then bending over a little, he goes and stands right next to Medora.

> Medora, thinking it is her lover, turns around, opening her arms to wrap them around his neck. [But] seeing the Pasha's face, she lifts her head away to the left. She puts her right hand on the Pasha's shoulder, then her left hand between her left cheek and the Pasha's face [to show that she is resisting him].

> The Pasha is holding her by the waist with his left hand.

Medora keeps her left hand on her left cheek to protect her from the Pasha's nearby face—a purposely awkward and melodramatic position—while at the same time dancing sixteen bars as the opening tune of the suite returns (see Ex. 6.35a).

Her steps include *petits ronds de jambe* and *petits battements*. She finally breaks away from the Pasha with *pas de basque*. The women take the Pasha upstage and dance around him as the orchestra swells to a *fortissimo* reprise of the same opening melody. Meanwhile, "the two lovers keep making almost imperceptible signs to each other."

A final coda passage begins in the score, featuring upward, rushing motives that suggest the desperation of the Pasha to reach Medora.

The Pasha leaves the ladies and hurries to Medora.

The Dervish goes back upstage.

The Pasha takes Medora to center, all cheerful and animated. He gets to his knees and kisses her hands.

The Dervish throws all manner of insults at him and runs to him, cursing him.

The Dervish comes up behind the Pasha and, in a comical choreographic expression of dominance, reaches over his head, takes Medora's hands, and assists her as she jumps and makes continual *cabrioles derrière* in a circle around the Pasha, who leans forward and, turning, looks into Medora's face as she is literally swung around him (and the Pasha is still not seeing the Dervish!). The other women dance joyously in pairs upstage of these shenanigans. The Dervish quickly takes his place among the four women, who move him upstage, as Medora moves stage left. The Pasha follows, takes her by the hand, and has her pass in front of him to center (the weaker position).

Justamant's drawing of the final group shows that the Dervish rushes back to Medora, who is supported in an *arabesque* by the Pasha. She leans her elbow on the Dervish's shoulder. The four women also pose in *arabesque*, upstage of the trio.

After the Pas du Derviche. At the beginning of No. 5 ("Final" in the Paris score), the Pasha is delighted and tells the Eunuch to take Medora up to his chambers. But Medora resists. The Dervish (Conrad) then makes a sign and takes off his monks' robes, his beard, and his hat. All the other dervishes (pirates) do the same and run toward the guards. A melee follows: The eunuch and the guard try to take Medora away by force; Birbanto, armed with his yatagan, strikes the guard and saves Medora. Now the Pasha sees Conrad for the first time and backs away from him.

Conrad: "Ha, you weren't expecting me, were you, now?"

Medora runs to throw herself into her lover's arms.

The ladies run away in all directions, chased by the pirates. [. . .]

[Gulnare approaches Conrad and asks for protection.]

Gulnare: "Ah, mercy, save me from this man who wants to take me. Protect me!"

Conrad: "Fear not, my men and I are fighting the Pasha, but not the women, and I take you under my protection."

Birbanto wants to say something, "But . . ."

Conrad: "Silence, and get out, get away from here."

Now Medora, seeing Birbanto, seems struck by a resemblance; he reminds her of something that happened; she cannot take her eyes off him. Birbanto goes back upstage slowly, saying to himself, "Oh well, it will have to end someday." Medora keeps watching him, examining him from head to toe and following his movements. She is realizing that Birbanto is the man who, wearing a veil, abducted her from the grotto!

She goes to Conrad and tells him the whole story of what transpired after he had been drugged by the lotus flower. The orchestra follows her closely, repeating the music of the original kidnapping scene as she narrates it (including the Lotus music, Ex. 6.13, and the music that sounds when Birbanto and his men creep into the room, Ex. 6.31).

> *Medora*: "Conrad, do you remember when you were taking me where you live, I gave you a flower and you kissed it, and suddenly you fell asleep. I stayed near you, on my knees, to watch over your sleep." (She kneels in the position she had held in the table scene of the 2nd tableau.)[99]
>
> "When I heard a noise, I stood up" (she stands up and turns upon herself on the left, with her back to the audience) "Great God!" She raises her arms and completes the turn, "I saw some men with a veil over their faces, then another" (she points to stage left), "I counted them" (she counts while walking with her back to the audience), "1, 2, 3 then a 4th, all of them armed. I was about to faint.
>
> I asked them what they wanted. One of them told me they wanted me to go away. I refused, because they wanted to kill you. I quickly wrote upon the tablets that I put in your hands, and taking your dagger, I stabbed his arm. When I saw the blood my heart grew faint, I begged them to let me stay with you and they refused. I collapsed, exhausted, and they put a gag on me and kidnapped me and took me away."

Conrad asks if she would be able to recognize her attacker. She points at Birbanto ("le voilà"); he denies everything. Conrad believes Birbanto's sworn denials until Medora recalls the wound she had inflicted on the veiled attacker. Sure enough, when she unrolls Birbanto's sleeve, the wound is visible.

> Birbanto is floored, and furious.
>
> Conrad, crazed with anger, to Birbanto, "It was true! Ah, wretched man, kneel in front of your victim!"
>
> Birbanto, turning to Medora, makes gestures of taking her and crushing her with his hands.
>
> Medora looks at him with a proud defiance.
>
> Conrad, even angrier, with a terrible look in his eyes, "Here, I tell you! Kneel right here!"
>
> Birbanto, mesmerized by his master's look, with his head between his hands, cries out, "Ah, well, yes," (going to Conrad) "it was I."

---

[99] Notably, in Justamant's manual, the penciled addition of the music staff and E-flat major key signature matches the revisions made by Delibes for the 1867 Paris revival, suggesting that Justamant may have revised his manual accordingly (see Chapter 8).

He kneels in front of Conrad.

Conrad briskly takes a pistol out of his belt, cocks it.

Medora looks at him with fear.

Conrad is about to shoot, but Medora tells him to spare Birbanto's life. Conrad tells him to "get away from here."

Birbanto quickly stands up and leaves, giving Conrad a furious look, filled with a desire for revenge.

Now Medora is overcome by emotion; she falls to her knees. Conrad and Gulnare take care of her. She puts her arms around Conrad's neck tenderly, and then steps away to thank the heavens for saving her lover.

The night is turning darker. Now Birbanto comes back, with guards, and takes advantage of this opportunity to abduct Medora. When Conrad tries to save her, he "finds a barrier of guns pointed at him." He turns to the other side and finds the same thing.

Now the Pasha arrives on the scene and is pleased to see that Conrad has been caught. He orders the guards to shoot Conrad on the spot. Gulnare pleads for mercy and calls for the ladies to come. Gulnare and the ladies all fall to their knees to supplicate the Pasha. In the background men with torches pass by, near the gardens. Bengal flames finish the tableau.

Act Three

Scene IV: The Pasha's apartment in an elegant Summer Palace

The window shows a view of the sea. An immense door at the back of the stage.[100]

According to Justamant's drawing, the stage area is walled in on three sides with a central opening in each wall (doors and windows in the Byzantine style). The openings at stage right and left are curtained; a staircase leads to a small door upstage left. A bell, on top of a small table, is downstage left. A bed, covered with a tasseled cloth, is situated at midstage right.

This scene features the least amount of dancing in the whole ballet: only a *scène dansante* for Medora and the Pasha.

Action scene: Conrad's death sentence; Gulnare hatches a scheme. The Pasha is sitting on his bed, and he appears to be thinking. Four dignitaries stand nearby in a row, awaiting his resolution. Now the Pasha gets up and declares to the dignitaries, "She must be my wife or Conrad must die." They bow and depart, and soon the Eunuch brings Medora in, and then leaves.

---

[100] This description, from the original Paris libretto (1856), matches up reasonably well with the drawing in Justamant, which depicts only one opening at the back of the stage without disclosing what is the view through that opening.

Pasha: (firmly) "Listen, you will be my wife, you will share my throne, or the one you love will die."

Medora: "I, your wife? Never."

Some soldiers, each with a gun on his shoulder, pass two-by-two behind the door in the back.

The Pasha approaches Medora, "There, look, it is your lover that they are taking to be executed."

The Pasha allows Medora the chance to speak with Conrad about the Pasha's proposal. He dispatches the soldiers, and leaves Medora and Conrad alone.

The door in the back closes.

Conrad and Medora fall into each other's arms and come downstage a little.

Medora: (with tears in her eyes) "So you are going to die, alas."

Conrad: "You are crying, dear one, ah, do not regret anything about me, I die, it is true, but I take your love away with me and that is my consolation."

Medora: "Ha, however, if you wanted it, you could escape death."

Conrad: "How?"

Medora: "If I agree to marry the pasha, you will go free."

Conrad: (indignant) "My freedom, at the price of your hand, no, never, never, [better] a thousand times death rather than seeing you in his arms."

Medora: "Death, then, but let us die together." They throw themselves in each other's arms.

All of a sudden, to the sounds of a happy cornet solo, Gulnare pokes her head through the doorway in the back. Conrad and Medora are surprised; they go upstage a little.

Gulnare comes down to them, after closing the door behind her.

Conrad and Medora: "What is going on?"

Gulnare: "I was listening, and I found a way to save you both."

Conrad AND *Medora*: "How?"

Gulnare: "First, you [Conrad] must stay alive, and you Medora must accept the Pasha's hand."

Conrad AND *Medora*: "Never, never."

But Gulnare smiles and whispers into Medora's ear, and then Conrad's. Medora listens with joy and says, "Oh, yes!" Conrad listens, and "something flashes in his eyes." They both agree to Gulnare's plan.

Now a pompous march in minor key is sounded. The door opens and the Pasha enters with two pistols in his belt and a dagger, and four guards. "The way he behaves shows that he is afraid of Conrad," according to Justamant. The Pasha approaches Medora and asks if Conrad shall live or die. The music changes to reflect the ensuing three-way conversation, with bits of melody in different ranges to reflect different voices.

Conrad: "I cannot fight with you, my love, and my life is not worth a throne. I accept that he will marry you and I resign myself."

Medora: "And I do, too."

The Pasha, filled with joy, turns toward the soldiers and says, "Ah, finally she made her decision."

As Gulnare congratulates the Pasha, Conrad secretly signals to Medora that at midnight he will return and come in "through this window" (presumably he indicates the window) and take her away with him. The Pasha orders a soldier to remove Conrad's chains; Conrad departs, a free man. Gulnare takes Medora by the hand and leads her to her chambers; the two are chatting as they walk.

After the soldiers have departed, the music changes: we now hear trumpet calls followed by a somewhat silly march. The happy Pasha goes to strike a little bell that sits on the small table, walks to midstage, and dances for joy, all alone. Then, after the women come in (presumably summoned by the bell), he tells them that he is getting married, and dances again briefly. His servants give boxes of gifts to the ladies, who open them to find "necklaces, bracelets, and fabrics; they show them to one another and find them beautiful."

The wedding ceremony. The dignitaries enter first, followed by two priests bearing a tripod, already lit up; a high priest, who remains behind the tripod; three more priests, one of them carrying the Bible; the Eunuch and some others (Ex. 6.9). When all the participants are in their places for the ceremony: Tableau.

The Pasha emerges from his chambers. Gulnare comes in from the other side, with two attendants; from time to time she lifts a corner of her veil and shows her face to the audience, then lowers it immediately. (Three blasts from the wind and strings in the orchestra were surely intended to reflect these veil-liftings.)

Now the Pasha, downstage with his back to the audience, takes Gulnare by the hand and leads her upstage toward the tripod. They kneel; the high priest prays to the heavens for the couple; crossing his arms in front of his chest, he turns to the Bible and reads from it. He bends over, and repeats that movement two or three times, then he tells the couple to stand, and they exchange rings.

The priest proclaims, "By the Koran and the heavens, you are now wed." The Pasha is delighted, and walks a few steps downstage, holding Gulnare's hand.

Addressing everyone, [the Pasha] shows Gulnare [and says], "From now on she is the queen of this palace." Then turning his back to the audience and talking to all present, "You can leave now."

Everyone leaves in silence: the guards, the priests, the ministers, and the ladies.

The Pasha follows them, thanking them.

Gulnare takes advantage of that moment to call Medora.

Medora enters, veiled like Gulnare.

Gulnare quickly runs into the chambers.

All the doors close.

Scène dansante: The wedding night encounter between the Pasha and Medora. Mazilier combines dance and action again in this *scène dansante*, during which Medora expertly disarms the Pasha, both literally and figuratively.

Accompanied by soft strings, the Pasha, looking at Medora, comes downstage. "Finally, she is alone with me, she belongs to me." He is delighted. He removes her veil and, stepping back a little, cries, "She is even more beautiful."

Suddenly the music perks up. A waltz introduction, punctuated by periodic accented bursts, conveys the Pasha's excitement and ardor. He goes to take Medora, who steps back and seems terrified.

Pasha: "What is wrong?"

Medora: "The sight of your dagger scares me."

Pasha: (smiling) "That is what it is." He removes it from his belt and gives it to her. "Here it is."

Medora takes it and with her eyes, says, "That is one."

She puts the belt down on the little table and begins to dance to a beguiling waltz, traveling across the front of the stage and back to the Pasha (Ex. 6.36).

The Pasha goes to her, giddy with happiness. He falls at her feet: "Ah, cruel woman, have mercy on me, I love you, I am mad about you."

Medora only smiles at him.

The Pasha stands up and partners Medora in a *tour de promenade* as she holds an *arabesque*. She holds her hand in front of her cheek to shield her face from her suitor, who leans forward as though trying to kiss her. Next, he supports her in another arabesque as she leans away, again using her arms to distance herself from the Pasha.

Ex. 6.36 *Scène dansante*; Act Three, Scene IV, *Suite de 4ieme tableau*, bars 26–33

Medora retreats upstage center. The Pasha follows, intending to seize her. Medora seems to want to caress him. She puts both hands around his neck and then rests her right elbow on his shoulder. The Pasha looks at her amorously.

They go downstage and Medora makes her next move. Posing *en attitude*, she removes a pistol from the Pasha's belt. He sees nothing. She does the same to remove his second pistol. She moves away, and the pasha tries to approach her, but Medora stops him in his tracks by aiming both pistols at him.

The Pasha puts his hands in front of his face and moves out of her line of fire, saying, "No, no, not that game." Medora plays along, still aiming at him and following the Pasha's movements when he goes upstage or down. Finally, she puts the pistols on the table and gets ready to dance. The Pasha breathes a sigh of relief.

Finally, after completely bewitching the Pasha with her dance, Medora kneels in front of him and says, "Ah, let's get wildly drunk." She surreptitiously glances at the window.

The pasha goes to seize her and she dances away from him, performing a final diagonal of *coupé, grand jeté en avant en tournant* four times and a *pas de basque* to finish.

The rescue. The Pasha, quite crazed now, cannot contain himself; he says, "This is it," and tells Medora that she must yield to his wishes. Horrified, she backs up. Seizing her by force, he pulls her toward the bed. She is overpowered, and the Pasha wants to push her onto the bed. Medora quickly gets her scarf.

"Hurry" music begins. The Pasha extends his hands to seize Medora; she takes his hands, and with a smile quickly ties them with her scarf. She is listening to the clock chiming. The Pasha doesn't resist at first, but then feels she is tying his hands too tightly and he falls at her knees. She coos at him and keeps looking at the window.

Suddenly the window opens, and Conrad appears. Medora cries out joyfully. The Pasha sees Conrad and stands up, shaking with fear and anger. He tries to break the bonds that bind his hands.

Conrad tells Medora to "come, quickly"; she runs toward him but then remembers the pistols; she runs to retrieve them. The Pasha, who has now freed his hands, approaches Medora. She points both pistols at his chest; "horrified, [he] backs up in fear, his heart filled with rage." She goes upstage walking backward, still aiming the pistols at the Pasha. But as she turns around to go up the stairs to the window, he runs in her direction. Now, she has reached the window and is next to Conrad. She aims the pistols at the pasha again. Dizzy and afraid, he falls backward on his bed. At that moment, Conrad disappears with Medora and closes the window.

The Pasha gets up from the bed and runs to the table, where he strikes the bell vigorously. Then he walks to center stage and all the doors open. Many people run in from every entrance, asking, "What is happening?" The Pasha, outraged, indicates the window and runs to it. Gulnare, covered with a veil, comes in from her chambers. The Pasha opens the window frantically and exclaims: "They are abducting my wife!"

Gulnare lifts her veil and says, "I am your wife, here is your ring." Stunned with surprise and rage, the Pasha refuses to recognize her. He is losing his mind; he cannot see; he cries, "Give me some air"; he suffocates and falls to the ground. Two dignitaries lift him up halfway; he falls again, suffocating.

Gulnare, showing her ring to everyone, tells them she is the queen and mistress. The women kneel down. Tableau. The curtain falls.

[End of Act Three, Scene IV]

(Justamant notes that the ship should be in place with only the foreground of the stage set up and ready to go.)

Before finishing our scene-by-scene account with Act Three, Scene V, let us pause to have a look at Justamant's detailed instructions for the machinists and the light operator responsible for the movements of the ship, manipulation of various curtains, and implementation of atmospheric lighting (and lightning strikes) that together achieved the effect of the magnificent storm and shipwreck that thrilled audiences and brought *Le Corsaire* to its stunning close. We list these instructions now (instead of placing them after the final curtain, as Justamant did in his manual).

Movements for the maneuver of the ship

No. 1   The trestles are removed, the sea gets more agitated

No. 2   The ship is rocked gently at first, then more and more until the end

No. 3   They get and attach the thread for the lightning

No. 4   The strips of water gradually rise

No. 5   The cloud at the forefront is lowered and the horizon background goes higher

No. 6   The ship starts going down while rocking, as soon as he [Conrad] sits down

No. 7   Lightning strikes (explosive sounds)

No. 8   Everyone exits the ship, the rails are taken down and they get the wires ready to lift up the large piece of fabric
The gauze curtains are lowered

No. 9   The ship's masts go down

No. 10   The ship is covered with the large piece of fabric

No. 11   The gauze curtains are lifted one after the other, the strips of water go down to their holding space

No. 13   The electrical light
The sea is continually agitated

For the light operator: Lightning lights up the sky after the horizon curtain is removed and until the end.

Act Three

Scene V: On board the ship

Justamant's drawing depicts the gentle waves of the sea covering the entirety of the stage. The audience is given a port-side view of the ship, which features two masts, two large sails, rigging, and a flag at the stern. The deck is filled with men and women.

At curtain-up, the audience hears an *andante sostenuto* in E-flat major that begins with ten bars of swelling tutti chords. The glorious sight of the pirate vessel in the ocean, however, is not seen at curtain-up, for a second curtain—looking like a cloud—is hiding it. Soon, as the audience is watching the cloud, the music switches to a $\frac{6}{8}$ that opens with a highly effective musical representation of slow rolling waves in a vast sea (Ex. 6.16). After sixteen bars, this cloud lifts to reveal the ship at last.

Ex. 6.37 Relaxing onboard ship; Act Three, Scene V, *Andante sostenuto*, bars 26–34

The audience now hears the sounds of a sweet flute melody with harp accompaniment (Ex. 6.37) and sees the following:

Medora is reclining on a bench, her head resting against the shoulder of a young female slave.

Conrad is standing behind Medora and gazing contentedly at her.

Some slaves are reclining against the men's shoulders, others talk among themselves, others seem to abandon themselves to the rhythm of the vessel.

A few men and sailor apprentices are about, here and there, sitting or standing, two of them on the prow are looking [out into the distance] with a spyglass.

Conrad joins Medora on the bench, she looks at him lovingly and puts her arms around his neck.

Medora: "Where were you while I was lying here?"

Conrad: "I was looking at you."

Medora: "And I was thinking about you."

Medora pours a drink for Conrad; after he drinks, the two lovers walk arm in arm from stern to bow. She climbs onto the bench, and Conrad, standing on the deck, hands a spyglass up to her so she can see if the shore is visible. After she has finished looking, she raises her right leg *à la seconde* as Conrad holds her hand in support. Behind Medora, the ladies place themselves "*en attitude* or in other groups." The music remains sweet and feminine.

After Conrad helps Medora step down from the bench, a mate approaches him (Ex. 6.23). As the music modulates into B minor and takes on a pirate style, he asks, "Captain, would you allow us to have a drink and dance a bit?" Conrad replies, "I allow it and welcome you to do so." He makes a sign. The sailors bring up a barrel of rum, pass cups around, and pour for Conrad and all the men. Everyone shouts, "To our captain's health!" "Thank you, young ones," says Conrad, and he drinks (Ex. 6.24).

The pirates each pair with a woman and dance a brief step. Standing face to face in what appears to be no particular formation—simply grouped casually on the deck of the ship—the pirates and women perform a "brisé soubressaut" on each foot, then repeat the step as they form a square (Ex. 6.20). They begin again and finish by jumping around randomly ("without order or figures").

During the musical transition to the next dance, Medora comes to center and says "I will dance, too. Come, Conrad!"

To the strains of a jaunty $^6_8$, Conrad joins Medora and they begin the dance with a short *pas de deux*: he lifts her overhead several times as she performs *cabriole derrière* into *arabesque allongée* then supports her in a *jeté, relevé à la seconde* (Ex. 6.21). This entire sequence is repeated. Meanwhile, eight of the women go to get four large blue scarves that will figure in the rest of the dance.

Two pairs of women, each pair holding a scarf between them, approaches from upstage left performing *glissade, jeté* twice. Arriving at center, "they drop and inflate their scarves by raising them," creating a billowing effect with the fabric.

Four more women enter and do the same thing. Eventually, the four pairs form a column at center. Medora comes to the top of the column and, one by one, each pair "snaps" their scarf into the air as Medora passes under it with a step forward and *relevé* (*sous-sus*). The women change position to form a lateral column across the stage. They "snap" up the scarves as Medora runs under all four scarves at once, and then they "snap" them up a second time as she returns under the scarves again, this time traveling backward.

The eight women next make a grouping at center in which the four who are closest to center continually exchange places with the four at the outermost points of the grouping. They form a circle—each women standing directly across from her scarf partner. They pull the scarves taut and then billow them into the air "and form a globe." After three "globes," Medora and Conrad enter the circle. As the eight women take

Ex. 6.38 Conrad and Medora enjoy a peaceful moment; Act Three, Scene V, *Suite du 5e tableau*, bars 7–14

Ex. 6.39 The storm; Act Three, Scene V, *Suite du 5e tableau*, bars 61–68

hands and kneel, Conrad lifts Medora by the waist, turns with her, and sets her down *en arabesque* twice.

The pirates join the group and lift their partners in the same way, making a half turn and then completing the turn with four small *glissades*, four times. The women give Medora one end of each scarf as the men bring a bench behind her. She steps onto it and raises her arms, holding the ends of the scarves overhead. Everyone joins the group as the dance ends.

At the beginning of the finale, Conrad helps Medora down as social groups are formed around the deck and people are chatting. To the strains of languid flute duet, Conrad enjoys a peaceful moment with his love (Ex. 6.38).

> Conrad: (to Medora) "Here comes the night, it is getting dark. Tomorrow we will reach our dwelling place, where you can rest from all your troubles, and where I will give you all my love."
>
> Medora: "Is that so, my Conrad?"
>
> Conrad: "In front of the heavens and the waters, I swear it to you." [Here Justamant notes in the margin of the page: "The trestle that supports the vessel is removed."]

The lights begin to dim. Faintly dissonant brass and tremolo strings make a far-off sound. A sailor alerts Conrad that a storm is coming; Conrad looks at the sky and dismisses the warning. The ship starts rocking. (Justamant notes: "The storm beings weakly, the sea becomes more agitated.") Conrad sits on the bench and takes Medora on his lap and looks at her happily.

The sky gets darker; the ship starts rocking harder. The agitation in the brass and strings begins to develop. Now seeing the danger, Conrad tells Medora to go inside.

("The lightning begins"). Conrad calls for his bullhorn and runs to place himself on the stern deck. He starts talking loudly. All the men run to their tasks and perform their maneuvers. The women are terrified. They are holding on to one another; some pray to the heavens. The music unleashes a *fortissimo* to match the storm (Ex. 6.39).

The ship now rocks up and down with a horrible violence. ("The horizon line is removed as the cloud [curtain] in the forefront is lowered.") Conrad continues to give orders.

The cloud on the forefront is slowly lowered, the "lightning thread" is attached. The water rises considerably. The boat slowly goes down. Thunder can be heard.

The sky is completely black; lightning strikes from stage right to stage left; we can only see the ship's masts and the men's arms, someone yells, and we can see everyone's arms and heads, they are running in all directions, then they disappear. (Layers of black gauze are lowered one after the other.) All we can see of the ship is the masts and even they go under. Lightning illuminates this disaster; an enormous wave covers the ship. As the ship goes down, the music modulates to B major for a *fortissimo* restatement of the flute theme heard at the beginning of the finale, here marked *pomposo*.[101]

The sea is "full of fury." The cloud curtain remains in the foreground. (The layers of gauze are lifted one after the other.)

The sea has calmed down and, in the distance, we can see Conrad holding Medora atop a broken piece of the ship, hands to the heavens. "Electricity shines its rays onto the couple." (The layers of fabric representing water are lowered into their holding space.)

[End of the ballet]

At the end of the long evening of the ballet's premiere—which had begun with the *régisseur*'s crisp recitation of the names of the ballet's creators and ended with the stunning shipwreck scene—the Opéra's director, François-Louis Crosnier, was brought to the Imperial Box to receive the praise of the Emperor Napoleon III and Empress Eugénie. "In all my life I have never seen, and probably never shall see, anything so beautiful or so moving," she is reputed to have said.[102] The ballet enjoyed a long run at the Opéra, and remained in place until Rosati left for Russia in 1858. Because it was difficult to find a ballerina who could equal Rosati in the role, the ballet was not revived till nearly a decade later, in 1867, when Mazilier came out of retirement to stage a new production with the brilliant young German ballerina Adèle Grantzow as Medora. For the new production, as we shall soon see, Adolphe Adam's original score was supplemented by his student Léo Delibes, who composed music for the new *Pas des fleurs* that Mazilier added.

Sadly, Adam did not live to see the new production, for he had died unexpectedly at the age of fifty-two, only five months into the run of the original *Le Corsaire*. After going to the Opéra on the night of 2 May 1856 to see *La Reine de Chypre*, he returned home, went to bed, and never woke up. Three days later, his funeral was held at his local parish church, Notre-Dame de Lorette; some three thousand mourners followed his coffin to the cemetery. A performance of *Le Corsaire* given that night at the Opéra was attended by the Emperor, who ordered that the receipts be given to the composer's widow.[103]

---

[101] Hilarion's death and the finale of *Swan Lake* are also accomplished in B major at *fortissimo*.

[102] Guest, *Second Empire 1847–1858*, 97. On the possible involvement of the Empress in the production, see Guest, *Second Empire 1847–1858*, 96–97, and Collins, *Le Corsaire*, 91–94.

[103] Guest, *Second Empire 1847–1858*, 101–102.

The first *Corsaire*, as we have seen in this chapter, is strikingly different from today's versions: a considerably larger amount of its running time is devoted to mime and action scenes, its title character (portrayed by a celebrated Italian mime and actor) barely dances at all, and the ballet ends with a lengthy and elaborately staged shipwreck scene that astounded nearly everyone who saw it. Some of the set pieces in the ballet tended toward the spectacular as well (in keeping with the Second Empire aesthetic), including the *Pas des éventails* in the grotto scene, the caravan of dervishes (complete with supernumerary camel), the *Pas des odalisques* performed for Zulmea, and the singing and dancing sailors on shipboard.

The diverse array of well-wrought action scenes in this ballet (some long gone) remind us, like the casting of the title role, of the importance in mid-century ballets at the Opéra of such scenes and their entertainment value—to name a few: the hand-to-hand fight between Conrad and Birbanto, the odalisques irreverently challenging the authority of Zulmea at the palace, the crazy wedding with the imposter bride. And the private and sexually charged encounter of Medora and Conrad in the grotto (involving "couch *cabrioles*" and a poisonous lotus blossom) was only one of several *pas d'action* that moved the plot forward with both acting and dancing—another sort of scene that has since declined in number.

Clearly, the practice of arranging a ballet around the scaffolding of a story was still alive and well when *Le Corsaire* was created in 1856, and the balance of dance and action fairly even. As we trace the ongoing life of the ballet in Russia, we shall see that dance came to assume a greater role.

7

Le Corsaire in St. Petersburg

With its combination of melodrama, humor, and exoticism culminating in a sensational shipwreck, *Le Corsaire* proved irresistible to the Imperial Theaters. Two years (nearly to the day) after its celebrated Paris premiere in 1856, the ballet was staged in St. Petersburg by Jules Perrot.

Like *Giselle*, *Corsaire* found a permanent home on the Russian stage, but the swash-buckler that eventually sailed into the twentieth century bore only partial resemblance to Mazilier and Adam's original. What had largely been a pantomime ballet, showcasing the acting talents of its original stars, became heavily populated with dances interpolated over decades. With one exception (Delibes's *Le pas des fleurs*), these were set to music inferior to that of the numbers they replaced, eroding the overall impact of Adam's score, which itself, as was customary, was surely reorchestrated for its Petersburg premiere. Moreover, the eventual omission of the ballet's fourth scene contributed to a loss of dramatic coherence in what had once been Saint-Georges's well-crafted albeit far-flung narrative.

New music for new dances. By the early years of the twentieth century, far more of the music added to *Le Corsaire* over time remained in the production than the music added to *Giselle*: only two interpolated variations for the title character (created for Adèle Grantzow and Elena Cornalba) ultimately became permanent fixtures of the latter score. Revisions made in *Corsaire*, however, were more numerous, and they materially impacted at least three of its five scenes. Dances were interpolated not only for Medora but for others as well. And most of these new dances replaced original numbers composed by Adam, significantly changing the musical landscape of the ballet.

Much of the interpolated music was composed by Cesare Pugni, who (before Minkus) was the official composer of ballet music for the St. Petersburg Imperial Theaters from 1850 until shortly before his death in 1870. His long tenure in Russia capped off a career that developed in London and Paris after he had received his training in Milan. Despite Pugni's ability to deliver music that was considered suitably *dansante* (that is, danceable) and the arguable merits of his other scores,[1] much of the music he composed for interpolation into *Le Corsaire* is stunningly vapid, harmonically unadventurous, and utterly predictable—evoking no emotions whatsoever—in contrast to the ballet scores by Adam and Deldevez that we have explored thus far. In particular, Pugni's limited melodic range, featuring a predominance of stepwise motion (made more tedious by frequent chromatic passing tones in the melodies), and simplistic harmonic rhythm contributed to a score that is a measurable downgrade from the one composed by Adam and enjoyed by Paris audiences.[2]

---

[1] Ivor Guest called for a reassessment of Pugni's substantial *oeuvre* in his article, "Cesare Pugni: A Plea for Justice," *Dance Research* 1, no. 1 (Spring 1983): 30–38.

[2] We acknowledge that our assessment of Pugni's music is based only on a two-violin *répétiteur* that provides little information about his instrumentation.

Five Ballets from Paris and St. Petersburg. Doug Fullington and Marian Smith, Oxford University Press.
© Oxford University Press 2024. DOI: 10.1093/oso/9780190944506.003.0008

Of the eight dances added to *Le Corsaire* in St. Petersburg that were recorded in Stepanov notation in the 1890s and the early years of the twentieth century—these include single numbers and multimovement dance suites, some of them revisions of pre-existing material by Adam—six of them are attributed to Pugni, as is a replacement overture for the ballet. The Act One *Pas de l'esclave* features music attributed primarily to Petr Georgievich of Oldenburg that is of the same ilk as Pugni's offerings. Only the divertissement by Léo Delibes, *Le pas des fleurs*, reaches the high bar set by Adam (see Chapter 8).

Whether of low quality or high, the handiwork of these other composers took up the space left by the expunging of Adam's numbers (and their choreography) that were part of the original Paris *Corsaire*, including the *pas de cinq* in Scene I and (eventually) the Scene V dances onboard ship. Newly composed music was fused into some of Adam's numbers, including the bacchanale in the opening scene (revised by Pugni), the *Pas des éventails* (performed periodically but ultimately cut) in the grotto scene, the *Pas des odalisques* (revised and enlarged by Pugni) and the *Pas du Derviche* (part of which was incorporated into the *Pas des trois des odalisques*) in Act Two.

Dramatic implications of the loss of narrative-driven dances and (eventually) the entirety of Scene IV. Another dance ultimately removed from the ballet was the *scène dansante* for Medora and the Pasha that was at the heart of Scene IV. (Recall that during this *pas d'action*, Medora charms the honeymoon-crazed Pasha into relinquishing his weapons, thereby setting the stage for Conrad to swoop in and rescue her in heroic fashion.) In fact, Scene IV in its entirety appears to have been omitted from the ballet when it was revived by Nikolai Sergeyev in 1914. The decision to expunge the scene that provides resolution for a fundamental conflict in the plot (Medora's oppression by the Pasha)—was it made because of the scene's dearth of dancing or to shorten the overall length of the ballet?—raises questions about contemporary attitudes toward dramatic coherence in ballet plots. Add to this the replacement of the *Pas du Derviche*, a genuine *pas d'action*, with the narrative-free *Le pas des fleurs* (titled *Le jardin animé* in St. Petersburg), and we see a further reduction of the amount of time devoted to the story in favor of pure dance. (This loss—perhaps recognized as problematic—was arguably mitigated somewhat in 1899 by the addition of the *Finesse d'amour* in the opening scene, a *pas d'action* in which Medora teases the Pasha.)

As we follow the journey of *Le Corsaire* in St. Petersburg from its first appearance in Perrot's 1858 production through the tenure of Petipa (who revived Perrot's staging four times over the course of thirty-seven years), we will tackle its complicated history of revisions, interpolations, and omissions in what we hope is the most straightforward way: by offering a chronicle of select performances. Then, as we have done in our chapters on the Petersburg *Giselle* and *Paquita*, we will provide a detailed scene-by-scene description of the ballet in its turn-of-the-century incarnation based on available sources.

St. Petersburg performance history

In tracing the constantly evolving *Le Corsaire* in the Petersburg repertory, we have consulted not only posters, programs, and other primary source material but also the work of scholars of the ballet. Ivor Guest's account of the first St. Petersburg *Corsaire*, found in his biography of Jules Perrot, provides an excellent starting point from which to follow the trail of interpolations that eventually and collectively remade *Le Corsaire* into a ballet that featured both action scenes (from the original ballet and using Adam's score) and interpolated or revised dances by other composers.[3] Additionally, we have relied on the research of Olga Fedorchenko, who has catalogued the various dances performed by Medora that came and went over the years, including recurring numbers that were recast and almost certainly rechoreographed.[4] We will also reference the recently published piano reduction of Le Corsaire edited by Yury Burlaka, that includes a lengthy appendix of numbers added to the ballet in the years following its 1856 Paris premiere.[5]

The 1858 St. Petersburg premiere

Le Corsaire made its St. Petersburg debut at the Bolshoi Theater on 9 January 1858 as a benefit performance for Perrot, who staged the production and performed the role of Seyd-Pasha. The balance of the cast featured the young Ekaterina Friedberg as Medora and Marius Petipa as Conrad, joined by Frédéric (Birbanto), Lubov Radina (Gulnare), Alexander Picheau (Lanquedem), Nadezhda Troitskaya (Zulma, as the character was called in Petersburg), and Timofei Stukolkin (the Eunuch, who in St. Petersburg was called "Keeper of Seyd-Pasha's harem").[6]

Although Friedberg received mixed reviews, the production was praised, particularly the shipwreck in the ballet's final moments:

> All the new scenery in Le Corsaire is good, but the scenery for the last scene, where a ship appears in front of the audience in the middle of a rough sea, is arranged with extraordinary skill. Storm, thunder, and lightning have been produced by new means, and very successfully. The doom of the ship in the waves and then the appearance on stage of Conrad and Medora, with lighting the likes of which has never been seen before, is the crown of the present art in ballet performances![7]

As Conrad, Petipa was in his element, performing a non-dancing role that showcased his dramatic abilities. Ekaterina Vazem, who would assume the role of Medora in the late 1860s, praised Petipa's acting prowess and vividly remembered his account of Conrad:

> The crowning glory of Petipa's art as a dancer was his miming ability. In this he was matchless. With his dark, burning eyes, his face mirroring a whole range of mood and emotion, and with broad, clear, convincing gestures and a deeply-penetrating understanding of his role (through which he achieved a veritable transformation into the character that he portrayed), Petipa attained the very pinnacle among "silent actors," and was equalled by only a very few of his colleagues. His acting excited the greatest admiration in his audience. . . . I danced with him in Le Corsaire in the spring of 1868, in my first season on the stage; this was, in fact, Petipa's last appearance as a dancer. His

[3] Guest, Jules Perrot, 304–308, 349.
[4] Olga Fedorchenko, "Balet 'Korsar': Evolyutsiya partii Medory v XIX veke" [The ballet "Korsar": The evolution of the part of Medora in the nineteenth century], Vestnik Akademii Russkogo baleta imeni A. Ya. Vaganovoy [Bulletin of the Academy of Russian Ballet named after A. Ya. Vaganova] 3 (2016): 94–101.
[5] See Chapter 6, note 74. The appendix is organized chronologically, both by the year a number was inserted into the ballet as well as the year the number was purportedly composed. This dual system of organization has resulted in some numbers being included twice in the appendix.
[6] Khronika III, 59–60.
[7] Severnaya pchela, 18 January 1858, qtd. in Khronika III, 60.

performance as Conrad, the corsairs' leader, was quite unforgettable: his every movement indicated that he was accustomed to rule and command. At the same time, one was conscious of his mastery of gesture and his complete confidence. He never employed meaningless gesticulation, as I have often witnessed in other dancers in the role of Conrad. One could learn a good deal from his acting, but not by slavish imitation, as Petipa put too much of his own artistry into his interpretation. Thus, in the courtship scene in the Grotto, Petipa, while making love to Medora, was so carried away that he embraced her, shaking and shuddering with emotion, and whispering: "Je t'aime, je t'aime. . . ." I was then a very young girl, and was shocked by this naturalistic acting. At rehearsals, when he was directing some scene, Petipa would act out every role, always with the utmost expressiveness.[8]

The Petersburg production of *Le Corsaire*, like that of *Paquita*, was not a restaging of the Paris original, although the story remained the same. Adam's score, likely reorchestrated using a *répétiteur*, was supplemented with music by Pugni, who received equal billing with Adam. Perrot was credited with new stagings of all the dances, although Ivor Guest assumed he had seen Mazilier's production and was naturally influenced by it.[9] We also note that, as in the case of Perrot's 1850 Petersburg *Giselle*, Petipa has recently been credited as the likely choreographer of at least some of the 1858 *Corsaire* dances (though, again, without firm evidence), perhaps in keeping with a trend among scholars of giving more credit to Petipa than to older choreographers whose creative work is less known today—in this case, Perrot.[10] In any event, the sources we consulted provide no evidence of Petipa's involvement in this production as a choreographer.

The poster for the 12 January 1858 performance reveals of mix of dance titles familiar from the Paris production and some new ones.[11] The opening scene in the Adrianople market featured Medora's entrance and the pirates' bacchanale, titled *Danse des Pirates, Ballabilli d'action*, which was performed by twenty-four women, half of them costumed in travesty, and "other dancers." A *pas Aragonnaise* was performed by the Polish dancer Wiktoria Koslovska (a guest from the Warsaw Opera), two student women, and three men.[12] The Paris *pas de cinq* of character dances was omitted. The grotto scene included the *Pas des éventails*—for Friedberg, two corps women, two student women, and "other women dancers"—and *scène dansante* for Friedberg and Petipa. The *Pas des éventails* was found to be "highly original" and full of "interesting groups composed by M. Perrot quite successfully."[13] The third scene's *Pas des odalisques* featured three dancers—Anna

<hr />

[8] Vazem, "Memoirs: Part 2," 18–19. The performance cited by Vazem was not Petipa's last; that came the following season, on 4 May 1869.

[9] Guest, *Jules Perrot*, 305.

[10] For example, Nathalie Lecomte suggests without citation that Petipa, in his capacity as Perrot's assistant, choreographed some or all of the dances in the 1858 production of *Le Corsaire*. Nathalie Lecomte, "Dans le sillage du *Corsaire*: de Paris (1856) à Saint-Petersbourg (1899)," *Slavica Occitania* 43 (2016): 158. And Yury Burlaka states that Pugni's 1858 revision of the pirates' bacchanale was made "on assignment for choreographer M. Petipa." Burlaka, ed., *Le Corsaire*, 267.

[11] We were unable to locate the poster for the premiere performance on 9 January 1858.

[12] Lecomte ascribes the music of the *pas Aragonnaise* to Pugni. See Lecomte, "Dans le sillage du *Corsaire*," 158. That the dance may have been performed to the Spanish variation from Adam's original *pas de cinq* seems unlikely because that number was quite short at only forty bars. Beaumont mentioned the dance in his volume of Russian ballet history (which is largely based on Pleshcheyev's *Nash Balet*): "The character dances [sic] by Kozlovskaya and the pupils Lyadova and Kosheva pleased the audience." Cyril W. Beaumont, *A History of Ballet in Russia (1613–1881)* (London: C.W. Beaumont, 1930), 90. The number seems to have been interpolated especially for Kozlovska; by April 4, 1858 (and perhaps earlier), it is no longer listed on the poster.

[13] M[avriky] Rappaport, *Teatral'nyy i muzyka'nyy vestnik*, 19 January 1858, no. 3, 28, qtd. in Fedorchenko, "Balet 'Korsar,' " 96.

Prikhunova and sisters Nadezhda and Anastasia Amosova, identified as "Pasha's slaves"; Prikhunova received a second call for her variation.[14] "Other women dancers" partook in this *pas* as well, suggesting that what would eventually become the *Pas de trois des odalisques*—with additional music by Pugni (Exx. 7.9a–c, below) and a repurposed number by Adam (Ex. 6.35b)—was already in development but had not yet reached its final form as a *pas* for just three dancers with no supporting corps de ballet.[15] The third scene also featured a *Scène de seduction* for Radina and Perrot (presumably performed to Ex. 6.4a) and a *Solo* for Friedberg that was possibly performed to Ex. 6.35b (if that number had not yet been appropriated for the *Pas des odalisques*). Scene IV included a *scène dansante* for Friedberg and Perrot (Medora's disarming of the Pasha), and Scene V featured Friedberg, Petipa, and "other women and men dancers" in what were likely the dances onboard the ship, though no titles are given for these dances on the poster.

As the production took its place in the repertory over the course of additional performances, dances were added for ballerinas new to roles. Some, such as Koslovska's Spanish *pas*, were short-lived while others found a more permanent home in the ballet. For example, Guest noted that by the end of the 1857–1858 season, Perrot had added a new dance to the opening scene for Marfa Muravieva, with music arranged by Pugni.[16] Originally titled *L'esclave, pas scenique*, the number was given slightly different names over the course of the many years it remained in the St. Petersburg production. (We will use these variant titles as they arise in our descriptions.)

On 23 April 1859, Moscow-based ballerina Praskovia Lebedeva performed the role of Medora in the second scene of *Le Corsaire* on a benefit program for Maria Surovshchikova-Petipa.[17] Lebedeva had already danced the role in Moscow, where *Corsaire* had premiered on 3 November 1858 in a staging of the Perrot production by Frédéric.[18] According to Burlaka, the *Finesse d'amour* (see Exx. 7.3a–d) that was added to the St. Petersburg production in 1899 (see later in this chapter) was first added to the Moscow production of *Le Corsaire* in 1858 for Lebedeva. The music, by Pugni, was taken from *Satanilla*, as staged by Jean Antoine Petipa and Marius Petipa.[19]

A revival of Perrot's staging, likely supervised by first ballet master Arthur Saint-Léon (who is not mentioned on the poster except as choreographer of a new dance), was given at the Bolshoi Theater on 8 November 1859. The production featured the first St. Petersburg performance of Carolina Rosati as Medora, another occasion of an original Paris interpreter reprising her role in the Russian capital, as Grisi had done in *Giselle* and *Paquita*. The cast included Petipa (Conrad), Nikolai Golts (Pasha), Felix Kshesinsky (Birbanto), Anna Kosheva (Gulnare), Picheau (Lanquedem), and Troitskaya (Zulma).[20] Saint-Léon's contribution, a dance added for Rosati in the third scene, was *La Musulmane*

---

[14] Guest, *Jules Perrot*, 308.

[15] Burlaka gives 1863 as the year Pugni made his revisions to the dance. See note 75, later in this chapter.

[16] Guest, *Jules Perrot*, 308. A poster for a performance given the next season on 8 November 1859 credits the choreography to Perrot and the arrangement of the music to Pugni. The performers were Muravieva, Nikolai Golts (Pasha), and Alexander Prosbin. (Burlaka attributes the choreography of the 1858 *L'esclave, pas scenique* to Petipa, despite the attribution to Perrot on the poster. Burlaka, ed., *Le Corsaire*, 275.)

[17] *Khronika III*, 73. The program also featured the premiere of Marius Petipa's one-act *Parisian Market* (also titled *Le Marché des innocents*) as well as *A Marriage during the Regency*, a ballet in two acts that had premiered the previous December.

[18] See Guest, *Jules Perrot*, 349.

[19] Burlaka, ed., *Le Corsaire*, 284. Lebedeva later performed the title role in Petipa's revival of Mazilier's *Satanilla* in St. Petersburg on 18 October 1866, for which Pugni provided supplemental music (according to the poster, "some numbers by M. Pugni"). See *Khronika III*, 120–121.

[20] *Khronika III*, 77.

(The Muslim woman), a "pas de caractère oriental." This was more a mime number than a dance; indeed, the critic Mavriky Rappaport, writing in *Teatralnaya letopis*, opined that Rosati danced little compared to her castmates, thereby rendering the role of Medora "inevitably pale":

> M. Saint-Léon depicted oriental bliss; all the poses were grouped by him with plasticity; but it is still not a dance, and in *Le Corsaire* this scene was unable to make a special impression on the public and seemed even boring. . . . Mlle Rosati, as elsewhere, is unusually graceful, but this is not new; we would like something more lively.[21]

Le Corsaire in St. Petersburg under Marius Petipa

As Petipa assumed control of subsequent stagings of *Le Corsaire*, he continued to do what Perrot and Saint-Léon had done before him by supplying each revival with a set of dances tailored to the strengths of the various ballerinas interpreting the role of Medora.

The 1863 revival. Petipa's first opportunity to supervise the Petersburg Corsaire came with the ballet's revival given on 24 January 1863 at the Bolshoi Theater. The ballet master continued to perform the role of Conrad, this time opposite his wife, Maria Surovshchikova-Petipa, who made her debut as Medora. Other members of the cast—including Frédéric, Picheau, and Troitskaya—revisited roles they had first performed in 1858. Golts and Kosheva also reprised their roles as the Pasha and Gulnare. Ivan Bocharov praised the broad accessibility of the production in Yakor: "Here is a ballet that absolutely pleases all ages and caters to all tastes."[22]

The poster notes that *Le Corsaire* was now given in four acts, though still in five scenes. Following a general acknowledgment of Saint-Georges and Mazilier, the credits state merely that the revival was newly staged by Petipa ("nouvellement mis en scène par M-r Petipa").

Two new dances are listed, both performed by Surovshchikova-Petipa in the grotto scene: a *pas de six* for the ballerina, Christian Johanson (as an unnamed cavalier), and four student women, and a *Pas du corsaire* for Surovshchikova-Petipa alone. (This latter dance, performed in travesty, would in later years be renamed *Petit Corsaire*.) The *Pas des éventails* was performed by soloist Alexandra Kemmerer, three student women, and "other dancers." No indication is given on the poster whether the choreography for this dance was new.

The 1868 revival. Just five years later, Petipa returned to *Le Corsaire* a second time with another revival presented on 25 January 1868 as a benefit performance for Adèle Grantzow. The highlight of the production was the addition of the divertissement *Le jardin animé* (with music by Léo Delibes) that had been added for the Paris revival of *Le Corsaire* a year earlier under the title *Le pas des fleurs*. Grantzow, who was praised especially for her miming abilities, was joined by Petipa (Conrad), Golts (Pasha), Kshesinsky (Birbanto), Lubov Radina (Gulnare), Picheau (Lanquedem), and Troitskaya (Zulma).[23]

Petipa's contributions are credited on the poster with greater specificity than the 1863 poster provided, suggesting that he made a more thorough revision of dances in his 1868

---

[21] *Teatralnaya letopis*, 1859, no. 45, qtd. in *Khronika III*, 77.
[22] Ivan Bocharov, *Yakor*, 14 September 1863, qtd. in *Khronika III*, 100.
[23] See *Khronika III*, 133–134.

revival than had been undertaken in 1863: "arrangée et mis en scène avec toutes les danses nouvellement composées par M-r Marius Petipa." The reviewer in *Golos* approved: "All of the dances in the revival of 'Le Corsaire' were composed anew by Petipa, and some of them are quite artistic."[24]

New dances listed on the poster include *Les Forbans, pas de caractère*, for three couples, in the opening scene, and *Le jardin animé*, featuring Grantzow, Radina, and seventy-eight dancers, including young students, in the third scene. (The two dances added for Surovshchikova-Petipa in 1863—the *pas de six* and *Pas du corsaire*—were not retained in the 1868 revival.) Some restructuring of the ballet is suggested by the poster's reference to "four acts and six scenes," the work having previously been divided into five scenes.

The 1868 revival was not only restructured to include six scenes but may have featured additional new or revised choreography: new titles are given for what appear to be dances and *pas d'action* included in earlier productions. The *Grand pas des éventails* in the grotto scene, for example, featured Grantzow, Petipa, four named women, and "24 women dancers." The new title and addition of Petipa to the cast suggest that the number (presumably using Adam's music) may have been rechoreographed for the 1868 revival, although the size of the female cast (four named dancers plus an ensemble) suggests similarity to the version danced in the Perrot production. The *Scène et danse de séduction* for Grantzow and Petipa in the same scene appears to have been the new name for the intimate *scène dansante*; *Golos* described Grantzow's "extremely daring leap onto the divan, on which she forms with Conrad a very original group in the grotto scene."[25] In the third scene, the *Scène de seduction* for Gulnare and the Pasha was renamed *Scène dansante* (with the Keeper of the Harem and "other women dancers" added to the cast list), and the *scène dansante* for Medora and the Pasha (now in the fifth scene—no dances are listed for whatever action comprised the fourth scene) was renamed *Pas scènique*. Finally, the dance in the last (here, sixth) scene was given a descriptive title: *Danse des Corsaires sur le navire*.

Cast numbers also suggest revisions to choreography included in previous productions. The poster notes the addition of four women to *L'Esclave* (the descriptive "pas scènique" having been dropped from the title) which featured Alexandra Shaposhnikova, still a student, and Lev Ivanov. The bacchanale gained a lead couple—Kshesinsky (Birbanto) and Anna Kosheva—who joined the twelve ensemble couples that continued to feature women in travesty. Finally, the mention of "other women dancers" was removed from the cast list for the *Pas des odalisques*; only the three soloists are listed, suggesting that by this time the dance had become a *pas de trois*.

Ekaterina Vazem made her debut as Medora, opposite Petipa's Conrad, on 7 April 1868 in a benefit performance for the dancer Nikolai Troitsky.[26] The ballet returned to its usual five scenes, but otherwise the list of dances on the poster is nearly identical to the revival danced by Grantzow—only the *Pas scènique* for Medora and the Pasha is omitted. Vazem recalled,

in this ballet, I was the last performer of the big "dance with fans" in the second act. After me, "Le Corsaire" was danced by the visiting ballerina [Henriette] Dor; another

---

[24] *Golos*, 27 January 1868, qtd. in *Khronika III*, 133.

[25] *Golos*, 27 January 1868, 2, qtd. in Fedorchenko, "Balet 'Korsar,'" 98.

[26] *Khronika III*, 136. The benefit artist performed the role of Nikez (Alain in the original French production) in the opening scene of the ballet *La Fille mal gardée*, presented after the complete *Corsaire*, according to the poster.

pas was staged for her, much less beautiful, which later remained in the ballet. In this "dance with fans," Petipa inserted for me a new variation of double pirouettes on the toe and other technical difficulties, which, as they said, I did very successfully.[27]

Dor made her St. Petersburg debut in the role of Medora on 3 September 1868, also dancing opposite Petipa. Writing in *Istoriya tantsev*, Sergei Khudekov noted how Dor's impressive technique prompted comparisons with recent interpreters of the role: "Adèle charmed, but Henriette amazed."[28]

The poster for Dor's debut reveals several changes to the list of dances, both major and minor. Medora's opening *Solo* was renamed *Entrée*. The first scene also included a *Pas Solo* for Dor. The second scene saw the return of the *Pas du corsaire*, renamed *Le petit corsaire* and danced by Alexandra Kemmerer. A *Pas de six (nouveau)* in the same scene, surely the *pas* mentioned by Vazem (above), featured Dor, Christian Johanson, and four women.

On 4 May 1869, Marius Petipa gave his final stage performance. The occasion was a benefit for Pugni. Petipa, at age fifty-one, performed the role of Conrad opposite Vazem's Medora.[29] Later that same year, Lev Ivanov assumed the role of Conrad on 18 September, with Dor as his Medora, and Timofei Stukolkin, the benefit artist, in the role of the Keeper of the Harem.[30] Alexander Pleshcheyev included mention of Dor's performance in *Nash Balet*: "At Stukolkin's benefit performance, on 18 September, Dor danced in *Corsaire*, in which she performed with inimitable perfection the variation and coda in the *pas de six* and poetic *le jardin animé*."[31]

For Vazem's benefit performance on 4 February 1873, Petipa added a new *Pas d'esclave* in the opening scene, performed by Vazem (Medora), Ivanov (Conrad), Picheau (Lanquedem), and Pavel Gerdt as a nameless cavalier. (We assume this number was completely different from *L'Esclave*, which is not listed on the poster.) The *Peterburgskaya gazeta* reported, "She [Vazem] showed all the strength of her talent in the exemplary performance of a new large *pas d'esclave* specially staged for her by M. Marius Petipa."[32] Vazem also performed a *pas de six* in the grotto scene. (The poster lacks the designation "nouveau" for this dance, indicating perhaps that this was the version first created for Surovshchikova-Petipa rather than the version made for Dor). We also note a revised credit for Petipa on the poster, acknowledging him as ballet master (Petipa had indeed become first ballet master of the St. Petersburg Imperial Ballet in 1870): "arrangé et mis en scene avec toutes les danses, composé par le maître de ballet M-r Marius Petipa."

The 1880 revival. Petipa revived *Corsaire* a third time on 30 November 1880 for the benefit performance of Evgenia Sokolova, who made her debut in the role of Medora. (In her later years, Sokolova prepared Tamara Karsavina for her own debut in the role.) The cast also featured Ivanov (Conrad), Johanson (Pasha), Kshesinsky (Birbanto), Marie Petipa (Gulnare), Picheau (Lanquedem), and Maria Zest (Zulma). The shipwreck

[27] Ekaterina Vazem, *Zapiski baleriny Sankt-Peterburgskogo Bol'shogo teatra, 1867–1884* [Memoirs of a Ballerina of the St. Petersburg Bolshoi Theatre, 1867–1884] (Leningrad and Moscow: Iskusstvo, 1937; St. Petersburg: Music Planet, 2021), 213. Citations refer to the Music Planet edition. About Petipa's new variation for Vazem, see note 75, later in this chapter.

[28] Sergei Khudekov, *Istoriya tantsev* [History of Dances], 4 vols. (St. Petersburg/Petrograd, 1913–1918), qtd. in *Khronika III*, 138–139.

[29] *Khronika III*, 143.

[30] Ibid., 145.

[31] Pleshcheyev, *Nash Balet (1673–1899)*, 277; also qtd. in *Khronika III*, 145.

[32] *Peterburgskaya gazeta*, 6 February 1873, qtd. in *Khronika III*, 166–167.

was deemed the "height of perfection" in a production that featured new scenery and costumes.[33]

This revival featured new dances as well as changes to existing *pas*, just as earlier productions had done. Sokolova danced a variation from the ballet *Météora* as her first entrance.[34] The grotto scene featured neither the *Pas des éventails* nor *pas de six* but rather a *Grand pas*. The cast listed on the poster for this number includes Sokolova, Gerdt, and nineteen women.[35] (A cast list for the same dance performed on 3 January 1881, however, lists Sokolova, Gerdt, Platon Karsavin, and eighteen women.[36]) This was followed by *Forban (characteristic dance)*, moved to the grotto scene from Scene I and performed by Kshesinsky, Radina, and two additional couples. Sokolova also performed *Le petit corsaire*, receiving a rapturous response, and the *scène dansante* with Ivanov.[37] In the third scene, *Le jardin animé* was reduced to sixty-eight dancers, down from the previous eighty.

The second act (grotto scene) of *Le Corsaire* was featured on a benefit performance for the Italian ballerina Emma Bessone on 22 November 1887. Although Ivanov performed the role of Conrad, Bessone danced a *pas de deux* with Enrico Cecchetti that she had performed at La Scala. According to *Minuta*, the ballerina did not live up to advance notices, but the *pas* revealed Cecchetti as an excellent dancer and able partner. The coda was particularly acrobatic: Cecchetti performed *pirouettes* at center as Bessone circled him with *jetés en tournant*.[38]

The 1899 revival. On 13 January 1899, Petipa revived *Le Corsaire* for a fourth and final time. The occasion was a benefit performance for the celebrated Italian ballerina Pierina Legnani, who only a year earlier had created the title role in Petipa's *Raymonda* (see Chapter 10). Here, she made her debut in the role of Medora, joined by Gerdt (Conrad), Alfred Bekefi (Pasha), Iosif Kshesinsky (Birbanto), Olga Preobrazhenskaya (Gulnare), Sergei Lukyanov (Lanquedem), and Nadezhda Petipa (Zulma).[39]

Though not acclaimed as an engaging dramatic artist, Legnani was praised for her technically superior dancing:

> As a dancer, Mlle. Legnani had tremendous success. All of her *pas*, from the first entrance (*entrée*) to the dance on the ship, drew unanimous applause, and many classical variations were repeated. Most of all, Mlle. Legnani captivated the audience with her technical talent in the *pas finesse d'amour* and in the *grand pas des éventails*.[40]

According to the printed program, Petipa made multiple revisions to *Corsaire* for the 1899 revival, much as he had in 1868. The ballet continued to be performed in four acts and five scenes. But the opening scene now featured a *Danse des Esclaves* for four women, followed by Legnani's *Entrée* and the *Pas de l'esclave* (we presume this was a version of the dance most recently titled *L'Esclave*). A number titled *Finesse d'amour*, for

---

[33] *Minuta*, 2 December 1880, qtd. in *Khronika III*, 209–210.
[34] Fedorchenko, "Balet 'Korsar,'" 94–95. Thanks to Olga Fedorchenko for additional information from the poster for 30 November 1880.
[35] Ibid., 97.
[36] Thanks to Peter Koppers for this information.
[37] Fedorchenko, "Balet 'Korsar,'" 98.
[38] *Minuta*, 24 November 1887, qtd. in *Khronika III*, 265–266.
[39] Bekefi had made his debut as the Pasha years earlier, replacing Johanson in a performance on 28 October 1884. See *Khronika III*, 233.
[40] *Teatr i iskusstvo*, 1899, no. 3, qtd. in *Khronika III*, 355.

Legnani, Gerdt, Bekefi, and Lukyanov, appeared for the first time. The concluding pirate dance had a slightly revised title: *Danse des Corsaires (ballabile d'action)*. More notable, perhaps, is the fact that the latter dance now featured twelve male-female ensemble couples, the men replacing the women in travesty.

The dances in the grotto scene included the *Danse des Forbans*, still for three couples, and the return of the *Grand pas des éventails*, performed by Legnani with Georgi Kyaksht, as an unnamed cavalier, and twelve women. The cast size for the latter number is different from previous versions, suggesting new choreography in whole or in part.[41] *Le petit corsaire* is not among the numbers performed in the grotto scene.

The third scene opened with an *Entrée des odalisques* for twelve women. The *scène dansante* for Gulnare and the Pasha was renamed *Scène d'espièglerie* (Scene of playfulness) and featured not only Preobrazhenskaya and Bekefi but also Nadezhda Petipa (Zulma), Dominika Solyannikova (Black woman, that is, Zulma's maid), and Nikolai Voronkov (Keeper of the Harem). The *Pas de trois des odalisques* and *Le jardin animé* maintained the same numbers of performers as in the 1880 production.

The first scene of the fourth act featured a *Scène dansante de caractère* (previously called *Pas scènique*) for Legnani and Bekefi, and the final scene included a *Danse à bord du vaisseau* for Legnani, Gerdt, Iosif Kshesinsky, four women, and five men.[42] The libretto for the 1899 revival also reveals, rather surprisingly, that Birbanto took part in the action of the final scene (more on this below).

Post-1899 performances in St. Petersburg. After Legnani's departure from St. Petersburg in early 1901, the role of Medora was taken up for several seasons by guest artists and also reclaimed by Petersburg ballerinas. For instance, the Moscow-based Lubov Roslavleva made her debut as Medora in the Petersburg production on 18 April 1901, with Gerdt as Conrad and Anna Pavlova as Gulnare, replacing Preobrazhenskaya.[43] And the Italian ballerina Enrichetta Grimaldi, also visiting from Moscow, essayed the role on 9 October 1902 with Gerdt as Conrad and Vera Trefilova as Gulnare.

St. Petersburg ballerina Julia Sedova made her debut as Medora earlier that same year in a matinee performance on 23 February 1902, having already danced the lead in *Le jardin animé* the previous December.[44] Gerdt was her Conrad, joined by Bekefi (Pasha), Iosif Kshesinsky (Birbanto), and Trefilova (Gulnare). The program reveals Sedova performed a *Variation* rather than the *Finesse d'amour* in the opening scene. In the grotto scene, she performed the *pas de six* (with Nikolai Legat), *Petit Corsaire* (as the travesty number was now called), and *scène dansante* (with Gerdt). *Le jardin animé* followed in the third scene. Reporting on a performance two years later, *Teatr i iskusstvo* noted that although "[t]he role of Medora is one of the most grateful in terms of wealth of material," Sedova had given a pallid performance both in dance and mime.[45]

[41] See also Fedorchenko, "Balet 'Korsar,'" 97.
[42] The editors of *Khronika III* state that the performance was "supplemented with an adagio and waltz to music by R[iccardo] Drigo," but these are not indicated in the program (or in the Rep or CN). *Khronika III*, 354
[43] *Khronika IV*, 18–19.
[44] Ibid., 26–27, 33.
[45] N. Fedorov, *Teatr i iskusstvo*, no. 16, 1906, qtd. in *Khronika IV*, 55–56.

Pavlova's debut as Medora came on 5 December 1904, with Gerdt as her Conrad, Alexander Shiryaev as Pasha, and Elizaveta Vill as Gulnare.[46] The program for the performance later that month on 28 December reveals that Pavlova performed a *pas de deux* in the grotto scene rather than the *pas de six*. Her partner was Sergei Legat, who also choreographed the duet. Reviewing the performance in *Birzhevye vedomosti*, Valerian Svetlov praised the diverse artistry which Pavlova brought to her interpretation of the role's many facets—a vivid contrast to Sedova's reception:

> The qualities of a top-ranking soloist were felt decisively yesterday in all her dances, beginning with the broad flights of the entrée . . . and in the *pas d'action*, which was performed with playful coquetterie and true artistic taste. She was matchless in the *pas de deux* . . . and performed a brilliant series of *fouettés en diagonale*—so much more attractive than the commonplace 'mechanical' *fouettés*. . . . Her image of Medora was chaste and moving, but for all that poetically beautiful.[47]

Despite these accolades, Pavlova gave a mere four performances as Medora between December 1904 and November 1905, and the role remained exclusively Sedova's until Tamara Karsavina made her auspicious debut nearly three years later, on 22 October 1908.

For her first performance as Medora, Karsavina was partnered by Gerdt (Conrad) and joined by Alexander Cherkrygin (Pasha), Alexander Monakhov (Birbanto), Vill (Gulnare), and Vasily Stukolkin (Lanquedem).[48] In the grotto scene, she danced a *pas de deux* with Samuil Andrianov. The choreography is unattributed in the printed program.

As Pavlova had made the role of Giselle distinctly her own, so did Karsavina claim the role of Medora, though she danced it only a few times. Writing in her autobiography, *Theatre Street*, the ballerina called *Corsaire* "an incontestable success of mine; I owed it greatly to Madame [Evgenia] Sokolova," who was her coach.[49] Karsavina's many descriptions of scenes in the ballet add greatly to our knowledge of the late-Imperial *Corsaire* in St. Petersburg. Her recollection of performing with Gerdt is particularly touching: "Gerdt, my darling Conrad, in the passionate embrace of the concluding scene, in a ventriloquist whisper, conveyed: 'Well done, god-daughter.'"[50]

Although Karsavina enjoyed success in the role of Medora, it is largely Pavlova's performance, along with parts of Sedova's, that Sergeyev documented in his notation of the ballet.

Sources

Before turning to our scene-by-scene account of the ballet, let us describe the performance sources we consulted—including Sergeyev's notations—in addition to the posters and programs already mentioned.

[46] *Khronika IV*, 62–63.
[47] *Birzhevye vedomosti*, 7 December 1904, tr. in Lazzarini, *Pavlova*, 73.
[48] About Karsavina's experience preparing and performing the role of Medora, see Karsavina, *Theatre Street*, 210–216, and Foster, *Karsavina*, 46–53. See also *Khronika IV*, 107, in which Samuil Andrianov is incorrectly listed as Conrad for Karsavina's debut performance.
[49] Karsavina, *Theatre Street*, 210.
[50] Ibid., 216.

Librettos. Like the St. Petersburg *Giselle* and *Paquita* librettos, the 1858 Petersburg *Le Corsaire* libretto (see Appendix E (b)) closely matches the story laid out in the 1856 Paris libretto, albeit more concisely. The 1899 Petersburg libretto is longer, restoring details that were omitted in the shorter 1858 libretto. It remains faithful to the Paris narrative with the exception of the return of Birbanto in the final scene.

Répétiteur. Among the holdings of the Sergeyev Collection is a microfilm of a manuscript *répétiteur* (Rep) of *Le Corsaire*. Arranged for two violins, the Rep comprises 254 pages, although fifty are missing from the microfilm (and, we assume, from the manuscript itself).[51] The title page reads "Ballet | *Korsar* | *Le Corsaire* | Music of Adam and of Mr Pugni" and is signed at the top by Nikolai Sergeyev. Although the Rep contains few annotations, it is a highly useful document—a compendium of original numbers by Adam and interpolations made over the course of the work's Petersburg performance history, spanning the years 1858 through, roughly, 1902 (the latter date arrived at by virtue of an interpolation in *Le jardin animé* for Sedova). In the absence of an orchestra score representing the Petersburg production, musical examples in this chapter will be drawn from the Rep.

Choreographic notation. The Sergeyev Collection's 160-page choreographic notation (CN) of *Le Corsaire* covers the first three of the ballet's five scenes, including a detailed notation of *Le jardin animé*, which we discuss separately in Chapter 8.[52] The rest of the CN is written in pencil, mostly on standard portrait-format notation paper, and is largely in Sergeyev's hand. Dancer names and dates included in the CN (as well as in other materials discussed in Chapter 8) suggest the complete body of notations spans roughly the years 1894 to 1906. Dancers named in the CN's action scenes include Pavlova (Medora), Gerdt (Conrad, who is sometimes identified as "Corsair"), Iosif Kshesinsky (Birbanto), Trefilova and Vill (Gulnare), Lukyanov (Lanquedem), and Ivan Voronkov (Caretaker of the Pasha's harem, identified as "Eunuch"—note that Ivan Voronkov replaced Nikolai Voronkov in this role during the 1900–1901 season).

Much like segments of the *Giselle* and *Paquita* CNs, the *Corsaire* CN offers only a sketch of the mimetic content of any given scene. Moreover, only the barest of details are recorded for some of the dances (Medora's first entrance, *Petit Corsaire*), and nothing of Scenes IV or V is documented at all. On the other hand, the manuscript does allow us to take a detailed look at a varied selection of danced numbers (*Pas de l'esclave, Finesse d'amour, Danse des Corsaires,* the *pas de six, Danse des Forbans,* the grotto *scène dansante, Le jardin animé, Scène d'espièglerie, Pas de trois des odalisques*).

Mime script. A four-page Russian-language mime script in Sergeyev's hand is filed at the beginning of the CN. The document contains mime conversations and a description of the action of parts of Scenes I and III.

Mariinsky Theater production documents. These pages, first prepared for the 1899 revival, provide prop lists, information about costume accessories, and drawings of stage settings that add to our understanding of the details included in the CN.[53]

A note on the division of scenes within acts: The Rep follows the 1858 format of three acts and five scenes, the same as the 1856 Paris production. The CN and 1899 libretto

[51] MS Thr 245 (270), Harvard Theatre Collection, Houghton Library, Harvard University. The missing pages are pages 89–104, 107–118, and 219–240.
[52] MS Thr 245 (1).
[53] St. Petersburg State Museum of Theatre and Music (GMTMI), GIK 16917, fols. 145v–150r. Folio 148, which presumably contained details for Scene III, is missing from the volume.

conform to the redistribution of scenes into four acts that appears to have been introduced in 1863.

Scene-by-scene description of the St. Petersburg
Le Corsaire as recorded in the Rep and CN

The following description is based on the Rep and CN, supplemented with information from posters, programs, and other primary and secondary sources. We refer to scenes rather than acts; scene titles are taken from the 1899 St. Petersburg program.

Because the present order of materials in the CN does not represent performance order and because the CN does not include all of the dances performed in 1899 or the several years following, we will use the Rep to establish the framework of scenes and numbers for this description. The Rep not only assists in determining performance order but also provides a glimpse of older productions through its inclusion of music for otherwise lost dances. Where the CN is silent, we will include details from the 1899 libretto.

Scene I
The Kidnapping of Medora

The Rep is divided into many more discrete numbers than the Paris score. Scene I comprises the following: Introduction, Nos. 1–5, *Pas de l'esclave*, No. 6, *Danse des Corsaires*, Finale.

Introduction. The brief introduction preserved in the Rep, which has been attributed to Pugni, is arranged for a single violin (the rest of the Rep is arranged for two violins).[54] The raucous music—descending diminished triads in the trumpets, punctuated by bass drum and followed by upward diminished arpeggios in the violins—creates an atmosphere of action that gives way to an eight-bar melody in D major, repeated four times in sequence at successively higher pitch (Ex. 7.1).

According to the Mariinsky Theater production documents, the stage floor of the Adrianople market setting is filled with "5 square hemp carpets," on which are stacked a number of cushions. Behind these is a large opening at upstage center, placed between the fourth and fifth wings. Lanquedem's balcony is set up at stage left.

No. 1. The curtain rises at bar 3 of No. 1, of which fifty-five of eighty-four bars are cut in the Rep. Although the CN makes no mention of it, the *Danse des Esclaves* for four women, listed in the program for the 1899 revival, was likely performed during this number, perhaps to the same music as the brief corresponding dance in the Justamant staging manual (see Chapter 6).

No. 2. The CN commences with No. 2 ("beginning"). (The CN's account of Scene I is dated 24 November 1904, less than two weeks prior to Pavlova's debut on 5 December.) The corsairs enter upstage left (Ex. 6.2). The group divides and the pirates move to each side of the stage. They are followed by Birbanto and finally Conrad, both of whom greet their comrades. Conrad approaches Birbanto and shakes his hand.

---

[54] According to Burlaka, "C[esare] Pugni composes [sic] the introduction to the ballet for the Petersburgian performance (1858) on assignment from choreographer J[ules] Perrot." Burlaka, ed., *Le Corsaire*, 264.

Ex. 7.1 Introduction (Pugni), bars 39–55

Conrad: "There is one beautiful girl, and I want to talk to her alone." He walks upstage left and addresses the other corsairs: "You all leave. I want to be here by myself." The corsairs depart.

No. 3. Medora appears on the balcony (Ex. 6.26a). She throws flowers—a *selam*, which the 1899 libretto explains is "a bouquet in which every flower has its own meaning"—to Conrad, who catches them. Lanquedem, who has joined Medora on the balcony, leads her back inside.

No. 4. Conrad (pointing to the bouquet): "This flower means she loves me." He kisses the *selam* and then claps his hands, calling the corsairs back to the stage (Ex. 6.25). They enter from all sides.

Conrad: "Everyone, listen. Here is one beautiful girl. I want to kidnap her. You will help me, yes?"

Corsairs: "Yes."

Conrad: "When you hear three claps, you come here." The corsairs leave the stage again.

As the music changes to ⁶⁄₈ meter, Medora enters down a staircase at stage left and circles upstage for her *Entrée* (as her entrance dance is called in the programs as early as Dor's debut in September 1868; Ex. 6.17). Her steps are written in prose rather than notated. Traveling down the diagonal, she performs "6 times | *glissade jeté*." She waltzes upstage right and repeats the diagonal to the other side, "4 times and turns," likely meaning four repetitions of *glissade*, *jeté* followed by turns on *pointe* (the Stepanov *pointe* symbol is drawn on the ground plan) that take Medora across the stage to the right. Karsavina recalled the challenge and purpose of this initial appearance:

> The first coming on of the ballerina in *Corsair* is very effective; traversing the stage in diagonal leaps, the dancer concludes her entrance with a series of difficult pirouettes. This first bit fetched loud applause; a link with the audience was established, the confidence of the public gained. Perhaps no other ballet offers such varied opportunities to the leading lady.[55]

[55] Karsavina, *Theatre Street*, 214–215. On Karsavina's experience rehearsing and performing the role of Medora, see Foster, *Karsavina*, 46–53.

Conrad comes forward, meeting Medora at center, where he embraces her (Ex. 6.18). *Conrad*: "This flower says you love me."

Lanquedem runs to the couple and separates them. Conrad, clasping his hands together, stomps his foot and charges at Lanquedem, who backs away. Conrad turns and walks downstage right.

No. 5. The Pasha is carried in on a litter from upstage right (Exx. 6.1a–b). He assesses the slave women, none of whom please him. A list in the CN, provided without further elaboration, appears to describe this bit of action and the various women who are presented:

     I. Dance of 4 women
    II. Black women are offered
  III. Big women are offered

Lanquedem brings forward a veiled woman (CN: "beautiful girl") for the Pasha to see. She is Medora. Lanquedem opens her veil, and the Pasha is astonished by her beauty. Conrad charges at the Pasha, who backs away then goes to sit down. This confrontation is interrupted by the *Pas de l'esclave*.

Pas de l'esclave. As discussed above, the dance that in 1899 was titled *Pas de l'esclave* (No. 5½ in the CN, where it is titled *Pas desclave*) appears to have first been added to the St. Petersburg *Corsaire* in 1858, when it was called *L'esclave, pas scènique*.[56] Choreographed by Perrot, the number featured a male-female couple and Lanquedem (by 1863 the latter's name was omitted from the poster). The composer of the entrée, adagio, and coda preserved in the Rep has been identified as Grand Duke Petr Georgievich of Oldenburg, whose short ballet, *The Rose, the Violet, and the Butterfly*, is the source of the music arranged for *Le Corsaire* by Pugni.[57] Various dates and sometimes conflicting details of the premiere of *The Rose, the Violet, and the Butterfly* have been put forward. A poster for a benefit performance given for the *régisseur* Ivan Marcel on 8 October 1857 at the Bolshoi Theater, St. Petersburg, provides the following information:[58]

[56] By the time the CN was made, the dance was titled *Pas d'esclaves* in printed programs.

[57] The music for this number is published twice in Burlaka, ed., *Le Corsaire*, 275–283 and 420–429): first, as *L'esclave* (as in 1858) in three movements: entrée, adagio, and coda; second, as *Pas d'esclaves* (as in 1899—although the title used in that production was *Pas de l'esclave*) in five movements: entrée, adagio, male variation (music by Tsybin, see below), female variation (music by Drigo, see below), and coda (a shorter version than the first and a semitone higher in E major).

[58] The program also included *Markitanka* (*La Vivandière*), the first act of Perrot's ballet *Faust*, and the second scene of *The Naiad and the Fisherman*. Other sources have stated the first performance took place at the Russian Imperial family's summer residence in Tsarskoe Selo. See *Khronika III*, 57. Ivor Guest suggested the choreography may have been by Petipa, citing the 1857 Tsarskoe Selo performance and a cast that included Marie Petipa, the student Matilda Madayeva, and Muravieva. See Guest, *Jules Perrot*, 303, 357. Finally, Konstantin Skalkovsky asserted the ballet, in the form of a large divertissement, premiered on 8 December 1857 in Peterhof. Nadine Meisner discusses this and the other possibilities in Meisner, *Marius Petipa*, 90–91, 301. Petr Georgievich, Duke of Oldenburg was the Tsar's cousin, grandson of Emperor Paul I, and an amateur composer.

For the 1st time:

THE ROSE, THE VIOLET, AND THE BUTTERFLY.
Choreographic interlude by Mr. Jules Perrot.

Characters:

The Rose	Mlle Radina.
The Violet	Mlle Amosova 2.
The Butterfly	Mlle MURAVIEVA.

Although the Rep does not name the composer of the *Pas de l'esclave*,[59] the words "Par Mlle Moravieva [sic]" link the number to *The Rose, the Violet, and the Butterfly*, in which Marfa Muravieva danced the role of the Butterfly.

The number preserved in the CN, dated 1905, represents the dance as it was performed in the early years of the twentieth century in what may have been an enlarged version of the 1858 original. The five-part structure of entrée, adagio, two variations, and coda reflects what we regard as traditional late-nineteenth-century *pas de deux* form. However, the frequent pantomime reminds us that the number was originally a *pas d'action* (recall the subtitle *pas scènique*), a combination of choreography and action that was a hallmark of Perrot's dancemaking. The pantomime recorded in the CN suggests that the dramatic premise of the dance involves a merchant attempting to persuade the Pasha to buy his slave.

Although an annotation at the end of the preceding No. 5 states, "Dance | Kyaksht and Legat S.," it is Varvara Rykhlyakova's performance, rather than Lydia Kyaksht's, that is notated.[60] And while Rykhlyakova was partnered by Nikolai Legat in the 1899 revival, the CN records his brother Sergei's performance.

Entrée. The entrée's static choreographic structure of repeated diagonals from upstage right (leading to the Pasha at downstage left) is broken up by brief scenes of pantomime, during which the merchant endeavors to interest the Pasha in his slave. The slave woman periodically approaches the Pasha alone, begging him to let her go.

Beginning upstage right, the couple travels down the diagonal with *cabriole derrière*, *assemblé, piqué en arabesque* three times, the woman partnered by the man, who "lifts [her] by the waist" (Ex. 7.2a). They run downstage right, where they continue with a *tour de promenade en piqué arabesque, piqué en arabesque* three times. The woman moves away with turns on *pointe*, while the man walks to the Pasha downstage, where the two engage in a "Scène" (*Stsena*; no further details are provided). Beginning again from upstage right, the woman performs a supported *grand jeté en avant, relevé fouetté* to *arabesque* three times. She moves away from her partner with turns on *pointe* while he promotes her to the Pasha: "Look, what a leg, what an arm." The dancers run upstage right for a third diagonal: two *glissades, sissonne* (the man "lifts the lady"), *relevé en arabesque*, again three times. Turns on *demi-pointe* for the woman complete the entrée.

Adagio. An annotation at the opening of the adagio, as documented in the CN, informs us that up until this time the ballerina has been wearing a veil. As she *bourrées*, making two circles in place, accompanied by a languid and leisurely melody spun out in compound meter, her partner removes ("unwraps") her veil (Ex. 7.2b). Traveling

---

[59] In the Rep, the number was originally titled *Pas d'Lesclave* but has been altered to read *Pas d'esclave*.
[60] Lydia Kyaksht and Sergei Legat performed the *Pas des esclaves* on 19 September 1904, the first performance of *Le Corsaire* in the 1904–1905 season. See *Ezhegodnik* (1904–1905), 107.

Ex. 7.2a *Pas de l'esclave*, Entrée (Oldenburg), bars 5–12

across the stage toward the Pasha, the merchant supports the woman in *glissade, piqué en arabesque, sissonne en arabesque* two times. She steps into a *double piqué tour en dehors*, her partner catching her by the waist. Then, performing a *glissade* and stepping into fourth position, she goes to the Pasha, whom she "asks not to"—presumably—buy her. She repeats the double turn then runs upstage right. Her partner supports her as they move across the stage with *glissade, développé à la seconde* to *attitude devant*, supported *double pirouette* to *arabesque* three times. At upstage left, they continue with a supported *arabesque* on *pointe* and *fouetté*, the working leg finishing ninety degrees *devant* as the woman leans far back, three times. She approaches the Pasha again, "stopping" or "pausing" then running back to her partner, who supports her in a final *double pirouette* to *arabesque*.

Variations. A four-bar transition (*Allegro moderato*, $\frac{6}{8}$) effects a modulation from G major to D major and leads to the solos.

The man's variation is not notated, and the strongly rhythmic number in $\frac{6}{8}$ meter that presumably accompanied it is unattributed in the Rep (Ex. 7.2c). Burlaka, whose edition of the *Pas de l'esclave* piano reduction includes the same male variation as the Rep, offers the following: "For the revival of 'Le Corsaire' in 1914 was used a new variation of a Slave on the music by the artist of the Mariinsky orchestra V[ladimir] Tsybin for the premier [of] P[etr] Vladimirov."[61] Indeed, in the program for the 21 December 1914 Mariinsky Theater performance of *Le Corsaire*, in which Vladimirov partnered Lubov Egorova in the *Pas d'esclaves*, the music for the male variation is credited to Tsybin.

The Rep informs us that the ballerina's solo is "from the ballet *Veṣṭalka* | Variation | Mlle Gorschenkova [sic]." Maria Gorshenkova danced the second ballerina role of Claudia in the 1888 premiere of Petipa's *The Vestal*, with music by Mikhail Ivanov. Burlaka attributes this variation to Riccardo Drigo, who conducted the premiere and is also credited with several numbers in the score (Ex. 7.2d).[62]

---

[61] Burlaka, ed., *Le Corsaire*, 424 and 446.
[62] Ibid., 396 and 426.

Ex. 7.2b *Pas de l'esclave*, Adagio (Oldenburg), bars 1–9

Ex. 7.2c *Pas de l'esclave*, Variation 1 (Tsybin), bars 2–9

Ex. 7.2d *Pas de l'esclave*, Variation 2 (attr. Drigo), bars 3–6, from *The Vestal*

Beginning at center, Rykhlyakova travels downstage right with *pas de basque, piqué tour en dehors* to *développé devant, tombé, emboîté derrière*. She repeats the enchaînement, beginning with the *piqué tour*, and continues by making a complete turn to the right as she performs *relevés petits passés*. She *bourrées* upstage left and repeats all of the material from the beginning of the variation. The second section (Rep: "meno") features a diagonal from upstage right: *entrechat cinq* to *demi-arabesque fondu, coupé dessous, piqué en arabesque, assemblé, entrechat cinq* to *demi-arabesque fondu, coupé dessous, piqué en arabesque, coupé dessous, jeté*. She continues with a series of *temps levés en demi-arabesque*, traveling downstage right, and a *bourrée en tournant*. Next, a series of *entrechat cinq, piqué en cou-de-pied devant* is followed by a *bourrée* that breaks into a run upstage left. The final section of the variation features two sets of three undesignated turns on the diagonal set to sixteen bars of an *allegro vivace*.

Coda. The extended coda (originally sixty-nine bars, not including repeats totaling twenty-four bars) is cut by half in the Rep (Ex. 7.2e), another apparent instance of a dance being altered over time. The CN begins with a solo passage for the ballerina, likely omitting an initial passage for the *danseur*. Traveling on the diagonal from upstage right, she performs a series of unusual *pas de basque* in which the first step of each is a *demi-gargouillade* traveling forward. She returns up the diagonal with *piqués de côté en cou-de-pied devant*. After repeating the *pas de basque* enchaînement, she "runs up to" her partner at center, where he supports her in *cabriole derrière, assemblé, entrechat six* three times to alternate sides as they travel in a zigzag pattern downstage.

Leaving the merchant, the slave woman runs to the Pasha and kneels in front of him, beseeching, "You, let me go," to which he answers, "Go!" She runs away to center and, after an initial "p[.] d. bu." (*pas de bourrée*), performs a series of six *demi-emboîtés derrière* and "3 *jeté*" three times to alternate sides. She approaches the Pasha a final time, performing *temps levés en demi-arabesque, pas de bourrée* six times to alternate sides. The Pasha bids her "Farewell, farewell," suggesting he has ultimately acquiesced and let her go.

Finesse d'amour. The subsequent "Pas d'action" in the CN is surely the comic *Finesse d'amour* that is found in the program's list of dances for the 1899 revival, during which Medora mockingly flirts with the Pasha. The interpolation of this *pas* in the opening

Ex. 7.2e *Pas de l'esclave*, Coda (Oldenburg), bars 2–9

scene afforded an additional dancing opportunity for Medora early in the ballet and also served to immediately establish the Pasha as a comedic character.

The heading in the Rep provides information about the provenance of the number: "From the ballet *Satanilla* | Variation | Mlle Lebedeva." (As noted above, the *Finesse d'amour* appears to have been added to the 1858 Moscow production of *Le Corsaire* before its addition to the St. Petersburg production in 1899.) As preserved in the Rep, the *Finesse d'amour* comprises four sections:

Allegro moderato, $\frac{2}{4}$, D major	41 bars, not including repeats of nearly all of the material
Moderato molto, $\frac{3}{4}$, G major	50 bars
Allegretto, $\frac{3}{4}$, C major	23 bars, not including several repeats, one of which is struck through
Allegro, $\frac{2}{4}$, C major	15 bars, not including a repeat; six bars are struck through

During the seven-bar introduction, Lanquedem approaches the Pasha: "She [Medora] will be dancing here." Medora begins at center, with the Pasha and Lanquedem downstage left and Conrad downstage right. She performs *piqué de côté en cou-de-pied devant*, *piqué en demi-arabesque*, *pas de bourrée* on *pointe* three times to alternate sides, stepping in time with the piquant melody—one of Pugni's more effective efforts—that complements the coquetry of the dance (Ex. 7.3a).

She *bourrées* directly downstage, then "runs on [*pointe* symbol]" to the Pasha. Taking him with her by pulling on his beard, Medora crosses the stage as she performs a variant of the opening enchaînement. She runs to center with the Pasha, *bourrées*—turning twice—then runs away upstage right. Arms open invitingly, she *bourrées* back toward the Pasha, who meets her at center. He kisses her hand, and she runs away again, this time toward Conrad at downstage right. The corsair takes Medora by the waist, supporting her in a *tour de promenade en arabesque*, *passé* to *attitude devant*. She runs upstage and *bourrées* toward the Pasha, allowing him again to kiss her hand. She returns to Conrad for a second supported *tour de promenade*, this one *en cou-de-pied devant*.

Ex. 7.3a *Finesse d'amour*, Variation from *Satanilla* (attr. Pugni), bars 10–17

Ex. 7.3b *Finesse d'amour* (attr. Pugni), bars 44–51

Running away to center, she begins a series of *temps levés en demi-arabesque* as she turns to the right, the working leg making a *grand rond de jambe en l'air* from *demi-attitude devant* to *demi-arabesque*. After making a complete turn, she brings the working leg to *cou-de-pied devant* and performs a *relevé double pirouette en dehors*, finishing in *plié en cou-de-pied devant*. This enchaînement is performed four times, bringing the first section of the dance to a close.

As a waltz begins, Medora walks a circle around the Pasha then runs to Conrad who supports her in an *arabesque* on *pointe* as she holds his shoulder and the hand of his outstretched arm (Ex. 7.3b).

After repeating these movements, Medora takes the Pasha's staff. She *bourrées* around him (a lone *arabesque à plat* is also notated at this point) then darts to the left as he moves right. She "takes the staff a second time" and *bourrées* in a circle; the Pasha steps in and recovers his staff. Medora travels away with three sets of *piqué en demi-arabesque, pas de bourrée*. After a fourth *piqué en demi-arabesque*, she moves upstage with *chassé, tour jeté*. She *bourrées* toward the Pasha and circles him as she "twirls the staff."

Ex. 7.3c *Finesse d'amour* (attr. Pugni), bars 92–99

Ex. 7.3d *Finesse d'amour* (attr. Pugni), bars 115–122

Medora leaves the Pasha again and goes to center to place herself for the third section of the dance: a solo (Ex. 7.3c).

Medora begins with three series of *relevés en cou-de-pied* on alternating legs, making a *double pirouette* on the fourth *relevé* of each series. Four *balancés* bring her upstage, then she travels back down in a zigzag pattern with *piqué en demi-arabesque* and four *demi-emboîtés devant* to alternate sides. *Balancés* bring her upstage right, and she returns on the diagonal with "4 *cabrioles*." As the music transitions to the final *allegro*, Medora begins a *manège*, performing "turns *en attitude*" (Ex. 7.3d). She concludes the *pas d'action* with turns on *pointe* at downstage right.

No. 6. At the beginning of the following "Scène" (Rep: "Après le pas"), the Pasha has made up his mind (Ex. 6.14a).

Pasha: (to Medora) "I am charmed by you. I like you very much, and I will buy you. I will give you jewelry—earrings, rings, and bracelets."

Medora: "I do not need that."

The Pasha calls for Lanquedem and asks how much money he wants for Medora. They bargain, while Medora "has a *scène* with the corsair," of which no details are given.

Pasha: (to Medora) "At last, you are mine. You will be rich and will live in the palace." (to Lanquedem) "You look after her, otherwise I will off with your head."

The Pasha gives Lanquedem money and signs papers as Conrad looks on. The transaction is complete. Preparing to depart, carried on his litter, the Pasha orders Lanquedem to bring Medora.

Introducing the final dance of the scene—which will create the necessary diversion to allow Medora to be abducted and saved from the Pasha—Conrad calls everyone and, throwing coins in the air, exclaims, "Drink and be merry!"

Here is the text of the mime script, which is based closely on the CN and summarizes the action of this scene from the point in which the Pasha begins to assess the slaves until his exit:

> They bring out the book. He [Pasha] looks at the slaves, does not like anyone. Dances of 4 ladies, then they offer Black women and then two big ones. After Lukyanov [Lanquedem] comes out and offers Medora, he [Pasha] looks and falls in love with her. The Corsair [Conrad] comes up and is jealous. He [Pasha] drives him away and they go and sit on the bench and watch the Dances of Legat and Rykhlyakova [*Pas de l'esclave*].
>
> Scene of Pasha and Medora [following the *Finesse d'amour*]. [Pasha:] "I am charmed by you. I like you very much, and I will buy you. I will give you all the jewelry." She [Medora] does not want this. He [Pasha] calls the Jew [Lanquedem] and asks, "How much money do you want," and bargains with him, and signs a contract. At this time, she [Medora] has a scene with the Corsair. Again he [Pasha] turns to her and says, "At last, you are mine. You will be rich, and you will live in the palace." Then he turns to the Jew and says, "You look after her, otherwise I will off with your head." He gets on a litter, and they carry him away.

Danse des Corsaires. As early as 1858, Pugni revised and enlarged Adam's *Bacchanale* (Ex. 6.28) by contributing new material early in the dance (Ex. 7.4a) and substituting a substantial polka coda (108 bars plus repeats) for the return of the opening theme (Ex. 7.4b). This version is represented in both the Rep (in which the new material in $\frac{3}{8}$ meter is struck through) and the CN.

The number is a vigorous and charming example of a nineteenth-century character dance. Unlike the dance preserved in the Justamant manual, the St. Petersburg version, which was classified from the beginning as a *ballabile d'action*, includes group pantomime encompassing romance, fighting, and working onboard ship. The choreography preserved in the CN features a lead couple (first incorporated into the dance in 1868) and twelve male-female ensemble couples (a change made in 1899 from the hitherto female-female couples that included women performing in travesty).

Vazem's recollections of celebrated character dancer Lubov Radina as the female lead give us an idea of the energy with which the dance was performed:

> Radina [who earlier in her career performed the role of Gulnare] also performed character dances, and towards the end of her career devoted herself entirely to this genre. She specialised in fiery, bravura character dances, which she performed with a rare brio and temperament; for example, her Indian dance in *La Bayadère* and her Pirate's

Ex. 7.4a *Danse des Corsaires* (rev. Pugni), bars 43–50

Ex. 7.4b *Danse des Corsaires* (rev. Pugni), bars 171–179

dance in *Le Corsaire* remain in the memory of those who saw them, if only once. Her success in these dances was unsurpassed.[63]

The CN is dated 12 May 1906. The dance is notated twice, once for the principal couple—the CN documents the performance of Ivan Kusov and Evgenia Eduardova—and a second time for the ensemble of pirates and slave women. Half of the couples are designated as "1st Blue" and the others "2nd Red," surely a reference to the color of their costumes. Ground plans are provided and annotated with details, but steps are rarely notated.

The blue group begins at center, arranged in two adjacent lines of three couples each. The couples travel directly downstage, where they make a single turn to the right. The two lines split and move to each wing as the red group, also from upstage center, travels downstage and makes a turn to the right. The red and blue women exchange places, dance briefly with their new partners, then return to their original cavaliers.

Next, the first action sequence commences as the women pose in a lunge position then run to the other side of their partner. The men mime: "You are very beautiful, I love you, and etc.," the CN providing what seem to be examples of a variety of phrases the pirates could express. This is performed four times to alternate sides.

As the opening theme returns, the principal couple appears from upstage left (their entrance is labeled "1st small piece") and travels downstage to center. The ensemble

[63] Ekaterina Vazem, "Memoirs of a Ballerina of the St. Petersburg Bolshoi Theatre: Part 3," tr. Nina Dimitrievich, *Dance Research* 5, no. 1 (Spring 1987): 36.

simultaneously performs the "first *pas* 4 times" as they move to the sides and travel upstage to form two rows, the women in front of the men. What is the "first *pas*"? The answer may be found in the first steps notated for the principal couple: a *temps levé en demi-arabesque* on each leg followed by three steps forward and a fourth step to bring the feet together. The couple performs this enchaînement three times then separates, traveling to opposite corners with three *temps levés* on alternate legs.

Here the reader is directed to "see 102" (the initial notation box is marked "101"), which can be found on a page of notation filed at the end of the dance that includes the balance of the steps that make up the principal couple's first entrance. Traveling back toward center with the "first *pas*," the couple meets and turns in place, performing multiple *temps levés en demi-attitude devant* on the left foot. (This turning enchaînement may be the same set of steps performed by the ensemble couples as they turn at the opening of the dance.) The couple separates again, returns to meet at center, then travels together downstage right, performing the "first *pas* 1 time" and finishing with *échappé en plié* and a spring into *demi-arabesque*.

Meanwhile, the ensemble has traveled directly downstage, performing the "first *pas*." As with the choreography for the principal couple, numbered notation boxes lead the reader from box 101 to boxes 102–103, which are notated on a separate page filed at the end of the dance. There, we find that the lines of dancers separate and return, then all face downstage as they perform the "first *pas*" (finally clearly notated for the ensemble) while the principal couple concludes its first entrance.

The second action sequence begins as the men kneel and the "ladies whisper in the cavalier's left ear." The men stand and perform *balancés* in place as the women split at center, waltz around each end of the men's row, and kneel in a row in front of the men. They make a "round movement with [their] body" while the "cavaliers move two hands 4 times." Traditionally, this has meant that the men mime the action of pulling ropes as one would onboard ship. The women stand and turn in place then the "two last plans [that is, the mimed movements and the women's turn] repeat 2 times." The couples split, run upstage along either side, turn, and form lines of six couples along each wing, the women inside of the men.

As the music transitions to the polka added by Pugni, the principal couple makes its second entrance (CN: "2nd small piece"). Facing each other, they hold one another by the waist or shoulders (the ground plan does not specify) and travel downstage sideways with *demi-valse*. Separating, they travel to opposite downstage corners with *temps levés en demi-arabesque, saut de basque* twice. They continue, repeatedly coming together for partnered movements then separating again. Most of the partnered movements are performed two times. At one point, the "cavalier gives [his] left hand and she turns 2 times." At another, the "cavalier holds [the woman] by the waist with both hands and they turn together while she leans back." Later, the woman runs to the man, the "cavalier gives [his] right hand and she gives [her] right hand," and they travel upstage on the diagonal with *demi-valse*. Finally, at center, they perform four *ballonnés de côté* on alternating legs and then run to opposite corners where they make a "small stop." All of this takes place downstage of the ensemble, which performs various combinations of *temps levé en demi-arabesque* and *demi-valse*.

The men run to center for the third action sequence. A series of steps in place is accompanied by the annotation, "cavaliers fighting." In current productions, the pirates engage in choreographed sword play at this point. Although no weapons are mentioned

Ex. 7.4c *Danse des Corsaires* (rev. Pugni), bars 236–243

in the CN, a photo of *Le Corsaire* featuring dancers Alexander Medalinsky and Fedor Vasiliev—both of whom performed in the *Danse des Corsaires* in the 1899 revival—may represent this third action sequence: the men face each other with sabers drawn and held overhead.[64] The women rush to retrieve the men, "jumping" as they travel to center. Holding onto each other, the couples turn in place before the women run back to the wings and the "three last plans [beginning with the men fighting] repeat 1 time." As the "cavaliers [are] fighting 4 times," the women travel upstage with *ballonnés* and return with *pas de valse en tournant*. They travel again to center, this time with multiple *précipités*, and pull their partners back to the wings. The pirates break free and resume their fighting. The "last 4 plans [from the men fighting and the women performing *ballonnés*] repeat 1 time." Finally, the pirates cross and recross twice at center ("cavaliers do 4 going over"—no step is given), while the women travel upstage with three *ballonnés*, *pas de bourrée* "3½ times."

To set up the fourth action sequence, the ensemble is instructed to "go into lines" upstage: two rows of women standing and holding each other by the waist are upstage of a semicircle of kneeling men. The principal couple, beginning their "3rd small piece," kneels in front of the group. As the ensemble women repeat a lunging movement that may be intended to resemble the waves of the sea, the others are "rowing 8 times," mimicking the actions of a crew propelling its boat forward to the strains of a new dotted theme in a relaxed tempo (Ex. 7.4c).

The ensemble returns to the wings, the men running, the women performing *temps levés en demi-arabesque* on alternate legs. The "cavaliers call each other to fight" and run to center, while the principal couple resumes a repeated series that consists of dashing to the corners and returning to center. The ensemble women waltz to center, and the entire group turns and moves upstage for their final enchaînement. They perform *temps levés* traveling downstage as the principal couple traces mirroring zigzags at the front of the group. In a final pose, the women are instructed to "fall on the cavalier's knees." The principal couple finish next to each other, but no final pose is given.

[64] GMTMI GIK 2016/57.

Finale. During the brief finale that follows the dance (Rep: "Finale 1er Tableaux"), Conrad, having propped a ladder against the balcony, climbs up, whistles, hits Lanquedem on the head, and runs away with Medora.

Scene II

The Conspirators

No. 1. The curtain rises on the grotto at bar 10 of No. 1 (Ex. 6.15). The stage plans preserved in the Mariinsky production documents indicate a rocky surround at the top of the third wing that is supported by four columns at stage right with a large opening at center. A curtained opening in the third wing at stage right hides a divan, seen in the overhead perspective. On stage left, another divan and small table are placed by the second wing.

This number is omitted in the CN.

No. 2. The subsequent *scène* begins with the "Entrance of students and slaves out of the compartment" (or "hold"; Ex. 6.22). Arrows drawn on the CN ground plan appear to indicate that the group enters through the central upstage opening. Conrad and Medora follow. The ground plan documenting their entrance also includes lines of six males along each wing who exit upstage left after Medora and Conrad walk downstage.

Medora: "What is all this?"

Conrad: "This is all mine, and I am your slave. You are tired. Go there and rest." Conrad walks with Medora toward stage right. She exits and he returns to center.

This brief exchange appears to be a truncated version of the longer conversation recorded in the 1899 libretto:

> Conrad, together with Medora, appears in the grotto. With curiosity and fear, she observes the slaves meeting her in the corsair's dwelling. Conrad tries to calm her, promising she will be mistress of all the untold treasures belonging to him as master of the seas.
>
> Medora gently thanks him for his love and promises, but asks him, precisely in the name of their love, to give up, from here on out, his dangerous exploits, to put down his weapons and live for her alone. Conrad swears to renounce wealth and glory for the sake of her glance, for even her one gentle word. In her turn, Medora promises to love Conrad until the end of her life. Casting a loving gaze on him, she leaves, giving him time to discuss his new intentions with his comrades.

Birbanto brings Lanquedem on stage. The merchant drops to his knees. Conrad shakes his finger at him threateningly.

Birbanto: "Slave women will be brought here." The women enter the stage.

The variety of dances performed during this scene routinely changed over the nearly sixty years that *Corsaire* was in the Petersburg repertory during the Imperial era. A survey of several configurations of dances demonstrates that they fluidly came and went, largely depending on the ballerina cast as Medora. Notably, an extra cavalier was often cast (as a sort of supplementary Conrad) to partner the ballerina in one of the dances. This was likely done in early years because Petipa (who performed the role of Conrad) did not excel at academic dance and in later years because Gerdt (who performed the role of Conrad regularly from 1899 onwards) was no longer dancing and limited himself to pantomime and partnering.

12 January 1858:
Pas des éventailles	Medora (Friedberg), 4 women plus other women
Scène dansante	Medora, Conrad (Petipa)

24 January 1863:
Pas de six	Medora (Surovshchikova-Petipa), Christian Johanson, 4 women
Pas d'éventails	Kemmerer, 3 women plus other women
Pas du corsaire	Medora
Scène dansante	Medora, Conrad (Petipa)

25 January 1868:
Grand pas des éventails	Medora (Grantzow), Conrad (Petipa), 4 women plus 24 women
Scène et danse de séduction	Medora, Conrad

3 September 1868:
Le petit Corsaire	Kemmerer
Pas de six (nouveau)	Medora (Dor), Christian Johanson, 4 women
Scène et danse de seduction	Medora, Conrad (Petipa)

30 November 1880:
Grand pas	Medora (Sokolova), Gerdt, 19 women (although possibly with the addition of Karsavin and with only 18 women; see reference above to the 3 January 1881 performance)
Forbans (characteristic dance)	3 women, 3 men
Le petit Corsaire	Medora
Scène dansante	Medora, Conrad (Ivanov)

13 January 1899:
Danse des Forbans	3 women, 3 men
Grand pas des éventails	Medora (Legnani), Georgi Kyaksht, 12 women
Scène dansante	Medora, Conrad (Gerdt)

7 April 1904:
Pas de six	Medora (Sedova), Nikolai Legat, 4 women
Danse des Forbans	3 women, 3 men
Petit Corsaire	Medora
Scène dansante	Medora, Conrad (Gerdt)

28 December 1904:
Pas de deux	Medora (Pavlova), Sergei Legat, choreographed by Sergei Legat
Danse des Forbans	3 women, 3 men, including Birbanto (Iosif Kshesinsky)
Petit Corsaire	Medora
Scène dansante	Medora, Conrad (Gerdt)

3 December 1908:
Pas de deux	Medora (Karsavina), Andrianov, choreography unattributed
Danse des Forbans	3 women, 3 men
Petit Corsaire	Medora
Scène dansante	Medora, Conrad (Gerdt)

21 December 1914:

Pas de six	Medora (Preobrazhenskaya), Vladimirov, 4 women
Danse des Forbans	3 women, 3 men, including Birbanto (Iosif Kshesinsky)
Petit Corsaire	Medora
Scène dansante	Medora, Conrad (Gerdt)

11 January 1915:

Pas d'action	Medora (Karsavina), Conrad (Andrianov), Anatole Obukhov, choreographed by Andrianov
Danse des Forbans	3 women, 3 men, including Birbanto (Iosif Kshesinsky)[65]
Petit Corsaire	Medora
Scène dansante	Medora, Conrad

From this list, we see that both the *Pas des éventails* and *Pas de six* were recurring numbers, the former presented under various titles and surely with revisions to its choreography, as the numbers of dancers listed suggest. The *scène dansante*, the central love scene of the ballet, was always included, though given a different title in 1868 (*Scène et danse de séduction*). The *Pas du corsaire*, eventually titled *Petit Corsaire*, was first introduced in 1868 and became a mainstay of the scene (although it was not danced by Legnani in the 1899 revival). Finally, the *Danse des Forbans*, first introduced in the opening scene in 1868 as *Les Forbans, pas de caractère*, was transferred to the grotto scene in 1899 and from thereon was a regular feature of the scene and sometimes led by the dancer performing the role of Birbanto.

Pas de six. Both the Rep and CN include the *pas de six* as the first danced number of the scene. (An earlier page in the CN lists a "Pas de deux," which could be a reference to the *pas de six* or to the 1904 *pas de deux* choreographed by Sergei Legat). First introduced in 1863, the *pas de six* was performed by Maria Surovshchikova-Petipa and Christian Johanson with four women students and set to a particularly banal suite of five movements, attributed to Pugni.[66] The Rep, in which the dance is titled *Pas de deux ou Pas de six*, lists the names "Mme Petipa, Mlle Vergina, Mlle Sokolova et Mlle Eugeni"; only "Mme Petipa" (Surovshchikova-Petipa) had been part of the original cast. Taking the Rep together with the CN, we find that the *pas* is made up of an entrée for the ensemble women, an adagio for Medora and her cavalier, a variation for the four women, a variation for Medora, and a coda for all.

Entrée. The entrée, a bright *allegro moderato*, comprises fifty-seven bars plus repeats, several of which are struck through in the Rep (Ex. 7.5a).

The four ensemble women begin upstage left, traveling down the diagonal with steps forward on *pointe*, the right leg raised in *demi-attitude devant* with each step on the left foot, followed by *tombé, chassé, tour jeté*. After repeating this to the other side, they return up the diagonal, traveling backward, with *temps levé* and *demi-arabesque fondu* separated by *pas de bourrée en arrière* on *demi-pointe*. They stop then run downstage right, repeat the phrase to the other side, and run downstage left. Next, they traverse the stage four times with multiple *piqués en demi-attitude* and *relevés double ronds de jambe en*

---

[65] Our copy of the program for 11 January 1915 includes manuscript annotations. For the *Danse des Forbans*, Kshesinsky's name is struck through and replaced with "[Ivan] Kusov."

[66] According to Burlaka, "C[esare] Pugni composes [sic] *Pas de six* (Medora, her partner and four female soloists) for the Petersburgian performance (1863) on assignment for choreographer M[arius] Petipa, for the ballerina M[aria] Surovshchikova-Petipa." Burlaka, ed., *Le Corsaire*, 299.

Ex. 7.5a *Pas de deux ou Pas de six*, Entrée (attr. Pugni), bars 1–9

l'air. They travel backward upstage with more *piqués* then split and move to the sides, finishing with a *pas de chat* as Medora and her cavalier enter upstage right.

Adagio. The adagio, a *pas de deux*, is made up of three sections. The first, by far the longest, features a lyrical melody in F major that modulates to C major and back to F over the course of forty-nine bars, eight of which are cut in the Rep (Ex. 7.5b). The opening enchaînement sees Medora supported by the cavalier, beginning with a *sous-sus*. She continues with *développé à la seconde* and a supported *pirouette* that opens to *arabesque*. The cavalier lifts Medora as she performs a *double rond de jambe*, and she completes the enchaînement with a *relevé en arabesque*.

Much of what follows is documented only with ground plans and sparse annotations. Eventually Medora begins a lengthy *bourrée* toward upstage left, where she turns in a circle before returning downstage along the diagonal. Turns on *demi-pointe* follow, and she finishes the phrase with a *relevé en arabesque*, likely supported by her cavalier. This passage may correspond to the second section of the music: seventeen bars of a dotted rhythm in B-flat major (Ex. 7.5c).

The final section of fifteen bars is a return to F major and the opening theme. Medora performs *glissade, relevé double rond de jambe en l'air*, and a supported *double pirouette* into another *double rond de jambe en l'air* opening *devant* three times. Then she "just walks" to her left and kneels beside her cavalier as he performs an *arabesque*. Medora next *bourrées* down the diagonal from upstage left, stopping at three points for a supported single *pirouette* that opens into *arabesque*. The couple moves to center to complete the adagio with "*poklon* [literally, bow or *révérence*] 4 times" and unspecified turns, possibly supported *pirouettes*.

Variation 1. The Rep continues with sixty-six bars of an *allegro giusto* waltz, marked "in one" (Ex. 7.5d).

Labeled "1st Coda | $\frac{3}{4}$" in the CN, the number features the ensemble women in solos and pairs and finally all together. (Because the actual coda is in $\frac{2}{4}$ meter throughout, we presume this dance in $\frac{3}{4}$ meter was performed to this particular piece of music, the only number in the *pas de six* that is in $\frac{3}{4}$ meter.) A first woman begins upstage right and travels down the diagonal with *cabriole derrière, pas de chat* twice. She repeats the enchaînement to the other side and finishes her entrée with turns on *demi-pointe*.

Ex. 7.5b *Pas de deux ou Pas de six*, Adagio (attr. Pugni), bars 2–9

Ex. 7.5c *Pas de deux ou Pas de six*, Adagio (attr. Pugni), bars 51–58

A second dancer travels downstage center with *ballonné, grand pas de basque* four times to alternate sides. The rest of her entrée, recorded in ground plans only, includes a turning step performed three times to alternate sides followed by turns toward downstage left.

The remaining pair dances together. From upstage left, they travel down the diagonal with *piqué en demi-arabesque, pas de bourrée* on *demi-pointe, cabriole devant* twice. They circle upstage with three *piqués en demi-arabesque en tournant* and run forward at center where they are joined by the other women. Together they travel downstage in a zigzag pattern then split and move to opposite downstage corners with turns on *demi-pointe*.

Ex. 7.5d *Pas de deux ou Pas de six*, Variation 1 (attr. Pugni), bars 3–10

Ex. 7.5e *Pas de deux ou Pas de six*, Variation 2 (attr. Pugni), bars 1–10

Variation 2. The entire "Variation | Madame Petipa," an *allegro* $\frac{2}{4}$ in F major, is struck through in the Rep (Ex. 7.5e) and unaccounted for in the CN.

Coda. The brief coda documented in the CN is hardly substantial enough to fill the lengthy music preserved in the Rep. The score features four sections (all in $\frac{2}{4}$ meter) for a total of 217 bars (not including repeats), of which fifty-five are struck through (Ex. 7.5f). The CN documents brief entrées for the ensemble and soloists before all come together for an equally short group finale.

Sergeyev opts for prose descriptions of most of the movements. The four women begin (CN: "2nd Coda"). They travel together on the diagonal from upstage left, moving downstage and back several times with a series of *cabrioles devant* and *derrière*, *arabesques*, and *jetés*. Finally, they run upstage right and travel down the diagonal with *demi-valse*, "waving hands."

Legat follows with a diagonal from upstage right. Medora (here, Sedova) is next, also traveling on the diagonal from upstage right, after which Legat makes a second pass on the same diagonal. No steps are documented for either dancer.

Ex. 7.5f *Pas de deux ou Pas de six*, Coda (attr. Pugni), bars 2–9

The four women return, zigzagging downstage with a series of "*glissade* and *jeté*" twice and "4 *brisé*." They split and *bourrée* to the sides followed by Sedova and Legat, who travel together down the diagonal from upstage left. Again no steps are given. They move to center as the women *bourrée* in from the sides and form a semicircle around the couple. At the end of the dance, Sedova performs a supported *double pirouette* from fourth position. No final pose is given.

Danse des Forbans. The Rep identifies the title, genre, and composer of the following dance: "*Forbans* | *Pas de Caractere* [sic] | Music by Pugni." ("Forbans" means "pirates.") The number is an extended mazurka comprising 177 bars (not including numerous repeats, some of which are struck through in the Rep) in C major, with excursions into A major and C minor and a contrasting middle section in A minor.

Like the *Danse des Corsaires*, the *Danse des Forbans* is a *pas d'action* as well as a character dance. Mime statements are peppered throughout, describing fighting and beautiful women—tropes of pirate life. Also similar to the *Danse des Corsaires* is the use of a signature step, a "1st *pas*," that is repeated throughout the dance.

The cast features a principal couple and two solo couples. The CN, in Chekrygin's hand, mostly documents the movements of the solo couples, suggesting that a second notation for the principal couple may have been planned or made, although such a document has not been preserved in the CN.

After an introduction of nine bars, the solo couples begin at opposite upstage corners as the main theme is introduced (Ex. 7.6a). Partners face each other as the couples travel down their respective diagonals, eventually crossing at center, performing the "1st *pas*": two *holubetz*—one to each side—a brief run, and a *sissonne ouverte*.[67] They repeat the enchaînement then perform it twice to the other side, again crossing at center. Arriving downstage, the women exchange places and circle the men "4 times" with *jetés* while the men perform *balancés* in place. The dancers continue in unison, traveling backward upstage with a *sissonne en demi-arabesque* on each leg and two *balancés* twice. Finally, they return downstage, again on opposite diagonals, performing "1st *pas*" and finishing at opposite downstage corners (CN: "end"), likely signaling the entrance of the

---

[67] For a description of the character step *holubetz*, see Chapter 5.

Ex. 7.6a *Danse des Forbans* (Pugni), bars 10–25

principal couple. The subsequent passage in the Rep, the recapitulation of the opening melody, includes the annotation "Entrance of [Olga] Fedorova 3 and [Boris] Romanov," who were among the cast of the *Danse des Forbans* in the 1914 revival. A second theme in A minor follows (Ex. 7.6b).

The second "piece" begins with a ground plan indicating three pirates running to center and the mime phrase, "I will kill him." A similar passage in modern performances—one that includes a clashing of sabers in the air when the trio comes together—coincides with the shift to A major (Ex. 7.6c). The solo women follow their partners to center and together they return to their respective downstage corners. This sequence is repeated.

The A minor passage returns and accompanies the solo women as they circle the stage in opposite directions, performing *pas de valse* and traveling around the principal couple at center (see Ex. 7.6b). A mime statement written below the ground plan reads, "I here will fight him. I will kill him."

As the main theme returns, the solo men repeat their meeting at center, but this time they are joined by the principal woman instead of the principal man. The CN provides more information this time: the mime phrase, "I go!" (or "I am coming!") and the annotations, "two strikes" and "third" written at the central meeting point, likely referring to "strikes" of the dancers' sabers. A review of the 1868 revival premiere praising the performance of Vera Lyadova, wife of Lev Ivanov, may refer to this particular moment in the choreography and suggests the principal woman brandished her partner's blade: "'Les Forbans' warranted the public's special approval, a very playful *pas* in which Miss Lyadova excelled, spryly fencing with sabres."[68] Again, the solo women approach center to retrieve their partners and return to their corners. The sequence is repeated.

[68] *Golos*, 27 January 1868, 2, tr. in Wiley, *Lev Ivanov*, 27.

Ex. 7.6b *Danse des Forbans* (Pugni), bars 58–73

Ex. 7.6c *Danse des Forbans* (Pugni), bars 74–89

Next, the solo couples turn three circles in place and return to center. The men face each other and travel directly upstage performing multiple *pas de valse en tournant*. An annotation instructs, "withdraws every time one saber | 6 times," suggesting, as seen in modern performances, that the pirates hit their swords together and withdraw them (or "whip" them "away," an alternative translation of the annotation). The women travel

Ex. 7.7 *Pas seul* (attr. Pugni), bars 17–24

alongside their partners. Reaching upstage, they turn and run to their respective down-stage corners and finish with *degagé de côté fondu* from fifth position *plié*.

The solo couples remain in the corners as the principal couple likely performs an entrée set to a repetitive, rhythmic passage in C minor. The men exclaim, "She is pretty!" and the women circle their partners. As the A major theme returns, now in C major, the couples travel upstage along the wings, facing each other and extending a flexed heel to the side. The ground plan includes the mimed phrase, "They are beautiful."

The pairs run downstage then circle back upstage, performing "1st *pas*" to the final return of the opening theme. The principal couple joins them at center. Arriving upstage in a single row, all three couples travel directly downstage with "1st *pas*" and conclude the dance with a pose in *demi-arabesque fondu*.

Petit Corsaire. The character number *Petit Corsaire* (Rep: "Pas Seul | pour Mme Petipa") is a folk-like polka, attributed to Pugni, that Medora dances in travesty, impersonating a corsair (Ex. 7.7).[69]

The CN records Pavlova's performance but offers little detail beyond a ground plan and a few annotations. No steps are notated. At one point, Medora is directed to mime while dancing as she crosses the stage from left to right.

Tamara Karsavina described this moment and others in the dance:

The romantic quality of Medora's part is set off by a little episode of spontaneous gaiety; Conrad is sombre, and to distract his mind Medora, in boy's apparel, dances for him. She seems to say by her frolicsome dance: "Alas, I have no moustache, but my heart is as valiant as a man's own." A never-failing effect comes at the end; Medora, through a speaking trumpet, cries words of nautical command.

The short, pleated skirt, bolero and fez of the costume that Maria Sergeyevna [Surovshchikova-]Petipa herself wore had been replaced by the ample trousers and turban of a Turkish boy. Madame Sokolova disapproved of the flagrant breach of tradition. The costume led me astray. Precepts of coy grace were forgotten; the trousers

⁶⁹ See Burlaka, ed., *Le Corsaire*, 313: "C[esare] Pugni composes a new character number 'Le petite corsaire' ('Little corsair') for the Petersburgian performance (1863) on assignment for choreographer M[arius] Petipa, for the ballerina M[aria] Surovshchikova-Petipa."

wanted me to leap and romp. From there the logical conclusion was not to apologise for the want of moustache, but to pull fiercely at an imaginary one. Encores told me of the success of my spontaneous inspiration.[70]

Remembering Karsavina's performance, Akim Volynsky described the *emboîtés derrière* that are the primary traveling steps in the dance:

> Her [Karsavina's] playfully comic variation, the Little Corsair, is a masterpiece of style, and her male impersonation caused quite a stir among the audience. She runs around the stage in long *emboîtés* back, accompanying the movement with a symmetrical and sprightly throwing about of her arms. This is simply an artistic gem.[71]

Fortunately, this jolly dance was filmed by Alexander Shiryaev, circa 1906–1909, documenting a performance by his wife, Natalia Matveyeva.[72] The entire dance is included in the Shiryaev documentary, *A Belated Premiere*.[73] By listening without sound (the added music is not synchronized with the movements), one can determine the pulse of the music and match steps to score. Doing so, we find the dance corresponds exactly to the Rep, which includes three repeated passages and one that is struck through near the end of the piece. Although Matveyeva performed on a small outdoor stage for the film, the ground plan of her dance matches the ground plan recorded in the CN. Likewise, her running steps are the same *emboîtés derrière* described by Volynsky, above.

Pas des creufailles. The Rep next includes the first and last pages of a "Pas des creufailles | Mlle Dor" (no composer is credited). We presume this is the score for the *Pas de six (nouveau)* that replaced the *Pas des éventails* and is listed on the poster for the 3 September 1868 performance featuring Henriette Dor—the same dance that Ekaterina Vazem deemed "much less beautiful" than her own *Pas d'éventails* (see above). This dance is not part of the CN, and we know next to nothing about its choreography beyond brief prose descriptions, such as the one in *Nash Balet*, wherein Alexander Pleshcheyev wrote that Dor "replaced the *pas des évantails* [sic] with the amazingly difficult *pas de deux* with M. [Christian] Johanson, astonishing the balletomanes with her so-called *pirouettes renversées*."[74]

From the Rep, we see that the dance began with an "Introduction" (Rep page 88), an *allegro moderato* in $\frac{3}{4}$, E major, and concluded with what was likely a coda in $\frac{2}{4}$, G major (Rep page 105; Ex. 7.8), suggesting the dance was a multimovement number. The intervening sixteen pages (Rep pages 89–104) are not part of the Sergeyev Collection's microfilm. We presume they were removed from the actual *répétiteur*, with the first and last pages left only as a reminder of the dance and its place in the score.

Pas des éventails. As we have seen, the *Pas des éventails* (see Exx. 6.29a–e and 6.19) was performed periodically throughout *Corsaire*'s Petersburg tenure—first by Friedberg (1858), then by Kemmerer (1863), Grantzow and Vazem (both 1868), and finally

---

[70] Karsavina, *Theatre Street*, 215–216.

[71] Volynsky, *Ballet's Magic Kingdom*, 127. The extensive writings about the Imperial Ballet in St. Petersburg by Akim Volynsky (1863–1926) cover the period when many of the dancers represented in the Stepanov notations made their careers at the Mariinsky. His often-precise descriptions of choreography at times relate directly to what was notated.

[72] See Beumers et al., *Alexander Shiryaev*, 24, 139, 144.

[73] *A Belated Premiere*, directed by Viktor Bocharov (Gosfilmfond Rossiyskoy Federatsii, 2003).

[74] Pleshcheyev, *Nash balet (1673–1899)*, 273.

Ex. 7.8 *Pas des creufailles*, excerpt from final page of what is likely the coda

Legnani (1899). Whether the same music accompanied the dance in each iteration, we cannot tell from the Rep.[75] As with the *Pas des creufailles*, only the first and last pages of Adam's *Pas des Éventailles* (sic) are preserved in the Rep.[76] The intervening twelve pages (Rep pages 107–118) are missing from the microfilm and were likely removed from the actual *répétiteur*. This dance is also omitted in the CN.

No. 3. Neither the Rep nor the CN contain a passage labeled No. 3, but neither has any music been cut from the score at this point. The action continues to the end of the scene with Nos. 4–12.

No. 4. "Apré [sic] Le Pas | 2de Tableau," as No. 4 is titled in the Rep, corresponds to the music that follows the *Pas des éventails* in Adam's Paris score (wherein it is marked "après le danse"). The corresponding material in the CN is headed "*Scène* | after all the dances."

Conrad, likely entering from the curtained opening at stage right, walks to center then goes back to stage right and returns with Medora (Ex. 6.10a). She begs him to free the slave women. Conrad acquiesces, but Birbanto objects (Ex. 6.10b).

Birbanto: "You want to let them go?"

Conrad: (nodding) "Yes."

Birbanto: "We do not agree to free them."

Conrad: "I want it." He goes to Medora and says, "I promised, and I will do it."

Brandishing a dagger, Birbanto charges Conrad, who grabs his hand. They struggle, Conrad forces Birbanto to his knee, and the dagger falls. Conrad kicks it and throws Birbanto to the side. According to the CN ground plan and annotations, all the pirates rush at Conrad, who fights them off or otherwise overpowers them. The pirates move away from him. Conrad approaches Birbanto and says, "I will not forget this, ever." He

---

[75] With regard to the version of the *Pas des éventails* performed by Vazem, the Burlaka piano reduction includes a thirty-seven-bar variation (*Allegro moderato*, 2/4, A major) with the following description: "The choreographer M[arius] Petipa staged a new variation of Medora on the music by C[esare] Pugni (*Pas des eventails*) for the Petersburgian performance (1868) to the debut of E[katerina] Vazem." Burlaka, ed., *Le Corsaire*, 389–390.

[76] The opening fifteen bars comprise Rep page 106. The number's final twenty-eight bars, which appear to be a revision of Adam's original ending, fill Rep page 119.

frees the slaves and they run offstage. A solitary corsair rushes at Conrad from stage left.[77] Conrad "throws him" toward stage right, then exits with Medora, likely into the stage right alcove.

No. 5. Labeled only "Scene with the Jew," nothing further is documented for No. 5 in the CN, and No. 6 is omitted.[78] We turn to the 1899 libretto for a description of the action:

> Having stayed in the grotto with some like-minded comrades, Birbanto sees Isaac, who has entered [Ex. 6.12]. Birbanto commands the Jew to immediately come to him, promising that if Isaac keeps certain conditions, he will return Medora, who has conquered the heart of their leader, to him. His first condition is that Isaac pay a significant ransom for her. The Jew swears that at the present moment he is completely bankrupt and sees no way to fulfill Birbanto's demand. The corsair does not believe him and declares to his comrades that the Jew has hidden his treasures. He commands that Isaac be searched. The corsairs throw themselves at the frightened prisoner, taking off his hat, from which sequins pour out; pulling off his overcoat, out of which fall pearls; and untying his scarf, out of which pour diamonds and other precious stones. Seeing all these treasures, the corsairs greedily gather them up and propose that Isaac take his Medora back. The surprised and frightened Jew asks them to show him in what way he can have his ward returned.
>
> Then Birbanto commands one of his comrades to bring him a bouquet from a vase [Ex. 6.13]. He takes a small bottle from his belt, sprays the flowers with it, and, carefully approaching one of the corsairs standing guard, allows him to smell the bouquet. The corsair quickly falls asleep. Pointing to the effect of the flowers, Birbanto gives Isaac the bouquet and commands him to bring it to Conrad. Isaac refuses, but, frightened by Birbanto's threats, fearfully takes the flowers and leaves, followed by the corsairs.

No. 7. The intimate *scène dansante* performed by Medora and Conrad may well be the romantic high point of the ballet. The value of Sergeyev's notation as a production document is nowhere more evident than in the pages preserving the *scène dansante*, with its detailed blocking, charming prose mime conversations, and notation of intricate *terre-à-terre enchaînements* for Medora (as performed by Pavlova with Gerdt).

The structure of the scene makes clear that the recurring musical refrain (Ex. 6.30) accompanies mime and action, while the intervening passages are intended for dance.

The lovers enter from the stage right alcove. As Conrad embraces Medora, they walk toward the divan and small table downstage left, stopping at center.

Conrad: "Do you love me?"

Medora: "Yes."

---

[77] The same notation box also includes the annotation, "Everyone rushes at Conrad."

[78] Lanquedem is referred to as "the Jew" instead of by his name throughout the CN: Sergeyev used both the derogatory *zhid* and the more neutral *yevrey*. Recall from Chapter 6 that Lanquedem is also referred to as "the Jew" in the Justamant staging manual.

Conrad: "If you cheat on me, I will kill myself." Medora stops Conrad's hand as he mimes killing himself.

Medora: "I love you." They continue walking then sit on the divan.

Conrad: "You are so beautiful. Your eyes are shining. I'm going to kiss you." Medora dodges his advances and runs away upstage right.

Traveling toward Conrad, Medora performs *piqué en demi-arabesque, pas de bourrée* on *pointe, demi-cabriole derrière*, and two more *pas de bourrée* on *pointe* (Ex. 6.26b). She repeats the enchaînement then *bourrées* to Conrad.

She takes a pitcher off the table then runs upstage and strikes a pose. She runs back toward Conrad and jumps on the divan. Next, lying on the couch, Medora pours Conrad a glass of wine. He gives her the glass and pours one for himself then she drinks and goes to center stage.

Medora's second entrée begins with *entrechat trois, double rond de jambe en l'air sauté, piqué en demi-arabesque* three times followed by *ballonné, pas de bourrée* on *pointe* twice as she travels downstage right. She returns toward the divan with a *tour jeté* to the knee twice. Conrad "opens her hands after the 2nd time" before she runs away downstage right.

"Calling [to] Gerdt" (who remains by the divan), Medora runs and sits on the divan before Gerdt lifts her onto it. She "lies down" then gets up again and runs upstage right for a third entrée.

Traveling again on the diagonal toward Conrad, Medora performs *pas de bourrée* on *demi-pointe, assemblé, relevé développé devant* four times followed by a series of turns traveling away from the divan: *glissade, piqué en demi-arabesque en tournant, pas de bourrée* on *pointe* either two times (per the notated staves) or four times (per the ground plan). Medora returns to the divan, performing "3 times *cabriole* and he catches her"—this is the "couch *cabriole*" that we encountered in the Justamant manual (see Chapter 6). Medora runs upstage left and concludes the *scène dansante* with a series of turns on *demi-pointe* traveling down the diagonal.

No. 8. Conrad asks for a kiss.

Medora: "Not here. Someone may see us." Conrad circles the stage, looking around.

Conrad: "No one is here. It's just me. Please kiss me." Medora does not want to kiss him, but he gets down on his knee and begs her. She kisses him and runs away. Conrad follows her, takes her by the waist, and leads her to the couch.

(Recall when Loys attempts to kiss Giselle in their *scène d'amour*—in the version recorded by Sergeyev—that she, too, runs away. At the end of the scene, like Medora, Giselle kisses her suitor and runs away again.)

No. 9. Lanquedem enters from upstage left accompanied by a young girl carrying Birbanto's bouquet. She approaches Medora.

Girl: "This flower is for you." She hands the gift to Medora and exits. Conrad sends Lanquedem away. Medora runs to center, holding the bouquet away from Conrad's view.

Conrad: "What are you hiding from me?"

Medora: "This flower."

Conrad: "For whom?"

Medora: "I am giving it to you."

Conrad: "Look at this flower, it is as pretty as your face." He kisses the bouquet and smells it then falls onto the divan, asleep.

No. 10. The "outlaws"—mutinous pirates—enter (Ex. 6.31). The first one approaches Medora from downstage right. She runs left, where her path is cut off by another. She runs upstage right and eventually to downstage center. She is surrounded.

Medora: "What do you want from me? What are you going to do?"

Birbanto: "I want you to get out."

Medora: "I will not go!" Far upstage, Lanquedem runs across the stage from left to right.

No. 11. Medora tries to wake Conrad. In desperation, she writes a note and puts it in his hand.

Medora: (again entreating) "What do you want from me?"

Birbanto: "I want to kill him."

Medora: "Please, do not!" She runs back to Conrad, tries again to wake him, and comes upon his dagger. She seizes it.

Medora: "If you dare to touch him, I will kill you." Birbanto laughs at Medora. Then he charges at her, and she stabs his right hand. She begs him to stop, but he grabs her by the hand and attempts to drag her downstage. She crawls on her knees.

No. 12. The CN provides only a sketch of the remainder of the act. The action recorded for No. 12 repeats some of what has already been described in No. 11, including Medora stabbing Birbanto and crawling on her knees. The last bit of action in the scene sees Medora being taken away by two pirates, who exit with her at upstage right.

Note: The beautiful and detailed notation of *Le jardin animé*, which we will examine in detail in Chapter 8, is inserted at this point in the CN, although it is performed near the end of Scene III.

Scene III

The Corsair's Captivity

The Mariinsky production documents contain no stage plan for the ballet's third scene, the setting of which is briefly described in the 1899 libretto as "The interior of the Pasha's palace on the banks of the Bosphorus."[79]

A brief *entr'acte*, a rowdy and dramatic *allegro vivace* in $\frac{3}{8}$ D minor, precedes the scene. (It will be heard again when Conrad and Medora are captured by the Pasha's guards at the end of Scene III.) The entr'acte is followed in the Rep by a passage titled *Apre le Pas* (sic), the same music that in the original Paris score (Act Two, No. 2) came after the *Pas des odalisques*.[80]

As in the previous scenes, the CN provides a spare outline of the action. Following the heading "3rd Act | Garden," surely a reference to *Le jardin animé*, the CN commences with the entry of a group of odalisques from upstage left—the program lists twelve women who perform an *Entrée des odalisques*. They form a diagonal line that reaches

[79] As mentioned earlier, the page that may have contained this information, page 148, has been removed from the production volume.

[80] Adam's *Pas des odalisques* become the entrée of the Petersburg *Pas de trois des odalisques*. By the time the Petersburg production came to be notated, the *pas de trois* was performed near the end of Scene III.

downstage right, where the Eunuch (Voronkov) appears to be seated. No steps are given, but the ground plan suggests an enchaînement that ends with a turn and is performed twice. Zulma and her maid enter next (Evgenia Makhotina and Antonina Yakovleva, respectively—this pair danced these roles with Vill as Gulnare in both performances of *Le Corsaire* during the 1906–1907 season.)

Gulnare (Vill) enters next, also from upstage left (Ex. 6.3). She travels down the diagonal with *glissade, jeté, pas de bourrée* on *pointe, piqué en arabesque* four times. She next moves toward stage left with *glissade, piqué de côté en cou-de-pied devant, fouetté* to *arabesque, pas de chat* four times. She changes directions with a *soutenu* and returns across the stage with *piqué en arabesque, pas de chat* three times before she *bourrées* the rest of the way, turning a circle in place when she arrives at stage right.

The following *scéne* begins with the annotation "All must bow to her," presumably a command from the Eunuch for the women to pay obeisance to Zulma. The mischievous odalisques form a circle around the Eunuch and, holding hands, turn in a clockwise direction (Exx. 6.33a and 6.33.b). Next, Gulnare teases the Eunuch as she *bourrées* backward away from him and he follows her.

The Pasha enters upstage left and all bow to him. The subsequent action, during which Zulma complains to the Pasha about the disrespect of the odalisques and they, in turn, complain of Zulma's unfairness, is documented in the CN with only ground plans. We turn to the mime script (lightly edited and formatted for clarity) to find greater detail (note that Trefilova was performing the role of Gulnare at the time the script was made):

The Pasha comes out and looks at his favorites and greets them. He sees a new favorite [Gulnare] and sees that she is pretty. His wife [Zulma] comes up to him. He kisses her hand and asks her, "What do you want to tell me?"

Zulma: "These slaves do not want to bow to me."
Pasha: "How, what is this?" He calls the Eunuch and says that they do not want to bow to her.

Eunuch: "Yes, they do not bow to her."
Pasha: "How do they not want to bow to her?" He comes up to them and makes them bow to her. Everyone bows.

Zulma: "This little one [Gulnare] in particular is not so good and does not want to bow to me." The Pasha approaches Trefilova [Gulnare].

Pasha: "How dare you not bow to her." She [Gulnare] goes to his wife [Zulma] but still does not want to bow to her.

The Pasha, seeing that she does not want to bow to her [Zulma], runs and wants to strike her [with his staff], but she runs under his arm. A second time again he wants to strike her, but she takes the staff from him.

/ Scene with staff and dancing /

Scène d'espièglerie. The playful polka danced by Gulnare as she teases the Pasha and further ingratiates herself to him, is headed "dance with staff" in the CN (Ex. 6.4a). The charm of this number is captured in a series of photos featuring Olga Preobrazhenskaya as Gulnare and Alfred Bekefi as the Pasha, the cast of the 1899 revival.[81]

Having commandeered the Pasha's staff before the polka begins, Gulnare, placed to the right of the Pasha, begins with *tendu devant fondu, relevé double petit battement* twice, finishing in a gently lunging fourth position before running behind the Pasha to his other side, where she repeats the enchaînement on the other leg. The annotation "Taps staff | 2 times | Pasha" tells us the Pasha has retrieved his staff and now—likely in time with the rhythmic *fortissimo* burst in the orchestra—taps it on the stage floor (Ex. 6.4b). Gulnare's movements are also described in an annotation: "2 times | Runs up to him and puts both hands on the staff, stopping him, while being on toes." This description is matched by the step notation: Gulnare performs a *piqué en demi-arabesque* followed by five hops on *pointe* in fifth position. Taking the annotations and step notation together with the ground plan that shows Gulnare approaching the Pasha then moving away from him, we might infer that the Pasha taps his staff on the floor (likely in frustration), Gulnare runs to him, performs a *pique en demi-arabesque* as she arrives, putting both hands on his staff to quell his irritation, and then backs away with hops on *pointe*, perhaps with her hands folded beseechingly as we see in one of the photos of Preobrazhenskaya and Bekefi.

With the return of the opening melody, Gulnare circles the Pasha with multiple *piqués en demi-arabesque* before beginning a diagonal from upstage left: *soutenu, jeté en avant,* and two *piqué tours en dehors* three times followed by turns on *demi-pointe*. She then pivots abruptly to the left, runs toward the Pasha, and finishes the dance next to him with a *pas de chat*.

The remaining action in the third scene is documented with only scant details in the CN, which continues with bits of information about the following:

> The Pasha's threat to decapitate the Eunuch
> Mischief with the handkerchief
> Arrival of Lanquedem with Medora
> Gulnare's befriending of Medora (when the Pasha asks if Medora will love him, Gulnare laughs and replies, "You are so old!")
> Brief danced passage for Gulnare (documenting Trefilova's performance)

Fortunately, the mime script describes the first three interactions on this list, beginning immediately after the *Scène d'espièglerie*:

> He [Pasha] takes her [Gulnare] by the hand and says that she is so beautiful, she has such nice eyes, and he likes her very much. Then the wife [Zulma] sees this, takes him by the hand, and drags him to the side. Then the other [Gulnare] drags him to the other side and says that the Eunuch pinches her and beats her.

> The Pasha is indignant, calls the Eunuch, and says, "How dare you beat her. On your knees." And he calls the executioner and says, "Chop off his head."

> But Trefilova [Gulnare] runs up and asks him not to kill the Eunuch. Then the Pasha sends her away and steps aside and says to Zulma, "Are you happy that I did that?"

---

[81] GMTMI GIK 5316/5031, 5316/5032, and 5316/5033.

Zulma: "Yes, yes."

Pasha: "Well, I will give you this handkerchief." He goes and hides [*pryachet*] the handkerchief.

Zulma: "You will give *me* this handkerchief," but he refuses her and goes on and sees Trefilova and throws her the handkerchief.

But the handkerchief is intercepted and finally the handkerchief gets to Trefilova. The Pasha, seeing this, is very happy, but she [Gulnare] hands the handkerchief to the Black woman, who happily runs toward the Pasha and shows him the handkerchief. When the Pasha sees this, he is angered, gives the handkerchief to his wife, and drives her [the Black woman] away. She runs to his wife, and she [Zulma] protects her.

Zulma: (to the Pasha) "Are you giving me this handkerchief?"

Pasha: "Of course, of course."

But the Pasha sees that Trefilova [Gulnare] is laughing, and he threatens her [perhaps wagging his finger], but again turns to his wife, takes her by the hand, and sees her off to the wings.

Everyone leaves, but the Pasha alone remains on the stage. He walks and thinks that this little one [Gulnare] is to blame: "But she is very pretty and I like her." He sits down and thinks.

At this time, the Eunuch runs in and says that a merchant [Lanquedem] has come and has brought one pretty one [Medora].

Pasha: "Where, here?"

Eunuch: "Yes, here."

Pasha: "Well, I must look." He goes . . . the Jew [Lanquedem] lifts the veil and the Pasha recognizes Medora. He feels ill. Everyone supports him, and he comes to his senses, takes her [Medora] by the hands and asks, "How did you get here?"

She points to the Jew and says that he tormented her and wants to sell her again.

Pasha: "If so, then good." He turns to the Jew and says, "You want to sell her to me?"

Lanquedem: "Yes."

Pasha: "Well, wait." He calls the Eunuch [and] speaks into his ear. He [the Eunuch] laughs and calls the others while the Pasha calls the Jew and says, "Go and get the money."

Then the Pasha goes and says that instead of [taking his] money, they will beat him. Then the Jew runs past the Pasha. The Pasha wants to strike him, but he jumps over the staff and runs away.

Medora sits and cries, then he [Pasha] comes up to her and calms her down. He calls his wives, everyone comes out, but he leaves. The wives look and do not know who she [Medora] is.

Returning to the CN, Conrad's subsequent entrance, in which he is disguised as a monk (*monakhov*), is recorded. Both Vill and Trefilova are designated as Gulnare in this scene.

Pasha: (to the monk) "What do you need?"

Conrad: "I came from afar and ask you to give me drink and food." He sees Gulnare (Vill), gives her a shawl to cover her exposed neck, and walks with her (now Trefilova) toward Medora at downstage right.

Seeing Medora, the monk calls everyone to prayer. As all assembled are praying, Medora approaches Conrad and he reveals his face. She is delighted.

Pas de trois des odalisques. The *Pas de trois des odalisques* follows in the Rep, although in the CN the pages documenting this dance are filed at the end of the scene and followed by additional variations and coda passages from *Le jardin animé* (these are discussed in Chapter 8). The *pas de trois* is a multimovement dance suite that combines music by Adam and Pugni in its five movements: the entrée and third variation are by Adam—numbers that were part of the original 1856 score but are here slightly revised—and the first two variations and coda are attributed to Pugni.[82] The CN documents the performances of Apollinaria Gordova, Agrippina Vaganova, and Elizaveta Vill.

Entrée. The entrée features trio, duet, and solo passages, all dovetailing smoothly from one to the next (see Ex. 6.32). The women begin upstage left and travel side by side down the diagonal with four *temps levés en demi-arabesque* on alternate legs, *assemblé, entrechat quatre*, all repeated to the other side. Zigzagging upstage to center, they continue with *glissade, piqué en demi-arabesque, glissade, pique en demi-attitude devant* four times to alternate sides. At center, they perform *pas de cheval, pas de bourrée* on *pointe, entrechat quatre, entrechat cinq* three times to alternate sides.

Gordova and Vill break away, traveling downstage right with *chaînés* on *demi-pointe*, as Vaganova performs the *pas de cheval* enchaînement a fourth time. She continues on her own with *degagé relevé enveloppé, piqué développé devant, tombé, pas de bourrée* on *pointe* four times to alternate sides as she zigzags downstage. She next travels upstage right with *"fouetté* and 2 *jeté"* three times and finishes her solo passage with turns on *demi-pointe*, traveling downstage left.

Vill and Gordova resume dancing together upstage left with *pas de bourrée* to fourth position *plié, relevé développé devant en tournant, pas de chat* three times. Vill finishes with *chaînes* on *demi-pointe* as Gordova continues with a fourth repetition of the enchaînement. She follows this with *glissade, relevé en demi-arabesque, entrechat trois* three times to alternate sides, traveling backward upstage, and concludes her solo passage with a run downstage left and *pas de chat*.

As the music introduces a new theme, Vaganova begins her solo passage with larger-scale steps from upstage left. Traveling on the diagonal, she performs *grand jeté en avant, assemblé, sissonne en arabesque* three times. She is joined by Vill downstage right and the pair travels backward up the diagonal with two *temps levés en arabesque, saut de basque* three times and two *balancés* as they arrive at center. Now mirroring each other as they dance side by side, the women perform a series of *temps levés en demi-arabesque, chassé*—exchanging places with each *chassé*—followed by two *entrechats quatre* and an *entrechat cinq*. This sequence is performed twice, after which the pair *bourrées* forward then travels to the right with three *piqué tours en dehors* that finish in fifth position on *pointe* and bring the entrée to a close.

---

[82] See Burlaka, ed., *Le Corsaire*, 290: "C[esare] Pugni revises the form of Adam's *Pas des odalisques* into *Pas des trois* for the Petersburgian performance (1863) on assignment for choreographer M[arius] Petipa, and writes also 1 and 2 odalisques variations and the general coda."

Ex. 7.9a *Pas de trois des odalisques*, Variation 1 (Pugni), bars 2–9

Variation 1. The sprightly first variation, performed by Gordova, begins at center (Ex. 7.9a). Traveling downstage in a zigzag pattern, she opens with three *brisés* and a *pas de bourrée* on *demi-pointe* (to change direction) four times then returns upstage with a series of *piqués de côté en cou-de-pied derrière* and a *bourrée* upstage left. She returns down the diagonal with *glissade, demi-cabriole devant, pas marché en arrière, entrechat trois* four times. Heading directly upstage backward, Gordova continues with a series of two *entrechats quatre*, two *échappés sur les pointes* four times. She repeats her diagonal enchaînement to the other side and concludes the variation with a sudden change of direction to the right and turns on *demi-pointe*.

Variation 2. Vill's performance is recorded in the second variation, a quick, piquant polka (Ex. 7.9b). Beginning upstage left, she travels sideways on the diagonal with *saut de basque, sissonne en demi-arabesque sur la pointe, pirouette* from fifth position that opens to *développé devant, tour en l'air* three times. A run downstage right sets her up to travel across the stage with *detourné* to the right, two consecutive *piqués en demi-arabesque, double demi-gargouillade, ballotté* three times. Another run, this one to downstage center, serves as preparation for a zigzag upstage with two *piqués de côté en cou-de-pied devant* and a series of three *temps levés en arabesque*, an enchaînement performed two and a half times. The final diagonal, from upstage left, includes two *piqué tours en dehors* followed by *chaînés* on *demi-pointe*.

Variation 3. Vaganova danced the final variation, set to music by Adam that originally accompanied Medora's solo during the suite of dances performed with Conrad in disguise as a dervish (see Ex. 6.35b). Beginning upstage center, she zigzags downstage with *glissade, entrechat cinq de volée, entrechat quatre, relevé développé devant* three times to alternate sides. She waltzes back to her starting point and travels the diagonal to downstage left with a series of *tour en l'air, piqué en arabesque* six times. She *bourrées* to center, where she performs alternating *pas de bourrée en avant* and *en arrière* on *pointe* in place, then travels upstage left to begin a final diagonal of unspecified turns on *demi-pointe*.

Coda. The brief coda builds continuous momentum with entries for two of the dancers leading to a final group passage that commences with the return of the main melody (Ex. 7.9c).

Gordova begins upstage left and travels down the diagonal *with sissonne ouverte double rond de jambe* into *ballotté, gargouillade* (with a single *rond du jambe* with each leg), and two sets of *glissade, piqué de côté en cou-de-pied devant*, all performed three

Ex. 7.9b *Pas de trois des odalisques*, Variation 2 (Pugni), bars 3–10

Ex. 7.9c *Pas de trois des odalisques*, Coda (Pugni), bars 2–9

times to alternate sides (the opening *sissonne* becomes a *double demi-gargouillade* for the second and third iterations of the enchaînement). She *bourrées* stage left where she waits for the others. Vill begins upstage center, zigzagging downstage with three *brisés*, *pas de bourrée* on *pointe* three times to alternate sides. She runs to meet Gordova, joined by Vaganova, who has entered downstage right.

Together, the trio travels toward upstage center with *ballotté*, *tour jeté* three times. They return downstage in a zigzag pattern with two *petits emboîtés*, *temps levé en demi-arabesque*, *glissade*, *jeté* three times. Rising onto *pointe*, they *bourrée* backward upstage then exchange places back and forth in a winding pattern (CN: "coming together [*musovka*] on [*pointe* symbol]"). They conclude the *pas de trois* by posing in *attitude à terre fondu*.

In the Rep, the *pas de trois* is followed directly by *Le jardin animé* and the tempestuous scene finale. The CN resumes after Conrad's identity has been revealed:

Conrad: (pushing away the Pasha) "She is mine, and you go away." He takes a pistol and aims it at the Pasha, who takes two steps back in fear. Conrad turns to Medora and says, "Now we run."

Birbanto (Kshesinsky) and Gulnare (Vill) run toward them. Gulnare begs Conrad to save her. Medora pauses, looks closely at Birbanto, then takes him by the hand and says, "Stay here."

Medora: (to Conrad—the CN labels this passage "Her story") "Do you remember I gave you a flower, you smelled it, and fell asleep?" (see Ex. 6.13). "Then I heard someone coming whose face was covered, then another" (see Ex. 6.31). "They wanted to kill you. I begged them not to, but they took me away."

Conrad: "Kill me? Who?"

Medora: "Do you want to know?" She takes Conrad to Birbanto and points at him.

Conrad: "There is no way! He is my only friend. It cannot be. Prove it."

Medora: (to Birbanto) "Swear!" Birbanto swears with his left hand. Medora pushes his hand and shows the wound on his right hand.

Conrad is astonished and calls Birbanto to come closer. Conrad takes his gun and shoots, intending to kill Birbanto, but Medora pushes Conrad's hand, and the shot is fired into the air.

The CN provides no further details of the ballet's action. As mentioned above, Scenes Four ("The Pasha's Wedding") and Five ("Storm and Shipwreck") are not included in the CN. The simple stage layout for Scene IV, depicted in a front-view sketch in the Mariinsky production documents, is set up downstage of the second wing (surely to allow the ship to be pre-set while the scene is being performed). A large arched opening at center dominates the shallow stage space. Stage left features an arched window next to the opening, stacks of cushions, and a small ottoman-style table. A divan is the sole piece of furniture at stage right.

The 1899 program lists a *Scène dansante de caractère* for Medora and the Pasha in Scene IV. The 1899 libretto describes the action that took place during this number:

> With her dances, Medora tries to seduce the Pasha, who is in love with her, but it is apparent that she is impatiently awaiting the desired hour of freedom. She expresses horror at the sight of a dagger in Seyd's belt and asks him to quickly take it off. The Pasha removes his dagger and gives it to Medora. But her fright becomes even greater at the sight of a pistol in the Pasha's belt. To finally calm her, Seyd takes out the pistol and gives it to her. He wants to gently embrace her, but she slips away from him with gentle dances. Seyd falls at her feet, begs her to love him, and gives her his handkerchief. As if joking, she ties his hands. Pleased, he laughs at her mischief.

By the end of 1904, the *Scène dansante de caractère* was no longer included in the ballet's list of dances, but a reference in the program for 28 December to Act Four, Scene II ("In the 4th act | 2nd scene | *Danse à bord du vaisseau*") suggests that Act Four, Scene I (that is, Scene IV of the ballet) remained part of the production. The program for 3 December 1908 (just weeks after Karsavina assumed the role of Medora on 22 October) includes this same reference to Act Four, Scene II, again suggesting that the ballet's fourth scene was still being performed.

The "5th Tableau" begins on Rep page 241 with wave music (Ex. 6.16). The Rep also includes the dances onboard ship—both the B minor dance in $\frac{6}{8}$ meter, labeled "Danse" (Ex. 6.20), and the D major dance in $\frac{6}{8}$ meter (Ex. 6.21), which is heavily cut. An overhead-perspective drawing of Scene V in the production documents reveals that the ship was placed at center stage, in the third wing, with what appears to be the prow of the ship facing stage right. Thus the audience would view the dances from the port side of the vessel.

The final Rep pages are either obscured or missing in the microfilm, but Karsavina's vivid recollections of the final scene help fill in the gap. (Her remarks suggest that the dances performed onboard ship were eliminated at some point after she began performing the role of Medora, although a program for a 21 April 1918 performance featuring Karsavina continues to list the *Danse à bord du vaisseau*.) Above all, they convey the thrill and excitement of the shipwreck scene felt by performers as well as audience:

> The last act did not require any dancing or histrionic skill, but was ever such fun for me. The whole of the scene represents a choppy sea. Under painted canvas hired sailors run on all fours. A storm breaks, and the sailors run on two legs. At the back, the corsairs' caravel pitches and rolls over a trap-door. Birbanto, leading a mutiny, treacherously attacks Conrad, and is killed by a pistol-shot. Medora, still in tarlatans, now looks through a telescope, now prays on her knees.
>
>   What the stage directions were I never quite knew, but we took them to be *ad libitum*, and, in the heat of make-believe, rather overacted this scene and played at shipwreck like excited children. Gerdt shouted orders through the megaphone; when the caravel split and sank in two tidy halves, my female attendants and I screamed. But screams, cannon, megaphone and orchestra were all drowned by the thunder and howling wind. The rebellious corsairs all perished with the ship, Gerdt and I, creeping low and making swimming movements, reached the wings. There I hastily put on a white chemise and let down my hair preparatory to appearing on a crag now jutting out of a quickly pacified sea. Up there, arms raised to thank Heaven for landing us on a desert rock, we struck the final group of the apotheosis.[83]

Karsavina's description reminds us that Birbanto made a dramatic reappearance in the final scene. In the librettos of the Paris 1856 and St. Petersburg 1858 productions, Birbanto is last seen at the end of Act Two when he rallies the Pasha's guards to recapture Medora. In the 1899 St. Petersburg libretto, however, he makes a final appearance as a prisoner onboard ship. While Karsavina recalls that Birbanto was shot and killed, the 1899 libretto describes a misfiring pistol, leading Conrad to throw the traitor overboard just before the storm breaks:

> A clear and quiet night. On the occasion of Medora's rescue from prison, a festival with dances is organized on the deck of the ship. The corsairs are pleased with such a happy end to their undertaking and rescue.
>
>   Only the unhappy Birbanto, bound in chains, does not take part in the merriment. Medora sees his unhappy situation and asks Conrad to forgive Birbanto, who himself joins in the pleading. After some indecision, Conrad forgives Birbanto, who joyfully asks permission to bring a small barrel of wine and treat his comrades. Conrad allows it. Birbanto brings wine and serves everyone.
>
>   The weather quickly changes, and a storm begins. Taking advantage of the confusion onboard, Birbanto once again stirs up the comrades and shoots at Conrad, but the

[83] Karsavina, *Theatre Street*, 216.

pistol misfires. Conrad involuntarily turns around at the sound of the pistol. Seeing the villain aiming at him, he grabs him and after a long fight throws him overboard.

Le Corsaire left the St. Petersburg repertory after the 1909–1910 season. After lying dormant for more than four years, the ballet was revived by Sergeyev for a benefit performance for the corps de ballet on 21 December 1914. The cast included Preobrazhenskaya, making her debut as Medora, with Gerdt (Conrad), Alexander Chekrygin (Pasha), Iosif Kshesinsky (Birbanto), Vill (Gulnare), and Vasily Stukolkin (Lanquedem). Lubov Egorova and Petr Vladimirov performed the *Pas d'esclaves*, and Elena Polyakova, Elizaveta Gerdt, and Alexandra Fedorova danced the *Pas de trois des odalisques*. The third act featured a *Valse* choreographed by Nikolai Legat and danced by Agrippina Vaganova as well as a *Danse de la bayadère* from Petipa's *Le Roi Candaule*, performed by Elena Smirnova and Boris Romanov.[84]

The list of dances in the program for the revival performance suggests that Act Four included just one scene (Scene V)—"In the 4th act | *Danse à bord du vaisseau*"—thus suggesting that Scene IV was omitted. Karsavina's statement, "The *Jardin Animé* practically terminated the responsibility of the leading part," also implies that at some point during the period in which she performed the role of Medora Scene IV had been eliminated from the ballet.[85]

Perhaps the strongest evidence of the omission of Scene IV, however, is its apparent removal from the Rep. Only the first page of Scene IV (Rep page 218) remains; the other twenty-two pages (219–240) have been removed. As with the music for the *Pas des creufailles* and *Pas des éventails*, the title page of the scene seems to have been left in the Rep as a sort of marker—a reminder that the music was once part of the performance score.

With the omission of Scene IV, the ballet's brief but stunning shipwreck conclusion followed Scene III, which ends with the recapture of Medora and Conrad in the Pasha's palace. One wonders how the narrative may have been altered to accommodate the loss of Scene IV, in which Medora and Conrad make their escape, enabling them to board the ship and sail away with the pirates and slave women before the fatal storm strikes.

The next performance of consequence was given on 11 January 1915 and featured Karsavina and Samuil Andrianov in the leading roles. The second scene featured the premiere of a *Pas d'action*—choreographed by Andrianov and danced by Karsavina, Andrianov, and Anatole Obukhov—that replaced the *pas de six* performed by Preobrazhenskaya less than a month earlier.[86] Smirnova made her debut as Medora on 21 January 1915. She also performed the new *pas d'action* with Andrianov and Obukhov.[87] The dance, which is not included in the Rep or CN, appears to have become a permanent replacement for the *pas de six* and all other predecessors. Reviewing a performance by Olga Spesivtseva as Medora in 1923, Volynsky wrote about the *pas d'action*:

> As I said, the first act of *Le Corsaire* came off absolutely faultlessly. The genuinely beautiful dancing, however, unfolded only in the second act. At one time in this act the

---

[84] *Khronika IV*, 176–177.

[85] Karsavina, *Theatre Street*, 216.

[86] Andrianov was credited as choreographer of the *Pas d'action* in printed programs for performances of *Le Corsaire* through the 1916–1917 season. See *Khronika IV*, 224.

[87] *Khronika IV*, 179. The editors identify Smirnova's debut as the performance that first featured the *pas d'action*, but the program for 11 January 1915 makes clear that the number was included in that performance.

complicated pas de six was performed with Olga Preobrazhenskaya. After her this old number was replaced by a more modest and compact dramatized duet in the production by the late Samuil Andriyanov. Precisely from that time a new tradition was established to which all ballet masters now adhere. The first part of the duet is constructed according to the usual plan. In Andriyanov's production, we had here a series of plastic motifs which depended on large effects. There were pirouettes of various kinds—with both open and closed falling into the partner's arms, and with the transferring of the female dancer—and they were generally effective and full of fervor. Dancing with Tamara Karsavina, the young ballet master with his magic antenna brought to the surface all of the charms of her exceptional feminine beauty. In the elevated arms of Andriyanov the ballerina's suppleness radiated and palpitated with the whole gamut of powers, inherent and acquired, in full bloom, in full light, and in excitable play.[88]

In 2007, Maria Babanina identified Andrianov's *pas d'action* as the origin of the so-called *Le Corsaire pas de deux* that became a popular showpiece in the twentieth century:

When speaking about the ballet "Le Corsaire," one immediately thinks of the beautiful famous *pas de deux*, a worldwide favourite of ballet galas and in almost all ballet competitions a compulsory piece. And invariably the programme reads "Pas de deux from the ballet 'Le Corsaire,' music by Adolphe Adam, choreography by Marius Petipa." In fact, neither Adam nor Petipa have anything to do with it. Furthermore, in 1915, five years after Petipa's death, it was choreographed as [a] *pas d'action* for three dancers. The cast list reads: "choreography by Samuel Andrianov." The music of the adage, the nocturne "Dreams of spring," is by Riccardo Drigo. The variation for the man was set to music by Julius Gerber, from the ballet "Trilbi" (1870), [and] Medora's variation is choreographed to music by Boris Fitinhof-Schell, from the ballet "Cendrillon" (1893). Shocking news, isn't it? Hotch-potch or musical diversity?

In any case, it is not quite unusual in ballet history. And the musical fate of Adam's "Le Corsaire" is a good example. Through the eclectic procedures of Jules Perrot, Marius Petipa, and later choreographers so many alien elements have been intermingled with Adam's music, that in certain versions we may find music by as many as twenty different composers.[89]

The subsequent evolution of the *pas d'action* is beyond the scope of this study, but it nevertheless serves as a potent reminder of the extent to which interpolations in *Le Corsaire* served to replace much of Adam's score over the nearly sixty years that the ballet was in the Petersburg repertory during the Imperial era. Recall, too, that the score was

---

[88] Akim Volynsky, *And then Came Dance: The Women Who Led Volynsky to Ballet's Magic Kingdom*, ed. and tr. Stanley J. Rabinowitz (New York: Oxford University Press, 2019), 229. Volynsky continues with a critique of choreographic elements added to the *pas* and suggestions for its improvement.

[89] Maria Babanina, "Prima la music, dopo la coreografia?—Prima la coreografia dopo la musica?" in *Le Corsaire* program book (Munich: Bayerisches Staatsballett, 2007), 31. The musical numbers cited by Babanina are published in Burlaka, ed., *Le Corsaire*, 450–460, along with a coda that Burlaka also attributes to Drigo. Burlaka gives both 1914 (page 440) and 1915 (page 450) as the year Andrianov's *Pas d'action* was added to the ballet.

Spring Dreams was a "choreographic scene," with music by Drigo, performed on 11 April 1910 at the Mariinsky Theater as part of an Imperial Theater School graduation performance. See E. M. Levasheva, ed., *Istoriya russkoy muzyki, Tom 10B, Kniga 1, 1890–1917, Khronograf* [History of Russian Music, vol. 10B, Book 1, 1890–1917, Chronograph], (Moscow: Yazyki Slavyanskikh kultur [Languages of Slavic Cultures], 2011), 485.

surely reorchestrated when the ballet was first performed in St. Petersburg. Thus, despite the ballet's longevity, the world has not heard Adam's *Le Corsaire* in the theater as he intended since the final curtain came down in 1858 at the close of the Paris production's initial two-year run.

As details of *Le Corsaire*'s narrative eroded over time due to the replacement of plot-driven *pas d'action* with divertissement-style numbers and the eventual excision of Scene IV, the ballet was eventually reshaped to resemble more recent creations, particularly ballets first produced in the 1890s. Some of these works—such as *Sleeping Beauty* and *The Nutcracker*—represented a new genre, the ballet-féerie, which favored dance and spectacle over story.[90] The second half of *Le Corsaire*, in particular, adhered to this model. When lacking its fourth scene, the ballet proceeded from the lavish divertissement *Le jardin animé* (which bore no relation to the plot) to the stunning shipwreck finale, omitting Conrad's and Medora's escape from the Pasha's clutches. The original Parisian incarnations of these two spectacles (*Le pas des fleurs* and the shipwreck), as glorious as they were reported to have been, contributed beauty and thrills to the production without overshadowing the detailed narrative that was delivered through extensive mime scenes and numerous *pas d'action*. But in St. Petersburg, where increasingly dance-heavy scenes were linked by a steadily diminishing plot and accompanied by a patchwork score, *Le Corsaire* became something of a disjointed catch-all—certainly an enjoyable romp but a much less cohesive work of art than the dramatic ballet-pantomime first envisioned by its original collaborators.

We will have occasion to return to the topics of style over substance and dance over narrative in our exploration of Petipa's *Raymonda*, produced in 1898, just one year before his final revival of *Le Corsaire*.

---

[90] About the ballet-féerie, see Scholl, *Petipa to Balanchine*, 18–20, 32–35, and Meisner, *Marius Petipa*, 195–198.

8

From *Le pas des fleurs* to *Le jardin animé*

When Joseph Mazilier added a new divertissement to the 1867 revival of *Le Corsaire*, he likely had little thought that his suite of dances would have a life beyond its current purpose, which was to feature a new ballerina in the lead role of Medora. That *Le pas des fleurs*—albeit redacted, rechoreographed, and renamed *Le jardin animé*—would be preserved in one of the most detailed documents of nineteenth-century dance notation was the happy result of Marius Petipa's curatorial approach to the repertory of the St. Petersburg Imperial Ballet.[1] Thanks to a variety of extant sources documenting this divertissement in its various iterations, we have the unique opportunity to follow the changes the ballet underwent through Petipa's evolutionary work over the course of nearly forty years. We also will encounter, for the first time in this study, complex choreographic polyphony, an important feature of Petipa's *oeuvre*.

But first we return to Paris.

The 1867 Paris revival of *Le Corsaire*

The revival of *Le Corsaire* at the Opéra on 21 October 1867 was produced near the end of the Exposition Universelle. Held in Paris from April through the beginning of November, this exposition was one of many such lavish public events staged by the Emperor Napoleon III, the Empress Eugénie, and a government determined to arouse and consolidate popular support for their regime.[2] It featured more than fifty thousand exhibitions and attracted more than six million visitors to the French capital, including the Ottoman Sultan Abülaziz, Otto von Bismarck of Prussia, a brother of the Tokugawa Shogun, the Khedive of Egypt Isma'il, and Franz Josef I of Austria, and Tsar Alexander II.[3] Rather than premiere a new ballet for the occasion as he did an opera (none other

---

[1] We use the term "curatorial approach" to mean Petipa's practice of maintaining revivals of older works in the repertory alongside new ones.

[2] Spectacular crown-sponsored displays included the baptism of the Prince Imperial in June 1856 (in a ceremony "worthy of a coronation" and costing 150,000 francs) and the welcoming home to France of a procession of 60,000 French soldiers (after a successful Italian campaign) who entered the city and walked to the Place Vendôme "under triumphal arches, and amidst trophies and decorations innumerable." Thomas Wright, *The History of France: From the Earliest Period to the Present Time*, vol. 3 (London: London Printing and Publishing Company, 1862), 823. Further, "[e]very new railway station built or boulevard opened up as part of [Napoleon III's] urban redevelopment scheme was celebrated with a ... wonderland of painted wood and canvas constructions." Yves Badetz, Guy Cogeval, Paul Perrin, and Marie-Paule Perrin, eds. "Spectaculaire Second Empire, 1852–1870," Musée d'Orsay, 2016–2017, https://www.musee-orsay.fr/fr/expositions/specta culaire-second-empire-1852-1870-196105.

And perhaps most controversially, Napoleon III reinstated the Feast of St-Napoleon, which had taken place every August 15 during the regime of Napoleon I (coinciding with the centuries-old Feast of the Assumption), and called for public display. Sudhir Hazareesingh, "Religion and Politics in the Saint-Napoleon Festivity 1852–70: Anti-Clericalism, Local Patriotism and Modernity," *English Historical Review* 119, no. 482 (2004): 621.

[3] Bela Menczer, "Exposition, 1867," *History Today* 17, no. 7 (July 1967): 429–436.

Five Ballets from Paris and St. Petersburg. Doug Fullington and Marian Smith, Oxford University Press.
© Oxford University Press 2024. DOI: 10.1093/oso/9780190944506.003.0009

than Giuseppe Verdi's *Don Carlos*), Émile Perrin, the Opéra's director, turned to recent works and reliable repertory: *La Source* (which had premiered the year before to mediocre reviews but became a genuine success when Adèle Grantzow assumed the title role in May 1867) and, in performances for visiting dignitaries, the second act of *Giselle*. He also commissioned a new production of the 1856 swashbuckler, *Le Corsaire*.

Mazilier was called out of retirement to stage the ballet. The cast featured Grantzow (Medora), Louis Mérante (Conrad), Edmond Cornet (Isaac Lanquedem), Eugène Coralli (Birbanto), and Angelina Fioretti (Gulnare).[4] Three artists reprised roles they had created in 1856: François Dauty (Seyd-Pasha), Louis Petit (Chief of the Eunuchs), and Louise Marquet (Zulmea). New scenery and costumes were designed and built, the originals having been destroyed in a warehouse fire in 1861. *Le Corsaire* was given ten performances in 1867 and five in 1868 before being permanently dropped from the repertory. Mazilier died on 10 May 1868 at the age of seventy, seven months after the revival.

Ivor Guest suggests Mazilier rechoreographed much of the production. Willa Collins, however, points out that because Mazilier was called in just five months before the premiere and had access to the original libretto and very likely a *répétiteur* for the first production and possibly other materials, the choreography may very well have resembled that of the original.[5]

The additions made to the new production, certainly added as vehicles for Grantzow, included a variation and a divertissement, *Le pas des fleurs*. Both were composed by relative newcomer Léo Delibes, a former student of Adam who recently had provided music for two scenes of *La Source* with success.[6] Various musical revisions were made to Adam's original score to accommodate *Le pas des fleurs*. Collins suggests that these as well as other musical changes were likely handled by Delibes.[7]

Because the ballet was a revival, the 1867 *Corsaire* received relatively little press. Nevertheless, in addition to extant musical scores, several sources offer details of what took place on stage. The libretto, for example, while including the same scenario as in 1856, provides a cast list for the revival and designates the insertion of the new divertissement into Act Two, Scene 6.[8] A single-page set of annotated humorous caricatures by Félix Rey, featuring highlights from the production, includes an image of a ballerina kneeling in front of a fan so large it covers all but the legs of the ensemble standing behind it.[9] That this grouping is similar to the final pose of the opening number of the *Pas des éventails* in Justamant's manual (see Chapter 6) strengthens the probability that at least some of the choreography from the 1856 production remained.

The idea of a *pas des fleurs*, performed by dancers carrying garlands or the like, was well established by 1867.[10] And in our study alone, we have seen a variety of references to

[4] Collins provides substantial biographies for Grantzow and Mérante. See Collins, *Le Corsaire*, 266–273.

[5] See Guest, *Second Empire 1858–1870*, 102, and Collins, *Le Corsaire*, 279.

[6] Adam died in 1856. About Delibes, see Collins, *Le Corsaire*, 273–277.

[7] For a description of the revisions made to the score of *Le Corsaire* for the 1867 revival, see Collins, *Le Corsaire*, 287–313.

[8] See Collins, *Le Corsaire*, 280–287, which includes reproductions of several pages of the 1867 libretto, including the title page, cast list, and list of dances.

[9] The document is signed "Félix Y." See Paris, Bibliotheque Nationale de France, Bibliothèque-Musée de l'Opéra, ESTAMPES SCENES Corsaire (3), "*Quelques croquis sur Le Corsaire a l'Opéra*—(1867): [estampe] / Félix Y. [sig.]," available online at https://gallica.bnf.fr/ark:/12148/btv1b8437126n.

[10] See Collins, *Le Corsaire*, 320–322. See also Lecomte, "Dans le sillage du *Corsaire*," 159–160. On garland dances, see Edmund Fairfax, "The Eighteenth-Century Garland Pose," *Eighteenth-Century Ballet* (blog), 18 October 2020, https://eighteenthcenturyballet.com/blog/, and Gutsche-Miller, *Parisian Music-Hall Ballet*, 104 and 316n28. For images and examples, see Madison U. Sowell and Debra H. Sowell, *Il Balletto Romantico: Tesori della Collezione Sowell* (Palermo: L'Epos, 2007), 65, 70–71, 76, 160.

flowers in both *Giselle* and *Paquita*. Flowers feature in the plot and—with the added divertissement in 1867—the choreography of *Le Corsaire* in crucial ways. We will find that flowers (garlands included) figure in *La Bayadère* and *Raymonda* as well.

The Music

The Library of Congress holds three items related to the 1867 revival of *Le Corsaire* as part of a large collection of Delibes manuscripts.[11] These include the variation composed for Grantzow, a revised passage of music by Adam, and *Le pas des fleurs*.[12]

The "Variation de Mlle Grantzow" comprises fifty-one bars, including six bars of introduction (Ex. 8.1).[13] Designated for "1er acte" in the autograph score, this number was added to the *Pas des éventails* in the ballet's second scene.[14] Perhaps following the lead of his teacher, whose full and rich orchestrations throughout *Le Corsaire* surely contributed to its success, Delibes employs the full orchestra for much of the number rather than opting for the light texture—a solo instrument accompanied by strings, for example—often employed for solo variations danced by women. The upward-leaping melody is syncopated throughout, giving a swing to the rhythmic phrases. These elements combine with Delibes's trademark harmonic chromaticism to imbue the variation with a lush grandeur.

The autograph score of Delibes's second and more significant contribution is titled "Divertissement pour Le Corsaire | Le pas des fleurs" and signed at the end in ink: "Leo Delibes | 7bre 67 [September 1867]." The divertissement consists of eight discrete sections, preceded by a four-bar introduction.[15]

The opening *mouvement de valse* (waltz) in A-flat major is one of two substantial numbers out of the eight, with a total of 146 bars. The tripping primary melody has a broad sweep in its rising and falling lines (Ex. 8.2a). A contrasting secondary melody features accents, syncopation, and a brief move to E major (Ex. 8.2b).

The waltz modulates at its end to introduce the subsequent *andante*, which serves as the divertissement's adagio movement. Over a light texture of harp and strings, including cellos divided four ways, a solo oboe plays a wide-ranging melody that Delibes would return to eight years later when composing the violin solo for the third act of his ballet *Sylvia* (Ex. 8.3). Generally soft throughout (despite the *mezzo forte* designated for the oboe at the beginning), the number builds only at the end, with a *crescendo* to *fortissimo* in the last three bars, scored for full orchestra.

---

[11] Léo Delibes music manuscripts, 1857–1890, ML96.D39, Library of Congress, Washington, DC.

[12] The three pages of revisions to Adam's score are from the end of Act Two, at the point in which Medora identifies Birbanto as her kidnapper. The Library of Congress pages match four pasted-over pages in the Paris full score of *Le Corsaire*, Act Two (A-590, vol. 2, 213–216). The pasted-over pages substitute for what is a fairly large cut in the score. See Collins, *Le Corsaire*, 301. The numbers are also included in the extant orchestra parts (see Chapter 6). The 1867 version of the score and the additions by Delibes are included on the Bonynge/English Chamber Orchestra recording of *Le Corsaire* (see Chapter 6, note 72).

[13] A piano reduction is published in Burlaka, ed., *Le Corsaire*, 349–350.

[14] The added variation is included in the copied full score, A-590 vol. 1, 295–306. See Collins, *Le Corsaire*, 288, 445.

[15] A piano reduction of the 1867 Paris score for *Le pas des fleurs* is published in Burlaka, ed., *Le Corsaire*, 318–336. For further analysis of *Le pas des fleurs*, see Collins, *Le Corsaire*, 329–364.

Ex. 8.1 *Variation de Mlle Grantzow*, bars 7–14

Ex. 8.2a *Le pas des fleurs*, Waltz, bars 5–11

Ex. 8.2b *Le pas des fleurs*, Waltz, bars 36–43

Ex. 8.3 *Le pas des fleurs*, *Andante*, bars 3–6

Ex. 8.4 *Le pas des fleurs*, Interlude 1, bars 3–13

The following section, forty-three bars in $\frac{3}{4}$ time, which we will call Interlude 1, serves as an extended introduction to the subsequent variation. Marked "1° tempo un peu plus animé" and based on the waltz melody, the interlude modulates several times, moving away from G major (the dominant of the preceding C major of the *andante*) to eventually settle on the dominant seventh of E-flat major (Ex. 8.4).

The fourth section is the first of two variations (Variation 1), this one comprising forty-nine bars and likely performed by Fioretti as Gulnare. With the melody in the flute doubled by clarinet an octave below, the scoring builds on the flute-solo genre we have seen in variations in *Giselle* and *Paquita* (Ex. 8.5).

Interlude 2, as we will call it, consists of twenty-six bars in E-flat major. Despite the languid quality of its opening, the tempo is *moderato sans lenteur* (Ex. 8.6). Like Interlude 1, this number serves to set up the following variation. Lyrical melodies in the violins and cellos lead to a staccato passage, followed by the return of the opening material in the winds and a modulation to C-flat major.

Variation 2, a thirty-three-bar *allegretto* in A-flat major, breaks Delibes's pattern of beginning the movements of the divertissement at a soft dynamic by opening forthrightly

Ex. 8.5 *Le pas des fleurs*, Variation 1, bars 1–6

Ex. 8.6 *Le pas des fleurs*, Interlude 2, bars 1–4

and with full orchestra playing *fortissimo* (Ex. 8.7a).[16] An annotation in the copied full score, "Granzow," confirms this variation was intended for Medora.[17] As with Grantzow's variation added for the grotto scene, also in $\frac{6}{8}$ meter, this solo projects strength and perhaps even a sense of majesty in its orchestration, dynamic, and sweep of phrase. A contrasting middle section maintains breadth while introducing lyricism (Ex. 8.7b). The variation ends with a brass fanfare and flourishes (Ex. 8.7c).

The seventh movement, a galop, comprises 160 bars in E-flat major and functions as a coda. Following fifteen bars of anticipatory introduction, the melody rushes forward in cascading phrases (Ex. 8.8a).

Typical of coda movements by Delibes, the number builds to a modulation featuring a broad melody that accompanies an entrée for a leading dancer. Here, the number modulates to C-flat major for eight bars, followed by a four-bar transition back to E-flat (Ex. 8.8b).

The final movement, a return to the opening waltz melody, may have been intended as a *sortie*, providing music to accompany a large group of dancers as they leave the stage. This number is preserved with two endings: both indicate a *diminuendo* just ahead of *fortissimo* final chords. The second ending is more substantial in impact by virtue of a *crescendo* preceding the final bars.[18]

Although the music is preserved in Act Three of the Paris full score, the new suite of dances appears to have been performed in Act Two, replacing No. 4 and No. 4 *bis*, the original divertissement in the second act.[19] This is confirmed by the placement of *Le pas des fleurs* in the extant orchestra parts.[20] The order of its various numbers in the Paris full score is the same as in Delibes's autograph: Waltz—*Andante*—Interlude 1—Variation

[16] "Allegretto" is struck through in the autograph score and replaced with *moderato marcato*.
[17] A-590, vol. 3, 153.
[18] Both endings are also included in the Paris full score.
[19] A-590, vol. 3, 65–223. See Collins, *Le Corsaire*, 316–317, 329n118.
[20] Collins, *Le Corsaire*, 477n60.

Ex. 8.7a *Le pas des fleurs*, Variation 2, bars 1–5

Ex. 8.7b *Le pas des fleurs*, Variation 2, bars 10–13

Ex. 8.7c *Le pas des fleurs*, Variation 2, bars 26–33

Ex. 8.8a *Le pas des fleurs*, Coda, bars 16–23

Ex. 8.8b *Le pas des fleurs*, Coda, bars 107–114

1 (presumably for Fioretti)—Interlude 2—Variation 2 (Grantzow)—Coda—*Sortie*. Whereas the original 1856 divertissement combined dance and action, *Le pas des fleurs*, which is twice as long, appears to have been a pure dance suite performed by Medora, Gulnare, and the Pasha's court after Conrad reveals his identity to Medora.

The libretto's cast list indicates sixty-two participants—Grantzow, Fioretti, twenty women, twenty extras (*comparses*), and twenty little boys[21]—however, an inventory list includes the names of twenty-five female dancers as part of the ensemble.[22] Sixty costumes were built for the divertissement.[23]

Several sources give us an idea of the scenery and properties used to depict a living garden on stage. Rehearsal notes refer to garlands, and accounting records list baskets as properties.[24] One of the caricatures by Félix Rey features a woman holding a garland, another depicts an elaborate configuration of what look to be flower baskets, a likely reference to the ground plan of the new *pas de fleurs*, and yet another shows a man (possibly an extra) with a small boy standing on the man's head.

A sketch by scenic designers Auguste Rubé and Philippe-Marie Chaperon reveals the plan for the onstage garden with greater clarity.[25] Collins describes the drawing, in

---

[21] According to the libretto, the boys portrayed "petits Nègres" (little Black males). See Collins, *Le Corsaire*, 285. In his 1868 and 1880 plans for *Le jardin animé*, Petipa refers to the roles of the student boys as "Nègres."

[22] Collins, *Le Corsaire*, 286–287.

[23] Ibid., 319–320n109.

[24] Ibid., 320.

[25] The set plan is preserved at the Archives Nationales, AJ[13] 506.

which a central circle is surrounded by two square formations, the second, larger square encompassing the first:

> The scenographers envisioned a garden, probably using geometric hedges similar to those found in the gardens of Versailles, filled with red peonies (*pivoines rondes*), pink and white rose bushes (*rosiers roses, fleurs blanches rosiers*), and an assortment of round, square, and oval baskets (*corbeilles ovales et carrés; corbeilles rondes*).[26]

Indeed, the sketch features components of formal seventeenth-century French garden design: the entirety is arranged around a central axis that is crossed by perpendicular alleyways (*allées*). Flower beds (*parterres*) of varying shapes are placed symmetrically around the axis and contain flowers of a limited range of colors, here pink, white, and red. Whether the garden was in place for the entire divertissement or assembled midway through, as we will find in the St. Petersburg production, these documents do not tell us.

From the sources consulted, we can know at what point during *Le Corsaire* the *pas des fleurs* was danced, how many performers participated, and that they wore newly made costumes, carried various properties, and danced within a specially designed stage framework that represented a well-manicured garden. However, we find little more than tantalizing mention about the dances themselves. Grantzow's name appears at two points within the divertissement in the Paris full score, suggesting a solo entrée and variation, and an early press notice announcing the revival commented on the pairing of Grantzow and Fioretti in the new *pas des fleurs*:

> In a *grand divertissement* added to the second act, a *pas de deux* will bring together Mlle. Granzow and Mlle. Fioretti, and will show us, in the most piquant way, a kind of contest between the two *danseuses*. It is M. Delibes, one of Adam's most distinguished pupils, who is responsible for writing the music of the *pas* and the added *divertissement*.[27]

The revival of *Le Corsaire* and its new *pas des fleurs* were well-received.[28] St. Petersburg, as always, was watching and would soon acquire the new divertissement for its own production.

Le jardin animé in St. Petersburg: 1868

Le pas des fleurs, renamed *Le jardin animé*, was first added to the St. Petersburg *Corsaire* as part of Petipa's revival presented on 25 January 1868, less than four months after its Paris premiere. The cast featured Grantzow as Medora joined by Lubov Radina, reprising the role of Gulnare. Surely Grantzow brought the divertissement with her from Paris to enhance her Petersburg debut in the role. Whether she danced choreography created for her by Mazilier or newly devised steps by Petipa, our sources

[26] Collins, *Le Corsaire*, 319.
[27] *Le Figaro*, 23 August 1867, 4.
[28] See Guest, *Second Empire 1858–1870*, 103.

do not reveal.[29] Whatever the case, *Le pas des fleurs* found a permanent home in St. Petersburg as *Le jardin animé* in the third scene of *Le Corsaire*.

The new dance was described in a review published in *Golos* that provides details about the staging and choreography:

> The audience was also impressed by the *pas* "Le jardin animé" (in the third scene), staged by M. Petipa to the rather colorless music of Delibes. In the *pas*, Mlle Grantzow simply does miracles: for example, she draws whole patterns with her feet, without leaving the flower garlands laid on the floor, then rushes across the stage with the swiftness of a doe, finally jumps onto a large basket filled with flowers, does an arabesque and, making several slow turns, standing on one leg, throws bouquets from the cornucopia. The masses of the corps de ballet (in very graceful costumes) here depict lively flowers and whole flower beds, illuminated by electric light, forming a real magical garden from *One Thousand and One Nights*. In general, the groups of the "lively

[29] Burlaka provides a second complete piano reduction of Delibes's divertissement which is intended to represent the music used by Petipa for *Le jardin animé* in his 1868 staging of *Le Corsaire* (pages 352–379) and is described by Burlaka as follows: "The choreographer M[arius] Petipa revises the form of *Pas des fleurs* by J[oseph] Mazilier into 'Le jardin animé' for the Petersburgian revival of [*Le Corsaire*] (1868) for the ballerina A[dèle] Grantzow. Petipa changes the form of the number and adds new variations." Burlaka, ed., *Le Corsaire*, 352. This mixed collection of numbers, not all of which Petipa appears to have used, includes compositions and arrangements that post-date 1868 (some of which are not found in the CN or the Rep). This second piano reduction, for which no source citations are provided, consists of the following numbers:

> *Grand Valzer* [Waltz]: While our sources indicate that Petipa used the opening waltz as composed by Delibes for the Paris production, Burlaka's reduction includes much of the piano solo version published in nineteenth-century Paris by Henri Heugel (no date), which features the incorporation of Variation 1 into the waltz. (See note 97 in this chapter for the citation of the Heugel publication, the cover of which is reproduced in the Burlaka volume on page 317.) No sources we consulted suggest that the Heugel arrangement of the waltz was used in the Petersburg *Le jardin animé*.
>
> *Grand Adagio* [Adagio]
>
> *Variation of Gulnare*: The music for this variation is printed twice in the volume (on pages 363–364 and 400–401). In the first instance, Burlaka writes that it was composed by "A[lbert] Zabel for the performance of the ballet 'Catarina ou la Fille du bandit' by C[esare] Pugni for the ballerina V[irginia] Zucchi in 1889" (page 363). (For an excerpt, see Ex. 8.15 in the present volume.) In the second instance, Burlaka adds that it was used in 1899 "as the variation of Gulnara in the divertissement 'Le Jardin Animé' with [Petipa's] new choreography." But in fact, the Rep includes an altogether different variation and it is for Olga Preobrazhenskaya, who danced the role of Gulnare in the 1899 revival (see Ex. 8.13). The *Catarina* variation appears to have been danced later by Vera Trefilova, possibly as early as 1901.
>
> *Female soloists' variation*: This variation is also included twice in the Burlaka piano reduction. On page 365, it is described as: "[Originally] written by R[iccardo] Drigo for the ballet 'La Esmeralda' by C[esare] Pugni for the ballerina A[nna] Johannson in 1899." On page 430, the variation is further described as: "For the revival of 'Le Corsaire' in 1899 choreographer M[arius] Petipa used the variation from the ballet 'La Esmeralda' on the music by R[iccardo] Drigo for the ballerina A[nna] Johannson as the female soloists' variation in the divertissement 'Le Jardin Animé' (III act) with his new choreography." Neither the music nor any choreography or description of this number is found in the sources we consulted.
>
> *Intermezzo I* [Interlude I]: Revised as in the Rep and CN.
>
> *Intermezzo II* [Interlude 2]: Revised as in the Rep, with two bars of introduction (see below).
>
> *Variation of Medora* [Variation 2]
>
> *Coda*: Revised with repeated bars as in the Rep and CN.
>
> *Finale* [we call this the *Sortie*]: While the version of this final movement included in the CN's *répétiteur* matches the Paris version (using the first of Delibes's two endings), the arrangement in the Burlaka edition includes an opening seven bars that are derived from Delibes's music for the ballet *La Source* (1866) and taken from Franz Doppler's 1878 arrangement of *Le pas des fleurs*, titled *Intermezzo (Pas des fleurs, grande valse) aus dem Ballet Naila*. See later in this chapter, especially note 94. As with the divertissement's opening waltz, nothing in the sources we consulted suggests that this arrangement was used in the Petersburg *Le jardin animé*.

garden," which include 80 artists . . . just ask for an artist's canvas and do honor to the choreographer who composed them.[30]

The reviewer confirms that eighty artists participated in the divertissement, garlands at one point were laid on the stage, and Grantzow threw bouquets from a large basket.[31] The "very graceful costumes" were designed by Adolf Charlemagne, whose sketches for the revival include designs for eleven different kinds of flowers.[32] Grantzow reigned supreme as "La Rose Centefeuilles" (The Rose of a Hundred Petals—or Leaves), as her costume design is titled. The other multi-colored, whimsical designs are labeled thus: "Le Gameriers | fleur des Alpes," "L'Astre," "La Rose," "La Campanule," "Le Bluet," "Le Coquelicot," "Le Liseron," "Le Muguet," "L'Eglantier," and "La Pensée." Alongside this visual luxury, the music of Delibes, a composer new to the St. Petersburg stage, was deemed "colorless"!

Ekaterina Vazem recounts Arthur Saint-Léon's own proposal of luxury, an indication that the ballet master was involved in the production:

> Saint-Léon liked to try out original ideas. For the Petersburg production of the divertissement *The Living Garden* (from the ballet *Le Corsaire*), which was so popular in Paris, he wanted to place enormous machines on stage to spray the audience with perfume, so that they would feel themselves transported into a garden with scented flowers. This, however, he was not allowed to do.[33]

Extant source material provides a rare opportunity to trace Petipa's ongoing conception of *Le jardin animé*, beginning with the 1868 revival of *Le Corsaire* and continuing into the first years of the twentieth century. Here we find early examples of the elaborate groupings Petipa devised that were so pleasing to his audience. We also discover passages of truly polyphonic choreography, featuring multiple groups of dancers performing different enchaînements simultaneously. Finally, we see Petipa's preference in working with groups of twelve dancers (or even twenty-four), something we have witnessed already in his productions of *Giselle* (twenty-four Wilis), *Paquita* (twelve couples in the *Pas des manteaux* and children's mazurka), and other dances in *Le Corsaire* (twelve ensemble couples in the *Danse des Corsaires* and twelve corps women in the 1899 *Grand pas des éventails* and *Entrée des odalisques*).

Notes and drawings in Petipa's hand help us understand his preparations for staging *Le jardin animé*.[34] Several of these appear to date from the 1868 production: the names of Grantzow and Radina are included in the sketches of ground plans.

[30] *Golos*, 27 January 1868, qtd. in *Khronika III*, 134. Italics added.

[31] In an 1868 letter to his colleague Karl Valts, Matvey Shishkov, decorator of the Imperial Theaters, described how Grantzow was lifted on a trap into the middle of a large flower basket, surrounded by the rest of the performers. See Yury Burlaka, "*Grand Pas iz baleta 'Pakhita' i Grand Pas 'Ozhivlennyy Sad' iz belta 'Korsar': Sravnitel'nyy analiz*" [*Grand Pas* from the ballet "Paquita" and *Grand Pas* "The Lively Garden" from the ballet "Korsar": A Comparative Analysis], *Vestnik Akademii Russkogo baleta imeni A. Ya. Vaganovoy* [Bulletin of the Academy of Russian Ballet named after A. Ya. Vaganova], 2 (2017): 77.

[32] St. Petersburg State Theatre Library (SPbGTB), inventory number Э1608.

[33] Vazem, "Memoirs of a Ballerina: Part 1," 9. Saint-Léon mentions *Le Corsaire* among the ballets contributing to his busy schedule in a letter to Charles Nuitter on 14 September 1869. Saint-Léon, *Letters from a Ballet Master*, 110.

[34] A.A. Bakhrushin State Central Theatre Museum (GTsTM) *fond* 205 (Marius Petipa archive), *op.* 1, *ed. khr.* 200–204 and 704–705. Our discussion will refer to a selection of the materials preserved.

Groupings. One drawing related to the 1868 production includes three groupings intended for the "adagio," Petipa's term for the *andante*.[35] At the top of the page, the "1er groupe de l'adage" bears the description "très joli." (This grouping corresponds to Group 1 of Petipa's later productions, discussed below.) Twenty-four *figurantes* (corps de ballet women) form a winding row across midstage.[36] Behind them are drawn a series of hoops—flower garlands were attached to stiff hoops in half-moon shapes, the ends of which were held in each hand. The hoops are clustered in a tight, central formation and likely represent the twelve men identified in subsequent groupings on the same page. Radina is at center, surrounded by what may be six student girls. On either side of Radina and her circle of students, three student boys are paired in rows with three *élèves* (student girls—an *élève* can be a boy or girl, but Petipa appears to indicate girls in this case). On either side of these pairs are nonsymmetrical formations of dancers: at stage right, two more boys are surrounded by eight "coryphées avec cerceaux" (though this number was likely six in performance, matching the six coryphées at stage left); at stage left, no descriptors are given, but the same symbols as those used for stage right indicate three boys surrounded by six "coryphées avec cerceaux." Finally, farthest downstage, three dancers flank a central figure on each side, with the annotation, "they give roses to Grantzow."

Petipa's description of the grouping drawn at the bottom of the page is similar to the one at the top—it is labeled "2me groupe de l'adage | très joli"—and corresponds to Group 2 of later productions. Here, rows of dancers line the upstage area. A row of twelve men and twelve corps women is farthest upstage. The men are represented by squares, which may indicate they are standing on tabourets, and the corps women ("12 f[igurantes]") are placed "au milieu des hommes." Twelve more corps women form a second row in front of the first: "12 f[igurantes] devant les hommes."

Downstage of these rows, three colonnades are formed by lines of paired dancers. The central colonnade is created by six pairs of dancers. Each holds one end of her own hoop and one end of her partner's hoop, thus creating an arbor between the "pillars" of the colonnade—in sum, they form an arcade. The hoops are drawn in a lowered position, their midpoints touching the floor at the center of the pathway. Though lacking descriptors, these dancers may be the coryphées designated in the first group, confirming their total number was twelve. Six additional "coryphées" are in diagonal rows, three women in each downstage corner (in later years, Petipa referred to these six women as "secondes danseuses"). Radina and Grantzow are placed at the upstage end of the central colonnade. The colonnades on each side are formed by six girls with hoops ("élèves de l'école | avec cerceaux") along the outside and six boys along the inside (the same + sign is used to denote the boys in this grouping as well as in the grouping at the top of this page). These pairs also form arcades by sharing hoops held high.

The grouping drawn in the middle of the page is labeled "4me figure," suggesting that the third adagio group is missing from the page.[37] Indeed, this grouping corresponds

---

[35] GTsTM *fond* 205, *op.* 1, *ed. khr.* 705. This drawing is reproduced in the exhibition catalog *Dva veka Petipa* [Two centuries of Petipa], ed. Sergey Konaev (Moscow: Ministry of Culture of the Russian Federation, A.A. Bakhrushin State Central Theatre Museum, 2018), 23.

[36] The accompanying annotation, "2 figurantes devant les grandes guirlandes," appears to support this reading but for the "2," which may have been intended to be "24."

[37] However, the grouping at the top of the page includes a large "2" at the center of the drawing, and the grouping at the bottom of the page includes a large "3" (albeit written just above a smaller "2") on the right side of the drawing. If the grouping formed at the end of the waltz, immediately preceding the adagio, is regarded as "1," then this numbering would follow.

most closely to Group 4 of later productions. Here, a circular formation at center is flanked by arcades on each side. Grantzow is at center surrounded by an inner circle of twelve dancers depicted by squares and an outer semicircle of another twelve dancers depicted by hoops. These may be "les 24 figurantes"—this annotation is written directly above the formation. "Radina gives her hand to Grantzow" is written in the space between the circle and semicircle. The arcades along each wing are formed by colonnades of six coryphées on the inside and six *hommes* on the outside. Each holds one end of their shared, raised hoops. Six undesignated dancers stand in a line within each arcade. (An annotation below the drawing, "12 men holding baskets," may refer to the "2me groupe," at the bottom of the page, although it is written just above the line separating the grouping drawn in the middle of the page from the one at the bottom.)

A subsequent page includes two more groupings in this series.[38] Petipa's "5me figure" also corresponds to Group 4 of later productions.[39] The men (*figurants*) stand upstage center in a square formation. Each side of the square is three men deep—they face outward, holding hoops. On either side of the men are two arcades situated on the diagonal from the upstage corners. The inside colonnades are made up of *figurantes* and the outside colonnades are formed by coryphées. As in the previous figures, the dancers in each colonnade share a raised hoop, creating an arcade. Another line of dancers, possibly the boys, stand under the hoops within each arcade. Radina is placed downstage of the men and Grantzow is even farther downstage. Below her name, the following is written: "The baskets in front of Grantzow or else with the student boys."[40] The second drawing on this page, labeled "6me figure," is similar to the other groupings but does not appear to exactly prefigure any single grouping from later productions (although it shares some formations with Group 2). The *figurantes* form two arcades upstage, made up of twelve dancers each. Between them are two colonnades labeled "Nèg[res] corbeilles." Downstage, an inverted "V" is formed by kneeling dancers who either hold hoops themselves or share them with other dancers (the student girls?) who appear to be sitting on the knees of the kneeling dancers. Farthest downstage is a "V" formed by six dancers (we presume those later referred to as "secondes danseuses"). At its apex is a drawing of what appears to be a large basket. (Neither Radina nor Grantzow are named in this drawing.)

A sketch on yet another page documents one more elaborate grouping, perhaps also from the adagio, but it is different in detail from those we will find in drawings and ground plans of later productions.[41] Here, two central arcades are formed by pairs of dancers who share hoops held aloft to form an arbor over what appear to be additional dancers placed within the arcades. Diagonal lines of dancers at the sides include men (*figurants*) standing and coryphées kneeling. Students (*élèves*) kneel downstage in a "V" formation, with Radina at its apex. More coryphées are placed behind the students. A solitary figure placed farthest downstage at center may represent Grantzow. Annotations below the drawing provide further information, either about the drawing above or subsequent action: "The *figurants* carry the boys on their shoulders, the boys hold the large hoops | a *figurante* is in front, the *figurant[e]* is holding her skirt very open."[42] Petipa concludes with a note to himself: "I have to see if this figure is good."[43]

---

[38] GTsTM *fond* 205, *op.* 1, *ed. khr.* 705.
[39] A second "5" at the top of the page is struck through in pencil and replaced with "3."
[40] "Les corbeilles devant Grantzow ou bien avec les nègres."
[41] GTsTM *fond* 205, *op.* 1, *ed. khr.* 705.
[42] "Les figurants portent les nègres sur les épaules, les nègres tiennent les grands cerceaux | une figurante est devant, le figurant [sic] tenant sa jupe très ouverte."
[43] "Je dois voir si cette figure est bien."

Stage design. Another drawing provides the layout of the flower beds on stage, a plan similar to the elaborate Paris set plan: four central beds form a square with their outside perimeter.[44] An open circular area at their inside central meeting point surrounds a circular bed or platform. The stage space around the platform is accessible by alleys between the beds. Pairs of rectangular beds line each side of the large square. This arrangement of flower beds will remain constant in Petipa's subsequent productions. Along the front of the stage, hoops—each representing a large flower petal—are placed on the stage floor, forming five large flowers of four petals each.

Annotations further our knowledge of the stage design, beginning with instructions at the top of the page explaining how the flower beds are to be brought on stage hidden from audience view: "[T]o place the garden, the *figurantes* hold their skirts very open to hide the garden."[45] Drawings of figures accompanied by the annotation "in front of the garden" show how the dancers (presumably placed far downstage) hold their skirts wide to block the audience's view of the stage as the flower beds are put in place, presumably by stage crew (later documents refer to "properties people"). Additional annotations describe the formation of the three central hoop flowers—"12 *figurantes* put these hoops on the floor"—and the hoop flowers on each side of the central three—"these 4 hoops placed outside by 4 boys," meaning four hoops are placed in the flower formation by the four student boys standing within it.[46] Annotations at the bottom of the page provide more detail: "The 6 coryphées [again, Petipa will later refer to these women as "secondes danseuses"] dance before. Then *figurants* and *figurantes* enter while the garden is set up as soon as possible. They quickly go into the 1st wing on the right and left. I must try to place the six dancers next to the coryphées."[47]

Cast size. Although the number of dancers depicted differs somewhat from group to group, the total cast represented in these drawings includes Grantzow, Radina, what appear to be eighteen coryphées (divided into two groups: twelve coryphées and what will be six *secondes danseuses*), twenty-four corps women (*figurantes*), twelve student girls (*élèves*), twelve men (*figurants* or *hommes*), and twelve student boys (*nègres*), for a total of eighty dancers, the same number as listed on the poster.

Taken together, the drawings reveal Petipa's plan for groups of dancers to create a literal "living garden" during the adagio by assembling multiple tableaux within which Medora and Gulnare would dance. Later in the divertissement, another garden is formed, this one with scenic pieces—flower beds—freeing the ensemble to dance within its alleyways, an entire bouquet of flowers coming to life, as it were.

The 1880 St. Petersburg revival of *Le Corsaire*

Petipa's next revival of *Le Corsaire* on 30 November 1880 featured Evgenia Sokolova as Medora and Marie Petipa as Gulnare.[48] Made in conjunction with this production were

---

[44] GTsTM *fond* 205, *op.* 1, *ed. khr.* 705.

[45] "[P]our faire mettre le jardin font sùr les figurantes tiennent leurs jupes tres ouvertes pour cacher le jardin."

[46] "12 figurantes mettent parterre ces cerceaux" and "ces 4 cerceaux sans placés par 4 nègres."

[47] "[A]vant les 6 coryphées dansant | ensuite les figurants et figurantes entrent en plançant sitot le jardin place | ils rentrent spontanement dans la 1ière coulisse a droite et à gauche. Les six danseuses je dois tacher de las places à côté des coryphées."

[48] See *Khronika III*, 209–210.

further detailed plans, also in Petipa's hand, that document the choreographer's revision of *Le jardin animé*.[49] Petipa's heading notes the timing of their preparation: "Benefit of Mme Sokolova | November 1880" and "I revised this *pas* for the rehearsal [*répété*] and finished the *pas* on 22 October 1880."[50] These statements confirm that Petipa revised *Le jardin animé* for the 1880 revival of *Corsaire* and that he completed his work in rehearsal five and a half weeks before the premiere. His written plans also reveal that the role of the divertissement's second ballerina (which Radina, as Gulnare, danced in the 1868 production) was performed not by Gulnare, the role performed by his daughter Marie, but by Vera Zhukova ("Jhukowa" in Petipa's plans).[51] This casting is confirmed by the poster.[52]

The plans also confirm the order of the divertissement, which represents a change from Delibes's original order: Waltz—Adagio (from hereon we adopt Petipa's term for Delibes's *Andante*)—Variation 1 (Zhukova)—Interlude 1—Interlude 2—Variation 2 (Sokolova)—Coda. The number of participants in the divertissement, twelve fewer than the 1868 production, can also be ascertained from symbols Petipa uses to indicate the various performers:

Performers:	Symbol:
Sokolova	"S"
Zhukova	Two oblique hash marks with a cross
6 *secondes danseuses*	"O" or stick figures
12 coryphées	"X"
12 *figurantes*	"O" or stick figures
12 student girls	"O", sometimes "X" or "small girls"
12 *figurants*	Squares
12 student boys	Filled-in circles

Total of 68 performers

Where the same symbols are used to depict multiple sets of dancers (*secondes danseuses*, *figurantes*, or student girls), Petipa provided prose descriptions as well. This additional prose primarily provides information about the order of entrances, the groupings of the dancers, the properties they hold, and occasionally the number of bars allocated to a given passage or grouping.

Petipa's drawing showing the placement of the flower beds on stage corresponds with his similar sketch from 1868.[53] The flower-shaped configuration of hoops placed on stage is omitted from the drawing, but other elements and references to performers are included: a large basket (*corbeille*) at center surrounded by *secondes danseuses*, coryphées along the wings, little girls (*petites*) in the side alleys, and Zhukova at downstage center.

---

[49] GTsTM *fond* 205, *op.* 1, *ed. khr.* 200–203.

[50] GTsTM *fond* 205, *op.* 1, *ed. khr.* 202, fol. 1r.

[51] Marie Petipa was not known for her abilities as a classical (academic) dancer. See Meisner, *Marius Petipa*, 128–135. For a contemporary assessment of Marie Petipa's abilities, see Vazem, "Memoirs of a Ballerina: Part 3," 39–40.

[52] Thanks to Olga Fedorchenko for providing this information.

[53] GTsTM *fond* 205, *op.* 1, *ed. khr.* 202, fol. 2v.

Because many of the details included in these plans are similar to those documented in the choreographic notation of *Le jardin animé*, we will discuss the two sources in tandem.

The Stepanov notation of *Le jardin animé*

The choreographic notation (CN) of *Le jardin animé* that is filed with the rest of the notation of *Le Corsaire* in the Sergeyev Collection is one of the most detailed and beautifully executed examples of Stepanov notation, indeed, of all nineteenth-century dance notation.[54] Much of it is written in ink using a formal, calligraphic script. The elaborate document, consisting of eighty-eight pages that are bound in three gatherings, includes a two-violin *répétiteur* (CN Rep, which we will distinguish from the *Corsaire* Rep, that is, the *répétiteur* of the entire *Le Corsaire* that was discussed in Chapter 7), ground plans, step notation—often with movements for the entire body—and detailed annotations.

The inclusion of a two-violin *répétiteur*, the use of ink, and the formal scribal hand suggest the notation is an early example of the practical use of the Stepanov system for ballet documentation, created at a time when enthusiasm for the project was high and effort was made to ensure that the notation document was itself a work of art. The paper is that used for the most detailed examples of Stepanov notation preserved in the Sergeyev Collection: oblong-format with two music staves at the top, below which are four sets of choreographic notation staves. Together, these staves create a complete system that includes music and can accommodate choreographic notation for up to four different groups of dancers performing simultaneously. Four boxes along the right margin of the page are intended for ground plans. The first bound gathering includes the Waltz; the second, the Adagio, Variation 1, and Interlude 1; and the third, Interlude 2, Variation 2, Coda, and *Sortie*. The lack of dancer names in the notation suggests the document may have been intended as a definitive record of the choreography rather than notes of a single cast's performance. Sadly, the initial scribes did not finish their work. The scribal hands for both the *répétiteur* and the choreography change after the second gathering; the *répétiteur* remains in ink, albeit in a heavier hand—likely Nikolai Sergeyev's—but the choreography, annotations, and ground plans are in pencil.

Why was *Le jardin animé* chosen to be notated? *Le Corsaire* was out of repertory during the 1890s and not revived in full until 1899, three years after Stepanov's death. The answer may lie on a page among the Bakhrushin Museum holdings that includes the following lone text in Petipa's hand: "I submit *le jardin animé* for a performance excerpt [*spectacle coupé*]. Mlles Johansson and Kulichevskaya. 4 Sept[ember] 1894 at Theatre Michel."[55] The *Yearbook of the Imperial Theaters* for the 1894–1895 season confirms the performance at the Mikhailovsky Theater on 4 September, which included the ballets *The Magic Flute*, *The Enchanted Forest*, *The Offerings to Cupid*, and a "Grand pas" from *Le Corsaire*.[56] Based on Petipa's written statement, the *Grand pas* appears to have been *Le jardin animé*. Rehearsals for this performance would have provided an opportunity for the divertissement to be notated, thus increasing the practical implementation of the Stepanov system.

---

[54] MS Thr 245 (1), Harvard Theatre Collection, Houghton Library, Harvard University.
[55] GTsTM *fond* 205, *op.* 1, *ed. khr.* 200, fol. 1r.
[56] *Ezhegodnik* (1894–1895), 3.

Who was the initial dance notator? Based on the sources we have consulted, we have not identified the scribe, although the primary scribal hand for the choreography is similar to that used to notate *The Awakening of Flora*, a ballet first performed on 25 July 1894. Also similar is the style and formatting of various features of the notation of *The Awakening of Flora*, a pencil notation that utilizes the same type of paper as *Le jardin animé*, includes a *répétiteur* in ink, was also unfinished by its initial scribe, and varies in level of detail provided throughout.[57]

We are tempted to attribute the notation of these two ballets to Stepanov himself. Based on the date of the performance of *Le jardin animé* that appears to have served as the model for the choreographic notation and the premiere of *The Awakening of Flora*, both in 1894, such attribution seems plausible.

The following number-by-number description is based on the CN, supplemented by notes from Petipa's 1880 plans.

The title page of the choreographic notation reads "*Le jardin animé* a[u] acte du Ballet *Corsaire*." Each member of the cast of sixty-eight dancers is assigned a number (separate sets of numbers are used for females and males). These are used both in the notation of the steps (dancers are identified by number in the margins next to the staves) and in the ground plans:

1	"Ballerina" (Medora)
2	"1st dancer" (Gulnare)
3–8	"6 dancers" (women, corresponding to Petipa's *secondes danseuses*)
9–20	12 student girls
21–32	12 coryphées (women)
33–44	12 corps de ballet women (corresponding to Petipa's *figurantes*)
1–12	12 student boys[58]
13–24	12 corps de ballet men (corresponding to Petipa's *figurants*)
Total	68 dancers (44 females, 24 males)

Each constituency is allotted its own set of staves unless two groups are dancing the same steps, in which case both groups are listed in the left margin next to the respective stave set. Where a group of dancers is divided between sides of the stage, the stage left side is notated; a box is drawn around the numbers corresponding to the dancers on stage right, indicating they should perform the steps to the opposite side and on opposite legs.

Nothing is notated for the four bars of introduction that precede the waltz.

---

[57] MS Thr 245 (45). Similar elements of style and formatting include the placement of annotations, stave headings, the format of ground plans, and the indication of dancers turning. In addition, the use of a rectangular (rather than circular) notehead for legs in "normal" position (that is, under the body) when a dancer is on *demi-pointe* or *pointe* is a feature of both the *Flora* and *Jardin* notations. The rectangular notehead is also used in this way in Stepanov's 1892 *Alphabet* and, with less regularity, in Gorsky's *Tablitsa znakov* [Table of Signs] but is changed to a round notehead in Gorsky's 1899 *Khoreografiia*: compare Stepanov's *Alphabet* (see *Alphabet*, tr. Lister, 31, examples 94–96) and Gorsky's *Tablitsa znakov* (*Table of Signs*, tr. Wiley, 20) with Gorsky's *Khoreografiia* (*Choreography*, tr. Wiley, 37–38 ff., examples 60 and 67, ff). The use of the rectangular notehead in this manner suggests that the notation of *Le jardin animé* was made prior to the publication of Gorsky's 1899 *Khoreografiia*.

[58] The CN refers to "student boys" and does not use the term "nègres" that Petipa had used in his plans for 1868 and 1880.

Waltz

"*Allegro*—beginning of the *pas* of *Corsaire*." So wrote Petipa in his 1880 plans.[59] Six cory-phées begin, three in a row at each downstage side. They travel toward center with *ballonné*, *piqué en arrière en cou-de-pied devant*, arms overhead, twice, followed by *pas de valse en tournant*. As the dancers reach center, a second group of six coryphées enters up-stage of the first group. As the first six repeat the opening enchaînement, traveling back toward the wings, the second six perform the same as they move toward center. Both groups repeat the sequence twice more, their rows crossing on their respective sides of the stage. All perform *pas de valse en tournant* to the wings during the final repetition and form a line along each side.

Next, twelve student girls enter upstage of the coryphées, six from each side, in two rows of three dancers each. All perform *pas de basque* as the girls travel to center and the coryphées move upstage and form a semicircle. After four *balancés* in place, they resume *pas de basque*, half of the girls turning and traveling upstage and back, the other half trav-eling downstage and back, the coryphées returning to the downstage sides.

Twelve student boys run in, six from each upstage corner, and a series of groupings follows. In the first, the boys form a large, inverted semicircle across the stage. The CN instructs, "they are sitting on the floor having brought under their legs." Behind them, the girls, in two lines, also form inverted semicircles, standing in first position, arms overhead. The coryphées line the wings, downstage of the boys, standing in *tendu croisé derrière*, arms in fourth position. All run to the second group, for which only a ground plan is given: the girls move upstage into two rows, the boys move to the sides, and the coryphées form a semicircle at center, their backs to the audience. The ground plan indi-cates the coryphées either hold hands or, if they are also kneeling, hold each other by the waist. All run back to the first group, where they remain for the duration of the waltz.

The rest of the number is given over to the "1st dancer" (we will refer to her as Gulnare) and "6 dancers." As the music transitions to a return of the opening melody, Gulnare enters upstage left. She performs a series of *piqués en arabesque* as she travels downstage on the diagonal. A *bourrée* brings her back to center, where she poses in *tendu croisé derrière*, arms overhead, until the waltz melody begins. The six dancers enter, three from each side, and form a line at each wing, opposite Gulnare. Petipa's annotations accom-panying his sketches confirm this order of events, beginning from the first grouping of students and coryphées: "1st [group] | 2nd [group] | Then to the 1st group again | Then the entrance of Mme Zhukova then the entrance of the six second *danseuses*."[60]

As the waltz resumes, Gulnare lowers her arms while performing a deep *fondu* in a lunging fourth position over the course of four bars. She waltzes in place, repeats the lunging pose, then waltzes upstage. She returns down center with three *pas de basque*, *piqué en arabesque*, arms overhead, twice. Throughout, Gulnare is flanked by the six dancers, who travel to center and return to the wings with a series of *pas de basque* and *piqué en arabesque*, *failli* then move upstage and back with a series of *pas de valse en tour-nant* and *ballonné*.

As the music approaches its final climax, Gulnare runs forward on the diagonal and performs *piqué en arabesque*, *failli*, wrists crossing overhead, then repeats the same to the other side, waltzes upstage, and repeats the entire enchaînement. The six dancers, having

[59] GTsTM *fond* 205, *op*. 1, *ed. khr.* 202, fol. 1r.
[60] GTsTM *fond* 205, *op*. 1, *ed. khr.* 202, fol. 1v.

formed a single row upstage of Gulnare, perform a series of *entrechat cinq, piqué degagé demi-seconde*, and *pas de valse en tournant* in place.

Gulnare travels directly downstage a final time with *pas de basque*, joined by the six dancers. The rest of the ensemble, including an additional twenty-four dancers who now enter from the wings at either side, moves into a grouping during the final chords of the waltz. The CN provides the following instructions for each set of dancers:

12 female corps de ballet dancers come on stage with baskets.

12 male corps de ballet dancers come on stage with garlands.

The girl students go behind the curtain past the people with the garlands [that is, they each get a garland in the wings] and they arrive and come to the group.

The boy students come straight to the group.

The coryphées go behind the curtain past the people with the garlands [that is, they each get a garland in the wings] and they arrive and come to the group.

The ground plan indicates a large semicircle upstage, four rows deep, the front row extended farther downstage by the addition of a line of six coryphées at each end. Detailed instructions are given for the group pose:

12 boy students [first row] sit having brought under their legs

12 girl students [second row] stand on one knee [that is, they kneel; they also hold garlands]

12 female corps dancers [third row] hold baskets

12 male corps dancers [fourth row] hold garlands

12 coryphées are holding garlands

At center, the six dancers surround Gulnare: "They stand [that is, kneel] on the left knee embracing one another around the waist." Gulnare stands within the circle in *tendu croisé derrière*, arms overhead. Petipa's sketches show a similar grouping, the only difference being the placement of the corps women and boys outside of the large semicircle, six of each on either side of the stage.[61] He also notes that the six dancers kneeling around Zhukova should hold each other's hands rather than waists.

At the final chord, "everyone goes to the first adagio group."

Adagio

The adagio features five elaborate groupings for the ensemble, within which Medora dances. Large groupings of dancers were a feature in many of Petipa's ballets as well as those of his predecessors. Groupings distinguished by a particular innovation—whether properties held by dancers, tabourets or other raised platforms on which they stood, a variety of participants, or the eccentricity or beauty of the costumes—were regularly

---

[61] GTsTM *fond* 205, *op.* 1, *ed. khr.* 201, fol. 2v.

noted in the press. We will encounter more such groupings in our surveys of *La Bayadère* and *Raymonda*.

The particulars of these groupings comprise the bulk of Petipa's notes and sketches relating to *Le jardin animé* in 1880. The CN also includes ground plans documenting the groupings. These are accompanied by charts, the columns of which detail the poses of each group of dancers using a combination of notation and prose descriptions. The number assigned to each dancer in the ground plans informs us of their placement in any given grouping, although their traveling path from one grouping to the next is not provided.

Group 1.[62] The first formation features three sets of dancers kneeling in circles who create three hoop flowers—the garland hoops they hold create the impression of petals. One hoop flower is placed at center (formed by six kneeling girls surrounding Gulnare, who stands with arms held overhead), the others at both downstage corners (each comprising six kneeling coryphées surrounding three boys—two kneeling, one standing). The rest of the ensemble is deployed symmetrically on stage. In a revision of Petipa's 1868 sketch, four lines of three men span the upstage area. In front of them, corps women stand in a semicircle holding baskets. On either side of the central hoop flower, three girls stand behind three kneeling boys. (In Petipa's 1868 plans, the boys are behind the girls;[63] according to his 1880 sketches, the girls sit on the boys' knees.[64]) At downstage center, the six dancers, each holding a "bouquet," stand in an inverted "V" formation. Medora enters downstage left and runs to its apex.

Taking the hand of the coryphée on either side of her, Medora steps onto the left *pointe* and raises her right leg in *attitude devant*. Lowering it, she *bourrées*, taking a flower from each of the two coryphées. She turns two circles in place as the others pass their bouquets farther up the line. She repeats the enchaînement, during which she presumably takes the rest of the bouquets from the coryphées. Petipa describes the action thus: "6 second *danseuses* have a rose in their hand. Sokolova runs to get on the 2 *pointes* in the middle, holding the 2 roses in each hand. The second [*danseuse*] on each side passes the rose to the 1st, who passes to Sokolova, who ends up having a bouquet [*qui finit par avoir un bouquet*]."

As Medora continues her *bourrée*, "everyone goes" to the next group. Medora runs upstage.

Group 2.[65] The coryphées form an arcade at center, each pair of dancers joining garlands together to create an arbor. Two more arcades are formed along each wing by the girls, standing on the inside and holding one end of their garlands, and the boys, kneeling and holding the other end of the girls' garlands (a reversal of their placement in 1868). Behind them, the corps women stand in a row across the stage in front of the men, who stand on tabourets. The six dancers, still in diagonal rows of three, have moved closer to each wing, opening up space downstage center. Gulnare is not included in the ground plan, but she is given two poses in the accompanying chart of notated poses and instructions for each set of dancers. Gulnare (Zhukova in 1880) is included in sketches from both 1868 and 1880, placed at the upstage end of the central arcade, next to Medora.[66]

[62] We use Petipa's system of numbering groups found in his sketches of the 1880 production. This group is labeled "I Group A" in the CN.

[63] GTsTM *fond* 205, *op.* 1, *ed. khr.* 705.

[64] GTsTM *fond* 205, *op.* 1, *ed. khr.* 201, fol. 2v.

[65] Labeled "II Group B" in the CN.

[66] GTsTM *fond* 205, *op.* 1, *ed. khr.* 705 and 200, fol. 2r, respectively.

Ex. 8.9 Adagio, bars 11–14 (source: *Corsaire* Rep)

The coryphées lower their garlands so that Medora, beginning upstage, can perform *jetés* over them as she travels through the arcade. (Petipa notes that Medora reaches the upstage end of the arcade by passing through it—garlands are raised—on *pointe*.) Reaching the downstage end, she performs a *piqué en arabesque* at the height of the musical phrase (Ex. 8.9, bar 12, beat 3).

As Medora performs her *arabesque*, the coryphées raise their garlands and the six dancers, who have been standing in *tendu effacé derrière*, change their hip direction and make the same pose on the other leg. Medora returns upstage by running beneath the raised garlands. (Again Petipa notes that Medora returns upstage beneath the raised garlands on *pointe*.) The entire enchaînement is repeated, after which "everyone goes" to the next group.

Group 3.[67] The third group features a diagonal formation, five dancers deep, at stage right. The ensemble is arranged in the following order: the girls (front row), "kneeling, having placed their own garlands on the floor" in front of them; the boys (second row), "standing, having crossed their arms on their chests"; the coryphées (third row), "holding their heads in the garlands," that is, holding their garlands in such a way that they frame their faces; the corps women (fourth row), "standing with baskets"; and the men (fifth row), "holding the garlands high." Three of the six dancers extend the third row downstage, while the three others stand in a row to the left of the upstage end of the diagonal. Gulnare waits for Medora downstage right. Petipa notes, "I must make a group in the middle with Sokolova-Zhukova and 6 second *danseuses*," although his sketch indicates both Sokolova and Zhukova at the upstage end of the diagonal and the six second *danseuses* in two rows of three at the downstage end.[68]

Beginning upstage as the music returns to its opening theme (see Ex. 8.3), Medora "goes through the garlands" laid on the floor by the girls. Holding her left arm overhead and her right arm side, she performs a *piqué en demi-arabesque* on the right foot in each of the first six garlands—one garland per bar of music. For the final six, she quickens her pace, performing a *piqué* on the left foot in each garland followed by a step on the right foot—one *piqué* per quarter note for two bars. Reaching the downstage end of the diagonal, Medora performs another *piqué en arabesque* on the right foot, "taking the

---

[67] Labeled "III Group C" in the CN.
[68] GTsTM *fond* 205, *op.* 1, *ed. khr.* 200, fol. 2v.

hand and shoulder of the 1st dancer," as "everyone goes" to the fourth group. Petipa's plans call for somewhat different choreography, in which Sokolova is partnered by Zhukova: "Sokolova does *petits battements* and holds the arm of a second *danseuse* [sic], and she goes down [downstage, that is, along the diagonal] on *pointe* while passing through the garlands after she does *petits battements*."

Group 4.[69] The fourth group features two arcades, formed by the boys kneeling on the outside and the coryphées standing on the inside, situated on the diagonal from each upstage corner. Their shared garlands form arbors under which six corps women stand in a line within each arcade. (According to Petipa's plans, the boys are placed within the arcades and the corps women hold one end of the garlands that create the arbors.) The men form a cross upstage center between the arcades, a configuration perhaps borrowed from the first adagio group of the 1868 sketches; three men make up each segment of the cross, all twelve facing away from its axis. Downstage, the girls kneel and form an inverted triangle. The six dancers flank the stage in rows of three by each wing, posing in *tendu effacé derrière fondu*.

Medora and Gulnare run to the downstage apex of the girls' triangle and pose together. Gulnare's body position is not notated, but the ground plan indicates she faces downstage. Medora, facing stage left and kneeling on her left knee, stretches her right leg behind her, her arms in fourth position. Her "body lies on the left knee of the 1st dancer," suggesting Gulnare kneels on her right knee. Petipa's plans present a different idea: Sokolova lies across the knees of six girls who are kneeling in a tight row, with Zhukova placed upstage of the other six girls, who also kneel and hold their garlands high.[70]

Group 5.[71] The ensemble forms the final group nine bars before the end of the adagio and maintains their pose until its conclusion. The ground plan indicates a square-shaped platform at center (no information is given as to how the platform is either brought on stage or raised from the stage floor) on which Medora stands in first position, facing right of center, arms held high, head turned left. Behind her, the men form a semicircle across the stage. In front of the men, the six dancers form a smaller semicircle. The corps women flank Medora in two rows of three on each side of the platform, facing inward and holding their baskets high. The rest of the ensemble forms three rows downstage of Medora. The coryphées stand, holding their garlands. In front of them, the girls kneel, their garlands framing their faces. Finally, the boys sit with crossed legs along the front of the stage. Gulnare kneels at center, the farthest downstage.

Petipa's sketches indicate an inverted semicircle involving all of the dancers except the men (who form a row upstage, as in the CN) and the six *danseuses* in the second group (in diagonal rows at either downstage corner, as in the CN's Group 4).[72] Sokolova is at center stage, but no platform is indicated. Petipa has drawn the coryphées (denoted with "X"s) as though they have crossed their arms, thus bending their hoops and creating a smaller circle with which they frame their faces.

---

[69] Labeled "II Group B" in the CN. This is the same label that was used for Group 2. If the scribe had continued the pattern used for labeling the first three groups, this group would have been labeled "IV Group D."

[70] GTsTM *fond* 205, *op.* 1, *ed. khr.* 201, fol. 2r.

[71] Labeled "V Group C" in the CN. If the scribe had continued the pattern used for labeling the first three groups, this group would have been labeled "V Group E."

[72] GTsTM *fond* 205, *op.* 1, *ed. khr.* 201, fol. 1v.

Ex. 8.10 Interpolated Variation 1 (attr. Pugni), bars 4–9 (source: CN Rep)

Variation 1

The first variation in the CN is not set to Delibes's music, but instead to a thirty-seven-bar interpolation by an unidentified composer (Ex. 8.10). (Burlaka attributes the variation to Pugni and sets its date of interpolation into *Le jardin animé* as 1869.[73]) The CN provides no information besides "Variation Mlle . . .," but Petipa confirms the variation performed at this point in the divertissement is intended for the "1st dancer" (Gulnare): "After this group [the final grouping of the preceding adagio]—comes the variation of the second *danseuse* [Zhukova]"[74]

During the three-bar introduction, "all disperse." Petipa's plans, however, suggest at least some of the dancers remained on stage: "Must have a group in place while Mme Zhukova dances her variation."[75]

Beginning upstage left and traveling on the diagonal, Gulnare performs *piqué en arabesque, pas de bourrée en avant* on *pointe, piqué en cou-de-pied devant*, two *entrechats quatre, soubresaut, relevé développé devant* twice. From this point, no further ground plans are provided for the variation.

She continues with *tour jeté, relevé à la seconde* on *demi-pointe, fouetté arabesque fondu* four times followed by small jumps in place: two *soubresauts* and four *demi-emboîtés devant*, all performed four times. At the return of the main melody, the jumping sequence becomes more complex: *glissade, entrechat cinq* twice then *assemble derrière, entrechat quatre*, and a quick *soubresaut* followed by *développé devant* with the right leg (the left leg *à plat*). Gulnare repeats the two *glissades* and *entrechats cinq* and, after a quick run, finishes the variation with *piqué en arabesque* and a pose in fourth position *fondu*.

Interlude 1

The first interlude, which now follows rather than precedes Variation 1, features the six dancers, who are later joined by the ensemble as the flower beds are put in place for the remainder of the divertissement.

Starting at opposite wings in lines of three, the dancers travel to center with *temps levés en arabesque*. Meeting at center in pairs, they circle each other and continue to the opposite wing with *demi-emboîtés devant*. They repeat the enchaînement from the beginning,

---

[73] "The choreographer M[arius] Petipa staged a new variation of Gulnara on the music by C[esare] Pugni (in the divertissement 'Le Jardin Animé') for the Petersburgian performance (1869)." Burlaka, ed., *Le Corsaire*, 388.

[74] GTsTM *fond* 205, *op.* 1, *ed. khr.* 201, fol. 1v.

[75] Ibid.

but arriving at center they cross and travel upstage, forming a single row. The dancers move directly downstage with *cabrioles derrière* and return upstage with *pas de valse en tournant* as the corps men and women enter in pairs, six couples from each upstage side, and travel toward center with *pas de basque*. Moving *en masse*, the group travels downstage with *pas de basque* as "the props people take out [presumably from the wings] the baskets and grassy beds [*kurtinki*]." Arriving downstage, the ensemble continues with four *balancés* in place before they "disperse to the sides and leave behind the wings."[76]

Petipa provides additional detail in his plans: "After Mme Zhukova's variation, the 6 second *danseuses* dance 20 measures alone. They finish at the back [upstage] and go downstage with the mass [ensemble]. The mass in 3 lines [rows] goes downstage for 12 measures, then they *balancé* in place for 8 [sic] measures and return to each side into the wings. (quickly) | 1st coryphées—1st wing. *Figurantes*, second wing. *Figurants*, 3rd wing. The 6 soloists return into the wings."[77]

The rest of the divertissement is danced within the framework of the flower beds. The garden's design in the CN matches those in Petipa's plans for both the 1868 and 1880 productions. The CN's ground plan for the garden indicates where twenty-four "baskets with flowers" are placed within the beds by denoting each of them with an "X."

Interlude 2

The girls, holding garlands, enter at midstage, six on each side.[78] They perform a series of *piqués en arabesque* on *demi-pointe* as they travel downstage through the side alleys then upstage through the central alley, returning down the side alleys and then across the front of the stage and back, passing each other twice.

At the same time, the six dancers enter from opposite downstage corners, three on each side. Performing the same steps as the girls, they enter the garden at downstage center, travel upstage, and circle around the back of the central platform. They perform a slight variation of their step four times in place then revert to the original step, exit the garden at midstage, and return downstage along the wings. Reaching the downstage corners, they perform *ballonnés* on *demi-pointe* then pose at the end of the number in *tendu effacé derrière*.

Meanwhile, the girls, having crossed the front of the stage twice, cluster in three groups of four and "put down the garlands," their hoops forming three flowers with four petals each. They "run away to the sides," where they stand in lines along the wings, awaiting Medora's entrance.

Here again the CN conforms to Petipa's plans. Under the heading "Variation of Mme Sokolova," Petipa writes: "1st coda [the subsequent description confirms he is referring to Interlude 2] | 12 little girls with garlands come downstage from the back to the middle of the path dancing—The 12 coryphées dance in the paths. The children finish the dance. The children place the hoops in front of the garden thus."[79] Here, Petipa has drawn three hoop flowers, each formed by four hoops. The stage is set for Medora's solo.

---

[76] A bar of music has been added to the end of Interlude 1 in both the *Corsaire* Rep and the CN Rep. The chords in the two preceding bars have been revoiced, but the harmony remains unchanged. The voicing of the chords is different in each Rep.

[77] GTsTM *fond* 205, *op.* 1, *ed. khr.* 200, fol. 1v.

[78] A single-bar introduction has been added to the CN Rep. Two identical bars of introduction are added to the *Corsaire* Rep, but the second bar is struck through.

[79] GTsTM *fond* 205, *op.* 1, *ed. khr.* 200, fol. 1v, and 201, fol. 1r.

Ex. 8.11a Variation 2, bars 23–26 (source: CN Rep)

Variation 2

Beginning stage left of the three hoop flowers, Medora runs and performs a *grand jeté en avant*, landing in *arabesque fondu* inside the first flower, followed by *relevé en cou-de-pied devant*. She repeats this enchaînement two more times as she leaps into the other flowers. Finishing at stage right, she runs back to the central flower.

The middle of the variation comprises a repeated series of *relevé pas de cheval* to *tendu devant fondu*. Medora extends her right leg into each hoop flower petal with each *tendu* and makes a quarter turn to the right with each *relevé*. After completing two full revolutions, she runs out of the central flower to far stage right for her final enchaînement, a more complex journey through the flowers. Running forward, she performs a *tour jeté*, landing inside the first flower in *arabesque fondu*, followed immediately by *relevé en arabesque*. After two more repetitions in the remaining flowers, she returns to the central flower. The CN Rep ends here, indicating that the music for the variation was cut short (Ex. 8.11a). Petipa's description of the variation, which calls for *cabrioles* rather than *jetés*, appears to suggest the same ending point: "Mme. Sokolova does *cabrioles* then passes into the hoops. She goes toward the middle making *cabrioles*, enters into the middle hoops, turns on two *pointes* and finishes in the middle of the hoops."[80]

Returning to the CN, however, we find that the bar in which the final pose would have been notated (that is, the final bar of Ex. 8.11a) has been struck through in red pencil. A subsequent page of notation includes five added bars of choreography and music, both of which appear to be written in the same hand as the rest of the variation (Ex. 8.11b). Here, remaining within the central flower, Medora perform steps in place on *pointe* whose rhythm matches the music: downbeats are punctuated by quick poses *en cou-de-pied* and rushing upward scales by *bourrées* and runs. During the first scale, Medora *bourrées* and turns in place; during the second, she runs out of the flower and finishes the variation, like Gulnare, with a *piqué en arabesque* and a pose in fourth position *fondu*.

Coda

The coda features a series of *entrées* for Gulnare and Medora, separated by the re-entry of the varied sets of dancers that make up the ensemble, until the entire cast of the divertissement is on stage together. Here we encounter the aforementioned choreographic polyphony, as the various groups of dancers perform discrete enchaînements simultaneously.

---

[80] GTsTM *fond* 205, *op*. 1, *ed. khr*. 201, fol. 1r.

Ex. 8.11b Variation 2, replacement bar 26 and bars 27–30 (source: CN Rep)

During the introduction, two short musical phrases and one longer one, the girls run from the sides to their respective garland hoops lying on the downstage floor, and "let themselves down to one knee." They "take the garlands," "get up from their knees," and return to their lines along each wing, traveling sideways on *demi-pointe*. Petipa writes: "2nd Coda | The little girls who have finished on each side arrive by 4 [inserted: "2 on each side"] in the middle taking the 4 hoops. The 4 on each side go near the hoops that they take—all turn and go to their places by 6 to each side."[81]

On the downbeat of the main theme, Gulnare begins a winding path around the downstage flower beds (Ex. 8.8a). Petipa writes: "Mme Zhukova must start the galop alone—for 24 measures." Starting in front of the central platform, she performs a sequence of *temps levés en arabesque* and *demi-emboîtés devant*. Twenty-four bars later, she finishes downstage center, posing in fourth position *fondu*, arms in fourth position, back arched.

The six dancers enter next to the accented chords of the second motif, three on each side of the stage, traveling downstage through the side alleys with a series of *temps levés en arabesque* (Ex. 8.12a). According to Petipa, "The 6 second *danseuses* dance in the paths for 31 measures—They finish in the paths near the wings." Indeed, the two trios meet downstage center and split again, forming a row behind the downstage flower beds on each side. Once there, they perform a repeated combination in place: *tombé de côté*, *fondu en cou-de-pied derrière*, and two steps *en arrière* on *demi-pointe*. Just before the return of the main theme, they *bourrée* to the downstage corners, forming a diagonal row at each side.

At the same time that the six dancers enter, the girls begin dancing in place in their rows along each wing. Facing each other across the stage, they begin with the *tombé* enchaînement performed by the six dancers before breaking into a rocking sequence alternating *temps levé en demi-arabesque* and *temps levé en demi-attitude devant*. They revert to the *tombé* enchaînement, joining the six dancers until the end of the passage.

At the return of the main theme, Medora begins her first entrée, entering the garden midstage right. She travels with *demi-emboîtés devant* along a diagonal path and

[81] Ibid.

Ex. 8.12a Coda, bars 40–47 (source: *Corsaire* Rep)

Ex. 8.12b Coda, bars 87–94 (source: *Corsaire* Rep)

performs a *grand jeté en avant*, leaping over the flower bed at downstage left. Tamara Karsavina recalled this unique moment in her description of the scene:

> The choreographic climax of *Corsair* was reached in the third act, called *Jardin Animé*. The curtain falls on the Pasha's seraglio. A short action goes on in front of the curtain. It is raised within a minute. The stage by now is a garden, complete with flower-beds. The *corps de ballet* in white tarlatans, wearing wreaths of roses, lead a graceful saraband. The daring effect is reserved for the ballerina, who ends a dance with a long leap over the front flower-bed. Naturally an impeccable line had to be kept in the air, or the effect would have smacked of the circus.[82]

Medora continues with *emboîtés*, traveling to midstage and then down the opposite diagonal, jumping over the bed at downstage right. She makes her way to center with more *emboîtés*, passing behind the central basket and finally posing in front of it in *arabesque fondu*, coinciding with a *fermata* added to the score in both Reps (Ex. 8.12b at bar 90). Petipa wrote: "Entrée of Mme Sokolova who jumps over the strips [that is, flower beds] and ends by turning around the basket, finishing in front *en arabesque*."[83]

To a third musical motif, the coryphées enter midstage, six from each side (Ex. 8.12b, bar 91 ff.). They travel to the central basket with a series of *ballonnés*. Having circled the basket, they perform *balancés* in place before resuming the traveling *ballonnés*, their circle revolving around the basket. These same steps are also performed by the six

[82] Karsavina, *Theatre Street*, 216.
[83] GTsTM *fond* 205, *op.* 1, *ed. khr.* 201, fol. 1v.

dancers, who travel back to the downstage beds before returning to their corners. The girls, meanwhile, have resumed their rocking *temps levés*, alternating with *balancés* in unison with the others.

At the fourth motif, this one in C-flat major (Ex. 8.8b), Gulnare begins her second entrée, performing a series of *cabrioles* and *demi-emboîtés devant* down the central alley in front of the large basket. After four *cabrioles*, she continues with *demi-emboîtés en tournant*, traveling downstage left, where she poses in fourth position *fondu*. Petipa's description, "The 12 coryphées—the 12 little girls[,] the 6 second *danseuses*[,] and Zhukova in a large group," once again corresponds to the CN.[84] The six dancers and coryphées perform *temps levés* and *emboîtés* in their respective formations, the six dancers at one point making two turns in place as they perform *demi-emboîtés devant*. The girls continue their *temps levés* and *balancés* throughout.

At this point, both the *Corsaire* Rep and the CN Rep designate a repeat of bars 71–118, beginning with the first return of the main theme. This repeat increases the length of the coda by forty-eight bars and affords Medora and Gulnare one additional entrance each.

At the repeat, Medora begins her second entrée. Traveling down the diagonal from midstage left, she performs *cabriole devant, piqué en arabesque* four times. She returns upstage with *demi-emboîtés devant*—doubling the tempo after the first four—and repeats the *cabriole* sequence. She continues with *emboîtés* to the downstage right corner, where her final pose—in *tendu effacé derrière*, left arm overhead, right arm side, back arched—again coincides with the added *fermata* (Ex. 8.12b).

At the repetition of the third motif, the six dancers and coryphées repeat their sequence of *ballonnés* and *balancés*, this time joined by the girls. The corps men and women are provided a set of notation staves in the CN at this point. Although the staves are empty—no steps are recorded—their presence informs us that the stage is now filled with an additional twenty-four dancers.

Gulnare returns for a near-repeat of her second entrée—her arms are held differently for the *cabrioles*, and she finishes with four *piqué tours en dedans*. Meanwhile, the ensemble continues with *ballonnés* and *balancés*, although the notation for the coryphées and girls ends just five bars into Gulnare's entrance.

From this point forward, only the six dancers are provided with notated steps. They continue for sixteen bars following the completion of Gulnare's third entrée. At bar 183, "general group" is written across the notation staves, followed by an erased annotation referencing the "Adagio," possibly suggesting that one of the adagio groupings may also have been the final grouping of the divertissement or served as its model (Ex. 8.12c).

Other erasures are also visible enough to decipher. These include erased steps for the "ballerina," notated on the staves above the six dancers' remaining steps, that reveal a final sixteen-bar entrée for Medora. These bars are followed by an additional sixteen bars of erased steps for the six dancers and an erased annotation, "general group," placed just ten bars before the end of the number, at bar 199.

The erased material continues the ever-increasing momentum of the dance. Like Gulnare's entrance before her, Medora's final entrée begins as a near-repeat of her previous one: *cabriole devant, piqué en arabesque* three times followed by "running," likely upstage. The *cabrioles* and *arabesques* are repeated another three times followed by *chaînés* on *pointe* and what appears to be a final pose (though the erased notations for it are indistinct).

---

[84] Ibid.

Ex. 8.12c Coda, bars 183–190 (source: CN Rep)

The six dancers continue with fast *demi-emboîtés devant* followed by turns in place that appear to resemble what today are called "paddle turns," a variant of *demi-valse*. The *emboîtés* and turns are repeated, and the CN concludes with the aforementioned annotation, "general group," for which no ground plan or further information is given.

Sortie

The CN Rep includes the complete final *sortie* (utilizing the first of Delibes's two endings), but no ground plans, steps, or other information are recorded.

The 1899 St. Petersburg revival of *Le Corsaire* and beyond

Petipa's final revival of *Le Corsaire* in 1899 (see Chapter 7) provided him with a further opportunity to revise *Le jardin animé*, and this he seems to have done to a certain extent. While the order of numbers in the divertissement appears to have been the same as documented in the CN, the *Corsaire* Rep includes a different interpolated variation for Gulnare, danced by Olga Preobrazhenskaya.

In addition to the three sets of bound folios that comprise the nearly complete notation of *Le jardin animé* (which from hereon we will call the "complete CN"), separate notations document much of the opening waltz, the students' choreography, three variations, and a coda entrance. The separate notations of the students' choreography include Pierina Legnani's name and suggest that in 1899 she may have danced the version of Medora's variation that is notated in the CN (or a version that incorporates the same framework of garland hoops on the stage floor). The additional notations of other variations interpolated into *Le jardin animé*, however, take us beyond 1899 and suggest yet another revision to the order of numbers in the divertissement.

Additional notation of the waltz. The additional waltz notation includes no dancer names that could assist with dating its creation. However, the notation appears to be in the same precise hand, which we believe to be that of Sergeyev, as the choreographic notation of *La Bayadère*. That notation mostly documents the performances of dancers in the December 1900 revival of *Bayadère*, nearly two years after the January 1899 revival of *Le Corsaire* (see Chapter 9). The similarity in scribal hands suggests these two notations were made within the same relative time period and therefore that the additional waltz notation represents the 1899 production of *Le Corsaire*.

The notation documents the beginning of the waltz up to the entrance of Gulnare then skips ahead (omitting material danced in bars 67–85) to the return of the opening melody, when the six dancers begin dancing with Gulnare. The notation continues up to the point when the larger ensemble enters and moves to the grouping at the end of the number (bar 140). The notation is detailed—providing movements for arms, head, and torso in addition to the lower body—and nearly identical in substance to what is notated in the complete CN.

Why was this careful and precise notation of *Le jardin animé* begun but not completed? Perhaps the waltz (in particular, the choreography of the ensemble) was the only part of *Le jardin animé* intended to be preserved in this notation project of 1899. Or, perhaps, after this document was begun, the older CN for *Le jardin animé* was rediscovered (or reconsidered) and determined to be sufficient to document the current production, resulting in the abandonment of this incomplete notation.

Additional notation of students' choreography. The content of the three additional pages of choreography for students suggests changes were made to the structure and steps of *Le jardin animé* in 1899. Medora's variation, however, continued to be danced in front of the garden, a feature of the divertissement we will see was later changed as evidenced by the order of music in the *Corsaire* Rep.

Labeled "b[allet] *Korsar* | *Garden* | Children," these three pages of notations are written in pencil on what are now very tattered sheets of oblong-format paper. The scribal hand appears to be Sergeyev's, suggesting the notations post-date the more formal complete CN that we suggest was made in 1894. This is confirmed by a reference to Legnani, who first performed the role of Medora in 1899. The notations consist mostly of ground plans followed by prose annotations and relatively few notated steps. Additionally, the ground plan perspective is reversed and drawn from the stage view rather than the audience view. That the notations contain only student choreography for the entire divertissement and that the information is crammed on the pages in an imprecise hand suggest the notations may have been made for use in rehearsal, where having the pertinent details of the choreography written on a few pages instead of many may have been a practicality.

The differences between what is found in these additional notations and the complete CN can be summarized briefly. Here, in the waltz, the girls enter in rows of six from opposite upstage wings. Their ground plan resembles that of the coryphées at the opening of the waltz: they move to center (here, with *temps levés en demi-arabesque*) and waltz back to the wings ("switching hands | one up then the other"). The groupings with the boys midway through the waltz are also different: at one point, the boys form a complete circle at center. When the students move to form the grouping at the end of the waltz, the boys join the girls by running into the wings, where they get baskets and the girls get garlands. When the boys and girls return to the stage, they perform *pas de basque* as they move to their places.

Five groupings are recorded for the adagio. While they are similar to those in the complete CN, there are differences. For example, in the second group, the side arcades are situated on the diagonal. They are formed in part by the girls, who make up the inside colonnades, kneeling and holding one end of the shared garland hoops. The boys sit in lines within the arcades. The fourth group is a repeat of the second group. In the fifth group, the students form rows across the stage. The boys are behind the girls, who kneel and hold their garlands around their faces.

The layout of the flower beds is likewise similar but not the same as that found in the complete CN. The girls perform a slightly different step as they move through the garden during what is presumably Interlude 2: their repeated *piqué en arabesque* is here a *piqué en demi-arabesque* preceded by a *pas de basque*. The girls end up in lines along either wing, where they perform a step forward into *relevé en demi-arabesque, fondu,* and a step back into a *pas de bourrée en tournant* on *demi-pointe*. An annotation above this sequence instructs, "4 times in place" in large letters, below which is written, in smaller script, "the garlands are lowered to the floor after counting to four." Two large question marks are drawn next to this annotation. Perhaps what is missing is an instruction for the girls to move downstage, where they presumably place their garlands on the floor for Medora's variation.

The subsequent ground plan indicates that the girls run downstage from their lines at the wings, presumably at the beginning of the coda. This is followed by the annotation, "running after Legnani's variation," and a ground plan showing the girls in four lines of three. Under this is written, "1st time turning to [toward] the middle and 2nd time from [away from] the middle | in front of the garden," accompanied by arrows indicating the girls turning in place. Next, the girls in the lines near the wings *bourrée* upstage on *pointe*, while those in the lines at center *bourrée* to their respective sides. This is followed by the annotation, "they run off in pairs with the motif." The first and second sets of turns may correspond to the first two phrases of the introduction to the coda, and the *bourrée* or "run" may correspond to the longer third phrase.

Does this information confirm that Legnani danced the variation notated in the complete CN, in which Medora dances in and around the garland hoops placed on the floor downstage of the garden? Not unequivocally, but it does seem to confirm—in agreement with the complete CN—that her variation was danced after the garden was installed on stage. The details provided here for the girls' movements, though incomplete, confirm that they placed their garlands on the floor, ran downstage of the garden following Legnani's variation, and returned to their lines along the wings.

The coda follows. After a trip around the side flower beds performing *demi-emboîtés devant*, the girls continue dancing in lines by the wings, much as they do in the complete CN. At one point, however, they perform four *pas de basque* as they travel downstage and meet at center, continuing with four *balancés* in place before repeating the entire enchaînement as they move back to the wings.

Two subsequent moments in the dance are preserved here that are not included in the complete CN: a final entrance for the boys and a final grouping for all the students. The ground plan indicates that the boys enter from the upstage corners, six boys from each side, with the annotation, "they run to the baskets [sic]," followed by "the girls do *balancé* in place." The final ground plan indicates that the twelve boys circle the central basket surrounded at a distance by the twelve girls, holding their garlands.

Before considering further additional notations, brief mention of the score of *Le jardin animé* as preserved in the *Corsaire* Rep is apt. The order of numbers in the divertissement, as preserved in the *Corsaire* Rep (Introduction—Waltz—Adagio—Variation 1—Variation 2—Interlude 1—Interlude 2—Coda), differs slightly from the order in the complete CN: here, Variation 2 precedes the interludes. Because the additional notation

Ex. 8.13 *Le jardin animé*, Interpolated Variation 1 (1899), from *The Adventures of Peleus* (likely Minkus), bars 7–14 (source: *Corsaire* Rep)

of the students' choreography suggests Legnani danced Variation 2 after Interlude 2, the order of numbers in the *Corsaire* Rep likely post-dates Legnani's performances as Medora in St. Petersburg, the last of which was given on 3 January 1901. As it was in earlier versions of the dance, the garden in the later version represented here was presumably in place by the end of Interlude 1 and remained in place during Interlude 2 and the coda. The final *sortie* is not included in the *Corsaire* Rep.

The music of *Le jardin animé*, like the rest of the score in the *Corsaire* Rep, is only sparsely annotated. For example, the adagio includes Roman numerals indicating the point at which groupings are formed. The numbers "II" (bar 11), "III" (bar 23), and "IV" (bar 35) correspond to the same group numbers and bars in the complete CN.

Interpolated Variation 1 in the 1899 production of Le Corsaire. Variation 1 in the *Corsaire* Rep is neither Delibes's original nor the variation preserved in the complete CN. Rather, it is an interpolated variation from Petipa's ballet *The Adventures of Peleus*, first presented in 1876 with a score by Ludwig Minkus. The ballet was revived by Petipa in a one-act version, retitled *Thetis and Peleus*, with additional music by Delibes, on 28 July 1897.[85] The performance was given on Holguin Island, Peterhof, with a cast that featured Matilda Kshesinskaya, Pavel Gerdt, and Olga Preobrazhenskaya. The heading given in the *Corsaire* Rep—"Variation | Mlle Preobrazhenskaya | from the ballet *The Adventures of Peleus*"—therefore suggests that Preobrazhenskaya repurposed her solo from *Thetis and Peleus* as a variation for Gulnare in the 1899 *Corsaire* revival.

The number begins with a four-bar introduction featuring a cadenza for solo violin. Forty-nine bars of a polka follow, eight of which are cut in the Rep (Ex. 8.13).[86] Though we have not had access to a full score of the variation, we assume from the introduction that it continues as a violin solo. And while no composer is credited, we note that the structure of the variation and writing style for the violin are similar to other Minkus violin solos discussed in this study (for example, the introduction to the *Paquita Grand pas* adagio and much of Nikia's variation in *La Bayadère*'s Kingdom of the Shades; see Exx. 9.43b and 9.43c).

[85] *Khronika III*, 340–341.
[86] A piano reduction of this variation is published in Burlaka, ed., *Le Corsaire*, 418–419.

Although no choreographic notation documenting Preobrazhenskaya's performance of this variation has been identified in the Sergeyev Collection, notation of a variation performed by Elizaveta Vill may represent choreography set to this music. Several factors support this possibility. The notation is part of the *Corsaire* CN, wherein it is labeled "Variation Vill | b[allet] *Korsar* | slave" and filed with two other variations identified as part of *Le jardin animé*. Librettos, posters, and programs as far back as 1858 consistently refer to Gulnare as the "Pasha's slave," suggesting this variation, with its annotation referring to "slave," may be intended for Gulnare.

Vill first performed the role of Gulnare on 19 September 1904. Her name is written in the *Corsaire* Rep at the end of bar 85 of the waltz, at the return of the main melody, corresponding to Gulnare's entrée. The presence of Vill's name in the Rep strengthens the likelihood that she danced Preobrazhenskaya's variation because no other musical option for the variation is provided in the *Corsaire* Rep.

Finally, the notated choreography matches the structure of the *Peleus* variation, although it would seem to require the inclusion of the previously mentioned eight bars that are struck through in the Rep. Beginning at upstage left, Vill runs down the diagonal then *bourrées* upstage, where she performs a *ballonné* on each foot, three *demi-emboîtés devant*, *tombé*. The *bourrée* and subsequent enchaînement are repeated twice, to alternate sides, after which Vill travels "simply on [*pointe* symbol]" toward upstage right.[87]

Zigzagging down the opposite diagonal at the beginning of the second section of the variation, Vill continues with *pas de chat*, *pas de bourrée* on *demi-pointe*, and *temps levé sur la pointe en demi-arabesque*. During the *temps levé*, her body is first leaned forward and then raised, back arched, as she lands the hop. This enchaînement is performed seven times on alternate legs. At the return of the opening melody, Vill travels upstage left with a series of *bourrées* and *demi-emboîtés devant*. Reaching the corner, she turns two circles in place on *pointe*. She begins her final diagonal with a series of steps that could be described as *ballotté par terre de côte*, continuing with two *piqué tours en dedans* and *chaînés* on *demi-pointe*. She finishes the variation with a pose in *tendu derrière*.

Interpolated Variation 2 danced by Julia Sedova. Variation 2 immediately follows Variation 1 in the *Corsaire* Rep, an indication that it was danced prior to the placement of the garden on stage and thus much more open stage space was available to the performer. Although we believe that Delibes's original variation for Medora may have been in use as late as 1901, it is replaced in the *Corsaire* Rep by a short variation from Petipa's ballet *The Cyprus Statue, or Pygmalion*, first presented in 1883 with a score by Ivan Trubetskoy.[88] After a brief introduction of two bars, the variation proceeds with sixteen bars in $\frac{6}{8}$ meter followed by a faster final section of sixteen bars in $\frac{2}{4}$ that are repeated with a second ending (Ex. 8.14). The first ending is struck through in the Rep, thus cutting half of the final section.

A choreographic notation labeled "Variation Sedova | b[allet] *Korsar* | Garden | mus[ic] from the b[allet] *Pygmalion*" matches the score in the *Corsaire* Rep. Sedova first danced the lead in *Le jardin animé* on 2 December 1901 when the divertissement was included on the program of a benefit performance for Olga Preobrazhenskaya.[89]

---

[87] The notation symbol denoting *pointe* is used in the quoted phrase.

[88] A piano reduction of this variation, titled "Variation of Galatea from the ballet 'THE CYPRUS STATUE, OR PYGMALION' for J[ulia] Sedova," is published in Burlaka, ed., *Le Corsaire*, 416–417. Burlaka asserts that the variation was interpolated into *Le jardin animé* for the 1899 revival.

[89] *Khronika IV*, 26–27. Burlaka states that the *Pygmalion* variation was interpolated into *Le jardin animé* earlier than 1901, indeed for the 1899 revival. Burlaka, ed., *Le Corsaire*, 416.

Ex. 8.14 *Le jardin animé*, Interpolated Variation 2 from *The Cyprus Statue, or Pygmalion* (Trubetskoy), bars 1–6 (source: *Corsaire* Rep)

Beginning upstage left, Sedova travels down the diagonal with a series of *grands jetés en avant, relevé grand battement en cloche*. She waltzes back to her starting point and continues with a zigzag downstage that includes *tombé, glissade, assemblé* four times to alternate sides. The third and final enchaînement, demonstrating the Italian influence in its extreme repetition, is a series of sixteen *ballonnés relevés* that travels across the stage from left to right on a shallow diagonal. Sedova finishes the variation on *pointe* with a final *relevé battement devant*.

Interpolated Variation 1 and coda entrées danced by Vera Trefilova. The final notated variation, labeled "b[allet] *Korsar* | 3rd Act | *Garden* | Trefilova," includes no mention of a composer and does not match any musical numbers within the sources we consulted. However, the choreography appears to fit a variation from Jules Perrot's ballet *Catarina, ou La Fille du bandit* that Burlaka has identified as being interpolated into *Le jardin animé*.[90] Attributed to Albert Zabel, solo harpist for the Imperial Ballet, the variation is believed to have been added to *Catarina* for the Italian ballerina Virginia Zucchi in 1889.[91] The notated choreography was danced by Vera Trefilova, who first performed the role of Gulnare on 22 April 1901.

Featuring solo harp, the number begins with a brief cadenza-like introduction followed by twenty-seven bars of an *allegro moderato* (Ex. 8.15).

From upstage left, Trefilova travels down the diagonal with a series of *piqués en arabesque* and *emboîtés sur les pointes*. Reaching center, she zigzags directly downstage with multiple *piqués en demi-arabesque* alternating with *pas de bourrée* on *pointe*. She *bourrées* left, turns a circle in place, and poses in *tendu derrière*. She continues, traveling

---

[90] See note 29 earlier in this chapter.

[91] Zucchi did not dance the role of Catarina during her years as guest artist at the St. Petersburg Imperial Theater, 1885–1888. However, she first performed the ballet in the Russian capital on 15 February 1889 at the Nemetti Theater in a production by her brother-in-law, the ballet master José Mendez, while on tour with an Italian troupe. See Guest, *Divine Virginia*, 121–132.

According to Maria Babanina, a Mariinsky Theater piano reduction of the variation is labeled, "Inserted variation in the ballet 'Korsar' | from the bal[let] 'Katerina' [sic] | Variation 'Zucci' [sic]." Personal communication.

Ex. 8.15 *Le jardin animé*, Interpolated Variation 1 (attr. Zabel), from *Catarina, ou La fille du bandit*, bars 3–7 (Source: courtesy of Maria Babanina, Bayerisches Staatsballett)

upstage on the diagonal with a *piqué tour en demi-arabesque* and *balancé*, the middle step of which is on *pointe*. After repeating this, she steps to fifth position on *pointe* twice—the first time facing downstage right, the second time facing downstage left—then *bourrées* downstage left. The CN indicates "the last three plans [beginning with the *piqué tour*] are repeated 2 times."

The final enchaînements travel across the front of the stage. Heading right, Trefilova steps forward into *tombé, coupé dessous, fouetté, chassé, tour jeté,* and two *pas marché sur les pointes*. The enchaînement is repeated to the other side, traveling left. The *tour jeté* is followed by *plié, sous-sus,* and a series of turns traveling right: the first several are on *pointe* followed by turns on *demi-pointe*. No final pose is given.

A "Coda I" is also notated for Trefilova that is similar to but longer than Gulnare's first coda entrée in the complete CN. After *demi-cabrioles derrière* that zigzag down-stage from midstage center, Trefilova runs back to her starting point and repeats the enchaînement. She runs upstage a second time and begins a final series of steps: traveling downstage left, she performs *piqué en cou-de-pied devant* on the left foot and *piqué en demi-arabesque* on the right foot followed by a run forward. This is repeated to the other side followed by turns on *demi-pointe*. After this entrée is the heading "2nd Coda," but nothing more is notated.

In sum, while we know next to nothing about Mazilier's choreography for the 1867 Paris *Le pas des fleurs*, we know a great deal about Petipa's incorporation of the divertisse-ment into the St. Petersburg *Corsaire* from his own notes as well as from the choreo-graphic notations and *répétiteurs* that are part of the Sergeyev Collection. Renamed *Le jardin animé*, the dance preserved much of the structure of its Paris progenitor. Although Delibes's music for the original variations came to be replaced by interpolations—we have seen this was a common practice as a ballet maintained its place in repertory over time—Petipa retained the majority of the music that had been expressly written for this divertissement. And his only change to the order of the numbers was to move both vari-ations ahead of the two interludes so that they could be danced on an open stage before the garden beds were put in place. Petipa also kept the Versailles-like formation of beds and alleyways seen in the set plan for the Paris revival. The orderly configuration surely appealed to his preference for symmetry and balance. Finally, we know that the cast size of the first 1868 Petersburg production of the divertissement was larger than that in Paris (eighty performers in Petersburg versus sixty-two in Paris—according to the 1867 Paris libretto), but by 1880 that number was reduced to a comparable sixty-eight.

The choreographic notations also reveal an important feature of Petipa's dance design in the coda of *Le jardin animé*: polyphonic choreography, a term we use to describe multiple enchaînements performed simultaneously by different groups of dancers. This represents a level of complexity we have not encountered in the work of Petipa's predecessors (at least as it has been preserved in the manuals of Justamant). In the next chapters we will discover it again in the character divertissements in the second acts of *La Bayadère* and *Raymonda*, though as we shall see, Petipa continued to favor unison choreography as well, sometimes combining it with polyphonic choreography when creating for large casts. In *Bayadère's* Kingdom of the Shades, the corps de ballet—forty-eight women strong—nearly always performs in unison (according to the notation representing the revival in 1900). And in *Raymonda's* first-act *Valse fantastique*, a cast of at least forty-four women and student girls (divided into five discrete groups) performs an array of varied enchaînements in succession that culminates in a brief passage of polyphonic choreography before the group joins together to end the dance with unison steps.

Finally, we can recognize how Petipa's careful preparation enabled his prolific output. He was a planner, preparing detailed notes in advance that would allow him to work efficiently in rehearsal. Alexander Shiryaev gives us an idea of Petipa's methods in his memoirs:

> Petipa managed his work as a *maître de ballet* as the perfect expert, which is certainly not surprising. He had developed this skill through some 10 years of regular work as *maitre de ballet*, a time when he developed his techniques of production. As a rule, Petipa went through the whole production of a new ballet at home, where he would usually call the pianist and the violinist. Forcing them to play several times over separate fragments of music, he planned the production on his table, using small dolls made from papier-mâché (especially for mass dances and groups). He moved them in various combinations, which he wrote down in detail, marking women with a zero and men with daggers, and different movements with arrows, hyphens, and lines, whose meaning only he knew. Thus, Petipa graphically created all his future productions.[92]

Shiryaev's account agrees with the detail we find in Petipa's sketches for *Le jardin animé*, which feature symbols denoting women, men, and students laid out in patterns and groupings. These are annotated with Petipa's prose notes, providing enough detail that we believe his meanings indeed can often be understood.

We will explore another selection of Petipa's preparatory notes as we turn in our next chapter to *La Bayadère*, the first of two original ballets by Petipa under examination in this volume. Here we will encounter his advance planning for mime scenes and processions as well as for dances. And while he was practical and methodical in working with a large ensemble, we will find that Petipa's contrasting spontaneity in choreographing for a soloist—a process that involved close collaboration with the featured artist—did not always proceed as smoothly.

---

[92] Beumers et al., *Alexander Shiryaev*, 108.

Postscript: The "Naïla" Waltz

One remaining topic having to do with Delibes's music composed for *Le Corsaire* is the so-called "Naïla" waltz, an amalgamation of several numbers from *Le pas des fleurs* that was arranged in the nineteenth century. "When, and how, the name of Naïla became associated with the waltz tune from Delibes's *Pas des fleurs divertissement*, composed for the 1867 Paris revival of *Le Corsaire*, is uncertain."[93] So wrote Thomas D. Dunn is his 1980 article concerning Delibes's contribution to *La Source*, a ballet created by Saint-Léon. Indeed, "Naïla waltz" is the name that has been most associated with the music of *Le pas des fleurs* since it was composed.

Naïla, the spirit of the spring, is the name of the lead character in *La Source*, first performed by the Italian ballerina Guglielmina Salvioni (the role originally was meant for Adèle Grantzow). Following its Paris Opéra premiere in 1866, *La Source* spent a decade in repertory and also found a home in other cities, including St. Petersburg, where it was staged in 1869 by Saint-Léon under the title *Le Lys*, and Vienna, where, on 4 October 1878, Saint-Léon staged the ballet for the Vienna Court Opera (Wiener Hofoper) under the title *Naïla, oder die Quellenfee*.[94]

An arrangement by Franz Doppler of the waltz from Delibes's *Le pas des fleurs* was published in 1878 by Berlin-based Adolph Fürstner and titled *Intermezzo (Pas des fleurs, grande Valse) aus dem Ballet "Naïla."* The work is credited thus: "by Léo Delibes | arranged and orchestrated for the K.K. Hofoperntheater in Vienna by Franz Doppler, K.K. Hofopern—Kapellmeister."[95] Doppler (1821–1883), a well-known flutist and composer (in addition to music for flute, he composed fifteen ballets), was conductor of the ballet orchestra of the Vienna Court Opera when Saint-Léon made his staging. The title of the arrangement seems to confirm that it was interpolated into the score of Saint-Léon's *Naïla, oder die Quellenfee*. The arrangement, in A major throughout, begins with an introduction based on a motif from *La Source* and continues with the entire waltz from *Le pas des fleurs*. Doppler's contributions include a countermelody that accompanies the main waltz theme as well as occasional melodic and rhythmic flourishes (Ex. 8.16). Instead of a transition to the subsequent *andante* at the end of the waltz, the arrangement features a *pianississimo* conclusion.

Other arrangements of the divertissement draw upon more of its numbers. For example, Paris-based Huegel published an uncredited piano arrangement titled *Grand Valse | Extraite du Pas des fleurs, Divertissement intercalé dans Le Corsaire*.[96] The arrangement begins with the *andante* in A-flat major, followed by the waltz in near entirety. A transition leads to Variation 1, arranged in waltz meter and in D-flat major. A second transition, consisting of newly composed material, ushers in a reprise of the waltz and a *fortissimo* finale.

---

[93] Thomas D. Dunn, "Delibes and *La Source*: Some Manuscripts and Documents," *Dance Chronicle* 4, no. 1 (1981): 9.

[94] On the Paris production, see Guest, *Second Empire 1858–1870*, 93–99. *Le Lys* premiered on 21 October 1869 at the Bolshoi Theater, St. Petersburg, with Adèle Grantzow in the leading role. See *Khronika III*, 145–146. The premiere date of *Naïla, oder die Quellenfee* is reported in *Musikalisches Wochenblatt* (published in Leipzig), 11 October 1878, 509. See also Dunn, "Delibes and *La Source*," 9.

[95] Léo Delibes and Franz Doppler, *Intermezzo (Pas des fleurs, grande valse) aus dem Ballet Naila* (Berlin: Fürstner, 1878).

[96] Léo Delibes, *Grand Valse | Extraite du Pas des fleurs, divertissement intercalé dans Le Corsaire*, Paris: Heugel, n.d. Plate H. 8198.

Ex. 8.16 *Intermezzo (Pas des fleurs, Grande valse) aus dem Ballet "Naïla"* (arr. Doppler), bars 32–47

These arrangements guaranteed Delibes's *Le pas des fleurs* a home in the repertory of salon music and light classical concert works. Moreover, Doppler's arrangement has been adopted for use in performances of *Le jardin animé* in *Le Corsaire* and other choreographies made to Delibes's music, and the Huegel arrangement was utilized by George Balanchine for his 1965 *Pas de Deux and Divertissement* (later incorporated into the 1969 revision of his *La Source*).[97] The manuscript sources held by the Library of Congress and Bibliothèque Nationale de France, however, provide us the opportunity to hear Delibes's original work in all of its colorful richness.

[97] Katz et al., eds. *Choreography George Balanchine*, 244–245 and 353.

9

La Bayadère

The two remaining ballets in our study were created in St. Petersburg: *La Bayadère* in 1877 and, twenty-one years later, *Raymonda* in 1898. While individually each was a product of its particular time and place, both perpetuated Parisian ballet traditions.

Set in India, *La Bayadère* is one of Marius Petipa's most popular and enduring "exotic" ballets, taking its place alongside the choreographer's other major exoticist works: *The Pharaoh's Daughter* (1862), set in Egypt, and *Le Roi Candaule* (1868), set in the ancient kingdom of Lydia. The story of *La Bayadère* was based in part on *Sacountala*, a ballet-pantomime produced in Paris two decades earlier by Petipa's brother, Lucien. *Giselle*, another ballet-pantomime, also served as inspiration for some of *La Bayadère*'s character relationships and scene details, particularly in the ghostly Kingdom of the Shades. The Orient was conjured by vivid costumes and scenic designs ("ethnographically true costumes," according to one review of the 1877 production), and character dances (which alternated with purely academic dances) evoked a European idea of local Indian color.[1] Academic dances, of course, were a staple of Petipa's choreography, not only in the Kingdom of the Shades, which has become one of classical ballet's most beloved scenes, but in the final act's *pas d'action*. All of these elements were supported by the well-crafted score composed by Ludwig Minkus, which is distinguished by its musical unity, achieved through recurring melodic and rhythmic motifs, and its representations of Indian and other "exotic" music using a variety of established techniques.

La Bayadère's plot and its precedents in earlier ballets. The authorship of the libretto has been the subject of discussion since the ballet's premiere. Current scholarship favors a collaboration between Petipa and the journalist and historian Sergei Khudekov.[2] While phrases from Petipa's preparatory notes for *La Bayadère* are quoted nearly verbatim in the libretto, other more erudite features likely were Khudekov's contribution. Indeed, Roland John Wiley suggests Khudekov "may have been responsible for the inclusion (and possible misuse) of Indian lore and Sanskrit terms."[3]

The melodramatic plot involves Nikia, a *bayadère* (an Indian temple dancer), who loves Solor, a great warrior. The two pledge eternal love, but Solor is obligated to marry the Rajah's daughter, Hamsatti, who with her father plots and murders Nikia.[4] Solor dreams of meeting Nikia in the "Kingdom of the Shades," where the bayadère warns him not to betray her. In the final wedding scene, the spirit of Nikia appears to Solor and, as he and Hamsatti are wed, the gods exact vengeance and the temple is destroyed by an

---

[1] *Golos*, 26 January 1877, 2, tr. in Wiley, *Tchaikovsky's Ballets*, 20.

[2] See Meisner, *Marius Petipa*, 141; Wiley, *Tchaikovsky's Ballets*, 18–19; and Sergey Konaev, "Der *Tigre Captif* und Gustave Doré: Marius Petipas Inspirations-Quellen" [The *Tigre captif* and Gustave Doré: Marius Petipa's sources of inspiration], in *La Bayadère* program book (Berlin: Staatsballett Berlin, 2018), 44.

[3] Wiley, *Century*, 291n2.

[4] We follow Petipa's spelling of "Hamsatti" instead of the more common "Gamzatti."

Five Ballets from Paris and St. Petersburg. Doug Fullington and Marian Smith, Oxford University Press.
© Oxford University Press 2024. DOI: 10.1093/oso/9780190944506.003.0010

earthquake and lightning, killing all within. Nikia and Solor are reunited, and together they fly over the peaks of the Himalayas.

Sergey Konaev has characterized this plot as a "revenge drama," in contrast to the "love drama," epitomized by *Giselle*.[5] Nevertheless, *La Bayadère* shares much with *Giselle* in its plot and characters.[6] Indeed, in his notes outlining the now-famous Kingdom of the Shades scene, Petipa referred to *Giselle* several times, as we shall see later in this chapter. And like *Giselle*, the story of *La Bayadère* centers on two love triangles. The first, made up of Solor, Nikia, and the Great Brahmin who loves her, can be seen as analogous to Albert, Giselle, and Hilarion; the second, including Solor, Nikia, and Hamsatti, is another version of Albert, Giselle, and Bathilde. However, as a "revenge drama," most of *Bayadère*'s characters are as aggressive as Hilarion in their attempts to steer the action toward their own purposes. But where Hilarion is ultimately contrite, the Brahmin is obdurate. Where Bathilde and Giselle find common ground, Hamsatti and Nikia quickly become enemies to the death in their quest to claim Solor as their own. Solor seems the exception. Whereas Albert is actively duplicitous, Solor becomes lost in his own dilemma. After an energetic opening scene, he recedes into inertia, conceding to stronger characters. Like *Giselle*, nearly half of *La Bayadère* takes place after its heroine has died. But once Nikia has met Solor in the afterlife, she returns to the real world to claim her vengeance. Unforgiving, she waits for Solor to die before claiming him, whereas Giselle saves her lover and returns him to his fiancée.[7]

In addition to *Giselle*, Lucien Petipa's *Sacountala*, produced in 1858 for the Paris Opéra, significantly influenced the story of *La Bayadère*. The libretto for that ballet, by Théophile Gautier, was based on Kalidasa's Sanskrit play *Shakuntala*, of which a French translation (of a 1789 English translation) had been published in 1803.[8] The title character is an Indian woman "of celestial origin" who enjoys the protection of the gods and falls in love with the King of India.[9] After overcoming a series of obstacles set up by the ballet's antagonists, the lovers are united. The plot is quite like that of *La Bayadère*, though it has a happy ending. The opening scene, in particular, is clearly the model for *Bayadère*'s "Festival of Fire," and some of the character names were borrowed as well (*Sacountala*'s Dushmata became *Bayadère*'s Dugmanta, Madhava became Madhavaya, and Hamsati was borrowed as Hamsatti).

The Western conception of the bayadère. La Bayadère and *Sacountala* are only two of many Western works of the period that drew from the Indian *devadasi* tradition. Molly Engelhardt has described the transformation of the *devadasi* into the bayadère (a French term taken from the Portuguese *bailadeira*, meaning female dancer), particularly "the origins of the bayadère story and how the *devadasi* tradition in India was appropriated and repackaged by poets, librettists, and choreographers for Western consumption."[10]

---

[5] Konaev, "Der *Tigre Captif*," 45.

[6] Tiziana Leucci has also drawn connections between *La Bayadère* and *Giselle*. See Tiziana Leucci, "Naslediye Romantizma i Oriyentalizma v Baletakh Mariusa Petipa s Indiyskim motivom: 'Bayaderka' (1877) i 'Talisman' (1889)" [The heritage of Romanticism and Orientalism in Ballets by Marius Petipa with Indian motives: "Bayaderka" (1877) and "Talisman" (1889)], *Vestnik Akademii Russkogo baleta imeni A. Ya. Vaganovoy* [Bulletin of the Academy of Russian Ballet named after A. Ya. Vaganova] 6 (2019): 27–28.

[7] See Scholl, *Petipa to Balanchine*, 5–7, for a discussion of features of Romantic ballet present in *La Bayadère*.

[8] *Sacountala, or the Fatal Ring . . . translated from the original Sanskrit and Prakrit* (Calcutta, 1789); *Sacontala, ou l'anneau fatal, drame traduit de la langue san-skrit en Anglais, par Sir W[illiam] Jones, et de l'Anglais, en Français par le citoyen A. Bruguière; avec des notes des traducteurs* (Paris, 1803). See Gautier's 19 July 1858 article on *Sacountala*, published in *Le moniteur universal* and tr. in Gautier, *Gautier on Dance*, 281–287.

[9] Beaumont, *Complete Book*, 363.

[10] Molly Engelhardt, "The Real Bayadère Meets the Ballerina on the Western Stage," *Victorian Literature and Culture* 42, no. 3 (2014): 511.

The elevated *devadasi*, a dedicated servant of god who ranked higher than men in her religious community and who enjoyed a variety of legal rights and certain sexual freedoms, was transformed into the bayadère, a subservient, fallen sinner in need of redemption.[11] (Nikia refers to herself as "a miserable bayadère.") This redefinition was largely accomplished by Goethe in his 1798 ballad *Der Gott und die Bajadere*, which served as an essential source for the 1830 Parisian opera-ballet of the same name, *Le Dieu et la Bayadère, ou La courtisane amoureuse*. A collaboration by composer Daniel Auber, librettist Eugène Scribe, and choreographer Filippo Taglioni, the work was a vehicle for Marie Taglioni, who danced the role of the Zoloé, a bayadère rewarded by the Hindu god Brahma for her self-sacrifice.[12] The libretto of *La Bayadère* assumes the merger of the *devadasi* and bayadère by defining the former as "bayadères of the first rank" then explaining that "bayadères are charged with looking after the pagodas; they live in the pagodas and study with the brahmins."[13]

Engelhardt also cites Jacob Haafner's *Reize in eenen Palanquin*, a travel narrative published in 1808, as an important source for the Western notion of the bayadère. She argues that this work influenced not only *Le Dieu et la Bayadère* but *La Sylphide* as well, "the ballet that dance historians agree marks the genesis of the form and pathos of the romantic ballet."[14] In his writings, "Haafner not only legitimizes the function of the *devadasi* [the financially independent temple prostitute who, as a servant of god, is rewarded with heaven] in his account, but he also praises the natural beauty of the Indian dancer and her affinity with nature in ways that anticipate European dance reviewers' celebration of the romantic form and the ballerinas who embodied it."[15] Giannandrea Poesio similarly described the bayadère's "double nature of priestess and dancer [which] epitomized the characteristic dichotomy of the Romantic female image: saint and sinner, angel and whore, unreachable and desirable."[16]

Gautier wrote with enthusiasm about the group of touring *devadasis* that performed in Paris in 1838. He acknowledged at the outset of his description that, in addition to whatever notions of "the East" the word bayadère would conjure in the mind,

> you will also be reminded of the slender legs of Mlle Taglioni beneath billowing clouds of muslin, the rosy shades of her tights plunging you into dreams of the same hue. Inevitably, the very unIndian bayadère of the Opéra will merge with the *devadasi* of Pondicherry and Chandernagore.[17]

At the end of his report, however, having recounted in great detail the bodies, dress, music, and dance of the Indian *devadasis*, Gautier concluded: "It is reported that the

---

[11] Ibid., 512.

[12] About Taglioni in *Le Dieu et la Bayadère*, see Guest, *Romantic Ballet in Paris*, 2nd ed., 102–105 and 233–235. For a discussion of *Le Dieu et la Bayadère*, see Smith, *Ballet and Opera*, 138–149.

[13] See Appendix F (i).

[14] Engelhardt, "The Real Bayadère," 513.

[15] Ibid.

[16] Giannandrea Poesio, "The Choreographer and the Temple Dancer: the origins of *La Bayadère*," *Dancing Times* 87, no. 1038 (March 1997): 527–528. Poesio suggests other stage works that may have served to inform Petipa's understanding of the bayadère and Orientalism more generally. These include Jean Coralli's ballet *La Péri* (1843) as well as two operas, Verdi's *Aida* and Gluck's *Orfeo ed Euridice*, both of which Petipa choreographed in the decade before creating *La Bayadère*. Nadine Meisner also points out the similarities in *Bayadère*'s plot to *La Péri* as well as to Saint-Léon's *Météora, or the Valley of the Stars* (originally, *Météora, ou Las Estrellas cadentas*). See Meisner, *Marius Petipa*, 140–141.

[17] Gautier, *La Presse*, 20 August 1838, tr. in Gautier, *Gautier on Dance*, 39.

Bayaderes will make their debut at the Variétés. Their proper place is at the Opéra, in *Le dieu et la bayadère*."[18]

Engelhardt notes the historical inaccuracies that resulted from this merger of diluted elements of Indian culture into the milieu of Western European academic dance theater:

> The backdrops of the ballets were not accurate—a little bit of Turkey here, a little bit of India there—and ballerinas wore their bouffant knee-length tutus slightly adjusted with an eastern trim. They still danced en pointe, pirouetted across the stage, and abided by the rules of classical ballet, using sensualist elements—scarves, earrings, darkened faces—as props for representing an exotic, non-specific east.[19]

Petipa's inspirations for La Bayadère. Within this context of imprecisions, Petipa had done his research in his usual fashion by looking to current events and visual arts for inspiration for his staging of *La Bayadère*. The Prince of Wales's visit to India in 1875 was covered extensively by European newspapers and periodicals. As Konaev has demonstrated, reports accompanied by evocative sketches published in one of Petipa's favorite French magazines, *L'Illustration*, as well as in the Russian magazine *Vsemirnaya Illustratsia* (*World Illustrated*), surely fueled the choreographer's imagination and inspired a number of particular moments in the ballet.[20] Petipa's efforts did not go unnoticed, as evidenced by this review of *La Bayadère* in the *Journal de Saint Pétersbourg*:

> Everything necessary to render the *couleur locale* exactly has been taken from engravings appearing in the *Graphic* and the *Illustrated London News* on the occasion of the Prince of Wales's journey. As a result, we see a series of scrupulously exact tableaux of the mores and costumes of the Indians, which naturally give the ballet an ethnographic interest quite exceptional and singularly fascinating.[21]

Despite these engaging visual components, balletomane Konstantin Skalkovsky reminded readers in *Novoe vremya* of the limits of realism in ballet:

> Mr. Petipa borrowed from India . . . only some external features, because the dances of this scene [the Festival of Fire] are little similar to the dances of the bayadères, which consist, as is well known, of some oscillations of the body and measured movements of the arms to the most doleful music.[22]

Finally, as Konaev notes, "Petipa's other source of inspiration and lifelong devotion were illustrations by Gustave Doré. There is innumerable evidence in Petipa's archives that he actively studied almost all the editions illustrated by Doré and then used them in his works."[23]

---

[18] Ibid., 46.
[19] Engelhardt, "The Real Bayadère," 510. See also Rajika Puri, "Im dienste der Gottheit: Die Indische Devadasi" [In the service of the deity: The Indian Devadasi], in *La Bayadère* program book (Berlin: Staatsballett Berlin, 2018), 11–13.
[20] Konaev, "Der *Tigre Captif*," 44–45.
[21] *Journal de Saint Pétersbourg*, 25 January 1877, no. 17, 2, tr. in Wiley, *Century*, 292.
[22] *Novoe vremya*, 26 January 1877, 2, tr. in Wiley, *Century*, 291.
[23] Konaev, "Der *Tigre Captif*," 45.

As we proceed through the ballet scene by scene, we will encounter Petipa's incorporation of these various inspirational sources.

Characters, in order of appearance

Roots of La Bayadère's *plot and characters in nineteenth-century Orientalist opera.* Before we introduce its individual characters, let us briefly contextualize the story of *La Bayadère* as a whole. Ralph Locke has identified a paradigmatic plot characteristic of Orientalist operas of the nineteenth and early-twentieth centuries that can be broadly applied to ballets of the same period.[24] This plot involves a white, European man (in opera, a tenor) who ventures into a brown- or black-skinned colony represented by alluring female dancers. There he both encounters an affectionate and sensitive woman (a lyric soprano) and incurs the wrath of a high priest or other tribal leader (a baritone or bass). While *La Bayadère* diverges somewhat from this paradigm (for instance, all of its characters are Indian Hindus—Locke makes the point that "an archetypal plot is not a rigid template"), we can identify within its characters and storylines elements that correspond to the paradigmatic archetypes and narrative tropes.[25]

The warrior **Solor** is the leading male character in *La Bayadère.* The libretto tells us he is a "wealthy and important kshatriya," that is, a high-ranking member of the Hindu military caste. Early in the ballet, Solor is both amicable and authoritative in his milieu—in his dealings with his peer Toloragva and also with the religious fakir Madhavaya. Although Solor is what Locke calls a "duty-bound male," he falls in love with Nikia, a bayadère who is bound to the temple.[26] Knowing they cannot be together in their current circumstances, Solor implores Nikia to run away with him. Yet, when the Rajah tells him he must marry his daughter Hamsatti (the two, in fact, have been promised to each other since childhood), Solor is ultimately unwilling to renounce her for Nikia. He spends the rest of the ballet dealing with his plight internally, revealing himself to be an *homme fragile,* which Locke defines as dreamy (literally, in this case) and under the spell of the female lead.[27]

Solor's comrade **Toloragva** is also a kshatriya.[28] According to the sources, he is active only in the opening scene, where he functions as a peer for Solor to converse with and leads the hunters in his absence. He is Solor's second-in-command.

Madhavaya.[29] Fakirs were holy men believed to possess miraculous powers, such as the ability to walk on fire, hence their inclusion in the opening scene's Festival of Fire. The fakir Madhavaya is a facilitator and informant for Solor, and he is kind and sympathetic toward the lovers. He is also smart, resourceful, and alert.

---

[24] Locke, *Musical Exoticism,* 181. Locke refers to the Orient in broad terms—encompassing Morocco on the western end to Japan on the eastern end. See ibid., 177.

[25] Ibid., 182.

[26] Locke discusses the "duty-bound male" in the context of Orientalist plot tropes. See Locke, *Musical Exoticism,* 186.

[27] Ibid., 192–196.

[28] The cast list in the libretto gives the spelling as "Taloragva," but the libretto text, 1877 poster, and subsequent programs give the spelling as "Toloragva."

[29] The cast list in the libretto and 1877 poster gives the spelling as "Madgavaya" (using Latin-alphabet transliteration), but "Magdavaya" is used in the libretto text and later programs. We have opted for the first spelling and, as with Hamsatti, we use the Roman the letter "h" instead of the more common "g" in place of the Cyrillic "г." Madhava is a Sanskrit name and another name for Vishnu, with references to sweetness and honey.

The **Great Brahmin** is the leader within a high-ranking priestly caste and the ballet's primary antagonist and catalyst for tragedy. He is the type described by Locke as the "brutal, intransigent priest." But as with the other principal players in *La Bayadère*, his character embodies complexities that go beyond stereotypes.[30] He desires Nikia for himself and uses his "coercive power" in an attempt to force her to submit to him.[31] When, out of jealousy, he exposes the romance of Solor and Nikia to the Rajah, he does not anticipate the Rajah's decision to have the bayadère killed and bitterly regrets his actions. But ultimately his pride—and what Locke refers to as the "fanatical rigidity and intolerance" of this character type—proves more powerful than any affection he feels for Nikia.[32]

As a bayadère, **Nikia's** dual nature of godly servant and alluring woman combine to make her both a *femme fragile* and *femme fatale*.[33] As the former, she returns Solor's affections and would rather die than be without him. She also fears that Solor, who is above her station, will abandon her. But as *femme fatale*, she continually and threateningly reminds her lover of his vow to her, does not hesitate to take up a dagger to kill a romantic interloper, and ultimately wreaks vengeance on the entire cast with the apparent blessing of the gods.

Rajah. Dugmanta, the rajah of Golconda, had carefully planned for the future of his kingdom by promising his daughter Hamsatti to the warrior Solor when they were both children.[34] As a ruler, he expects his will to be done and does not tolerate deviation or opposition. When he learns from the Great Brahmin that Solor plans to marry Nikia, he immediately resolves to have her killed, regardless of her religious status.

As the daughter of the Rajah, **Hamsatti** wields power and influence, making her more *femme fatale* than *femme fragile*. She believes herself entitled and is willing to kill to get what she believes should be hers. She is guilty of "personally vindictive violence" against Nikia, another trope cited by Locke.[35] But she also suffers from feelings of insecurity and is unsure that Solor will find her attractive or love her. The similarities between Nikia and Hamsatti as *femmes fatales* are suggested by the title of the ballet's second scene, "The Two Rivals." But because Hamsatti is "earthly," whereas Nikia is "heavenly," she ultimately loses out to divine intervention.

Aiya. The term *aiya*, of Malay origin, refers to a maid or nursemaid. Hamsatti's *aiya* is described as a "young girl" in the libretto but was portrayed by an adult woman in Imperial Ballet productions.[36] In modern productions, the character is sometimes interpreted by an older woman, suggesting a close, familial relationship between princess and nanny. Young or old, Hamsatti's *aiya* cares deeply for her and defends her from Nikia's attack.

Depictions of people of color. The hierarchy of performers within the Imperial Ballet demonstrates an imperialist model of depicting race: lower-ranking members of the company and school had their skin darkened by make-up and costuming. Cast photographs of the revival in 1900 and its subsequent performances show that these artists included male supernumeraries (the most inconsequential of roles) in Act One as well

---

[30] Locke, *Musical Exoticism*, see 181.

[31] Ibid., 196.

[32] Ibid., 198.

[33] See Locke's discussion of these character types in Orientalist opera in *Musical Exoticism*, 184–192.

[34] Golconda was a territory in southwestern India.

[35] Locke, *Musical Exoticism*, 196.

[36] *Khronika III* lists A[lexandra] Natarova as the *aiya* in 1877; however, because Alexandra Natarova was born in 1869 and "Natarova" listed on the poster is not designated as a student, it seems likely that the role was played by Varvara Natarova, a member of the corps de ballet since 1867. See *Khronika III*, 189.

as the young boy students (in roles akin to the "nègres" in *Le jardin animé* and the Arab boys in Act Two of *Raymonda*—Petipa's twelve exotic boys within a larger ensemble) and the men carrying large fans in the Act Two divertissement. (The roles for the boys and men in Act Two also feature the ballet's most basic step vocabulary in comparison to the more complex choreography for other roles.[37])

The drummer in the Hindu dance appears to have been another type of performer presented with darkened skin: a leading but nameless character in a divertissement. A color caricature drawn by Nikolai and Sergei Legat depicts Vasily Stukolkin as the drummer in the Act Two Hindu dance, the wildest exotic number in the festival divertissement.[38] Stukolkin's costume features a dark brown leotard, dark brown face make-up, and dark brown slippers that suggest bare feet. Other exotic elements include large hoop earrings, bracelets worn on his wrists and arms, a large necklace crossing his chest, bells on his ankles, and exaggerated features—long black hair and large red lips.

In contrast, the highest-ranking performers (including the ballerinas and *premier danseur*) and performers of roles with governmental or religious authority (including those portraying the Rajah and Great Brahmin) do not appear to have had their skin darkened.[39]

Dance and exoticist spectacle in La Bayadère. Roland John Wiley has placed *La Bayadère* in the broader context of Petipa's *oeuvre*: "*La Bayadère* illustrates the continuing vitality of the *ballet à grand spectacle* on oriental motifs, of which *The Pharaoh's Daughter* was prototype: extravagant tableaux interspersed with episodes of an active, melodramatic love story."[40] Indeed, melodrama fills *La Bayadère*, particularly its first two scenes, which are primarily exposition with little dancing. "Extravagant tableaux" form the bases of two subsequent scenes, one a religious festival and the other the Kingdom of the Shades, set in the spiritual realm. The ballet also includes depictions of "Eastern ceremoniality"—several rituals and numerous processions—which Locke identifies as "the most prominent markers of an Eastern society" in operas.[41] Such rituals and processions, of course, could easily be included in ballets, which—whether set in the East or West— often called for processions anyway, followed by suites of dances (in which rituals or other observances could be enacted). Opportunities for dance are also built into the various ceremonies and are often centered around Nikia, who, as a bayadère, both conforms to Orientalist stereotypes and fulfills Romantic ballet's requirement of a modicum of verisimilitude: she is a dancer. Group dances also have rationales: they are part of religious rituals or festival celebrations, or they represent a natural expression of the characters' nature—the shades of dead bayadères, for example.[42]

---

[37] For example, see the supernumeraries on the steps of the pagoda in the cast photo of Act One (St. Petersburg State Museum of Theatre and Music [GMTMI], 3240/48, circa 1900, available online at https://goskatalog.ru/portal/#/collections?id=12631641), the student boys (sitting with their legs crossed) and the supernumeraries (holding large fans at the rear of the stage) in the cast photo of Act Two, Scene III (GMTMI GIK 2705/160, circa 1900, available online at https://goskatalog.ru/portal/#/collections?id=7655664), and the later photo (circa 1917) of Petr Vladimirov as Solor with two boys from the Act Two divertissement (GMTMI GIK 17937/4299, available online at https://goskatalog.ru/portal/#/collections?id=31691539).

[38] This and many other caricatures were published in Nikolai and Sergei Legat, *Russkiy balet' v karrikaturakh'* [sic] [Russian ballet in caricatures] (St. Petersburg: 1902–1905).

[39] See GMTMI GIK 2705/160. See also the photo (circa 1901) of Julia Sedova (Hamsatti), Nikolai Aistov (Dugmanta), and Pavel Gerdt (Solor). GMTMI GIK 2037/99, available online at https://goskatalog.ru/portal/#/collections?id=12631653.

[40] Wiley, *Century*, 291. See also Wiley, *Tchaikovsky's Ballets*, 17.

[41] Locke, *Musical Exoticism*, 196.

[42] See Smith, *Ballet and Opera*, 65–67.

A list of *La Bayadère*'s scenes (with the titles given in the libretto) and their various components demonstrates this amalgam of exoticist elements, traditional features of the *ballet à grand spectacle*, and opportunities for justifiable dance:

Act One, Scene I: The Festival of Fire
  Festival of Fire (mysterious religious ceremony)
  Procession-like entrance of the Great Brahmin, munis, *rsi*, *brahmacarins*, gurus
  Dance of the bayadères
  Dance of the fakirs

Act Two, Scene II: The Two Rivals
  Procession-like entrance of Rajah, *kshatriyas*
  Djampe dance to entertain the Rajah

Act Two, Scene III: The Bayadère's Death
  Procession of Badrinata
  Large festival divertissement comprising multiple dances and groupings

Act Three, Scene IV: The Appearance of the Shade
  Dance of snake charmers (described in libretto)/Dance of astrologers (listed on poster: *Sakodusa*) performed to calm and distract Solor

Act Three, Scene V: The Kingdom of the Shades
  Extended classical *pas* featuring large, female corps de ballet comprising multiple dances

Act Three, Scene VI: Solor's Awakening

Act Four, Scene VII: The Gods' Wrath
  Procession-like entrance of warriors, brahmins, bayadères, Hamsatti, Rajah and retinue, Solor
  Pas d'action comprising entrée, adagio, variations, coda for relatively small cast of eight performers
  Wedding ceremony
  Natural event precipitated by religious ceremony: lightning, earthquake

Apotheosis

The Music

Turning next to the music, we will examine the only complete score by Ludwig Minkus encountered in our study. Wiley, who has delineated the role of the ballet composer in late-nineteenth century Russia, concludes that Minkus's score for *La Bayadère* is "varied and subordinate but competent" and "stands directly in the specialist tradition," a tradition that called for composers to hew to the needs of the ballet master, to complement with their music the visual component of the ballet and "vivify" the dance as well, and to provide the right orchestral colors at the right times.[43] As Wiley puts it, "The right choice [of sonority] had to be made for numerous solo obbligatos, and mime scenes were to be made suitably characterful by including descriptive elements appropriate to the action."[44]

Yet no matter how difficult the task, nor how successfully the specialist ballet composer met its challenges, Russian "serious" composers tended to look down on ballet music (until Tchaikovsky started composing it) and were likely unsympathetic to ballet lovers of the time who, as Wiley notes,

> liked the works of specialist composers (and they still do today), possibly because they experienced them in the theatre and grew familiar with them in their proper setting.[45]

In any case, Minkus, who appears to have begun composing for ballet as early as 1857, served successfully as court ballet composer of the Imperial Theaters in St. Petersburg from 1872 to 1885.[46] He enjoyed a particularly fruitful relationship with Petipa, beginning with their initial collaboration on *Don Quixote*, which premiered in Moscow in 1869. During his tenure, Minkus wrote the scores for the large majority of Petipa's new works, with *Don Quixote* and *La Bayadère* becoming the two most famous ballets resulting from their partnership.

Among Petipa's plans for *La Bayadère* is a page detailing the numbers in Act Four that the ballet master noted he had given to Minkus (see below). That the specificity in the description of music and action is far less than what Petipa provided for Tchaikovsky may be an indication of Minkus's familiarity with the ballet master's working process, a familiarity he no doubt developed during their many years of collaboration.[47]

Several musical sources allow us to both describe Minkus's score and coordinate it with information found in other sources, including choreographic notations and mime scripts.

A microfilm of a two-violin *répétiteur* (Rep) is preserved in the Sergeyev Collection.[48] At 312 pages, its contents appear to span at least the period 1877 to 1901 and provide a record of changes made to the score during that time—cuts, interpolations, and changes in order—and a handful of annotations. In addition, a manuscript piano reduction (PR), also an Imperial-era document (as its scribal hand suggests), is held by the Royal Opera House, London.[49] Comprising 228 pages, it includes a variety of brief annotations in Russian and English (often entrances) which confirm its use through the mid-twentieth

---

[43] Wiley, *Tchaikovsky's Ballets*, 23; see also 1–10 for his full discussion of the skills and challenges of the specialist composer. Robert Letellier provides a more positive assessment of Minkus's work. See Robert Ignatius Letellier, *The Ballets of Ludwig Minkus* (Newcastle, UK: Cambridge Scholars Publishing, 2008), 24–34. For a discussion of Parisian traditions, see Smith, *Ballet and Opera*, especially 3–18.

[44] Wiley, *Tchaikovsky's Ballets*, 7.

[45] Ibid., 6.

[46] About Minkus, see Letellier, *Ludwig Minkus*, 5–17.

[47] Petipa's notes for Tchaikovsky for *Sleeping Beauty* and *The Nutcracker* are reproduced and translated in Wiley, *Tchaikovsky's Ballets*, 354–359 and 371–376, respectively.

[48] MS Thr 245 (272), Harvard Theatre Collection, Houghton Library, Harvard University.

[49] Royal Opera House score courtesy of Lars Payne. No shelf mark has been provided. The piano reduction of Act Four is reproduced in Ludwig Minkus, *La Bayadère*, ed. Robert Ignatius Letellier (Newcastle upon Tyne, UK: Cambridge Scholars Publishing, 2009), 298–331. This publication also includes a reproduction of "a repetiteur's piano score from Kiev (1981)" of the complete ballet, representing twentieth-century Soviet-era productions, and additional excerpts.

century.[50] Additional piano reductions and an orchestra score of the Kingdom of the Shades (discussed below) are also held at Harvard. These scores appear to have been copied (and likely orchestrated) during Sergeyev's years in Riga (as were similar scores for *Giselle* and *Paquita*).[51]

The musical examples that follow in this chapter are drawn from both the Rep and PR, but their numbering and barring follow the Rep. For some examples, we have combined annotated details regarding instrumentation, as well as dynamics and phrase marks, from both sources. We have also corrected obvious errors and edited lightly for consistency.

Recurring motifs

As is the case for all of the ballets in our study, Minkus's score for *La Bayadère* is made up of many discrete and fairly short numbers. Most of these numbers in *La Bayadère* are built on phrases of four, eight, or sixteen bars, and rather than following the action in a literal way—for example, by underscoring particular physical gestures with descriptive musical ones—they provide atmospheric music appropriate to the action or the emotions being expressed.

One of Minkus's most effective and oft-deployed devices is the short rhythmic or melodic motif. Most notable, perhaps, is a rhythm first heard in the Great Brahmin's motif. This rhythm also appears in numerous subsequent melodic motifs, thereby providing continuity to much of the action music throughout the ballet. This rhythmic motif also appears in select dance melodies, often those accompanying Nikia, perhaps to demonstrate that her fate is tied to the Brahmin's actions. Other motifs appear only in a single act or scene, providing short-term continuity between music and action.

Great Brahmin's motif. The heavy, descending motif Minkus composed to represent the Great Brahmin accompanies the priest's initial entrance. Marked *maestoso* (majestic) in the Rep, the stark, stately theme makes clear the Brahmin's authoritative station and exemplifies the rigidity of the high priest character type (Ex. 9.1a).[52] The motif returns when the jealous Brahmin visits the Rajah to inform him of Solor's pledge of love to Nikia, underscoring the gravity of the situation (Act Two, Scene II, No. 6).

A shorter, inverted statement of the motif is introduced shortly thereafter, in the same number (Ex. 9.1b), and it recurs at several points throughout the ballet as a portent of Nikia's doom: when the Brahmin orders Nikia to be summoned following the bayadères' dance (Act One, No. 4); as Solor is made aware that the Rajah intends for him to marry Hamsatti (Act Two, Scene II, No. 5, in a slight variant); while the Brahmin offers Nikia an antidote to the snake venom (Act Two, Scene III, No. 16); and just before the destruction of the temple at the end of the ballet (Act Four, Scene VII, No. 6).

The Brahmin's rhythmic figure. More pervasive still is the rhythmic figure, ♩ ♩. ♪ ♩ (long—long—short—long), drawn from the Brahmin's motif (Ex. 9.1a, see brackets). This figure is employed by Minkus throughout the ballet, both in mime scenes and in dances performed by leading characters and is often associated with the Brahmin's power

[50] For example, the manuscript annotations "Rudi" and "Margot" are references to Rudolf Nureyev and Margot Fonteyn, who first performed the roles of Solor and Nikia together in the "Kingdom of the Shades" scene in 1965, in a staging by Nureyev for The Royal Ballet.

[51] See Wiley, "Dances from Russia," 99.

[52] See Locke, *Musical Exoticism*, 198.

Ex. 9.1a Great Brahmin's motif; Act One, No. 2, bars 1–8

Ex. 9.1b Shortened, inverted version of the Brahmin's motif; Act One, No. 2, bars 17–20

Ex. 9.1c Brahmin's rhythmic figure; Act Two, Scene II, No. 4, bars 30–33

and authority. The figure is presented in a variety of ways and informs a broad collection of melodies. For example, in the second act the figure is paired with a descending melody that shares the oppressive weight of the Brahmin's motif as the Rajah tells his daughter that she is to be married to Solor (Ex. 9.1c).

Use of upward semitone neighbor note. The pairing of the rhythmic figure with a melody characterized by an upward semitone neighbor note also recurs throughout the ballet. First presented shortly before the final curtain in Act One, the phrase is the first in a series of related motifs associated with Nikia and her fate (Ex. 9.1d).

The most substantial iteration of this phrase becomes Nikia's Act Three motif, first heard in Act Three, Scene IV, as Solor is visited in his chamber by the shade of his beloved bayadère. The motif is stated twice at the beginning of an extended passage (Ex. 9.2a, bars 67–70). According to Locke, the combination of flute and harp that is present here

Ex. 9.1d Rhythmic figure paired with upward semitone neighbor note (see brackets); Act One, Scene I, No. 13, bars 170–177

"was one of the standard French-operatic markers of ancient or exotic religiosity."[53] We will return to further expressions of exoticism presently.

The latter half of this excerpt (bars 75–78) is foreshadowed in the previous act after Nikia is bitten by the snake. In that case, the phrase is followed by a descending scale that spans an entire octave (presumably as the poison takes hold), heard just before the Brahmin offers Nikia an antidote, which she stubbornly refuses (Act Two Scene III, No. 16, bars 190–202).

The motif returns in the subsequent Kingdom of the Shades scene at Nikia's first appearance as a shade (Act Three, Scene V, No. 4) and is incorporated as the second phrase of the violin solo in No. 10 (Ex. 9.5c, bars 4–5) that accompanies the first meeting of the lovers in the afterlife.

The *Grand Adage* of the Kingdom of the Shades scene features both the upward semitone and the rhythmic figure in its opening phrase (Ex. 9.2b), and the rhythmic figure is repeated throughout the number, infusing this famous scene with reminders both of the Brahmin's treachery and of Nikia's doomed fate.

Chromatic appoggiatura. Two motifs representing Nikia (in the opening scene) and Hamsatti are related by their shared chromatic appoggiatura (which, perhaps in both cases, represents their longing for fulfillment). Nikia's first entrance in the ballet is accompanied by a melody incorporating a chromatic appoggiatura as well as the Brahmin's rhythmic figure (Ex. 9.3a; for the latter, see brackets in bars 1–2 and 3–4).

A less florid version of this motif is introduced in the previous number (possibly to accompany a mimed mention of Nikia or the actions of those going to fetch her from the pagoda), which is struck in the Rep and omitted in the PR (Ex. 9.3b). An augmented version of the motif appears again, two numbers later, in Act One, No. 8, after the Brahmin declares his love for Nikia (Ex. 9.3c).

A similar downward chromatic inflection is found at the midpoint of Hamsatti's motif, first introduced at her initial entrance in Act Two, Scene II. Like Nikia's motif in Act One, this melody also incorporates the Brahmin's rhythmic figure as part of an upward melodic gesture, adding a hint of martial quality to depict Hamsatti, who after all is the Rajah's daughter (Ex. 9.4, see brackets). Hamsatti's motif returns in Act Three, Scene IV (No. 3), when the hopeful bride visits her troubled groom in his chamber.

As the rhythmic figure informs further melodies, so can the chromatic appoggiatura of Nikia's and Hamsatti's motifs be found in other melodies later in the score. Minkus's musical depiction of Hamsatti's despair upon learning Solor is pledged to Nikia includes the chromatic appoggiatura as well as rising fifths and descending scales, both features

[53] Ibid., 197.

Ex. 9.2a Nikia's Act Three motif; Act Three, Scene IV, No. 3, bars 67–78 (Source: Rep)

of the Brahmin's motif (Ex. 9.5a). The appoggiatura phrase, in retrograde, opens the *pas de trois* in the Kingdom of the Shades (Ex. 9.5b), perhaps as a reference to the altogether different setting. Minkus employs the same retrograde phrase at the beginning of the subsequent violin solo (Ex. 9.5c).

Solor's motifs. The rhythmic figure also informs the Act Three motif of Solor that opens the act and is featured in both of its scenes (Ex. 9.6). This turbulent melody reflects

Ex. 9.2b Brahmin's rhythmic figure, incorporating upward semitone, in *Grand Adage*, Act Three, Scene V, No. 11, bars 3–6

Ex. 9.3a Nikia's Scene I motif: her first entrance, featuring a chromatic appoggiatura and the Brahmin's rhythmic figure; Act One, No. 6, bars 1–4

Ex. 9.3b Less florid version of Nikia's Scene I motif; Act One, No. 5, bars 1–4

the warrior's inner conflict. Of all the recurring motifs Minkus employs in *La Bayadère*, Solor's is the most thoroughly developed, though its use is limited to Act Three.

Contrasting sharply with this stormy motif is a consonant one that is heard in the first two scenes of the ballet, representing Solor as a stately, assured warrior and ruler (Ex. 9.7).

Ascending line. Several dance melodies associated with bayadères and Nikia include an ascending line that directly contrasts with the descending line of the Brahmin's motif. The first occurrence is heard in the bayadères' dance in Act One (Ex. 9.8a).

This ascending line returns when Nikia arrives to visit Hamsatti (Act Two, Scene II, No. 9), confirming its association with bayadères. A rising line also figures prominently

Ex. 9.3c Augmented version of Nikia's Scene I motif, after the Brahmin declares his love for her; Act One, No. 8, bars 89–95

Ex. 9.4 Hamsatti's motif; Act Two, Scene II, No. 4, bars 14–21 (bar numbering from PR)

Ex. 9.5a Hamsatti's despair, featuring her motif that includes a chromatic appoggiatura, rising fifths, and chromatic scales; Act Two, Scene II, No. 8, bars 1–8

Ex. 9.5b Kingdom of the Shades, *Pas de trois*, featuring the appoggiatura phrase in retrograde (bar 1); Act Three, Scene V, No. 6, bars 1–4

Ex. 9.5c Kingdom of the Shades, violin solo, featuring the appoggiatura phrase in retrograde (bars 2 and 6); Act Three, Scene V, No. 10, bars 2–9

Ex. 9.6 Solor's Act Three motif, representing his inner conflict; Act Three, Scene IV, No. 1, bars 1–4

Ex. 9.7 Solor's Act One motif, representing him as a stately, assured warrior and ruler; Act One, Scene I, No. 1, bars 76–91

Ex. 9.8a Ascending line in the bayadères' dance; Act One, Scene I, No. 3, bars 13–16

Ex. 9.8b Ascending line in Nikia's mournful solo; Act Two, Scene III, No. 16, bars 16–23

in Nikia's mournful solo at the end of Act Two, Scene III (Ex. 9.8b), as she laments Solor's impending marriage to Hamsatti.

The upward scale returns in the waltz section of the Act Four *Pas de Guirlandes* (garland dance) performed as a divertissement by students, at the end of which Nikia is said to have appeared by rising out of a trap in the stage (Ex. 9.8c).

Ex. 9.8c Rising scale in the *Pas de Guirlandes*; Act Four, Scene VII, No. 2, bars 46–53

Ex. 9.8d Rising scale in the finales of Acts Three and Four; Act Three, Scene VI, No. 16, bars 274–277

The aspirational ascending line becomes the antithesis of the dooming descent of the Brahmin's motif and has the final say in the drama. The extended major-key finale that concludes both Acts Three and Four features a rising melody—yet again incorporating the Brahmin's pervasive rhythmic figure—that reaches heavenward (Ex. 9.8d). If the descending scale is interpreted as representing Nikia's doom and that of all the major characters, the ascending melody, in contrast, signifies the happiness the lovers ultimately find together in the afterlife. D major, also the predominant key in the Kingdom of the Shades, emerges as the key of final resolution.

Musical depictions of India, Elsewhere, and Otherness

Minkus depicts India and, more broadly, Elsewhere, by employing several devices that Locke has identified as typical of Western music meant to sound exotic.[54] These include the use of solo instruments and melodic styles intended to represent the *vina*, an Indian stringed instrument that is played by Nikia. The *vina* has historically been represented in Western music by winds or strings playing extended melismatic solo lines perceived as "arabesque"-like, a term that here refers not to a ballet position but to a "decorative,

---

[54] Ibid., 51–54.

Ex. 9.9a   A flute imitates the sounds of the *turti* and the *vina*; Act One, Scene I, No. 7, bars 1–9

Ex. 9.9b   Coda of Nikia's first dance; Act One, Scene I, No. 7, bars 25–30

curvaceous" melodic line intended to depict the atmosphere of Arabic architecture and, more broadly, the Orient.[55]

The Indian vina. Solo flute accompanies Nikia's first dance in the ballet's opening scene (Act One, Scene I, No. 7). The libretto names the accompanying instruments: "Then the sounds of the *turti* (bagpipes) and the *vina* (a small guitar) served to accompany the graceful and languorous movements of the bayadère." After an introductory bar, in which the flute emulates the droning of the *turti* (presumably related to the *titti*, an Indian bagpipe made of goat skin), a long, winding solo begins that combines references to drones with quick scales and rising arpeggios (Ex. 9.9a). The solo concludes with a fast coda that blends the leaps of the drone motif with the running sixteenth notes often employed for the ending of a traditional ballet variation (Ex. 9.9b).

[55] Ibid., 53, 60. On Locke's use of the terms Orient and Orientalism, see 177–178.

The flute serves the dual function of both a signifier of exoticism and a typical instrument used to accompany female ballet solos (compare variations for Giselle and the Peasant *pas de deux* soloist in Act One of *Giselle* and one of the female solos in the second act *pas de deux* in *Paquita*). Moreover, the flute is associated with Nikia throughout the ballet as it is with Giselle.

Later in the scene, "[t]he pleasant sounds of the vina (guitar) are heard" as Nikia is about to appear from the pagoda again, this time for her rendezvous with Solor: "The window opens and Nikia appears in it, holding a guitar. The fakir [Madhavaya] crawls along some branches and places a plank beneath the window, along which the bayadère descends, illuminated by the moonlight." This atmospheric scene is also accompanied by a *vina*-inspired flute solo that is introduced by harp. The solo, even more than the first, embodies the "decorative, curvaceous" lines of the arabesque, performed over a rhythmic ostinato accompaniment, yet another signifier of exoticism identified by Locke (Ex. 9.10).[56]

In the second act, Minkus depicts the *vina* using a solo cello to accompany Nikia's mournful dance at the end of Scene III. As the libretto tells us, "Nikia comes out of the crowd with her little guitar. Her face is covered by a veil. She plays the same melody she played in Act 1." Though Minkus did not actually repeat the Act One melody, he did compose a melismatic tune with a somber, singing quality (Ex. 9.8b) that is not unlike the brief cello solo that gives voice to Albert's grief at Giselle's grave (Ex. 9.11).

Elsewhere and Otherness. More broadly, Minkus depicts Elsewhere using a combination of musical features, including short, disjunct melodic phrases, rhythmic ostinato, extensive repetition, and asymmetry. Locke describes such features as "not distinctive (not inherently marked as to origin)" but nonetheless able to suggest Otherness "by their rigid insistence."[57] These elements, emphasized through repetition, are found in the music accompanying the actions (Ex. 9.12a) and dances of the fakirs (Ex. 9.12b) as well as in the dance of the bayadères in the opening Festival of Fire, with its insistent repeated sixteenth-notes that conclude each two-bar phrase (Ex. 9.8a).

These features play a particular role in connection to the choreography in the divertissement of Scene III, wherein Minkus assigns these signifiers to dances performed using character steps, not on *pointe*, or dances intended to represent Indian life, such as the *Manu* dance, which is performed on *pointe* (Ex. 9.13). As the divertissement progresses and the dances begin to include more steps from the classical vocabulary, Minkus employs more traditional-sounding melodies made up of longer phrases that are either conjunct or legato and sometimes both (Ex. 9.14).

The character dances are intended to suggest local color—Indian dance—without any specific connection to actual Indian dancing beyond the broadest suggestion. Minkus likewise employs disjunct melodic contour, staccato articulation, and short phrase length to convey Otherness without direct reference to Indian music. The resulting mechanistic quality of these musical numbers, combined with the limited step vocabulary of their choreography (we will discuss this below) can cause the dancers to seem doll-like and

---

[56] Ibid., 52.
[57] Ibid. The devices Minkus uses to depict Elsewhere are among those listed by Locke under the following heading: "Departures from normative types of continuity or compositional patterning and forward flow. These departures may include 'asymmetrical' phrase structure, 'rhapsodic' melodic motion, sudden pauses or long notes (or, quick notes), and intentionally 'excessive' repetition (of, for example, short melodic fragments using a few notes close together; or of accompanimental rhythms." Locke, *Musical Exoticism*, 53.

Ex. 9.10 "Decorative, curvaceous" lines in the melody; Act One, Scene I, No. 10, bars 8–20

caricatured, simpler and perhaps two-dimensional, in comparison to the dancers who perform classical step vocabulary of far greater variety.

Minkus's use of these exoticist techniques was not a new feature of ballet scores in St. Petersburg. His predecessor at the Imperial Ballet, Cesare Pugni, employed these same broad signifiers to depict Otherness. Take, for example, Pugni's variation for the "Hong Ho" river (Huang Ho, or Yellow River) in China that is part of the famous underwater scene in *The Pharaoh's Daughter*. Over a simple chordal accompaniment in $\frac{6}{8}$ meter, Pugni has written a disjunct, staccato melody made up of two-bar phrases (Ex. 9.15).

Finally, we cannot lose sight of the fact that Minkus's score was deemed successful and served its purpose well, as summed up by Vazem in her recollections about *La Bayadère*:

Ex. 9.11 *Giselle*, Act Two, *Entrée d'Albert et de Wilfride* (Adam), bars 17–21

Ex. 9.12a Actions of the fakirs; Act One, Scene I, No. 4, bars 13–16

Ex. 9.12b Dancing of the fakirs; Act One, Scene I, No. 8, bars 1–4

Ex. 9.13 *Manu* dance; Act Two, Scene III, No. 14, bars 15–22 (Source: Rep)

Ex. 9.14 Ensemble dance with a traditional-sounding melody; Act Two, Scene III, No. 6, bars 1–8

Ex. 9.15 *The Pharaoh's Daughter*, *Pas des fleuves*, Variation 5 (Pugni), bars 6–14

Of all of my created roles, Nikia was my favourite. I liked this ballet for its beautiful and very theatrical libretto, its interesting and colourful dances in various genres and for its music by Minkus, highly successful in its melodies and appropriate to the choreography and to every scene.[58]

Early performance history

La Bayadère, grand ballet in four acts and seven scenes with apotheosis, with a libretto by Marius Petipa and Sergei Khudekov, music by Ludwig Minkus, and choreography by Petipa, premiered on 23 January 1877 at the Bolshoi Theater, St. Petersburg. The occasion was a benefit performance for Ekaterina Vazem, who danced the lead role of Nikia alongside Lev Ivanov as Solor and Maria Gorshenkova as Hamsatti. Veterans Christian Johanson, Nikolai Golts, and Nikolai Troitsky took the roles of the Rajah, Great Brahmin, and the fakir Madhavaya, respectively. Pavel Gerdt, as a nameless cavalier, performed a "Classical dance" with Gorshenkova in the third scene's divertissement and the Act Four *pas d'action*.[59]

The production was a great success, particularly for Vazem. "It is difficult to evaluate that perfection with which the benefit artist, Mlle Vazem, performed all the dances of her new role, both classical and character," wrote the critic for *Golos*.[60] Vazem herself, despite difficulties working with Petipa (see below), admitted, "The reception given me by the public was magnificent."

Petipa's attention to detail paid off. *Golos* effused: "Everything, beginning with the superb décor of Messrs Roller, Wagner, Shishkov, and Bocharov, the lavish, ethnographically true costumes, and ending with the tiniest accessory details, glitters with magnificence, novelty, originality, and produces an enchanting impression on the audience."[61]

La Bayadère immediately became the ballet of choice for further benefit performances in 1877: for Alexei Bogdanov, chief director of the ballet troupe, on 30 January; for Lubov Radina, who danced the lead in the third scene's "Hindu dance," on 5 February; for the corps de ballet on 13 February; and for the soloist Alexandra Kemmerer on 20 February.[62] A subsequent benefit for Troitsky on 31 March 1877 was attended by Alexandre Benois, whose memories provide details about the first production.[63] Select passages from the ballet were soon featured on other special programs. For example, on 29 April 1877, the second act was performed on a program benefiting the Red Cross Society.[64]

On 19 October 1880, a benefit performance for Timofei Stukolkin, the first three acts of *La Bayadère* were given, omitting the fourth act. Although the final act would eventually be dropped from the ballet in the early twentieth century, the omission here was likely made to accommodate the benefit artist: Stukolkin was featured in a revival of Saint-Léon's *Graziella*, which followed the three acts of *La Bayadère*.[65]

---

[58] Vazem, "Memoirs: Part 4," 33.
[59] *Khronika III*, 188–189. See also Wiley, *Century*, 291–293, and Wiley, *Tchaikovsky's Ballets*, 20.
[60] *Golos*, 26 January 1877, 2, tr. in Wiley, *Tchaikovsky's Ballets*, 20.
[61] Ibid.
[62] *Khronika III*, 190.
[63] *Khronika III*, 190. See also Alexandre Benois, *Reminiscences of the Russian Ballet*, tr. Mary Britnieva (London: Putnam, 1941), 42–45.
[64] *Khronika III*, 191.
[65] Ibid., 208.

Marie Petipa made her debut in the role of Hamsatti on 21 October 1882, dancing opposite Vazem. A mediocre review in *Novoe vremya* deemed her miming abilities satis-factory, but observed, "When she started dancing in the sixth scene, something curious happened: neither legs nor hands obeyed."[66] This report suggests Marie may not have performed Hamsatti's "Classical dance" in Act Two, Scene III.

Following Vazem's retirement, Anna Johanson made her debut as Nikia on 16 September 1884, with Gerdt as Solor and Marie Petipa as Hamsatti. Ivanov moved into the role of the Rajah and Alfred Bekefi made his debut as Madhavaya.[67] Pavel Gershenzon has called this production a restaging and notes several changes made to the order of dances and the cast size of various numbers. Close inspection of the poster, however, reveals no men-tion of a revival or restaging and just two significant differences from the earlier poster of 1877. First, the "Classical dance" in the third scene is omitted. Second, the 1884 poster states that the ballet is given in six scenes, rather than the original seven, because the very short "Solor's Awakening" scene is cut. But the poster mistakenly retains the title "Solor's Awakening" and applies it to the ballet's closing scene, which should be called "The Wrath of the Gods." (The 1900 revival program includes the same number of scenes with the same titles as in 1884, including the mis-titled final scene.) On 1 February 1885, the third scene of *La Bayadère* was presented as part of the farewell benefit of Lubov Radina, who reprised her role in what Pleshcheyev called the "spectacular Hindu dance."[68]

Petipa revived *La Bayadère* a final time on 3 December 1900 at the Mariinsky Theater. The occasion was the benefit performance of Pavel Gerdt, in observance of forty years of service. The production featured new scenery and costumes as well as the debuts of Matilda Kshesinskaya as Nikia and Olga Preobrazhenskaya as Hamsatti. Gerdt remained in the role of Solor with Nikolai Legat taking over duties as the nameless cavalier in Act Four. Marie Petipa was featured in the Hindu dance.[69]

Petipa took the opportunity in this revival to make further revisions. Many of the pro-duction's dances were meticulously recorded in Stepanov notation at this time or shortly thereafter. In a separate document, the mime conversations of (at least) the ballet's opening two scenes, as performed by the revival cast, were also recorded in detail. Both of these documents will presently serve as main sources for our description of the ballet.

With *La Bayadère* once again in repertory as of 1900, more debuts followed. Moscow ballerina Ekaterina Geltser danced the role of Nikia at the Mariinsky Theater on 21 October 1901, with Gerdt as Solor and Julia Sedova in her debut as Hamsatti.[70]

But the most important debut in this new production of *La Bayadère* was Anna Pavlova's in the role of Nikia on 28 April 1902, with Gerdt as her Solor and Sedova as Hamsatti. Wearing new costumes designed by Alexander Golovin, Pavlova achieved tremendous success as the bayadère.[71] As she would do the following year for *Giselle* with her interpretation of the title character, Pavlova's performance as Nikia revived the public's interest in *La Bayadère*, injecting new life into the ballet that contributed signifi-cantly to its maintenance in the repertory.

---

[66] *Novoe vremya*, 23 October 1882, qtd. in *Khronika III*, 220.
[67] *Khronika III*, 232. Pavel Gershenzon noted that the "Classical dance" was omitted by at least 1884. See Gershenzon, "*La Bayadère*," 17.
[68] Pleshcheyev, *Nash Balet (1673–1899)*, qtd. in *Khronika III*, 237.
[69] *Khronika III*, 372–373.
[70] *Khronika IV*, 25.
[71] *Khronika IV*, 35, and Lazzarini, *Pavlova*, 55. Photographs of Pavlova as Nikia taken by Karl Fischer in 1902 are reproduced in Lazzarini, *Pavlova*, 54–57.

Sources

In addition to the libretto, poster, programs, and music scores, sources documenting choreography, mime, action, and the stage plan allow us to assemble a description of the Imperial-era *La Bayadère*. These include the sources mentioned above: a choreographic notation in the Stepanov method, a mime script for the ballet's first two scenes, and a selection of Petipa's preparatory notes.

Choreographic notation. The choreographic notation (CN) of *La Bayadère* is one of the Sergeyev Collection's most detailed documents, including movements for the entire body— not just legs and feet—for many of the dances.[72] However, only dances are included in this notation, and nearly all of them are ensemble dances (exceptions are the *Manu* dance and the solos for the three Shades in Scene V). This reminds us that the earliest extant examples of Stepanov notation in the Imperial Theaters (of which this is one) appear to have been intended to document dance—in particular, ensemble dances—rather than action and mime.

The CN documents the performance of a single cast, that of the 1900 revival, with two exceptions (Vera Trefilova as the first Shade soloist and Nikolai Legat as the cavalier in the Act Four *pas d'action*).[73] This is confirmed by the dancer names listed in the CN:

Solor	Pavel Gerdt
Madhavaya	Alfred Bekefi
Great Brahmin	Alexei Bulgakov
Nikia	Matilda Kshesinkaya
Dugmanta	Nikolai Aistov
Hamsatti	Olga Preobrazhenskaya
Shades	Vera Trefilova, Varvara Rykhlyakova, Anna Pavlova
Cavalier	Nikolai Legat

Moreover, the notation score appears to be a finished product that was based on an earlier draft. An annotation in the Scene III "Crooked Dance" referring to a "rough draft" reflects the amount of care taken to produce a legible, accurate accounting of the ballet's ensemble choreography, the restaging of which would pose the greatest challenge to a *régisseur*.

The CN was made by a single scribe—almost certainly Nikolai Sergeyev. The time period during which the notation must have been made favors this attribution: recall that Gorsky was already working in Moscow as of September 1900 (that is, during the rehearsal period for the *Bayadère* revival). Further, Sergeyev was not provided with notation assistants until after his appeal to Vladimir Telyakovsky, director of the Imperial Theaters, in May 1903.[74] Sergeyev's script is tidier here than we see in most of the notations that comprise the Harvard collection, but the hand, as well as the method of notating certain steps, appears similar to notations in which Sergeyev's authorship can be identified with

---

[72] MS Thr 245 (105).

[73] Julia Sedova danced the first Shade variation in the 1900 revival. When she debuted as Hamsatti on 21 October 1901, Vera Trefilova replaced her as a solo Shade. Georgi Kyaksht was the extra cavalier in the revival cast. When Nikolai Legat replaced him is uncertain, but Legat was dancing the role at least by 28 April 1902 when Pavlova made her debut as Nikia.

[74] See Konaev, "My vse visim v vozdukhe . . .," 556–557.

certainty.[75] (This tidier hand crops up from time to time in other notations, for example, in parts of *Sleeping Beauty*.[76]) But regardless of the identity of the scribe, the notation of *La Bayadère* certainly belongs to the early period of the Stepanov method's use, during which notations were prepared in greater detail than in subsequent years.

The 141 pages of choreographic notation are written on oblong-format sheets that include two musical staves (not utilized here) above four systems of notation staves. Four boxes in the right margin are used by Sergeyev for annotations. Ground plans are written on the staves ahead of each corresponding passage of notated steps. Pencil is used throughout. The sheets are bound in a single volume, now fragile, with tape at the binding. An inside page at the beginning of the volume lists the notated ballets included in the Sergeyev Collection.

Manuscript mime script. A set of manuscript pages containing a mime script for Act One and the first scene of Act Two is preserved in the Gorsky archive at the Museum of the State Academic Bolshoi Theater.[77] This document comprises a cover page (bearing the title "Ballet 'Bayaderka' | (Plot) | Author's manuscript") followed by eleven pages of script written in ink in Cyrillic cursive in a neat, legible hand that we also believe to be that of Nikolai Sergeyev. (Comparison with the mime scripts for *Giselle*, *Paquita*, and *Le Corsaire* that are preserved in the Sergeyev Collection confirms this.)[78] Unlike several of the scripts preserved in the collection, however, the *Bayadère* mime script is a discrete document rather than a compilation of annotations found in the CN. This suggests that in the initial stages of documenting the steps and action of the Imperial Ballet repertory, choreography and mime were intended to be recorded separately. But as we have seen, the early, prescriptive examples of Stepanov choreographic notation (such as this one for *La Bayadère*) gave way to the descriptive, less polished examples that make up most of the notations preserved in the Sergeyev Collection, in which both choreography and mime are included in a single document.

The script is particularly valuable as evidence that the complexity of the mime conversations in the action scenes of *La Bayadère*—and, therefore, likely other ballets in the Imperial Ballet repertory—was similar to those preserved in the Justamant staging manuals. Further, the abundance of mime recorded here for these two scenes seems to confirm that the mime documented in many of the Sergeyev Collection's choreographic notations represents abbreviated versions of what were likely more detailed conversations.[79] As in the case of the CN, the artist names included in the mime script (Kshesinskaya, Bekefi, etc.) confirm that the document was prepared in conjunction with the 1900 revival.

Mariinsky Theater production documents and Yearbook of the Imperial Theaters. As we have done for the other St. Petersburg productions in our study, we will reference the Mariinsky Theater's production documents that include stage plans for each scene of the ballet as well as descriptions of props and other elements. The production documents

---

[75] See Introduction, note 55.

[76] MS Thr 245 (204). See, for example, the notation of the *Dance of the Maids of Honor and Pages* in Act One, in which the scribal hand used for notation, ground plans, and annotations matches the hand in the *Bayadère* CN.

[77] Museum of the State Academic Bolshoi Theatre (GABT), KP 3949 *fond* 1, *op.* 1, item 78, pp. 1–8, courtesy of Alexei Ratmansky. Two pages of the manuscript are reproduced in Churakova et al., *Aleksandr Gorskiy*, 103.

[78] See Chapter 3, note 74.

[79] We note that while inclusion of mime conversations in the choreographic notation documents resulted in briefer descriptions of what characters said—sometimes seeming to provide only a distillation of more detailed dialogue—it also came with the benefit of a ground plan showing how characters move onstage during mime scenes.

for *La Bayadère* were initially prepared for the 1900 revival.[80] In addition, the *Yearbook of the Imperial Theaters* for the season 1900–1901 features a lengthy entry on the revival. Although the prose in the *Yearbook* is essentially a distillation of the libretto and thus offers no new information in that regard, it is illustrated with numerous photographs of stage designs (as well as the cast), allowing for comparison with the stage drawings included in the production documents.[81]

Petipa's preparatory notes. A selection of Petipa's preparatory notes for *La Bayadère* is held by the Russian State Archive of Literature and Arts in Moscow.[82] Written in French in Petipa's hand, these include scene descriptions (notes for Act One appear to be lost) and two lists of participants in the extensive procession that opens Act Two, Scene III.[83] That several phrases in the libretto seem to be taken near verbatim from Petipa's notes supports the supposition that Petipa coauthored the libretto with Khudekov.[84]

La Bayadère: A scene-by-scene description

We will use these various sources to assemble a composite description of *La Bayadère*, drawing freely on primary and secondary sources that shed light on various elements of the production, be they music, dance, mime, or action.[85] As with the music examples, our description will follow the numbering found in the Rep.

Act One
Scene I: The Festival of Fire

Introduction. The two-part introduction is comprised of passages from the fast, rhythmic Act One *Danse des Fakirs* (Ex. 9.12b) and the stately *Grand Adage* from Act Three, Scene V (see Ex. 9.2b). This binary form, in which the aggressive music of the rough, earthy fakirs contrasts with that of the gentle, heavenly shades, is the same used in introductions to *Giselle* and *Sleeping Beauty*, the latter beginning with the stormy, chromatic motif of the fairy Carabosse followed by the consonant, flowing theme of the Lilac Fairy. Here, Minkus presents an Orientalist version of the form, juxtaposing some of the score's most exoticist music with some of the least.

In the absence of Petipa's notes for Act One, we rely primarily on the detailed mime script for a description of the action.[86] In reproducing the text (in translation), we have retained words and phrases that may seem redundant or otherwise unnecessary to the reader, but which refer to the various mime gestures used to convey the meaning of the

[80] GMTMI GIK 16917, fols. 176r–182r.
[81] *Ezhegodnik* (1900–1901), 157–173, available online at https://archive.org/details/ezhegodnikimpera1900diag/mode/2up.
[82] Russian State Archive of Literature and Arts (RGALI) *fond* 1657, *op.* 3, *ed. khr.* 122, 132, and 133, courtesy of Alexei Ratmansky.
[83] Some of these have been translated into Russian, with commentary by Fedor Lopukhov. See *Marius Petipa. Materialy, vospominaniya, stat'i* [Marius Petipa. Materials, Recollections, Articles], ed. Yury Slonimsky et al. (Leningrad: Iskusstvo, 1971), 169–175.
[84] See note 2 in this chapter.
[85] Gershenzon provides a summary and comparison of the 1877, 1884, and 1900 productions. See Gershenzon, "*La Bayadère*," 16–19.
[86] Lopukhov explains that Petipa's extant notes begin with the second scene. *Marius Petipa. Materialy*, 169.

prose. We also retain dancer names when they appear in the manuscript and accompany them, at least at first use, with their character's name. The script refers to "Dugmanta" rather than "Rajah"; we will use both names interchangeably in our description. We also have frequently substituted "Nikia" for "bayadère" and "Madhavaya" for "fakir" for greater clarity. Finally, we will refer to select musical motifs as they occur in the score.

The opening scene introduces the first love triangle: Solor, Nikia, and the Great Brahmin. Exotic features abound: a mysterious temple, a fire pit of unknown spiritual significance with wild-looking men jumping through its flames, attractive bayadères who emerge from the temple, and a menacing high priest.

The production documents reveal an outdoor scene, set up downstage of the fifth wing. The temple façade is placed at a slight angle upstage left, with a central, curtained opening. A small staircase leads from a raised entrance down to the stage floor. A fire pit is at center and behind it a raised platform that appears to support a carved image. The scene is framed by tall trees and lush foliage.

No. 1. The curtain rises at the second bar of No. 1. Short, staccato phrases and dotted rhythms over a pulsing bass immediately create an atmosphere of suspense (Ex. 9.16).

The libretto adds detail to the sketches in the production documents: "The stage represents a consecrated forest; branches of bananas, amras, madhavis, and other Indian trees are intertwined. At the left a pond designated for ablutions. In the distance, the peaks of the Himalayas. The wealthy *kshatriya* Solor (a famous warrior) enters with a bow in his hand." He is joined by Toloragva and a group of hunters.

Solor: (aside) "I will not go hunting with them, I will stay here alone, in order to"—pointing to a window in the pagoda "—see and talk to a beauty, whom I love" [Ex. 9.7]. (to the hunters) "You all go hunting there and try to kill the tiger."

Toloragva: "Are you not going with us?"

Solor: "No! I will stay here, bow, and pray before this pagoda."

Toloragva: (to the hunters) "Go!" All exit.

Alone, Solor looks over the entire stage. He points again to the window in the pagoda.

Ex. 9.16 Suspenseful music at curtain-up; Act One, Scene I, No. 1, bars 1–10

Solor: "Right there is one beauty whom I love with a passion; but I see her so little, that I even suffer for her" [Solor's motif; Ex. 9.7]. "But I very much would like to speak with her. But how to call her here, I do not know. Anyway, I will ask the fakir about it." He claps his hands to call the fakir Madhavaya, who runs in and bows to Solor.

Madhavaya: "What can I do for you?"

Solor: "Listen. In there is one beauty whom I would like to see and speak with. But how to call her here? Can you think of something?"

Madhavaya: "I have an idea. When everyone comes out of there to here and will be bowing to this fire here, I will also be stabbing myself with this dagger and fall in exhaustion. Then she will come and give me to drink. At the same time, I will whisper to her to come when she hears three claps of the hand."

Solor: (with exuberance) "Good! What a great idea. Wonderful!"

Madhavaya: (pointing to the pagoda) "Footsteps can be heard there. Let us run."

Solor runs off stage, while Madhavaya runs up to the doors of the pagoda, hears footsteps, and runs away.

No. 2 ("Priest"). The Brahmin enters from the pagoda, walking softly, his hands crossed on his chest (Ex. 9.1a). After him walk the other brahmins.

Brahmin: "One beauty I love passionately. I am a priest."

He calls the fakirs, who come up to the fire and pray. Bekefi (Madhavaya) walks up to the Brahmin, hands raised up, and falls before him.

According to Locke, "Eroticism mingles with mysterious ceremoniality in various dances of priestesses in French exotic operas."[87] The dance for twelve bayadères, choreographed with the onstage fire pit as its central focus, fits this paradigm hand in glove.[88]

No. 3 ("Entrance of the Bayadères"). The "Bayadères' dance" is the only notated passage of the opening scene. Twelve bars facilitate the entrance of the women, followed by a piquant, staccato melody in waltz time (Ex. 9.8a). The CN offers an unusual amount of logistical detail: "12 women corps de ballet bayadères come out of the temple and fold arms over chest crosswise. Walk quietly." They form lines of six on either side of the stage. The fire pit near center is labeled "holy fire" and "priest | Bulgakov" is indicated by an "X" at downstage left. In bars 11–12, the "priest says, You dance here." Sergeyev has noted, "left side written down," that is, the steps for the women on stage left are notated, and those on stage right should perform them on the opposite foot and to the opposite side. The dance is not performed on *pointe*.

Traveling upstage to encircle the fire pit, the women perform a variant of *demi-valse*— the front leg rising to *demi-attitude devant* with each step—alternating legs with each bar, the same arm overhead as the leg raised in *attitude*. Backs are arched, heads are turned downstage. The women are joined by the Brahmin, who stands upstage of the fire, facing the audience. Again they arch their backs and necks, their arms overhead, then bow forward, crossing their arms on their chests. After repeating this ritualistic gesture,

[87] Locke, *Musical Exoticism*, 196.
[88] The program for the 1900 revival lists only six women participating in the Festival of Fire, but the CN records choreography for twelve, in agreement with the 1877 poster and other programs for performances after the revival, including the program for Pavlova's debut on 28 April 1902.

they travel away from the pit and back, rotate in a circle around it, and move out to the wings and back, all with variants of *demi-valse*. They repeat the ritual gesture a third time then form a row across the downstage. "The priest walks away from the fire | stepping quietly" and moves downstage right. After the bayadères travel upstage and back, they return to the sides and the dance comes to a conclusion.

No. 4 (Brahmin's inverted motif; see Ex. 9.1b).

Brahmin: "The one who is beautiful is not here."

He commands Nikia to be called, and Madhavaya goes to the pagoda to summon the bayadère. The Brahmin calls the fakirs to pray. They run up and eat (*kushayut*) the sacred fire (Ex. 9.12a). Others then jump through the fire.

No. 5. All but the final three bars of No. 5 are cut in the Rep (Ex. 9.3b).[89]

No. 6 ("1st Entrance of the Bayadère"). Nikia enters from the pagoda, her face covered with a veil (Ex. 9.3a).

Brahmin: [to the others; he wishes to speak with Nikia privately] "You pray over there."

Nikia bows to the fire and then to the Brahmin. The Brahmin walks up to Nikia and lifts her veil. He is stunned by her beauty.

Brahmin: "How beautiful she is." (to Nikia) "You dance here."

Writing in 1922, Akim Volynsky recalled Pavlova's affecting first appearance as Nikia:

[Pavlova] entered covered with a veil. She stopped on top of the staircase, which led to the entrance of the Indian temple, for only a few seconds. But this already signified a feature of her passionate and brilliant art. You need to know how to stand while the music is playing, the strings roaring, the violins singing, and the orchestra waving and sighing. Descending from the stair in a slow step, the dancer came out to the proscenium and, pausing for several new measures, threw off the dark veil covering her face. A storm was set off in the theater. But the peal of acclaim quickly died away and the audience became still at the first signs of the dance theme. How wonderful Pavlova was at this moment![90]

No. 7 ("La Danse"). As are most solo dances in the ballet, Nikia's variation (Exx. 9.9a and 9.9b) is absent from the CN.[91] We turn again to Volynsky for a description, this one of Pavlova's final performance at the Mariinsky in 1913:

The Bayadère begins her dance with a graceful andante, starting with her leg back in *tendu croisé*, in the spirit of an arabesque. Throwing her arms about in an oblique line, she bends her body in a low bow, with her face to the public. Then, within a second, she rises on her toes and dances to the beat of the orchestra, acting with her hands and saucily lifting them sideways. The picture here is unparalleled in the curvature of forms, which convey the sensation of enthusiasm. This was one of the dancer's most remarkable entrances.[92]

---

[89] This sixty-bar number (not including repeats) is structured in a similar way as No. 4: twelve slow bars are followed by a longer, faster section in $\frac{3}{8}$ meter that is an extended version of the second half of No. 4.

[90] Volynsky, "Marius Petipa (*Baiaderka*)," *Zhizn' iskusstva*, 21 March 1922: 2, tr. in *Ballet's Magic Kingdom*, 65.

[91] The libretto (but not the 1877 poster) refers to this dance as "*Djampo*."

[92] Volynsky, "Proshchal'nyi spektakl' A. P. Pavlovoi (*Baiaderka*)" [Farewell performance by A. P. Pavlova (*La Bayadère*)], *Birzhevye vedomosti*, 25 February 1913, 5, tr. in *Ballet's Magic Kingdom*, 49.

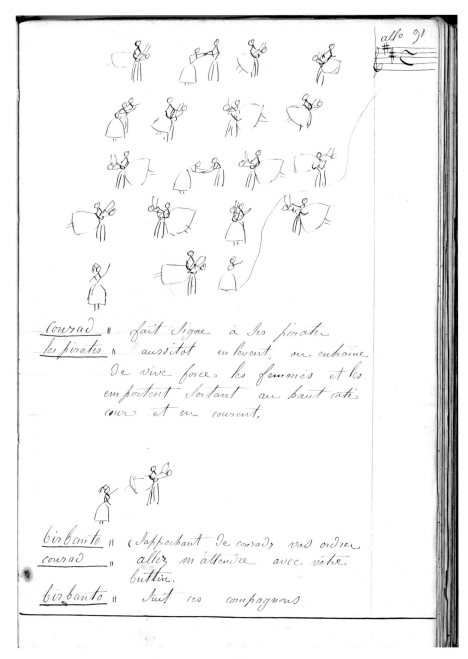

Conrad || fait signe à ses pirate

les pirates || aussitot enlevent, ou entraine
de vive force les femmes et les
emportent sortant au haut coté
cour et en courent.

Birbanto || (s'approchant de conrad) vas ordrer
conrad || allez m'attendre avec votre
buttin.

Birbanto || suit ses compagnons

Figure 35. Henri Justamant's staging manual for *Le Corsaire*, circa 1857. Act One, Scene I, depicting the final chaotic pose of the *Bacchanale des Corsaires* as they seize the women.

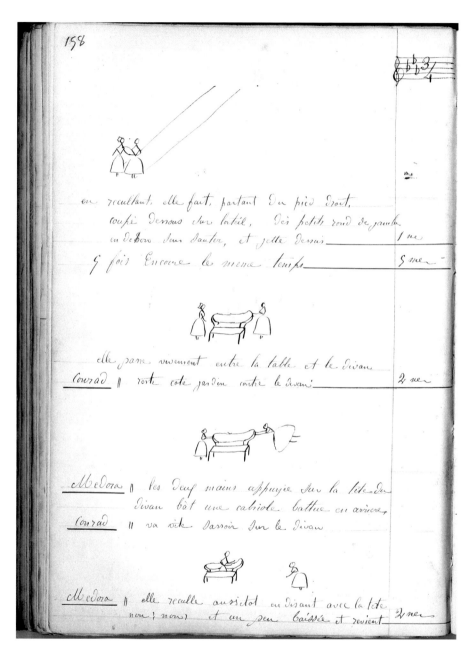

Figure 36. Justamant staging manual for *Le Corsaire*, circa 1857. Act One, Scene II, depicting Medora's "couch *cabriole*" (third drawing from top) during her *Scène de la table* with Conrad.

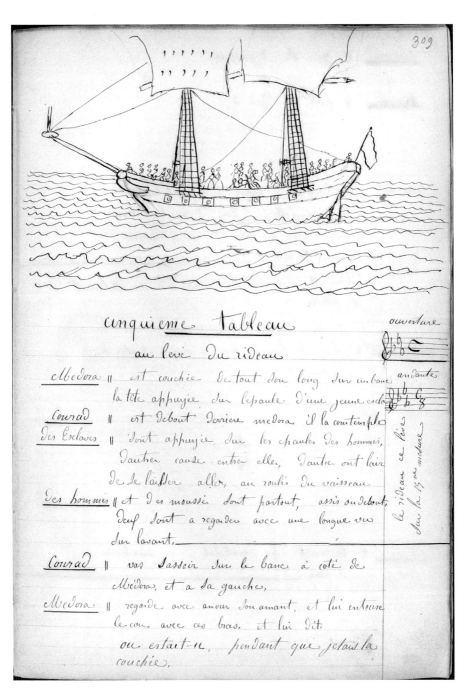

cinquieme tableau

au levé Du rideau

Medora ‖ est couchée De tout Son long Sur un banc
la tête appuyée Sur lepaule D'une jeune esclave

Conrad ‖ est Debout Derriere medora il la contemple

Des Esclaves ‖ Sont appuyée Sur les chaules Des hommes,
Dautre cause entre elle, Dautre out l'air
De Se laisser aller, au roulis Du vaisseau

Des hommes ‖ et Des moussé Sont partout, assis ou debout,
Deux Sont a regardee avec une longue vu
Sur lavant,

Conrad ‖ vas Sassoir Sur le banc à coté de
Medora, et a Sa gauche,

Medora ‖ regarde avec amour Son amant, et lui entoure
le cou avec ses bras, et lui Dit,
ou estait=ile, pendant que jetais la
couchée,

ouverture

andante

le rideau se leve
Sur la 15 me mesure

Figure 37. Justamant staging manual for *Le Corsaire*, circa 1857. Act Three, Scene V, depicting the ship on the water at the opening of the scene.

Figure 38. "Quelques croquis" [Some sketches], caricatures of *Le Corsaire* signed by Félix Y., including an anti-semitic drawing of Lanquedem, a pose with feathers from the *Pas d'eventails*, the Black maidservant with a handkerchief, Medora pointing pistols at the Pasha, and a Black boy standing on top of a man's head (likely a depiction of *Le pas des fleurs*), Paris, 1867.

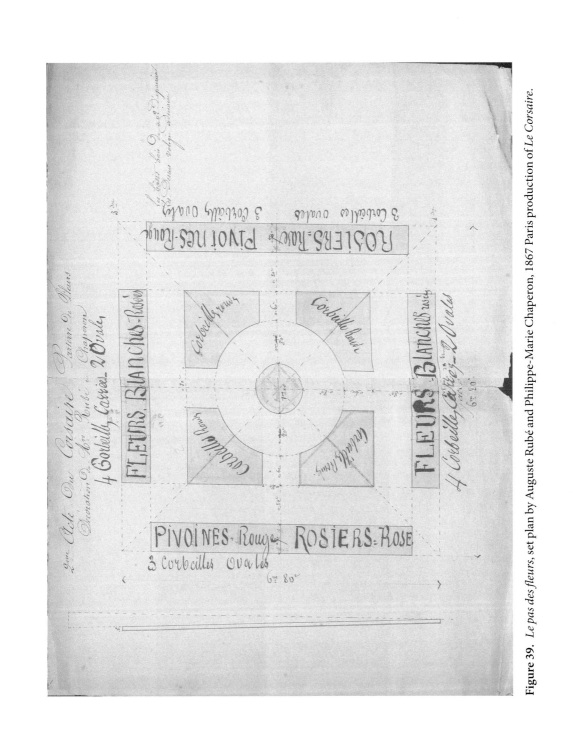

Figure 39. *Le pas des fleurs*, set plan by Auguste Rubé and Philippe-Marie Chaperon, 1867 Paris production of *Le Corsaire*.

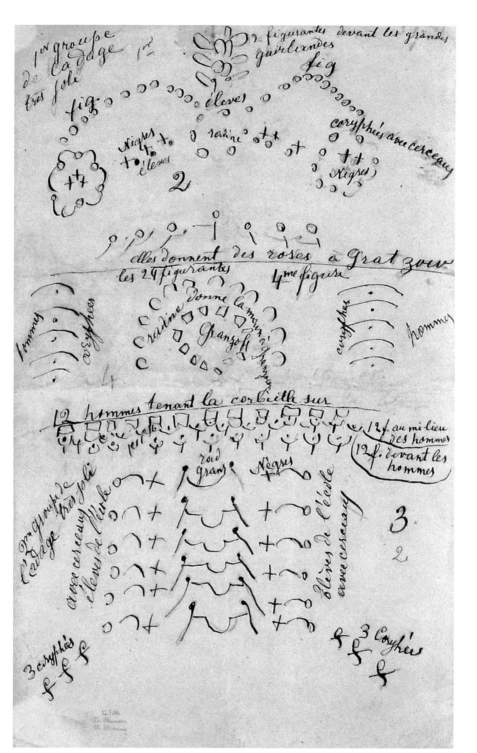

Figure 40. Marius Petipa's preparatory sketch for *Le jardin animé*, 1868 St. Petersburg production.

Figures 41–43. Adolf Charlemagne, costume designs for *Le jardin animé* in *Le Corsaire*, 1867 (for 1868 St. Petersburg production).

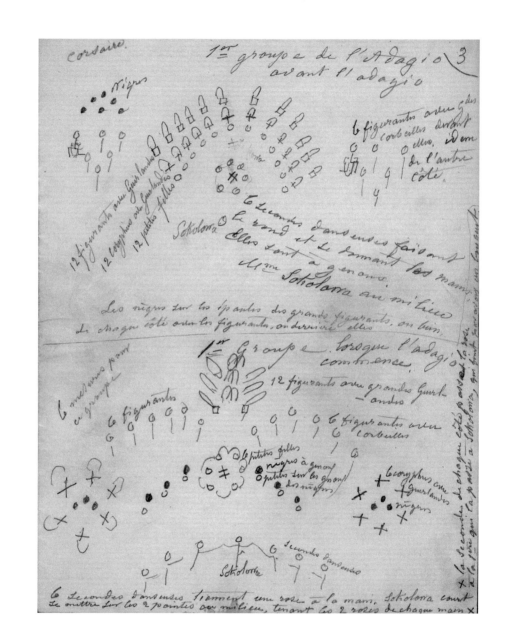

Figure 44. Marius Petipa's preparatory notes for *Le jardin animé* in *Le Corsaire*, 1880 St. Petersburg production.

Figures 45–47. *Le Corsaire*, Act Three, *Scène d'espièglerie* with Olga Preobrazhenskaya (Gulnare) and Alfred Bekefi (Seyd-Pasha), Mariinsky Theater, 1899.

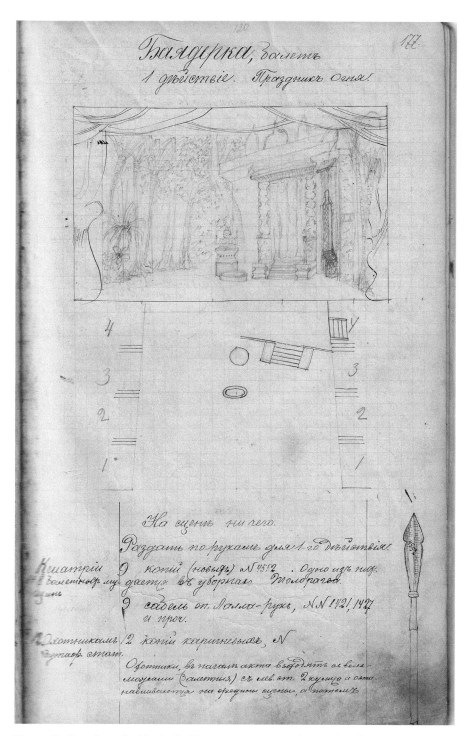

Figure 48. Page from the Mariinsky Theater manuscript volume of production documents describing the stage setting and properties for *La Bayadère*, Act One, Scene I, 1900.

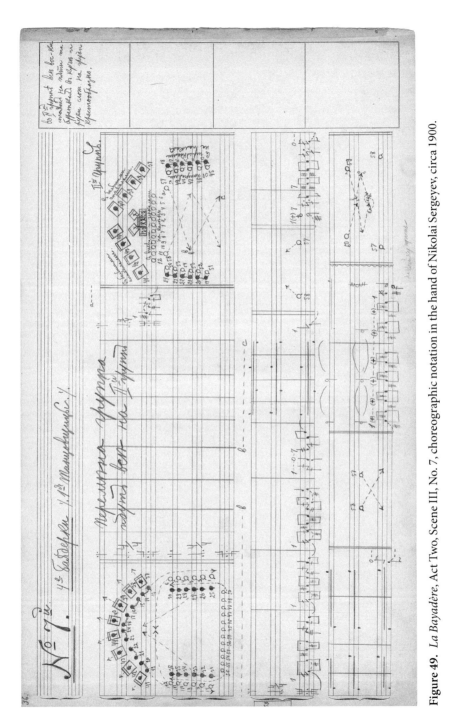

Figure 49. *La Bayadère*, Act Two, Scene III, No. 7, choreographic notation in the hand of Nikolai Sergeyev, circa 1900.

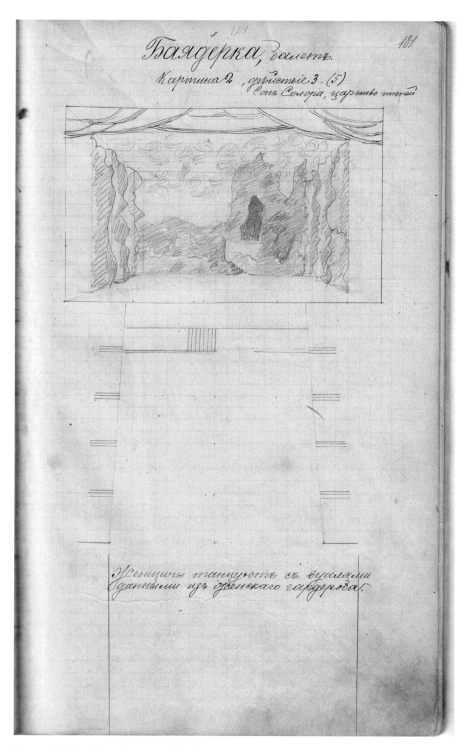

Figure 50. Page from the Mariinsky Theater manuscript volume of production documents describing the stage setting and properties for *La Bayadère*, Act Three, Scene V, 1900.

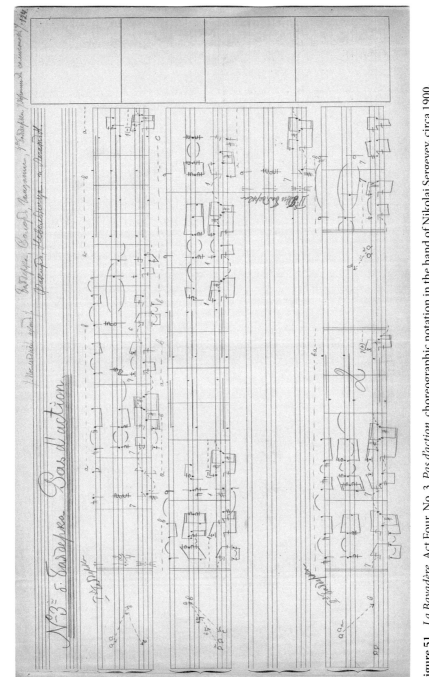

Figure 51. *La Bayadère*, Act Four, No. 3, *Pas d'action*, choreographic notation in the hand of Nikolai Sergeyev, circa 1900.

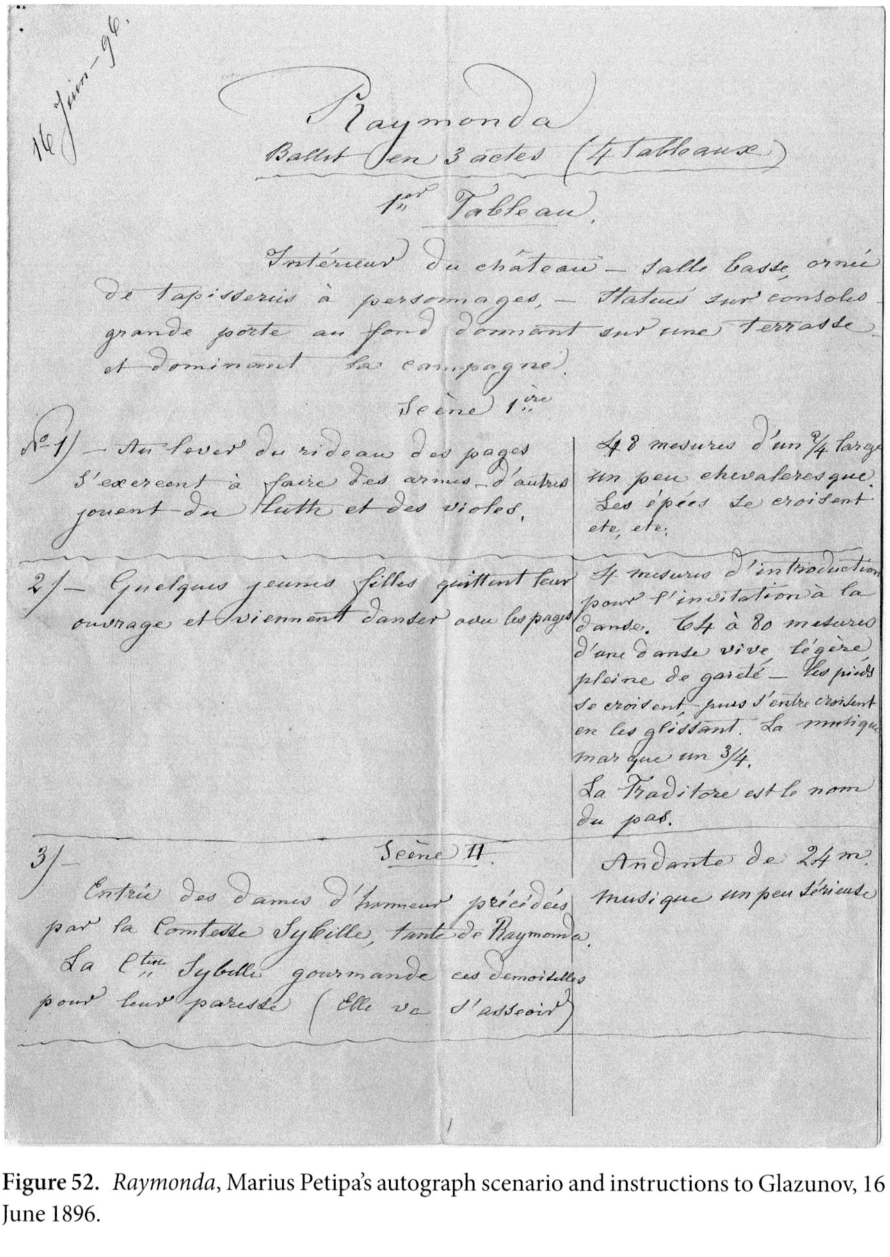

16 Juin – 96.

Raymonda
Ballet en 3 actes (4 tableaux)
1er Tableau.

Intérieur du château – salle basse, ornée de tapisseries à personnages, – Statues sur consoles grande porte au fond donnant sur une terrasse et dominant la campagne.

Scène 1ère

No 1/ – Au lever du rideau des pages s'exercent à faire des armes, d'autres jouent du luth et des violes.	48 mesures d'un 3/4 large un peu chevaleresque. Les épées se croisent etc, etc.
2/ – Quelques jeunes filles quittent leur ouvrage et viennent danser avec les pages	4 mesures d'introduction pour l'invitation à la danse. 64 à 80 mesures d'une danse vive, légère pleine de gaîté – les pieds se croisent, puis s'entrecroisent en les glissant. La musique marque un 3/4. La Traditore est le nom du pas.
3/ – Scène II. Entrée des dames d'honneur précédées par la Comtesse Sybille, tante de Raymonda. La Ctesse Sybille gourmande ces demoiselles pour leur paresse (Elle va s'asseoir)	Andante de 24 m. musique un peu sérieuse

Figure 52. *Raymonda*, Marius Petipa's autograph scenario and instructions to Glazunov, 16 June 1896.

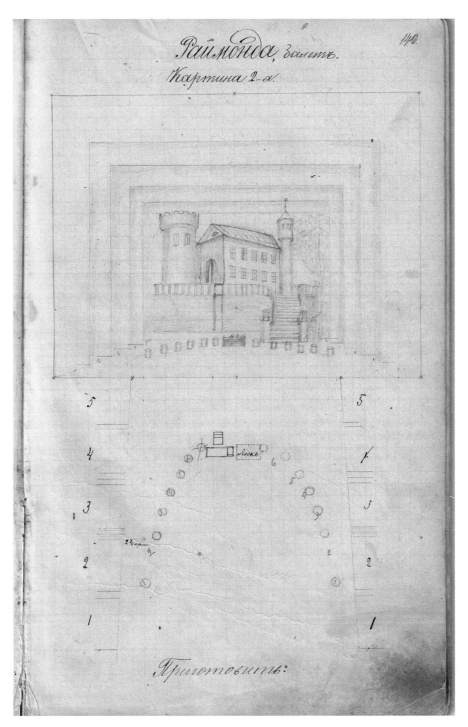

Figure 53. Page from the Mariinsky Theater manuscript volume of production documents describing the stage setting and properties for *Raymonda*, Act One, Scene II, 1898.

Figure 54. Karl Brozh, scene from *Raymonda*, Act One, Scene II, depicting the White Lady and Raymonda's double observing the *pas de deux* of Raymonda and Jean de Brienne. Published in *Vsemirnaya Illyustratsiya* [*World Illustrated*], 1898.

Volynsky was still praising Pavlova's "dance of fire" in 1922, comparing her performance to that of Elizaveta Gerdt:[93]

> The dance of fire begins—a ritual in the full sense of the word as regards the beauty of its lines and the inspiration of its poses and gestures—with a smooth and tranquil andante. The dance figures are not compact in their design; indeed, the dancing is even somewhat cumbersome in its individual nuances, but it nonetheless constitutes one of Petipa's masterpieces. The dancer nervously tosses up first one knee, then the other, each bent in the air, and she traverses the stage on pointe, drawing with them countless circles in all directions.
>
> Among the figures of the dance of fire there is one that is exceptionally wonderful. Extending the leg back at full length, the dancer must lightly turn from a pose where she is rolled up in a ball to full height. This is a slow turn with the whole body to the protracted tempo of the violins, as if the body were going through the complete cycle of its growth and suddenly becomes erect, like a wonderfully strong sapling, before the audience's eyes.... In Pavlova's interpretation this figure produced an enormous impression.[94]

No. 8. The *Danse des Fakirs* follows, an extended scene juxtaposing the fakirs' dancing at the fire pit with the Brahmin's passionate declaration of love to Nikia and her rejection of his advances. The number opens with the frenetic melody first heard in the introduction (Ex. 9.12b). According to Benois, "The stage was occupied by a pyre whose long tongues of flame leapt high into the air while wild-looking, bearded people, dressed in brown tights and red slips and wearing high turbans, fearlessly jumped over it."[95] Although this is a group dance, it is not included in the CN. Perhaps the nature of the movement performed by the "wild looking" fakirs was such that it was felt it did not warrant documentation or could not be adequately notated with the Stepanov system.

The Brahmin seizes the opportunity to make his confession to Nikia.

Brahmin: [to the fakirs and bayadères] "All of you pray!" The fakirs run up to the fire. [aside] "I will tell her now." He goes to Nikia, takes her by the hand, and brings her out into the center of the stage. The general scene continues, that is, the fakirs and bayadères pray.

Brahmin: "You listen to me, what I will tell you. I love you. Love me and I will protect you and make you the first bayadère."

Nikia: "[Oh] God!"

Brahmin: "If you return my love, I will make you the first bayadère above all."

Nikia: "I do not love you and will never love you."

Brahmin: "Ah! You do not love me?" He moves a little to the side. "Then I will force you to love me!" [Ex. 9.3c]

After their prayer, the fakirs fall to the ground in exhaustion. The Brahmin commands the bayadères to bring water and give the fakirs a drink. They do so. Kshesinskaya (Nikia) gives Bekefi a drink, and when he has had enough, Kshesinskaya makes to goes away, but Bekefi stops her.

[93] Elizaveta Gerdt made her debut as Nikia on 11 March 1922. *Khronika IV*, 263.
[94] Volynsky, "Marius Petipa (*Baiaderka*)," tr. in *Ballet's Magic Kingdom*, 65.
[95] Benois, *Reminiscences*, 42–43.

Ex. 9.17 Conversation between Madhavaya and Solor; Act One, Scene I, No. 9, bars 17–21 (Source: Rep)

Madhavaya: "One noble soldier wishes to see you and wants to speak with you. At night he will come here, and when you hear three claps of the hand, then come out."

Just then, the Brahmin, having noticed the fakir Bekefi talking to Nikia, commands her to leave and then commands everyone to leave. All exit.

No. 9. This next number sets up the meeting of the lovers. The conversation between Madhavaya and Solor is accompanied by one of Minkus's most affecting musical ideas, in which plaintive, two-part counterpoint represents two voices in conversation (Ex. 9.17).

Madhavaya: (alone) "They all left and there is no one here." He gets up and calls Solor, who enters.

Solor: "Well? Did you see the bayadère? What did you say to her?"

Madhavaya: "Wait. I will tell you now. From there they came here to pray before this fire. I also prayed and stabbed myself and fell in exhaustion. Then the Brahmin commanded the bayadère to give me a drink. The bayadère brought water and gave me a drink. I told her you will come here at night. When she hears three claps, then she will come here."

Solor: "Good! Good! Now go and keep watch so that no one sees us."

Madhavaya goes and watches so that no one sees them.

No. 10. At this time in the pagoda one can hear the bayadère playing on an instrument. According to the libretto, "The pleasant sounds of a vina (guitar) are heard" (Ex. 9.10).

Solor: "Oh God! these sounds of hers, how good they are! My heart is aching for her, for her. I love her so much and want to take her to myself. She must be mine, oh yes! yes! she is mine."

No. 11. This number begins with Solor's three hand claps, his signal to Nikia to come and meet him. These are clearly expressed in the score with three accented chords (Ex. 9.18) and are followed by rising sighing figures that describe Solor's breathless anticipation. Nikia enters. A forward-moving, lyrical melody accompanies the first meeting of the lovers (Ex. 9.19).

Nikia: "Why did you call me here?"

Solor: "I did not go hunting [but] stayed here in order to see you and say that I love you. You are so beautiful that I am beside myself."

Ex. 9.18 Solor claps three times to summon Nikia; Act One, Scene I, No. 11, bars 1–4
(Source: Rep)

Ex. 9.19 The meeting of the lovers; Act One, Scene I, No. 11, bars 16–23

No. 12 (Allegro appassionata).

Nikia: "You, listen! There is a brahmin there. He also told me he loves me. We need to be careful."

Solor: "How did he? How did he dare to say that to you? But listen—" (pointing to the pagoda) "—leave all this and we will run away to my home. Are you not willing?"

Nikia: "I cannot go there with you."

Solor: (in dismay) "How? Why?"

Nikia: "You are a noble warrior, and what am I? a miserable bayadère in this costume. You will abandon me and push me away from yourself."

Solor: "I will abandon you? Never . . . I will love you eternally and you will be my wife!"

Nikia: "All right! but swear right in front of this fire that you love me and will be my husband."

Solor: (getting on one knee before the fire) "I swear to love you eternally. I swear you will be my wife." (The Brahmin eavesdrops on Solor's oath.) "Now you must believe me. You are mine now. Come to me, come to my arms." He embraces and kisses Nikia. "I am your slave."

Nikia: "But do not forget your oath."

Solor swears again and sits Nikia on his knee.

The lovers' conversation bears strong resemblance to the similar exchange between Paquita and Lucien, in which Paquita refuses Lucien's request to go with him because she recognizes "the distance separating a poor *gitana* and an officer."[96] Here, however, Nikia quickly shifts the focus of the conversation to Solor's oath, a subject she will return to with insistence throughout the ballet.

No. 13. At the return of the hunters, Minkus reprises the act's opening march (see Ex. 9.15).

Madhavaya: (running in) "I hear footsteps. Someone is coming. Hide."

Nikia and Solor run and hide behind the temple. The bayadères come out for water in pairs. At the same time, Nikia runs into the temple. Solor blows a kiss after her.

The hunters enter. Solor meets them and asks them about the hunt and whether they killed the tiger.

Toloragva: I saw the tiger there, and he was coming toward me and pounced on me, and I killed him." He points with his hand to the dead tiger.

Solor goes and looks at the dead tiger, thanks them, and tells everyone to go home.

Solor: "I will follow you." All depart. Solor blows another kiss to Nikia [toward the temple], but Madhavaya stops him and points to the window, where Nikia has appeared. Solor runs into her arms.

Nikia: "You remember your oath" [Ex. 9.1d].

Solor: "I swear. I swear! But it is already getting light, and I must leave. Farewell!" He runs to the wings with Madhavaya as the Brahmin watches them again.

Brahmin: "I will have vengeance!" He gestures threateningly as Solor exits.

Act Two

Scene II: The Two Rivals

The second scene introduces the second love triangle: Solor, Hamsatti, and Nikia. First, Solor admits to the Rajah that he cannot fulfill his obligation to marry his daughter but quickly realizes that the Rajah will not take "no" for an answer. Solor retreats into his thoughts as the women emerge as the aggressors.

No. 1. The act opens with a march that will return at the beginning of Act Four. A driving, pulsing melody creates anticipation for curtain-up, which takes place at bar 32 (Ex. 9.20). Nobles enter what the libretto describes as "a magnificent hall in the palace of the rajah Dugmanta." The production documents record a stage setting that is again set up downstage of the fifth wing. A partition extending from the first wing at stage left serves as a backdrop for a chessboard and five low seats set up at the edge of the stage. The nobles are followed by the Rajah himself.

Dugmanta: (coming forward and greeting his guests) "What joy, today my daughter will be married. How happy I am!" Addressing a particular guest, [he continues,] "You,

---

[96] *Paquita*, 1846 Paris libretto, Act One, scene VIII. See Appendix D (i).

Ex. 9.20 Curtain-up and entrance of the Rajah and his men; Act Two, Scene II, No. 1, bars 32–39 (Source: Rep)

there, play chess with me. Please sit!" [They sit and he commands the *kshatriyas* to bring in dancers:] "You, from there, call them to come here and dance."

No. 2. The *Djampe* dance (Rep, CN: "Dance with veils") is a two-part number for "two second *danseuses* and eight coryphées" with "veils tied to the right leg." Photographs confirm the other end of the long veil was held in both hands, and the CN, in which movements for arms are recorded, indicates that one or both arms are often held overhead. Sergeyev explains, "Left side written down and right side does with the other leg and in the other direction." A ground plan indicates seven *kshatriyas* situated behind a table downstage right. Two men sit on either side of the table; Aistov (Dugmanta) sits on the side closest to the wing.[97]

The first half of the number features a precise, marked melody over a martial accompaniment with the feel of a polonaise in duple time (Ex. 9.21a).

The dance is built on a variety of Petipa's favorite traveling steps—*ballonné, emboîté,* and, most often used for character dance, *demi-valse*—the simplicity of which focuses the attention on the patterns the dancers make *en masse*, whether it be a serpentine line, intersecting diagonals or circles, or block formations. The dance is not performed on *pointe*.

The eight coryphées advance downstage in a single row with a series of two *ballonnés, tombé, pas de bourrée* and turn a circle to the left with *demi-valse*. After returning upstage, they travel back down with multiple *temps levé en attitude devant* then split and travel to the side with *demi-valse*. The women traverse the stage four times with a series of *temps levé en arabesque* and *temps levé en demi-attitude devant* then perform alternating *emboîtés derrière à terre* in place. They kneel as the two soloists enter upstage left.

The soloists travel backward downstage in mirroring zigzags, performing two *demi-valse, tombé, pas de bourrée* four times. Downstage and turning to face front, they continue with *pas de cheval, pas de bourrée* six times to alternate sides. After moving out to opposite corners with *demi-valse* then back up toward center with a series of turning

[97] A photograph in the *Yearbook* for the season 1900–1901 shows three kshatriyas seated at the table, with two more standing beside it. *Ezhegodnik* (1900–1901), 157.

Ex. 9.21a *Djampe* dance; Act Two, Scene II, No. 2, bars 1–5

temps levés en demi-attitude devant, tombé, pas de bourrée, they hold each other by the waist and travel downstage with fifteen consecutive *temps levés en arabesque*, left arms overhead, right arms side. They release each other and travel backward upstage with alternating *emboîtés derrière à terre*, finishing at center with *tombé, pas de bourrée* to *tendu croisé derrière*.

No. 3. The second part of the dance is a coda-like variant of No. 2, a *presto* polka in A major, that follows on directly; the CN is marked "attacca" (Ex. 9.21b).

The soloists continue at center with two *temps levés*—the first with the working leg in *demi-attitude devant*, the second with the *attitude* leg passing to *demi-arabesque fondu*—*pas de bourrée* four times, the coryphées beginning to dance midway through the sequence with *demi-valse*, turning in place. The entire group repositions itself, the coryphées moving upstage, still in two groups of four, the soloists moving slightly to the side. Together, the ten women travel downstage in mirroring zigzags that cross at center. They perform repeated *temps levés en demi-attitude devant*, with *tombé, pas de bourrée* used to change direction. Repositioning upstage once again with a series of *temps levés* and *petits emboîtés*, they turn four circles in place, performing multiple *temps levés en*

Ex. 9.21b *Djampe* dance coda; Act Two, Scene II, No. 3, bars 1–8

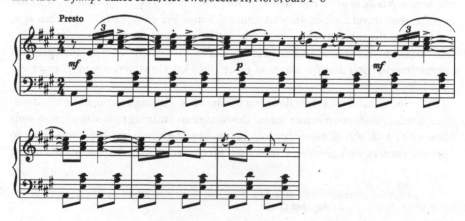

Ex. 9.22 Act Two, Scene II, *Pas Dzheni*, bars 1–6 (Source: Rep)

arabesque. As the music begins to die away, they travel all the way upstage with *demi-valse* then turn left and, like the children in the *Paquita* mazurka, dance into the wings.

Pas Dzheni. The Rep indicates, "Segue No. 4." However, mention must be made of an interpolation at this point in the Rep. For the ballet's sixth performance on 20 February 1877, Petipa added a *Pas Dzheni* for the soloist Alexandra Kemmerer. Gershenzon, who refers to the number as a demi-character dance, explains that it was first part of the large divertissement in Act Two, Scene III before being moved a scene earlier, where we find it in the Rep, in 1884.[98] The two folios that comprise the number, which has been struck though, are interpolated after the *Djampe* dance. At sixty-one bars (plus repeats), the *Pas Dzheni* is a substantial number (Ex. 9.22). Its middle section features rising and falling staccato lines that remind us of the opening bayadères' dance (Ex. 9.7a). The variation ends with a typical fast section (in D major) filled with sixteenth-note scales and octave leaps.

Our sources do not indicate how long the *Pas Dzheni* remained in the production. For the 1900 revival, a "Hindu dance" was performed in Scene II by Maria Rutkovskaya and Alexander Shiryaev, presumably immediately following the *Djampe* dance. No additional music is provided for this dance in the Rep, and the *Pas Dzheni*, as mentioned above, is struck through. By the following season the new "Hindu dance" was retitled "Dance of a bayadère with a Hindu." The dance appears to have been performed sporadically throughout the first years of the twentieth century.

No. 4 ("Après la danse"). After the dances, Dugmanta sets his dagger on the table, stands up, and calls a slave [*aiya*], who runs in and bows.

Dugmanta: "Call my daughter to come here." The slave goes to summon Hamsatti, [while] Dugmanta addresses his guests: "I thank you, my lords. Now you may leave." The guests depart and the *aiya* returns, running.

Aiya: "Your daughter is coming here!"

Dugmanta: "Good!"

The *aiya* invites the young woman into the room. Hamsatti enters with two ladies of the court [Ex. 9.4]. She greets her father, who embraces her and kisses her forehead. They walk forward.

Hamsatti: "Why did you call me from there?"

Dugmanta: "You listen to me. I will tell you. I called you from there to tell you. You remember there was one [young man], who has now grown up, and you are to be wed to him."

[98] Gershenzon, "*La Bayadère*," 15.

Hamsatti: "I am to be married! . . . to whom! . . . I do not know him!" [Ex. 9.1c].

Dugmanta: "Calm down. He is one of ours. He has a brave heart, and you will meet him!"

Hamsatti: "He has not seen me?"

No. 5.

Dugmanta: "Just wait. He will see you, your figure, your face. He will fall in love for certain" [variant of Solor's theme; see Ex. 9.7]. (addressing the *kshatriya*) "Call him from there to come here." The *kshatriya* leaves. (to Hamsatti) "Just wait, you will see; he will come here."

The kshatriya invites Solor to enter. The warrior walks into the room and bows to Dugmanta.

Solor: "You called me here. I am waiting. What do you command? I am at your service."

Dugmanta: "You fought very well and battled the enemy. You are a brave warrior and I protect you." He puts his hand on Solor, who bows down. "You remember that from childhood you were chosen as the groom for my daughter."

Solor: "Me, a groom?"

Dugmanta: "Yes!"

Solor: "I am a groom." He walks to the side, suffering. "[Oh] God, what should I do? I swore my love to one beauty and suddenly I have to marry another. What should I do? How should I act?" He approaches Dugmanta. "But I have never seen your daughter."

Dugmanta: "Oh, be at ease! You will see her now." He walks up to his daughter and removes her veil. "There, look!" He reassures Hamsatti. "You see, he is in love and he likes you."

Seeing her face, Solor is struck by Hamsatti's beauty [variant of the Brahmin's inverted theme; see Ex. 9.1b].

Solor: (aside) "[Oh] God, how beautiful!" He approaches Dugmanta in bewilderment. "I do not know if she loves me. Can we not put off our wedding and wait for some time?"

Dugmanta: "No! I want it so badly. She is as beautiful as this pearl. I give her to you."

Solor: "Oh yes! She is simply a beauty." He comes up to Hamsatti and bows.

Dugmanta: "Oh, how happy I am! He will marry her."

No. 6.

Aiya: [to Dugmanta] "The priest is coming here and wishes to speak with you" [variant of the Brahmin's motif; see Ex. 9.1a].

Dugmanta: "The priest, here, why? Tell him to come in and speak to me." The slave goes to ask the Brahmin to come in. The priest enters and bows to Dugmanta, [who inquires,] "Why have you come?"

Brahmin: "I came to tell you something alone and in secret, with no one else around."

Dugmanta: "Alone? Strange. All right, all of you leave," he commands, and all depart. Hamsatti [wonders], "Why alone?" She hides and eavesdrops on the conversation between the priest and her father. Leaving, Solor looks at the Brahmin as at an adversary. "We are here alone, so tell me, what?" [asks Dugmanta again]. Hamsatti runs to her *aiya* and says, "I will stay here to listen."

Brahmin: "Is your daughter to be married?"

Dugmanta: (nodding) "Yes!"

Brahmin: "She is getting married to him?" [He perhaps indicates the portrait of Solor that figures later in the scene.]

Dugmanta: (nodding again) "Yes!"

Brahmin: "Does he love her?"

Dugmanta: (with his hand) "Yes!"

Brahmin: "That is impossible!"

Dugmanta: "You dare to speak!"

No. 7. Rushing upward scales and accented chords in C minor, followed by descending chromatic tremolos, express the Rajah's indignation.

Brahmin: "I saw at night how he spoke to her [Nikia] about love. He gave her an oath, there before the fire, that he will marry her and steal her and take her away." At this point, Hamsatti, hearing what the Brahmin is saying, sends her slave to fetch Nikia, whom she wants to see for herself, and find out the truth.

From this point onward, Petipa's extant notes describe the rest of the scene—the fallout from the Brahmin's disclosure of the secret love between Solor and Nikia:

The Rajah is revolted by the conduct of his future son-in-law.
He says to the Great Brahmin that the bayadère must die.
The Brahmin, who does not want the death of his beloved bayadère, but wants Solor to be punished, says to the Rajah that killing the bayadère of the pagoda would put Vishnu against them.
The Rajah does not want to hear anything and tells the Brahmin that during the great festival, that [blank space in the manuscript].
At these words, the great Brahmin shudders.
Hamsatti, who has heard everything, [and] wants to know and talk to this bayadère, orders her slave to go and look for her.
The Rajah, quite satisfied with this revenge, exits with the Brahmin.[99]

We return to the mime script, which follows Petipa's plan:

[99] RGALI *fond* 1657, *op.* 3, *ed. khr.* 122, fol. 2r.

Dugmanta: "What am I hearing? He will steal her, that beauty. I will destroy her!"

Brahmin: "No! No! She belongs to God and to do that is impossible."

Dugmanta: "No, she has insulted me. I will destroy her, that is my will. Let us go." [He makes to leave.] Seeing that the Brahmin is not coming, he repeats, "Let us go."

Brahmin: "Ah! what have I done! It is I that have killed her. What should I do!" [*piano* variant of the Brahmin's motif]. At the second call of Dugmanta, he also makes to depart. "Let us go."

Petipa's notes describe the subsequent confrontation between Hamsatti and Nikia:

Hamsatti, weakened from what she heard, cries, sobbing, but she wants to know from the bayadère's mouth if Solor really loves her.

Her slave runs up and announces to her the arrival of the bayadère.

Nikia, bowing, approaches Hamsatti.

Hamsatti looks at her and finds her very beautiful.

She tells her that she is getting married and that she wants her to dance for her wedding.

The bayadère is very happy to have this honor.

Hamsatti also wants her to know her fiancé and shows her the large portrait of Solor.[100]

At this sight, Nikia goes mad. She tells the Rajah's daughter that Solor has sworn his eternal love [to her].

Hamsatti orders Nikia to abandon Solor. Never! Nikia answers, [I would] rather die!

Hamsatti offers [Nikia] her jewelry and gold on condition that she leave the country.[101] Nikia snatches Hamsatti's jewelry from her hands and throws it at her feet.

Hamsatti begs the bayadère to give up Solor. At her words, Nikia takes a dagger which she finds near her and rushes toward Hamsatti.

The slave, who has followed Nikia's movements, rushes forward and covers her mistress with her body. Distraught, Nikia runs away.

Hamsatti gets up and says: now she must die.[102]

The mime script again fulfills Petipa's plan:

No. 8.

Hamsatti: "Oh my god! my god! What have I heard? He will not marry me. He does not love me." She falls on the table and cries [Ex. 9.5a].

---

[100] Petipa added an annotation on the side of the page: "I know that the Hindus did not have these portraits, but I have allowed myself this anachronism to make the subject clearly understood." This comment is quoted nearly verbatim in the published libretto: "I know very well that Indians did not have portraits, and used this anachronism only to make the comprehension of the story easier. (Author's note.)"

[101] The libretto specifies the jewels as "diamonds and gold." The Golconda region was famous for its diamonds.

[102] RGALI *fond* 1657, *op.* 3, *ed. khr.* 122, fols. 2r and 3v.

No. 9.

Aiya: (running in) "The bayadère is coming here" [melodic reference to the bayadères' dance; see Ex. 9.8a].

Hamsatti: "Let her come in." The slave leaves. "I will look at her here." The slave asks Nikia to enter. She comes in and bows to the Rajah's daughter.

Hamsatti: "You may get up." She looks at Nikia. "Oh! how beautiful she is."

Nikia: "You called me from there. Why?"

Hamsatti: "I called you from there to say you must dance at my wedding."

Nikia: (with joy) "I am willing to dance at your wedding." She makes a great bow. Hamsatti wishes to know what Nikia's reaction will be if she shows her a portrait of the groom.

Hamsatti: "Look at my groom! Here he is." She points to the portrait. Nikia looks. Seeing the image of Solor, she is terribly stricken.

No. 10. Rushing scales in C minor, similar to those that accompanied the Rajah's consternation in No. 7, here depict Nikia's outrage.

Nikia: "He! (pointing with her hand to the portrait) is your groom?"

Hamsatti: "Yes!"

Nikia: "Do you love him?"

Hamsatti: "Yes!"

Nikia: "You, his bride. His bride, never."

Hamsatti: "Listen to me, what I will tell you. I love him, love him terribly. I am asking you, leave." But the bayadère does not want to listen to Hamsatti.

Nikia: "I, leave here? No! You are great, and I am nothing—a simple bayadère—and he swore to love me."

Hamsatti: "I will reward you, and I will protect you. I am asking you to leave him."

Nikia: "No!"

Hamsatti: "I pray you, I pray." She takes Nikia by the hand and falls on her knees. "Here, take it," she says, giving her jewelry, rings, and other valuables. Nikia takes everything and throws it to her feet. She runs and falls on the table. Seeing the dagger, she has a thought to kill Hamsatti. She grabs the dagger, goes, and raises it. At the same time, the slave, seeing the whole picture, when the bayadère wants to strike a blow with the dagger, at the last moment gets between them and parries the blow. Hamsatti falls, and Nikia in horror throws the dagger away and runs away. Hamsatti stands and says to all, "Now she must die."

By at least 1902, the dramatic action we have just described was listed in the program as "Scene of jealousy" (*Stsena revnosti*), featuring Nikia, Hamsatti, Solor, the Brahmin, and Dugmanta.

Scene III: The Bayadere's Death

The love triangles and central conflict now established, the remaining scenes feature long stretches of dancing: a combination of character and classical dance in Scene III, and classical dance in both Scene V's Kingdom of the Shades and Scene VII's children's dance and *pas d'action*. Mime is used sparingly and efficiently in these scenes to move the narrative forward to the next danced segment.

The libretto describes the perspective scenery viewed by the audience as the curtain rises on the third scene:

> The stage represents the façade of the rajah's palace from the side of a garden, with masses of huge flowers and broad-leaved trees. In the distance—the tower of the large pagoda of Megatshada, which reaches almost to the heavens.[103] In the background, the light blue of the heavens themselves. The Himalayas are thinly covered with silvery snow.

The stage setting preserved in the production documents reveals a raised platform across the entirety of the fifth wing, piled high with cushions for seating. A narrow staircase at stage right connects the platform to the stage. High above the platform, a "stone" canopy supported by pillars is situated on the diagonal and projects from the upstage right corner. As with Scene I, trees and foliage frame the stage.

The occasion is a celebration in honor of Badrinata, one of the many names for the Hindu deity Vishnu and the name associated with the Hindu temple dedicated to Vishnu that is located in the town of Badrinath in Uttarakhand, India. Petipa's notes demonstrate the splendor and richness he planned for the opening procession. The first of two lists, which includes 178 participants, is the more concise:

3rd tableau ballet Bayadère

The Rajah
Solor
Great Brahmin
8 Priests
4 Gurus [*Gourons*]
8 Hindu men—same costumes[104]
6 women of the people—same costumes
12 Hindus pulling a cart—*Statistes* [Extras]
8 Penitents armed with red-hot irons—*Statistes*
16 Hindus who carry idols and palanquins—*Statistes*
12 Hindus with lances—they are minding a tiger[105]
9 Kshatriyas of the Rajah's retinue—same costumes
2 Noble women of Hamsatti's retinue

---

[103] "Megatshada" may refer to the ancient kingdom of Magadha in eastern India.

[104] We presume "same costumes" means these characters were meant to wear the same costumes they wore in a previous scene.

[105] Konaev suggests an image published in 1876 in the French newspaper *L'illustration*, of which Petipa was an avid reader, may have provided inspiration for inclusion of the tiger in the procession. Titled "Tigre captive amené devant le Prince, à Baroda" and published in connection with the Prince of Wales's recent visit to India, the image depicts a chained tiger in procession, surrounded by men holding lances. See Konaev, "Der *Tigre Captif*," 43–45.

1 Slave of Hamsatti

8 Religious pilgrims—*Statistes*

8 fanatical Hindu men of the people—they put themselves under the wheels of the cart

9 Hindus—second *danseurs* (*Pas de Radina*)[106]

12 young girls, second *danseuses*

4 Hindu students } *pas*[107]

12 *figurants* [corps de ballet men]

12 little Black boys

12 1st coryphées

12 2nd coryphées[108]

A second list provides further detail. Petipa wrote "c'est bon" at the top of the page, suggesting his satisfaction. Multiple strike-throughs, shown below, represent changes made in the manuscript; our notes are in brackets.

Procession

3rd Tableau

1	12 Second coryphées | The torch bearers are on the stage before the entry of the procession
2	4 Gurus
3	4 Priests
4	1 Great Brahmin
5	4 Priests
6	12 Little Black boys
7	1 Hamsatti's slave
8	2 Hamsatti's noble ladies
9	1 Hamsatti on a palanquin [litter]
	4 men who carry the palanquin 1st
~~10~~ 12	12 *danseuses* [replaces "2 second coryphées"]
11	~~12~~ 6 *figurants* [corps de ballet men], they come back a second time
~~12~~ 10	12 coryphées [replaces "2 young girls who dance the *pas*"]
13	~~9~~ 4 Kshatriyas
14	1 The Rajah on a palanquin
	4 men who carry the palanquin and who return to take Solor for his entrance
	4 who are near the palanquin with fans
15	~~5~~ 2 Kshatriyas—they go up and go behind the stage to come back with Solor
16	5 male *figurants* [corps de ballet men]
17	4 they carry an idol
18	9 Hindus second *danseurs*. Picheau and the 8.[109]
	6 second coryphées they come back
19	8 Hindu men [–] same costumes
20	6 women of the people—same costumes

[106] Lubov Radina was in the original cast of the Hindu dance.

[107] Twelve women and four male students made up the cast of the 1877 Slave Dance (also known as the Crooked Dance of the Slaves). The same cast numbers are represented in the CN.

[108] RGALI *fond* 1657, *op.* 3, *ed. khr.* 122, fol. 5r.

[109] Alexander Picheau was in the original cast of the Hindu dance.

21	4 Hindus [–] students
22	6 coryphées	4 idols [replaces "4 that carry an idol"]
23	8 6 fanatical Hindu men of the people [–] they throw themselves under the wheels
24	8 Penitents armed with branding-irons *statistes* [extras] (fanatics)
25	12 Hindus pulling the cart ["chariot"]
26	8 Religious pilgrims, *statistes* [extras]

Those who return before Solor's entry[:]

27	8 Hindu men [–] same costumes
28	6 women of the people [–] same costumes
29	4 Hindus [–] students.
30	8 who carried the two idols [see 17 and 22]
31	4 Kshatriyas who return in front of Solor
32	1 The Fakir, slave of Solor Troitsky[110]
33	1 Solor on a palanquin—the same palanquin that served the Rajah	Solor comes down and orders that the tiger be brought back
	4 that he presents to Hamsatti
	4 near the palanquin with large fans
34	6 *figurants* [corps de ballet men] of No. 11 who return a second time
35	12 who hold the tiger captive

The tiger is dragged off the stage

The Rajah [possibly struck through, with "Solor" written above] orders that the celebration begin.

Also put near Hamsatti's palanquin 4 or 2 men with fans from *corsaire* [*Le Corsaire*] or the other larger ones.[111]

Taking revisions into account, the procession envisioned here numbers up to 221 participants—far more than appeared in, for example, the hunting procession in the 1841 Paris production of *Giselle* (which called for about thirty participants) or the Pasha's procession in Act One of *Le Corsaire* in its original Paris production of 1856 (which called for as many as forty-two participants).[112]

No. 1. According to the poster, the act begins with a "Solemn Procession in Honor of the Idol Badrinata." The march that accompanies this massive procession is notated twice in the Rep. The two versions are nearly the same, but not identical. The first is completely struck through. The second, which appears to supersede the first and whose pages have been added to the Rep between the final two pages of the first, comprises 288 bars,

---

[110] Nikolai Troitsky was in the cast in the role of the fakir Madhavaya in 1877.

[111] RGALI *fond* 1657, *op.* 3, *ed. khr.* 133, fols. 62r–v and 63r.

[112] This information comes from the original Paris librettos for *Giselle* and *Le Corsaire* (see Appendices C (i) and E (i), respectively). More numerous casts appeared in opera processions at the Opéra in the 1830s and 1840s, and featured members of the ballet company. The closing act of *Gustave III, ou Le bal masqué* (1833), for instance, called for the entire ballet company to appear on stage in the "Marche et fin general": "Tout le personnel du ballet, premiers danseurs, corps de ballets et élèves." Eugène Scribe, *Gustave III, ou Le bal masqué* (Paris: Jonas), 1833. On the increasing numbers of onstage characters in operas at the Paris Opéra in the nineteenth century, see Arnold Jacobshagen, "Analyzing Mise-en-Scène: Halévy's *La Juive* at the Salle Le Peletier," in *Music, Theater, and Cultural Transfer: Paris, 1830–1914*, eds. Annegret Fauser and Mark Everist (Chicago: University of Chicago Press, 2009), 176–194.

Ex. 9.23 Processional march; Act Two, Scene III, No. 1, bars 1–8

offering six distinct melodic ideas, plus a fifty-four-bar coda (Ex. 9.23). Plentiful internal repeats (usually in sixteen-bar periods) allow for maximum flexibility.

Benois described with enthusiasm the procession he witnessed as a child in 1877:

> The curtain soon rose again and I found myself in a magnificent tropical park with palm trees and baobabs growing in profusion. In the distance one could see a procession approaching; it consisted at first of tiny cardboard figures, but soon the real ones filed across the stage to disappear in the opposite wing and then form a group in the background. The appearance of the bejeweled elephant caused me to clap my hands with delight, but the innumerable heads and arms of the gilt idols made me feel distinctly uncomfortable, and I could hardly keep my seat at the sight of the "royal tiger" nodding his head from side to side. He was so convincing.

> But what enchanted me more than anything—more than the warriors in their golden armour, more than the beautiful veiled maidens whose arms and ankles jiggled with bracelets, was the group of blackamoors who approached dancing, twirling and tinkling their bells. The winding lines of little blackamoors so amazed and delighted me—principally because they were of my own size—that during the following days I shamelessly lied and boasted to my little friends in the kindergarten that I had actually taken part in that dance. I got so used to this lie that I actually began to believe it myself.[113]

The CN confirms Benois's recollection of procession participants who first cross the stage before re-entering. Under the title "March," entrances for six such groups are notated. Here the ground plans are drawn from the stage perspective rather than that of the audience. Groups enter in pairs at stage right, cross, and exit stage left. Each has a characteristic step notated in $\frac{2}{4}$ meter. In all, the CN accounts for eighty-four bars of the march. Identifiers for the first four groups are written in the left margin by their respective notation systems. Some of the words are cut off in the CN binding.

The first group of twelve women holds "fans or mirrors in hand." They will dance No. 5, below. Their traveling step combination begins with a *temps levés en demi-attitude devant* on each leg followed by a variant of *demi-valse*, the left leg rising to *demi-seconde* with each step.

[113] Benois, *Reminiscences*, 43.

The second group, also twelve women, is labeled "Crooked *pas*," indicating those who will dance Nos. 2 and 3, below. Their appropriately halting enchaînement consists of a *temps levé en demi-arabesque* and a *balancé*, stepping backward on the second step.

The third group holds "garlands on sticks." The ground plan indicates twelve men, again in pairs. A wavy line drawn between each pair likely depicts the garlands that are attached to the end of the pikes they hold. An annotation confirms: "stick for garland in hand." These men perform the same enchaînement as the first group of women.

Yet another group of twelve women, the fourth group, holds "on pointer finger a parrot" as they move across the stage with a *temps levé en demi-arabesque* and three quick steps forward. They will dance No. 6, below.

The five men making up the fifth group (one man leads the other four, in pairs) perform consecutive *temps levés en attitude devant*, the left arm held directly overhead, the elbow bent ninety degrees, and the right arm held forty-five degrees behind the body. No annotation is provided to offer further description.

The sixth and final group includes four men holding pikes who perform the same enchaînement as the first group. An annotation explains that their right arm should be "behind the pike" and the "end of the pike pushes into his side" (that is, one end of the pike is balanced against the hip). Instead of exiting into the opposite wing, this group travels downstage left.

The divertissement commences immediately following the procession. Returning to Volynsky's review of Pavlova's farewell performance in 1913, we find a summary of the dances that is in agreement with the order found in the Rep, PR, and CN:

> The third scene constitutes a mosaic of dances of various configurations. The so-called Crooked Dance of Slaves [Nos. 2 and 3], with its organized asymmetry, in which equal groups of the corps disperse up- and downstage, is followed by the Fan Dance [No. 5] and Parrot Dance [No. 6], with the four Bayadères [Nos. 7 and 9] with low take-offs and entrechats quatres, and with Manu's dance [No. 14] in which Elsa Vill performs, having inherited this number—with descending grades of vivid execution—from Vera Trefilova and Tamara Karsavina. Immediately, Alexander Orlov, Vasily Stukolkin, and Olga Fedorova rush across the stage in a feverishly rhythmic Indian dance [No. 14½]. Stukolkin whirls in a vortex, beating the drum with his foot from the bottom up. And Fedorova, among the multicolored ribbons, rushes toward the footlights like a hurricane. The act concludes with the solo number of the Bayadère [No. 16], who dances in the final moment with a basket of flowers in a passionate arabesque upward, with her darkened eyes directed toward the audience.[114]

The organization of the dances reflects a similar, hierarchical pattern observed by Tim Scholl in the dances of the first act of *Sleeping Beauty*:

> The usual Petipa proprieties are observed in Act I: the dances move from low genre to high, from folk dancing in wooden shoes (the knitters) to grand ballabile with props (garlands, flowers, children), to the summit of the ballet's academic choreography, the adagio for Aurora and her four cavaliers.[115]

---

[114] Volynsky, "Proshchal'nyi spektakl' A. P. Pavlovoi (*Baiaderka*)," tr. in *Ballet's Magic Kingdom*, 49.
[115] Scholl, *Sleeping Beauty*, 42.

Ex. 9.24 Dance of the Slaves (part one); Act Two, Scene III, No. 2, bars 1–8

Here in *La Bayadère*, the divertissement begins with dances for various ensembles performing relatively simple steps that graduate to more complicated dances for smaller, select groups. The choreography increases in *danse d'école* vocabulary, and in 1877 culminated in a classical *pas* for Hamsatti and a cavalier. After this classical *pas* was eliminated, however, the low-to-high progression was disrupted and the order of the dances was rearranged, as we will see in the later revivals.

No. 2. The two-part "Dance of the Slaves" (or "Crooked Dance of Slaves" as Volynsky called it; recall the similar reference in the CN, above) is characterized by the mixed meters of its opening section: fifty bars of disjunct melody using a combination of $\frac{2}{4}$, $\frac{3}{4}$, and $\frac{4}{4}$ meters (Ex. 9.24). This metrical asymmetry complements the asymmetrically "crooked" nature of the choreography, the main feature of which is a variant of *demi-valse* in which the working leg makes repeated *degagés demi-seconde*, resulting in a hobbling gait.

In agreement with the 1877 poster, the CN shows that the performers include twelve women and four student men. The women enter upstage left in pairs, flanked by the men, who carry pikes and are instructed to "hold onto the middle of the pike, and the end of it stick into one's right side," much as they did when entering in the opening procession (see above).

All perform a series of *temps levés en demi-attitude devant* on each leg and the *demi-valse* variant. Arriving downstage center, the men continue the enchaînement as they move toward the wings while the pairs of women separate into two lines, each circling upstage as the women alternate six *demi-emboîtés derrière* with the same *demi-valse*. Forming a single row upstage, the women circle in place before turning to each other in pairs and exchanging places several times as the men approach from the wings and form a row upstage of the women. With bounding *jetés en avant*, the men and half of the women (those on stage right) turn and travel upstage as the women on stage left perform the same steps moving downstage. Returning to center, the entire ensemble travels upstage and back with *jetés de côté* and more *demi-valse*, posing in *attitude devant fondu* (the working leg bent ninety degrees) at the end of the number.

No. 3. The second part of the dance, a polka, features a variety of short, repeated phrases of the sort Minkus employs for other character dances in this scene (Ex. 9.25).

Ex. 9.25 Dance of the Slaves (part two); Act Two, Scene III, No. 3, bars 1–8

The steps include the usual *temps levés* and *demi-valse* as well as some variety; for instance, the men begin with *échappé* followed by three *demi-emboîtés devant*. Later, pairs face each other, holding one another by the waist with the left arm, and circle in place four times performing multiple *temps levés en attitude devant*. The dancers repeatedly cover the stage in circles and lines, moving upstage and down, to the wings and back to center, all with a similar small-scale movement vocabulary. The men remain upstage of the women.

. At one point, lining the wings and upstage, the dancers pause: "Pose | refer to rough draft" is written in the CN across the respective five bars, reminding us of the care that was taken in creating this neat and precise copy that has survived.

Finally, the ensemble travels directly downstage in rows. Performing *emboîtés devant*, the women hold each other by the waist and the men hold their pikes in their right hand and the waist of their partner with their left. The final pose is nearly the same as that for No. 2: *attitude devant fondu*, the extended leg bent just forty-five degrees rather than ninety.

Beginning with No. 4 in the CN, Sergeyev has assigned each participant in the divertissement a number that is notated on the ground plan and also used alongside the notation staves to indicate whether the performer is dancing. (We encountered a similar numbering system in the notation of *Le jardin animé* in Chapter 8.) The numbers not only allow us to keep track of which performers participated in the various dances but also their placement in the groupings. (The dancers participating in Nos. 2 and 3—Dance of the Slaves—are not numbered in the CN and do not appear to participate in the subsequent dances.)

No. 4. The *Danse infernale* is struck through in the Rep and copied again later in the act. ("Segue No. 5" is written at the end of No. 3.) However, the 1877 poster, in which the number is titled *Hindu dance*, confirms its original position at this point in the divertissement, following No. 3. This suggests the Rep dates as far back as the premiere production. The cast list in the poster includes a lead male-female couple and seven men, a slight revision from the nine men Petipa listed in both of his procession plans (see "Pas de Radina" in his shorter list and entry 18 in his longer list, above). The program for the 1900 revival includes a cast of the same size and confirms the dance was moved to the end of the divertissement, just before the coda.

Ex. 9.26 Grand Indian Dance; Act Two, Scene III, No. 5, bars 1–8

No. 5. The "Grand Indian Dance" features "12 women corps de ballet | in their hands fans and mirrors | and 12 men with garlands on sticks" as well as twelve student boys. Sergeyev notes, "left side is written down."

Like the dances that precede it, this piquant waltz features the kind of short, disjunct, staccato phrases with which Minkus signifies character dance (Ex. 9.26).

The twelve corps women (numbered 1–12 in the CN) begin, entering six from each side, performing similar steps as those for the Crooked Dance (and also not on *pointe*): *temps levé* and *demi-valse*. Reaching downstage center, they add *pas de basque*, moving away from and back to a central row. Meanwhile, the men enter in pairs (numbered 13–24), six from each side. They carry the same pikes mentioned above, with garlands attached. The adults are soon joined by twelve small boys (numbered 25–36). Much like their Crooked Dance counterparts, the dancers move about the stage in pairs, rows, and lines. *Pas de basque* and *balancé* are their primary steps. At one point, the boys form two rows downstage while the adults form a large circle upstage. The women travel backward toward its center and turn in place before heading toward the downstage wings as the men and boys form a long column at center. Each boy places both hands on the shoulders of the boy in front of him. They dance in place as the men's pairs split away and move toward opposite wings and back. The women travel toward center and back to the wings. The dance ends abruptly with a final *échappé en plié* and a spring to *demi-attitude devant* for the women.

No. 6. The ensemble spends the first four bars of No. 6 moving into a grouping (Ex. 9.14). The boys split and travel to either wing with *pas de basque*. There they form lines next to the corps women. The men, also traveling with *pas de basque*, form a semicircle upstage. Behind them, "on stools stand 8 men with large fans" (numbered 37–44 in the CN).[116]

Twelve women (numbered 45–56) enter at midstage, six from either side. Each holds a parrot, which "sits on the pointer finger." Here Minkus returns to more traditional melodic fare, complementing choreography that includes *pointe* work. To the strains of a

---

[116] The production documents include four diagrams detailing the positioning of the stools in the various groupings formed during the divertissement.

broad sweeping melody in waltz rhythm, the women travel in their lines with a series of *temps levés en demi-arabesque* followed by three steps forward. They form a column of two lines at center that transforms into two rows and eventually into one row across the stage. Steps include *demi-cabrioles derrière, piqués de côté en cou-de-pied devant*, and multiple *temps levés en demi-arabesque* while turning. Traveling steps include *pas de basque, balancé*, and a series of *temps levés sur la pointe* in *demi-attitude devant*. Similar to previous dances, the final pose is in *attitude devant*, this time on *demi-pointe*.

From here on in the divertissement, the corps de ballet yields to soloists. The 1877 poster lists several dances for pairs or trios of performers:

7) Two bayadères	2 student women
8) *Nautch*[117]	2 women
9) Classical dance	Hamsatti and Solor
10) *Manu*	1 woman and 2 student girls

The dance for two bayadères became a dance for four by 1900, and the CN thus records the number as a *pas de quatre*. The *Manu* dance is also notated, but as No. 14 in the CN and Rep. How the other two dances correspond to the intervening numbers in the Rep is uncertain. Out of a possible eight numbers (Nos. 7 through 14), the Rep contains just five, the CN three. The PR also includes just three numbers, but an annotation after the third—"No dance *Manu* and beginning of Indian"—refers to missing pages that included the entire *Manu* and the opening of the Hindu dance.

No. 7. The nine bars of introduction at the beginning of No. 7 allow time for the ensemble to form a second grouping, which is similar to the first but with additional dancers upstage. The twelve men switch places with the boys and pose with the women along the wings who are holding parrots. The boys "stand on five stools in a circle and arms folded on chest crosswise" behind a row formed by the women holding fans and mirrors, who kneel. In contrast to the groupings Petipa devised for the adagio in *Le jardin animé*, which filled the entirety of the stage and within which the leading performers danced, the groupings here frame the stage, leaving an open, central space for dancing.

The dance begins with the entrance of a pair of bayadères (numbered 57 and 58, the CN refers to them as "1st dancers"), one at each upstage corner. They travel down their respective diagonals to a light, staccato—yet mostly conjunct—melody made up of eight-bar phrases (Ex. 9.27). Their steps include multiple *pas de bourrée* on *demi-pointe, glissade, jeté* once to each side. The pair returns backward up the diagonal with *piqué en demi-arabesque* and two hops on *pointe* in fifth position three times. They finish with six *chaînés* on *demi-pointe*, traveling to opposite corners, crossing at center.

A second pair of bayadères (numbered 59 and 60) also begins from opposite upstage corners. They zigzag downstage with *pas de bourrée, jeté en avant, cabriole derrière* three times. The women circle each other with *piqués de côté en cou-de-pied devant* then travel

---

[117] Pallabi Chakravorty defines *nautch* as "a distortion of the word *naach*, or dance, which is derived from the Sanskrit *nritya* through the Prakrit *nachcha*." Historically, nautch dancers were "predominantly Muslim women who were trained in north Indian music and dance and once held high status in the royal courts." The term "nautch" was coined as a catch-all term during British rule to define this northern style as well as various regional dance styles of southern India. By the end of the nineteenth century, nautch dancers had become associated with "low culture and women of loose morals." See Pallabi Chakravorty, "Dancing into Modernity: Multiple Narratives of India's Kathak Dance," *Dance Research Journal* 38, no. 1/2 (Summer–Winter, 2006): 116–117.

Ex. 9.27 Bayadères' dance; Act Two, Scene III, No. 7, bars 10–17

Ex. 9.28 Transition passage accompanying the move to the next formation; Act Two, Scene III, No. 8, bars 1–8

directly downstage with a series of *piqués sur les pointes* and *pas de bourrée*, all on *pointe*. They finish their entrée with a *temps levé en tournant*, traveling upstage, and *glissade, assemblé*. During this last enchaînement, the first pair of bayadères travels upstage on the diagonal with *piqués de côté en cou-de-pied devant* and joins the second pair, forming a single row at center.

Together the bayadères conclude their dance with a unison passage of walks backward on *pointe*, *temps levé*, *pas de bourrée*, *arabesque fondu*, *assemblé* three times followed by five *pirouettes* from fifth position and *pas de chat*.

No. 8. The first half of No. 8 is a lengthy transition passage. The CN instructs, "In 29 bars all change group." The music builds throughout, from *piano* to *fortissimo*, creating a sense of anticipation as the dancers move around the stage to assume their next formation. (Ex. 9.28).

The third grouping is depicted in a ground plan that lacks performers' numbers and yet is detailed enough to allow for identification of the various constituents. The upstage platforms, of which there are now twelve, are again placed in a semicircular formation.

Ex. 9.29 Act Two, Scene III, No. 8 (Variation 1), bars 32–39

Ex. 9.30 Bayadère's dance (polka); Act Two, Scene III, No. 9 (Variation 2), bars 2–9

The men with pikes and garlands stand on them. The eight men with fans stand in a broad semicircle at the base of the platforms. In front of them, eight boys stand on eight stools, also positioned in a semicircle. The remaining four boys stand in a row in the center of the space within this formation; each pair shares a garland or similar prop (the CN does not specify). The women with mirrors and fans remain in lines of six at each side, positioned on a slight diagonal. Those with parrots stand in a row at center, in front of the four boys, positioned to face slightly inward on the diagonal.

No. 8 in the Rep continues with "Variation 1," thirty bars (not including internal repeats) of running eighth notes that are similar to the preceding transition music (Ex. 9.29). The entire variation is struck through. Whether or not this is the *Nautch* dance listed on the poster our sources do not tell us.[118]

No. 9. "Variation 2" in the Rep, also labeled No. 9, is a polka that corresponds to a thirty-two-bar passage titled "4 bayadères" in the CN (Ex. 9.30).

The four soloists (57–60) remain in a single row throughout the dance. They cover the available stage space with steps that include *entrechat quatre, changement, échappé*

118 Gershenzon, "*La Bayadère*," 17.

Ex. 9.31 Act Two, Scene III, No. 10, bars 10–18

on *pointe* followed by a spring to fifth position on *pointe*, runs forward on *pointe*, and *bourrées*. Further into the number, they perform *cabriole devant, piqué en arabesque, jeté en avant*, and hops on *pointe* in fifth position After a series of *chaînés* on *demi-pointe*, the dancers finish downstage right.

No. 10. Nine bars of *forte* introduction to No. 10 lead to sixty-four bars of a waltz whose lush melody is reminiscent of No. 6 (Ex. 9.31). This dance is not included in the CN.

Following a double bar line at the end of the number, a second twenty-nine-bar transition passage facilitates the ensemble's move to a fourth grouping. The women with parrots join the women with fans and mirrors in lines at each side: "In 29 bars, the women with parrots walk away to the sides and all others stand in their places." Here, the ground plan includes numbers assigned to all participants, which helps confirm their placement in the previous group. The music is a repeat of the earlier transition passage (Ex. 9.29) with four additional bars that are struck through.

Neither the Rep nor the CN includes Nos. 11, 12, and 13, and neither are any additional numbers included in the PR.[119]

No. 14. The popular *Manu* dance features a milk seller and two young girls who want a drink from the jug she carries on her head.[120] This gentle polka, which bears resemblance to the earlier polka that is No. 9, is punctuated throughout its first half by pauses at the end of upward scales that accompany passages of *bourrées* (Ex. 9.13). Once again Minkus uses a disjunct melodic line and chromaticism to suggest the exoticism of the vignette and its locale.

Volynsky reminisced about the dance in 1922:

> This [the *Manu* dance] is a combination of various patterns on the floor: pas de bour-
> rée, polka which earlier were performed by Trefilova and Karsavina. Karsavina pro-
> vided such a splash of fragrant colors and florescent charm that one can never forget

---

[119] Gershenzon suggests the following possibilities for these numbers: "11) Variation of 2 bayadères? (Allegro non troppo ⁴₄) | 1884 & 1900: Omitted; 12) Pas Classique of Gamzatti [Hamsatti] and danseur noble (Allegro ⁶₈) | 1884 & 1900: Omitted; 12a) Variations of the Pas Classique? | Omitted 1884 & 1900; 13) Corps de ballet? (Allegro con fuoco ²₄) | 1884 & 1900: Omitted." Gershenzon, "*La Bayadère*," 17.

[120] *Manu* is a Sanskrit term that carries various meanings in Hinduism, referring in early writing to the archetypal, or first, man.

it. A mother is playing with her children [this is Volynsky's interpretation of the dance and its characters]. With one hand she supports a pitcher on her head, and the other she waves around freely as if to ward off the hopping little chicks who are clinging to her legs. These circles on the floor depicted by the legs are extended in all directions of the stage, now to the outer wings and now to the edge of the lighted ramp, everywhere following after two Lebanese Cedars of extraordinary beauty.[121]

Volynsky's description agrees with the ground plan of the CN, which confirms that circles, small and large, are a feature of the lead dancer's trajectory on stage. Entering from upstage, the soloist (numbered 61 in the CN) dances alone for thirty-eight bars. Nearly always on *pointe*, she performs *relevés en demi-arabesque*, *piqués en demi-arabesque*, *piqués sur les pointes*, *temps levés sur la pointe*, and *bourrées* on *pointe*. (All of the *bourrées* in this dance, for the soloist and the students, are notated in fifth position, as *pas de bourrée couru en cinquième*, rather than first position, *pas de bourrée couru en première*.)

After turning a circle at center, she travels downstage left where she is met by the first young girl (62), who runs up to her. Stopping, the soloist asks, "What is needed?" "Give me a drink," demands the girl. "No," the milk seller replies, and she runs across the stage. There she is met by a second young girl (63). They repeat the exchange the seller had with the first girl. Circling around to upstage center, the soloist is joined by the girls, who are also on *pointe*. The trio dances for twenty-eight bars, their steps including more *bourrées*, walks and skips on *pointe*, *relevés en demi*-arabesque, and *relevés petits passés*.

The final hijinks begin. Traveling downstage left with two *piqués en demi-arabesque* separated by a *pas de bourrée*, the soloist is followed by one of the girls, who moves quickly with four successive *piqués en arabesque*. The girl "with two hands drags the milk seller by the skirt"—as both dancers *bourrée*, the girl pulls the soloist backward and upstage toward center. The soloist "with the right hand hits the hands of the girl student," who "takes [her] hands away and threatens her," possibly with a wagging finger. The same scenario is played out with the second girl on stage right, but this time the soloist allows herself to be pulled to center. Joining together once again, the trio travels backward upstage with walks and skips on *pointe*. They return, alternating steps into fifth position and *bourrées*, remaining on *pointe* throughout. The soloist breaks away, circling the girls in a counterclockwise pattern with more steps and skips on *pointe*. Finally, to a stream of continuous sixteenth notes, and with all three dancers performing a continuous *bourrée*, the girls chase the soloist across the stage, the soloist traveling backward as she faces the girls. All stop just short of the downstage left wing at the conclusion of the number. The CN is silent regarding any action that may accompany the final moments of the dance. An added annotation after the final bar in the CN reads, "Run backstage. End."

No. 14½. The "Hindu dance" (as it is called in its new position in the Rep) follows, untitled, in the CN. The popularity of this number, which featured leading character artists in the company, and the removal of the classical dance for Hamsatti and Solor are possible reasons for moving the Hindu dance to "pride of place" in the divertissement: the last dance before the coda. Led by Lubov Radina and Felix Kshesinsky in 1877 and Marie Petipa and Sergei Lukyanov in 1900, the dance was fast, pulsing, loud, and physically aggressive. Except for brief moments of respite, the dancers performed repeated small jumps throughout. Active torsos leaned forward and back, while arms were repeatedly held behind the body and then raised up.

---

[121] Volynsky, "Marius Petipa (*Baiaderka*)," tr. in *Ballet's Magic Kingdom*, 68.

Ex. 9.32a Hindu dance: A man enters with a drum; Act Two, Scene III, No. 14½, bars 1–8 (Source: Rep)

A man (numbered 64 in the CN) "enters with a drum" from stage left. He is the physical embodiment of the drum we hear in the score from the outset (Ex. 9.32a). He is followed by six more men (65–70) who circle the stage with a series of *temps levé en attitude devant*. They form a diagonal line downstage left, where they continue with multiple *temps levés en demi-arabesque* with a slightly bent knee alternating with *temps levé en arabesque* with a stretched knee, bending forward during the latter. These various *temps levés* comprise much of the choreography of the dance. Alexander Shiryaev explained, "The 'Hindu Dance' in *La Bayadère* is based on *grand battements*," referring to the lifting of the leg to the front or back during the small jumps on one leg.[122] Connecting the dance to imagery illustrating the Prince of Wales's tour to India, Sergey Konaev has observed that "La danse infernale à Ceylon," published in *L'illustration* in 1876, in which dancing men are depicted in a position similar to the *temps levé en attitude devant*, may have inspired the choreography for this dance.[123]

The men travel upstage and form a row in pairs, whose partners circle each other, the CN instructing, "Do this nose to nose. Close to each other." The dancers circle the stage once more, this time forming a diagonal line at stage right, where they stand in a fourth position lunge, arms side, torso leaned forward.

The lead couple (71 and 72) enters upstage left (Ex. 9.32b). Like the men before them, they circle the stage with multiple *temps levés en attitude devant*. Arriving at center, each dancer turns a circle away from the other and, again facing front, continues with *échappé en plié* and three *demi-emboîtés devant* twice, a series of *temps levés en attitude devant* on the same leg, and alternating *demi-emboîtés derrière*. They turn a circle away from each other again before traveling on the diagonal toward downstage left with multiple *ballonnés* as they are joined by the men, who travel on the diagonal toward upstage left performing the same step. Both groups return on their respective diagonals with *temps levés en demi-arabesque en tournant*, making two full turns. The entire traveling enchaînement is repeated, then the dancers pause at a *fermata* in the score.

---

[122] Beumers et al., *Alexander Shiryaev*, 109.
[123] Konaev, "Der *Tigre Captif*," 44–45.

Ex. 9.32b Hindu dance: Entrance of the lead couple; Act Two, Scene III, No. 14½, bars 69–76

At the return of the opening drumbeat, the couple travels again to the downstage left corner, where they turn to watch the men, who take center stage. The men form a circle that rotates in a counterclockwise direction as they perform a series of *temps levés en attitude devant* on the inside leg. The ground plan suggests the men hold the shoulder of the dancer in front of them with their inside arm. The circle opens into a single row, and the men travel directly downstage with alternating *demi-emboîtés derrière* and back up with *temps levés en demi-arabesque en tournant*.

The lead couple joins the men; they perform a series of *balancés* and *temps levés en arabesque* as they exchange places, while the men, in pairs, repeat their earlier enchaînement danced "nose to nose." The nonstop intensity of the dance continues, the lead couple eventually moving upstage before the entire ensemble travels downstage together with *demi-emboîtés derrière*. On the final downbeat, all perform *échappé en plié*. The woman and the ensemble men spring to *attitude devant fondu*, while the lead man holds his *échappé* position, body forward, head looking up.

After his initial entrance at the beginning of the number, the drummer is omitted from the CN. Fortunately, a film of the dance was made by Shiryaev, this one using three-dimensional puppets captured in stop-motion.[124] The three-minute film, made during the period 1906–1909, features seven puppet dancers: the drummer, lead couple, and four (rather than six) ensemble men. The dance clearly held meaning for Shiryaev, who had fond memories of Radina's performance and danced the male lead himself, both at the Mariinsky and on tour.[125]

No. 15. The concluding "Coda" (Rep: "Corps de Ballet"; 1877 poster: "General Final Dance") features a similarly strong musical pulse but in waltz tempo (Ex. 9.33). The ground plan drawn in the CN suggests the ensemble spends the nine introductory bars reconfiguring the stage space to create additional room for dancing.

The women holding fans and mirrors and the women holding parrots line the wings, with six of each group on either side. As the buoyant waltz begins, pairs of dancers

[124] The film is included in *A Belated Premiere*, dir. Viktor Bocharov. See Beumers et al., *Alexander Shiryaev*, 27–30, 46–51.

[125] Beumers et al., *Alexander Shiryaev*, 95–96, 137.

Ex. 9.33 Divertissement coda; Act Two, Scene III, No. 15, bars 10–17

take turns traveling to center with *temps levés sur la pointe en demi-attitude devant* and returning with *piqués de côté en cou-de-pied devant* and *pas de basque*, while the others perform *balancés* in place. The boys move downstage in lines on either side, nearest the wings, performing *pas de basque*. They return upstage, traveling backward with *balancés*. By the end of the first thirty-two bars, the women have formed two rows across the stage, where they pose briefly in *tendu croisé derrière fondu*.

The boys traverse the stage, their lines crossing at center, with a series of *temps de flèche devant*. Meanwhile, the women perform a series of *relevés battements devant*, six *emboîtés devant à terre*, and a *pirouette* from fifth position, *pas de bourrée*, and two *balancés*. The boys, having formed a row upstage of the women, continue by first circling in place with *pas de basque* then performing *demi-emboîtés derrière* in pairs as they "hold each other by the hands" and turn another circle. The rows of women interact by each advancing toward the other and back with *demi-emboîtés devant*.

The mass of dancers reconfigures, traveling with *pas de basque*. The boys return to lines at the wings, and the women's rows regroup at center as the four bayadères enter downstage right and move to center. Dancing in unison, all of the women perform a series of *pas de basque en tournant*, with a *balancé* to finish the turn, *cabriole devant*, *balancé*, before dispersing to the sides and upstage. The boys perform two *grand pliés* in fifth position followed by four *pas de basque* as they move away from their lines and back.

The full dancing contingent now having entered, the lines and rows move upstage and down, toward center and back to the wings in varying configurations, traveling with *demi-emboîtés*, *pas de basque*, and *balancés* (as the boys travel forward, they maintain an open second position). Ten bars before the end, all move to the final grouping with *pas de basque*. Arriving at the penultimate bar, the ensemble forms a fifth and final grouping. The women and boys form rows across the stage in front of the men (13–24, with pikes and garlands, and 37–44), who "stand on stools"—a row of four farthest upstage and sixteen more in four lines. No pose is given for the women, who are facing slightly inward in their rows. The boys have their "arms folded on chest crosswise" and "sit in the Turkish manner" (that is, legs crossed).

The CN includes nothing further from this act.

No. 16. Nikia's mercurial dance monologue concludes the scene, taking us seamlessly from divertissement back to dramatic plot. Titled "With snake" in the Rep and labeled with the annotation "Bayadère's dance with flowers" in the PR, this number comprises

Ex. 9.34a Nikia's dance monologue: A brief, sweet *pianissimo*; Act Two, Scene III, No. 16, bars 56–63

four danced sections, each with a different affect and each increasing in tempo. The act concludes with action music accompanying Nikia's death.

In the absence of choreographic notation for Nikia's dance, we turn to the libretto for a description of the action:

> At the end of the dances, the rajah commands the beautiful Nikia to come in, and he orders her to entertain the public.
>
> Nikia comes forward out of the crowd with her little guitar. The bayadère's face is hidden by a veil.
>
> She plays the same melody she played in the first act [this detail was not realized in the score].
>
> Solor, who the whole time is near the rajah's throne, listens carefully to this harmonious melody and recognizes his beloved. He looks at her with love.
>
> With suppressed malice the Great Brahmin watches him, hardly concealing his wrath.
>
> During the bayadère's dance the rajah's jealous daughter uses all her strength to conceal her state of mind. Smiling, she comes down from the balcony and orders a basket with flowers to be presented to the graceful Nikia.
>
> Nikia takes the basket and continues her dance, admiring the pensive Sólor.
>
> Suddenly a snake crawls out of the basket and strikes the bayadère in the heart. Its bite is deadly.

Following a fourteen-bar introduction of rising lines and a continuous *crescendo*, the first section features a melancholy cello solo (Ex. 9.8b), which represents Nikia's *vina* ("her little guitar"). A repeat of the introductory material is followed by a brief, sweet *pianissimo* (Ex. 9.34a) leading to a quick polka, a two-bar diminution of the previous melody followed by a rushing upward scale (Ex. 9.34b). The polka moves directly to a concise recapitulation of the scene's opening march melody (see Ex. 9.23), culminating in the snakebite, after which action music takes over until the end of the scene.

Ex. 9.34b Nikia's dance monologue: Polka; Act Two, Scene III, No. 16, bars 77–84

The libretto tells us that Nikia "appeals to Solor for help, and he embraces her." But whereas Giselle professed her love for Albert as she died, Nikia reminds Solor of his promise: "'Do not forget your vow,' she gasps. 'You are sworn to me ... I am dying ... Farewell!'" Having rejected the Brahmin's offer of an antidote, Nikia dies, claiming innocence in her last breath.

Volynsky describes the impression Pavlova made during this number:

> Pavlova danced this variation with a basket of flowers in such a remarkably strong and expressive way that the theater broke out in wild applause as soon as the music died down. The dancer died at the footlights, falling headfirst to the ground, and lying flat with her entire body. The enchanted audience froze for several moments and awakened from the artistic spell only when the curtain finally fell.[126]

Act Three

Scene IV: The Appearance of the Shade

The opening scene of the third act provides a transition to the dream world of the Kingdom of the Shades. Benois's description, beginning with the previous act's finale, takes us from the scene of Nikia's death and conveys us into the sober atmosphere of Solor's chamber:

> A dark fate hung over the ballerina: the charming girl fell down dead, struck by a snake emerging from a basket of flowers, to the skirling sound of a pipe. From now on she was a shadow. Her silhouette would suddenly flit upon the background of a wall or she would appear to her lover looking like her old self and lure him to the sad, dimly-lighted world beyond the grave, which I identified as "our heaven"—where all the good people went after their death.[127]

[126] Volynsky, "Marius Petipa (*Baiaderka*)," tr. in *Ballet's Magic Kingdom*, 67.
[127] Benois, *Reminiscences*, 44.

Ex. 9.35 *Sakodusa*; Act Two, Scene IV, No. 2 (*Pas comique*), bars 3–10

The production plans reveal that the scene is set up in what appears to be the first wing. A number of columns, connected with draperies, frame the scene, with an opening between two columns at upstage right. A hookah (*kal'yan'*) is placed next to the opening, and a divan is placed downstage left.

In our description below, we have assigned the nine numbered entries from Petipa's notes to the four numbers that comprise the scene in the Rep and have also allotted bar numbers where possible in order to provide a detailed account of the action. (This scene is not recorded in the CN.)

No. 1. The act opens with Solor's new motif (Ex. 9.6). The curtain rises at bar 17. The descriptive heading at the top of Petipa's page matches that in the libretto:

> Order of the 1st tableau of the 3rd act
> Solor's chamber in the Rajah's palace

1 Entrance of Solor, sad, then he places himself on a divan [bars 17–45].
2 Entrance of the fakir [presumably Madhavaya]. He sees Solor is sad and has the idea of bringing people who will remove the bad spirit [*mauvaise esprit*] that he has in the body. He calls the snake charmers [bars 46–66].

No. 2. The 1877 poster indicates that the *Sakodusa* dance (Rep: "Pas comique") was performed by three Indian astrologers, one of whom was Madhavaya, rather than by the snake charmers planned by Petipa and described in the libretto (Ex. 9.35).

3 Entrance of the snake charmers. Dance of the serpent woman and one who plays the clarinet. Comic dance.

No. 3.

4 Solor returns to his senses and angrily chases away the entertainers [*saltimbanques*].
5 The Fakir announces to Solor the visit of his fiancée Hamsatti.

Ex. 9.36 "Shadow Dance" for Nikia and Solor; Act Two, Scene IV, No. 4, bars 49–56 (Source: Rep)

6 Entrance of Hamsatti, with two maids of honor, who remain languorous during this scene [bar 22, Hamsatti's theme; see Ex. 9.4]. There are during this scene of coquetry two appearances of the shade [bars 67 and 112; Ex. 9.2a]. Then Hamsatti departs with Solor's promise to marry the next day. The maids of honor follow Hamsatti. Solor remains alone.

No. 4.

7 Solor goes and looks near the door and the wall to see if he can see the shade of his bayadère [bar 14].
8 The bayadère makes an entrance while dancing, then a small scene between her and Solor. [The 1877 poster includes a "Shadow Dance" for Nikia and Solor, likely bars 49–74; Ex. 9.36]. The bayadère disappears and Solor remains alone.
9 Solor goes to place himself on the divan and falls asleep. The clouds descend.[128]

A harp cadenza introduces the following scene.

Scene V: The Kingdom of the Shades

The Kingdom of the Shades, Solor's encounter with Nikia in the afterlife, surrounded by a multitude of deceased bayadères, or shades, is the most famous scene in *La Bayadère* and includes its most concentrated passages of classical dance. The long, winding entrance

---

[128] RGALI *fond* 1657, *op.* 3, *ed. khr.* 132, fol. 2v. Although neither Petipa's plan nor the libretto mention that opium was the catalyst for Solor's subsequent dream, the inclusion of a hookah in the stage setting preserved in the Mariinsky production documents suggests this may indeed have been the case.

of the corps de ballet, in particular, has become iconic. Four sources provide various details about this legendary scene: Petipa's notes, the libretto, the Rep, and the CN. The 1877 poster simply lists all of the performers under one heading, "Dances of the Shades." Further sources, including reviews and memoirs, suggest changes were made between the 1877 premiere and the 1900 revival. We will not attempt to sort through what the changes may have been, but where we can suggest connections between the sources, we will do so.

Beginning with Petipa's notes, we find that he mapped out the scene in his usual detail. His description includes mentions of *Giselle* as well as *A Midsummer Night's Dream*, presumably a reference to his one-act ballet of the same name that premiered in July 1876, with Mendelssohn's music arranged by Minkus.[129] The page bears the heading, "On 25 November 1876 I agreed with Mssr. Roller at the grand theater the evening of the opera *La Juive* for the plan of the 3rd act of the shades of the new ballet. This is what we have agreed upon."[130]

1   As the curtain rises, it is light for the effect of the decoration of Mssr. Wagner.

2   The stage becomes a bit dark.

3   Entrée of the ensemble [*masse*].

4   Entrée of 4 or 6 or 8 *danseuses* dancing in poses [*danse au posés*].

5   Entrée of Solor.

6   Entrée of the ensemble [*masse*].

7   Vazem is seen high up in the grass (*A Midsummer Night's Dream*). Solor goes near her—The shade disappears.

8   The dancers encircle [*en tourent*] Solor.

9   The shade passes as in *Giselle*.

10   The dancers circle Solor again and all the dancers disappear. Solor remains.

11   The stage is dark. Solor alone—the shade passes very quickly. Solor seems to faint.

11bis   An entrée for Vazem [and] Solor on stage[;] it is very good [*très bien*] like *Giselle*.

12   The ensemble comes on stage and the shades under the gauze form groups along the wings. At that point, Vazem appears in the water. Several colors should be there.

13   The stage becomes light[;] the shade throws herself into Solor's arms, grand adagio.

14   During the adagio, the shades by the wings must come once again.[131]

At the bottom of the page, Petipa concluded, "Then I will see for the rest."

The ballet master's notes refer to numerous familiar elements of the Kingdom of the Shades—the entrance of the corps, an entrée for a smaller number of *danseuses*, an entrance for Solor followed by an appearance by Nikia, and, of course, a "grand adagio." Other features are unfamiliar, including the shade of Nikia passing quickly by Solor as in *Giselle*, the dancers encircling Solor, and Nikia appearing "in the water."

Petipa's plan makes no reference to the conversation between the lovers that is recorded in the libretto:

[129] See Wiley, *Tchaikovsky's Ballets*, 4.
[130] See Chapter 6, p. 333.
[131] RGALI *fond* 1657, *op.* 3, *ed. khr.* 132, fol. 2r.

"I died innocent," says Nikia's shade, "I remained true to you; behold then everything around me here. Is it not magnificent! . . . The gods have granted me all possible blessings. I lack only you!"

"What must I do to belong to you?" Solor asks her.

"Do not forget your vow! You promised to be faithful to me! . . . The melody which you are hearing now will come to protect you. . . . and my shade to guard you. . . . I shall be with you in misfortune."

"If you do not betray me," Nikia continues, "then your spirit shall find rest here, in this kingdom of the shades."

Neither do the notes describe a moment that was hampered by issues of timing during the 1877 premiere. According to Wiley, "During Solor's dream Nikia was to show him a castle in the sky, but in the performance the appearance of the castle was not accurately co-ordinated with Nikia's gesture, and the dancers faced [upstage] to look at it only after it had disappeared."[132]

The Rep preserves some unfamiliar music, including two numbers near the beginning of the scene (Nos. 8 and 9, see below). And while much of the rest of the music is familiar from performances today, we are left guessing as to when certain of the less familiar elements described by Petipa may have taken place within this music, assuming, that is, that all of Petipa's plans were realized. Strikethroughs in the Rep suggest various cuts that bring the scene more into alignment with present-day performance. Whether these cuts were made after the 1877 premiere and therefore represent changes made in subsequent productions, our sources do not say.

The collection of dances preserved in the CN, though it does not include all of the choreography to which we are accustomed today, does suggest that by 1900 present-day order was more or less in place. Passages not documented in the CN include the brief action scene that features the initial appearances of Solor and Nikia (No. 7—only the first two bars are accounted for), the lovers' first *pas de deux*, and Nikia's variation.

The following list is a comparison of numbers found in the Rep and CN for Act Three, Scene V:

Rep	CN
No. 5. Entrance of the shades	No. 5. "Shades"
No. 6. "3 Solistes (Dames)"	No. 6. "Three soloists"
No. 7. Entrance of Solor; appearance of Nikia	No. [blank] "Scène"; two bars only
No. 8. Brief reprise of No. 6; cut indicated from end of No. 7. to beginning of No. 10	Omitted
No. 9. 21 bars struck through; cut indicated from end of No. 7. to beginning of No. 10	Omitted

---

[132] Wiley, *Tchaikovsky's Ballets*, 20.

Rep	CN
No. 10. "Violino Solo"	Omitted
No. 11. "Grand Adage"	No. 11. "2nd Adagio"
No. 12. "1. Variation"	No. 12. "Variation"
No. 13. "2. Variation"	No. 13. "Variation"
No. 14. "3. Variation"	No. 14. "Variation"
No. 15. "4th Variation"	Omitted
No. 16. "Coda"	No. 16. "Coda"

Taking these various sources together, we can now describe the Kingdom of the Shades.

No. 5. Titled "Shades" (or "Shadows") in the CN, the famous entrance of the corps de ballet begins far upstage, somewhat left of center. An annotation provides details: "Coming in, one after another | 48 ladies" is written at the top of the page. Indeed, forty-eight women enter the stage on an elevated ramp and trace a wide serpentine line as they descend to stage level and make their way downstage.[133] While details of the ramp, intended to create the effect of descent from the mountains of the Himalayas, are not given in the CN, they are preserved in the production documents: an upstage-left opening in the mountainous rock façade that surrounds the stage gives onto a platform leading dancers toward stage right. Turning around to the left, the bayadères would step onto the next section of the platform which took them to center stage and a short flight of steps that led down to the stage floor, where they continued their serpentine trajectory. The drawing does not indicate any degree of incline in either ramp.

Next to number "3" in his notes, above, Petipa had drawn a similar winding line that then transforms into more of a spiral. This resembles, in part, the path taken by the shades as they made their initial appearance. Such patterns are found among Doré's numerous engravings that illustrate the 1868 publication of Dante's *Purgatorio* and *Paradiso* from his *Divine Comedy*. Some feature multitudinous angels arranged in scrolling lines and circles, while others depict them on a staircase that descends from the heavens.[134]

Vazem recalled the scene's initial reception and confirmed the Doré artwork as a source of Petipa's inspiration:

Apart from the last act [of *La Bayadère*], there was much applause for "The Kingdom of the Shades," where Petipa's choreography was most successful. In this scene, all the group dances and solo variations are imbued with poetry.

The group poses were copied by Petipa from Gustave Doré's "Paradise" from his illustrations for Dante's *Divine Comedy*.[135]

---

[133] The poster for the 1877 premiere includes Nikia, three soloists, Solor, thirty-eight *corps de ballet* women, eleven female students, sixteen small student girls, and twelve small student boys in the list of "Shades Dances." Gershenzon notes the 1884 production included thirty-six corps de ballet women and twelve "senior girls." This total of forty-eight Shades is the number employed in the 1900 production. See Gershenzon, "*La Bayadère*," 16.

[134] Dante Alighieri, *Il purgatorio e il paradiso (colle figure di G. Doré.)* (Paris: L. Hachette e Cia, 1868).

[135] Vazem, "Memoirs: Part 4," 35.

Ex. 9.37a Entrance of the Shades; Act Three, Scene V, No. 5, bars 1–4

In his 1925 *Book of Exaltations*, Volynsky explained how the costumes of the shades brought Dante's world to life:

> The attire of the female dancers is unlike anything else. White skirts with white veils, the ends of which are held in the dancers' hands, produce a fantastic impression. Before us are shadows of the world beyond the grave, rocking and swaying, undulating and whirling, with the aerial lightness of Dante's visions.[136]

Returning to the CN, we find the dancers' entrance enchaînement fills one bar of music—*arabesque à plat* on the right foot, *tendu devant* with the right foot as the torso bends back and to the left, arms overhead (Volynsky's "rocking and swaying"), *cou-de-pied derrière* with the left foot, and two steps forward. (We note that the *arabesque* is not notated as an *arabesque fondu*.) The ground plan indicates every second dancer performs this combination of steps on the opposite leg. The annotation "first forward, second back, etc." refers to the direction each dancer faces as she performs the *cambré*, the bending and arching of the torso: the first woman turns her body to the left, toward the audience (that is, "forward"); the second woman bends her body to the right, or upstage (that is, "back"). When the dancers change direction and move toward stage left, the subsequent annotation "first back, second forward, etc." now means the first woman's *cambré*, bending to the left, faces upstage (that is, "back"), and the second woman's *cambré*, bending to the right, faces downstage (that is, "forward").

The enchaînement is repeated thirty-nine times for a total of forty iterations set to the opening forty bars of the number, which begins with a languid, slowly descending melody that matches the trajectory of the dancers (Ex. 9.37a). Because only forty bars are allotted to this opening step and the ensemble is made up of forty-eight women, we must

[136] Volynsky, *Kniga likovanii* [The Book of Exaltations] (1925), tr. in *Ballet's Magic Kingdom*, 252.

Ex. 9.37b Entrance of the Shades (B section); Act Three, Scene V, No. 5, bars 17–20

presume that during the final bars of this passage the balance of the ensemble makes its way on stage. Finally, the shades form four rows of twelve across the stage.

Moving in unison to a new melody, this one in B minor, the women make a *développé à la seconde* with the right leg, the arms held to the side (Ex. 9.37b). They next stand in *arabesque* on the right leg, facing downstage right. "Quietly lowering to the knee," they kneel on the left leg and extend the right leg to the front, arms overhead, torso bent left, back arched. "Quietly rising from the knee," they perform *sous-sus en croisé* on *pointe* and *bourrée* upstage for four bars, arms overhead. Remaining on *pointe*, they return downstage for three bars, lowering their left arm to the side.

Facing downstage right, they step forward into *arabesque à plat* on the left leg. Lowering the right leg to *tendu croisé derrière*, they perform *détourné* to the right, facing downstage left, and continue with *arabesque à plat* on the right leg. They *bourrée*, turning a circle to the left, followed by *glissade*, *arabesque à plat* on the left leg, again facing downstage left, and a repeat of the *bourrée* turn and *arabesque*.

As the opening melody returns, the ensemble *bourrées* upstage again. This time, individual arrows drawn on the ground plan for each row suggest the rows travel upstage one at a time over the course of six bars. Finally, facing downstage right, the women kneel once again on the left leg, extending the right leg forward, arms overhead, torso bent left, back arched, a position they hold until the end of the number.

Originally performed on a fully lit stage, the ambience of the Kingdom of the Shades appears to have been changed in 1900, when the scene played out against the dark and craggy Himalayas of Petr Lambin's new design, lit to resemble what Tamara Karsavina referred to as "a blue transparency of night."[137] Karsavina tells of further scenic elements, as well as the practicalities involved in deploying forty-eight moving dancers on stage, and how these enhanced the magical effect of the corps de ballet's entrance:

> The supernatural element of Romanticism needed also certain contrivances to lend credence to the plot. Thus in the original production [although Petipa mentions gauze in his notes (see above), this may be a description of the 1900 revival], several thicknesses of gauze at the proscenium eerily dimmed the descending shapes. One by one

137 Tamara Karsavina, "'A Blue Transparency of Night,'" *Dancing Times* 54, no. 641 (February 1964): 239. See also Wiley, *Tchaikovsky's Ballets*, 20.

the veils lifted, but the light on the stage remained a blue transparency of night. I remember, too, that the dancers were more closely welded in their ranks, so the spectator took in, not the separate figures, but a chain of shapes that might have been likened to a slow swirling mist, the effect enhanced by the full tarlatans.[138]

The CN suggests the ensemble's subsequent movement toward the wings is performed during the Rep's transitional "Cadenza ad libitum Arpa," a passage facilitating a key change to G major. "Rising from the knee," the women split at center and *bourrée* to opposite sides. Eighteen women line each wing, and twelve women form a row across the upstage.

No. 6. "The soloists are running in" refers to the three women who will dance the subsequent *pas de trois* accompanied by the corps de ballet. Later in the scene, each will dance a solo variation. The trio will unite again in the coda.

The harp cadenza serves as both an introduction and transition, and the women begin dancing on the downbeat of the subsequent waltz in $\frac{6}{8}$ meter (Ex. 9.5b). Traveling on the diagonal from upstage left, they perform *cabriole derrière, sous-sus* four times. They continue on the opposite diagonal with *glissade, relevé développé écarté devant, entrechat cinq*, landing in *demi-arabesque fondu*, three times. Circling upstage to center, they perform *cabriole derrière*, the ground plan indicating they make a full turn to the left, *assemblé*. Meanwhile, the corps repeats a majority of the soloists' steps in their places at the sides and back of the stage.

Next, the soloists and ensemble form trios by joining right hands at the center of seventeen three-person pinwheels. Rotating to the right, the trios perform two *temps levés en arabesque* before moving away from each other with a *tour jeté*. They run back, join hands, and repeat the enchaînement two times. As the corps repeats the sequence a fourth time, the soloists travel directly downstage with *grand jeté en avant, piqué pirouette en dedans* twice.[139]

Continuing downstage, now in a zigzag pattern, the soloists perform *glissade, temps levé en arabesque, relevé passé* to *développé devant* four times to alternate sides, the corps performing the same in place. The soloists return upstage, traveling backward with a series of *pas de bourrée* punctuated by *tombé* and *fouetté*, the working leg passing through *demi-seconde*. They make a final zigzagging pass downstage with *sissonne ouverte, assemblé, relevé en arabesque* four times as the corps complements their movements with *assemblé, sissonne ouverte*, and two *emboîtés derrière*.

Finally, all of the women rise on *pointe* and *bourrée* to center, the corps forming four rows of twelve behind the soloists as the melody winds upward to a gentle conclusion. All finish with a pose in *arabesque à plat*, each row facing opposite sides of the stage.

A second harp cadenza, this one facilitating a key change to A minor, is struck through in the Rep.

No. 7. Titled "Scène," No. 7 is a brief action number represented in the CN only by the ensemble's exit: the group splits at center to "run behind the wings," the soloists exiting downstage right.[140]

---

[138] Karsavina, "Blue Transparency."

[139] The CN indicates that the corps perform the enchaînement twice more, but this would fill four more bars than are allotted to the soloists at this point.

[140] Although listed as "No. 7" in the Rep, an "8" is written in light pencil in the CN where Sergeyev had left a blank space after "No."

Ex. 9.38 Scherzo; Act Three, Scene V, No. 9, bars 1–24 (Source: Rep)

The number comprises three sections and may have accompanied the brief conversation between the lovers that is included in the libretto (quoted above). The first fifteen bars reprise Solor's motif (see Ex. 9.6). The next twelve bars feature Nikia's motif played by solo flute, which may have accompanied Nikia's mime and represented the melody she references in her speech (Ex. 9.2a). This is followed by twenty-eight bars of agitated music that perhaps prefigures the impending "misfortune."

Nos. 8 and 9. The next two numbers are cut in the Rep. No. 8 is a brief thirty-one-bar reprise of the *pas de trois* waltz, now in A major (see Ex. 9.5b). No. 9 is a 139-bar A minor *allegro* in $\frac{3}{8}$ meter (Ex. 9.38).[141] This fleet scherzo sounds more like Mendelssohn's *A Midsummer Night's Dream* than anything else in the scene. (Whether Petipa was referring in his notes to the Mendelssohn score or a moment in his ballet based on Shakespeare's play is unclear.) An indication of a cut and the annotation in the Rep at the end of No. 7 confirm the omission of Nos. 8 and 9: "Grande Pause | Violino Solo," a reference to No. 10.

No. 10. What is known today as the first *pas de deux* for Nikia and Solor is not included in the CN. Whether the sixty-eight-bar violin solo (Ex. 9.5c) served this purpose in 1877 is something our sources do not reveal. However, because the subsequent number is titled "2nd Adagio" in the CN, this number appears to have been the first adagio at least by 1900. Volynsky referenced the double adagio in 1913, writing of "Pavlova's adagio with Samuil Andriyanov, so beautiful in style but divided into two parts. The artist performs the second one among the corps de ballet, who are lying on the floor in a semicircle and accompanying her to the beat of the orchestra with the waving of their veils."[142]

---

[141] This does not include a repeat of eight bars or a cut of twenty-one bars.
[142] Volynsky, "Proshchal'nyi spektakl' A. P. Pavlovoi (*Baiaderka*)," tr. in *Ballet's Magic Kingdom*, 50.

In his 1972 *Khoreograficheskie otkrovennosti* (Choreographic Revelations), Fedor Lopukhov analyzes the Kingdom of the Shades as an example of choreographic "sonata form," a reference to the long-established form used for the first movement of multi-movement Western instrumental compositions. In the course of his analysis, Lopukhov offers a partial description of this first *pas de deux* that resembles what is commonly performed today:

> The waltz is followed by the adagio of Nikia and Solor, where the ballerina, supported by her partner, performs a saut de basque, a développé into ecarté à la seconde followed by a turn into arabesque. These gently flowing movements . . . form the basis of the soloists' adagio. Then, with a series of jetés, one after the other, the ballerina disappears into the wings, while her partner follows slowly behind her.[143]

No. 11. Titled "Grand Adage" in the Rep, this eighty-seven-bar *andante* accompanies a second *pas de deux* for Nikia and Solor enhanced by the corps of forty-eight women who provide an active frame for the duet. Rarely only posing, save for the opening groupings, the ensemble is constantly in motion.

As the *adage* begins, Solor is downstage center. The corps de ballet enters from either side through the first wing during the two-bar introduction. During the next sixteen bars, they form two groupings (Ex. 9.2b). For the first, the entire ensemble is directed to "stand in two columns, one behind the other." The dancers form groups of four, all standing in *arabesque à plat*. The pair in front hold each other by the waist with one arm, while the couple behind holds hands. Each dancer grasps one end of a veil in her outside hand. The two dancers on the left of the quartet share a veil as do the dancers on the right.

After six bars, the ensemble spends two bars changing poses. Here, the same groups of four form circles, the dancers holding each other by the hand. The dancer farthest upstage stands, facing the audience, while the others kneel. The dancers on each side face inward, while the dancer farthest downstage faces the audience. After six bars, the dancers take two bars to move to the sides, where they form lines of twenty-four along each wing. Nikia runs in from upstage right, meeting Solor at center.

The CN provides a full set of staves for both Nikia and Solor as well as for the corps de ballet. Annotations provide generous partnering instructions for both leads. Solor and Nikia begin with movements that mirror each other and, in turn, are mirrored by the corps: *degagé de côté* followed by *grand port de bras*. Nikia continues with *pas de bourrée en tournant, relevé rond de jambé en l'air en tournant* to *arabesque*. Solor catches her by the waist with his right hand. Nikia puts her left hand on Solor's shoulder and brings her working foot through *passé* to *attitude devant*, as the corps *bourrées* in place, arms overhead. Solor lifts Nikia by the waist in two *sissonnes ouverte* as they travel backward on the diagonal toward upstage left. The corps kneels and extends a leg forward as the dancers did during their entrée (No. 5). Solor and Nikia walk back to their starting point, the corps stands, and the opening enchaînement is repeated.

Next the entire ensemble changes position—Nikia and Solor walk downstage right as the corps walks to form a large semicircle encompassing three sides of the stage. The women lie on their sides, supported by an elbow, the other arm held overhead. Solor

---

[143] Sonata form, simply put, calls for an opening section of music (exposition) that returns as the last section of music (recapitulation). Fedor Lopukhov, *Writings on Dance and Music*, ed. Stephanie Jordan, tr. Dorinda Offord (Madison: University of Wisconsin Press, 2002), 178.

Ex. 9.39 *Grand Adage*: Solo passage for Nikia; Act Three, Scene V, No. 11, bars 47–54

lifts Nikia: as she makes a *plié* in fifth position, arms overhead, Solor "takes her with both hands and places her on his right side." In other words, as Nikia faces Solor, she is lifted and placed on his right hip, maintaining a straight body position, facing upward, her back arched slightly so her face is visible to the audience. Her arms are overhead and her legs are crossed with knees slightly bent. Once he has her in place, Solor holds Nikia with only his right hand, extending his left arm to the side as he walks backward on the diagonal. Reaching center, Solor kneels, with Nikia still in a supine position. He "puts the lady on her leg and himself rises from the knee."

A new musical section introduces a brief solo passage for Nikia (Ex. 9.39). Traveling on the diagonal from upstage left as Solor walks downstage left, Nikia performs two *piqué tours en dehors, relevé detourné* three times. After running downstage left to meet Solor, she next travels across the stage with two unsupported *piqué tours en dehors* and a supported single *pirouette en dehors* from fourth position to *arabesque*, leaning far forward over Solor's left arm, two times. Repeating the enchaînement a third time, she concludes with a *double* (rather than a single) *pirouette* to *arabesque*, back arched, arms in fourth position. Solor holds her by the waist with both hands, standing in a lunging fourth position.

The dancers of the corps, who have been raising and lowering their free arm in time with the music, next stand and *bourrée* to form five rows of eight across the stage. Nikia performs an unsupported *tour de promenade* in *arabesque*, followed by a supported *relevé* (Solor takes her left hand with his left hand), the working leg passing to *développé devant*. This is repeated, the corps keeling at Nikia's second *relevé*, then the couple walks downstage left.

Standing behind Nikia, who faces away from her partner, Solor lifts her by the waist and extends his arms overhead. Nikia's arms are also held overhead, and her legs are crossed and slightly bent. Solor traces a serpentine pattern as he walks backward upstage toward center, alternating his orientation (and Nikia's, who moves her legs from side to side) between downstage corners. As they travel, the corps—each row facing opposite downstage corners—slowly stands and repeats a combination of kneeling followed by a slow rise, their arms passing through positions from side to overhead to opposite side. The gentle up-and-down motion, each line moving opposite the other, creates a wave-like effect, remembered by Karsavina when it was absent from a twentieth-century

Ex. 9.40 Variation 1; Act Three, Scene V, No. 12, bars 1–10

revival: "With my mind's eye I can clearly see the horizontal lines of dancers, semi-reclining, in *arabesque allongé à terre* while my partner carried me high in his arms in and between those lines."[144]

Nearing the conclusion of the adagio, Nikia and Solor walk side by side directly downstage as the corps *bourrées* toward the wings. The couple joins hands, interlocking arms, and makes a circle to the left. The corps kneels, each dancer facing the near down-stage corner. Slowly rising from the knee, they pose in *tendu effacé devant* then raise the working leg to *arabesque* as they turn to face the opposite wing. Solor kneels in *effacé*, facing downstage left, back arched, left arm overhead. The position of his right arm is not given, and nothing is notated for Nikia.

The CN provides a record of the first three of the four variations that follow. Whether the corps de ballet remained on stage for these solos is not indicated. Each notated variation features distinct vocabulary—turns in the first, *cabrioles* in the second, *sissonnes doublée* in the third. They share similarities as well: each variation features plenty of *pointe* work, both *relevé* and *piqué* steps.

No. 12. The CN records the performance of Vera Trefilova in the first variation, a pi-quant fifty-bar polka (Ex. 9.40). The choreography differs from modern productions particularly in the number of repetitions of its combinations and in its final enchaîne-ment, in which the sequence of traveling *relevés en arabesque* is broken up with a *bourrée* upstage.

Beginning upstage right, Trefilova travels down the diagonal with *piqué de côté en ar-abesque, tendu devant fondu,* two running steps on *pointe, glissade* four times. Traveling across the downstage, she continues with three quick *temps levés sur la pointe en arabesque* followed by a *bourrée*, the hips now facing downstage left even as she continues traveling to the right, three times. She runs upstage to center for the middle section, marked *poco meno* in the Rep, and performs *pas de chat, pas de bourrée* on *pointe, piqué arabesque en tournant, pas de chat, pas de bourrée* on *pointe, double pirouette en dehors* from fourth po-sition three times. She runs upstage left for a final diagonal, the music gaining in tempo (Rep: "Poco più mosso"): six *relevés en arabesque* followed by a *bourrée* during which she

---

[144] Karsavina, "Blue Transparency."

Ex. 9.41 Variation 2; Act Three, Scene V, No. 13, bars 5–12

travels back upstage, four more *relevés en arabesque* continuing downstage—the music becoming ever faster (Rep: "cresc. accell. al Fine")—and seven *chaînés* on *demi-pointe*, finishing *tendu croisé derrière*, the body leaning forward, head left.

No. 13. The second variation, thirty-six bars of a swinging $\frac{6}{8}$, is punctuated by pauses allowing for briefly held poses on *pointe* (Ex. 9.41). The CN documents the performance of Varvara Rykhlyakova. Of the four variations, this one has changed the least over time.

After an annunciatory introduction of four bars, Rykhlyakova begins upstage left and travels down the diagonal with *cabriole devant, temps levé en demi-arabesque* three times, finishing the enchaînement with *assemblé, relevé en arabesque,* right arm up, left arm side. A *fermata* allows her to briefly hold this position. She continues with *tombé, relevé pirouette en dehors développé devant, tombé, glissade* twice followed by a run upstage left and a repeat from the beginning of the variation, after which she runs downstage left.

Volynsky assessed Agrippina Vaganova's performance in 1913 with a description of the opening enchaînement: "With the technical perfection available only to her, Vaganova does four [sic] cabrioles with leaps of increasing elevation, terminating them with a fading arabesque on pointe."[145]

Returning to Rykhlyakova, she next travels toward upstage center on the diagonal: turning to the right, she performs *demi-cabriole devant* and two *demi-emboîtés derrière* twice, followed by *relevé en arabesque, pas de bourrée* on *demi-pointe* to each side. All of this is repeated from the *demi-cabriole* through the first *relevé en arabesque,* after which she runs upstage center for the return of the opening melody.

Traveling directly down center, Rykhlyakova performs a series of seven *relevés en attitude effacé* on alternating legs. Turning to the left, she continues with *demi-cabriole devant, pas de bourrée* on *demi-pointe* twice before turning abruptly to the right for a final enchaînement: *saut de basque* and three *chaînés* on *demi-pointe,* finishing with *soussus,* arms overhead.

No. 14. The CN of the third variation records the performance of Anna Pavlova. Performed slowly today, the variation in the Sergeyev Collection's orchestra score (discussed below) includes a metronome marking of ♪ = 120, with an *accelerando* only during

---

[145] Volynsky, "Proshchal'nyi spektakl' A.P. Pavlovoi (*Baiaderka*)," tr. in *Ballet's Magic Kingdom*, 50.

Ex. 9.42 Variation 3; Act Three, Scene V, No. 14, bars 1–9

the final phrase; in modern performances, an *accelerando* occurs halfway through the thirty-three-bar number. The Rep does not include metronome marking but confirms the *accelerando* occurs just five bars before the end. The skipping rhythm of the opening phrase characterizes the entire number (Ex. 9.42).

Beginning upstage right and traveling down the diagonal, Pavlova performs *sissonne doublée, pirouette* from fifth position, *relevé rond de jambe en l'air* four times. Crossing the stage to the right, she continues with *relevé développé devant, relevé en arabesque, pas de bourrée piqué en tournant* three times. After running downstage right, she travels backward on the diagonal, alternating steps on *pointe* with two single *pirouettes en de-dans*, the working leg carefully notated with the knee bent 135 degrees, three times. Her final diagonal begins with *pas de bourrée couru en première*, traveling the length of the stage, and finishes with *pas de chat, relevé en arabesque* on the right leg, right arm overhead, left arm side.

No. 15. The fourth variation, a violin solo in three sections of increasing virtuosity, is Nikia's solo. Accounts tell us the variation was danced with a scarf that flew upward, likely at the end of the opening *legato* section (see below). Both the use of solo violin and the scarf helps to set Nikia's variation apart from those preceding and make it special. Vazem remembered: "I had a tremendous success with my variation with a veil, danced to a violin solo by Leopold Auer, with the veil flying up to the sky at the end."[146] Karsavina also recalled "the scarf in the ballerina's solo, flying away into the skies on the last upward arabesque."[147] (In most performances today, the first half of Nikia's variation is performed as a *pas de deux* with Solor. The dancers are connected by a long tulle scarf, each of them holding one end.)

Lopukhov provides details about each of the variation's three sections. While we cannot know how closely his description may resemble what Vazem, Kshesinskaya, or Pavlova may have danced, much that he includes is supported by earlier references. We quote here only his step descriptions and not his accompanying analysis:

> The variation begins with turns—*demi-tours* in attitude. . . . The descent from pointe to the sole of the foot and the immediate rise back to pointe for the next demi-tour is

146 Vazem, "Memoirs: Part 4," 35.
147 Karsavina, "Blue Transparency."

Ex. 9.43a Variation 4: Nikia's solo variation (first part); Act Three, Scene V, No. 15, bars 4–7

Ex. 9.43b Variation 4: Nikia's solo variation (second part); Act Three, Scene V, No. 15, bars 20–23

performed as if it were a single continuous movement. . . . Petipa reinforced the impression created by the slow *demi-tours* by placing in the ballerina's hands a piece of tulle that would fly upward at the end of the first part of the variation [Ex. 9.43a].[148]

The second part of the variation is based on the *jeté* that first appeared in the exposition [Lopukhov's analytic designation for Nos. 5, 6, 10, and 11]. Here the *jeté* is performed in a different alignment, toward the back of the stage. After the *jeté*, there follows by way of preparation a *pas de bourrée* on *pointe* and a double *tour en dehors* that again comes to a halt in an arabesque, but with the ballerina facing the audience. . . . The choreographic phrase is repeated twice in succession [Ex. 9.43b], and then comes the transition to the third part of the variation—again a walk/run.[149]

The third part of the variation consists of a walk on *pointe*, a *pas de bourrée* that comes to a halt on one supporting leg, then on the other. This is a progressive movement. It is repeated twice, after which the variation finishes like the third variation: there is a

---

[148] Lopukhov, *Writings on Dance and Music*, 181–182.
[149] Ibid., 182–183.

Ex. 9.43c Variation 4: Nikia's solo variation (third part); Act Three, Scene V, No. 15, bars 28–31

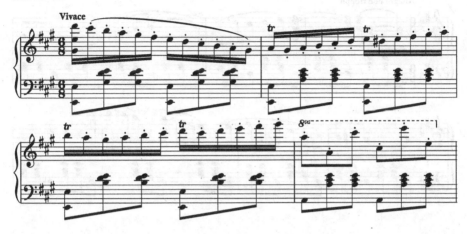

forceful *pas de bourrée* with open arms, not this time down the diagonal but toward the front of the stage, and the ballerina comes to an unexpected halt, not with a *pas de chat* but in an attitude [Ex. 9.43c].[150]

Volynsky offered a summary of the variation in 1913 that is not dissimilar from Lopukhov's description: "Pavlova's variation, of the terre-à-terre kind, is based on graceful pliés, on pirouettes en dehors, on semi-leaps, on dances across a slanted line to the accompaniment of the sonorous sounds of the violin, and on the marvelous turns of the body with bended leg which invariably changes to arabesque."[151]

No. 16. The coda brings the entire cast together. Beginning with the trio of solo shades and the corps de ballet, the number continues with entrances for Nikia and Solor, the CN providing rare examples of solo choreography for Nikia. Her final entrée is completely different from what is performed today. Likewise, the corps steps are different from most modern versions, which often retain the ground plan and spacing of the 1900 production but not its choreography. In particular, the varying orientations of the body, often directed toward upstage corners while performing steps *en effacé*, have largely disappeared.

The number opens with 115 bars of a broad, swinging $\frac{6}{8}$ featuring an expansive melody (Ex. 9.44a). Seventy-three of these bars are cut in the Rep, including a soft, chromatic middle section punctuated by sudden *sforzandi*.

With the corps de ballet again lining the wings, twenty-four on each side, the three soloists begin upstage right. Traveling on the diagonal, they perform *brisé, pas de chat* to fourth position *plié*, five more *brisés, sissonne ouverte changé en avant*. Traveling upstage, they continue with *chassé, tour jeté* twice, followed by *assemblé, entrechat six*. Having reached upstage left, they repeat their entrée from the beginning to the other side. The corps, meanwhile, performs its own choreography in place: *piqué* steps and *bourrées en tournant*.

[150] Ibid., 183.
[151] Volynsky, "Proshchal'nyi spektakl' A.P. Pavlovoi (*Baiaderka*)," tr. in *Ballet's Magic Kingdom*, 50.

Ex. 9.44a Coda: Soloists and corps de ballet; Act Three, Scene V, No. 16, bars 3–10

Ex. 9.44b Coda: Entrance of Nikia and Solor; Act Three, Scene V, No. 16, bars 116–123

The soloists finish at center as the corps runs to form four rows across the stage. All continue in unison with *entrechat quatre, relevé petit passé* twice, followed by *échappé* on *pointe* in *plié*, a spring to fifth position on *pointe*, a *bourrée* forward, and four *relevés en arabesque* alternating with *relevés en demi-arabesque en tournant*. This enchaînement is repeated followed by five sets of *chassé, cabriole derrière* to alternate sides. The ensemble splits at center and *bourrées* toward the wings, the soloists traveling downstage right, where they finish in *attitude à terre*.

A new musical theme, heavily marked, introduces Nikia and Solor, who begin upstage left (Ex. 9.44b).

The Romantic trope of the elusive woman is vividly brought to life in this passage, in which Solor pursues the shade of Nikia, catching her in a lift only to lose her again. Traveling on the diagonal, Nikia performs *temps levé en demi-arabesque* three times and an *assemblé* as Solor walks beside her, perhaps following slightly behind her. Indeed, with each jump, Nikia turns her head left, to the downstage side, as though to beckon her beloved Solor. He lifts her by the waist as she beats her legs, arms overhead. This is performed three times along the same diagonal. Nikia next runs across to downstage left as

Solor "stands and looks at the bayadère." She begins a *manège—saut de basque, grand jeté en avant, petits jetés en tournant* three times—followed by three *chaînés* on *demi-pointe* on the diagonal toward downstage right, finishing with *sous-sus,* arms overhead.

The CN continues with the corps de ballet. No repeated music is indicated in either the CN or the Rep, although it is customary today for Solor to dance a solo passage to a repeat of the same twenty-four bars that have just accompanied his entrée with Nikia and her subsequent brief solo. Lopukhov asserts that the same was done during Gerdt's early years performing the role:

> I talked to Gerdt, and he confirmed that the danseur's coda was based on the musical repetition of Nikiya's coda and that the movements consisted of a cabriole derrière preceded by a *tombé* (preceded directly by a *tombé,* without a step before the *cabriole*), followed by a step forward into an arabesque. In the course of the *cabriole,* the dancer would move forward, and the greater his progress, the more beautiful the appearance of the movement. This combination would be performed twice, followed by an *entrechat six.*[152] The whole sequence would be repeated using the other leg.[153] Then came the *saut de basque* in a circle, as performed earlier by Nikiya.[154]

Continuing, Lopukhov bemoans changes made to the choreography of *La Bayadère* and offers further detail that may explain why this passage for Solor is omitted in the CN:

> I should mention that in this scene from *La Bayadère,* as in Petipa's other ballets, unacceptable changes are sometimes made. Because they do not grasp the essence of the work, dancers performing the role of Solor replace the *cabriole* and the *saut de basque* in the coda with movements they are better able to perform, their main concern being their own perceived success and not the meaning of the work as a whole. They often justify their action by pointing out that Pavel Gerdt omitted the male coda when he danced the role of Solor. However, Gerdt gave up performing the *cabriole* and the *saut de basque* in the coda because of age and with Petipa's permission. When he was younger, he performed all the movements and never replaced them with others that were his own particular favorites. He did what the dénouement of this work demanded, as it was set by Petipa.[155]

While we are unable to confirm Lopukhov's assertions, several of his descriptions of choreography match what is found in the CN. These include elements that are no longer part of many current performances, for instance, Nikia's coda *manège* enchaînement that begins with a *saut de basque.* We therefore believe his descriptions could inform the revival of choreography for this scene that is omitted in the CN, particularly Nikia's variation and Solor's coda entrée.

Returning now to the coda, a new passage begins—a *più mosso, quasi presto* in $\frac{2}{4}$ meter (Ex. 9.44c). More than half of the one hundred bars (not including repeats) allotted to the corps in this passage are cut in the Rep. As the music builds with a *crescendo,* the corps performs a sort of vamping step in place that resembles a combination of *demi-valse* and

---

[152] We presume the *cabriole* and *arabesque* would be performed three times, mirroring Nikia's three *temps levés.*

[153] Here again, three repetitions of this enchaînement would more closely mirror Nikia's choreography.

[154] Lopukhov, *Writings on Dance and Music,* 184.

[155] Ibid.

Ex. 9.44c Coda: Corps de ballet; Act Three, Scene V, No. 16, bars 148–155

Ex. 9.44d Coda: Nikia's final entrance; Act Three, Scene V, No. 16, bars 240–247

balancé. This continues as the four women farthest upstage on each side travel toward center with seven *précipités*. Having formed a row across the stage, they continue with multiple *échappés* on *pointe* as the next four women on each side move toward center with *précipités*. This pattern continues: the third group consists of eight women from each side traveling toward center in two rows of four, followed by the last four women from each side, those farthest downstage.

Having formed five rows of eight women each, the corps continues with rhythmic runs forward on *pointe* (*taqueté*) and *arabesque voyagée* traveling backward. These are repeated, followed by *cabriole derrière, assemblé, entrechat six* twice. The ensemble splits at center and *bourrées* to the sides for four bars as "Kshesinskaya enters into the center of the stage [at the] 4th measure."

Traveling directly downstage, Nikia performs *piqué double rond de jambe en l'air, sissonne ouverte en avant*, landing on *pointe* in *demi-arabesque*, eight times to alternate sides, while the corps performs *cabriole devant* (facing the opposite upstage corner) and *piqué en arabesque* (turning and facing the near downstage corner) four times in place along the sides (Ex. 9.44d).

Nikia travels backward on the diagonal toward upstage left with two hops on *pointe* in fifth position *effacé, échappé en plié*, and a spring back to fifth position on *pointe* six times as the corps performs two *relevés en demi-arabesque* (facing the opposite downstage corner), four *demi-emboîtés devant* (turning *en face* and then toward the near downstage corner) three times.

Nikia returns downstage along the same diagonal with *demi-emboîtés devant* and presumably meets Solor (he is not mentioned at this point in the CN), who supports her in a *double pirouette* finishing on *pointe* in *cou-de-pied devant*, left arm side, right arm bent 135 degrees at the elbow (suggesting her hand is placed over her heart), leaning left and back from the waist, torso twisted left. The corps, which has run in from the sides toward center, kneels facing the opposite upstage corner, arms in fourth position, leaning back and toward downstage from the waist, twisting their torsos downstage. No final ground plan is given.

Thus ends the Kingdom of the Shades in the CN.[156] The subsequent forty-two-bar scene is untitled in the Rep, but we assume it constitutes Scene VI: Solor's Awakening, described in the libretto:

> Solor is lying on his divan. His dream is troubled. The fakir enters, stops beside his master, and looks at him sadly.
> Solor awakens suddenly. He thought he was in Nikia's embrace.
> Servants of the rajah bring in expensive gifts and announce to Solor that all preparations are completed for his wedding to the rajah's daughter.
> All exit.
> Solor, obsessed with his thoughts, follows them.

Various cuts in the Rep shorten this already brief scene, which ends with music often used today as an epilogue to conclude the Kingdom of the Shades (Ex. 9.8d).

Act Four

Scene VII: The Gods' Wrath

The final act affords Nikia the opportunity to turn the tables and reclaim her errant lover and also provides the audience with an exciting dénouement. In addition, the scene serves as a reminder that Petipa did not always end his ballets with a large-scale divertissement. Although there are elements of a divertissement in the act, which opens with a procession followed by a delightful children's dance, the main event is a *pas d'action*, performed by a small cast, that thrusts the plot forward to its thrilling conclusion. The act is concise and fast-moving, a welcome and strategic change after several sprawling scenes.

According to our performance sources, Petipa's plans for the final act were realized with few revisions. The balletmaster noted at the top of the page detailing the final scene, "Order [*Marche*] of the 4th act that I gave to Minkus":

Act 4

All is being prepared for the celebration of the marriage of Solor and Hamsatti.

---

[156] Two sets of eight-bar repeats are cut in the Rep near the end of the coda, and additional cuts are made in its final bars.

Entry of the warriors, nobles, Brahmins and Bayadères, then the Rajah and his
daughter and Solor.
After the arrival of the two fiancés, the rajah orders that the celebration begin.

Pas des Lotus de Delhi
by the young girls

Pas d'action

Allegro—the 4 *danseuses* enter by one and by two, or [only?] by two.
Then Hamsatti with Gerdt, and while they dance Mme. Vazem circles around
Solor. The end of the *allegro* is done together and ends this first piece (*allegro*).

Adagio

During the adagio, the 4 young ladies offer bouquets to the bride, and the shade
always comes between Solor and Hamsatti. Hamsatti gives Solor a flower,
and the shade takes the flower and throws it away.
3 variations—one for the 4 *danseuses*, a second for Gerdt, a 3rd for Hamsatti.

Coda. In this coda, there are 2 entrées needed for the shade as if we hear the
breeze of the wind.
At the end of the coda—while the shade dances its last entrée, the 4 dancers offer
a basket to Hamsatti, who pushes it away with horror, for it reminds her of the death
of the bayadère. Next, she sees the shade in front of her like a specter. Hamsatti
throws herself into her father's arms, begging him to speed up the marriage.
Thunder is heard a little when the bride sees the specter.
Next comes the wedding.
Then the lightning [*éclair*], the rain, the bursts of thunder and lightning
[*foudre*] that engulf everyone.

Apotheosis[157]

The libretto tells us, "The stage represents a large hall with columns in the rajah's palace,"
a description matched by the stage plan in the production documents: a seemingly endless hall—an effect created by forced perspective—is flanked by columns and set on a
raised platform reached by a short set of stairs at upstage center. Seating in long rows is
placed upstage right and along stage left. Primary seating, probably for the Rajah and the
nuptial couple, is placed in the second wing at stage left.

No. 1. The act opens with a reprise of the march first heard at the beginning of Act
Two, bringing with it references to the Rajah's palace (see Ex. 9.20). The music accompanies the wedding preparations envisioned by Petipa and the entrance of the nuptial
guests.[158] The libretto is in agreement with Petipa's list of attendees: "Warriors enter, together with brahmins, bayadères, and others. Hamsatti appears, followed by her father
and his retinue. When the young warrior Solor appears, the rajah orders the festival to
begin." The libretto, 1877 poster, and 1900 program all refer to the wedding celebration

---

[157] RGALI *fond* 1657, *op.* 3, *ed. khr.* 122, fol. 7r/v.
[158] The Rep includes 148 bars (not including many internal repeats), of which twenty-three are cut. An additional eight bars serve as a transition and modulation to No. 2.

as *sipmanadi*. This term may refer to *saptapadi*, Sanskrit for "seven steps," a reference to the ritual steps taken by the couple during the Hindu marriage ceremony that symbolize their journey together through life.

No. 2. The *Pas de Guirlandes*, Petipa's *Pas des Lotus de Delhi*, is a two-part dance for twenty-four student girls, all of them on *pointe*. The CN provides particulars that agree with Petipa's brief description: "No. 2 | 4th Act, Scene 5. Anger of the gods. | Dance of the lotuses—24 student girls," and further, "12 average girl students and in their hands garlands | 12 little girl students | All in all only 12 hard garlands," that is, garlands strung on hoop frames, as they were for *Le jardin animé*. (We note that the posters for the 1877 premiere and 1884 revival list two named students in addition to the ensemble of twenty-four student girls. By 1900, the program lists only "Girl students of the Imperial Theater School.")

The first part of the dance is made up of poses and groupings. To the benign strains of an *andantino*, the students enter, six couples in lines from each upstage side (Ex. 9.45). Presumably, each couple includes an average (we will call them "tall") girl standing upstage of a small girl. Each holds one end of a shared garland. The CN instructs, "garlands are lifted up," that is, held aloft. Meeting at center in a row that spans the stage, the students form a "1st Group" in which the small girls kneel and the tall girls pose in *arabesque à plat*.

The grouping dissolves as the students run downstage to form the "2nd Group"—"all run into 2 columns like the two first pairs"—the arrows in the ground plan designate the path of the central couples who form the downstage end of the two columns. The tall girls stand outside of the small girls and again pose in *arabesque*; the small girls stand in *attitude à terre*.

As they move to the "3rd Group," the tall girls take the garlands and *bourrée* upstage, as the small girls walk in two lines that loop around the tall girls. They reassemble into their columns, the small students kneeling with their "arms on chest crosswise," the tall girls posing in *arabesque* as they encircle their smaller partners with the garlands.

Sharing garlands once again and holding each other by the waist, the pairs *bourrée* across the stage sideways, their columns intersecting as they pass. They pose in *arabesque* by the wings then *bourrée* back to center, form a single column of pairs, and pose again in *arabesque*.

Ex. 9.45 *Pas de Guirlandes*; Act Four, Scene VII, No. 2, bars 2–5

The central column dissolves as every other pair *bourrées* toward opposite sides then runs upstage where the ensemble forms a single row. Here, couples face each other on the diagonal—tall girls facing downstage left, small girls facing upstage right. Holding both ends of the garlands, the tall girls encircle their partners, who hold their counterparts by the waist. They *bourrée* directly downstage in this position then kneel and pose for three bars. Finally, they run to form an inverted semicircle of three rows at center. The tall girls form the two upstage rows, and the small girls, who "hold each other by the waist," form a single row in front. The tall girls lower their garlands—the CN instructs, "with the middle of garland touch the floor"—then "lift up the garlands" on the second beat of the last bar, corresponding to a final *sforzando* chord, as the two downstage rows kneel.

Between the two sections of the dance, the students form lines of twelve along each wing: six tall girls with garlands stand upstage of six small girls.

The second half of the number is a waltz that begins as the small girls travel to center with a *temps levé en arabesque* and *demi-emboîtés derrière* twice (Ex. 9.8c). Arriving, they perform *relevés petits passés* then return to the wings as they came. Meanwhile, the tall girls perform *balancés* in place. The small girls run to center and form a circle, kneeling. They are joined by the tall girls, who travel to center with *pas de basque* and form an outer circle. Placing their garlands on the floor, the tall girls move away from the circle with two *ballonnés* and turn in place with two *pas de basque*. Returning to the circle, they repeat the enchaînement then move away and back one more time. They pick up their garlands, and all move to form two columns as in the first part of the dance.

The girls travel downstage with *emboîtés sur les pointes*. They continue with two *temps levés en demi-arabesque* in place then repeat the enchaînement, traveling farther downstage. Each column becomes a single row with each small girl standing in front of her taller partner. The tall girls hold their garlands high over the small girls, who reach up and grasp the middle of the garland with both hands. Traveling in this position with a series of *temps levés* and *demi-emboîtés derrière*, the two lines cross at center then travel upstage and back.

The small girls release the garlands, and all run to reassemble into their double circles. Holding their garlands high, the tall girls perform *balancés* in place, while the small girls travel away from the circle with *pas de basque*, passing between the tall girls, then run to form a larger outside circle, where they perform *sous-sus* as the tall girls lower their garlands. They repeat the enchaînement as the small girls return to their inside circle and then repeat the entire figure again. On their final return to the inside circle, the small girls delay their *sous-sus* until the second beat of the final bar, coinciding again with the last chord of the music, as the tall girls kneel, their garlands lowered. A final annotation in the CN reads, "End [*Fine*] and all walk off to the sides."

We see in Petipa's choreography steps similar to those given to the garland-wielding students in *Le jardin animé*—*balancé, emboîté, pas de basque, ballonné*—the latter two favored as traveling steps along with *bourrées*. At the same time, we find in his dance architecture the similar columns and circles he would return to four years after the premiere of *La Bayadère* when choreographing the mazurka in *Paquita*, a dance that also featured twenty-four students.

In his commentary accompanying a Russian translation of Petipa's plans, Lopukhov describes an appearance by Nikia at the end of the garland dance and a subsequent variation, neither of which are part of the sources we evaluated: "In the finale [of the Lotus dance], the children formed a tight circle in the middle of the stage and, scattering to the sides, they revealed the shade of Nikia, who rose from the hatch [a trapdoor]. Nikia performed a very difficult variation, set in the style of the shades scene of the previous act."[159] While the CN makes clear that the girls are indeed in a circular formation at center at the end of the dance, it is silent with regard to an appearance at this point by Nikia and a subsequent variation. Neither the Rep nor the PR include a variation or annotations about Nikia's appearance. That being said, a program for a 4 September 1905 performance of *La Bayadère* included a "Solo" for Pavlova (as Nikia) that followed the "Lotus Dance." No such solo is included in the program for Pavlova's 1902 debut in the role.

No. 3. The concluding *pas d'action* is choreographed for just eight dancers: Hamsatti, Solor, Nikia, four bayadères, and a nameless cavalier, who both dances and partners, whereas Solor is documented in the CN as a partner only. Whether the same distribution of duties was observed in 1877, we cannot say, but the poster confirms Pavel Gerdt as the nameless cavalier in the original *pas d'action.* By 1900, Gerdt had long since replaced Ivanov as Solor, and Georgi Kyaksht (and later Nikolai Legat) served as the extra cavalier. In a sense, there are two Solors participating in the *pas d'action,* and sometimes they are on the stage together; for example, during the coda, Solor partners Hamsatti while the cavalier nearly simultaneously partners Nikia.

Petipa envisioned the *pas d'action* as a multimovement suite of dances: entrée, adagio, three variations, and coda. The ensemble dances combine choreography with action and mime sequences. The limited number of dancers serves to focus attention more intensely on the main players in the drama. Between dance passages for the four bayadères, Hamsatti and the alt-Solor (the cavalier) make their entrance as bride and groom. The shade of Nikia appears, visible only to Solor (having stepped in to replace the cavalier), and separates the couple. Hamsatti, sensing something is amiss, becomes increasingly apprehensive. She attempts to distract Solor with her dancing and briefly succeeds, but the shade of Nikia persists and eventually Solor partners her, if only figuratively (she dances with the alt-Solor cavalier). He is torn between duty and love.

The CN includes only the entrée and coda, omitting the adagio and the interpolated variations that are part of the Rep. The CN confirms the participants on the first page of the entrée: "No. 3 | b[allet] Bayaderka | *Pas d'action* | Last act | Bayadère, Solor, Hamsatti, 4 bayadères | from the good soloists | Fakir, Slave, and Legat N[ikolai]."[160] The movements and actions of the fakir and slave, likely Madhavaya and the *aiya,* are not documented in the CN.

Entrée. The entrée is the most substantial number of the *pas d'action,* comprising 157 bars.[161] Three piquant musical motifs, presented in sixteen-bar periods, are eventually interrupted by a series of increasingly chromatic passages that accompany the intrusion of Nikia in the wedding proceedings.

The bayadères begin. Starting upstage right, a first pair travels down the diagonal with two *temps levés en arabesque, cabriole derrière,* two *demi-emboîtés derrière,* all repeated to the other side (Ex. 9.46a). Traveling backward up the diagonal from downstage right, they continue with *tour jeté, relevé développé devant* three times and return downstage with *temps levé en demi-arabesque* and *pas de chat.*

---

[159] *Marius Petipa. Materialy,* 175.

[160] According to the program for the 1900 revival premiere, the four soloists were Julia Sedova, Anna Pavlova, Evgenia Obukhova, and Lubov Egorova. See Appendix F (iii).

[161] The CN does not include repeats of twenty-four bars, eight of which are struck through in the Rep. An additional eight bars are also struck through.

Ex. 9.46a Act Four, Scene VII, No. 3, Entrée (first motif), bars 1–10

Ex. 9.46b Act Four, Scene VII, No. 3, Entrée (second motif), bars 19–22

Ex. 9.46c Act Four, Scene VII, No. 3, Entrée (third motif), bars 35–38

As the second motif is introduced, the second pair of bayadères begins upstage right and travels on the diagonal with *cabriole derrière, grand jeté en avant* three times (Ex. 9.46b). Returning upstage, they continue with *temps levé en tournant* and *assemblé*. Reaching center, they dance in place: *entrechat quatre* and *relevé rond de jambe en l'air* to each side, *temps levé en arabesque* to each side, and more *entrechats quatre* and *relevés ronds de jambe en l'air*. They run downstage where they are joined by the first pair of bayadères.

To the third motif, the quartet travels upstage and back with steps that include *entrechat trois, piqué derrière degagé devant to attitude devant* (though *retiré* may be the intended position because the knee is bent 135 degrees), *pirouette en dehors* from fifth position, *temps levé en demi-arabesque, assemblé, changement,* and *relevé à la seconde* (Ex. 9.46c).

The second motif returns and the bayadères travel upstage and back again, this time with *relevé en arabesque* alternating with *pas de bourrée* on *pointe* and *ballonné*

Ex. 9.46d Act Four, Scene VII, No. 3, Entrée (Nikia's entrance), bars 82–90

to *demi-arabesque* alternating with *pas de bourrée* on *demi-pointe*. The quartet splits at center, and the pairs move to opposite sides with *chaînés* on *demi-pointe*.

At the return of the opening melody, Hamsatti and her cavalier (Legat) enter upstage right. Having waited through three acts, Hamsatti will dance for the first time in this entrée. Traveling down the diagonal, the pair performs *temps de flèche derrière* to *arabesque fondu, chassé en tournant*. Hamsatti continues with *relevé en arabesque* as the cavalier performs *pas de chat*. This enchaînement is performed three times, then they run to midstage center.

The couple mirrors each other with *cabriole devant*, Hamsatti crossing in front of her cavalier. They change direction with *jeté en tournant* and cross each other again with *grand jeté en avant*. After three times, Hamsatti travels downstage right with four *piqué tours en dehors* as her cavalier walks beside her. They return up the diagonal, Hamsatti with a series of *piqué de côté en cou-de-pied devant* and *piqué tour en dehors en arabesque*, the cavalier with multiple *tours jetés, assemblés, relevés développé devant*, as "all walk to the group," setting up Nikia's entrance. The pair runs run forward at center, where they are flanked by the bayadères, and Gerdt steps in for Legat, who remains slightly upstage.

To a tripping melody followed by a sequence of short upward flourishes, the vengeful ghost of the bayadère enters downstage left and circles the stage clockwise with five *grands jetés en avant* on alternating legs (Ex. 9.46d). Nikia next crosses the stage left to right with a diagonal of five *piqué tours en dehors* then circles upstage of the bayadères and cavalier, moving toward center with three more *grands jetés en avant*. Arriving, she "roughly pushes through Hamsatti and Solor," then continues downstage left with six more *piqué tours en dehors* before running into the wings. The music pauses suddenly at the height of a *crescendo*.

This particular entrée is claimed by Vazem to have been borne of a confrontation between Petipa and the ballerina during the creation process ahead of the 1877 premiere. Vazem wrote at length about the episode in her memoirs, recalling the steps first choreographed for this entrance:

We began rehearsing the last act, in which Solor celebrates his wedding to Princess Gamzatti; the ceremony is interrupted by the spectre of Nikia, killed at the bride's behest to prevent her hindering the marriage. Nikia's intervention is expressed in a *Grand pas d'action*, danced by Solor, Gamzatti and soloists: the Bayadère's spectre appears among them, but is seen only by the bridegroom. I was dancing the spectre, and Petipa once again composed an unsuitable variation, consisting of very small movements. Without much ado, I turned down this composition—which did not suit the music or the whole conception of the dance. The spectre's appearance during the festivities demanded something more imposing than the "petits riens" [little nothings] created by Petipa.[162]

Such was the argument between Vazem and Petipa that the ballerina left the rehearsal. Taking up the subject again the next day, the two still could not agree on a suitable entrée. Vazem claims she determined the steps she would dance after Petipa taunted her by suggesting she perform choreography danced by Maria Gorshenkova, in the role of Hamsatti, whose jumping prowess Petipa had exploited in her earlier entrée with the cavalier. Vazem was not a jumper:

> "Very well," I replied, "but, for the sake of variety, I shall dance these *jetés* entering from the wing nearest the footlights, not from the one at the back." This is much more diffi-cult, as the visual effect of the jumps is not helped by the rake of the stage.
> On the day of the first orchestra rehearsal. . . . The rehearsal proceeded as usual. At last we reached the last act and the moment for the *Pas d'action*; I stood in the first wing, waiting for my entrance. I was on fire, anxious to teach this conceited Frenchman a lesson, to show him what a "talent" I was. The moment for my entrance arrived and, at the opening strains of my music, I gathered up all my strength, which seemed to be infinitely greater than usual, and literally flew onto the stage, even jumping over some kneeling dancers. Covering the stage in three leaps, I stopped. Everyone on the stage and in the audience greeted me with thunderous applause. Petipa, who was on the stage, realised his unfair treatment. He came up to me and said: "Madame, forgive, I am 'durak' (a fool).'[163]

All of this being said, the resulting choreography fulfilled Petipa's intent expressed in his sketches: "Then Hamsatti with Gerdt [in his role as the cavalier in 1877], and while they dance Mme. Vazem circles around Solor."

Returning to the CN, the third motif returns strongly as the bayadères resume danc-ing in a row at center with *pas de chat, relevé fouetté double rond de jambe* to *arabesque*, three *demi-emboîtés derrière* four times, traveling downstage. This is followed by *relevé développé devant, assemblé, entrechat cinq* three times traveling upstage. As before, the dancers split at center and move to the wings in pairs with *chaînés* on *demi-pointe*.

Solor (Gerdt this time) and Hamsatti begin a second entrée at center as the second motif returns. Hamsatti zigzags downstage with *double ronds de jambe jetés* and *piqués en arabesque*. She is "holding the shoulder of Solor," as she performs the *piqués* (after the *jeté*, she turns around for the *piqué*), and he is "holding the waist of Hamsatti" with his right hand as he stands in a slightly lunging fourth position, his left arm extended to the side. This enchaînement is performed four times to alternate sides. The last time,

[162] Vazem, "Memoirs: Part 4," 34.
[163] Ibid., 34–35.

Ex. 9.47a Act Four, Scene VII, No. 3, Adagio, bars 2–5

Hamsatti poses in *arabesque* as Nikia runs in from upstage left and again "roughly pushes through Solor and Hamsatti." The music, suddenly soft, features tremolos beneath rapid upward chromatic scales. Nikia performs a *piqué en arabesque*, supported by Solor, her body leaning far forward. Hamsatti runs back to Solor and embraces him, displacing Nikia, who runs around the couple to the right. As Solor returns Hamsatti's embrace, Nikia pushes them apart again and performs a *piqué en arabesque*, supported at the waist by Solor. She breaks away, performing *chaînés* toward downstage right as Solor follows. Hamsatti runs toward them.

Nikia exits into the downstage wing as Hamsatti reaches her groom and performs a *piqué en arabesque*. She mimes, "You watch how I will dance." Solor agrees and, to the *fortissimo* return of the third motif, Hamsatti travels backward on the diagonal with *tour jeté*, *assemblé*, *relevé développé devant* four times. Solor walks beside her and "admires the dances of his bride." The bayadères join Hamsatti, dancing in pairs on either side: *saut de basque*, *cabriole derrière* four times to alternate sides.

Solor and Hamsatti reach center and the bayadères pose in pairs as Nikia makes her third entrance, accompanied by a rising, florid, chromatic melody. Running down from upstage right, she "roughly pushes through" each pair of bayadères. "In horror [they] walk off to the side [that is, split apart] and again run up [to each other] and stand in a pose." Meanwhile, Solor and Hamsatti "exchange pleasantries" until Nikia, circling around to center, "grasps the waist of Hamsatti with her right hand." Taking the bride with her, Nikia spins ("simply turning on two legs") on the diagonal toward downstage right. Solor walks beside the two women. As Nikia releases Hamsatti and runs into the wings, Solor supports his bride in a final pose—*demi-attitude devant* on *pointe*, her hands crossed on her chest—bringing the tumultuous entrée to a close.

Writing in 1913, Volynsky captured the dramatic quality of the dance: "In the last act, Pavlova glides and flashes across the stage, breaking the tempos of her flight with movements on pointe, circling the bride and groom and whirling with them in a delirium of dream movement."[164]

---

[164] Volynsky, "Proshchal'nyi spektakl' A.P. Pavlovoi (*Baiaderka*)," tr. in *Ballet's Magic Kingdom*, 50.

Ex. 9.47b Act Four, Scene VII, No. 3, Adagio, bars 26–29

Adagio. Although the adagio is missing from the CN, we find it in the Rep: forty-six bars in compound quadruple meter. As in the entrée, three melodic motifs are followed by a passage of chromatic scales that may have accompanied an interruption by the shade of Nikia, an appearance planned by Petipa (Ex. 9.47a).[165] He also envisioned the four bayadères offering bouquets to Hamsatti during the adagio. His further plan for the shade to take a flower from Solor and toss it away is yet another resemblance to *Giselle* that we find in *La Bayadère*. This may have been the action accompanied by the return of the third motif, *pianissimo* and transposed to A-flat major, before a recapitulation of the main melody in the home key of C major (Ex. 9.47b).

Variations. The three variations planned by Petipa are not part of the CN or PR.[166] At the conclusion of the adagio, an annotation in the PR states merely, "Follow 2 No. No. [sic] | Inserted Variations | Men's and Ladies.'" Turning to the Rep, however, we find two variations interpolated from other ballets.

Titled "Variation | From the ballet *Babochka* [The Butterfly]," the first variation was presumably danced by the cavalier. *The Butterfly* is an 1874 ballet by Petipa, with music by Minkus, based on Marie Taglioni's 1860 *Le Papillon*. Letellier identifies the variation as that for Prince Djalma, the male lead of *Le Papillon*.[167] Our sources do not reveal at what point the variation was added to *La Bayadère* or indicate whether or not Kyaksht danced it in the 1900 revival.

A brief number at twenty-five bars, the variation is in ABA form, with a strong, swinging A section bookending a gentler B section (Ex. 9.48).

More information is provided for the second variation: "From the ballet *Vestalka* Cornalba | Variation Mlle Sedova | Music by Drigo." The inclusion of Sedova's name confirms the variation is for Hamsatti: Sedova first performed the role on 21 October 1901.

Petipa created *The Vestal* for Elena Cornalba in 1888.[168] Sedova performed one of Cornalba's variations from *The Vestal* when she made her debut as Teresa in Petipa's *Halt*

---

[165] The bars containing the chromatic scales are omitted from the PR.

[166] Gershenzon states that neither these numbers nor later interpolations are found in the Mariinsky sources. Gershenzon, "La Bayadère," 15–16, 28.

[167] Letellier, *Ludwig Minkus*, 110.

[168] The premiere was given at the Mariinsky Theater on 17 February 1888. See *Khronika III*, 269. The libretto has been translated into English, with an introduction, by Wiley in *Century*, 323–349.

Ex. 9.48 Act Four, Scene VII, No. 3, Interpolated Variation, from *The Butterfly* (Minkus), bars 1–5

Ex. 9.49 Act Four, Scene VII, No. 3, Interpolated Variation, from *The Vestal* (Drigo), bars 5–9

of the Cavalry on 26 September 1899.[169] Whether or not that variation and this one interpolated into *La Bayadère* are one and the same, our sources are silent. We are also left uncertain as to the variation Preobrazhenskaya may have danced in 1900.

Sedova's variation is a more substantial number than the cavalier's variation. The form is ABAC, with the return to A serving as a brief transition to C, which features seventeen bars of *Tempo di galop* following an *accelerando* (Ex. 9.49).

Coda. A swinging ⁶₈ meter creates momentum throughout the concise coda.[170] The dance proceeds as a series of entrées. The four bayadères begin in a row upstage left. One at a time, each dancer travels down the diagonal performing the same enchaînement to Minkus's jaunty tune: *glissade*, *saut de basque* three times and two *chaînés* on *demi-pointe* (Ex. 9.50a). Having all arrived downstage right, the bayadères continue in unison, traveling backward up the diagonal with *pirouette en dehors développé devant*, *pas de chat* three times. They run upstage to center and continue with two *pas de bourrée* on *pointe*,

---

[169] *Khronika III*, 361–362.
[170] The coda comprises 151 bars, not including several internal repeats, two of which are cut. Forty-five of the bars are clearly cut in the Rep. The remaining bars total a greater number than are accounted for in the CN. For clarification, we look to the PR. Here, the bars cut in the Rep are omitted altogether, as are bars on two pages of the Rep that follow the beginning of a cut that lacks a corresponding end. The remaining ninety bars (we ignore the PR's own cuts and added repeats) match the CN exactly.

Ex. 9.50a Act Four, Scene VII, No. 3, Coda, bars 3–10

Ex. 9.50b Act Four, Scene VII, No. 3, Coda, bars 35–42

entrechat quatre, entrechat cinq three times. Splitting into pairs, they travel to opposite downstage corners with five *chaînés* on *demi-pointe*.

Hamsatti begins her entrée traveling directly down center with *pas de cheval, pas de bourrée* on *demi-pointe* six times to alternate sides, followed by a *bourrée* upstage left. She continues with a diagonal of *piqué en demi-arabesque* and two *pas de bourrée* on *pointe* making a complete turn six times, finishing with four *chaînés* on *demi-pointe*.

The cavalier is next, joined by the four bayadères, flanking him in pairs. In a "V" formation at center stage, they perform seven *cabrioles derrière* on alternate legs, each separated by a *chassé*. The heavy beat of the new motif complements this series of jumps (Ex. 9.50b). After running downstage left, they hold each other by the waist in a row, the cavalier at center, and travel backward up the diagonal with twelve *entrechats quatre*. They run back downstage and finish with *temps levé en cou-de-pied devant, pas de bourrée en avant* on *demi-pointe*, and a pose in *arabesque à plat fondu*. They run upstage left, where the bayadères presumably exit and the cavalier awaits his next entrée.

Hamsatti and Solor (Gerdt) enter downstage right. Facing her groom, who holds her left hand in his, Hamsatti *bourrées* backward across the stage, finishing with a *piqué en*

Ex. 9.51 Destruction of the temple and bolts of lightning; Act Four, Scene VII, No. 6, bars 29–36

demi-arabesque, supported at the waist by Solor. Nikia and the cavalier follow. Of Petipa's two planned entrées for Nikia in the coda ("as if we hear the breeze of the wind"), this is the only one documented in the CN. Traveling down the diagonal from upstage right, the cavalier lifts her by the waist in a *grand jeté en avant* followed by a supported *double pirouette* from fourth position, her hands crossed on her chest. They perform this enchaînement three times then run upstage left and travel down the opposite diagonal. The cavalier lifts Nikia in four *sissonnes ouverte* to *à la seconde*, her arms overhead. Reaching downstage right, he performs six *pirouettes* as the bayadère travels across the stage with four *piqués de côté en cou-de-pied devant* before running into the wings.

Petipa contrasts the earthly Hamsatti with the heavenly Nikia: the former is given *terre à terre* steps while the bayadère is lifted in movements that create the impression of flight. (Assuming the same or similar steps were performed in 1877, this distinction seems ironic given that Gorshenkova was a jumper and Vazem was not.)

After the *pas d'action*, the plot moves swiftly to its conclusion.[171] The CN provides the briefest account of the remaining action and apotheosis: "After the *pas d'action* begins the last scene, i.e., the wedding of Solor and Hamsatti. When the priest joins their hands, all collapses and all fall dead. Except Solor, who kneels, the bayadère standing behind him." Despite the narrative in the CN, the libretto, in agreement with Petipa's notes, confirms Solor's death and provides further detail: four young girls (Petipa envisioned these to be the four soloists) offer a basket of flowers to Hamsatti (Petipa planned this action to occur during the coda of the *pas d'action*). Horrified by the recollection of Nikia's death and the snake that bit her, Hamsatti rejects the basket then sees the shade of Nikia standing in front of her. Petipa called for an ominous reaction from the sky: "The thunder is heard a little when the bride sees the specter." Hamsatti begs her father to begin the wedding ceremony. As he joins the hands of his daughter and Solor, thunder is heard, an earthquake follows, and lightning strikes the temple, which collapses, leading to the demise of

---

[171] The finale comprises a mere seventy-two bars (not including two internal repeats), of which eighteen are cut in the Rep. This final bar count matches the PR with the exception of four bars omitted in the latter that are not cut in the Rep (where they are repeated).

everyone inside. Minkus provides descending chromatic scales to accompany the fall of the temple and quick upward flourishes to depict the bolts of lightning (Ex. 9.51).

Konaev suggests Petipa took inspiration for the destruction of the temple from yet another Doré drawing, *The Death of Samson*.[172] This gravure, created in 1866 for an illustrated Bible, depicts the legendary strongman pushing apart the pillars that hold him captive. They break and topple in much the same way as those depicted in a photograph of the *Bayadère* apotheosis.[173]

The apotheosis features a reprise of the passage that follows the Kingdom of the Shades and concludes Act Three (see Ex. 9.8d).[174] Evoking a sense of calm resolution, the music accompanies a final image of Solor and Nikia, described in the libretto: "Through the rain the peaks of the Himalayas are visible. Nikia's shade glides through the air; she is triumphant, and tenderly looks at her beloved Solor, who is at her feet." Recounting his impressions years after the fact, Benois described a special effect employed in the apotheosis: "For the last time, through a shower of golden rain, we see *la bayadère* who has now become a celestial being. The trick of the golden rain was much admired and even commented on in the newspapers."[175]

As *La Bayadère* continued to hold its place in the St. Petersburg repertory during the years following the 1900 revival, important debuts were made in the role of Nikia alongside Pavlova, who continued to perform the role until her last Mariinsky performance. Moreover, the Kingdom of the Shades emerged as a favorite scene chosen for special performances.

The Shades scene was performed at a costume ball held at the Winter Palace on 11 February 1903, at which guests wore seventeenth-century Russian costumes: Emperor Nikolai II and Empress Alexandra Feodorovna were dressed as Tsar and Tsarina. Pavlova danced the role of Nikia, to the chagrin of Kshesinskaya.[176] On 12 February 1906, Pavel Gerdt's forty-five years of service were celebrated with a benefit performance that included the third and fifth scenes of *La Bayadère*. As Solor, he partnered Pavlova as Nikia, with Evgenia Obukhova as Hamsatti.[177] Gerdt finally relinquished the role to Mikhail Fokine on 19 September 1907.[178]

A complete rendition of *La Bayadère* was given at a benefit performance for Pavlova marking her ten years of service on 15 November 1909. She was partnered by Samuil Andrianov as Solor and joined by Sedova (Hamsatti), Gerdt (Rajah), and Olga Fedorova, who made her debut in the Hindu dance.[179] Just over three years later, having firmly established her reputation in the West, Pavlova danced Nikia for her final performance at the Mariinsky Theater on 24 February 1913. She was partnered once again by Andrianov, with Egorova as Hamsatti and Gerdt as the Rajah.[180]

---

[172] Konaev, "Der Tiger Captif," 45. See *La Sainte Bible selon la Vulgate. Traduction nouvelle avec les dessins de Gustave Doré*, 2 vols. (Tours: Alfred Mame et fils, 1866).

[173] The photograph is reproduced in the Staatsballett Berlin *La Bayadère* program book (2018), 62–63.

[174] The Rep includes forty-two bars, of which twenty-four are cut; the PR includes just eighteen bars, matching the Rep after cuts.

[175] Benois, *Reminiscences*, 44.

[176] See *Khronika IV*, 43.

[177] *Khronika IV*, 82.

[178] Until this date, Gerdt had performed the role Solor in every performance of *La Bayadère* since the 1900 revival, with the exception of a single performance by Sergei Legat on 4 September 1905. Thanks to Andrew Foster for this information.

[179] *Khronika IV*, 121.

[180] Ibid., 161.

Several seasons earlier, Andrianov had partnered a new Nikia in an auspicious debut: Tamara Karsavina danced the leading role for the first time to great acclaim on 10 February 1910 after several seasons as a successful *Manu* soloist.[181] Gerdt was her Rajah, Egorova danced Hamsatti, and Vaganova, Vill, and Elena Smirnova performed the solo shades.[182] Another important debut was made shortly before the Revolution at a charity performance for the benefit of the Elizabethan Society of Sisters of Mercy, given on 16 April 1916. The program featured a duet from the Kingdom of the Shades and marked the first (albeit excerpted) performances in the roles of Nikia and Solor by Olga Spesivtseva and Anatole Obukhov.[183] Spesivtseva would dance the role in the West in Sergeyev's reduced version of the Kingdom of the Shades (of which more will be said later in this chapter).

The elimination of Act Four from the St. Petersburg (then Petrograd) production in the 1920s has long been the subject of speculation. When did it happen and why? Natalia Zozulina recently has determined that the final act was permanently dropped in 1924 for a confluence of reasons that includes, among others, the inexperience of the ballerinas performing *La Bayadère*'s leading roles, the condition of the décor (which may have sustained water damage in 1924), and the entire ballet itself, which was considered by the theater management to lack artistic value.[184] Certainly the loss of the ballet's climactic scene changed its dramatic trajectory significantly, despite the fact that certain segments of the *pas d'action* from Act Four were eventually subsumed into the Act Two divertissement. Petipa's version of the final act would not be restored in St. Petersburg until the earlier years of the twenty-first century.[185]

In *La Bayadère* we encounter a structure somewhat different from the ballets we have thus far discussed. Instead of a series of scenes that balance mime and action with set dances and *pas d'action*, as we found in *Giselle* and *Le Corsaire* as well as much of *Paquita*, *La Bayadère* is frontloaded with two lengthy expository mime scenes—the Festival of Fire and the Two Rivals—that feature little dancing. These are followed by three scenes consisting mostly of dance and little mime—the festival of Badrinata, the Kingdom of the Shades, and the wedding of Solor and Hamsatti. Petipa programmed a single, modestly cast *pas d'action* (in his favored format of entrée, adagio, variations, and coda), but he strategically placed it in the ballet's final scene in order to create an exciting dénouement that combined dance and mime. (The eventual excision of this final scene robbed the ballet of this carefully calculated ending.)

Petipa's *pas d'action* featured an element that was not uncommon in the repertory of the St. Petersburg Imperial Ballet but would likely be incomprehensible today—an

---

[181] Karsavina made her debut in the *Manu* dance on 3 September 1906. See *Khronika IV*, 85, and Foster, *Karsavina*, 105.

[182] *Khronika IV*, 128, and Foster, *Karsavina*, 105.

[183] *Khronika IV*, 195.

[184] Natalia Zozulina, "'Bayaderka' M. Petipa: K voprosu o chetvertom akte baleta" [M. Petipa's *Bayaderka*: To the Question about the Fourth Act of the Ballet], *Vestnik Akademii Russkogo baleta imeni A. Ya. Vaganovoy* [Bulletin of the Academy of the Russian Ballet named after A. Ya. Vaganova] 5 (2018): 36. Zozulina writes: "Thus, if we have managed to correctly build the system of arguments, the answer to the question, when was the last time Petipa's *La Bayadère* went on the stage of the Mariinsky Theater in four acts, there will be two dates in 1924: either 21 September or 10 December." See also Boris A. Illarionov, "'Bayaderka': Chetyre ili tri?" [*Bayaderka*: Four or Three?], *Vestnik Akademii Russkogo baleta imeni A. Ya. Vaganovoy* [Bulletin of the Academy of Russian Ballet named after A. Ya. Vaganova] 4 (2017): 28–39.

[185] For details about Sergei Vikharev's 2002 production of *La Bayadère* for the Mariinsky Ballet, see Gershenzon, "*La Bayadère*."

additional cavalier who served as an alt-Solor and who was sometimes onstage at the same time as the real Solor. This arrangement, while requiring the suspension of narrative coherence on the part of the audience, served the purpose of allowing the aging Pavel Gerdt to assume the mime and most of the partnering duties of the leading man (at which he excelled) while relieving him of the rigors of virtuosic dancing, which were entrusted to the younger, nameless cavalier.

A feature of *La Bayadère* that contrasts strongly with the earlier ballets we have discussed is its near complete lack of humor. Aside from the witty and charming *Manu* dance in Scene III and the comic *Sakodusa* (about which we know little) in the fourth scene, *Bayadère* is every inch a serious drama, with jealousy, revenge, broken vows, and forbidden love driving its plot.

We have already studied Petipa's handling of a large cast of adults and children in the divertissement *Le jardin animé*. In *La Bayadère*, we find further examples. The festival scene in the 1900 revival featured seventy-two performers that included corps de ballet, children, and non-dancing participants. In addition to their own dances, the ensemble formed elaborate groupings that framed the stage for soloists and small-group dances. And as we found in the coda of *Le jardin animé*, the festival coda included polyphonic choreography as the different groups of dancers performed discrete enchaînements simultaneously. All of this was preceded by a procession for which Petipa had originally planned to include more than two hundred participants, some of whom (according to the CN) were given danced entrances. In the Kingdom of the Shades, the dancers in the large corps de ballet—forty-eight women strong—are not divided into various groups but instead all represent the same character (a shade) and perform unison steps *en masse*. Not only do they frame the stage during the dances of Nikia and the other soloists, but they also mirror their choreography, thereby amplifying the visual impact of the movement.

The constellation of available source documents allows us to follow the development of Petipa's initial plans into a libretto and then into mime scripts (the latter document including far more detail than the preceding two) and a choreographic notation. Moreover, the precise and detailed source material that preserves the mime and choreography for much of the production in separate, finished documents provides a tantalizing example of the way other St. Petersburg productions might have been recorded if time and resources had been available. In particular, the mime scripts for *Bayadère's* opening scenes confirm that mime exchanges in Imperial Ballet productions were real conversations, similar to those recorded by Justamant in his staging manuals.

These elements—dance and mime—are supported by Minkus's specialist score, which is characterized by exoticist tropes familiar in many nineteenth-century works. More significant, however, are Minkus's simple yet effective recurring melodies and rhythmic figure and his use of them to create continuity.

Finally, we note that Petipa's plans for the Kingdom of the Shades describe a scene that is more magical and fantastical—with its references to *Giselle* and imagery of Nikia "in the water"—than the one that has been handed down over time. Moreover, the libretto for the scene provides only a scant narrative, and the choreographic notation of it, documenting Petipa's revival in 1900, records what is essentially a series of academic dances. Perhaps this emphasis on pure dance has contributed to the longevity of the Kingdom of the Shades, allowing it to transcend changing tastes and become part of the canon of classical ballet.

La Bayadère in the West

Both character and classical dances from *La Bayadère* began to make their way West during the early decades of the twentieth century, long before the celebrated performance of the Kingdom of the Shades by the Kirov Ballet in Paris in 1961. For instance, the raucous Hindu dance (No. 14½) from Scene III made for an energetic closing number of a divertissement. Its relatively small cast combined with high-energy character choreography was an appealing choice for inclusion on touring programs that often catered to music hall audiences. The dance was likely the final item on the program of divertissements offered by the "Famous Russian Dancers" during its May 1910 season at London's Coliseum. There the number was titled "Indian Dance," with music credited to Minkus and a cast of one woman and six men.[186] Similarly, a "Danse Hindu" from *La Bayadère* was on Anna Pavlova's program for her tour of Britain in 1911 that included Alexander Shiryaev among its dancers.[187]

But it was the Kingdom of the Shades that was the jewel of *La Bayadère* and a personal favorite of Nikolai Sergeyev. Jane Pritchard and Sergey Konaev have chronicled Sergeyev's various attempts—both successes and failures—to stage the Kingdom of the Shades in the West.[188] While still in Petrograd, he requested that it be programmed for his farewell benefit performance in September 1917, but the performance itself was denied.[189] Once in the West, Sergeyev was no less enthusiastic. Konaev puts it plainly: "Of the corps de ballet dances by Petipa, Sergeyev especially valued the 'Shades,' which he was ready to stage no matter what plot was used as a pretext."[190] Accordingly, he fashioned the three scenes of the third act of *La Bayadère* into a one-act ballet with a slender, exoticist narrative to accompany the dances. He called it *Le Songe du Rajah*, but it was sometimes presented with a variant title, such as *Le Rêve du radjah*. A variety of source materials preserved in the Sergeyev Collection contributes to our knowledge of this little-known redaction from *La Bayadère*. We will discuss them in the context of its diverse stagings.

Sergeyev first set the Kingdom of the Shades in the West for the Latvian National Ballet. The one-act version premiered on 28 November 1923 in Riga on a program that also featured Sergeyev's staging of *The Magic Flute*, a two-act ballet with music by Drigo and choreography by Ivanov.[191] Ten performances were given.[192]

Several of Harvard's music holdings relating to *Le Songe du Rajah* appear to have originated in connection with these Riga performances. They include an orchestra score, several piano reductions, and orchestra parts. The 116-page manuscript orchestra score,

[186] Pritchard, "Bits of Bayadere."
[187] Beumers et al., *Alexander Shiryaev*, 137.
[188] See Pritchard, "Bits of Bayadere," and Konaev, "My vse visim v vozdukhe . . ."
[189] St. Petersburg newspapers chronicled Sergeyev's request and its subsequent denial: "Troubles about a benefit performance. At the next general meeting of the ballet troupe's artists, the issue of granting the former chief regisseur Mr. Sergeyev a farewell benefit will be put on the agenda. Mr. Sergeyev asked for a benefit performance on 22 October and chose *La Bayadère*. According to rumors, the male staff of the troupe spoke out against the benefit performance for Mr. Sergeyev, finding that all his past activities did not deserve a reward." *Petrogradskaya gazeta*, 22 September 1917, no. 223, 5. The denial was reported in the *Petrogradsky golos* on 10 May 1918: "The former chief regisseur of the ballet, Mr. Sergeyev, turned to the troupe committee with a request to give him a benefit performance. The issue was discussed at a general meeting of artists and was decided negatively by a majority of several votes." Thanks to Sergey Belenky for providing these citations.
[190] Konaev, "My vse visim v vozdukhe . . ." 560.
[191] Konaev, "My vse visim v vozdukhe . . .," 580n63 (the year in the essay should read "1923" instead of "1924").
[192] See Stals, *Lettische Ballett*, 51.

dated 7 March 1923, is in the same hand and format as other scores in the Sergeyev Collection that indicate they were copied (and likely arranged) in Riga during Sergeyev's years there as ballet master.[193] Titled *Le Songe du Rajah* (The Rajah's Dream), the score includes the entirety of *La Bayadère* Act Three with minor adjustments. These include cuts in Scene IV (likely corresponding to cuts in the Rep) and an added transition to bridge Scenes V and VI. Markings in crayon, ink, and pencil include annotations in French and English, suggesting the score was used for subsequent performances in France and England. Of particular interest among the otherwise expected musical annotations are metronome markings for the danced numbers.[194] Ideally, these tell us the tempi at which Sergeyev intended the numbers to be danced. The score is also annotated with cues for entrances and lighting. Supplementing this score are three annotated manuscript piano reductions (two in ink, one in pencil) and a set of manuscript orchestra parts.[195] A manuscript synopsis of *Le Songe du Rajah* in French and signed by Sergeyev is also among the holdings.[196]

In 1926 Sergeyev staged a version of the Kingdom of the Shades in Paris using the title *Le Songe du radjah*. The performance was given on 26 July 1926 at the Cercle Interalliée (Le Cercle de l'Union Interalliée, a political club) for the Moroccan Sultan Moulay Youseff (Mulai Yusef), who was visiting Paris to open a new mosque. The reduced cast featured Olga Spesivtseva and Serge Peretti in the leading roles, joined by an ensemble of eight women.[197] An enthusiastic notice in *Excelsior* provided a summary of the event:

THE "DREAM OF THE RAJAH" UNDER THE EYES OF THE SULTAN

During the beautiful celebration that took place on Monday evening at the Union Interalliée, in honor of S. M. Moulay-Youssef, a ballet, "le Songe de radjah" [sic], of a perfect grace, very prettily costumed, after the sketches of prince A. Shervaschidze, and perfectly arranged by M.N. Sergueeff to music by Mincus, was danced by Mlle. O. Spessivtzewa, of the Opéra, by M. Peretti, also of the Opéra, and by Mlles. Petri, Tikanoff, Berry, Oulianovskaia, Soumarokoff, Alexeeva, Kirova and Tomina.[198]

---

[193] MS Thr 145 (111). See Wiley, "Dances from Russia," 99.

[194] The metronome markings are listed here as they correspond to the numbering in the Rep:

No. 5 ♩ = 60
No. 6 ♩. = 72
No. 10 ♩ = 60
No. 11 ♩. = 60
No. 12 ♩ = 108; middle section, ♩ = 80; final section, ♩ = 136
No. 13 ♩. = 72
No. 14 ♪ = 120; last five bars, ♩ = 88
No. 16 ♩. = 80; corps de ballet after Nikia and Solor entrance, ♩. = 144; final bars, preceding an
  allargando, ♩. = 180

[195] MS Thr 245 (107): *Le Songe du Rajah*, manuscript piano reduction, 41 pages, pencil, includes a list of orchestra parts (see item 113); (110): *Le Songe du Rajah*, manuscript piano reduction, 36 pages, ink; (112): *Le Songe du Rajah*, manuscript piano reduction, ink, in a similar hand and with a similar layout to item 110; (113): 37 manuscript orchestra parts, ink. The score and parts are marked to indicate that Variation 3 was to be played before Variation 2, indicating that in at least one performance or set of performances the variations were reordered.

[196] MS Thr 245 (112). The text is reproduced in Wiley, "Dances from Russia," 101. Item 262 is another copy of the synopsis in French, unsigned.

[197] For further details about the performance, see Konaev, "My vse visim v vozdukhe . . .," 583n75.

[198] *Excelsior*, 28 July 1926, 2. Alexander Konstantinovich Shervashidze (Chachba) was an Abkhaz artist, painter, art historian, and critic. Sergeyev had commissioned the designs from him. See Konaev, "My vse visim v vozdukhe . . .," 562, 566, 569–570, 572.

One of two photos accompanying the notice includes the entire cast of the ballet in costumes similar in style to the 1900 Mariinsky production, complete with veils.

The printed program, from which the information in the *Excelsior* notice was drawn, was laid out as follows.

Soirée en l'honneur de Sa Majesté le Sultan du Maroc

"LE SONGE DU RADJAH"

Costumes d'aprés les Maquettes
du Prince A. Shervaschidze

Réglé par M.N. Sergueeff
Musique de Mincus

L'Ombre Fiancée du Solor	Mlle O. Spessivtzewa, *de l'Opéra*
Radjah—Solor	M. Peretti, *de l'Opéra*
Les Ombres	Mlles Petri, Tikanoff, Oulianovskaïa, Soumarokoff, Alexeeva, Kirova, Tomina

ARGUMENT

Dans le château de SOLOR règne le silence; les chants se sont éteints, toutes joies ont disparu depuis le temps où l'esclave favorite est morte. Le Radjad puissant s'afflige et ses rêves l'emportent vers la jolie femme trépassée dont la voix était tellement magique.

La flute et les danses atteignent les limites les plus hautes. Les Fakirs voyant leur Radjad accablé veulent le guérir au moyen d'une conjuration.

Le Radjad, au comble du désespoir, enjoint à tous de se retirer. Il fume de l'opium, s'assoupit et se trouve transporté dans le monde de la fantaisie; des nuages s'approchent de lui et, lentement, provenant d'eux, se dessinent des ombres au milieu desquelles, le Radjad reconnaît son esclave bien aimée, qui l'emmène dans son royaume.[199]

Under the title *Le Rêve du radjah*, Sergeyev staged his ballet a second time in Paris for a performance given in observance of the second anniversary of Anna Pavlova's death on 23 January 1933 at the Théâtre des Champs-Elysées.[200] This time the leading roles were performed by Sergeyev's wife Evgenia Poplavskaya and Henry Taneyev.[201]

A folder of choreographic notations in the Sergeyev Collection gives us an idea of the choreography Sergeyev staged for his various productions of *Le Songe du Rajah*.[202] The folder includes two title pages: one headed "Bayaderka" and the other "Song-Radjah | 1930—Paris | NS." The dances are documented on plain paper that Sergeyev divided into a grid of eight squares. Stepanov symbols are used to notate movements for the legs and feet (on handwritten staves), as well as the direction of the hips, below corresponding ground

---

[199] Program for *Soirée en l'honneur de Sa Majesté le Sultan du Maroc* courtesy of Lynn Garafola.

[200] Pavlova died in The Hague on 23 January 1931.

[201] For an example of a press announcement of the event, see *Le petit journal*, 21 November 1932, 4, wherein the ballet is attributed to Sergeyev.

[202] MS Thr 245 (106).

plans. These pages, in Sergeyev's hand, reveal how he revised the third act for an ensemble of dancers that was far smaller in number than the forces available at the Mariinsky.

The entrance of the shades is arranged for twelve women. After the opening serpentine entrance, the women dance in pairs then form two circles that eventually consolidate into one large circle that contracts, expands, and rotates. The following *pas de trois* with corps de ballet is an exact copy of the dance recorded in the *Bayadère* CN. Next, a second version of the shades' entrance, this one for ten corps and three soloists, is struck through. An "Adagio" follows, comprised of various poses and groupings for twelve women. Some of the ground plans are similar to those of No. 11, the *Grand Adage*, suggesting this represents Sergeyev's reworking of the ensemble choreography performed during Nikia and Solor's second *pas de deux*. (As with the *Bayadère* CN, the first adagio is not included.)

Corps de ballet groupings accompanying the four variations follow: for Variation 1, a chain of five dancers on each side of the stage, placed upstage; for Variation 2, similar chains but positioned downstage; for Variation 3, a diagonal line from upstage left; and for Variation 4, a line of dancers along each wing. The solo variations are also notated, duplicating what is found in the *Bayadère* CN for legs and feet. Variation 4 is not among the notations.

The coda begins as in the *Bayadère* CN: the corps' movements are notated below ground plans that also include the three soloists. The "ballerina and cavalier" make their same diagonal entrance; their choreography is also notated. When the corps begins to dance again (see Ex. 9.44c), we encounter some revisions. Sergeyev brings the three soloists back. They traverse the stage in a pattern similar to their first coda entrance, while the corps continues to dance by the wings. Eventually the corps forms two rows behind the soloists and perform steps familiar from the *Bayadère* CN: *cabriole derrière*, *assemblé*, *entrechat six* twice. The ensemble *bourrées* to the sides just before the ballerina makes her final entrance—the same as in the *Bayadère* CN—accompanied by the corps. The end of the coda is not documented.

The final pages of the folder comprise a collection of various parts of *Le Songe de Rajah* plus an additional dance. Two pages look as though they may be a rough draft of Variation 1 from the Kingdom of the Shades that was eventually recopied in finished form in the *Bayadère* CN. The scribal hand is the same, but the ground plans are drawn from the stage perspective, movements for arms, head, and torso are omitted, and a straight edge is not used for bar lines and some note stems as it is in the finished copy. Although the steps are essentially the same as in the final draft, some details differ. For example, *pas de bourrée* that are notated on *pointe* in the *Bayadère* CN are notated here on *demi-pointe*, and *pas de chat* in the finished copy are *glissades* in the incomplete version. If the hand of the potential rough draft is indeed Sergeyev's, that fact would support the notion that Sergeyev made the finished notation as well. That this page is among Sergeyev's papers is also support for his authorship. The final two numbers in the folder are a "Hindu dance" in $\frac{3}{4}$ meter for a solo woman (not on *pointe*) and a *pas de trois* in $\frac{2}{4}$ meter for three women (on *pointe*)—"'Mirlitons' mus[ic by] Tchaikovsky"—presumably from *The Nutcracker*.

Wiley has observed that with *Le Songe du Rajah* Sergeyev "was trying to exploit the Parisians' [and, by extension, Western Europeans'] long-standing fascination with Russian art, in particular the Russian variety of Orientalism that Diaghilev first popularized there in 1909." Citing *Cléopâtre* and *Shéhérezade* for comparison, he notes that the ballet's scenario "is highly derivative in plot and language from the scenarios of works featured in Diaghilev's early seasons."[203] Despite these narrative similarities, however, Sergeyev was working with music composed in the 1870s, which certainly was regarded as passé compared with the new works commissioned and championed by Diaghilev. Likewise, the character choreography of the "Fakir's dance" (see below), and perhaps even the strictly academic step vocabulary of the Kingdom of the Shades, must have seemed outdated in contrast to the freshness of new works by Fokine, Nijinsky, and other Ballets Russes protégés.

Perhaps due to such perceptions in Paris, most of Sergeyev's attempts to stage the Kingdom of the Shades in England were thwarted. The English dancer Harcourt Algeranoff recounted Sergeyev's attempt to stage the scene for Anna Pavlova's company in 1927:

> A few days after the tour [of England] started Nicolai Sergueeff arrived to stage *La Bayadère* for the Company. Pavlova began rehearsing the *pas de deux*, and I can see her now as she held the *à la seconde* on *pointe*, while [Laurent] Novikov left her and then returned to her and took her hand. The *corps de ballet* had very dull work, and Sergueef, who could not speak in English at all at that time, kept trying to make the character dancers do the classic work. The English girls tried to say "*Ya Charakternaya*" but to no effect. Then he started rehearsing the Fakir's dance, with John Sergeieff and Aubrey Hitchins. It was so *démodé* that the Company were having hysterics—only Sergueeff was serious. Pavlova saw it, and then she realised that it was no good trying to revive this old monstrosity which had once been good in Russia; the Fakir's dance settled it. Sergueeff was paid and returned to Paris. No diplomacy could soothe his hurt. "*The Rajarh's Drim*," as he often called it in later years, was a great favorite of his (twenty years later he gave the choreography to Mona Inglesby as a wedding present!). He never spoke kindly of Pavlova afterwards.[204]

In the early 1930s Sergeyev tried to persuade Marie Rambert to let him stage *Le Songe du Rajah* for her Ballet Club. Her response seems representative of the times:

> Nicholas Sergueeff, who had been ballet-master at the Maryinsky, was now working as ballet-master at Sadler's Wells. Every time I met him he told me there was something very important he wanted to talk to me about. So I invited him and his wife to lunch, and he told me all about a ballet he wanted to put on. It was a terribly trite story about a Rajah or a Sultan and all his wives. He insisted on telling me every trivial detail.
> So I said, "In what way can I help you?"
> "Well," he replied, "I thought you might like to put it on at your theatre."
> "Why not at Sadler's Wells?"
> "Oh, that's much too small!"[205]

It took forming his own company to allow Sergeyev the opportunity to stage the Kingdom of the Shades again. Opening on 5 March 1934, Sergeyev's Russian Ballet gave eight performances of *The Rajah's Dream* at Bournemouth Pavilion while on tour in England.[206] The leading roles were again danced by Poplavskaya and Taneyev, the same

---

[203] Wiley, "Dances from Russia," 100.

[204] Harcourt Algeranoff, *My Years with Pavlova* (London: William Heinemann, 1957), 165. See also Pritchard, "Bits of Bayadere."

[205] Marie Rambert, *Quicksilver* (New York: St. Martin's Press, 1972), 138. See also Pritchard, "Bits of Bayadere."

[206] Pritchard, "Bits of Bayadere," 1121.

cast as for the Paris performance the year before. This time, the ballet included a *Danse Orientale* in its opening scene, performed by a female dancer to music likely composed by Lischke.[207] (This may be the music for the solo "Hindu dance" included in the choreographic notation described above.) The rest of the cast included two fakirs and eleven shades. The designs were by the Russian painter Konstantin Korovin.[208]

The brief scenario included in the program is essentially a translation of the earlier French synopsis, with a sentence added for the *Danse Orientale*:

> The Rajah "Solor" surrounded by his wives and slaves, mourns the death of his beautiful wife with the enchanted voice. One of his slaves, wishing to distract him, dances before him; the Rajah sleeps; the flute and the dances continue becoming more and more splendid. The Fakirs, seeing the Rajah so prostrate, wish to cure him by means of a spell. The Rajah, overwhelmed with despair, tells them all to go away; he smokes opium, falls asleep and finds himself transported into the world of Fantasy. The stars spin round, the clouds growing larger, come towards him, throwing shadows, among which the Rajah recognises his beloved slave, who takes him away at last into her kingdom.[209]

One final attempt to present the Kingdom of the Shades ended in disappointment for Sergeyev. In 1947, after working with International Ballet for six years, Sergeyev persuaded Mona Inglesby to allow him to stage his one-act Kingdom of the Shades. Rehearsals progressed, with Nana Gollner and Paul Petrov in the principal roles, but the production never made it to the stage.[210] Various reasons were given, but it is likely that post-war tastes had moved beyond Sergeyev's outdated aesthetics.[211] While sympathetic to Sergeyev's desires and understanding of his disappointment, Mona Inglesby let the project go: "Personally, I found the choreography of *La Bayadère* quite enchanting in spite of the old fashioned music, and I was very sad that the ballet never came to be performed by International Ballet."[212] Sergeyev, who died four years later in Nice, had seen the last of his beloved shades.

---

[207] A manuscript full score for oboe and strings (*Danse Orientale* with "Mus[ic] de C. Lischké | Paris," ink) and manuscript piano reduction ("K. Lischke. Oriental. For Mr. Sergeev," in Russian, pencil) are part of the Sergeyev Collection. See MS Thr 245 (108) and (109), respectively.

[208] Sketches of three male costumes and two scenic designs by Konstantin Korovin that may represent this production are also part of the Sergeyev Collection. See Ms Thr 245 (249) and (250), respectively.

[209] MS Thr 245 (283), qtd. in Pritchard, "Bits of Bayadère," 1121.

[210] The orchestra score, MS 245 Thr (111), includes names of International Ballet dancers among its annotations: "Sandra [Vane] & Domini [Callaghan], Herida [May]" and "Jack S[purgeon] & Bayadere."

[211] See Inglesby, *Ballet in the Blitz*, 96–98.

[212] Ibid., 98.

10

Raymonda

"Glazunov's music for *Raymonda* contains some of the finest ballet music we have," wrote George Balanchine. "And Petipa's original choreography, which I remember from student appearances at the Maryinsky Theatre, was superb."[1] In three acts and four scenes, with an apotheosis, *Raymonda* was set in the Middle Ages on a "subject taken from knightly legends," as the libretto tells us. Several of its characters were even based on historical figures, though their relationships to one another are likely the invention of the librettist, Lydia Pashkova.

Raymonda was Marius Petipa's last evening-length ballet to achieve longevity. The work featured a score by the acclaimed young Russian composer Alexander Glazunov, and Ivan Vsevolozhsky, the Francophile director of the Imperial Theaters, designed the costumes. Created to showcase the talents of the great Italian virtuosa Pierina Legnani, *Raymonda* calls upon the title character to appear in all four of the ballet's scenes and dance in a variety of styles, performing a wide-ranging step vocabulary. The plot, with its elaborate celebrations as well as the presence of denizens of a medieval court in Provence joined by visitors from Arabia, Spain, and Hungary, provided opportunities aplenty for both character and classical dance, and indeed the ballet favors dance over story.

The premiere on 7 January 1898 at the Mariinsky Theater was met with great approbation. Legnani received rapturous notices in the press, and Petipa was lauded with the respect due an octogenarian who had led the Imperial Ballet in St. Petersburg to unprecedented heights of artistic achievement.[2] Yet despite *Raymonda*'s initial success and continuing presence on the stage, its slight narrative led to frequent criticism throughout the twentieth century.

Raymonda's *plot, exoticism, and nineteenth-century Crusade narratives.* The story told in Pashkova's relatively brief libretto centers around the countess Raymonda, who apparently lives in Provence and is engaged to the knight Jean de Brienne. Awaiting his return home from the Crusades, she is warned in a dream of danger ahead and then wooed by Abderrakhman, a Middle Eastern Muslim warrior, who ultimately attempts to kidnap her.[3] Jean de Brienne arrives in the nick of time to save his fiancée by felling Abderrakhman in a duel, and the happy couple's wedding is celebrated in the presence of King Andrei II of Hungary, in whose honor a Hungarian-themed divertissement is performed.

---

[1] Balanchine and Mason, *Complete Stories*, 500.

[2] *Khronika III*, 343–345. The performance was a benefit for Legnani. See Wiley, *Century*, 393. Perhaps in deference to Petipa at his advanced age—he was nearly eighty years old when *Raymonda* premiered— newspaper writers focused on the totality of Petipa's career-long contributions rather than the specifics of his work in *Raymonda*.

[3] The sources frequently use the term Saracen to describe Abderrakhman and members of his entourage. Saracen, from the Greek *sarakenos* (meaning "Easterner"), was used pejoratively by medieval Christian writers to refer to Muslim people (including Arabs, Turks, and others), who were regarded as enemies of Christianity. We will use the term in this chapter only as it is used in the sources.

Five Ballets from Paris and St. Petersburg. Doug Fullington and Marian Smith, Oxford University Press.
© Oxford University Press 2024. DOI: 10.1093/oso/9780190944506.003.0011

Let us enumerate the various circumstances that call for the stage to be populated with picturesquely costumed characters, both children and adults: a celebration involving ladies and pages of the court, vassals, and forty-eight dancers of the *Valse provençale* (Act One, Scene I); a dream sequence calling for knights and *farfadets* (Act One, Scene II);[4] a performance at Abderrakhman's behest intended to impress Raymonda with the glories of the Muslim "Orient," in which Moriscos, sixty-one Saracen slaves, and eighteen dancers of the *Panadéros* dance (Act Two) participate;[5] and Raymonda's wedding, at which appear multitudinous performers of the *Rapsodie, Palotás,* and mazurka (Act Three). Lending an air of fantasized reality to the proceedings is the setting in Provence as well as the presence of historical figures, including the celebrated troubadour Bernard de Ventadour (Bernat de Ventadorn, in old Occitan spelling), the crusader Jean de Brienne, the Countess Sybil, King Andrew of Hungary, and, possibly, Raymonda herself.[6] The White Lady, the supernatural patroness of Raymonda's family, appears to have been lifted directly from the pages of Sir Walter Scott's 1820 novel *The Monastery,* in which a character of the same name is the supernatural guardian of the House of Avenal.[7]

The Muslim antagonist Abderrakhman is not based on a particular historical figure, but rather represents a generalized bad-acting "Oriental" man onto whom unfavorable characteristics are projected: he is evil and barbaric, in stark contrast to the refined, righteous, and courtly Christians who are the heroes of the plot. The librettists' approach to the story, then, is quite in keeping with nineteenth-century Western, Islamophobic accounts of the Crusades—including Chateaubriand's—which held that the crusaders were "armed pilgrims who merely avenged the violence of 'Omar's descendents' and liberated Jesus' grave in Jerusalem."[8] Therefore, when Jean de Brienne fells Abderrakhman

---

[4] *Farfadets* are creatures of French folklore, resembling sprites or pixies.

[5] Moriscos refers to Muslims converted or coerced into converting to Christianity after Spain outlawed the practice of Islam in the early sixteenth century. While the term post-dates the Crusades by several centuries, its use broadly reinforces the Spanish connection to Arab peoples depicted in the plot of *Raymonda.*

[6] Bernart de Ventadorn (1135–1194) was a Provençal troubadour who lived at the court of Eleanor of Aquitaine and then at Toulouse. John of Brienne (c. 1170–1237) became king of Jerusalem (1210–1225) and Latin emperor of Constantinople (1231–1237) and was active in the Fifth Crusade, whose first contingent was led by his contemporary, Andrew II (1175–1235), king of Hungary. Sibyl (1160–1190) was queen of Jerusalem (1186–1190), reigning alongside her husband, Guy of Lusignan. (She was also countess of Jaffa and Ascalon.) Perhaps the only medieval counterpart of the character of Raymonda heretofore identified is Raymonde, daughter of Raymond VI (1194–1222), count of Toulouse, who became a nun at the monastery of Espinasse. See Claude Devic and Joseph Vaissette, *Histoire Générale de Languedoc,* vol. 5, ed. Alexandre Du Mège (Toulouse: J.-B. Paya, 1842), 404: "Nous apprenons d'un ancien monument que Raymond VI, comte de Toulouse, eut un hlle [sic] nommée Raymonde, qu'il aimoit beaucoup, et qu'il fit religieuse dans le monastere de l'Espinasse de l'ordre de Fontevraud au diocése de Toulouse . . ." [We learn from an ancient monument that Raymond VI, count of Toulouse, had a daughter named Raymonde, whom he loved very much, and whom he made a nun in the monastery of Espinasse of the order of Fontevraud in the diocese of Toulouse].

Note further that another character in the libretto, "Béranger, a troubadour of Aquitaine," may have been inspired by Berengueir de Palazol, a Catalan troubadour (fl. 1160–1209) or the nineteenth-century poet Laurent-Pierre Béranger (1749–1822). Finally, Abderrakhman and the troubadours Béranger and Bernard de Ventadour all are mentioned in Théophile Gautier's travel account, *Voyage en Espagne* (Paris: Charpentier, 1845).

[7] Walter Scott, *The Monastery. A Romance. By the Author of "Waverley."* In Three Volumes. Vol. I (II–III) (Edinburgh: Archibald Constable and John Ballantyne; London: Longman, Hurst, Rees, Orme, and Brown, 1820).

[8] Matthias Schwerendt and Ines Guhe, "Describing the Enemy: Images of Islam in Narratives of the Crusades," in *FrancoGerman Perspectives International Workshop—Research Group "Myths of the Crusades,"* Eckert.Dossiers 4 (2011): 5, https://repository.gei.de/bitstream/handle/11428/129/ED_2011_04_04_Schwerendt_Guhe_Describing_the_Enemy_Images_of_Islam.pdf?sequence=7&isAllowed=y. See François-René Chateaubriand, *Itinéraire de Paris à Jérusalem et de Jérusalem à Paris . . .* (Paris: Le Normant, 1811), and another Islamophobic account, Joseph-François Michaud and Jean-Joseph François Poujoulat, *Histoire des croisades, abrégée à l'usage de la jeunesse* (Tours: Mame, 1899). On the influences of Muslim artists in European courts of the Middle Ages, see W.S. Merwin, *The Mays of Ventadorn* (Washington, DC: National

at the end of Act Two, he does so remorselessly, and the Christian characters soon there-after, without qualms, take part in a joyous wedding celebration.

The presence of a Muslim character, too (whether good or evil), follows a pattern that Petipa had turned to before. As Nadine Meisner has pointed out, the plot of *Raymonda*, with its love triangle involving a Muslim character, bears similarities to the plots of two earlier Petipa ballets, *Roxana, the Beauty of Montenegro* (1878) and *Zoraiya, the Moorish Girl in Spain* (1881), both with librettos by Sergei Khudekov and Petipa.[9] *Roxana* is described by Meisner as "a patriotic response to the Russo-Turkish War of 1877–1878."[10] (Indeed, the ballet premiered just weeks before the end of the war.) The story depicts Slav Montenegrins under the rule of Muslim Ottomans (and even incorporates Wilis, who are, after all, Slavic!).[11] The Christian hero Ianko, who loves the orphan Roxana, disposes of his rival, the Muslim Radivoi, by throwing him off a bridge. In *Zoraiya*, set during the Granada-based Moorish occupation of Spain, both hero and heroine are Muslim. Abu Soliman (son of Caliph Abderraman) and the African tribal leader Ali-Ben-Tamarat vie for the hand of Zoraiya, who ultimately saves Soliman from the murderous Tamarat. Both *Roxana* and *Zoraiya* featured Muslim characters in serious, dramatic plots in con-trast to *Le Corsaire*, in which Islamic culture was largely depicted comedically. And in *Raymonda*, Abderrakhman is presented as a genuine threat to the heroine's safety.

A minor Russian novelist, journalist, and avid traveler, Pashkova had already written two librettos before creating *Raymonda: Cinderella* in 1893 and *Bluebeard* in 1896.[12] Her libretto for *Raymonda* has received much of the blame for the ballet's perceived inade-quacies.[13] In his critique of *Raymonda*, published nearly forty years after the premiere, Prince Peter Lieven summed up what he believed was the ballet's great shortcoming:

> I myself . . . could never follow the story of *Raymonda*. It has a wicked Saracen, a noble knight betrothed, a Hungarian king, a duel, a goblet with magic drink, and of course Raymonda herself, who, it appears, does not want to marry the Saracen; it has a finale and a *divertissement*—in a word, it has everything but meaning.[14]

Laying blame solely at Pashkova's feet, however, would be to overlook the contri-butions to the libretto by both Petipa and Vsevolozhsky. While authorship is ascribed

---

Geographic Society, 2002), Chapter 7. Nineteenth-century accounts of the Crusades are explored at length in Georg-Eckert-Institut für internationale Schulbuchforschung, ed., *European Receptions of the Crusades in the Nineteenth Century. Franco-German Perspectives International Workshop—Research Group "Myths of the Crusades,"* Eckert.Dossiers 4 (2011), https://repository.gei.de/bitstream/handle/11428/129/ED4_Crusades.pdf?sequence=3&isAllowed=y.

[9] Meisner, *Marius Petipa*, 249.

[10] Ibid., 120.

[11] Note the addition of a paragraph explaining the Slavic origins of the Wilis in the 1842 St. Petersburg *Giselle* libretto. See Appendix C (ii).

[12] On Lydia Pashkova (1850–1917), see Sergey Konaev's comments in Alastair Macaulay, Doug Fullington, and Sergey Konaev, "'Raymonda' and Ballet Herstory: historians Doug Fullington and Sergey Konaev on Lydia Pashkova, Ivan Vsevolozhsky, Marius Petipa and the Russian Imperial Theatres. A 'Raymonda' ques-tionnaire." *Alastair Macaulay* (blog), 21 January 2022, https://www.alastairmacaulay.com/all-essays/byq3y65 60y798jcrlmiwp4s4su9ii6. See also Wiley, *Lev Ivanov*, 157–158, and Meisner, *Marius Petipa*, 249.

[13] Mary Clarke and Clement Crisp refer to the "foolish and incomprehensible story." See Mary Clarke and Clement Crisp, *Ballet: An Illustrated History* (New York: Universe Books, 1973), 98. The author of the *Raymonda* entry in the *International Encyclopedia of Dance* refers to "the flaws of its libretto." See Karina L. Melik-Pashayeva, "Raymonda," in *International Encyclopedia of Dance*, vol. 5 (New York and Oxford: Oxford University Press, 1998), 321. Further, Arlene Croce found the score "lacking in theatrical momentum." Arlene Croce, *Afterimages* (New York: Knopf, 1977), 168.

[14] Prince Peter Lieven, *The Birth of the Ballets-Russes* (London: George Allen & Unwin, 1936), 71.

solely to Pashkova, Vsevolozhsky—himself an experienced librettist—had obtained the manuscript and sent it to Petipa. On 22 October 1895, he wrote to the choreographer, signaling his readiness to alter the libretto according to Petipa's instructions: "Dear Mr Petipa! Attached to this is Mme. Pashkova's manuscript. You could do something with it. There is little dance; on the other hand, there is too much pantomime. When you have a moment of time, you will tell me what to do."[15] Over the next year, both Vsevolozhsky and Petipa made significant revisions to Pashkova's scenario. Citing a variety of correspondence between the two and between Petipa and Glazunov during this period, Pavel Gershenzon concluded, "It is clear from this correspondence that Ivan Vsevolozhsky personally reworked Lydia Pashkova's scenario for *Raymonda*. As a result, it was this variant on which Glazunov's and Petipa's work was based."[16]

The structure of Raymonda: *emphasis on spectacle and dance.* The ballet is spread over four scenes, and its division of action and dance within scenes is much like that in *Sleeping Beauty* (1890): each of the ballet's scenes is centered around a suite of dances (or two, as in the case of *Raymonda's* second act). The emphasis on dance is made clear from the beginning: the expository opening scene is dominated by a dance sequence (the *Valse provençale*) and the ballet even opens with dancing at curtain-up: we are introduced to Raymonda's friends first as dancers rather than characters with personalities. The plot is thin, and spectacle—large-scale dance suites filled with prop-wielding performers, appearances and disappearances through trapdoors in the stage, and a lavish apotheosis featuring knights astride horses—replaces action. Roland John Wiley explains:

> *Raymonda* stresses ceremony over substance, dancing over story. The exhaustive list of dances and performers and the fussy subdivisions of the text in the libretto call attention to individual numbers at the expense of the story-line. . . . Petipa emphasized dancing for its own sake in ballets subsequent to *Raymonda*, continuing his turn away from narrative dramas on which he had built his reputation towards brief, plotless ballets of a kind later taken up by Fokine. *Raymonda* and *The Magic Mirror* [1903] are exceptional because a scanty narrative is spread over a long time span, and executed choreographically in the grand manner associated with the dramatic ballets of previous decades.[17]

Tim Scholl concurs on the matter of Petipa's tendency away from narrative dramas: "The quality and quantity of the choreography in *Raymonda* evidenced Petipa's interest in dancing, rather than narrative, late in his career."[18] *Raymonda* therefore may be viewed as a step toward abstraction, its plot serving primarily as the means to connect the ballet's various dance suites.[19] That being said, recall that Petipa was working with a ballerina (Legnani) who was far more a technician than an actor and therefore was much more suited to dance than mime. Her strengths as a virtuoso dancer were many and her range

---

[15] Quoted in Pavel Gershenzon's excellent annotated timeline detailing the genesis of *Raymonda*, "Cronografia di *Raymonda*: Lettere, documenti, recensioni, commenti," tr. Carla Muschio, in *Raymonda* program book (Milan: Teatro alla Scala, 2011), 47.

[16] Gershenzon, "Cronografia di *Raymonda*," 51.

[17] Wiley, *Century*, 392.

[18] Scholl, *Petipa to Balanchine*, 139n19.

[19] For a discussion of the move toward abstract dance in Russian ballet at the turn of the twentieth century, see Scholl, *Petipa to Balanchine*, 11–12, 40–43, and 144n25.

broad. Therefore the ballet becomes a showcase for the ballerina: Raymonda performs no fewer than fourteen numbers that demonstrate her mastery of many types of classical dance as well as elements of Hungarian character dance (or at least a flavor of it in her *Pas classique hongrois*).

Mime and action in Raymonda. Continuing a comparison of *Raymonda* with *Sleeping Beauty* by looking to the ballets' lead characters: Raymonda is more assertive than Aurora, and Jean de Brienne, obliged to rescue Raymonda from the dire situation in which she eventually finds herself, is arguably more active than Désiré. But even so, the characters in *Raymonda* are not developed through mime and action to the degree of those populating the Parisian ballets under discussion in this volume or *La Bayadère*. Raymonda communicates little about herself through mime other than her joy in receiving the news of Jean de Brienne's return from the Crusades and her distress at Abderrakhman's advances. And while she partakes in a *scène dramatique* and *pas d'action* with Abderrakhman, she and Jean de Brienne have no mimed interactions—at least none that are recorded in the libretto or the choreographic notation of the ballet—no love scene, no *scène dansante*. (In fact, Jean de Brienne is given relatively little stage time, and much of that is spent as a cavalier supporting Raymonda as she dances.) This minimization of dialogue between the romantic leads distinguishes the couple from their predecessors—Giselle/Albert, Paquita/Lucien, Medora/Conrad, and Nikia/Solor—all of whom participate in extensive mime conversations with each other (and with other characters as well). By contrast, Abderrakhman does communicate via mime and is thereby more closely related to the other antagonists we have encountered—Hilarion, Inigo, Birbanto, and the Great Brahmin. Still, his desires are ultimately carried out within the context of danced scenes: he attempts to woo Raymonda during the *Grand pas d'action* in Act Two and then tries to kidnap her during the subsequent divertissement's coda. And the character of Raymonda is developed in her dance numbers (which demonstrate her grace, strength, and authority) rather than in her mime scenes, an approach surely chosen by Petipa because of Legnani's technical skills. In sum, dance in *Raymonda* is the primary focus, and dance, as much as mime, drives the action forward.

This is not to say that *Raymonda*'s mime scenes are skimpy in number. Though the ballet's characters are not as developed through mime conversations than their counterparts in the ballets thus far discussed, plenteous mime scenes are still to be found in the ballet and, in general, serve mainly to move the action quickly forward to the next occasion for dance.

Characters, in order of appearance

Raymonda's four friends—Clémence, Henriette, and the troubadours Bernard de Ventadour and Béranger—are her constant companions at the castle. Though little is disclosed in the ballet about these four as individuals—some in the audience may have recognized Bernard as an actual twelfth-century troubadour—we can be certain that Raymonda enjoys her friends' company and they hers: she plays the lute as they dance after which they invite her to dance for them. During the second act, they dance by her side as Abderrakhman presses Raymonda for her hand. At Raymonda's wedding, Bernard and Béranger are participants with the bride and groom in the *Pas classique hongrois*.

Countess Sybille is Raymonda's aunt. She lives with her niece in Raymonda's castle. Not only a countess, Sybille also is a canoness (and therefore unwed).[20] Not surprisingly then, and like Berthe in *Giselle*, she discourages idleness and encourages hospitality.

Raymonda is the Countess of Doris. She lives with her aunt, the Countess Sybille, in a castle likely in Provence, and is engaged to the knight Jean de Brienne. Delighted at the prospect of marriage, and truly in love with her betrothed, Raymonda shares her joy with not only her aunt but also her four close friends, two of whom are troubadours whose very presence calls to mind "the habits of taste, pleasure, and admiration" known to have prevailed in Provençal courts of the period.[21] She delights in her four friends' company and engages in music-making and dancing with them, and she also enjoys the company (and dancing) of her tenants, who congratulate her on her name day in the ballet's opening scene. Like the other leading female characters considered in this volume, Raymonda is assertive (though to a lesser extent, due in part to the minimization of mime, discussed above), and her actions drive the ballet's narrative. She repeatedly shuns the advances of the Abderrakhman (saying she would rather die than love him), she orders a *cour d'amour* to celebrate the homecoming of her fiancé, and she enthusiastically cheers him on when he enters a duel with his rival.[22]

In her two entrées, three adagios, five variations, and four codas, Raymonda receives ample opportunity to express herself through dance. But the focus of her role is less an exploration of the character and intrigues of a medieval countess than the presentation of the consummate classical ballerina—all her dances are performed on *pointe* and only those in the final act include a character quality—embodying a Russian fusion of French and Italian technique and style: Legnani at the height of her powers.

Abderrakhman is a Muslim knight and the ballet's exotic antagonist, a role created by the Imperial Ballet's senior male *danseur*, Pavel Gerdt. A non-dancing character (though he partners Raymonda in the second act), Abderrakhman is the ballet's primary mime. He madly desires Raymonda, tries to woo her with gifts and impress her with his vast entourage, and is even prepared to kidnap her if she will not go with him willingly. He is charismatic and passionate whereas Jean de Brienne is bland and dutiful. His violent behavior in Raymonda's dream reinforces his depiction as barbaric.

The White Lady, "protector of the House of Doris," is a ghostly ancestress of Raymonda's family. Akin to a patron saint, she rewards diligence, punishes idleness, and warns of danger. A statue of the White Lady in the hall of Raymonda's castle is a testament to the esteem in which she is held. The White Lady appears in three of the ballet's four scenes.

Jean de Brienne is a celebrated French knight of the Crusades marching under the banner of King Andrei II of Hungary and Raymonda's fiancé. For much of the ballet, he is en route to his lover's castle and therefore offstage, but Pashkova and Petipa managed to bring him into the action before his actual return to France by including him in Raymonda's dream in the ballet's second scene. His narrative role is primarily ceremonial, calling for him to defend Raymonda's honor and marry her upon his return, and

---

[20] Countess Sybille likely was a secular canoness, that is, she lived with other aristocrats and was not committed to a life of poverty.

[21] Merwin, *Mays of Ventadorn*, 108ff.

[22] *Cours d'amour*, or courts of love, were medieval courtly games, organized as tribunals. Discussions of love and law were presided over by aristocratic women and expressed in poetry by troubadours. *Cours d'amour* were particularly popular in Provence. See Alicia C. Montoya, *Medievalist Enlightenment from Charles Perrault to Jean-Jacques Rousseau* (Cambridge, UK: D.S. Brewer, 2013), 102.

his dancing role is limited: he partners and dances with Raymonda in the dream scene adagio and coda as well as in the final act's *Pas classique hongrois*, in which he also performs a *pas de quatre* with Raymonda's friends.

Andrei II is King of Hungary and a Crusader under whose banner Jean de Brienne rides. He arrives with Jean de Brienne at the House of Doris as Abderrakhman is attempting to kidnap Raymonda. Notably, King Andrei is presented as an authority figure who brings order to the ensuing chaos and suggests Jean de Brienne and Abderrakhman fight a duel. Finally, he is the guest of honor and the impetus for the Hungarian-themed divertissement performed at the wedding of Jean and Raymonda.

The Music

The score for *Raymonda* was the first by a Russian composer of international stature after the death of Tchaikovsky in 1893 and can be seen as an attempt to replicate the collaboration between celebrated choreographer and composer that produced *Sleeping Beauty* (1890) and *The Nutcracker* (1892).[23] Glazunov, whose early nationalist focus (he was a pupil of Rimsky-Korsakov and considered the heir to the Mighty Handful) became increasingly international (he was later influenced by Liszt and Wagner as well as by Tchaikovsky), must have have seemed an ideal choice for the similarly cosmopolitan Vsevolozhsky. Glazunov began composing the score of *Raymonda* after receiving Petipa's instructions for the ballet's opening numbers, dated 16 June 1896.[24] He finished both the composition and its orchestration on 21 October 1897, noting "I spent a year orchestrating it."[25]

Recurring motifs

The lush, expansive, and colorful score of *Raymonda*, in which Glazunov deployed his masterly orchestration skills to great advantage, creates an ever-changing kaleidoscope of sound that complements the diverse content of Petipa's ballet, in which interest was maintained through variety (mime, classical dance, character dance, processions, groupings, and so on). Yet it is Glazunov's *pervasive* use of recurring motifs that sets *Raymonda* apart from other nineteenth-century ballet scores, in which descriptive music had hewed closely to the action on stage. Here, multiple motifs, repeated frequently and often developed—melodically, rhythmically, and through change in instrumentation—create continuity and guide the listener through the ballet's narrative. Glazunov took the additional step of transforming several motifs into melodies for danced numbers, creating an unwavering cohesion between action scenes and the dance.

Following the lead of his predecessors—Adam, Minkus, Delibes, and Tchaikovsky—Glazunov provided motifs for no fewer than six characters, including two for Raymonda (the first in Act One and another in Act Two), and one each for Jean de Brienne, Abderrakhman, the White Lady, Countess Sybille, and King Andrei II. Another motif

---

[23] Vsevolozhsky wrote to Petipa about Glazunov and his musical style on 30 May 1896, stating, "It's Delibes fused with Tchaikovsky. He's definitely the man we have been looking for to compose ballets." Tr. in Meisner, *Marius Petipa*, 247.

[24] About Petipa's instructions to Glazunov, see notes 63–64 in this chapter.

[25] Gershenzon, "Cronografia di *Raymonda*," 48–50, 60.

Ex. 10.1a Raymonda 1 motif; Introduction, bars 1–2

Ex. 10.1b Raymonda 1 motif, inversion of semitone into interval of a seventh; Introduction, bars 8–9

denotes Jean de Brienne's return from the Crusades. (Exx. 10.1–8 present each motif in its first appearance in the score.)

The motifs permeate several pivotal dance numbers. For example, the Raymonda Act One motif becomes the melody for the heroine's entrance dance, Jean de Brienne's motif is developed into the *Grand Adagio* of Scene II, and Abderrakhman's motif provides the melodic basis for the *Grand pas d'action* in Act Two. Such a tightly organized score does not easily lend itself to the sort of alterations *Raymonda* has undergone since its premiere, as we shall see later in this chapter.[26]

The languid quality of the rhythm of Raymonda's Act One motif (which we will call Raymonda 1; Ex. 10.1a) combines with inconclusive harmonic resolution to suggest a character in an irresolute state: Raymonda in Act One is anxiously awaiting the return of her fiancé. Her motif and its subsequent development are most often presented in sequences that pass restlessly through multiple key areas.

After three statements of the Raymonda 1 motif, Glazunov inverts the semitone of its recurring neighbor-tone figure into the interval of a seventh (Ex. 10.1b, bars 8–10). Glazunov subsequently combines the original motif and its interval inversion in Raymonda's entrance music later in the scene (Ex. 10.1c).

The interval of a seventh remains when the Raymonda 1 motif appears as an ostinato above the first statement of Jean de Brienne's motif (Jean's motif is in the top voice of the left hand in Ex. 10.2a). As the plot unfolds further, the interval of a seventh reappears in Raymonda 1 at moments of heightened emotion in the narrative, be it joy or terror.

---

[26] For additional (florid) musical analysis, see Rodney Stenning Edgecombe, "Internationalism, regionalism, and Glazunov's *Raymonda*," *Musical Times* 149, no. 1902 (Spring 2008): 47–56. See also Yuri Slonimsky's lengthy discussion of the score, number by number, " 'Raimonda': Put' Glazunova k baletnomu tvorchestvu" ["Raymonda": Glazunov's Path to Ballet Creativity], in *Aleksandr Glazunov. Issledvaniia, materialy, publikatsii, pis'ma* [Alexander Glazunov. Research, materials, publications, letters], vol. 1, ed. M[ark] O[sipovich] Yankovsky (Muzgiz: Leningrad, 1959), 377–503.

Ex. 10.1c Raymonda's entrance; Act One, *Scène IV*, bars 1–4

Ex. 10.2a Jean de Brienne's motif (top voice of left hand); Introduction, bars 14–18

This continues through the entirety of Act One and into Act Two. Finally, the rising seventh becomes the primary interval in the Act Three *entr'acte* and the ballet's apotheosis, reminding the listener of Raymonda's journey as the score is about to reach its final resolution. In contrast, Jean de Brienne's motif is rhythmically and harmonically sturdy. If played at a brisk tempo, it could serve as a march or fanfare.

Jean de Brienne's motif returns, transformed, as an adagio for solo violin in the dream scene (Ex. 10.2b).

The Countess Sybille's simple motif (Ex. 10.3) is essentially a three-note pattern, repeated several times at successively higher pitch levels. This creates a feeling of insistence that matches her persona as keeper of decorum, defender of duty, and upholder of hospitality.

Ex. 10.2b Act One, Scene II, *Grand Adagio*, bars 3–6

Ex. 10.3 Countess Sybille's motif; Act One, *Le récit de la Comtesse*, bars 1–4

Glazunov employed a fanfare-like melody (Ex. 10.4) at the mention (or thought) of Jean de Brienne's imminent return. The rising lines echo the upward motion of Jean de Brienne's motif.

The sweet and gentle quality of the White Lady's motif (see brackets in Ex. 10.5) stands in contrast to the stern image of the patroness offered by the Countess. The melody, whose rhythm is similar to Raymonda 1, more aptly depicts Raymonda's dreamlike state when first encountering the White Lady.

Abderrakhman's motif (Ex. 10.6a) also resembles Raymonda 1 in its recurring triplet figure that also suggests the meandering, decorative quality of Nikia's *vina* music in *La Bayadère* (see Exx. 9.9a–10).

When the motif is developed in the adagio of the *Grand pas d'action* in Act Two, the "exotic" augmented second between the flattened sixth scale degree and raised seventh is thoroughly exploited by Glazunov (Ex. 10.6b).

Raymonda's second motif (we will call this Raymonda 2; Ex. 10.7a), which makes its first appearance in the *entr'acte* preceding Act Two, is stalwart and resolute, in contrast to the restless Raymonda 1. The motif adopts the fanfare-like qualities of both Jean de Brienne's motif and the Homecoming motif and may be seen as a commentary on

Ex. 10.4 Homecoming motif; Act One, *Le récit de la Comtesse*, bars 45 (beat 2)–51

Ex. 10.5 The White Lady's motif: Act One, *Scène VII*, bars 20–23

Ex. 10.6a Abderrakhman's motif; Act One, *Scène IX*, bars 8–9

Ex. 10.6b Act Two, *Grand pas d'action*, bars 2–5

Ex. 10.7a Raymonda 2 motif; Act Two, *Entr'acte*, bars 1–8

Raymonda's categorical rejection of Abderrakhman's advances and her anticipation of Jean de Brienne's imminent return.

The horn returns as a solo instrument at the beginning of Raymonda's variation in the same act, in which Glazunov offers a more concise statement of the motif (Ex. 10.7b).

With the final motif (Ex. 10.8a), representing King Andrei II of Hungary, Glazunov begins a series of borrowings freely culled from Lizst's *Hungarian Rhapsodies*, which appear to have served as building blocks for the dances of Act Three (see later in this chapter).[27] Writing about that act's *Grand pas hongrois*, Yuri Slonimsky noted,

---

[27] Franz Liszt, *Hungarian Rhapsodies*, S.244, R.106, is a set of nineteen works for solo piano based on Hungarian themes, composed and published mostly between 1846 and 1853. Several were later orchestrated by the composer. The works were popular and emulated by composers of subsequent generations. For a discussion of Liszt's rhapsodies and Hungarian-Roma style, see Locke, *Musical Exoticism*, 135–149. Glazunov had met Liszt in Weimar, where the senior musician conducted Glazunov's First Symphony (1881) in 1884. Two years later, Glazunov dedicated his Second Symphony to Liszt's memory.

Ex. 10.7b Act Two, Variation IV, bars 5–8

Ex. 10.8a King Andrei II's motif; Act II, *Scène III*, bars 27–30, quoting Liszt's *Hungarian Rhapsody* No. 14 and incorporating repeated chords similar to those in *Hungarian Rhapsody* No. 8

"Glazunov's music created the theatrical counterpart to Lizst's Hungarian music."[28] Here, in the first two bars of King Andrei's motif, Glazunov quotes from *Hungarian Rhapsody* No. 14 (Ex. 10.8b), whose opening theme is itself based on the Hungarian folk song "Magasan repül a daru."[29] The music is magisterial in its harmonic consonance and strong rhythm; Locke observes that the "syncopated, symmetrical rhythm," found in bar 26 of Liszt's rhapsody (long-short-short-long), is "typical of various Hungarian-Gypsy and other European dances."[30] A possible model for the strongly repeated tonic chords in the third and fourth bars of King Andrei's motif (representing a harmonic solidity not found in the twisting melody of Abderrakhman's motif) can be found near the end of Liszt's *Hungarian Rhapsody* No. 8 (Ex. 10.8c).

Act Three opens with *Le cortège hongrois*, in which Glazunov extends his quotation of *Hungarian Rhapsody* No. 14 as he develops King Andrei's motif into the procession of wedding guests (Ex. 10.8d).

Dance genres

Glazunov also gave close attention to the historic, national, and exotic dance genres that fill *Raymonda*'s score. Like Pashkova's cast of characters, the origins of these dances span multiple centuries and disparate regions, and some reflect tropes created to represent cultures about which Europeans knew little.

---

[28] Slonimsky, " 'Raimonda,' " 479.

[29] Michael Saffle, *Franz Liszt: A Guide to Research* (New York: Routledge, 2004), 328. See Locke's analysis of No. 14 in *Musical Exoticism*, 144–148.

[30] Locke, *Musical Exoticism*, 144–145.

Ex. 10.8b Liszt, *Hungarian Rhapsody* No. 14, bars 25–32

Ex. 10.8c Liszt, *Hungarian Rhapsody* No. 8, bars 151–158

Historic dances. The ballet's opening scene includes several examples of French court dance, a category of Petipa's choreographic output largely forgotten today. The composers with whom he collaborated on such dances provided pastiches—imitating the structures and modes of earlier music but using nineteenth-century instrumentation—which Petipa complemented with pastiche quasi-historical choreography, usually performed in period dress with low heels.[31]

La Traditrice. The first dance in *Raymonda*, *La Traditrice* (literally, "the traitor"), is a galliard, a triple-time dance popular among the gentry in late-medieval France and

[31] In addition to the genres and forms discussed here, Edgecombe has referred to Raymonda's Act One *pizzicato* variation as a gavotte, though no such identification is provided by choreographer or composer. Originating in the fourteenth century as a peasant dance in Pays de Gap region of southeastern France near Provence, the gavotte is a dance in $\frac{4}{4}$ time that eventually became a popular court dance. Glazunov's *pizzicato* is in $\frac{2}{4}$ time, complicating its identification as a gavotte, which according to common practice commences on the third beat of an anacrusic bar. See Edgecombe, "Internationalism," 52.

Ex. 10.8d Act Three, *Le cortège hongrois*, bars 1–8, further quoting *Hungarian Rhapsody* No. 14

also a term describing a young man full of high spirits. The sixteenth-century composer Thoinot Arbeau published the galliard "La traditore mi fa morire" in his 1589 *Orchésographie*, a collection of French social dances.[32] Arbeau described the galliard dance: "In the beginning it was danced more discreetly: the dancer and his damosel, after making their bows, performed a turn or two simply. Then the dancer, loosing his damosel, danced apart to the end of the room. . . . Young people are apter to dance it than old fellows like me."[33]

Glazunov provided a galliard in $\frac{3}{8}$ time in response to Petipa's instructions: "From 64 to 80 measures of lively, light, gay dancing. Feet cross and recross in a gliding pas. Music in $\frac{3}{4}$. Name of dance La Traditore."[34]

La Romanesca. Raymonda's four friends dance a romanesca for her as they relax together in the evening following her name-day celebrations.[35] The antique sound of the music is perhaps derived in part from its resemblance to a gavotte with its opening half-bar upbeats, but it also bears a connection to the romanesca (a melodic-harmonic structural formula used in the sixteenth and seventeenth centuries for singing of poetry with instrumental accompaniment) insofar as it uses repeating melodic and harmonic sequences. Too, at the beginning at least, this romanesca calls for Raymonda to play the lute—a harp solo prelude in the orchestra, which establishes the antique-sounding

[32] "Orchéosographie, par Thoinot Arbea [sic], 1588" is handwritten on the back of a sheet of paper listing the ballets represented in the documents comprising the Sergeyev Collection. The folder of loose sheets in which this document is filed includes a list of historical figures in dance. See MS Thr 245 (280), Harvard Theatre Collection, Houghton Library, Harvard University.

[33] Thoinot Arbeau, *Orchésographie* (Langres, 1588). For an early-twentieth-century discussion of the history of the galliard, see Philip Hale's program note for the Boston Symphony Orchestra performances on 20–21 December 1907, Boston Symphony Orchestra program, season 1907–1908 (Boston: C.A. Ellis, 1907), 666–679.

[34] [Marius Petipa], "'Raymonda': Scenario by Marius Petipa," tr. Debra Goldman, *Ballet Review* 5, no. 2 (1975–1976) [hereafter: Goldman, "*Raymonda*"]: 38. Here, Petipa uses the Italian, "La Traditore."

[35] Name-day celebrations, distinct from birthday celebrations, observe the day associated with one's given name. Raymonda, a feminine form of Raymond, meant "counsel" and also came to mean "protection." Protection is a primary theme in *Raymonda*: The White Lady is the protectress of the House of Doris.

harmony. The music is broadly in AABA form, and its sweet and gentle mood matches that of Raymonda and her friends on this pleasant evening.

Une fantaisie. Raymonda's subsequent solo, *Prélude et Variation*, is titled *Une fantaisie* in the libretto's list of dances. A fantaisie is an improvisatory musical form; the term was first used in the sixteenth century, where it is found in the lute tablature of several Western European countries, including France. Here, Glazunov's solo harp replaces the lute. Like the romanesca, the dance itself is preceded by a brief prelude. The pervasive arpeggios contribute to the improvisatory character of the dance, as does the length of tulle held by Raymonda throughout.

Exotic and national dances. In composing the Act Two suite of exotic dances, Glazunov unsurprisingly responded to Petipa's list of dances and spare musical requirements (usually a few words to describe the performers, number of bars, and meter) in much the same way that Minkus did in composing *La Bayadère*—by employing well-used musical tropes to depict people and cultures of Elsewhere, in this case, the Arabic and Moorish peoples of the medieval Middle East, northern Africa, and Spain (compare Exx. 9.9a–9.10, 9.12a–9.13, and 9.35).

The opening *Entrée des jongleurs* features a mostly pentatonic melody played on the xylophone in compound $\frac{6}{8}$ meter followed by two numbers that feature modal melodies and drones on open fifths. The first, *Danse des garçons Arabes*, features short, two-bar phrases over an insistent drone of repeated eighth notes. In the second, *Entrée des Sarrazins*, a similar accompaniment (highlighted by tamburo and tambourine) supports a winding then rising melody in the oboe that is quickly taken up by the full orchestra. All of these features are among those identified by Locke as hallmarks of exoticism in Western music: modes and harmonies, "gapped" scales (such as pentatonic), bare textures, repeated rhythmic or melodic patterns, arabesque-like wind solos, and the use of foreign-sounding instruments (such as the xylophone).[36]

Danse orientale. Glazunov borrowed the accompaniment figure for his *Danse orientale* from Tchaikovsky's *Danse arabe* in *The Nutcracker*. For the middle section of the dance, he also drew from the melody of Tchaikovsky's B section (a melody based on three rising notes), which in turn is based on a Georgian lullaby that was transcribed and sent to Tchaikovsky by Mikhail Ippolitov-Ivanov.[37] But the opening and closing melodies of the dance are in the same broadly meandering vein as Nikia's Act One solo in *La Bayadère* (see Ex. 9.10). More precisely, they resemble the melodic motifs incorporated by Mily Balakirev into his Georgian art songs. Adalyat Issiyeva has demonstrated how Balakirev blended elements of actual Georgian songs (for example, melismatic turns based on a five-note motif) with exoticist tropes (here, triplet figures, drones) in a manner similar to the melodic contours of Glazunov's *Danse orientale*.[38]

Panadéros. The Spanish dance, initially meant to depict the Moors in Granada, ultimately became a *panadéros* (literally, bakers), a dance originating in Seville that is traditionally performed as a duet (Petipa's cast features a lead couple and corps de ballet).[39]

---

[36] See Locke, *Musical Exoticism*, 51–54.

[37] Wiley, *Tchaikovsky's Ballets*, 234. The lullaby was quoted by Mikhail Ippolitov-Ivanov in the second movement ("Berceuse") of his *Caucasian Sketches, Suite No. 2*, op. 42, "Iveria" (1896).

[38] Adalyat Issiyeva, *Representing Russia's Orient: From Ethnography to Art Song* (New York: Oxford University Press, 2021), 178–181.

[39] See Matteo Marcellus Vittucci and Carola Goya, *The Language of Spanish Dance* (Norman: University of Oklahoma Press, 1993), 142–143.

Ex. 10.9a Act Three, *Grand pas hongrois*, bars 1–8, drawing from *Hungarian Rhapsody* No. 6

Like his *Dance orientale*, Glazunov's *Panadéros* also owes a debt to its sister dance in *The Nutcracker*: both are in triple time and in E-flat major.

In Act Three, Glazunov transitions to another exotic style—Hungarian-Roma—which he first signaled at the end of Act Two with the arrival on stage of Andrei II (Ex. 10.8a, above) and which informs the works that make up the divertissement performed at Raymonda's wedding celebration in honor of the Hungarian king.[40] Here Glazunov continues to glean material from Liszt's *Hungarian Rhapsodies*, as examples drawn from the following numbers will illustrate.

Grand pas hongrois. The *Grand pas hongrois* is a czardas titled *Palotás* in the libretto's list of dances and subsequent programs. The *palotás*, or "palace" dance, was a fifteenth-century Hungarian court dance traditionally performed in the presence of the king that eventually became the traditional opening dance of Hungarian balls. The czardas developed in the nineteenth century and is considered to be the national dance of Hungary. In two-part form, it begins with the slow *lassú* and concludes with the fast *friss*.[41] Glazunov precedes these two sections of his czardas with a stately opening section in ABA form. For this, he incorporates phrases similar to those used in *Hungarian Rhapsodies* Nos. 6 and 8 (Exx. 10.9a–b, 10.10a–b).

The slow *lassú* draws from the famous *Hungarian Rhapsody* No. 2 (Exx. 10.11a–b). Here Glazunov employs a distinctive scale—termed "*verbunkos*-minor" by Shay Loya—that features the interval of an augmented second between the third and fourth and the sixth and seventh scale degrees.[42] The beginning of the fast *friss* clearly seems to be

[40] See Locke, *Musical Exoticism*, 135–174. See also Bellman, *Style Hongrois*.

[41] See Locke, *Musical Exoticism*, 144.

[42] Shay Loya, "Beyond 'Gypsy' Stereotypes: Harmony and Structure in the *Verbunkos* Idiom," *Journal of Musicological Research* 27 (2008): 254–280, cited in Locke, *Musical Exoticism*, 142.

Ex. 10.9b Liszt, *Hungarian Rhapsody* No. 6, bars 5–10

Ex. 10.10a Act Three, *Grand pas hongrois*, bars 25–28, drawing from *Hungarian Rhapsody* No. 8

Ex. 10.10b Liszt, *Hungarian Rhapsody* No. 8, bars 64–67

inspired by *Hungarian Rhapsody* No. 8 (Exx. 10.12a–b; note the three-bar phrases in each example).

Rapsodie. The third-act *Danse des enfants* is titled *Rapsodie* in the libretto and subsequent programs, a term that came to define a large-scale nationalist orchestral work in the second half of the nineteenth century, a prime example of which is Liszt's orchestration of his own *Hungarian Rhapsody* No. 2.[43] For the students in *Raymonda*, Glazunov

[43] See John Rink, "Rhapsody," *Oxford Music Online* (2001), https://doi.org/10.1093/gmo/9781561592630.article.23313.

Ex. 10.11a Act Three, *Grand pas hongrois*, bars 37–40, drawing from *Hungarian Rhapsody* No. 2

Ex. 10.11b Liszt, *Hungarian Rhapsody* No. 2, bars 11–18

Ex. 10.12a Act Three, *Grand pas hongrois*, bars 61–66, inspired by *Hungarian Rhapsody* No. 8

Ex. 10.12b Liszt, *Hungarian Rhapsody* No. 8, bars 140–145

Ex. 10.13 *Bokázó* cadence; Act Three, *Danse des enfants* (*Rapsodie*), bars 3–6

provides an orchestral miniature, distinguished by the melodic and rhythmic inflections of the Hungarian-Roma style, including *bokázó* cadences. The dotted *bokázó* rhythm, also found throughout the previous *Grand pas hongrois*, was often used at ends of phrases (see the bracketed cadence in bar 6 of Ex. 10.13). We will encounter the heel-clicking choreography that accompanies *bokázó* cadences in the dances described below.[44]

Pas classique hongrois. Glazunov continues his incorporation of Hungarian-Roma style in this multimovement dance suite, which comprises an entrée, adagio, four variations, and coda. The adagio and fourth variation (the one danced by Raymonda) feature winding, arabesque-like melodies of the kind we have found in *La Bayadère* and in the second-act exotic suite of dances in *Raymonda* (Exx. 10.14a–b). Both numbers are based in part on the *verbunkos*-minor scale.

In the opening of the coda, Glazunov appears to draw from the opening of the *friss* of *Hungarian Rhapsody* No. 13 (Exx. 10.15a–b); in the second section of the coda (Ex. 10.16a), he quotes directly from another source, as Jonathan Still has shown: the folk czardas *Hullámzó Balaton* (The waves of the Balaton), a tune that is also quoted in Jenő Hubay's 1887 *Scènes de la Csarda* for violin and piano (Ex. 10.16b).[45]

Less than three years after *Raymonda*'s premiere, Lev Ivanov choreographed Lizst's *Hungarian Rhapsody* No. 2 for interpolation into a performance of Saint-Léon's *Little Humpbacked Horse* on 11 October 1900 at the Mariinsky Theater. Wiley suggests the dance was created—and we suggest that the music may have been chosen—"possibly in

[44] Describing the features of the *Hungarian Rhapsodies*, Locke explains, "Many of the tunes end with one of several equally distinctive melodic-rhythmic cadential patterns. These *bokázó* cadences often give the impression of firmly 'closing off' a phrase, much the way that the steps of various Hungarian folk dances, notably the *csárdás*, end a section with a sharp clicking of the heels." Locke, *Musical Exoticism*, 143. See also Bellman, *Style Hongrois*, 93–130, and Loya, "Verbunkos," 263–268.

[45] Jonathan Still, "Glazunov, *Raymonda*, and *Hullámzó Balaton*," *Jonathan Still, ballet pianist* (blog), 12 May 2010, http://jonathanstill.com/2010/05/12/raymonda-and-hullamzo-balaton/.

Ex. 10.14a Act Three, *Pas classique hongrois*, bars 2–5

Ex. 10.14b Act Three, *Pas classique hongrois*, Variation IV, bars 3–7

Ex. 10.15a Act Three, *Pas classique hongrois*, Coda, bars 1–4, drawing from *Hungarian Rhapsody* No. 13

Ex. 10.15b Lizst, *Hungarian Rhapsody* No. 13, bars 101–104

Ex. 10.16a Act Three, *Pas classique hongrois*, bars 65–80, quoting the tune *Hullámzó Balaton*

Ex. 10.16b Hubay, *Hullámzó Balaton* from *Scènes de la csarda*, no. 5, op. 33 (1887), bars 68–75 (violin part)

response to the successful divertissement on Hungarian motifs that Petipa had created in Act III of *Raymonda*."[46] The number enjoyed great success.[47]

Raymonda's solo dances

Finally, Glazunov's score also supports and reinforces the extensive ballerina role in all of its variety. Each of Raymonda's five solo variations, as well as her vision scene *pas de deux* with Jean de Brienne, features a different solo instrument or a specialty instrumental technique:

Act One, Scene I *pizzicato*	Pizzicato strings
Act One, Scene I variation	Harp
Act One, Scene II *pas de deux*	Violin
Act One, Scene II original variation[48]	Flute
Act Two variation	Horn
Act Three variation	Piano

Collaboration between Glazunov and Petipa

Glazunov's pervasive use of motifs and lush orchestration was carried out within the parameters set by Petipa in his instructions for the composition of each number in the ballet. The ballet master dictated details of genre, number of bars, tempo, and occasionally orchestration as well as the action the composer was meant to complement with his score.[49] With regard to the length of each number, Glazunov followed Petipa's instructions more closely in *Raymonda* than Tchaikovsky had done in *Sleeping Beauty* and *The Nutcracker*, but his autonomous approach to the project nonetheless created frustration for the choreographer.[50] Petipa complained about both Glazunov's reluctance to make requested revisions—revisions that were fully expected of Petipa's former specialist composers, Pugni and Minkus—and his publication of *Raymonda* (in both full score and piano reduction) by Glazunov's publisher Belaieff in versions that did not reflect all of the changes made before the premiere, that is, the choreographer's final intentions.[51] (Owing to his stature as a major composer, Glazunov was accustomed to having his compositions published as he saw fit.) Because neither the printed piano reduction nor the printed orchestra score matches the performance score (or each other, for that matter), they do not reflect the variety of revisions made as the ballet went into production.[52] Any

---

[46] Wiley, *Lev Ivanov*, 203. See also Slonimsky, "'Raimonda,'" 479–480.

[47] See Wiley, *Lev Ivanov*, 203–205.

[48] The interpolated variation that replaced the original one features solo violin.

[49] See notes 63–64, later in this chapter.

[50] On Petipa's collaboration with Tchaikovsky on *Sleeping Beauty* and *The Nutcracker*, see Wiley, *Tchaikovsky's Ballets*, 109–111 and 193–200. For Petipa's instructions to Tchaikovsky for *Sleeping Beauty* and *The Nutcracker*, see Wiley, *Tchaikovsky's Ballets*, 354–359 and 371–376, respectively.

[51] Petipa's complaints, made in a letter to an unknown recipient, are quoted in Gershenzon, "Cronografia di *Raymonda*," 63–64.

[52] Comparison of the printed piano reduction and orchestra score with the annotated PR in the Sergeyev Collection reveals the following omissions from the published sources: The printed piano reduction is missing the eight bars added for Abderrakhman's Act One, Scene I, entrance; repeated bars in the *Valse fantastique*; an additional six bars of introduction to the *Danse des garçons Arabes*; and repeated bars in the *Baccanal*. All

of Petipa's irritations, however, no doubt paled in comparison to his satisfaction with the overwhelmingly positive reception of the ballet at its premiere.

The score was well received and recognized as a key component of the ballet's success. "*Raymonda* is indebted to a very significant degree to Mr. Glazunov's score," wrote the ballet critic Nikolai Bezobrazov.[53] The music critic Vladimir Frolov was more direct, praising the music at the expense of the story:

> Despite the subject's paucity and its almost total absence of content, Mr. Glazunov has nevertheless known how to bring to it much imagination, taste, and beautiful, animated music, with rhythmic diversity, and interest, orchestrated sonorously and effectively.[54]

Brief performance history

In addition to Legnani, the 1898 premiere cast featured a mix of seasoned veterans, artists approaching leading-dancer status, and youthful newcomers. Sergei Legat, just twenty-two years old, created the role of Jean de Brienne. Dancing opportunities equal or greater to those of Jean de Brienne were given to Raymonda's male friends, Bernard de Ventadour and Béranger—roles created by Georgi Kyaksht and Nikolai Legat, respectively—who danced in the Act Two *Grand pas d'action* as well as the Act Three men's *pas de quatre*. Henriette (Olga Preobrazhenskaya) and Clémence (Klavdiya Kulichevskaya), Raymonda's girlfriends, were also given variations among other dancing duties. Pavel Gerdt created the role of Abderrakhman, with Giussepina Cecchetti and Nikolai Aistov in the smaller roles of Countess Sybille and King Andrei. Lydia Svirskaya created the role of the White Lady. Marie Petipa was also featured, performing the lead in the *Panadéros* and in the interpolated mazurka in Act Three.[55]

Raymonda remained in repertory after Legnani's departure in 1901. Moscow ballerina Ekaterina Geltser assumed the title role on 25 April 1901, with Sergei Legat and Gerdt reprising their roles. Raymonda's friends were danced by Lubov Egorova (Clémence), Vera Mosolova (Henriette), Mikhail Fokine (Bernard), and Mikhail Obukhov (Béranger).[56]

On 21 September 1903, Olga Preobrazhenskaya made her debut as Raymonda, joined by Tamara Karsavina in her first performance of Henriette. Preobrazhenskaya had a great success in the role, which was tailored to her strengths by Petipa (more on this below). When the ballet came to be recorded in Stepanov notation, much of the 1903 cast was represented.

Further casts featured dancers familiar from revivals of the other ballets in our study. At a benefit for the corps de ballet on 10 December 1906, Matilda Kshesinskaya danced the title role in a performance of the third act, partnered by Nikolai Legat. Anna Pavlova performed the *Panadéros*, having made her debut in the dance, just weeks earlier, on 29

---

of these passages are included in the printed orchestra score with the exception of the bars added in Act One, Scene I, for Abderrakhman's entrance (Ex. 10.17).

[53] Nikolai Bezobrazov, *Peterburgskaya gazeta*, 8 January 1898, 4, tr. in Meisner, *Marius Petipa*, 248.
[54] Vladimir Frolov, *Peterburgskiy listok*, 8 January 1898, 4, tr. in Meisner, *Marius Petipa*, 248.
[55] Marie Petipa performed these same dances for her farewell benefit on 11 November 1907. See *Khronika IV*, 95, and *Ezhegodnik* (1907–1908), 99–100.
[56] *Khronika IV*, 19.

October 1906.[57] Karsavina made her debut as Raymonda in the complete ballet, part-nered by Nikolai Legat, on 12 September 1909.[58] Lubov Egorova followed a year later, making her debut on 26 December 1910, also partnered by Legat.[59]

Sources

Published scores. As mentioned above, the orchestra score (OS) and piano reduction (PR) of *Raymonda* were published at Glazunov's behest by Belaieff in 1898.[60] (Because these scores are accessible online, we have provided fewer musical examples in this chapter.) Printed stage directions in the OS and PR are quoted from Petipa's scenario sent to Glazunov with the choreographer's instructions for composing the score. The Sergeyev Collection holds a copy of the printed piano reduction that is annotated in Russian and includes manuscript music interpolations.[61] Its primary importance is that it likely indi-cates which passages were cut and which were added to the score for performances at the Mariinsky Theater.[62]

Petipa's scenario and instructions to Glazunov. Petipa's instructions to Glazunov for *Scènes I–IV* (through Raymonda's first entrance) are held in the Glazunov archive at the National Library of Russia.[63] Instructions for other scenes were sent to the composer over a period of time, through spring 1897. These are preserved among several other institutions, including the A.A. Bakhrushin State Central Theatre Museum, and some appear to have been lost.[64]

---

[57] *Khronika IV*, 86–87. See also Lazzarini, *Pavlova*, 80.

[58] *Ezhegodnik* (1909–1910, vol. 6), 66, 92, 97. The editors of *Khronika IV* give both 26 November 1917 and 17 February 1918 as Karsavina's debut dates. See *Khronika IV*, 212–213 and 217, respectively.

[59] *Khronika IV*, 138.

[60] Alexander Glazunov, *Raymonda* (Leipzig: M.P. Belaieff, 1898). The piano reduction is arranged by the composer and Alexander Winkler. Both the piano reduction and orchestra score are available online at https://imslp.org/wiki/Raymonda,_Op.57_(Glazunov,_Aleksandr).

[61] MS Thr 245 (69).

[62] The following is a list of cuts, changes, and interpolations made in the printed piano reduction housed in the Harvard Theatre Collection, MS Thr 245 (69):

Act One

 Scène V, 35–36: replaced by eight added bars; MS page of PR is taped over printed page 22 (Ex. 10.17, below).

 Valse fantastique, 81–95, 97–112: MS annotations indicate a repeat of these bars to match repeats in printed orchestra score.

 Variation III: cut. MS annotation, "Violin solo." Interpolated in its place is an MS piano reduction of *Valse* from Glazunov's *Scènes de Ballet*, op. 52, 1894.

 Ronde des follets et des farfadets, 1–32: cut.

Act Two

 Grand Coda, 65–80: cut.

 Danse des garçons Arabes: six bars added at beginning, bringing the music into agreement with the published full score. A two-violin *répétiteur* score of these bars is pasted at the top of the page.

 Grand pas espagnol, 1–8: cut.

 Baccanal: 101–115: repeated, with MS notes added.

Act Three

 Danse des enfants: reordered to follow *Le cortège hongrois*.

 Grand pas hongrois: a double-sided MS page containing a piano reduction of bars 123–163 (that is, all of page 141) is inserted at page 141.

 Entrée: an MS page including a piano reduction of the *Entrée* is inserted at page 141.

 Variation II: 46–49: cut.

 Variation III: cut.

[63] National Library of Russia, *fond* 187, item 1426, pp. 1–4 (p. 4 is blank).

[64] Pavel Gershenzon has included the instructions (translated into Italian) in "Cronografia di *Raymonda*," 48–58. The instructions were translated into Russian by A[lexander] Grigorievich] Movshenson and pub-lished, with commentary, in *Aleksandr Glazunov*, 543–555. The instructions are also published in Russian

Yearbook of the Imperial Theaters and Mariinsky Theater production documents. In addition to the libretto and early performance programs, a lengthy illustrated description of *Raymonda* in the *Yearbook of the Imperial Theaters* for the 1897–1898 season provides further details about the original production (for instance, 106 performers are listed by name for the Act Three galop).[65] The Mariinsky Theater production volume includes stage plans for each scene and lists of properties and costume pieces.[66]

Choreographic notation. Additional sources relating to early performances of *Raymonda* are part of the Sergeyev Collection. Chief among them is a choreographic notation (CN), consisting of 190 numbered pages (on portrait-format paper) that are nearly all in Sergeyev's hand.[67] Additional pages in other hands (on oblong-format paper) are inserted throughout. For the most part, Sergeyev provides only ground plans and movements for feet and legs, with occasional notations for arms, hands, head, and body. The additional notations of a number of variations and some group dances that are interspersed throughout the CN are mostly complete, that is, in addition to ground plans, movements for the entire body are notated. Although music is not included on the notation scores, Sergeyev often noted rehearsal numbers from the OS and sometimes provided the number of measures a particular section of choreography is meant to cover, both of which greatly increase the ability to coordinate dance and action with music.

An assessment of the names of dancers listed in the CN allows us to date the manuscript to the period around 21 September 1903, when Preobrazhenskaya made her debut in the title role. The CN records the performance of Preobrazhenskaya (for whom Petipa rechoreographed some of the ballet)[68] as well as Sergei Legat in his original role as Jean de Brienne and Pavel Gerdt in his original role as Abderrakhman. The four friends are Tamara Karsavina (Henriette), Lubov Egorova (Clémence), Mikhail Fokine (Bernard de Ventadour), and Mikhail Obukhov (Béranger). Nadezhda Petipa is Countess Sybille.

Other items relating to *Raymonda* in the collection include additional choreographic notations of single dances or sections of a dance, manuscript *répétiteurs* and piano reductions for individual numbers, and printed programs from two performances (12 October 1903 and 12 May 1918).[69]

Raymonda: A scene-by-scene description

The following description of *Raymonda* is based primarily on the CN, taken together with information from the other sources listed above and augmented by period criticism and commentary.

---

translation in *Marius Petipa. Materialy*, 145–151, and in English translation by Debra Goldman (without source citations) in "*Raymonda*," 38–44. We will cite Goldman's translations throughout this chapter.

[65] *Ezhegodnik* (1898–1899), 250–270, available online at https://archive.org/details/ezhegodnikimpera1898diag.

[66] St. Petersburg State Museum of Theatre and Music (GMTMI), GIK 16917, fols. 140r–145r.

[67] MS Thr 245 (67).

[68] On 19 September, Petipa noted in his diary: "At the school I rehearsed *Raymonda*. Recomposed some variations and the coda, as well as some movements [*des temps*] in the adagio for Mlle. Preobrazhenskaya." See Garafola, ed., *Diaries*, 18.

[69] See MS Thr 245 (68, 70, 227, 228, and 247).

Act One

Scene I

Raymonda's Name Day

Introduction. Glazunov's brief introduction begins with Raymonda 1 (Ex. 10.1a), which soon intertwines with Jean de Brienne's motif at bar 14 (Ex. 10.2a), introducing to the listener the lovers at the heart of the story.

Scène I. The curtain rises at rehearsal number (RN) 4 to reveal a hall in the castle of Raymonda, Countess of Doris, in medieval Provence. Petipa described the setting in his scenario: "The interior of a castle. A hall with a low ceiling, decorated with tapestries with human figures. There are sculptures on pedestals. At the rear a large door, opening onto a terrace with a view of the surrounding country."[70] The Mariinsky Theater production documents confirm the large entrance upstage center flanked by two large, elevated sculptures on each side. Seating frames the stage, with two high-backed chairs downstage left and a high-backed *chaise longue* downstage right.

On stage are Raymonda's girlfriends, Henriette and Clémence, troubadours Bernard de Ventadour of Provence and Béranger of Aquitaine, and six student couples. The male students, pages, are practicing fencing and playing lutes and viols, and the female students are sewing and embroidering. The seneschal (the CN records the performance of Alexei Bulgakov), steward of the house, enters upstage right and issues orders regarding Raymonda's name-day celebrations. "Games," written in the CN, may refer to the pages' fencing. At RN 7, Glazunov included Petipa's instruction in the score, "Les pages s'exercent." The program refers to this scene as "Jeux et danses."

The CN provides the ballet's first danced steps, performed by the four friends (RN 9). The choreography here is in Petipa's faux-antique style that he used for pastiche eighteenth-century court dances. Henriette and Clémence wear floor-length dresses and low-heeled shoes. Their opening enchaînement, in which they are joined by Bernard and Béranger, consists of two *tendu devant*, *tombé*, three *pas de bourrée* performed alternately by the couples as they travel downstage. The girl students join the friends and perform similar choreography (RN 10).[71]

La Traditrice. Petipa was already envisioning *La Traditrice* when writing his instructions to Glazunov: "Feet cross and recross in a gliding pas."[72] Akim Volynsky described the choreography in similar terms: "The dancing is innocent, gliding along straight and broken lines, and interwoven with the fleeting movements of the mazurka."[73]

The girls bow and the boy students walk up to them and ask them to dance.[74] The student couples travel in pairs upstage and down, then cross the stage. The girls move to center, circle around each other, and return to their partners. They pose—three couples on each side of the stage—while the friends join (likely at RN 15). Obukhov and Karsavina begin, traveling downstage, where he lifts her by the waist. They return upstage, perform another lift, then travel down again and finish with a complete turn to the

---

[70] Goldman, "*Raymonda*," 38.

[71] The choreography for the students (for both *Scène I* and the subsequent *La Traditrice*) is notated twice. The more detailed of the two notations provides movements for torso, head, and arms. See MS Thr 245 (227).

[72] Goldman, "*Raymonda*," 38.

[73] Volynsky, "*Raimonda*," *Birzhevye vedomosti*, 12 November 1912, 5–6, tr. in *Ballet's Magic Kingdom*, 33–34. In agreement with Volynsky, "mazurka" is indeed written into both notations of the students' dances.

[74] Petipa asked Glazunov for "4 bars of prelude of the invitation to dance." Goldman, "*Raymonda*," 38.

left. Egorova and Fokine repeat the entire enchaînement to the other side. The students join the friends, and finally all perform the lift sequence, ending with another complete turn as the men hold the women by the waist. According to the CN, the students move upstage left as the music segues into *Scène II*.

Scène II. Countess Sybille (Nadezhda Petipa), canoness and Raymonda's aunt, enters with the seneschal, followed by eight women of the court. The girl students bow to the Countess then join the boy students and four friends in diagonal lines on either side of the stage, the women in front of the men.

The subsequent action and short passages of dance appear to be recorded out of order in the CN when compared to the scenario and score. Some of the notation boxes are numbered by Sergeyev (101–104) to indicate their intended order (the box numbered 102 precedes the box numbered 101, hence the need for the numbering). We will describe the material in the CN according to this numbering and compare it to the libretto and Petipa's scenario.

The Countess, standing at center, orders the boys to stop playing the mandolin (box 101, which does not include a RN). According to the libretto, this action occurred in the later *Scène mimique*, and instead, the Countess "reproaches the girls for their idleness."

Reprise de la danse. Petipa's scenario describes the action: "All her [the Countess's] efforts are in vain. Just one or two [of the girls] return to their work, as the others throw aside their sewing and embroidery and start dancing again."[75] Petipa asked for sixteen bars of dance music; Glazunov wrote only eight. The notated choreography in box 101, however—three *piqués de côté en cou-de-pied devant*, *pas de bourrée*, all on *pointe*, four times to alternate sides, performed by the women in their diagonal lines near the wings— seems to correspond more accurately to the later passage titled *La danse* (see below).

Scène mimique. According to the scenario, OS, and PR at RN 22, the Countess "pounces on the pages and orders them to put away their viols and lutes in order to break off the dance." CN box 102 references RN 22 but offers only a ground plan showing the Countess standing opposite the four friends and half of the students, all at stage right.

La récit de la Comtesse. Accompanied by a sober setting of her motif (Ex. 10.3), the Countess indicates a statue in the hall and explains it is a likeness of their ancestor, the Countess of Doris (subsequently called the White Lady), who appears from beyond to warn the House of Doris of impending danger and to punish those who do not fulfill their duties. The libretto provides the following narrative (Petipa's scenario mirrors this account closely):

> Countess: "Take care . . . Countess de Doris, famous by the name of the White Lady, will punish you for disobedience; do you see this statue? This is our revered ancestor. She appears from the other world to warn the house of Doris every time one of its members is in danger, and punishes those who do not fulfill their responsibilities."

The narrative in the CN is written on the page following the one with the numbered notation boxes. It is titled "Story" and is likely based on the Countess's actual pantomime gestures:

> Countess: "You listen to me. When night comes, this White Lady comes out and looks around to see what is happening, and if she sees you dancing a lot, then she becomes

75 Goldman, "*Raymonda*," 39.

angry. If you are calm, then she will be our patron. Let's go bow to her." Everyone walks and venerates the White Lady. "Everything I told you, everything is truth."[76]

As one can see, the Countess's tale in the CN differs from her story in the libretto and scenario in tone and content, demonstrating how narrative in a libretto could change when it was translated into mime gestures. According to the CN, the appearance of the White Lady is not precipitated by dangers, and dancing is condemned as a vice. The CN narrative also requires all to bow to the statue.

The somber mood is broken by four measures of an *allegro* $\frac{2}{4}$ that introduce "La danse," during which, according to the scenario, the "[Y]oung ladies and pages laugh at the gullible countess, make a circle and draw her in to a circle dance (*khovorod*)." Here, the girl students surely perform the enchaînement notated in notation box 101 (labeled "a little piece of dance on [*pointe* symbol]," see above), traveling downstage and back twice in their lines. The Countess, out of breath, falls heavily into a chair. The ground plan in the notation box numbered 103 indicates the four friends circling the Countess twice then traveling upstage left. In the box numbered 104, they surround the seated Countess, action that corresponds to the scenario: "The countess, out of breath, falls heavily into a chair."

At RN 29, a "trumpet behind the curtain" signals the arrival of visitors (Homecoming motif; Ex. 10.4).

Scène III. The seneschal enters the hall to announce the arrival of Jean de Brienne's messenger, who has brought a letter from the knight to his fiancée, Raymonda. The Countess leaves to fetch her niece, while the seneschal gives last-minute instructions to the guests and the student girls lay flowers on the ground in a pathway for the ballerina in preparation for her entrance. The CN explains: "Girl students put flowers down on the floor in a diagonal line." The ground plan indicates with an "X" where each flower should be placed. The boys and girls form a diagonal line on stage left, next to the flowers. The Countess, having returned, stands at the downstage end of the line. (The four friends are unaccounted for in this part of the CN.)

Scène IV. Entrée de Raymonda. At the height of a crescendo, under which the brass repeats the Homecoming motif, Raymonda enters, "beside herself with joy," traveling downstage through the flowers with a *bourrée* on *pointe* (RN 33). The melody here is a variant of Raymonda 1 (Ex. 10.1c), Petipa having requested "lively, sparkling, happy music," words that provide insight into his conception of Raymonda's character. He added parenthetically for Glazunov, "You must pay special attention to this entrance. It is for the prima ballerina."[77]

After moving across the stage with alternating *piqués en demi-arabesque* and *piqués de côté en cou-de-pied devant*, Raymonda returns to the downstage end of the flower line. "Traveling backward over the flowers," as the CN explains, she "takes flowers off the floor." The notated combination of steps for this action includes leaning forward in fourth position *plié* (presumably to pick up a flower), a *relevé en arabesque*, and a *bourrée* backward on *pointe*. This sequence is repeated four times to alternate sides, thereby allowing the ballerina to return upstage, traveling backward through the line of flowers

[76] The Countess's "Story" is written in prose on a separate page in the CN. Following the narrative, the action resumes on the previous notation page and then returns to the narrative page, where RN 21 is written in the fifth notation box.

[77] Goldman, "*Raymonda*," 39.

and picking them up as she goes. (Whether Raymonda picks up one or two flowers with each repetition is not indicated.) After a series of two *pirouettes* from fifth position, *demi-emboîtés devant*, *assemblé* followed by a *manège* of turns ("everything on [*pointe* symbol]"), Raymonda concludes with an *arabesque* on *pointe* at center, flanked and supported by two women—traditionally, Clémence and Henriette, though they are not named in the CN.

Scène V. Scène mimique. Her entrée concluded, Raymonda receives Jean de Brienne's letter. She reads it, shares its good news with her aunt, and exudes the joy that is a dominant characteristic of her personality. Petipa's instructions to Glazunov underscore the emotion of the scene: "She is joyful. Likewise the rhythm. More lively and expressive. It ends with a happy, passionate, animated crescendo."[78]

Here again, the CN appears to present some of the action out of order and also provides redundant detail. By reordering the notation boxes based on information from the score, we can determine what seems to be the intended order of action.

The printed annotations in the OS present the action thus (corresponding musical motifs are given in parentheses):

Bars 1–8 (Homecoming)
The messenger kneels and delivers the letter.
Bars 9–14 (Raymonda 1)
Raymonda reads the letter . . .
Bars 15–18 (Raymonda 1 with rising sevenths)
. . . and says, "The knight Jean de Brienne returns home covered in glory."
Bars 19–24 (Jean de Brienne)
"Tomorrow Brienne will return to the house of Doris to celebrate his wedding with Raymonda."
Bars 25–28 (Countess)
She [Raymonda] shows the letter to the Countess, who is delighted.
Bars 29–33 (Raymonda 1 followed by a crescendo leading to entrance of vassals and peasants)

The CN provides additional detail that we have allotted to bars of music based on musical motifs and the annotations in the score:

Bars 1–8
The seneschal announces, "From there to here one knight comes from your groom." Raymonda replies, "Oh, how happy I am."
Preobrazhenskaya says "Hello" to the the knight [Alexander Medalinsky in the role of the Cavalier of Jean de Brienne], who enters and says, "One who is noble [King Andrei II] sent you a letter from the knight [Jean de Brienne]." He kneels when he reaches Raymonda. Preobrazhenskaya takes the letter with excitement.
Bars 9–14
She reads the letter and says, "Ah, he is here." She presses the letter to her heart and turns to the knight, saying, "You may go." She reads the letter again.
Bars 15–24
[Raymonda's recounting of the letter to the court is omitted in the CN.]

[78] Ibid., 40.

Bars 25–28

The Countess [until this point in the CN she is referred to as "Petipa" or "Petipa 2,"
but here she erroneously is called "Mother" and Raymonda her "daughter"] walks
to Raymonda, kisses her on the head, and says, "You are so beautiful, and I congratulate you."

Bars 29–33

The seneschal re-enters to announce the arrival of a new guest.

Scène VI: Entrée des vassaux et des paysans. Here, Petipa made a late change to the narrative, introducing the antagonist Abderrakhman earlier than originally planned.[79] The
libretto, revised in time to accommodate Petipa's alteration, offers a lengthy explanation
of the action, which involves the Muslim knight presenting gifts to Raymonda and the
revelation of his plot to abduct her. Glazunov, on the other hand, now required to introduce Abderrakhman's motif an entire scene earlier than planned, wrote a scant eight
extra bars of additional music (replacing the original first two bars of *Scène VI*) to facilitate this addition to the action (Ex. 10.17).

A page of mime script details the action of this added encounter, the length of which
suggests that at least some of the mime exchange spilled over into the music intended for
the subsequent entrance of the vassals:

Enter Gerdt, [who] bows and says [to Raymonda], "I heard about your beauty from
afar and now find that they say the truth. You are a beauty; I ask that you accept from
me a gift." He gives a sign with his hand and they [unidentified] present a box with gifts.

She [Raymonda]: I do not accept these presents.

He is in despair. She takes the letter [sent from Jean de Brienne] and reads. "My
fiancé will come here." Gerdt eavesdrops and says, "She will never marry; she must
be mine."

The Countess comes up and asks the Saracen to go and sit near her. He thanks her
for the invitation and goes and sits.

Waltz.

The name-day festivities continue, now with Abderrakhman on stage. Eight vassals
enter (their entrance was originally intended for RN 41 but may have been delayed
until the action detailed above was complete). They greet and congratulate Raymonda.
According to the printed annotation in the score, "They bring barrels [of wine], cakes,
and flowers." Petipa explained to Glazunov, "The music is happy, but when the vassals drink, sparkling." In response, the composer provided a march with a fanfare-like
melody (Ex. 10.17, last two bars) that builds to a "sparkling" crescendo, accompanied by
trills in the woodwinds. According to the CN, "Lords come out and [peasants] dance a
waltz. Props people bring fruit onto the stage" (two bars before RN 43).

Four bars before RN 44, twenty-four peasant couples enter.

[79] Petipa had planned Abderrakhman's first appearance as a surprise plot twist during Raymonda's dream
in the second scene and then ensured that he dominated the ballet's second act. But before the premiere, the
choreographer added a brief entrance for him in the opening scene. Pavel Gershenzon suggests this was done
to give Gerdt more stage time. See Sergey Konaev and Pavel Gershenzon, "Commenti a *Raymonda*," tr. Carla
Muschio, in *Raymonda* program book (Milan: Teatro alla Scala, 2011), 118–119.

Ex. 10.17 *Scène VI: Entrée des vassaux et des paysans*, eight added bars (replacing original bars 1–2) followed by original bars 3–4 (Source: MS Thr 245 [69])

Grande Valse. Addressing the seneschal, Raymonda says, "You to them here, command to dance." The seneschal relays the instruction to the peasants, and the waltz commences (RN 47).

The *Valse provençale* (as it is called in the libretto's list of dances) is reminiscent of the Act One *Valse villageoise* in *Sleeping Beauty*, but without children. This massed dance mainly features its performers in block formation, sometimes with couples side by side, other times alternating rows of women and men. According to the CN, which includes far more annotations than notated steps, garlands and wreaths are the principal properties, with *balancé* and *pas de basque* the principal steps. Dancers travel downstage and back, traverse the stage, and eventually coalesce into a grouping in which some of the dancers form a circle at center, performing *ballonné* and *balancé*, while the rest of the women perform *piqués degagés de côté* and *emboîtés sur les pointes* in several lines along each downstage side. After returning to their block formation with *pas de basque*, the ensemble travels downstage as the "Ladies lift their hands up and hold onto the wreaths and the Cavaliers hold the garlands by the ends."

"*Pizzicato.*" The waltz leads directly into the *pizzicato*, a variation for Raymonda, the corps de ballet having formed a large semicircle upstage in two rows, the women in front of the men. Raymonda's dance is made up of steps mostly on *pointe* and choreographed in the Italian style that we have so far identified as featuring multiple repetitions of movements, often featuring hops on *pointe*.

Raymonda begins upstage center and travels directly downstage with *pas de bourrée* on *pointe*, *piqué en demi-arabesque*, *précipité*, *piqué en arabesque* three times to alternate sides. After a walk backward toward upstage left, she continues with a diagonal of *pas de chat*, *assemblé*, *relevé en arabesque* three times, a *bourrée* upstage right, and a repeat of the enchaînement to the other side. A *bourrée* upstage left precedes a diagonal of hops on the left *pointe*—an enchaînement performed three times: *piqué en demi-arabesque* followed by four *temps levés sur la pointe en demi-arabesque*, one *en cou-de-pied devant*, and another as the working leg moves to *développé devant*, all on the left foot. (During this enchaînement, the corps women rise from their knee in preparation for the reprise of the waltz.) A final walk backward on *pointe* introduces another enchaînement of hops on the left *pointe* from upstage right: twenty-two *temps levés ballonnés sur la pointe*.[80] The variation ends with a repeat of *pas de chat*, *assemblé*, *relevé en arabesque* followed by a *bourrée* traveling farther downstage left. No final pose is given.

Volynsky described the *pizzicato* in detail, praising the ballerina: "Preobrazhenskaya's genius shines here. She performs her leaps with feline lightness and gracefulness.... The *pizzicato* ends with a marvelous *pas*. The dancer crosses the stage diagonally doing jumps on the toes of one foot, doing *battements* with the other."[81]

Reprise de la valse. During the four-bar introduction to the reprise, the corps performs *pas de basque* as the dancers make their way back to center and resume a block formation, this time comprising four rows of six couples each. The group moves forward with *pas de valse en tournant*, then the "ladies bend [their] body backward and the cavaliers hold them with two hands and kneel." They travel upstage then down with more *pas de valse* and upstage once again where they pose as Raymonda makes a final entrance (RN 62). She travels downstage in a zigzag pattern performing *jeté* to *demi-attitude devant*, *pas de bourrée* on *demi-pointe* six times to alternate sides. The corps joins with *pas de basque* downstage followed by *balancé* upstage two times as Raymonda traverses the stage from right to left with alternating *pas de bourrée en avant* and *piqués en demi-attitude devant*, all on *pointe*. She circles upstage with a *manège* of *piqué tours en dehors*. The final ground plan shows Raymonda posing between two men who each hold the end of a garland. The men are flanked by women, and an annotation explains, "holds wreath with garland."

Scène mimique. At RN 65, an annotation in the score states, "Raymonda wants the reception of her fiancé to be brilliant and gives orders for the next day to organize a *cour d'amour* in his honor." Perhaps Raymonda's instructions to the seneschal may instead

---

[80] The music appears to allow for only twelve repetitions of this step.
[81] Volynsky, "*Raimonda*," tr. in *Ballet's Magic Kingdom*, 34.

have begun at RN 66, at which point a statement of the Raymonda 1 motif builds over the course of fourteen bars and several key modulations. According to the libretto, Raymonda's orders further incite Abderrakhman's anger, though no music was added to depict his reaction.

At RN 68, the music used to bring on the vassals is repeated underneath a triple-time ostinato based on Raymonda 1. This builds to RN 69, at which point a score annotation states, "The vassals withdraw, salutations, etc." A manuscript annotation at the corresponding point in the PR reads, "Everyone leaves." After another musical climax at RN 70, the music softens and relaxes over the course of another fourteen bars.

The CN mostly documents the various departures of those on stage: "The peasants do bows [to Raymonda and the Countess] and all leave" (RN 65) followed by "Gerdt and his suite leave." All exit upstage right. The Countess (here referred to as "Aunt") kisses Raymonda on the forehead and suggests they depart together. Raymonda replies, "No, I ask you to leave me alone and to dream." The Countess says, "Good," kisses Raymonda's forehead a second time, proposes that the pages also depart, and exits upstage right.

The musical landscape changes at RN 72 to a depiction of a moonlit night—a score annotation explains, "Evening has come and the moon is shining." Petipa's musical instructions ask for "the tender music of dusk" and "rather poetic music."[82]

Raymonda (to her four friends): "I ask you to remain with me here. Ah! look, what a wonderful night. Give me a guitar [lute] and I'll play."

One of the men hands a lute to Raymonda. She takes it and goes to the *chaise longue* at stage right where she sits.

Prélude et la Romanesca. Raymonda plays the lute at RN 74 and the two couples begin to dance at RN 75. Volynsky, in a review of a performance in 1912, described the features of the dance: "The *Romanesque* is restrained, in the style of the eighteenth century. The music has a courtly character and is somewhat weighty and majestic. Agrippina Vaganova and Elsa Vill dance beautifully, with aristocratic elegance."[83]

Few steps are notated, but the ground plan indicates that the couples dance together, traveling upstage then back, before separating and performing *pas de bourrée en tournant* followed by a bow. This enchaînement is repeated several times. Next each couple joins hands and turns in place then travels upstage on the diagonal, performing alternating *pas de bourrée* and *chassé*. Near the end of the dance, the couples travel downstage, side by side, performing steps similar to those performed in the opening scene of the ballet (see *Scène I*, above). They finish the dance with a bow.

Prélude et Variation. During the prelude to her next variation (*Une fantaisie*), Raymonda approaches her friends and says, "You dance beautifully." They respond by asking her to dance.

Raymonda passes the lute to Clémence and performs to the accompaniment of solo harp while holding a scarf (alternately referred to as "veil" and "tulle" in the CN).[84] Volynsky described the opening movements: "Preobrazhenskaya performs the gentle fantasy with its broken chords. She gently extends her leg sideways to waist height and then she changes over to an arabesque with a graceful turn."[85] Indeed, the opening enchaînement begins with *relevé à la seconde*, *fouetté* to *arabesque à plat*. After a *pas*

[82] Goldman, "*Raymonda*," 40.
[83] Volynsky, "*Raimonda*," tr. in *Ballet's Magic Kingdom*, 34.
[84] See MS Thr 245 (70) for a manuscript copy of the solo harp part for this variation.
[85] Volynsky, "*Raimonda*," tr. in *Ballet's Magic Kingdom*, 34.

de bourrée on *pointe*, Raymonda continues with three *piqués en arrière*, decorated with *petits battements* in the working leg, and another *pas de bourrée* on *pointe*. After repeating this enchaînement, Preobrazhenskaya travels backward again with more *piqués en arrière* leading to a *pas de chat*, during which she "throw[s] the veil," and a series of *temps levés en demi-arabesque* as she makes a full turn to the right, finishing with *relevé en arabesque*, all performed twice. Next she zigzags backward upstage with *tendu devant fondu*, *passé* to *tendu derrière fondu*, and two steps on *pointe* three times. A *bourrée* or run on *pointe* directly down center ends with the annotation "throw the tulle" and a final pose in fourth position *plié*.

Scène mimique. The following scene begins with an annotation in the score: "Finally, tired of the emotions of the day [here, Glazunov quotes a melody from the *Grande Valse* danced earlier in the act], she [Raymonda] stretches on a carpet and her pages fan her, while a lady plays her a languorous air." The libretto tells us that it is Clémence who continues to play the lute.

The CN provides a different account. Raymonda, taking the "tulle" and walking toward stage left, says, "I will dream of the one I love." A female "friend" (Henriette?) brings Jean de Brienne's letter to Raymonda, who takes it and offers thanks. She sits in a chair at stage left and kisses the letter. The friends ask to take their leave: "Let us go and fall asleep." They cross the stage to the *chaise longue*.

By the end of the scene, the friends are still on stage: "Everyone lies down and falls asleep."

Scène VII: Apparition de la Dame blanche (Ex. 10.5). The CN carries the caption "White Lady" at the top of the first page of the next scene. According to annotations in the PR, the action unfolds as follows: "The White Lady descends from a pedestal, lit by a ray of the moon. Raymonda looks at her, petrified with terror. Nonchalantly, Raymonda stands up. A mysterious force constrains her to obey—she is drawn to the terrace, following the apparition who calls her. The curtain slowly falls." The descent of the White Lady (Svirskaya) to the stage from the pedestal seems to have been made possible by a stage mechanism, after which she walks downstage. "Preobrazhenskaya awakens [though according to the libretto, Raymonda had not fallen asleep] and follows the white woman." The ground plan shows that Raymonda follows the White Lady out of the hall at upstage center. The CN for Scene I ends here.

From this point, Petipa left musical decisions to Glazunov: "All of this passage will show your inspiration to advantage. From beyond the large staircase up which she climbs, I cannot give you an exact count of measures."[86] The White Lady's motif is first heard at RN 87. At RN 88, the Raymonda 1 motif returns, now outlining downward sevenths. In the PR, the third bar of this passage carries the manuscript annotation, "They are walking." The White Lady's motif returns to bring the scene to a close.

The opening scene contains the bulk of the ballet's mime, which serves to introduce the characters and set up the plot. Though lacking the multimovement dance sequences of subsequent scenes, this part of the ballet features plenty of dancing, beginning with the curtain-up court dance and including a lively entrance for the ballerina, an extended ensemble waltz with a variation for Raymonda and an entrée for her within the waltz reprise, a *pas de quatre* for the soloists, and a second variation for the ballerina.

---

[86] Goldman, "*Raymonda*," 41. The staircase is not mentioned in the scenic descriptions in the OS or PR, nor is it visible in extant images depicting Act One, Scene I.

Scene II

Visions

The second scene features a suite of classical dances: adagio, ensemble waltz, three variations, and coda. Action and dance are notably less integrated here than in the opening scene: the various classical dances are followed by an extended mime sequence, and the scene concludes with a brief danced passage for children.

Entr'acte—Scène VIII. Following an *entr'acte* based on Clémence's "sleep" music, the curtain rises on a park outside the castle. The stage set-up documented in the Mariinsky production book includes a simplified sketch of scenic designer Petr Lambin's castle, in front of which is an open outdoor space accessed from the castle terrace by a large staircase at stage right. Twelve round tabourets are arranged in a semicircle on either side of a raised *chaise longue* behind which is a small platform with several steps. A trapdoor (*lyuk*) is located on the stage-left side of the *chaise longue.*

The White Lady walks on the castle terrace, followed by Raymonda's double. (The ballerina performing the part of Raymonda dances in the vision scene, while the double looks on with the White Lady.[87]) The park is briefly clouded in mist, which clears to reveal a vision of Jean de Brienne, twelve knights, and an ensemble of allegorical figures: forty-eight corps de ballet women—one representing fame and renown (*La renommée*), and the forty-seven others representing glory (*Gloire*)—as well as twelve student girls as *Les amours*. According to the libretto, Jean de Brienne and his knights are "encircled by girls putting crowns [likely laurel wreaths, see next section] on their heads." Raymonda runs to her lover's arms.

Grand Adagio. The CN for Scene II begins with the adagio for Raymonda and Jean, the music for which is an elaborate development of Jean de Brienne's motif for solo violin (Ex. 10.2b). The majority of the properties employed in the adagio—palm leaves, laurel wreaths (which may be the "crowns" mentioned in the previous section), shields, a sword—represent popular Crusades imagery, symbolizing military victory, martyrdom, and honor.

The danced duet is framed by six large groupings—or groups (*gruppy*)—motionless tableaux that are formed by the ensemble. The drawings of the groups preserved in the CN are rough sketches and do not appear to account for all dancers on stage in each group, but they nevertheless provide a significant amount of information. The groups are not always symmetrical formations, yet they balance the stage space. The men and some of the women stand on the tabourets, which are moved around the stage as subsequent groups are formed, though the CN does not indicate whether they are moved by members of the stage crew, supernumeraries, or dancers.[88] Each group is identified by a Roman numeral, marked in manuscript annotations in the PR, that indicates when each group is to be formed.

---

[87] The original cast list for the *scène dramatique* near the end of the act includes "Mlle Legnani, M. Gerdt. *The White Lady and Raymonda's Double."* A drawing of Scene II by the illustrator Karl Brozh, showing Raymonda's double standing alongside the White Lady, was published in *Vsemirnaya Illyustratsiya* [World Illustrated], 59, no. 1513 (1898): 106.

[88] According to author and historian Vera Krassovskaya, the dancers portraying knights moved the tabourets during the vision scene adagio. See Vera Krassovskaya, *Vaganova: A Dance Journey from Petersburg to Leningrad,* tr. Vera Siegel (Gainesville: University of Florida Press, 2005), 35.

Group I (bar 1) is made up of rows of dancers on the diagonal at stage right, with a back row of women standing on tabourets. The knights also may stand on the tabourets; the drawing lacks clarity, but one of several annotations reads, "men by ladies." Some of the women carry wreaths, others carry palm leaves, some carry shields, and still others hold garlands. What may be a single row of dancers at stage left balances the larger group at stage right. Two students kneel downstage right in front of the diagonal rows of dancers. Raymonda and Jean de Brienne appear to be upstage center, surrounded by six women.

Group II assembles at bar 11. Here, the dancers form rows in a semicircle around the stage. Ten tabourets again create a raised back row, with two more tabourets farther upstage at center. The drawing shows that women ("with shields") stand on the tabourets, each holding one end of a garland; the other end is held by a student standing on the stage floor in front of each tabouret. In addition, the knights sit on the tabourets. The next two rows include women holding palms (wreaths are not mentioned); those in the innermost semicircle are lying down. Three women flank the two tabourets that are farthest downstage at each side. Raymonda and Jean de Brienne are unaccounted for in the drawing of this grouping.

Group III (bar 19) features three lines of women at both stage right and left; the women in the central lines carry palm leaves, while the others carry wreaths. As in the second group, pairs of women flank the downstage ends of the triple lines. A semicircle of women and men on tabourets is at stage right. The students stand in two symmetrical diagonal lines at center, and between them stand four male-female couples. And again, the placement of the lovers is not indicated in the drawing.

Group IV coalesces at bar 27, with the majority of the dancers again at stage right, including a row of knights on tabourets behind three rows of women, all on the diagonal.[89] The dancers in the row farthest downstage kneel; their row is balanced by another row of kneeling women opposite them on stage left. In front of the kneeling dancers are two pairs of women, one at stage right and one at stage left, likely holding each other by the waist. Two trios of women flank them on either side. A central upstage couple may represent Raymonda and Jean de Brienne; they are also flanked by pairs of women. The students stand downstage of them in two lines at center.

Group V (bar 35) bears the heading, "Like 3rd group." The only difference in the drawing of this group from the third is the addition of two women, one standing with each of the centerstage couples.

Lastly, group VI forms at bar 49. This tableau is completely symmetrical, with dancers in both diagonal and straight lines on either side of the stage. Each knight stands in front of a woman in diagonal lines along each wing; both knights and women appear to be on tabourets. This drawing features the addition of "[Ekaterina] Burmistrova [representing *La renommée*, fame and renown] with a trumpet," standing far upstage at center. Raymonda and Jean de Brienne are once again not indicated.

The *pas de deux* itself is sparsely notated, with nowhere near the detail found in the notated second *pas de deux* of the Kingdom of the Shades scene in the *La Bayadère* CN. Moreover, as is the case for most *pas de deux* notated in the Stepanov system, this one lacks indications of metered rhythm for the steps. That said, the CN is rich with

---

[89] "Group IV" is written in bar 17 and again at bar 27. That the third grouping is indicated at bar 19 suggests the annotation in bar 17 may be an error.

annotations describing quasi-ceremonial actions and giving an idea of the unusual details of the dance.

Having asked Glazunov for "heavenly music, poetic, expressive, lively, passionate," Petipa surely intended to imbue his choreography with these characteristics.[90] The duet begins with Raymonda sitting on Jean de Brienne's knee (RN 102). After some standard poses, lifts, and balances (including one in which Jean de Brienne holds Raymonda by the bodice with one hand as she holds a *demi-arabesque* on *pointe*), Raymonda again sits on her lover's knee. They walk downstage left, where he asks her to bring him his sword. She carries it over her head while walking toward him on *pointe*. An annotation explains, "She sticks [or pierces] the sword into the floor and takes the wreath off head [presumably Jean de Brienne's head] and puts it on the sword handle." As Raymonda *bourrées* toward stage left, Jean de Brienne goes upstage and takes a palm leaf from one of the knights. The leaf is featured in the subsequent choreography. For example, near the end of the *pas*, the CN instructs Jean de Brienne to put the palm branch around Raymonda's waist and hold each end while making a clockwise *tour de promenade* as Raymonda stands on *pointe* in *arabesque*. Next, "they walk [upstage] and Legat takes the wreath off the [his] head and places [it] on the floor" before partnering Raymonda by the hand in a final *tour de promenade en arabesque*—the CN appears to indicate two full revolutions— followed by two turns, likely supported *pirouettes*.[91]

Volynsky's brief description of the *pas de deux* is in agreement with the conclusion of the dance as documented in the CN: "Preobrazhenskaya and Nikolai Legat's adagio is thematically beautiful; charmingly performed arabesques alternate with attitudes. The dancing ends with two pirouettes on the left foot."

Valse fantastique. The light and gentle *Valse fantastique* is notated for corps de ballet, coryphées, soloists, and students, though the exact number of dancers involved is difficult to determine from the CN.

The dance begins with twelve corps de ballet women dancing in pairs (RN 110). They perform *balancés* in place, forward and back, before tracing circular patterns around the stage. Two soloists (identified as "[Elizaveta] Vill and [Evgenia] Snetkova" in the CN, although "Vill" is struck through and "[Elena] Makarova" has been added) enter together at upstage center (RN 114). Traveling downstage together, they perform *piqué en demi-arabesque* three times (the enchaînement appears to be notated in incomplete form) followed by *chaînés* on *demi-pointe* to opposite downstage wings.

Twelve more corps women enter (identified as "1st corps de ballet"), moving in two groups of six (RN 115). Traveling on opposite diagonals (they cross at center), the groups perform *piqué de côté en cou-de-pied devant* four times followed by *pas de valse en tournant* and *pas de bourrée*. The entire enchaînement is repeated to the other side. Next, they travel upstage with *temps levé en demi-arabesque*, *assemblé* then *bourrée* on their return. This is repeated to the other side as they travel downstage and back, then the entire sequence is danced one more time.

Twelve "2nd corps de ballet" women begin at RN 116 in an upstage row. They travel down center performing *glissade*, *cabriole devant*, *coupé dessous* on *demi-pointe*, *tombé* three times then turn a circle in place with *demi-valse*. Backward walks on *pointe* bring them upstage, then they split and move to the sides with *pas de basque*. Two upstage rows of six student girls each follow at RN 117.[92] They perform "*cabr[iole]* back [*derrière*] 6

[90] Goldman, "*Raymonda*," 41.

[91] Volynsky, "*Raimonda*," tr. in *Ballet's Magic Kingdom*, 34.

[92] The Harvard PR includes the manuscript annotation "Coryphée" at RN 117, at odds with the CN.

times" as they travel downstage then split at center, return upstage, and form lines along the wings.

An unspecified number of coryphées (entrances in the subsequent coda indicate six women) enters at RN 118. They travel downstage in a single line performing *cabrioles derrière* to either side (half the women to the left, the other half to the right) then a *saut de basque* (as they return to the line) three times to alternate sides. More *pas de basque* bring them downstage, where they form a single row. They perform a series of *relevés en demi-arabesque* alternating with *relevés en attitude devant* then split and move to the sides as the "Corps dc ballet walks to the middle" and everyone on stage resumes dancing. Although no steps are notated at this point, the ground plan indicates that the soloists and coryphées traverse the stage in two groups, passing each other at center, while traveling groups of three corps women each trace an intricate pattern upstage among pairs of corps women dancing in place.

Near the end of the waltz, thirty-two women (not including the students) are accounted for in the CN.[93] An annotation states, "Everyone in place *pas* 12 times," matching the notation of twelve *relevés*, again alternating *demi-arabesque* and *attitude devant*. The women turn a circle on *pointe* before the final grouping, in which the dancers are "on [*pointe* symbol] and on the knee."

Three variations for women follow. The music for each conjures the same light and airy sound world as the dreamy *Valse fantastique*.

The existence of multiple similar yet distinct notations of each of these variations—like those we found in the variants of the *Paquita Grand pas* variations (see Chapter 5) or Medora's Act Two variation in the Justamant manual for *Le Corsaire* (see Chapter 6)—reminds us that the choreography of a given solo dance may have differed, even slightly, from dancer to dancer. In the case of differences between notations documenting the steps of the same dancer, perhaps the dancer herself was allowed leeway in her choices from rehearsal to rehearsal or performance to performance.

Variation I. The CN for the first variation, a gentle $\frac{2}{4}$ in D-flat major featuring the celesta, documents the performance of Agrippina Vaganova.[94] Beginning at center, she performs two *relevés en arabesque, sissonne doublée*, and steps on *pointe* backward (returning to her starting position) two times to alternate sides. She continues with more *relevés en arabesque* followed by a *piqué double rond de jambe en l'air* three times to alternate sides, then she *bourrées* downstage left. Changing direction, Vaganova *bourrées* backward on the diagonal as she zigzags upstage, punctuating each segment with an *entrechat six*. Reaching upstage right, she returns on the diagonal with *relevé en arabesque*—swinging the working leg from a *développé devant fondu* to *arabesque*—*pas de chat* six times. The variation concludes with *chaînés* on *demi-pointe*, crossing the stage to the right. No final pose is given.

A second notation of this variation, providing movements for the entire body (the first version indicates only feet and legs), is preserved in the collection's miscellaneous files.[95] In this version, for which no dancer's name is given, *temps levés sur la pointe en demi-arabesque* are substituted for the initial *relevés*. The variation continues like Vaganova's version until the final diagonal, which consists of a *pirouette* from fifth position, *coupé*

[93] The Harvard PR includes the MS annotation "girl students" at RN 119. The group of thirty-two women likely includes the two groups of twelve corps de ballet dancers, six coryphées, and two soloists.
[94] The meter of this variation is $\frac{2}{4}$, but the PR includes the annotation $\frac{4}{8}$ at the top of the page, suggesting the conductor might beat four in each bar. Varvara Rykhlyakova danced the first variation in the 1898 premiere.
[95] MS Thr 245 (228), 16–17.

dessous, assemblé six times. The subsequent turning sequence across the stage appears to begin with *piqué tours en dehors* (the "+" sign indicating a turn to the right is missing) followed by *chaînés* on *demi-pointe*.

Variation II. The CN of the contrasting second variation—a sprightly, running $\frac{6}{8}$ featuring rapidly descending melodic scales—records the performance of Elena Polyakova.[96] Instead of the smooth *relevés* of the first variation, this one opens with a diagonal of *cabriole derrière* and two *pas de bourrée* three and a half times from upstage left. Polyakova returns up the diagonal with *chassé, tour jeté, relevé en arabesque* three times followed by a run downstage left. Traveling backward up the opposite diagonal, she performs *entrechat six, échappé sur les pointes*, and three hops in fifth position on *pointe* three times. After another run, this time downstage right, she travels across the stage with *glissade, jeté*, and *temps levés sur la pointe* on the left foot as the right leg makes a *grand fouetté* to *arabesque fondu* followed by a *pas de bourrée* on *demi-pointe*, all performed twice. She continues with multiple *pas de bourrée* on *pointe*, punctuated by *piqués en demi-attitude devant*, then changes direction to finish the variation with *chaînés* on *demi-pointe* to downstage right.

A second, more detailed notation of this variation, also a recording of Polyakova's performance and largely in agreement with the first version, is filed within the main CN.[97] This superb notation is signed by Alexandra Konstantinova, a student at the time the several extant notations bearing her name appear to have been made, and is written on oblong-format paper of the kind that Wiley suggests may have been used for classroom exercises (formatted with staves only, without boxes for ground plans).[98] A third notation of this variation is written in the same hand as the alternate version of *Variation I* and is also part of the collection's miscellaneous files.[99]

Variation III. Before the first performance, Petipa appears to have discarded the music Glazunov had composed for the original third variation for Raymonda and replaced it with a new variation for solo violin—an arrangement of the *Valse* from the composer's *Scènes de ballet* (Ex. 10.18)[100] The dance is recorded twice by Sergeyev and a third time by Konstantinova. All three versions record the performance of Preobrazhenskaya and are filed within the main CN. The version filed first (by Sergeyev) includes a ground plan and notated movements for legs and feet; the second version (also by Sergeyev) is fragmentary and appears to have been abandoned midway through; the third version (by Konstantinova—it is signed and dated 22 March 1905) is complete, with movements given for the entire body. The steps in Konstantinova's version are nearly identical to those in Sergeyev's (we will list differences below).

Preobrazhenskaya begins at center with a series of alternating *piqués en arabesque* and *piqués en cou-de-pied devant*, creating a gentle rocking motion that ends in *pas de bourrée*

---

[96] The second variation was danced by Ekaterina Geltser in the 1898 premiere.

[97] This notation—which includes movements of the head, torso, arms, and hands—matches the choreography included in the main CN with one significant difference: instead of running downstage right following the third combination (*entrechat six, échappé sur les pointes*, and hops on *pointe*), here the dancer makes her way downstage performing multiple *temps levés en demi-arabesque* on alternate feet. These conclude with an *assemblé* leading to the *temps levés sur la pointe*, traveling across the stage from right to left. A final pose is also given: *relevé en demi-attitude devant*.

[98] Wiley, "Dances from Russia," 107n36.

[99] MS Thr 245 (228), 17. Here, in the second enchaînement, the *échappé* precedes the *entrechat six*, and the final *chaînés* are performed on *pointe*.

[100] Alexander Glazunov, *Scènes de ballet*, op. 52, 1894. Here, the solo violin of the *Valse* replaces the solo flute of the original third variation. A two-violin *répétiteur* of the interpolated and arranged waltz variation for Raymonda is part of the Sergeyev Collection, MS Thr 245 (69).

Ex. 10.18 Interpolated Variation 3, based on *Valse* from *Scènes de ballet* (Glazunov)

on *pointe*. A continuous *bourrée* on *pointe* (only recorded by Konstantinova) takes her upstage left to begin a diagonal of *glissade, relevé enveloppé, tombé, piqué en cou-de-pied devant, pas de bourrée* on *pointe* three and a half times, culminating in two fast *pas de bourrée* that coincide with a fast-rising line in the violin and a half cadence.

The middle section of the variation features *renversé, pas de bourrée en tournant* six times as Preobrazhenskaya travels across the front of the stage. After a *bourrée* upstage (on *demi-pointe* in Sergeyev's notation and on *pointe* in Konstantinova's), the final section features a speedy zigzag comprised of *piqué en attitude devant, pas de bourrée en avant* on *pointe, piqué en attitude devant, pas de bourrée couru en première, tendu de côté fondu, assemblé, relevé en attitude devant* three times. In Sergeyev's version, the variation ends with a final *renversé, pas de bourrée* on *pointe*, a run on *pointe* directly downstage, and a *piqué en demi-arabesque* to the knee. Konstantinova's account of the concluding *enchaînement* differs slightly from Sergeyev's: fourth position, *relevé en arabesque, pas de bourrée en tournant* on *pointe, pas de bourrée couru en première, relevé en attitude devant*, arms overhead.

Volynsky described Preobrazhenskaya's performance as

full of difficulties. But the rotations of the whole body [*renversé*], which end in the wide fourth position of the legs, are full of poetry. Preobrazhenskaya does them effortlessly. She performs her movements first whirling around, then giving them up to the whim of her fantasy. The variation concludes after the dance on *pointe* in a straight line, with a new and delicate rotation [perhaps a reference to the final repeat of the *renversé*].[101]

Coda. The coda (also based on Jean de Brienne's motif) involves all participants. Vill and Snetkova (Vill's name is again struck through and Makarova's added) begin from

---

[101] Volynsky, "*Raimonda*," tr. in *Ballet's Magic Kingdom*, 34–35.

opposite upstage corners. They travel on the diagonal with *temps levé en demi-arabesque*, *temps levé en tournant* four times, then change direction for four more repetitions, this time crossing paths at center. They move upstage backward with a series of *piqués de côté en cou-de-pied devant, glissade, jeté,* then head to their nearest downstage corners with *chaînés* on *demi-pointe* as twelve corps de ballet women run in from the upstage sides. This group travels directly downstage in two rows of six with a series of *tendu devant fondu, relevé en cou-de-pied devant, glissade.* They next turn two circles in place as they *bourrée* on *pointe* before traveling backward upstage with a series of walks on *pointe* and *temps levés sur la pointe en demi-arabesque.* They move to the sides with multiple *précipités* and a *pas de bourrée* on *pointe* to finish. The six coryphées are next, first traveling directly downstage in a single row with *précipités* before moving on to larger-scale steps: *développés devant, cabrioles derrière,* and *grands jetés en avant.* After their row splits at center and they run to the sides, concluding with *pas de chat,* twelve more corps women enter from either side and perform a lengthy series of *demi-emboîtés devant* in various formations and patterns followed by *piqués de côté en cou-de-pied devant* and *relevés petits passés.*

Raymonda follows at RN 137.[102] She begins with *temps levé en arabesque, piqué tour en dehors, développé devant* six times. After retracing her path backward with *arabesques voyagées,* she returns down the diagonal with what is likely a repeat of her initial enchaînement. This is followed by a run to the downstage left corner and a *manège* of this same "first pas," as the step is designated in the CN. She finishes with undesignated turns on *demi-pointe.*

After the fermata just before RN 140, the students enter, performing multiple *pas de chat, pas de bourrée* as they travel in a single row directly downstage before running back to their starting point.[103] Polyakova and Vaganova, the two variations soloists, enter together from opposite upstage corners and perform a series of *glissade, saut de basque* on the diagonal (RN 141). The corps re-enters from each upstage side (CN: "Corps de ballet in long dresses"), as the soloists briefly pause then continue to dance: they cross paths at center then move upstage with multiple *temps de flèche* (RN 142). Traveling in two lines, the corps traces symmetrical circular patterns around the stage, after which all "walk into groups," suggesting the end of the dance for the ensemble.

A "Coda II | Preobrazhenskaya and Legat" follows, forty bars before the end of the dance (RN 143). Traveling on the diagonal from upstage left, Raymonda performs *glissade, piqué en arabesque, pas de bourrée* on *pointe* twice. An annotation directs, "Legat lifts," although lifts are not clearly indicated until the next enchaînement: running around to center, Preobrazhenskaya performs *sissonne ouverte* (lifted at the waist by Legat), *assemblé, relevé en arabesque* four times. She next passes in front of Legat, moving to his right side. He picks her up with his right arm, carrying her "to the side" (that is, on his side), and walks backward on the diagonal toward upstage center, where they make their final pose. The CN instructs one or both of them to kneel; perhaps Legat knelt and Preobrazhenskaya sat on his knee.

The coda is a masterful summation of this multimovement dance suite, featuring all of its various constituencies: corps de ballet in multiple groups, coryphées, waltz soloists,

---

[102] This entrance is headed, "Preobrazhenskaya for the second time," although an earlier entrance is not indicated in the CN. The PR includes a printed annotation, "Solo de Raymonda," at RN 138.

[103] The PR includes the annotation "girl students" at RN 140. The fermata is written in the CN at the end of Raymonda's entrée and matches the fermata in the PR in the bar preceding RN 140.

variations soloists, students, and, of course, Raymonda, first in a solo entrée then part-nered by Jean de Brienne.

The next notation page begins with the annotation, "like 1st Group," which may suggest the ensemble returns to the first grouping of the adagio. As the orchestra plays a sort of epilogue to the coda (a restatement of Jean de Brienne's theme in a warm D-flat major), Raymonda, according to Petipa's scenario, approaches the White Lady, who says, "Look, and learn what awaits you." Raymonda runs to Jean de Brienne but instead finds herself face to face with Abderrakhman, "who has taken the place of her fiancé."[104]

Scène IX—Scène mimique. The CN ground plan indicates that Preobrazhenskaya approaches the upstage, raised *chaise longue* (RN 147). Gerdt is shown next to it, where the trapdoor is indicated in the production drawing. According to the scenario, "All the heavenly maidens have disappeared, just as Jean de Brienne has." An extended *scène dra-matique* ensues, in which Abderrakhman declares his love for Raymonda, who continu-ally rejects him.

Petipa described the surprise meeting and subsequent dramatic scene in detail for Glazunov:

> Chromatic scale. Two measures when Raymonda runs to Jean and a fairly shrill sound (high) when she comes face to face with Abder-Rakhman. Pause. And then two beats tremolo. Abder-Rakhman speaks to her of his love, which Raymonda rejects in terror. This is almost a dramatic scene, contrasting with the scene of Raymonda and Jean de Brienne. Music of a passionate, violent, sharp character. The terror of Raymonda. At the end, fortissimo $\frac{2}{4}$ for 84 bars.[105]

Glazunov gave Petipa much of what he requested: A rising scale leads to the mo-ment that Raymonda meets Abderrakhman, although the scale is more diatonic than chromatic and ends on a high D-flat. This is followed by the ballet's first statement of Abderrakhman's motif (disregarding his added entrance in Scene I; Ex. 10.6a) and a pause (fermata) as the final note is held. String tremolos follow, underscoring repetitions of the motif that soften before another pause.

The passage proceeds *con moto*, alternating Abderrakhman's motif with Raymonda 1 (which features frequent leaps of a seventh), as the music becomes increasingly "pas-sionate, violent, and sharp."[106] Returning to the CN, we find that Abderrakhman appears to advance upon Raymonda as "she, fearful, retreats," traveling backward downstage, her arms held in front of her. The subsequent mime scene, in which Abderrakhman becomes increasingly physically aggressive, is described in detail:

Abderrakhman: "I ask you not to leave. I love you." He wants to embrace her. Raymonda "drives [him] out."

Abderrakhman: "Do not drive me out. I love you." He wants to embrace her again. Raymonda runs away under his arms as they cross paths at center.

Abderrakhman: "She wants to leave. She is mine."

---

[104] Goldman, "*Raymonda*," 41.

[105] Ibid., 42.

[106] At RN 148, the OS includes the designation *Scène mimique.* This is missing from the PR, in which all of the musical material comprising the *Scène mimique* is part of *Scène XI.*

He takes Raymonda by the hands and turns her around. Still holding her hands, he pulls her across the stage. She kneels and begs to be saved. Seeing her begging, Abderrakhman steps away. Running upstage, Raymonda attempts to escape. Abderrakhman follows and takes her by the waist. She twists free and pushes him away, making multiple turns as she travels downstage.

Raymonda: "I hate you. Just kill me—and I will not love you."

Abderrakhman: "You do not want to love me. I will kill you with this dagger." He lunges at her, lifting the dagger, but seeing her beauty, he drops the weapon and takes her again by the waist. Raymonda twists free with more turns and runs away. Pursuing her and this time taking her by the neck, Abderrakhman pulls Raymonda upstage to center. Breaking free one last time, she runs downstage only to be lifted by Abderrakhman and carried upstage to the trapdoor.

At the same time, another character, performed by "[Alexandra] Mikhailova," approaches the trapdoor from upstage left. Mikhailova may have been cast as Raymonda's double, a role listed among the participants of the *Scène dramatique*. (We know she was not the White Lady, a role Mikhailova never performed.) The CN instructs, "Gerdt and Mikhailova fall through the trapdoor." If indeed Mikhailova performed as Raymonda's double, her disappearance through the trapdoor with Abderrakhman appears to have been the solution for dispatching the body double at the end of Raymonda's dream.

Scène X—Ronde des follets et des farfadets. Students portraying will-o-the-wisps and goblins (*dukhi*, or "spirits," in the CN) run onto the stage, first boys then girls (RN 154). Their dance is very sparsely notated. After running into a circle formation around Raymonda, they surround her in a box formation along three sides of the stage (sides and front); the ground plan suggests the boys travel in circles around the girls.[107] Next, the *dukhi* travel downstage in rows—two rows of girls followed by a row of boys. Finally, annotations listing Roman numerals I through V suggest division of the students into five groups, the first of which carries the instruction, "Girl students come near." Nothing is indicated for the other four groups, but at the end of the list another annotation instructs, "and all together." According to an annotation in the scores, "Raymonda falls with a cry and faints; everyone disappears."

The order of events just described based on the CN differs from the libretto, wherein Abderrakhman's final attempt to abduct Raymonda occurs after the entrance of the *dukhi*.

Scène XI. This atmospheric scene depicts the sunrise and, musically, is a development of themes accompanying Raymonda's first glimpse of Jean de Brienne combined with short statements of the White Lady's motif and followed by a reminder of Raymonda's scarf variation from Scene I (*Une fantaisie*).[108] Glazunov employs all of these themes to transfer the action from the twilight of Raymonda's dreams back to the daylight reality of her courtly life.

Scène XII. The final annotation in the CN for Act One reads, "Entrance of girl pupils and boy pupils from the castle" in search of their missing mistress. The number of students, or whether the four friends are involved, is not indicated. The music imitates

---

[107] The circular ground plans remind us of the choreography for the young students that make up the court of Oberon's kingdom during the opening of George Balanchine's *A Midsummer Night's Dream* (1962).

[108] Petipa asked for "16 bars of music expressive of the situation." Goldman, "*Raymonda*," 42.

running steps, followed by a quick crescendo, culminating in a final statement of the sunrise theme from *Scène XI* as the curtain falls.

Act Two

Cour d'amour

Act Two includes two complete dance suites, one a classical *pas d'action* and the other a diverse collection of mostly exotic character dances. Brief mimed passages introduce each suite. The final bacchanale dovetails into the conclusion of the act, which features the denouement: the return of Jean de Brienne and his triumph over Abderrakhman.

Entr'acte—Scène I. Marche. Following a second *entr'acte*, which introduces the Raymonda 2 motif, the opening march brings on knights, lords, ladies, troubadours, minstrels, and others who have been invited to the *cour d'amour*, which is set in an interior courtyard of Raymonda's castle. The scenic design by Konstantin Ivanov features a central entrance with rounded doors upstage at the top of a short, broad staircase. Bench seating is set up along each wing. The CN instructs, "All of them enter from the left side," that is, from upstage right rather than through the central doors. Everyone congratulates Raymonda, who is distracted by her concern that Jean de Brienne has not yet arrived. Trumpets, played *sur la scène*, announce special guests.[109]

Scène II: Entrée d'Abdérame. The seneschal (Bulgakov) reports, "A knight comes" (RN 186).[110] Expecting Jean de Brienne, Raymonda is met once again by Abderrakhman, who enters at RN 187, bringing his entourage with him. Raymonda is upset as she recognizes the Muslim knight of her dream.[111] Seeing Raymonda, Abderrakhman bows to her.

Abderrakhman: "I come here for your celebration. Allow me to introduce my suite." He presents his entourage then crosses to stage right.

Abderrakhman: [aside] "She is beautiful. I will propose that she take my hand."

Crossing back to stage left, he extends his hand to Raymonda, but she withdraws her own hand with disdain. According to an annotation in the scores, the Countess "calms Raymonda in the name of hospitality," and the *pas d'action* begins.

Glazunov, drawing on Abderrakhman's motif as presented in the vision scene, here provides the strongest statement of the antagonist's motif thus far. This may have been in response to Petipa's request in this scene for a return of earlier music: "From 16 to 24 bars of music in an Arabian spirit. *Forte* for entrance of Abder-Rakhman. He bows before Raymonda and shows his retinue to her. Music should be somewhat reminiscent of the scene in the previous act."[112]

---

[109] Glazunov included a final chord in G minor (first inversion) at the end of the *Marche*, following the onstage fanfare. This isolated chord serves, musically, to bridge the abrupt transition from the E-flat major of the *Marche* to the A minor of *Scène II*. It also functions as a scene-changing chord, creating a momentary suspense, not dissimilar to the brief scene-changing chords Adam provided in the second act of *Giselle* just prior to Albert's entrance.

[110] The score annotation states that Abderrakhman enters at RN 186, but the CN makes clear that his entrance does not come until RN 187, coinciding with a *forte* statement of his motif.

[111] The annotation in the score states, "Raymonda lets out a cry as she recognizes Abderrakhman from her vision."

[112] Goldman, "*Raymonda*," 42. Italics added.

Grand pas d'action: Grand Adagio. The dramatic adagio continues the development of Abderrakhman's motif (Ex. 10.6b). Choreographed for three women and three men—Raymonda, Clémence, Henriette, Abderrakhman, Bernard, and Béranger—the dance calls for Abderrakhman to make advances toward Raymonda. (Countess Sybille, undoubtedly an interested onlooker, is included in the cast list for the *pas d'action*.) Petipa pointed out the contrasting emotions expressed in the scene in his instructions to Glazunov: "Music is begun expressing tenderness. However, for the depiction of the Saracen, it is *forte*."[113] His scenario is poetic in its description of the dance:

> Abder-Rakhman, captivated by the beauty of Raymonda, speaks to her of his love. But she prefers the madrigals of the other lords. Abder-Rakhman becomes all the more insistent: "You should belong to me, beautiful countess"—he says—"you will be surrounded by luxury and delights if you stay with me."[114]

Far less clear in this case is the CN—the document capable of providing concrete details of what occurred on stage—which offers a series cluttered ground plans filled with annotations, numerous arrows indicating direction of travel, and strike-throughs that require careful deciphering in order to determine what the actual movements and choreography may have been. This is our reading of it:

Raymonda, at center, begins the dance with an *arabesque* on *pointe*. The ground plan suggests she supports herself by holding Clémence's shoulder. Abderrakhman approaches Raymonda, who moves away from him in a clockwise circle around the stage, as he mimes, "You, do not leave." Raymonda rejoins her two girlfriends at center and mimes in reply, "No! Nobody." The women take hold of each other at the waist and, standing on *pointe*, move their leg "forward and back" three times—that is, they pass their working leg from ninety degrees *devant* to *arabesque* three times. The girlfriends on either side of Raymonda hold the hands of Fokine (Bernard) and Obukhov (Béranger), who flank the trio and face upstage.

Raymonda runs downstage where she is again confronted by Abderrakhman, who mimes, "Listen to me." She refuses, and Obukhov lifts her and carries her back to center, as Fokine partners the two girlfriends at upstage right. Abderrakhman follows. Partnered by Obukhov, Raymonda poses on the left *pointe* (her right foot in *cou-de-pied derrière*) and arches her back to lean away from Abderrakhman. She runs from him again, and he approaches her, declaring, "I love you." Abderrakhman continues to move alongside Raymonda as she *bourrées* across the front of the stage. She steps into a *piqué tour en dehors* that ends *à la seconde* as Obukhov steps in to partner her. Raymonda continues with a *glissade* and *piqué en arabesque* on the right foot then crosses the stage again with *bourrées*, followed by what is likely another *piqué tour en dehors*—the ground plan indicates a turn. (Perhaps she was partnered by Fokine, as Obukhov had partnered her at stage right, although an annotation mentioning Fokine's name is struck through.) Raymonda runs upstage left. The girlfriends *bourrée* to meet her.

At the climactic point in the music, Obukhov "carries" Preobrazhenskaya "with both hands," preceded by the girlfriends, who continue to *bourrée*. The group travels on the diagonal. When they reach downstage right, "Gerdt wants to grab her, but she runs past him under his arm" toward stage left where Fokine partners her in a *tour de*

[113] Ibid. Italics added.
[114] Ibid.

promenade as she poses in *arabesque* on *pointe*. She pulls in for a single *pirouette* that opens to *arabesque* as she leans forward. Meanwhile, Obukhov partners both Egorova (Clémence) and Karsavina (Henriette) at stage right as Fokine had done earlier in the dance. Preobrazhenskaya continues with Fokine, who partners her in a *double piqué tour en dehors* opening to *arabesque* as Gerdt, who has crossed to stage left, again declares, "I love you."

In preparation for the finale, the girlfriends run downstage left to their mistress. They *bourrée* ("all three on [*pointe* symbol]") to midstage—Preobrazhenskaya to center (where she *bourrées* around Obukhov), Karsavina to stage right (where Gerdt has walked via upstage to meet her), and Egorova at stage left (paired with Fokine). Annotations instruct, "Obukhov spins Preobrazhenskaya 2 circles"; the notation calls for three turns on the right *pointe*: the first *en arabesque*, the second *en cou-de-pied devant*, and the third again *en arabesque*. Preobrazhenskaya next *bourrées* forward for a preparatory fourth position and supported *double pirouette*, finishing *en cou-de-pied devant*. In this final pose, she faces downstage left, away from Abderrakhman (who, despite partnering Karsavina in an *arabesque*, faces directly toward Raymonda), her head turned even farther to the left.

Four variations follow—one for each of Raymonda's girlfriends, one for a male dancer, and one for Raymonda.[115]

Variation I. The first variation, an *allegretto*, $\frac{2}{4}$ in D-flat major, features a tripping melody that rises and falls with a continual sense of forward motion. The CN documents the performance of Egorova as Clémence. She begins at center with a series of *pas de bourrée* and *relevés* that alternate *demi-attitude devant* and *demi-arabesque* positions in place. Although the facing position of the hips is not given, the progression of steps suggests the *relevés* were all performed *en effacé*. After traveling upstage right, alternating *pas de bourrée en avant* and *en arrière* on *pointe* while traveling sideways, Egorova returns down the diagonal, still moving sideways, with *pas de chat, pas de bourrée* on *pointe, relevé en arabesque, sissonne changée, pas de chat* four times. The next enchaînement, which travels across the front of the stage, may be missing one bar of steps: Egorova begins with two *échappés battus*. (What follows immediately after the *échappés battus* may be missing from the enchaînement.) The next bar documents an *à la seconde* position on the right *pointe*; the left foot then lowers to *cou-de-pied derrière*. These three bars are repeated to the other side as Egorova moves upstage left on the diagonal. A final diagonal features two *relevés petits passés* and two *pas de chat* four times followed by a series of *glissades* and *piqués de côté en cou-de-pied derrière* across the front of the stage. After an abrupt change of direction, Egorova travels back across the stage with unspecified turns, first on *pointe* then on *demi-pointe*.

Variation II. The second variation, for Henriette as danced by Karsavina, is a lyrical $\frac{6}{8}$ in B-major. Like Egorova's variation, this one also relies heavily on *pointe* work. Karsavina begins with *piqué fouetté* to *arabesque effacé, pas de bourrée* on *pointe* on each foot followed by a gentle *bourrée* that zigzags downstage. After two *glissades*, an abbreviated annotation appears to call for *rond de jambe* on *pointe*. This enchaînement is repeated then followed by two *pas de cheval* to *tendu devant fondu* and hops on *pointe* in

---

[115] An additional notation of a brief (possibly incomplete) female variation that we have not yet identified is written on the oblong-format paper associated with student notation work and included within the Act Two pages of the CN. No ballerina's name is given, the notation is not signed, and the heading reads merely, "Variation for ballet 'Raymonda.' Music by Glazunov."

fifth position as Karsavina makes two complete turns to the right. All of these movements are repeated, beginning from the two *glissades*.

The rest of the variation features travel up and down the diagonal to and from upstage left. Karsavina first moves backward up the diagonal with repeated *relevés en arabesque* then downstage with eight *entrechat six, relevé développé devant*. She travels up again with *piqués en demi-arabesque* and finally returns downstage with a *bourrée* backward that ends with a *pas de basque*, making a half turn and finishing in fourth position *plié*.

A second, more detailed notation of this variation (filed with the main CN) records the performance of Anna Pavlova as Henriette.[116] While all of the bars of music do not appear to be accounted for, this notation provides greater detail than the first, particularly for the unusual steps preceding the hops on *pointe*: three quick *grands battements*—the working leg moving from fifth position *demi-pointe* to *attitude devant* and back— beginning with three with the right foot, then three with the left foot, and then three with the right again, all performed as the dancer makes a complete turn to the right. She concludes the enchaînement with an *assemblé* before continuing with the hops on *pointe*. Other differences between the notated versions include the opening enchaînement: instead of two *piqué fouettés effacé*, Pavlova performs only one followed by *coupé dessous* on *pointe* and *pas de basque* into *piqué en arabesque, fondu*. What seems to be a truncated or incomplete final section of Pavlova's variation concludes with a string of *piqué tours en dehors* that finish with *sous-sus*.

Variation III. The sole male variation in Raymonda, an *allegro* $\frac{2}{4}$ featuring trumpets that imbue it with a martial quality, sadly is not included in the CN.

Variation IV. Raymonda's variation is based on the Raymonda 2 motif and begins with a horn solo that lends a heroic quality to her dance (Ex. 10.7b). As in the preceding variations, the emphasis is on *pointe* work. Preobrazhenskaya begins with a diagonal downstage right from center: *pas de cheval* to *tendu effacé devant fondu, assemblé, pirouette* from fifth position followed by three *piqués petits passés* twice. Next, traveling backward and to the side across the stage, she performs *entrechat cinq, piqué en cou-de-pied devant, glissade en arrière, piqué de côté*, the working leg extended forty-five degrees *devant* then brought in to *cou-de-pied devant*, three times. After a *bourrée* that brings her back to downstage right, Preobrazhenskaya returns up the diagonal with a *piqué tour en arabesque* to *tendu effacé devant* followed by a *bourrée* three times. She continues to *bourrée*, tracing a circle, and arrives upstage center for the climactic phrase: two hops in fifth position on *pointe* followed by a hop to *demi-arabesque* on *pointe, plié* six times to alternate sides, traveling directly down center. A variant of this phrase, notated alongside the first option, calls for *changements de pieds* on *pointe*. After a series of *piqués en cou-de-pied* on alternating feet traveling sideways as Preobrazhenskaya makes her way downstage right, she travels backward up the diagonal with a step we have previously described as *ballotté par terre de côté* (see Chapter 8). She returns with *chaînés* on *demi-pointe* and finishes the variation in fifth position on *pointe*.

A second, incomplete notation of this variation (the second enchaînement is missing) appears to be in the same hand as the second notation of *Variation II*. The notation is filed with the main CN, written on oblong-format paper, and also documents Preobrazhenskaya's performance, providing movements for the torso, head, arms, and hands. The *changement* hops are the only option given, and the final *chaînés* are replaced

---

[116] We have not identified the notator. The scribal hand and oblong-format paper suggest that this notation may be the work of a student.

by ten *piqué tours en dedans*. Volynsky described these final turns, although his account suggests a *manège* instead of a diagonal:

> In the *pas d'action* of the second act, Preobrazhenskaya again dances a complicated variation. In particular, she does a circle of jumps with turns on her left leg, bringing her turned-out right foot above the arch of the left foot first in the front [the notated *coup de pied* position of the right foot], then in the back [the position of the foot when the dancer steps on the right foot before the next turn].[117]

The notation confirms the final step in the variation is *sous-sus*.

Coda. The coda brings all participants together and includes solo passages for the three women and Obukhov (Béranger), suggesting the earlier male variation may have been danced by Fokine (Bernard).[118]

Béranger and Clémence begin upstage left with a diagonal of *cabrioles derrière, temps levé passé* to *tombé croisé*, passing the working leg from *arabesque* to forty-five degrees *devant*, three times (RN 211). The ground plan's drawing of the dancers' extended arms suggests the two may have performed the steps in unison while Obukhov held Egorova by the waist, Egorova held Obukhov by the shoulder, or both. On the return diagonal upstage, Clémence's *bourrées* are punctuated by lifts—*sissonnes* landing in *arabesque fondu*. This initial entrée concludes with *chaînés* on *demi-pointe* for Clémence, traveling back down the diagonal as Béranger walks alongside her.

Henriette follows, traveling downstage at center with *glissade, entrechat cinq de volée* to each side, and four *sissonnes fermé* twice (RN 212). She *bourrées* backward toward upstage right and returns on the diagonal with *piqué tours en dehors* followed by turns on *demi-pointe*.

Béranger is next, the CN providing a rare example of male coda steps. His first *enchaînement*, traveling down the diagonal from upstage right, comprises *tombé, glissade, assemblé, relevé à la seconde, temps de flèche derriére*, likely performed two times. He returns up the diagonal with *pas de bourrée en tournant, assemblé, entrechat quatre, entrechat cinq* three times. His final *enchaînement*, traveling again down the diagonal, is not notated but may have been a repeat of his opening *enchaînement*.

Preobrazhenskaya enters upstage right at RN 216. After a run forward on *pointe*, traveling on the diagonal, she performs *relevé en arabesque, pas de bourrée* on *demi-pointe*, and a fleeting pose in *relevé en attitude devant*, arms overhead, back arched, and head to the left (thereby seen in profile by the audience), three times. She changes direction, running downstage right, and travels up the diagonal with *arabesque fondu* and three steps backward on *pointe* performed six times to alternate sides. She returns down the diagonal with a final *enchaînement* of two *relevés développé devant*, three *demi-emboîtés devant, assemblé* three and a half times followed by turns on *demi-pointe* as the melody rises to a climactic *fermata*, one bar before RN 219.

Henriette and Clémence continue, dancing side by side as they travel directly downstage at center with "*fouetté [sauté]* and [*piqué en*] *arabesque*" twice to alternate sides

---

[117] Volynsky, "*Raimonda*," tr. in *Ballet's Magic Kingdom*, 35.

[118] Fokine appears to confirm this in his memoirs. After lamenting a lack of roles in his early years as a dancer, he explains, "The exception in my repertoire was the role of Bernard de Ventadour in *Raymonda*, one of the best of Petipa's ballets, to the music of Alexander Glazunov. This role I acquired my very first year in service. It contained many dances and two classic variations, one in the third [scene, the *pas d'action*] and another in the fourth act [that is, the fourth scene, the dance for four cavaliers]." Fokine, *Memoirs*, 43–44.

(RN 219). They continue with *chassé, tour jeté* followed by a run forward into *grand jeté en avant* twice. They head downstage left with a rapid enchaînement of two *piqués en demi-attitude devant* and two *pas de bourrée*, all on *pointe*, twice. Finally, changing direction, the pair crosses the stage with *pas de cheval, jeté, saut de basque* three times followed by *chaînés* on *demi-pointe*.

Preobrazhenskaya returns for a second, brief entrée—a run directly downstage on *pointe* (RN 221), after which she runs upstage to join her companions. Raymonda allows herself to be partnered briefly by Abderrakhman at center, flanked by the two couples. The CN directs, "everyone forward," the women performing *demi-emboîtés devant* and finishing with supported *double pirouettes*. At the end, Raymonda "runs away," exiting downstage right (therefore she remains in character, is appalled by Abderrakhman, and breaks the convention of waiting for applause at the end of a dance).

Scène mimique. Abderrakhman presents his retinue to Raymonda, who has returned to the stage. Following a brief mime exchange, a suite of character dances is performed.

According to the libretto, Abderrakhman entreats, " 'You must be mine, beautiful countess.' . . . 'I offer you a life of magnificence and pleasure.' He calls his slaves to entertain Raymonda."

The CN provides the following narrative:

Abderrakhman: "She left. I love her madly. She must be mine. Oh! What a thought [that is, I have an idea]! I am calling my slaves." [to a male servant] "You call them here and they shall dance here."

The "Saracens" run in and Raymonda approaches Abderrakhman at center.

Abderrakhman: [to Raymonda] "You look. I led them here. They here will dance for you."

Together, Raymonda and Abderrakhman walk downstage left to watch the divertissement.

With the following suite of character dances performed by Abderrakhman's entourage, the audience is thrust into the exotic, imagined world of the medieval Middle East and the Islamic stronghold in Spain.

Comparison of Petipa's general descriptions of the dances in his instructions to Glazunov with the names of the dances eventually printed in the program reveals that as Petipa created the choreography, he sometimes deviated from his original plans:

> *Entrée des jongleurs*, which Petipa described as an "entrée of slaves, jugglers, and others" became *Pas des esclaves sarrasins*
>
> "Entrée of Saracens" became a dance for a dozen Arab boys called *Pas des moriscos*
>
> "Entrée of Moorish women with cymbals" became *Danse sarrasine*, a duet performed by a male-female couple
>
> "Entrée of the Spaniard from Granada (Moor) with castanets" became *Panadéros*, a Spanish-flavored ensemble dance led by a second male-female couple that was joined by an all-female ensemble, half of whom performed in travesty

Petipa's choreographic choices for this suite of dances were similar to those he made for the dances in *La Bayadère's* festal third scene: when depicting peoples whose dance traditions were essentially unknown to him (the exception here is the Spanish *Panadéros*), Petipa employed a short list of relatively simple, ballet-based steps—*emboîtés, temps levés, soubresauts, pas de basque*, and the like—often combined with non-academic or character dance movements for the upper body. Such dances frequently employ props (for example, sticks in the *Pas des esclaves sarrasins* and coconut shells in the *Pas des moriscos*).

The step vocabulary for two numbers in this set of exotic dances makes understandable Shiryaev's later assertion that Petipa's approach to character choreography was based more on academic dance than on national dance steps. He explained, "I shall give some examples: the 'Saracen Dance' (*Danse sarrasine*) in *Raymonda* is based on the classical movements of the *pas de basque* and *ballonné*; the Spanish *Panadéros* in the same ballet is based on the very same *pas de basque*."[119] While Shiryaev's assessment is relatively accurate for the exotic character dances in Act Two, we will find that the Act Three dances employ a greater number of national dance steps.

Entrée des jongleurs. Although the ensemble dance of Saracen slaves was first performed by thirty couples, the CN accounts for only sixteen.[120] An annotation below the heading "Saracens" explains, "The cavaliers hold sticks in their hands." Before the dancing begins, Raymonda and Abderrakhman walk across the stage to join Countess Sybille at downstage left.

The ensemble commences in a block formation comprised of four rows of couples. The group runs directly downstage, then the women move to the sides in two lines. They travel back toward the men (also arranged in two lines) at center with six *demi-emboîtés devant*, arms overhead, followed by six *demi-emboîtés derrière*, bodies leaned forward, arms reaching behind, then out to the sides and repeat the enchaînement. The men likely perform similar steps: according to the CN, "Cavaliers walk after 4th time" and arrange themselves into four lines.

As the men perform multiple *soubresauts* in place, their arms lifted overhead and opening to the side with each jump, the women travel toward them with a *temps levé en demi-arabesque* then change direction with a *pas de basque*. The ensemble next forms a dense, semicircular grouping upstage, the women flanking a central group of men. The cavaliers "hit the floor with the sticks," while the women, kneeling, perform a repeating *port de bras*, arms finishing overhead. After more *pas de basque* for the women and *demi-emboîtés devant* and *derrière* for the men, the group travels downstage—annotations include, "everyone walks forward," as well as, "7 *pas de basque*." Assembling once again into a block formation—lines of women alternating with lines of men—the ensemble performs a series of *temps levés en attitude devant* in place on alternating legs. At the conclusion of the dance, the women kneel as the men spring from *échappé en plié* to a pose in *demi-attitude devant*.

Danse des garçons Arabes. The dance of the Arab boys features twelve students and is notated twice; each notation also includes the boys' entrée in the final *Baccanal*. The more detailed record, in Rakhmanov's hand, includes movements for the entire body.

---

[119] Beumers et al., *Alexander Shiryaev*, 109.
[120] To be exact, the 1898 premiere program lists thirty-one women and thirty men; a program for 12 October 1903 lists seventeen women and twenty men.

The boys enter upstage, six from each side. Annotations inform us of an exotic property added to the dance: coconut shells. The boys "run and hit coconuts on their knees."
The more detailed CN explains: "in the hands, half-spheres with which they hit the same
ones on their legs," that is, the boys hold a half coconut shell in each hand; the other
halves are attached to their legs just above the knee. Holding their hands in front of them
at waist height, palms down, they run. As they lift their knees, the two halves of the coconut meet and make a percussive noise in time with the quarter-note pulse of the music.

Meeting at center, the boys form two rows and travel forward. The front row turns
toward the back row, and the boys switch places with their counterparts in the opposing
row: they jump toward each other with a *temps levé en demi-attitude derrière*, complete
the turn with a *temps levé en demi-attitude devant*, and dance in place, facing front, with
three *emboîtés devant*. They perform this enchaînement four times then resume their
high-knee running as they "align into two columns, clapping [the coconuts] on the
knees." Next, pairs of boys, one boy behind the other, "face the audience" and perform
"do-za-do" four times—switching places as they perform two *soubresauts* then returning
to their original places with two more.

The boys resume their "run and clap on the knees." The two lines circle toward opposite sides and meet farther upstage in a single row. As the dance approaches its conclusion, the boys travel downstage then "sit down in the Turkish manner" (that is, with legs
crossed) on the final chord. As the music for the next dance begins, they "stand up" and,
splitting at center, "just run" to opposite sides (the more detailed CN calls for *temps levés
en demi-arabesque*), where they sit in lines along the wings.

Entrée des Sarrazins. The CN for this lively duet danced by a Saracen couple records
the performance of Evgenia Obukhova and Vasily Stukolkin.[121] The notated choreography includes the *pas de basque* and *ballonnés* described by Shiryaev. The pair begins
upstage left and speeds down the diagonal with a series of *pas de basque*. Retracing their
path, the dancers move "backward in *échappé*." Reaching center, they circle in place away
from each other with a series of four *temps levés en demi-arabesque* followed by a spring
from *échappé en plié* into *demi-attitude devant fondu* and a *pas de bourrée en tournant*
(which also ends in *demi-attitude devant fondu*) twice.

The couple repeats its opening *pas de basque* enchaînement, the dancers crossing
paths as they travel to opposite downstage corners, then "runs sideways" on *demi-pointe*
to center. The man holds the woman's waist as they travel sideways and diagonally upstage left performing *pas de bourrée* punctuated by *battements degagés en demi-attitude
devant* twelve times. Both raise their left arm overhead with each *battement* as their head
is thrown back and twisted left. Arriving upstage left, they circle away from each other in
place with *pas de basque* finishing in fifth position on *demi-pointe*. Returning downstage
on the diagonal, they "turn the head right and left" as they perform eight *ballonnés* on
alternate legs. Next, the cavalier "pushes the lady" as she performs a pose in fifth position
on *demi-pointe*—arms overhead, body bent back, head to the left—followed by a *tombé*
and a run forward four times, crossing the stage left to right.

Preparing for their final steps, the couple travels backward on the diagonal toward
center with *temps levés en demi-arabesque*, the working leg rising to full *arabesque* when
landing the jump. They advance toward the footlights with their opening *pas de basque*,
turn away from each other with a circle in place of *temps levés en demi-attitude devant*,

---

[121] An annotation at the end of the previous boys' dance notes another pairing: "Dance of [Alexander]
Shiryaev and Obukhova."

then run forward for a final pose in which "the cavalier holds the lady by her head" as she poses in *tendu derrière fondu*, arms extended to the side, back arched, and head turned left.

Grand pas espagnol. With the Spanish dance—*Panadéros*—Petipa returns to step vocabulary and movements we encountered in some of the dances in his *Paquita*. Too, the dance features a lead couple and sixteen women, half of whom perform in travesty, as in the *Pas des manteaux*. The CN records the performance of the original lead interpreters, Marie Petipa and Sergei Lukyanov, separately from the ensemble. (We note that studio photographs of Marie Petipa in this role show her holding a large tambourine, a prop not mentioned in the CN.[122])

The eight bars of transitional music that precede the dance are struck through in the PR. The lead couple enters upstage left at bar 29 and circles the stage for sixteen bars performing undesignated steps.[123] Arriving at center, the couple stamps their feet (likely an *appel*), performs a *double rond de jambe en l'air fondu* and "*balancé* 4 times" as they travel backward upstage. What follows is made somewhat uncertain due to strikethroughs in the ground plan: The couple separates, traveling downstage on opposite diagonals, then crosses paths as each dancer traverses the stage in turns (annotations call for *pas de basque* and "stamp the foot") before the woman "turns in place and gets on the knee and bends." More *pas de basque* bring the dancers back to center, where the woman kneels and her partner poses "over her." A *fermata* in the CN may correspond to bar 45, which includes three *tenuto* chords marked *passionato* in the score.

The dancers continue with two Spanish *glissades* (see Chapter 5)—an annotation instructs, "extend the leg"—and *saut de basque*, performed three times to alternate sides. They run forward, crossing paths, and pose—"she is over him." The man continues with two *pas de basque* and a *pirouette*, performed three-and-a-half times, while the woman performs *pas de basque*, traveling away from the man, then runs back toward him and strikes an undesignated pose. She performs this set of movements three times.

The couple next performs eight *pas de basque*, traveling downstage left, then separates and traverses the stage in opposing circular patterns, while they "extend the leg" (that is, perform a Spanish *glissade*)—four times for her, two times and more *pas de basque* for him. Reaching opposite sides of the stage, they conclude the dance by running toward each other and meeting at center stage for a single *pirouette*, ending on the knee.

As mentioned, the ensemble choreography is notated separately. Beginning in two rows, the "men" (those performing in travesty) behind the women, they travel forward with *pas de basque*. Arriving downstage, they perform "in place *pas*" (*plié* in fifth position followed by an extension of the right foot diagonally forward on *demi-pointe* four times), then the men "turn 2 times" (a *piqué tour en dehors* to fourth position *plié*, performed twice) as the women kneel. The rows split and the dancers move to either side of the stage with *pas de basque* and form lines of couples. Partners face each other as the "ladies gradually go down on the knees" while the "men" echo this movement with an increasing lunge position. The couples continue dancing in lines along the wings. The CN instructs them to "stamp the feet" (they perform four *appels*) "and *bal[ancé]*" (they

---

[122] See, for example, two photographs preserved in the A.A. Bakhrushin State Central Theatre Museum (KP 325094/7 and KP 252504/779), available online at https://goskatalog.ru/portal/#/collections?id=24140124 and https://goskatalog.ru/portal/#/collections?id=24501507, respectively.

[123] A manuscript annotation in the PR at bar 29 reads, "Beginning [Anna] Pavlova," suggesting the principal couple begins dancing at this point. Pavlova made her debut as the female lead in the *Panadéros* on 29 October 1906. See Lazzarini, *Pavlova*, 80.

perform two *balancés en avant*). After further enchaînements involving *pas de basque* and various poses, the lines travel upstage with Spanish *glissades* and return with *pas de basque* several times. At one point, the "ladies are on the knee and bend the body backward," while the "cavaliers stand over the ladies." At the end of the dance, both lines run upstage, meet at center, and run forward in two rows. For their final pose, the "men" stand behind the women, who kneel.

Danse orientale. The twenty-two-bar *Danse orientale* is something of a puzzle. The score indicates this number is a variation for Raymonda, but no such variation is included in the CN or listed among the dances in the program or the *Yearbook of the Imperial Theaters*, suggesting the number may have been cut. Nevertheless, the dance remains intact in the annotated PR, which otherwise appears to account for cuts and additions to the performance score.[124]

Baccanal. The *Baccanal* functions as both a coda for the suite of character dances and a *pas d'action*. Each group of character performers makes a final danced appearance, and at the end of the bacchanale, Abderrakhman, with the help of his slaves, attempts to abduct Raymonda.

A number of separately notated passages must be collated and reconciled to arrive at an accurate picture of the controlled chaos that defines the *Baccanal*. These include two pages of notation that serve as an outline for the placement onstage of the various ensemble groups as well as separate notations for girl students, boy students, Saracen corps, and Spanish corps plus an entrance for Raymonda and four entrances for the Spanish lead couple (two labeled "1st coda" and two labeled "2nd coda").

Musically, Glazunov complements the dance with a raucous main theme characterized by dissonance and off-rhythms, a metaphor for the wild exoticism surprisingly unleashed into Raymonda's comparatively sedate *cour d'amour* (the theme is a duple-meter variant of the triplet figure from Abderrakhman's motif). Themes from previous numbers are restated, including Raymonda's *pas d'action* variation (Raymonda 2), the Arab boys' dance, and the *Panadéros* (now in duple meter). The Saracen couples' dance is not among the reprises, although it is difficult to imagine they did not take part in the bacchanale.

Our description is based on the variety of notated passages in the CN as well as printed and manuscript annotations in the scores. The latter are offered with the caveat that printed score annotations represent early plans that may have been changed during the creation of the ballet. That being said, it is nevertheless a printed annotation in the score that sets the action in motion: "After the character dances, Abderrakhman calls out servants who fill goblets with intoxicating drinks." The CN references "Girl students with goblets" and "$\frac{2}{4}$" meter without further elaboration. An additional notation, however—preserved in the collection's miscellaneous files and labeled "Grandees with goblets (girl students)"—provides a ground plan and choreography for twelve students, with some steps notated on *pointe*.[125] An annotation in this additional CN tells us that the students hold a goblet in their right hand. Standing in a row across the stage, they run downstage and drink out of their goblets. They next form a column of two lines at center, drink again, and so on. Eventually forming two rows, they perform a series of *temps levés*, both *en demi-arabesque* and *en demi-attitude devant*, and *demi-valse*. Further steps include

---

[124] Slonimsky suggests the music was performed but without providing details of the action. Slonimsky, "'Raimonda,'" 473.

[125] MS Thr 245 (227), 2–4.

"dos-a-dos" in couples and *assemblés soutenus sur les pointes* that alternate with more *demi-valse*. The students finish in lines along the wings, where they dance in place "until the end" of their entrée.

At bar 77 (RN 256), Glazunov reintroduces the Raymonda 2 motif. The main CN provides choreography for Raymonda, who joins in the fray.[126] Raymonda, "with a goblet in her hand," performs "*saut de basque* twice" then "drinks" while performing a *piqué en demi-arabesque* four times as she zigzags downstage. She circles around to center with three more *sauts de basque* then travels downstage right performing "turns on [*pointe* symbol]." She stops beside Abderrakhman, who "takes the goblet."

Here follow the two pages of the main CN, labeled "Coda," that provide an outline and ground plans for the remainder of the *Baccanal*.[127] At RN 258 (though possibly sixteen bars earlier to coincide with the reprise of the *Panadéros* music), Abderrakhman and Raymonda walk across the stage. The student girls are lined up on either side performing *balancé*, and the Spanish ensemble dances in a row upstage: two Spanish *glissades*, *saut de basque* four times.[128] The Spanish dancers next travel downstage with *pas marché* and *temps levé battement degagé devant* for twelve bars then split and moves to the sides with *pas de basque*. The Spanish leads, "Petipa [and] Lukyanov," are also listed but not shown in the ground plan. Of their several separately notated coda entrées, the two labeled "1st coda" complement the ground plan of the Spanish ensemble. In the version filed first in the CN, the solo pair runs on upstage right then travels downstage and up with a series of *temps levés battement degagé devant* and Spanish *glissades*. As the ensemble moves downstage, the soloists travel downstage right with four *pas de basque*. The man kneels while the woman circles around him performing *pas de basque* and what may be a cachucha step (she stretches her left leg out in *tendu devant* before pulling it back into fifth position). The other notated entrances feature *pas de basque*, Spanish *glissades* (Sergeyev again writes, "extend the leg"), "do-za-do," and the cachucha step. The CN does not indicate when the Spanish couple's second entrée was performed or provide further detail about the various notated Spanish entrées. Neither does the CN mention an entrée for the Saracen couple, although a notated "Coda" that appears to fill twenty-four bars is filed after the notation of their solo duet (*Entrée des Sarrazins*, above).[129]

The CN continues with a brief passage (sixteen bars) during which the Saracen corps joins the Spanish corps, which now lines the wings inside of the student girls. This section may coincide with the second half of the Spanish couple's entrée—the Saracen corps appears to remain in the top half of the stage, leaving the downstage area open. After running forward in four rows of couples, the Saracen corps men perform a series of four *temps levés en demi-arabesque* followed by four *demi-emboîtés devant* four times

[126] Though he applied the following idea to the earlier *Danse orientale*, David Vaughan suggested Raymonda's willingness to join in the dance might be based on reasoning similar to that found in the ballet *Sylvia*, in which the title character, a huntress of Diana, pretends to go along with the scheme of Orion by drinking wine with him, thereby buying herself time in a dangerous situation. David Vaughan, "Nureyev's 'Raymonda,'" *Ballet Review* 5, no. 2 (1975–1976): 35.

[127] A second, detailed notation (in an unidentified hand) of the *Baccanal* entrée for thirty-two Saracens (sixteen couples) is part of the CN.

[128] The Spanish reprise comprises thirty-bars in the OS but only sixteen bars in the PR. Manuscript annotations in the PR indicate a repeat of the sixteen bars, bringing the PR into agreement with the OS.

[129] After running directly down center, the couple performs multiple *demi-emboîtés devant* followed by a four *pas de basque*, which they perform as they make a complete turn to the right and exchange places. After repeating this enchaînement, they move upstage with a variant of *demi-valse* followed by three *temps levés* on *demi-pointe* as they make a complete turn three and a half times. They finish at center with a pose in *tendu derrière*.

(nothing is notated for the women), while the Spanish corps performs two Spanish *glissades*, *battement degagé de côté* four times. As the Arab boys run in upstage from either side, the corps (the notated steps do not designate a particular group) continues with more *temps levés en demi-arabesque* as well as *temps levés en demi-attitude devant*, which the couples perform as they turn—an annotation directs the men to "circle together with lady."

The Arab boys' theme returns for a mere sixteen bars, but the entrée preserved for them fill twenty-four bars. After eight bars of their signature high-knee run, during which they enter upstage from either side (this entrance may be performed during the eight bars preceding the return of their theme music), the boys form a column of two lines at center. Performing *soubresauts*, they jump away from the line and back two times over the course of eight bars. They make a half turn on the last jump, landing with their backs to the audience. They resume running and head upstage, where they form a single row and "stand."

The Spanish and Saracen ensembles continue dancing throughout. In the final box of notated steps, the mass of dancers that fills the stage in rows is identified as "Saracens, boy students, Spanish." Two additional pages of notation in an unidentified hand document the *Baccanal* choreography for the Saracen corps in detail. The pages conclude with three ground plans for which no steps are provided. In the first, the ensemble travels downstage: "16 bars they move hitting with sticks"; in the second, "move backward [upstage] also hitting with sticks all the time"; in the third, "stand in place and continue hitting with sticks until soldiers surround them."

The final annotation in the main CN states, "Gerdt carries away Preobr[azhenskaya]," an instruction that agrees with an annotation in the scores at RN 265, when the music has reached fever pitch: "Taking advantage of the wild, noisy dance, Abderrakhman abducts Raymonda with the help of his slaves."

Glazunov's musical scheme for the *Baccanal*, which as we have seen includes the Raymonda 2 motif and incorporation of melodies from the preceding dances in the character suite, can be compared to the choreographic structure of the dance as deduced from the CN, PR, and OS. Indeed, the music serves as a map for ordering the choreography of this complex dance number.

Rehearsal number	Section/Motif	Bars	Bars per section/motif
251	Introduction	12 bars	21 bars
252		9 bars	
253	*Baccanal* theme	16 bars	48 bars
254		16 bars	
255		16 bars	
256	Raymonda 2	9 bars	17 bars
257		8 bars	
	Panadéros	16 bars	32 bars
258		16 bars	
259	Arab boys	16 bars	16 bars
260	*Baccanal* theme	8 bars	8 bars
261	Abderrakhman	8 bars	8 bars
262	*Baccanal* theme	8 bars	8 bars
	Raymonda 2	4 bars	40 bars

263	20 bars	
264	12 bars	
265	4 bars	
Baccanal theme	8 bars	16 bars
266	8 bars	

Scène III. Jean de Brienne and King Andrei II of Hungary arrive suddenly on the scene with their retinue. According to the libretto, "Jean de Brienne frees Raymonda from the clutches of the slaves and attacks Abderrakhman." The CN for this act concludes with Jean de Brienne's entrance, though the word "Duel" heads a subsequent page that is otherwise blank.

Although the CN does not include ground plans for this final section, the stage directions included in the scores and the explicitness of the music—motifs and other descriptive devices, such as the dissonance that suggests the clashing of weapons—offer detailed clues about the action.

We turn to Petipa's scenario for a description of the remaining narrative:

> The king waves a hand to calm the excitement [Ex. 10.8a]. He has everyone gather in a circle and suggests to the knight de Brienne and Abder-Rakhman that they settle their fight in hand-to-hand combat. They agree. The armor-bearers arm them and stand alongside their respective lords. Raymonda throws her scarf to the knight Jean de Brienne.[130]

An annotation in the scores adds, "Enraged by this, Abderrakhman attacks the knight."

Le combat. The duel, which comprises three attacks, is expressed musically through a combination of Jean's and Abderrakhman's motifs along with tense dissonance in the brass. After the second attack, the White Lady appears in protection of Jean—her motif is heard clearly in the score—who then delivers a mortal wound to Abderrakhman.[131] The scenario continues: "All the ladies, lords, and servants express their joy and surround Raymonda. The king takes her hand and puts it into the hand of the knight Jean."[132]

Hymne. The final *Hymne* is based on Jean de Brienne's motif. The White Lady's motif also makes an appearance, as does the signature triplet of Abderrakhman's motif, before more onstage brass fanfares signal the end of the act.[133] The intertwining of these motifs provides a summation of the second act's conflict and its resolution—Abderrakhman's defeat at the hands of the victor, Jean de Brienne, assisted by the intercession of the White Lady.

---

[130] Goldman, "*Raymonda*," 43.

[131] According to Petipa's scenario, Abderrakhman did not die, but rather was "put in chains" while "[w]ith sabres the army of King Andrei II pursues Abder-Rakhman's retinue." Goldman, "*Raymonda*," 43. The change had been made by the time the libretto was printed: "Abderrakhman received his mortal wound and his retinue did not escape, but was surrounded by King Andrei's sword-bearers."

[132] Goldman, "*Raymonda*," 43.

[133] Petipa considered a final, post-battle appearance of the White Lady, which may explain the presence of her motif in the *Hymne*. His notes to Glazunov state, "Possible: In a cloud, the White Lady promises them happiness." Goldman, "*Raymonda*," 44.

Act Three

Le festival des noces

The final act of *Raymonda* features the wedding divertissement, including the *Pas classique hongrois*, the celebrated dance suite whose very name tells us that it is an amalgam of classical and character dance. The CN for Act Three is the sparsest of the entire ballet (prose descriptions and step names often replace actual step notation), but it preserves enough information to show that many of today's productions match much of what was notated.

Entr'acte. The sweeping *entr'acte* that precedes Act Three includes repetition of motifs from Acts One and Two—Raymonda 2, the White Lady, the Homecoming motif, and the pervasive rising seventh from the development of Raymonda 1—reminding the listener of the main action of the plot.

Le cortège hongrois. The curtain rises on the wedding feast of Raymonda and Jean de Brienne in the gardens of Jean's castle "on the slope of an Alpine peak" (Ex. 10.8d).[134] The scenic design by Petr Lambin features a castle perched on a summit that is accessible by a wide winding pathway. This is viewed through a large stone archway framed by trees. The production documents indicate smaller arched openings in the third wing on either side of the stage (presumably through which dancers will enter and exit), surrounded by bench seating. According to Petipa's notes to Glazunov, the *cortège hongrois* (Hungarian procession) brings on the following: pages and arms-bearers of the King, King Andrei II, Hungarian knights, Countess Sybille, the seneschal, distinguished ladies and their pages, French knights with their arms-bearers, troubadours, and finally Raymonda and Jean, both of whom wear formal dress (they will change costume before dancing the *Pas classique hongrois*). "The newlyweds take their place on the rostrum with King Andrei and accept congratulations from their guests."[135]

Although Sergeyev's documentation of dances in this act features some notated movements, he just as often accompanied his ground plans with prose descriptions of choreography or simply the name of a dance step; many of the steps named are from the customary step vocabulary of Hungarian and Polish theatrical dance. As we did for our description of the children's mazurka and other dances in *Paquita*, we will refer to the 1939 *Fundamentals of Character Dance* (FCD) in order to fill out the details of these steps. A number of the movements and steps described in the CN can be matched with steps described in the FCD:

> "Hungarian" (*vengerka*) in the CN is first encountered in the *Danse des enfants* and refers to the FCD's *verevochka*, or "hopping in place"—a skipping step that can also be described as a small *temps levé petit passé*. As used in the CN, "Hungarian" is usually performed as a traveling step, often as the dancers move backward upstage.[136]
>
> "In place *pas*" is used in a variety of CNs to indicate any number of steps that are performed in place, that is, without traveling. In *Raymonda* Act Three, steps

---

[134] Goldman, "*Raymonda*," 44.
[135] Ibid.
[136] Lopukhov et al., *Character Dance*, 88–89, see especially entry number 20, "Verevochka. No. 3. Moving Backwards."

performed "in place" often include a *bokázó*—a type of "break" (or "finishing") step featuring a clip (or click) of the heels (recall the musical figure that accompanies this step; see Ex. 10.13). A *bokázó* is customarily performed at the end of a sequence of steps. The *bokázó* notated most often in the CN is identified in the FCD as "A more Elaborate Bokazo. Break No. 3," and features a turning in of the left foot, a turning in of the right foot, and a heel "clip" (see *holubetz*, next paragraph) as the knees are turned outwards.[137] This particular step is both referred to in the ground plan ("in place *pas*") and notated for the first time for the soloists near the beginning of the *Grand pas hongrois*.

"Holubetz" (*golubets*) refers to a heel clip; the men performing these dances traditionally wore boots and the women heeled shoes.[138] The Stepanov notators used a symbol (a combination of circle and cross) to denote the clip. The FCD authors explain: "Such steps [*holubetz*] mean that one foot is *clipped* against the other and is distinguished from the more classical *cabriole* in that both legs take part equally and the legs are directly under the body."[139] *Holubetz* is both written in the ground plan and notated the first time for the soloists near the beginning of the *Grand pas hongrois*.

"Side *pas*" does not precisely resemble any step in the FCD. Using ballet terminology, we would describe this step as a *pas de bourrée degagé de côté*. It could be considered a stylized version of the FCD's *balancé holubetz*, whose movements include steps to either side, but with "side *pas*" the legs are lifted from the floor and the heels are not clipped as the legs come together under the body.[140] Although the term "side *pas*" is frequently written in the *Raymonda* ground plans, it is not once notated in Stepanov symbols. To find the notation, one must look at the choreographic notation of the czardas in *Swan Lake*, where the step is both notated and labeled "Side *pas*."[141]

"Czardas" is first written in the CN as a title for the notation of the ensemble choreography in the *Grand pas hongrois*. To find actual notation of the czardas step, one must again consult the choreographic notation of the *Swan Lake* czardas. The step documented there closely matches the FCD description of "Promenade No. 1," in which two steps are followed by a *battement développé* on each foot.[142]

"Chassé" (*shosse*) is first written in the CN for the entrance of the soloists in the interpolated mazurka. This traveling step is not notated in the *Raymonda* CN, but the term *chassé* may refer to one or more of the standard Polish dance steps described in the FCD, particularly the "Pas-chassé coupé for Boys" and possibly various *pas marché* steps for both men and women.[143] Later in the mazurka, the soloists are instructed to perform "mazurka chassé," again suggesting the *pas-chassé* step, which is described in the FCD as a "variant of *pas marché* (that is, Mazurka on one foot)."[144]

---

[137] Ibid., 91, see especially No. 26.
[138] Ibid., 50–51, and 83–85.
[139] Ibid., 83.
[140] Ibid., 97–98, entry number 11: "Balancé Holubetz in Krakoviak No. 2."
[141] See MS Thr 186 (11).
[142] Lopukhov et al., *Character Dance*, 80–81.
[143] Ibid., 93–95, nos. 1–4.
[144] Ibid., 94.

"Mazurka" is the opening step for the ensemble of the interpolated mazurka, and later in the dance it is performed by the soloists. As with "side *pas*" and "chassé," the mazurka step is not notated in the *Raymonda* CN (although the ground plan indicates the couples hold hands while performing the step). However, the step is notated in the choreographic notation of the *Paquita* children's mazurka (see Chapter 5) as well as in the notation of the *Swan Lake* mazurka.[145]

The first three dances of Act Three (*Danse des enfants*, *Grand pas hongrois*—a *czardas*— and the interpolated mazurka) draw heavily from national dance step vocabulary. The *Pas classique hongrois*, on the other hand, features mostly classical steps, the women wearing pointe shoes and the men ballet slippers. Taken together, these dances demonstrate a variety of ways in which Petipa choreographed and featured character dance.

Danse des enfants. The CN for this act begins with a children's dance for twelve student couples.[146] Although in the published musical scores the divertissement begins with the *Grand pas hongrois* (below), the opening number in the libretto's list of dances (where it is called *Rapsodie*) is also the *Danse des enfants*.

Volynsky writes, "At the beginning of the act the little children dance charmingly and youthfully, accompanied by the whirlwind of large, leaping notes."[147] The sparely notated dance begins with the students coming forward in three rows of four couples each (Ex. 10.13).[148] The couples take hands and turn a circle to the left, after which the "girl students spin around in place," while the "boy students clap their hands, standing in place." These opening turning passages are repeated, then the couples perform a *do-si-do* pattern followed by a spin as they hold each other by the front of the waist. These latter steps are also repeated after which the block of dancers reassembles into three circles, the largest at upstage center with two smaller circles at either side and farther downstage. Holding hands, the students rotate their circles in a counterclockwise direction then disperse and form two lines of six students at either sides of the stage and a row of twelve students upstage. As the central row travels downstage and splits, each half moving toward opposite wings, the students on the sides move upstage center and form a new row of twelve. This pattern is repeated after which the couples who finish on the sides take each other by the waist and, making three clockwise turns, travel to form a single row across the front of the stage. The annotation "obertas," written next to the turns in the ground plan, is the name of a Polish folk dance that features turning steps for a pair of dancers.[149] Those in the upstage row travel downstage to meet them, and the two rows move together, upstage and down, the CN providing no indication of steps other than "Hungarian" for the final movement upstage. The dance ends with two rows of students at center. No final pose is given.

Grand pas hongrois. Titled *Palotás* in the libretto's list of dances,[150] the *Grand pas hongrois* is a czardas for a solo couple and twenty ensemble couples (later reduced to

---

[145] See MS Thr 186 (11).

[146] The *Danse des enfants* bears the heading "Czardas" in the CN.

[147] Volynsky, "*Raimonda*," tr. in *Ballet's Magic Kingdom*, 35.

[148] Elizaveta Gromova includes a detailed account of the *Danse des enfants* in *Detskie tantsy iz klassich-eskikh baletov*, 221–233, that is similar in its minute level of detail to her description of the *Paquita* children's mazurka (see Chapter 5).

[149] See Lopukhov et al., *Character Dance*, 99.

[150] See description of *palotás* earlier in this chapter.

twelve).[151] The dance was originally led by Olga Preobrazhenskaya and Alfred Bekefi, the latter dancer being the artist whose style and technique informed the codification of Hungarian dance steps in the FCD.[152]

The choreography for the soloists and ensemble is notated separately. The ensemble enters first, traveling in procession by pairs from upstage left (Ex. 10.9a). They perform a promenade step, in which movements forward are made with a low *battement dével-oppé devant*, then continue with "simply Hungarian."[153] The dancers form rows of four couples across the stage. The men and women of each couple change places ("cross") four times, sliding their feet on the floor as they perform a *detourné* (a complete turn) with each crossing.

The block of dancers moves upstage backward while performing "Hungarian" then change to a czardas step as they return downstage and disperse to the sides, where they again perform "Hungarian" as they travel upstage and back (Ex. 10.10a). Next, they "simply stand"—"Bekef[i]" is written on this same ground plan, likely indicating the soloists' entrance.

Despite the reference to Bekefi in the notation of the ensemble's dance, the CN records the performances of Maria Rutkovskaya and Nikolai Kremnev. After walking to center, holding hands, the couple clicks heels and travels in a zigzag pattern downstage with a "promenade" step, finishing with a *bokázó* break (the steps are notated and the ground plan contains the annotation "in place *pas*"). Making a *soutenu* turn to opposite sides, they step to *demi-arabesque* then move back to center with two *holubetz* (Ex. 10.11a). This enchaînement is performed three times and concludes with two more *holubetz* that bring the couple slightly upstage, where they perform another *bokázó* break ("in place *pas*").

The cavalier offers a scarf to the lady. Each dancer holds one end with their upstage hand as they first turn away from each other into a lunging *arabesque par terre* then turn back with a small *temps levé* and *demi-arabesque fondu* followed by another *bokázó* break ("in place *pas*"). This is performed three times. Next, after a series of "Hungarian" steps, performed as the couple travels backward upstage, they begin a diagonal enchaînement of "2 czardas and *cabriole* and in place *pas*" three times. A short series of *pas marché* to alternating sides (bringing the feet together with each step) brings the *lassú* to a close.

The *friss*, marked "All[egr]o" in the CN, begins with the cavalier holding the woman by the waist as the two travel backward upstage at center (Ex. 10.12a). They perform "Hungarian" and a "break" step three and a half times followed by a series of "side *pas*" as they move around the stage—sometimes switching places, other times facing each other—often holding hands or waists. Various combinations of "side *pas*" and "Hungarian" follow—at one point, the dancers extend and flex their foot with the heel touching the floor. At the end, following another "side *pas*" sequence, the couple holds right hands as the woman makes a turn.

---

[151] A printed program for a performance of *Raymonda* at the Mariinsky Theater on 12 October 1903 lists twelve women and twelve men who danced in the *Palotás* ensemble. See MS Thr 245 (247).

[152] "Although the characteristics of Hungarian dance are very obvious, those appearing in the old classical ballets are very much influenced by the technique of A[lfred] Bekefi, the great character dancer, who performed at the Mariinsky from 1883–1914 as well as with Diaghilev and then taught until his death. He was Hungarian by birth and his particular style was greatly envied and copied. It is those steps which were so associated with his dancing that are given here." Lopukhov et al., *Character Dance*, 80.

[153] See Lopukhov et al., *Character Dance*, 80–83, nos. 1–4, for various examples of "promenade" steps.

Meanwhile, the ensemble dances at the sides for the remainder of the *Grand pas hongrois*. Their steps include "Hungarian," czardas, and *holubetz* combined with academic vocabulary—*soutenu* turns, *temps levés en demi-arabesque*, and *balancés*. At the end, mirroring the soloists, the men turn the women by the hand.

Mazurka. At this point in the divertissement, Petipa inserted an existing mazurka by Glazunov. Like the added waltz in Scene II, this is a movement from Glazunov's *Scènes de ballet.* The addition of this dance provided Petipa an opportunity to feature his daughter Marie, who was paired with Iosif Kshesinsky, son of Felix Kshesinsky. (The elder Kshesinsky, "king of the mazurka," had brought the house down at the premiere of the revival of *Swan Lake* three years earlier, in which both the mazurka and czardas had great success.[154])

Like the previous *Grand pas hongrois*, the mazurka was danced by a solo couple and an ensemble (here, twelve couples), and their choreography is again notated separately. The CN provides clear ground plans that nearly always include the number of bars allotted to each notation box. Fewer steps are notated than for the preceding *Grand pas hongrois*, with Sergeyev relying almost exclusively on step names written in the ground plan.

The ensemble begins with mazurka steps as couples travel downstage in lines along each wing. Having formed two rows across the stage, they travel upstage performing unspecified turns before returning to the sides with *pas de basque* and leaving the center of the stage open for the soloists' entrance.

The soloists begin sixteen bars into the dance. Their steps include primarily *chassé* and mazurka, but in one instance also *holubetz* for the woman. Annotations in the CN suggest an active rapport between the couple—she calls him, he gives her his hand, and she turns in place—reminiscent of Birbanto calling his partner in Petipa's *Danse des Corsaires* (see Chapter 7). Later, in a flirtatious exchange, "He gives her his hand, but she says no. Two times she gives her hand. He tries to catch it, but she takes it away."

The ensemble, meanwhile, is positioned in lines on each side of the stage, where the couples perform *cabrioles* to either side before traveling upstage and down, alternating mazurka and turns. When they stop traveling, the men and women exchange places four times with a turning figure, then all perform *balancés* in place. The women move toward center and back, then the men join them for the same pattern. After returning to the sides, the women cross the stage and back twice, and eventually the couples circle the stage. Again at the sides, the ensemble performs turns, *balancés*, *holubetz*, and *cabrioles* before changing to mazurka and forming two rows behind the soloists. Finally, everyone travels downstage together with turns in the air and *temps levés en demi-arabesque* before striking a final pose, the ground plan suggesting they hold each other around the waist.

Pas classique hongrois is both the collective title used in the program to indicate Petipa's seven-movement suite of classical-cum-character dances for Raymonda, Jean de Brienne, and an ensemble of eight couples as well as the title in the musical score for the second number in this sequence (the adagio).

---

[154] About the *Swan Lake* premiere, the critic Nikolai Bezobrazov wrote, "The appearance of Mr. [Felix] Kshesinsky I, the king of the mazurka, created an absolute sensation." Both the mazurka, led—in the words of another critic—by "the incomparable mazurist Kshesinsky I," and the czardas were repeated. Nikolai Bezobrazov, *Sanktpeterpurgskie vedomosti*, 17 January 1895, 3, tr. in Wiley, *Tchaikovsky's Ballets*, 266. About Felix Kshesinsky, the FCD authors write, "The elements of Polish Dance as used in the late nineteenth century ballets were greatly influenced by the famous character dancer Kshessinsky [sic], whose brilliant performances inspired so many artists and audiences. The importance of his work was to insist on the exact timing and phrasing of the various steps thus ensuring that the dancers preserved most of the characteristics exclusive to Polish folk dance." Lopukhov et al., *Character Dance*, 93.

Entrée. The first number ("Entrée" in the score, "Grand Hungarian *pas*" in the CN) is begun by four couples who are joined by four more couples and finally Raymonda and Jean de Brienne. These entrances set up the subsequent *Pas classique hongrois*, the adagio danced by all nine couples.

The opening enchaînement performed by the first four couples is not notated at the beginning of the dance. However, they likely performed the same steps notated for Raymonda and Jean de Brienne in their later entrance: *temps levé en demi-arabesque* and two steps forward. A pair of couples begins from each upstage corner. The quartets cross once at center while traveling downstage in a zigzag pattern, performing their enchaînement three and a half times to alternate sides. They next form two rows, the men behind the women, and exchange places two times before the rows split and two couples move to each side. A second group of four couples makes a similar entrance, but instead of tracing a zigzag pattern, the dancers pass each other at center and make a circular sweep of the stage. Like the first group, they form two rows. After being lifted by the men, the women perform an "in place *pas*," this time an enchaînement of classical steps: *entrechat six*, single *pirouette* from fifth position, and three *relevés petits passés*. The lift and enchaînement are repeated. The men next "lift the lady 2 times," the ground plan indicating that they make a complete turn as they lift, followed by another "in place *pas*"—*tombé, chassé, cabriole devant, tombé*, two steps forward, *jeté en avant*. Finally, the dancers perform *holubetz* and a turn as they move to the sides to join the first group.

Raymonda and Jean de Brienne enter upstage left and make a counterclockwise circle around the stage as they performed repeated *temps levés en demi-arabesque* on alternate legs. When they reach center, all nine couples perform three *tours jetés* as they travel upstage. The ensemble assembles upstage of Raymonda and Jean de Brienne, and all run forward. No final pose is given.

Pas classique hongrois (the adagio). Like the *Entreé*, the adagio is sparsely notated, but the information given in the CN corresponds in large part to the choreography as it has been handed down by oral tradition and seen in modern productions. The dance begins with *sous-sus* and a supported *développé à la seconde* to *attitude croisé devant* for the women (Ex. 10.14a). The cavaliers next lift the women, who draw up their legs slightly, and lower them to their knee before lifting them again. This time, carrying the women "on the side" (that is, each woman is lifted and held against the side of the man's body), the men walk backward upstage.

Next, at least three women—only three are drawn on the CN ground plan—hold each other around the waist as they perform "arabesque," after which all run to the side. Raymonda poses with her hands behind her head before performing a supported *double pirouette* from fourth position. The dancers at the sides now cross the stage, the men again lifting the women, while Raymonda performs a supported *sissonne ouverte* to *arabesque fondu* followed by *relevé fouetté* to *effacé devant*. The movements of Raymonda and the ensemble are repeated, then the ensemble forms a semicircle—the men in a row in front of the women—as Raymonda holds a supported *arabesque* on *pointe*. All of the women run around their cavaliers then perform a *pas de chat* to fourth position *plié*.

Accompanied by solo flute, Raymonda *bourrées* downstage in a zigzag pattern punctuated by *double pirouettes*, in which she is supported by the nearest cavalier. The fourth time, she is supported by Jean de Brienne downstage left. She then "simply walks" to center for a supported *double pirouette* from fourth position, followed by what appears to be an unsupported *tour de promenade à plat*—during which she moves her working leg from *arabesque* to *à la seconde* to *devant*—followed by a *relevé*. She finishes the dance with a supported *tour de promenade à la seconde* on *pointe* and a supported *double pir-ouette* from fourth position as the ensemble continues to frame Raymonda and Jean de Brienne in a semicircle.

Variations. Four variations follow. The first is recorded twice, documenting the performances of Olga Chumakova (the CN includes ground plans, annotations, and notation for legs and feet) and Evgenia Obukhova (the CN includes the sparest of ground plans and only a few annotations). As with earlier variations in the ballet, *pointe* work is strongly featured, although here turned-in movements and step vocabulary already performed in the preceding *Grand pas hongrois* are combined with academic dance. The opening enchaînement highlights this fusion: traveling downstage on the diagonal, Chumakova extends her right foot to the side—turned in and on *demi-pointe*—before bringing it front to *tendu devant*, now with a turned-out leg. She continues with *relevé en cou-de-pied devant, tombé, piqué en cou-de-pied devant, tombé,* and *pas de bourrée* on *demi-pointe* to fifth position *plié*. The entire enchaînement is performed four times.

Traveling backward on the same diagonal, she does *pas de bourrée en arrière* on *pointe* four times, raising the working leg to *cou-de-pied* on the first step of each *pas de bourrée,* then moves forward with four *piqués en demi-arabesque,* all performed twice. Arriving at center, she performs multiple *relevés petits passés,* traveling upstage in what could be considered a variation of "Hungarian." She travels directly downstage with "side *pas*"[155] then returns upstage with a further variation on "Hungarian": *entrechat quatre* alternating with *relevé petit passé* six times.

The final enchaînement, during which the dancer traces a zigzag pattern from upstage left, begins with *holubetz* followed by a *temps levé en demi-arabesque* on the right foot, *pas de bourrée, temps levé en demi-arabesque* on the left foot, three steps forward into first position (which may be a variation on a *bokázó* "finishing" step), and a final series of unspecified turns on *pointe*.

The second variation is the well-known men's *pas de quatre*. While not notated in the CN, the dance is included in a list of the three variations that follow the adagio: "2nd Variation 4 Cavaliers."[156] Rather than dancing a solo variation, Jean de Brienne performed as one of the four men in this *pas de quatre,* joined by Bernard and Béranger, and a fourth cavalier who was drawn from the ensemble (Alexander Gorsky in the 1898 premiere).

The third variation, intended for a female dancer, was cut by Petipa, likely before the premiere.

The famous piano variation for Raymonda is the fourth and final variation of the *Pas classique hongrois*. The Hungarian-Roma style of its music and the improvisatory quality of Petipa's choreography were tangible features that were likely not lost on the dancers who performed it.[157] In an interview late in her life, Alexandra Danilova recalled this particular number: "I remember this variation exactly how it was done in Russia. It is a beautiful variation. But you have to give the style—the Hungarian style. It's like talking to all the gypsies around you."[158]

[155] The ground plan calls for "side *pas* 6 times," while an annotation on the notation staff indicates "side *pas* 8 times."

[156] Volynsky noted "Viktor Semenov's femininely light turns in the air." Volynsky, "*Raimonda*," tr. in *Ballet's Magic Kingdom*, 35.

[157] Volynsky: "Preobrazhenskaya's variation is built entirely on dancing à terre without any particular choreographic difficulties." Volynsky, "*Raimonda*," tr. in *Ballet's Magic Kingdom*, 35.

[158] Doug Fullington, "Alexandra Danilova on Raymonda," *Ballet Review* 26, no. 4 (Winter 1998): 74. Danilova's final sentence in this quotation is from an unpublished conversation with Doug Fullington.

The variation is characterized by long, continuous *bourrées* that trace patterns around the stage, complementing the winding lines of the solo piano, which are clearly meant to evoke the sound and style of Hungarian-Roma cimbalom music (Ex. 10.14b).[159] The CN provides a clear ground plan and notated choreography for feet and legs. After an opening zigzag and circle of *bourrées*, Raymonda comes down the diagonal with *pas de bourrée* punctuated by *piqués en demi-attitude devant* (CN: "throws leg sideways"). She runs downstage right and performs *sous-sus*, arms opened to the sides. The *bourrées* begin again. This time she travels diagonally upstage, tracing small circles in a clockwise direction as her "[b]ody leans forward and up." The ongoing *bourrées* are next decorated with *soutenu* turns as Raymonda again travels downstage right.

Midway through the variation, the music gains in intensity and rhythmic impulse, and Petipa responded with a complementary enchaînement: four *piqués de côté en cou-de-pied devant* and *fondu, pas de bourrée* on *demi-pointe* twice, all performed two times. Raymonda moves backward toward upstage left with a series of *piqués de côté en demi-arabesque* alternating with *piqués en arrière*. Her final diagonal comprises what the CN calls "Hungarian forward" (three *relevés petits passés*), *battement degagé de côté, pirouette* from fifth position, *tombé, pas de bourrée* on *demi-pointe* three times—a brilliant final amalgam of classical and character dance. The variation concludes with *chaînés* on *demi-pointe*. (We note that the traditional claps that Raymonda performs at the beginning and end of the variation are not mentioned in the CN.)

Danilova summarized the ballerina role in her memoir: "*Raymonda* contains marvelous dancing. For a ballerina, it's a wonderful opportunity to show every facet of your talent, with several variations in widely differing styles."[160] This final variation represents the culmination of a wonderfully comprehensive role.

Coda. The sparsely notated coda is danced by all nine couples. Four couples begin, as they did for the *Entrée*, with the quartets crossing and recrossing in a zigzag pattern before forming two rows upstage then traveling downstage and to the side (Ex. 10.15a). Two more pairs enter. They trace a similar pattern, but this time their steps are notated: a variant of *demi-valse* is followed by two *holubetz* and a variant on the "finishing" step that is similar to the one performed by Chumakova in her variation. They continue with *temps levé en demi-arabesque en tournant, ballotté, saut de basque*. The entire enchaînement is repeated, then they continue with more *holubetz* as they move to the sides. A seventh couple enters upstage left and performs "side *pas*" and *saut de basque* on the diagonal toward downstage right. The eighth ensemble couple enters upstage right and repeats the same steps to the other side.

Finally, Raymonda and Jean de Brienne ("Preob[razhenskaya] and Legat") make their entrance, but only Raymonda is shown on the ground plan (Jean is included later, just before the end of the number). From downstage center, she performs "Hungarian backward 24 times" followed by "side *pas*" as she returns downstage (Ex. 10.16a). Next, traveling upstage on the diagonal, she performs four turns to the right—these are indicated on the ground plan, while a variant of *demi-valse* is notated on the stave below. She returns downstage once more with "side *pas*" then finishes her first coda entrance with turns on *demi-pointe*.

Recalling the *Entrée* again, everyone performs what appears from the ground plan to be two *tours jetés* traveling upstage, where the ensemble forms two rows, women in front

---

[159] Liszt similarly evokes this sound in his *Hungarian Rhapsody* No. 2, bars 143–178.
[160] Danilova, *Choura*, 160.

of men. All travel downstage with "side *pas*" and return upstage with "Hungarian." Next, the women move downstage and to the sides with "side *pas*" and turns, and the men perform an unspecified "in place *pas*" twice to alternate sides. The women run to join them "after the 2nd time" for unspecified "turns with cavalier."

The ensemble disperses to the sides as Raymonda and Jean make their second entrance at center stage. They (or possibly only Raymonda) perform *pas de cheval, pas de bourrée* on *demi-pointe* to each side as the ensemble performs "side *pas*" while moving to center. Encircled by the couples, "Legat lifts Preobrazhenskaya and holds her on his chest"—he "lifts her by the waist" as she draws her knees up slightly. The ensemble moves upstage from its circle formation and forms two rows behind Raymonda and Jean de Brienne.

The final moments are sparsely notated. The ground plan and annotations suggest Raymonda (possibly joined by the ensemble women) walks "around [her] cavalier," while holding his hand. All travel upstage with "Hungarian" then run forward. Raymonda performs a supported *double pirouette* downstage center to end the dance.

Galop. The final galop is a *danse générale* for all participants (106 of them are listed by name in the *Yearbook of the Imperial Theaters*).[161] Two lines of couples flank the sides of the stage (RN 369). Each line circles the stage in a mirror image of the other, performing "chassé" (we assume this refers to the galop step), and eventually forms two circles that travel in clockwise motion. After they disperse to the sides, another group of couples enters (RN 372). After circling the stage, they perform turns as they move to the sides, where they join the other couples in lines. The dancers now cross to the opposite sides of the stage and back, then the women form five rotating circles, leaving the men in their lines. Next, the men form five rotating circles, and eventually all dancers return to the sides of the stage. The couples travel in two opposing lines, crossing downstage as they move around the stage in a circular pattern, then assemble in a block formation of four rows. The group travels downstage and back two times. No final pose is given as the ballet's final dance comes to its conclusion.

Apothéose. The brief apotheosis, with music based on the theme of the Act Three *entr'acte*, depicts a tournament (it is subtitled *Le tournoi* in the score), a final reminder of the heraldry and ceremony that laced the ballet's fragile narrative. The episode is omitted in the CN, but a sketch by Petr Lambin (dated 1899) that was published in the *Yearbook of the Imperial Theaters* features at least six knights holding jousting lances astride horses that are rearing and pawing.[162] The production documents detail the lavish costumes and properties for four men on horses as well as for additional men who took part (the number of men on horses was apparently reduced by half in 1900):

For the apotheosis is prepared:

On the right side: 2 horses with knights[:][163]

1) White horse, *drap de dames* blanket with lilies, on the knight a helmet and steel cuirass with wool [*garusniye*] feathers, in his hands a lance. No. 567

2) Piebald horse, green blanket; on the knight a white costume, steel cuirass and helmet with feathers, in his hands a lance. No. 565

161 *Ezhegodnik* (1897–1898), 266–267.
162 Ibid., 270.
163 In the right-hand margin: "From 1900 is given one horse per side."

Ballet men:

2 shields [from the] op[era] *Aldona* (with eagles)

2 swords from the same opera without scabbards

1 gray spear

1 yellow banner [from the] op[era] *Faust*

On the left side: 2 horses [with knights]:

1) Black horse, golden brocade [*glazet*] blanket, on the knight a costume of the same kind, steel leg cuffs and handcuffs, helmet with horns and a lion. No. 568.

2) Black horse, blanket out of brown *drap de dames*, costume on the knight of golden brocade [*glazet*]; copper leg cuffs and handcuffs, helmet the same. No. 566.

[Ballet men:]

1 sword [from the] op[era] *Aldona* crosspiece

1 shield the same

1 banner [from the] op[era] *Faust*

1 marshal's baton with a small lily

Raymonda in the West

Raymonda was popular with the younger generation of Mariinsky dancers—the ballet was new, included multiple substantive solo roles, and was felt to have a superior score in the music of Glazunov.[164] Many who received performance opportunities in *Raymonda*'s early seasons were among the host of Imperial Ballet dancers who eventually toured and emigrated to the West, bringing the Russian repertory with them. For example, the ensemble that danced the *Pas classique hongrois* in the 11 November 1907 Mariinsky performance of *Raymonda*, featuring Preobrazhenskaya and Fokine, included Karsavina and Egorova as well as Elizaveta Vill, Lydia Kyaksht, Elena Smirnova, Ludmilla Schollar, Vaslav Nijinsky, Adolph Bolm, and Leonid Leontiev, all of whom would go on to have careers in Western Europe, the United States, and elsewhere.

Raymonda came West in excerpted form, and the complete ballet was not performed outside of Russia until thirty-five years after its St. Petersburg premiere. Serge Diaghilev wanted to present the complete *Raymonda* in Paris during the Ballets Russes' première season at the Théâtre du Châtelet in Paris in 1909, and he invited Gerdt to reprise his role as Abderrakhman. Those plans fell through, but even though Diaghilev abandoned the idea of mounting the entire ballet, he did include the Act Three *Pas classique hongrois* as part of *Le Festin*, a pastiche of dances from several ballets.[165] Vera Karalli and Mikhail

---

[164] Within an otherwise bitter review of his early Imperial Ballet roles, Mikhail Fokine allowed, "The exception in my repertoire was the role of Bernard de Ventadour in 'Raymonda,' one of the best of Petipa's ballets, to the music of Alexander Glazounov." Fokine, *Memoirs*, 43.

[165] The *Pas classique hongrois* was added to *Le Festin* for the company's second performance on 21 May 1909. Thanks to Andrew Foster for this information. About Diaghilev's plans to present *Raymonda*, see Sergey Laletin, " 'Raymonda' i S.P.Dyagilev: nesostoyavshayasya postanovka baleta M.I. Petipa v 'Russkikh sezonakh' 1909 goda" ["Raymonda" and S.P. Diaghilev: the failed production of the ballet by M.I. Petipa in the "Russian Seasons" in 1909] (Moscow: 2018), available online at https://theatremuseum.ru/naukpubl/laletin.

Mordkin danced the leading roles joined by an ensemble of sixteen that included Nijinsky, Bolm, Bronislava Nijinska, Alexandra Baldina, and Schollar.[166]

Anna Pavlova performed the fiery *Panadéros* on tour in Helsinki in 1908 and Berlin in 1909.[167] Several years later, she and her Ballet Russe premiered a two-act production of *Raymonda* at the Century Opera House in New York on 2 February 1915. Staged by Ivan Clustine after Petipa, the ballet included both scenes from Act One.[168]

The first complete production of *Raymonda* in Western Europe was toured by the Ballet of the Lithuanian National Opera in 1933.[169] The choreography was attributed to Petipa and arranged by Nicolas Zvereff, the troupe's ballet master, who also performed the role of Abderrakhman. The printed cast list and libretto (given in both French and English) for a performance in Monte Carlo on 18 January 1935 closely match the Mariinsky's Petipa production, albeit without the children's dances or the Act Three mazurka. The variation cut by Petipa in Act Three before the premiere also appears to have been included. Vera Nemtchinova danced the role of Raymonda, partnered by Anatole Obukhov as Jean de Brienne.[170]

George Balanchine retained a special affection for *Raymonda*. As a student in St. Petersburg/Petrograd, he performed the role of an Arab boy in Act Two, and he likely performed other roles during his years in Russia and his tours with the Ballets Russes.[171] He may have choreographed the *Grand pas espagnol* as a *pas de deux* in 1923,[172] and he restaged the Act Three divertissement for Diaghilev in 1925.[173] Too, Balanchine staged and choreographed four ballets using music, and sometimes elements of Petipa's choreography, from *Raymonda*. These included a nearly full-length *Raymonda* staged with Alexandra Danilova for the Ballet Russe de Monte Carlo in 1946 and three one-act ballets choreographed for New York City Ballet: *Pas de dix* (1955), *Raymonda Variations* (1961, originally titled *Valses et variations*), and *Cortège hongrois* (1973).[174] Although Balanchine did not produce a full-length *Raymonda* during his New York City Ballet years, he choreographed most of the ballet's dance numbers. The one-act ballets demonstrate his preference for distilling story ballets into short, plotless works.

The 1946 Ballet Russe de Monte Carlo production staged by Balanchine and Danilova featured choreography based on Petipa. (This was the pair's first collaborative revival of a nineteenth-century ballet—the second was their 1974 staging of *Coppélia* for New York

---

[166] *Le Festin* also included a "Czardas," presumably also from Act Three, featuring Sophia Fedorova and Mikhail Mordkin dancing choreography by Alexander Gorsky. See Boris Kochno, Diaghilev and the Ballets Russes, tr. Adrienne W. Foulke (New York: Harper & Row, 1970), 30. *Le Festin* was an umbrella title used by the Diaghilev company throughout its twenty-year existence. The excerpted ballets and short numbers that were presented under the title *Le Festin* varied, but the *Pas classique hongrois* from *Raymonda* was often among them.

[167] Thanks to Andrew Foster for this programming information.

[168] Pavlova had danced the role of Henriette as well as the lead in the Spanish dance at the Mariinsky. See Lazzarini, *Pavlova*, 52, 80, 156–157. See also Sergey Konaev, "*Raymonda* dopo Petipa," tr. Carla Muschio, in *Raymonda* program book (Milan: Teatro alla Scala, 2011), 93.

[169] The production also toured to Monte Carlo and London. For a brief discussion of this and other post-Petipa productions of *Raymonda*, see Vaughan, "Nureyev's 'Raymonda,'" 32. See also Anton Dolin, Ballet Go Round (London: Michael Joseph, 1938), 144–149.

[170] Printed program courtesy of the collection of Robert Greskovic.

[171] Katz et al., eds., *Choreography by George Balanchine*, 320.

[172] Ibid., 60.

[173] Ibid., 172–173.

[174] On the 1946 *Raymonda*, see Lynn Garafola, "*Raymonda*, 1946," *Ballet Review* 47, nos. 1–2 (Spring–Summer 2019): 151–160. For a description of Balanchine's *Raymonda* ballets, see Doug Fullington, "*Raymonda* at 100," *Ballet Review* 26, no. 4 (Winter 1998): 77–86. See also Katz et al., eds., *Choreography by George Balanchine*.

City Ballet.) Much of the mime was eliminated, the story abbreviated, and some new choreography added by Balanchine.[175]

This "complete" *Raymonda* was performed by Ballet Russe de Monte Carlo for three seasons, but danced numbers and pantomime were deleted bit by bit, as was the character of the White Lady. By the 1949–1950 season, only the third act remained, and the full-length version was dropped from the repertory. The company was still performing Act Three as late as the early 1960s.[176]

Raymonda in twentieth-century Russia

Discussing *Raymonda* as it stood in the early years of the Soviet Union, dance historian Elizabeth Souritz wrote, "Created on the threshold between two centuries, the ballet belonged to the past, and this affected its fate. Despite its extraordinary music[,] *Raymonda* was performed more rarely and reworked more often."[177] Indeed, in both St. Petersburg (later, Petrograd then Leningrad) and Moscow, the layering on of material created by subsequent choreographers and stagers grew thick.[178]

Moscow. Two years after its Petersburg premiere, *Raymonda* was performed in Moscow on 23 January 1900. This restaging of Petipa's production was directed by Ivan Clustine and Alexander Gorsky (that is, they were responsible for the *mise-en-scène*).[179] Eight years later, on 30 November 1908, Gorsky staged his own *Raymonda*, incorporating some of Petipa's choreography in a production that stressed naturalism and impressionism.[180] On 7 April 1945, Moscow's Bolshoi Theater presented Leonid Lavrovsky's production, which incorporated choreography by both Petipa and Gorsky and a scenario by Sergei Kobuladze.[181] Finally, on 29 June 1984 the Bolshoi presented Yuri Grigorovich's production, which like Lavrovsky's, incorporated material by both Petipa and Gorsky.[182]

St. Petersburg/Petrograd/Leningrad. Petipa's production held the stage in St. Petersburg/Petrograd through the first two decades of the twentieth century. On 29 October 1922, Fedor Lopukhov staged a revival based on Petipa's choreography but

---

[175] The Ballet Russe de Monte Carlo program book for the season 1946–1947, includes the following: "*Raymonda* was first presented at the Maryinsky Theatre, St. Petersburg, in 1898 and the present version differs from the original merely in the omission of long passages of miming for dramatic action and fascinating and demanding choreography. The current version is the result of collaboration of Alexandra Danilova and George Balanchine both of whom appeared in the Russian production of this ballet some years back. The story of this ballet is concerned with a girl named Raymonda, who is betrothed to a knight of the Crusades. After his departure to war, the unexpected arrival of a Saracen Knight is heralded. The Saracen Knight pays court to Raymonda, and when she refuses him, he attempts to carry her off—just as Raymonda's fiancé arrives and kills the Saracen Knight. There is a wedding and colorful divertissements ensue. The score of Alexander Glazounov, famous Russian composer, was written especially for this ballet, and beautifully supports the brilliant choreography of Petipa. The sumptuous designs of décor and costumes are by Alexander Benois of Diaghileff fame, and the dean of Russian theatrical art."

[176] A large number of items relating to the Balanchine-Danilova *Raymonda* are housed in the Jerome Robbins Dance Division of the New York Public Library for the Performing Arts, including substantial filmed excerpts of the ballet.

[177] Elizabeth Souritz, *Soviet Choreographers in the 1920s*, ed. Sally Banes, tr. Lynn Visson (Durham, NC: Duke University Press, 1990), 23. See also Konaev, "Raymonda dopo Petipa," 91–99.

[178] For discussions of the major productions of *Raymonda*, see Konaev, "Raymonda dopo Petipa"; Melik-Pashayeva, "Raymonda"; Souritz, *Soviet Choreographers*, 23–24, 32–33; and Vaughan, "Nureyev's 'Raymonda.'"

[179] Konaev, "*Raymonda* dopo Petipa," 91–92.

[180] Ibid., 92–93.

[181] Ibid., 95.

[182] Ibid., 98–99.

"made corrections" in the ballet.[183] For instance, Lopukhov fashioned his own version of the Act Two finale, where according to Alexandre Benois, "Petipa left an obvious 'blank' ... which urgently needed to be 'filled.'" Souritz explains, "to do this, the events that took place after Raymonda's fiancé's victory over Abderâme had to somehow be portrayed to the magnificent music of the apotheosis. In Benois's opinion, Lopukhov did this 'superbly,' not allowing himself anything that would destroy the conventional style of that ballet.'"[184] Agrippina Vaganova staged her own production in 1931 and fourteen years later, on 22 March 1938, Leningrad's Kirov Ballet presented Vasily Vainonen's version of Raymonda, using some of Petipa's choreography (actually Petipa cum Lopukhov's choreography) and a scenario by Yuri Slonimsky and Vainonen.[185]

Another important production, premiering on 30 April 1948, was created by Konstantin Sergeyev for the Kirov Ballet. This production retained much of the original plot but, as Rudolf Nureyev would do two decades later, Sergeyev altered the focus of the action. Based on a redaction of Pashkova's libretto prepared by Slonimsky, the plot allowed Raymonda to choose between Jean de Brienne and Abderrakhman.[186] The program book from the Kirov's 1964 United States tour includes the following note:

> Mr. Sergeyev staged a revised version of Raymonda in 1948 in which he preserved the musical and choreographic richness of the work, and re-created a number of dance scenes staged by Petipa with rare splendor and virtuosity. In addition, he painted the principal characters more vividly and boldly introduced new scenes that enriched the expressiveness of the dance. On July 16, 1964, Sergeyev made further revisions in a new production designed by Ivan Sevastianov.[187]

This promotional description makes clear that Konstantin Sergeyev's revisions were considered to be improvements to Petipa's original work.

The production made by Nureyev in 1964 (first performed by the Royal Ballet Touring Company) and later altered several times called for the majority of the ballet's action to be presented as a figment of the heroine's imagination and the dramatic tensions therein as psychosexual.[188] This approach inevitably sharpened the ballet's focus on the three principal characters—Raymonda, Jean de Brienne, and Abderrrakhman—but it also minimized the secondary characters who originally played important roles in the drama.

The source documents afford us an invaluable opportunity to discover Petipa's original plans for Raymonda. They help us to understand Raymonda's place in Western dance history as a pivotal work, with one foot in the tradition-steeped nineteenth century and the other in the twentieth, with its growing interest in what would become the plotless ballet.

Raymonda maintains the traditional balance of classical dance, character dance, and mime. But the story is told in a streamlined fashion: mime conversations are not long, and a greater proportion of the ballet's running time is filled with dance sequences, both

[183] Souritz, Soviet Choreographers, 258.
[184] Souritz, Soviet Choreographers, 259, quoting Alexandre Benois, "Pietet ili koshchunstvo?" [An homage or blasphemy?], in Ezhenedelnik gosudarstvennikh petrogradskikh akademicheskikh teatrov [Weekly of the State Academic Theaters] 11 (1922): 34–35. See also Konaev, "Raymonda dopo Petipa," 93–94.
[185] Konaev, "Raymonda dopo Petipa," 94–95.
[186] Konaev, "Raymonda dopo Petipa," 96–97.
[187] Kirov Ballet souvenir program.
[188] See Vaughan, "Nureyev's 'Raymonda.'"

character and classical. Indeed, Petipa's amalgamation of classical and character dance in the last act can be seen as a further development of the kind of synthesis we encountered in parts of the *Paquita Grand pas.*

Yet the action of the ballet is not superfluous. In her miming as well as her dancing, *Raymonda* is revealed as a character of stature and a worthy heir to her older sisters— Giselle, Paquita, Medora, Nikia. She experiences joy, fear, love, and anger; she is both stalwart and faithful. That the expression of these emotions is not as overtly presented through mime does not diminish Raymonda's personality, but it does place the ballet *Raymonda* farther along the continuum of aesthetic change—change embraced by a French ballet master in his eightieth year.

Conclusion

Our examination of original source documents has allowed us to learn a great deal about the history and original substance—musical, choreographic, and narrative—of five important nineteenth-century French and Russian ballets. But before we make our closing remarks about the five ballets, let us sum up the general conclusions we reached about nineteenth-century ballet history in France and Russia—conclusions that challenge, clarify, and fill in gaps in received ballet-history narratives.

First, the Paris Opéra exerted a strong influence on ballet in St. Petersburg throughout the nineteenth century and up through the end of Petipa's tenure during the first decade of the twentieth century.[1] It is true that dance scholars have long known that the St. Petersburg Imperial Ballet had Francophile proclivities, big money, a hunger for ballets, and French ballet masters: Titus (who followed Didelot and others), then Perrot, Mazilier (for a single season), Saint-Léon, and Petipa. And it is well known that the Imperial Ballet imported many of the Opéra's ballets. And as noted many times in this volume, they kept these ballets alive with new casts, revisions, and updates.[2] But the crucial contributions made by Petipa's French ballet-master predecessors both in France and in Russia, which are plain to see in the manuscripts, have not heretofore received their due recognition. Neither has it been acknowledged that Petipa followed the principles of their dance design and used much of the same step vocabulary.

A case in point: Petipa's role in revising *Giselle* has been misrepresented. In keeping with custom, Petipa made adjustments and created fresh choreography when tastes and styles changed and new ballerinas took to the stage. But he did not entirely remake *Giselle* or even alter the version he inherited nearly as much as we had all thought—a fact that came as quite a surprise to us when we first saw Justamant's *Giselle* manual, which showed explicitly how much of the ballet as it looked in France in the 1850s resembled the ballet as it exists today. Petipa—and his predecessors—kept the Act One waltz (choreographed by Coralli) mostly intact. He retained mime scenes. He did not "expand" the Wilis' dance (as numerous historians have averred). He kept some of the bold geometric floor-pattern shapes that help ensure the strong impact of the Wilis' menacing behavior. That is, he kept what he liked, made alterations as he saw fit, and presented to the public an amalgam of old and new, some of it matching *Giselle*'s earliest incarnations as Titus and Justamant recorded them. This is important because it illuminates the contributions made by Petipa's forebears in France and offers deeper understanding of Petipa's working method, which involved not only creating, but assembling.

---

[1] Regarding French influence in St. Petersburg in years in the nineteenth century before the focus period of this book, see Wiley, *Century*.

[2] To be sure, the Paris Opéra was still staging new ballets and reviving old ones, too, but it did not have nearly as high a demand for ballet repertory in the last four decades of the century or as aggressive a curatorial approach as did the Imperial Ballet, where many older ballets mixed regularly with new ones in a repertory that expanded to twenty-six works (not including opera ballets or divertissements) by the turn of the twentieth century. *Ezhegodnik* (1899–1900), 46–47.

Five Ballets from Paris and St. Petersburg. Doug Fullington and Marian Smith, Oxford University Press.
© Oxford University Press 2024. DOI: 10.1093/oso/9780190944506.003.0012

Second: we have been able to discern how the three ballets made in France compare in step vocabulary and choreography to the two Russia-made ones. First, *petit allegro* step combinations (made up of many small jumps) were the staple of the French ballets. We know that the Russian ballets called for *petit allegro*, too, for we find them in the Stepanov manuscripts—though with the influx of Italian dancers and teachers the step vocabulary came to include larger jumps and more turns for men and increased *pointe* work for women, often featuring many consecutive repetitions of the same step. Some of these new additions may have come at the expense of the "filigree work" whose loss—post-Saint-Léon—was lamented by Vazem.[3]

As for *pas de deux*: Some may find it surprising that in the French productions of *Giselle, Paquita,* and *Le Corsaire,* the man lifted the woman, sometimes overhead, and supported her as she posed. (The lifts were often done to change direction near the side of the stage or to carry her upstage.) He did the same in *La Bayadère* and *Raymonda* (and the later Petersburg productions of the French works), and he added the skill of supporting the ballerina in turns. But the unison side-by-side dancing that characterized many French *pas de deux* eventually gave way in Russia to an increase in supported movements for the ballerina, assisted by her cavalier.[4] Thereby the French *pas de deux* partnership can be considered to have been more equal between partners than in *La Bayadère* and *Raymonda,* in which the man's primary purpose was to assist the woman.

Ensemble numbers often featured simpler steps than those for soloists, reflecting the hierarchy of performers. When the entire cast performed together, the ensemble often framed the stage, and therefore the leading dancers, in formations of lines, rows, and semicircles.

Broadly, we find in the French ballets a more natural interweaving of dance and mime, a less formalized succession of numbers that allowed the story to remain paramount as the dances were performed as a consequence of the narrative action.

Third, there is of course the constancy of change. As we have noted countless times in the foregoing pages, alterations were made to ballets on a regular basis and were most typically applied to the solos and small ensembles. This speaks to the vibrancy of the ballet, its flexibility, its carefully maintained currency, its fit to the ballerina. But we must also point out that many of the components that complemented the danced segments, including the stories and mime scenes, stayed mostly *intact* until the twentieth century, contributing immeasurably to ballet's success. (What happened in the twentieth century is another matter, as we note below.)

Fourth, we offer some summarizing comments about what the sources have told us about Petipa's career and the histories thereof. The sources reveal, first of all, that he has been credited with accomplishments that likely pre-date and certainly post-date his tenure as first ballet master at the Imperial Ballet, which began in 1870 and effectively ended in 1905. That is, some scholars have assumed without confirmation (as noted above) that Petipa created new dances for revivals earlier in his career than the written records can prove—assumptions that overlook the fact that the fully capable first ballet master in charge would likely have created the new dances himself. It is also a regular practice today to attribute many choreographies to Petipa (or say they are "after Petipa")

---

[3] See Chapter 1, p. 44, note 97.

[4] On eighteenth-century precedents for side-by-side unison dancing in the *pas de deux*, see Sandra Noll Hammond, "Windows into Romantic Ballet, Part Two: Content and Structure of Four Early Nineteenth Century *Pas de Deux*," in *Proceedings, Society of Dance History Scholars* (1998), 47–53.

that were heavily revised or newly made after he died (for example, Andrianov's 1915 *pas d'action* in *Le Corsaire* that eventually became the so-called *Le Corsaire pas de deux*). Fortunately, the Stepanov notations provide a record against which such post-Petipa versions of the ballets can be compared.

Given Petipa's uncontested genius and his extraordinarily long and fruitful tenure at the Imperial Ballet—and the fact that his name is attached to most of the nineteenth-century ballets at the core of today's classical canon (*Giselle, Sleeping Beauty, Swan Lake*, and so forth)—it is not surprising that, as a sort of default, he would receive credit even when it is not due. But he is not a man whose reputation needs burnishing. His accomplishments, as the sources confirm them, are nothing short of astonishing. He maintained a large repertory of ballets, opera ballets, and divertissements for more than thirty years as first ballet master, building on his twenty-plus years' "apprenticeship" that had begun in St. Petersburg in 1847. (He served the Imperial Theaters for well over a half-century.) He was not only endlessly creative but—as his preparatory notes and instructions to composers attest—practical and well organized. Despite suffering the inevitable failures that creative every artist must, Petipa was able, year after year, to put works on the stage that were both pleasing to his audiences and artistically distinguished. He developed the *pas d'action* into the more expansive multimovement dance suite that we know today. He excelled as a maker of polyphonic choreography. He responded to the influx of Italian dancers and teachers in St. Petersburg by incorporating their technique and steps into the vocabulary of French classical ballet. And he must also be lauded for his curatorial approach to repertory, for he conserved older ballets at the same time he was creating new ones in the amassing of the St. Petersburg Imperial Ballet's large body of works. A simple fact illustrates the scope of his achievement: the Yearbook for the 1901–1902 season lists an astonishing twenty-seven ballets in the active repertory (not including opera ballets or divertissements), including all five of the ballets explored in this volume.[5]

Finally, let us turn to the five ballets and share our conclusions about what we observed about their essential elements.

What the five ballets have in common: Essential elements

Despite the differences among them, and the long time-span within which they were created, the five ballets we have described in this volume have in common several essential elements.

Story and character. The sources have made clear the paramountcy of story and the presence of characters with distinct personalities in the French ballets we have examined. Indeed, *Giselle, Paquita*, and *Le Corsaire* could almost be seen as mimed plays with danced segments, for the running time for each of them is split at roughly half and half between action and dance. Dancing took up more time in the two Russian-made ballets (*La Bayadère* and *Raymonda*), and though the stories were still important—especially in *La Bayadère*—they were relatively less complex, and their action sometimes intended

---

[5] *Ezhegodnik* (1901–1902), 46–47: *La Bayadère* (four performances), *Giselle* (three performances), *Le Corsaire* (two performances plus one performance of Acts 1–3), *Paquita* (three performances), *Raymonda* (two performances).

mainly to set up dancing scenes. Nonetheless, it can be said that story and character drove all five of the ballets.

As for the characters, far from being the cardboard cut-outs that some of them have become, in both Paris and St. Petersburg they had human traits and tendencies that one could easily recognize from real life. The music assisted in communicating the story and creating the characters in a multitude of ways, not the least of which was giving them a voice when the action called for it by supplying appropriate melodies to be played by carefully chosen instruments. Plenteous mime scenes and *pas d'action* put the characters' personalities on display and at the same time helped round out the action and give the audience a deeper feel for the ballet's setting and atmosphere. Take, for instance, Inigo's rehearsal scene in *Paquita* in which he instructs the "kiddos" (*moutards*) who are to perform at the festival; *Le Corsaire*'s loving *scène dansante* performed by Medora and Conrad in the pirates' grotto; the opening scene of *La Bayadère* during which Madhavaya helps Solor arrange his secret rendezvous with Nikia outside the pagoda; and even the pleasant conversation of Raymonda and her friends that leads to their moonlit dance as she accompanies them on the lute and then dances a solo herself. Many such personalizing scenes for principal characters were removed over the course of the twentieth century when they were made superfluous by the shift in emphasis that favored dancing over story and character.

Compelling female leads. By supplying the mime scripts and showing how the characters moved around the stage in relationship to others, the staging manuals and choreographic notations have shown us, first of all, how powerful and strong the female lead characters could be in the French ballets. To be sure, they all sought to settle down with a man and presumably to marry him in conventional, societally sanctioned fashion. But despite that constraining frame, these women were self-confident, industrious, quick-witted, ingenious, and defiant when necessary; their desires and actions drove the plot. Though they could be polite, none of them struck us as mild-mannered. Giselle was vivacious, fun-loving, courageous, a bit rebellious, and the only character in the ballet strong enough to stand up to Myrtha. Paquita was resourceful, daring, even audacious, and clever enough to thwart the evildoers who obstructed her path to happiness. Medora was overtly sensuous, goal-driven, a loyal and warm friend to her female peers, and unafraid when it came to stabbing a male adversary or two.

Nikia and Raymonda were not strong in the way the women mentioned above were. It is true that Nikia made Solor swear his love to her and held him to his oath even in death, but she was a single-focused zealot who lacked the charm and versatility of her French forebears in *Giselle*, *Paquita*, and *Le Corsaire*. Raymonda, for her part, may have had a little pluck, but she was more victim than instigator. Powerless in the face of Abderrakhman's threats, she needed to be saved by Jean de Brienne. However, both of these characters commanded the attention of audiences—Nikia through the intensity of her dramatic narrative arc and Raymonda by the sheer technical brilliance of her dancing.

Spectacle and variety. All of the ballets we have studied in this book offered the audience some sort of spectacle or special effect. And clearly such offerings increased in scope and number as the century wore on. *Giselle*, the shortest of our five ballets, featured in Act One the impressive and lengthy entrance of the noble hunting procession (complete with onstage trumpets blaring and two live horses) as well as the breathtaking flights of Giselle in Act Two. *Paquita* offered (after the manner of the super-popular Danseuses Viennoises) the *Pas des manteaux* with its "thick red mantle[s] now folded around the figure[s], now extended wide," the show-stopping dancing of Paquita in the *Pas des tam-bourins*, and the final ballroom scene whose onlookers were French officers wearing rep-licas of Napoleonic uniforms.[6] Then there was *Le Corsaire* with its lavish harem scenes, the parade of dervishes with its (fake) camel, and of course the terrifying storm and ship-wreck that ended the ballet.

The Russian ballets in our study demonstrate an even higher level of spectacle and dazzlement, reflecting the tastes and budget of the Imperial court and, eventually, the influence of the popular ballet-féerie. In *La Bayadère*, we find the procession and festival of Badrinata (including a tiger) and the opium dream that places the audience in the fan-tastical Kingdom of the Shades. And in *Raymonda*, we encounter successive large-scale divertissements that culminate in a final galop involving more than a hundred partic-ipants and an apotheosis that featured live horses. Some of these spectacles were car-ried out with an over-the-top extravagance that most theaters have today ceded to the cinema.

Variety, however, was just as important, and ballets were sure to feature distinctly different and recognizable movement styles—mime, classical dance, character dance, social dance—as well as characters of various sorts and ages and national origins, and scene types of several kinds. Small-ensemble danced numbers were certain to figure into the action, as were close encounters in mime scenes. Solo expressions in the manner of an opera aria—doleful, happy, or otherwise—were also typical. Other options included comic interchanges (as seen in our three French-made ballets, like Giselle's spat with Hilarion; Paquita's teasing of Inigo; Gulnare's face-off with Zulmea), the appearance on stage of animals (real or fake), prop dances, the presence of children, and entertainments for onstage audiences (like the Roma troupe in *Paquita*, the scarf dancers in *Le Corsaire*, the troupe of Arab boys that Abderrakhman brings to Provence to perform a coconut dance to go along with the stick dance and Spanish dance from Grenada). All of these types of scenes, including the entertainments, were arranged in a way that kept the bal-let's pace up, made for highs and lows, and sustained the audience's attention for the full length of the ballet. Thus were these ballets unashamedly grand variety shows, aiming at high entertainment value.

Above, we have listed the elements we found to be essential to nineteenth-century ballet. We did not include racism on the list for the reason that many of that century's ballets (including *Giselle*, *Coppélia*, *Sleeping Beauty*, *Swan Lake*) were not dependent on racist themes. At the same time the sources do disclose, beyond a shadow of doubt and in granular detail, that a good many nineteenth-century ballets did make racist depictions of characters they chose to deem as Others, who were presented as stupid, immoral, or cruel, or all three (for instance, Inigo in *Paquita*, Lanquedem and the Pasha in *Le Corsaire*, and Abderrakhman in *Raymonda*). This should give pause to propo-nents of revivals that embrace the cultural beliefs of the original libretto to a tee. Such orthodoxy could lead, for instance, to a virulently Islamophobic *Raymonda* revival—an unacceptable prospect. To alleviate problems of this sort, of course, ballet directors in some instances have overseen alterations of the stories and replaced old characters with new ones in order to bring the stories more closely into alignment with the values of their own times.

---

[6] *Times* of London, 4 June 1846, qtd. in Beaumont, *Complete Book*, 190.

What was lost in the twentieth century

As we read through the manuscript descriptions of the five ballets, we could not help but think about how much was lost in the twentieth century of the essential elements we have identified.[7] And it occurred to us that a restoration of emphasis on these elements could be beneficial in today's productions, be they full-out historically informed revivals or otherwise.

Spectacle and variety. The decline of spectacle in these five ballets (including special effects) would surely be the most difficult to reverse on today's stages, for the trap doors and fireworks, the devices that allowed for dancers to fly in the air and glide on the stage, the machinery that made the stunning effects of the shipwreck in *Le Corsaire* possible, are now rarely available. Nor can most companies afford the vast numbers of performers who used to fill the stage for festivals and parades; such large casts have given way to smaller groups which, by dint of their dwindled numbers, are unlikely to impress audiences with their presence alone. The decline of the onstage equine population is notable, as well, though we cannot argue that *Giselle*'s or *Raymonda*'s effectiveness has suffered greatly for it. (The lushness of the *Giselle* Act Two set is another matter; an abundance of trees, flowers, a lake, and aquatic plants could help create the luxuriant and sumptuous natural setting in which the Wilis hold their nightly rounds; rushes and reeds are needed for Giselle to peek through at her lover; a well-flowered tree is needed for Myrtha to select her two blossoms from.[8])

A greater loss, we would aver, is that many supporting characters were cut out or their roles significantly reduced, and with them the star turns by performers celebrated for their charisma and stage presence. Such characters had not only supplied variety, but enlivened the action, broadened the range of age and personality type of the population on stage, and lightened the burden placed on the principal characters. So in many productions we lost such snapshots of humanity as the offbeat heroism of the Old Man who leads the villagers to safety in *Giselle*, the eccentric postures of the Eunuch and the irreverent wit of Gulnare in *Le Corsaire*, the helpful ingenuity of Madhavaya in *La Bayadère*; the commitment to duty and hospitality of Countess Sybille in *Raymonda*.[9] Other defining character traits that are perhaps not completely lost but that could be reinvigorated include the wisdom of Wilfride, sincere kindness of Bathilde, feistiness of Giselle, haughtiness of Zulmea, insecurity of Hamsatti, righteous zeal of Nikia, joy of Raymonda. (Portayals of Giselle, especially, have strayed quite far from the person the manuscripts describe.)

---

[7] This calls to mind what Arlene Croce wrote after reading Roland John Wiley's dissertation on *Swan Lake* in 1979, in which he discusses the original production. "Recently, I was asked how many times I had seen *Swan Lake*. Incredulity usually lurks in this question—an implied 'How can you stand it?' Yet the answer is not 'Because I love it.' Like so many others, I go to *Swan Lake* not to re-see a ballet but hoping to see the ballet beyond the ballet. That performance is only the occasion for meditating on what might have been." Arlene Croce, "'Swan Lake' and Its Alternatives," in *Going to the Dance* (New York: Knopf, 1982), 186.

[8] Venuso writes, "The scenography [for *Giselle*] of Pierre Cicéri, acclaimed for the use of gas lighting (recently introduced in theaters) and author of the décor for *Robert le diable*, depicts a dense forest, imposing trees, a pond, water lilies and moonlight. Giselle's tomb is almost hidden in the midst of so much vegetation, a very exotic spot according to the romantic taste. Today the scenography has lost this connotation." Maria Venuso, *'Giselle' e il teatro musicale*, 153.

[9] Here, we note that Frederick Ashton's *La Fille mal gardée* retained such character elements in his remake of the ballet (1960); Denmark never lost its characters or mime tradition, both of which continue to thrive into the present day.

Another sort of variety was compromised over the course of the twentieth century with the de-emphasis of character dance, which was relegated sometimes to the status of an afterthought as ballet became more and more reliant on classical dance. Nowadays, few ballet companies offer character classes on a regular basis (favoring brush-up coaching before particular ballets are performed), so dancers cannot be expected to have mastered the nuance, the flair, and strong projections of character (or even a hint at an untold back story) that comes with intensive exposure and training. In this regard, we recall these words from a *New York Times* article of 1983:

> The self-assurance, pride, and daring that come with character training are often reflected in the quality of a dancer's other roles. Mr. [Mikhail] Baryshnikov says, "Many of the best classical dancers, from Alexandra Danilova and Felia Doubrovska to Rudolf Nureyev, had character training. They get to cheat, play with the audience, because they are so aware of what they are doing."[10]

Certainly some character dance remains in place (though often with new choreography), including character numbers in the Tchaikovsky ballets. But these are often performed in a mostly-classical style (and sometimes in *pointe* shoes) and do not necessarily provide the striking contrast to classical style or evoke the wildly enthusiastic audience responses that newspaper accounts of nineteenth-century ballet performances describe.

The general loss of so much character dance has resulted in the near-complete primacy of classical dance, and yet classical dance itself has seen a reduction in step variety that has resulted in a certain choreographic homogeneity. Manifestations of this trend range from the obvious (such as the ubiquity of *fouetté* turns) to the subtle (for instance, the loss of connecting steps, often replaced by walks or runs). A strong preference for *croisé* positions over *effacé* (seen throughout the Stepanov notations but now often considered unflattering) has also resulted in reduced options for orienting the body on stage, and therefore an erasure of certain varieties of physical perspective (the Shades frequently danced en *effacé* facing upstage corners on the diagonal—a feature that has largely disappeared). And while the Italian influence remains strong, with acrobatic jumps and turns and extreme repetition filling many dances, the speed and verve that surely accompanied Vazem's "filagree work"—suggested by the sheer number of steps dancers performed within any given musical passage—has given way to slower tempos, a preference for smooth movements and balances, and, ultimately, fewer steps performed.

Story and character. In many twentieth-century revivals, mime scenes were de-emphasized or cut out altogether. And if the music for such scenes were kept intact (or restored at some point along the way), choreographers added new dances to fill the time, or even—because the conversations in the old mime scenes had been entirely forgotten—created new action that failed to contribute meaningfully to the building of story or character (for instance, in one production, Hilarion brings a fish to place on Berthe's cottage door in the opening scene of *Giselle*).[11]

---

[10] Alan Jones, "Character Dance Returns with Panache," *New York Times*, 19 June 1983, Section H, 20.

[11] An instance of an effective reinterpretation of a bit of mime music in *Giselle* may be found in the Royal Ballet version. As jaunty music is played (shortly after Berthe has frightened all of the village girls except Giselle by describing the Wilis), Giselle (according to Adam's autograph score) says "I'll always dance" and (according to Justamant) says "I don't believe any of that" and crosses the stage, dancing. In the Royal Ballet version, this passage of jaunty music is instead given to Berthe, who imitates the jaunty walk of a man with a feather in his cap, entering into the Wilis' territory (soon thereafter to be threatened by them, as Berthe explains through mime). That is, though the original action was forgotten, someone rechoreographed it in

Contributing to the deterioration of the mime scene was the fact that ballet-makers and performers (understandably, given the fact that the manuscripts are not easy to gain access to) collectively forgot, over the course of the twentieth century, about the ambient sounds and bursts of mood expression that composers often helpfully embedded in the music for the express purpose of helping the performers convey action and character to the audience. This obliviousness has made it harder to stage action and mime scenes and led to unintended mismatches of sound and action; for example, shortly after the curtain rises in *Giselle* Act One, the music tells us that Albert has come onstage, accompanied by Wilfride, and that the two of them are engaged in a big argument.[12] But in some productions this scene is performed mostly by Albert alone, with Wilfride offstage for much of it, the two men's musical "voices" and flashing mood changes going unused, with the result that an opportunity for characterization and plot-building is lost.

The erosion of mime scenes has made for shallower characters, for in losing their "voices" they also lost the chance to disclose much at all in the way of ideas or motivations; they became far less inclined to argue or joke with other characters; they relinquished their ability to divulge the nuances of their feelings and emotions. And, somehow they lost permission (with rare exceptions) to address the audience directly.

Strong female leads. One of the most disappointing consequences of this general weakening of the characters is that the lead female characters—the center of the action—lost much of the power, determination, and spirit that made them so appealing in the nineteenth century.

This undermining of personality in general—not just of the lead female—can limit the engagement of some spectators (as we have seen first-hand) who, try as they might, cannot find characters they can relate to. They are thus less likely to be moved by the story or to care about its outcome. Also, without well-presented mime and action scenes that explain the reasons for the dancing, a story ballet might be rendered incomprehensible. (Yes, certain ballet plots are far-fetched, but no more so than those of operas, films, and plays, wherein story and character are carefully attended to.)

We hasten to acknowledge that French and Russian story ballets did survive and thrive through the twentieth century, and continue today to draw enthusiastic crowds in opera houses and theaters around the world. Yet at the same time we argue that the twentieth-century cutbacks and revisions to ballet's stories have not always worn well. In this regard, the written record (miraculously extant) has much to offer as remedy and advice. For it reflects the work of experienced creative artists who possessed profound knowledge of theatricality, narrative, and dance. As a great repository of practical ballet knowledge, this written record could profitably supplement the vital person-to-person training by which ballet is passed down through the generations—and even allow today's practitioners to tap further back into this memory-based art form than living memory can allow.

An acquaintance with the written record, too, might help ballet directors to restore some of the old, effective-but-lost qualities to story ballet, but through new means. For instance, to promote comprehensibility, super-titles could be projected during mime

a manner that responded directly to the music. (There is also a chance that Giselle's blithe contradiction of her mother was replaced with the little story about the jaunty man to support a recasting of Giselle as a meek person.)

[12] For a description of this scene as described in the Titus *répétiteur*, see Chapter 2, pp. 93–94.

scenes. To expand the range of movement styles, specialist dancers from outside the ballet world could be brought in to perform as the plots call for it.[13] To draw from familiar practices of real life, choreographers (as they did in the nineteenth century) could include current popular dances in divertissements—dances that audience members are likely to recognize and may even have done themselves.

Further study of the manuscripts will doubtless lead to many more findings and insights. Justamant's wide-ranging manuals, which record the works of multiple choreographers whose work has been thought to have vanished forever (including Mazilier and Perrot), as well as ballets for venues outside the opera house, offer great potential for expanding our picture of nineteenth-century ballet and its theatrical contexts far beyond the usual boundaries. These manuals, as well as the Stepanov notations, may also beckon to choreographers and performers wishing to stage scenes or mount revivals, and to shape story and character in effective ways. They may also inspire a greater awareness of revisions made to the ballets since their first heyday.

But—further manuscript study aside—we believe that the present volume in itself can be useful to a wide constituency, including dance makers devising altogether new works and theater-goers who may not be drawn to nineteenth-century story ballets but who may seek answers therein about what can make for effective drama or what cultural forces can help animate a stage work. Our readers, we hope, in learning about what audiences saw and heard when the curtain went up on *Giselle*, *Paquita*, *Le Corsaire*, *La Bayadère*, and *Raymonda*, can benefit from knowing more about what made these works prosper and perhaps imagine how a deeper understanding of ballet's past and present can lead to a compelling sense of what its future can be.

---

[13] Recall that Balanchine hired the Spanish dancers Rosita Ortega and César Tapià (after spotting Ortega performing Spanish dances in a nightclub floor show) to appear in *Carmen* in 1937 at the Metropolitan Opera. See Marian Smith, "The Metropolitan Balanchine," *Ballet Review* 41, nos. 1–2 (Spring–Summer 2019): 125–140. Information from the program at which these dancers made their Met debut may be found at http://archi ves.metoperafamily.org/archives/scripts/cgiip.exe/WService=BibSpeed/fullcit.w?xCID=122060.

In 1830 Gautier, in vain, exhorted the Paris Opéra to do something similar: "In my opinion the Opéra should seek out the finest dancers in the world, anyone with a reputation in this field. Can one believe, for example, that a bayadere role would not assume a very lively attraction if performed by a genuine bayadere from Calcutta or Masulipatam? Why not have almehs in the theatre [at the Opéra]? [. . .] [A]n innovation such as this [to the choreographic art . . .] can only add spice to the deadly boring framework of ballet. The saltarello and the tarantella danced by Romans and Neapolitans, the cachucha, the jota argonesa and the zapateado by Spaniards, and the scarf dances of almehs and bayaderes would surely offer an attraction that is lacking when they are performed by ordinary dancers." *La Charte de 1830*, 18 April 1837, tr. in Gautier, *Gautier on Dance*, 8.

Selected List of Ballets and Operas Cited

This selected list of eighty-eight ballets and operas cited in the previous chapters includes performance history and production credits for works performed by the Paris Opéra and the St. Petersburg Imperial Ballet. Data has been drawn from a variety of sources listed in this volume's bibliography, including:

Boglacheva, Mirovana, Zozulina, eds., *Peterburgskiy balet. Tri veka: khronika*, vols. II–IV

Beaumont, *Complete Book of Ballets*

Garafola, ed., *The Diaries of Marius Petipa*

Gautier (ed. Guest), *Gautier on Dance*

Guest, *Ballet of the Second Empire 1858–1870*; *Jules Perrot*; *Letters from a Ballet Master*; *The Paris Opéra Ballet*; *The Romantic Ballet in Paris*, 2nd ed.

Letellier, *The Ballets of Ludwig Minkus*

Meisner, *Marius Petipa*

Smith, *Ballet and Opera in the Age of Giselle*

Wiley, *A Century of Russian Ballet*; *The Life and Ballets of Lev Ivanov*; *Tchaikovsky's Ballets*

Additional sources consulted include:

Girard, Pauline. *Léo Delibes: Itinéraire d'un musicien, des Bouffes-Parisiens à l'Institut.* Paris: Vrin, 2018.

Lajarte, Théodore. *Bibliothèque musicale du théâtre de l'Opéra. catalogue historique, chronologique, anecdoctique.* Paris: Librairie des Bibliophiles, 1878.

Loewenberg, Alfred. *Annals of Opera, 1597–1940.* Totowa, NJ: Rowman and Littlefield, 1978.

Volf, A[bram] I[akovlevich]. *Khronika peterburgskikh teatrov s kontsa 1826 do nachala 1855 goda* [Chronicle of St. Petersburg Theaters from the End of 1826 to the Beginning of 1855]. St. Petersburg, 1877.

Wiley, Roland John. "Dances in Opera: St. Petersburg." *Dance Research* 33, no. 2 (Winter 2015): 227–257.

We also cite English translations of librettos, synopses, and substantial or notable discussions of some of the ballets. We note that Wiley's forthcoming monograph on Petipa, *The Petersburg Noverre: Marius Petipa in Russia* (London: Anthem Press, 2024), contains additional translations of librettos and discussions of the works of Petipa.

Digitized copies of many French-language librettos and other source documents are available online at Gallica, the digital library of the Bibliothèque Nationale de France, https://gallica.bnf.fr/.

The National Library of Russia site provides links to digitized Russian-language librettos for select ballets by Petipa at http://expositions.nlr.ru/ex_manus/petipa/program.php.

Printed sources of Russian-language librettos include:

Burlaka, Yury, and Anna Grutsynova, eds., *Antologiya baletnogo libretto. Rossiya 1800–1917. Sankt-Peterburg. Blash, Val'berkh, Didlo, Dyupor, Sen-Leon, Le Pik, Malavern', Perro, Tal'oni, Tityus* [Anthology of Ballet Librettos. Russia 1800–1917.

St. Petersburg. Blache, Walberch, Didelot, Duport, Saint-Léon, Le Pic, Malavergne, Perrot, Taglioni, Titus]. St. Petersburg: Planet Music, 2021.

Burlaka, Yury, and Anna Grutsynova, eds. *Antologiya baletnogo libretto. Rossiya 1800– 1917. Sankt-Peterburg. Gerdt, Ivanov, Koppini, Kulichevskaya, N. Legat, S. Legat, Petipa, Romanov, Fokin, Chekketti* [Anthology of Ballet Librettos. Russia 1800– 1917. St. Petersburg. Gerdt, Ivanov, Coppini, Kulichevskaya, N. Legat, S. Legat, Petipa, Romanov, Fokine, Cecchetti]. St. Petersburg: Planet Music, 2021.

Burlaka, Yury, and Anna Grutsynova, eds. *Libretto baletov Mariusa Petipa | Rossiya 1848–1904* [Librettos of Ballets by Marius Petipa | Russia 1848–1904]. St. Petersburg: Compozitor, 2018.

Burlaka, Yury, and Marina Leonova, eds., *Balety M.I. Petipa v Moskve* [Ballets by M.I. Petipa in Moscow]. Moscow: Progress-Tradition, 2018.

* * * * *

The Adventures of Peleus

Mythological ballet in three acts and five scenes, libretto by Marius Petipa, music by Ludwig Minkus, choreography by Petipa, first performed by the Imperial Ballet on 18 January 1876 at the Bolshoi Theater, St. Petersburg, with Evgenia Sokolova and Pavel Gerdt in leading roles. Revived by Petipa, in a one-act version titled *Thetis and Peleus*, with additional music by Léo Delibes and score supervised by Riccardo Drigo, on 28 July 1897 at Holguin Island, Peterhof, St. Petersburg, with Matilda Kshesinskaya, Pavel Gerdt, and Olga Preobrazhenskaya in leading roles. Synopsis: Letellier, *Ludwig Minkus*, 112–113.

L'Africaine

Opera in five acts, libretto by Eugène Scribe, music by Giacomo Meyerbeer, choreography by Arthur Saint-Leon, first performed by the Paris Opéra on 28 April 1865 at the Théâtre Impérial de l'Opéra (Salle Le Peletier). First performed by the Imperial Italian Opera on 7 January 1866 at the Bolshoi Theater, St. Petersburg, with dances staged by Arthur Saint-Léon.

Aida

Opera in four acts and seven scenes, libretto by Antonio Ghislanzoni, music by Giuseppe Verdi, first performed on 24 December 1871 at the Khedivial Opera House, Cairo. First performed by the Imperial Italian Opera on 19 November 1875 at the Mariinsky Theater, St. Petersburg, with dances choreographed by Marius Petipa. First performed by the Paris Opéra on 22 March 1880 at the Théâtre National de l'Opéra (Palais Garnier).

Aldona

See *I Lituani*.

The Awakening of Flora

Anacreontic ballet in one act, libretto by Marius Petipa and Lev Ivanov, music by Riccardo Drigo, choreography by Petipa, first performed by the Imperial Ballet on 28 July 1894, at Peterhof, St. Petersburg, with Matilda Kshesinskaya in the title role. Synopsis: Wiley, *Lev Ivanov*, 257–258; see also 166–169.

The Bandits

Ballet in two acts and five scenes, with prologue, libretto, and choreography by Marius Petipa, music by Ludwig Minkus, first performed by the Imperial Ballet on 26 January 1975 at the Bolshoi

Theater, St. Petersburg, with Ekaterina Vazem in a leading role. Synopsis: Letellier, *Ludwig Minkus*, 110–111; see also 111–112. See *Khronika III*, 178–179.

La Bayadère

Ballet in four acts and seven scenes with apotheosis, libretto by Sergei Khudekov and Marius Petipa, music by Ludwig Minkus, choreography by Petipa, first performed by the Imperial Ballet on 23 January 1887 at the Bolshoi Theater, St. Petersburg, with Ekaterina Vazem, Lev Ivanov, Maria Gorshenkova, Christian Johanson, and Nikolai Golts in leading roles. Revived by Petipa on 3 December 1990 at the Mariinsky Theater, St. Petersburg, with Matilda Kshesinskaya, Pavel Gerdt, Olga Preobrazhenskaya,. Nikolai Aistov, and Felix Kshesinsky in leading roles. Libretto: Appendix F (i) and Wiley, *Century*, 291–303.

Betty

Ballet-pantomime in two acts, music by Ambroise Thomas, choreography by Joseph Mazilier, first performed by the Paris Opéra on 10 July 1846 at the Théâtre de l'Académie Royale de Musique (Salle Le Peletier), with Sofia Fuoco and Lucien Petipa in leading roles. Synopsis: Beaumont, *Complete Book*, 190–196. See Gautier, *Gautier on Dance*, 175–177, and Guest, *Romantic Ballet in Paris*, 255–257.

Bluebeard

Ballet-féerie in three acts and seven scenes, with apotheosis, libretto by Lydia Pashkova, music by Petr Schenk, choreography by Marius Petipa, first performed by the Imperial Ballet on 8 December 1896 at the Mariinsky Theater, St. Petersburg, with Pavel Gerdt and Pierina Legnani in leading roles. Synopsis: Beaumont, *Complete Book*, 443–448.

The Butterfly

Fantastic ballet in four acts, libretto by Henri Vernoy de Saint-Georges and Marius Petipa, music by Ludwig Minkus, choreography by Petipa, first performed by the Imperial Ballet on 6 January 1874 at the Bolshoi Theater, St. Petersburg, with Ekaterina Vazem, Lev Ivanov, and Alexei Bogdanov in leading roles. Synopsis: Letellier, *Ludwig Minkus*, 108–109; see also 109–110. See *Khronika III*, 172–174. See also *Le Papillon*.

Camargo

Ballet in three acts and nine scenes, libretto by Jules-Henri Vernoy de Saint-Georges and Marius Petipa, music by Ludwig Minkus, choreography by Petipa, first performed by the Imperial Ballet on 17 December 1872 at the Bolshoi Theater, St. Petersburg, with Adèle Grantzow in the title role. Revived with additional dances by Lev Ivanov on 28 January 1901 at the Mariinsky Theater, St. Petersburg, with Pierina Legnani in the title role. Synopsis: Beaumont, *Complete Book*, 410–416.

Carmen

Opéra-comique in four acts, libretto by Henri Meilhac and Ludovic Halévy, music by Georges Bizet, first performed by the Opéra-Comique on 3 March 1875 at the Théâtre National de l'Opéra-Comique (Salle Favart), Paris. First performed by the Imperial Italian Opera on 16 February 1878 at the Bolshoi Theater, St. Petersburg, with dances choreographed by Marius Petipa. See *Khronika III*, 194–195. Additional dances have been attributed to Petipa in connection with a performance given on 29 October 1882 at the Mariinsky Theater. See Wiley, "Dances in Opera: St. Petersburg," 232–234.

Catarina, ou La fille du bandit

Grand ballet in three acts and four scenes, libretto by Jules Perrot, music by Cesare Pugni, choreography by Perrot, first performed on 3 March 1846 at Her Majesty's Theatre, London, with Lucile Grahn and Perrot in leading roles. First performed by the Imperial Ballet, in a staging by Perrot, on 4 February 1849 at the Bolshoi Theater, St. Petersburg, with Fanny Elssler, Christian Johansson, and Perrot in leading roles. See Guest, *Jules Perrot*, 155–165 and 184–190. Revived by Marius Petipa on 1 November 1870 at the Bolshoi Theater, St. Petersburg, with Adéle Grantzow in the title role. Revived by Enrico Cecchetti in a version with two acts and five scenes, with additional music by Riccardo Drigo, on 25 September 1888 at the Mariinsky Theater, St. Petersburg, with Luigia Algisi in the title role. Synopsis: Beaumont, *Complete Book*, 254–262.

Le Chalet

Opéra-comique in one act, libretto by Eugène Scribe and Mélesville, music by Adolphe Adam, first performed by the Opéra-Comique on 25 September 1834 at the Salle de la Bourse, Paris. First performed by the Imperial Russian Opera in 1835 in St. Petersburg.

Cinderella

Ballet fantastique in three acts, libretto by Lydia Pashkova, music by Boris Fitinghoff-Schell, choreography by Marius Petipa, Enrico Cecchetti, and Lev Ivanov, first performed by the Imperial Ballet on 5 December 1893 at the Mariinsky Theater, St. Petersburg, with Pierina Legnani and Pavel Gerdt in leading roles. Libretto: Wiley, *Lev Ivanov*, 251–256; see also 159–165.

Coppélia, ou La fille aux yeux d'émail

Ballet in two acts and three scenes, libretto by Charles Nuitter, music by Léo Delibes, choreography by Arthur Saint-Léon,, first performed by the Paris Opéra on 25 May 1870 at the Théâtre Impérial de l'Opéra (Salle Le Peletier), Paris, with Giuseppina Bozzacchi and Eugénie Fiocre in leading roles. Synopsis: Beaumont, *Complete Book*, 483–487; see also 487–489. See Guest, *Second Empire 1858-1870*, 107–131, and Girard, *Léo Delibes*, 72–78. First performed by the Imperial Ballet on 25 November 1884 at the Bolshoi Theater, St. Petersburg, choreography by Marius Petipa, with Varvara Nikitina and Pavel Gerdt in leading roles.

Le Corsaire

Ballet-pantomime in three acts, libretto by Jules-Henri Vernoy de Saint-Georges, music by Adolphe Adam, choreography by Joseph Mazilier, first performed by the Paris Opéra on 23 January 1856 at the Théâtre Impérial de l'Opéra (Salle Le Peletier), with Carolina Rosati and Domenico Segarelli in leading roles. Revived by Mazilier, revised and with additional music by Léo Delibes, on 21 October 1867, with Adèle Grantzow and Louis Mérante in leading roles. First performed by the Imperial Ballet in a staging by Jules Perrot, with additional music by Cesare Pugni, on 9 January 1958 at the Bolshoi Theater, St. Petersburg, with Ekaterina Friedberg and Marius Petipa in leading roles. Petipa revived *Le Corsaire* four times in St. Petersburg: on 24 January 1863, at the Bolshoi Theater, with Maria Surovshchikova Petipa and Marius Petipa in leading roles; on 25 January 1868, with additional music by Léo Delibes, at the Bolshoi Theater, with Adéle Grantzow and Petipa in leading roles; on 30 November 1880, at the Bolshoi Theater, with Evgenia Sokolova and Lev Ivanov in leading roles; and on 13 January 1899, at the Mariinsky Theater, with Pierina Legnani and Pavel Gerdt in leading roles. Librettos: Paris 1856, see Appendix E (i); St. Petersburg 1858, see Appendix E (ii).

The Cyprus Statue, or Pygmalion

Ballet in four acts and six scenes, with apotheosis, libretto, and music by Prince Nikolai Trubetskoi, choreography by Marius Petipa, first performed by the Imperial Ballet on 11 December 1883 at the Bolshoi Theater, St. Petersburg, with Evgenia Sokolova, Felix Kshesinsky, Pavel Gerdt, and Lubov Radina in leading roles.

Le Délire d'un peintre

Divertissement, music by Cesare Pugni, choreography by Jules Perrot, first performed on 3 August 1843 at Her Majesty's Theatre, London, with Fanny Elssler and Perrot in leading roles. See Guest, *Romantic Ballet in England*, 68. First performed by the Imperial Ballet, staged by Perrot as *Le Rêve du peintre*, on 3 October 1853 at the Bolshoi Theater, St. Petersburg, with Louise Fleury and Perrot in leading roles. Presented in a new version (based on Perrot) on 29 July 1887 at the Arcadia Theater, St. Petersburg, music by Madolio, choreography by Enrico Cecchetti, with Cecchetti and Giovannina Limido in leading roles. See *Khronika III*, 261–262.

Les Deux pigeons

Ballet in two acts and three scenes, libretto by Henry de Régnier, music by André Messager, choreography by Louis Mérante, first performed by the Paris Opéra on 18 October 1886 at the Théâtre de l'Opéra (Palais Garnier), with Rosita Mauri and Marie Sanlaville in leading roles. Synopsis: Beaumont, *Complete Book*, 508–512.

Le Diable amoureux

Ballet-pantomime in three acts and eight scenes, libretto by Jules-Henri Vernoy de Saint-Georges, music by François Benoist and Napoléon Henri Réber, choreography by Joseph Mazilier, first performed by the Paris Opéra on 23 September 1840 at the Théâtre de l'Académie Royale de Musique (Salle Le Peletier), with Pauline Leroux, Louise Fitzjames, and Mazilier in leading roles. See Guest, *Romantic Ballet in Paris*, 191–195. First performed by the Imperial Ballet as *Satanilla, or Love and Hell*, staged by Marius Petipa and Jean Antoine Petipa, and orchestrated by Konstantin Lyadov and Fedor Rahl, on 10 February 1848 at the Bolshoi Theater, St. Petersburg, with Elena Andreanova, Tatiana Smirnova, and Marius Petipa in leading roles. Revived by Marius Petipa on 18 October 1866 at the Bolshoi Theater, St. Petersburg, with Alexandra Prikhunova, Praskovia Lebedeva, and Lev Ivanov in leading roles. Synopsis: Beaumont, *Complete Book*, 169–177. See Selma Jeanne Cohen, "In Search of Satanella: An Adventure Prompted by *The Children of Theater Street*," *Dance Research Journal* 11, nos. 1–2 (1978–1979): 25–30, and Simon Morrison, "Still in Search of Satanilla," *19th Century Music* 46, no. 1 (2022): 3–38.

Le Diable à quatre

Ballet-pantomime in two acts, libretto by Adolphe de Leuven, music by Adolphe Adam, choreography by Joseph Mazilier, first performed by the Paris Opéra on 11 August 1845 at the Théâtre de l'Académie Royale de Musique (Salle Le Peletier), with Carlotta Grisi, Lucien Petipa, and Mazilier in leading roles. See Gautier, *Gautier on Dance*, 277–278; Guest, *Romantic Ballet in Paris*, 246–250; and Guest, *Second Empire 1858–1870*, 54–55. First performed by the Imperial Ballet as *The Willful Wife*, in a staging by Jules Perrot, with additional music by Cesare Pugni, on 14 November 1850 at the Bolshoi Theater, St. Petersburg, with Grisi, Marius Petipa, Elena Andreanova, and Perrot in leading roles. Restaged by Mazilier on 18 October 1851 at the Bolshoi Theater, St. Petersburg, with the same leading couple as in 1850 but with Mazilier performing in place of Perrot. Marius Petipa restaged *The Willful Wife*, with additional music by Ludwig Minkus, on 23 January 1885 at the Bolshoi Theater, St. Petersburg, with Maria Gorshenkova and Pavel Gerdt in leading roles. Synopsis: Beaumont, *Complete Book*, 177–183.

Le Diable boiteux

Ballet-pantomime in three acts and ten scenes, libretto by Burat de Gurgy and Adolphe Nourrit, music by Casimir Gide, choreography by Jean Coralli, first performed by the Paris Opéra on 1 June 1836 at the Théâtre de l'Académie Royale de Musique (Salle Le Peletier), with Fanny Elssler, Legallos, Leroux, Joseph Mazilier, and Jean-Baptiste Barrez in leading roles. Synopsis: Beaumont, *Complete Book*, 114–122. See Théophile Gautier, "Notice sur *Le Diable Boiteux*," in *Les beautés de l'Opéra*, and Gautier, *Gautier on Dance*, 37 and 79–81.

Le Dieu et la Bayadère, ou La courtisane amoureuse

Opera-ballet in two acts, libretto by Eugène Scribe, music by Daniel François-Esprit Auber, first performed by the Paris Opéra on 13 October 1830 at the Théâtre de l'Académie Royale de Musique (Salle Le Peletier), with dances staged by Filippo Taglioni and Maria Taglioni in the leading role. First performed by the Imperial Russian Opera as *The Amorous Bayadère* (*Vlyublennaya bayaderka*) on 12 November 1835 at the Alexandrinsky Theater, St. Petersburg, with dances staged by Antoine Titus. For a discussion of *Le Dieu et la Bayadère*, see Smith, *Ballet and Opera*, 138–149. About Taglioni in *Le Dieu et la Bayadère*, see Guest, *Romantic Ballet in Paris*, 102–105, 233–235.

Don Carlos

Opera in five acts, libretto by Joseph Méry and Camille du Locie, music by Giuseppe Verdi, first performed by the Paris Opéra on 11 March 1867 at the Théâtre Impérial de l'Opéra (Salle Le Peletier), with dances staged by Lucien Petipa. First performed by the Imperial Italian Opera on 20 December 1868 at the Bolshoi Theater, St. Petersburg.

Don Quixote

Ballet in four acts and eight scenes, with a prologue, libretto (after the novel by Cervantes) and choreography by Marius Petipa, music by Ludwig Minkus, first performed by the Imperial Ballet on 14 December 1869 at the Bolshoi Theater, Moscow, with Anna Sobeshchanskaya and Sergei Sokolov in leading roles. First performed in St. Petersburg in a revised version staged by Petipa on 9 November 1871 at the Bolshoi Theater, with Alexandra Vergina and Lev Ivanov in leading roles. Synopsis: Beaumont, *Complete Book*, 405–410. See Meisner, *Marius Petipa*, 153–156.

The Enchanted Forest

Ballet fantastique in one act, music by Riccardo Drigo, choreography by Lev Ivanov, first performed on 24 March 1887 at the Imperial Theater School, St. Petersburg, with student Alexandra Vinogradova in the leading role. First performed by the Imperial Ballet on 3 May 1887 at the Mariinsky Theater, St. Petersburg, with Varvara Nikitina in the leading role. Synopsis: Wiley, *Lev Ivanov*, 226–227; see also 84–91.

Euryanthe

Opera in three acts, libretto by Helmina von Chézy, music by Carl Maria von Weber, first performed on 25 October 1823 at the Theater am Kärntnertor, Vienna. First performed at the Paris Opéra on 6 April 1831 at the Théâtre de l'Académie Royale de Musique (Salle Le Peletier). First performed by the German troupe of the Imperial Theaters in St. Petersburg during the 1839–1840 season.

An Extraordinary Journey to the Moon

See *Le Voyage dans la lune*.

Faust

Grand ballet in three acts with libretto and choreography by André Jean-Jacques Deshayes, music by Adolphe Adam, first performed on 16 February 1833 at the King's Theatre, London. See Kristin Rygg, "Faust Goes Dancing," in *The Oxford Handbook of Faust in Music*, eds. Lorna Fitzsimmons and Charles McKnight (New York: Oxford University Press, 2019), 461–482, available online at doi: 10.1093/oxfordhb/9780199935185.013.24.

Faust

Opera in five acts, libretto by Jules Barbier and Michel Carré, music by Charles Gounod, first performed as an opera-comique by the Théâtre Lyrique on 19 March 1859 at the Théâtre Historique, Paris. First performed by the Paris Opéra in a revised version, with recitatives added as well as ballet music for the *Walpurgisnacht* scene, on 3 March 1869, at the Théâtre Impérial de l'Opéra (Salle Le Peletier), with dances staged by Henri Justamant. First performed by the Imperial Italian Opera on 31 December 1863 at the Bolshoi Theater, St. Petersburg. Revived on 19 November 1882 at the Bolshoi Theater, St. Petersburg, with the addition of the *Walpurgisnacht* scene staged by Marius Petipa.

La Favorite

Opera in four acts, libretto by Alphonse Royer and Gustave Vaëz, music by Gaetano Donizetti, first performed by the Paris Opéra on 2 December 1840 at the Théâtre de l'Académie Royale de Musique (Salle Le Peletier), with dances by Albert. First performed by the Imperial Russian Opera in St. Petersburg during the 1842–1843 season.

Fiammetta, ou L'amour du diable

Ballet fantastique in two acts, four scenes, with prologue, libretto by Henri Meilhac and Ludovic Halévy, choreography by Arthur Saint-Léon, music by Ludwig Minkus, first performed by the Imperial Ballet on 13 February 1864 at the Bolshoi Theater, St. Petersburg, with Marfa Muravieva in the title role. (The ballet was a re-working of Saint-Léon's *Love's Flame, or The Salamander*, first performed in Moscow on 12 November 1863.) A revised version, titled *Néméa, ou L'amour vengé*, ballet-pantomime in two acts, was first performed by the Paris Opéra on 11 July 1864 at the Théâtre Impérial de l'Opéra (Salle Le Peletier), with Muravieva in the title role. See Gautier, *Gautier on Dance*, 297–308 and 319, and Guest, *Second Empire 1858–1870*, 75–79. Marius Petipa revived *Fiammetta*, with additional music by Riccardo Drigo, on 6 December 1887 at the Mariinsky Theater, St. Petersburg, with Elena Cornalba in the title role. Synopsis: Beaumont, *Complete Book*, 347–351, and Letellier, *Ludwig Minkus*, 67–75.

La Fille mal gardée

Ballet-pantomime in two acts and three scenes, libretto and choreography by Jean Dauberval, music drawn from popular songs and arias, first performed on 1 July 1789 at the Grand Théâtre, Bordeaux, with Mlle Théodore and Eugène Hus in leading roles. First performed by the Imperial Ballet as *Deceived* [or, *Vain*] *Precautions* (*Obmanutyye predostorozhnosti*), staged by Charles Didelot, after Dauberval, on 13 September 1809, at the Bolshoi Theater, St. Petersburg, with Josephine Sainte-Claire and Louis-Antione Duport in leading roles. See *Khronika II*, 36. First performed by the Paris Opéra, staged by Jean-Louis Aumer (after Dauberval), with music by Ferdinand Hérold, on 17 November 1828 at the Théâtre de l'Académie Royale de Musique (Salle Le Peletier), with Pauline Montessu and Marinette Launer in leading roles. See Guest, *Romantic Ballet in Paris*, 88–91, and Gautier, *Gautier on Dance*, 244–246. Restaged by Jules Perrot, after Dauberval, with music by François Joseph Hérold, on 3 November 1853 at the Bolshoi Theater, St. Petersburg, with Rose Marie Girod and Christian Johanson in leading roles.

See *Khronika III*, 29. Restaged by Lev Ivanov and Marius Petipa on 15 December 1885 at the Bolshoi Theater, St. Petersburg, with Virginia Zucchi and Pavel Gerdt in leading roles. Revived on 25 September 1894 at the Mariinsky Theater, St. Petersburg, with Hedwige Hantenberg and Pavel Gerdt in leading roles. See Wiley, *Lev Ivanov*, 73–84 and 280–285. Synopsis: Beaumont, *Complete Book*, 2–5.

La Gipsy

Ballet-pantomime in three acts and five scenes, libretto by Jules-Henri Vernoy de Saint-Georges, music by François Benoist, Ambroise Thomas, and Count Marco Urelio Marliani, choreography by Joseph Mazilier, first performed by the Paris Opéra on 28 January 1839 at the Théâtre de l'Académie Royale de Musique (Salle Le Peletier), with Fanny Elssler, Thérèse Elssler, and Mazilier in leading roles. Synopsis: Beaumont, *Complete Book*, 160–168. See Gautier, *Gautier on Dance*, 58–65.

Giselle, ou Les wilis

Ballet fantastique in two acts, libretto by Jules-Henri Vernoy de Saint-Georges and Théophile Gautier, music by Adolphe Adam, with additional music by Friederich Bürgmuller, choreography by Jean Coralli and Jules Perrot, first performed by the Paris Opéra on 28 June 1841 at the Théâtre de l'Académie Royale de Musique (Salle Le Peletier), with Carlotta Grisi, Lucien Petipa, and Adèle Dumilâtre in leading roles. First performed by the Imperial Ballet, in a staging by Antoine Titus, on 18 December 1842 at the Bolshoi Theater, St. Petersburg, with Elena Andreanova, Irakli Nikitin, and Tatiana Smirnova in leading roles. A production supervised by Jules Perrot was first performed on 8 October 1850 at the Bolshoi Theater, St. Petersburg, with Grisi, Christian Johanson, and Elizaveta Nikitina in leading roles. A production supervised by Arthur Saint-Léon was first performed on 8 November 1862 at the Bolshoi Theater, St. Petersburg, with Marfa Muravieva, Johanson, and Nikitina in leading roles. Revived by Marius Petipa on 5 February 1884 at the Bolshoi Theater, St. Petersburg, with Maria Gorshenkova, Pavel Gerdt, and Sofia Petrova in leading roles. Librettos: Paris 1841, Appendix C (i); St. Petersburg 1842 (reprinted in 1889), Appendix C (ii).

Graziella, ou Les dépits amoureux (Graziella ou, La querelle amoureuse)

Demi-caractére ballet in two acts, libretto and choreography by Arthur Saint-Léon, music by Cesare Pugni, performed by the Imperial Ballet on 11 December 1860 at the Bolshoi Theater, St. Petersburg, with Carolina Rosati and Saint-Léon in leading roles. (Previously performed at the Gachina Theater, St. Petersburg.) Revived in one act by Lev Ivanov on 12 April 1900 at the Mariinsky Theater, St. Petersburg, with Vera Trefilova and Sergei Legat in leading roles. See Guest, *Letters from a Ballet Master*; 146.

Gretna-Green

Ballet-pantomime in one act, libretto by Charles Nuitter, music by Ernest Guiraud, choreography by Louis Mérante, first performed by the Paris Opéra on 5 May 1873 at the Théâtre de l'Opéra (Salle Le Peletier), with Léontine Beaugrand and Mérante in leading roles.

Gustave III, ou Le bal masqué

Opéra historique in five acts, libretto by Eugène Scribe, music by Daniel Auber, first performed by the Paris Opéra on 27 February 1833 at the Théâtre de l'Académie Royale de Musique (Salle Le Peletier), with dances by Filippo Taglioni. See Guest, *Romantic Ballet in Paris*, 124–126. First performed by the Imperial Russian Opera as *Gonzago* on 2 February 1860 at the Alexandrinsky Theater, St. Petersburg.

The Haarlem Tulip
Ballet fantastique in three acts and four scenes, libretto and choreography by Lev Ivanov, music by Boris Fitinhof-Schell, first performed by the Imperial Ballet on 4 October 1887 at the Mariinsky Theater, St. Petersburg, with Emma Bessone and Pavel Gerdt in leading roles. Revived on 16 April 1903 at the Mariinsky Theater, St. Petersburg, with Vera Trefilova and Pavel Gerdt in leading roles. Libretto: Wiley, *Lev Ivanov*, 228–239; see also 92–112.

The Halt of the Cavalry
Character ballet in one act, libretto and choreography by Marius Petipa, music by Johann Armsheimer, first performed by the Imperial Ballet on 21 January 1896 at the Mariinsky Theater, St. Petersburg, with Pierina Legnani, Pavel Gerdt, and Marie Petipa in leading roles. Synopsis: Beaumont, *Complete Book*, 441–443.

Hamlet
Opera in five acts, libretto by Michel Carré and Jules Barbier, music by Ambroise Thomas, first performed by the Paris Opéra on 9 March 1868 at the Théâtre National de l'Opéra (Salle Le Peletier), with dances staged by Lucien Petipa. First performed by the Imperial Italian Opera on 14 October 1872 at the Bolshoi Theater, St. Petersburg, with dances choreographed by Marius Petipa.

Harlequinade (Les millions d'arlequin)
Harlequinade in two acts, libretto and choreography by Marius Petipa, music by Riccardo Drigo, first performed by the Imperial Ballet on 10 February 1900 at the Hermitage Theater, St. Petersburg, with Matilda Kshesinskaya, Georgi Kyaksht, Olga Preobrazhenskaya, Sergei Lukyanov, and Enrico Cecchetti in leading roles. See Alexei Ratmansky, "Staging Petipa's *Harlequinade* at ABT," *Ballet Review* 47, nos. 1–2 (Spring–Summer 2019): 45–55.

La Jolie fille de Gand
Ballet-pantomime in three acts and nine scenes, libretto by Jules-Henri Vernoy de Saint-Georges, music by Adolphe Adam, choreography by Albert Decombe, first performed by the Paris Opéra on 22 June 1842 at the Théâtre de l'Académie Royale de Musique (Salle Le Peletier), with Carlotta Grisi, Louise Fitzjames, and Lucien Petipa in leading roles. Synopsis: Beaumont, *Complete Book*, 149–159. See Gautier, *Gautier on Dance*, 103–111, 140–145, and 155–158.

Jovita, ou Les boucaniers
Ballet-pantomime in three scenes, libretto and choreography by Joseph Mazilier, music by Théodore Labarre, first performed by the Paris Opéra on 11 November 1853 at the Théâtre de l'Opéra, with Carolina Rosati and Louis Mérante in leading roles. See Gautier, *Gautier on Dance*, 259–264, and Guest, *Second Empire 1847–1858*, 75–78. First performed by the Imperial Ballet, in a staging by Arthur Saint-Léon, on 13 September 1859 at the Bolshoi Theater, St. Petersburg, with Carolina Rosati and Christian Johanson in leading roles. Synopsis: Beaumont, *Complete Book*, 204–208.

La Juive
Opera in five acts, libretto by Eugène Scribe, music by Fromental Halévy, first performed by the Paris Opéra on 23 February 1835 at the Théâtre de l'Académie Royale de Musique (Salle Le Peletier), with dances staged by Filippo Taglioni. See Philarète Chasles, "Notice sur *La Juive*," in *Les beautés de l'Opéra*, First performed by the German troupe of the Imperial Theaters, as *The Cardinal's Daughter*, on 11 October 1837 at the Mikhailovsky Theater, St. Petersburg.

King Candaules (Le Roi Candaule)

Grand ballet in four acts and six scenes, libretto by Jules-Henri Vernoy de Saint-Georges and Marius Petipa, music by Cesare Pugni, choreography by Petipa, first performed by the Imperial Ballet on 17 October 1868 at the Bolshoi Theater, St. Petersburg, with Henriette Dor, Felix Kshesinsky, Lev Ivanov, and Anna Kuznetsova in leading roles. Revived by Petipa on 24 November 1891 at the Mariinsky Theater, St. Petersburg, with Carlotta Brianza, Pavel Gerdt, Alexander Oblakov, and Giuseppina Cecchetti in leading roles, and on 9 April 1903 at the Mariinsky Theater, St. Petersburg, with Julia Sedova, Sergei Legat, Nadezhda Petipa, and Gerdt in leading roles. Synopsis: Beaumont, *Complete Book*, 400–405. See Meisner, *Marius Petipa*, 150–153.

The King's Command

Grand ballet in four acts and five scenes, libretto by Marius Petipa and Albert Vizentini (after Edmond Gondinet), music by Vizentini, choreography by Petipa, first performed on 14 February 1886 at the Bolshoi Theater, St. Petersburg, with Virginia Zucchi and Pavel Gerdt in leading roles. Revived by Petipa in a shortened version (two acts), titled *The Pupils of Dupré*, on 14 February 1900 at the Hermitage Theater, St. Petersburg, with Pierina Legnani in a leading role. See Meisner, *Marius Petipa*, 203–205.

Lida, or The Swiss Milkmaid

See *Nathalie, ou La laitière suisse.*

The Little Humpbacked Horse, or The Tsar-Maiden

Magic ballet in four acts and nine scenes, libretto and choreography Arthur Saint-Léon, music by Cesare Pugni, first performed by the Imperial Ballet on 3 December 1864 at the Bolshoi Theater, St. Petersburg, with Marfa Muravieva in a leading role. Revived by Marius Petipa on 6 December 1895 at the Mariinsky Theater, St. Petersburg, with Pierina Legnani, Alexander Shiryaev, and Felix Kshesinsky in leading roles. Libretto: Wiley, *Century*, 238–249; see also 250–275.

I Lituani (Aldona)

Opera in three acts with prologue, libretto by Antonio Ghislanzoni, music by Amilcare Ponchielli, first performed on 7 March 1874 at La Scala, Milan. First performed by the Imperial Italian Opera, in a revised version titled *Aldona*, on 8 November 1884 at the Mariinsky Theater, St. Petersburg, with dances staged by Marius Petipa.

The Magic Flute

Comic ballet in one act, music by Riccardo Drigo, choreography by Lev Ivanov, first performed on 10 March 1893 at the Imperial Theater School, St. Petersburg, with Stanislava Belinskaya, Mikhail Fokine, Sergei Legat, and Agrippina Vaganova in leading roles. First performed by the Imperial Ballet at the Mariinsky Theater, St. Petersburg, on 11 April 1893, with Anna Johansson, Pavel Gerdt, and Timofei Stukolkin in leading roles. Synopsis: Beaumont, *Complete Book*, 514–516, and Wiley, *Lev Ivanov*, 247–250; see also 150–155.

The Magic Mirror

Ballet fantastique in four acts and seven scenes, libretto by Marius Petipa and an unnamed collaborator (likely Ivan Vsevolozhsky), music by Arseny Koreshchenko, choreography by Marius

Petipa, first performed by the Imperial Ballet on 9 February 1903 at the Mariinsky Theater, St. Petersburg, with Matilda Kshesinskaya, Sergei Legat, Pavel Gerdt, and Marie Petipa in leading roles. Libretto: Wiley, *Century*, 408–416. See Meisner, *Marius Petipa*, 269–275.

The Magic Pills

Ballet-féerie in three acts and thirteen scenes, libretto by Ferdinand Laloue, Anicet Bourgeois, and Clément Laurent, music by Ludwig Minkus, choreography by Marius Petipa, first performed by the Imperial Ballet on 9 February 1886 at the Mariinsky Theater, St. Petersburg, with Varvara Nikitina in a leading role. Synopsis: Letellier, *Ludwig Minkus*, 148–150.

Le Marché des innocents

See *The Parisian Market*.

Météora, ou Las estrellas cadentas

Ballet fantastique in three acts and four scenes, libretto and choreography by Arthur Saint-Léon, music orchestrated by Santos Pinto, first performed on 9 May 1856 at the Teatro de São Carlos, Lisbon. First performed by the Imperial Ballet, as *Météora, or the Valley of the Stars*, with music attributed to Saint-Léon, Pinto, and Cesare Pugni, on 23 February 1861 at the Bolshoi Theater, St. Petersburg, with Nadezhda Bogdanova in the title role.

A Midsummer Night's Dream (Balanchine)

Ballet in two acts and six scenes, music by Felix Mendelssohn, choreography by George Balanchine, first performed by New York City Ballet on 17 January 1962 at City Center of Music and Drama, New York, with Melissa Hayden, Edward Villella, and Arthur Mitchell in leading roles. Synopsis: Balanchine and Mason, *Complete Stories*, 359–361.
See the *Balanchine Catalogue*, https://balanchine.org/see-also/cat-319/.

A Midsummer Night's Dream (Petipa)

Fantastic ballet in one act, libretto (after Shakespeare) and choreography by Marius Petipa, music by Felix Mendelssohn, with additional music by Ludwig Minkus, first performed by the Imperial Ballet on 14 July 1876 at Peterhof, St. Petersburg, with Evgenia Sokolova and Pavel Gerdt in leading roles. See *Khronika III*, 186, and Letellier, *Ludwig Minkus*, 113–114.

The Mikado's Daughter

Ballet fantastique in three acts, libretto by Vladimir Langhammer, music by Vasily Wrangell, choreography by Lev Ivanov, first performed by the Imperial Ballet on 9 November 1897 at the Mariinsky Theater, St. Petersburg, with Matilda Kshesinskaya and Pavel Gerdt in leading roles. Libretto: Wiley, *Lev Ivanov*, 270–279; see also 188–201.

Mlada

Fantastic ballet in four acts and nine scenes, libretto by Stepan Gedeonov, music by Ludwig Minkus, choreography by Marius Petipa, first performed by the Imperial Ballet on 2 December 1879 at the Bolshoi Theater, St. Petersburg, with Evgenia Sokolova, Felix Kshesinsky, and Maria Gorshenkova in leading roles. Synopsis: Letellier, *Ludwig Minkus*, 134–138; see also 138–140. See *Khronika III*, 204.

Les Mohicans

Ballet-pantomime in two acts, libretto by Léon Halévy, music by Adolphe Adam, choreography by Antonio Guerra, first performed by the Paris Opéra on 5 July 1837 at the Théâtre de l'Académie Royale de Musique (Salle Le Peletier), with Nathalie Fitzjames, Guerra, Joseph Mazilier, and Georges Elie in leading roles. See Gautier, *Gautier on Dance*, 9–14.

La Muette de Portici

Opera in five acts, libretto by Germain Delavigne (revised by Eugène Scribe), music by Daniel Auber, first performed by the Paris Opéra on 29 February 1828 at the Théâtre de l'Académie Royale de Musique (Salle Le Peletier), with dances staged by Jean-Louis Aumer and with Lise Noblet in the title role. First performed, as *Fenella*, by the German troupe of the Imperial Theaters on 13 January 1834 at the Alexandrinsky Theater, St. Petersburg, with dances staged by Antoine Titus and with Ekaterina Teleshova in the title role. Revived by the Imperial Ballet on 20 January 1887, with dances staged by Marius Petipa, at the Mariinsky Theater, St. Petersburg, with Virginia Zucchi in the title role. See Guest, *The Divine Virginia*, 106–107.

The Naiad and the Fisherman

See *Ondine, ou La naïade*.

Nathalie, ou La laitière suisse

Ballet in two acts, choreography by Filippo Taglioni, music by Adalbert Gyrowetz, first performed as *Das Schweizer Milchmädche* on 8 October 1821 at the Theater am Kärntnertor, Vienna. First performed by the Paris Opéra, with Gyrowetz's score revived by Michele Carafa, on 7 November 1932 at the Théâtre de l'Académie Royale de Musique (Salle Le Peletier), with Marie Taglioni, Pauline Leroux, and Joseph Mazilier in leading roles. See Gautier, *Gautier on Dance*, 20–21. First performed by the Imperial Ballet, staged by Antoine Titus as *The Swiss Milkmaid*, on 13 April 1832 at the Bolshoi Theater, St. Petersburg, with Laura Peysar in the leading role. Revived by Titus (with a new dance scene staged by Jules Perrot), as *Lida, or The Swiss Milkmaid*, on 4 December 1849 at the Bolshoi Theater, St. Petersburg, with Fanny Elssler in the title role. Synopsis: Beaumont, *Complete Book*, 86–92.

Néméa

See *Fiammetta, ou L'amour du diable*.

The Nutcracker

Ballet-féerie in two acts and three scenes, libretto by Marius Petipa (borrowed from the stories of E.T.A. Hoffman), music by Pyotr Tchaikovsky, choreography by Lev Ivanov, first performed by the Imperial Ballet on 6 December 1892 at the Mariinsky Theater, St. Petersburg, with Antonietta Dell-Era and Pavel Gerdt in leading roles. Libretto: Wiley, *Lev Ivanov*, 240–246; see also 132–149. See Wiley, *Tchaikovsky's Ballets*, 193–241, and Meisner, *Marius Petipa*, 229–233.

Les Nymphes amazones

Ballet in two acts, choreography by Henri Justamant, music by Joseph Luigini, first performed on 26 May 1864 at the Théâtre Royal de la Monnaie, Brussels.

Les Offrandes à l'amour, ou Le bonheur est d'aimer (The Offerings to Cupid, or The Joys of Love)

Allegorical ballet in one act, libretto and choreography by Marius Petipa, music by Ludwig Minkus, first performed by the Imperial Ballet on 22 July 1886 at Peterhof, St. Petersburg, with

Maria Gorshenkova, Marie Petipa, Evgenia Sokolova, and Pavel Gerdt in leading roles. See Letellier, *Ludwig Minkus*, 150. Revived by Lev Ivanov on 26 September 1893 at the Mariinsky Theater, St. Petersburg, with Varvara Rykhlyakova, Olga Preobrazhenskaya, Elizaveta Kuskova, and Nikolai Legat in leading toles. Synopsis: Wiley, *Lev Ivanov*, 158; see also 157–159.

Ondine, ou La naïade

Ballet in six scenes, libretto and choreography by Jules Perrot (after Friedrich de la Motte Fougué), music by Cesare Pugni, first performed on 22 June 1843 at Her Majesty's Theater, London, with Fanny Cerrito, Perrot, and Marie Guy-Stéphan in leading roles. See Philarète Chasles, "Notice sur *Ondine*," in *Les beautés de l'Opéra*, and Guest, *Perrot*, 98–108. First performed by the Imperial Ballet, staged by Perrot as *The Naiad and the Fisherman*, ballet fantastique in three acts and five scenes, on 30 January 1851 at the Bolshoi Theater, St. Petersburg, with Carlotta Grisi, Perrot, and Elena Andreanova in leading roles. See Guest, *Jules Perrot*, 254–259. The first act of the ballet was revived by Marius Petipa on 31 January 1871 at the Bolshoi Theater, St. Petersburg, with Ekaterina Vazem and Pavel Gerdt in leading roles. Complete ballet revived by Petipa on 27 October 1874 at the Bolshoi Theater, St. Petersburg, with Evgenia Sokolova and Gerdt in leading roles. Revived again by Petipa on 20 September 1892 at the Mariinsky Theater, St. Petersburg, with Varvara Nikitina and Pavel Gerdt in leading roles. Revived by Alexander Shiryaev on 7 December 1903 at the Mariinsky Theater, St. Petersburg, with Anna Pavlova and Sergei Legat in leading roles. Synopsis: Beaumont, *Complete Book*, 237–241.

Orfeo ed Euridice

Opera in three acts, libretto by Ranieri de' Calzabigi, music by Christoph Willibald Gluck, first performed on 5 October 1762 at the Burgtheater, Vienna. First performed by the Paris Opéra, as *Orphée et Eurydice*, drame héroïque in three acts, libretto by Pierre-Louis Moline (after Calzabigi), on 2 August 1774 at the Théâtre de l'Académie Royale de Musique (Seconde Salle du Palais-Royal). First performed by the Italian opera troupe of the Imperial Theaters on 24 November 1782 at the Theater at the Winter Palace, St. Petersburg, with dances staged by Ivan Stackelberg. Revived by the Imperial Italian Opera on 15 April 1868 at the Bolshoi Theater, St. Petersburg, with dances staged by Marius Petipa.

Le Papillon

Ballet-pantomime in two acts and four scenes, with a libretto by Henri Vernoy de Saint-Georges, music by Jacques Offenbach, choreography by Marie Taglioni, first performed by the Paris Opéra on 26 November 1860 at the Théâtre Impérial de l'Opéra (Salle Le Peletier), with Emma Livry, Louis Mérante, and Louise Marquet in leading roles. Synopsis: Beaumont, *Complete Book*, 289–295. See also Guest, *Second Empire 1858–1870*, 17–25. See also *The Butterfly*.

Paquita

Ballet-pantomime in two acts and three scenes, libretto by Paul Foucher, music by Édouard Deldevez, choreography by Joseph Mazilier, first performed by the Paris Opéra on 1 April 1846 at the Théâtre de l'Académie Royale de Musique (Salle Le Peletier), with Carlotta Grisi, Lucien Petipa, and Georges Elie in leading roles. First performed in St. Petersburg, staged by Frédéric and Marius Petipa, on 26 September 1847 at the Bolshoi Theater, with Elena Andreanova, Petipa, and Frédéric in leading roles. Revived by Petipa, with additional music by Ludwig Minkus, on 27 December 1881 at the Bolshoi Theater, St. Petersburg, with Ekaterina Vazem, Pavel Gerdt, and Felix Kshesinsky in leading roles. Librettos: Paris 1946, Appendix D (i); St. Petersburg 1847, Appendix D (ii).

The Parisian Market

Ballet comique in one act, libretto and choreography by Marius Petipa, music by Cesare Pugni, first performed on 23 April 1859 at the Bolshoi Theater, St. Petersburg, with Maria

Surovshchikova-Petipa and Marius Petipa in leading roles. First performed by the Paris Opéra, staged by Marius Petipa as *Le Marché des innocents*, ballet-pantomime in one act, on 29 May 1861 at the Théâtre de l'Opéra (Salle Le Peletier), with Maria Surovshchikova-Petipa and Louis Mérante in leading roles. See Guest, *Second Empire 1858–1870*, 46–49. Revived by Petipa on 8 January 1895 at the Mariinsky Theater, St. Petersburg, with Maria Anderson and Sergei Litavkin in leading roles. Synopsis: Beaumont, *Complete Book*, 388–391. See Guest, *Second Empire 1858–1870*, 46–49, and Meisner, *Marius Petipa*, 92–93, 96–97, 113–114.

La Péri

Ballet fantastique in two acts and three scenes, libretto by Théophile Gautier, music by Friedrich Burgmüller, choreography by Jean Coralli, first performed by the Paris Opéra on 17 July 1843 at the Théâtre de l'Académie Royale de Musique (Salle Le Peletier), with Carlotta Grisi and Lucien Petipa in leading roles. First performed by the Imperial Ballet, in a staging by Frédéric, on 20 January 1844 at the Bolshoi Theater, St. Petersburg, with Elena Andreanova and Christian Johanson in leading roles. Synopsis: Beaumont, *Complete Book*, 137–143. See Gautier, *Gautier on Dance*, 112–121 and 161–162, and Guest, *Romantic Ballet in Paris*, 221–225.

Petrushka

Scènes burlesque in four scenes. libretto by Alexander Benois and Igor Stravinsky, music by Stravinsky, choreography by Michel [Mikhail] Fokine, first performed by Serge Diaghilev's Ballets Russes on 13 June 1911 at the Théâtre du Châtelet, Paris, with Vaslav Nijinsky, Tamara Karsavina, Alexander Orlov, and Enrico Cecchetti in leading roles. Synopsis: Beaumont, *Complete Book*, 586–591.

The Pharaoh's Daughter

Grand ballet in three acts and nine scenes, with prologue and epilogue, libretto by Jules-Henri Vernoy de Saint-Georges, music by Cesare Pugni, choreography by Marius Petipa, first performed by the Imperial Ballet on 18 January 1862 at the Bolshoi Theater, St. Petersburg, with Carolina Rosati in the title role. Revived by Petipa on 10 November 1885 at the Bolshoi Theater, St. Petersburg, with Virginia Zucchi and Pavel Gerdt in leading roles, and on 21 October 1898 at the Mariinsky Theater, St. Petersburg, with Matilda Kshesinskaya and Gerdt in leading roles. Libretto: Wiley, *Century*, 217–237. See Meisner, *Marius Petipa*, 99–106.

Prince Igor

Opera in four acts with prologue, libretto and music by Alexander Borodin (completed by Nikolai Rimsky-Korsakov and Alexander Glazunov), first performed by the Imperial Russian Opera on 23 October 1890 at the Mariinsky Theater, St. Petersburg, with dances staged by Lev Ivanov. See Wiley, *Lev Ivanov*, 121–125. The "Polovtsian Dances" from Act Two of the opera were first performed under the title *Prince Igor* by Serge Diaghilev's Ballets Russes, choreography by Michel [Mikhail] Fokine, on 19 May 1909 at the Théâtre du Châtelet, Paris. Fokine's choreography was first performed by the Imperial Ballet on 22 September 1909 at the Mariinsky Theater, St. Petersburg. Synopsis: Beaumont, *Complete Book*, 560–564.

The Pupils of Dupré

See *The King's Command*.

Pygmalion

See *The Cyprus Statue, or Pygmalion*.

Raymonda

Ballet in three acts and four scenes, with apotheosis, libretto by Lydia Pashkova (from knightly legends), music by Alexander Glazunov, choreography by Marius Petipa, first performed by the Imperial Ballet on 7 January 1898 at the Mariinsky Theater, St. Petersburg, with Pierina Legnani, Sergei Legat, and Pavel Gerdt in leading roles. Libretto: Appendix G (i) and Wiley, *Century*, 392–401.

Le Rêve du peintre

See *Le Délire d'un peintre.*

Robert le diable

Opera in five acts, libretto by Eugène Scribe and Germain Delavigne, music by Giacomo Meyerbeer, first performed by the Paris Opéra on 21 November 1831 at the Théâtre de l'Académie Royale de Musique (Salle Le Peletier), dances staged by Filippo Taglioni. First performed by the Imperial Russian Opera on 14 December 1834 at the Alexandrinsky Theater, St. Petersburg, dances staged by Antoine Titus. Dances staged by Marius Petipa were first performed in the production by the Imperial Italian Opera on 27 September 1882 at the Mariinsky Theater, St. Petersburg. See Ann Hutchinson Guest and Knud Arne Jürgensen, *Robert le Diable: The Ballet of the Nuns* (Amsterdam: Gordon & Breach, 1997), and Robert Ignatius Letellier, *Meyerbeer's Robert le Diable: The Premier Opéra Romantique* (Newcastle upon Tyne, UK: Cambridge Scholars Publishing, 2012).

Le Roi Candaule

See *King Candaules.*

The Rose, the Violet, and the Butterfly

Choreographic interlude, music by Petr, Duke of Oldenburg. The first performance by the Imperial Ballet may have been given on 8 October 1857 at the Bolshoi Theater, St. Petersburg, as part of a benefit program for the *régisseur* I. Marcel, with libretto and choreography by Jules Perrot and with Lubov Radina as the Rose, Nadezhda Amosova as the Violet, and Marfa Muravieva as the Butterfly. Other sources state that this performance was given at the Grand Duke's summer residence in Tsarskoe Selo. See *Khronika III,* 57. Ivor Guest suggested the choreography may have been by Marius Petipa, who produced the work during the summer of 1857 at Tsarskoe Selo with a cast including Marie Surovshchikova-Petipa, the student Matilda Madayeva, and Muravieva. See Guest, *Jules Perrot,* 303, 357. Finally, Konstantin Skalkovsky claimed the ballet, a large divertissement, premiered on 8 December 1857 at Peterhof, St. Petersburg. See Meisner, *Marius Petipa,* 90–91.

Roxana, the Beauty of Montenegro

Fantastic ballet in four acts, libretto by Sergei Khudekov and Marius Petipa, music by Ludwig Minkus, choreography by Petipa, first performed by the Imperial Ballet on 29 January 1878 at the Bolshoi Theater, St. Petersburg, with Evgenia Sokolova and Pavel Gerdt in leading roles. See *Khronika III,* 192–193, and Letellier, *Ludwig Minkus,* 131.

Sacountala

Ballet-pantomime in two acts, libretto by Théophile Gautier, music by Ernest Reyer, choreography by Lucien Petipa, first performed by the Paris Opéra on 14 July 1858 at the Théâtre Impérial de l'Opéra (Salle Le Peletier), with Amalia Ferraris and Lucien Petipa in leading roles. Synopsis: Beaumont, *Complete Book,* 361–365. See Gautier, *Gautier on Dance,* 281–287.

Satanilla, or Love and Hell
See *Le Diable amoureux.*

Serenade
Classic ballet in four parts, music by Pyotr Tchaikovsky, choreography by George Balanchine, first performed by students of the School of American Ballet on 10 June 1934 at Woodlands, Hartsdale, New York, and then on 8 December 1934 by the Producing Company of the School of American Ballet at the Avery Memorial Theatre, Hartford, Connecticut. First performed by the American Ballet on 1 March 1935 at the Adelphi Theater, New York, with Kathryn Mullowney, Heidi Vossler, and Charles Laskey in leading roles. See the *Balanchine Catalogue*, https://balanchine.org/catalo gue/141-serenade-1935/.html. See also Balanchine and Mason, *Complete Stories*, 530–533.

Sleeping Beauty
Ballet-féerie in three acts, with prologue, libretto by Ivan Vsevolozhsky, music by Pyotr Tchaikovsky, choreography Marius Petipa, first performed by the Imperial Ballet on 3 January 1890 at the Mariinsky Theater, St. Petersburg, with Carlotta Brianza, Pavel Gerdt, Marie Petipa, and Enrico Cecchetti in leading roles. Libretto: Wiley, *Century*, 360–372; see also 373–391. See Wiley, *Tchaikovsky's Ballets*, 102–192, and Meisner, *Marius Petipa*, 224–229.

La Source
Ballet in three acts and four scenes, libretto by Charles Nuitter, music by Ludwig Minkus and Léo Delibes, choreography by Saint-Léon, first performed by the Paris Opéra on 12 November 1866 at the Théâtre Impérial de l'Opéra (Le Peletier), with Guglielmina Salvioni, Eugenie Fiocre, and Louis Mérante in leading roles. See Gautier, *Gautier on Dance*, 320–323; Guest, *Second Empire 1858–1870*, 93–99. First performed by the Imperial Ballet on 21 October 1869, in a revised version by Saint-Léon, titled *Le Lys*, at the Bolshoi Theater, St. Petersburg, with Adèle Grantzow in the leading role. Also performed in Vienna in a staging by Saint-Léon in 1878. First performed by the Vienna Court Opera (Wiener Hofoper) on 4 October 1848 in a staging by Saint-Léon with the title *Naïla, oder die Quellenfee* (Naïla, or the Waternymph). Selections from *La Source* were choreographed by George Balanchine for a divertissement of the same name that was first performed with the title *Pas de Deux: La Source* by New York City Ballet on 23 November 1668 at the New York State Theater, New York, with Violette Verdy and John Prinz in leading roles. Synopsis: Beaumont, *Complete Book*, 354–359, and Letellier, *Ludwig Minkus*, 75–77; see also 77–80.

The Star of Granada
Divertissement, music by Cesare Pugni, choreography by Marius Petipa (uncredited), first performed by the Imperial Ballet on 22 January 1855 at the Mikhailovsky Theater, St. Petersburg, with Maria Surovshchikova-Petipa in the leading role. See Meisner, *Marius Petipa*, 301.

Swan Lake
Grand ballet in four acts, libretto by Vladimir Begichev, music by Pyotr Tchaikovsky, choreography by Wenzel Reisinger, first performed by the Imperial Ballet on 20 February 1877 at the Bolshoi Theater, Moscow, with Polina Karpakova and Stanislav Gillert in leading roles. 1877 libretto and poster: Wiley, *Tchaikovsky's Ballets*, 321–327 and 342–344; see also 25–91 and 242–274. See also Sergey Konaev and Boris Mukosey (eds.), *Lebedinoe Ozero, balet v 4-kh deystviyakh: Postanovka v Moskovskom Bol'shom Teatre 1875–1883: Skripchniy repetitor i drugiye dokumenty* [Swan Lake, ballet in 4 acts: Staged at the Moscow Bolshoi Theater 1875–1883: Violin *répétiteur* and other documents] (St. Petersburg: Compozitor, 2015). The ballet's second scene, choreographed by Lev Ivanov, was performed by the Imperial Ballet on 17 February 1894 at the Mariinsky Theater, St.

Petersburg. The complete ballet, ballet fantastique in three acts and four scenes, with music revised by Riccardo Drigo and with choreography by Marius Petipa and Ivanov, was first performed by the Imperial Ballet on 15 January 1895 at the Mariinsky Theater, St. Petersburg, with Pierina Legnani and Pavel Gerdt in leading roles. 1895 libretto: Wiley, *Lev Ivanov*, 259–264; see also 170–183. See Wiley, *Tchaikovsky's Ballets*, 25–101, and Meisner, *Marius Petipa*, 239–243.

La Sylphide

Ballet-pantomime in two acts, libretto by Adolphe Nourrit, music by Jean Schneitzhoeffer, choreography by Filippo Taglioni, first performed by the Paris Opéra on 12 March 1832 at the Théâtre de l'Académie Royale De Musique (Salle Le Peletier), with Marie Taglioni in the title role. See Jules Janin, "Notice sur *La Sylphide*," in *Les beautés de l'Opéra*; Gautier, *Gautier on Dance*, 51–55, 78, 131–133, 140–143; and Guest, *Romantic Ballet in Paris*, 112–117. First performed by the Imperial Ballet, in a staging by Antoine Titus, on 28 May 1835 at the Bolshoi Theater, St. Petersburg, with Luisa Croisette in the title role. Revived by Marius Petipa, with additional music by Riccardo Drigo, on 19 January 1892 at the Mariinsky Theater, St. Petersburg, with Varvara Nikitina in the title role. Libretto: Marian Smith, ed., *La Sylphide*, 316–323. (Note: this entry does not include reference to the 1836 production of *La Sylphide* by August Bournonville.)

Sylvia, ou La nymphe de Diane

Ballet in three acts and four scenes, libretto by Jules Barbier, music by Léo Delibes, choreography by Louis Mérante, first performed by the Paris Opéra on 14 June 1876 at the Théâtre National de l'Opéra (Palais Garnier), Paris, with Rita Sangalli and Mérante in leading roles. Synopsis: Beaumont, *Complete Book*, 489–496. See Pauline Girard, *Léo Delibes: Itinéraire d'un musicien, des Bouffes-Parisiens à l'Institut* (Paris: Vrin, 2018), 151–169. First performed by the Imperial Ballet on 2 December 1901 at the Mariinsky Theater, St. Petersburg, choreography by Lev Ivanov (completed by Pavel Gerdt and Alexander Shiryaev). See Wiley, *Lev Ivanov*, 206–209.

Tancrède

Tragédie lyrique in five acts with prologue, libretto by Antoine Danchet, music by André Campra, first performed on 7 November 1702 at the Théâtre de l'Académie Royale de Musique (Théâtre du Palais-Royal), Paris.

La Tarentule

Ballet-pantomime in two acts, libretto by Eugène Scribe, music by Casimir Gide, choreography by Jean Coralli, first performed by the Paris Opéra on 24 June 1839 at the Théâtre de l'Académie Royale de Musique (Salle Le Peletier), with Fanny Elssler, Joseph Mazilier, and Jean-Baptiste Barrez in leading roles. Synopsis: Beaumont, *Complete Book*, 122–128. See Gautier, *Gautier on Dance*, 66–75 and 79–81.

Thetis and Peleus

See *The Adventures of Peleus*.

The Traveling Dancer

Episode in one act, libretto and choreography (some of both possibly borrowed from Paul Taglioni's 1849 *La Prima Ballerina, ou l'Embuscade*) by Marius Petipa, music by Cesare Pugni, first performed by the Imperial Ballet on 4 November 1865 at the Bolshoi Theater, St. Petersburg, with Maria Surovshchikova-Petipa, Lubov Radina, and Timofei Stukolkin in leading roles. Petipa had prepared a revival of *The Traveling Dancer* (along with his last ballet, *The Romance of the Rosebud and the Butterfly*) for a performance at the Hermitage Theatre, St. Petersburg, on 23 January 1904. The performance was canceled, but Olga Preobrazhenskaya performed *The Traveling Dancer* as part of her benefit program on 9 January 1905 at the Mariinsky Theater, St. Petersburg, for which Petipa composed a new variation for the ballerina. See Meisner, *Marius Petipa*, 278–280 and 287.

Les Tribulations d'une balerine

Ballet-pantomime in two scenes by Henri Justamant, performed in 1860 at the Grand Théâtre, Lyon.

Vert-Vert

Ballet-pantomime in three acts, libretto by Adolphe de Leuven, music by Édouard Deldevez and Jean-Baptiste-Joseph Tolbecque, choreography by Joseph Mazilier (completed by Arthur Saint-Léon?), first performed by the Paris Opéra on 24 November 1851 at the Théâtre de l'Opéra (Salle Le Peletier), Paris, with Adeline Plunkett and Olimpia Priora in leading roles. See Gautier, *Gautier on Dance*, 230–233, and Guest, *Second Empire 1847–1858*, 58–61. First performed by the Imperial Ballet on 8 January 1852 at the Bolshoi Theater, St. Petersburg, staged by Mazilier, with Carlotta Grisi, Sofia Radina, Mazilier, and Jules Perrot in leading roles. Synopsis: Beaumont, *Complete Book*, 197–204.

The Vestal

Ballet in three acts and four scenes, libretto by Sergei Khudekov, music by Mikhail Ivanov, choreography by Marius Petipa, first performed by the Imperial Ballet on 17 February 1888 at the Mariinsky Theater, St. Petersburg, with Elena Cornalba, Maria Gorshenkova, Felix Kshesinsky, Pavel Gerdt, and Anna Johanson in leading roles. Libretto: Wiley, *Century*, 323–349. See Meisner, *Marius Petipa*, 212–218.

Le Voyage dans la lune (The Extraordinary Journey to the Moon)

Opera féerie in four acts and twenty-three scenes, libretto by Albert Vanloo, Eugène Leterrier, and Arnold Mortier, music by Jacques Offenbach, choreography (two ballets) by Henri Justamant, first performed on 26 November 1875 at the Théâtre de la Gaîté, Paris.

The Willful Wife

See *Le Diable à quatre*.

Zoraiya, the Moorish Girl in Spain

Grand ballet in four acts and seven scenes, libretto by Sergei Khudekov, choreography by Marius Petipa, music by Ludwig Minkus, first performed by the Imperial Ballet on 1 February 1881 at the Bolshoi Theater, St. Petersburg, with Ekaterina Vazem and Pavel Gerdt in leading roles. Synopsis: Beaumont, *Complete Book*, 417–422.

APPENDIX B
Justamant Staging Manuals Listed by Repository

Henri Justamant's personal library of books, staging manuals, musical scores, and other items was put up for auction in Paris in 1893. Items were listed in an auction catalog:

> Catalogue de livres anciens et modernes et des manuscrits originaux des ballets et divertissement de M. Henri Justamant: (vente à Paris, Hôtel des commissaires-priseurs, salle 10, 15 mai 1893, Mr. Maurice Delestre, commissaire-priseur)

> [Catalog of old and modern books and original manuscripts of ballets and entertainment by M. Henri Justamant: (sale in Paris, Hôtel des commissaires-auctioneers, room 10, 15 May 1893, Mr. Maurice Delestre, auctioneer)]

A digitized copy of the auction catalog is available online at available online at http://catalogue.bnf.fr/ark:/12148/cb36537250g.

Repositories:

   (i) Theaterwissenschaftliche Sammlung der Universität Köln, Schloß Wahn (The Theater Studies Collection of the University of Cologne, at Wahn Castle)
   (ii) Bibliothèque Nationale de France, Bibliothèque-Musée de l'Opéra, Paris
   (iii) Bibliothèque Nationale de France, Département des Arts du Spectacle, Paris
   (iv) The New York Public Library for the Performing Arts, Jerome Robbins Dance Division
   (v) Deutsches Tanzarchiv Köln

Many of the staging manuals contain newspaper clippings, theater posters and tickets, and images of dancers in stage costumes (photographs, lithographs, watercolors, and other media) that are not enumerated in the descriptions below.

The entries below represent abbreviated listings, lightly edited for spelling, punctuation, and consistency and to remove redundancies.

(i) Theaterwissenschaftliche Sammlung der Universität Köln, Schloß Wahn (TWS)

Almaviva et Rosine
Ballet in three acts [with a libretto] by Blache Pére [Jean-Baptiste Blache]. Revived at the Grand Théâtre de Lyon on [n.d.]. *Mise en scéne* and dances by Justamant. Includes list of dancers for the seasons 1854–1855, 1855–1856, 1856–1857.
TWS Inventory Number 70-435

Les Amadryades
Ballet Feérie in two scenes by Mr. H. Justamant, performed for the first time in Brussels at the Théâtre Royal de La Monnaie in December 1863. Includes "Analyse du ballet."
TWS Inventory Number 70-436

Le Bal Travesti | Les Saltimbanques
Two Ballets *Divertissements*. 1. *Le Bal Travesti*. 2. *Les Saltimbanques*.
Un Bal Travesti. Ballet . . . *Divertissement* in one scene by Mr. H. Justamant, performed for the first time at the Grand Théâtre, Lyon, in 1851. *Les Saltimbanques*. Ballet *Divertissement* in one scene, performed for the first time at the Grand Théâtre de Lyon in 1853.
TWS Inventory Number 70-483

Le Baptême du Tropique

Ballet Fantaisie in one act by Mr. H. Justamant. Music by Mr. Métra. Performed for the first time in Paris at the Théatre des Folies Bergéres [sic] on 22 March 1873. Includes accessories list.
TWS Inventory Number 70-437

Les Conscrits espagnols, ou Le Recrutement forcé

Ballet Comique in one act by Mr. H. Justamant. Music by Mr. Jozet. Performed for the first time in Lyon at the Grand Théàtre in March 1851. Performed at the Théàtre Royal de la Monnaie in Brussels on [n.d.].
TWS Inventory Number 70-438

Les Contrebandiers

Ballet-pantomime in two scenes by Mr. H. Justamant. Music by Mr. Jozet. Performed for the first time in Lyon at the Grand Théàtre in 1850. Theater directed by Mr. Delestang.
TWS Inventory Number 70-439

Le Corsaire

Ballet in three acts and five scenes by MM. de St George and Mazilier. Music by Mr. A. Adam. Performed for the first time at the Grand Théàtre de Lyon on 17 February 1857. *Mise en scène* by Mr. H Justamant. Theater directed by Mr. Halanzier-Dufrenoy. Includes libretto of Paris premiere performance on 23 January 1856 as well as a list of the movements of the ship in the final scene and an accessories list.
TWS Inventory Number 70-441

Les Cosaques, ou La Ferme Finlandaises

Ballet in two acts and four scenes by Mr. H. Justamant. Music by Mr. Rozet. Performed for the first time in Lyon at the Grand Théàtre on 23 April 1854. Theater directed by Mr. Delestang.
TWS Inventory Number 70-442

Les Dentelles

Divertissement du Pas des Dentelles by Justamant composed in Brussels for the Théàtre Royal de la Monnaie [in] 186[-]. Music by Mr. Calendini.
TWS Inventory Number 70-446

Le Diable à quatre

Ballet in two acts and four scenes. Revived at the Grand Théàtre de Lyon in 1853. *Mise en scène* by Mr. Justamant.
TWS Inventory Number 70-443

Le Diable amoureux

Ballet in three acts and ten scenes by MM. de St-George and Mazilier. Music by MM. Benoist, (1st and 3rd acts), Réber (2nd act). Performed for the first time at l'Académie Royale de Musique on 23 September 1840. Performed for the first time at the Grand Théàtre de Lyon on 4 October 1854. *Mise en scéne* and dances by Mr. Justamant. Theater directed by Mr. Lefebvre.
TWS Inventory Number 70-453

Le Dieu et la Bayadère

Ballets from *Le Dieu et la Bayadère*. Staged by Mr. H. Justamant, performed at the Grand Théâtre de Lyon. *Mise en scène* of the *pas* and ballets of the role of Zoloé. Includes information about seasons 1853–1854 and 1854–1855.
TWS Inventory Number 70-445

L'étoile de Messine

Ballet-pantomime in two acts and five scenes by MM. Paul Foucher and [Pasquale] Borri. Music by Mr. Le Comte Gabrielli. Performed for the first time in Paris at the Théâtre Imperial de l'Opéra on 20 November 1861. Performed for the first time in Brussels at the Théâtre Royal de la Monnaie in 1864 with changes in the piece and in the dances by Mr. Justamant (at the request of Mme [Amalia] Ferraris).
TWS Inventory Number 70-447

Faust

Divertissements from *Faust*. Staged by Mr. Justamant. Performed for the first time at the [Théâtre de] l'Académie Impériale de Musique on 3 March 1869.
TWS Inventory Number 70-454

La Favorite

Divertissements from *La Favorite*. Staged by Mr. Justamant. Performed for the first time at the [Théâtre de] l'Académie Impériale de Musique on 18 October 1869. *Divertissements* from *La Favorite* by Mr. H. Justamant, performed at the Grand Théâtre de Lyon. Includes detailed cast list.
TWS Inventory Number 70-448

La Fille du Ciel

Ballet in four scenes by Mr. H. Justamant. Music by Mr. J. Luidgini [sic]. Scenery by Mr. Devoir. Performed for the first time in Lyon at the Grand Théâtre on November 1858. Theater directed by Mr. Delestang. Performed at the Théâtre [Royal] de la Monnaie in Brussels on 1 September 1861. Theater directed by Mr. Letellier.
TWS Inventory Number 70-449

Flamma, la Fille du Diable

Ballet fantastique in two acts by Mr. H. Justamant. Performed for the first time in Lyon at the Grand Théâtre on 12 December 1860. Theater directed by Mr. Delestang. Performed in Brussels at the Théâtre Royal de la Monnaie on 19 December 1863. Theater directed by Mr. Letellier. Includes costume lithograph.
TWS Inventory Number 70-455

Fleurs et Papillons

Ballet from *Fleurs et Papillons*. *Ballet-féerie* in one act and two scenes by M. Justamant. Scenery by M. Devoir. Costumes by M. Blot. Machines by M. Tonny. Performed for the first time at the Grand Théâtre de Lyon on 22 October 1860. Includes printed program from Lyon premiere.
TWS Inventory Number 70-452

La Forêt Noir

Pantomime in three acts *à grand spectacle*, [libretto] by [Jean-François] Arnould, given at the Théâtre de l'Ambigu-Comique, with new scenes, on 20 Frimaire, Year X and 9 February 1807.

Music arranged by Mr. Guaisain. Ballet by Mr. Richard, pensionnaire of the Académie Impériale de Musique. Exact copy of the *livret*, (Justamant). Revived in Lyon at the Grand Théâtre on 18 February 1855, theater directed by Monsieur Lefebvre. *Mise en scéne* and arrangement [adaptation] by Mr. Justamant, *Maitre de Ballet*.
TWS Inventory Number 70-451

Guillaume Tell

Ballets from *Guillaume Tell*. Staged by Mr. H. Justamant, performed at the Grand Théâtre de Lyon. Theater directed by Mr. Delestang.
TWS Inventory Number 70-456

Gustave III

Grand Ballet from *Gustave III*. Composed and staged by Mr. H. Justamant, performed at the Grand Théâtre de Lyon in 1855.
TWS Inventory Number 70-457

La houri

Ballet-féerie in one act, arrangement in the first act of the *Royaume des Fleurs* by Justamant. Performed at the Grand Théâtre de Lyon on 6 January 1859. Theater directed by Mr. Delestang.
TWS Inventory Number 70-459

Les Huguenots

Divertissements from *[Les] Huguenots*. Staged by Mr. Justamant. Performed for the first time at the [Théâtre de] l'Académie Impériale de Musique on 13 November 1868.
TWS Inventory Number 70-458

Jérusalem

Divertissement. Composed and staged by Mr. H. Justamant. Performed at the Grand Théâtre de Lyon, 1849. Includes four divertissements:
1. *Pas de Quatre* staged by Mr. Justamant for the Grand Théâtre de Lyon, 1849
2. *Pas de Deux* staged by Mr. Justamant for the Grand Théâtre de Lyon, 1849, in *Jérusalem*
3. *Pas des harpes* staged by Mr. Justamant for the Grand Théâtre de Lyon, 1857
4. *Pas de Quatre* staged by Mr. Justamant for the Théâtre Royal de la Monnaie in Brussels, 1864

TWS Inventory Number 70-460

Le Joueur de Biniou, ou Le Guerz enchanté

Ballet in one act by Mr. H. Justamant. Music by Mr. Bertou. Performed for the first time in Lyon at the Grand Théâtre in November 1850. Theater directed by Mr. Delestang. Performed in Brussels at the Théâtre Royal [de la Monnaie] in 1863. Theater directed by Mr. Letellier.
TWS Inventory Number 70-462

La Juive

Ballets in *La Juive*, staged by Mr. H. Justamant. Performed at the Grand Théâtre de Lyon. Theater directed by Mr. Delestang.
TWS Inventory Number 70-461

Lore-Ley, La Fée du Rhin
Ballet in four scenes by MM Justamant and Montlouis. Music by Mr. J. Luigini. Décors de Mr. Savette. Performed for the first time at the Grand Théâtre de Lyon on 23 January 1856.
TWS Inventory Number 70-463

Le Magicien
Ballet chinoiserie in two acts and two scenes by Mr. Justamant. Music by Mr. Jozet. Dècors de Mr. Devoir. Costumes de Mr. Blot. Machines de Mr. Conny. Performed for the first time at the Grand Théâtre de Lyon in September 1860. Performed for the first time at the Théâtre [Royal] de la Monnaie in Brussels on 30 September 1861.
TWS Inventory Number 70-464

Les Martyrs | La Favorite
Ballets in Les Martyrs, staged by Mr. H. Justamant. Performed at the Grand Théâtre de Lyon in November 1856. Ballets in in La Favorite, staged by Mr. H. Justamant. Performed at the Grand Théâtre de Lyon, 1855.
TWS Inventory Number 70-466

La Muette [de Portici]
Role of Fenella and dances. Staged by Justamant for the Grand Théâtre de Lyon, 1849.
TWS Inventory Number 70-467

Les Néréides, ou Le Lac enchanté
Ballet-féerie in two acts and four scenes by M. Justamant. Music by Jules Ward. Performed for the first time at the Grand Théâtre de Lyon on 11 March 1861.
TWS Inventory Number 70-468

Les Nymphes Amazones
Ballet in two acts by Mr. Justamant, music by Mr. J[oseph] Luigini. Performed for the first time at the Théâtre Royal de la Monnaie in Brussels on 26 May 1864.
TWS Inventory Number 70-469

Obéron
Divertissement from Obéron. Staged by Justamant in Brussels for the Théâtre Royal de la Monnaie, 1863.
TWS Inventory Number 70-470

Ondine
Ballet in two acts and four scenes by Mr. [Jules] Perrot. Music by Mr. [Cesare] Pugni. Mise en scène written by Mr. Justamant in Brussels, 1863.
TWS Inventory Number 70-471

L'orco | Les Templiers

Ballets in *L'orco* and *Les Templiers*. Composed by Mr. H Justamant. Performed at the Théâtre Royal de la Monnaie, Brussels.

    1. Choirs danced [*Choeurs dansé*] in the opera *[L'o]rco* staged in Brussels for the Théâtre Royal de la Monnaie, 1864
    2. *Pas de quatre* danced in *L'orco* staged in Brussels at the Théâtre Royal de la Monnaie, 1864
    3. *Valse* of the opera *L'orco* staged in Brussels at the Théâtre Royal de la Monnaie, 1864
    4. *Pas de quatre* in *[L]es Templiers*, music by Mr. Hensens

TWS Inventory Number 70-472

Orphée aux Enfers—Mise en Scène

Opéra Bouffe-féerie, [libretto] by Mr. H. Crémieux. Music by Mr. Jacques Offenbach. *Mise en scène* by Mr. Henri Justamant after that of Paris. *Orphée aux Enfers. Mise en scène* by Henri Justamant. Performed for the first time in London at the Royal [sic] Alhambra Theatre on 30 April 1877. Theater directed by Mr. Leader. Includes a program from the Alhambra Theatre, 1877, and a French program that cites the 1858 premiere at the Théâtre des Bouffes-Parisiens, Paris and 1874 revival at the Théâtre de la Gaîté, Paris.

TWS Inventory Number 70-475

Orphée aux Enfers—Ballets

Ballets in *Orphée aux Enfers*. Composed and staged by H. Justamant. Performed for the first time in London at the Royal [sic] Alhambra Theatre on 30 April 1877. Monsieur Leader, Director. Performed at the Théâtre de la Gaîté in Paris for the revival of *Orphée [aux Enfers]* on 19 January 1878. Monsieur A. Vizentini, Theater Director.

TWS Inventory Number 70-473

Orphée aux Enfers—Costumes of the Ballets

Costumes of *Orphée aux Enfers*. Includes dozens of watercolor drawings, photographs, and lithographs as well as a theater bill from the Royal Alhambra Theatre, dated 30 April 1877.

TWS Inventory Number 70-474

Paquita

Ballet in two acts and three scenes by MM. Paul Foucher and [Joseph Mazilier, music by Mr. [Éduoard] Deldevez, performed for the first time at the Théâtre de l'Académie Royale de Musique on 1 April 1846. Performed at the Grand Théâtre de Lyon on 6 December 1854. *Mise en scène* and dances by M. Justamant. Theater directed by Monsieur Lefebvre. Includes a program from the Paris premiere, dated 1 April 1846, and accessories list.

TWS Inventory Number 70-479

La Permission de Dix Heures

Ballet in two acts, performed in Lyon.

TWS Inventory Number 70-476

Le Prophéte—Ballets

Ballets in *Le Prophète*. Staged by Mr. H. Justamant. Performed for the first time in Lyon at the Grand Théâtre.

TWS Inventory Number 70-481

Le Prophéte—Divertissements

Divertissements of [Le] Prophéte. Staged by Mr. Mabile [when] performed for the first time. Revived at the same Théâtre on 28 June 1869 with a Scène Nouvelle des Patineurs staged by Mr. Justamant.
TWS Inventory Number 70-482

Quasimodo, ou La bohémienne

Ballet d'actions [sic] in three acts and six scenes by M. Justamant. Music by M. Luigini. Scenery by M. Devoir, Costumes de M. Blod. Mise en scène and detailed notes about everything in the work [sur tout a que contient l'ouvrage]. Performed for the first time at the Grand Théâtre de Lyon, 1859.
Inventory Number 70-484

La Reine de Saba

Divertissements from La Reine de Saba. Composed by Justamant in Brussels for the Théâtre Royal de la Monnaie according to the cuts made to the music by the author, 186[-].
TWS Inventory Number 70-477

Robert le Diable

Divertissement from Robert le Diable opera. Staged by Justamant in Brussels for the Théâtre Royal de la Monnaie, 1863.
TWS Inventory Number 70-480

Les Sept Merveilles

Ballets des Sept Merveilles. Composed and staged by Mr. H. Justamant. Performed at the Grand Théâtre de Lyon.
TWS Inventory Number 70-465

Les Songes

Ballet divertissement féerie in one act by Mr. Justamant. Performed for the first time in Brussels at the Théâtre Royal de la Monnaie in Décembre 1862.
TWS Inventory Number 70-478

Les Tribulations d'une Ballerine

Ballet-pantomime in two scenes by Mr. H. Justamant, performed at the Grand Théâtre de Lyon in 1860.
TWS Inventory Number 70-487

Le Trouvère

Dances in Le Trouvère, composed by Mr. H. Justamant, performed at the Grand Théâtre de Lyon on 3 April 1857. Dances of Trouvère opera composed by Justamant for the Théâtre Royal de la Monnaie in Brussels, 1861.
TWS Inventory Number 70-486

Les Vépres Siciliennes

Ballets in Les Vépres Siciliennes, staged by Mr. H. Justamant, performed at the Grand Théâtre de Lyon.
TWS Inventory Number 70-485

(ii) Bibliothèque Nationale de France, Bibliothèque-Musée de l'Opéra, Paris

Divers pas nobles | composed by Mr. H. Justamant | *pas* with groups
1. *Pas de deux*, music by Réthaler, danced by Mr. Herbin and Mme. Tell Duleau
2. *Pas de deux*, music by Bertou
3. *Pas de deux*, adagio, with a piston solo, danced by Mr. Mège and Mlle. Delechaux
4. *Pas de deux, ou Pas de la Couronne*, adagio
5. *Pas de deux*, music by Massip, dancec by Mr. Herbin and Mlle. Saline
6. *Pas de Mlle Carlotta Devecchi*, inserted in *Paquita*
7. *Pas de deux*, music by Mr. Adam, danced in *Le Carnaval* by Mr. Tell and Mlle. Duriez
8. *Pas de deux*, music by Massip, danced by Mr. Herbin and Mlle. Saline
9. *Pas de deux*, music from *Paquita*, danced by Mlles. Navare and Leblanc

B-217 (1)

Divers pas nobles | composed by Mr. H. Justamant | *pas* with groups
1. *Pas de deux*, on a motif by Gustave Wasa, danced by the 1st [danseur] and 1st danseuse
2. *Gustave III, pas de deux*, music from *[Zerline, ou] La corbeille d'oranges*, danced by Mr. Herbin, Bertoto, Mlle. Saline and Camille, [Grand Théâtre de Lyon, 1855]
3. *Pas de deux*, music by Massip, by the Sultan and the Reine des fées
4. *Pas de deux*, [music by Massip], danced by Mr. Mazillier and Mlle. Devecchi
5. *Pas de cinq*, music by d'Halévy, 1st danseuses, Mlle. Bertin, Navare, Vernet, Girod
6. *Pas de deux*, [music by Massip], 2nd danseur and Lélia
7. *Pas de Bacchantes*, music by d'Halévy, staged for Mlles. Delechaux, Girod, Wesmael
8. *Pas de deux*, music by Massip, staged for Mr. Gredelu et Mlle. Dor
9. *Pas de deux*, music by Devecchi, staged for Mr. Vincent, Mlle. Dor, et four third danseuses
10. *Pas de deux*, music by Bertou, staged for Mlle. Delechaux and Mr. Guillemin
11. *Pas de deux*, staged for Madame Ferraris, two adagios
12. *Pas de deux, de Madame Ferraris*

B-217 (2)

Pas de genres | [composed by Henri Justamant]
1. *Tarentelle* with three danseuses including two *en travesties*
1bis. *Polka Mazourka à 6*, music by Jules Massip
2. *Mazourka, bal travesti, à 4*, music by Rozet, danced by Mlles. Hortense, Marquita, Vinay, and Lise
3. *La Norvégienne, pas de deux, de genre*, music from *[Zerline, ou] La corbeille d'oranges*, in *Gustave III*, [Grand Théâtre de Lyon, 1855]
4. *Crakovienne, coda, à 2*, music from *[Zerline, ou] La corbeille d'oranges*, in *Gustave III*
5. *Redowa crakovienne*, music by Mr. Rozet, danced by Mlle. Bertin, Vernet, and Girod
6. *Mazourka à 6*, music by Rhétaler
7. *La Matelott*
8. *Arlequinade, scène* and *pas de huit*, Polichinelle, Arlequin, Pierrot, Arlequine, Polichinelle, Pierrette
9. *Anglaise*, music by Massip, danced by two women
10. *Anglaise*, music by Mr. Massip, danced by two men and two women
11. *Pas des momies, ou Pas chinois*, music from *[Zerline, ou] La corbeille d'oranges*, in *Gustave III*, 16 danseurs
12. *Pas de marquis, ou Pas d'enfants*, music from *[Zerline, ou] La corbeille d'oranges*, in *Gustave III*, 16 danseurs
Unbound cahier: Évolutions for 8 men and 16 women, composed by Justamant

B-217 (4)

Ballets and the role of Fiametta | of *[Le t]imbre d'argent* | staged by Mr. H. Justamant | performed for the first time in Paris at the Théâtre National Lyrique | [23] February 1877 | music by Mr. de Saint-Saëns | Mr. Albert Vizentini, theater director
B-217 (5)

Ballet | of *[Le] Bravo* | by Mr. H. Justamant | music by Mr. Salvayre | performed for the first time in Paris at the Théâtre National Lyrique | 18 April 1877 | Mr. Albert Vizentini, theater director
B-217 (6)

Ballets of *Obéron* | Paris | staged by Mr. Justamant | performed for the first time in Paris at the Théâtre National Lyrique | the old [Théâtre de la] Gaité | 8 June 1876 | Mr. Albert Vizentini, theater director
Includes accessories list.
The revival of *Oberon*, *opéra fantastique* by Carl Maria von Weber, premiered in 1857 at the Théâtre Lyrique.
B-217 (7)

Ballets of *Dimitri* | staged by Mr. H. Justamant | music by Mr. V. Joncières | performed for the first time in Paris at the Théâtre National Lyrique | old [Théâtre de la] Gaité | 5 May 1876 | Mr. Albert Vizentini, theater director
Includes accessories list. At the beginning of the volume, an autograph letter signed by Victorin Joncières addressed to Henri Justamant, Paris, May 6, 1876 (expresses his satisfaction to him the day after Dimitri's premiere), and a printed leaflet containing the casting.
B-217 (8)

Ballets in *Madame Thérèse* | composed and staged by Mr. H. Justamant | performed for the first time in Paris at the Théâtre du Châtelet | 9 October 1882 | Mr. Floury, theater director
Includes a printed program.
B-217 (9)

Ballets | staged by H. Justamant | for the *féerie Peau d'âne* | performed at the Théâtre de la Renaissance in Nantes | performed 3 October 1868
Includes a leaflet announcing the first performance of *Peau d'âne*, shelf mark B-217 (10,2).
Tournée of the Théâtre de la Gaîté, where the work was created in 1863.
B-217 (10,1)

Ballets | *[Les f]ugitifs* | composed and staged by Mr. H. Justamant | performed for the first time | in Paris at the Théâtre du Châtelet | 6 February 1875 | Mr. Fischer, theater director . . .
Drame created at the Théâtre de l'Ambigu-Comique, then revived at the Théâtre de la Gaîté and Théâtre du Châtelet
Includes accessories list with drawings and costume details.
B-217 (11)

Pas, valse | *et mixte* | [composed by Henri Justamant]
    1. *Valse à cinq*, music by Bartoloti
    2. *Valse, corps de ballet*, musique des *[Anita, ou Les] Contrebandiers*, staged in Brussels for the Théâtre Royal de la Monnaie, 1861, music by Rozet
    3. *Pas valse*, by Justamant, composed in Brussels for the Théâtre Royal de la Monnaie, music by Mr. Calendini, 1862
    4. *La Styrienne nouvelle*, music by Roze
    5. *Nouvelle Styrienne, bal travesti*, danced by Mr. Justamant, Mlle. Duleau and Génat, music by Rozet
    6. *Styrienne à deux, ou Pas styrien*, music from *[Zerline, ou] La corbeille d'oranges*, in *Gustave III*, [danced] by M. Tell and Mlle. Duleau [Grand Théâtre de Lyon, 1855]
    7. *Valses à trois*, danced by Mr. Elisée, Mlles. Vernet and Girod
    8. *La Mecklembourgeoise*, danced by M. Baptistin, Mlles. Génat, Moulin, and Gibbert
    9. *La Viennoise*
B-217 (12)

Les forges infernales | ballet | composed and staged by Mr. H. Justamant | music by Mr. Hubans | performed for the first time in Paris at the Théâtre du Châtelet, in the revival of the *féerie Peau d'âne* | . . . July 1883.
B-217 (13)

Ballets | *[L]es fleurs guerrières* | and | *[L]es flocons de neige* | by Mr. H. Justamant | music by Mr. Lajarte | costumes by Mr. Landolf | performed in Paris in [the *ballet-féerie*] *Le Pied de Mouton* at the Eden-Théâtre | 16 September 1888 | Mr. Bertrand, theater director
B-217 (14)

La vague | ballet in two scenes | by Mr. H. Justamant | music by MM. Métra and Roger | performed for the first time in Paris | at the Palace Théâtre, 10 April 1883.
B-217 (15)

Théâtre | de la Renaissance | dances of *opéras bouffes* | by Mr. H. Justamant
1. Dances in *La Camargo*, composed and staged by M. H. Justamant, performed in Paris at the Théâtre de la Renaissance [in 1878]
2. Divertissement in *Kosiki*, composed and staged by Mr. H. Justamant, performed for the first time in Paris at the Théâtre de la Renaissance [in 1876]
3. Divertissement in *Le Saïs*, composed and staged by Mr. H. Justamant, performed for the first time in Paris at the Théâtre de la Renaissance, 17 December 1881
4. *Scène et danse* staged by Mr. H. Justamant in *La bonne aventure*, opéra bouffe, performed for the first time in Paris at the Théâtre de la Renaissance, 3 November 1882; Mr. Gravière, theater director

B-217 (16)

Ballet | *des bohémiens et soldats* | by Mr. H. Justamant | music by Mr. Lecocq | inserted in *Le petit duc* | performed at the Eden-Théâtre | 30 November 1888 | Mr. Bertrand, theater director
B-217 (17)

Le carnaval de Venise | ballet in three acts and four scenes | by Mr. Millon, music by MM. Persuis and Kreutzer | revived in Lyon . . . 1850 | *mise en scène* by Mr. Justamant | Mr. Delestang, theater director
Includes casting of dancers from 1850 to 1857.
B-217 (18)

Divertissements | of *opéras comiques* | with coryphées and women of the corps de ballet
1. Divertissements from *Juagarita [l'indienne]*, staged by Mr. H. Justamant, performed for the first time in Lyon at the Grand Théâtre, 1856 to 1857, Mr. Halanzier, theater director
2. Divertissements from *L'étoile du nord*, staged by Mr. H. Justamant, performed for the first time at the Grand Théâtre de Lyon, 1854 to 1855, Messieurs George Hail and Lefèbvre, theater directors
3. *Danse de Giralda*, staged by Mr. H. Justamant, performed at the Grand Théâtre de Lyon, 1852; Mr. Delestang, theater director
4. *Danse du Roi des Halles*, staged by Mr. H. Justamant, performed at the Grand Théâtre de Lyon, 1854; Mr. Delestang, theater director
5. Divertissements from *[Le p]ré aux clercs*, staged by Mr. H. Justamant, revival, performed at the Grand Théâtre de Lyon, 1859 to 1860; Mr. Delestang, theater director
6. *La Bamboula*, dance in *Paul et Virginie*, opera, staged by Mr. H. Justamant, performed for the first time in Paris at the Théâtre National Lyrique, the old [Théâtre de la] Gaité, on 15 November 1876; Mr. Albert Vizentini, theater director
Juagarita l'indienne, music by Fromental Halévy, was created at the Théâtre-Lyrique in 1855.
B-217 (19)

Dances // from *opéras comiques* | [composed by Henri Justamant]
1. *Grand pas* in *La fée aux roses*, to music by Mr. Halévy, stage by Mr. H. Justamant, performed at the Grand Théâtre de Lyon in 1849
2. Divertissement in *Le cheval de bronze*, composed and staged by Mr. H. Justamant, performed at the [Théâtre] Royal[de la Monnaie in Brussels in 1862
3. Dance in *Le médecin malgré lui*, staged by Mr. H. Justamant, performed at the Théâtre Royal de la Monnaie in Brussels in 1863
B-217 (20)

Divertissements | from *opéras comiques* | with *sujets secondaires* | [composed by Henri Justamant]

1. *Ballet de Martha*, composed by Mr. H. Justamant, performed for the first time, in revival, in Paris at the Théâtre National Lyrique, the old [Théâtre de la] Gaité, on 16 January 1877, music by Mr. Flotow, placed in *Stradella*, opera, Mr. Halanzier, theater director

2. *Danse* in *Si j'étais roi*, staged by Mr. H. Justamant, performed at the Grand Théâtre de Lyon in 1853

3. Divertissement from *[Les a]mours du Diable*, staged by Mr. H. Justamant, performed for the first time at the [Grand] Théâtre de Lyon, November 1857, Mr. Delestang, theater director

4. Divertissement in *Lalla-Roukh*, staged by Mr. H. Justamant, performed for the first time at the Théâtre [Royal] de la Monnaie in Bruxelles in 1862; Mr. Letellier, theater director

B-217 (22)

La fiancée du magot | *ballet chinoiserie* in two scenes | by Mr. H. Justamant | performed for the first time in Bordeaux at the Grand Théâtre in September 1847 | performed in Lyon at the Grand Théâtre in 1850 | performed in Brussels at the Théâtre [Royal] de la Monnaie in 1861.
Includes a manuscript synopsis and a gravure: "Pagode à neuf étages."
B-217 (23)

Grand pas | composed by Mr. H. Justamant | performed in Marseille and Brussels | 1. La cypriote, [in] *La reine de Chypre* [music by Fromental Halévy] | 2. *Satyres et bacchantes*, [in] *Herculanum* [music by Félicien David] | 3. *Pas de Diane*

1. *Cypriote*, M. Bertoto and Mlle. Navare and the corps de ballet

2. *Pas des satyres et des bacchantes*, danced in *Herculanum*

3. *Pas de Diane*, music by Mr. Calandini, staged by Justamant, danced by Mlles. Delechaux, Girod, Wesmael, four coryphées and eight women of the corps de ballet in Brussels, 1862

First presentation of *Herculanum* at [the Théàtre Royal de l]a Monnaie, 29 November 1860
B-217 (24)

Les meuniers | *ballet comique bouffe* | [libretto] by Mr. Blache père [Jean-Baptiste Blache] | performed for the first time at | the Grand Théâtre in Bordeaux | *mise en scène* according to the | old traditions | exact score of the music of the time | of the creation of the ballet | score of the *valse comique* | *répétiteur* of the ballet
Includes two musical scores: a ballet *répétiteur* and a *partition des meuniers*.
Henri Justamant was a ballet master in Bordeaux around 1846, according to *Le Théâtre Illustré*, no. 26bis, March 1869.
B-217 (25)

Le royaume des fleurs, *ballet-féerie* in two acts, by M. Justamant, music by M. Bertou | performed for the first time in Marseille at the Grand Théâtre in 1845 | performed in Lyon at the Grand Théâtre in June 1849 | performed in Brussels at the Théâtre Royal [de la Monnaie] on 19 December 1863.
Includes a printed *livret*, shelf mark B-217 (27).
B-217 (26)

Le fils de l'alcade, ou Les deux chasseresses | ballet comique in one act | by Mr. H. Justamant | performed for the first time at the Grand Théâtre de Marseille in 1843.
Includes manuscript synopsis.
B-217 (28)

1. *Le puits qui chante* | 2. *La reine Carotte* | 3. *Les griffes du Diable*

1. Divertissements in *[Le p]uits qui chante*, staged by Mr. Justamant, performed for the first time in Paris at the Théâtre des Menus-Plaisirs on 23 September 1871, Mr. de Jallais, theater director (First divertissement, *Pas des almées*, music by Luigini and

Bertou; second divertissement, *Les deux salamandres*, music by Fossey, et *Les fulgurins*, music by Massip)

2. Divertissement in *La reine Carotte*, stage by Mr. Justamant, specially for Mlle. Thérésa, performed for the first time in Paris at the Théâtre des Menus-Plaisirs on 13 January 1872, Mr. de Jallais, theater dirextor; la pièce est de MMrs. Clairville, Bernard, et Koning

(Spanish music, the *Jaléo de Jérez ou Jaléo de Geres*, the *Gadagala* or *Gala gada*, the *Séguedille*)

3. Divertissements in *[Les g]riffes du diable*, staged by Mr. Justamant, performed for the first time in Paris at the Théâtre des Menus-Plaisirs on 18 April 1872, pièce de MMrs. Clairville et Gabet, Mr. de Jallais, theater director

B-217 (29)

Ballet des Amours | divertissement from *Boudoir de Vénus* | composed and staged by Mr. Justamant | music by Mr. Diaz | performed for the first time at the Théâtre du Château-d'eau in Paris on 8 September 1872 | Mr. Hypolite Cognard, theater director
Includes cast list, accessories list and sketches of the set and scenery.
B-217 (30)

Divertissement of *Qui veut voir la Lune* | staged by Mr. Justamant | music by Mr. Diaz | performed for the first time at the | Théâtre du Château d'Eau, 24 December 1871 in Paris | Mr. Hypolite Cognard, theater director
Includes cast list and a printed *livret*, shelf mark B-217 (32).
B-217 (32–33)

La Fille du Feu. Ballet in four scenes by Mr. H. Justamant. Music by Mr. [. . .] Costumes by Mr. [. . .] Scenery by Mr. Grixves, performed for the first time at the Theater Alhambra Royal [sic] in London, 28 December 1869: ballet in four scenes | by Henri Justamant
B-217 (34)

Fairys-home | *ballet-féerie* in four scenes | and apotheosis | by Mr. H. Justamant | music by Mr. G. Jacobi | scenery by Mr. Cal. Cott | costumes by Mlle. Fisher | machines by MM. Stoman *frères* | accessories by Mr. Buckley | performed for the first time in London at the Théâtre Royal Alhambra, 26 December | 1876 | Mr. Leader, theater director, and company
B-217 (35)

Divertissements, ballets of *Sept corbeaux* | composed and staged by Mr. Justamant | performed for the first time at the Théâtre Victoria | in Berlin, 3 October 1874 | *féerie* in four acts | by Mr. Emile Pohl | scenery by Mrs. [Brückner] *frères* | machines by Mr. Brandt | costumes by Mr. Happel | Mr. Hahn, theater director
Includes cast list and accessories list with drawings.
B-217 (36)

Ballet of *La belle au bois dormant* | composed and staged | by Mr. H. Justamant | performed for the first time in Paris | at the Théâtre National du Châtelet | 4 April 1876 | music by Mr. H. Litolff | Mr. Hostein, theater director | duration of the ballet 19 minutes | note, the ballet was performed in Berlin | at the Théâtre Victoria, 3 October 1874 | in the *féerie Les sept corbeaux*
Includes accessories list and a colored drawing of the stage plan: "Groupe général des suspensions."
B-217 (37)

Ballets Pantomime by Mr. H. Justamant
Includes:
    1. *Le Fils de L'alcade* in 1843 ballet in 1 act, Marseille.
    2. *La Fiancée du Magot*, 1849, *ballet choreographique* in 2 scenes, Lyon.

    3. *Le Guerz enchanté*, 1850, ballet in 1 act, Lyon.

    4. *Les Conscrits Espagnols*, 1850, ballet in 1 act, Lyon.

    5. *Les Contrebandiers Bohêmiens*, 1852, ballet in 2 acts, Lyon.

    6. *La permission de dix heures*, 1852, *ballet comique* in 2 acts, Lyon.

    7. *Quasimodo*, 1859, Lyon.

    8. *Les tribulations d'une Balerine*, 1859, *ballet-féerie* in 2 acts, Lyon.

    9. *Le Magicien*, 1860, ballet in 2 scenes, Lyon.

Collection of 9 ballets, including 7 manuscript autographs.

All indications regarding the dates of the ballets have been added, in pencil, by the author.

C-891 (1-9)

(iii) Bibliothèque Nationale de France, Département des Arts du Spectacle, Paris

Collection Georges Douay

Bequest of Georges Douay, 1919

Finding aid available online at https://archivesetmanuscrits.bnf.fr/ark:/12148/cc1116632.

In addition to manuscripts in the hand of Henri Justamant (listed below), the collection includes numerous printed programs of ballets choreographed and staged by Justamant.

La Sylphide: ballet in 2 acts. *Mise en scène* and dances staged by M. Justamant

MS-DOUAY-180

Ballet militaire: in 1 scene

MS-DOUAY-181

Dans le soleil: ballet in 2 acts and 4 scenes

Includes manuscript synopsis.

MS-DOUAY-182 and 183

Dans le soleil: ballet in 2 acts and 4 tableaux

Proposed replacement titles: *Une Fille du soleil*; *Un Rayon de soleil*.

Includes manuscript synopsis with the proposed replacement title: *Un Rayon d'or*.

MS-DOUAY-184 and 185

France et Russie ou Deux grands peuples amis: *divertissement* [*choréographique*]

Includes a summary of the synopsis.

MS-DOUAY-186

Noël: *divertissement* in 1 scene

[ca 1886?]

Single page includes:

Front: list of characters and beginning of the synopsis.

Back: draft of a letter addressed to the administration of the Théâtre des Folies-Bergère, dated 14 December1886.

MS-DOUAY-187

Les Filles d'azur: ballet

Third act only, subtitled: "Défilé des muses et des grosses têtes."

MS-DOUAY-188

La Esmeralda: ballet in 3 scenes, taken from the novel [*Notre-Dame de Paris*] by Victor Hugo

Includes manuscript synopsis.

MS-DOUAY-189 and 190

Ballets de la statue
MS-DOUAY-191

La Bouquetière du Roi: *ballet-divertissement*
MS-DOUAY-192 and 193

Les Filles [sic] du ciel: *ballet-fantaisie* in 1 scene
La Fille du ciel, ballet in 3 acts by Henri Justamant, music by Luigini
Includes manuscript synopsis.
MS-DOUAY-198

L'Amour d'une fée ou La Reine des sept planètes: *féerie* in 22 scenes, based on the tale *La Fée aux crumbs* by Charles Nodier
MS-DOUAY-202

Les Nations à Paris: *ballet d'actualité* in 3 scenes. Music: Louis Desormes. Costumes: Landolf
Item 213 is a copy intended for Landolf, comprising the synopsis, list of characters, and list of accessories.
MS-DOUAY-211, 212, and 213

Dans l'inconnu: ballet in 1 act. Music: [Louis] Desorme[s]. Costumes: Landolf. Performance: Paris, Folies-Bergère, September 1888
[ca. 1888?]
MS-DOUAY-214

Les Pieuvres: *ballet-fantaisie* in 1 scene
MS-DOUAY-216

Les Deux bossus: *ballet-féerie-fantaisie*, in 5 tableaux
[ca. 1876?]
Title page cites Paris, 10 August 1876.
MS-DOUAY-217 and 218

Une Fête villageoise (en Espagne ou autre village): ballet in 1 scene. [Music: Bartolotti].
Performance: Brussels, Théâtre Royal de la Monnaie, 1861
[ca 1861?]
Manuscript scenario only.
MS-DOUAY-232

Introduction à la Fête villageoise: divertissement staged in Brussels for the Théâtre Royal de la Monnaie, 1861. Music by Bartoloti
MS-DOUAY-233

Les Circassiennes: equestrian ballet-pantomime with divertissement, for racetrack and circus
Includes manuscript synopsis.
MS-DOUAY-234 and 235

Le Diamant, l'or et l'argent: ballet in 2 scenes
Includes manuscript synopsis.
MS-DOUAY-236 and 237

Les Souris blanches: ballet in 2 scenes
Includes manuscript synopsis.
MS-DOUAY-238 and 239

Tableaux vivant[s]: *Les Saisons: l'Yvert, le Printemps, l'Eté [et] l'Automne*: in 4 scenes and 10 groups
MS-DOUAY-240

Joujou: ballet in 2 scenes
Manuscript scenario only.
MS-DOUAY-241

Alpha, la fée mendiante: féerie in 21 scenes
Includes author's note regarding the persons to whom the manuscript was entrusted in 1880.
MS-DOUAY-242

Les Automates: *ballet-folie* in 2 scenes
Includes manuscript synopsis.
MS-DOUAY-243 and 244

Le Duel du vin et de la bière: ballet in 1 tableau. Music: Hervé
Includes manuscript synopsis.
MS-DOUAY-245 and 246

(iv) The New York Public Library for the Performing Arts, Jerome Robbins Dance Division

Lincoln Kirstein Collection
Scenarios, *mise-en-scènes*, choreographic notes and drawings for 16 ballet divertissements [by Henri Justamant]
*MGRN-Res. 73-259

Vol. 1

Ballets in *Les parisiens à Londres*. 1866.

Choreography by Henri Justamant, play by Louis François Nicolaïe Clairville. First French performance in Paris at the Théâtre de la Porte Saint-Martin, 29 September 1866.

Vol. 2

Divertissements of *La tour de Nesles*, and of *Bossu*, drames. 1867.

La tour de Nesle, with choreography for the incidental dances by Henri Justamant and music by A. Artus and Mons. Bessac, was first performed in March 1867 at the Théâtre de la Porte Saint-Martin, Paris. *Le bossu*, with choreography for the incidental dances by Henri Justamant and music by A. Artus and Calendini. was first performed circa 1867 at the Théâtre de la Porte Saint-Martin, Paris.

Vol. 3

Ballets de *La revue 1867*. 1867.

Play with music by Albert Vizentini, Bessac, Jozet, and others, and choreography by Henri Justamant, first performed on 28 December 1867 at the Théâtre de la Porte Saint-Martin, Paris.

Vol. 4

Ballets in *Salvator Rosa*, drame. 1868.

Drame with libretto by Eugène Grangé and Henri Trianon, music by Jules Duprato, and choreography for the incidental dances by Henri Justamant (music by Jozet), first performed in 1868 at the Théâtre de la Porte Saint-Martin, Paris.

Vol. 5

Divertissements of *Gilbert Danglars*. 1870.

Drame in five acts and ten scenes with choreography for the incidental dances by Henri Justamant (music by Jonas), first performed on 12 March 1870 at the Théâtre de la Gaîté, Paris.

Vol. 6

Divertissements of *La chatte blanche*. 1870.

Play with choreography for the incidental dances by Henri Justamant (music by Jonas), first performed on 16 April 1870 at the Théâtre de la Gaîté, Paris.

Vol. 7

Le bourgeois gentilhomme, intermedès de danses. 1876.

Play by Molière with with choreography for the incidental dances by Henri Justamant (music by J.-B. Lully), performed on 23 January 1876 at the Théâtre de la Gaîté, Paris.

Vol. 8

Monsieur de Pourceaugnac, intermedès de danses. 1876.

Play. First performed in Paris, Théâtre de la Gaîté, April 2, 1876, with choreography for the incidental dances by Henri Justamant; music by Lully.

Vols. 9–10

Ballet in *Cendrillon*. 1879. *Mise-en-scène* of *Cendrillon, feërie*. 1879.

Play by Henri Monnier, Louis Clairville and Ernest Blum, music by Victor Chéri, and choreography for the incidental dances by Henri Justamant, first performed on 20 September 1879 at the Théâtre de la Porte Saint-Martin, Paris.

Vol. 11

Ballets in *Le voyage de la lune*. 1879.

Opéra-féerie in four acts and twenty-three scenes with libretto by Eugène Leterrier, Albert Vanloo, and Arnold Mortier, music by Jacques Offenbach, and choreography for the incidental dances by Henri Justamant, first performed on 26 October 1879 at the Théâtre de la Gaîté, Paris.

Vol. 12

Grand ballet du Royaume de Noël. 1880.

Play by Eugène Leterrier, Albert Vanloo, and Arnold Mortier, first performed in Paris, Théâtre de la Porte Saint-Martin, 6 October 1880, with choreography for the incidental dances by Henri Justamant. Music for the play by Alexandre Lecocq and Lonati, for the ballet, Georges Jacobi; scenery by Jules Chéret and Robecchi; costumes by Mare, Grévin, and Jules Draner.

Vol. 13

Scenes 1–14, *mise en scène* of *L'arbre de Noël, feërie.* 1880?

Féerie in three acts and thirty scenes with libretto by Eugène Leterrier, Albert Vanloo, and Arnold Mortier, music by Alexandre Lecocq and Georges Jacobi, and choreography for the incidental dances by Henri Justamant, performed on 4 October 1880 at the Théâtre de la Porte Saint-Martin, Paris. [The Bibliothèque Nationale de France gives the premiere date as 5 October 1880.]

Vol. 14

Ballet . . . in . . . *Les chevaliers du Brouillard.* 1881.

Play with music by Lonati and Massif and choreography for the incidental dances by Henri Justamant, first performed in February 1881 at the Théâtre de la Porte Saint-Martin, Paris.

Vols. 15–16

Ballets of *La biche au bois.* 1881. *Mise en scène* of *La biche au bois.* 1881.

Play by Ernest Blum and Raoul Toché [Frimousse] after Hippolyte and Théodore Cogniard, with music by A. Artus, Jozet and others, performed on 10 September 1881 at the Théâtre de la Porte Saint-Martin, Paris.

Vols. 17–18

Ballets of *Petit Faust.* 1882. *Mise en scène* of *Petit Faust.* 1882.

Opera with libretto by Hector Crémieux and Adolphe Jaime, music by Hervé, and choreography for the incidental dances by Henri Justamant was performed on 15 February 1882 at the Théâtre de la Porte Saint-Martin, Paris.

Vol. 19

Les folies espagnoles, ballet. 1885.

Ballet with music by Gerard von Brucken Fock and choreography by Henri Justamant, first performed on 30 April 1885 at the Théâtre de la Gaîté, Paris.

Ballet des Erynnies | staged by Mr. Justamant; music by Mr. Massenet, performed for the first time in Paris at the Théâtre de la Gaité (the new [Gaité-]Lyrique) on 19 May 1876; Mr. Albert Vizentini, theater director.
*MGRN-Res.+ 94-2734

Les fugitifs: drame
Divertissements des *[Les f]ugitifs* by H. Justamant. Performed for the first time at the Théâtre de la Gaité in Paris, 17 July 1868. Mr. Victor Honning, theater director. Music by Léon Fossey.
*MGRN-Res.+ 94-2733

(v) Deutsches Tanzarchiv Köln

Giselle

Mise en scène of Giselle | by Mr. Justamant
Giselle | *Ballet Fantastique* in two acts | by MM de St [G]eorge, [T]héophile [G]autier, and
[C]orally | Music by Mr. A. [A]dam | performed for the first time in Paris at the Théatre de
l'Académie Royal de Musique | 28 June 1841
Item Number 52915

Published in facsimile as:

Giselle ou Les Wilis: Ballet Fantastique en deux actes. Faksimile der Notation von Henri Justamant
aus den 1860er Jahren. Edited with an introduction by Frank-Manuel Peter. Hildesheim: Georg
Olms Verlag, 2008.

Includes drawings of the stage plan for both acts and additional choreography at the back of the
volume: "*Giselle* | *Groupes* of the pas de deux of the second act | staged by Justamant | for Mme
[Amalia] Ferraris | Brussels 1864"—the adagio and coda.

APPENDIX C

Giselle

(i) *Giselle* libretto, Paris, 1841

GISELLE

OU

LES WILIS,

Ballet fantastique in two Acts,

by

MM. DE SAINT-GEORGES, THÉOPHILE GAUTIER AND CORALY;

MUSIC BY M. ADOLPHE ADAM,

Scenery by Mr Cicéri.

PERFORMED FOR THE FIRST TIME ON THE STAGE OF THE THÉATRE DE L'ACADÉMIE
ROYALE DE MUSIQUE, MONDAY 28 JUNE 1841.

Paris.
Mme Widow Jonas, Publisher, Opéra Bookstore.
1841.

FIRST ACT.

CHARACTERS	ACTORS	
DUKE ALBERT OF SILESIA, in the attire of a villager	MM.	PETIPA.
THE PRINCE OF COURLANDE		QUÉRIAU.
WILFRIDE, the Duke's Squire		CORALLI.
HILARION, the Game-keeper		SIMON.
AN OLD PEASANT MAN		L. PETIT.
BATHILDE, the Duke's Fiancée	Mlles	FORSTER.
GISELLE, a Peasant Girl		CARLOTTA GRISI.
BERTHE, Giselle's Mother		ROLAND.
MYRTHA, Queen of the Wilis		ADÈLE DUMILATRE.
ZULMÉ, ⎫ Wilis		SOPHIE DUMILATRE.
MOYNA, ⎭		CARRÉ.

DANCE NUMBERS.

PAS DE DEUX. M. Mabille; Mlle Nathalie Fitzjames.
PAS DE DEUX. M. Petipa; Mlle Grisi.

CORYPHÉES.
M. Desplaces 2me.

Mmes	Dimier.	Mmes	Marquet 1re.
	Breistroff.		Laurent 1re.
	Wiéthof.		Fleury.
	Caroline.		Robert.

VINEGATHERER WOMEN.

MM.	Isambert.	MM.	Renauzy.
	Millot.		Chatillon.
	Lefevre.		Constant.
	Célarius.		Gourdoux.
	Duhan.		Cornet 2me.
	Dugit.		Rouyet.
	Fromage.		Souton.
	Dimier.		Scio.

VINEGATHERER MEN.

Mmes	Saulnier 1re.	Mmes	Dubignon.
	Leclercq.		Galby.
	Lacroix.		Bénard 1re.
	Marivin.		Athalie.
	Colson.		Dabas 1re.
	Gougibus.		Josset.
	Robin.		Courtois.
	Bouvier.		Marquet 2me.

MUSICIANS.

MM.	Ernest.	MM.	Maujin.
	Petit-Alix.		Wiéthof 1re.

VILLAGER CHILDREN.

MM.	Hardy.	MM.	Peaufert.
	Liger.		Albrié.
	Minart.		Wiéthof 2me.

Mlles	Masson.	Mlles	Toulain.
	Cassan.		Vioron.
	Devion.		Hunter.
	Debas 2me.		Favre.
	Franck.		Passerieux.
	Jeunot.		Jeandron 2me.
	Laurent 2me.		Vaudras.
	Chambret.		Voisin.
	Cluchar.		Feugère.

LORDS.

MM.	Lenfant.	MM.	Darcour.
	Cornet 1re.		Feltis.
	Grénier.		Jesset.
	Martin.		Lénoir.

LADIES.

Mmes	Rodriguez.	Mmes	Léoni.
	Cartembert.		Petit.
	Clément.		Deuénil.
	Richard.		Coupotte.

PAGES.

Mmes	Pèche.	Mmes	Bourdon.
	Julien.		Pézée.

HUNTERS, WHIPPERS-IN, VALETS.

ACT TWO.

WILIS.

Mmes	Carré.	Sophie Dumilatre.	Adèle Dumilatre.

CORYPHÉES.

Mmes	Dimier.	Mmes	Marquet 1re.
	Breistroff.		Laurent 1re.
	Wiéthof.		Fléury.
	Caroline.		Robert.

Mmes	Robin.	Mmes	Saulnier 1re.
	Athalie.		Gougibos.
	Galby.		Bouvier.
	Dubignon.		Colson.
	Marivin.		Leclercq.
	Bénard 1re.		Toussaint.
	Courtois.		Danse.
	Josset.		Lacoste.
	Dabas 1re.		Jeandron 1re.
	Chévalier.		Drouet.
	Perés.		Potier.

The Actors of the first act. — THE VINEGATHERER MEN, THE NOBLEMEN.

GERMAN TRADITION

FROM WHICH THE PLOT OF THE BALLET GISELLE OR THE WILIS IS TAKEN.

There exists a tradition of the night-dancer, who is known in Slavic countries under the name Wili. — Wilis are young brides-to-be who die before their wedding day. The poor young creatures cannot rest peacefully in their graves. In their stilled hearts and lifeless feet, there remains a love for dancing which they were unable to satisfy during their lifetimes. At midnight they rise out of their graves, gather together in troupes on the roadside, and woe be unto the young man who comes across them! He is forced to dance with them until he dies.

Dressed in their wedding gowns, with wreathes of flowers on their heads and glittering rings on their fingers, the *Wilis* dance in the moonlight like *Elves*. Their faces, though white as snow, have the beauty of youth. They laugh with a joy so hideous, they call you so seductively, they have an air of such sweet promise, that these dead *bacchantes* are irresistible.

HEINRICH HEINE (de l'Allemagne).

THE WILIS.

ACT ONE.

The setting represents a pleasant Valley in Germany. In the distance, vine-covered hills, across which runs a road leading into the Valley.

SCENE I.

A tableau of grape-harvesting on the Thuringian slopes in the early morning. The vinegatherers depart to continue the harvest.

SCENE II.

Hilarion appears, and glances around, as though looking for someone: then, he points lovingly at Giselle's cottage, and angrily at Loys's cottage. *It's there that his rival lives. If he can ever avenge himself, he will do so gladly.* The door to Loys's cottage opens mysteriously; Hilarion hides himself so he can see what will happen next.

SCENE III.

The young Duke Albert of Silesia, under the name Loys and wearing humble attire, emerges from his cottage, accompanied by his squire Wilfride. Wilfride appears to be imploring the Duke to renounce some secret project, but Loys persists, pointing to Giselle's dwelling place. This simple roof shelters the one he loves, the object of his unique affection... He orders Wilfride to leave him alone. Wilfride is still hesitant, but at a gesture from his master, Wilfride salutes him respectfully and then departs.

Hilarion is left stupefied by seeing a fine lord like Wilfride evince such high regard for his rival, a simple peasant. He appears to conceive suspicions that he will clear up later.

SCENE IV.

Loys, or rather the duke Albert, approaches Giselle's cottage and knocks lightly on the door. Hilarion remains hidden. Giselle immediately emerges and runs into the arms of her beloved. Transports of delight and happiness of the two young people. Giselle recounts her dream to Loys: She was jealous of a beautiful lady whom Loys loved, whom he preferred to Giselle.

Loys, troubled, reassures her: he doesn't—he will never—love anyone but her. *If you ever betrayed me,* the young girl says to him, *I can feel it, I would die.* She places his hand over her heart as though to tell him that she often suffers from this. Loys reassures her with spirited caresses.

She picks some daisies, and strips away the petals, to assure herself of Loys's love. — The test succeeds, and she falls into her beloved's arms.

Hilarion, no longer able to restrain himself, runs up to Giselle and reproaches her for her conduct. He was there; he saw everything! *Ah! what does it matter to me?* Giselle airily responds. *I am not ashamed, and I will never love anyone but him....* then she brusquely turns her back to Hilarion, laughing in his face, while Loys pushes him, threatening him with his wrath if he doesn't cease his amorous pursuit of Giselle. *Fine,* says Hilarion with a menacing gesture. *Later, we'll see.*

SCENE V.

A troupe of young vinegatherer girls comes to fetch Giselle for the vintage. Day has broken and duty calls; but Giselle, passionately fond of dancing and diversion, forestalls her companions. Dancing is, after Loys, the thing she loves most in the world. She proposes to the young girls that they indulge in pastimes instead of going to work. She dances alone at first, in order to persuade them. Her gaiety, her joyous ardor—her steps, so full of joy and enthusiasm, and infused with her love for Loys, are soon imitated by the vinegatherers. They throw down the baskets, the staffs, the instruments of their labor, and thanks to Giselle, everyone joins in boisterously. Berthe, Giselle's mother, then emerges from her cottage.

SCENE VI.

— *You will always dance*, she says to Giselle... *Evening..... morning..... it's truly a passion... and all that, instead of working, instead of doing household chores.*

— *She dances so well!* says Loys to Berthe.

— *It's my only pleasure*, Giselle responds, *just as he*, she adds, pointing out Loys, *he is my sole happiness!!!*

— *Bah!* says Berthe. *I am sure that if this foolish little thing died, she would become a Wili, and dance even after her death, like all the girls who love dancing too much!*

— *What do you mean?...* the young village girls cry out with fright, pressing closely to one another.

Berthe then, to a lugubrious music, appears to depict an apparition of dead people returning to the world and dancing together. The terror of the village girls is at its height. Giselle alone laughs, and responds gaily to her mother that she is incorrigible and that, dead or alive, she will always dance.

— *Nevertheless*, Berthe adds, *it's not good for you... It concerns your health, and your life, perhaps!!!*

She is very fragile, she says to Loys, *fatigue and excitement could be fatal to her, the doctor has told her; it could do her harm.*

Loys, troubled by this disclosure, reassures her good mother, and Giselle, taking Loys's hand, presses it to her heart, and appears to say that as long as she is with him, *she is never in fear of danger*.

The fanfares of the hunt are heard in the distance. Loys, worried by this sound, quickly gives the signal to depart for the harvest and hurries the peasant girls away. Meanwhile Giselle, forced to return to her cottage with her mother, blows a farewell kiss to Loys, who departs, following everyone else.

SCENE VII.

As soon as Hilarion finds himself alone, he explains his project. He wishes, at any price, *to discover the secret of his rival; to find out who he is...* Assuring himself that no one can discover him, he furtively gains entry to Loys's cottage... At this moment, the fanfares come near again, and the whippers-in and valets of the hunt appear on the hillside.

SCENE VIII.

The Prince and Bathilde, his daughter, soon appear on horseback, accompanied by a numerous suite of lords, ladies, and falconers with falcons on their fists. The heat of the day is overpowering them; they have come to find a favorable spot for repose. A huntsman points out Berthe's cottage to the Prince; he knocks on the door, and Giselle appears at the threshold, followed by her mother. The Prince gaily calls for hospitality from the young vinegatherer; she invites him into the cottage, though it is a poor place in which to receive so fine a lord!

During this time, Bathilde approaches Giselle; she observes her and finds her charming. Giselle exerts herself to the utmost to do the honors of her modest dwelling, she bids Bathilde be seated, and offers her fruit and milk. Bathilde, charmed by Giselle's graces, removes a gold chain from her own neck and clasps it around that of the young girl, who is both proud and shy at this gift.

Bathilde asks Giselle about her work and her pleasures.

— *She is happy! She has neither sorrows or cares; in the morning, work; in the evening, dancing!...* — *Yes!* says Berthe to Bathilde, *especially dancing... It is her obsession.*

Bathilde smiles and asks Giselle if her heart has spoken; if she loves someone? ... — *Oh! yes!* cries the young girl while pointing out Loys's cottage: *the one who lives there! My beloved, my fiancé...! I would die if he loved me no more!* Bathilde seems to take a lively interest in the young girl... They are in the same situation, because she too will soon be married, to a young and handsome lord!... She will give a dowry to Giselle, who seems to please her more and more..... Bathilde wants to see Giselle's fiancé, and she goes back into the cottage, followed by her father and Berthe, while Giselle goes to find Loys.

The Prince makes the sign for his retinue to continue the hunt; he is tired and desires to rest for awhile. He will sound the horn when he wishes them to return.

Hilarion, who appears at the door of Loys's cottage, sees the Prince and hears the orders he gives. The Prince goes with his daughter into Berthe's cottage.

SCENE IX.

While Giselle goes to look down the road to see if she can find her beloved, Hilarion re-emerges from Loys's cottage, holding a nobleman's sword and mantle; he finally knows who his rival is! He is a great lord! Now he is sure of it... he is a seducer in disguise! He can now take revenge and wants to destroy his rival in the presence of Giselle and the entire village. He hides Loys's sword in a bush, waiting until all of the vinegatherers are assembled for the festival.

SCENE X.

Loys appears in the distance... he looks worriedly about, and assures himself that the hunt is far away.

Giselle sees him and flies into his arms! At this moment joyous music is heard.

SCENE XI.

A march commences. The harvest is over. A wagon, decorated with grape leaves and flowers, slowly comes into view, followed by all the peasants of the valley, their baskets full of grapes. A little Bacchus is carried triumphally astride a cask, in keeping with an old country tradition.

Everyone gathers around Giselle. She is named Queen of the vintage... They crown her with flowers and vine leaves. Loys is more in love than ever with his pretty vinegatherer. All the peasants are soon possessed with a most joyous abandon.

It is the festival of the vintage!... Giselle can now abandon herself to her favorite pastime; she leads Loys to the middle of the troupe of vinegatherers and dances with him, surrounded by the entire village, who soon join in with the young lovers, whose dance ends with a kiss that Loys bestows on Giselle... At this sight, the fury, the jealousy of the envious Hilarion knows no bounds... he throws himself into the middle of the crowd and declares that Loys *is a deceiver, a seducer,* A NOBLEMAN IN DISGUISE!... Giselle, at first taken aback, responds to Hilarion that he knows not what he is saying; that he has dreamed it all up... Ah! I dreamed it up, continues the gamekeeper... Well! See for yourself, he cries while revealing Loys's sword and mantle for the villagers to see. Here is what I found in his cottage... this is sufficient proof, I trust.

Albert, furious, lunges toward Hilarion, who hides behind some villagers.

Giselle, struck with surprise and sadness at this revelation, appears to have sustained a terrible blow, and leans against a tree, unsteady and on the verge of collapse.

All the peasants pause, in a state of consternation! Loys, or rather Albert, rushes up to Giselle, and still believing he can deny his rank, tries to reassure her, to calm her with protestations of tenderness. *This is a mistake,* he says to her, *he is just her Loys, a simple peasant, her sweetheart, her fiancé!!!*

The poor girl asks nothing more than to believe him. Already hope seems to return to her heart; happy and confident, she accepts the embrace of the perfidious Albert, when Hilarion, seeking his vengeance, and recalling the Prince's order to his suite to return at the sound of the horn, seizes one of the noblemen's horns, which is attached to a tree, and blows it forcefully... At this signal the entire hunting party is seen rushing in, and the Prince exits Berthe's cottage. Hilarion points out to the Prince's suite the sight of Albert on his knees before Giselle. Everyone, upon recognizing the young duke, overwhelms him with salutations and deference. Giselle, on seeing this, can no longer doubt her misfortune nor Albert's high station.

SCENE XII.

The Prince steps forward in his turn, recognizes Albert, doffs his hat in salutation, and immediately asks him for an explanation of his strange conduct and the costume he is wearing.

Albert rises, stupefied and confounded by this encounter.

Giselle has seen everything! She is sure then of fresh betrayal by the one she loves; her sorrow is boundless; she appears to make an effort to control herself, and withdraws from Albert with feelings of fear and terror. Then, as though horror-stricken by this new blow, she runs toward the cottage and falls into the arms of her mother, who emerges therefrom at this moment, accompanied by the young Bathilde.

SCENE XIII.

Bathilde advances briskly toward Giselle and questions her with a touching interest about the agitation she feels. Giselle's sole response is to point out Albert, distressed and confounded.

What do I see?... says Bathilde.... The Duke in this costume!... But he is the one I am going to marry... He's my fiancé!... she adds, pointing out the engagement ring she wears on her finger.

Albert approaches Bathilde and tries in vain to prevent her from finishing this terrible avowal; but Giselle has heard everything and understood all! The deepest horror is now manifested on the features of the poor child; her mind becomes confused, a horrible and dark delirium consumes her, as she sees herself betrayed, lost, dishonored!... Her reason is lost, tears begin to fall... then she laughs a nervous laugh. She takes Albert's hand, places it on her heart, and then quickly pushes it away with fear. She seizes Loys's sword, resting on the ground, first of all playing mechanically with this weapon, and is about to let herself fall on its sharp point when her mother hurries toward her and grabs it away. The love of dance returns to the poor girl's memory: she believes she hears the music of her dance with Albert... She lunges forward and begins to dance with ardor, with passion. So many sudden sorrows, so many cruel blows, together with this latest effort, have finally exhausted her dwindling resources... Life seems to abandon her... Her mother takes her in her arms... A last sigh escapes from the heart of poor Giselle... She glances sadly at Albert in despair, *and her eyes close forever!*

Bathilde, kind and generous, melts in tears. Albert, forgetting everything, tries to revive Giselle with burning caresses. He puts his hand on the young girl's heart and with horror assures himself that it has ceased to beat.

He seizes his sword to kill himself; the Prince stops him and takes his weapon. Berthe embraces the body of her ill-starred daughter. Albert is led away, crazed with love and despair.

The peasants, the noblemen, the entire hunting party, gather round and complete this sad picture.

END OF ACT ONE.

ACT TWO.

The setting represents a forest on the banks of a small lake. A damp and chilly spot where rushes, reeds, clumps of wildflowers, and aquatic plants grow. Birch trees, aspens, and weeping willows droop their pale foliage to the ground. To the left, beneath a cypress, stands a white marble cross on which Giselle's name is engraved. The tomb is overgrown with the thick vegetation of grasses and wildflowers. The bluish gleam of a very bright moon gives a cold and misty appearance to the scene.

SCENE I.

Several gamekeepers arrive by different paths in the forest; they seem to be seeking a favorable spot for setting up an observation post and are about to do so by the bank of the pool when Hilarion comes rushing in.

SCENE II.

Hilarion evinces the liveliest fear upon divining the plans of his comrades. *It's a cursed spot,* he tells them, *it's the circle where the Wilis dance!* He shows them the tomb of Giselle ... of Giselle who was always dancing. He points it out by the crown of vine-leaves Giselle wore on her brow during the festival, and which is attached to the marble cross.

At this moment, midnight is heard striking in the distance: it is the gloomy hour when, according to local tradition, the Wilis gather in their ballroom.

Hilarion and his companions listen to the chimes with terror, trembling; they look about, expecting to see the apparition of the airy phantoms. *Let us flee,* says Hilarion, *the Wilis are pitiless; they surround travelers and force them to dance with them until they die of exhaustion or are engulfed in the lake that you see here.*

A fantastic music then commences; the gamekeepers grow pale, staggering and fleeing on all sides, showing the greatest fright, pursued by will-o'-the-wisps that appear all around them.

SCENE III.

A sheaf of bullrushes slowly opens, and from the depths of the humid foliage the airy Myrtha, *the Queen of the Wilis,* a pale and transparent shade, is seen darting forth. She carries with her a mysterious radiance that suddenly illuminates the forest, piercing the shadows of the night. It is thus every time the Wilis appear; on the white shoulders of Myrtha, trembling and fluttering, are the diaphanous wings in which the Wili can envelop herself as though in a gauzy veil.

This tangible apparition cannot stay in place and leaps now to this tuft of flowers, now to a willow branch, flying here and there, traversing and appearing to explore her tiny empire whither she comes each night to reclaim possession. She bathes herself in the water of the lake, then suspends herself from the willow branches and swings to and fro.

After a solo dance, she plucks a branch of rosemary and in turn touches it to each plant, each bush, each tuft of foliage.

SCENE IV.

Scarcely has the Wili queen's flowery scepter rested on an object, a plant, a flower, a bush than it opens up, letting escape a new Wili who joins, in her turn, the graceful group that surrounds Myrtha, like bees around their queen. This last named, hearing the azure wings of her subjects, then gives them the signal to dance. Several Wilis present themselves, in turn, before their sovereign.

First Moyna, the Odalisque, executing an oriental step; then Zulmé, the Bayadère, who displays her Indian poses, then two French women, dancing a sort of bizarre minuet; then the German women, waltzing among themselves.... Then, finally, the entire troupe of Wilis, all of whom died for loving dancing too much, or perished too early in life before sufficiently gratifying this foolish passion, to which they appear to surrender themselves furiously in their new graceful metamorphosis.

Before long, at a sign from the queen, the fantastic ball comes to a close.... She announces to her subjects the arrival of a new sister. All arrange themselves around the queen.

SCENE V.

A vivid, bright ray of moonlight shines on Giselle's tomb; the flowers that cover it rise up and straighten themselves on their stems, as if to form a passageway for the pale creature they cover.

Giselle appears, wrapped in her thin shroud. She advances toward Myrtha, who touches her with her rosemary branch; the shroud falls off... Giselle is transformed into a Wili. Her wings grow and unfold... her feet skim the ground. She dances, or rather she flutters in the air, like her graceful sisters, joyfully recalling and showing the steps that she danced in the first act before her death.

A sound is heard in the distance. All the Wilis disperse and hide themselves in the rushes.

SCENE VI.

Young villagers returning from a festival in the neighboring village gaily cross the scene, led by an old man. They are going to depart when a bizarre music, the Wilis' dance music, is heard. The peasants, in spite of themselves, seem to feel a strange desire to dance. The Wilis soon surround them, twine about them, and fascinate them with their voluptuous poses.

Each of the Wilis seeks to detain the men, to please them with the figures of their native dance... The villagers, deeply affected, are about to succumb to this seduction, to dance and die, when the old man throws himself in their midst and tells them with fright of the risk they run and rescues them all, chased by the Wilis, who are furious at seeing their prey escape.

SCENE VII.

Albert appears, followed by Wilfride, his faithful squire. The Duke is sad and pale; his garments are in disorder; his reason is nearly gone, as a result of Giselle's death. He slowly approaches the cross as if seeking a memory, as though he wished to collect his confused thoughts.

Wilfride entreats Albert to accompany him, and not to linger near the fatal tomb, which recalls so many sorrows... Albert bids him depart... Wilfride again insists, but Albert orders him away with such vigor that Wilfride is forced to obey. He departs, promising himself to make one last effort to induce his master to leave this fatal spot.

SCENE VIII.

Scarcely is he left alone than Albert gives vent to his sorrow. His heart is torn to pieces; he melts in tears. All of a sudden, he grows pale; his gaze fixes on a strange object that takes shape before his eyes. He remains stricken with surprise and very nearly with terror, on recognizing Giselle, who looks lovingly at him.

SCENE IX.

A prey to the most violent delirium, the most lively anxiety, he still doubts and dares not believe in what he sees. For it is no longer the pretty Giselle, the one he adored, but Giselle the Wili, in her new and strange metamorphosis, who remains motionless before him. The Wili seems only to invite him with a look. Albert, believing himself in the thrall of a sweet illusion, approaches her with slow steps and cautiously, like a child wishing to capture a butterfly poised on a flower. But at the moment when he extends his hand toward Giselle, quicker than lightning, she darts away from him to take flight and traverse the air like a frightened dove to alight elsewhere, whence she throws him loving glances.

This dance, or rather this flight, is repeated several times, to the great despair of Albert, who vainly attempts to join with the Wili, who flees several times above him like a wisp of mist.

Sometimes, however, she makes him a loving gesture, throws him a flower, which she plucks from its stem, throwing him a kiss; but, as intangible as a cloud, she disappears just as he thinks she is in his grasp.

At last he gives up! He kneels before the cross and joins his hands together before her, in a prayerful attitude. The Wili, as if attracted by this mute sorrow, so full of love, bounds lightly alongside her lover: he touches her; already drunk with love and delight, he goes to embrace her. But when he is gliding gently between her arms, she vanishes among the roses; while Albert clasps his arms together, embracing nothing more than the cross of the tomb.

The deepest despair seizes him; he rises and is about to leave this place of sorrow, when the strangest spectacle appears before his eyes and fascinates him to the point that he is transfixed, frozen, and forced to witness the strange scene that unfolds in front of him.

SCENE X.

Hidden behind a weeping willow, Albert sees the wretched Hilarion, pursued by the entire band of Wilis.

Pale, trembling, frightened nearly to death, the gamekeeper collapses at the foot of a tree, and seems to implore the pity of his demented foes! But the Queen of the Wilis touches him with her scepter and forces him to rise and imitate the dance movement which she herself begins to dance around him... Hilarion, impelled by a magic force, dances despite himself with the beautiful Wili until she gives way to one of her companions, who in turn cedes her place to another, and so on, up to the last of all!

Just when the hapless wretch believes his torment ended with his wearied partner, she is replaced with another, more vigorous one. Exhausted by unimaginable effort, to the rhythms of an ever-quickening tempo, he finishes by staggering and feeling overwhelmed by weariness and woe.

He takes a desperate action, finally, and tries to flee; but the Wilis surround him in a vast circle, which contracts little by little, closing in on him and then changing into a fast waltz movement, in which a supernatural power obliges him to partake. A giddiness seizes the gamekeeper, who leaves the arms of one waltzing Wili only to fall into those of another.

The victim, completely enmeshed in this graceful and deadly web, soon feels his knees giving way beneath him. His eyes close, he can no longer see... and he dances, however, with an ardent frenzy. The queen of the Wilis seizes him and makes him turn and waltz one last time with her, until the poor devil, the last link in the chain of waltzers, arrives at the water's edge, opens his arms, expecting to find the next waltzer, and goes tumbling into the abyss! The Wilis commence a joyous bacchanale, led by their triumphant queen, when one of them comes to discover Albert, still stunned by what he had just seen, and leads him to the center of their magic circle.

SCENE XI.

The Wilis seem to applaud the discovery of another victim; their cruel troupe has already begun to hover around this new prey; but at the moment when Myrtha is about to touch Albert with her magic scepter, Giselle darts forward and restrains the queen's arm, which is raised toward Giselle's lover.

SCENE XII.

Flee, says Giselle to the one she loves, *flee, or you will die, as Hilarion has,* she adds, pointing toward the lake.

Albert is frozen with terror for an instant at the idea of sharing the frightful fate of his gamekeeper. Giselle profits from this moment of indecision to seize Albert's hand; they glide together by the force of a magical power toward the marble cross, and she indicates this sacred symbol as his only salvation!...

The queen and all the Wilis chase him up to the tomb; but Albert, ever protected by Giselle, arrives at the cross, which he embraces; and at the moment when Myrtha is about to touch him with her scepter, the enchanted branch breaks in the hands of the queen, who stops short, as do all the Wilis, struck with surprise and dismay.

Furious at thus having their cruel hopes dashed, the Wilis encircle Albert, and frequently dart toward him, each time repelled by a power greater than their own. The queen, then, wishing to avenge herself on the one who robbed her of her prey, extends her hand toward Giselle, whose wings soon open, and who begins dancing with the strangest, most graceful ardor, as though transported by an involuntary delirium.

Albert, motionless, watches her, overwhelmed and astounded at this bizarre scene!!! But soon the Wili's graces and ravishing poses attract him despite himself; this is what the queen wanted; he leaves the holy cross that protects him from death, and approaches Giselle, who pauses with dismay, and begs him to go back to the sacred talisman. But the Queen touches her anew, forcing her to continue her seductive dance. This scene is replayed several times, until finally, ceding to the passion that consumes him, Albert abandons the cross and rushes toward Giselle... He seizes the enchanted branch and wishes to die, so he can rejoin the Wili and never again be separated from her!!!...

Albert seems to have wings; he skims the ground and hovers around the Wili, who from time to time tries to restrain him.

But soon compelled by her newfound nature, Giselle is forced to join her lover. A rapid, airborne, frenetic dance begins between them. They seem to vie with each other in grace and agility: at times they pause to fall into each other's arms, then the fantastic music lends them new strength and a fresh ardor!!!...

The entire group of Wilis intermingles with the two lovers, framing them in voluptuous poses.

A deadly weariness seizes Albert. It is clear that he still struggles, but his powers are beginning to abandon him. Giselle approaches him, stops for an instant, her eyes full of tears; but a sign from the queen obliges her to take flight anew. After a few seconds, Albert is about to perish from weariness and exhaustion, when dawn begins to break... The first rays of the sun illuminate the silvery ripples of the lake.

The fantastic and tumultuous round of the Wilis slows down as the night fades away.

Giselle seems inspired by a new hope on seeing the disappearance of the terrible enchantment that was leading Albert to his doom.

Little by little, and under the bright rays of the sun, the entire band of Wilis sinks and collapses; one by one they can be seen staggering, expiring, and falling in a tuft of flowers, or on the stem that witnessed their birth, like flowers of the night that die at the approach of dawn.

During this graceful tableau, Giselle, subject like her airy sisters to the influence of daylight, slowly gives herself up to Albert's enfeebled embrace; she goes back to her tomb, as though drawn toward it by fate.

Albert, conscious of the doom that threatens Giselle, carries her in his arms far from her tomb and puts her down on a knoll, amidst a clump of flowers. Albert kneels by her and gives her a kiss, as though to infuse her with his spirit and restore her to life.

But Giselle, pointing to the sun, which is now shining brightly, seems to tell him that she must obey her fate and leave him forever.

At this moment, loud fanfares are heard from the depths of the woods. Albert hears them with fear, and Giselle, with a sweet joy.

SCENE XIII.

Wilfride comes running up. The faithful squire is ahead of the Prince, Bathilde, and a numerous retinue; he leads them to Albert, hoping that their efforts will be more effective than his own in inducing Albert to leave this place of sadness.

Everyone stops on seeing him. Albert leaps toward his squire to hold him back. During this time, the Wili nears her last moments; already the flowers and the grasses that surround her have begun to rise and cover her with their tender stems... already partly concealing the graceful apparition.

Albert comes back, and remains spellbound with surprise and sorrow on seeing Giselle sink slowly, little by little, into this verdant tomb; then, with the arm that she still keeps free, she points Albert toward the trembling Bathilde, on her knees a few steps away and stretching out her hand in a gesture of entreaty.

Giselle appears to tell her lover to give his heart and soul to this sweet young girl... it's her only wish, her last prayer, from *her* who can no longer live in this world, then, wishing him a sad and eternal adieu, she disappears in the midst of the flowery grasses which now completely engulf her.

Albert rises heartbroken; but the Wili's command to him seems sacred... He gathers some of the flowers that cover Giselle, and lovingly presses them to his heart, to his lips. Weak and staggering, he falls into the arms of those who surround him and reaches out his hand to Bathilde!!!

Tableau.

END OF THE BALLET.

Printed by Pollet. rue St-Denis, 380

Translation by Marian Smith.

Authors' note: This translation relies on that of Cyril Beaumont in *The Ballet Called Giselle* (pp. 39–52) and is more faithful to the original libretto in its details but less poetic than Beaumont's.

(ii) *Giselle* libretto, St. Petersburg, 1889 reprint of 1842 libretto

GISELLE
ou
LES WILIS

Fantastic ballet in two acts.

Composed by MM. Coralli and T. Gautier.

Music by M. Adam.

PRESENTED FOR THE FIRST TIME AT THE BOLSHOI THEATER
18 DECEMBER 1842.

St. Petersburg.
PUBLISHED BY THE PRINTING HOUSE OF THE IMPERIAL ST. PETERSBURG THEATERS.
(DEPARTMENT OF INDEPENDENT PRINCIPALITIES). 1889.[1]

PERMITTED BY THE CENSOR, ST. PETERSBURG, 19 OCTOBER 1889.

TYPOGRAPHER OF THE IMPERIAL SPB. THEATERS (DEPARTMENT OF INDEPENDENT
PRINCIPALITIES), MOKHOVAYA, 40.

CHARACTERS.

Duke Albert, disguised in the clothes of a simple peasant Loys.
German sovereign prince.
Wilfride, squire of Duke Albert.
Hans, a forester.
Old peasant man.
Bathilde, fiancée of Duke Albert.
Giselle, a young peasant girl.
Berthe, mother of Giselle.
Myrtha, lady of the Wilis.

The Duke's retinue, hunters, pages, settlers, and Wilis.

GERMAN FOLKLORE
from which is composed the ballet
"GISELLE, OU LES WILIS".

In Germany there exists a tradition of a night dancer, called the *Wili.*
Wilis—are brides who have died before their wedding. Their graves did not calm them. Dancing is their element even after death; and often at midnight they go out on a large road, whirl, dance—in a word, indulge in their invincible passion. Woe to the young traveler who meets them; they will spin him, torture him with frantic dances, and his death is inevitable.
In wedding dresses, with wedding rings on their hands, wearing flower wreaths, Wilis, like Norman Elves, dance charmingly in the moonlight. Their faces are pale, but youthfully lovely.

---

[1] The 1889 St. Petersburg libretto was a reprint of the 1842 St. Petersburg libretto. See Yury Burlaka and Anna Grustynova, comps., *Libretto baletov Mariusa Petipa: Rossiya, 1848–1904* [Librettos of ballets by Marius Petipa: Russia, 1848–1904] (St. Petersburg: Compozitor, 2018), 379n1.

Their laugh is treacherous, their greetings tempting; their gaze is so attractive that rarely can anyone resist them.

This tradition is taken from the Slavic and, even closer, from the Serbian myth about exactly the same unearthly creatures, called *Vily*. The main difference of their character consists in the fact that Serbian Vily are creatures transformed (*métamorphosés*): they were brides and became sepulchral toilers of dancing. Serbian Vily are not evil, but punish a person only for an evil deed and more often than not for arrogance and pride. They do this with knowledge, with dignity, as befits creatures of higher intelligence, although they also passionately love dancing. For them, to whirl some braggart-hunter or a haughty knight—is more than pleasure.

ACT I.

THE THEATER PRESENTS A MERRY VALLEY, HILLS COVERED WITH VINEYARDS ARE VISIBLE; A MOUNTAINOUS ROAD DESCENDS INTO A VALLEY.

SCENE I.

Day is breaking. The people gather grapes.

SCENE II.

Hans enters; looks around, as if looking for someone; then looks with love at Giselle's hut and turns with anger to Loys's dwelling: here is his rival and he is ready to avenge him with pleasure. The door of Loys's hut quietly opens. Hans hides and spies.

SCENE III.

Loys—is the young Duke Albert, hiding in the clothes of a simple peasant; he comes together with his squire Wilfride. Wilfride attempts to persuade the duke to abandon his secret intention; Loys disagrees and points to Giselle's hut: there, under a simple poor roof, lives the object of his love... He orders Wilfride to leave. Wilfride hesitates; but at another imperative sign from the duke, he respectfully bows and leaves.

Hans wonders why Wilfride gives so much respect to a simple peasant and already begins to develop certain suspicions.

SCENE IV.

Loys walks over to Giselle's hut and knocks quietly on the door: Hans observes everything. Giselle runs out and throws herself into Loys's embrace. A scene of heartfelt effusions and delights of love. Giselle tells Loys her dream: she saw Loys, but a Loys unfaithful to her,—a Loys who preferred some lady of high society to her.

Embarrassed, Loys calms her, assures her that he loves and will always love only her. "Make sure you don't lie to me," says Giselle: "I feel that I will die then out of despair"—and puts a hand to her heart, as if expressing the doubts with which her soul languishes. Loys tries even harder to comfort her with his caresses.

Giselle picks a daisy; starts fortune-telling: "He loves me, he loves me not.... he loves me, he loves me not... he loves me!... " and she throws herself into the arms of her beloved.

Hans, out of patience, runs up to Giselle and showers her with reproaches.

"Yes, I love him, and will always love, and am not ashamed of my love," Giselle replies gaily, and turning away from Hans, laughs at him. Hans leaves, promising to avenge the insult.

SCENE V.

Morning. Giselle's friends come, they call her to gather grapes; but Giselle is a bad worker: she just wants to have fun; love for Loys and for dancing—are her only thoughts; she holds her friends back, persuades them to dance instead of work; spins, winds in front of them; turns to Loys as well and with her carefree playfulness she captivates everyone. Baskets and shears are abandoned: all are busy dancing, which soon turns into a loud, unanimous delight. Enter Berthe, Giselle's mother.

SCENE VI.

"It seems you will spend your whole life dancing, Giselle," she says to her daughter, "instead of working and looking after the farm."

"But she dances so beautifully!" replies Loys.

"Dancing and Loys—are my only delight," adds Giselle,—"in them only lies my happiness!!!"

"I'm sure," says Berthe, "that this fool, when she dies, will become a Wili and will dance even after death, like all lovers of dancing!"

"What are you saying?" the girls scream with horror and huddle in fear next to each other.

Berthe, paying no attention to them, speaks, accompanied by gloomy music, about the appearance of the Wilis or dead brides—from the otherworld—and about their terrible dances. The horror of the peasant girls gradually increases. Only Giselle laughs and responds boldly to her mother, that she will always dance, both alive and dead.

"It's all of no concern to you," Berthe adds. . . "but here is a question of your health, perhaps even your life!!—My Giselle is so delicate," she says, turning to Loys, "and the doctor told me that all these powerful movements and sensations are very bad for her."

A frightened Loys reassures the kind mother; Giselle takes his hand, presses it to her heart, and says to him: "I'm not afraid of anything with you."

Hunting horns are heard in the distance. Loys is alarmed and tries to quickly send away the peasant girls. Giselle, too, goes into her hut against her will and blows a farewell kiss to Loys; Loys leaves with the others.

SCENE VII.

Hans, alone, expresses his intention. He wishes by all means, at any cost, to penetrate the secret of his rival and find out who he is. . . Inspecting everything around to make sure that nobody is on the watch for him, he enters stealthily into Loys's hut. . . The hunting horns are heard still clearer; hunters appear on the hill.

SCENE VIII.

The sovereign prince and his daughter Bathilde arrive on the stage on horseback; behind them is their retinue, cavaliers, ladies, and hunters. The midday heat has exhausted them, and they seek shelter for rest. One of the hunters points the prince to Berthe's hut: he knocks on the door; Giselle appears in the doorway, her mother is behind her. The prince cheerfully asks for their hospitality, and Berthe offers him her poor hut.

Bathilde calls Giselle to her, scrutinizes her, admires her; Giselle hosts and takes care of her guest; invites Bathilde to sit down; treats her with milk, fruits; Bathilde is absolutely charmed; she takes a golden chain off herself and puts it around embarrassed Giselle's neck.

Bathilde asks Giselle what she does, what her pleasures are.

"She is very happy; she has no sorrow, no concerns: in the morning—she works, in the evening—she dances!. . . And dancing—is her passion," says Berthe.

Bathilde smiles and asks Giselle, does she love anyone? "Oh! but of course . . . " Giselle answers: "Here lives my bridegroom . . . " and points to Loys's hut: "I love him very much, I will die if he ceases to love me." Bathilde sympathizes with her; their fate is the same, —she is also getting married. Bathilde promises to give Giselle a dowry. . . and certainly wants to see her groom. Giselle runs to get Loys.

The prince, meanwhile, orders his retinue to continue the hunt; he himself is tired and wants to rest in the hut: "I will blow the horn," he says to the retinue, "when I need you."

Hans appears in the doorway of Loys's hut; he sees the prince and hears his last order. The prince leaves with Bathilde and Berthe.

SCENE IX.

Giselle runs out on the road and awaits Loys. Hans appears on the stage, too; in his hands are a sword and a hat; he finally knows his rival: he is a nobleman and, according to Hans, he is surely a disguised seducer! Hans wants to expose him before Giselle and before the whole village. He hides Loys's sword in a bush and waits for all the peasants to gather for the celebration.

SCENE X.

Loys appears upstage... He looks around anxiously and sees that the whole hunting party has already retired.

Giselle sees him; throws herself into his arms! At this time cheerful music sounds.

SCENE XI.

A march. The grapes have been harvested. Peasant men and women appear on the stage with baskets full of grapes; a small Bacchus rides solemnly on a barrel.

All surround Giselle and proclaim her queen of the festival, crown her with flowers and grape leaves. Loys falls in love with her even more. All are having fun.

Celebration! Giselle can now freely indulge in her passion; she takes Loys and starts dancing with him; peasants join them; Giselle's kiss ends the dance. Hans loses his temper; tormented by jealousy and rage, he rushes into the middle of the crowd and announces to Giselle that Loys is a deceiver, a seducer, that he is a disguised nobleman. Giselle is abashed; replies to Hans that he does not know what he is saying, that he is delirious... "Ah! I'm delirious," the forester continues... "So see for yourself, be assured"—and he shows the peasants the sword and Loys's hat. "I found them in his hut, and it seems they can be sufficient evidence of his deception."

Albert furiously lunges at Hans; he hides behind the peasants.

Giselle is stricken by this discovery; she is ready to faint from exhaustion.

The peasants in surprise, Loys runs to Giselle, tries to reassure and comfort her with still new caresses, new expressions of his tenderness. "You are being deceived," he says: "I'm your Loys, I'm a simple peasant, I'm your groom!"

And Giselle believes, hopes; she is again happy and trustingly throws herself into the arms of the treacherous Albert. But Hans takes revenge; he remembers the order that the prince gave to his retinue; takes a horn and starts to blow... The entire retinue comes running; the prince comes out of the hut; Hans points to Albert, who is kneeling in front of Giselle; everyone recognizes the young duke and bows respectfully to him. Giselle sees this and no longer doubts the deception of her bridegroom.

SCENE XII.

The prince also approaches Albert, recognizes him, and demands an explanation.

Albert stands in embarrassment. Giselle sees everything; she is very bitter, but she overcomes her weakness and walks away from Albert with fear. Suddenly some new thought strikes her; she runs to the hut and falls into her mother's arms, who at this time comes out together with Bathilde.

SCENE XIII.

Bathilde turns to Giselle with concern; asks her why she is so alarmed; instead of an answer, she points at Albert.

"What do I see?" says Bathilde... "The duke is here and in such a costume! Giselle! This is my bridegroom..." and shows her the engagement ring.

Albert approaches Bathilde, —wants to stop her, prevent her from telling his secret; but Giselle already heard everything, understood everything. She loses her mind, cries, laughs; takes Albert by the hand, presses it to her heart; then pushes it away with horror; raises his sword from the ground, first mechanically, then wants to throw herself at the blade; Loys lunges at her and takes the weapon away. After a short pause, Giselle seems to remember the dancing, she hears that cheerful music to which she so recently danced with Loys. Some strange delight animates her; she again indulges her passion, dancing, jumping, whirling; but an instant—and her strength is exhausted... life leaves her, she falls into her mother's arms, and the last dying breath flies out of poor Giselle's chest. She glances once more at Albert and dies.

The kind, generous Bathilde cries; Albert forgets everything, tries to revive Giselle with his caresses... puts his hand to her heart: the heart does not beat.

He wants to stab himself; the prince holds him back and takes away his sword. Berthe supports the body of her daughter. Albert is taken away.

The peasants and the entire retinue surround the body of Giselle. General scene.

END OF FIRST ACT.

ACT II.

THE THEATER PRESENTS A FOREST ON THE SHORE OF A LAKE, NEAR WHICH
ARE CANE, REED, AND WATER PLANTS. TO THE LEFT IS A STONE WITH
THE INSCRIPTION "GISELLE"; THE GRAVESTONE IS ALL OVERGROWN WITH
GRASS AND WILDFLOWERS. THE MOON FAINTLY ILLUMINATES [THE SCENE].

SCENE I.

Hunters come out of the forest and search for the best place to set up an ambush; they occupy the shore of the lake; Hans runs in.

SCENE II.

Hans is horrified, seeing the intention of his comrades. "This is a cursed place"—he says: "Here the Wilis dance." He shows them the tomb of Giselle, then the wreath of grape leaves with which she was crowned at the festival. Now [we see] the same wreath, but not on Giselle, but on the marble tombstone.

The clock strikes midnight; it is said that at this mysterious hour the Wilis flock.

Hans and his companions watch with fear; they constantly look around and await the appearance of ghosts. "Let us run," says Hans, "the Wilis are ruthless: they captivate all wanderers, forcing them to dance with them. Languor, torment, and finally death in the waves of the lake— that is the consequence of this terrible dance."

Fantastic music begins; the hunters pale and in horror run in all directions; everywhere wandering lights appear and pursue them.

SCENE III.

Myrtha appears,—a transparent pale shadow—the lady of the Wilis. She carries with her a mysterious light and suddenly illuminates the entire forest.

The shadow does not remain a single minute in one place: it flies through flowers, among branches; patrols her small domain; flies above the lake, and then swings on a branch.

After a single dance, she breaks off a rosemary branch and touches it to every plant, to every shrub, to every clump of leaves.

SCENE IV.

Plants, flowers, shrubs open and from them emerge the Wilis. Dancing begins. The Wilis appear before their lady one by one.

They all died because they loved dancing too much; death kidnapped them prematurely; they had not yet had enough time to completely satisfy their insane passion, and here, in their graceful rebirth, they again indulge in it with the same frenzy.

But now, at a sign from their lady, the fantastic dances cease. She announces to her subjects that she has chosen them another sister [podrugu].

SCENE V.

A moonbeam falls on the tomb of Giselle.

Giselle comes out; approaches Myrtha; the lady touches her with a rosemary branch... and Giselle turns into a Wili. Wings grow; she barely touches the ground; she flies in the air and delightedly recalls all the pas which she danced before her death.

Noise is heard in the distance. The Wilis run away and hide in the reeds.

SCENE VI.

A crowd of cheerful young villagers passes; they are returning from a festival from a nearby village; with them is an old man; fantastic music sounds again, it lures the poor villagers, and they are ready to dance. The Wilis surround them and charm them even more with their magnificent poses.

In order to please them more, to attract them more strongly, the Wilis dance their characteristic native dance... The villagers are delighted; ready to dance and die, the old man rushes between them; reveals their impending danger; they flee; the Wilis pursue them.

SCENE VII.

Albert enters with his faithful squire Wilfride. The duke is sad, pale; his clothes are in disarray; in all his movements some kind of strangeness is noticeable. The death of Giselle almost deprived him of reason. Going quietly to the tombstone, he thinks, as if trying to recall the past.

Wilfride implores him to follow him, not to stop at this fatal tomb, which reminds him of so much grief... Albert asks him to leave; Wilfride insists even more; but Albert orders him, and Wilfride obeys, although in his heart he gives himself his word that he will definitely remove his comrade from this sad place.

SCENE VIII.

Albert is alone and at liberty surrenders to sadness; he cries... suddenly turns pale, his eyes stop, fixed; a wondrous vision is drawn before his eyes: he recognizes in this ghost Giselle, who looks at him with love.

SCENE IX.

Albert still doubts; does not believe his eyes. And to be sure: this is not the same rosy, flowery Giselle, whom he loved so much, this is Giselle reborn, Giselle-Wili. Giselle remains motionless before him, she beckons him with glances alone, and an enchanted Albert quietly approaches her, like a child to a moth resting on a flower. But at the very time when he extends his hand to her, Giselle, like lightning, slips away from him; flies in the air, and already from another place beckons him to her with the same look of passion.

This is repeated several times. In vain Albert catches her; she is incorporeal, like a cloud; like light steam, she descends, then rises above him. The flowers that she throws to him, the glances, smiles, kisses on the fly just further incite his desire; finally exhausted, he kneels in front of the tombstone and again turns to her with a pleading look.

Giselle pities Albert; she quietly drops to him, and his hands have already touched her waist; he is ready to grab her, hug her; Giselle dodges and disappears, and Albert embraces only the tombstone.

Albert is desperate, gets up, wants to leave, but an unexpected sight appears before his eyes and holds him.

SCENE X.

Albert hides behind a tree; a miserable Hans runs in; the Wilis pursue him.

The pale, frightened forester falls before a tree and begs them! But the lady of the Wilis touches him with her staff, forces him to stand and dance with her... Hans obeys the power of magic and dances against his will with the beautiful Wili; then she passes him to her friend, she to another, and so on, to the last.

Hans becomes exhausted, wants to run, the Wilis surround him; at first they make a wide circle, then crowd more and more toward him, surround him completely, the waltz begins, and Hans, as if obeying some kind of supernatural force, spins with them all one by one.

But soon the forces leave him a completely unfortunate victim; his knees bend, his eyes close; he sees nothing, but dances still with terrible frenzy. The lady herself takes him, takes him in a waltz to the lake; leaves him and he falls into the abyss! An exuberant bacchanale begins, led by the triumphant lady. One Wili notices Albert and leads him into the magic circle.

SCENE XI.

The Wilis are delighted, Myrtha raises her magic staff over Albert, but Giselle rushes to her and holds back her arm.

SCENE XII.

"Run," says Giselle to Albert, "run away from here: otherwise you will die just like Hans."

Albert is frightened by the thought alone that he might share the fate of Hans. Giselle, taking advantage of the general confusion, takes Albert by the hand and leads him to her grave. "Here is your protection," she says, pointing to the tombstone.

The lady and all the Wilis pursue them all the way to the grave; Albert grabs the tombstone; Myrtha extends her staff to him; the magic branch breaks in her hands; she stops in wonder and with her all the Wilis.

They surround Albert, lunge at him; but some invisible force pushes them away. Then the lady addresses Giselle, the very culprit of this misfortune; her wings spread and she begins to dance.

Albert stares at her, motionless; but the grace and sumptuous poses of the Wilis enthrall him; he leaves the tombstone and walks up to Giselle; she begs him to return to his place again.

The lady forces her to dance her seductive dance. Finally, Albert gives in to his passion and rushes to Giselle... He grabs the enchanted branch himself, wants to die, wants to unite forever with the Wili!!!

Albert is as if on wings, barely touching the ground; he flies around Giselle, but Giselle is trying still to stop him.

In vain, she herself soon takes a fancy to her new assignment. They whirl, flit, suddenly stop, and again, excited by the music, continue their dance.

All the Wilis join them.

Albert tires; he struggles, but his strength leaves him; Giselle comes to him, cries and again flies away at the sign of the inexorable lady. A few more seconds and Albert will certainly die from fatigue. It is dawn, and the first rays of sun gild the mirror-like surface of the lake.

The noisy dance subsides little by little.

Giselle is happy...

The Wilis gradually weaken from the sun's rays; life goes out of them and they descend to the places from which they came.

Giselle experiences the same effect of daylight and quietly bends into the embrace of Albert, while trying to get closer to her grave.

Albert guesses the fate of Giselle and carries her in his arms farther from the grave; lays [her] on the ground on a flower bed; kneels in front of her and kisses her.

Giselle points to the sun and says that she must obey her fate and leave him forever.

From the depths of the forest sounds of horns are heard. Albert listens with fear, Giselle with quiet pleasure.

SCENE XIII.

Wilfride comes running; behind him the prince, Bathilde, and all the retinue; the faithful horseman led everyone to Albert to take him out of this dismal place.

All stop, seeing Albert.

Giselle points to Bathilde, who is kneeling a few steps away from him and extending her arms to him with a pleading look.

Giselle persuades Albert to love Bathilde again... This is her final request; she can no longer love anyone; says goodbye to Albert, and, dying, disappears in the flowers.

THE END

Translation by Anastasia Shmytova.

(iii) Giselle poster, St. Petersburg, 18 December 1842

AT THE BOLSHOI THEATER.

On Friday 18 December,

the court ballet dancers
will present

for the benefit of balletmaster
M. TITUS,

for the first time:

G I S E L L E
ou
LES WILIS.

Fantastic ballet in two acts, by MM. Coralli and Théophile Gautier; put on the local stage by the balletmaster M. Titus; music by A. Adam; scenery and machines by M. Roller; new costumes by M. Mathieu.

Will dance in the first act: Mlle Andreanova 2 and M. Nikitin—*pas de deux*; Mlle Shlefokht and M. Emile Gredelue—*pas de deux*; Mlles Danilova, Gravert, Milova, Beleutovtseva, Students Nikitina, Yakovleva, Gorina and Kostina.

In the 2nd act: Mlle Smirnova—*solo*; Mlle Andreanova 2 and M. Nikitin—*pas de deux*; Mlles Danilova, Gravert, Milova, Students Nikitina, Yakovleva, Gorina, Konstina and Bormotova.

CHARACTERS:

Duke Albert, *disguised in the clothes of a common peasant Loys*	M. Nikitin.
German sovereign Prince	M. Frédéric.
Wilfride, *squire of Duke Albert*	M. Spiridonov 2.
Hans, *a forester*	M. Fleury.
Old Man, *a peasant*	M. Spiridonov 1.
Bathilde, *fiancée of Duke Albert*	Mlle Maximova.
Giselle, *a young peasant*	Mlle Andreanova 2.
Berthe, *mother of Giselle*	Mlle Savitskaya.
Myrtha, *lady of the Wilis*	Mlle Smirnova.

The duke's suite, pages, hunters, village men, village women, and wilis.

STARTS AT 7:30.

Individuals who wish to have a ticket for this performance
are pleased to send for them at the box office of the Bolshoi Theater.

(iv) *Giselle* program, St. Petersburg, 30 April 1903

Price 5 kopecks.

1903

MARIINSKY THEATER.

On Wednesday, 30 April,
35TH SUBSCRIPTION PERFORMANCE.

The Artists of the Imperial theaters will present:

I

FOR THE 9TH TIME IN REVIVAL:

GISELLE

Fantastic ballet in 2 acts, composed by **St. Georges,
T. Gautier and Coralli.** Music by **Adolphe Adam.**

Staged by the soloist of HIS MAJESTY, balletmaster
M. Petipa.

Scenery 1st and 2nd act—M. Bocharov; costumes based on drawings by M. Ponomarev:
men's—M. Caffi, women's—Mlle Ofitserova; headwear: men's—M. Bruneau, women's—Mlle
Termain; wigs—M. Pedder; accessories—sculptor M. Kamensky.

Machinist-mechanic—M. Berger.

The role of "Hans" will be performed by M. **Gerdt**, soloist of
HIS MAJESTY.

In the 1st act:
CHARACTERS:

Giselle	*Mlle Pavlova 2.*
Count Albert	*M. N. Legat.*
Berthe, *mother of Giselle*	*Mlle Yakovleva 1.*
Hans, *a forester*	*M. Gerdt.*
Duke	*M. Gillert.*
Mathilde, *fiancée of Count Albert*	*Mlle Petipa 2.*
Squire of Count Albert	*M. Kusov.*

Ladies of the court, gentlemen, pages, peasant men, peasant women, and hunters.

WILL DANCE:

1) **Entrée**—Mlle Pavlova 2.

2) **Valse**—Mlle Pavlova 2 and N. Legat, Mlles Bakerkina 1, Vasilieva, Erler 2, Slantsova, Kasatkina, Golubeva, Konetskaya, Ilyina 3, Dorina, Rykhlyakova, Sazonova, Urakova, Spryshinskaya, Stepanova 2, Leonova 2, Chernyatina.

3) **Scène dansante**—Mlle Pavlova 2 and N. Legat.

4) **Fête des vendanges**—Mlles Snetkova, Goncharova, Fedorova 2, Matveyeva, Alexne, Lopukhova, Karlson, Rykhlyakova 2, Chernyatina, Sazonova, Spryshinskaya, Konetskaya, Urakova, Erler 2, Stepanova 2, Leonova 2, Golubeva, Dorina, Ilyina 3 and other women and men dancers.

5) **Solo**—Mlle Pavlova 2.

6) **Final**—Everyone.

7) **Pas-de-deux**—Mlle Karsavina and M. Fokine.

8) **Galop**—Everyone.

In the 2nd act:

CHARACTERS:

Wili	*Mlle Pavlova 2.*
Count Albert	*M. N. Legat.*
Myrtha, lady of the wilis	*Mlle Sedova.*
Zulme ⎫	*Mlle Kyaksht.*
Moyna ⎬ wilis	*Mlle Polyakova.*
Hans, a forester	*M. Gerdt.*
Squire of Count Albert	*M. Kusov.*

WILL DANCE:

1) **Apparition et danse de la reine des willis**—Mlle Sedova.

2) **Pas des willis**—Mlles Sedova, Kyaksht, Polyakova, Slantsova, Vasileva, Lits, Matveyeva, Konetskaya, Erler 2, Leonova 2, Matyatina, Ilina 3, Rykhlyakova 2, Stepanova 2, Spryshinskaya, Golubeva, Tsalison, Sazonova, Stepanova 3, Lobanova, Niman, Frank, Bakerkina 2, Bastman, Chernetskaya, Levenson 2, Kuzmina, Erler 1, Alexieva.

3) **Solo**—Mlle Pavlova 2.

4) **Pas-de-deux**—Mlle Pavlova 2 and N. Legat.

The viola solo will be performed by the soloist of the Court of HIS IMPERIAL MAJESTY M. **Auer.**

Also performing a solo:
On the oboe—M. **Liebstein.**

[*Giselle* was followed on the program by *The Awakening of Flora.*]

APPENDIX D

Paquita

(i) *Paquita* libretto, Paris, 1846

PAQUITA

BALLET-PANTOMIME IN TWO ACTS,

BY MM. PAUL FOUCHER AND MAZILIER,

MUSIC BY M. DELDEVEZ,

PRESENTED FOR THE FIRST TIME

at the Theatre de l'Académie Royale de Musique,

THE 1st OF APRIL 1846.

The Scenery of the 1st act is by MM. PHILASTRE and CAMBON,
Those of the 2nd act are by
MM. DIÉTERLE, SÉCHAN and DESPLECHIN.

Paris,
Mme Widow Jonas, bookseller-publisher of the Opéra,
Passage du Grand-Cerf, 52.
1846.

DISTRIBUTION.

Characters.		*Actors.*
LUCIEN D'HERVILLY	MM.	PETIPA.
INIGO, leader of a band of Gitanos		ÉLIE.
DON LOPEZ DE MENDOZA, Spanish Governor of the province		CORALLI.
THE COUNT D'HERVILLY, French General, father of Lucien		MONET.
A SCULPTOR		PETIT.
PAQUITA	Mmes	CARLOTTA GRISI.
DONA SÉRAPHINA		ZÉLIE PIERSON.
THE COUNTESS, Mother of the General		DELAQUIT.
A YOUNG GITANA		DABAS 1re.

The action takes place in Saragossa and the surrounding area.

DANCE.

FIRST ACT.

GITANOS.
MM. Théodore, Toussaint, Cornet, Chatillon, Clément, Gondoin, Minar, Wiethof 2me, Beauchet.
Mmes Émarot, Robert, Barré, Drouet, Dabas 1re, Dabas 2me, Hecmanus, Duriez.

PAS DE TROIS.
M^{MES} ÉMAROT, ROBERT, BARRÉ.

PAS SEUL.
MLLE GRISI.

MAYOS.
MM. Josset, Wells; Mmes Robin, Gougibus.

SPANISH VILLAGE MEN.
MM. Lenfant, Guiffart, Isambert, Lenoir, Rouget, Maujin, Wiethof 1er, Vandris, Deschamps, Alexandre, Archinar, Pinguely, Darcour.

CHILDREN.
MM. Beauchet, Dieul 1er, Dieul 2me, Frapar, Belleville, Nettre, Levavasseur, Charonsonnet, Billard.

SPANISH VILLAGE WOMEN.
Mmes Saulnier, Baillet, Julien, Vaslin, Petit, Bourdon, Pézée, Lenoir, Rosa, Cluchar, Favre, Maréchalle, Passérieux, Maujin, Glinelle, Giraudier, Gayot.

CHILDREN.
Mlles Monpérin 1er, Cassegrain, Delahaye 1re, Delahaye 2me, Bertin, Vigier, Jourdan, Péréda, Landelle, Pierron, Hennecar, Baron, Legrain, Monpérin 2me.

CORPS DE DANSE.
M^{MES} CAROLINE, DIMIER.

IN MEN'S [COSTUMES].
MM [sic]. Marquet 3me, Jeandron, Laurent 2me, Faugère, Chambret, Toutain, Rousseau, Savelle, Gallois, Mayé.

IN WOMEN'S [COSTUMES].
Mmes Paget, Devion, Marquet 2me, Courtois, Franck, Josset, Jeunot, Nathan, Danse, Lacoste.

SECOND ACT.

SENIOR OFFICERS.
MM. QUÉRIAU, PETIT.

OFFICERS OF DIFFERENT FRENCH CORPS
MM. Wells, Rouget, Josset, Pinguely, Deschamps, Lefèvre, Carri, Lenfant,
Isambert, Archinar, Maujin, Millot, Vandris.

SPANISH OFFICERS.
MM. Darcour, Lenoir, Weithof 1er, Alexandre, Guiffard.

HUSSARDS.
Mmes Baillet, Toussaint, Maujin, Gallois, Laurent 2me, Marquet 3me, Toutain,
Maréchalle.

LADIES OF THE COURT.
Mmes Dabas 1re, Dabas 2me, Drouet, Frank.
Robin, Saulnier, Gougibus, Rosa, Laurent 1er, Petit, Julien, Vaslin, Devion,
Bourdon, Pézée, Passérieux, Glinelle, Giraudier.

CHILDREN.
Mlles Hecmanus, Monpérin 1re, Tassin, Savel, Cassegrain, Delahaye 1re,
Delahaye 2me, Bertin, Dedieu, Vigier, Duriez, Quériau, Jourdan, Pérada,
Landelle, Pierron, Baron, Hennecar, Legrain, Monpérin 2me.

CORPS DE DAMES DANSANT.
Mmes Danse, Nathan, Jeunot, Rousseau, Lacoste, Cluchar, Chambret,
Jeandron, Paget, Courtois, Fengère, Marquet 2me.

GAVOTTE.
MM. Théodore, Toussaint; Mmes Célestine Émarot, Caroline.

PAS DE DEUX.
Mmes A. Dumilatre, Plumkett [sic].

PAS SEUL.
Mlle Carlotta Grisi.

VALSE.
M. Petipa, Mlle Carlotta Grisi.

PAQUITA,
BALLET-PANTOMIME IN TWO ACTS.

FIRST ACT.

The Valley of the Bulls near Saragossa. Large roughly carved stone bulls line the hills in the background. To the right, still at the bottom, huge rocks with a natural staircase carved into the stone. On the right, to the side, a tent prepared for the Gitanos.

FIRST SCENE.

A sculptor is busy engraving an inscription on a marble tablet. Groups of Spanish peasants are nonchalantly stretched out in the sun. The French general appears, accompanied by the Spanish governor and his sister Séraphina; Lucien's grandmother is on his arm. The General is presented with the inscription, which reads thus:

TO THE MEMORY OF MY BROTHER,
CHARLES D'HERVILLY,
ASSASSINATED, WITH HIS WIFE AND HIS DAUGHTER
25 MAY 1795.

In a mimed recitative, the General relates this sad episode, which occurred during one of his trips to the peninsula. Having become all-powerful in Spain owing to the French victories there, he wishes that this inscription be carved in stone at the exact place where his brother perished at the hands of bandits. Lucien and his grandmother share the count's emotion. The Governor distracts them from these sad thoughts by telling them that a big village festival will take place on this day, in this place. After the festival, the General's pious intentions will be carried out. Don Lopez gestures ceremonially in the Spanish style to the family to which he is allying himself; the General, for his part, takes Dona Séraphina's hand and places it in his son's hand. Dona Sérafina gives her consent, but the Spanish Governor makes it clear that he considers this a political marriage imposed by the invasion and ostensibly accepted by him, but far from being concluded. The Governor secretly harbors one of those national hatreds which have produced so many deaths during the Spanish wars.

The grandmother quietly asks her grandson: does he love his young fiancée? — No, he answers; but at least my heart is free. The good lady appears to add: — Love will come later. Don Lopez de Mendoza bids his guests take advantage of the beautiful day by visiting the nearby sites. Everyone departs.

SCENE II.

Lively and joyful music announces a troupe of gitanos. They come down from the mountains. Carts loaded with their bags, musical instruments, etc., approach from the valley. These nomadic *danseuses* promise much pleasure and the success of the festival, but Inigo, the head of the troupe, glancing at his *Corps de ballet*, sees that Paquita is missing—his prettiest and best pupil. He orders that they go back to look for her. But at that moment, Paquita appears on the mountaintop, her sad eyes mechanically focused on a bouquet of flowers that she holds in her hands. She comes down from the mountain and gives her friends the flowers that had drawn her off the path. Inigo is furious at the delay; he can scarcely be contained. He orders everyone to prepare for the festival. The gitanos all go into the tent.

SCENE III.

However, he detains Paquita. Alone with her, he explains to her that if she so desires, he will cease being such a terrible master and instead become her most obedient slave. But Paquita still prefers servitude to the sort of degrading love that he proposes. Instead of answering Inigo, she rushes forward and begins to dance, as if to escape her troubles for a moment through the intoxication of dance. Inigo tries in vain to stop her from dancing. Exasperated, he raises his hand to her. Paquita gives him a withering look, her indignation bringing out the sparkle of her native nobility. She slips away from him again, and Inigo walks away, confused by the power his captive Paquita exercises over him.

SCENE IV.

Paquita, who remains alone, takes a medallion portrait from her bosom that she has kept since childhood. The portrait doesn't indicate the nationality or station of the person portrayed. With an inexpressible gentleness, she looks at the features of the person to whom she surely owes her existence, and dreams of the delights of family life. Then, as she gets ready to join her friends, suddenly—casting her eyes around the surrounding landscape—she believes she recognizes the site of a terrible event that she only barely remembers. Yes, it was here that she saw the dying officer fall; the one who had held her in his arms; it was here that she felt herself being carried away by unknown hands. But the crowd of people who approach her from all sides bring her back to her sad present-day life. She goes into the tent that serves as the shelter of the gitanos.

SCENE V.

The stage fills up. The General, the grandmother, Séraphina, and the Governor return and take allotted places. The gitanos come out of their tent wearing the costumes they have donned for the festival.

BALLET.

After the dancing, Inigo orders Paquita to collect money. He is counting on her pretty face to bring out generous donations. Paquita obeys reluctantly and makes the rounds amongst the audience. As she passes by Lucien, she makes a vivid impression on him. But despite the officer's generous offering, the result of the collection doesn't satisfy Inigo's greed: Paquita must dance to achieve the sum that he desires. More sad and defiant than ever, Paquita refuses. Inigo gets angry; Lucien rushes in to protect Paquita and energetically pushes Inigo away. Then he reassures the young girl, and in gazing at her, he notices the foreign charm of her appearance and the whiteness of her complexion, which contrasts with the bronzed faces of the gitanos. He takes her over to his grandmother, who looks at her with interest, and like Lucien is surprised by this peculiarity. Lucien asks Inigo who this *jeune fille* is; Inigo answers that she's his relative. You are lying, the officer appears to say; she cannot be related to you. He asks the *jeune fille*: Who is your family? She answers that she has only one clue, a portrait, and she looks for it on her person. But Inigo, seeing the turn the conversation had taken, had adroitly snatched the medallion from Paquita's pocket. She is very distressed when she sees that it is gone. She blames Inigo. Lucien wants to arrest him; his family and the Governor intervene to calm him down. But Lucien tells Inigo to stop forcing poor Paquita to dance. Inigo, who has begun to feel jealous, is glad to obey this order. But Paquita is so happy at the interest her protector has shown her that she wants to thank him in the only way she can. She wishes to shine for the young man whose friendly affinity for her has already drawn her to him. Inigo opposes the idea; but the Governor, for reasons of his own, obliges Inigo to give free rein to the young gitana.

Electrified by Lucien's presence, Paquita dances with a ravishing inspiration; the young officer's incipient love turns into a delirium, and Mendoza notes this turn of events with satisfaction. He invites the French family to a meal before they depart—the meal is about to be served, as the comings and goings of the servants show. His guests precede him to the banquet; as for him, he must remain to watch the end of the festival.

SCENE VI.

Remaining alone with Inigo, the Governor asks him questions. You are furious, surely, with this officer? -- I certainly am. — Well! If you would like to get rid of him with a good stab of a dagger, I promise to pardon you. — Me, get rid of him, your future brother-in-law? That's why I'm siding with you... so that the marriage doesn't take place ... — But you seem to be helping Paquita get closer to him. — That's because she's the one who must be the involuntary instrument of our revenge.

SCENE VII.

Paquita reappears... Mendoza goes to look for his guests. Inigo tells Paquita that he wants to set out again. He leaves to go collect his troupe together.

SCENE VIII.

Scarcely has Paquita found herself alone than Lucien rushes quickly onto the stage.... unconquerable desire draws him to the young gitana; — he compliments her for her beauty and offers her a richly decorated little purse. Paquita refuses it. Lucien is upset that he doesn't know how to better reward a woman of her social class who combines such unselfishness with such attractiveness. But, at the very least, he doesn't want to leave Paquita under the yoke of the brutal Inigo. He assures Paquita of a better fate if she wishes to follow him... Paquita refuses again. She is all too willing to listen to Lucien, but she knows the distance separating a poor gitana and an officer, and she knows that her low station alone could increase the gap. Therefore she tears herself away from Lucien's entreaties. He asks her permission to come look for her in the future, and begs her to give him her bouquet as a sign of hope. Paquita refuses; Lucien departs, very sad. Then Paquita no longer has the strength to let him go... She rushes after him to give him the flowers he desired so much.

SCENE IX.

But instead she runs into the jealous and smirking figure of Inigo, who stops her short. Unseen, he was present—and spying—at the end of the preceding scene... Paquita's thought of a dangerous trap awaiting Lucien makes her glad that she had resisted the young officer's attempts to woo her.

SCENE X.

The Governor comes back, followed by his guests. Inigo tells him about the conversation between the two young people, the story of Paquita's refusal to give her bouquet to Lucien. The Governor comes up with a plan and announces the departure of the French general. Pretending to hold the French general in the highest regard, the Governor orders all of the young village women to gather their bouquets together and offer them to this valiant ally of Spain. Paquita guilelessly gives up her bouquet. But instead of throwing it into the basket [along with the other bouquets], the Governor secretly hands it to a gitana and gives her certain instructions.

SCENE XI.

The General, the grandmother, and the young Séraphina prepare to depart. Lucien is ready to follow them; the young gitana approaches him and in a mysterious manner hands him Paquita's bouquet, which she says she was charged with giving him. Joyfully, Lucien recognizes it. — He questions the young gitana, who tells him how to find Paquita, whose home is not far away. The young man, exhilarated, informs his relatives that he is going alone into town on horseback. They admonish him not to be late getting back because the General is giving a ball that very night to celebrate the wedding planned for the next day. Lucien promises to be on time, and reassures his grandmother, who is already terribly worried about him. Wrapping himself up in a cape that his servant brings him, Lucien kisses one hundred times the flowers that have given him hope. The village women form a merry circle around the Governor's guests, while the caravan of gitanos, Inigo and Paquita at its head, winds up the craggy cliffs. Lucien rushes after them. The curtain falls.

END OF THE FIRST ACT.

SECOND ACT.

First Tableau.

Interior of a small dwelling place of Gitanos. At the back, a fireplace. A little to the left, a cabinet; between the cabinet and the fireplace, a shuttered window. Table to the right at the front of the stage. A door to the side, on the right; a rustic clock, chair, etc.

FIRST SCENE.

PAQUITA.

She comes in alone, very agitated. She sighs, dreaming of the handsome officer whom, doubtless, she will never see again. At this moment, a noise is heard outside. She opens the shutters and is astonished to see a masked man dressed in a cape approaching the house. She hears him enter, and suspecting some mystery, hides behind the cabinet.

SCENE II

INIGO *enters with* THE GOVERNOR, *who is wearing a mask.*

They arrive only moments before the victim, who is about to fall into their trap. Don Lopez takes off his mask and orders Inigo to strike Lucien without mercy. Inigo needs no such encouragement and shows the Governor a narcotic substance [in a wine bottle] he is going to give to the traveler to render him defenseless. He then hides this wine in the cabinet, which he locks. Paquita, a witness to the plot being hatched, shudders. The Governor departs, his vengeance assured, giving Inigo a purse, which Inigo does not forget to demand. Inigo then calls out the window to four men who will be lending him a hand in the assassination. He gives them a share of the money. Midnight is the time set for the premeditated murder. Inigo has two men hide behind the wall of the fireplace, which rotates and can open up to the outside; at this moment Paquita makes it clear by her gestures that she noticed how this sinister trick fireplace works, and that she will make every effort to warn the victim, whoever it is. She comes out of her hiding place and moves stealthily, close to the wall. But just as she is about to exit through the door, she trips on a chair. Inigo turns around, and runs to her. There will be trouble for Paquita if she is aware of the plot that is afoot! But Paquita protests that she has just arrived. Inigo is reassured. One of his men goes out the window and posts himself there; the other goes out through the door, and acts as a sentinel outside. At this moment, there is a knock at the door. They are hopeful [that everything is unfolding as planned].

SCENE III.

LUCIEN *appears.*[1]

His joy upon seeing Paquita. Her unspeakable terror on seeing that the intended victim is Lucien. Lucien asks if he may stay the night. Inigo welcomes him with great demonstrations of humility. What are you doing here? Paquita seems to be saying to Lucien. Lucien's answer is to show her the bouquet—which he believes to have been sent by Paquita—hidden under his cloak. Denial of Paquita. Inigo orders Paquita to serve the traveler. The latter gives his sword to Inigo, who hides it, and his coat to the *jeune fille*. Paquita throws the cloak over Inigo's head and then warns Lucien, through gestures, about the fate that awaits him. But the latter, carried away by his love and full of confidence in his brothers-in-arms (who have fought the war alongside him), refuses to believe in this danger. Inigo humbly invites Lucien to be kind enough to sup; he goes out to get everything ready, taking Paquita, who is still trying to persuade Lucien to be cautious.

SCENE IV.

Lucien, left alone, begins to find something strange in everything that is happening; he goes to the window, which is locked; also, the doors are double locked... He then realizes that his sword has been hidden... He looks around for something he can use to defend himself... but at this moment he hears someone enter...

SCENE V.

Paquita is the first to reappear, carrying plates; Inigo follows her... They serve supper... Then Inigo seems to be getting ready to go out. Paquita signals to Lucien to hold him back and not lose sight of him. Lucien asks Inigo to join him at supper. The latter accepts with humility and gratitude... Inigo pours a drink from a first bottle for his guest. Paquita signals to Lucien that he can drink, and even while waiting on both men removes the pistols from Inigo's holster, then removes the ammunition from them. Inigo, whom she caresses, invites the officer to watch her perform a dance, then goes to get Paquita's castanets. New signs of communication between the two lovers. At that moment Inigo finishes pouring out the first bottle into Lucien's glass, while his is still full... Then he slaps his head as if an idea has just occurred to him: he will look

---

[1] The libretto erroneously says here, "JULIEN *paraît.*"

in the cupboard for the best wine for the officer. Paquita signals to Lucien that it is the prepared bottle. Inigo pours this wine for Lucien; invites Lucien to drink with him. The officer is about to refuse... but Paquita drops a stack of plates with a loud crash. Inigo turns and angrily gets up to inspect the damage, and Paquita meanwhile swaps their wine glasses. Inigo sits down again, and the officer, turning the tables by using his own wiles, ironically invites Inigo to clink glasses with *him*. Inigo drinks, and believing his ploy has succeeded, gives Paquita the signal to dance. He himself performs a national step with her. Paquita, as she dances, uses signs to communicate the number of bandits and the time of the attack. But Lucien is too lovestruck to see the danger he is in, and anyway is unafraid of death when Paquita keeps passing close by as she dances—which only makes him think of stealing a kiss from her at every moment. Paquita, however, signals to Lucien to feign sleep. Lucien obeys; with a gesture Inigo makes fun of his rival, who has seemingly been vanquished without even putting up a defense. But at the same time, Inigo's mouth opens, his eyes close; his demeanor shows that he has been seized by the conquering power of sleep. He tries to overcome this perfidious drowsiness. To get a breath, he loosens his clothing, which causes him to drop the medallion he had taken from Paquita, who quickly snatches it back. Inigo sinks into the chair and his head falls to the table. Then Paquita tells Lucien to get up... The fatal hour is about to strike... Paquita, finally, can tell him openly the extent of the peril that they are in. The officer seizes Inigo's pistols. Paquita dolefully tells him that in order to protect his life she has removed the ammunition. Lucien is desperate, but while looking about the room, he discovers his saber, which had been hidden by Inigo! Finally he can fight, but Paquita makes him understand the futility of resistance against four bandits with firearms! What to do?... Midnight strikes... The fireplace begins to revolve; an idea occurs to Paquita! Perhaps God will allow the trap set by the bandits to be used to *save* the victims instead! She and Lucien stand against the wall, which—when it rotates—deposits the two lovers outside at the same time it brings the two gitanos into the room... Two more [of the would-be assassins] appear, one through the window, the other through the door; they see with astonishment Inigo alone and asleep; they wake him up by shouting loudly. Despair and fury of Inigo seeing that his victims have escaped. — The curtain falls.

Second Tableau.

A magnificent ballroom in the home of the French commander in Saragossa. — Moorish architecture decorated in the style of the Empire period. — A large portrait of an officer is in the foreground of the room. — Tableau of a period ball. Soldiers of all ranks, old generals, young hussars, dragoons, soldiers of the light brigade, etc.; in sum, all the magnificent uniforms of the Empire. Among these brilliant representatives of Napoleon's army, Frenchwomen attired in the grand court costume of the ladies of the Empire. — The Spanish nobility, in national costume, also figure in this ball. When the curtain rises, French contredanse and the gavotte classique.

The Count d'Hervilly appears with his future daughter-in-law and the Governor. The grandmother, who accompanies them, is surprised at Lucien's lateness. The father reassures her and urges her to put on her best demeanor. — He resumes the interrupted quadrille. However, the grandmother, who does not see her dear Lucien, becomes more and more alarmed, and the Count begins to share the venerable dowager's worries. Suddenly the crowd parts in astonishment: it is Lucien, who is dishevelled, and he is bringing Paquita into the ballroom with him... The Count and his mother are joyful, and then surprised in equal measure when Lucien tells them that, in the night, he was surrounded in an isolated house that was guarded by brigands. — Barely concealed fury of the Governor. Lucien owed his salvation to courage, to devotion, to the love of this young woman. — To love? responds the General with astonishment. — Yes, to her love, which I share, Lucien seems to say; my whole life belongs to my liberator. But Paquita refuses this marriage proposal, knowing that her social standing is far below his... The joy of saving Lucien's life is enough for her. She wants to take her leave. Lucien detains her; if she flees, he will follow her... The Count and his mother try to appease Lucien: they will forever be thankful to their child's guardian angel... But the Count did give his word to the Governor, who pretended to accept it eagerly. Suddenly Paquita's gaze falls on Don Lopez Mendoza, whom she hadn't noticed at first. — She recoils with fear... and points to him... It is he, and he alone, who, disguised and masked, ordered the murder and paid for it. The ring of truth in her words confounds the Spaniard. His sword is taken away from him. — He is led away; his sister goes with him. — Paquita remains in the arms of Lucien and his grandmother.... Paquita still refuses the path to happiness; but making a movement to flee, she finds herself face to face with a portrait placed in the front of the stage... She hurriedly draws her medallion from her bosom. There can be no more doubt: the same image appears in both paintings. This officer is her father; she herself is the kidnapped child who escaped the massacre and was raised by Inigo. But as the Count's niece, she belonged to his family by blood even before she proved herself worthy of joining the family by her devotion. The General kisses Paquita, lovingly welcoming her to the family. The grandmother leads her new child away in order to adorn her [for the ball]. The Count orders the ball to resume.

DIVERTISSEMENT

At the end of which Paquita reappears in the costume of her true homeland, and dances a step in which all the characters of the party unite in a final ensemble.

Translation by Marian Smith.

Authors' note: This translation draws from the translations of Cyril Beaumont in the *Complete Book of Ballets* (pp. 183–190) and of the Bayerisches Staatsballett, Munich.

(ii) *Paquita* libretto, St. Petersburg, 1847

PAQUITA.

Pantomime ballet in three acts,
composed by MM. Foucher and Mazilier,
produced on the local stage by MM. Frédéric and Petipa.
Music by M. Deldevez,
with instrumentation for orchestra by M. Lyadov.
With a new galop of his composition.

Saint Petersburg.
By the Printer I. Glazunov and Comp.
1847.

Dramatis personae:

Characters	Artists
Lucien d'Hervilly	M. Petipa.
Inigo, *chief of a band of gitanos*	M. Frédéric.
Don Lopez de Mendoza, *Spanish governor of the province*	M. Spiridonov.
Count d'Hervilly, *French general, father of Lucien*	M. Golts.
A Sculptor	M. Artemiev.
Paquita	Mlle Andreanova.
Doña Seraphina, *promised to Lucien and sister of Don Lopez*	Mlle Samoilova.
The Countess, *mother of Count d'Hervilly*	Mlle Hammer.
A Young Gitana	Mlle Sokolova (student).

The action takes place in Saragossa and its environs.

The Dances of Act I.

Solo—Mlle Andreanova.

Pas de trois—M. Johanson, Mlles Smirnova and Yakovleva.

Pas de[s] manteaux:

In men's costumes:

Mlles Nikitina, Panova, Makarova, Ryukhina, Dushkina 1, Korostenskaya 2, Bormotova, Apolonskaya (student), Zakaspiskaya 2, Baranova, Golovanova 1, Kozlovskaya, Radina, Stefanova, Ushakova 1, Gopshtok.

In women's costumes:

Mlles Prikhunova, Grigorieva, Sysoyeva, Misheva, Gorina, Kostina, Beleutovtseva, Gundurova, Shulgina (student), Malysheva (student), Vasilieva, Terekhova (student), Sergeyeva (student), Varentsova, Golovanova 2 (student), Petrova (student).

Pas de neuf.

Mlles Andreanova, Sokolova 1 (student) Amosova 1 (student), Nikulina, Amosova 2 (student), Radina (student), Vinogradskaya (student), MM. Kuznetsov, Reinshausen.

The Dances of Act II.

Contredanse française—Mlles Ryukhina and Makarova.
Gavotte—MM. Kuznetsov, Reinshausen, Mlles Ryukhina, Makarova.
Pas de fleurs—Thirty-two little girls of the Theater School.
Waltz pas de la folie—Mlle Andreanova, M. Petipa.
Pas de cinq—Mlles Nikitina, Prikhunova, Panova, Amosova 1, Sokolova.
El Haleo de Cadix—Mlle Andreanova, M. Petipa.

Galop général.

Mlles Andreanova, Prikhunova, Nikitina, Ryukhina, Panova, Amosova 1, Sokolova; MM. Petipa, Frédéric, Kuznetsov, Reinshausen, and all the men and women dancers of the corps de ballet.

PAQUITA.

Pantomime-Ballet in Three Acts.

ACT I.

The Valley of the Bulls [*La vallée des Taureaux*] near Saragossa. Large, roughly crafted stone bulls are seen sculpted in the distant hills. At the right, still at a distance, huge cliffs rise up, with a natural staircase cut into the stone. Also at the right, a tent for the gitanos.

SCENE 1.

A sculptor is cutting an inscription into a marble slab. Spanish peasants are lying and standing around in groups. A French general appears with the governor of the Spanish province and his sister Seraphina. Lucien is helping his old grandmother along. The general directs the sculptor to show him the inscription, which reads:

IN MEMORY OF MY BROTHER
CHARLES D'HERVILLY,
KILLED WITH HIS WIFE AND DAUGHTER
25 MAY 1795.

Looking at it, he recalls in a mimed narration this sad event, which occurred on his last trip to Spain. As a Frenchman and a conquerer in this country, and having therefore the right to rule, he has ordered the inscription to be cut into the rocks at the very place where his brother was killed by a robber's knife. Lucien and his old grandmother share his sorrowful feelings. The governor, wishing to lessen their sorrow somewhat, announces to them that a big village cele- bration is scheduled for that day, and after the festival, promises to fulfill the general's intentions with respect to his deceased brother's memorial. Don Lopez, as host, looks after his newly arrived guests, all the more since he has in mind effecting a family alliance with them. The general has no objection to this union, and with Seraphina's consent, takes her hand and joins it with Lucien's. The governor meanwhile lets it be known that he only seems to agree to this marriage, forced by political circumstances and the conqueror's superiority of power, and that he is far from agreeing to it in his heart. As a Spaniard, the governor nurtures within him a hatred for the French, a hatred which was repeatedly the cause of much killing in the latest Spanish wars.

Meanwhile the grandmother quietly asks her grandson if he loves his intended. "No," he answers, "but at least my heart is still free." "You'll manage! You'll manage to fall in love, there is still time," the old woman says, and all three, at Don Lopez's invitation, go out to admire the pic- turesque environs of Saragossa.

SCENE 2.

Lively and merry music announces the arrival of a band of gitanos. They are coming down from the mountains. Covered wagons, litters with belongings, instruments, etc., slowly make their way across the plain. Everyone is joyous and merry in expectation of the impending celebration, but Inigo, their leader, casting his glance about, notices that Paquita, his first, most beautiful and most skillful dancer, is not there. At his order several gitanos retrace the route to find her, but just then she appears on the mountain. Not lifting her downcast eyes from the bouquet she is holding, Paquita slowly descends. Going over to her friends, she shares with them the flowers she has gathered along the way. Inigo is angry and loses his temper at her being late; the others hold him back with difficulty. He gives various orders relating to the celebration, and all go into the tent.

SCENE 3.

Keeping Paquita back, alone with her—he tells her of his feelings, says that on her depends whether he is transformed from a proud and indomitable master into her most devoted slave. Oppressed by her servitude, Paquita nevertheless prefers it to the love Inigo is offering. She recoils, runs, circles, dances in some kind of distraction, as if trying to stifle both Inigo's proposals and the sad feelings which they cast over her. Inigo tries in vain to stop her, and in a rage wants to hit her, but Paquita restrains him with one look, which shows both her indignation and the nobility which she senses within her. Disconcerted, Inigo withdraws.

SCENE 4.

Alone, Paquita takes out a miniature concealed in her bosom, which she has kept since earliest childhood. It gives neither the name nor the country of the person it represents. But to Paquita it seems that the portrait depicts the dear features of the person to whom she is obliged for her life, and with whom she associates all the joys and pleasures of quiet family happiness. Intending to go find her girlfriends, she glances at the surrounding landscape and suddenly stops, as if recognizing in horror the place where bloody events occurred before her very eyes, of which she preserves a faint recollection. It was here, in this very place, that the officer who had been carrying her in his arms fell dead; then unfamiliar people seized her and took her away . . . then . . . But the noise and the gathering crowd of spectators and participants in the celebration upset and disturb Paquita's dreamlike mood and remind her of her sad obligation to her present fate. She goes into the gitano tent.

SCENE 5.

The stage fills up. The general, his mother, Seraphina, and the governor all return and take the places prepared for them. Gitanos dressed for the celebration come out of the tent.

Dances.

Afterwards Inigo, reckoning on Paquita's beauty, orders her to walk among the audience and collect money. Paquita obeys, but timidly, sadly, reluctantly. Passing Lucien, she makes a strong impression. The collection finished, the greedy Inigo is not content despite the young officer's generosity. He wants to increase the take, and reckoning on Paquita again, orders her to begin a dance. But Paquita is not up to it. Less than ever is she disposed to dance; she is sad, she is weary; she refuses. Inigo loses his temper and is about to force her, but Lucien steps forward to protect her and repulses him. Calming Paquita, he studies her more intently. The tenderness of her face, her light complexion, and her nobility astonish him. It all clearly tells him that she is not a gitana, that her life and origins conceal some fateful secret. Lucien takes Paquita to his grandmother, who is likewise astonished at her features and expresses her sympathy. Lucien asks Inigo who she is, and Inigo answers that she is a relative of his. Lucien does not believe him, and asks Paquita herself. Paquita says that one thing can explain as much as anything about who she is and where she came from, a portrait. She begins to look for it, but alas. . . the portrait has disappeared. Inigo foresaw what turn this explanation would take, and frightened by its consequences, stole the medal—he took it from her pocket. In sorrow and despair Paquita blames Inigo. Lucien orders him taken, but the governor and Lucien's relatives intervene and free the gitano. Lucien insists, however, that Paquita not be forced to dance again. The jealous Inigo hardly protests. But Paquita, wishing somehow to express her gratitude for the young officer's sympathy and protection, responding to him with her feelings, and moved by the irresistible instinct of a woman's innocent and most natural desire to be coquettish—Paquita herself now wants to dance. Inigo objects again. Then the governor steps in and orders that Paquita not be hindered in doing what she wants.

Animated by Lucien's presence, she dances with inexpressible charm and fire. Lucien is ever more inflamed with love, and Mendoza, having conceived something fearsome, gladly follows the progress of this passion. Meanwhile he invites the general and his family to dinner, about which his entering servants inform him. The guests depart, but the governor stays behind for a time on the pretext that he must oversee the end of the celebration.

SCENE 6.

One on one with Inigo, he asks him if he is angry with Lucien. "Yes of course," replies Inigo. "And what if I promised not to prosecute you if you killed him?" "Him? Your future brother-in-law?"... "Yes, my future... but that he not be my brother-in-law is why I am putting you up to killing him ... " "But aren't you helping him get together with Paquita?" "There is a point in this," answers Mendoza, "Let Paquita be the unwitting instrument of our vengeance."

SCENE 7.

Paquita comes back, Mendoza goes to his guests. Inigo tells Paquita that he wants to leave, and withdraws into the tent to press his entire band to leave immediately.

SCENE 8.

Paquita is alone, but hardly a moment has passed before Lucien runs in. The young people have fallen in love with each other passionately since their first meeting. Lucien, still taking her for a simple and thus mercenary gitana, offers her money, but Paquita, insulted, refuses it with dignity. Lucien promises to settle her fate in another way, to free her from her bondage, and asks her to come away with him, but this Paquita also refuses, seeing the difference in their stations—the aristocratic Lucien and herself of lowly origin. Lucien begs her at least to let him see her, and as a pledge of this permission asks for the bouquet of flowers she is holding. But Paquita refuses him this also. Chagrined, Lucien withdraws; Paquita feels sorry for him; she repents her cruelty; she runs after him and wants to grant his wish ...

SCENE 9.

But she meets instead with Inigo's derisive and jealous look. He was here, he saw everything, he observed their last declarations. Paquita stops, as if having a premonition that death is threatening Lucien, and wishing under no circumstances to be its cause, she is contented with her conduct, with her unyielding stance from the preceding scene.

SCENE 10.

The governor enters. Inigo tells him of the young people's meeting and the bouquet Paquita refused to give Lucien. The governor immediately conceives a sure plan for Lucien's death, and meanwhile announces the departure of the French general. As if concerned only with seeing him off, he gives various instructions in this regard, and incidentally orders all the peasants to gather flowers and bouquets and present them to his guests as a sign of special esteem to such worthy allies of Spain. Paquita's bouquet, however, he keeps out of the common basket and secretly gives to a young gitana, having instructed her in advance what to do with it.

SCENE 11.

The general, the elderly Countess accompanied by Lucien and Seraphina, all arrive. During the presentation of the bouquets, the young gitana comes up to Lucien and secretly gives him the bouquet. Lucien, delighted, recognizes it as Paquita's. He questions the gitana, who confirms this, and having indicated where Paquita lives, adds that he can see her at any time. Unable to contain himself, Lucien wants immediately to go to the city alone on horseback, and announces this to his relatives. The general and the old Countess do not hold him back, but ask only that he not be late to the forthcoming ball, at which his wedding to Seraphina is to be celebrated. Lucien is hastening to leave, dons a cape for the road, bids farewell and departs. Peasant women surround the governor's guests, while the band of gitanos, led by Inigo and Paquita, also set out on their way. Lucien follows them at a distance. The curtain falls.

END OF THE FIRST ACT.

ACT II.

The interior of a small gitano dwelling. On the left a cupboard; between the cupboard and the hearth a window with closed shutters. A table to the right at the front of the stage. A side door to the right. A clock on the wall, chairs, etc.

SCENE 1.

Paquita enters, sad and pensive. She is dreaming about Lucien. Will she ever see him again?... Suddenly a noise, Paquita opens the shutters; a masked stranger is approaching the house and then walks up the staircase. Suspecting no good, Paquita hides behind the cupboard.

SCENE 2.

The governor, masked, enters with Inigo. The governor is plotting the death of the victim they have marked, who will arrive in just a few minutes. Inigo needs neither advice nor inducement: he has already laid in a narcotic which he shows the governor and which he will mix with the drink of the expected traveler, and at that point he considers that certain death is awaiting Lucien. Inigo hides the drink in the cupboard and locks it, not suspecting that Paquita is following his every move. The governor leaves, giving Inigo a purse for services to be rendered. After this Inigo hails four comrades through the window, who are to be his accomplices in the bloody deed; he gives them part of the payment he received. The crime is to be committed at midnight. Meanwhile Inigo hides two of his comrades behind the wall of the hearth, which moves and rotates to face the courtyard on the other side. Suddenly Paquita, wishing to leave and warn the unfortunate victim against whom this crime is being plotted, brushes against a chair, makes a noise and thus unwittingly reveals her presence. Inigo turns around to see Paquita and takes her by the arm ... death to her if she overheard the secret.... But Paquita claims she only just entered, and Inigo, reassured, lets her go. At this moment someone knocks at the door. There is no longer hope for rescue; the marked victim—Lucien—comes in.

SCENE 3.

Lucien's joy at meeting Paquita; Paquita's horror, convinced that Lucien is the person threatened with death... Lucien asks for lodging for the night. With feigned servility, Inigo thanks him for this honor. Something quite different is to be noted in Paquita's movements and the signs she makes. She asks, as if to say "What are you doing here? Why are you going to your death[?] ... " In response Lucien shows her the bouquet that he thought she sent him. Paquita disclaims it, but in vain. Lucien does not believe and does not understand her. Inigo orders Paquita to serve the guest. Lucien gives Inigo his sabre and Paquita his cloak. As if by accident Paquita throws it in Inigo's face, and meanwhile explains to Lucien the danger which threatens him, but as before, Lucien is indifferent to her admonitions; he sees and thinks only of her, casting caution to the winds. Meanwhile Inigo offers dinner to Lucien, and leaving to make arrangements for it takes Paquita with him, who withdraws still making signs to Lucien—to be careful and prepare for the most imminent danger.

SCENE 4.

By himself, Lucien notices that there really is something strange and suspicious about the house itself and about his host. He goes to the window—it is locked—and to the doors—likewise. He recalls that he had a saber and hunts for it, but it has been hidden. As he thinks of a means of defending himself, the others enter the room again.

SCENE 5.

Paquita enters first with table settings and dishes. Inigo follows. Dinner is prepared. Inigo makes to leave. Paquita signals Lucien to keep him there and not to lose sight of him for a moment. Lucien bids Inigo to eat with him. After lengthy ceremony and servility, Inigo agrees. He pours a glass of wine for Lucien. Paquita gives a sign that he can drink and Lucien heeds it. Meanwhile Paquita, waiting on them, manages to steal Inigo's pistols and removes the priming charges. Not noticing this, but only Paquita's affections and obliging attentions toward him, Inigo proposes that she dance for Lucien. While he goes out for castanets, the young people manage to exchange a number of warning signs. Returning, Inigo pours the remainder of the bottle into Lucien's glass at the same time that his own is still full. As if remembering something, he slaps himself on the forehead, goes to the cabinet and takes out the poisoned bottle as if it were the very best vintage, to which he wanted to treat the young officer. Paquita gives Lucien to know that the bottle is poisoned. Having poured, Inigo invites his guest to drink—but Lucien refuses. At this moment Paquita drops some dishes. Inigo turns around and angrily goes to see what was broken, while Paquita manages to switch the glasses. Everything grows calm, but the roles have been exchanged. Now Lucien invites Inigo to drink with him, to drain the glass at one draught. Inigo, suspecting nothing, agrees. After this, fully certain that his trick and the sleeping draught will succeed as nothing else, he invites Paquita to dance and even dances a native gitano [*tsyganskuyu*] dance with her. During the dance Paquita manages to give Lucien a sign about the number of killers and the hour set for the murder. Moreover, she orders him to pretend he is falling asleep. Lucien obeys and Inigo triumphs, seeing his rival completely in his hands, but suddenly he himself stops, yawns, and unwillingly closes his eyes. In vain he tries to overcome the sleeping draught's effect; he unbuttons his coat, hoping to get some air, and in the meantime he drops Paquita's medallion, which she immediately picks up; then, reeling, he walks over to the table, drops into a chair and falls asleep. At that point Paquita signals Lucien that there is no time to lose and explains the impending danger in detail. Lucien seizes the pistols but alas! they have no priming charges. Lucien looks for his saber, finds it, but what good is it against four killers armed with pistols? While midnight is striking and the hearth begins to turn, a happy thought: Paquita takes Lucien by the hand and runs with him to the hearth; they lean against it, and as it rotates they are carried outside the room—to safety. Meanwhile the killers appear and murder Inigo, mistaking him for Lucien.

END OF THE SECOND ACT.

ACT III.

A magnificent hall in the home of the French commandant of Saragossa. Moorish architecture, furnished in the style of the Empire. A large portrait, with a lifesize figure of an officer in full dress uniform, is hanging at the front of the hall. A ball is in progress after the fashion of the time. Military men of all ranks and ages, courtiers of all classes and both sexes, in the most brilliant dress uniforms and costumes of the Empire period. Besides Frenchmen, there are a few Spaniards in their national dress. At the rise of the curtain they are dancing a French quadrille and a classical gavotte.

Count d'Hervilly enters with his future daughter-in-law and her brother, the governor. The Countess, also present, is astonished at Lucien's long absence. The Count calms her and persuades her not to be alarmed. At his wish the quadrille is begun again. The old woman is still anxious, and by now the Count shares her apprehension. But suddenly the crowd parts, Lucien enters, upset, leading Paquita by the hand. Lucien's tale of the dangers which he escaped arouses general astonishment and joy, and the governor's horror. Meanwhile Lucien explains to whom he is indebted for his rescue, and their feelings for each other. Lucien asks that nothing stand in the way of their union, yet Paquita herself does not wish it, knowing the difference in their stations and social rank. She is content with having managed to save Lucien and wants to leave. Lucien holds her back; in the event of objection he is prepared to follow her everywhere. The Count and the elderly Countess try to dissuade Lucien, especially as the governor is present and is prepared to demand that they keep their word that Lucien will marry Seraphina. But horrors! Paquita looks intently at the governor and clearly recognizes him as the stranger who put Inigo up to the murder. The governor's dismay confirms the truth still more; he is arrested and taken away; Seraphina follows him. Still Paquita will not accept the happiness being offered to her, but again wishing to leave, her eyes happen upon the portrait; she looks at it carefully, takes out her medallion, compares it with the portrait, and—oh joy! oh rapture!—they are both likenesses of her father, and she is the child who escaped death during the frightful occurrence in 1795, to be raised in Inigo's gitano band. The general kisses Paquita; the Countess leads her away. Paquita changes dress. The general gives a signal and the ball recommences.

DIVERTISSEMENT.

Quadrille.
Gavotte.
Pas de fleurs, performed by children.
Pas de cinq.
El Haleo de Cadix.
Galop général.

THE END.

Publication permitted, and upon printing an agreed-upon number of copies to be presented to the Censorship Committee. St. Petersburg, 24 September 1847.

Censor A. Ochkin.

Translation by Roland John Wiley.

Authors' note: The Russian *tsygan* and its declensions (Cyrillic transliterations of the pejorative French *tzigane* and *tziganes*) have been translated using the Spanish *gitano* and its declensions.

(iii) *Paquita* poster, St. Petersburg, 26 September 1847

AT THE BOLSHOI THEATER.
On Friday 26 September,
The court ballet dancers will present:

For the benefit of the dancer M. Frédéric.

For the first time:

PAQUITA.

Grand ballet in three acts; composed by MM. Mazilier and Foucher, produced on the local stage by MM. Frédéric and Petipa; music composed by M. Delvedez and orchestrated by M.K. Lyadov; a new galop of his own composition; — new scenery: 1st and 2nd acts M. Jourdelle, 3rd act M. Wagner; new costumes M. Mathieu.

In this ballet the dancer M. PETIPA, committed to this Theater, for his first debut will play the role of Lucien. The role of Paquita will be played by Mlle ANDREANOVA, for the first time upon her return from Paris.

Dancing in the first act: Mlle Andreanova *Solo*; M. Johanson, Mlles Smirnova and Yakovleva *pas de trois*; Mlles Prikhunova, Grigorieva, Nikitina, Panova, Makarova, Rukhina, Gorina, Kostina, Misheva, Sysoeva, Bormotova, Dushkina 1, Korostenskaya 2, Beleutivtseva and other students and corps de ballet dancers *pas de[s] Manteaux*. — Mlles Andreanova, (students) Sokolova 1, Amosova 1, Radina, Amosova 2, Vinogradskaya 1, Mlle Nikulina and MM. Kusietsov and Rensgausen *pas de neuf*.

In the second act: Mlle Andreanova *Solo*.

In the third act: Mlles Rukhina and Makarova (student) *Contredanse française*; MM. Kusietsov, Reinshausen, Mlles Rukhina and Makarova (student) *la Gavotte*; 32 Small students of the Theater school will dance *pas de fleurs*; M. Petipa and Mlle Andreanova, *Valse pas de la folie*; Mlles Nikitina, Prikhunova (student), Panova (student), Sokolova 1 (student) and Amosova 1 (student) *pas de cinq*; M. Petipa and Mlle Andreanova *El haleo de Cadix*; MM. Petipa, Frédéric and Mlles Andreanova, Prikhunova (student), Nikitina, Panova, Amosova 1 (student), Sokolova 1 (student), Rukhina, Makarova (student) and others (students), corps de ballet women and men *GENERAL GALOP*.

CHARACTERS:

Lucien d'Hervilly	M. Petipa.
Paquita	Mlle Andreanova.
Inigo, the leader of a group of gitanos	M. Frédéric.
Count d'Hervilly, a French general	M. Golts.
Don Lopez de-Mendoza, governor of a province in Spain	M. Spiridonov.
Dona Serafina, fiancée of Lucien	Mlle Samoylova.
The Countess, Lucien's [grand]mother	Mlle Gammer.
Sculptor	M. Artemyev.
Young gitana	Mlle Sokolova (student).

The action takes place in Saragossa and its surroundings.

[*Paquita* was preceded on the program by the one-act vaudeville *The Schoolteacher, or Teaching fools is like healing the dead* by Joseph Philippe Simon, called Lockroy.]

(iv) *Paquita* libretto (excerpt), St. Petersburg, 27 December 1881

PAQUITA.

Pantomime-ballet
in three acts

composed by
MM. PAUL FOUCHER AND MAZILIER.

Produced on the stage by MARIUS PETIPA;
dances put together by the same.

Music by
MM. DELDEVEZ and MINKUS.

St. Petersburg.
Published by Eduard Hoppé,
Typographer of the Imperial Spb. theaters.
1881.

AT THE BOLSHOI THEATER.
On Sunday, 27th December.

BENEFIT OF
Mlle VAZEM.

For the 1st time in revival,
PAQUITA.

Grand ballet in 3 acts, composed by Mazilier and Foucher, revived by the balletmaster
M. M. Petipa; music by Deldevez; instrumentation by K. Lyadov; some numbers newly
composed by M. Minkus; scenery 1st and 3rd acts M. Wagner, 2nd—MM. Egorov and
Lupanov; costume drawings by M. Charlemagne, Mlle Ofitserova
and M. Jurus.

The role of **Paquita** will be performed for the 1st time by Mlle **Vazem**.

Characters:

Paquita	Mlle **Vazem**.
Inigo, the leader of a group of gitanos	M. **Kshesinsky**.
Lucien d'Hervilly	M. **Gerdt 1**.
Count d'Hervilly, a French general, his father	M. **Geltser**.
Don Lopez de Mendoza, governor of a province in Spain	M. **L. Ivanov**.
Dona Serafina, niece of Mendoza, fiancée of Lucien	Mlle **Zest**.
The Countess, Lucien's [grand]mother	Mlle **Legat**.
A sculptor	M. **Chistyakov**.
Gitanos 1	M. **Lukianov**.
2	M. **Voronkov**.
3	M. **Tatarinov**.
4	M. **Orlov**.

Officers, women, cavaliers, peasant women and men, gitanas and gitanos.

The action takes place in Saragossa and its surroundings.

In the 1st act will dance:

ENTRÉE – Mlle Vazem.
SCÈNE DANSANTE – Mlle Vazem and M. Kshesinsky.
PAS DE TROIS – Mlles Johanson, Petrova and M. Karsavin 2.

PAS DE[S] MANTEAUX.

In men's costumes:
Mlles Alexandrova, Vorobyeva, Sokolova 2, Kuzmina 3,
Selesneva, Potaikova, Gruzdovskaya, Predtechina, Olgina,
Nikonova, Ogoleit 2 and Bunyakina.

In women's costumes:
Mlles Zaitseva 2, Kulichevskaya, Matveyeva, Solovieva, Vlekh,
Leonova, Zhukova 2, Nesterenko, Lvova, Andreyeva,
Ogoleit 3, Zakrzhevskaya.

PAS DE SEPT BOHÉMIEN. – Mlles Vazem, Kruger, Nedremskaya,
Simskaya 2, Frolova, Fedorova 2, Troitskaya; MM. Kshesinsky
and Lukyanov.

In the 2nd act.

SOLO – Mlle Vazem.
PAS SCÉNIQUE – Mlle Vazem, MM. Kshesinsky and Gerdt 1.

In the 3rd act:

CONTREDANSE – Mlles Savitskaya, Zest, Kuzmina 1, Polonskaya,
Ushakova, Fedorova 1, Dolganova, Ivanova, Shamburskaya 2,
Leonova, Stepanova, Prokofieva, Menshikova, Potaikova;
MM. Oblakov, Leonov, Picheau 3, Puchkov, Belov, Litvinov, Genzel,
Dyadichkin, Konstantinov, Tatarinov, Kamishev, Akentiev, Lusteman
and Bogdanov.

LA GAVOTTE – Mlles Savitskaya, Zest; MM. Leonov and Oblakov.

MAZURKA:

Girl students:
Shebert, Tatarinova, Isayeva, Sadovskaya, Urban, Slantsova, Stepanova,
Ryabova, Labunskaya, Kuskova, Troitskaya and Vinogradova.

Boy students:
Dorofeyev, Voskresensky, Fridman, Stepanov, Voronkov 1, Fedorov,
Kshesinsky, Petrov, Ivanov, Shiryaev, Navatsky and Gavlikovsky.

VALSE DE LA FOLIE. – Mlle Gorshenkova 1 and M. Manokhin.

GRAND PAS – Mlles Vazem, Shaposhnikova, Zhukova 1, Nikitina,
Johanson, Petrova, Petipa, Ogoleit 1, Simskaya 2, Nedremskaya,
Frolova, Fedorova 2, Grusdovskaya, Zhukova 2, Zaitseva 2,
Glagoleva and M. Gerdt 1 and other women and men dancers, girl
and boy students.

Performing solos:
On the violin – soloist of the court of His Imperial Majesty, M. Auer.
On the flute – M. Keller.

Beginning at 8 o'clock.

[The subsequent libretto is nearly identical in content to the 1847 St. Petersburg libretto but with different prose. Dona Seraphina is now the niece, rather than the sister, of Mendoza. In the first act, "Ballet" replaces "Dances" as the designator of the divertissement. Inigo remains alive at the end of second act, which concludes as follows:]

What to do now?. . . Midnight strikes. The interior wall of the hearth begins to turn. . . A thought occurs to Paquita! The Lord makes it possible for all these snares to serve the victims' good! They push on the wall, and the wall, in its rotation, draws the lovers behind it at the same time it allows the two gitanos to enter the room. . . The two others also enter, one from the window, the other through the doors; astonished, they see Inigo by himself and asleep; they awaken him, shaking him with all their might. Inigo's fury and despair, when he sees that his victims have evaded him. The curtain falls.

[In the third act, the following text is printed after "Divertissement":]

Paquita returns in the costume of her true nationality and dances a *pas* in which all present take part. General finale.

The End.[2]

---

[2] Libretto narrative excerpts translated by Roland John Wiley. See Petipa, M., Ivanov, L., *Imperatorskiy Sankt-Peterburgskiy Bol'shoy teatr, Mariinskiy teatr,* & John Milton Ruth Neils Ward Collection. (1875). *Collection of 36 ballet scenarios, chiefly from the St. Petersburg Imperial Ballet, in the collection of J.M. Ward, [1875–1907]*, Harvard Library, Theatre Collection, GEN TS 5000.10.

Le Corsaire

(i) *Le Corsaire* libretto, Paris, 1856

LE CORSAIRE

BALLET-PANTOMIME IN THREE ACTS

by
MM. DE SAINT-GEORGES AND MAZILIER

Music by
M. A. ADAM

Set designs by
MM. DESPLÉCHIN, CAMBON, THIÉRY AND MARTIN

STAGE MACHINERY BY M. SACRÉ

Performed for the first time in Paris at the Imperial Opera Theater,
23 January 1856.

Price: 1 franc.

PARIS
Mme Widow Jonas, Publisher and Bookseller of the Opera
4, rue Mandar

MICHEL LÉVY FRÈRES	TRESSE, PALAIS-ROYAL
2 bis, rue Vivienne.	Galerie de Chartres.

1856

CHARACTERS.

CONRAD, the Corsair	MM.	SEGARELLI.
SEYD, Pasha of the Isle of Cos		DAUTY.
ISAAC LANQUEDEM, master of a bazaar at Adrianople		BERTHIER.
BIRBANTO, first Lieutenant of the Corsairs		FUCHS.
CHIEF OF THE EUNUCHS of Seyd-Pasha's Harem		PETIT.
SECOND EUNUCH		CORNET.
MÉDORA, a young Greek girl	Mmes	ROSATI.
ZULMÉA, favorite Sultana of the Pasha		L. MARQUET.

GULNARE, Slave of the Pasha of the Isle of Cos	CUCCHI.[1]
MOLDAVIAN WOMAN	CAROLINE.[2]
ITALIAN WOMAN	NATHAN.
FRENCH WOMAN	QUÉNIAUX.
ENGLISH WOMAN	LEGRAIN.
SPANISH WOMAN	L. MARQUET.
BLACK WOMAN	ALINE.[3]
YOUNG SLAVE	CELLIER.
Idem	POUSSIN.
Idem	TROISVALLETS.
ALMEH	PIERRON.
Idem	VILLIERS.
Idem	SAVEL.
Idem	ROUSSEAU.

Eunuchs, Corsairs, Slaves, Imams, Merchants, Buyers, Guards, Sailors, Almehs, Odalisques, etc., etc.

DIVERTISSEMENT.

ACT ONE.

PAS DE CINQ.
Mlles Caroline, Nathan, Quéniaux, Legrain, Marquet.

BACCHANALE DES CORSAIRES.
M. Fuchs; Mlles Pierron, Villiers, Savel, Rousseau.

PAS DES ÉVENTAILS.
Mmes Rosati, Pierron, Villiers, Savel, Rousseau.

ACT TWO.
PAS DE Mme ROSATI.

[ACT THREE.]

DANSES A BORD.
Mme Rosati and the Coryphées.

ACT I.

FIRST TABLEAU.

TWELVE ALMEHS.
Mlles Mercier, Troisvallets, Schlosser, Maupérin, Dieul, Simon, Gaujelin, Poussin, Mathet, Ynemer, Cellier, Pilvois.

---

[1] The French use the phonetic spelling "Couqui" for Claudina Cucchi's name.
[2] Mme Caroline Dominique-Venettozza, born Caroline Lassiat, danced under the name Mlle. Caroline prior to and after her marriage to violinist Dominique Venettozza. As a dance professor at the *Conservatoire de danse*, she was known as Mme Dominique. See AJ[13] 195, personnel de danse.
[3] AJ[13] 193, personnel de danse. Aline Dorsay *dit* Mlle Aline.

TWELVE MUSLIM WOMEN.

Mlles Giraud, Danse, Chambret, Cassegrain, Daufeld, Erivaud, Vibon, Maloubier, Marchand, Gallois, Boin, Villeroy.

FOUR RUSSIAN WOMEN.

Mlles Dujardins, Chatenay, Baratte, Parent.

FOUR CIRCASSIAN WOMEN.

Mlles Chassaignes, Lefèvre, Ducimetière, Mortier.

FOUR ITALIAN WOMEN.

Mlles Fontaine, Jousse, Letourneur,[4] Potier.

FOUR ARMENIAN WOMEN.

Mlles Crétin, Lamy, Gambelon, Devaux.

THREE SLAVE MERCHANTS.

MM. Millot, Monfallet, Bion.
First Buyer, M. Lefèvre.

SIXTEEN CORSAIRS.

MM. Charansonnay, Raimond, Caron, Dieul, Duhamel, Gendron, Libersac, Gilles, Scio, Pisarello, Estienne, Darcount, Faucher, Meunier, Gondoin, Caré.

SIX FEMALE SLAVES.

Mlles Malgorne 2, Corinne,[5] Meunier, Letellier, Dubelly, Decamps, Prévot.

FOUR VEILED WOMEN.

Mlles Garcy, Dufour, Collet, Rossi.

EIGHT YOUNG MOORISH BOYS.[6]

MM. Barbier, Bretonneau, Moutet, Andrieux, Letourneur 1, Letourneur 2, Letourneur 3, Agasse.

SIXTEEN YOUNG MOORISH WOMEN.[7]

Mlles Marcus 1, Toutain, Tarlé, Delionaix, Brach 1, Piogue, Rebard, Hairivau, Fiocre 2, Thibert, Porral, Andrieu, Pilatre, Robert, Baugrand, Marcus 2.

ELEVEN BLACK MALES.[8]

MM. Michand, Lefèvre 2, Duhamel 3, Barbier, Leroi, Mami, Duport, Bertrand, Gabillot, Carey, Rousseau.

---

[4] Élise-Anaïs Tourneur, dite Letourneur, AJ¹³ 491, personnel de danse.

[5] Aimée Meunier, dite Corinne, AJ¹³ 491, personnel de danse.

[6] Personnel records suggest that the cast members listed here are boys from the ballet school. Also, one of the entries in the costume ledger is for "Ballets garçons Musulmans." Unfortunately, the list does not indicate a specific number. See AJ¹³ 196, 479, 490, and 500.

[7] The costume list for these characters in AJ¹³ 500 is probably one containing a scribal error. The copyist wrote "Coryphées 16 Nymphs," crossed out the word "nymphs," but made no correction. Furthermore, the word "nymphs" reappears in the recapitulation pages, however there are no nymphs in this ballet. Additionally, according to the personnel records, these were students from the school between twelve and sixteen years of age. See AJ¹³ 490, 491.

[8] The costume list in AJ¹³ 500 for this role indicates both men and boys. The costume drawing and the personnel records, suggest that all of these were boys from the school. See AJ¹³ 197, 490, and Bibliothèque-musée de l'Opéra D 216 (21) ff. 37.

SIX YOUNG EUNUCHS.[9]
Mlles Malgorne 1, Sibillisse, Dulert, Fontaine, Motteaux, Julien.

FOUR MERCHANTS, TEN BUYERS, TWENTY CORSAIR GUARDS.[10]

Danse des Corsaires.
M. Fuchs; Mlles Pierron, Villers, Savel, Rousseau; MM. Charansoney, Raimond, Caron, Duhamel, Gendron, Libersac, Dieul, Gilles, Siot, Pissard, Estienne, Darcourt, Faucher, Meunur, Gondoin, Caré.

[SECOND TABLEAU.]

THIRTY-TWO WOMEN.
Mlles Mercier, Troisvallets, Schossler, Maupérin, Simon, Gaujelin, Poussin, Mathet, Ynemer, Cellier, Giraud, Pilevois, Danse, Chambret, Cassegrain, Danfeld, Dieul, Erivaud, Vibon, Dujardins, Chassaigne, Lefèvre, Ducimetière, Mortier, Maloubier, Crétin, Gallois, Boin, Marchand, Fontaine, Jousse, Letourneur, Potier, Lamy, Gambelon.

Pas d'Éventail[s].
Mmes Rosati, Pierron, Villiers, Savel, Rousseau, Mercier, Troisvallets, Schossler, Maupérin, Simon, Gaujelin, Poussin, Mathet, Ynemer, Cellier, Giraud, Pilvois.

[ACT II.]

Danse des Odalisques.
Mlles Mercier, Troisvallets, Schossler, Maupérin, Simon, Gaujelin, Poussin, Mathet, Ynemer, Cellier, Giraud, Pilevois, Danse, Chambret, Cassegrain, Danfeld, Dieul, Erivaud, Vibon, Dujardins, Chassaigne, Lefèvre, Ducimetière, Mortier, Maloubier, Crétin, Gallois, Boin, Marchand, Fontaine, Jousse, Letourneur, Potier, Lamy, Baratte, Gambelon, Chatenay, Villeroy, Devaux, Parent, Marcus, Toutin, Tarlé.

SIXTEEN HAREM BATHERS[11]
Mlles Malgorne 1, Garry, Julien, Dufour, Rossi, Malgorne 2, Collet, Bulies, Corinne, Fontaine, Letellier, Prévost, Dubelly, Moteny, Sivelisse, Decamps.

Pas de Mme ROSATI.
Mlles Gaujelin, Mathet, Ynemer, Giraud, Pilvois, Danse, Chambret, Danfeld.

TWENTY DERVISHES.
MM. Charansonney, Raimond, Caron, Duhamel, Gendron, Libersac, Dieul, Gilles, Scio, Millot, Monfalet, Pissarello, Estienne, Darcourt, Faucher, Bion, Meunier, Gondoin, Lefèvre, Caré.

FOUR BLACK MALES.
MM. Michand, Carret, Duhamel, Barbier

---

[9] This is a travesty role, and according to AJ[13] 500 these are *figurants*, or extras. Personnel records suggest these were also students from the school. See AJ[13] 490, 491.

[10] The number of corsair guards is uncertain. AJ[13] 500 contains a costume list for sixteen corsairs, but no list for corsair guards. There is, however, a list for twenty dervish costumes, and most likely the same cast members dressed as corsairs in Act One were disguised as dervishes in Act Two. Therefore, the number of corsair guards is probably four and not twenty.

[11] Personnel records suggest that these were *figurantes* and students around sixteen years of age. See AJ[13] 490 and 491.

TWENTY-FOUR GUARDS OF THE PASHA,[12] TWENTY PILGRIMS,
TWO CAMEL DRIVERS, FOUR GIAOURS.[13]
Extras.

[ACT III.]

[FIRST TABLEAU.]

TEN BLACK MALES.
MM. Duhamel, Barbier, Carret, Leroy, Mamy, Bertrand, Gabillo, Rousseau, Lefèvre.

TEN GUARDS OF THE PASHA, FOUR THURIFERS, SIX PRIESTS.
Extras.

[SECOND TABLEAU.]

TWENTY CORSAIRS.
Men of the Corps de Ballet.

FIFTEEN CABIN BOYS.
Students from the Classes.

SIXTEEN SLAVES.
Women Coryphées.

LE CORSAIRE

BALLET-PANTOMIME IN THREE ACTS.

ACT ONE.

FIRST TABLEAU.

A square in the city of Adrianople. In the center, a slave market.

FIRST SCENE.

Beautiful slave women are lying on mats and couches.

Turks, Greeks, and Armenians are smoking in the middle of the square as Egyptian dancers [*Almehs*] dance in front of them.

Merchants display splendid fabrics.

SCENE II.

A troupe of Greek corsairs, preceded by Conrad, their chief, enters the market.

Conrad tells his men to maintain silence and sobriety; he seems to be looking for someone in the bazaar.

A veiled woman comes out onto the balcony of one of the houses in the square.

It is the beautiful Medora, the ward of an old renegade Jew, Isaac Lanquedem, master of the bazaar.

---

[12] According to costume report in AJ[13] 500, there are twelve guards of the Pasha.
[13] There is no costume listing for the camel drivers or the *giaours* in AJ[13] 500.

When she sees the handsome corsair, the young lady partially opens her veil, then removes flowers from her hair and bodice and forms them into a *selam*, or speaking bouquet, in which each flower translates a thought or sentiment.

She throws the bouquet to Conrad, who expresses his joy in reading therein Medora's love.

The young lady leaves the balcony.

Conrad gathers his corsairs and gives them secret orders.

SCENE III.

Isaac and Medora appear in the bazaar; the Jew examines his different clients and haggles over some slaves, which he himself also sells.

Meanwhile, Conrad and Medora exchange knowing looks.

SCENE IV.

A march is heard, and from a sumptuous litter emerges the Pasha from the Isle of Cos.

Seyd-Pasha is a worn-out, blasé, and powerfully rich old man. He's coming to replenish his harem, and he looks at the slaves with the eye of a connoisseur.

To attract the rich amateur, the merchants have women from all countries dance before him. But the Pasha remains unmoved; nothing pleases him. One is too fat, another is too thin, this one is too tall, that one is too short. He is getting ready to leave when he sees Medora.

All of a sudden his face lights up.

She and she alone is the one he wants to buy.

The Jew refuses to sell his ward.

[*Pas de cinq.*]

The Pasha offers him treasures, and the renegade seems to capitulate to his conscience.

Conrad follows this scene with a worried expression. He seizes his tablets, writes a few words on them, and slips them to Medora to inform her of the dangers threatening her.

Medora becomes upset when she reads; but with an energetic gesture, Conrad reassures her he will watch over her; he will save her!

The Pasha, who is increasingly smitten with the beautiful Greek woman, offers the renegade Isaac so much gold and precious stones that he decides to conclude the shameful transaction.

The Pasha leaves to gather his servants in order to take Medora away. But, before leaving the bazaar, he approaches her, pays her compliments, and leaves looking at her longingly.

Fearfully, the young Greek woman rushes to Conrad; she feels that with him there is refuge, a protection for her!

Conrad signals his pirates to surround Isaac, and they obey, while overwhelming the Jew with comic politeness.

Meanwhile, the Corsair swears to Medora that he will take her away from the old master to whom she is being given. He throws some gold to the young Almehs and gives a sign for a joyous and animated dance between them and the corsairs. Then, leading Medora, they both join with the other dancers.

The Jewish woman participates, laughing, despite Isaac's protestation and the Pasha's displeasure when he has returned looking for his captive.

[*Danse des Corsaires.*]

All of a sudden, the Corsair takes off his gold serape, which he flashes in the eyes of his companions. When they see this, the corsairs seize the beautiful dancers in their arms and quickly carry them away, fleeing to all sides.

Conrad takes possession of Medora, whom he presses to his heart in defiance of the Pasha.

The Jew comes running after his niece. — *What difference does it make,* says the Corsair, *take him away also!* indicating the Jew to his men.

Some of the corsairs take Isaac away despite his resistance and flee with their prey, while the Pasha remains alone with his stunned and dismayed eunuchs.

SECOND TABLEAU.

A subterranean palace, a vast and magnificent dwelling, where there are piles of dazzling riches: precious armor, splendid fabrics, jewels of all kinds, and vases of gold and silver.

FIRST SCENE.

Black men burn perfumes and prepare everything for the entrance of their lord and master.

SCENE II.

Conrad appears bringing the beautiful Medora, his charming conquest.

The young girl examines everything with a curiosity mingled with fear.

Conrad reassures her. He will make her queen of this subterranean place, just as he himself is king of the sea and waters. He expresses to her his passion, his happiness.

— *But why*, says Medora, *a state so terrible? Why is death always in your heart? The dagger in your hand?*

Won't you now live for the one who loves you?

Conrad responds that for her he can renounce everything, his savage glory, his riches that he augments every day.

— *I would give all that*, he says to the beautiful Greek woman, *for one word from your mouth, for one look from your eyes!* . . .

— *In that case, my lips will open only to bless you*, replies Medora, *and my eyes will only look at you with tenderness and gratitude.*

Conrad leaves with Medora.

SCENE III.

Birbanto, the chief pirates, and the renegade Isaac brought along by them, come settle down around the grotto.

The captive old Jew is pale and trembling.

A crimson curtain rises to reveal Conrad the Corsair, half-lying on a tiger-skin bed.

Medora is at his feet.

Conrad smokes his chibouque, his arm wrapped around Medora's neck as she looks at him with love.

SCENE IV.

The captives taken away from the Adrianople market and from other shores, who consist of Greek, Spanish, Italian, and Muslim women, are brought to the Corsair.

The women process in front of the chief, who looks at them with indifference, as he only has eyes for his love, the charming Medora.

The weeping young girls throw themselves at Conrad's knees and beg him for mercy.

But the pirate pushes them away and orders them to join Medora in a brilliant dance that the beautiful Greek prepares to dance for him.

Pas des éventails.

Medora takes advantage of the Corsair's admiration by asking him to free the beautiful prisoners.

Conrad has a moment of indecision, but he cannot resist the pleas of the one he loves. He orders that the women be granted their freedom.

But Birbanto, the lieutenant, gathering the chief corsairs around him, argues that these women are part of their booty and that they have a right to divvy them up.

They all move threateningly toward Conrad.

The Corsair's look becomes terrible.

He forces back the mutineers with a powerful gesture.

These fierce men are ready to revolt.

But Conrad grabs the arm of Birbanto, who is the boldest of them all, forces the rebel to bend down in front of him, and throws him to his knees.

At this act of strength, the pirates acknowledge their master and bow down before him.

On a signal from Conrad, all of the grotto doors open at once, and the joyous prisoners rush outside like a flock of birds returning to their freedom.

Conrad leaves embracing Medora and is followed by the humbled and repentant pirate chiefs.

SCENE V.

Birbanto and some of the corsairs remain alone in the grotto with Isaac, who is terrified by this somber group . . .

— *Come here*, says Birbanto to Isaac. *You have nothing to fear from us; on the contrary, you must take back your ward, this enchantress who already has too much power over our chief's heart. You must deliver us from her; in a word, buy her back from us.*

— *How horrible*, cries the dismayed Jew, *sell my own ward to myself!*

— *You wanted to sell her to Seyd-Pasha! . . .*

— *She was my property.*

— *She's ours now, since we stole her from you.*

— *But how can you sell her to me? I have nothing, I'm broke, ruined! . . .*

— *You're lying*, says Birbanto, *and you're hiding what you possess.*

They take off his hat and coins fall out of it.

Pearls fall out as they take off his gown, and diamonds cascade out when they take off his sash.

— *Now*, says Birbanto, laughing at him, *here is the payment for your captive. She is yours, we give her back to you.*

— *And how can that be?* cries Isaac with surprise.

— *Look*, the pirate says to him, *and don't move! . . .*

The pirate picks a bouquet of *lotus flowers* from the shrubs that decorate the grotto.

Then, mysteriously showing the renegade a small gold bottle, which he pulls from his breast pocket, *he pours the contents from the bottle on the lotus flowers.*

He then approaches a pirate standing guard at the door and makes him smell his bouquet.

The pirate immediately shows signs of sleepiness.

He spreads out his arms, closes his eyes, collapses, and falls asleep.

— *See!* says Birbanto to the astonished renegade, *now come*, he adds, rapidly leading him away, *the beautiful Medora is yours! . . .*

SCENE VI.

It is time for Conrad's supper.

A splendidly appointed table is brought into the room.

The Corsair reappears with Medora, shows her the table, and invites her to sit down.

But first, he dismisses his slaves in order to be alone with his beloved.

A love scene commences between them.

Medora refuses to sit next to Conrad.

It is she who will serve him.

Increasing her efforts around her lord, she refills his glass, presents him with sorbet, and brings in his chibouque.

All this attention is intertwined with gracious dancing and kisses the Corsair steals from her.

A curtain silently rises.

A young girl appears, carrying on a gold dish the *fatal lotus bouquet*, on which Birbanto has poured his powerful sleeping potion.

The young girl, guided by Isaac, approaches Medora, asks that she give the Corsair the bouquet, and leaves right away.

Medora takes the fatal bouquet.

She presses it for a moment against her heart, as if to give it greater value in the eyes of her lover.

She then presents it to the Corsair.

Conrad accepts it with love.

He presses the bouquet onto his lips and deliciously inhales the perfume.

But no sooner does Conrad smell the fatal aroma, than his entire body becomes languid.

He passes his hand over his eyes as if to drive away the sleep invading him.

But the urge to sleep is stronger.

Little by little Conrad succumbs, and his head falls back onto the ottoman cushions.

Medora looks at him with tenderness.

She will keep watch over her lover while he sleeps.

Soon a faint noise is heard.

The beautiful Greek woman listens, and sees, with fear, two men with veiled faces appear at one of the grotto doors.

She gets up, nervous and troubled.

Two new men come in by a second door, then two more men.

Filled with dread, Medora rushes to the Corsair, whom she tries in vain to awaken.

But Conrad's sleep is beyond her efforts.

The men advance, threatening her with their daggers.

— *What do you want from me?* she asks.

— *To take you away from this man*, they reply, pointing to Conrad.

— *You will never separate me from him!* cries Medora, grabbing the dagger of the sleeping Conrad.

Bold Birbanto tries to disarm [Medora], who stabs him in the arm, making a deep and painful wound.

Birbanto, still more enraged at the sight of his blood, is about to rush toward his prey again. But he thinks he hears a noise, forcing him, like his companions, to go check at the back of the grotto that there are no witnesses to their crime.

Medora takes advantage of this moment to hastily write a few lines on the tablets that Conrad had given her at the market on the Isle of Cos, and to place them under the sleeping Conrad's hand.

The pirates return, surround the young girl, throw a veil over her head, and take her away despite her efforts, followed by Isaac, who rubs his hands together and appears delighted by the success of the ruse.

Meanwhile, the sleeping Conrad brings the lotus bouquet that Medora had given him close to his lips and kisses the flowers with love.

END OF ACT ONE.

ACT TWO.

The Pasha's palace on the Isle of Cos. — The baths of the Pasha's women, in the middle of magnificent gardens. — The view of the baths is obscured by immense draperies.

FIRST SCENE.

The Pasha's women get out of the bath and finish dressing.

Some are braiding their long hair; others, seated in front of mirrors held up by slaves, crown their heads with flowers and pearls.

Others, wrapped in their vast dressing gowns, choose their apparel from among the tunics presented to them, while others frolic among themselves.

Zulmea, the favorite sultana, is in the midst of the odalisques and receives their attention haughtily. The odalisques express their resentment at being forced to obey the imperious sultana.

[Danse des Odalisques.]

SCENE II.

After this mixed tableau of dances, Gulnare, Zulmea's young rival in the Pasha's heart, comes in.

All of the odalisques prefer the charming Gulnare to the arrogant sultana; they laugh at the orders she gives them, and also make fun of the eunuch by dancing around him.

— *This is a complete revolt*, says the furious eunuch; *thanks to this hothead here*, he adds pointing to Gulnare; *but the Pasha will restore order.*

SCENE III.

Seyd-Pasha appears, surrounded by his ministers.

He is still furious about his mishap at the Adrianople bazaar; he wants to take his anger out on everyone.

He walks in, scowling and his face infuriated.

The first eunuch comes complaining to the Pasha about the revolt by the women in the harem.

Zulmea, for her part, also complains about the insolent Gulnare, who has failed to show respect to the favorite sultana.

The women take turns complaining about the favorite sultana's arrogance.

The poor Pasha doesn't know to whom to listen.

Stunned by all this arguing, he consults his ministers.

— *Should I cut off their heads?* he says. *After that, I'd have to look for others, and it would be the same thing all over again.*

He has the rebels approach; they advance with a proud and mocking expression, encouraged by the young Gulnare.

The Pasha orders them to bow down in his presence, and to pay homage to his favorite sultana, who looks at them with a triumphant expression.

Initially intimidated by their master's fury, they all bow their heads before the sultana, except the foolish Gulnare, who laughs in the Pasha's face, stands up to him, and seems to defy her master.

Far from being afraid, she dances gaily around the sultan, who is stunned by her audacity.

But the old man, charmed in spite of himself by the young girl's attractions, gradually softens, decides against the first eunuch and Zulmea, and in his admiration for the pretty slave, offers her the head of the first eunuch. . . a gift that Gulnare hastens to refuse.

Zulmea takes offence at her master's preference; she loses her temper, the sultan laughs at her, and, attracted, seduced, and swept away by Gulnare's coquettishness, he throws his handkerchief to her, to the delight of the harem and even greater fury of the sultana Zulmea.

Gulnare picks up the precious handkerchief with a false humility, then throws it back to one of her companions, who throws it back to another and, bouncing and ricocheting, the handkerchief ends up arriving thus at an old Black woman, who is amazed at such an honor.

Zulmea is avenged on her unfaithful lover.

The Pasha furiously moves toward Gulnare, but she makes an ironic bow and briskly runs off with her crazed companions. The Pasha foams with anger. . . he does not know whom to blame, and orders the beating of the poor eunuch, who is trembling with fear.

SCENE IV.

Zulmea's triumph is short-lived, because no sooner does the Pasha begin to become pleasant to her again than a slave merchant is announced, and the old renegade Isaac appears bringing by force a veiled woman.

This woman is Medora.

The Pasha is overjoyed at being reunited with the beautiful Greek woman who had been taken away by the corsairs.

Zulmea notices with fear the Pasha's intense emotion. From this moment onwards Medora has acquired another enemy.

Medora demands justice, from the Pasha, from the despicable Isaac. . . . But when she sees the Jew receive the price of her freedom, she grabs the Pasha's dagger, and goes to stab the renegade. . . She is immediately disarmed, and the frightened Isaac flees, while the Pasha roars with laughter at the poor wretch's terror.

SCENE V.

Gulnare and the Pasha's women come to examine with curiosity their new companion, finding a thousand flaws in her, and criticizing her beauty. But when she sees tears in the eyes of the new captive, Gulnare quickly rushes to her, takes her hand, and reassures her. Meanwhile, as the Pasha gives orders to his eunuchs, the two young women come to understand one another, become friends, and seem to join forces against their common master.

The Pasha shows his new slave to Gulnare and tells her that Medora is the one he will love henceforth.

— *She will love you no more than I do*, replies Gulnare, *neither her heart nor mine belong to you.*

— *We will see about that*, says Seyd.

He has chests full of jewelry and precious fabrics brought to Medora, but Medora refuses them all, rejecting everything, to the great joy of Gulnare, and even greater anger of the Pasha.

SCENE VI.

The scene is interrupted by lots of activity that is taking place in the harem gardens . . .

A long caravan of pilgrims and dervishes on their way to Mecca process across the back of the gardens.

The chief of the caravan is an old man, a pious dervish who comes to ask the Pasha for hospitality for himself and his men.

The pious dervish appears quite troubled when he sees himself surrounded by the harem women.

He modestly lowers his eyes and turns them away from the seductive beauties! . . .

Old Seyd, amused by the holy man's comic embarrassment, commands his women to raise their veils before this worthy [pious man].

He quickly moves away from them with indignation.

The Pasha laughs even more and allows the caravan to rest in his gardens.

Then, he finds it amusing to continue his test of the holy dervish's virtue; he wants to show him all the joys of the harem.

At his command, a ballet commences.

Gulnare dances with her companions before the dervish, who becomes increasingly nervous.

Then comes Medora's turn, who refuses to join in this game.

But a mysterious sign from the dervish has changed her resolve; she has recognized her lover; joy replaces despair; intoxicated with happiness, she dances in turn, fluttering around the dervish, whose attention toward the beautiful odalisque immensely entertains the Pasha.

[Pas de Mme Rosati.]

But the scene soon changes.

Night approaches, and Seyd orders his eunuchs to take away Medora, his new favorite.

They come forward to seize her, when, seeing that Medora is about to faint, the dervish lets the gown covering him fall, and reveals himself as Conrad, the Corsair.

"We see his chainmail and shine the lightning of his sword. His sparkling eyes, his gloomy face, make him appear in the eyes of his enemies as an infernal genius, the blows of which it is impossible to escape."[14]

The Corsair rushes toward the back of the stage, grabs the horn he carries in his belt, and blows it, producing a brilliant sound.

At this signal, the pilgrims, the dervishes, and the entire fake caravan strip off their pious clothes, and appear, like their chief, dressed in combat attire.

The corsairs' daggers are drawn, muskets shine in their hands . . .

[14] This quotation is from a French prose translation of *The Corsair*. However, the librettists omitted the equivalent of the second line of the original poem: "His close but glittering casque, and sable plume." Byron, *The Corsair*, Canto II/4.

Chaos reigns everywhere, one fray commences in the middle of the gardens.

Seyd runs away, frantic, full of terror, followed by his women and his court.

Conrad clasps Medora, who is dying of fear and happiness, to his heart.

She holds on to him and implores him to follow her... But the Corsair resists; he will only leave the battle after victory.

At this moment, a frightened woman, pursued by Birbanto, rushes up to Conrad and begs him to protect her.

It is the young Gulnare.

Tearful Gulnare comes looking for a refuge with the victorious Corsair.

Conrad, touched by Gulnare's tears, reassures her and takes her under his protection. He is not waging war with the women, but against the person who wanted to take Medora away from him!

During this scene, and at the sight of Birbanto, Medora, struck by a dreadful memory, seems to recognize in the lieutenant of the pirates a resemblance to the masked bandit who had kidnapped her from the grotto.

Medora circles around the bandit and examines him carefully. His height, his looks, all strike her, all make her shudder with horror.

Her suspicions increase at this examination, and the desire for a just revenge appears in Medora's expression.

Her decision is made; she will reveal the traitor to Conrad's anger.

The Corsair has just ordered Birbanto to leave.

But just as the bandit is getting ready to depart, he finds himself face to face with Medora, pale with contempt and anger.

Medora detains the scoundrel and brings him back trembling before Conrad.

She explains to the Corsair about her kidnapping and the cruel threats to which she had yielded.

She recalls the terrible scene in which she was overpowered by her kidnappers and ends by designating Birbanto as the chief of these villains.

Conrad's eyes fill with rage; he orders Birbanto to justify himself.

He brazenly denies the crime of which he is accused.

— Well then! says Medora, *dare to swear it before the heavens, which will crush you if you are lying.*

The bandit hesitates for a moment, then he comes to a decision; and lifting his hand, he makes the oath demanded of him.

Medora grabs the arm of the perjurer to stop him; but when she puts pressure on his arm, the bandit feels a sharp pain; it is the arm that Medora had stabbed.

— *It is he! It is he!* cries Medora; and quickly lifting the scoundrel's sleeve, she shows Conrad the wound that she had given him in the grotto.

Dismayed, trembling, the convicted bandit acknowledges his crime.

— *On your knees,* Conrad then says to him, *on your knees before your victim, you wretch!* and forces him to fall at Medora's feet.

Pulling a pistol from his belt, he points it at the bandit's forehead and is getting ready to fire... when Gulnare and Medora hold back his arm. And the bandit, getting up quickly, takes advantage of this moment of respite to flee, while making menacing gestures at them.

SCENE VII.

Exhausted by so many different emotions, Medora is ready to faint into the arms of her lover; but Gulnare's attentions, and the Corsair's tenderness help her overcome this moment of weakness. She is getting ready to leave with Conrad, when Seyd-Pasha's guards, rallied by the traitor Birbanto, slip into the gardens, surround Medora, and rapidly carry her away, while the Corsair receives the gratitude of the young Gulnare for having snatched her away from his men.

Conrad soon realizes his new misfortune; he is about to run, to rush after Medora's kidnappers... but the number of his enemies overwhelms him.

The Pasha, glowing with happiness, grabs his formidable enemy, who stands disarmed in the midst of a circle of rifles where his chest is the center.

—*Spare him!* cries Gulnare, falling to Seyd's knees.

Impervious to her prayers, and to those of all the harem women surrounding him, Seyd-Pasha orders that his enemy prisoner be put to death, and Conrad leaves throwing Seyd looks of contempt.

TABLEAU.

END OF ACT TWO.

ACT THREE.

FIRST TABLEAU.

The Pasha's apartment, in an elegant pavilion. The window shows a view of the sea. An immense door at the back of the stage.

FIRST SCENE.

Seyd-Pasha is holding court, surrounded by his great dignitaries.

He orders the first eunuch to bring Medora to him.

SCENE II.

Seyd-Pasha has Medora come forward.

— *Choose between my throne, my hand, and the life of the one you love*, he says to her.

Medora refuses this shameful agreement.

A lugubrious march is heard, and Conrad is seen walking in chains on his way to his execution.

Medora rushes toward the Corsair and begs the Pasha to postpone the execution.

— *I'll agree to it*, says Seyd; *Tell him my conditions; his fate is in your hands.*

On a sign from the Pasha, the condemned man is brought forward; and Seyd leaves, giving Medora one last threat.

SCENE III.

The Corsair and Medora fall into each other's arms.

— *Why this reprieve of my execution?* he asks Medora.

— *So that you can live, if you want*, she replies to him.

Conrad is astonished when she explains the price that Seyd is putting on his salvation.

Conrad prefers death one hundred times to the infidelity of the one he loves.

— *Well then*, Medora says to him, *we will die together, because I will not outlive you!*

SCENE IV.

The end of this scene is overheard by Gulnare, who has slipped into the pavilion.

She then comes closer and tells the lovers that there is another course of action to take, another way of saving them.

— *It is you who protected me against your treacherous pirates*, she says to Conrad. *The time has come to show you my gratitude.*

Accept the life that Seyd-Pasha offers you, noble Conrad; accept his proposal, beautiful Medora, and you shall not be less happy.

The Corsair and Medora are astonished.

But Gulnare takes them each aside and confides something mysterious to them.

An expression of joy and hope immediately shines on their faces, and they clasp in turn the hands of their benefactress angel with deep gratitude.

SCENE V.

Seyd reappears.

— *Should he live or should he die?...* he asks Medora, pointing to Conrad.

— *I cannot fight you*, Conrad says to him, *my love and my roaming life are not worth the throne that you are offering her.*

Medora makes a sign of submission.

The Pasha is intoxicated with joy and conveys his happiness to those surrounding him.

Meanwhile, Conrad, Gulnare, and Medora have conferred among themselves.

After a new oath to take care of them, made by Gulnare to the two lovers, Conrad tells Medora that at midnight he will rescue her from her captivity.

— *At midnight*, he repeats to her; *until then, keep watch over my happiness.*

— *Let him go*, says Seyd, pointing to Conrad, *and let no one dare to make an attempt on his life.*

Conrad leaves, along with [the guards] surrounding him, and repeats, by a sign to Medora, the promise of his return.

SCENE VI.

Everything takes on a festive air.

Gulnare accompanies Medora, whom the Pasha lovingly designates as the queen of these premises.

As soon as the two young girls have left, the Pasha orders the preparations for his wedding.

He then has chests full of riches brought in, the contents of which he joyfully distributes to his odalisques.

SCENE VII.

Joyous music is heard; it is the wedding march.

Ministers, eunuchs, and odalisques come gather around the Pasha.

First, young Almehs enter throwing flowers before them, then thurifers carrying fragrant incense burners, followed by the priests, the imams leading the Pasha's fiancée.

The young girl is covered by a long muslin veil, embroidered with silver, which covers her completely. But, when she walks in front of the audience, she quickly lifts the veil, and lets the audience see that it is Gulnare, who has taken the place of Conrad's beloved.

The Pasha leads her before the great mufti, who is situated close to a portable Oriental-style altar, and on which burns the sacred fire.

He utters prayers over the bowed couple, as the Almehs dance around them.

The young odalisque presents her hand to the Pasha, her face still hidden under her long veil, and Seyd places the wedding ring on the finger of his new wife.

He then offers her his hand to lead her back to his living quarters.

SCENE VIII.

Everything is being prepared for the wedding night.

The Pasha hopes to demonstrate his love by the sumptuous preparations.

Vases of flowers are carried in, along with lit incense burners. A gentle darkness prevails in the pavilion, and it is with a heart full of love and tender emotion that Seyd awaits the hour, so desired, for his happiness.

SCENE IX.

A door curtain mysteriously rises, and the young Almehs lead in the beautiful fiancée, still covered by her thick veil.

Seyd orders the young women to leave.

He remains alone with his new wife, or rather with the one he believes he married.

He lovingly comes close to her and wants to lift the veil that hides her from him.

The young girl modestly refuses.

But Seyd insists, and soon the veil falls to his bride's feet.

But it is no longer Gulnare hiding from the attentions of the amorous Pasha; it is Medora herself in the most seductive attire.

Her scarcely hidden charms intensify Seyd's passion.

The light creature flutters and leaps around the transported Pasha.

From time to time, she reveals her impatience at seeing the time pass so slowly. But the hour of her deliverance has not yet chimed.

Suddenly she seems struck with terror when she sees the sumptuous dagger that Seyd carries in his belt. She shows it to the Pasha and feigns the greatest fear.

The gallant Pasha offers it to her right away; but Medora's terror seems to increase at the sight of Seyd's pistols.

He places them, like the dagger, in the beautiful Greek woman's hands.

He then goes to seize her; but she flees from him again, and her dancing becomes still more brilliant and lively.

The Pasha falls to Medora's feet, clasping his hands together, begging her to listen to him at last.

Medora seems struck by a foolish and charming idea when she sees Seyd stretch his hands out to her.

She quickly takes off the gold gauze sash wrapped around her slender waist, and, laughing, she tightens it like a bond to tie her admirer's hands.

At first, the Pasha laughs at this folly, but he thinks the knot chaining him is tied a little too tight.

At this moment the clock strikes midnight, the window spontaneously opens, and Conrad appears at the window, his eyes terrible and menacing.

Seyd, pale and trembling at this sudden apparition, sees with fear the dagger that he was carrying offered to the Corsair by Medora.

Seyd is about to rush to the back of the stage and call for help, when Medora seizes the Pasha's pistols, points them at him, and threatens him with death if he makes a move or lets out a cry.

Then, protecting thus the flight of the Corsair who carries her to the window, they rush to safety through it. The window closes all of a sudden behind them.

Seyd-Pasha, who has successfully freed his tied hands, runs to his bronze bell, and strikes it with fury.

At this noise, all of the doors open.

SCENE X.

Rushing from all sides, the guards and all of the harem women appear at the same time.

The Pasha shows the window to his guards.

The window is violently opened; but the balcony is empty, and the sound of three canon shots is heard in the distance.

The fugitives have disappeared. They are returning to the pirate ship that calls and waits for them.

Seyd-Pasha's fury is at its peak; they are taking away the one he loves, in essence, his wife, even!

— *Your wife*, says Gulnare, who appears to him, and shows him her ring, *it is I!... I am your wife and the queen of these premises.*

At this revelation, the astonished Pasha falls crushed with anger and astonishment, while all of the harem women bow and kneel down before Gulnare, who proudly shows them her wedding ring.

SECOND TABLEAU.

The sea.

The sky at the horizon.

An immense ship, the pirate vessel, floats in the midst of waves barely stirred by the evening breeze.

Conrad is sitting on the bridge of the ship, holding his beloved in his arms.

A few female slaves are lying here and there.

Seamen and corsairs are smoking on the bow of the ship.

A beautiful and pleasant evening presides over this moment of happiness purchased by Conrad and Medora at the cost of so many storms.

They are saved at last and are returning to their blessed grotto.

Conrad shows Medora the land off in the distance.

Pirates and sailors appear on the bridge, summoned by Conrad.

He wants to celebrate, by a party on board, his and Medora's fortunate deliverance.

He distributes gold to his pirates, has a barrel of rum brought to the bridge, and the joyous sailors draw full cups from the barrel.

This celebration of drinking is followed by a more gracious one.

Young Greek women surround Medora, and an aerial and poetic dance replaces the corsairs' drunken merriment.

[*Danses à bord.*]

Conrad, transported anew by the grace and charms of his beloved, presses her against his heart and pledges to her his eternal love, surrounded by his crew who bear witness to this solemn vow.

At this moment, clouds slowly descend over the water and extinguish the last of the evening light.

Thunder dully rumbles.

Conrad grabs his megaphone and summons his crew to the bridge.

The thunderstorm is moving closer across the sky, carrying with it threat and terror.

Flashes of lightening illuminate the seagoing vessel with their sinister glow!

Everyone springs into action for the common good!

They run to the sails, the mast, and the rudder.

The tempest increases . . . the sea lifts its waves toward the sky!

The sinister sound of the alarm canon is heard.

The ship rises and falls with a horrible violence.

Cries of agony and horror resound.

Lightening explodes and strikes the ship, breaking it partially open.

Next, a horrible scene commences. With their arms lifted toward the heavens that they have so often cursed, the pirates ask God for help and mercy.

But God wants to engulf this hoard of bandits in a single blow.

A fearful snap is heard.

The ship fills with water. . . the waves wash over the sides.

Conrad and Medora, all of the pirates, their wives with their children in their arms, hurled from front to back, tossed about by the tempest, see with despair the ship sinking little by little into the great abyss, and they soon disappear with it into the depths of the ocean that closes above them.

EPILOGUE.

The sea has subsided! The waves have engulfed the formidable ship and its terrible occupants.

The wave has covered everything like a vast shroud.

A clear and brilliant moon appears coating the sea in silver from its shining reflection, and from this vivid and fantastic light, the last debris from the submerged vessel is seen.

It is a floating piece of debris, lost in the midst of the immense wave.

Two human creatures are still attached to it, clinging hard to each other.

It is Conrad; it is Medora, who have miraculously escaped from the shipwreck.

Their pure love has without a doubt touched the one before whom they swore eternal love.

The wind blows them toward the shore, where a protective lighthouse shines.

They reach it at last and fall to their knees to give thanks to the heavens.

From this day onward, the terrible Corsair is never seen again;[15] love has inspired him to repent... repentance, undoubtedly, has given him peace and happiness!

THE END.

Translation and footnotes by Willa Collins.

Authors' note: The libretto and notes below represent a lightly edited version of the translation in Willa J. Collins, *Adolphe Adam's Ballet Le Corsaire at the Paris Opéra, 1856–1868: A Source Study* (PhD diss., Cornell University, 2008), 404–429.

Translator's note: In translating the *Corsaire* livret [libretto], I have made some modifications to give a clearer understanding of the contents than the original 1856 publication. For example, there are certain spelling inconsistencies in the front matter, which produced various spellings of cast members' names. Thus, whenever possible, dancers' names have been verified from personnel records at the [Paris] Archives Nationales (AJ[13] 193–194, 477–480, 485–486, 490–491). Additionally, since some of the names on the personnel files and the documents therein are not always spelled consistently either, I have spelled the names according to the dancers' signatures in their contracts. Names of cast members with various spellings that I was unable to verify, or who did not have a personnel file in the Archives Nationales, have been left as they appear in the printed livret. All dancers are listed by surnames as they appear in the livret, unless provided with an explanatory footnote. Dancers with the same surname are ranked in the order in which they were hired, (i.e., Parent 1; Parent 2; Parent 3, etc.).

---

[15] "And Conrad came not, came not since that day..." Byron, *The Corsair*, Canto III/24.

(ii) *Le Corsaire* libretto, St. Petersburg, 1858

LE CORSAIRE,

PANTOMIME BALLET

in three acts
and
five scenes,

MM. SAINT-GEORGES AND MAZILIER.

Put on stage by Imperial St. Petersburg Theater Balletmaster
M. Perrot.

THE DANCES ARE NEWLY COMPOSED BY HIM.

Music
Adam and M. Pugni.

Scenery: 1st Act 1st scene M. Roller, 2nd scene M. Wagner, 2nd act M. Roller,
3rd act 1st scene Petrova, 2nd scene M. Wagner. Machines M. Roller.

SAINT PETERSBURG
By the publishing house of N. P. Bogdanov.
1858.

PRINTING IS ALLOWED:

In order that, after printing, the legal number of copies would be presented to the Censoring
Committee. Saint Petersburg. 4 January 1858.
Censor *V. Beketov.*

LE CORSAIRE.

Pantomime Ballet.

CHARACTERS:

Conrad, Corsair	*M. Petipa.*
Seyd, Pasha	*M. Perrot.*
Isaac Lanquedem, the bazaar owner	*M. Picheau.*
Birbanto, one of the main Corsairs	*M. Frédéric.*
Caretaker of Seyd Pasha's harem	*M. Stukolkin 1.*
Medora, a young Greek woman	*Mlle Friedberg.*
Zulma, the Pasha's beloved Sultana	*Mlle Troitskaya.*
Gulnara, the Pasha's Slave	*Mlle Radina.*
Black woman	*Mlle Gundorova.*
Slaves	*Mlles Prikhunova,*
	Amosova 1,
	Amosova 2 and the rest.

LE CORSAIRE.

ACT I.

FIRST SCENE.

Eastern bazaar.

SCENE I.

Buyers and sellers watch the women dance.

SCENE II.

Enter a crowd of corsairs and their leader, Conrad. Medora, the ward of the owner of the bazaar, the Jew-renegade Isaac, shows herself on the balcony.[16] She opens her veil and, seeing the Corsair, puts together a *selam* (a so-called explanatory bouquet, in which each flower has the meaning of a particular word) and throws the bouquet to Conrad. Reading Medora's love in it, he becomes ecstatic and gives secret commands to his companions.

SCENE III.

Isaac and Medora come to the bazaar, and while her guardian trades slave girls for resale, Medora and Conrad exchange glances.

SCENE IV.

Seyd-Pasha, the chief of the island, appears at the bazaar to buy slave women for his harem. The traders force their slave women to showcase their skill in dances, but not one of them attracts the Pasha's attention. Only at the sight of Medora does an expression of joy appear on his face. He wants to buy her. At first the Jew refuses, but the Pasha's offers are so enormous that he begins to waver and finally agrees to sell his ward.

Conrad and Medora observe the Pasha and the Jew. The corsair calms Medora with the promise that he will steal her from the old admirer. At his command, the corsairs begin a merry dance with the women. To the great displeasure of the Pasha, Conrad and Medora also join in the dance.

At a sign from Conrad, the corsairs abduct Medora and the dancers. The Jew runs after his ward...

"In that case, take him, too," commands Conrad. Isaac is whisked away, and the Pasha is left in grief with his entourage.

SECOND SCENE.

The Corsair's Dwelling.

SCENE I.

The servants, waiting for their master, make preparations for his arrival.

SCENE II.

Very soon Conrad and Medora appear. Medora looks over Conrad's abode with curiosity and some apprehension. Conrad encourages her, promising that she will be the mistress of these underground places, just as he is master of seas. "But for what?" objects Medora, "to live always with a dagger in your hands? Live now for me alone!" Conrad answers that for her sake he is ready to renounce his dangerous fame and his riches, which grow greater every day, and will gladly give it all up for only one word from her, for only her glance. "If that is so, I will bless you," answers Medora... They both exit.

---

[16] The libretto text uses the pejorative "zhid" for "Jew."

SCENE III.

Birbanto and the rest of the corsairs bring in Isaac, who is beside himself with fear. A curtain opens and Conrad and Medora are seen behind it.

SCENE IV.

The corsairs bring in the stolen slave women, who beg Conrad for mercy. He orders them to begin dancing.

Fan dance.

Taking advantage of Conrad's delight, Medora asks him for the release of the slave women. He agrees, but Birbanto and his comrades rebel against his decision, demanding that the slave girls and the rest of the booty be shared.

In a terrible rage, Conrad forces Birbanto to beg forgiveness. The corsairs bow before him, open the doors, and the slave women run free.

Conrad exits with Medora, accompanied by the corsairs who are loyal to him.

SCENE V.

Birbanto and a few corsairs stay behind with Isaac.

"Come here, Isaac," says Birbanto, "you have nothing to fear. We want to return your ward to you. Give us a ransom for her." "How is that possible?" exclaims the Jew. "You want to sell me my own property." "But you sold her to the Pasha." "But she is mine." "She was yours and now she is ours. We stole her from you." "But what money can I buy her with? I'm broke. I have nothing left!" "You lie," says Birbanto. "You have hidden your riches."

They take off his hat and coins pour out; they tear off his caftan and pearls fall out; they untie his belt and diamonds pour out.

"There is your ransom. Take Medora!" "But how?" protests Isaac... "Look," says Birbanto... and, plucking a bouquet of flowers, he takes out a small glass apothecary's bottle and sprinkles the bouquet. When he offers it to a pirate standing watch, he immediately falls asleep.

"Did you see?" says Birbanto. "Come with me: Medora is yours."

SCENE VI.

A table set for supper is carried in. Conrad, entering with Medora, dismisses the slave women, and remaining alone with her, invites her to sit next to him, but she prefers to serve him, and bringing him drink, sherbet, and a pipe, dances next to him.

A slave girl enters with Isaac, and offering a bouquet of flowers, asks Medora to give it to Conrad. He takes the bouquet from the hands of his beloved, but the smell of the flowers suddenly makes him fall asleep. Soon Medora hears footsteps. Suddenly two men appear at one of the entrances. She gets up from the couch in confusion. Another two men enter from another door, then another few. She wants to wake Conrad, but his sleep cannot be overcome. The men who have entered threaten her with daggers.

"What do you want with me?" asks Medora.

"We want to take you away from him."

"No, I will never leave him!" shouts Medora, grabbing the dagger of the still-sleeping Conrad.

Bold Birbanto wants to disarm her, but she wounds him.

The enraged Birbanto throws himself at his prey, but hearing some noise, exits with his comrades.

Taking advantage of the moment of freedom, Medora writes down a few words and puts a note into the hand of sleeping Conrad.

The bandits return and carry away Medora. Isaac rejoices at this success.

ACT II.

The garden at the Pasha's Palace.

SCENE I.

The Pasha's wives, coming out of the baths, finish their toilette. Zulma, the Pasha's favorite wife, is the one who commands the slave girls, who are unhappy with her proud manner.

SCENE II.

Gulnare, her competitor, enters. The slave girls surround her, laughing at Zulma's anger.

SCENE III.

At the entrance of Seyd-Pasha, Zulma and the keeper of the harem complain to him about the slave girls, who in their turn complain about Zulma.

The Pasha orders the slave girls to submit to Zulma, but Gulnare, unafraid of threats, enchants the Pasha with her cheerfulness; now he blames Zulma and the keeper, and, to calm Gulnare down, he offers to cut off the keeper's head, but she does not agree to this.

Zulma is enraged. The Pasha, carried away by the enchantments of Gulnare, throws her a handkerchief, to the general delight of the harem.

Gulnare, picking up the handkerchief, throws it to one of her friends, who in her turn passes it to one of her friends, and so on. The handkerchief, going from hand to hand, finally arrives at an old Black woman.

Zulma is avenged.

The Pasha, in terrible anger, approaches Gulnare, but she laughs at him and runs away with her friends.

The Pasha's anger falls on the poor keeper.

SCENE IV.

Zulma's triumph does not last: the Pasha has scarcely turned to her when a servant reports the arrival of a slave-girl trader. Old Isaac enters and shows him Medora. The Pasha delightedly sees the return of the slave who was stolen by the corsairs. Medora begs the Pasha... but seeing that he rewards Isaac, she tears the Pasha's dagger away from him and throws herself at Isaac, who runs away in fear. Medora is disarmed; the Pasha laughs at the Jew's fright.

SCENE V.

Gulnare and the other women run in to see their new companion. First they feel jealousy, but seeing Medora's tears, Gulnare, in a gesture of friendship, treats her kindly.

The Pasha announces that he is in love with Medora. "She will not love you, just as I do not," says Gulnare. "We will see ...," retorts the Pasha, and he offers Medora costly gifts, but she refuses everything, to the joy of Gulnare and the great anger of Seyd.

SCENE VI.

A caravan traveling to Mecca appears in the garden. The leader of the caravan, an old dervish, asks to spend the night. The Pasha allows the caravan to stay in the garden and, amused by the embarrassment of the dervish, who has been surrounded by odalisques, commands them to take off their veils in front of the servant of Mohammed and begin dancing. Gulnare and her friends fulfill the command of their master; only Medora does not want to take part in the fun, but, recognizing the old dervish as her beloved, she joyfully submits to the wish of the Pasha. Soon, however, Seyd commands his new slave girl to be taken to the inner chambers. Medora is ready to faint, but Conrad and his comrades, throwing off their dervish costumes, cause the Pasha and his servants and slave girls to take flight.

A woman runs in, pursued by Birbanto. It is Gulnare. Triumphant Conrad, touched by her tears, announces that he has armed himself not against women, but against the abductor of Medora!

Medora, looking closely at Birbanto, who, seeing her, tries to escape, and recognizing in him her abductor, catches hold of him and tells Conrad about his act of betrayal.

Birbanto refutes her accusations, but Medora shows Conrad the bandit's wound, which she delivered with her own hand.

Conrad wants to shoot the robber; Medora and Gulnare hold him back, and Birbanto runs away, threatening Medora with vengeance.

SCENE VII.

Exhausted Medora is ready to faint, but with the help of Gulnare and Conrad she comes to [her senses] and already wants to follow them, when suddenly Seyd's guards, rallied by the betrayer Birbanto, surrounding Medora, abduct her again, and Conrad is unable to defend her against such a force on his own.

The Pasha, ignoring Gulnare's pleas, commands Conrad be taken to be executed.

ACT III.

SCENE I.

The Pasha's room, with a view to the sea.

SCENE I.

Seyd-Pasha, surrounded by his cronies, demands that Medora be brought to him.

SCENE II.

He proposes that Medora become his wife in order to save Conrad from death. She refuses his proposal with contempt.

Conrad is being taken to be executed. Medora begs Seyd to postpone the execution. "All right," he says, "but his fate is in your hands."

SCENE III.

Conrad flings himself into Medora's arms. She explains to him on what condition the Pasha has agreed to pardon him.

Conrad prefers death.... "So then let us die together," exclaims Medora. "I won't outlive you."

SCENE IV.

Gulnare, hearing their conversation and approaching the lovers, says that she has a way to save them and tells them to agree to the Pasha's demand. She secretly tells each of them her plan and they are convinced by her words.

SCENE V.

Seyd returns and asks what their decision is.

Conrad announces that, being unable to resist, he must agree to the Pasha's proposal.

Medora is also ready to submit. The Pasha is triumphant and gives the command to free Conrad, who walks away from those who surround him, promising with signs that he will help free Medora.

SCENE VI.

The Pasha commands preparations for his wedding; both friends [Medora and Gulnare] walk away; with joy, the Pasha gives jewelry to the odalisques.

SCENE VII.

Wedding procession. Imams lead the bride; she is veiled, but as she passes the audience, she opens her veil so that, instead of Conrad's beloved, they see that the bride is Gulnare.

After the ceremony, the Pasha leaves with the supposed Medora to his rooms.

SCENE VIII.

Soon female servants enter and after them the Pasha with his new companion, still under the same veil. At the command of Seyd, all leave. Remaining alone with his wife, he wishes to remove her veil; after some resistance, the veil falls and instead of Gulnare, Medora appears beneath the gaze of the Pasha.

She entrances the Pasha with dances, but at times it is noticeable how impatiently she waits for the hour of her deliverance. Suddenly she is horrified by the sight of a dagger at Seyd's waist. The Pasha, in love, happily hands it over to Medora, and when her fright grows at the sight of his pistols, he gives them to her as well. Seyd wants to embrace his bride, but she slips away from him in gentle dances. Seyd falls at her feet, and she, as if jokingly, takes off her sash and uses it to tie the hands of her admirer, who, at first, laughs at her antics. Midnight strikes, the window opens suddenly, and Conrad appears.

Seyd is horrified, seeing Medora give his dagger to Conrad. He wants to call for help, but Medora, aiming the pistols at him, threatens him with death for the slightest shout and exits through the window with Conrad.

Seyd-Pasha, finally untangling the sash binding his hands, rings, and all the doors open.

SCENE IX.

All of Seyd's house runs in. The Pasha points at the window. They open it, but the balcony is empty. In the distance, three cannon shots are heard. Seyd is furious: his beloved wife has been stolen.

"I am your wife," says Gulnare, "here is your ring!" Seyd is in shock.

SCENE II.

The Sea.

The corsair's ship; Conrad and his beloved are on the deck.

The night is lovely.

Conrad wants to joyfully celebrate Medora's deliverance. The young slave girls surrounding Medora begin to dance.

Soon the sky is covered with clouds, thunder rumbles, lightning flashes, the sea rages. All fall to their knees, praying for salvation, but providence is just and wants to simultaneously punish all of the offenders. Lightning strikes the ship, and it sinks beneath the waves.

EPILOGUE.

The sea has calmed. By the light of the moon the floating wreckage of the ship is seen, and on one of the pieces, two living figures.

It is Conrad, it is Medora, miraculously saved from the general disaster.

Their pure love softened the anger of the heavens.

They come ashore and, falling to their knees, offer thanksgiving for their salvation.

Translation by Stephan Sveshnikov.

(iii) *Le Corsaire* poster, St. Petersburg, 12 January 1858

PERFORMANCE *No.* 38.
On Sunday 12 January,[17]
The court ballet dancers will present:
FOR THE SECOND TIME:

LE CORSAIRE.

Grand ballet pantomime in 3 acts and 5 scenes by MM. Saint-Georges and Mazilier (after the poem by Lord Byron), staged and all dances newly composed by balletmaster M. Perrot; music by Adam and M. Pugni; new scenery for the 1st and 3rd scenes by M. Roller, for the 2nd and 5th by M. Wagner, for the 4th by M. Petrova; machines by M. Roller, new costumes by M. Calvert; electro-galvanic illumination and lightning by M. Shishko, chemist of the Imperial Theaters.

Will dance in the 1st scene: Mlle Katerina Friedberg *Solo*; Mlle Victoria Kozlovskaya, students Lyadov, Kosheva; MM. Bogdanov, Volkov and Troitsky—Spanish *pas Aragonnaise*. In women's costumes: Mlles Lapshina, Apolonskaya, Kostina, Sheryaeva 2, Petrova 2, Fedorova 2, Vasilieva 2, Pavlova 1, Shishko, Bochenkova, Pavlova 2, Godovikova; in men's costumes: Mlles Ignatieva, Pukhina 2, Pribilova, Fedorova 1, Sokolova 2, Pavlova 3, Shulgina, Korostinskaya, Liadova 1, Zenkova, Shebert, Nikolaevskaya and other dancers—*Danse des Pirates, Ballabilli d'action*.

In the second scene: Mlles Katerina Friedberg, Nikitina, Efremova, students Lyadova, Kosheva and other dancers *pas des eventailles*; Mlle Katerina Friedberg and M. Petipa *Scène dansante*.

In the third scene: Mlles Prikhunova, Amosova 1, Amosova 2, and other dancers *Pas des odalis-ques*; Mlle Radina 3 and M. Perrot *scène de seduction*; Mlle Katerina Friedberg *Solo*.

In the fourth scene: Mlle Katerina Friedberg and M. Perrot *scène dansante*.

In the fifth scene: Mlle Katerina Friedberg, M. Petipa and other women and men dancers.

CHARACTERS:

Conrad, a corsair	*M. Petipa.*
Medora, a young Greek woman, ward of Isaac	*Mlle Kat[erina] Friedberg.*
Seyd-Pasha	*M. Perrot.*
Birbanto, one of the chief corsairs	*M. Frédéric.*
Zulma, the beloved sultana of the Pasha	*Mlle Troitskaya.*
Gulnare, the Pasha's slave	*Mlle Radina 3.*
Isaac Lanquedem, owner of the bazaar	*M. Picheau.*
Keeper of Seyd-Pasha's harem	*M. Stukolkin.*
Black woman	*Mlle Gundorova.*
Slaves of the Pasha	*Mlle Prikhunova.*
	Mlle Amosova 1.
	Mlle Amosova 2.

Merchants selling slaves, corsairs, slaves, Arabs, Mauritanians, etc.

STARTS AT 7 O'CLOCK.

---

[17] The poster for the premiere performance on 9 January 1858 could not be located.

(iv) *Le Corsaire* program, St. Petersburg, 13 January 1899

1899

MARIINSKY THEATER

PROGRAM.

On Wednesday, 13th January,
BENEFIT of Mlle PIERINA LEGNANI.

The Artists of the Imperial theaters will present:

FOR THE 1ST TIME IN REVIVAL:

LE CORSAIRE

Ballet in 4 acts (five scenes), by MM. St-Georges and Mazilier.
(plot based on the poem by Lord Byron).

Music by Adam and C. Pugni.

Dances and production newly staged by balletmaster M. Petipa.

Act 1 — "The Kidnapping of Medora". Act 2 — "The Conspirators".
Act 3 — "The Corsair's Captivity". Act 4, Scene 1 — "The Pasha's
Wedding". Scene 2 — "Storm and Shipwreck".

SCENERY: 1ST ACT—M. ALLEGRI; 2ND ACT—M. SURENYANTS; 3RD
ACT—EXECUTED BY MM. SHIRYAEV AND LUPANOV AFTER DRAWINGS BY M.
LAMBIN. 4TH ACT, 1ST SCENE—M. VOROBYEV; 2ND SCENE—M. LAMBIN.
MACHINIST—M. BERGER.

COSTUMES BASED ON SKETCHES BY M. PONOMAREV; SCULPTOR'S ACCESSORIES BY
M. KAMENSKY.

The role of "Medora" will be performed Mlle Pierina Legnani.

CHARACTERS:

Conrad, a corsair	*M. Gerdt.*
Medora, a young Greek woman, ward of Isaac	*Mlle Legnani.*
Seyd-Pasha	*M. Bekefi.*
Birbanto, one of the chief corsairs	*M. Kshesinsky 2.*
Zulma, beloved sultana of the Pasha	*Mlle N. Petipa 2.*
Gulnare, the Pasha's slave	*Mlle Preobrazhenskaya.*
Isaac Lanquedem, owner of the bazaar	*M. Lukyanov.*
Caretaker of Seyd-Pasha's harem	*M. Voronkov 1.*
Black woman	*Mlle Solyannikova.*
Mufti	*M. Solyannikov 2.*

Merchants: *MM. Marzhetsky and Fedorov 1.*

Corsairs, slaves, eunuchs, Turkish officers and soldiers,
imams, merchants, buyers, sailors, cabin boys, Black people, almehs, odalisques
and others.

WILL BE DANCED:

In the 1st act:

1) **Danse des esclaves:** Mlles Pavlova, Slantsova, Bakerkina and Vasilieva.
2) **Entrée:** Mlle Legnani.
3) **Pas de l'esclave:** Mlle Rykhlyakova 1 and M. Legat 1.
4) **Finesse d'amour:** Mlle Legnani; MM. Gerdt, Bekefi and Lukyanov.
5) **Danse des corsaires** (ballabile d'action): *Slaves:* Mlles Kshesinskaya 1, Slantsova, Pavlova, Bakerkina, Vasilieva, Shchedrina, Kasatkina, Lits, Porokhovnikova, Rubtsova, Konetskaya, Grupilyon, Goncharova; *Corsairs:* MM. Kshesinsky 2, Kusov, Medalinsky, Fedulov, Smirnov 1, Oglev, Ivanov 2, Titov, Kiselev, Romanov, Vasiliev, Aolin, Presniakov.

In the 2nd act:

6) **Danse des Forbans:** Mlles Skorsyuk, Trefilova, Borkhardt; MM. Shiryaev, Obukhov, Osipov.
7) **Grand pas des éventails:** Mlle Legnani and M. Kyaksht; Mlles Nikolaidis, Dorina, Urakova, Levina, Porokhovnikova, Shtikhling, Legat, Golubeva 2, Stepanova 3, Vsevolodskaya, Sazonova, Ilyina 3.
8) **Scène dansante:** Mlle Legnani and M. Gerdt.

In the 3rd act:

9) **Entrée des odalisques:** Mlles Nikolaidis, Urakova, Dorina, Levina, Egorova 1, Porokhovnikova, Yakovleva 2, Grupilyon, Radina, Ryabova, Shtikhling, Golubeva 1.
10) **Scène d'espièglerie:** Mlles Preobrazhenskaya, Petipa 2, Solyannikova; MM. Bekefi and Voronkov 1.
11) **Pas de trois des odalisques:** Mlles Sedova, Gordova, Egorova 2.
12) **Le jardin animé:** (Music by L. Delibes) Mlles: Legnani, Preobrazhenskaya, Trefilova, Borkhardt, Chumakova, Ofitserova, Vaganova, Fonareva, Kasatkina, Bakerkina, Pavlova, Matveyeva 3, Rykhlyakova 2, Vasilieva, Konetskaya, Erler 2, Stepanova 2, Ilyina 3, Golubeva 2, Sazonova, Sitnikova, Erler 1, Bastman, Mikhailova, Alexandrova 2, Pakhomova, Semenova 2, Stepanova 4, Simonova, Rakhmanova, Postolenko, Goryacheva; MM. Kristerson, Legat 2, Maksimov, Balashev, Alekseyev, Tikhomirov 2, Smirnov 2, Ponomarev, Ivanov 3, Voronkov 2, Levinson, Maslov. Girl and boy students of the Imperial Theater School.

In the 4th act:

1ST SCENE:

13) **Scène dansante de caractère:** Mlle Legnani and M. Bekefi.

2ND SCENE:

14) **Danse à bord du vaisseau:** Mlle Legnani, M. Gerdt; Mlles Svirskaya, Grigorieva, Simonova, Maslova; Messrs. Kshesinsky 2, Kusov, Aslin, Medalinsky, Presnyakov and Vasiliev.

Will perform solo: on violin — *M. Kruger.*
On French horn — *M. Solsky.*
Conductor *R. DRIGO.*
Beginning at 8 pm.

For the convenience of the public, the Directorate of the IMPERIAL theaters
humbly asks all ladies occupying seats in the chairs and amphitheaters
to take off their hats when entering the auditorium.

Typographer of the Imperial SPb. theaters, Mokhovaya, 40

La Bayadère

(i) *La Bayadère* libretto, St. Petersburg, 1877

LA BAYADÈRE.

BALLET

IN FOUR ACTS AND SEVEN SCENES

with

APOTHEOSIS,

BY M. Petipa.
MUSIC BY M. Minkus.

Presented for the first time at the IMPERIAL Spb.
Bolshoi Theater on 23 January 1877.

St. Petersburg.

EDITIONS EDOUARD HOPPE,

Typographer of the Imperial Spb. Theaters.

1877.

Dramatis personae:

Dugmanta, rajah of Golconda.
Hamsatti, his daughter.
Solor, a wealthy and important *kshatriya* [a warrior of the royal caste].
Nikia, a bayadère.
The Great Brahmin.
Madgavaya, a fakir.[1]
Taloragva, a warrior.[2]
Four fakirs.
Six kshatriyas.
Two attendants of Hamsatti.
A slave woman.

Brahmins, Brahmacarins, Sudras (servants of the rajah) warriors, bayadères, fakirs, pilgrims, Indian people, musicians and hunters.

Permitted by the censor, St. Petersburg, 12 January 1877.

---

[1] The cast list in the libretto and 1877 poster give the spelling as "Madgavaya" (using Latin-alphabet transliteration), but "Magdavaya" is used in the libretto text and later programs.
[2] The cast list in the libretto gives the spelling as "Taloragva," but the libretto text, poster, and subsequent programs give the spelling as "Toloragva."

ACT ONE.

Scene I.

The Festival of Fire.

The stage represents a consecrated forest, branches of bananas, amlas, magdavis and other Indian trees are intertwined among each other. At the left a pond designated for ablutions. In the distance, the peaks of the Himalayas.

The wealthy kshatriya Solor (a famous warrior) enters with a bow in his hand. Hunters are pursuing a tiger. At a sign from Solor, they run across the stage and are lost in the depths of the forest.

Solor lingers for a time and commands the fakir Magdavaya not to leave this place, that he might find occasion to say a few words to the beautiful Nikia, who lives in a [nearby] pagoda.

Then Solor exits.

The doors of the pagoda open and from the temple the Great Brahmin emerges triumphantly; behind him follow munis [monastic wise men], rsi [seers], Brahmacarins (Indian priests), and finally gurus in long linen garments. All the priests wear [pendants made of] cords on their foreheads—a sign of brahminesque rank.

From the pagoda also emerge *devadasis* (bayadères of the first rank).[*]

They are making preparations for the festival of fire. By the side of the pagoda, and on its very galleries gather fakirs, yogas, *fadins* (wandering holy people).

— "Where now is our modest bayadère Nikia?" the Great Brahmin asks. "I do not see her here. Order her to be called. She must adorn our spiritual procession with her dances."

Several bayadères go out after Nikia. Penitents handle the iron and the fire, touching them to their bodies. Some have daggers, sabres, knives and other sharp instruments which they brandish; others hold burning torches.

The fakir Magdavaya also takes part in the dance, but in doing so never stops looking for the beautiful Nikia.

At last the bayadère appears in the doors of the pagoda, wrapped in a veil.

Illuminated by the reddish light of the torches, she attracts the general attention.

The Great Brahmin walks up to her, lifts her veil and orders her to take part in the dances.

Nikia comes down from the steps of the pagoda and begins to dance.

The dance "Djampo".

Then the sounds of the turti (bagpipes) and the vina (a small guitar) serve to accompany the graceful and languorous movements of the bayadère. These movements become more lively and fast, the orchestra positively thunders, and the previous dance is taken up again.

During this time the Great Brahmin does not take his enamoured gaze from the beautiful bayadère.

While she is dancing he walks up to her and says:

— "I love you... I am going mad with love for you... do you want me to protect you?... I will make you first in our temple... I shall force all the people to worship you!... You will be the goddess of all India... Only... return my love!"

Nikia takes from him his brahmin's cord.

— "You are forgetting who you are!" she says, "look at this cord!... It is a sign of the high rank which you hold... I do not love you and never will."

---

[*] Bayadères are charged with looking after the pagodas; they live inside these pagodas and study with the brahmins.

In horror she pushes him back.

— "Ah!" the Great Brahmin exclaims... "Mark well that I shall never forget this insult... this terrible offense!... I shall use all my powers to take revenge on you!... And my vengeance will be frightful! ... "

Nikia tries to get away. She goes with the other bayadères and, like them, fills her vase from the sacred pond and gives drink to weary travelers and those who took part in the dances.

The fakir Magdavaya continues his original dance and his fanatical flagellation.

Nikia goes up to him and offers water to cool him.

The fakir takes advantage of the opportunity and says to the bayadère:

— "Solor is nearby... He wants to see you."

Nikia is delighted with this news.

— "Let him approach as soon as the celebration ends," she answers. "I will be at the window... Knock three times, and I will come out."

— "Fine, I understand. Only quiet! They can hear us."

The fakir resumes his tortured dance, and Nikia walks away as if nothing had happened.

The ceremony ends. The brahmins order the bayadères back into the temple. Everyone leaves the stage.

The moon comes up. The windows of the pagoda are dark.

Solor enters with the fakir, sits down on a pile of rocks and anxiously awaits the appearance of his beloved bayadère.

A light appears in one of the windows of the pagoda.

The pleasant sounds of a vina (guitar) are heard.

Solor approaches the window slowly and knocks three times. The window opens and Nikia appears in it, holding a guitar.

The fakir crawls along some branches and places a plank beneath the window, along which the bayadère descends, illuminated by the moonlight.

Solor falls at her feet, then embraces her. They are happy.

— "I love you," Nikia says, "you are courageous!... What grief it is that we cannot see each other often! ... "

— "I cannot live without you," Solor answers, "You are the air I breathe... my life! ... "

— "Yes, but what is to be done?... Look at these garments, I am a bayadère! I must keep order in the pagoda. I was destined for this calling since childhood. I cannot give it up... You are my only consolation in life."

The Great Brahmin appears in the doors of the pagoda. He finds the lovers embracing. In a burst of jealousy and wrath he wants to rush over to them but holds back, promising vengeance. He hides and listens to their conversation, then exits.

— "I have found a way we can attain happiness," says Solor. "Let us flee. In a few days I shall come for you... I am rich... You have only to agree! ... "

— "I cannot refuse you... I agree! Only swear to me before this temple that your heart will never belong to anyone else but me, that you will love me your whole life! ... "

— "This I swear to you, and I call on Brahma and Vishna as witness, that I shall remain true to you my whole life! ... "

— "Wonderful, remember your vow... If you forget it, all possible misfortune will pursue you."

— "Look though, it is beginning to dawn; we must part."

At this moment the fakir runs in with the news that the hunters are returning.

The doors of the pagoda open, and the bayadères come out to the pond for water.

Unnoticed, Nikia hurriedly enters the pagoda, and Solor watches as she appears again at the window. Having heard the girls approach, Solor hides among the trees.

The hunters in triumph bring in a tiger they have killed. The kshatriya Toloravga tells Solor how they managed to fell the wild animal, but Solor listens distracted, and looks pensively at his beloved's window.

Finally he orders the hunters to return home and goes with them, reckoning on returning soon.

Nikia throws Solor a kiss from her window, and on her instrument begins to play the same melody as before.

The Great Brahmin again appears in the doors of the pagoda. He calls on all the gods as witness to his future vengeance.

ACT TWO.

Scene II.

THE TWO RIVALS.

The stage represents a magnificent hall in the palace of the rajah Dugmanta.

The rajah is sitting on a tiger skin, on pillows. He orders the bayadères to be called to entertain him, and proposes to one of the *kshatriyas* to play a round of chess.

During the rajah's play at chess—a *divertissement*.

After the dances, the rajah sends for his daughter Hamsatti, who enters with her girlfriends.

— "Today, my child," says Dugmanta, "the day of your marriage with the brave warrior Solor will be decided. It is time for you to marry."

— "I agree, Father... Only I have yet to see my bridegroom... and I am not sure if he will love me."

— "He is my subject!... He is obliged to fulfil my commands!... Call him!"

A few minutes later Solor appears. When he enters, the rajah's daughter covers her face with a veil.

— "It seems you have long known already," says the rajah turning to him, "that in a few days your marriage to my daughter will take place."*

— "But sire," Solor answers in confusion, "I am not yet prepared to do this."

— "In childhood you were proclaimed Hamsatti's bridegroom, and now you must marry her. Come here, my daughter!"

The girl walks up to her father, and he removes her veil.

— "Behold, Solor!... Is she not beautiful!... Is she not the finest pearl in the universe!... I am sure you will be happy with her."

Solor looks, and is indeed struck by the girl's beauty, but recalling his beautiful bayadère, to whom he swore eternal love, he suddenly turns away.

— "You are a brave *kshatriya*," the rajah continues. "I entrust to you the fate of my lovely child, and am certain that you, as no other could, will carry out your duty as it relates to your future wife, marriage with whom shall be your happiness."

Solor is deeply troubled by the impending marriage.

The rajah's daughter looks in perplexity at her betrothed, losing herself in conjecture as to what is causing his grief.

— "He does not love me!... I do not please him," she says. "But he will nevertheless be my husband... Not for nothing am I the daughter of a rajah... My will must be done!..."

— "Sire," Solor says in a meek voice, approaching the rajah, "the news which you have announced to me is astounding. I openly confess that I cannot fulfil your desire."

— "What!? You make bold to take exception to your rajah's command!... I repeat my will to you: in three days you will marry my daughter. Do you understand?"

Solor knows that it is impossible to propitiate the rajah, and feels utterly destroyed by this fateful command.

A Sudra (servant) announces the arrival of the Great Brahmin.

— "Let him enter," says the rajah.

---

* Marriages among Indians are contracted when girls are no less than seven and no more than nine years old, and boys are from twelve to fourteen. After a long wedding ceremony, at which a brahmin is present, the bride usually returns to her parents' home, where she stays until maturity. At that point there is another marriage ceremony, with other formalities.

The brahmin enters and bows down before the worldly sovereign.

— "I know a great secret!. . . I must tell you about it in private," he whispers into the rajah's ear, looking hatefully at the young Solor.

— "All leave!" the rajah commands, "and you, Solor, see that you do not forget my order."

All exit; the brahmin and the rajah remain alone.

The rajah's daughter hides behind the portière and listens to their conversation.

In a lively narrative the Great Brahmin describes what happened on the preceding night.

He declares that Solor does not love Hamsatti, but adores the bayadère with whom he is seen every night, and wants to run away with her.

The rajah is indignant at the behaviour of his future son-in-law, and tells the Great Brahmin of his intention to destroy the bayadère.

The brahmin, wishing only Solor's death, is frightened at the thought of the serious danger to which he has exposed his beloved bayadère, and tells the rajah that her death will incense the god Vishna and will set the god against them.

The rajah, however, does not want to hear it and declares to the brahmin that tomorrow, during the celebration in honour of Badrinat, Nikia will, as usual, dance with flowers. In one of the baskets of flowers a serpent will be concealed which will crawl out, frightened at the dancer's movements, and bite her, causing her death.

At these words the brahmin's whole body shudders.

Hamsatti, who has heard everything from behind the portière, wants to see the bayadère, and commands her slave girl to fetch her straightaway.

The rajah, completely satisfied with the vengeance he has planned, exits with the brahmin.

Hamsatti sobs and cries in sorrow. She wants to hear from the bayadère herself if it is true that Solor adores her.

The slave woman runs in with word of Nikia's arrival.

Bowing, the bayadère approaches the rajah's daughter. Hamsatti looks at her and finds her beautiful. She tells Nikia of her impending wedding and invites her to dance in her presence on that day.

Nikia is flattered by such an honor.

Hamsatti wants to see what kind of impression it will make on the bayadère if she knows the identity of her betrothed, and points to a portrait of Solor.[*]

Nikia all but loses her head from grief. She declares that Solor swore eternal love to her, and that his marriage to the rajah's daughter will never take place.

Hamsatti insists that Nikia renounce Solor.

— "Never!" answers Nikia, "I would sooner die!"

At that moment Hamsatti offers her diamonds and gold and tries to persuade her to go off to another land.

Nikia rips away the jewels that the rajah's daughter is offering to her and throws them on the floor.

Hamsatti beseeches the bayadère to let her have Solor, and then to leave.

With these words Nikia takes a dagger which has happened into her hand, and rushes at her rival.

The slave woman, who has anxiously followed the bayadère's movements and intentions, defends her mistress with her body. Nikia, meanwhile, disappears from the palace.

Hamsatti gets up and says: "Now she must die!"

Scene III.

THE BAYADÈRE'S DEATH.

The stage represents the façade of the rajah's palace from the side of a garden. There are masses of huge flowers and broad-leaved trees. In the distance—the tower of the large pagoda of Megatshada,

---

[*] I know very well that Indians did not have portraits, and used this anachronism only to make the comprehension of the story easier. —*Author's note.*

which reaches almost to the heavens. In the background, the light blue of the heavens themselves. The Himalayas are thinly covered with silvery snow.

At the rise of the curtain the great procession of Badrinat is being presented. Brahmins pass, then four classes of bayadères (devadasis, natche, vestiatrissas, kansenissas), finally pagoda servants, various Indian castes, and others.

Penintents appear with burning hot irons. The rajah, his daughter, Solor and other rich Indians are brought in on palanquins.

The rajah takes his place on a platform and orders that the festival begin.

At the end of the dances, the rajah commands the beautiful Nikia to come in, and he orders her to entertain the public.

Nikia comes forward out of the crowd with her little guitar. The bayadère's face is hidden by a veil.

She plays the same melody she played in the first act.

Solor, who the whole time is near the rajah's throne, listens carefully to this harmonious melody and recognizes his beloved. He looks at her with love.

With suppressed malice the Great Brahmin watches him, hardly concealing his wrath.

During the bayadère's dance the rajah's jealous daughter uses all her strength to conceal her state of mind. Smiling, she comes down from the balcony and orders a basket with flowers to be presented to the graceful Nikia.

Nikia takes the basket and continues her dance, admiring the pensive Solor.

Suddenly a snake crawls out of the basket and strikes the bayadère in the heart. Its bite is deadly.

Continuing her dance, the beautiful girl appeals to Solor for help, and he embraces her.

— "Do not forget your vow," she gasps. "You are sworn to me... I am dying... Farewell!"

The Great Brahmin runs up to the dancer and offers her an antidote which will save her. But Nikia refuses the flagon and throws herself once again into Solor's arms.

— "Farewell Solor!... I love you!... I die innocent!..."

These are the bayadère's last words, after which she falls and dies.

The rajah and his daughter triumph.

As if through mist a shade is seen, behind which follow will-o'-the wisps. This shade grows pale and vanishes in the icecaps of the Himalayas.

ACT THREE.

Scene IV.

THE APPEARANCE OF THE SHADE.

Solor's room in the rajah's palace.

At the rise of the curtain Solor is walking around the stage like a madman, now slowly, now in wild haste. He is apparently trying to remember something. Then he falls, exhausted, onto a divan.

The fakir Magdavaya watches him with a look of profound pity, then orders snake charmers to be brought in (a man and a woman), to drive the evil spirit from Solor's body. (*Comic dance.*)

Solor orders the fakir to send them away.

There is a knock at the door. The fakir opens it. Hamsatti enters, the rajah's daughter, with a crowd of women retainers.

She is dressed magnificently, all covered in gold and pearls.

She turns to Solor with reproaches.

The fakir points out to her that he requires healing, not quarrels.

At that moment Hamsatti wants to divert him, and is extremely obliging.

She sits down next to him, caresses him and tries in every way to attract his attention.

Solor at last revives, and takes her by the hand. At this moment the melancholy strains of the bayadère's song are heard.

The shade of the weeping Nikia appears on the wall. Solor trembles.

— "Oh! Now my misfortunes will begin," he says, "I forgot my vow! Remorse shall pursue me my whole life."

— "Calm down!. . . What's the matter?" Hamsatti says, and tries to console him.

— "I beg of you. . . leave me alone. . . Tomorrow we shall see each other again!. . . Tomorrow is our wedding. . . I do not feel well now. . . I must rest! . . . "

Hamsatti, sorrowful, withdraws from the room, bidding him farewell until the morrow.

Solor goes over to the wall, but the shade is already gone; it appears only at moments when his imagination is deranged.

— "You forgot your vow, unhappy man!"—it is as if the shade were speaking to him—"you intend to marry Hamsatti, and by this to disturb my peace beyond the grave! But I still love you!"

In vain Solor tries to seize Nikia's elusive shade.

— "And I love you," answers Solor. "I did not forget you and love you as before."

The shade at last disappears.

Solor falls unconscious on the divan. A dream takes possession of him, and he falls asleep, never ceasing to think about the shade.

Clouds descend.

Scene V.

THE KINGDOM OF THE SHADES.

An enchanted place. Soft, harmonious music is heard.

Shades appear at the sounds of this music—Nikia first, then Solor.

DANCES.
Plastic groupings.

— "I died innocent," says Nikia's shade, "I remained true to you; behold then everything around me here. Is it not magnificent!. . . The gods have granted me all possible blessings. I lack only you!"

— "What must I do to belong to you?" Solor asks her.

— "Do not forget your vow! You promised to be faithful to me!. . . The melody which you are hearing now will come to protect you. . . and my shade to guard you. . . I shall be with you in misfortune."

— "If you do not betray me," Nikia continues, "then your spirit shall find rest here, in this kingdom of the shades."

A large concluding dance of the shades.

Clouds descend.

Scene VI.

SOLOR'S AWAKENING.

Solor's room, as before.

Solor is lying on his divan. His dream is troubled. The fakir enters, stops beside his master and looks at him sadly.

Solor awakens suddenly. He thought he was in Nikia's embrace.

Servants of the rajah bring in expensive gifts and announce to Solor that all preparations are completed for his wedding to the rajah's daughter.

All exit.

Solor, obsessed with his thoughts, follows them.

ACT FOUR.

Scene VII.

THE GODS' WRATH.

The stage represents a large hall with columns in the rajah's palace.

Preparations are underway for the celebration of sipmanadi (marriage) of Solor and Hamsatti.

Warriors enter, together with brahmins, bayadères and others.

Hamsatti appears, and behind her her father with his retinue.

When the young warrior Solor appears, the rajah orders the festival to begin.

During the dances the shade pursues Solor and reminds him of his vow.

Hamsatti, meanwhile, does everything in her power to please her bridegroom, who grieves the whole time and never stops thinking of Nikia.

Four young girls present a basket to the bride exactly similar to the one given to the bayadère, and from which crawled the snake that bit her.

In horror Hamsatti rejects the basket, as it reminds her of her rival—the cause of all her unhappiness.

The recollection of the basket resurrects the poisoned bayadère in Hamsatti's memory.

The shade appears before her, the spectre of the bayadère appears to Hamsatti's troubled mind.

The rajah's daughter flees from it and rushes into her father's arms, begging him to hasten the wedding.

Just then the rajah orders the ritual to begin.

The Great Brahmin takes bride and groom by the hand.

With the beginning of the ceremony the sky darkens, lightning flashes, thunder crashes, and it begins to rain.

At the very moment when the brahmin takes the hands of Solor and Hamsatti to join them, there is a fearful thunderclap followed by an earthquake. Lightning strikes the hall, which collapses and covers in its ruins the rajah, his daughter, the Great Brahmin and Solor.

APOTHEOSIS.

Through the rain the peaks of the Himalayas are visible. Nikia's shade glides through the air; she is triumphant, and tenderly looks at her beloved Solor, who is at her feet.

THE END.

Typographer of the Imperial Spb. Theaters (Eduard Hoppe),
Voznesenskii prosp., No. 58.

Translation by Roland John Wiley.

Authors' note: A nearly identical translation of this libretto is included in Roland John Wiley, *A Century of Russian Ballet* (New York: Oxford University Press, 1990), 293–303.

(ii) *La Bayadère* poster, St. Petersburg, 23 January 1877

1877
Imperial Spb. Theaters

IN THE BOLSHOI THEATER.
On Sunday, 23 January.

BENEFIT OF DANCER
Mlle VAZEM.

For the 1st time:
LA BAYADÈRE

Grand ballet in 4 acts and 7 scenes with apotheosis, by balletmaster M. Marius Petipa; music by
M. Minkus; machines by M. Roller; costumes by M. Jurus and Mme Ofitserova, after designs
by M. Panov; accessories by M. Gavrilov, headwear and flowers by Mme Magnus, wigs by
M. Malishev, women's hairstyles by M. Michel, chemical lighting by M. Shishko.

MLLE VAZEM will perform the role of NIKIA.

Scene 1: THE FESTIVAL OF FIRE.
Scenery by M. Bocharov.

Scene 2: THE TWO RIVALS.
Scenery by M. Shishkov.

Scene 3: THE DEATH OF THE BAYADÈRE.
Scenery by M. Shishkov.

Scene 4: THE APPEARANCE OF THE SHADE.
Scenery by M. Andreyev.

Scene 5: SOLOR'S DREAM.
THE KINGDOM OF THE SHADES.
Scenery by M. Wagner.

Scene 6: SOLOR'S AWAKENING.
Scenery by M. Andreyev.

Scene 7: THE WRATH OF THE GODS.
Scenery by M. Roller.

APOTHEOSIS.
Scenery by M. Roller.

Dances will be:

In the 1st scene:
1) FESTIVAL OF FIRE—Mlle VAZEM; Mlles: Predtechina, Zhukova 2, Tistrova,
Olgina, Lezenskaya, Freytag, Gruzdovskaya, Kruger 2, Sokolova 2, Nikonova, Kuzmina 4 and
Leonova; MM. Troitsky, Gerdt 2, Leonov, Bystrov, Nidt, Bizukin, Didichkin, Orlov, Litvinov 1,
Students: Lukyanov, Voronkov, Konstantinov, Tatarinov, and other women and men dancers.

In the 2nd scene:

2) DJAMPE—Mlles: Madaeva, Tistrova, Zhukova 2, Kuzmina 4, Predtechina, Sokolova 2, Olgina, Nikonova and Lezenskaya.

In the 3rd scene:

3) SOLEMN PROCESSION IN HONOR OF THE IDOL BADRINATH.

4) SLAVE DANCE—Mlles: Tistrova, Olgina, Gruzdovskaya, Freytag, Nikonova, Lvova, Selezneva, Sokolova 2, Leonova, Kuzmina 4, Ogoleit 2 and Lezenskaya; Students: Bogdanov, Konstantinov, Voronkov and Puchkov.

5) HINDU DANCE—Mlle Radina 1; MM. Kshesinsky, Picheau, Leonov, Bystrov, Gerdt 2, Nidt; Students: Tatarinov and Lukyanov.

6) GRAND INDIAN DANCE—Mlles: Menshikova 1, Ushakova, Shamburskaya 2, Geltser, Kuzmina 1, Ivanova 3, Zhebeleva, Kemmerer 2, Kenchikova 2, Lomanovskaya, Larionova, Polonskaya, Stepanova, Kuzmina 2, Dolganova, Tsvetkova, Pavlovskaya, Shukelskaya, Prokofieva, Niman, Antonio, Savina, Sidova, Marzhetskaya, 12 small student boys, 12 medium student boys and 12 adult male corps de ballet dancers

7) TWO BAYADÈRES—Students: Petrova and Nikitina.

8) NATU—Mlles Ogoleit 1 and Glagoleva.

9) CLASSICAL DANCE—Mlles Gorshcnkova and M. Gerdt 1.

10) MANU—Mlle Zhukova 1, Students Vishnevskaya and Nedremskaya.

11) GENERAL FINAL DANCE.

12) THE BAYADÈRE—Mlle VAZEM.

In the 4th scene:

13) SAKODUSA—DANCE OF THE INDIAN ASTROLOGISTS: MM. Troitsky, Bizukin and Tomas.

14) SHADOW DANCE—Mlle VAZEM and M. L. Ivanov.

In the 5th scene:

15) SHADES DANCES—Mlles: Vazem, Prikhunova, Shaposhnikova 1, Zhukova 1, M. L Ivanov, Mlles Alexandrova, Zaitseva 2, Zest, Selezneva, Sokolova 2, Nesterenko, Zhukova 2, Tistrova, Gredtechina, Gruzdovskaya, Olgina, Kruger 2, Leonova, Ushakova, Geltser, Kemmerer 2, Menshikova 1, Ivanova 3, Shamburskaya 2, Niman, Polonskaya, Menshikova 2, Kuzmina 1, Zhebeleva, Lomanovskaya, Larionova, Pavlovskaya, Stepanova, Dolganova, Kuzmina 2, Tsvetkova, Shukelskaya, Prokofieva, Sidova, Zhikhareva, Olshevskaya, Ogoleit 2, Efimova, girl students: Andreyeva, Fedorova 2, Simskaya, Moksheva, Vorobieva, Aleksandrova, Matveyeva, Potaikova, Kurbanova, Gorshenkova, Bunyakina and 16 small student girls, 12 small student boys.

In the 7th scene:

16) SIPMANADI: Wedding celebration.

17) LOTUS DANCE—Students: Voronova, Fedorova 1 and 24 small student girls.

18) PAS D'ACTION—Mlles Vazem, Gorshenkova, Ogoleit 1 and Glagoleva, students: Petrova, Nikitina; MM. L. Ivanov, Gerdt 1, Johanson, Golts and Troitsky.

Will perform solo:
On violin—Soloist of His Imperial Majesty's Court
M. Auer

CHARACTERS:

Dugmanta, rajah of Golconda	M. Johanson.
Hamsatti, his daughter	Mlle Gorshenkova.
Solor, a rich and famous warrior	M. L. Ivanov.
Nikia, a Bayadère	Mlle VAZEM.
Great Brahmin	M. Golts.
Madgavaya, a fakir	M. Troitsky.
Toloragva, a warrior	M. Geltser.

Fakirs	M. Gerdt 2.
	M. Leonov.
	M. Bystrov.
	M. Nidt.
Kshatriyas	M. Chistyakov.
	M. Vishnevsky.
	M. Shcherbakov.
	M. Khamarberg.
	M. Stukolkin 2.
	M. Zelensky.
Attendants of Hamsatti	Mlle Nikulina.
	Mlle Shamburskaya 1.
Aiya, a slave	Mlle Natarova.

Brahmins, brahmacarins, sudras, servants, warriors, bayadères, fakirs, pilgrims, Indian people, musicians and hunters.

The action takes place in India, on the slopes of the Himalayan mountains.

Starting at 7½ o'clock.

Tickets can be obtained at the Bolshoi theater box office from 9 a.m.

(iii) *La Bayadère* program, St. Petersburg, 3 December 1900

1900

MARIINSKY THEATER

On Sunday, 3rd December,

BENEFIT
P. A. GERDT
(for 40 years of service).

Artists of the IMPERIAL theaters will present:

FOR THE 1ST TIME IN REVIVAL:

LA BAYADÈRE

Ballet in 4 acts and 6 scenes, with apotheosis,
by **MARIUS PETIPA**, soloist of HIS MAJESTY.

Music by M. **Minkus**.

New Scenery:

1st act, scene 1.
THE FESTIVAL OF FIRE.
Scenery by M. A. Kvapp.

2nd act, scene 2.
THE TWO RIVALS.
Scenery by M. K. Ivanov.

Scene 3.
THE DEATH OF THE BAYADÈRE.
Scenery by M. P. Lambin.

3rd act, scene 4.
THE APPEARANCE OF THE SHADE.
Scenery by O. Allegri.

Scene 5.
SOLOR'S DREAM. THE KINGDOM OF THE SHADES.
Scenery by M. P. Lambin.

4th act, scene 6.
SOLOR'S AWAKENING.[3]

---

[3] The program states that the ballet is given in six scenes, rather than the original seven, because the very short "Solor's Awakening" scene is cut. But the program mistakenly retains the title "Solor's Awakening" and applies it to the ballet's closing scene, which should be called "The Wrath of the Gods." This error seems to have first been made on the 1884 poster (see Chapter 9). The *Yearbook of the Imperial Theaters* for the 1900–1901 season nevertheless states that the ballet was given in seven scenes, as it was in 1877. *Ezhegodnik* (1900–1901), 161. The action of the omitted scene at the end of Act Three is described in the summary of the ballet's story on pp. 171–172.

Scenery by K. Ivanov.

APOTHEOSIS.

Scenery by K. Ivanov.

MACHINES: MACHINIST-MECHANIC N. A. BERGER. ACCESSORIES: SCULPTOR P. KAMENSKY. NEW COSTUMES BASED ON DRAWINGS BY STAFF ARTIST E. P. PONAMAREV. WOMEN'S—E. OFITSEROVA, MEN'S—D. CAFFI. HEADWEAR: WOMEN'S—MLLE TERMAIN, MEN'S—M. BRUNEAU. SHOES BY MLLE LEVSTEDT, WIGS BY G. PEDDER, METALWORK M. INGINEN, TIGHTS BY L. DOBROVOLSKAYA.

WILL PLAY THE ROLES:

"Nikia"—Mlle **Kshesinskaya 2**, "Hamsatti"—Mlle **Preobrazhenskaya**,
"Great Brahmin"—M. **Kshesinsky 1**, merited artist of the
IMPERIAL Theaters, "Solor"— M. **Gerdt**.

CHARACTERS:

Dugmanta, rajah of Golconda	*M. Aistov.*
Hamsatti, his daughter	*Mlle Preobrazhenskaya.*
Solor, a famous warrior	*M. Gerdt.*
Nikia, a bayadère	*Mlle Kshesinskaya 2.*
Great Brahmin	*M. Kshesinsky 1.*
Magdavaya	*M. Bekefi.*
Toloragva, a warrior	*M. Gillert.*
Kshatriyas	*M. Barychistov.*
	M. Volonin.
	M. Voronkov 2.
	M. Kiselev.
	M. Oblakov.
	M. Solyannikov.
	M. Titov.
	M. Yakovlev.
Aiya, slave	*Mlle Solyannikova.*

Kshatriyas, Brahmacarins, Sudras, fakirs, servants, warriors, bayadères, pilgrims,
Indian people, musicians and hunters.

The action takes place in India, on the slopes of the Himalayan mountains.

WILL DANCE:

In the 1st scene:

1) THE FESTIVAL OF FIRE—Mlle Kshesinskaya 2, Lits, Shchedrina, Yakovleva 2, Shtikhling, Sprishinskaya, Georgievskaya; MM. Trudov, Gavlikovsky, Loboyko, Nikitin, Fedulov, Novikov, Stukolkin, Fedorov 1, Pashchenko 1, Smirnov 1, Fedorov 2.

In the 2nd scene:

2) DJAMPE—Mlles Ofitserova, Chumakova, Slantsova, Bakerkina, Vasilieva, Pavlova 1, Goncharova, Kasatkina, Konetskaya, Ilyina 3.

3) HINDU DANCE—Mlle Rutkovskaya and M. Shiryaev.

In the 3rd scene:

4) SOLEMN PROCESSION IN HONOR OF THE IDOL BADRINATA.

5) DANCE OF THE SLAVES—Mlles Fonareva, Borkhardt, Gordova, Vaganova, Makarova, Belinskaya, Renina, Nesterovskaya, Vill, Matveyeva, Przhebyletskaya, Snetkova; MM. Alexandrov, Vasiliev, Medalinsky and Aslin.

6) GREAT INDIAN DANCE—Mlles Kshesinskaya 1, Bakerkina, Slantsova, Vasilieva, Pavlova 1, Kasatkina, Konetskaya, Shchedrina, Lits, Goncharova, Ilyina 3, Chernyavskaya, Dyuzhikova, Leonova 2, Dorina, Levina, Legat, Yakovleva 2, Stepanova 3, Georgievskaya, Radina, Sazonova, Shtikhling, Golubeva 2 and other female dancers, male dancers and boy students of the IMPERIAL Theater school.

7) BAYADÈRES—Mlles Leonova 1, Egorova 2, Mosolova and Andrianova.

8) MANU—Mlle Trefilova; Students: Lezgilye and Nesterovskaya.

9) HINDU DANCE—Mlle Petipa 1; MM. Lukyanov, Gavlikovsky, Novikov, Trudov, Nikitin, Loboyko, Chekrygin, Stukolkin.

10) GENERAL FINAL DANCE.

11) THE BAYADÈRE—Mlle Kshesinskaya 2.

In the 4th scene:

12) SAKODUSA—dance of the Indian astrologers. MM. Bekefi and Solyannikov.

13) LOVE SCENE—Mlle Preobrazhenskaya and M. Gerdt.

NIKIA'S SHADE—Mlle Kshesinskaya 2.

In the 5th scene:

14) DANCES OF THE SHADES – Mlle Kshesinskaya 2, Rykhlyakova 1, Pavlova 2, Sedova, Slantsova, Vasilieva, Bakerkina, Kasatkina, Goncharova, Lits, Shchedrina, Konetskaya, Erler 2, Leonova 2, Chernyavskaya, Urakova, Dorina, Golubeva 2, Stepanova 3, Legat, Levina, Radina, Chernetskaya, Sprychinskaya, Dyuzhikova, Rykhlyakova 2, Ilyina 3, Isaeva 1, Fedorova 1, Laktionova, Przhebyletskaya, Frank, Sazonova, Yakovleva 2, Georgievskaya, Erler 1, Golubeva 1, Peters, Shtikhling, Picheau, Levenson 2, Golovkina, Isaeva 2, Bastman, Pakhomova, Alexandrova 2, Vertinskaya, Ilyina 2, Lobanova, Niman, Matyatina and girl students of the IMPERIAL Theater Schools.

In the 6th scene:

15) SIPMANADI: Wedding festival.

16) LOTUS DANCE—Girl students of the IMPERIAL Theatre School.

17) PAS D'ACTION: Mlles Kshesinskaya 2, Preobrazhenskaya, Sedova, Pavlova 2, Obukhova, Egorova 2; MM. Gerdt, Kyaksht and Bekefi.

Will perform solo:
Court Soloists of HIS IMPERIAL MAJESTY.
On violin—M. **Auer.**
On harp—M. **Zabel.**

Also will perform solo:
On violoncello—M. **Loganovsky.**
On flute—M. **Stepanov.**

Conductor *R. Drigo.*

Beginning at 8 p.m.

APPENDIX G

Raymonda

(i) *Raymonda* libretto, St. Petersburg, 1898

RAYMONDA.

BALLET IN 3 ACTS (4 SCENES).

(Subject borrowed from knightly legends).

by Mme L. **Pashkova**.

Music by A.K. GLAZUNOV.

Dances and production by balletmaster M. I. PETIPA.

The role of "Raymonda" will be performed by Mlle Pierina Legnani.

New decorations: Act I, Scene 1, M. **Allegri**; Act I, Scene 2, Act III and the apotheosis, M. **Lambin**; Act II, M. **Ivanov**. Machinist, M. **Berger**. Costumes: women's, Mme **Ofitserova**; men's, M. **Caffi**; Headwear: women's, Mme **Termain**; men's, M. **Bruneau**. Accessories: **P.P. Kamensky**. Wigs and coiffures, M. **Pedder**. Footwear, Mme **Levstedt**. Metalwork, M. **Inginen**. Tricot, Mlle **Dobrovolskaya**. Flowers, Mlle **Revenskaya**.

Produced for the first time on the stage of the Imperial Maryinsky Theater 7 January 1898 (for the benefit performance of Mlle Pierina Legnani).

St. Petersburg.
Typographer of the Imperial Theatres, Mokhovaya, 40.
1898.

Permitted by the censor. St. Petersburg, 3 January 1898.

DRAMATIS PERSONAE:

Raymonda, Countess de Doris	*Mlle Legnani.*
The Countess Sybil, canoness, aunt of Raymonda	*Mme Cecchetti.*
The White Lady, protector of the home of Doris	*Mlle Svirskaya.*
Clémence ⎱ girlfriends of Raymonda	*Mlle Kulichevskaya.*
Henriette ⎰	*Mlle Preobrazhenskaya.*
Knight Jean de Brienne, fiancé of Raymonda	*M. Legat 3.*
Andrei II, King of Hungary	*M. Aistov.*
Abderrakhman, a Saracen knight	*M. Gerdt.*
Bernard de Ventadour, a troubadour of Provence	*M. Kyaksht.*
Béranger, a troubadour of Aquitaine	*M. Legat 1.*
Seneschal in charge of the castle of Doris	*M. Bulgakov.*
Cavalier in the retinue of de Brienne	*M. Yakovlev.*
A Hungarian knight	*M. Gillert.*
Saracen knights:	*M. Tatarinov.*
	M. Voronin.
	M. Baltser.
	M. Bykov.

Women, vassals; Hungarian and Saracen knights; heralds, moors,
citizens of Provence, royal soldiers and servants.

In the First Act, First Scene:
LA FÊTE DE RAYMONDE.

1) **Jeux et danses:** Mlles Kulichevskaya, Preobrazhenskaya; MM. Legat 1, Kyaksht. Girl students: Petipa 1, Sedova, Belinskaya, Egorova, Andrianova, Grupilion. Boy students: Obukhov, Osipov, Fokine, Ogniev, Barïshistov, Ivanov.

2) **Entrée:** Mlle Legnani.

COURTLY WOMEN: Mlles Natarova, Alexandrova 2, Postolenko, Kil, Antonova, Efimova, Goryacheva, Semenova 2.

VASSALS: MM. Navatsky, Kunitsky, Solyannikov 2, Marzhetsky, Alexeyev, Fomichev, Panteleyev, Sosnovsky.

3) **Valse provençale:** Mlles Kasatkina, Erler 2, Bakerkina, Pávlova, Chernyavskaya, Kunitskaya, Vaganova, Matveyeva 3, Yakovleva 2, Vasilieva, Golubeva 2, Leonova 2, Yakovleva 1, Radina, Ilyina 3, Dyuzhikova, Shtikhling, Rykhlyakova 2, Przhebyletskaya, Erler 1, Sazonova, Stepanova 2, Stepanova 3, Matyatina; MM. Kusov, Gavlikovsky, Nikitin, Pashchenko 1, Fedulov, Fedorov 1, Aslin, Presnyakov, Voronkov 3, Chekrygin, Fedorov 2, Medalinsky, Sergeyev, Martyanov, Loboiko, Ponomarev, Maslov, Mikhailov, Smirnov, Kristerson, Ivanov 1, Balashev, Levinson, Dmitriev.

4) **Pizzicato:** Mlle Legnani.

5) **La romanesque:** Mlles Kulichevskaya, Preobrazhenskaya; MM. Kyaksht and Legat 1.

6) **Une fantaisie:** Mlle Legnani.

In the Second Scene:
VISIONS.

Mlle Legnani, M. Legat 3; **La renommée:** Mlle Nikolaidis; **Gloire:** Mlles Rykhlyakova 1, Geltser, Leonova 1, Mosolova, Ofitserova, Borkhardt, Trefilova, Chumakova, Repina, Vaganova, Chernyavskaya, Nikolaeva, Kasatkina, Pavlova, Kshesinskaya 1, Kuskova, Shchedrina, Kunitskaya, Lits, Egorova 2, Bakerkina, Kunitskaya, Erler 2, Ogoleit 2, Oblakova, Vasilieva, Leonova 2,

Golubeva 1, Dorina, Konetskaya, Tsalison, Ilyina 3, Matveyeva 3, Slantsova, Golubeva 2, Andreyeva, Radina, Urakova, Levina, Dyuzhikova, Stepanova 2, Vsevolodskaya, Stepanova 3, Yakovleva 2, Przhebyletskaya, Lobanova, Rosh.

Les chevaliers: MM. Alexandrov, Titov, Romanov, Ivanov 2, Voronkov 2, Plessyuk, Vasiliev, Rykhlyakov, Voskresensky, Chernikov, Oblakov 2, Terpilovsky. *Les amours*: students of the Imperial Theater School.

Scène dramatique: Mlle Legnani, M. Gerdt. THE WHITE LADY AND RAYMONDA'S DOUBLE.

Farfadets: Girl and boy students of the Imperial Theater School.

In the Second Act:
COUR D'AMOUR.

1) **Pas d'action:** Mlles Legnani, Cecchetti, Kulichevskaya, Preobrazhenskaya: MM. Gerdt, Legat 1, Kyaksht.

2) **Pas des esclaves sarrasins:** Mlles Matveyeva 3, Savitskaya, Konetskaya, Leonova 2, Sheberg, Isaeva 1, Legat, Ilyina 3, Dyuzhikova, Nikolaidis, Yakovleva 2, Erler 1, Ryabova, Lobanova, Peters, Mikhailova, Yakovleva 1, Golubeva 2, Niman, Kuzmina, Ilyina 2, Golovkina, Rosh, Pakhomova, Kusterer, Levinson 2, Gorskaya, Temireva, Matyatina, Rakhmanova, Ilyina 1; MM. Nikitin, Kusov, Fedorov 1, Alexandrov, Gavlikovsky, Voronkov 2, Trudov, Fedulov, Usachev, Aslin, Ivanov 1, Loboiko, Chekrygin, Balashhev, Vasiliev, Romanov, Novikov, Pashchenko 2, Medalinsky, Kristerson, Rykhlyakov, Mikhailov, Levinson, Presnyakov, Pechatnikov, Fedorov 2, Dmitriev, Martyanov, Smirnov, Maslov.

3) **Pas des Moriscos:** Boy students of the Imperial Theater School.

4) **Danse sarrasine:** Mlle Skorsyuk and M. Gorsky.

5) **Panadéros:** Mlle Petipa 1, M. Lukyanov; Mlles Kshesinskaya 1, Makhotina, Lits, Kuskova, Shchedrina, Bakerkina, Radina, Urakova, Borkhardt, Kasatkina, Chernyavskaya, Pavlova, Vasilieva, Tsalison, Ogoleit 3, Vaganova.

6) **Coda:** all participants.

LES ÉCHANSONS: Girl students of the Imperial Theater School.

7) **Entrée:** Mlle Legnani.

8) **Ensemble:** All participants.

9) **Dénouement:** Mlles Legnani, Cecchetti, Kulichevskaya, Preobrazhenskaya; MM. Gerdt, Legat 3, Aistov and others. THE WHITE LADY.

In the 3rd Act:
LE FESTIVAL DES NOCES.

1) **Rapsodie:** Boy and girl students of the Imperial Theater School.

2) **Palotás:** Mlle Preobrazhenskaya and M. Bekefi; Mlles Slantsova, Pavlova, Kasatkina, Kunitskaya, Bakerkina, Chernyavskaya, Tsalison, Golubeva 2, Radina, Dyuzhikova, Leonova 2, Egorova 2, Ilyina 2, Peshkova, Starostina, Peters, Gorshenkova, Tselikhova, Shtikhling, Kil; MM. Fedorov 1, Rakhmanov, Ivanov 1, Levinson, Kristerson, Loboiko, Martyanov, Smirnov, Medalinsky, Trudov, Pashchenko 1, Novikov, Balashev, Fomichev, Baltser, Voronkov 3, Usachev, Pashchenko 2, Legat 2, Panteleyev.

3) **Mazurka:** Mlle Petipa 1, M. Kshesinsky 2; Mlles Tatarinova, Nikolaeva, Ogoleit 2, Ogoleit 3, Kshesinskaya 1, Kuskova, Shchedrina, Urakova, Levina, Konetskaya, Golubeva 1, Nikolaidis; MM. Voronkov 2, Fedulov, Alexandrov, Yakovlev, Vasiliev, Titov, Ivanov 2, Ponomarev, Aslin, Presnyakov, Romanov, Rykhlyakov.

4) **Pas classique hongrois:** Mlles Legnani, Johanson, Rykhlyakova 1, Obukhova, Geltser, Ofitserova, Borkhardt, Chumakova, Vaganova; MM. Legat 3, Kyaksht, Oblakov 1, Legat 1, Gorsky, Kusov, Gavlikovsky, Nikitin and Sergeyev.

5) **Final:** All participants.

APOTHEOSIS.
TOURNEY.

Soloists of the Court of His Imperial Highness:
On the violin—*M. Auer.*
On the harp—*M. Zabel.*
Other soloists: on the harp—*Mlle Virginia Charlione*; on the celesta and pianoforte—*M. Griben.*

Conductor *M. Drigo.*

RAYMONDA

ACT I.

First Scene.

A hall in the castle of Countess de Doris.

Tableau 1.
The seneschal issues orders concerning the imminent celebration of Raymonda's name-day. Bernard de Ventadour, Beranger, and several pages are fencing, others are playing on lutes, viols, etc.; several young girls from Raymonda's retinue, attracted by the general liveliness, cease their work and begin to dance with the pages.

Tableau 2.
Courtly ladies enter, preceded by Countess Sybil; she reproaches the girls for their idleness, but in vain—some have hardly sat back down to work when others begin to dance.
Then the countess turns to Bernard, Beranger, and the pages and commands them to take up lutes and viols. "Take care," she says to the girls, "Countess de Doris, famous by the name the White Lady, will punish you for disobedience; do you see this statue? This is our revered ancestor, she appears from that world to warn the house of Doris every time one of its members is in danger, and punishes those who do not fulfil their responsibilities." The young girls laugh at Countess Sybil's superstition, and distract her into dancing. The sound of a horn is heard, which proclaims the arrival of guests.

Tableau 3.
The seneschal rushes into the hall and announces the arrival of a runner from the knight Jean de Brienne bringing a letter to his bride. Countess Sybil goes over to tell her niece.
The seneschal, hurriedly giving last instructions before the arrival of Raymonda, directs the meeting of the guests, who are arriving with congratulations for Raymonda; meanwhile the girls scatter flowers along the path by which Raymonda will enter.

Tableau 4.
Raymonda enters. She admires the flowers that pages bring in for her.

Tableau 5.
Kneeling, the runner hands her the letter from her fiancé, Jean de Brienne. It informs Raymonda that King Andrei II of Hungary, under whose banners knight de Brienne does battle, is returning, covered in glory, to his native land. Not later than tomorrow de Brienne will arrive at the castle of Doris for his wedding to Raymonda. She is delighted. At this moment the seneschal reports the arrival of the Saracen knight Abderrakhman; Raymonda and her aunt are astonished, although Countess Sybil orders that the guest be invited in.

Tableau 6.

Abderrakhman enters, greeting the entire company with great dignity. He explains that word has reached him of Raymonda's remarkable beauty and of the regal hospitality of the castle of Doris. He made bold to come and congratulate the charming name-day celebrant and to present her several gifts. Puzzled by this unexpected turn of events, Raymonda, concealing her indignation with difficulty, declines the gifts, which brings Abderrakhman to despair. Meanwhile the seneschal requests permission of Countess Sybil to introduce the vassals. Abderrakhman, leading his first swordbearer to the side, confides in him his secret to kidnap Raymonda.

Raymonda rereads and kisses the letter from her fiancé. Countess Sybil offers Abderrakhman a place at her side to watch the forthcoming dances. The Saracen accepts her invitation, but the proceedings little interest him, as his thoughts are lost in dreams of Raymonda, whom he admires the whole time.

Tableau 7.

The vassals come on, noisily greeting and congratulating Raymonda.

Valse.

After the dances Raymonda commands the seneschal to prepare with all possible magnificence the reception of her fiancé, and to prepare a *cour d'amour* in his honor. Hearing this, Abderrakhman finally decides to abduct Raymonda. He exits, accompanied, at Countess Sybil's order, by the seneschal; the vassals and other guests also withdraw.

It is getting dark, the moon illuminates the terrace.

Tableau 8.

Only Raymonda's closest friends and troubadours remain with her. She plays the lute (*Romanesque*, performed by 2 pairs). Raymonda hands the lute to one of her friends and shows them a new dance (*Fantaisie*). Finally, tired from the day's excitements, she lies down on the carpet, the pages wave fans over her, and Clémence gives pleasure to Raymonda's ear with a tender melody on the lute. Suddenly a magic torpor comes over those present: the pages and everyone else fall asleep, except Raymonda, who looks at them with astonishment. The White Lady appears; illuminated by moonlight Raymonda, frightened, looks closely at her. With an imperious gesture the White Lady beckons to her to follow. Obedient to some mysterious, unknown power, Raymonda submissively follows the White Lady.

Second Scene.

A shady park. In the depth of the park, the high terrace of Countess de Doris's castle.

Tableau 1.

The White Lady moves silently around the terrace, Raymonda, as if in a trance, follows her. At a sign from the White Lady the garden is enshrouded in darkness for a time. The mists gradually disperse, revealing the figure of Jean de Brienne.

Tableau 2.

Visions.

Jean de Brienne and his knights, encircled by girls putting crowns on their heads.

A Large Grouping.

The White Lady points Raymonda toward her fiancé;—delighted, she throws herself into the knight's embrace.

Dances and Groupings.

Raymonda expresses her delight to the White Lady, who, however, disenchants her. "Have a look, and know what still awaits you," the White Lady tells her. Raymonda wants to return to her fiancé, but comes face-to-face with Abderrakhman, who appears in the knight's place.

The stage darkens.

Tableau 3.
Abderrakhman declares his love to Raymonda, but she rejects him indignantly.

Tableau 4.
Apparitions appear from all sides. Raymonda implores the White Lady to save her. At this moment Abderrakhman is about to abduct Raymonda; she falls, unconscious. The apparitions, dancing, encircle the motionless Raymonda.

Dawn comes; the first rays of the coming day replace the moonlight
The apparitions disappear with Abderrakhman and the White Lady.

Tableau 5.
A castle servant and Raymonda's friends and pages run onto the terrace, and noticing her lying in a faint, attempt to revive her.

ACT II.

Cour d'amour.

An interior court of Countess de Doris's castle.

Tableau 1.
Entrance of the knights, cavaliers, owners of neighboring castles, noblewomen, minstrels, and others invited to be present at the *Cour d'amour*. Then follow the seneschal, Raymonda and Countess Sybil. Raymonda greets the assembled company and expresses pleasure at the furnishings of the court and reception which has been prepared for her fiancé. But Raymonda cannot conceal her uneasiness at the delay in Jean de Brienne's arrival.

Tableau 2.
Abderrakhman enters with his retinue. In confusion Raymonda orders the seneschal to send away the uninvited guest, but Countess Sybil persuades her that on this day no one should be denied hospitality.

Grand Pas d'action.

Abderrakhman, struck by Raymonda's beauty, indicates his passion for her, but she is afraid and evades it. "You must be mine, beautiful countess,"—he says to her—"I offer you a life of magnificence and pleasure." Abderrakhman calls his slaves to entertain Raymonda.

Tableau 3.
"See how agile and diverting my slaves are,"—he says. (The slaves enter dancing.) Raymonda, as before, rejects contemptuously. He commands his slaves to dance.

Tableau 4.
Cupbearers fill the cups of those present with wine.

BACCHANALE.

During this dance Abderrakhman and his slaves make attempt to abduct Raymonda and steal off with her.

Tableau 5.

Suddenly the knight de Brienne appears with King Andrei II and his retinue. Jean de Brienne frees Raymonda from the clutches of the slaves and charges Abderrakhman, but the king commands the rivals to settle their quarrel with a duel. They agree. Swordbearers bring in arms. Raymonda rushes to her beloved's embrace, but the king takes Raymonda to one side, after which the opponents engage in battle. First Jean de Brienne attacks. The spectre of the White Lady appears in the depth of the stage. With a stroke of the sword to the head, he delivers the Saracen his mortal wound. The latter's seconds carry him out; meanwhile Abderrakhman's slaves try to steal away, but at a sign from the king, as if a ring, the royal swordbearers surround them. The king joins the hands of the young couple—Raymonda and Jean de Brienne.

ACT III.

Garden in the castle of the knight de Brienne.

A wedding feast at which King Andrei II is present. In honor of the highborn guest a grand Hungarian divertissement is given.

APOTHEOSIS.

TOURNEY.

Translation by *Roland John Wiley*.

Authors' note: A nearly identical translation of this libretto is included in Roland John Wiley, *A Century of Russian Ballet* (New York: Oxford University Press, 1990), 393–401.

Selected Bibliography

Adam, Adolphe. *Giselle*. Piano reduction by V. Cornette, Paris: Meissonier, n.d. [1841?].

Adam, Adolphe. *Giselle, ou, Les wilis: ballet-pantomime en deux actes de Théophile Gautier et Saint-Georges. Revision et arrangement de Henri Busser* [piano reduction]. Paris: Editions Max Eschig, 1943.

Adam, Adolphe. *Le Corsaire*. Richard Bonynge and the English Chamber Orchestra. Decca 430 2862, 1990. Re-released: Eloquence Classics (Decca 4828605), 2018.

Adam, Adolphe. *Le Corsaire*. Edited by Yuri Burlaka. St. Petersburg, Compozitor: 2021.

Adice, Léopold. *Histoire et théorie de la danse théâtrale*, 6 vol. manuscript (unpublished), 1873. Bibliothèque Nationale de France, Bibliothèque-Musée de l'Opéra, RES-1184 (1–6).

Adice, Léopold. *Théorie de la gymnastique de la danse théâtrale*. Paris: Chais, 1859.

Aldrich, Elizabeth Aldrich. "Nineteenth Century Social Dance." Washington, DC: Library of Congress: 1998. https://www.loc.gov/collections/dance-instruction-manuals-from-1490-to-1920/articles-and-essays/western-social-dance-an-overview-of-the-collection/nineteenth-century-social-dance/.

Aldrich, Elizabeth, Sandra Noll Hammond, and Armand Russell. *The Extraordinary Dance Book T B. 1826: An Anonymous Manuscript in Facsimile*. Dance and Music Series, no. 11, general editor Wendy Hilton. Stuyvesant, NY: Pendragon Press, 2000.

Aleksandr Glazunov: Issledvaniia, materialy, publikatsii, pis'ma [Glazunov: Research, materials, publications, letters]. Vol. 1. Edited by M[ark] O[sipovich] Yankovsky. Muzgiz: Leningrad, 1959.

Algeranoff, Harcourt. *My Years with Pavlova*. London: William Heinemann, 1957.

Alighieri, Dante. *Il purgatorio e il paradiso. (colle figure di G. Doré)*. Paris: L. Hachette e Cia, 1868.

Anderson, Jack. *The One and Only: The Ballet Russe de Monte Carlo*. New York: Dance Horizons, 1981.

Arbeau, Thoinot. *Orchésographie*. Langres, 1588.

Arkin, Lisa C., and Marian Smith. "National Dance in the Romantic Ballet." In *Rethinking the Sylph: New Perspectives on the Romantic Ballet*, edited by Lynn Garafola, 11–68, 245–252. Hanover, NH: University Press of New England, 1997.

Arsenault, Natalie, and Christopher Rose. *Africa Enslaved*. Austin: University of Texas, 2006. https://liberalarts.utexas.edu/hemispheres/curriculum/africa-enslaved.html.

Au, Susan. "Giselle." In *International Encyclopedia of Dance*, edited by Selma Jeanne Cohen, vol. 3, 177–184. New York and Oxford: Oxford University Press, 1998.

Au, Susan. "Joseph Mazilier." In *International Encyclopedia of Dance*, edited by Selma Jeanne Cohen, vol. 4, 339–343. New York and Oxford: Oxford University Press, 1998.

Babanina, Maria. "Prima la music, dopo la coreografia?—Prima la coreografia dopo la musica?" In *Le Corsaire* program book, edited by Wolfgang Oberender, 31–37. Munich: Bayerisches Staatsballett, 2007.

Babsky, Monique. "Lucien Petipa." In *International Encyclopedia of Dance*, edited by Selma Jeanne Cohen, vol. 5, 148–149. New York and Oxford: Oxford University Press, 1998.

Badetz, Yves, Guy Cogeval, Paul Perrin, and Marie-Paule Perrin, eds. *Spectaculaire Second Empire, 1852–1870*. Paris: Musée d'Orsay, 2016–2017. https://www.musee-orsay.fr/fr/expositi ons/spectaculaire-second-empire-1852-1870-196105.

Balanchine, George, and Francis Mason. *Balanchine's Complete Stories of the Great Ballets*. Rev. ed. Garden City, NY: Doubleday, 1977.

The Ballet Annual. Second Issue. Edited by Arnold L. Haskell. London: A. & C. Black, 1948.

Banducci, Antonia. "Staging a *tragédie en musique*: A 1748 Promptbook of Campra's 'Tancrède.'" *Early Music* 21, no. 2 (May 1993): 180–190.

Barnett, Dene. *The Art of Gesture: The Practices and Principles of 18th Century Acting*. Heidelberg: C. Winter, 1987.

Barzel, Ann. "Elizabetta Menzeli." *Dance Chronicle* 19, no. 3 (1996): 277–288.

Beaumont, Cyril W. *The Ballet Called "Giselle."* 2nd ed. London: Beaumont, 1945. Reprint, London: Dance Books, 1996.

Beaumont, Cyril W. *Complete Book of Ballets*. Garden City, NY: Garden City Publishing, 1941.

Beaumont, Cyril W. *A History of Ballet in Russia (1613–1881)*. London: C.W. Beaumont, 1930.

A Belated Premiere. Directed by Viktor Bocharov. Gosfilmfond Rossiyskoy Federatsii, 2003.

Bellman, Jonathan. *The Style Hongrois in the Music of Western Europe*. Boston: Northeastern University Press, 1993.

Bennett, Alexander. "Regarding the 1835 Brussels Manuscript of *La Sylphide* (the 'Bartholomin score')." In *La Sylphide: Paris 1832 and beyond*, edited by Marian Smith, 334–336. Alton, UK: Dance Books, 2012.

Benois, Alexandre. *Reminiscences of the Russian Ballet*. Translated by Mary Britnieva. London: Putnam, 1941.

Beumers, Birgit, Victor Bocharov, and David Robinson. *Alexander Shiryaev: Master of Movement*. Pordenone: Le Giornate del Cinema Muto, 2009.

Bindman, David, and Henry Louis Gates Jr., gen. eds., Karen C.C. Dalton, assoc. ed. *The Image of the Black in Western Art*. 10 vols. Cambridge, MA: Harvard University Press, 2010–2012.

Binney 3rd, Edwin. *Les ballets de Théophile Gautier*. Paris: Librairie Nizet, 1965.

Boglacheva, Irina, ed. *Peterburgskiy balet. Tri veka: khronika. Tom II. 1801-1850* [The Petersburg ballet. Three centuries: A chronicle. Volume II. 1801-1850]. St. Petersburg: Academy of Russian Ballet named after A.Y. Vaganova, 2014.

Boglacheva, Irina, ed. *Peterburgskiy balet. Tri veka: khronika. Tom III. 1851-1900* [The Petersburg Ballet. Three Centuries: A Chronicle. Volume III. 1851-1900]. St. Petersburg: Academy of Russian Ballet named after A.Y. Vaganova, 2015.

Brenner, C.D. "The Eighteenth-Century Vogue of 'Malbrough' and Marlborough." *Modern Language Review* 45, no. 2 (April 1950): 177–180.

Brown, Ismene. "Time to Get Authentic." *Dance Now* 16, no. 1 (Spring 2007): 34–39.

Buckle, Richard, *Diaghilev*. London: Weidenfeld and Nicolson, 1979.

Burlaka, Yuri, ed. *Classical Repertoire for Ballet Competitions: Pas de Deux and Duets*. 13 vols. St. Petersburg: Compozitor, 2017.

Burlaka, Yuri. "*Grand Pas iz baleta 'Pakhita' i Grand Pas 'Ozhivlennyy Sad' iz belta 'Korsar': Sravnitel'nyy analiz*" [*Grand Pas* from the ballet "Paquita" and *Grand Pas* "The Lively

Garden'" from the ballet "Korsar".: A Comparative Analysis]. *Vestnik Akademii Russkogo baleta imeni A. Ya. Vaganovoy* [Bulletin of the Academy of Russian Ballet named after A. Ya. Vaganova] 2 (2017): 69–79.

Burlaka, Yuri, and Anna Grutsynova, eds. *Libretto baletov Mariusa Petipa* [Librettos of ballets by Marius Petipa]. St. Petersburg: Compozitor, 2018.

Cellarius, Henri. *La danse des salons*, 2nd ed. Paris: [Chez l'Auteur], 1849. Translated into English and published as *Fashionable Dancing*. London: David Bogue, 1847.

Chakravorty, Pallabi. "Dancing into Modernity: Multiple Narratives of India's Kathak Dance." *Dance Research Journal* 38, no. 1/2 (Summer–Winter, 2006): 115–136.

Chane-Yue-Chiang, Linièle. *Pas en variations: Henri Justamant, entrée dans une écriture singulièr: Partitions en Cinétographnie Laban*. [Paris]: Linièle Chane-Yue-Chiang, 2015.

Chapman, John V. "Joseph Mazilier." In *International Dictionary of Ballet*, edited by Martha Bremser, vol. 2, 934–937. Detroit: St. James Press, 1993.

Chapman, John V. "Jules Janin and the Ballet." *Dance Research* 7, no. 1 (Spring 1989): 65–77.

Chapman, John V. "Jules Janin: Romantic Critic." In *Rethinking the Sylph: New Perspectives on the Romantic Ballet*, edited by Lynn Garafola, 197–241. Hanover, NH: University Press of New England, 1997.

Chateaubriand, François-René. *Itinéraire de Paris à Jérusalem et de Jérusalem à Paris . . .* Paris: Le Normant, 1811.

Churakova, Ekaterina, Elena Frolova, Tatiana Saburova, and Sergey Konaev. *Aleksandr Gorskiy: baletmeyster, khudozhnik, fotograf* [Alexander Gorsky: choreographer, artist, photographer]. Moscow: Kuchkovo Pole, 2018.

Clarence-Smith, William Gervase. *Islam and the Abolition of Slavery*. London: Hurst & Company, 2006.

Clark, Maribeth. "Bodies at the Opéra: Art and the Hermaphrodite in the Dance Criticism of Théophile Gautier." In *Critics Reading Critics: Opera and Ballet Criticism in France from the Revolution to 1848*, edited by Roger Parker and Mary Ann Smart, 237–253. New York: Oxford University Press, 2001.

Clark, Maribeth. "The Quadrille as Embodied Musical Experience in 19th-Century Paris." *Journal of Musicology* 19, no. 3 (Summer 2002): 503–526.

Clark, Maribeth. *Understanding French Grand Opera through Dance*. PhD diss., University of Pennsylvania, 1998.

Clarke, Mary, and Clement Crisp. *Ballet: An Illustrated History*. New York: Universe Books, 1973.

Clarke, Mary. *The Sadler's Wells Ballet: A History and an Appreciation*. New York: Da Capo Press, 1977.

Cohen, H. Robert, ed. *The Original Staging Manuals for Twelve Parisian Operatic Premières*. Stuyvesant, NY: Pendragon Press, 1991.

Collins, Willa J. *Adolphe Adam's Ballet* Le Corsaire *at the Paris Opéra, 1856–1868: A Source Study*. PhD diss., Cornell University, 2008.

Contant, Clément, and Joseph de Filippi. *Parallèle des principaux théâtres modernes de l'Europe et des machines théâtrales français, allemandes et anglaises*. Paris: A. Levy, 1860.

Crisp, Clement. "*Giselle* Revived." *Dance Research* 13, no. 2 (Winter 1995): 47–61.

Croce, Arlene. *Afterimages*. New York: Knopf, 1977.

Cruz, Gabriela. *Grand Illusion: Phantasmagoria in Nineteenth-Century Opera*. New York: Oxford University Press, 2020.

Dacko, Karen. "La Source." In *International Dictionary of Ballet*, edited by Martha Bremser, vol. 2, 1330–1332. Detroit: St James Press, 1993.

Danilova, Alexandra. *Choura: The Memoirs of Alexandra Danilova*. New York: Knopf, 1986.

Day, David A. "An Inventory of Manuscript Scores at the Royal Opera House, Covent Garden." *Notes, the Quarterly Journal of the Music Library Association*, Second Series, vol. 44, no. 3 (March 1988): 456–462.

Day, David A. *The annotated* violon répétiteur *and early Romantic ballet at the Theatre Royal de Bruxelles (1815–1830)*. PhD diss., New York University, 2007.

Day, David A. "Digital Opera and Ballet: A Case Study of International Collaboration." *Fontes Artis Musicae* 61, no. 2 (April–June 2014): 99–106.

Dean, Alexander. *Fundamentals of Play Directing*. New York: Farrar & Rinehart, 1941.

De Garmo, Wm. B. *The Dance of Society a Critical Analysis of All the Standard Quadrilles, Round Dances, 102 Figures of Le Cotillon ("the German"), &C., Including Dissertations upon Time and Its Accentuation, Carriage, Style, and Other Relative Matter*. New York: W.A. Pond, 1875. https://www.loc.gov/item/05035056/.

de la Tour, Charlotte. *Le Langage des Fleurs*. 7th ed. Paris: Garnier, 1858.

Deldevez, Edouard Marie Ernest. *Mes Mémoires*. Lu Puy: Marchessou Fils, 1890.

Delibes, Léo. "Grand Valse | *Extraite du Pas des Fleurs, Divertissement intercalé dans Le Corsaire*." Paris: Huegel, n.d. (circa 1895). Plate H. 8198.

Delibes, Léo, and Franz Doppler, F. *Intermezzo (Pas de fleurs, grande valse) aus dem Ballet Naila*. Berlin: Fürstner, 1878.

De Valois, Ninette. *Come Dance with Me: A Memoir, 1898–1956*. London: Hamish Hamilton 1957.

Devic, Claude, and Joseph Vaissette, *Histoire Générale de Languedoc*, vol. 5, edited by Alexandre Du Mège. Toulouse: J.-B. Paya, 1842.

di Tondo, Ornella. "The Italian *Silfide*." In *La Sylphide: Paris 1832 and Beyond*, edited by Marian Smith, 170–232. Alton, Hampshire, UK: Dance Books, 2012.

Dolin, Anton. *Ballet Go Round*. London: Michael Joseph, 1938.

Drescher, Seymour. *Abolition: A History of Slavery and Antislavery*. Cambridge, UK: Cambridge University Press, 2009.

Dunn, Thomas D. "Delibes and *La Source*: Some Manuscripts and Documents." *Dance Chronicle* 4, no. 1 (1981): 1–13.

Edgecombe, Rodney Stenning. "Internationalism, Regionalism, and Glazunov's *Raymonda*." *Musical Times* 149, no. 1902 (Spring 2008): 47–56.

Edgecombe, Rodney Stenning. "A Ragbag of Ballet Music Oddments." *Brolga* 23 (December 1, 2005): 12–21. https://ausdance.org.au/articles/details/a-ragbag-of-ballet-music-oddments.

Eliot, Karen. "Adèle Dumilâtre." In *Dancing Lives: Five Female Dancers from the Ballet d'Action to Merce Cunningham*, 33–59. Champaign: University of Illinois Press, 2007.

Eliot, Karen. "Dancing the Canon in Wartime: Sergeyev, de Valois, and Inglesby and the Classics of British Ballet." In *Dance on Its Own Terms*, edited by Melanie Bales and Karen Eliot, 13–42. New York: Oxford University Press, 2013.

Engelhardt, Molly. "The Real Bayadère Meets the Ballerina on the Western Stage." *Victorian Literature and Culture* 42, no. 3 (2014): 509–534.

Ezhegodnik Imperatorskikh Teatrov [Yearbook of the Imperial Theaters]. St. Petersburg/Petrograd, 1890–1915.

Fairfax, Edmund. "The Eighteenth-Century Garland Pose." *Eighteenth-Century Ballet* (blog). 18 October 2020. https://eighteenthcenturyballet.com/blog/.

Fedorchenko, Olga. "Balerina Adel' Grantsova: 'Zakonnaya naslednitsa' talanta Tal'oni" [Ballerina Adèle Grantzow: "Rightful Heiress" of Taglioni's Talent]. *Muzykal'nyy teatr: spektakl', rol', obraz* [Musical theater: performance, role, image] 1 (2019): 92–106. https://artcenter.ru/wp-content/uploads/2019/11/Ряпосов_сборник.pdf.

Fedorchenko, Olga. "*Balet 'Korsar': Evolyutsiya partii Medory v XIX veke*" [The Ballet "Corsaire": The Evolution of the Part of Medora in the 19th Century]. *Vestnik Akademii Russkogo baleta imeni A. Ya. Vaganovoy* [Bulletin of the Academy of Russian Ballet named after A. Ya. Vaganova] 3 (2016): 94–101.

Fedorchenko, Olga. "*Zhozef Mazil'ye v Peterburge (1851–1852): novyye dokumenty i fakty*" [Joseph Mazilier in St. Petersburg (1851–1852): New Documents and Facts]. *Vestnik Akademii Russkogo baleta imeni A. Ya. Vaganovoy* [Bulletin of the Academy of Russian Ballet named after A. Ya. Vaganova] 5 (2020): 36–45.

Fiske, Roger. *Ballet Music*. London: George G. Harrap, 1958.

Fokine, Michel. *Fokine: Memoirs of a Ballet Master*. Edited by Anatole Chujoy, translated by Vitale Fokine. Boston: Little, Brown, 1961.

Foster, Andrew. "Kschessinska versus Nijinsky" [part one]. Dancing *Times* 111, no. 1324 (December 2020): 24–27; [part two]. *Dancing Times* 111, no. 1325 (January 2021): 20–23.

Foster, Andrew. *Tamara Karsavina: Diaghilev's Ballerina*. London: Andrew Foster, 2010.

Fullington, Doug. "Alexandra Danilova on *Raymonda*." *Ballet Review* 26, no. 4 (Winter 1998): 73–76.

Fullington, Doug. "Elementos de danza española en dos producciones de 'Paquita.'" In *Marius Petipa: Del Ballet Romántico al Clásico*, edited by Laura Hormigón, 105–120. Madrid: Asosiación de Directores de Escena de España, 2020.

Fullington, Doug. "Finding the Balance: Pantomime and Dance in Ratmansky's New/Old Sleeping Beauty." *Oxford Handbooks Online* (August 2017). DOI: 10.1093/oxfordhb/9780199935321.013.169.

Fullington, Doug. "*Raymonda* at 100." *Ballet Review* 26, no. 4 (Winter 1998): 77–86.

Galkin, Andrei. "Choreographic Notations from 'N.G. Sergeyev's Collection' as a Source of Reconstruction of Ballet Performance." In *Marius Petipa on the World Ballet Stage: Materials of the International Conference*, edited by V. V. Chistiakova and N. A. Chistiakova, 35–44. St. Petersburg: St. Peterburg State Museum of Theatre and Music, 2018.

Garafola, Lynn, ed. and trans. *The Diaries of Marius Petipa*. Studies in Dance History, vol. 3, no. 1 (Spring 1992). Pennington: a cappella books, 1992.

Garafola, Lynn, ed. and trans. *La Nijinska: Choreographer of the Modern*. New York: Oxford University Press, 2022.

Garafola, Lynn, ed. and trans. "*Raymonda*, 1946." *Ballet Review* 47, nos. 1–2 (Spring–Summer 2019): 151–160.

Garafola, Lynn, ed. and trans. "Russian Ballet in the Age of Petipa." In *The Cambridge Companion to Ballet*, edited by Marion Kant, 151–163. Cambridge: Cambridge University Press, 2007.

Gautier, Théophile, Jules Janin, Jean-Baptiste Giraldon, and Philarète Chasles. *Les beautés de l'Opéra*. Paris: Soulié, 1844. Published in English as *Beauties of the Opera and Ballet*. Edited by Charles Heath. London: David Bogue, 1845.

Gautier, Théophile. *Gautier on Dance*. Edited and translated by Ivor Guest. London: Dance Books, 1986.

Gautier, Théophile. *The Romantic Ballet as Seen by Théophile Gautier*. Translated by Cyril W. Beaumont. Rev. ed. London: C.W. Beaumont, 1947.

Gautier, Théophile. *Voyage en Espagne*. Paris: Charpentier, 1845.

Genné, Beth. "Creating a Canon, Creating the 'Classics' in Twentieth-Century British Ballet." *Dance Research* 18, no. 2 (Winter, 2000): 132–162.

Gershenzon, Pavel. "Cronografia di *Raymonda*: Lettere, documenti, recensioni, commenti." Translated by Carla Muschio. In *Raymonda* program book, 47–79. Milan: Teatro alla Scala, 2011.

Gershenzon, Pavel. "*La Bayadère*: The Wrath of the Gods Restored." *Ballet Review* 30, no. 3 (Fall 2002): 15–28.

Glazunov, Alexander. *Raymonda*. Leipzig: M.P. Belaieff, 1898. Available online at https://imslp. org/wiki/Raymonda,_Op.57_(Glazunov,_Aleksandr). The orchestral score and piano reduction were published separately.

Gorsky, Alexander. *Tablitsa znakov dlia zapisyvaniia dvizhenii chelovecheskago tela po sisteme V.I. Stepanova* [Table of Signs for the Notation of Movements of the Human Body According to the System of the Artist of the Imperial St. Petersburg Theaters V.I. Stepanov]. Imperial St. Petersburg Theater School [n.d]. *Khoreografiia, primery dlia chteniia* [Choreography: Examples for Reading]. Imperial St. Petersburg Theater School. Installment I. 1899. Published in English as *Two Essays on Stepanov Dance Notation by Alexander Gorsky*. Translated by Roland John Wiley. New York: Congress on Research in Dance, 1978.

Grant, Gail. *Technical Manual and Dictionary of Classical Ballet*. 3rd ed. New York: Dover, 1982.

Grigoriev, S[erge] L[eonidovich]. *The Diaghilev Ballet: 1909–1929*. Edited and translated by Vera Bowen. Middlesex, UK: Penguin, 1960.

Gromova, Elizaveta. *Detskie tantsy iz klassicheskikh baletov s notnym prilozheniem* [Children's Dances from Classical Ballets with Musical Scores], 2nd ed. St. Petersburg: Music Planet, 2010.

Guest, Ann Hutchinson. *Choreo-Graphics: A Comparison of Dance Notation Systems from the Fifteenth Century to the Present*. New York: Gordon and Breach, 1989.

Guest, Ann Hutchinson. *Fanny Elssler's "Cachucha."* London: Dance Books, 1981.

Guest, Ivor. *The Ballet of the Enlightenment: The Establishment of the Ballet d'Action in France, 1770–1793*. London: Dance Books, 1996.

Guest, Ivor. *Ballet of the Second Empire 1847–1858*. London: Adam and Charles Black, 1955.

Guest, Ivor. *Ballet of the Second Empire 1858–1870*. London: Adam and Charles Black, 1953.

Guest, Ivor. "Cesare Pugni: A Plea for Justice," *Dance Research* 1, no. 1 (Spring 1983): 30–38.

Guest, Ivor. *The Divine Virginia: A Biography of Virginia Zucchi*. New York: Marcel Dekker, 1977.

Guest, Ivor. *Fanny Cerrito: The Life of a Romantic Ballerina*. 2nd ed. London: Dance Books, 1974.

Guest, Ivor. *Fanny Elssler*. Middletown, CT: Wesleyan University Press, 1970.

Guest, Ivor. "Théophile Gautier on Spanish Dancing." *Dance Chronicle* 10, no. 1 (1987): 1–104.

Guest, Ivor. "Jean Coralli and the Influence of Eugène Scribe at the Porte Saint-Martin Theatre." In *Prima la danza! Festschrift für Sybille Dahms*, edited by Gunhild Oberzaucher-Schüller, Daniel Brendenberg, and Monika Woitas, 253–257. Würzburg: Königshausen Nermann, 2004.

Guest, Ivor. *Jules Perrot: Master of the Romantic Ballet*. London: Dance Books, 1984.

Guest, Ivor. *The Paris Opéra Ballet*. Alton, UK: Dance Books, 2006.

Guest, Ivor. *The Romantic Ballet in England*. Rev. ed., 1972. Reprint, Hampshire, UK: Dance Books, 2014.

Guest, Ivor. *The Romantic Ballet in Paris*. 2nd ed. London: Dance Books, 1980; 3rd ed. Alton, UK: Dance Books, 2008.

Gutsche-Miller, Sarah. "Liberated Women and Travesty Fetishes: Conflicting Representations of Gender in Parisian Fin-de-Siècle Music-Hall Ballet." *Dance Research* 35, no. 2 (2017): 187–208.

Gutsche-Miller, Sarah. *Parisian Music-Hall Ballet 1870–1913*. Rochester, NY: University of Rochester Press, 2015.

Hallman, Diana R. *Opera, Liberalism, and Antisemitism in Nineteenth-Century France: The Politics of Halévy's* La Juive. Cambridge: Cambridge University Press, 2002.

Hammond, Sandra Noll. "Ballet's Technical Heritage: The *Grammaire* of Léopold Adice." *Dance Research* 13 (Summer 1995): 33–58.

Hammond, Sandra Noll. "Dancing *La Sylphide* in 1832: Something Old or Something New?" In *La Sylphide: Paris 1832 and Beyond*, edited by Marian Smith, 31–56. Alton, Hampshire, UK: Dance Books, 2012.

Hammond, Sandra Noll. "The 'Gavotte de Vestris': A Dance of Three Centuries." In *Proceedings*, 202–208. Society of Dance History Scholars, 1984.

Hammond, Sandra Noll. "History of Ballet Technique: Ballet in the Late Eighteenth and Early Nineteenth Centuries," and "History of Ballet Technique: Ballet since the Mid Nineteenth Century." In *International Encyclopedia of Dance*, edited by Selma Jeanne Cohen, vol. 1, 344–349. New York and Oxford: Oxford University Press, 1998.

Hammond, Sandra Noll. "*La Sténochorégraphie* by Saint-Léon: A Link in Ballet's Technical History." In *Proceedings*, 148–154. Society of Dance History Scholars, 1982.

Hammond, Sandra Noll. "Steps Through Time: Selected Dance Vocabulary of the Eighteenth and Nineteenth Centuries." *Dance Research* 10, no. 2 (1992): 93–108.

Hancock, Ian. *The Pariah Syndrome: An Account of Gypsy Slavery and Persecution*. Open Library: Karoma, 1987. http://www.oocities.org/~patrin/pariah-contents.htm.

Hazareesingh, Sudhir. *The Legend of Napoleon*. London: Granta UK, 2005.

Hazareesingh, Sudhir. "Napoleonic Memory in Nineteenth-Century France: The Making of a Liberal Legend." *Modern Language Notes* 120, no. 4 (September 2005): 747–773.

Hazareesingh, Sudhir. "Religion and Politics in the Saint-Napoleon Festivity 1852–70: Anti-Clericalism, Local Patriotism and Modernity." *English Historical Review* 119, no. 482 (2004): 614–649.

Hilton, Wendy. "Loure." In *International Encyclopedia of Dance*, edited by Selma Jeanne Cohen, vol. 4, 231–232. New York and Oxford: Oxford University Press, 1998.

Holm, Bent. *The Taming of the Turk: Ottomans on the Danish Stage 1596–1896*. Vienna: Hollitzer, 2014.

Homans, Jennifer. *Apollo's Angels: A History of Ballet*. New York: Random House, 2010.

Hormigón, Laura. *Marius Petipa en España 1844–1847: Memorias y otros materiales*. Madrid: Danzarte Ballet, 2010.

Hormigón, Laura. "Petipa in Spain." *Ballet Review* 47, nos. 3–4 (Fall–Winter 2019): 69–72.

Hugo, Victor. "Funérailles de l'empereur Napoléon: détails circonstanciés des actes qui ont signalé la journée du 15 décember, 1840." Genève: imprimerie de Vaney, 1840.

Hugo, Victor. "Fantômes," from *Les Orientales*. Paris: Charles Gosselin, 1829. Critical edition by Élisabeth Barineau. Vol. 2, 134–137. Paris: Librairier Marcel Didier, 1968. Published in English in *Translations from the Poems of Victor Hugo*, 61–65. Translated by Henry Carrington. London: Walter Scott, 1887.

Illarionov, Boris A. " 'Bayaderka': Chetyre ili tri?" ["Bayaderka": Four or Three?]. *Vestnik Akademii Russkogo baleta im. A. YA. Vaganovoy* [Bulletin of the Academy of Russian Ballet named after A. Ya. Vaganova] 4 (2017): 28–39.

Inglesby, Mona, with Kay Hunter. *Ballet in the Blitz*. Suffolk, UK: Groundnut, 2008.

Issiyeva, Adalyat. *Representing Russia's Orient: From Ethnography to Art Song*. New York: Oxford University Press, 2021.

Jacobshagen, Arnold. "Analyzing Mise-en-Scène": Halévy's *La Juive* at the Salle Le Peletier." In *Music, Theater, and Cultural Transfer: Paris, 1830–1914*, edited by Annegret Fauser and Mark Everist, 176–194. Chicago: University of Chicago Press. 2009.

Jennings, Lawrence C. *French Antislavery: The Movement for the Abolition of Slavery in France, 1802–1848*. New York: Cambridge University Press, 2000.

Jeschke, Claudia. "Choreo-graphing Spectacularity." In *de-archiving movement #3*, edited by Rose Breuss and Claudia Jeschke, 28–40. Munich: epodium, 2017. https://www.epodium.de/e-zine.

Jeschke, Claudia, and Robert Atwood. "Expanding Horizons: Techniques of Choreo-Graphy in Nineteenth-Century Dance." *Dance Chronicle* 29, no. 2 (2006): 195–214.

Jeschke, Claudia, Gabi Vettermann, and Nicole Haitzinger. *Les Choses Espagnoles: Research into the Hispanomania of 19th Century Dance*. Munich: epodium, 2009.

Jeschke, Claudia, and Helmut Zedelmaier, eds. *Fremde Körper, andere Bewegungen*. Münster: Lit, 2005.

Join-Diéterlé, Catherine. *Les décors de scène de l'Opéra de Paris à l'époque romantique*. Paris: Picard, 1988.

Jürgensen, Knud Arne. *The Verdi Ballets*. Parma: Instituto nazionale di studi verdiani, 1995.

[Justamant, Henri.] *Giselle, ou, Les wilis: Ballet fantastique en deux actes*. Edited by Frank-Manuel Peter. Hildesheim: Georg Olms Verlag, 2008.

Kalman, Julie. *Rethinking Antisemitism in Nineteenth-Century France*. New York: Cambridge University Press, 2010.

Kane, Angela, and Jane Pritchard. "The Camargo Society Part I." *Dance Research* 12, no. 2 (Autumn 1994): 21–65.

Karsavina, Tamara. "A Blue Transparency of Night." *Dancing Times* 54, no. 641 (February 1964): 239.

Karsavina, Tamara. "Lost Steps! I. – 'Giselle.'" *Dancing Times* New Series, no. 517 (October 1953): 9–10; "Lost Steps (II): Second Act Of Giselle." *Dancing Times* New Series, no. 518 (November 1953): 75; "Lost Steps (III): Giselle's Character." *Dancing Times* New Series, no. 519 (December 1953): 139; "Lost Steps (V): Stage Illusions." *Dancing Times* New Series, no. 521 (February 1954): 281–282.

Karsavina, Tamara. *Theatre Street: The Reminiscences of Tamara Karsavina*. Rev. ed. London: Dance Books, 1981.

Katz, Leslie George, Nancy Lassalle, and Harvey Simmonds, eds. *Choreography by George Balanchine: A Catalog of Works*. Viking: New York, 1984.

Kendall, Elizabeth. *Balanchine and the Lost Muse*. New York: Oxford University Press, 2013.

Kochno, Boris. *Diaghilev and the Ballets Russes.* Translated by Adrienne W. Foulke. New York: Harper & Row, 1970.

Koegler, Horst. "Wenn die Musik die gehorsame Tochter des Tanzes zu sein hat" [When Music Must Be the Obedient Daughter of Dance]. In *Prima la danza. Festschrift für Sibylle Dahms*, edited by Gunhild Oberzaucher-Schüller, Daniel Brandenburg, and Monika Woitas, 373–378. Würzburg: Königshausen und Neumann, 2004.

Konaev, Sergey. "Der *Tigre Captif* und Gustave Doré: Marius Petipas Inspirations-Quellen" [The *Tigre Captif* and Gustave Doré: Marius Petipa's Sources of Inspiration]. In *La Bayadère* program book, edited by Annegret Gertz, 42–45. Berlin: Staatsballett Berlin, 2018.

Konaev, Sergey, ed. *Dva veka Petipa* [Two centuries of Petipa]. Moscow: Ministry of Culture of the Russian Federation, State Central Theatre Museum named after A.A. Bakhrushin, 2018.

Konaev, Sergey. "Khronika osnovnykh postanovok s vstavnymi variatsiami (1841–1924)" [Chronicle of main productions with inserted variations (1841–1924)]. In *Giselle* program book, edited by Sergey Konaev, 80–101. Moscow: Bolshoi Theater, 2019.

Konaev, Sergey, ed. "My vse visim v vozdukhe … Pis'ma N.G. Sergeyeva k A.K. Shervashidze (1921–1933)" [We Are All Hanging in the Air … Letters from N.G. Sergeev to A.K. Shervashidze (1921–1933)]. *Mnemozina* 6 (2014): 555–584. http://teatrlib.ru/Library/Mnemozina/Mnemoz_6/Mnemoz_.

Konaev, Sergey. "*Raymonda* dopo Petipa." Translated by Carla Muschio. In *Raymonda* program book, 91–99. Milan: Teatro alla Scala, 2011.

Konaev, Sergey, and Pavel Gershenzon. "Commenti a *Raymonda*." Translated by Carla Muschio. In *Raymonda* program book, 113–126. Milan: Teatro alla Scala, 2011.

Krassovskaya, Vera. *Vaganova: A Dance Journey from Petersburg to Leningrad.* Translated by Vera Siegel. Gainesville: University of Florida Press, 2005.

Kschessinska, Mathilde. *Dancing in Petersburg: The Memoirs of Kschessinska.* Translated by Arnold Haskell. Garden City, NY: Doubleday, 1961.

Kuehn, Julia. "Exotic Harem Paintings: Gender, Documentation, and Imagination." *Frontiers: A Journal of Women Studies* 32, no. 2 (2011): 31–63.

Laletin, Sergey. "'Raymonda' i S.P.Dyagilev: nesostoyavshayasya postanovka baleta M.I.Petipa v 'Russkikh sezonakh' 1909 goda" ["Raymonda" and S.P. Diaghilev: The Failed Production of the Ballet by M.I. Petipa in the 'Russian Seasons' in 1909]. Moscow: 2018. https://theatremuseum.ru/naukpubl/laletin.

Lathers, Marie. "Posing the 'Belle Juive': Jewish Models in 19th-Century Paris." *Woman's Art Journal* 21, no. 1 (2000): 27–32.

Lazzarini, John, and Roberta Lazzarini. *Pavlova: Repertoire of a Legend.* New York: Schirmer Books, 1980.

Lecomte, Nathalie. "Dans le sillage du *Corsaire*: de Paris (1856) à Saint-Petersbourg (1899)." *Slavica Occitania* 43 (2016): 149–166.

Legat, Nicolas. *Ballet Russe: Memoirs of Nicolas Legat.* Translated by Sir Paul Dukes. London: Methuen, 1939. Legat's memoirs have been republished in *The Legat Legacy*. Edited by Mindy Aloff. Gainesville: University of Florida Press, 2020.

Letellier, Robert Ignatius. *The Ballets of Ludwig Minkus.* Newcastle, UK: Cambridge Scholars Publishing, 2008.

Leucci, Tiziana. "Naslediye Romantizma i Oriyentalizma v Baletakh Mariusa Petipa s Indiyskim motivom: 'Bayaderka' (1877) i 'Talisman' (1889)" [The Heritage of Romanticism and Orientalism in Ballets by Marius Petipa with Indian Motives: "La Bayadère" (1877) and

"Talisman" (1889)]. *Vestnik Akademii Russkogo baleta imeni A. Ya. Vaganovoy* [Bulletin of the Academy of Russian Ballet named after A. Ya. Vaganova] 6 (2019): 22–32.

Levasheva, E.M., ed. *Istoriya russkoy muzyki, Tom 10B, Kniga 1, 1890–1917, Khronograf* [History of Russian Music, Vol. 10B, Book 1, 1890–1917, Chronograph]. Moscow: *Yazyki Slavyanskikh kultur* [Languages of Slavic Cultures], 2011.

Levy, Morris S., and John Milton Ward. *Italian Ballet 1637–1977 from the John Milton and Ruth Neils Ward Collection*. Cambridge, MA: Harvard University Press, 2005.

Lieven, Prince Peter. *The Birth of the Ballets-Russes*. London: George Allen & Unwin, 1936.

Lifar, Serge. *Apothéose du ballet romantique*. Paris: Albin Michel, 1942.

Lifar, Serge. *La Danse: les grands courants de la danse académique*. Paris: Denoël, 1938.

Ligore, Bruno. "Le lettere di Louis Henry e di Élise Henry-Vallier." In *Danza e ballo a Napoli, un dialogo con l'Europa (1806–1861)*, edited by Paologiovanni Maione and Maria Venuso, 171–190. Napoli: Turchini Edizioni, 2020.

Ligore, Bruno. "Violin Conductor's Scores and Pantomimic Encoding in the First Half of the Nineteenth Century: Some Methodological Approaches." In *Times of Change: Artistic Perspectives and Cultural Crossings in Nineteenth-Century Dance*, edited by Irene Brandenburg, Francesca Falcone, Claudia Jeschke, Bruno Ligore, 305–330. Bologna: Massimiliano Piretti Editore, 2023.

Locke, Ralph P. *Music and the Exotic from the Renaissance to Mozart*. Cambridge: Cambridge University Press, 2015.

Locke, Ralph P. *Musical Exoticism: Images and Reflections*. New York: Cambridge University Press, 2009.

Longino, Michèle. *Orientalism in French Classical Drama*. Cambridge: Cambridge University Press, 2002.

Lopukhov, Fedor. *Writings on Dance and Music*. Edited by Stephanie Jordan, translated by Dorinda Offord. Madison: University of Wisconsin Press, 2002.

Lopukhov, A[ndrei] V[asilievich], A[lexander] V[iktorovich] Shiryaev, and A[lexander] I[lyich] Bocharov. *Osnovy kharakternogo tantsa* [The Fundamentals of Character Dance]. Leningrad: Iskusstvo, 1939. Published in English as *Character Dance*. Translated by Joan Lawson. London: Dance Books, 1986.

Loya, Shay. "Beyond 'Gypsy' Stereotypes: Harmony and Structure in the *Verbunkos* Idiom." *Journal of Musicological Research* 27 (2008): 254–280.

Ludwig, Paul. *Henri Justamant (1815–1890), Kommentiertes Bestandsverzeichnis seiner Ballett-Notationen in der Theaterwissenschaftlichen Sammlung Schloß Wahn, Gefördert von der Fritz Thyssen Stiftung, Köln, und der Studienstiftung Niessen*. Köln: Universität zu Köln, Theaterwissenschaftliche Sammlung Schloss Wahn, 2005.

Macaulay, Alastair. "Further Annals of *The Sleeping Beauty*: A Questionnaire." *Ballet Review* 43, no. 4 (Winter 2015–2016): 83–109.

Macaulay, Alastair, Doug Fullington, Maina Gielgud, Jane Pritchard, Alexei Ratmansky, and Marian Smith. "Giselle: Questions and Answers." *Alastair Macaulay* (blog). 10 October 2020. https://www.alastairmacaulay.com/all-essays/giselle-questions-answers.

Macaulay, Alastair, Doug Fullington, and Sergey Konaev. "'Raymonda' and Ballet Herstory: historians Doug Fullington and Sergey Konaev on Lydia Pashkova, Ivan Vsevolozhsky, Marius Petipa and the Russian Imperial Theatres. A 'Raymonda' Questionnaire." *Alastair Macaulay* (blog). 21 January 2022. https://www.alastairmacaulay.com/all-essays/byq3y6560y798jcrlmi wp4s4su9ii6.

Manela, Aaron. "Arthur Saint-Leon's *The Little Humpbacked Horse* in Context." Master's thesis, University of Oregon, 2011.

Marion, Sheila, with Karen Eliot. "Recording the Imperial Ballet: Anatomy and Ballet in Stepanov's Notation." In *Dance on Its Own Terms*, edited by Melanie Bales and Karen Eliot, 309–340. New York: Oxford University Press, 2013.

Marius Petipa. Materialy, vospominaniya, stat'i [Marius Petipa. Materials, Recollections, Articles]. Edited by Yury Slonimsky et al. Leningrad: Iskusstvo, 1971.

Marsh, Carol G. "Gavotte." In *International Encyclopedia of Dance*, edited by Selma Jeanne Cohen, vol. 3. 123–125. New York and Oxford: Oxford University Press, 2003.

Mason, Francis. *I Remember Balanchine*. New York: Doubleday, 1991.

Matache, Margareta. "The Legacy of Gypsy Studies in Modern Romani Scholarship." *FXB Center for Health & Human Rights at Harvard University* (blog). 14 November 2016. https://fxb.harv ard.edu/2016/11/14/the-legacy-of-gypsy-studies-in-modern-romani-scholarship/.

McGarry, Aidan. *Romaphobia: The Last Acceptable Form of Racism*. London: Zed Books, 2017. https://www.zedbooks.net/shop/book/romaphobia/.

Meisner, Nadine. *Marius Petipa: The Emperor's Ballet Master*. New York: Oxford University Press, 2019.

Melik-Pashayeva, Karina L. "Raymonda." In *International Encyclopedia of Dance*, edited by Selma Jeanne Cohen, vol. 5, 320–322. New York and Oxford: Oxford University Press, 1998.

Menczer, Bela. "Exposition, 1867." *History Today* 17, no. 7 (July 1967): 429–436.

Merwin, W[illim] S[tanley]. *The Mays of Ventadorn*. Washington, DC: National Geographic Society, 2002.

Michaud, Joseph-François, and Jean-Joseph François Poujoulat. *Histoire des croisades, abrégée à l'usage de la jeunesse*. Tours: Mame, 1899.

Minkus, Aloysius Ludwig, and Alphonse Victor Marius Petipa. *Bol'shoye klassicheskoye pa iz baleta Pakhita* [Grand Pas Classique from the Ballet "Paquita"]. Edited by Yuri Burlaka, choreographic text and musical material assembled and prepared by G.N. [Herman Nikolayevich] Pribylov. Moscow: Planeteum, 2000.

Minkus, Ludwig. *La Bayadère*. Edited by Robert Ignatius Letellier. Newcastle upon Tyne, UK: Cambridge Scholars Publishing, 2009.

Mitchell, Robin. *Vénus Noire: Black Women and Colonial Fantasies in Nineteenth-Century Franc*. Athens: University of Georgia Press, 2020.

Montoya, Alicia C. *Medievalist Enlightenment from Charles Perrault to Jean-Jacques Rousseau*. Cambridge, UK: D.S. Brewer, 2013.

Nijinska, Bronislava. *Early Memoirs*. Translated and edited by Irina Nijinska and Jean Rawlinson. New York: Holt, Rinehart and Winston, 1981.

Nochlin, Linda. *The Politics of Vision: Essays on Nineteenth-Century Art and Society*. London: Thames and Hudson, 1991.

Olevesi, Vannina. "Entre discretion et quête de reconnaissance: Jean Coralli à l'Opéra, une ascension professionnelle au défi de la standardization du ballet (1830–1854)." In *Giovanni Coralli, l'autore di Giselle*, edited by José Sasportes and Patrizia Veroli, 123–233. Canterano: Aracne editrice, 2018.

Peabody, Sue. "*There Are No Slaves in France*": *The Political Culture of Race and Slavery in the Ancien Régime*. New York: Oxford University Press, 1997.

Pendle, Karin, and Stephen Wilkins. "Paradise Found: The Salle le Peletier and French Grand Opera." In *Opera in Context: Essays on Historical Staging from the Late Renaissance to the Time of Puccini*, edited by Mark A. Radice, 171–207. Portland, OR: Amadeus Press, 1998.

[Petipa, Marius.] " 'Raymonda': Scenario by Marius Petipa." Translated by Debra Goldman. *Ballet Review* 5, no. 2 (1975–76): 38–44.

Pleshcheyev, Alexander. *Nash Balet (1673–1899)* [Our Ballet (1673–1899)]. 2nd, supplemented ed. St. Petersburg: Th. A. Pereyaslavtsev and A.A. Pleshcheyev, 1899. Reprint, St. Petersburg: Music Planet, 2009.

Poesio, Giannandrea. "The Choreographer and the Temple Dancer: the origins of *La Bayadère*." *Dancing Times* 87, no. 1038 (March 1997): 527–531.

Poesio, Giannandrea. *The Language of Gesture in Italian Dance from Commedia Dell'arte to Blasis*. PhD. diss., University of Surrey, 1993.

Pougin, Arthur. *Adolphe Adam: Sa vie, sa carrière, ses mémoires artistiques*. Paris: Charpentier, 1877. Available online at https://gallica.bnf.fr/ark:/12148/bpt6k64572131/f7.item.texteImage.

Pritchard, Jane, with Caroline Hamilton. *Anna Pavlova: Twentieth Century Ballerina*. Rev. and extended ed. London: Booth-Clibborn, 2013.

Pritchard, Jane. "Bits of Bayadere in Britain." *Dancing Times* 79, no. 948 (September 1989): 1120–1121.

Pritchard, Jane. "Nicholas Sergeyev." In *International Dictionary of Ballet*, edited by Martha Bremser, vol. 2, 1275–1277. Detroit: St. James Press, 1993.

Prod'homme, J[acques]-G[abriel]. "Napoleon, Music and Musicians." Translated by Frederick H. Martens. *Musical Quarterly* 7, no. 4 (October 1921): 579–605.

Puri, Rajika. "Im dienste der Gottheit: Die Indische Devadasi" [In the Service of the Deity: The Indian Devadasi]. In *La Bayadère* program book, edited by Annegret Gretz, 11–13. Berlin: Staatsballett Berlin, 2018.

Rambert, Marie. *Quicksilver*. New York: St. Martin's Press, 1972.

Ratmansky, Alexei. "Staging Petipa's *Harlequinade* at ABT." *Ballet Review* 47, nos. 1–2 (Spring–Summer 2019): 45–55.

Ratner, Leonard. *Classic Music: Expression, Form, and Style*. New York: Schirmer, 1980.

Ratner, Leonard. *Romantic Music: Sound and Syntax*. New York: Schirmer, 1992.

Reflections of a Dancer: Alexandra Danilova. Directed by Anne Belle. Public Broadcasting Service, 1980.

Roslavleva, Natalia. *The Era of Russian Ballet*. London: Victor Gollancz, 1966.

Rousseau, Jean-Jacques. *Dictionnaire de musique*. Paris: Chez le Veuve Duchesne, 1785.

Rygg, Kristin. "Faust Goes Dancing." In *The Oxford Handbook of Faust in Music*, edited by Lorna Fitzsimmons and Charles McKnight, 461–482. New York: Oxford University Press, 2019. Doi: 10.1093/oxfordhb/9780199935185.013.24.

Saffle, Michael. *Franz Liszt: A Guide to Research*. New York: Routledge, 2004.

Saint-Léon, Arthur. *La sténochorégraphie, ou L'art d'écrire promptement la danse*. Paris, 1852.

Saint-Léon, Arthur. *Letters from a Ballet Master: The Correspondence of Arthur Saint-Léon*. Edited and translated by Ivor Guest. London: Dance Books, 1981.

Scholl, Tim. *From Petipa to Balanchine*. New York: Routledge, 1994.

Scholl, Tim. *Sleeping Beauty: A Legend in Progress*. New Haven and London: Yale University Press, 2004.

Sasportes, José, and Patrizia Veroli. *Giovanni Coralli, l'autore di Giselle*, eds. Canterano: Gioacchino Onorati editore, 2018.

Schwerendt, Matthias, and Ines Guhe. "Describing the Enemy: Images of Islam in Narratives of the Crusades." In *European Receptions of the Crusades in the Nineteenth Century: Franco-German Perspectives*. Edited by Georg-Eckert-Institut für internationale Schulbuchforschung, Eckert.Dossiers 4, 1–13. Braunschweig: Georg-Eckert-Institut, 2011. https://repository.gei.de/bitstream/handle/11428/129/ED4_Crusades.pdf?sequence=3&isAllowed=y.

Scott, Walter. *The Monastery. A Romance*. By the Author of "Waverley." Vol. I (II–III). Edinburgh: Archibald Constable and John Ballantyne; London: Longman, Hurst, Rees, Orme, and Brown, 1820.

Semmens, Richard. *The "Bals publics" at the Paris Opera in the Eighteenth Century*. Hillsdale, NY: Pendragon Press, 2004.

Sensuality & Nationalism in Romantic Ballet. DVD. Directed by Claudia Jeschke. Dallas: Dancetime Publications, 2012.

Slonimsky, Yuri. " 'Raimonda': Put' Glazunova k baletnomu tvorchestvu" ["Raymonda": Glazunov's path to ballet creativity]. In *Aleksandr Glazunov: Issledvaniia, materialy, publikatsii, pis'ma* [Glazunov: Research, materials, publications, letters], vol. 1, edited by M[ark] O[sipovich] Yankovsky, 377–503. Muzgiz: Leningrad, 1959.

Smith, Marian. *Ballet and Opera in the Age of Giselle*. Princeton, NJ: Princeton University Press, 2000.

Smith, Marian. "The Disappearing Danseur." *Cambridge Opera Journal* 19, no. 1 (2007): 1–25.

Smith, Marian. "Le Disposizioni Sceniche delle Opere Francesi negli Anni Parigini di Donizetti." In *Atti del Convegno Internazionale di Studio 1992*, edited by Francesco Bellotto, 371–394. Bergamo: Assessorato allo Spettacolo, 1992.

Smith, Marian. "The Earliest *Giselle*? A Preliminary Report on a St. Petersburg Manuscript." *Dance Chronicle* 23, no. 1 (2000): 29–48.

Smith, Marian. "The Metropolitan Balanchine." *Ballet Review* 47, nos. 1–2 (Spring–Summer 2019): 125–140.

Smith, Marian. "New Life for Character and Story in *Sleeping Beauty*." *Oxford Handbooks Online*, March 2017. Doi: 10.1093/oxfordhb/9780199935321.013.172.

Smith, Marian. "Processions in French Grand Opera." In *Bild und Bewegung im Musiktheater. Interdisziplinäre Studien im Umfeld der Grand Opéra*. [Image and Movement in Music Theatre. Interdisciplinary Studies around Grand Opéra], edited by Roman Brotbeck, Laura Moeckli, Anette Schaffer, and Stephanie Schroedter, 43–50. Schliengen: Argus 2018.

Smith, Marian, ed. *La Sylphide: Paris 1832 and Beyond*. Alton, Hampshire, UK: Dance Books, 2012.

Souritz, Elizabeth. *Soviet Choreographers in the 1920s*. Edited by Sally Banes, translated by Lynn Visson. Durham: Duke University Press, 1990.

Sowell, Madison U., and Debra H. Sowell. *Il Balletto Romantico: Tesori della Collezione Sowell*. Palermo: L'Epos, 2007.

Sowell, Madison U. "Nineteenth-Century Ballet in Paris: A Tale of Two Alines." In *Toute littérature est littérature comparée: Études de littérature et de linguistique offertes à Roy Rosenstein par ses collègues, ses disciples et ses amis*, edited by Danielle Buschinger, Martine Marzloff, Patricia Gillies, and Marie-Geneviève Grossel, 569–582. Amiens: Centre d'Études Médiévales de Picardie, 2021.

Sparti, Barbara, Judy Van Zile, Elsie Ivancich Dunin, Nancy Heller, and Adrienne L. Kaeppler, eds. *Imaging Dance: Visual Representations of Dancers and Dancing*. Hildensheim: Georg Ohms, 2011.

Spencer, Helena Kopchick. "Le divertissement dansé." In *L'histoire de l'opéra français, vol. 2, Du Consulat aux débuts de la Troisième République*, edited by Hervé Lacombe, 316–324, 364–365. Paris: Fayard, 2020.

Spencer, Helena Kopchick. *The* Jardin des femmes *as Scenic Convention in French Opera and Ballet*. PhD diss., University of Oregon, 2014.

Spencer, Helena Kopchick. "Louisiana Imagined: Gender, Race and Slavery in Le Planteur (1839)." In *America in the French Imaginary, 1789–1914: Music, Revolution and Race*, edited by Diana Hallman and César Leal, 50–99. Woodbridge, UK: Boydell & Brewer, 2022.

Spencer, Helena Kopchick, Sarah Gutsche-Miller, and Marian Smith. "Justamant's *Le Bossu* and Depictions of Indigenous Americans in Nineteenth-Century French Ballet." In *America in the French Imaginary, 1789–1914: Music, Revolution and Race*, edited by Diana Hallman and César Leal, 49–99. Woodbridge, UK: Boydell & Brewer, 2022.

Stals, Georgs. *Das Lettische Ballett des Rigaer Oper*. Riga: J. Kadili Verlag, 1943.

Stepanov, V[ladimir] I[vanovich]. *Alphabet des mouvements du corps humain; essai d'enregistrement des mouvements du corps humain au moyen des signes musicaux*. Paris: Impr. M. Zouckermann [Librairie P. Vigot], 1892. Published in Russian as *Tablitsa znakov dlya zapisyvaniya dvizhenii chelovecheskogo tela po sisteme Artista Imperatorskikh S.-Peterburgskikh Teatrov, V.I. Stepanova* [Table of Signs for the Notation of the Movements of the Human Body According to the System of the Artist of the Imperial St. Petersburg Theaters, V.I. Stepanov]. St. Petersburg [n.d.]. Published in English as *Alphabet of Movements of the Human Body*. Translated by Raymond Lister. Cambridge, UK: Golden Head Press, 1958.

Still, Jonathan. "Glazunov, Raymonda, and Hullámzó Balaton." *Jonathan Still, Ballet Pianist* (blog). 12 May 2010. http://jonathanstill.com/2010/05/12/raymonda-and-hullamzo-balaton/.

Strobel, Desmond F. "Quadrille." In *International Encyclopedia of Dance*, edited by Selma Jeanne Cohen, vol. 5, 285–287. New York and Oxford: Oxford University Press, 1998.

Svetlov, Valerian. *Terpsikhora: Stat'i ocherki i zametk* [Terpsichore: Articles, essays, and notes]. St. Petersburg: 1906.

Swack, Jeanne. "Anti-Semitism at the Opera: The Portrayal of Jews in the 'Singspiels' of Reinhard Keiser." *Musical Quarterly* 84, no. 3 (2000): 389–416.

Taburetkina, Irina V. "The Central Music Library of the St. Petersburg State Academic Mariinsky Theatre." *Fontes Artis Musicae* 53, no. 3 (July–September 2006): 170–172.

Tamvaco, Jean-Louis. *Les Cancans De L'opéra: Chroniques de L'académie Royale de Musique et du Théâtre, à Paris sous les Deux Restaurations: Première Édition Critique Intégrale Du Manuscrit Les Cancans De L'opéra, ou, Le Journal D'une Habilleuse, de 1836 à 1848*, vol. 2. Paris: CNRS Editions, 2000.

Telyakovsky, V[ladimir] A[rkadievich] "Memoirs: Part 2." Translated by Nina Dimitrievitch. *Dance Research* 9, no. 1 (Spring 1991): 26–39.

Troven, Carol. "Innocents Abroad: American Painters at the 1867 Exposition Universelle, Paris." *American Art Journal* 16, no. 4 (Autumn 1984): 32–29.

Tulard, Jean. "Le retour des cendres." In *Les lieux de mémoire*, edited by Pierre Nora, part 2: *La nation*, vol. 3, 81–110. Paris: Gallimard, 1986.

Urista, Dawn. "Giselle's Mad Scene: A Demonstration and Comparison of 21st Century and 19th Century Paris Opéra Stagings." Master's project, University of Oregon, 2011.

Vaillat, Léandre. *La Taglioni, ou la Vie d'une danseuse*. Paris: A. Michel, 1942.

Van Dyk, Garritt. "The Embassy of Soliman Aga to Louis XIV: Diplomacy, Dress, and Diamonds." In *Cosmopolitan Moments: Instances of Exchange in the Long Eighteenth Century*, edited by Jennifer Milam, 1–19, *emaj*, Special Issue 9, no. 1 (December 2017). http://emajartjournal. com/cosmopolitan-moments/.

Vaughan, David. "Nureyev's 'Raymonda.'" *Ballet Review* 5, no. 2 (1975–76): 30–37.

Vazem, Ekaterina. "Memoirs of a Ballerina of the St Petersburg Bolshoi Theatre." Translated by Nina Dimitrievitch. Part 1: *Dance Research* 3, no. 2 (Summer 1985): 3–22; Part 2: *Dance Research* 4, no. 1 (Spring 1986): 3–28; Part 3: *Dance Research* 5, no. 1 (Spring 1987): 21–41; Part 4: *Dance Research* 6, no. 2 (Autumn 1988): 30–47.

Vazem, Ekaterina. *Zapiski baleriny Sankt-Peterburgskogo Bol'shogo teatra, 1867–1884* [Memoirs of a Ballerina of the St. Petersburg Bolshoi Theatre, 1867–1884]. Leningrad and Moscow: Iskusstvo, 1937. Reprint, St. Petersburg: Music Planet, 2021.

Venuso, Maria. *Giselle e il teatro musicale: nuove visioni per la storia del balletto.* Firenze: Polistampa, 2021.

Veroli, Patrizia. "La dernière étoile de Diaghilev dans la Russie en émigration. Serge Lifar de 1929 à 1939," *Reherches en danse* 5 (2016): 1–15. https://doi.org/10.4000/danse.1419.

Veroli, Patrizia. "Serge Lifar as a Dance Historian and the Myth of Russian Dance in 'Zarubezhnaia Rossiia' (Russia Abroad) 1930–1940." *Dance Research: The Journal of the Society for Dance Research* 32, no. 2 (2014): 105–143.

Vittucci, Matteo Marcellus, and Carola Goya. *The Language of Spanish Dance*. Norman: University of Oklahoma Press, 1993.

Volkov, Solomon. *Balanchine's Tchaikovsky*. Translated by Antonina W. Bouis. New York: Simon and Schuster, 1985.

Volynsky, Akim. *Ballet's Magic Kingdom*. Edited and translated by Stanley J. Rabinowitz. New Haven and London: Yale University Press, 2008.

Volynsky, Akim. *And Then Came Dance: The Women Who Led Volynsky to Ballet's Magic Kingdom.* Edited and translated by Stanley J. Rabinowitz. New York: Oxford University Press, 2019.

Walker, Kathrine Sorley. "The Camargo Society." *Dance Chronicle* 18, no. 1 (1995): 1–114.

Walsh, John. "The Grand Opera of Paris." *American Quarterly Review* XXI (June 1837): 183–184.

Wilberg, Rebecca. *The* mise en scène *at the Paris Opéra-Salle Peletier (1821–1873) and the staging of the first French Grand Opera: Meyerbeer's* Robert le diable. PhD diss., Brigham Young University, 1990.

Wild, Nicole. *Dictionnaire des Théâtres Parisiens au XIXe Siècle*. Paris: Aux Amateurs de Livres, 1989.

Wiley, Roland John. *A Century of Russian Ballet*. New York: Oxford University Press, 1990.

Wiley, Roland John. "A Context for Petipa," *Dance Research* 21, no. 1 (Summer 2003): 42–52.

Wiley, Roland John. "Dances from Russia: An Introduction to the Sergejev Collection." *Harvard Library Bulletin* 24, no. 1 (1976): 96–112.

Wiley, Roland John. *The Life and Ballets of Lev Ivanov*. Oxford: Clarendon Press, 1997.

Wiley, Roland John. *Tchaikovsky's Ballets*. New York: Oxford University Press, 1985.

Wolff, Larry. *The Singing Turk: Ottoman Power and Operatic Emotions on the European Stage from the Siege of Vienna to the Age of Napoleon*. Stanford, CA: Stanford University Press, 2016.

Wright, Thomas. *The History of France: From the Earliest Period to the Present Time*. Vol 3. London: London Printing and Publishing Company, 1862.

Zhiltsova, Maria. "Jean Coralli au Théâtre de la Porte-Saint-Martin (1825–1829)." In *Giovanni Coralli, l'autore di Giselle*, edited by José Sasportes and Patrizia Veroli, 105–122. Canterano: Gioacchino Onorati editore, 2018.

Zozulina, Natalia. "'Bayaderka' M. Petipa: K voprosu o chetvertom akte baleta" [M. Petipa's *Bayaderka*: To the Question about the Fourth Act of the Ballet]. *Vestnik Akademii Russkogo baleta imeni A. Ya. Vaganovoy* [Bulletin of the Academy of the Russian Ballet. A. Ya. Vaganova] 5 (2018): 26–39.

Zozulina, Natalia. "S oglyadkoy na istoriyu (N.G. Sergeyev i zapisi russkikh baletov iz garvardskoy kollektsii)" [With an Eye to History (N.G. Sergeyev and Recordings of Russian Ballets from the Harvard Collection)]. *Baletom i Operoy* [Ballet and Opera] (online forum). February 18, 2001. http://forum.balletfriends.ru/viewtopic.php?t=3510.

Zozulina, Natalia, and V.M. Muronova, eds. *Peterburgskiy balet. Tri veka: khronika. Tom IV. 1901-1950* [The Petersburg Ballet. Three Centuries: a Chronicle. Volume IV. 1901-1950]. St. Petersburg: Academy of Russian Ballet named after A.Y. Vaganova, 2015.

Index

Digital users please note: indexed terms that span two pages (e.g., 52–53) may, on occasion, appear on only one of those pages.

Footnotes are indicated with a lowercase n, as in 4n.6, meaning page 4, footnote 6. Except in main headings, Paris Opéra has been abbreviated PO, and St. Petersburg has been abbreviated SPb. Petipa refers to Marius Petipa unless otherwise noted. Titles and names found in Appendix A are included in the index.

Figures are indicated by *f* following the page number.